IUCN ACADEMY OF ENVIRONMENTAL LAW RESEARCH STUDIES

Compendium of Sustainable Energy Laws

Energy law – up until today – has addressed only how to generate electricity, mine coal, extract oil and gas, and distribute energy sources. With contemporary concerns for climate modification due to emissions from burning fossil fuels, new energy trading systems have emerged to encourage the use of solar, wind, geothermal, and other renewable sources, as well as hydrological sources. In addition, laws today manage demand for energy, not just supply. This book sets forth the legal instruments – at international and national levels – that are in use today to govern energy efficiency, demand-side management, and sustainable use of energy.

Richard L. Ottinger is Dean Emeritus and Professor of Law at Pace Law School in White Plains, New York. He is a member of the IUCN Commission on Environmental Law and Chair of its Climate and Energy Specialist Group. He served for 16 years in the U.S. Congress, chairing the House Subcommittee on Energy, Conservation and Power.

Nicholas Robinson is Gilbert and Sarah Kerlin Distinguished Professor of Environmental Law at Pace University and has developed environmental law since 1969 when he was named to the Legal Advisory Committee of the President's Council on Environmental Quality. He has practiced environmental law in law firms, for municipalities, and as former general counsel of the N.Y.S. Department of Environmental Conservation. He chairs the IUCN Commission on Environmental Law.

Victor Tafur is a staff attorney for the Pace Energy Project. He is representing environmental and community interests in proceedings involving the siting of energy facilities in New York State. He was Deputy Director of Operations for the President of Colombia and a legal counsel and environmental advisor on energy projects in Colombia.

IUCN ACADEMY OF ENVIRONMENTAL LAW RESEARCH STUDIES

Compendium of Sustainable Energy Laws

Edited by

RICHARD L. OTTINGER
Pace University

NICHOLAS ROBINSON
Pace University

VICTOR TAFUR
Pace University

CAMBRIDGE
UNIVERSITY PRESS

CAMBRIDGE UNIVERSITY PRESS
Cambridge, New York, Melbourne, Madrid, Cape Town, Singapore, São Paulo

Cambridge University Press
40 West 20th Street, New York, NY 10011-4211, USA

www.cambridge.org
Information on this title: www.cambridge.org/9780521845267

First published 2005

Printed in the United States of America

A catalog record for this publication is available from the British Library.

Library of Congress Cataloging in Publication Data

ISBN-13 978-0-521-84526-7 hardback
ISBN-10 0-521-84526-2 hardback

Contents

Acknowledgments

The editors gratefully acknowledge the contributions of a number of individuals who have assisted in the compilation of this set of primary references on sustainable energy law. Nancy Kong and Elena Roffman, law students at Pace University School of Law, have reviewed a wide range of energy law resources to come up with the legal instruments selected here. The Director of the Pace University School of Law Library, Professor Marie Newman, and her able colleagues Jack McNeill and Cynthia Pittson, provided invaluable assistance. The Director of the Pace Energy Project, Professor Fred Zalcman, lent his expertise to the effort, as did the Specialist Group on Energy Law of the IUCN Commission on Environmental Law, in particular Professor Adrian Bradbrook (Adelaide University, Australia). The support of the IUCN Environmental Law Centre, Bonn, Germany, and John Scanlon, head of the centre, and Maria Socorro Manguiat, IUCN's legal counsel for energy and climate issues, is gratefully acknowledged. The editors are grateful to Cambridge University Press, and John Berger, for their outstanding professional support in publishing this compendium.

Introduction

This volume contains the first compendium of legal instruments ever prepared on the emerging field of the "law of sustainable energy." Admittedly, no such field of law exists today, but it is fast emerging and will of necessity become a recognized legal discipline. Energy issues were not much featured in *Agenda 21*, adopted by the United Nations Conference on Environment and Development in 1992. In contrast, the Johannesburg Plan of Implementation adopted in 2002 at the United Nations World Summit for Sustainable Development, featured energy efficiency and energy choice issues as a key element of sustainable development.

The World Energy Assessment (WEA) definies "sustainable energy" as follows: "Energy produced and used in ways that support human development in all its social, economic and environmental dimensions is what is meant by sustainable energy" (page 3, World Energy Assessment: Energy and the Challenge of Sustainability). The WEA was prepared for the United Nations Department of Economic and Social Affairs, the UN Development Programme, and the World Energy Council. Assembled by Professor Thomas Johansson, it is an outstanding survey of worldwide energy supply and demand issues. Before there can be a recognized field of sustainable energy law, there needs to be a global view of the *energy problemmatique.* The WEA provides that worldview, and its "Overview" chapter sets forth that understanding as the filter for the selection of the legal instruments that are published together here.

At present, energy supply is governed essentially by national laws. The International Energy Agency provides for some collective management of petroleum supplies for developed economies, and by inference for other oil-dependent economies. Traditionally, the only legal concerns for energy address how to ensure a supply, not how to curb wasteful use or manage its externalities. Regulatory utility commissions exist in many nations to ensure that the price of electricity is set at a fair rate, with an affordable price for the consumer, a return sufficient to sustain the generating and distribution facilities, and a reasonable profit for the investors who own or invest in the electrical utility. In situations of gasoline or heating oil shortage, states have intervened to govern prices. Gradually, laws have emerged on the siting of new electrical generating facilities, whether they be for fossil fuel plants or dams or wind farms. Siting laws attempt to deal with the environmental consequences of locating, building, and operating new energy supply systems.

What is missing in all of this pattern of legal development is any attention to the management of demand for energy, or the governance of the efficiency of energy generation and use. Demand side management (DSM) and the economic and other regulatory means for encouraging or mandating DSM have become a primary focus of sustainable energy law. This is a long overdue legal development, since to regulate only supply and not demand is a grossly unbalanced approach to the issues of energy supply and use. When supply was plentiful, it was allocated without regard for the efficiency of use. Now that supply is more problematic, and not always plentiful where needed, the policy and legal focus has turned to DSM.

If nations all understood the common worldview of sustainable energy as advanced by the WEA, the next step would be to understand the range of legal instruments that can be used to implement a sustainable energy system. Many of the elements of a legal framework for sustainable energy have been described by the authors published in Bradbrook, Lyster, Ottinger, and Wang, *The Law of Energy for Sustainable Development* (Cambridge University Press, 2005). This compendium is intended as a reference of primary sources to serve as a companion volume to that book.

No single nation today uses all the legal elements assembled here. Nations with abundant energy resources, such as the geothermal resource of Iceland or the petroleum resources of West Asia, may have less urgent present need for the different legal tools provided here. Most nations, however, have a pressing and real need to study and deploy appropriate legal innovations to redress their energy supply and demand issues. Nations that lack a national policy on sustainable energy law are coasting toward the disruptions in their economies that blackouts and brownouts and shortages entail. Nations that fail to integrate their economic energy policy with the other two of the three pillars of sustainable development, environmental protection and social equity, will find their energy policy and law drag down and frustrate sustainable growth rather than advance it. This volume provides examples of legal innovations that nations can study and select from to adapt to forge their own sustainable energy policies.

The elements of a sustainable energy law will need to include environmental impact assessment, a technique that is admittedly used very inadequately today to guide the planning and implementation of energy supply regimes. Nations will need to provide a regulatory forum to adjust pricing of electricity and other sources of energy. Until distributed energy systems, such as hydrogen fuel cells, become a widespread reality, the distribution of electricity is a "natural monopoly" and requires some equitable form of market regulation. This, in turn, requires use of meters to measure the use of electricity, management of the grid for distribution to govern the wheeling of electricity across different supply regions, and the associated pricing of the sources of power.

States acknowledge that they have common but differentiated responsibilities to cooperate together to ensure that sustainable development can be attained. Their common responsibility is to develop a common worldview on energy and share knowledge about how to manage the supply and demand of energy resources to meet the needs of their people and their environmental conditions and economies. This volume provides a basis for understanding the various options for framing the legal reforms that a nation may need to advance toward the goal of sustainable energy.

Innovations in sustainable energy law are moving rapidly. At the present rate of legislative innovation, there will be a need to update this sort of compendium no less than every five years. Slower is the pace of the progressive development of international energy law, but that arguably can only come after the common worldview is more widely embraced and the majority of states have begun to apply their own national laws for sustainable energy.

States will enact different elements of sustainable energy laws, as they do have differentiated responsibilities depending on their stage of economic development, environmental problems, or natural resource endowments. Their common duty, throughout, is to enact an appropriate set of sustainable energy laws. It is the editors' hope, shared by the IUCN Academy of Environmental Law, that this volume of references may materially further those endeavors.

The Editors

World Energy Assessment: United Nations Development Programme, United Nations Department of Economic and Social Affairs, World Energy Council, World Energy Assessment and the Challenge of Sustainability (2000)

World Energy Assessment (New York, UNDP) 2000

http://www.undp.org/seed/eap/activities/wea/drafts-frame.html

One way of looking at human development is in terms of the choices and opportunities available to individuals. Energy can dramatically widen these choices. Simply harnessing oxen, for example, multiplied the power available to a human being by a factor of 10. The invention of the vertical waterwheel increased productivity by another factor of 6; the steam engine increased it by yet another order of magnitude. The use of motor vehicles greatly reduced journey times and expanded human ability to transport goods to markets.

Today the ready availability of plentiful, affordable energy allows many people to enjoy unprecedented comfort, mobility, and productivity. In industrialised countries people use more than 100 times as much energy, on a per capita basis, as humans did before they learned to exploit the energy potential of fire.[1]

Although energy fuels economic growth, and is therefore a key concern for all countries, access to and use of energy vary widely among them, as well as between the rich and poor within each country. In fact, 2 billion people – one-third of the world's population – rely almost completely on traditional energy sources and so are not able to take advantage of the opportunities made possible by modern forms of energy (World Bank, 1996; WEC-FAO, 1999; UNDP, 1997).[2] Moreover, most current energy generation and use are accompanied by environmental impacts at local, regional, and global levels that threaten human well-being now and well into the future.

In Agenda 21 the United Nations and its member states have strongly endorsed the goal of sustainable development, which implies meeting the needs of the present without compromising the ability of future generations to meet their needs (WCED, 1987, p. 8).[3] The importance of energy as a tool for meeting this goal was acknowledged at every major United Nations conference in the 1990s, starting with the Rio Earth Summit (UN Conference on Environment and Development) in 1992.[4] But current energy systems, as analysed in this report and summarised here, are not addressing the basic needs of all people, and the continuation of business-as-usual practices may compromise the prospects of future generations.

Energy produced and used in ways that support human development over the long term, in all its social, economic, and environmental dimensions, is what is meant in this report by the term *sustainable energy*. In other words, this term does not refer simply to a continuing supply of energy, but to the production and use of energy resources in ways that promote – or at least are compatible with – long-term human well-being and ecological balance.

Many current energy practices do not fit this definition. As noted in Agenda 21, "Much of the world's energy . . . is currently produced and consumed in ways that could not be sustained if technology were to remain constant and if overall quantities were to increase substantially" (UN, 1992, chapter 9.9).[5] Energy's link to global warming through greenhouse gas emissions (most of which are produced by fossil fuel consumption) was addressed by the United Nations Framework Convention on Climate Change, adopted in 1992. And in 1997 a United Nations General Assembly Special Session identified energy and transport issues as being central to achieving a sustainable future, and set key objectives in these areas.

The energy industry also recognises the need to address energy issues within a broad context. For example, the conclusions and recommendations of the 17th Congress of the World Energy Council discuss the need to provide commercial energy to those without it, and to address energy-linked environmental impacts at all levels (WEC, 1998).[6]

Although there seem to be no physical limits to the world's energy supply for at least the next 50 years, today's energy system is unsustainable because of equity issues as well as environmental, economic, and geopolitical concerns that have implications far into the future. Aspects of the unsustainability of the current system include:

- Modern fuels and electricity are not universally accessible, an inequity that has moral, political, and practical dimensions in a world that is becoming increasingly interconnected.
- The current energy system is not sufficiently reliable or affordable to support widespread economic growth. The productivity of one-third of the world's people is compromised by lack of access to commercial energy, and perhaps another third suffer economic hardship and insecurity due to unreliable energy supplies.
- Negative local, regional, and global environmental impacts of energy production and use threaten the health and well-being of current and future generations.

More specific – and more quantifiable – elements of sustainability are identified below in the section on energy scenarios. Before looking into the future, however, some basic features of energy and its relationship to economic development are described, and the linkages between energy and major global challenges are analysed.

PART 1. ENERGY AND MAJOR GLOBAL ISSUES

Part 1 analyses the linkages between energy and the economy, social and health issues, environmental protection, and security, and describes aspects of energy use that are incompatible with the goal of sustainable development. It shows that:

- Affordable, modern energy supplies – including gaseous and liquid fuels, electricity, and more efficient end-use technologies – are not accessible by 2 billion people. This constrains their opportunities for economic development and improved living standards. Women and children are disproportionately burdened by a dependence on traditional fuels.
- Wide disparities in access to affordable commercial energy and energy services are inequitable, run counter to the concept of human development, and threaten social stability.
- Unreliable supplies are a hardship and economic burden for a large portion of the world's population. In addition, dependence on imported fuels leaves many countries vulnerable to disruptions in supply.
- Human health is threatened by high levels of pollution resulting from energy use at the household, community, and regional levels.
- The environmental impacts of a host of energy-linked emissions – including suspended fine particles and precursors of acid deposition – contribute to air pollution and ecosystem degradation.
- Emissions of anthropogenic greenhouse gases, mostly from the production and use of energy, are altering the atmosphere in ways that may already be having a discernible influence on the global climate.

Finding ways to expand energy services while simultaneously addressing the environmental impacts associated with energy use represents a critical challenge to humanity. The resources and options available to meet this challenge – energy efficiency, renewables, and advanced energy technologies – are analysed in the next sections.

AN INTRODUCTION TO ENERGY

An energy system is made up of an energy supply sector and energy end-use technologies. The object of the energy system is to deliver to consumers the benefits that energy offers. The term *energy services* is used to describe these benefits, which in households include illumination, cooked food, comfortable indoor temperatures, refrigeration, and transportation. Energy services are also required for virtually every commercial and industrial activity. For instance, heating and cooling are needed for many industrial processes, motive power is needed for agriculture, and electricity is needed for telecommunications and electronics.

The energy chain that delivers these services begins with the collection or extraction of primary

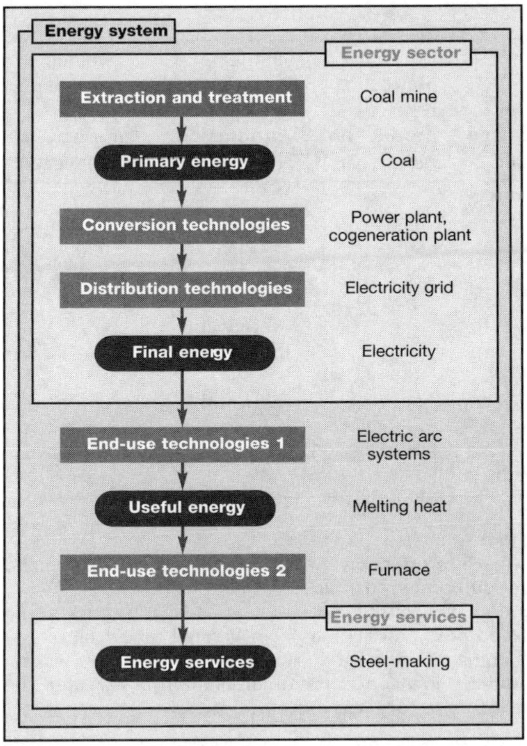

Figure 1: An example of the energy chain from extraction to services. *Source:* Adapted from Chapter 6.

energy that, in one or several steps, may be converted into energy carriers, such as electricity or diesel oil, that are suitable for end uses. Energy end-use equipment – stoves, light bulbs, vehicles, machinery – converts final energy into useful energy, which provides the desired benefits: the energy services. An example of an energy chain – beginning with coal extraction from a mine (primary energy) and ending with produced steel as an energy service – is shown in figure 1.

Energy services are the result of a combination of various technologies, infrastructure (capital), labour (know-how), materials, and primary energy. Each of these inputs carries a price tag, and they are partly substitutable for one another. From the consumer's perspective, the important issues are the economic value or utility derived from the services. Consumers are often unaware of the upstream activities required to produce energy services.

Per capita consumption of primary energy in the United States was 330 gigajoules in 1995, more than eight times as much as used by an average Sub-Saharan African (who used 40 gigajoules that year when both commercial and traditional energy are included). Many people in the least developed countries use much less. Figure 2 shows commercial and non-commercial energy consumption in various regions.

In most low-income developing countries, a small, affluent minority uses various forms of commercial energy in much the same way as do most people in the industrialised world. But most people in low-income developing countries rely on traditional, non-commercial sources of energy using inefficient technologies such as unventilated stoves or open fires. Traditional energy sources are generally not reflected in energy statistics. Analysis based on per capita consumption of commercially distributed energy resources is common because the data are much easier to collect. The resulting analysis, however, does not accurately reflect the world's energy situation, which is why estimates of non-commercial energy use are included in table 1 and figure 2. Though less well documented, non-commercial energy is very significant globally, and is used far more widely than commercial energy in rural areas of many developing countries, particularly the least developed countries.

The rate of global commercial energy consumption is thousands of times smaller than the energy flows from the sun to the earth. Primary energy

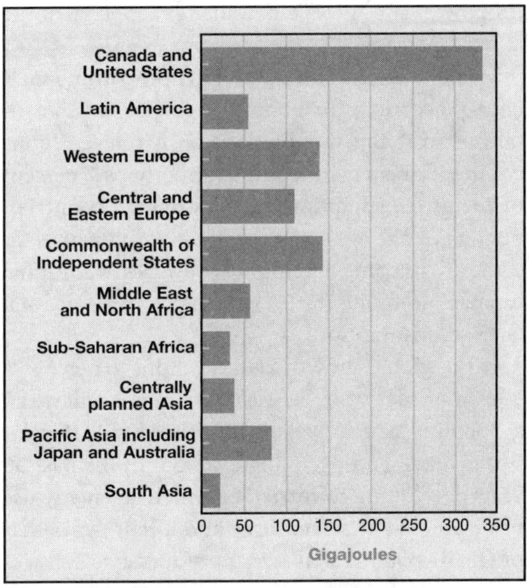

Figure 2: Primary per capita energy consumption (commercial and non-commercial) by region, 1995. *Source:* World Bank, 1997; WRI, 1998.

Table 1: World primary energy consumption, 1998

Source	Primary energy (exajoules)	Primary energy (10^9 tonnes of oil equivalent)	Percentage of total	Static reserve-production ratio (years)[a]	Static resource base-production ratio (years)[b]	Dynamic resource base-production ratio (years)[c]
Fossil fuels	320	7.63	79.6			
Oil	142	3.39	35.3	45	~200	95
Natural gas	85	2.02	21.1	69	~400	230
Coal	93	2.22	23.1	452	~1,500	1,000
Renewables	56	1.33	13.9			
Large hydro	9	0.21	2.2		Renewable	
Traditional biomass	38	0.91	9.5		Renewable	
'New' renewables[d]	9	0.21	2.2		Renewable	
Nuclear	26	0.62	6.5			
Nuclear[e]	26	0.62	6.5	50[f]	>>300[f]	
Total	**402**	**9.58**	**100.0**			

[a] Based on constant production and static reserves.
[b] Includes both conventional and unconventional reserves and resources.
[c] Data refer to the energy use of a business-as-usual scenario – that is, production is dynamic and a function of demand (see chapter 9). Thus these ratios are subject to change under different scenarios.
[d] Includes modern biomass, small hydropower, geothermal energy, wind energy, solar energy, and marine energy (see chapter 7). Modern biomass accounts for about 7 exajoules, and 2 exajoules comes from all other renewables.
[e] Converted from electricity produced to fuels consumed assuming a 33 percent thermal efficiency of power plants.
[f] Based on once-through uranium fuel cycles excluding thorium and low-concentration uranium from seawater. The uranium resource base is effectively 60 times larger if fast breeder reactors are used.
Source: Chapter 5.

consumption is reliant on fossil fuels (oil, natural gas, and coal), which represent nearly 80 percent of the total fuel mix (table 1). Nuclear power contributes slightly more than 6 percent, and hydropower and new renewables each contribute about 2 percent.

World-wide, traditional (often non-commercial) energy accounts for about 10 percent of the total fuel mix. But the distribution is uneven: non-commercial energy accounts for perhaps 2 percent of energy consumption in industrialised countries, but an average of 30 percent in developing ones. In some low-income developing countries, traditional biomass accounts for 90 percent or more of total energy consumption.

If the global growth rate of about 2 percent a year of primary energy use continues, it will mean a doubling of energy consumption by 2035 relative to 1998, and a tripling by 2055. In the past 30 years developing countries' commercial energy use has increased at a rate three and a half times that of OECD countries, the result of life-style changes made possible by rising personal incomes, coupled with higher population growth rates and a shift from traditional to commercial energy. On a per capita basis, however, the increase in total primary energy use has not resulted in any notable way in more equitable access to energy services between industrialised and developing countries. Clearly, more energy will be needed to fuel global economic growth and to deliver opportunities to the billions of people in developing countries who do not have access to adequate energy services.

However, the amount of additional energy required to provide the energy services needed in the future will depend on the efficiencies with which the energy is produced, delivered, and used. Energy efficiency improvements could help reduce financial investments in new energy supply systems, as they have over the past 200 years. The degree of interdependence between economic activity and energy use is neither static nor uniform across regions. Energy intensity (the ratio of energy demand to GDP) often depends on a country's stage of development. In OECD countries, which enjoy abundant energy services, growth in energy demand is less tightly linked to economic productivity than it was in the past (figure 3).

The trend towards a reduction in energy intensity as economic development proceeds can be

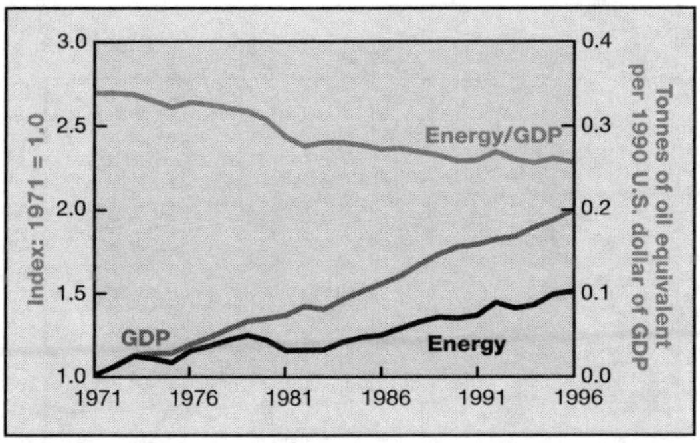

Figure 3: GDP and primary energy consumption in OECD countries, 1971–96. *Source:* IEA, 1999.

discerned over a long historical period, as shown in figure 4, which includes the developing country examples of China and India. A detailed, long-term analysis of energy intensity for a number of countries reveals a common pattern of energy use driven by the following factors:

• The shift from non-commercial to commercial forms of energy, industrialisation, and motorisation initially increase the commercial energy-GDP ratio. (In the 1990s this ratio increased in transition in economies, mainly because of slower economic growth.)

• As industrialisation proceeds and incomes rise, saturation effects, as well as an expansion of the service sector (which is less energy intensive), decrease the ratio of commercial energy to GDP after it reaches a peak. This maximum energy intensity has been passed by many countries, but not by low-income developing countries.

• As a result of world-wide technology transfer and diffusion, energy efficiency improvements can be the main limiting factor in the growth of energy demand arising from increasing populations and growing production and incomes.

• The more efficient use of materials in better-quality, well-designed, miniaturised products, the recycling of energy-intensive materials, and the saturation of bulk markets for basic materials in industrialised countries contribute to additional decreases in energy intensity.

• In developing countries, technological leapfrogging to the use of highly efficient appliances, machinery, processes, vehicles, and transportation systems offers considerable potential for energy efficiency improvements.

These drivers are leading to a common pattern of energy use per unit of GDP in industrialised and developing countries.

Energy prices influence consumer choices and behaviour and can affect economic development and growth. High energy prices can lead to increasing import bills, with adverse consequences for business, employment, and social welfare. High energy prices can also stimulate exploration and development of additional resources, create a pull for innovation, and provide incentives for efficiency improvements.

Although some impacts of energy prices are fairly steady, others are more transient. For example, different absolute price levels have had little effect on economic development in OECD European countries or Japan relative to the much lower energy prices in the United States and some developing countries. What affected economic growth in all energy-importing countries were the price hikes of the 1970s. It appears that economies are more sensitive to price changes than to prices per se.

Capital investment is a prerequisite for energy development. Energy system development and structural change are the results of investment in plants, equipment, and energy system infrastructure. Difficulties in attracting capital for energy investment may impede economic development, especially in the least developed countries. Scarce public funds, especially in developing countries, are needed for many projects – ranging from rural development, education, and health care to energy supplies. Because energy supply, more than any other alternative, is often seen as more readily capable of generating early revenues, energy investments are increasingly viewed as a private sector affair. Yet private funds are not flowing into many developing countries for a variety of reasons, especially risks to investors.

Foreign direct investment approached $400 billion in 1997 – up from $50 billion in 1984 – and represents an increasing share of international investment flows.[7] Foreign direct investment is generally commercially motivated, and investors not only expect to recover the initial capital but also count on competitive returns. These outcomes cannot be guaranteed in developing countries with potentially fragile governments or without free markets. In fact, very little foreign direct investment reaches the least developed countries.

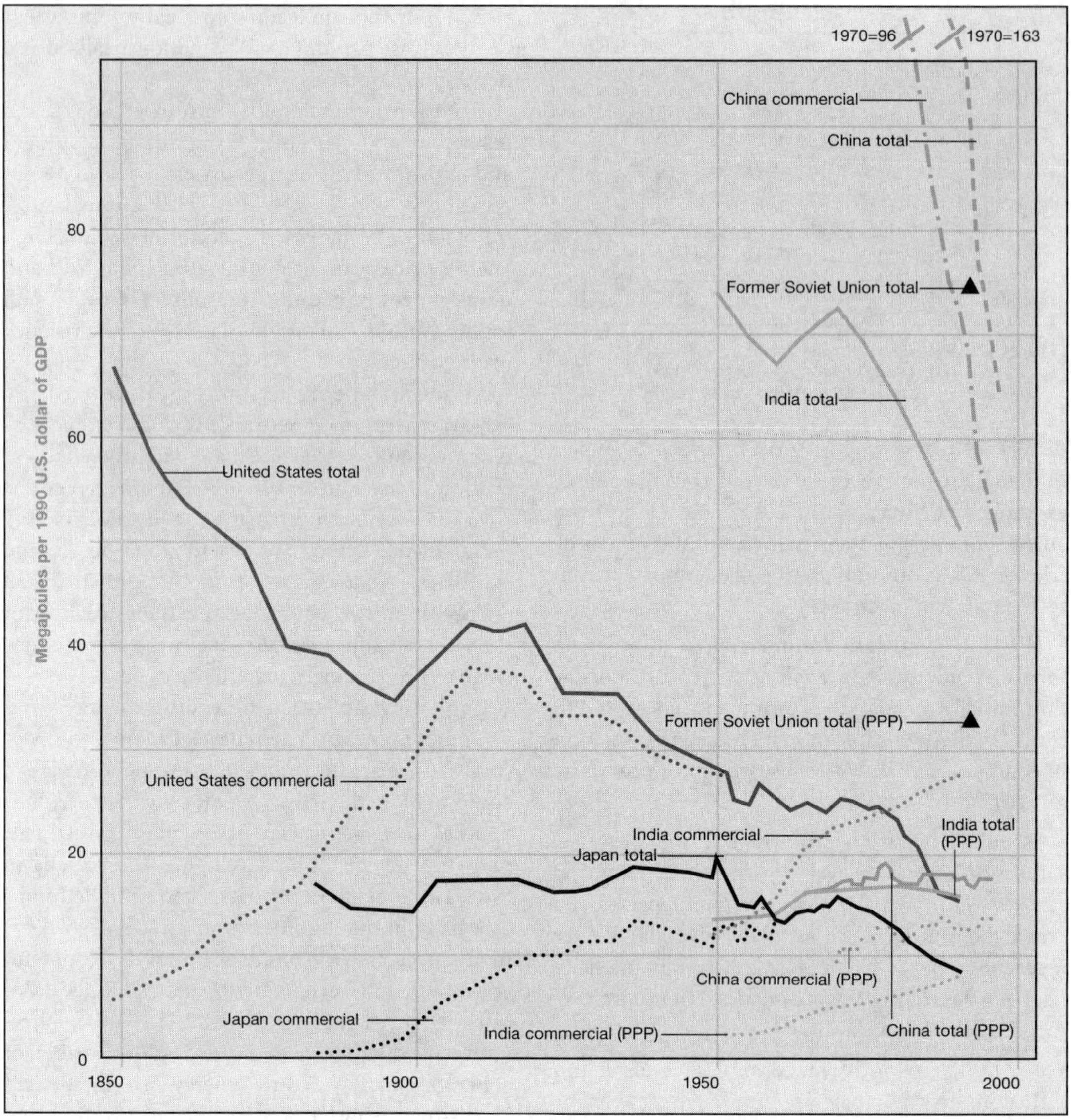

Figure 4: Primary energy intensities in various countries, 1850–2000. Two energy intensity paths are shown for Japan and the United States, one based on total energy consumption from all sources and the other only on commercial energy. The paths converge where traditional sources have been replaced by commercial energy. Because of distortions from market fluctuations, energy intensity paths for China and India are calculated in two ways: using total and commercial energy divided by GDP measured at market exchange rates (as with Japan and the United States), and divided by GDP measured at purchasing power parities (PPP). Energy intensities for the former Soviet Union, derived using both market exchange rates and PPP, are data points only. *Source:* Nakićenović, Grübler, and McDonald, 1998.

Unlike foreign direct investment, official development assistance has remained flat relative to gross world product. In 1997 it totaled $56 billion, or 0.25 percent of the GDP of OECD countries – which have agreed in principle to a target of 0.7 percent of GDP.[8] Against this backdrop, financing is inadequate for energy projects in developing countries. Until the economic risks to foreign investors can be managed (for example, through clear and stable rules for energy and financial markets, steady revenue generation through bill collection, and profit transfers), most developing countries may have to continue to finance their energy development from domestic savings.

Although energy investment as a share of total investment varies greatly among countries and at different stages of economic development, on balance, 1.0–1.5 percent of GDP is invested in the energy sector. This ratio is expected to remain relatively stable. Based on these rules of thumb, current energy supply sector investment totals $290–430 billion a year. But this does not include investment in end-use energy efficiency.

ENERGY AND SOCIAL ISSUES

Energy use is closely linked to a range of social issues, including poverty alleviation, population growth, urbanisation, and a lack of opportunities for women. Although these issues affect energy demand, the relationship is two-way: the quality and quantity of energy services, and how they are achieved, have an effect on social issues as well.

Poverty is the overriding social consideration for developing countries. Some 1.3 billion people in the developing world live on less than $1 a day. Income measurement alone, however, does not fully capture the misery and the absence of choice that poverty represents. The energy consumption patterns of poor people – especially their reliance on traditional fuels in rural areas – tend to keep them impoverished.

World-wide, 2 billion people are without access to electricity and an equal number continue to use traditional solid fuels for cooking. As shown in the next section, cooking with poorly vented stoves has significant health impacts. In addition, hundreds of millions of people – mainly women and children – spend several hours a day in the drudgery of gathering firewood and carrying water, often from considerable distances, for household needs. Because of these demands on their time and energy, women and children often miss out on opportunities for education and other productive activities.

Lack of electricity usually means inadequate illumination and few labour-saving appliances, as well as limited telecommunications and possibilities for commercial enterprise. Greater access to electricity and modern fuels and stoves for cooking can enable people to enjoy both short-term and self-reinforcing, long-term advances in their quality of life. Table 2 summarises some of the specific improvements that may result.

Limited income may force households to use traditional fuels and inefficient technologies. Figure 5 shows the average primary energy demand for various fuels as a function of income levels in Brazil. For low-income households, firewood is the dominant fuel. At higher incomes, wood is replaced by commercial fuels and electricity, which offer much greater convenience, energy efficiency, and cleanliness. Because convenient, affordable energy can contribute to a household's productivity and income-generating potential, its availability can become a lever for breaking out of a cycle of poverty.

Although population growth tends to increase energy demand, it is less widely understood that the availability of adequate energy services can lower birth rates. Adequate energy services can shift the relative benefits and costs of fertility towards a lower number of desired births in a family. An acceleration of the demographic transition to low mortality and low fertility (as has occurred in industrialised countries) depends on crucial developmental tasks, including improving the local environment, educating women, and ameliorating the extreme poverty that may make child labour a necessity. All these tasks have links to the availability of low-cost energy services.

The growing concentration of people in urban centres is another key demographic issue linked to energy. Although the general trend towards urbanisation has many components and may be inevitable, providing more options to rural residents through energy interventions could potentially slow migration and reduce pressure on rapidly growing cities. Although the negative externalities associated with energy use in urban areas can be severe, various strategies can mitigate their effects and promote energy conservation. Taking energy into consideration in land-use planning, and in designing physical infrastructure, construction standards, and transportation systems, can reduce some of the growth in energy demand that accompanies rapid urbanisation.

Transportation systems may be especially important in this regard, given the rapid growth in the number of motor vehicles world-wide. Since about 1970 the global fleet has been increasing by 16 million vehicles a year, and more than 1 billion cars will likely be on the road by 2020. Most of these cars will be driven in the cities of the developing world, where they will create more congestion, aggravate

Table 2: Energy-related options to address social issues

Social challenge	Energy linkages and interventions
Alleviating poverty in developing countries	• Improve health and increase productivity by providing universal access to adequate energy services – particularly for cooking, lighting, and transport – through affordable, high-quality, safe, and environmentally acceptable energy carriers and end-use devices. • Make commercial energy available to increase income-generating opportunities.
Increasing opportunities for women	• Encourage the use of improved stoves and liquid or gaseous fuels to reduce indoor air pollution and improve women's health. • Support the use of affordable commercial energy to minimise arduous and time-consuming physical labour at home and at work. • Use women's managerial and entrepreneurial skills to develop, run, and profit from decentralised energy systems.
Speeding the demographic transition (to low mortality and low fertility)	• Reduce child mortality by introducing cleaner fuels and cooking devices and providing safe, potable water. • Use energy initiatives to shift the relative benefits and costs of fertility – for example, adequate energy services can reduce the need for children's physical labour for household chores. • Influence attitudes about family size and opportunities for women through communications made accessible through modern energy carriers.
Mitigating the problems associated with rapid urbanization	• Reduce the 'push' factor in rural-urban migration by improving the energy services in rural areas. • Exploit the advantages of high-density settlements through land planning. • Provide universal access to affordable multi-modal transport services and public transportation. • Take advantage of new technologies to avoid energy-intensive, environmentally unsound development paths.

Source: Adapted from chapter 2.

urban pollution, and undermine human health – even with optimistic projections about efficiency improvements and alternative fuels.

In developing countries, addressing the energy needs of the poor, who represent a large majority,

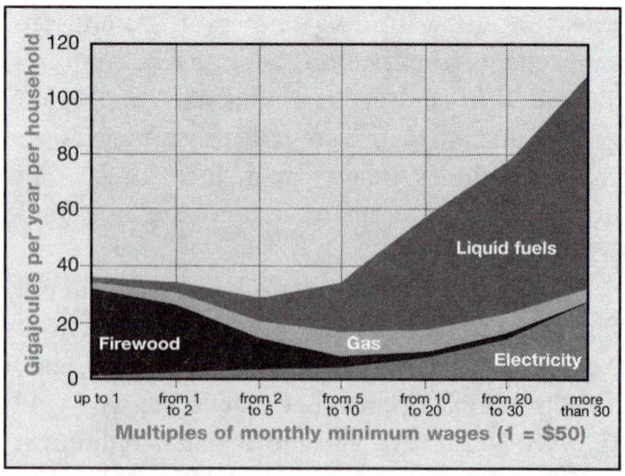

Figure 5: Average energy demand by income segment in Brazil, 1988. *Source:* De Almeida and de Oliveira, 1995.

will require major structural changes. On the other hand, in industrialised countries adequate access to affordable energy is problematic only for a minority, and thus more amenable to social policy solutions. Throughout the world, however, poor households pay a larger fraction of their incomes for energy than do the rich, and so are vulnerable to rapid increases in the price of energy. Increases in the price of oil in the winter of 1999/2000, for example, posed a hardship for many people, even in some industrialised countries.

Eradicating poverty is a long-term goal of development. But long before that goal is achieved, convenient and affordable energy services could dramatically improve living standards and offer more opportunities to people. Today's inequity is unsustainable. Satisfying the energy needs of the poor with modern technologies has the potential to improve standards of living and health, and to create new jobs and business opportunities. Allowing one-third of the world's population to continue to endure the constraints associated with traditional energy is unacceptable from a humanitarian and moral standpoint. Making commercial energy more widely available makes sense from a political perspective as well. The wave of democratisation sweeping the world is putting political power in the hands of the economically disenfranchised. Societies with grave inequalities and disparities tend to be unstable, and large populations below the poverty line are fertile ground for social upheavals.

ENERGY, THE ENVIRONMENT, AND HEALTH

The environmental impacts of energy use are not new. For centuries, wood burning has contributed to the deforestation of many areas. Even in the early stages of industrialisation, local air, water, and land pollution reached high levels. What is relatively new is an acknowledgement of energy linkages to regional and global environmental problems and of their implications. Although energy's potential for enhancing human well-being is unquestionable, conventional energy[9] production and consumption are closely linked to environmental degradation. This degradation threatens human health and quality of life, and affects ecological balance and biological diversity.

The environment-energy linkage is illustrated in table 3, which shows the share of toxic emissions and other pollutants attributable to the energy supply. The human disruption index is the ratio of the human-generated flow of a given pollutant (such as sulphur dioxide) to the natural, or baseline, flow. Thus, in the case of sulphur, the index is 2.7, which means that human-generated emissions of 84 million tonnes a year are 2.7 times the natural baseline flow of 31 million tonnes a year. The table indicates that, together with other human activities, energy systems significantly affect the global cycling of important chemicals. Although by itself the index does not demonstrate that these emissions translate into negative impacts, their magnitudes provide warning that such impacts could be considerable. Some impacts, as discussed below, are already significant.

Just in the course of the past 100 years, during which the world's population more than tripled, human environmental insults[10] grew from local perturbations to global disruptions. The human disruptions of the 20th century – driven by more than 20-fold growth in the use of fossil fuels, and augmented by a tripling in the use of traditional energy forms such as biomass – have amounted to no less than the emergence of civilisation as a global ecological and geochemical force. In other words, the accelerating impact of human life is altering the world at the global level.

At every level (local, regional, global), the environmental consequences of current patterns of energy generation and use make up a significant fraction of human impacts on the environment. At the household level, solid fuel use for cooking and heat has significant health impacts. Poor air quality – at the household, local, and regional levels – is associated with increased sickness and premature death. About 2 million premature deaths a year – disproportionately of women and children – are estimated to occur from exposure to indoor air pollution caused by burning solid fuels in poorly ventilated spaces. Particulate matter (which is both emitted directly and formed in the air as the result of the emissions of gaseous precursors in the form of oxides of sulphur and nitrogen) and hydrocarbons are growing concerns world-wide. They are especially troublesome in many parts of the developing world, where dirtier fuels predominate with little emissions abatement. No safe threshold level for exposure to small particulate matter has been established.

Fossil fuel combustion is problematic on several levels (although natural gas produces significantly fewer harmful emissions than do oil or coal). The main pollutants emitted in the combustion of fossil fuels are sulphur and nitrogen oxides, carbon monoxide, and suspended particulate matter. Ozone is formed in the troposphere from interactions among hydrocarbons, nitrogen oxides, and sunlight. Energy-related emissions from fossil fuel combustion, including in the transport sector, are major contributors to urban air pollution. Precursors of acid deposition from fuel combustion can be precipitated thousands of kilometres from their point of origin – often crossing national boundaries. The resulting acidification is causing significant damage to natural systems, crops, and human-made structures; and can, over time, alter the composition and function of entire ecosystems. In many regions acidification has diminished the productivity of forests, fisheries, and farmlands. Large hydropower projects often raise environmental issues related to flooding, whereas in the case of nuclear power, issues such as waste disposal raise concern.

Table 3: Environmental insults due to human activities by sector, mid-1990s

Insult	Natural baseline (tones per year)	Human disruption index[a]	Share of human disruption caused by: Commercial energy supply	Traditional energy supply	Agriculture	Manufacturing, other
Lead emissions to atmosphere[b]	12,000	18	41% (fossil fuel burning, including additives)	Negligible	Negligible	59% (metal processing, manufacturing, refuse burning)
Oil added to oceans	200,000	10	44% (petroleum harvesting, processing, and transport)	Negligible	Negligible	56% (disposal of oil wastes, including motor oil changes)
Cadmium emissions to atmosphere	1,400	5.4	13% (fossil fuel burning)	5% (traditional fuel burning)	12% (agricultural burning)	70% (metals processing, manufacturing, refuse burning)
Sulphur emissions to atmosphere	31 million (sulphur)	2.7	85% (fossil fuel burning)	0.5% (traditional fuel burning)	1% (agricultural burning)	13% (smelting, refuse burning)
Methane flow to atmosphere	160 million	2.3	18% (fossil fuel harvesting and processing)	5% (traditional fuel burning)	65% (rice paddies, domestic animals, land clearing)	12% (landfills)
Nitrogen fixation (as nitrogen oxide and ammonium)[c]	140 million (nitrogen)	1.5	30% (fossil fuel burning)	2% (traditional fuel burning)	67% (fertiliser, agricultural burning)	1% (refuse burning)
Mercury emissions to atmosphere	2,500	1.4	20% (fossil fuel burning)	1% (traditional fuel burning)	2% (agricultural burning)	77% (metals processing, manufacturing, refuse burning)
Nitrous oxide flows to atmosphere	33 million	0.5	12% (fossil fuel burning)	8% (traditional fuel burning)	80% (fertiliser, land clearing, aquifer disruption)	Negligible
Particulate emissions to atmosphere	3,100 million[d]	0.12	35% (fossil fuel burning)	10% (traditional fuel burning)	40% (agricultural burning)	15% (smelting, non-agricultural land clearing, refuse)
Non-methane hydrocarbon emissions to atmosphere	1,000 million	0.12	35% (fossil fuel processing and burning)	5% (traditional fuel burning)	40% (agricultural burning)	20% (non-agricultural land clearing, refuse burning)
Carbon dioxide flows to atmosphere	150 billion (carbon)	0.05[e]	75% (fossil fuel burning)	3% (net deforestation for fuelwood)	15% (net deforestation for land clearing)	7% (net deforestation for lumber, cement manufacturing)

Note: The magnitude of the insult is only one factor determining the size of the actual environmental impact.

[a] The human disruption index is the ratio of human-generated flow to the natural (baseline) flow.

[b] The automotive portion of human-induced lead emissions in this table is assumed to be 50 percent of global automotive emissions in the early 1990s.

[c] Calculated from total nitrogen fixation minus that from nitrous oxide.

[d] Dry mass.

[e] Although seemingly small, because of the long atmospheric lifetime and other characteristics of carbon dioxide, this slight imbalance in natural flows is causing a 0.4 percent annual increase in the global atmospheric concentration of carbon dioxide.

Source: Chapter 3.

Fossil fuel combustion produces more carbon dioxide (CO_2) than any other human activity. This is the biggest source of the anthropogenic greenhouse gas emissions that are changing the composition of the atmosphere and could alter the global climate system, including the amount and pattern of rainfall. Achieving a stable atmospheric CO_2 concentration at any level would require that CO_2 emissions eventually be cut by more than half from current levels. Stabilising CO_2 at close to the present concentration would require reducing emissions to half of current levels within the next few decades. Instead, CO_2 emissions continue to increase. Current CO_2 emission trends, if not controlled, will lead to more than a doubling of atmospheric concentrations before 2070, relative to pre-industrial levels. Changes have been observed in climate patterns that correspond to scientific projections based on increasing concentrations of greenhouse gases. The balance of evidence, according to the Intergovernmental Panel on Climate Change, suggests that there is already a discernible human influence on global climate.

Because, by definition, sustainable energy systems must support both human and ecosystem health over the long term, goals on tolerable emissions should look well into the future. They should also take into account the public's tendency to demand more health and environmental protection as prosperity increases.

Although the scope of environmental problems related to energy may seem overwhelming, numerous 'win-win' strategies could simultaneously benefit the environment (at several levels), the economy, and human well-being. For example, the replacement of solid fuels for cooking with gaseous or liquid fuels could have significant environmental benefits at the local, community, regional, and global scales, with attendant benefits for health and productivity.

ENERGY SECURITY

Energy security means the availability of energy at all times in various forms, in sufficient quantities, and at affordable prices. These conditions must prevail over the long term if energy is to contribute to sustainable development.

Attention to energy security is critical because of the uneven distribution both of the fossil fuel resources on which most countries currently rely and of capacity to develop other resources. The energy supply could become more vulnerable over the near term due to the growing global reliance on imported oil. For example, the oil dependence (net imports as a share of total demand) of OECD countries is expected to grow from 56 percent in 1996 to 72 percent in 2010.

In addition, although energy security has been adequate for the past 20 years, and has in fact improved, the potential for conflict, sabotage, disruption of trade, and reduction in strategic reserves cannot be dismissed. These potential threats point to the necessity of strengthening global as well as regional and national energy security. Options to enhance energy security include:

- Avoiding excessive dependence on imports by increasing end-use efficiency and encouraging greater reliance on local resources (particularly those whose development will have other positive externalities such as job creation, capacity building, and pollution reduction), provided these do not involve disproportionate costs or waste scarce resources.
- Diversifying supply (including both suppliers and energy forms).
- Fostering greater political stability through international cooperation and long-term agreements among energy-importing countries and between importing and exporting countries. Examples might include wider adoption – and more effective implementation of – the Energy Charter Treaty,[11] as well as increased sharing of infrastructure for transporting natural gas.
- Encouraging technology transfers (for example, through joint ventures and public-private partnerships) to developing countries so they can develop local resources and improve energy efficiencies.
- Increasing national and regional strategic reserves of crude oil and oil products through increased investment and advanced exploration technologies.

Although markets play a prominent role in securing energy supply in OECD countries, their role is modest in some developing countries and absent in others. Where markets do not flourish, the security of supply and services depends almost solely on government action and multinational companies, which may not serve the best interests of consumers. In such situations, energy security can be enhanced by encouraging the development of frameworks that allow markets to contribute to the allocation of energy resources.

Because of small fuel requirements, nuclear power contributes to the diversity of supply and to supply security. But public concerns about economic necessity, reactor safety, and radioactive waste transport and disposal – as well as weapons proliferation – have curbed nuclear energy development in many countries. A nuclear accident anywhere in the world or a proliferation incident linked to nuclear power could further reduce support for nuclear power programmes, with long-term loss in the diversity of the energy supply mix. But if generally accepted responses could be found to the above concerns, nuclear energy could contribute significantly to secure electricity generation in many parts of the world.

Individuals and commercial enterprises are also vulnerable to disruptions of energy supply. Although the trend towards the liberalisation of energy markets generally has enhanced energy security by offering more options, supplies, and competition, it has also raised concerns that those who are impoverished will be left out of the process, resulting in continued energy insecurity for some individuals.

PART 2. ENERGY RESOURCES AND TECHNOLOGICAL OPTIONS

Physical resources and technical opportunities are available – or could become available – to meet the challenge of sustainable development. Without policy changes, cost differentials may favour conventional fuels for years to come. Options for using energy in ways that support sustainable development, which requires addressing environmental concerns, include:

- More efficient use of energy, especially at the point of end use in buildings, electric appliances, vehicles, and production processes.
- Increased reliance on renewable energy sources.
- Accelerated development and deployment of new energy technologies, particularly next-generation fossil fuel technologies that produce near-zero harmful emissions – but also nuclear technologies, if the problems associated with nuclear energy can be resolved.

All three options have considerable potential, but realising this potential will require removing obstacles to wider diffusion, developing market signals that reflect environmental costs, and encouraging technological innovation.

ENERGY RESOURCES

Careful analysis of the long-term availability of energy resources, starting with conventional and unconventional oil and gas, indicates that these resources could last another 50–100 years – and possibly much longer – with known exploration and extraction technologies and anticipated technical progress in upstream operations. Coal resources and nuclear materials are so abundant that they could, respectively, last for centuries or millennia. Moreover, although fossil fuel prices may rise slowly over time, the large, cost-driven increases in energy prices projected in the 1970s and 1980s will not take place in the foreseeable future.

As evidenced by rising oil prices in the winter of 1999/2000, however, prices are subject to volatility. This may occur, for example, if cartels set prices independent of production costs. Some fluctuations in prices can also be expected, especially during the transition to a large-scale use of unconventional oil and gas resources, because the timing of investments in upstream production capacities may not correspond with demand. Other cost-pushing factors could arise from the environmentally more challenging extraction of unconventional oil resources.

Renewable resources are more evenly distributed than fossil and nuclear resources, and energy flows from renewable resources are more than three orders of magnitude higher than current global energy use. But the economic potential of renewables is affected by many constraints – including competing land uses, the amount and timing of solar irradiation, environmental concerns, and wind patterns.

Although there are no real limitations on future energy availability from a resource point of view, the existence of resources is of little relevance without consideration of how these can contribute to the supply of (downstream) energy services. Rather, the key concerns are: Can technologies to extract, harvest, and convert these vast energy stocks and flows be developed in time? Will these processes have adverse implications? Will the energy services eventually generated from these resources be affordable? Historical evidence suggests that these concerns may be at least partly offset by technological progress, but that such progress needs to be encouraged – by regulations to improve market performance, temporary subsidies, tax incentives, or other mechanisms – if it is to occur in a timely fashion.

ENERGY END-USE EFFICIENCY

The quadrupling of oil prices in the 1970s, the growing awareness of energy-related pollution, and the possibility of climate change have all contributed to a re-evaluation of energy use. The result has been an improvement in the efficiency with which energy is used in industry and power generation as well as in lighting, household appliances, transportation, and heating and cooling of buildings. This more efficient use of energy is a major factor contributing to the improvements in energy intensity that have occurred historically in almost all OECD countries, and more recently in many transition economies, as well as in some in fast-growing developing countries such as Brazil and China.

Today the global energy efficiency of converting primary energy to useful energy is about one-third (see figure 1). In other words, two-thirds of primary energy is dissipated in the conversion processes, mostly as low-temperature heat. Further significant losses occur when the useful energy delivers the energy service. Numerous and varied economic opportunities exist for energy efficiency improvements, particularly in this final conversion step from useful energy to energy services. Taking advantage of these opportunities, which have received relatively little attention, has the largest potential for cost-effective efficiency improvements. It would mean less costly energy services and lower energy-related pollution and emissions.

Over the next 20 years the amount of primary energy required for a given level of energy services could be cost-effectively reduced by 25–35 percent in industrialised countries (the higher figure being achievable by more effective policies). These reductions are mostly in the conversion step of useful energy to energy services in the residential, industrial, transportation, public, and commercial sectors. Reductions of more than 40 percent are cost-effectively achievable in transition economies. And in most developing countries – which tend to have high economic growth and old capital and vehicle stocks – the cost-effective improvement potentials range from 30 to more than 45 percent, relative to energy efficiencies achieved with existing capital stock.[12]

The improvements of about 2 percent a year implied by the above figures could be enhanced by structural changes in industrialised and transition economies, by shifts to less energy-intensive industrial production, and by saturation effects in the residential and transportation sectors. These combined effects, made up by efficiency improvements and structural changes, could lead to decreases in energy intensity of 2.5 percent a year. How much of this potential will be realised depends on the effectiveness of policy frameworks and measures, changes in attitudes and behaviour, and the level of entrepreneurial activity in energy conservation.

The next few decades will likely see new processes, motor systems, materials, vehicles, and buildings designed to reduce useful energy demand. Because the demand for cars is expected to grow rapidly in the developing world, gaining greater efficiencies in this area will be very important. In addition, rapidly industrialising countries could greatly profit from the introduction of radically new and more efficient technologies in their energy-intensive basic materials processing. Because these countries are still building their physical infrastructure, they have a growing demand for basic materials. This opens a window of opportunity to innovate and improve efficiencies of production, particularly in countries undergoing market reform. The opportunities are larger at the point of new investment, relative to retrofitting.

Over the long term, additional and dramatic gains in efficiency are possible at all stages of energy conversion, particularly from useful energy to energy services. Analysis shows that current technologies are not close to reaching theoretical limits, and that improvements of an order of magnitude for the whole energy system may eventually be achieved.[13]

For a number of reasons the technical and economic potentials of energy efficiency, as well as its positive impact on sustainable development, have traditionally been under-realised. Achieving higher end-use efficiency involves a great variety of technical options and players. Because it is a decentralised, dispersed activity, it is a difficult issue for which to organise support. And because it has little visibility, energy efficiency is not generally a popular cause for politicians, the media, or individuals looking for recognition and acknowledgement. In addition, significant barriers – primarily market imperfections that could be overcome by targeted policy instruments – prevent the realisation of greater end-use efficiencies. These barriers include:

- Lack of adequate information, technical knowledge, and training.
- Uncertainties about the performance of investments in new and energy-efficient technologies.
- Lack of adequate capital or financing possibilities.
- High initial and perceived costs of more efficient technologies.
- High transaction costs (for searching and assessing information and for training).
- Lack of incentives for careful maintenance.
- The differential benefits to the user relative to the investor (for example, when energy bills are paid by the renter rather than the property owner).
- External costs of energy use, not included in energy prices.
- Patterns and habits of consumers, operators, and decision-makers, which may be influenced by many factors, including ideas of social prestige and professional norms.

Realising cost-effective energy efficiency potentials will be beneficial not only for individual energy consumers, but also for the economy as a whole. For example, saved energy costs can be used to produce energy-saving domestic goods and services. And as cost-effective energy improvements are realised, additional profitable opportunities for improvement will continue to open up as a result of research and development, learning curves, and economies of scale. That means that continual cost-effective energy efficiency improvements can be expected.

Energy efficiency policies that use direct or indirect price mechanisms (such as the removal of subsidies and the incorporation of externalities) are effective in lowering consumption trends in price-sensitive sectors and applications. But even without changing the overall price environment, energy efficiency policies should be pursued to address market failures. For example, efficiency standards, appliance and product labelling, voluntary agreements, and professional training or contracting can increase GDP growth by improving environmental and economic performance, using a given quantity of energy. Legal standards; well-informed consumers, planners, and decision-makers; motivated operators; and an adequate payments system for energy are central to the successful implementation of energy efficiency improvements.[14]

RENEWABLE ENERGY TECHNOLOGIES

Renewable energy sources (including biomass, solar, wind, geothermal, and hydropower) that use indigenous resources have the potential to provide energy services with zero or almost zero emissions of both air pollutants and greenhouse gases. Currently, renewable energy sources supply 14 percent of the total world energy demand. The supply is dominated by traditional biomass used for cooking and heating, especially in rural areas of developing countries. Large-scale hydropower supplies 20 percent of global electricity. Its scope for expansion is limited in the industrialised world, where it has nearly reached its economic capacity. In the developing world, considerable potential still exists, but large hydropower projects may face financial, environmental, and social constraints.

Altogether, new renewable energy sources contributed 2 percent of the world's energy consumption in 1998, including 7 exajoules from modern biomass and 2 exajoules for all other renewables (geothermal, wind, solar, and marine energy, and small-scale hydropower). Solar photovoltaics and grid-connected wind installed capacities are growing at a rate of 30 percent a year. Even so, it will likely be decades before these new renewables add up to a major fraction of total energy consumption, because they currently represent such a small percentage.

Substantial price reductions in the past few decades have made some renewables competitive with fossil fuels in certain applications in growing markets. Modern, distributed forms of biomass seem particularly promising for their potential to provide rural areas with clean forms of energy based on the use of biomass resources that have traditionally been used in inefficient, polluting ways. Biomass can be economically produced with minimal or even positive environmental impacts through perennial crops. Wind power in coastal and other windy regions is promising as well.

Unlike hydropower and conventional thermal power sources, wind and solar thermal or electric sources are intermittent. Nevertheless, they can be important energy sources in rural areas where grid extension is expensive. They can also contribute to grid-connected electricity supplies in appropriate hybrid configurations. Intermittent renewables can reliably provide 10–30 percent of total electricity supplies if operated in conjunction with hydropower- or fuel-based power generation. Emerging storage possibilities and new strategies for operating grids offer promise that the role of intermittent technologies could be considerably larger.

Significant barriers, which could be overcome by appropriate frameworks and policies, stand in the way of the accelerated development of renewable technologies. These barriers include economic risks, regulatory obstacles, limited availability of products, information and technology gaps, and lack of investment. The greatest challenge is financial, even though costs have come down significantly over the past several decades. Table 4 summarises the status of various renewable technologies, and also provides information on trends in cost and capacity.

Many renewable technologies, because they are small in scale and modular, are good candidates for continued cost-cutting as a result of field experience. The cost reductions of manufactured goods, which are typically rapid at first and then taper off as the industry matures, are called experience curves. These curves resulted in industry-wide cost declines of about 20 percent for each cumulative doubling of production for solar photovoltaics, wind generators, and gas turbines – due to learning effects, marginal technological improvements, and economies of scale (figure 6). Similar declines are expected for other small-scale renewables.

A rapid expansion of renewable-based energy systems will require actions to stimulate the market in this direction. This expansion can be achieved by finding ways to drive down the relative cost of renewables in their early stages of development and commercialisation, while still taking advantage of the economic efficiencies of the marketplace. Pricing based on the full costs of conventional energy sources (including phasing out subsidies and internalising externalities) will make renewables more competitive. Because internalising external costs may be controversial for some time, 'green' pricing of electricity and heat (which lets consumers pay more for environmentally benign energy supplies if they choose) may be an immediate option in industrialised countries.

ADVANCED ENERGY TECHNOLOGIES

Fossil Energy

Sustainability goals indicate the importance of evolving fossil energy technologies towards the long-term goal of near-zero air pollutant and greenhouse gas emissions without complicated end-of-pipe control technologies. Near-term technologies and strategies should support this long-term goal.

The technological revolution under way in power generation, where advanced systems are replacing steam turbine technologies, does support this long-term goal. Natural-gas-fired combined cycles offering low costs, high efficiency, and low environmental impacts are being chosen wherever natural gas is readily available – in some countries even displacing large new hydropower projects. Cogeneration is more cost-effective and can play a much larger role in the energy economy – if based on gas turbines and combined cycles rather than on steam turbines.

Reciprocating engines and emerging microturbine and fuel cell technologies are also strong candidates for cogeneration at smaller scales, including commercial and apartment buildings. Coal gasification by partial oxidation with oxygen to produce syngas (mainly carbon monoxide and hydrogen) makes it possible to provide electricity through integrated gasifier combined cycle (IGCC) plants with air pollutant emissions nearly as low as for natural gas combined cycles. Today power from IGCC cogeneration plants is often competitive with power from coal steam-electric plants in either cogeneration or power-only configurations.

Although synthetic liquid fuels made in single-product facilities are not competitive, superclean syngas-derived synthetic fuels (such as synthetic middle distillates and dimethyl ether) produced in polygeneration facilities that make several products simultaneously may soon be. Syngas can be produced from natural gas by steam reforming or other means or from coal by gasification using oxygen, as noted. Expanding markets for clean synthetic fuels are likely to result from toughening air pollution regulations. Synthetic fuels produced through

Table 4: Current status and potential future costs of renewable energy technologies

Technology	Increase in installed capacity in past five years (percent a year)	Operating capacity, end 1998	Capacity factor (percent)	Energy production, 1998	Turnkey investment costs (U.S. dollars per kilowatt)	Current energy cost	Potential future energy cost
Biomass energy							
Electricity	≈ 3	40 GWe	25–80	160 TWh (e)	900–3000	5–15 ¢/kWh	4–10 ¢/kWh
Heat[a]	≈ 3	>200 GWth	25–80	>700 TWh (th)	250–750	1–5 ¢/kWh	1–5 ¢/kWh
Ethanol	≈ 3	18 billion litres		420 PJ		8–25 $/GJ	6–10 $/GJ
Wind electricity	≈ 30	10 GWe	20–30	18 TWh (e)	1100–1700	5–13 ¢/kWh	3–10 ¢/kWh
Solar photovoltaic electricity	≈ 30	500 MWe	8–20	0.5 TWh (e)	5000–10000	25–125 ¢/kWh	5 or 6–25 ¢/kWh
Solar thermal electricity	≈ 5	400 MWe	20–35	1 TWh (e)	3000–4000	12–18 ¢/kWh	4–10 ¢/kWh
Low-temperature solar heat	≈ 8	18 GWth (30 million m^2)	8–20	14 TWh (th)	500–1700	3–20 ¢/kWh	2 or 3–10 ¢/kWh
Hydroelectricity							
Large	≈ 2	640 GWe	35–60	2510 TWh (e)	1000–3500	2–8 ¢/kWh	2–8 ¢/kWh
Small	≈ 3	23 GWe	20–70	90 TWh (e)	1200–3000	4–10 ¢/kWh	3–10 ¢/kWh
Geothermal energy							
Electricity	≈ 4	8 GWe	45–90	46 TWh (e)	800–3000	2–10 ¢/kWh	1 or 2–8 ¢/kWh
Heat	≈ 6	11 GWth	20–70	40 TWh (th)	200–2000	0.5–5 ¢/kWh	0.5–5 ¢/kWh
Marine energy							
Tidal	0	300 MWe	20–30	0.6 TWh (e)	1700–2500	8–15 ¢/kWh	8–15 ¢/kWh
Wave	–	exp. phase	20–35	Unclear	1500–3000	8–20 ¢/kWh	Unclear
Current	–	exp. phase	25–35	Unclear	2000–3000	8–15 ¢/kWh	5–7 ¢/kWh
OTEC	–	exp. phase	70–80	Unclear	Unclear	Unclear	Unclear

Note: The cost of grid-supplied electricity in urban areas ranges from 2–3 (c/kWh (off-peak) to 15–25c/kWh) (peak). See chapter 11.
[a] Heat embodied in steam (or hot water in district heating), often produced by combined heat and power systems using forest residues, black liquor, or bagasse.
Source: Chapter 7.

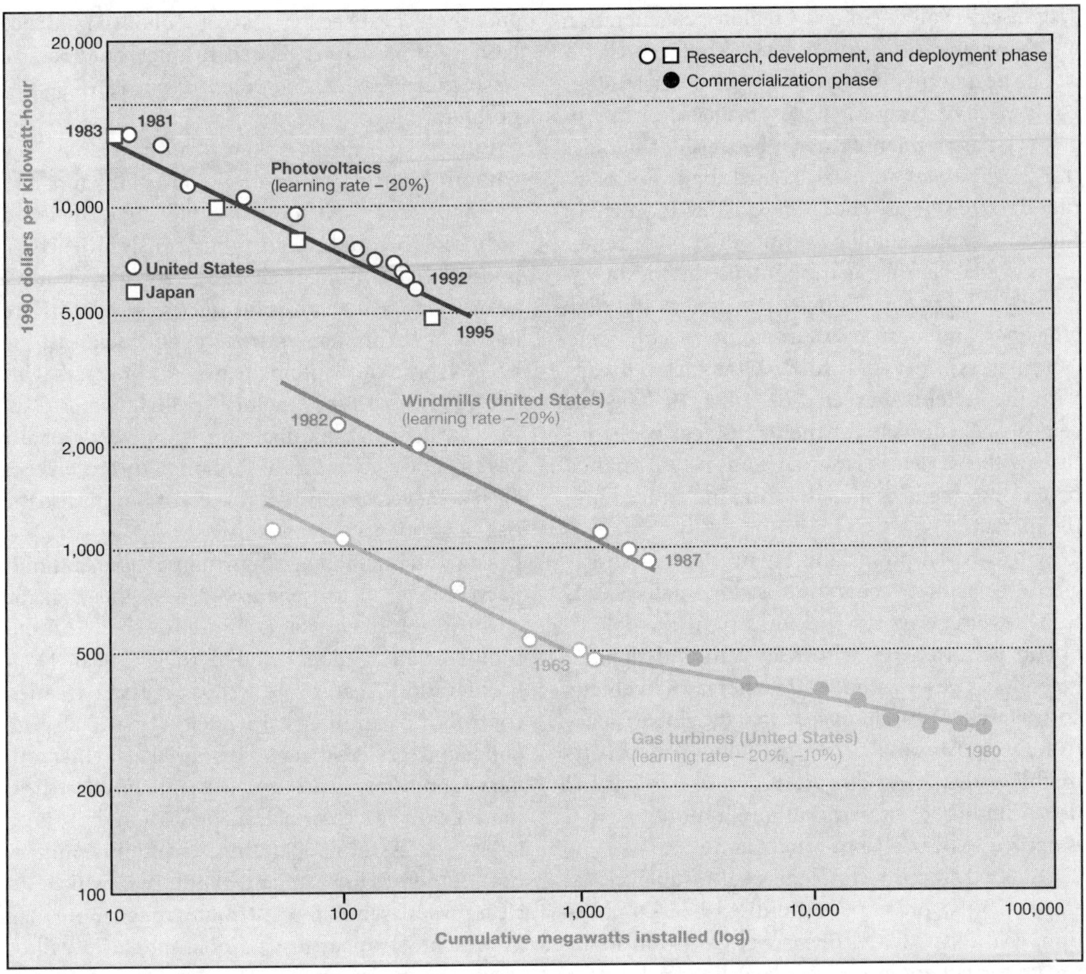

Figure 6: Experience curves for photovoltaics, windmills, and gas turbines in Japan and the United States. Technology performance and costs improve with experience, and there is a pattern to such improvements common to many technologies. The specific shape depends on the technology, but the persistent characteristic of diminishing costs is termed the 'learning' or 'experience' curve. The curve is likely to fall more sharply as technologies first seek a market niche, then full commercialisation, because lower costs become increasingly important for wider success. *Source:* Nakićenović, Grübler, and McDonald, 1998.

polygeneration will be based on natural gas if it is readily available. Synthetic middle distillates so produced are likely to be competitive where low-cost natural gas is available (as at remote developing country sites); the technology might facilitate exploitation of relatively small remote natural gas fields.

In natural-gas-poor, coal-rich regions, polygeneration based on coal gasification is promising. Such systems might include production of extra syngas for distribution by pipelines to small-scale cogeneration systems in factories and buildings – making possible clean and efficient use of coal at small as well as large scales. Rapidly growing polygeneration activity is already under way in several countries based on the gasification of low-quality petroleum feedstocks – activity that is helping to pave the way for coal-based systems.

Barriers to widespread deployment of advanced cogeneration and polygeneration systems are mainly institutional. Most systems will produce far more electricity than can be consumed on-site, so achieving favourable economics depends on being able to sell co-product electricity at competitive prices into electric grids. Utility policies have often made doing so difficult, but under the competitive market conditions towards which electric systems are evolving in many regions, cogeneration and polygeneration systems will often fare well.

The near-term pursuit of a syngas-based strategy could pave the way for widespread use of hydrogen (H_2) as an energy carrier, because for decades the cheapest way to make H_2 will be from fossil-fuel-derived syngas. The successful development of fuel cells would facilitate the introduction of H_2 for energy. Fuel cells are getting intense attention, especially for transportation, because they offer high efficiency and near-zero air pollutant emissions. Automakers are racing to develop fuel cell cars, with market entry targeted for 2004–10. The fuel cell car will compete for the role of 'car of the future' with the hybrid internal combustion engine/battery powered car already being introduced into the market.

Syngas-based power and H_2 production strategies also facilitate separation and storage of CO_2 from fossil energy systems, making it possible to obtain useful energy with near-zero emissions of greenhouse gases without large increases in energy costs. Recent research suggests that the global capacity for secure disposal of CO_2 in geological reservoirs might be adequate to dispose of CO_2 from fossil fuel use for hundreds of years, although more research is needed to be sure about this.

Other advanced technologies (ultrasupercritical steam plants, pressurised fluidised-bed combustion, coal IGCC based on partial oxidation in air for power generation, direct coal liquefaction for synthetic fuels production) offer benefits relative to conventional technologies. But unlike syngas-based technologies, such options in the near term would not offer clear paths to the long-term goal of near-zero emissions without significant increases in costs for energy services.

Nuclear Energy

World-wide, nuclear energy accounts for 6 percent of energy and 16 percent of electricity. Although nuclear energy dominates electricity generation in some countries, its initial promise has not been widely realised. Most analysts project that nuclear energy's contribution to global energy will not grow – and might decline during the initial decades of the 21st century. Nuclear power is more costly than originally projected, competition from alternative technologies is increasing, and there has been a loss of public confidence because of concerns related to safety, radioactive waste management, and potential nuclear weapons proliferation.

But because nuclear power can provide energy without emitting conventional air pollutants and greenhouse gases, it is worth exploring if advanced technologies could offer simultaneously lower costs, boost public confidence in the safety of nuclear reactors, assure that peaceful nuclear programs are not used for military purposes, and demonstrate effective nuclear waste management practices. Unlike Chernobyl-type reactors, the light water reactors (LWRs) that dominate nuclear power globally have a good safety record – although this record has been achieved at considerable cost to minimise the risk of accidents.

The potential linkage between peaceful and military uses of nuclear energy was recognised at the dawn of the nuclear age. Efforts to create a non-proliferation regime through the Nuclear Non-Proliferation Treaty and a series of regional treaties, controls on commerce in nuclear materials and goods and services that might be used to further military ambitions, and safeguards applied to nuclear materials in peaceful nuclear applications have been largely successful in separating peaceful and military uses. If there is to be an energy future in which nuclear power eventually contributes much more than at present, stronger institutional measures will be needed to maintain this separation. These measures should be complemented by technological advances aimed at limiting opportunities to acquire nuclear weapons under the guise of peaceful nuclear energy applications and to steal weapons-usable nuclear materials.

Reactor development activity for the near term has involved both evolutionary LWRs and new concepts. Reactor vendors now offer several evolutionary LWRs with improved safety features and standardised designs, for which there can be a high degree of confidence that performance and cost targets will be met. Another evolutionary activity involves modifying LWRs to make them more proliferation resistant through a denatured uranium or thorium fuel cycle. One concept being revisited, the pebble bed modular reactor, offers the potential for a high degree of inherent safety without the need for complicated, capital-intensive safety controls. A pebble bed modular reactor could also be operated on a proliferation resistant denatured uranium- or thorium fuel cycle.

Access to low-cost uranium supplies could constrain nuclear power development based on LWRs. The plutonium breeder reactor, which requires reprocessing spent fuel to recover plutonium for recycling in fresh fuel, was once thought to be a viable option for addressing this challenge. But electricity costs for breeders would probably be higher than for LWRs, at least until late in the 21st century, and preventing proliferation is much more challenging with reprocessing and plutonium recycling than with LWRs operated on once-through fuel cycles.

Other long-term options for addressing the nuclear resource constraint are alternative breeder concepts – including particle-accelerator-driven reactors, uranium from seawater, and thermonuclear fusion. The prospective costs, safety, and proliferation resistance features of such alternative breeder concepts are uncertain, and the concepts would take decades to develop. Recent research suggests it might be feasible, at relatively low cost, to extract uranium from seawater, where its concentration is low but total quantities are vast. If the technology could be deployed at globally significant scales, it might be feasible to avoid making major commitments to nuclear fuel reprocessing and plutonium recycling. Fusion could provide an almost inexhaustible energy supply, but it will probably not be commercially available before 2050.

Radioactive waste by-products of nuclear energy must be isolated so that they can never return to the human environment in concentrations that could cause significant harm. Although the safety of long-term waste disposal has not been proven, the technical community is confident that this objective can be realised – largely because of the small volumes of wastes involved. But in most countries there is no social consensus on the goals and standards for radioactive waste disposal and on strategies (both interim and long-term) for implementing them. The issues involved are only partly technical. The current social stalemate on waste disposal not only clouds prospects for nuclear expansion, it also has made spent fuel reprocessing a de facto interim nuclear waste management strategy in some countries. This has happened even though fuel reprocessing does not offer economic gains and does not solve the waste disposal problem – it merely buys time and is creating large inventories of plutonium that must be disposed of with low proliferation risk.

PART 3. ARE SUSTAINABLE FUTURES POSSIBLE?

Analysis using energy scenarios indicates that it is possible to simultaneously address the sustainable development objectives set forth in part 1 using the resources and technical options presented in part 2. The scenarios exercise and subsequent sections suggest that:

- Continuing along the current path of energy system development is not compatible with sustainable development objectives.
- Realising sustainable futures will require much greater reliance on some combination of higher energy efficiencies, renewable resources, and advanced energy technologies.
- A prerequisite for achieving an energy future compatible with sustainable development objectives is finding ways to accelerate progress for new technologies along the energy innovation chain, from research and development to demonstration, deployment, and diffusion.
- Providing energy services to rural areas poses particular challenges. But it also offers considerable opportunity for improving the lives of billions of people within a relatively short period. Promising approaches include decentralized solutions, appropriate technologies, innovative credit arrangements, and local involvement in decision-making.

ENERGY SCENARIOS

Energy scenarios provide a framework for exploring future energy perspectives, including various combinations of technology options and their implications. Many scenarios in the literature illustrate the degree to which energy system developments will affect the global issues analysed in part 1. Some describe energy futures that are compatible with sustainable development goals. Key developments in sustainable scenarios include increases in energy efficiencies and the adoption of advanced energy supply technologies. Sustainable development

Table 5: Summary of three energy development cases in 2050 and 2100 compared with 1990

		Case A High growth	Case B Middle growth	Case C Ecologically driven
Population (billions)	1990	5.3	5.3	5.3
	2050	10.1	10.1	10.1
	2100	11.7	11.7	11.7
Gross world product (trillions of 1990 dollars)	1990	20	20	20
	2050	100	75	75
	2100	300	200	220
Gross world product (annual percentage change)	1990–2050	High	Medium	Medium
	1990–2100	2.7	2.2	2.2
		2.5	2.1	2.2
Primary energy intensity (megajoules per 1990 dollar of gross world product)	1990	19.0	19.0	19.0
	2050	10.4	11.2	8.0
	2100	6.1	7.3	4.0
Primary energy intensity improvement rate (annual percentage change)	1990–2050	Medium	Low	High
	1990–2100	−0.9	−0.8	−1.4
		−1.0	−0.8	−1.4
Primary energy consumption (exajoules)	1990	379	379	379
	2050	1041	837	601
	2100	1859	1464	880
Cumulative primary energy consumption, 1990–2100 (thousands of exajoules)	Coal	8.9–30.7	15.3	7.1–7.2
	Oil	27.6–15.7	15.3	10.9
	Natural gas	18.4–28.7	15.8	12.2–12.9
	Nuclear energy	6.2–11.2	10.5	2.1–6.2
	Hydropower			
	Biomass	3.7–4.2	3.6	3.6–4.0
	Solar energy	7.4–14.3	8.3	9.1–10.1
	Other	1.8–7.7	1.9	6.3–7.4
	Global total	3.0–4.7	4.3	1.4–2.2
		94.0–94.9	77.2	56.9
Energy technology cost reductions (through learning)	Fossil	High	Medium	Low
	Non-fossil	High	Medium	High
Energy technology diffusion rates	Fossil	High	Medium	Medium
	Non-fossil	High	Medium	Medium
Environmental taxes (excluding carbon dioxide taxes)		No	No	Yes
Sulphur dioxide emissions (millions of tonnes of sulphur)	1990	58.6	58.6	58.6
	2050	44.8 – 64.2	54.9	22.1
	2100	9.3 – 55.4	58.3	7.1
Carbon dioxide emission constraints and taxes		No	No	Yes
Net carbon dioxide emissions (gigatonnes of carbon)	1990	6	6	6
	2050	9–15	10	5
	2100	6–20	11	2
Cumulative carbon dioxide emissions (gigatonnes of carbon)	1990–2100	910–1450	1000	540
Carbon dioxide concentrations (parts per million by volume)	1990	358	358	358
	2050	460–510	470	430
	2100	530–730	590	430
Carbon intensity (grams of carbon per 1990 dollar of gross world product)	1990	280	280	280
	2050	90–140	130–60	70–10
	2100	20–60		
Investments in energy supply sector (trillions of 1990 dollars)	1990–2020	15.7	12.4	9.4
	2020–50	24.7	22.3	14.1
	2050–2100	93.7	82.3	43.3
Number of scenarios		3	1	2

The three cases unfold into six scenarios of energy system alternatives: three case A scenarios (A1, ample oil and gas; A2, return to coal; and A3, non-fossil future), a single case B scenario (middle course), and two case C scenarios (C1, new renewables; and C2, new renewables and new nuclear). Some of the scenario characteristics, such as cumulative energy consumption, cumulative carbon dioxide emissions, and decarbonisation, are shown as ranges for the three case A and two C scenarios.
Source: Nakićenović, Grübler, and McDonald, 1998.

Table 6: Characteristics of sustainability in three energy development scenarios in 2050 and 2100 compared with 1990

Indicator of sustainability	1990	Scenario A3	Scenario B	Scenario C1
Eradicating poverty	Low	Very high	Medium	Very high
Reducing relative income gaps	Low	High	Medium	Very high
Providing universal access to energy	Low	Very high	High	Very high
Increasing affordability of energy	Low	High	Medium	Very high
Reducing adverse health impacts	Medium	Very high	High	Very high
Reducing air pollution	Medium	Very high	High	Very high
Limiting long-lived radionuclides	Medium	Very low	Very low	High
Limiting toxic materials[a]	Medium	High	Low	High
Limiting GHG emissions	Low	High	Low	Very high
Raising indigenous energy use	Medium	High	Low	Very high
Improving supply efficiency	Medium	Very high	High	Very high
Increasing end-use efficiency	Low	High	Medium	Very high
Accelerating technology diffusion	Low	Very high	Medium	Medium

[a] For this row only, the qualitative indicators are not based on quantitative features of the scenarios, but were specified by the authors on the basis of additional assumptions.
Source: Chapter 9.

scenarios are characterised by low environmental impacts (local, regional, and global) and equitable allocation of resources and wealth.

The three cases of alternative global developments presented in chapter 9 suggest how the future could unfold in terms of economic growth, population trends, and energy use. The challenge is formidable. For example, by 2100, 6–8 billion additional people – significantly more than today's world population – will need access to affordable, reliable, flexible, and convenient energy services.[15] All three cases achieve this through different energy system developments, but with varying degrees of success in terms of sustainability (table 5).

A middle-course, or reference, case (B) includes one scenario and is based on the general direction in which the world is now headed. This scenario assumes the continuation of an intermediate level of economic growth and modest technological improvement, and it leads to adverse environmental impacts, including regional acidification and climate change. Although this middle-course scenario represents a substantial improvement relative to the current situation, it falls short of achieving a transition towards sustainable development. The other two scenarios and their variants lead to higher economic development with vigorous improvement of energy technologies. They both – and especially the ecologically driven case (C) – achieve, to a much higher degree, a transition towards sustainable development (table 6).

For instance, one of the three high-growth case A scenarios (A3) achieves some goals of sustainable development, primarily through rapid economic growth and a shift towards environmentally more benign energy technologies and options. In this scenario, higher levels of affluence result from impressive technological development, including a significant role for clean fossil, renewable, and nuclear energy. Dedicated decarbonisation of the energy system contributes to environmental sustainability. Two other variants of this high-growth case are also considered. Both lead to higher dependence on carbon-intensive fossil fuels, resulting in high energy-related emissions. Consequently, they are unsustainable from an environmental point of view.

A third case (C) includes two scenarios and is ecologically driven, with high growth in developing countries (towards being rich and 'green'). The difference between the two scenarios is that one, C1, assumes a global phase-out of nuclear energy by 2100, whereas the other, C2, does not. Both assume the introduction of carbon and energy taxes directed at promoting renewables and end-use efficiency improvements. The revenues from carbon and energy taxes are assumed to be used to enhance economic growth and promote renewables and end-use efficiency, rather than to reduce other taxes in industrialised regions.

Both case C scenarios assume decentralisation of energy systems and reliance on local solutions. They also require considerably lower supply-side investments than the others. They would, however, require substantial investments in the end-use sector, which is not captured in the scenarios. Ambitious

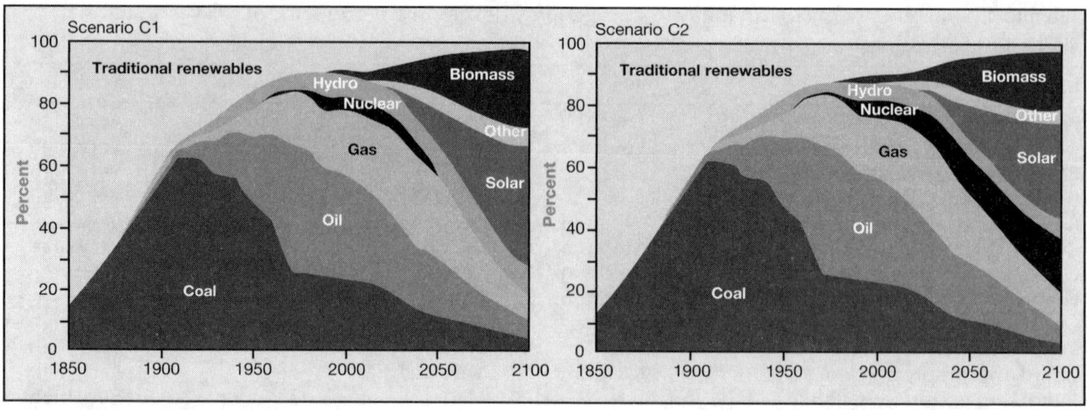

Figure 7: Primary energy shares, 1850–1990, and in scenarios C1 and C2 to 2100. *Source:* Nakićenović, Grübler, and McDonald, 1998.

policy measures control local and regional pollutants, and a global regime results in reduced greenhouse gas emissions. Of the three cases considered, case C is the most compatible with the aims of sustainable development, as analysed in part 1 (table 6). In scenario C1 this occurs through a diminishing contribution of coal and oil to the primary energy mix, with a large increase in the share of solar and biomass energy by 2100 (figure 7).

Also shown for illustrative purposes is the primary energy mix for scenario C2, in which nuclear energy could play a large role if the problems associated with it (cost, safety, waste disposal and weapons proliferation) can be adequately resolved.

The considerable differences in expected total energy consumption among the scenarios reflect different approaches to addressing the needs for energy services in the future, and they demonstrate clearly that policy matters (figure 8). Achieving the two scenarios with characteristics of sustainable development will require a substantial increase in private and public research, development, and deployment efforts to support new energy technologies. Otherwise, most clean fossil and renewable technologies, as well as many energy-efficient end-use technologies, may not reach competitiveness. (The mix of needed efforts may vary depending on the maturity of the specific technology.) Significant technological advances will be required, as will incremental improvements in conventional energy technologies.

In terms of their expected high growth in energy demand, developing countries are well-positioned to take advantage of innovations in energy technologies and policies that support them. In general, scenarios A3, C1, and C2 require significant policy and behavioural changes within the next several decades to achieve more sustainable development paths. Taken together, the outcomes of these changes, which are described in more detail in part 4, represent a clear departure from a business-as-usual approach.

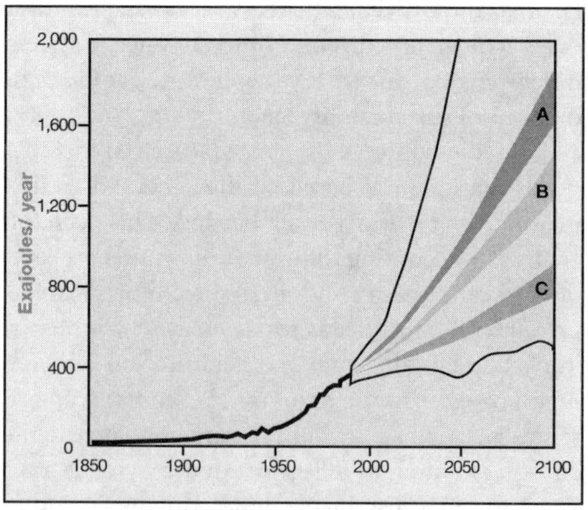

Figure 8: Global primary energy requirements, 1850–1990, and in three cases, 1990–2100. The figure also shows the wide range of future energy requirements for other scenarios in the literature. The vertical line that spans the scenario range in 1990 indicates the uncertainty across the literature of base-year energy requirements. *Source:* Nakićenović, Grübler, and McDonald, 1998; Morita and Lee, 1998; Nakićenović, Victor, and Morita, 1998.

Another crucial prerequisite for achieving sustainability in the scenarios is near-universal access to adequate, affordable energy services and more equitable allocation of resources. Finally, environmental protection – from indoor pollution to climate change – is an essential characteristic of sustainable development in these scenarios. The resolution of these future challenges offers a window of opportunity between now and 2020. The nature of the decisions made during this time will largely determine whether the evolution of the energy system is consistent with current practices (along the lines of the B scenario), or whether it achieves the transition towards more sustainable development paths (along the lines of the A3, C1, and C2 scenarios).

Because of the long lifetimes of power plants, refineries, steel plants, buildings, and other energy-related investments such as transportation infrastructure, there is not sufficient turnover of such facilities to reveal large differences among the alternative scenarios presented here before 2020. But the seeds of the post-2020 world will have been sown by then. Thus choices about the world's future energy systems are relatively wide open now. This window of opportunity is particularly significant where much infrastructure has yet to be installed, offering the possibility of a rapid introduction of new, environmentally sound technologies.

Once the infrastructure is in place, a phase of largely replacement investments begins. Changes can be made in this phase, but they take much longer to affect average system performance. If wise decisions are not made during the next few decades, we will be locked into those choices, and certain development opportunities might not be achievable. Thus the achievement of sustainable development demands a global perspective, a very long time horizon, and the timely introduction of policy measures.

RURAL ENERGY IN DEVELOPING COUNTRIES

Between 1970 and 1990 about 800 million additional people were reached by rural electrification programmes. Some 500 million saw their lives improve substantially through the use of better methods for cooking and other rural energy tasks, particularly in China. Despite these enormous efforts to improve energy services to rural populations in the past 20–30 years, the unserved population has remained about the same in absolute numbers – 2 billion people.

Although the unavailability of adequate energy services in rural areas is probably the most serious energy problem confronting humanity in the near future, rural energy remains low on the list of priorities of most government and corporate planners. And the increased demands of the more influential (and rapidly growing) urban population will make it more difficult to keep rural development on the agenda.

An effective strategy to address the energy needs of rural populations is to promote the climbing of the 'energy ladder'. This implies moving from simple biomass fuels (dung, crop residues, firewood) to the most convenient, efficient form of energy appropriate to the task at hand – usually liquid or gaseous fuels for cooking and heating and electricity for most other uses. Such climbing involves not only a shift to modern fuels but is often also complemented by the synergistic use of modern, more efficient endtrsuse devices such as cooking stoves.

Climbing the energy ladder does not necessarily mean that all the rungs used in the past should be re-climbed. In the case of cooking, for example, users do not have to go from fuelwood to kerosene to liquefied petroleum gas (LPG) or electricity. What users should do – whenever possible – is leapfrog directly from fuelwood to the most efficient end-use technologies and the least polluting energy forms (including new renewables) available. Because of the emergence of new technologies, it is also possible to introduce new rungs on the energy ladder, and gain even greater efficiencies and environmental acceptability.

The energy-related sustainable development goals for rural areas are to:

- Satisfy basic human needs by providing all households with minimally adequate amounts of electricity for uses such as lighting and fans, in addition to cleaner cooking fuels. Specifically, all households should move away from unprocessed solid fuels (biomass and coal) for cooking and heating to modern energy forms, which may potentially be derived from renewable sources (biomass and solar) or fossil fuels.

- Provide electricity that is sufficiently affordable to support industrial activity in rural areas, which can provide employment and help curb urban migration.

In many cases the rural poor are willing and able to pay for energy services if appropriate financing options are offered to help them meet high first costs. The economics of providing basic electricity to rural households should be evaluated according to the costs of supplying comparable energy services through less efficient carriers. In most cases home solar photovoltaic systems can provide energy services at a lower cost than the kerosene and batteries they replace and can be an economically viable source of rural household power, even at relatively low levels of service provision.

The availability of affordable and adequate energy services in rural areas could lead to significant improvements in living conditions and to the fulfilment of basic human needs over a relatively short time frame. The amount of energy needed to provide such services in rural areas is relatively small. Modern ways of using biomass more efficiently could go a long way towards achieving this objective. Experience has shown that to find the most viable and appropriate solutions to rural energy, the active participation of the people who will use it is a must.

The challenge is to find ways to make modern energy carriers affordable to satisfy the basic needs of all rural residents – which may, at least initially, require subsidies. The key is to introduce market efficiencies if possible to use the smallest subsidy needed to achieve social objectives. If a subsidy is required, it might be provided as an integral part of a new social contract, whereby energy providers serve rural energy needs while simultaneously, highly competitive conditions are created in the energy sector (a key element of energy reforms). One way to finance the subsidies that might be needed would be to complement the creation of competitive markets with the establishment of a public benefits fund generated by non-bypassable wire and pipe charges on electricity and on gas providers. Such funds have been adopted or are under consideration in several countries as a means of protecting public benefits under competitive market conditions. Other options include carefully designed economic incentives, perhaps using tax regimes.

Specifically, some of these revenues could be used to subsidise the very poorest households until they are able to work themselves out of poverty. This strategy could be made entirely consistent with a shift to greater reliance on market forces to efficiently allocate resources. If, for example, a rural energy concession was the preferred approach for bringing adequate energy services at a set price to a particular rural area, and if the concession was awarded competitively, market forces would be brought into play to find the least costly mix of energy technologies with the least amount of subsidy to satisfy the concessionaire's obligation to provide affordable energy services to all.

PART 4. WHERE DO WE GO FROM HERE?

Part 4 identifies key strategies and policies for achieving both economic growth and sustainable human development. They include:

- Setting the right framework conditions – including continued market reforms, consistent regulations, and targeted policies – to encourage competition in energy markets, reduce the cost of energy services to end users, and protect important public benefits.
- Sending accurate price signals, including phasing out subsidies to conventional energy and internalising externalities.
- Removing obstacles or providing incentives, as needed, to encourage greater energy efficiency and the development and diffusion to wider markets of new sustainable energy technologies.

The challenge of sustainable energy will require a concerted effort from national governments, the energy community, civil society, the private sector, international organisations, and individuals. Whatever the difficulties of taking appropriate action, they are small relative to what is at stake. Because today's world is in a dynamic and critical period of economic, technological, demographic, and structural transition, and because energy systems take decades to change, the time to act is now.

ENERGY AND ECONOMIC PROSPERITY

The demand of industrialised and transition economies for energy services is likely to grow, although increasing efficiency in conversion and end uses may result in a levelling off or even a reduction in the demand for primary energy. In developing countries, however, primary energy demand is expected to grow at about 2.5 percent a year as industrialisation and motorisation proceed and living standards improve.

Meeting these projected demands will be essential if developing countries are to achieve economic prosperity. It will require considerable investment – on the order of 2.0–2.5 percent of the GDP of developing countries over the next 20 years. This is close to historical norms and, with good financial and economic policies, should be affordable. In the past, energy investments in developing countries rested heavily – and unnecessarily – on government subsidies, and too little on the financial resources that would be generated by real cost-based pricing, regulatory policies, and efficient management.

In general, there is no reason the energy sector should not be financially self-sufficient in the following sense: appropriate pricing and regulatory policies would raise revenues to cover operating costs and generate returns on investment sufficient to attract largescale private finance and investment. Indeed, one of the primary aims of market liberalisation and the new forms of regulation introduced in many countries in the 1990s was precisely this: to reduce the need for government subvention and to attract private capital and investment to the energy sector. The other aims were to encourage innovation, cost-effectiveness, and managerial efficiency.

But temporary government subsidies may be needed to help people who are excluded from the market by extreme poverty. Just as poor areas in today's industrialised countries benefited in the past from non-market energy policies, such options should be still available, when justified, in developing countries. Moreover, the poor may need to be shielded from economic hardships caused by trends over which they have no control. In some developing countries, for instance, the oil price increases of the 1970s and early 1980s contributed to large increases in external debt – up to 50 percent in some cases.[16] The effects of that debt – impoverishment of the country and widespread unemployment – were particularly hard on the poor, even though their main source of fuel was and continues to be firewood rather than oil. The debt burden from the 1970s persists in many developing countries.

Although there seem to be no physical limitations on total energy resources, potentially severe problems are likely if appropriate economic, technological, and environmental policies are not developed in a timely manner. Rational energy pricing is part of what is needed, but so is a willingness to prompt markets to find technological solutions to problems before they begin exacting high societal and environmental costs. Finding ways to curb energy-related greenhouse gas emissions and to address other environmental problems, while still expanding energy services, will require enlightened research, development, and demonstration policies. Much therefore will depend on the energy and environmental policies that are introduced, and on their relationship to the forces of globalisation and liberalization (discussed below).

Thanks to technological advances and better information on impacts, developing countries are in a position to address local and regional environmental problems early in the 21st century, and at an earlier stage of development than industrialised countries did. By addressing these negative externalities of energy generation and use early on, developing countries would find their overall economic well-being and the prospects of their people improved, not diminished. The issue of global climate change, however, may prove more difficult to reconcile with high levels of economic growth.

Overall, however, the analysis in this report suggests that there are no fundamental technological, economic, or resource limits constraining the world from enjoying the benefits of both high levels of energy services and a better environment. This is not to suggest that these benefits are to be expected – only that they are achievable. As the scenarios discussed above demonstrate, sustainable futures depend on ambitious policy measures and support for technological innovation.

In analysing appropriate policies, it is important to keep in mind key features of the political and economic environment in which new energy systems will evolve:

- *The broad structure of macroeconomic and development policies* – particularly those for education and broad-based growth. Below a certain level of per capita income, subsistence needs other than energy dominate household budgets and priorities. Income growth among groups without access is the most important determinant of whether they will be willing to pay for energy services (and thus provide the demand required for markets to work effectively).

This, in turn, depends on policies beyond the control of energy industries.

- *The widespread liberalisation of energy markets and the restructuring of the energy sector.* These changes are driven by inefficient monopolies, government budget constraints, and expanding technological opportunities – especially in electric power generation. Liberalisation and restructuring can lower costs and generate the finance required for the expansion and extension of supplies (as long as it is profitable to do so). But in restructured energy markets, cross-subsidies will not be available to increase access in areas that are not attractive to investors, unless restructuring is accompanied by policy measures that specifically address such concerns.

- *Globalisation and the transformations of the information age.* Related to the liberalisation of markets is globalisation – the world-wide expansion of major companies and their acquisition of, or partnership with, local companies. Procurement of materials and services from distant and foreign sources has become common. New technologies are also diffusing at rates faster than ever before, spurred by world-wide access to the Internet and other information technologies. This expansion can expedite the awareness of sustainable energy options and the deployment of new technologies.

ENERGY POLICIES FOR SUSTAINABLE DEVELOPMENT

The scenarios exercise showed that, although energy can contribute to sustainable development, its performance in this respect will depend on a range of factors. These include attitudes and behaviour, information and technologies, the availability of finance and supporting institutions, and – in particular – policies and policy frameworks that encourage change in the desired direction. The current path of energy development, and the rate of change, are not compatible with key elements of sustainable development. The divergence of alternative futures that becomes apparent in the scenarios after about 20 years reflects the long-term nature of energy systems. It also indicates that if governments, corporations, and international institutions do not introduce appropriate policies and measures now, critical windows of opportunity are likely to close. It will then become even more difficult to change course.

The most critical issues that sustainable energy strategies and the policies derived from them need to address are how to widen access to reliable and affordable modern energy supplies, and how to ease the negative health and environmental impacts of energy use.

Given proper frameworks, pricing signals, and regulatory regimes, markets can efficiently deliver on the economic objectives of sustainable development. But markets alone cannot be expected to meet the needs of the most vulnerable groups and to protect the environment. Where markets fail to protect these and other important public benefits, targeted government policies and consistent regulatory approaches will be needed. The problem is that government interventions are usually less efficient than market approaches. Government intervention may have unintended consequences at odds with its original aims. For that reason, there is a need to try different approaches and learn from the experiences of other countries.

Policies and policy frameworks in support of sustainable development should focus on widening access, encouraging energy efficiency, accelerating new renewable energy diffusion, and expanding the use of advanced clean fossil fuel technologies, while keeping open the nuclear option. These policy areas, as well as related decisions on private-public transportation and city planning, have the greatest relevance to the environmental and safety problems associated with conventional fuels.

The broad strategies for encouraging sustainable energy systems are straightforward. But achieving them will require wide acknowledgement of the challenges we face and stronger commitment to specific policies. The strategies are largely aimed at harnessing market efficiencies to the goal of sustainable development and using additional measures to speed up innovation, overcome obstacles and market imperfections, and protect important public benefits. Among the basic strategies, six stand out.

Making Markets Work Better

Driven by the forces of competition, markets do a better job than administered systems in allocating resources. But the marketplace fails to adequately account for the social and environmental costs of energy provision and use. Policies that reduce market distortions – that level the playing field – would give sustainable energy (renewable sources, energy efficiency measures, new technologies with nearzero emissions) a considerably better market position relative to current uses and practices.

Market distortions can be reduced by phasing out permanent subsidies to conventional energy (estimated at $250–300 billion a year in the mid-1990s) and by including social and environmental costs in prices. Several countries have experimented with energy and environment taxes as a way to address the latter. In many cases incentives will be needed to induce or accelerate changes. One such option is a targeted, time-limited (through a 'sunset clause') subsidy. Where energy markets cannot function effectively because of absolute poverty, additional resources, including official development assistance, are required.

Another aspect of making markets work better is finding ways to overcome obstacles to energy end-use efficiency measures. Even in the absence of subsidies, market barriers – such as lack of technological knowledge, different interests of investors and users, and high transaction costs of individual investors – keep energy efficiency measures from reaching their cost-effective potential. Options to overcome these barriers include voluntary or mandatory standards (effectively applied) for appliances, vehicles, and buildings, labeling schemes to better inform consumers, procurement policies to achieve higher standards and economies of scale, technical training in new energy efficiency technologies and their maintenance, and credit mechanisms to help consumers meet higher first costs.

Complementing Energy Sector Restructuring with Regulations that Encourage Sustainable Energy

The ongoing, world-wide restructuring of the energy industry – largely driven by the increasing globalisation of the economy – will lead to more economically efficient energy markets. This restructuring presents a window of opportunity for ensuring that the energy-related public benefits needed for sustainable development are adequately addressed in emerging policies for energy market reform. The process could be enhanced if governments set goals that define the performance characteristics of qualifying sustainable energy technologies (for example, by specifying air pollution emission limits or minimum standards on plants, machinery, and vehicles).

These goals for suppliers can be complemented by mechanisms that favour sustainable energy technologies in energy market choices. Other regulatory approaches supportive of sustainable energy include mandating that a certain percentage of energy comes from renewable sources, requiring that energy grids be open to independent power producers, and ensuring that rural populations are served. Such regulations are based on the recognition that energy market restructuring in itself may not help achieve sustainable development.

Mobilising Additional Investments in Sustainable Energy

Energy markets in many countries are rapidly becoming more competitive. For that reason, successful sustainable energy policies, whether involving financing, incentives, taxes, or regulations, must engage the private sector and catalyse private investment on a large scale. But for political or institutional reasons, many of the transition and developing economies that most need investment have problems attracting private enterprise and gaining access to financial markets. Reliable commercial legislation and jurisdiction, as well as incentives, may be needed to encourage private companies to invest in sustainable energy – or to defray the risks associated with such investments.

Official developement assistance may also need to play a greater role in the least developed countries, especially in those where the conditions that attract private sector investment are lacking. Political stability, application of the rule of law, avoidance of arbitrary intervention, and the existence of institutions that facilitate savings and investment are generally important for promoting investment. Supportive financial and credit arrangements (including microcredit arrangements like those now in existence) will be needed to introduce commercial energy to people excluded from markets, especially in rural areas.

Encouraging Technological Innovation

Currently applied technologies are not adequate and profitable enough to deliver the energy services that will be needed in the 21st century and simultaneously protect human health and environmental stability. Adequate support for a portfolio of promising advanced and new technologies is one way to help ensure that options will be available as the need for them becomes more acute. Energy innovations face barriers all along the energy innovation chain (from research and development, to demonstration projects, to cost buy-down, to widespread diffusion). Some of these barriers reflect market imperfections, some inadequacies in the public sector, and some different views about needs, corporate priorities, relevant time horizons, and reasonable costs.

The public support needed to overcome such barriers will vary from one technology to the next, depending on its maturity and market potential. Obstacles to technology diffusion, for example, may need to be given higher priority than barriers to innovation. Direct government support is more likely to be needed for radically new technologies than for incremental advances, where the private sector usually functions relatively effectively. Options to support technological innovation, while still using competition to keep down costs, include tax incentives, collaborative research and development ventures, government or cooperative procurement policies, 'green' labelling schemes, and market transformation initiatives.

Supporting Technological Leadership and Capacity Building in Developing Countries

Because most of the projected growth in energy demand will occur in the developing world, innovation and leadership in energy technologies could be highly profitable for developing countries in economic, environmental, and human terms. Developing economies need to further develop their resources – human, natural, and technological – so they can create energy systems appropriate to their own circumstances. But they also need assistance with technology transfer, financing, and capacity building.

The declining share of official development assistance relative to required investment capital suggests that much of this investment will need to be led by the private sector or private-public partnerships. International industrial collaboration offers one means by which the private sector could gain markets while fostering the private research institutes, and regional institutes that provide training in technological management offer additional possibilities for furthering technology sharing and capacity building.

Encouraging Greater Cooperation at the International Level

The ongoing process of globalisation means that ideas, finances, and energy flow from one country to another. Productive ways of moving forward might include combining national efforts, for example, in the procurement of renewable energy technologies. Other options include international harmonisation of environmental taxes and emissions trading (particularly among industrialised countries), as well as energy efficiency standards for mass-produced products and imports of used machinery and vehicles. The need for concerted action on energy is clear from Agenda 21, which emerged from the 1992 Earth Summit.

The challenge of sustainable energy includes crucial enabling roles for governments, international organisations, multilateral financial institutions, and civil society, including nongovernmental organisations and individual consumers. Partnerships will be required, based on more integrated, cooperative approaches and drawing on a range of practical experience. A common denominator across all sectors and regions is setting the right framework conditions and making public institutions work effectively and efficiently with the rest of society and other economic actors to reach beneficial, shared objectives.

Clearly, energy can serve as a powerful tool for sustainable development. Redirecting its power to work towards that overarching goal, however, will require major changes of policy within an enabling overall framework. Poverty, inequity, inefficiency, unreliable service, immediate environmental priorities, a lack of information and basic skills, and an absence of needed institutions and resources – require changes to be made. Unless these changes occur within the next few decades, many of the opportunities now available will be lost, the possibilities for future generations diminished, and the goal of sustainable development unrealised.

References

De Almeida, E., and A. de Oliveira. 1995. "Brazilian Life Style and Energy Consumption". In *Energy Demand, Life Style Changes and Technology Development.* London: World Energy Council.

IEA (International Energy Agency). 1999. *Energy Balances of OECD Countries.* Paris.

Morita, T., and H.-C. Lee. 1998. "IPCC SRES Database, Version 0.1, Emission Scenario". Database prepared for IPCC Special Report on Emissions Scenarios, http://www.cger.nies.go.jp/ cger-e/db/ipcc.html.

Nakićenović, N., A. Grübler, and A. McDonald, eds. 1998. *Global Energy Perspectives.* Cambridge: Cambridge University Press.

Nakićenović, N., N. Victor, and T. Morita. 1998. "Emissions Scenarios Database and Review of Scenarios". *Mitigation and Adaptation Strategies for Global Change* 3 (2–4): 95–120.

UN (United Nations). 1992. *Earth Summit Agenda 21: The United Nations Programme of Action from Rio.* New York.

UNDP (United Nations Development Programme). 1997. *Energy after Rio.* New York.

WCED (World Commission on Environment and Development). 1987. *Our Common Future.* Oxford: Oxford University Press.

WEC (World Energy Council). 1998. *Round Up: 17th Congress of the World Energy Council.* London.

______. 2000. *Statement 2000: Energy for Tomorrow's World – Acting Now!* London.

WEC-FAO (World Energy Council and Food and Agriculture Organization of the United Nations). 1999. *The Challenge of Rural Energy Poverty in Developing Countries.* London.

World Bank. 1996. Rural Energy and Development: Improving Energy Supplies for Two Billion People. Washington, D.C.

______. 1997. World Development Indicators 1997. Washington, D.C.

WRI (World Resources Institute). 1998. *A Guide to the Global Environment.* Oxford: Oxford University Press.

Notes

1. In this report the term *industrialised countries* refers primarily to highincome countries that belong to the Organisation for Economic Cooperation and Development (OECD). *Developing countries* generally refers to lower income countries that are members of the G-77 and China. Although many *transition economies* also have a high degree of industrialisation, they are often considered and discussed separately because of their specific development requirements.

2. In this report the terms *traditional energy* and *non-commercial energy* are used to denote locally collected and unprocessed biomass-based fuels, such as crop residues, wood, and animal dung. Although traditional energy sources can be used renewably, in this report the term *new renewables* refers to modern biofuels, wind, solar, small-scale hydropower, marine, and geothermal energy.

3. The Brundtland Report, as the World Commission on Environment and Development report is commonly known, set forth a global agenda for change.

4. Energy's links to sustainable development were most recently acknowledged by the UN General Assembly Special Session on Small Island Developing States in 1999. The major conferences that noted the importance of energy issues were the UN Conference on Population and the UN Conference on Small Island Developing States in 1994, the Copenhagen Social Summit and the Beijing Fourth World Conference on Women in 1995, and the World Food Summit and HABITAT II in 1996. The energy issues emerging from these conferences are summarised in chapters 1 and 2 of UNDP (1997).

5. Agenda 21 is the plan of action for sustainable development adopted at the Rio Earth Summit.

6. Means for achieving these objectives are discussed in more detail in WEC (2000).

7. Unless otherwise noted, all prices are in U.S. dollars.

8. This target was reaffirmed in 1992 (in chapter 33 of Agenda 21).

9. In this report the term *conventional energy* is used to refer to fossil fuel, nuclear energy, and large-scale hydropower.

10. In this report the word *insult* is used to describe a physical stressor produced by the energy system, such as air pollution. The word *impact* is used to describe the resulting outcome, such as respiratory disease or forest degradation.

11. The Energy Charter Treaty, together with a protocol on energy efficiency and related environmental aspects, entered into force in 1998. It has been signed by about 50 countries, including the members of the European Union and the Commonwealth of Independent States, Australia, and Japan.

12. Analysis of efficiency potentials in end-use sectors in the next 20 years appears in chapter 6 of this report and is based on detailed techno-economic studies and examples of best practices.

13. Conventionally, energy efficiency has been defined on the basis of the first law of thermodynamics. The second law of thermodynamics recognises that different forms of energy have different potentials to carry out specific tasks. For example, a gas boiler for space heating may operate at close to 100 percent efficiency (in terms based on the first law of thermodynamics). This seems to suggest that limited additional efficiency improvements are possible. But by extracting heat from the ground or other sources, a gas-driven heat pump could generate considerably more low-temperature heat with the same energy input. The

second example illustrates the potential for energy efficiency improvements according to the second law of thermodynamics.

14. An adequate payments system means using meters and payment collection to ensure that all energy services have a price that is paid by all users on a regular basis.

15. Both figures include the 2 billion currently without access to commercial energy. UN population projections were revised downwards in 1998, after the scenarios described here were developed. Although the population assumption used for the scenarios described here (11.7 billion by 2100) is slightly higher than the UN medium scenario (10.4 billion), the two are not inconsistent.

16. The policies of industrialised countries and inflationary pressures from petro-dollars could also have contributed to debt levels.

United Nations Conference on Environment and Development: Framework Convention on Climate Change

31 I.L.M. 849 (1992)
1771 UNTS 107 (1992)

http://unfccc.int/resource/conv/conv.html

The Parties to this Convention,

Acknowledging that change in the Earth's climate and its adverse effects are a common concern of humankind,

Concerned that human activities have been substantially increasing the atmospheric concentrations of greenhouse gases, that these increases enhance the natural greenhouse effect, and that this will result on average in an additional warming of the Earth's surface and atmosphere and may adversely affect natural ecosystems and humankind,

Noting that the largest share of historical and current global emissions of greenhouse gases has originated in developed countries, that per capita emissions in developing countries are still relatively low and that the share of global emissions originating in developing countries will grow to meet their social and development needs,

Aware of the role and importance in terrestrial and marine ecosystems of sinks and reservoirs of greenhouse gases,

Noting that there are many uncertainties in predictions of climate change, particularly with regard to the timing, magnitude and regional patterns thereof,

Acknowledging that the global nature of climate change calls for the widest possible cooperation by all countries and their participation in an effective and appropriate international response, in accordance with their common but differentiated responsibilities and respective capabilities and their social and economic conditions,

Recalling the pertinent provisions of the Declaration of the United Nations Conference on the Human Environment, adopted at Stockholm on 16 June 1972,

Recalling also that States have, in accordance with the Charter of the United Nations and the principles of international law, the sovereign right to exploit their own resources pursuant to their own environmental and developmental policies, and the responsibility to ensure that activities within their jurisdiction or control do not cause damage to the environment of other States or of areas beyond the limits of national jurisdiction,

Reaffirming the principle of sovereignty of States in international cooperation to address climate change,

Recognizing that States should enact effective environmental legislation, that environmental standards, management objectives and priorities should reflect the environmental and developmental context to which they apply, and that standards applied by some countries may be inappropriate and of unwarranted economic and social cost to other countries, in particular developing countries,

Recalling the provisions of General Assembly resolution 44/228 of 22 December 1989 on the United Nations Conference on Environment and Development, and resolutions 43/53 of 6 December 1988, 44/207 of 22 December 1989, 45/212 of 21 December 1990 and 46/169 of 19 December 1991 on protection of global climate for present and future generations of mankind,

Recalling also the provisions of General Assembly resolution 44/206 of 22 December 1989 on the possible adverse effects of sea-level rise on islands and coastal areas, particularly low-lying coastal areas and the pertinent provisions of General Assembly resolution 44/172 of 19 December 1989 on the implementation of the Plan of Action to Combat Desertification,

Recalling further the Vienna Convention for the Protection of the Ozone Layer, 1985, and the Montreal Protocol on Substances that Deplete the Ozone Layer, 1987, as adjusted and amended on 29 June 1990,

Noting the Ministerial Declaration of the Second World Climate Conference adopted on 7 November 1990,

Conscious of the valuable analytical work being conducted by many States on climate change and of the important contributions of the World Meteorological Organization, the United Nations Environment Programme and other organs, organizations and bodies of the United Nations system, as well as other international and intergovernmental bodies, to the exchange of results of scientific research and the coordination of research,

Recognizing that steps required to understand and address climate change will be environmentally, socially and economically most effective if they are based on relevant scientific, technical and economic considerations and continually re-evaluated in the light of new findings in these areas,

Recognizing that various actions to address climate change can be justified economically in their own right and can also help in solving other environmental problems,

Recognizing also the need for developed countries to take immediate action in a flexible manner on the basis of clear priorities, as a first step towards comprehensive response strategies at the global, national and, where agreed, regional levels that take into account all greenhouse gases, with due consideration of their relative contributions to the enhancement of the greenhouse effect,

Recognizing further that low-lying and other small island countries, countries with low-lying coastal, arid and semi-arid areas or areas liable to floods, drought and desertification, and developing countries with fragile mountainous ecosystems are particularly vulnerable to the adverse effects of climate change,

Recognizing the special difficulties of those countries, especially developing countries, whose economies are particularly dependent on fossil fuel production, use and exportation, as a consequence of action taken on limiting greenhouse gas emissions,

Affirming that responses to climate change should be coordinated with social and economic development in an integrated manner with a view to avoiding adverse impacts on the latter, taking into full account the legitimate priority needs of developing countries for the achievement of sustained economic growth and the eradication of poverty,

Recognizing that all countries, especially developing countries, need access to resources required to achieve sustainable social and economic development and that, in order for developing countries to progress towards that goal, their energy consumption will need to grow taking into account the possibilities for achieving greater energy efficiency and for controlling greenhouse gas emissions in general, including through the application of new technologies on terms which make such an application economically and socially beneficial,

Determined to protect the climate system for present and future generations,

Have agreed as follows:

ARTICLE 1 DEFINITIONS*

For the purposes of this Convention:

1. "Adverse effects of climate change" means changes in the physical environment or biota resulting from climate change which have significant deleterious effects on the composition, resilience or productivity of natural and managed ecosystems or on the operation of socio-economic systems or on human health and welfare.

2. "Climate change" means a change of climate which is attributed directly or indirectly to human activity that alters the composition of the global atmosphere and which is in addition to natural climate variability observed over comparable time periods.

3. "Climate system" means the totality of the atmosphere, hydrosphere, biosphere and geosphere and their interactions.

4. "Emissions" means the release of greenhouse gases and/or their precursors into the atmosphere over a specified area and period of time.

5. "Greenhouse gases" means those gaseous constituents of the atmosphere, both natural and

* Titles of articles are included solely to assist the reader.

anthropogenic, that absorb and re-emit infrared radiation.

6. "Regional economic integration organization" means an organization constituted by sovereign States of a given region which has competence in respect of matters governed by this Convention or its protocols and has been duly authorized, in accordance with its internal procedures, to sign, ratify, accept, approve or accede to the instruments concerned.

7. "Reservoir" means a component or components of the climate system where a greenhouse gas or a precursor of a greenhouse gas is stored.

8. "Sink" means any process, activity or mechanism which removes a greenhouse gas, an aerosol or a precursor of a greenhouse gas from the atmosphere.

9. "Source" means any process or activity which releases a greenhouse gas, an aerosol or a precursor of a greenhouse gas into the atmosphere.

ARTICLE 2 OBJECTIVE

The ultimate objective of this Convention and any related legal instruments that the Conference of the Parties may adopt is to achieve, in accordance with the relevant provisions of the Convention, stabilization of greenhouse gas concentrations in the atmosphere at a level that would prevent dangerous anthropogenic interference with the climate system. Such a level should be achieved within a time-frame sufficient to allow ecosystems to adapt naturally to climate change, to ensure that food production is not threatened and to enable economic development to proceed in a sustainable manner.

ARTICLE 3 PRINCIPLES

In their actions to achieve the objective of the Convention and to implement its provisions, the Parties shall be guided, INTER ALIA, by the following:

1. The Parties should protect the climate system for the benefit of present and future generations of humankind, on the basis of equity and in accordance with their common but differentiated responsibilities and respective capabilities. Accordingly, the developed country Parties should take the lead in combating climate change and the adverse effects thereof.

2. The specific needs and special circumstances of developing country Parties, especially those that are particularly vulnerable to the adverse effects of climate change, and of those Parties, especially developing country Parties, that would have to bear a disproportionate or abnormal burden under the Convention, should be given full consideration.

3. The Parties should take precautionary measures to anticipate, prevent or minimize the causes of climate change and mitigate its adverse effects. Where there are threats of serious or irreversible damage, lack of full scientific certainty should not be used as a reason for postponing such measures, taking into account that policies and measures to deal with climate change should be cost-effective so as to ensure global benefits at the lowest possible cost. To achieve this, such policies and measures should take into account different socio-economic contexts, be comprehensive, cover all relevant sources, sinks and reservoirs of greenhouse gases and adaptation, and comprise all economic sectors. Efforts to address climate change may be carried out cooperatively by interested Parties.

4. The Parties have a right to, and should, promote sustainable development. Policies and measures to protect the climate system against human-induced change should be appropriate for the specific conditions of each Party and should be integrated with national development programmes, taking into account that economic development is essential for adopting measures to address climate change.

5. The Parties should cooperate to promote a supportive and open international economic system that would lead to sustainable economic growth and development in all Parties, particularly developing country Parties, thus enabling them better to address the problems of climate change. Measures taken to combat climate change, including unilateral ones, should not constitute a means of arbitrary or unjustifiable discrimination or a disguised restriction on international trade.

ARTICLE 4 COMMITMENTS

1. All Parties, taking into account their common but differentiated responsibilities and their specific national and regional development priorities, objectives and circumstances, shall:

(a) Develop, periodically update, publish and make available to the Conference of the Parties, in accordance with Article 12, national inventories of anthropogenic emissions by sources and removals by sinks of all greenhouse gases not controlled by the Montreal Protocol, using comparable methodologies to be agreed upon by the Conference of the Parties;

(b) Formulate, implement, publish and regularly update national and, where appropriate, regional programmes containing measures to mitigate climate change by addressing anthropogenic emissions by sources and removals by sinks of all greenhouse gases not controlled by the Montreal Protocol, and measures to facilitate adequate adaptation to climate change;

(c) Promote and cooperate in the development, application and diffusion, including transfer, of technologies, practices and processes that control, reduce or prevent anthropogenic emissions of greenhouse gases not controlled by the Montreal Protocol in all relevant sectors, including the energy, transport, industry, agriculture, forestry and waste management sectors;

(d) Promote sustainable management, and promote and cooperate in the conservation and enhancement, as appropriate, of sinks and reservoirs of all greenhouse gases not controlled by the Montreal Protocol, including biomass, forests and oceans as well as other terrestrial, coastal and marine ecosystems;

(e) Cooperate in preparing for adaptation to the impacts of climate change; develop and elaborate appropriate and integrated plans for coastal zone management, water resources and agriculture, and for the protection and rehabilitation of areas, particularly in Africa, affected by drought and desertification, as well as floods;

(f) Take climate change considerations into account, to the extent feasible, in their relevant social, economic and environmental policies and actions, and employ appropriate methods, for example impact assessments, formulated and determined nationally, with a view to minimizing adverse effects on the economy, on public health and on the quality of the environment, of projects or measures undertaken by them to mitigate or adapt to climate change;

(g) Promote and cooperate in scientific, technological, technical, socio-economic and other research, systematic observation and development of data archives related to the climate system and intended to further the understanding and to reduce or eliminate the remaining uncertainties regarding the causes, effects, magnitude and timing of climate change and the economic and social consequences of various response strategies;

(h) Promote and cooperate in the full, open and prompt exchange of relevant scientific, technological, technical, socio-economic and legal information related to the climate system and climate change, and to the economic and social consequences of various response strategies;

(i) Promote and cooperate in education, training and public awareness related to climate change and encourage the widest participation in this process, including that of non-governmental organizations; and

(j) Communicate to the Conference of the Parties information related to implementation, in accordance with Article 12.

2. The developed country Parties and other Parties included in Annex I commit themselves specifically as provided for in the following:

(a) Each of these Parties shall adopt national1 policies and takecorresponding measures on the mitigation of climate change, by limiting its anthropogenic emissions of greenhouse gases and protecting and enhancing its greenhouse gas sinks and reservoirs. These policies and measures will demonstrate that developed countries are taking the lead in modifying longer-term trends in anthropogenic emissions consistent with the objective of the Convention, recognizing that the return by the end of the present decade to earlier levels of anthropogenic emissions of carbon dioxide and other greenhouse gases not controlled by the Montreal Protocol would contribute to such modification, and taking into account the differences in these Parties' starting points and approaches, economic structures and resource bases, the need to maintain strong and sustainable economic growth, available technologies and other individual circumstances, as well as the need for equitable and appropriate contributions by each of these Parties to the global effort regarding that objective. These

Parties may implement such policies and measures jointly with other Parties and may assist other Parties in contributing to the achievement of the objective of the Convention and, in particular, that of this subparagraph;

(b) In order to promote progress to this end, each of these Parties shall communicate, within six months of the entry into force of the Convention for it and periodically thereafter, and in accordance with Article 12, detailed information on its policies and measures referred to in subparagraph (a) above, as well as on its resulting projected anthropogenic emissions by sources and removals by sinks of greenhouse gases not controlled by the Montreal Protocol for the period referred to in subparagraph (a), with the aim of returning individually or jointly to their 1990 levels these anthropogenic emissions of carbon dioxide and other greenhouse gases not controlled by the Montreal Protocol. This information will be reviewed by the Conference of the Parties, at its first session and periodically thereafter, in accordance with Article 7;

(c) Calculations of emissions by sources and removals by sinks of greenhouse gases for the purposes of subparagraph (b) above should take into account the best available scientific knowledge, including of the effective capacity of sinks and the respective contributions of such gases to climate change. The Conference of the Parties shall consider and agree on methodologies for these calculations at its first session and review them regularly thereafter;

(d) The Conference of the Parties shall, at its first session, review the adequacy of subparagraphs (a) and (b) above. Such review shall be carried out in the light of the best available scientific information and assessment on climate change and its impacts, as well as relevant technical, social and economic information. Based on this review, the Conference of the Parties shall take appropriate action, which may include the adoption of amendments to the commitments in subparagraphs (a) and (b) above. The Conference of the Parties, at its first session, shall also take decisions regarding criteria for joint implementation as indicated in subparagraph (a) above. A second review of subparagraphs (a) and (b) shall take place not later than 31 December 1998, and thereafter at regular intervals determined by the Conference of the Parties, until the objective of the Convention is met;

(e) Each of these Parties shall:

(i) Coordinate as appropriate with other such Parties, relevant economic and administrative instruments developed to achieve the objective of the Convention; and

(ii) Identify and periodically review its own policies and practices which encourage activities that lead to greater levels of anthropogenic emissions of greenhouse gases not controlled by the Montreal Protocol than would otherwise occur;

(f) The Conference of the Parties shall review, not later than 31 December 1998, available information with a view to taking decisions regarding such amendments to the lists in Annexes I and II as may be appropriate, with the approval of the Party concerned;

(g) Any Party not included in Annex I may, in its instrument of ratification, acceptance, approval or accession, or at any time thereafter, notify the Depositary that it intends to be bound by subparagraphs (a) and (b) above. The Depositary shall inform the other signatories and Parties of any such notification.

3. The developed country Parties and other developed Parties included in Annex II shall provide new and additional financial resources to meet the agreed full costs incurred by developing country Parties in complying with their obligations under Article 12, paragraph 1. They shall also provide such financial resources, including for the transfer of technology, needed by the developing country Parties to meet the agreed full incremental costs of implementing measures that are covered by paragraph 1 of this Article and that are agreed between a developing country Party and the international entity or entities referred to in Article 11, in accordance with that Article. The implementation of these commitments shall take into account the need for adequacy and predictability in the flow of funds and the importance of appropriate burden sharing among the developed country Parties.

4. The developed country Parties and other developed Parties included in Annex II shall also assist the developing country Parties that are particularly vulnerable to the adverse effects of climate change in meeting costs of adaptation to those adverse effects.

5. The developed country Parties and other developed Parties included in Annex II shall take all practicable steps to promote, facilitate and finance, as appropriate, the transfer of, or access to, environmentally sound technologies and know-how to other Parties, particularly developing country Parties, to enable them to implement the provisions of the Convention. In this process, the developed country Parties shall support the development and enhancement of endogenous capacities and technologies of developing country Parties. Other Parties and organizations in a position to do so may also assist in facilitating the transfer of such technologies.

6. In the implementation of their commitments under paragraph 2 above, a certain degree of flexibility shall be allowed by the Conference of the Parties to the Parties included in Annex I undergoing the process of transition to a market economy, in order to enhance the ability of these Parties to address climate change, including with regard to the historical level of anthropogenic emissions of greenhouse gases not controlled by the Montreal Protocol chosen as a reference.

7. The extent to which developing country Parties will effectively implement their commitments under the Convention will depend on the effective implementation by developed country Parties of their commitments under the Convention related to financial resources and transfer of technology and will take fully into account that economic and social development and poverty eradication are the first and overriding priorities of the developing country Parties.

8. In the implementation of the commitments in this Article, the Parties shall give full consideration to what actions are necessary under the Convention, including actions related to funding, insurance and the transfer of technology, to meet the specific needs and concerns of developing country Parties arising from the adverse effects of climate change and/or the impact of the implementation of response measures, especially on:

(a) Small island countries;

(b) Countries with low-lying coastal areas;

(c) Countries with arid and semi-arid areas, forested areas and areas liable to forest decay;

(d) Countries with areas prone to natural disasters;

(e) Countries with areas liable to drought and desertification;

(f) Countries with areas of high urban atmospheric pollution;

(g) Countries with areas with fragile ecosystems, including mountainous ecosystems;

(h) Countries whose economies are highly dependent on income generated from the production, processing and export, and/or on consumption of fossil fuels and associated energy-intensive products; and

(i) Land-locked and transit countries.

Further, the Conference of the Parties may take actions, as appropriate, with respect to this paragraph.

9. The Parties shall take full account of the specific needs and special situations of the least developed countries in their actions with regard to funding and transfer of technology.

10. The Parties shall, in accordance with Article 10, take into consideration in the implementation of the commitments of the Convention the situation of Parties, particularly developing country Parties, with economies that are vulnerable to the adverse effects of the implementation of measures to respond to climate change. This applies notably to Parties with economies that are highly dependent on income generated from the production, processing and export, and/or consumption of fossil fuels and associated energy-intensive products and/or the use of fossil fuels for which such Parties have serious difficulties in switching to alternatives.

ARTICLE 5 RESEARCH AND SYSTEMATIC OBSERVATION

In carrying out their commitments under Article 4, paragraph 1(g), the Parties shall:

(a) Support and further develop, as appropriate, international and intergovernmental programmes and networks or organizations aimed at defining, conducting, assessing and financing research, data collection and systematic observation, taking into account the need to minimize duplication of effort;

(b) Support international and intergovernmental efforts to strengthen systematic observation and national scientific and technical research capacities and capabilities, particularly in developing countries, and to promote access to, and the exchange of, data and analyses thereof obtained from areas beyond national jurisdiction; and

(c) Take into account the particular concerns and needs of developing countries and cooperate in improving their endogenous capacities and capabilities to participate in the efforts referred to in subparagraphs (a) and (b) above.

ARTICLE 6 EDUCATION, TRAINING AND PUBLIC AWARENESS

In carrying out their commitments under Article 4, paragraph 1(i), the Parties shall:

(a) Promote and facilitate at the national and, as appropriate, subregional and regional levels, and in accordance with national laws and regulations, and within their respective capacities:

(i) The development and implementation of educational and public awareness programmes on climate change and its effects;

(ii) Public access to information on climate change and its effects;

(iii) Public participation in addressing climate change and its effects and developing adequate responses; and

(iv) Training of scientific, technical and managerial personnel.

(b) Cooperate in and promote, at the international level, and, where appropriate, using existing bodies:

(i) The development and exchange of educational and public awareness material on climate change and itseffects; and

(ii) The development and implementation of education and training programmes, including the strengthening of national institutions and the exchange or secondment of personnel to train experts in this field, in particular for developing countries.

ARTICLE 7 CONFERENCE OF THE PARTIES

1. A Conference of the Parties is hereby established.

2. The Conference of the Parties, as the supreme body of this Convention, shall keep under regular review the implementation of the Convention and any related legal instruments that the Conference of the Parties may adopt, and shall make, within its mandate, the decisions necessary to promote the effective implementation of the Convention. To this end, it shall:

(a) Periodically examine the obligations of the Parties and the institutional arrangementsunder the Convention, in the light of the objective of the Convention, the experience gained in its implementation and the evolution of scientific and technological knowledge;

(b) Promote and facilitate the exchange of information on measures adopted by the Parties to address climate change and its effects, taking into account the differing circumstances, responsibilities and capabilities of the Parties and their respective commitments under the Convention;

(c) Facilitate, at the request of two or more Parties, the coordination of measures adopted by them to address climate change and its effects, taking into account the differing circumstances, responsibilities and capabilities of the Parties and their respective commitments under the Convention;

(d) Promote and guide, in accordance with the objective and provisions of the Convention, the development and periodic refinement of comparable methodologies, to be agreed on by the Conference of the Parties, inter alia, for preparing inventories of greenhouse gas emissions by sources and removals by sinks, and for evaluating the effectiveness of measures to limit the emissions and enhance the removals of these gases;

(e) Assess, on the basis of all information made available to it in accordance with the provisions of the Convention, the implementation of the Convention by the Parties, the overall effects of the measures taken pursuant to the Convention, in particular environmental, economic and social effects as well as their cumulative impacts and the extent to which progress towards the objective of the Convention is being achieved;

(f) Consider and adopt regular reports on the implementation of the Convention and ensure their publication;

(g) Make recommendations on any matters necessary for the implementation of the Convention;

(h) Seek to mobilize financial resources in accordance with Article 4, paragraphs 3, 4 and 5, and Article 11;

(i) Establish such subsidiary bodies as are deemed necessary for the implementation of the Convention;

(j) Review reports submitted by its subsidiary bodies and provide guidance to them;

(k) Agree upon and adopt, by consensus, rules of procedure and financial rules for itself and for any subsidiary bodies;

(l) Seek and utilize, where appropriate, the services and cooperation of, and information provided by, competent international organizations and intergovernmental and non-governmental bodies; and

(m) Exercise such other functions as are required for the achievement of the objective of the Convention as well as all other functions assigned to it under the Convention.

3. The Conference of the Parties shall, at its first session, adopt its own rules of procedure as well as those of the subsidiary bodies established by the Convention, which shall include decision-making procedures for matters not already covered by decision-making procedures stipulated in the Convention. Such procedures may include specified majorities required for the adoption of particular decisions.

4. The first session of the Conference of the Parties shall be convened by the interim secretariat referred to in Article 21 and shall take place not later than one year after the date of entry into force of the Convention. Thereafter, ordinary sessions of the Conference of the Parties shall be held every year unless otherwise decided by the Conference of the Parties.

5. Extraordinary sessions of the Conference of the Parties shall be held at such other times as may be deemed necessary by the Conference, or at the written request of any Party, provided that, within six months of the request being communicated to the Parties by the secretariat, it is supported by at least one third of the Parties.

6. The United Nations, its specialized agencies and the International Atomic Energy Agency, as well as any State member thereof or observers thereto not Party to the Convention, may be represented at sessions of the Conference of the Parties as observers. Any body or agency, whether national or international, governmental or non-governmental, which is qualified in matters covered by the Convention, and which has informed the secretariat of its wish to be represented at a session of the Conference of the Parties as an observer, may be so admitted unless at least one third of the Parties present object. The admission and participation of observers shall be subject to the rules of procedure adopted by the Conference of the Parties.

ARTICLE 8 SECRETARIAT

1. A secretariat is hereby established.

2. The functions of the secretariat shall be:

(a) To make arrangements for sessions of the Conference of the Parties and its subsidiary bodies established under the Convention and to provide them with services as required;

(b) To compile and transmit reports submitted to it;

(c) To facilitate assistance to the Parties, particularly developing country Parties, on request, in the compilation and communication of information required in accordance with the provisions of the Convention;

(d) To prepare reports on its activities and present them to the Conference of the Parties;

(e) To ensure the necessary coordination with the secretariats of other relevant international bodies;

(f) To enter, under the overall guidance of the Conference of the Parties, into such administrative and contractual arrangements as may be required for the effective discharge of its functions; and

(g) To perform the other secretariat functions specified in the Convention and in any of its protocols and such other functions as may be determined by the Conference of the Parties.

3. The Conference of the Parties, at its first session, shall designate a permanent secretariat and make arrangements for its functioning.

ARTICLE 9 SUBSIDIARY BODY FOR SCIENTIFIC AND TECHNOLOGICAL ADVICE

1. A subsidiary body for scientific and technological advice is hereby established to provide the

Conference of the Parties and, as appropriate, its other subsidiary bodies with timely information and advice on scientific and technological matters relating to the Convention. This body shall be open to participation by all Parties and shall be multidisciplinary. It shall comprise government representatives competent in the relevant field of expertise. It shall report regularly to the Conference of the Parties on all aspects of its work.

2. Under the guidance of the Conference of the Parties, and drawing upon existing competent international bodies, this body shall:

(a) Provide assessments of the state of scientific knowledge relating to climate change and its effects;

(b) Prepare scientific assessments on the effects of measures taken in the implementation of the Convention;

(c) Identify innovative, efficient and state-of-the-art technologies and know-how and advise on the ways and means of promoting development and/or transferring such technologies;

(d) Provide advice on scientific programmes, international cooperation in research and development related to climate change, as well as on ways and means of supporting endogenous capacity-building in developing countries; and

(e) Respond to scientific, technological and methodological questions that the Conference of the Parties and its subsidiary bodies may put to the body.

3. The functions and terms of reference of this body may be further elaborated by the Conference of the Parties.

ARTICLE 10 SUBSIDIARY BODY FOR IMPLEMENTATION

1. A subsidiary body for implementation is hereby established to assist the Conference of the Parties in the assessment and review of the effective implementation of the Convention. This body shall be open to participation by all Parties and comprise government representatives who are experts on matters related to climate change. It shall report regularly to the Conference of the Parties on all aspects of its work.

2. Under the guidance of the Conference of the Parties, this body shall:

(a) Consider the information communicated in accordance with Article 12, paragraph 1, to assess the overall aggregated effect of the steps taken by the Parties in the light of the latest scientific assessments concerning climate change;

(b) Consider the information communicated in accordance with Article 12, paragraph 2, in order to assist the Conference of the Parties in carrying out the reviews required by Article 4, paragraph 2(d); and

(c) Assist the Conference of the Parties, as appropriate, in the preparation and implementation of its decisions.

ARTICLE 11 FINANCIAL MECHANISM

1. A mechanism for the provision of financial resources on a grant or concessional basis, including for the transfer of technology, is hereby defined. It shall function under the guidance of and be accountable to the Conference of the Parties, which shall decide on its policies, programme priorities and eligibility criteria related to this Convention. Its operation shall be entrusted to one or more existing international entities.

2. The financial mechanism shall have an equitable and balanced representation of all Parties within a transparent system of governance.

3. The Conference of the Parties and the entity or entities entrusted with the operation of the financial mechanism shall agree upon arrangements to give effect to the above paragraphs, which shall include the following:

(a) Modalities to ensure that the funded projects to address climate change are in conformity with the policies, programme priorities and eligibility criteria established by the Conference of the Parties;

(b) Modalities by which a particular funding decision may be reconsidered in light of these policies, programme priorities and eligibility criteria;

(c) Provision by the entity or entities of regular reports to the Conference of the Parties on its funding operations, which is consistent with the requirement for accountability set out in paragraph 1 above; and

(d) Determination in a predictable and identifiable manner of the amount of funding necessary and available for the implementation of this Convention and the conditions under which that amount shall be periodically reviewed.

4. The Conference of the Parties shall make arrangements to implement the above-mentioned provisions at its first session, reviewing and taking into account the interim arrangements referred to in Article 21, paragraph 3, and shall decide whether these interim arrangements shall be maintained. Within four years thereafter, the Conference of the Parties shall review the financial mechanism and take appropriate measures.

5. The developed country Parties may also provide and developing country Parties avail themselves of, financial resources related to the implementation of the Convention through bilateral, regional and other multilateral channels.

ARTICLE 12 COMMUNICATION OF INFORMATION RELATED TO IMPLEMENTATION

1. In accordance with Article 4, paragraph 1, each Party shall communicate to the Conference of the Parties, through the secretariat, the following elements of information:

(a) A national inventory of anthropogenic emissions by sources and removals by sinks of all greenhouse gases not controlled by the Montreal Protocol, to the extent its capacities permit, using comparable methodologies to be promoted and agreed upon by the Conference of the Parties;

(b) A general description of steps taken or envisaged by the Party to implement the Convention; and

(c) Any other information that the Party considers relevant to the achievement of the objective of the Convention and suitable for inclusion in its communication, including, if feasible, material relevant for calculations of global emission trends.

2. Each developed country Party and each other Party included in Annex I shall incorporate in its communication the following elements of information:

(a) A detailed description of the policies and measures that it has adopted to implement its commitment under Article 4, paragraphs 2(a) and 2(b); and

(b) A specific estimate of the effects that the policies and measures referred to in subparagraph (a) immediately above will have on anthropogenic emissions by its sources and removals by its sinks of greenhouse gases during the period referred to in Article 4, paragraph 2(a).

3. In addition, each developed country Party and each other developed Party included in Annex II shall incorporate details of measures taken in accordance with Article 4, paragraphs 3, 4 and 5.

4. Developing country Parties may, on a voluntary basis, propose projects for financing, including specific technologies, materials, equipment, techniques or practices that would be needed to implement such projects, along with, if possible, an estimate of all incremental costs, of the reductions of emissions and increments of removals of greenhouse gases, as well as an estimate of the consequent benefits.

5. Each developed country Party and each other Party included in Annex I shall make its initial communication within six months of the entry into force of the Convention for that Party. Each Party not so listed shall make its initial communication within three years of the entry into force of the Convention for that Party, or of the availability of financial resources in accordance with Article 4, paragraph 3. Parties that are least developed countries may make their initial communication at their discretion. The frequency of subsequent communications by all Parties shall be determined by the Conference of the Parties, taking into account the differentiated timetable set by this paragraph.

6. Information communicated by Parties under this Article shall be transmitted by the secretariat as soon as possible to the Conference of the Parties and to any subsidiary bodies concerned. If necessary, the procedures for the communication of information may be further considered by the Conference of the Parties.

7. From its first session, the Conference of the Parties shall arrange for the provision to developing country Parties of technical and financial support, on request, in compiling and communicating information under this Article, as well as in identifying the technical and financial needs associated with proposed projects and response measures under Article 4. Such support may be provided by other Parties, by competent international organizations and by the secretariat, as appropriate.

8. Any group of Parties may, subject to guidelines adopted by the Conference of the Parties, and to prior notification to the Conference of the Parties, make a joint communication in fulfilment of their obligations under this Article, provided that such a communication includes information on the fulfilment by each of these Parties of its individual obligations under the Convention.

9. Information received by the secretariat that is designated by a Party as confidential, in accordance with criteria to be established by the Conference of the Parties, shall be aggregated by the secretariat to protect its confidentiality before being made available to any of the bodies involved in the communication and review of information.

10. Subject to paragraph 9 above, and without prejudice to the ability of any Party to make public its communication at any time, the secretariat shall make communications by Parties under this Article publicly available at the time they are submitted to the Conference of the Parties.

ARTICLE 13 RESOLUTION OF QUESTIONS REGARDING IMPLEMENTATION

The Conference of the Parties shall, at its first session, consider the establishment of a multilateral consultative process, available to Parties on their request, for the resolution of questions regarding the implementation of the Convention.

ARTICLE 14 SETTLEMENT OF DISPUTES

1. In the event of a dispute between any two or more Parties concerning the interpretation or application of the Convention, the Parties concerned shall seek a settlement of the dispute through negotiation or any other peaceful means of their own choice.

2. When ratifying, accepting, approving or acceding to the Convention, or at any time thereafter, a Party which is not a regional economic integration organization may declare in a written instrument submitted to the Depositary that, in respect of any dispute concerning the interpretation or application of the Convention, it recognizes as compulsory ipso facto and without special agreement, in relation to any Party accepting the same obligation:

(a) Submission of the dispute to the International Court of Justice, and/or

(b) Arbitration in accordance with procedures to be adopted by the Conference of the Parties as soon as practicable, in an annex on arbitration.

A Party which is a regional economic integration organization may make a declaration with like effect in relation to arbitration in accordance with the procedures referred to in subparagraph (b) above.

3. A declaration made under paragraph 2 above shall remain in force until it expires in accordance with its terms or until three months after written notice of its revocation has been deposited with the Depositary.

4. A new declaration, a notice of revocation or the expiry of a declaration shall not in any way affect proceedings pending before the International Court of Justice or the arbitral tribunal, unless the parties to the dispute otherwise agree.

5. Subject to the operation of paragraph 2 above, if after twelve months following notification by one Party to another that a dispute exists between them, the Parties concerned have not been able to settle their dispute through the means mentioned in paragraph 1 above, the dispute shall be submitted, at the request of any of the parties to the dispute, to conciliation.

6. A conciliation commission shall be created upon the request of one of the parties to the dispute. The commission shall be composed of an equal number of members appointed by each party concerned and a chairman chosen jointly by the members appointed by each party. The commission shall render a recommendatory award, which the parties shall consider in good faith.

7. Additional procedures relating to conciliation shall be adopted by the Conference of the Parties, as soon as practicable, in an annex on conciliation.

8. The provisions of this Article shall apply to any related legal instrument which the Conference of the Parties may adopt, unless the instrument provides otherwise.

ARTICLE 15 AMENDMENTS TO THE CONVENTION

1. Any Party may propose amendments to the Convention.

2. Amendments to the Convention shall be adopted at an ordinary session of the Conference of the Parties. The text of any proposed amendment to the Convention shall be communicated to the Parties by the secretariat at least six months before the meeting at which it is proposed for adoption. The secretariat shall also communicate proposed amendments to the signatories to the Convention and, for information, to the Depositary.

3. The Parties shall make every effort to reach agreement on any proposed amendment to the Convention by consensus. If all efforts at consensus have been exhausted, and no agreement reached, the amendment shall as a last resort be adopted by a three-fourths majority vote of the Parties present and voting at the meeting. The adopted amendment shall be communicated by the secretariat to the Depositary, who shall circulate it to all Parties for their acceptance.

4. Instruments of acceptance in respect of an amendment shall be deposited with the Depositary. An amendment adopted in accordance with paragraph 3 above shall enter into force for those Parties having accepted it on the ninetieth day after the date of receipt by the Depositary of an instrument of acceptance by at least three fourths of the Parties to the Convention.

5. The amendment shall enter into force for any other Party on the ninetieth day after the date on which that Party deposits with the Depositary its instrument of acceptance of the said amendment.

6. For the purposes of this Article, "Parties present and voting" means Parties present and casting an affirmative or negative vote.

ARTICLE 16 ADOPTION AND AMENDMENT OF ANNEXES TO THE CONVENTION

1. Annexes to the Convention shall form an integral part thereof and, unless otherwise expressly provided, a reference to the Convention constitutes at the same time a reference to any annexes thereto. Without prejudice to the provisions of Article 14, paragraphs 2(b) and 7, such annexes shall be restricted to lists, forms and any other material of a descriptive nature that is of a scientific, technical, procedural or administrative character.

2. Annexes to the Convention shall be proposed and adopted in accordance with the procedure set forth in Article 15, paragraphs 2, 3 and 4.

3. An annex that has been adopted in accordance with paragraph 2 above shall enter into force for all Parties to the Convention six months after the date of the communication by the Depositary to such Parties of the adoption of the annex, except for those Parties that have notified the Depositary, in writing, within that period of their non-acceptance of the annex. The annex shall enter into force for Parties which withdraw their notification of non-acceptance on the ninetieth day after the date on which withdrawal of such notification has been received by the Depositary.

4. The proposal, adoption and entry into force of amendments to annexes to the Convention shall be subject to the same procedure as that for the proposal, adoption and entry into force of annexes to the Convention in accordance with paragraphs 2 and 3 above.

5. If the adoption of an annex or an amendment to an annex involves an amendment to the Convention, that annex or amendment to an annex shall not enter into force until such time as the amendment to the Convention enters into force.

ARTICLE 17 PROTOCOLS

1. The Conference of the Parties may, at any ordinary session, adopt protocols to the Convention.

2. The text of any proposed protocol shall be communicated to the Parties by the secretariat at least six months before such a session.

3. The requirements for the entry into force of any protocol shall be established by that instrument.

4. Only Parties to the Convention may be Parties to a protocol.

5. Decisions under any protocol shall be taken only by the Parties to the protocol concerned.

ARTICLE 18 RIGHT TO VOTE

1. Each Party to the Convention shall have one vote, except as provided for in paragraph 2 below.

2. Regional economic integration organizations, in matters within their competence, shall exercise their right to vote with a number of votes equal to the number of their member States that are Parties to the Convention. Such an organization shall not exercise its right to vote if any of its member States exercises its right, and vice versa.

ARTICLE 19 DEPOSITARY

The Secretary-General of the United Nations shall be the Depositary of the Convention and of protocols adopted in accordance with Article 17.

ARTICLE 20 SIGNATURE

This Convention shall be open for signature by States Members of the United Nations or of any of its specialized agencies or that are Parties to the Statute of the International Court of Justice and by regional economic integration organizations at Rio de Janeiro, during the United Nations Conference on Environment and Development, and thereafter at United Nations Headquarters in New York from 20 June 1992 to 19 June 1993.

ARTICLE 21 INTERIM ARRANGEMENTS

1. The secretariat functions referred to in Article 8 will be carried out on an interim basis by the secretariat established by the General Assembly of the United Nations in its resolution 45/212 of 21 December 1990, until the completion of the first session of the Conference of the Parties.

2. The head of the interim secretariat referred to in paragraph 1 above will cooperate closely with the Intergovernmental Panel on Climate Change to ensure that the Panel can respond to the need for objective scientific and technical advice. Other relevant scientific bodies could also be consulted.

3. The Global Environment Facility of the United Nations Development Programme, the United Nations Environment Programme and the International Bank for Reconstruction and Development shall be the international entity entrusted with the operation of the financial mechanism referred to in Article 11 on an interim basis. In this connection, the Global Environment Facility should be appropriately restructured and its membership made universal to enable it to fulfil the requirements of Article 11.

ARTICLE 22 RATIFICATION, ACCEPTANCE, APPROVAL OR ACCESSION

1. The Convention shall be subject to ratification, acceptance, approval or accession by States and by regional economic integration organizations. It shall be open for accession from the day after the date on which the Convention is closed for signature. Instruments of ratification, acceptance, approval or accession shall be deposited with the Depositary.

2. Any regional economic integration organization which becomes a Party to the Convention without any of its member States being a Party shall be bound by all the obligations under the Convention. In the case of such organizations, one or more of whose member States is a Party to the Convention, the organization and its member States shall decide on their respective responsibilities for the performance of their obligations under the Convention. In such cases, the organization and the member States shall not be entitled to exercise rights under the Convention concurrently.

3. In their instruments of ratification, acceptance, approval or accession, regional economic integration organizations shall declare the extent of their competence with respect to the matters governed by the Convention. These organizations shall also inform the Depositary, who shall in turn inform the Parties, of any substantial modification in the extent of their competence.

ARTICLE 23 ENTRY INTO FORCE

1. The Convention shall enter into force on the ninetieth day after the date of deposit of the fiftieth instrument of ratification, acceptance, approval or accession.

2. For each State or regional economic integration organization that ratifies, accepts or approves the Convention or accedes thereto after the deposit of the fiftieth instrument of ratification, acceptance, approval or accession, the Convention shall enter into force on the ninetieth day after the date of deposit by such State or regional economic integration organization of its instrument of ratification, acceptance, approval or accession.

3. For the purposes of paragraphs 1 and 2 above, any instrument deposited by a regional economic integration organization shall not be counted as additional to those deposited by States members of the organization.

ARTICLE 24 RESERVATIONS

No reservations may be made to the Convention.

ARTICLE 25 WITHDRAWAL

1. At any time after three years from the date on which the Convention has entered into force for a Party, that Party may withdraw from the Convention by giving written notification to the Depositary.

2. Any such withdrawal shall take effect upon expiry of one year from the date of receipt by the Depositary of the notification of withdrawal, or on such later date as may be specified in the notification of withdrawal.

3. Any Party that withdraws from the Convention shall be considered as also having withdrawn from any protocol to which it is a Party.

ARTICLE 26 AUTHENTIC TEXTS

The original of this Convention, of which the Arabic, Chinese, English, French, Russian and Spanish texts are equally authentic, shall be deposited with the Secretary- General of the United Nations.

IN WITNESS WHEREOF the undersigned, being duly authorized to that effect, have signed this Convention.

DONE at New York this ninth day of May one thousand nine hundred and ninety-two.

Kyoto Protocol to the United Nations Framework Convention on Climate Change

37 I.L.M. 22 (1998)

http://unfccc.int/resource/docs/convkp/kpeng.html

The Parties to this Protocol,

Being Parties to the United Nations Framework Convention on Climate Change, hereinafter referred to as "the Convention",

In pursuit of the ultimate objective of the Convention as stated in its Article 2,

Recalling the provisions of the Convention,

Being guided by Article 3 of the Convention,

Pursuant to the Berlin Mandate adopted by decision 1/CP.1 of the

Conference of the Parties to the Convention at its first session,

Have agreed as follows:

ARTICLE 1

For the purposes of this Protocol, the definitions contained in Article 1 of the Convention shall apply. In addition:

1. "Conference of the Parties" means the Conference of the Parties to the Convention.

2. "Convention" means the United Nations Framework Convention on Climate Change, adopted in New York on 9 May 1992.

3. "Intergovernmental Panel on Climate Change" means the Intergovernmental Panel on Climate Change established in 1988 jointly by the World Meteorological Organization and the United Nations Environment Programme.

4. "Montreal Protocol" means the Montreal Protocol on Substances that Deplete the Ozone Layer, adopted in Montreal on 16 September 1987 and as subsequently adjusted and amended.

5. "Parties present and voting" means Parties present and casting an affirmative or negative vote.

6. "Party" means, unless the context otherwise indicates, a Party to this Protocol.

7. "Party included in Annex I" means a Party included in Annex I to the Convention, as may be amended, or a Party which has made a notification under Article 4, paragraph 2(g), of the Convention.

ARTICLE 2

1. Each Party included in Annex I, in achieving its quantified emission limitation and reduction commitments under Article 3, in order to promote sustainable development, shall:

(a) Implement and/or further elaborate policies and measures in accordance with its national circumstances, such as:

(i) Enhancement of energy efficiency in relevant sectors of the national economy;

(ii) Protection and enhancement of sinks and reservoirs of greenhouse gases not controlled by the Montreal Protocol, taking into account its commitments under relevant international environmental agreements; promotion of sustainable forest management practices, afforestation and reforestation;

(iii) Promotion of sustainable forms of agriculture in light of climate change considerations;

(iv) Research on, and promotion, development and increased use of, new and renewable forms of energy, of carbon dioxide sequestration technologies and of advanced and innovative environmentally sound technologies;

(v) Progressive reduction or phasing out of market imperfections, fiscal incentives, tax and duty exemptions and subsidies in all greenhouse gas emitting sectors that run counter to the objective of the Convention and application of market instruments;

(vi) Encouragement of appropriate reforms in relevant sectors aimed at promoting policies and measures which limit or reduce emissions of greenhouse gases not controlled by the Montreal Protocol;

(vii) Measures to limit and/or reduce emissions of greenhouse gases not controlled by the Montreal Protocol in the transport sector;

(viii) Limitation and/or reduction of methane emissions through recovery and use in waste management, as well as in the production, transport and distribution of energy;

(b) Cooperate with other such Parties to enhance the individual and combined effectiveness of their policies and measures adopted under this Article, pursuant to Article 4, paragraph 2(e)(i), of the Convention. To this end, these Parties shall take steps to share their experience and exchange information on such policies and measures, including developing ways of improving their comparability, transparency and effectiveness. The Conference of the Parties serving as the meeting of the Parties to this Protocol shall, at its first session or as soon as practicable thereafter, consider ways to facilitate such cooperation, taking into account all relevant information.

2. The Parties included in Annex I shall pursue limitation or reduction of emissions of greenhouse gases not controlled by the Montreal Protocol from aviation and marine bunker fuels, working through the International Civil Aviation Organization and the International Maritime Organization, respectively.

3. The Parties included in Annex I shall strive to implement policies and measures under this Article in such a way as to minimize adverse effects, including the adverse effects of climate change, effects on international trade, and social, environmental and economic impacts on other Parties, especially developing country Parties and in particular those identified in Article 4, paragraphs 8 and 9, of the Convention, taking into account Article 3 of the Convention. The Conference of the Parties serving as the meeting of the Parties to this Protocol may take further action, as appropriate, to promote the implementation of the provisions of this paragraph.

4. The Conference of the Parties serving as the meeting of the Parties to this Protocol, if it decides that it would be beneficial to coordinate any of the policies and measures in paragraph 1(a) above, taking into account different national circumstances and potential effects, shall consider ways and means to elaborate the coordination of such policies and measures.

ARTICLE 3

1. The Parties included in Annex I shall, individually or jointly, ensure that their aggregate anthropogenic carbon dioxide equivalent emissions of the greenhouse gases listed in Annex A do not exceed their assigned amounts, calculated pursuant to their quantified emission limitation and reduction commitments inscribed in Annex B and in accordance with the provisions of this Article, with a view to reducing their overall emissions of such gases by at least 5 per cent below 1990 levels in the commitment period 2008 to 2012.

2. Each Party included in Annex I shall, by 2005, have made demonstrable progress in achieving its commitments under this Protocol.

3. The net changes in greenhouse gas emissions by sources and removals by sinks resulting from direct human-induced land-use change and forestry activities, limited to afforestation, reforestation and deforestation since 1990, measured as verifiable changes in carbon stocks in each commitment period, shall be used to meet the commitments under this Article of each Party included in Annex I. The greenhouse gas emissions by sources and removals by sinks associated with those activities shall be reported in a transparent and verifiable manner and reviewed in accordance with Articles 7 and 8.

4. Prior to the first session of the Conference of the Parties serving as the meeting of the Parties to this Protocol, each Party included in Annex I shall provide, for consideration by the Subsidiary Body for Scientific and Technological Advice, data to establish its level of carbon stocks in 1990 and to enable an estimate to be made of its changes in carbon stocks in subsequent years. The Conference of the Parties serving as the meeting of the Parties to this Protocol shall, at its first session or as soon as practicable thereafter, decide upon modalities, rules and guidelines as to how, and which, additional human-induced activities related to changes in greenhouse gas emissions by sources and removals by sinks in the agricultural soils and the land-use change and forestry categories shall be added to, or subtracted from, the assigned amounts for Parties included in Annex I, taking into account uncertainties, transparency in reporting, verifiability, the methodological work of the Intergovernmental Panel on Climate Change, the advice provided by the Subsidiary Body for Scientific and Technological Advice in accordance with Article 5 and the decisions of the Conference of the Parties. Such a decision shall apply in the second and subsequent commitment periods. A Party may choose to apply such a decision on these additional human-induced activities for its first commitment period, provided that these activities have taken place since 1990.

5. The Parties included in Annex I undergoing the process of transition to a market economy whose base year or period was established pursuant to decision 9/CP.2 of the Conference of the Parties at its second session shall use that base year or period for the implementation of their commitments under this Article. Any other Party included in Annex I undergoing the process of transition to a market economy which has not yet submitted its first national communication under Article 12 of the Convention may also notify the Conference of the Parties serving as the meeting of the Parties to this Protocol that it intends to use an historical base year or period other than 1990 for the implementation of its commitments under this Article. The Conference of the Parties serving as the meeting of the Parties to this Protocol shall decide on the acceptance of such notification.

6. Taking into account Article 4, paragraph 6, of the Convention, in the implementation of their commitments under this Protocol other than those under this Article, a certain degree of flexibility shall be allowed by the Conference of the Parties serving as the meeting of the Parties to this Protocol to the Parties included in Annex I undergoing the process of transition to a market economy.

7. In the first quantified emission limitation and reduction commitment period, from 2008 to 2012, the assigned amount for each Party included in Annex I shall be equal to the percentage inscribed for it in Annex B of its aggregate anthropogenic carbon dioxide equivalent emissions of the greenhouse gases listed in Annex A in 1990, or the base year or period determined in accordance with paragraph 5 above, multiplied by five. Those Parties included in Annex I for whom land-use change and forestry constituted a net source of greenhouse gas emissions in 1990 shall include in their 1990 emissions base year or period the aggregate anthropogenic carbon dioxide equivalent emissions by sources minus removals by sinks in 1990 from land-use change for the purposes of calculating their assigned amount.

8. Any Party included in Annex I may use 1995 as its base year for hydrofluorocarbons, perfluorocarbons and sulphur hexafluoride, for the purposes of the calculation referred to in paragraph 7 above.

9. Commitments for subsequent periods for Parties included in Annex I shall be established in amendments to Annex B to this Protocol, which shall be adopted in accordance with the provisions of Article 21, paragraph 7. The Conference of the Parties serving as the meeting of the Parties to this Protocol shall initiate the consideration of such commitments at least seven years before the end of the first commitment period referred to in paragraph 1 above.

10. Any emission reduction units, or any part of an assigned amount, which a Party acquires from another Party in accordance with the provisions of Article 6 or of Article 17 shall be added to the assigned amount for the acquiring Party.

11. Any emission reduction units, or any part of an assigned amount, which a Party transfers to another Party in accordance with the provisions of Article 6 or of Article 17 shall be subtracted from the assigned amount for the transferring Party.

12. Any certified emission reductions which a Party acquires from another Party in accordance with the provisions of Article 12 shall be added to the assigned amount for the acquiring Party.

13. If the emissions of a Party included in Annex I in a commitment period are less than its assigned amount under this Article, this difference shall, on request of that Party, be added to the assigned amount for that Party for subsequent commitment periods.

14. Each Party included in Annex I shall strive to implement the commitments mentioned in paragraph 1 above in such a way as to minimize adverse social, environmental and economic impacts on developing country Parties, particularly those identified in Article 4, paragraphs 8 and 9, of the Convention. In line with relevant decisions of the Conference of the Parties on the implementation of those paragraphs, the Conference of the Parties serving as the meeting of the Parties to this Protocol shall, at its first session, consider what actions are necessary to minimize the adverse effects of climate change and/or the impacts of response measures on Parties referred to in those paragraphs. Among the issues to be considered shall be the establishment of funding, insurance and transfer of technology.

ARTICLE 4

1. Any Parties included in Annex I that have reached an agreement to fulfil their commitments under Article 3 jointly, shall be deemed to have met those commitments provided that their total combined aggregate anthropogenic carbon dioxide equivalent emissions of the greenhouse gases listed in Annex A do not exceed their assigned amounts calculated pursuant to their quantified emission limitation and reduction commitments inscribed in Annex B and in accordance with the provisions of Article 3. The respective emission level allocated to each of the Parties to the agreement shall be set out in that agreement.

2. The Parties to any such agreement shall notify the secretariat of the terms of the agreement on the date of deposit of their instruments of ratification, acceptance or approval of this Protocol, or accession thereto. The secretariat shall in turn inform the Parties and signatories to the Convention of the terms of the agreement.

3. Any such agreement shall remain in operation for the duration of the commitment period specified in Article 3, paragraph 7.

4. If Parties acting jointly do so in the framework of, and together with, a regional economic integration organization, any alteration in the composition of the organization after adoption of this Protocol shall not affect existing commitments under this Protocol. Any alteration in the composition of the organization shall only apply for the purposes of those commitments under Article 3 that are adopted subsequent to that alteration.

5. In the event of failure by the Parties to such an agreement to achieve their total combined level of emission reductions, each Party to that agreement shall be responsible for its own level of emissions set out in the agreement.

6. If Parties acting jointly do so in the framework of, and together with, a regional economic integration organization which is itself a Party to this Protocol, each member State of that regional economic integration organization individually, and together with the regional economic integration organization acting in accordance with Article 24, shall, in the event of failure to achieve the total combined level of emission reductions, be responsible for its level of emissions as notified in accordance with this Article.

ARTICLE 5

1. Each Party included in Annex I shall have in place, no later than one year prior to the start of the first commitment period, a national system for the estimation of anthropogenic emissions by sources and removals by sinks of all greenhouse gases not controlled by the Montreal Protocol. Guidelines for such national systems, which shall incorporate the methodologies specified in paragraph 2 below, shall be decided upon by the Conference of the Parties serving as the meeting of the Parties to this Protocol at its first session.

2. Methodologies for estimating anthropogenic emissions by sources and removals by sinks of all greenhouse gases not controlled by the Montreal Protocol shall be those accepted by the Intergovernmental Panel on Climate Change and agreed upon by the Conference of the Parties at its third session. Where such methodologies are not used, appropriate adjustments shall be applied according to methodologies agreed upon by the Conference of the Parties serving as the meeting of the Parties to this Protocol at its first session. Based on the work of, *inter alia*, the Intergovernmental Panel on Climate Change and advice provided by the Subsidiary Body for Scientific and Technological Advice, the Conference of the Parties serving as the meeting of the Parties to this Protocol shall regularly review and, as appropriate, revise such methodologies and adjustments, taking fully into account any relevant decisions by the Conference of the Parties. Any revision to methodologies or adjustments shall be used only for the purposes of ascertaining compliance

with commitments under Article 3 in respect of any commitment period adopted subsequent to that revision.

3. The global warming potentials used to calculate the carbon dioxide equivalence of anthropogenic emissions by sources and removals by sinks of greenhouse gases listed in Annex A shall be those accepted by the Intergovernmental Panel on Climate Change and agreed upon by the Conference of the Parties at its third session. Based on the work of, *inter alia*, the Intergovernmental Panel on Climate Change and advice provided by the Subsidiary Body for Scientific and Technological Advice, the Conference of the Parties serving as the meeting of the Parties to this Protocol shall regularly review and, as appropriate, revise the global warming potential of each such greenhouse gas, taking fully into account any relevant decisions by the Conference of the Parties. Any revision to a global warming potential shall apply only to commitments under Article 3 in respect of any commitment period adopted subsequent to that revision.

ARTICLE 6

1. For the purpose of meeting its commitments under Article 3, any Party included in Annex I may transfer to, or acquire from, any other such Party emission reduction units resulting from projects aimed at reducing anthropogenic emissions by sources or enhancing anthropogenic removals by sinks of greenhouse gases in any sector of the economy, provided that:

(a) Any such project has the approval of the Parties involved;

(b) Any such project provides a reduction in emissions by sources, or an enhancement of removals by sinks, that is additional to any that would otherwise occur;

(c) It does not acquire any emission reduction units if it is not in compliance with its obligations under Articles 5 and 7; and

(d) The acquisition of emission reduction units shall be supplemental to domestic actions for the purposes of meeting commitments under Article 3.

2. The Conference of the Parties serving as the meeting of the Parties to this Protocol may, at its first session or as soon as practicable thereafter, further elaborate guidelines for the implementation of this Article, including for verification and reporting.

3. A Party included in Annex I may authorize legal entities to participate, under its responsibility, in actions leading to the generation, transfer or acquisition under this Article of emission reduction units.

4. If a question of implementation by a Party included in Annex I of the requirements referred to in this Article is identified in accordance with the relevant provisions of Article 8, transfers and acquisitions of emission reduction units may continue to be made after the question has been identified, provided that any such units may not be used by a Party to meet its commitments under Article 3 until any issue of compliance is resolved.

ARTICLE 7

1. Each Party included in Annex I shall incorporate in its annual inventory of anthropogenic emissions by sources and removals by sinks of greenhouse gases not controlled by the Montreal Protocol, submitted in accordance with the relevant decisions of the Conference of the Parties, the necessary supplementary information for the purposes of ensuring compliance with Article 3, to be determined in accordance with paragraph 4 below.

2. Each Party included in Annex I shall incorporate in its national communication, submitted under Article 12 of the Convention, the supplementary information necessary to demonstrate compliance with its commitments under this Protocol, to be determined in accordance with paragraph 4 below.

3. Each Party included in Annex I shall submit the information required under paragraph 1 above annually, beginning with the first inventory due under the Convention for the first year of the commitment period after this Protocol has entered into force for that Party. Each such Party shall submit the information required under paragraph 2 above as part of the first national communication due under the Convention after this Protocol has entered into force for it and after the adoption of guidelines as provided for in paragraph 4 below. The frequency of subsequent submission of information required under this Article shall be determined by

the Conference of the Parties serving as the meeting of the Parties to this Protocol, taking into account any timetable for the submission of national communications decided upon by the Conference of the Parties.

4. The Conference of the Parties serving as the meeting of the Parties to this Protocol shall adopt at its first session, and review periodically thereafter, guidelines for the preparation of the information required under this Article, taking into account guidelines for the preparation of national communications by Parties included in Annex I adopted by the Conference of the Parties. The Conference of the Parties serving as the meeting of the Parties to this Protocol shall also, prior to the first commitment period, decide upon modalities for the accounting of assigned amounts.

ARTICLE 8

1. The information submitted under Article 7 by each Party included in Annex I shall be reviewed by expert review teams pursuant to the relevant decisions of the Conference of the Parties and in accordance with guidelines adopted for this purpose by the Conference of the Parties serving as the meeting of the Parties to this Protocol under paragraph 4 below. The information submitted under Article 7, paragraph 1, by each Party included in Annex I shall be reviewed as part of the annual compilation and accounting of emissions inventories and assigned amounts. Additionally, the information submitted under Article 7, paragraph 2, by each Party included in Annex I shall be reviewed as part of the review of communications.

2. Expert review teams shall be coordinated by the secretariat and shall be composed of experts selected from those nominated by Parties to the Convention and, as appropriate, by intergovernmental organizations, in accordance with guidance provided for this purpose by the Conference of the Parties.

3. The review process shall provide a thorough and comprehensive technical assessment of all aspects of the implementation by a Party of this Protocol. The expert review teams shall prepare a report to the Conference of the Parties serving as the meeting of the Parties to this Protocol, assessing the implementation of the commitments of the Party and identifying any potential problems in, and factors influencing, the fulfilment of commitments. Such reports shall be circulated by the secretariat to all Parties to the Convention. The secretariat shall list those questions of implementation indicated in such reports for further consideration by the Conference of the Parties serving as the meeting of the Parties to this Protocol.

4. The Conference of the Parties serving as the meeting of the Parties to this Protocol shall adopt at its first session, and review periodically thereafter, guidelines for the review of implementation of this Protocol by expert review teams taking into account the relevant decisions of the Conference of the Parties.

5. The Conference of the Parties serving as the meeting of the Parties to this Protocol shall, with the assistance of the Subsidiary Body for Implementation and, as appropriate, the Subsidiary Body for Scientific and Technological Advice, consider:

(a) The information submitted by Parties under Article 7 and the reports of the expert reviews thereon conducted under this Article; and

(b) Those questions of implementation listed by the secretariat under paragraph 3 above, as well as any questions raised by Parties.

6. Pursuant to its consideration of the information referred to in paragraph 5 above, the Conference of the Parties serving as the meeting of the Parties to this Protocol shall take decisions on any matter required for the implementation of this Protocol.

ARTICLE 9

1. The Conference of the Parties serving as the meeting of the Parties to this Protocol shall periodically review this Protocol in the light of the best available scientific information and assessments on climate change and its impacts, as well as relevant technical, social and economic information. Such reviews shall be coordinated with pertinent reviews under the Convention, in particular those required by Article 4, paragraph 2(d), and Article 7, paragraph 2(a), of the Convention. Based on these reviews, the Conference of the Parties serving as the meeting of the Parties to this Protocol shall take appropriate action.

2. The first review shall take place at the second session of the Conference of the Parties serving as

the meeting of the Parties to this Protocol. Further reviews shall take place at regular intervals and in a timely manner.

ARTICLE 10

All Parties, taking into account their common but differentiated responsibilities and their specific national and regional development priorities, objectives and circumstances, without introducing any new commitments for Parties not included in Annex I, but reaffirming existing commitments under Article 4, paragraph 1, of the Convention, and continuing to advance the implementation of these commitments in order to achieve sustainable development, taking into account Article 4, paragraphs 3, 5 and 7, of the Convention, shall:

(a) Formulate, where relevant and to the extent possible, cost-effective national and, where appropriate, regional programmes to improve the quality of local emission factors, activity data and/or models which reflect the socio-economic conditions of each Party for the preparation and periodic updating of national inventories of anthropogenic emissions by sources and removals by sinks of all greenhouse gases not controlled by the Montreal Protocol, using comparable methodologies to be agreed upon by the Conference of the Parties, and consistent with the guidelines for the preparation of national communications adopted by the Conference of the Parties;

(b) Formulate, implement, publish and regularly update national and, where appropriate, regional programmes containing measures to mitigate climate change and measures to facilitate adequate adaptation to climate change:

(i) Such programmes would, *inter alia,* concern the energy, transport and industry sectors as well as agriculture, forestry and waste management. Furthermore, adaptation technologies and methods for improving spatial planning would improve adaptation to climate change; and

(ii) Parties included in Annex I shall submit information on action under this Protocol, including national programmes, in accordance with Article 7; and other Parties shall seek to include in their national communications, as appropriate, information on programmes which contain measures that the Party believes contribute to addressing climate change and its adverse impacts, including the abatement of increases in greenhouse gas emissions, and enhancement of and removals by sinks, capacity building and adaptation measures;

(c) Cooperate in the promotion of effective modalities for the development, application and diffusion of, and take all practicable steps to promote, facilitate and finance, as appropriate, the transfer of, or access to, environmentally sound technologies, know-how, practices and processes pertinent to climate change, in particular to developing countries, including the formulation of policies and programmes for the effective transfer of environmentally sound technologies that are publicly owned or in the public domain and the creation of an enabling environment for the private sector, to promote and enhance the transfer of, and access to, environmentally sound technologies;

(d) Cooperate in scientific and technical research and promote the maintenance and the development of systematic observation systems and development of data archives to reduce uncertainties related to the climate system, the adverse impacts of climate change and the economic and social consequences of various response strategies, and promote the development and strengthening of endogenous capacities and capabilities to participate in international and intergovernmental efforts, programmes and networks on research and systematic observation, taking into account Article 5 of the Convention;

(e) Cooperate in and promote at the international level, and, where appropriate, using existing bodies, the development and implementation of education and training programmes, including the strengthening of national capacity building, in particular human and institutional capacities and the exchange or secondment of personnel to train experts in this field, in particular for developing countries, and facilitate at the national level public awareness of, and public access to information on, climate change. Suitable modalities should be developed to implement these activities through the relevant bodies of the Convention, taking into account Article 6 of the Convention;

(f) Include in their national communications information on programmes and activities undertaken pursuant to this Article in accordance with relevant decisions of the Conference of the Parties; and

(g) Give full consideration, in implementing the commitments under this Article, to Article 4, paragraph 8, of the Convention.

3. The developed country Parties and other developed Parties in Annex II to the Convention may also provide, and developing country Parties avail themselves of, financial resources for the implementation of Article 10, through bilateral, regional and other multilateral channels.

ARTICLE 11

1. In the implementation of Article 10, Parties shall take into account the provisions of Article 4, paragraphs 4, 5, 7, 8 and 9, of the Convention.

2. In the context of the implementation of Article 4, paragraph 1, of the Convention, in accordance with the provisions of Article 4, paragraph 3, and Article 11 of the Convention, and through the entity or entities entrusted with the operation of the financial mechanism of the Convention, the developed country Parties and other developed Parties included in Annex II to the Convention shall:

(a) Provide new and additional financial resources to meet the agreed full costs incurred by developing country Parties in advancing the implementation of existing commitments under Article 4, paragraph 1(a), of the Convention that are covered in Article 10, subparagraph (a); and

(b) Also provide such financial resources, including for the transfer of technology, needed by the developing country Parties to meet the agreed full incremental costs of advancing the implementation of existing commitments under Article 4, paragraph 1, of the Convention that are covered by Article 10 and that are agreed between a developing country Party and the international entity or entities referred to in Article 11 of the Convention, in accordance with that Article.

The implementation of these existing commitments shall take into account the need for adequacy and predictability in the flow of funds and the importance of appropriate burden sharing among developed country Parties. The guidance to the entity or entities entrusted with the operation of the financial mechanism of the Convention in relevant decisions of the Conference of the Parties, including those agreed before the adoption of this Protocol, shall apply *mutatis mutandis* to the provisions of this paragraph.

ARTICLE 12

1. A clean development mechanism is hereby defined.

2. The purpose of the clean development mechanism shall be to assist Parties not included in Annex I in achieving sustainable development and in contributing to the ultimate objective of the Convention, and to assist Parties included in Annex I in achieving compliance with their quantified emission limitation and reduction commitments under Article 3.

3. Under the clean development mechanism:

(a) Parties not included in Annex I will benefit from project activities resulting in certified emission reductions; and

(b) Parties included in Annex I may use the certified emission reductions accruing from such project activities to contribute to compliance with part of their quantified emission limitation and reduction commitments under Article 3, as determined by the Conference of the Parties serving as the meeting of the Parties to this Protocol.

4. The clean development mechanism shall be subject to the authority and guidance of the Conference of the Parties serving as the meeting of the Parties to this Protocol and be supervised by an executive board of the clean development mechanism.

5. Emission reductions resulting from each project activity shall be certified by operational entities to be designated by the Conference of the Parties serving as the meeting of the Parties to this Protocol, on the basis of:

(a) Voluntary participation approved by each Party involved;

(b) Real, measurable, and long-term benefits related to the mitigation of climate change; and

(c) Reductions in emissions that are additional to any that would occur in the absence of the certified project activity.

6. The clean development mechanism shall assist in arranging funding of certified project activities as necessary.

7. The Conference of the Parties serving as the meeting of the Parties to this Protocol shall, at its first session, elaborate modalities and procedures with the objective of ensuring transparency, efficiency and accountability through independent auditing and verification of project activities.

8. The Conference of the Parties serving as the meeting of the Parties to this Protocol shall ensure that a share of the proceeds from certified project activities is used to cover administrative expenses as well as to assist developing country Parties that are particularly vulnerable to the adverse effects of climate change to meet the costs of adaptation.

9. Participation under the clean development mechanism, including in activities mentioned in paragraph 3(a) above and in the acquisition of certified emission reductions, may involve private and/or public entities, and is to be subject to whatever guidance may be provided by the executive board of the clean development mechanism.

10. Certified emission reductions obtained during the period from the year 2000 up to the beginning of the first commitment period can be used to assist in achieving compliance in the first commitment period.

ARTICLE 13

1. The Conference of the Parties, the supreme body of the Convention, shall serve as the meeting of the Parties to this Protocol.

2. Parties to the Convention that are not Parties to this Protocol may participate as observers in the proceedings of any session of the Conference of the Parties serving as the meeting of the Parties to this Protocol. When the Conference of the Parties serves as the meeting of the Parties to this Protocol, decisions under this Protocol shall be taken only by those that are Parties to this Protocol.

3. When the Conference of the Parties serves as the meeting of the Parties to this Protocol, any member of the Bureau of the Conference of the Parties representing a Party to the Convention but, at that time, not a Party to this Protocol, shall be replaced by an additional member to be elected by and from amongst the Parties to this Protocol.

4. The Conference of the Parties serving as the meeting of the Parties to this Protocol shall keep under regular review the implementation of this Protocol and shall make, within its mandate, the decisions necessary to promote its effective implementation. It shall perform the functions assigned to it by this Protocol and shall:

(a) Assess, on the basis of all information made available to it in accordance with the provisions of this Protocol, the implementation of this Protocol by the Parties, the overall effects of the measures taken pursuant to this Protocol, in particular environmental, economic and social effects as well as their cumulative impacts and the extent to which progress towards the objective of the Convention is being achieved;

(b) Periodically examine the obligations of the Parties under this Protocol, giving due consideration to any reviews required by Article 4, paragraph 2(d), and Article 7, paragraph 2, of the Convention, in the light of the objective of the Convention, the experience gained in its implementation and the evolution of scientific and technological knowledge, and in this respect consider and adopt regular reports on the implementation of this Protocol;

(c) Promote and facilitate the exchange of information on measures adopted by the Parties to address climate change and its effects, taking into account the differing circumstances, responsibilities and capabilities of the Parties and their respective commitments under this Protocol;

(d) Facilitate, at the request of two or more Parties, the coordination of measures adopted by them to address climate change and its effects, taking into account the differing circumstances, responsibilities and capabilities of the Parties and their respective commitments under this Protocol;

(e) Promote and guide, in accordance with the objective of the Convention and the provisions of this Protocol, and taking fully into account the relevant decisions by the Conference of the Parties, the development and periodic refinement of comparable methodologies for the effective implementation of this Protocol, to be agreed on by the Conference of the Parties serving as the meeting of the Parties to this Protocol;

(f) Make recommendations on any matters necessary for the implementation of this Protocol;

(g) Seek to mobilize additional financial resources in accordance with Article 11, paragraph 2;

(h) Establish such subsidiary bodies as are deemed necessary for the implementation of this Protocol;

(i) Seek and utilize, where appropriate, the services and cooperation of, and information provided by, competent international organizations and intergovernmental and non-governmental bodies; and

(j) Exercise such other functions as may be required for the implementation of this Protocol, and consider any assignment resulting from a decision by the Conference of the Parties.

5. The rules of procedure of the Conference of the Parties and financial procedures applied under the Convention shall be applied *mutatis mutandis* under this Protocol, except as may be otherwise decided by consensus by the Conference of the Parties serving as the meeting of the Parties to this Protocol.

6. The first session of the Conference of the Parties serving as the meeting of the Parties to this Protocol shall be convened by the secretariat in conjunction with the first session of the Conference of the Parties that is scheduled after the date of the entry into force of this Protocol. Subsequent ordinary sessions of the Conference of the Parties serving as the meeting of the Parties to this Protocol shall be held every year and in conjunction with ordinary sessions of the Conference of the Parties, unless otherwise decided by the Conference of the Parties serving as the meeting of the Parties to this Protocol.

7. Extraordinary sessions of the Conference of the Parties serving as the meeting of the Parties to this Protocol shall be held at such other times as may be deemed necessary by the Conference of the Parties serving as the meeting of the Parties to this Protocol, or at the written request of any Party, provided that, within six months of the request being communicated to the Parties by the secretariat, it is supported by at least one third of the Parties.

8. The United Nations, its specialized agencies and the International Atomic Energy Agency, as well as any State member thereof or observers thereto not party to the Convention, may be represented at sessions of the Conference of the Parties serving as the meeting of the Parties to this Protocol as observers. Any body or agency, whether national or international, governmental or non-governmental, which is qualified in matters covered by this Protocol and which has informed the secretariat of its wish to be represented at a session of the Conference of the Parties serving as the meeting of the Parties to this Protocol as an observer, may be so admitted unless at least one third of the Parties present object. The admission and participation of observers shall be subject to the rules of procedure, as referred to in paragraph 5 above.

ARTICLE 14

1. The secretariat established by Article 8 of the Convention shall serve as the secretariat of this Protocol.

2. Article 8, paragraph 2, of the Convention on the functions of the secretariat, and

Article 8, paragraph 3, of the Convention on arrangements made for the functioning of the secretariat, shall apply *mutatis mutandis* to this Protocol. The secretariat shall, in addition, exercise the functions assigned to it under this Protocol.

ARTICLE 15

1. The Subsidiary Body for Scientific and Technological Advice and the Subsidiary Body for Implementation established by Articles 9 and 10 of the Convention shall serve as, respectively, the Subsidiary Body for Scientific and Technological Advice and the Subsidiary Body for Implementation of this Protocol. The provisions relating to the functioning of these two bodies under the Convention shall apply *mutatis mutandis* to this Protocol. Sessions of the meetings of the Subsidiary Body for Scientific and Technological Advice and the Subsidiary Body for Implementation of this Protocol shall be held in conjunction with the meetings of, respectively, the Subsidiary Body for Scientific and Technological Advice and the Subsidiary Body for Implementation of the Convention.

2. Parties to the Convention that are not Parties to this Protocol may participate as observers in the proceedings of any session of the subsidiary bodies. When the subsidiary bodies serve as the subsidiary bodies of this Protocol, decisions under this Protocol shall be taken only by those that are Parties to this Protocol.

3. When the subsidiary bodies established by Articles 9 and 10 of the Convention exercise their functions with regard to matters concerning this Protocol, any member of the Bureaux of those subsidiary bodies representing a Party to the Convention but, at that time, not a party to this Protocol, shall be replaced by an additional member to be elected by and from amongst the Parties to this Protocol.

ARTICLE 16

The Conference of the Parties serving as the meeting of the Parties to this Protocol shall, as soon as practicable, consider the application to this Protocol of, and modify as appropriate, the multilateral consultative process referred to in Article 13 of the Convention, in the light of any relevant decisions that may be taken by the Conference of the Parties. Any multilateral consultative process that may be applied to this Protocol shall operate without prejudice to the procedures and mechanisms established in accordance with Article 18.

ARTICLE 17

The Conference of the Parties shall define the relevant principles, modalities, rules and guidelines, in particular for verification, reporting and accountability for emissions trading. The Parties included in Annex B may participate in emissions trading for the purposes of fulfilling their commitments under Article 3. Any such trading shall be supplemental to domestic actions for the purpose of meeting quantified emission limitation and reduction commitments under that Article.

ARTICLE 18

The Conference of the Parties serving as the meeting of the Parties to this Protocol shall, at its first session, approve appropriate and effective procedures and mechanisms to determine and to address cases of non-compliance with the provisions of this Protocol, including through the development of an indicative list of consequences, taking into account the cause, type, degree and frequency of non-compliance. Any procedures and mechanisms under this Article entailing binding consequences shall be adopted by means of an amendment to this Protocol.

ARTICLE 19

The provisions of Article 14 of the Convention on settlement of disputes shall apply *mutatis mutandis* to this Protocol.

ARTICLE 20

1. Any Party may propose amendments to this Protocol.

2. Amendments to this Protocol shall be adopted at an ordinary session of the Conference of the Parties serving as the meeting of the Parties to this Protocol. The text of any proposed amendment to this Protocol shall be communicated to the Parties by the secretariat at least six months before the meeting at which it is proposed for adoption. The secretariat shall also communicate the text of any proposed amendments to the Parties and signatories to the Convention and, for information, to the Depositary.

3. The Parties shall make every effort to reach agreement on any proposed amendment to this Protocol by consensus. If all efforts at consensus have been exhausted, and no agreement reached, the amendment shall as a last resort be adopted by a three-fourths majority vote of the Parties present and voting at the meeting. The adopted amendment shall be communicated by the secretariat to the Depositary, who shall circulate it to all Parties for their acceptance.

4. Instruments of acceptance in respect of an amendment shall be deposited with the Depositary. An amendment adopted in accordance with paragraph 3 above shall enter into force for those Parties having accepted it on the ninetieth day after the date of receipt by the Depositary of an instrument of acceptance by at least three fourths of the Parties to this Protocol.

5. The amendment shall enter into force for any other Party on the ninetieth day after the date on which that Party deposits with the Depositary its instrument of acceptance of the said amendment.

ARTICLE 21

1. Annexes to this Protocol shall form an integral part thereof and, unless otherwise expressly provided, a reference to this Protocol constitutes at the same time a reference to any annexes thereto. Any

annexes adopted after the entry into force of this Protocol shall be restricted to lists, forms and any other material of a descriptive nature that is of a scientific, technical, procedural or administrative character.

2. Any Party may make proposals for an annex to this Protocol and may propose amendments to annexes to this Protocol.

3. Annexes to this Protocol and amendments to annexes to this Protocol shall be adopted at an ordinary session of the Conference of the Parties serving as the meeting of the Parties to this Protocol. The text of any proposed annex or amendment to an annex shall be communicated to the Parties by the secretariat at least six months before the meeting at which it is proposed for adoption. The secretariat shall also communicate the text of any proposed annex or amendment to an annex to the Parties and signatories to the Convention and, for information, to the Depositary.

4. The Parties shall make every effort to reach agreement on any proposed annex or amendment to an annex by consensus. If all efforts at consensus have been exhausted, and no agreement reached, the annex or amendment to an annex shall as a last resort be adopted by a three-fourths majority vote of the Parties present and voting at the meeting. The adopted annex or amendment to an annex shall be communicated by the secretariat to the Depositary, who shall circulate it to all Parties for their acceptance.

5. An annex, or amendment to an annex other than Annex A or B, that has been adopted in accordance with paragraphs 3 and 4 above shall enter into force for all Parties to this Protocol six months after the date of the communication by the Depositary to such Parties of the adoption of the annex or adoption of the amendment to the annex, except for those Parties that have notified the Depositary, in writing, within that period of their non-acceptance of the annex or amendment to the annex. The annex or amendment to an annex shall enter into force for Parties which withdraw their notification of non-acceptance on the ninetieth day after the date on which withdrawal of such notification has been received by the Depositary.

6. If the adoption of an annex or an amendment to an annex involves an amendment to this Protocol, that annex or amendment to an annex shall not enter into force until such time as the amendment to this Protocol enters into force.

7. Amendments to Annexes A and B to this Protocol shall be adopted and enter into force in accordance with the procedure set out in Article 20, provided that any amendment to Annex B shall be adopted only with the written consent of the Party concerned.

ARTICLE 22

1. Each Party shall have one vote, except as provided for in paragraph 2 below.

2. Regional economic integration organizations, in matters within their competence, shall exercise their right to vote with a number of votes equal to the number of their member States that are Parties to this Protocol. Such an organization shall not exercise its right to vote if any of its member States exercises its right, and vice versa.

ARTICLE 23

The Secretary-General of the United Nations shall be the Depositary of this Protocol.

ARTICLE 24

1. This Protocol shall be open for signature and subject to ratification, acceptance or approval by States and regional economic integration organizations which are Parties to the Convention. It shall be open for signature at United Nations Headquarters in New York from 16 March 1998 to 15 March 1999. This Protocol shall be open for accession from the day after the date on which it is closed for signature. Instruments of ratification, acceptance, approval or accession shall be deposited with the Depositary.

2. Any regional economic integration organization which becomes a Party to this Protocol without any of its member States being a Party shall be bound by all the obligations under this Protocol. In the case of such organizations, one or more of whose member States is a Party to this Protocol, the organization and its member States shall decide on their respective responsibilities for the performance of their obligations under this Protocol. In such cases, the organization and the member States shall not be

entitled to exercise rights under this Protocol concurrently.

3. In their instruments of ratification, acceptance, approval or accession, regional economic integration organizations shall declare the extent of their competence with respect to the matters governed by this Protocol. These organizations shall also inform the Depositary, who shall in turn inform the Parties, of any substantial modification in the extent of their competence.

4. For the purposes of this Article, any instrument deposited by a regional economic integration organization shall not be counted as additional to those deposited by States members of the organization.

ARTICLE 25

1. This Protocol shall enter into force on the ninetieth day after the date on which not less than 55 Parties to the Convention, incorporating Parties included in Annex I which accounted in total for at least 55 per cent of the total carbon dioxide emissions for 1990 of the Parties included in Annex I, have deposited their instruments of ratification, acceptance, approval or accession.

2. For the purposes of this Article, "the total carbon dioxide emissions for 1990 of the Parties included in Annex I" means the amount communicated on or before the date of adoption of this Protocol by the Parties included in Annex I in their first national communications submitted in accordance with Article 12 of the Convention.

3. For each State or regional economic integration organization that ratifies, accepts or approves this Protocol or accedes thereto after the conditions set out in paragraph 1 above for entry into force have been fulfilled, this Protocol shall enter into force on the ninetieth day following the date of deposit of its instrument of ratification, acceptance, approval or accession.

ARTICLE 26

No reservations may be made to this Protocol.

ARTICLE 27

1. At any time after three years from the date on which this Protocol has entered into force for a Party, that Party may withdraw from this Protocol by giving written notification to the Depositary.

2. Any such withdrawal shall take effect upon expiry of one year from the date of receipt by the Depositary of the notification of withdrawal, or on such later date as may be specified in the notification of withdrawal.

3. Any Party that withdraws from the Convention shall be considered as also having withdrawn from this Protocol.

ARTICLE 28

The original of this Protocol, of which the Arabic, Chinese, English, French, Russian and Spanish texts are equally authentic, shall be deposited with the Secretary-General of the United Nations.

DONE at Kyoto this eleventh day of December one thousand nine hundred and ninety-seven.

IN WITNESS WHEREOF the undersigned, being duly authorized to that effect, have affixed their signatures to this Protocol on the dates indicated.

Convention on the Organisation for Economic Co-operation and Development

Paris 14th December 1960

http://www.oecd.org/document/7/0,2340,en_2649_201185_1915847_1_1_1_1,00.html

THE GOVERNMENTS of the Republic of Austria, the Kingdom of Belgium, Canada, the Kingdom of Denmark, the French Republic, the Federal Republic of Germany, the Kingdom of Greece, the Republic of Iceland, Ireland, the Italian Republic, the Grand Duchy of Luxembourg, the Kingdom of the Netherlands, the Kingdom of Norway, the Portuguese Republic, Spain, the Kingdom of Sweden, the Swiss Confederation, the Turkish Republic, the United Kingdom of Great Britain and Northern Ireland, and the United States of America;

CONSIDERING that economic strength and prosperity are essentiel for the attainment of the purposes of the United Nations, the preservation of individuel liberty and the increase of general well-being;

BELIEVING that they can further these aims most effectively by strengthening the tradition of co-operation which has evolved among them;

RECOGNISING that the economic recovery and progress of Europe to which their participation in the Organisation for European Economic Co-operation has made a major contribution, have opened new perspectives for strengthening that tradition and applying it to new tasks and broader objectives;

CONVINCED that broader co-operation will make a vital contribution to peaceful and harmonious relations among the peoples of the world;

RECOGNISING the increasing interdependence of their economies;

DETERMINED by consultation and co-operation to use more effectively their capacities and potentialities so as to promote the highest sustainable growth of their economies and improve the economic and social well-being of their peoples;

BELIEVING that the economically more advanced nations should co-operate in assisting to the best of their ability the countries in process of economic development;

RECOGNISING that the further expansion of world trade is one of the most important factors favouring the economic development of countries and the improvement of international economic relations; and

DETERMINED to pursue these purposes in a manner consistent with their obligations in other international organisations or institutions in which they participate or under agreements to which they are a party;

HAVE THEREFORE AGREED on the following provisions for the reconstitution of the Organisation for European Economic Co-operation as the Organisation for Economic Co-operation and Development:

ARTICLE 1

The aims of the Organisation for Economic Co-operation and Development (hereinafter called the "Organisation") shall be to promote policies designed:

(a) to achieve the highest sustainable economic growth and employment and a rising standard of living in Member countries, while maintaining financial stability, and thus to contribute to the development of the world economy;

(b) to contribute to sound economic expansion in Member as well as non-member countries in the process of economic development; and

(c) to contribute to the expansion of world trade on a multilateral, non-discriminatory basis in accordance with international obligations.

ARTICLE 2

In the pursuit of these aims, the Members agree that they will, both individually and jointly:

(a) promote the efficient use of their economic resources;

(b) in the scientific and technological field, promote the development of their resources, encourage research and promote vocational training;

(c) pursue policies designed to achieve economic growth and internal and external financial stability and to avoid developments which might endanger their economies or those of other countries;

(d) pursue their efforts to reduce or abolish obstacles to the exchange of goods and services and current payments and maintain and extend the liberalisation of capital movements; and

(e) contribute to the economic development of both Member and non-member countries in the process of economic development by appropriate means and, in particular, by the flow of capital to those countries, having regard to the importance to their economies of receiving technical assistance and of securing expanding export markets.

ARTICLE 3

With a view to achieving the aims set out in Article 1 and to fulfilling the undertakings contained in Article 2, the Members agree that they will:

(a) keep each other informed and furnish the Organisation with the information necessary for the accomplishment of its tasks;

(b) consult together on a continuing basis, carry out studies and participate in agreed projects; and

(c) co-operate closely and where appropriate take co-ordinated action.

ARTICLE 4

The Contracting Parties to this Convention shall be Members of the Organisation.

ARTICLE 5

In order to achieve its aims, the Organisation may:

(a) take decisions which, except as otherwise provided, shall be binding on all the Members;

(b) make recommendations to Members; and

(c) enter into agreements with Members, non-member States and international organisations.

Decision of the Council

Establishing an International Energy Agency of the Organisation

(Adopted by the Council at its 373rd Meeting on 15th November, 1974. The Delegates for Finland, France and Greece abstained)

The Council,

Having regard to the Convention on the Organisation for Economic Co-operation and Development of 14th December, 1960 (hereinafter called the "Convention") and, in particular, Articles 5(a), 6, 9, 12, 13 and 20 of the Convention;

Having regard to the Financial Regulations of the Organisation and, in particular, to Articles 5, 10, 14(b) and 16(b) thereof;

Having regard to the Regulations, Rules and Instructions for Council Experts and Consultants of the Organisation;

Noting that the Governments of certain Member countries have declared their intention to enter into a separate Agreement on an International Energy Program which is attached to document C(74)204 of 6th November, 1974, and Corrigendum 1 thereto, which is circulated for reference and is hereinafter referred to as the "Agreement";

Having regard to the Recommendation of the Council of 29th June, 1971 on Oil Stockpiling [C(71)113(Final)];

Having regard to the Decision of the Council of 14th November, 1972 on Emergency Plans and Measures and Apportionment of Oil Supplies in an Emergency in the OECD European Area [C(72)201(Final)];

Having regard to the Recommendation of the Council of 10th January, 1974 on the Supply of Bunker Fuels for Shipping and Fishing [C(73)257(Final)];

Having regard to the Recommendation of the Council of 10th January, 1974 on the Supply of Fuel for Civil Aircraft [C(73)258(Final)];

Having regard to the Note by the Secretary-General of 6th November, 1974 concerning the International Energy Program [C(74)203 and Corrigendum 1];

DECIDES:

ARTICLE 1

An International Energy Agency (hereinafter called the "Agency") is hereby established as an autonomous body within the framework of the Organisation.

ARTICLE 2

Participating Countries of the Agency are:

(a) Austria, Belgium, Canada, Denmark, Germany, Ireland, Italy, Japan, Luxembourg, the Netherlands, Spain, Sweden, Switzerland, Turkey, the United Kingdom and the United States;

(b) other Member countries of the Organisation which accede to this Decision and to the Agreement in accordance with its terms.

ARTICLE 3

This Decision will be open for accession by the European Communities upon their accession to the Agreement in accordance with its terms.

ARTICLE 4

A Governing Board composed of all the Participating Countries of the Agency shall be the body from which all acts of the Agency derive, and shall have the power to make recommendations and to take decisions which shall, except as otherwise provided, be binding upon Participating Countries, and to delegate its powers to other organs of the Agency.

The Governing Board shall adopt its own rules of procedure and voting rules.

ARTICLE 5

The Governing Board shall establish such organs and procedures as may be required for the proper functioning of the Agency.

ARTICLE 6

(a) The Governing Board shall decide upon and carry out an International Energy Program for co-operation in the field of energy, the aims of which are:

(i) development of a common level of emergency self-sufficiency in oil supplies;

(ii) establishment of common demand restraint measures in an emergency;

(iii) establishment and implementation of measures for the allocation of available oil in time of emergency;

(iv) development of a system of information on the international oil market and a.framework for consultation with international oil companies;

(v) development and implementation of a long-term co-operation programme to reduce dependence on imported oil, including: conservation of energy, development of alternative sources of energy, energy research and development, and supply of natural and enriched uranium;

(vi) promotion of co-operative relations with oil producing countries and with other oil consuming countries, particularly those of the developing world.

The Governing Board may adopt other measures of co-operation in the energy field which it may deem necessary and otherwise amend the Program by unanimity, taking into account the constitutional procedures of the Participating Countries.

(b) Upon the proposal of the Governing Board of the Agency the Council may confer additional responsibilities upon the Agency.

ARTICLE 7

(a) The organs of the Agency shall be assisted by an Executive Director and such staff as is necessary who shall form part of the Secretariat of the Organisation and who shall, in performing their duties under the International Energy Program, be responsible to and report to the organs of the Agency.

(b) The Executive Director shall be appointed by the Governing Board on the proposal or with concurrence of the Secretary-General.

(c) Consultants to the Agency may be appointed for a period exceeding that provided in Regulation 2(b) of the Regulations and Rules for Council Experts and Consultants of the Organisation.

ARTICLE 8

The Governing Board shall report annually to the Council on the activities of the Agency. The Governing Board shall submit, upon the request of the Council or upon its own initiative, other communications to the Council.

ARTICLE 9

The Agency shall co-operate with other competent bodies of the Organisation in areas of common interest. These bodies and the Agency shall consult with one another regarding their respective activities.

ARTICLE 10

(a) The budget of the Agency shall form part of the Budget of the Organisation and expenditure of the Agency shall be charged against the appropriations authorised for it under Part II of the Budget which shall include appropriate Budget estimates and provisions for all expenditure necessary for the operation of the Agency. Each Participating Country's share in financing such expenditure shall be fixed by the Governing Board. Special expenses incurred by the Agency in connection with activities referred to in Article 11 shall be shared by the Participating Countries in such proportions as shall be determined by unanimous agreement of those countries. The Governing Board shall designate an organ of the Agency to advise the Governing Board as required on the financial administration of the Agency and to give its opinion on the annual and other budget proposals submitted to the Governing Board.

(b) The Governing Board shall submit the annual and other budget proposals of the Agency to the Council for adoption by agreement of those Participating Countries of the Agency which voted in the Governing Board to submit the proposals to the Council.

(c) Notwithstanding the provisions of Article 14(b) of the Financial Regulations, the Governing Board may accept voluntary contributions and grants as well as payments for services rendered by the Agency.

(d) Notwithstanding the provisions of Article 16(b) of the Financial Regulations of the Organisation, appropriations in respect of the special activities referred to in Article 11 of this Decision, for which no commitment has been entered into before the end of the Financial Year for which they were appropriated, shall be automatically carried forward to the budget for the ensuing year.

ARTICLE 11

Any two or more Participating Countries may decide to carry out within the scope of the Program special activities, other than activities which are required to be carried out by all Participating Countries under the Agreement. Participating Countries who do not wish to take part in such activities shall abstain from taking part in such decisions and shall not be bound by them. Participating Countries carrying out such activities shall keep the Governing Board informed thereof.

ARTICLE 12

In order to achieve the objectives of the Program, the Agency may establish appropriate relationships with countries which are not Participating Countries, international organisations, whether Governmental or non-Governmental, other entities and individuals.

ARTICLE 13

(a) A Participating Country for which the Agreement shall have ceased to be in force or to apply provisionally shall be deemed to have withdrawn from the Agency.

(b) Notwithstanding the provisions of paragraph (a), a Country whose Government shall have signed the Agreement may, upon written notice to the Governing Board and to the Government of Belgium to the effect that the adoption of the Program by the Governing Board is binding on it pursuant to this Decision, remain a Participating Country of the Agency after the Agreement shall have ceased to apply for it, unless the Governing Board decides otherwise. Such a Country shall have the same obligations and the same rights as a Participating Country of the Agency for which the Agreement shall have entered definitively into force.

ARTICLE 14

The present Decision shall enter into force on 15th November, 1974.

IEP AGREEMENT

Explanatory Note:

Set out below is the text of the IEP Agreement of 18 November 1974, as amended to the present time, with particular reference to amendments to Article 62.

Subsequent to signature by the original Member countries indicated at the end of the Agreement, the following Member countries acceded to the I.E.P Agreement: Australia, Czech Republic, Finland, France, Greece, Hungary, Korea, New Zealand and Portugal.

Norway participates in the Agency as a Member under a special agreement.

The Commission of the European Communities also takes part in the work of the Agency pursuant to the Supplementary Protocol No. 1 to the OECD Convention.

Agreement on an International Energy Program

(As Amended)

THE GOVERNMENTS OF THE REPUBLIC OF AUSTRIA, THE KINGDOM OF BELGIUM, CANADA, THE KINGDOM OF DENMARK, THE FEDERAL REPUBLIC OF GERMANY, IRELAND, THE ITALIAN REPUBLIC, JAPAN, THE GRAND DUCHY OF LUXEMBOURG, THE KINGDOM OF THE NETHERLANDS, SPAIN, THE KINGDOM OF SWEDEN, THE SWISS CONFEDERATION, THE REPUBLIC OF TURKEY, THE UNITED KINGDOM OF GREAT BRITAIN AND NORTHERN IRELAND, AND THE UNITED STATES OF AMERICA,

DESIRING to promote secure oil supplies on reasonable and equitable terms,

DETERMINED to take common effective measures to meet oil supply emergencies by developing an emergency self-sufficiency in oil supplies, restraining demand and allocating available oil among their countries on an equitable basis,

DESIRING to promote co-operative relations with oil producing countries and with other oil consuming countries, including those of the developing world, through a purposeful dialogue, as well as through other forms of co-operation, to further the opportunities for a better understanding between consumer and producer countries,

MINDFUL of the interests of other oil consuming countries, including those of the developing world,

DESIRING to play a more active role in relation to the oil industry by establishing a comprehensive international information system and a permanent framework for consultation with oil companies,

DETERMINED to reduce their dependence on imported oil by undertaking long term co-operative efforts on conservation of energy, on accelerated development of alternative sources of energy, on research and development in the energy field and on uranium enrichment,

CONVINCED that these objectives can only be reached through continued co-operative efforts within effective organs,

EXPRESSING the intention that such organs be created within the framework of the Organisation for Economic Co-operation and Development,

RECOGNISING that other Member countries of the Organisation for Economic Co-operation and Development may desire to join in their efforts,

CONSIDERING the special responsibility of governments for energy supply,

CONCLUDE that it is necessary to establish an International Energy Program to be implemented through an International Energy Agency, and to that end,

HAVE AGREED as follows:

Article 1

1. The Participating Countries shall implement the International Energy Program as provided for in

this Agreement through the International Energy Agency, described in Chapter IX, hereinafter referred to as the "Agency".

2. The term "Participating Countries" means States to which this Agreement applies provisionally and States for which the Agreement has entered into and remains in force.

3. The term "group" means the Participating Countries as a group.

CHAPTER I

EMERGENCY SELF-SUFFICIENCY

Article 2

1. The Participating Countries shall establish a common emergency self-sufficiency in oil supplies. To this end, each Participating Country shall maintain emergency reserves sufficient to sustain consumption for at least 60 days with no net oil imports. Both consumption and net oil imports shall be reckoned at the average daily level of the preceding calendar year.

2. The Governing Board shall, acting by special majority, not later than 1st July, 1975, decide the date from which the emergency reserve commitment of each Participating Country shall, for the purpose of calculating its supply right referred to in Article 7, be deemed to be raised to a level of 90 days. Each Participating Country shall increase its actual level of emergency reserves to 90 days and shall endeavour to do so by the date so decided.

3. The term "emergency reserve commitment" means the emergency reserves equivalent to 60 days of net oil imports as set out in paragraph 1 and, from the date to be decided according to paragraph 2, to 90 days of net oil imports as set out in paragraph 2.

Article 3

1. The emergency reserve commitment set out in Article 2 may be satisfied by:

- oil stocks,
- fuel switching capacity,
- stand-by oil production,

in accordance with the provisions of the Annex which forms an integral part of this Agreement.

2. The Governing Board shall, acting by majority, not later than 1st July, 1975, decide the extent to which the emergency reserve commitment may be satisfied by the elements mentioned in paragraph 1.

Article 4

1. The Standing Group on Emergency Questions shall, on a continuing basis, review the effectiveness of the measures taken by each Participating Country to meet its emergency reserve commitment.

2. The Standing Group on Emergency Questions shall report to the Management Committee, which shall make proposals, as appropriate, to the Governing Board. The Governing Board may, acting by majority, adopt recommendations to Participating Countries.

CHAPTER II

DEMAND RESTRAINT

Article 5

1. Each Participating Country shall at all times have ready a program of contingent oil demand restraint measures enabling it to reduce its rate of final consumption in accordance with Chapter IV.

2. The Standing Group on Emergency Questions shall, on a continuing basis, review and assess:

- each Participating Country's program of demand restraint measures,
- the effectiveness of measures actually taken by each Participating Country.

3. The Standing Group on Emergency Questions shall report to the Management Committee, which shall make proposals, as appropriate, to the Governing Board. The Governing Board may, acting by majority, adopt recommendations to Participating Countries.

CHAPTER III

ALLOCATION

Article 6

1. Each Participating Country shall take the necessary measures in order that allocation of oil

will be carried out pursuant to this Chapter and Chapter IV.

2. The Standing Group on Emergency Questions shall, on a continuing basis, review and assess:

- each Participating Country's measures in order that allocation of oil will be carried out pursuant to this Chapter and Chapter IV,
- the effectiveness of measures actually taken by each Participating Country.

3. The Standing Group on Emergency Questions shall report to the Management Committee, which shall make proposals, as appropriate, to the Governing Board. The Governing Board may, acting by majority, adopt recommendations to Participating Countries.

4. The Governing Board shall, acting by majority, decide promptly on the practical procedures for the allocation of oil and on the procedures and modalities for the participation of oil companies therein within the framework of this Agreement.

Article 7

1. When allocation of oil is carried out pursuant to Article 13, 14, or 15, each Participating Country shall have a supply right equal to its permissible consumption less its emergency reserve drawdown obligation.

2. A Participating Country whose supply right exceeds the sum of its normal domestic production and actual net imports available during an emergency shall have an allocation right which entitles it to additional net imports equal to that excess.

3. A Participating Country in which the sum of normal domestic production and actual net imports available during an emergency exceeds its supply right shall have an allocation obligation which requires it to supply, directly or indirectly, the quantity of oil equal to that excess to other Participating Countries. This would not preclude any Participating Country from maintaining exports of oil to non-participating countries.

4. The term "permissible consumption" means the average daily rate of final consumption allowed when emergency demand restraint at the applicable level has been activated; possible further voluntary demand restraint by any Participating Country shall not affect its allocation right or obligation.

5. The term "emergency reserve drawdown obligation" means the emergency reserve commitment of any Participating Country divided by the total emergency reserve commitment of the group and multiplied by the group supply shortfall.

6. The term "group supply shortfall" means the shortfall for the group as measured by the aggregate permissible consumption for the group minus the daily rate of oil supplies available to the group during an emergency.

7. The term "oil supplies available to the group" means

- all crude oil available to the group,
- all petroleum products imported from outside the group, and
- all finished products and refinery feedstocks which are produced in association with natural gas and crude oil and are available to the group.

8. The term "final consumption" means total domestic consumption of all finished petroleum products.

Article 8

1. When allocation of oil to a Participating Country is carried out pursuant to Article 17, that Participating Country shall

- sustain from its final consumption the reduction in its oil supplies up to a level equal to 7 per cent of its final consumption during the base period,
- have an allocation right equal to the reduction in its oil supplies which results in a reduction of its final consumption over and above that level.

2. The obligation to allocate this amount of oil is shared among the other Participating Countries on the basis of their final consumption during the base period.

3. The Participating Countries may meet their allocation obligations by any measures of their own choosing, including demand restraint measures or use of emergency reserves.

Article 9

1. For purposes of satisfying allocation rights and allocation obligations, the following elements will be included:

- all crude oil,
- all petroleum products,

• all refinery feedstocks, and

• all finished products produced in association with natural gas and crude oil.

2. To calculate a Participating Country's allocation right, petroleum products normally imported by that Participating Country, whether from other Participating Countries or from non-participating countries, shall be expressed in crude oil equivalents and treated as though they were imports of crude oil to that Participating Country.

3. Insofar as possible, normal channels of supply will be maintained as well as the normal supply proportions between crude oil and products and among different categories of crude oil and products.

4. When allocation takes place, an objective of the Program shall be that available crude oil and products shall, insofar as possible, be shared within the refining and distributing industries as well as between refining and distributing companies in accordance with historical supply patterns.

Article 10

1. The objectives of the Program shall include ensuring fair treatment for all Participating Countries and basing the price for allocated oil on the price conditions prevailing for comparable commercial transactions.

2. Questions relating to the price of oil allocated during an emergency shall be examined by the Standing Group on Emergency Questions.

Article 11

1. It is not an objective of the Program to seek to increase, in an emergency, the share of world oil supply that the group had under normal market conditions. Historical oil trade patterns should be preserved as far as is reasonable, and due account should be taken of the position of individual non-participating countries.

2. In order to maintain the principles set out in paragraph 1, the Management Committee shall make proposals, as appropriate, to the Governing Board, which, acting by majority, shall decide on such proposals.

CHAPTER IV

ACTIVATION

Article 12

Whenever the group as a whole or any Participating Country sustains or can reasonably be expected to sustain a reduction in its oil supplies, the emergency measures, which are the mandatory demand restraint referred to in Chapter II and the allocation of available oil referred to in Chapter III, shall be activated in accordance with this Chapter.

Article 13

Whenever the group sustains or can reasonably be expected to sustain a reduction in the daily rate of its oil supplies at least equal to 7 per cent of the average daily rate of its final consumption during the base period, each Participating Country shall implement demand restraint measures sufficient to reduce its final consumption by an amount equal to 7 per cent of its final consumption during the base period, and allocation of available oil among the Participating Countries shall take place in accordance with Articles 7, 9, 10 and 11.

Article 14

Whenever the group sustains or can reasonably be expected to sustain a reduction in the daily rate of its oil supplies at least equal to 12 per cent of the average daily rate of its final consumption during the base period, each Participating Country shall implement demand restraint measures sufficient to reduce its final consumption by an amount equal to 10 per cent of its final consumption during the base period, and allocation of available oil among the Participating Countries shall take place in accordance with Articles 7, 9, 10 and 11.

Article 15

When cumulative daily emergency reserve drawdown obligations as defined in Article 7 have reached 50 per cent of emergency reserve commitments and a decision has been taken in accordance with Article 20, each Participating Country shall take the measures so decided, and allocation of available oil among the Participating Countries shall take place in accordance with Articles 7, 9, 10 and 11.

Article 16

When demand restraint is activated in accordance with this Chapter, a Participating Country may substitute for demand restraint measures use of emergency reserves held in excess of its emergency reserve commitment as provided in the Program.

Article 17

1. Whenever any Participating Country sustains or can reasonably be expected to sustain a reduction in the daily rate of its oil supplies which results in a reduction of the daily rate of its final consumption by an amount exceeding 7 per cent of the average daily rate of its final consumption during the base period, allocation of available oil to that Participating Country shall take place in accordance with Articles 8 to 11.

2. Allocation of available oil shall also take place when the conditions in paragraph 1 are fulfilled in a major region of a Participating Country whose oil market is incompletely integrated. In this case, the allocation obligation of other Participating Countries shall be reduced by the theoretical allocation obligation of any other major region or regions of the Participating Country concerned.

Article 18

1. The term "base period" means the most recent four quarters with a delay of one quarter necessary to collect information. While emergency measures are applied with regard to the group or to a Participating Country, the base period shall remain fixed.

2. The Standing Group on Emergency Questions shall examine the base period set out in paragraph 1, taking into account in particular such factors as growth, seasonal variations in consumption and cyclical changes and shall, not later than 1st April, 1975, report to the Management Committee. The Management Committee shall make proposals, as appropriate, to the Governing Board, which, acting by majority, shall decide on these proposals not later than 1st July, 1975.

Article 19

1. The Secretariat shall make a finding when a reduction of oil supplies as mentioned in Article 13, 14 or 17 has occurred or can reasonably be expected to occur, and shall establish the amount of the reduction or expected reduction for each Participating Country and for the group. The Secretariat shall keep the Management Committee informed of its deliberations, and shall immediately report its finding to the members of the Committee and inform the Participating Countries thereof. The report shall include information on the nature of the reduction.

2. Within 48 hours of the Secretariat's reporting a finding, the Committee shall meet to review the accuracy of the data compiled and the information provided. The Committee shall report to the Governing Board within a further 48 hours. The report shall set out the views expressed by the members of the Committee, including any views regarding the handling of the emergency.

3. Within 48 hours of receiving the Management Committee's report, the Governing Board shall meet to review the finding of the Secretariat in the light of that report. The activation of emergency measures shall be considered confirmed and Participating Countries shall implement such measures within 15 days of such confirmation unless the Governing Board, acting by special majority, decides within a further 48 hours not to activate the emergency measures, to activate them only in part or to fix another time limit for their implementation.

4. If, according to the finding of the Secretariat, the conditions of more than one of the Articles 14, 13 and 17 are fulfilled, any decision not to activate emergency measures shall be taken separately for each Article and in the above order. If the conditions in Article 17 are fulfilled with regard to more than one Participating Country any decision not to activate allocation shall be taken separately with respect to each Country.

5. Decisions pursuant to paragraphs 3 and 4 may at any time be reversed by the Governing Board, acting by majority.

6. In making its finding under this Article, the Secretariat shall consult with oil companies to obtain their views regarding the situation and the appropriateness of the measures to be taken.

7. An international advisory board from the oil industry shall be convened, not later than the activation of emergency measures, to assist the Agency in ensuring the effective operation of such measures.

Article 20

1. The Secretariat shall make a finding when cumulative daily emergency reserve drawdown obligations have reached or can reasonably be expected to reach 50 per cent of emergency reserve commitments. The Secretariat shall immediately report its finding to the members of the Management Committee and inform the Participating Countries thereof. The report shall include information on the oil situation.

2. Within 72 hours of the Secretariat's reporting such a finding, the Management Committee shall meet to review the data compiled and the information provided. On the basis of available information the Committee shall report to the Governing Board within a further 48 hours proposing measures required for meeting the necessities of the situation, including the increase in the level of mandatory demand restraint that may be necessary. The report shall set out the views expressed by the members of the Committee.

3. The Governing Board shall meet within 48 hours of receiving the Committee's report and proposal. The Governing Board shall review the finding of the Secretariat and the report of the Management Committee and shall within a further 48 hours, acting by special majority, decide on the measures required for meeting the necessities of the situation, including the increase in the level of mandatory demand restraint that may be necessary.

Article 21

1. Any Participating Country may request the Secretariat to make a finding under Article 19 or 20.

2. If, within 72 hours of such request, the Secretariat does not make such a finding, the Participating Country may request the Management Committee to meet and consider the situation in accordance with the provisions of this Agreement.

3. The Management Committee shall meet within 48 hours of such request in order to consider the situation. It shall, at the request of any Participating Country, report to the Governing Board within a further 48 hours. The report shall set out the views expressed by the members of the Committee and by the Secretariat, including any views regarding the handling of the situation.

4. The Governing Board shall meet within 48 hours of receiving the Management Committee's report. If it finds, acting by majority, that the conditions set out in Article 13, 14, 15 or 17 are fulfilled, emergency measures shall be activated accordingly.

Article 22

The Governing Board may at any time decide by unanimity to activate any appropriate emergency measures not provided for in this Agreement, if the situation so requires.

DEACTIVATION

Article 23

1. The Secretariat shall make a finding when a reduction of supplies as mentioned in Article 13, 14 or 17 has decreased or can reasonably be expected to decrease below the level referred to in the relevant Article. The Secretariat shall keep the Management Committee informed of its deliberations and shall immediately report its finding to the members of the Committee and inform the Participating Countries thereof.

2. Within 72 hours of the Secretariat's reporting a finding, the Management Committee shall meet to review the data compiled and the information provided. It shall report to the Governing Board within a further 48 hours. The report shall set out the views expressed by the members of the Committee, including any views regarding the handling of the emergency.

3. Within 48 hours of receiving the Committee's report, the Governing Board shall meet to review the finding of the Secretariat in the light of the report from the Management Committee. The deactivation of emergency measures or the applicable reduction of the demand restraint level shall be considered confirmed unless the Governing Board, acting by special majority, decides within a further 48 hours to maintain the emergency measures or to deactivate them only in part.

4. In making its finding under this Article, the Secretariat shall consult with the international advisory board, mentioned in Article 19, paragraph 7, to obtain its views regarding the situation and the appropriateness of the measures to be taken.

5. Any Participating Country may request the Secretariat to make a finding under this Article.

Article 24

When emergency measures are in force, and the Secretariat has not made a finding under Article 23, the Governing Board, acting by special majority, may at any time decide to deactivate the measures either wholly or in part.

CHAPTER V

INFORMATION SYSTEM ON THE INTERNATIONAL OIL MARKET

Article 25

1. The Participating Countries shall establish an Information System consisting of two sections:

- a General Section on the situation in the international oil market and activities of oil companies,
- a Special Section designed to ensure the efficient operation of the measures described in Chapters I to IV.

2. The System shall be operated on a permanent basis, both under normal conditions and during emergencies, and in a manner which ensures the confidentiality of the information made available.

3. The Secretariat shall be responsible for the operation of the Information System and shall make the information compiled available to the Participating Countries.

Article 26

The term "oil companies" means international companies, national companies, non-integrated companies and other entities which play a significant role in the international oil industry.

GENERAL SECTION

Article 27

1. Under the General Section of the Information System, the Participating Countries shall, on a regular basis, make available to the Secretariat information on the precise data identified in accordance with Article 29 on the following subjects relating to oil companies operating within their respective jurisdictions:

(a) Corporate structure;

(b) Financial structure, including balance sheets, profit and loss accounts, and taxes paid;

(c) Capital investments realised;

(d) Terms of arrangements for access to major sources of crude oil;

(e) Current rates of production and anticipated changes therein;

(f) Allocations of available crude supplies to affiliates and other customers (criteria and realisations);

(g) Stocks;

(h) Cost of crude oil and oil products;

(i) Prices, including transfer prices to affiliates;

(j) Other subjects, as decided by the Governing Board, acting by unanimity.

2. Each Participating Country shall take appropriate measures to ensure that all oil companies operating within its jurisdiction make such information available to it as is necessary to fulfil its obligations under paragraph 1, taking into account such relevant information as is already available to the public or to Governments.

3. Each Participating Country shall provide information on a non-proprietary basis and on a company and/or country basis as appropriate, and in such a manner and degree as will not prejudice competition or conflict with the legal requirements of any Participating Country relating to competition.

4. No Participating Country shall be entitled to obtain, through the General Section, any information on the activities of a company operating within its jurisdiction which could not be obtained by it from that company by application of its laws or through its institutions and customs if that company were operating solely within its jurisdiction.

Article 28

Information provided on a "non-proprietary basis" means information which does not constitute or relate to patents, trademarks, scientific or manufacturing processes or developments, individual sales, tax returns, customer lists or geological and geophysical information, including maps.

Article 29

1. Within 60 days of the first day of the provisional application of this Agreement, and as appropriate thereafter, the Standing Group on the Oil Market

shall submit a report to the Management Committee identifying the precise data within the list of subjects in Article 27, paragraph 1, which are required for the efficient operation of the General Section, and specifying the procedures for obtaining such data on a regular basis.

2. The Management Committee shall review the report and make proposals to the Governing Board which, within 30 days of the submission of the report to the Management Committee, and acting by majority, shall take the decisions necessary for the establishment and efficient operation of the General Section.

Article 30

In preparing its reports under Article 29, the Standing Group on the Oil Market shall

- consult with oil companies to ensure that the System is compatible with industry operations;
- identify specific problems and issues which are of concern to Participating Countries;
- identify specific data which are useful and necessary to resolve such problems and issues;
- work out precise standards for the harmonization of the required information in order to ensure comparability of the data;
- work out procedures to ensure the confidentiality of the information.

Article 31

1. The Standing Group on the Oil Market shall on a continuing basis review the operation of the General Section.

2. In the event of changes in the conditions of the international oil market, the Standing Group on the Oil Market shall report to the Management Committee. The Committee shall make proposals on appropriate changes to the Governing Board which, acting by majority, shall decide on such proposals.

SPECIAL SECTION

Article 32

1. Under the Special Section of the Information System, the Participating Countries shall make available to the Secretariat all information which is necessary to ensure the efficient operation of emergency measures.

2. Each Participating Country shall take appropriate measures to ensure that all oil companies operating within its jurisdiction make such information available to it as is necessary to enable it to fulfil its obligations under paragraph 1 and under Article 33.

3. The Secretariat shall, on the basis of this information and other information available, continuously survey the supply of oil to and the consumption of oil within the group and each Participating Country.

Article 33

Under the Special Section, the Participating Countries shall, on a regular basis, make available to the Secretariat information on the precise data identified in accordance with Article 34 on the following subjects:

(a) Oil consumption and supply;

(b) Demand restraint measures;

(c) Levels of emergency reserves;

(d) Availability and utilisation of transportation facilities;

(e) Current and projected levels of international supply and demand;

(f) Other subjects, as decided by the Governing Board, acting by unanimity.

Article 34

1. Within 30 days of the first day of the provisional application of this Agreement, the Standing Group on Emergency Questions shall submit a report to the Management Committee identifying the precise data within the list of subjects in Article 33 which are required under the Special Section to ensure the efficient operation of emergency measures and specifying the procedures for obtaining such data on a regular basis, including accelerated procedures in times of emergency.

2. The Management Committee shall review the report and make proposals to the Governing Board which, within 30 days of the submission of the report to the Management Committee, and acting by majority, shall take the decisions necessary for the establishment and efficient operation of the Special Section.

Article 35

In preparing its report under Article 34, the Standing Group on Emergency Questions shall

- consult with oil companies to ensure that the System is compatible with industry operations;
- work out precise standards for the harmonization of the required information in order to ensure comparability of the data;
- work out procedures to ensure the confidentiality of the information.

Article 36

The Standing Group on Emergency Questions shall on a continuing basis review the operation of the Special Section and shall, as appropriate, report to the Management Committee. The Committee shall make proposals on appropriate changes to the Governing Board, which, acting by majority, shall decide on such proposals.

CHAPTER VI

FRAMEWORK FOR CONSULTATION WITH OIL COMPANIES

Article 37

1. The Participating Countries shall establish within the Agency a permanent framework for consultation within which one or more Participating Countries may, in an appropriate manner, consult with and request information from individual oil companies on all important aspects of the oil industry, and within which the Participating Countries may share among themselves on a co-operative basis the results of such consultations.

2. The framework for consultation shall be established under the auspices of the Standing Group on the Oil Market.

3. Within 60 days of the first day of the provisional application of this Agreement, and as appropriate thereafter, the Standing Group on the Oil Market, after consultation with oil companies, shall submit a report to the Management Committee on the procedures for such consultations. The Management Committee shall review the report and make proposals to the Governing Board, which, within 30 days of the submission of the report to the Management Committee, and acting by majority, shall decide on such procedures.

Article 38

1. The Standing Group on the Oil Market shall present a report to the Management Committee on consultations held with any oil company within 30 days thereof.

2. The Management Committee shall consider the report and may make proposals on appropriate co-operative action to the Governing Board, which shall decide on such proposals.

Article 39

1. The Standing Group on the Oil Market shall, on a continuing basis, evaluate the results of the consultations with and the information collected from oil companies.

2. On the basis of these evaluations, the Standing Group may examine and assess the international oil situation and the position of the oil industry and shall report to the Management Committee.

3. The Management Committee shall review such reports and make proposals on appropriate co-operative action to the Governing Board, which shall decide on such proposals.

Article 40

The Standing Group on the Oil Market shall submit annually a general report to the Management Committee on the functioning of the framework for consultation with oil companies.

CHAPTER VII

LONG TERM CO-OPERATION ON ENERGY

Article 41

1. The Participating Countries are determined to reduce over the longer term their dependence on imported oil for meeting their total energy requirements.

2. To this end, the Participating Countries will undertake national programs and promote the adoption of co-operative programs, including, as appropriate, the sharing of means and efforts, while concerting national policies, in the areas set out in Article 42.

Article 42

1. The Standing Group on Long Term Co-operation shall examine and report to the Management Committee on co-operative action. The following areas shall in particular be considered:

(a) Conservation of energy, including co-operative programs on

- exchange of national experiences and information on energy conservation;
- ways and means for reducing the growth of energy consumption through conservation.

(b) Development of alternative sources of energy such as domestic oil, coal, natural gas, nuclear energy and hydro-electric power, including co-operative programs on

- exchange of information on such matters as resources, supply and demand, price and taxation;
- ways and means for reducing the growth of consumption of imported oil through the development of alternative sources of energy;
- concrete projects, including jointly financed projects;
- criteria, quality objectives and standards for environmental protection.

(c) Energy research and development, including as a matter of priority co-operative programs on

- coal technology;
- solar energy;
- radioactive waste management;
- controlled thermonuclear fusion;
- production of hydrogen from water;
- nuclear safety;
- waste heat utilisation;
- conservation of energy;
- municipal and industrial waste utilisation for energy conservation;
- overall energy system analysis and general studies.

(d) Uranium enrichment, including co-operative programs

- to monitor developments in natural and enriched uranium supply;
- to facilitate development of natural uranium resources and enrichment services;
- to encourage such consultations as may be required to deal with international issues that may arise in relation to the expansion of enriched uranium supply;
- to arrange for the requisite collection, analysis and dissemination of data related to the planning of enrichment services.

2. In examining the areas of co-operative action, the Standing Group shall take due account of ongoing activities elsewhere.

3. Programs developed under paragraph 1 may be jointly financed. Such joint financing may take place in accordance with Article 64, paragraph 2.

Article 43

1. The Management Committee shall review the reports of the Standing Group and make appropriate proposals to the Governing Board, which shall decide on these proposals not later than 1st July, 1975.

2. The Governing Board shall take into account possibilities for co-operation within a broader framework.

CHAPTER VIII

RELATIONS WITH PRODUCER COUNTRIES AND WITH OTHER CONSUMER COUNTRIES

Article 44

The Participating Countries will endeavour to promote co-operative relations with oil producing countries and with other oil consuming countries, including developing countries. They will keep under review developments in the energy field with a view to identifying opportunities for and promoting a purposeful dialogue, as well as other forms of co-operation, with producer countries and with other consumer countries.

Article 45

To achieve the objectives set out in Article 44, the Participating Countries will give full consideration to the needs and interests of other oil consuming countries, particularly those of the developing countries.

Article 46

The Participating Countries will, in the context of the Program, exchange views on their relations with oil producing countries. To this end, the Participating Countries should inform each other of co-operative action on their part with producer countries which is relevant to the objectives of the Program.

Article 47

The Participating Countries will, in the context of the Program

- seek, in the light of their continuous review of developments in the international energy situation and its effect on the world economy, opportunities and means of encouraging stable international trade in oil and of promoting secure oil supplies on reasonable and equitable terms for each Participating Country;
- consider, in the light of work going on in other international organisations, other possible fields of co-operation including the prospects for co-operation in accelerated industrialisation and socio-economic development in the principal producing areas and the implications of this for international trade and investment;
- keep under review the prospects for co-operation with oil producing countries on energy questions of mutual interest, such as conservation of energy, the development of alternative sources, and research and development.

Article 48

1. The Standing Group on Relations with Producer and other Consumer Countries will examine and report to the Management Committee on the matters described in this Chapter.

2. The Management Committee may make proposals on appropriate co-operative action regarding these matters to the Governing Board, which shall decide on such proposals.

CHAPTER IX

INSTITUTIONAL AND GENERAL PROVISIONS

Article 49

1. The Agency shall have the following organs:
   - a Governing Board
   - a Management Committee
   - Standing Groups on
     - Emergency Questions
     - The Oil Market
     - Long Term Co-operation
     - Relations with Producer and Other Consumer Countries.

2. The Governing Board or the Management Committee may, acting by majority, establish any other organ necessary for the implementation of the Program.

3. The Agency shall have a Secretariat to assist the organs mentioned in paragraphs 1 and 2.

GOVERNING BOARD

Article 50

1. The Governing Board shall be composed of one or more ministers or their delegates from each Participating Country.

2. The Governing Board, acting by majority, shall adopt its own rules of procedure. Unless otherwise decided in the rules of procedure, these rules shall also apply to the Management Committee and the Standing Groups.

3. The Governing Board, acting by majority, shall elect its Chairman and Vice-Chairmen.

Article 51

1. The Governing Board shall adopt decisions and make recommendations which are necessary for the proper functioning of the Program.

2. The Governing Board shall review periodically and take appropriate action concerning developments in the international energy situation, including problems relating to the oil supplies of any

Participating Country or Countries, and the economic and monetary implications of these developments. In its activities concerning the economic and monetary implications of developments in the international energy situation, the Governing Board shall take into account the competence and activities of international institutions responsible for overall economic and monetary questions.

3. The Governing Board, acting by majority, may delegate any of its functions to any other organ of the Agency.

Article 52

1. Subject to Article 61, paragraph 2, and Article 65, decisions adopted pursuant to this Agreement by the Governing Board or by any other organ by delegation from the Board shall be binding on the Participating Countries.

2. Recommendations shall not be binding.

MANAGEMENT COMMITTEE

Article 53

1. The Management Committee shall be composed of one or more senior representatives of the Government of each Participating Country.

2. The Management Committee shall carry out the functions assigned to it in this Agreement and any other function delegated to it by the Governing Board.

3. The Management Committee may examine and make proposals to the Governing Board, as appropriate, on any matter within the scope of this Agreement.

4. The Management Committee shall be convened upon the request of any Participating Country.

5. The Management Committee, acting by majority, shall elect its Chairman and Vice-Chairmen.

STANDING GROUPS

Article 54

1. Each Standing Group shall be composed of one or more representatives of the Government of each Participating Country.

2. The Management Committee, acting by majority, shall elect the Chairmen and Vice-Chairmen of the Standing Groups.

Article 55

1. The Standing Group on Emergency Questions shall carry out the functions assigned to it in Chapters I to V and the Annex and any other function delegated to it by the Governing Board.

2. The Standing Group may review and report to the Management Committee on any matter within the scope of Chapters I to V and the Annex.

3. The Standing Group may consult with oil companies on any matter within its competence.

Article 56

1. The Standing Group on the Oil Market shall carry out the functions assigned to it in Chapters V and VI and any other function delegated to it by the Governing Board.

2. The Standing Group may review and report to the Management Committee on any matter within the scope of Chapters V and VI.

3. The Standing Group may consult with oil companies on any matter within its competence.

Article 57

1. The Standing Group on Long Term Co-operation shall carry out the functions assigned to it in Chapter VII and any other function delegated to it by the Governing Board.

2. The Standing Group may review and report to the Management Committee on any matter within the scope of Chapter VII.

Article 58

1. The Standing Group on Relations with Producer and other Consumer Countries shall carry out the functions assigned to it in Chapter VIII and any other function delegated to it by the Governing Board.

2. The Standing Group may review and report to the Management Committee on any matter within the scope of Chapter VIII.

3. The Standing Group may consult with oil companies on any matter within its competence.

SECRETARIAT

Article 59

1. The Secretariat shall be composed of an Executive Director and such staff as is necessary.

2. The Executive Director shall be appointed by the Governing Board.

3. In the performance of their duties under this Agreement the Executive Director and the staff shall be responsible to and report to the organs of the Agency.

4. The Governing Board, acting by majority, shall take all decisions necessary for the establishment and the functioning of the Secretariat.

Article 60

The Secretariat shall carry out the functions assigned to it in this Agreement and any other function assigned to it by the Governing Board.

VOTING

Article 61

1. The Governing Board shall adopt decisions and recommendations for which no express voting provision is made in this Agreement, as follows:

(a) by majority:

- decisions on the management of the Program, including decisions applying provisions of this Agreement which already impose specific obligations on Participating Countries
- decisions on procedural questions
- recommendations

(b) by unanimity:

- all other decisions, including in particular decisions which impose on Participating Countries new obligations not already specified in this Agreement.

2. Decisions mentioned in paragraph 1 (b) may provide:

(a) that they shall not be binding on one or more Participating Countries;

(b) that they shall be binding only under certain conditions.

Article 62

1. Unanimity shall require all of the votes of the Participating Countries present and voting. Countries abstaining shall be considered as not voting.

2. When majority or special majority is required, the Participating Countries shall have the following voting weights:

	General voting weights	Oil consumption voting weights	Combined voting weights
Australia	3	1	4
Austria	3	1	4
Belgium	3	1	4
Canada	3	4	7
Czech Republic	3	1	4
Denmark	3	1	4
Finland	3	1	4
France	3	6	9
Germany	3	8	11
Greece	3	0	3
Hungary	3	1	4
Ireland	3	0	3
Italy	3	5	8
Japan	3	14	17
Korea (Republic of)	3	1	4
Luxembourg	3	0	3
The Netherlands	3	1	4
New Zealand	3	0	3
Portugal	3	0	3
Spain	3	2	5
Sweden	3	2	5
Switzerland	3	1	4
Turkey	3	1	4
United Kingdom	3	5	8
United States	3	43	46
Totals	75	100	175

3. Majority shall require 60 per cent of the total combined voting weights and 50 per cent of the general voting weights cast.

4. Special majority shall require:

(a) 60 per cent of the total combined voting weights and 36 general voting weights for:

- the decision under Article 2, paragraph 2, relating to the increase in the emergency reserve commitment;
- decisions under Article 19, paragraph 3, not to activate the emergency measures referred to in Articles 13 and 14;

• decisions under Article 20, paragraph 3, on the measures required for meeting the necessities of the situation;

• decisions under Article 23, paragraph 3, to maintain the emergency measures referred to in Articles 13 and 14;

• decisions under Article 24 to deactivate the emergency measures referred to in Articles 13 and 14.

(b) 66 general voting weights for:

• decisions under Article 19, paragraph 3, not to activate the emergency measures referred to in Article 17;

• decisions under Article 23, paragraph 3, to maintain the emergency measures referred to in Article 17;

• decisions under Article 24 to deactivate the emergency measures referred to in Article 17.

5. The Governing Board, acting by unanimity, shall decide on the necessary increase, decrease, and redistribution of the voting weights referred to in paragraph 2, as well as on amendment of the voting requirements set out in paragraphs 3 and 4 in the event that

• a Country accedes to this Agreement in accordance with Article 71, or

• a Country withdraws from this Agreement in accordance with Article 68, paragraph 2, or Article 69, paragraph 2.

6. The Governing Board shall review annually the number and distribution of voting weights specified in paragraph 2, and, on the basis of such review, acting by unanimity, shall decide whether such voting weights should be increased or decreased, or redistributed, or both, because a change in any Participating Country's share in total oil consumption has occurred or for any other reason.

7. Any change in paragraph 2, 3 or 4 shall be based on the concepts underlying those paragraphs and paragraph 6.

RELATIONS WITH OTHER ENTITIES

Article 63

In order to achieve the objectives of the Program, the Agency may establish appropriate relations with non-participating countries, international organisations, whether governmental or non-governmental, other entities and individuals.

FINANCIAL ARRANGEMENTS

Article 64

1. The expenses of the Secretariat and all other common expenses shall be shared among all Participating Countries according to a scale of contributions elaborated according to the principles and rules set out in the Annex to the "OECD Resolution of the Council on Determination of the Scale of Contributions by Member Countries to the Budget of the Organisation" of 10th December, 1963. After the first year of application of this Agreement, the Governing Board shall review this scale of contributions and, acting by unanimity, shall decide upon any appropriate changes in accordance with Article 73.

2. Special expenses incurred in connection with special activities carried out pursuant to Article 65 shall be shared by the Participating Countries taking part in such special activities in such proportions as shall be determined by unanimous agreement between them.

3. The Executive Director shall, in accordance with the financial regulations adopted by the Governing Board and not later than 1st October of each year, submit to the Governing Board a draft budget including personnel requirements. The Governing Board, acting by majority, shall adopt the budget.

4. The Governing Board, acting by majority, shall take all other necessary decisions regarding the financial administration of the Agency.

5. The financial year shall begin on 1st January and end on 31st December of each year. At the end of each financial year, revenues and expenditures shall be submitted to audit.

SPECIAL ACTIVITIES

Article 65

1. Any two or more Participating Countries may decide to carry out within the scope of this Agreement special activities, other than activities which are required to be carried out by all Participating Countries under Chapters I to V. Participating

Countries which do not wish to take part in such special activities shall abstain from taking part in such decisions and shall not be bound by them. Participating Countries carrying out such activities shall keep the Governing Board informed thereof.

2. For the implementation of such special activities, the Participating Countries concerned may agree upon voting procedures other than those provided for in Articles 61 and 62.

IMPLEMENTATION OF THE AGREEMENT

Article 66

Each Participating Country shall take the necessary measures, including any necessary legislative measures, to implement this Agreement and decisions taken by the Governing Board.

CHAPTER X

FINAL PROVISIONS

Article 67

1. Each Signatory State shall, not later than 1st May, 1975, notify the Government of the Kingdom of Belgium that, having complied with its constitutional procedures, it consents to be bound by this Agreement.

2. On the tenth day following the day on which at least six States holding at least 60 per cent of the combined voting weights mentioned in Article 62 have deposited a notification of consent to be bound or an instrument of accession, this Agreement shall enter into force for such States.

3. For each Signatory State which deposits its notification thereafter, this Agreement shall enter into force on the tenth day following the day of deposit.

4. The Governing Board, acting by majority, may upon request from any Signatory State decide to extend, with respect to that State, the time limit for notification beyond 1st May, 1975.

Article 68

1. Notwithstanding the provisions of Article 67, this Agreement shall be applied provisionally by all Signatory States, to the extent possible not inconsistent with their legislation, as from 18th November, 1974 following the first meeting of the Governing Board.

2. Provisional application of the Agreement shall continue until:

- the Agreement enters into force for the State concerned in accordance with Article 67, or
- 60 days after the Government of the Kingdom of Belgium receives notification that the State concerned will not consent to be bound by the Agreement, or
- the time limit for notification of consent by the State concerned referred to in Article 67 expires.

Article 69

1. This Agreement shall remain in force for a period of ten years from the date of its entry into force and shall continue in force thereafter unless and until the Governing Board, acting by majority, decides on its termination.

2. Any Participating Country may terminate the application of this Agreement for its part upon twelve months' written notice to the Government of the Kingdom of Belgium to that effect, given not less than three years after the first day of the provisional application of this Agreement.

Article 70

1. Any State may, at the time of signature, notification of consent to be bound in accordance with Article 67, accession or at any later date, declare by notification addressed to the Government of the Kingdom of Belgium that this Agreement shall apply to all or any of the territories for whose international relations it is responsible, or to any territories within its frontiers for whose oil supplies it is legally responsible.

2. Any declaration made pursuant to paragraph 1 may, in respect of any territory mentioned in such declaration, be withdrawn in accordance with the provisions of Article 69, paragraph 2.

Article 71

1. This Agreement shall be open for accession by any Member of the Organisation for Economic Co-operation and Development which is able and willing to meet the requirements of the Program. The Governing Board, acting by majority, shall decide on any request for accession.

2. This Agreement shall enter into force for any State whose request for accession has been granted on the tenth day following the deposit of its instrument of accession with the Government of the Kingdom of Belgium, or on the date of entry into force of the Agreement pursuant to Article 67, paragraph 2, whichever is the later.

3. Until 1st May, 1975, accession may take place on a provisional basis under the conditions set out in Article 68.

Article 72

1. This Agreement shall be open for accession by the European Communities.

2. This Agreement shall not in any way impede the further implementation of the treaties establishing the European Communities.

Article 73

This Agreement may at any time be amended by the Governing Board, acting by unanimity. Such amendment shall come into force in a manner determined by the Governing Board, acting by unanimity and making provision for Participating Countries to comply with their respective constitutional procedures.

Article 74

This Agreement shall be subject to a general review after 1st May, 1980.

Article 75

The Government of the Kingdom of Belgium shall notify all Participating Countries of the deposit of each notification of consent to be bound in accordance with Article 67, and of each instrument of accession, of the entry into force of this Agreement or any amendment thereto, of any denunciation thereof, and of any other declaration or notification received.

Article 76

The original of this Agreement, of which the English, French and German texts are equally authentic, shall be deposited with the Government of the Kingdom of Belgium, and a certified copy thereof shall be furnished to each other Participating Country by the Government of the Kingdom of Belgium.

ANNEX (TO THE IEP)

EMERGENCY RESERVES

Article 1

1. Total oil stocks are measured according to the OECD and EEC definitions, revised as follows:

A. Stocks included: crude oil, major products and unfinished oils held

- in refinery tanks
- in bulk terminals
- in pipeline tankage
- in barges
- in intercoastal tankers
- in oil tankers in port
- in inland ship bunkers
- in storage tank bottoms
- in working stocks
- by large consumers as required by law or otherwise controlled by Governments.

B. Stocks excluded:

(a) crude oil not yet produced

(b) crude oil, major products and unfinished oils held

- in pipelines
- in rail tank cars
- in truck tank cars
- in seagoing ships' bunkers
- in service stations and retail stores
- by other consumers
- in tankers at sea
- as military stocks.

2. That portion of oil stocks which can be credited toward each Participating Country's emergency reserve commitment is its total oil stocks under the above definition minus those stocks which can be technically determined as being absolutely unavailable in even the most severe emergency. The Standing Group on Emergency Questions shall examine this concept and report on criteria for the measurement of absolutely unavailable stocks.

3. Until a decision has been taken on this matter, each Participating Country shall subtract 10 per

cent from its total stocks in measuring its emergency reserves.

4. The Standing Group on Emergency Questions shall examine and report to the Management Committee on:

(a) the modalities of including naphtha for uses other than motor and aviation gasoline in the consumption against which stocks are measured,

(b) the possibility of creating common rules for the treatment of marine bunkers in an emergency, and of including marine bunkers in the consumption against which stocks are measured,

(c) the possibility of creating common rules concerning demand restraint for aviation bunkers,

(d) the possibility of crediting towards emergency reserve commitments some portion of oil at sea at the time of activation of emergency measures,

(e) the possibility of increasing supplies available in an emergency through savings in the distribution system.

Article 2

1. Fuel switching capacity is defined as normal oil consumption that may be replaced by other fuels in an emergency, provided that this capacity is subject to government control in an emergency, can be brought into operation within one month, and that secure supplies of the alternative fuel are available for use.

2. The supply of alternative fuel shall be expressed in terms of oil equivalent.

3. Stocks of an alternative fuel reserved for fuel switching purposes may be credited towards emergency reserve commitments insofar as they can be used during the period of self-sufficiency.

4. Stand-by production of an alternative fuel reserved for fuel switching purposes will be credited towards emergency reserve commitments on the same basis as stand-by oil production, subject to the provisions of Article 4 of this Annex.

5. The Standing Group on Emergency Questions shall examine and report to the Management Committee on:

(a) the appropriateness of the time limit of one month mentioned in paragraph 1,

(b) the basis of accounting for the fuel switching capacity based on stocks of an alternative fuel, subject to the provisions of paragraph 3.

Article 3

A Participating Country may credit towards its emergency reserve commitment oil stocks in another country, provided that the Government of that other country has an agreement with the Government of the Participating Country that it shall impose no impediment to the transfer of those stocks in an emergency to the Participating Country.

Article 4

1. Stand-by oil production is defined as a Participating Country's potential oil production in excess of normal oil production within its jurisdiction

- which is subject to government control, and
- which can be brought into use during an emergency within the period of self-sufficiency.

2. The Standing Group on Emergency Questions shall examine and report to the Management Committee on:

(a) the concept of and methods of measurement of stand-by oil production as referred to in paragraph 1,

(b) the appropriateness of "the period of self-sufficiency" as a time limit,

(c) the question of whether a given quantity of stand-by oil production is of greater value for purposes of emergency self-sufficiency than the same quantity of oil stocks, the amount of a possible credit for stand-by production, and the method of its calculation.

Article 5

Stand-by oil production available to a Participating Country within the jurisdiction of another country may be credited towards its emergency reserve commitment on the same basis as stand-by oil production within its own jurisdiction, subject to the provisions of Article 4 of this Annex provided that the Government of that other country has an agreement with the Government of the Participating Country that it shall impose no impediment to the supply of oil from that stand-by capacity to the Participating Country in an emergency.

Article 6

The Standing Group on Emergency Questions shall examine and report to the Management Committee on the possibility of crediting towards a Participating Country's emergency reserve commitment mentioned in Article 2, paragraph 2, of the Agreement, long term investments which have the effect of reducing the Participating Country's dependence on imported oil.

Article 7

1. The Standing Group on Emergency Questions shall examine and report to the Management Committee regarding the reference period set out in Article 2, paragraph 1, of the Agreement, in particular taking into account such factors as growth, seasonal variations in consumption and cyclical changes.

2. A decision by the Governing Board to change the definition of the reference period mentioned in paragraph 1 shall be taken by unanimity.

Article 8

The Standing Group on Emergency Questions shall examine and report to the Management Committee on all elements of Chapters I to IV of the Agreement to eliminate possible mathematical and statistical anomalies.

Article 9

The reports from the Standing Group on Emergency Questions on the matters mentioned in this Annex shall be submitted to the Management Committee by 1st April, 1975. The Management Committee shall make proposals, as appropriate, to the Governing Board, which, acting by majority, not later than 1st July, 1975, shall decide on these proposals, except as provided for in Article 7, paragraph 2, of this Annex.

Universal Declaration of Human Rights

G.A. res. 217A (III), U.N. Doc A/810 at 71 (1948)

http://www.un.org/Overview/rights.html

On December 10, 1948 the General Assembly of the United Nations adopted and proclaimed the Universal Declaration of Human Rights the full text of which appears in the following pages. Following this historic act the Assembly called upon all Member countries to publicize the text of the Declaration and "to cause it to be disseminated, displayed, read and expounded principally in schools and other educational institutions, without distinction based on the political status of countries or territories."

PREAMBLE

Whereas recognition of the inherent dignity and of the equal and inalienable rights of all members of the human family is the foundation of freedom, justice and peace in the world,

Whereas disregard and contempt for human rights have resulted in barbarous acts which have outraged the conscience of mankind, and the advent of a world in which human beings shall enjoy freedom of speech and belief and freedom from fear and want has been proclaimed as the highest aspiration of the common people,

Whereas it is essential, if man is not to be compelled to have recourse, as a last resort, to rebellion against tyranny and oppression, that human rights should be protected by the rule of law,

Whereas it is essential to promote the development of friendly relations between nations,

Whereas the peoples of the United Nations have in the Charter reaffirmed their faith in fundamental human rights, in the dignity and worth of the human person and in the equal rights of men and women and have determined to promote social progress and better standards of life in larger freedom,

Whereas Member States have pledged themselves to achieve, in co-operation with the United Nations, the promotion of universal respect for and observance of human rights and fundamental freedoms,

Whereas a common understanding of these rights and freedoms is of the greatest importance for the full realization of this pledge,

Now, Therefore THE GENERAL ASSEMBLY **proclaims** THIS UNIVERSAL DECLARATION OF HUMAN RIGHTS as a common standard of achievement for all peoples and all nations, to the end that every individual and every organ of society, keeping this Declaration constantly in mind, shall strive by teaching and education to promote respect for these rights and freedoms and by progressive measures, national and international, to secure their universal and effective recognition and observance, both among the peoples of Member States themselves and among the peoples of territories under their jurisdiction.

ARTICLE 1

All human beings are born free and equal in dignity and rights. They are endowed with reason and conscience and should act towards one another in a spirit of brotherhood.

ARTICLE 2

Everyone is entitled to all the rights and freedoms set forth in this Declaration, without distinction of any kind, such as race, colour, sex, language, religion, political or other opinion, national or social origin, property, birth or other status. Furthermore, no distinction shall be made on the basis of the political, jurisdictional or international status of the country or territory to which a person belongs, whether it be independent, trust, non-self-governing or under any other limitation of sovereignty.

ARTICLE 3

Everyone has the right to life, liberty and security of person.

ARTICLE 4

No one shall be held in slavery or servitude; slavery and the slave trade shall be prohibited in all their forms.

ARTICLE 5

No one shall be subjected to torture or to cruel, inhuman or degrading treatment or punishment.

ARTICLE 6

Everyone has the right to recognition everywhere as a person before the law.

ARTICLE 7

All are equal before the law and are entitled without any discrimination to equal protection of the law. All are entitled to equal protection against any discrimination in violation of this Declaration and against any incitement to such discrimination.

ARTICLE 8

Everyone has the right to an effective remedy by the competent national tribunals for acts violating the fundamental rights granted him by the constitution or by law.

ARTICLE 9

No one shall be subjected to arbitrary arrest, detention or exile.

ARTICLE 10

Everyone is entitled in full equality to a fair and public hearing by an independent and impartial tribunal, in the determination of his rights and obligations and of any criminal charge against him.

ARTICLE 11

(1) Everyone charged with a penal offence has the right to be presumed innocent until proved guilty according to law in a public trial at which he has had all the guarantees necessary for his defence.

(2) No one shall be held guilty of any penal offence on account of any act or omission which did not constitute a penal offence, under national or international law, at the time when it was committed. Nor shall a heavier penalty be imposed than the one that was applicable at the time the penal offence was committed.

ARTICLE 12

No one shall be subjected to arbitrary interference with his privacy, family, home or correspondence, nor to attacks upon his honour and reputation. Everyone has the right to the protection of the law against such interference or attacks.

ARTICLE 13

(1) Everyone has the right to freedom of movement and residence within the borders of each state.

(2) Everyone has the right to leave any country, including his own, and to return to his country.

ARTICLE 14

(1) Everyone has the right to seek and to enjoy in other countries asylum from persecution.

(2) This right may not be invoked in the case of prosecutions genuinely arising from non-political crimes or from acts contrary to the purposes and principles of the United Nations.

ARTICLE 15

(1) Everyone has the right to a nationality.

(2) No one shall be arbitrarily deprived of his nationality nor denied the right to change his nationality.

ARTICLE 16

(1) Men and women of full age, without any limitation due to race, nationality or religion, have the right to marry and to found a family. They are entitled to equal rights as to marriage, during marriage and at its dissolution.

(2) Marriage shall be entered into only with the free and full consent of the intending spouses.

(3) The family is the natural and fundamental group unit of society and is entitled to protection by society and the State.

ARTICLE 17

(1) Everyone has the right to own property alone as well as in association with others.

(2) No one shall be arbitrarily deprived of his property.

ARTICLE 18

Everyone has the right to freedom of thought, conscience and religion; this right includes freedom to change his religion or belief, and freedom, either alone or in community with others and in public or private, to manifest his religion or belief in teaching, practice, worship and observance.

ARTICLE 19

Everyone has the right to freedom of opinion and expression; this right includes freedom to hold opinions without interference and to seek, receive and impart information and ideas through any media and regardless of frontiers.

ARTICLE 20

(1) Everyone has the right to freedom of peaceful assembly and association.

(2) No one may be compelled to belong to an association.

ARTICLE 21

(1) Everyone has the right to take part in the government of his country, directly or through freely chosen representatives.

(2) Everyone has the right of equal access to public service in his country.

(3) The will of the people shall be the basis of the authority of government; this will shall be expressed in periodic and genuine elections which shall be by universal and equal suffrage and shall be held by secret vote or by equivalent free voting procedures.

ARTICLE 22

Everyone, as a member of society, has the right to social security and is entitled to realization, through national effort and international co-operation and in accordance with the organization and resources of each State, of the economic, social and cultural rights indispensable for his dignity and the free development of his personality.

ARTICLE 23

(1) Everyone has the right to work, to free choice of employment, to just and favourable conditions of work and to protection against unemployment.

(2) Everyone, without any discrimination, has the right to equal pay for equal work.

(3) Everyone who works has the right to just and favourable remuneration ensuring for himself and his family an existence worthy of human dignity, and supplemented, if necessary, by other means of social protection.

(4) Everyone has the right to form and to join trade unions for the protection of his interests.

ARTICLE 24

Everyone has the right to rest and leisure, including reasonable limitation of working hours and periodic holidays with pay.

ARTICLE 25

(1) Everyone has the right to a standard of living adequate for the health and well-being of himself and of his family, including food, clothing, housing and medical care and necessary social services, and the right to security in the event of unemployment, sickness, disability, widowhood, old age or other lack of livelihood in circumstances beyond his control.

(2) Motherhood and childhood are entitled to special care and assistance. All children, whether born in or out of wedlock, shall enjoy the same social protection.

ARTICLE 26

(1) Everyone has the right to education. Education shall be free, at least in the elementary and fundamental stages. Elementary education shall be compulsory. Technical and professional education shall be made generally available and higher education shall be equally accessible to all on the basis of merit.

(2) Education shall be directed to the full development of the human personality and to the strengthening of respect for human rights and fundamental

freedoms. It shall promote understanding, tolerance and friendship among all nations, racial or religious groups, and shall further the activities of the United Nations for the maintenance of peace.

(3) Parents have a prior right to choose the kind of education that shall be given to their children.

ARTICLE 27

(1) Everyone has the right freely to participate in the cultural life of the community, to enjoy the arts and to share in scientific advancement and its benefits.

(2) Everyone has the right to the protection of the moral and material interests resulting from any scientific, literary or artistic production of which he is the author.

ARTICLE 28

Everyone is entitled to a social and international order in which the rights and freedoms set forth in this Declaration can be fully realized.

ARTICLE 29

(1) Everyone has duties to the community in which alone the free and full development of his personality is possible.

(2) In the exercise of his rights and freedoms, everyone shall be subject only to such limitations as are determined by law solely for the purpose of securing due recognition and respect for the rights and freedoms of others and of meeting the just requirements of morality, public order and the general welfare in a democratic society.

(3) These rights and freedoms may in no case be exercised contrary to the purposes and principles of the United Nations.

ARTICLE 30

Nothing in this Declaration may be interpreted as implying for any State, group or person any right to engage in any activity or to perform any act aimed at the destruction of any of the rights and freedoms set forth herein.

Millennium Declaration

GA Res. A/Res/55/2, 8 Sept. 2000

http://www.un.org/millennium/declaration/ares552e.htm

The General Assembly

Adopts the following Declaration:

United Nations Millennium Declaration

I. VALUES AND PRINCIPLES

1. We, heads of State and Government, have gathered at United Nations Headquarters in New York from 6 to 8 September 2000, at the dawn of a new millennium, to reaffirm our faith in the Organization and its Charter as indispensable foundations of a more peaceful, prosperous and just world.

2. We recognize that, in addition to our separate responsibilities to our individual societies, we have a collective responsibility to uphold the principles of human dignity, equality and equity at the global level. As leaders we have a duty therefore to all the world's people, especially the most vulnerable and, in particular, the children of the world, to whom the future belongs.

3. We reaffirm our commitment to the purposes and principles of the Charter of the United Nations, which have proved timeless and universal. Indeed, their relevance and capacity to inspire have increased, as nations and peoples have become increasingly interconnected and interdependent.

4. We are determined to establish a just and lasting peace all over the world in accordance with the purposes and principles of the Charter. We rededicate ourselves to support all efforts to uphold the sovereign equality of all States, respect for their territorial integrity and political independence, resolution of disputes by peaceful means and in conformity with the principles of justice and international law, the right to self-determination of peoples which remain under colonial domination and foreign occupation, non-interference in the internal affairs of States, respect for human rights and fundamental freedoms, respect for the equal rights of all without distinction as to race, sex, language or religion and international cooperation in solving international problems of an economic, social, cultural or humanitarian character.

5. We believe that the central challenge we face today is to ensure that globalization becomes a positive force for all the world's people. For while globalization offers great opportunities, at present its benefits are very unevenly shared, while its costs are unevenly distributed. We recognize that developing countries and countries with economies in transition face special difficulties in responding to this central challenge. Thus, only through broad and sustained efforts to create a shared future, based upon our common humanity in all its diversity, can globalization be made fully inclusive and equitable. These efforts must include policies and measures, at the global level, which correspond to the needs of developing countries and economies in transition and are formulated and implemented with their effective participation.

6. We consider certain fundamental values to be essential to international relations in the twenty-first century. These include:

- **Freedom.** Men and women have the right to live their lives and raise their children in dignity, free from hunger and from the fear of violence, oppression or injustice. Democratic and participatory governance based on the will of the people best assures these rights.
- **Equality.** No individual and no nation must be denied the opportunity to benefit from development. The equal rights and opportunities of women and men must be assured.
- **Solidarity.** Global challenges must be managed in a way that distributes the costs and burdens

fairly in accordance with basic principles of equity and social justice. Those who suffer or who benefit least deserve help from those who benefit most.

- **Tolerance.** Human beings must respect one other, in all their diversity of belief, culture and language. Differences within and between societies should be neither feared nor repressed, but cherished as a precious asset of humanity. A culture of peace and dialogue among all civilizations should be actively promoted.

- **Respect for nature.** Prudence must be shown in the management of all living species and natural resources, in accordance with the precepts of sustainable development. Only in this way can the immeasurable riches provided to us by nature be preserved and passed on to our descendants. The current unsustainable patterns of production and consumption must be changed in the interest of our future welfare and that of our descendants.

- **Shared responsibility.** Responsibility for managing worldwide economic and social development, as well as threats to international peace and security, must be shared among the nations of the world and should be exercised multilaterally. As the most universal and most representative organization in the world, the United Nations must play the central role.

7. In order to translate these shared values into actions, we have identified key objectives to which we assign special significance.

II. PEACE, SECURITY AND DISARMAMENT

8. We will spare no effort to free our peoples from the scourge of war, whether within or between States, which has claimed more than 5 million lives in the past decade. We will also seek to eliminate the dangers posed by weapons of mass destruction.

9. We resolve therefore:

- To strengthen respect for the rule of law in international as in national affairs and, in particular, to ensure compliance by Member States with the decisions of the International Court of Justice, in compliance with the Charter of the United Nations, in cases to which they are parties.

- To make the United Nations more effective in maintaining peace and security by giving it the resources and tools it needs for conflict prevention, peaceful resolution of disputes, peacekeeping, post-conflict peace-building and reconstruction. In this context, we take note of the report of the Panel on United Nations Peace Operations and request the General Assembly to consider its recommendations expeditiously.

- To strengthen cooperation between the United Nations and regional organizations, in accordance with the provisions of Chapter VIII of the Charter.

- To ensure the implementation, by States Parties, of treaties in areas such as arms control and disarmament and of international humanitarian law and human rights law, and call upon all States to consider signing and ratifying the Rome Statute of the International Criminal Court.

- To take concerted action against international terrorism, and to accede as soon as possible to all the relevant international conventions.

- To redouble our efforts to implement our commitment to counter the world drug problem.

- To intensify our efforts to fight transnational crime in all its dimensions, including trafficking as well as smuggling in human beings and money laundering.

- To minimize the adverse effects of United Nations economic sanctions on innocent populations, to subject such sanctions regimes to regular reviews and to eliminate the adverse effects of sanctions on third parties.

- To strive for the elimination of weapons of mass destruction, particularly nuclear weapons, and to keep all options open for achieving this aim, including the possibility of convening an international conference to identify ways of eliminating nuclear dangers.

- To take concerted action to end illicit traffic in small arms and light weapons, especially by making arms transfers more transparent and supporting regional disarmament measures, taking account of all the recommendations of the forthcoming United Nations Conference on Illicit Trade in Small Arms and Light Weapons.

- To call on all States to consider acceding to the Convention on the Prohibition of the Use, Stockpiling, Production and Transfer of Anti-personnel Mines and on Their Destruction, as well as the amended mines protocol to the Convention on conventional weapons.

10. We urge Member States to observe the Olympic Truce, individually and collectively, now and in the future, and to support the International Olympic Committee in its efforts to promote peace and human understanding through sport and the Olympic Ideal.

III. DEVELOPMENT AND POVERTY ERADICATION

11. We will spare no effort to free our fellow men, women and children from the abject and dehumanizing conditions of extreme poverty, to which more than a billion of them are currently subjected. We are committed to making the right to development a reality for everyone and to freeing the entire human race from want.

12. We resolve therefore to create an environment – at the national and global levels alike – which is conducive to development and to the elimination of poverty.

13. Success in meeting these objectives depends, *inter alia*, on good governance within each country. It also depends on good governance at the international level and on transparency in the financial, monetary and trading systems. We are committed to an open, equitable, rule-based, predictable and non-discriminatory multilateral trading and financial system.

14. We are concerned about the obstacles developing countries face in mobilizing the resources needed to finance their sustained development. We will therefore make every effort to ensure the success of the High-level International and Intergovernmental Event on Financing for Development, to be held in 2001.

15. We also undertake to address the special needs of the least developed countries. In this context, we welcome the Third United Nations Conference on the Least Developed Countries to be held in May 2001 and will endeavour to ensure its success. We call on the industrialized countries:

- To adopt, preferably by the time of that Conference, a policy of duty- and quota-free access for essentially all exports from the least developed countries;
- To implement the enhanced programme of debt relief for the heavily indebted poor countries without further delay and to agree to cancel all official bilateral debts of those countries in return for their making demonstrable commitments to poverty reduction; and
- To grant more generous development assistance, especially to countries that are genuinely making an effort to apply their resources to poverty reduction.

16. We are also determined to deal comprehensively and effectively with the debt problems of low- and middle-income developing countries, through various national and international measures designed to make their debt sustainable in the long term.

17. We also resolve to address the special needs of small island developing States, by implementing the Barbados Programme of Action and the outcome of the twenty-second special session of the General Assembly rapidly and in full. We urge the international community to ensure that, in the development of a vulnerability index, the special needs of small island developing States are taken into account.

18. We recognize the special needs and problems of the landlocked developing countries, and urge both bilateral and multilateral donors to increase financial and technical assistance to this group of countries to meet their special development needs and to help them overcome the impediments of geography by improving their transit transport systems.

19. We resolve further:

- To halve, by the year 2015, the proportion of the world's people whose income is less than one dollar a day and the proportion of people who suffer from hunger and, by the same date, to halve the proportion of people who are unable to reach or to afford safe drinking water.
- To ensure that, by the same date, children everywhere, boys and girls alike, will be able to complete a full course of primary schooling and that girls and boys will have equal access to all levels of education.
- By the same date, to have reduced maternal mortality by three quarters, and under-five child mortality by two thirds, of their current rates.
- To have, by then, halted, and begun to reverse, the spread of HIV/AIDS, the scourge of malaria and other major diseases that afflict humanity.

• To provide special assistance to children orphaned by HIV/AIDS.

• By 2020, to have achieved a significant improvement in the lives of at least 100 million slum dwellers as proposed in the "Cities Without Slums" initiative.

20. We also resolve:

• To promote gender equality and the empowerment of women as effective ways to combat poverty, hunger and disease and to stimulate development that is truly sustainable.

• To develop and implement strategies that give young people everywhere a real chance to find decent and productive work.

• To encourage the pharmaceutical industry to make essential drugs more widely available and affordable by all who need them in developing countries.

• To develop strong partnerships with the private sector and with civil society organizations in pursuit of development and poverty eradication.

• To ensure that the benefits of new technologies, especially information and communication technologies, in conformity with recommendations contained in the ECOSOC 2000 Ministerial Declaration, are available to all.

IV. PROTECTING OUR COMMON ENVIRONMENT

21. We must spare no effort to free all of humanity, and above all our children and grandchildren, from the threat of living on a planet irredeemably spoilt by human activities, and whose resources would no longer be sufficient for their needs.

22. We reaffirm our support for the principles of sustainable development, including those set out in Agenda 21, agreed upon at the United Nations Conference on Environment and Development.

23. We resolve therefore to adopt in all our environmental actions a new ethic of conservation and stewardship and, as first steps, we resolve:

• To make every effort to ensure the entry into force of the Kyoto Protocol, preferably by the tenth anniversary of the United Nations Conference on Environment and Development in 2002, and to embark on the required reduction in emissions of greenhouse gases.

• To intensify our collective efforts for the management, conservation and sustainable development of all types of forests.

• To press for the full implementation of the Convention on Biological Diversity and the Convention to Combat Desertification in those Countries Experiencing Serious Drought and/or Desertification, particularly in Africa.

• To stop the unsustainable exploitation of water resources by developing water management strategies at the regional, national and local levels, which promote both equitable access and adequate supplies.

• To intensify cooperation to reduce the number and effects of natural and man-made disasters.

• To ensure free access to information on the human genome sequence.

V. HUMAN RIGHTS, DEMOCRACY AND GOOD GOVERNANCE

24. We will spare no effort to promote democracy and strengthen the rule of law, as well as respect for all internationally recognized human rights and fundamental freedoms, including the right to development.

25. We resolve therefore:

• To respect fully and uphold the Universal Declaration of Human Rights.

• To strive for the full protection and promotion in all our countries of civil, political, economic, social and cultural rights for all.

• To strengthen the capacity of all our countries to implement the principles and practices of democracy and respect for human rights, including minority rights.

• To combat all forms of violence against women and to implement the Convention on the Elimination of All Forms of Discrimination against Women.

• To take measures to ensure respect for and protection of the human rights of migrants, migrant workers and their families, to eliminate the increasing acts of racism and xenophobia in many societies and to promote greater harmony and tolerance in all societies.

- To work collectively for more inclusive political processes, allowing genuine participation by all citizens in all our countries.

- To ensure the freedom of the media to perform their essential role and the right of the public to have access to information.

VI. PROTECTING THE VULNERABLE

26. We will spare no effort to ensure that children and all civilian populations that suffer disproportionately the consequences of natural disasters, genocide, armed conflicts and other humanitarian emergencies are given every assistance and protection so that they can resume normal life as soon as possible.

We resolve therefore:

- To expand and strengthen the protection of civilians in complex emergencies, in conformity with international humanitarian law.

- To strengthen international cooperation, including burden sharing in, and the coordination of humanitarian assistance to, countries hosting refugees and to help all refugees and displaced persons to return voluntarily to their homes, in safety and dignity and to be smoothly reintegrated into their societies.

- To encourage the ratification and full implementation of the Convention on the Rights of the Child and its optional protocols on the involvement of children in armed conflict and on the sale of children, child prostitution and child pornography.

VII. MEETING THE SPECIAL NEEDS OF AFRICA

27. We will support the consolidation of democracy in Africa and assist Africans in their struggle for lasting peace, poverty eradication and sustainable development, thereby bringing Africa into the mainstream of the world economy.

28. We resolve therefore:

- To give full support to the political and institutional structures of emerging democracies in Africa.

- To encourage and sustain regional and subregional mechanisms for preventing conflict and promoting political stability, and to ensure a reliable flow of resources for peacekeeping operations on the continent.

- To take special measures to address the challenges of poverty eradication and sustainable development in Africa, including debt cancellation, improved market access, enhanced Official Development Assistance and increased flows of Foreign Direct Investment, as well as transfers of technology.

- To help Africa build up its capacity to tackle the spread of the HIV/AIDS pandemic and other infectious diseases.

VIII. STRENGTHENING THE UNITED NATIONS

29. We will spare no effort to make the United Nations a more effective instrument for pursuing all of these priorities: the fight for development for all the peoples of the world, the fight against poverty, ignorance and disease; the fight against injustice; the fight against violence, terror and crime; and the fight against the degradation and destruction of our common home.

30. We resolve therefore:

- To reaffirm the central position of the General Assembly as the chief deliberative, policy-making and representative organ of the United Nations, and to enable it to play that role effectively.

- To intensify our efforts to achieve a comprehensive reform of the Security Council in all its aspects.

- To strengthen further the Economic and Social Council, building on its recent achievements, to help it fulfil the role ascribed to it in the Charter.

- To strengthen the International Court of Justice, in order to ensure justice and the rule of law in international affairs.

- To encourage regular consultations and coordination among the principal organs of the United Nations in pursuit of their functions.

- To ensure that the Organization is provided on a timely and predictable basis with the resources it needs to carry out its mandates.

- To urge the Secretariat to make the best use of those resources, in accordance with clear rules and procedures agreed by the General Assembly, in the interests of all Member States, by adopting the best management practices and technologies available and by concentrating on those tasks that reflect the agreed priorities of Member States.

• To promote adherence to the Convention on the Safety of United Nations and Associated Personnel.

• To ensure greater policy coherence and better cooperation between the United Nations, its agencies, the Bretton Woods Institutions and the World Trade Organization, as well as other multilateral bodies, with a view to achieving a fully coordinated approach to the problems of peace and development.

• To strengthen further cooperation between the United Nations and national parliaments through their world organization, the Inter-Parliamentary Union, in various fields, including peace and security, economic and social development, international law and human rights and democracy and gender issues.

• To give greater opportunities to the private sector, non-governmental organizations and civil society, in general, to contribute to the realization of the Organization's goals and programmes.

31. We request the General Assembly to review on a regular basis the progress made in implementing the provisions of this Declaration, and ask the Secretary-General to issue periodic reports for consideration by the General Assembly and as a basis for further action.

32. We solemnly reaffirm, on this historic occasion, that the United Nations is the indispensable common house of the entire human family, through which we will seek to realize our universal aspirations for peace, cooperation and development. We therefore pledge our unstinting support for these common objectives and our determination to achieve them.

8th plenary meeting
8 September 2000

Stockholm Declaration of the United Nations Conference on the Human Environment

Stockholm, 16 June 1972

U.N. Doc.A/Conf.48/14

http://www.unep.org/Documents/Default.asp?DocumentID=97&ArticleID=1503

The United Nations Conference on the Human Environment, having met at Stockholm from 5 to 16 June 1972, having considered the need for a common outlook and for common principles to inspire and guide the peoples of the world in the preservation and enhancement of the human environment,

Proclaims that:

1. Man is both creature and moulder of his environment, which gives him physical sustenance and affords him the opportunity for intellectual, moral, social and spiritual growth. In the long and tortuous evolution of the human race on this planet a stage has been reached when, through the rapid acceleration of science and technology, man has acquired the power to transform his environment in countless ways and on an unprecedented scale. Both aspects of man's environment, the natural and the man-made, are essential to his well-being and to the enjoyment of basic human rights the right to life itself.

2. The protection and improvement of the human environment is a major issue which affects the well-being of peoples and economic development throughout the world; it is the urgent desire of the peoples of the whole world and the duty of all Governments.

3. Man has constantly to sum up experience and go on discovering, inventing, creating and advancing. In our time, man's capability to transform his surroundings, if used wisely, can bring to all peoples the benefits of development and the opportunity to enhance the quality of life. Wrongly or heedlessly applied, the same power can do incalculable harm to human beings and the human environment. We see around us growing evidence of man-made harm in many regions of the earth: dangerous levels of pollution in water, air, earth and living beings; major and undesirable disturbances to the ecological balance of the biosphere; destruction and depletion of irreplaceable resources; and gross deficiencies, harmful to the physical, mental and social health of man, in the man-made environment, particularly in the living and working environment.

4. In the developing countries most of the environmental problems are caused by under-development. Millions continue to live far below the minimum levels required for a decent human existence, deprived of adequate food and clothing, shelter and education, health and sanitation. Therefore, the developing countries must direct their efforts to development, bearing in mind their priorities and the need to safeguard and improve the environment. For the same purpose, the industrialized countries should make efforts to reduce the gap themselves and the developing countries. In the industrialized countries, environmental problems are generally related to industrialization and technological development.

5. The natural growth of population continuously presents problems for the preservation of the environment, and adequate policies and measures should be adopted, as appropriate, to face these problems. Of all things in the world, people are the most precious. It is the people that propel social progress, create social wealth, develop science and technology and, through their hard work, continuously transform the human environment. Along with social progress and the advance of production, science and technology, the capability of man to

improve the environment increases with each passing day.

6. A point has been reached in history when we must shape our actions throughout the world with a more prudent care for their environmental consequences. Through ignorance or indifference we can do massive and irreversible harm to the earthly environment on which our life and well being depend. Conversely, through fuller knowledge and wiser action, we can achieve for ourselves and our posterity a better life in an environment more in keeping with human needs and hopes. There are broad vistas for the enhancement of environmental quality and the creation of a good life. What is needed is an enthusiastic but calm state of mind and intense but orderly work. For the purpose of attaining freedom in the world of nature, man must use knowledge to build, in collaboration with nature, a better environment. To defend and improve the human environment for present and future generations has become an imperative goal for mankind-a goal to be pursued together with, and in harmony with, the established and fundamental goals of peace and of worldwide economic and social development.

7. To achieve this environmental goal will demand the acceptance of responsibility by citizens and communities and by enterprises and institutions at every level, all sharing equitably in common efforts. Individuals in all walks of life as well as organizations in many fields, by their values and the sum of their actions, will shape the world environment of the future.

Local and national governments will bear the greatest burden for large-scale environmental policy and action within their jurisdictions. International cooperation is also needed in order to raise resources to support the developing countries in carrying out their responsibilities in this field. A growing class of environmental problems, because they are regional or global in extent or because they affect the common international realm, will require extensive cooperation among nations and action by international organizations in the common interest.

The Conference calls upon Governments and peoples to exert common efforts for the preservation and improvement of the human environment, for the benefit of all the people and for their posterity.

Principles

States the common conviction that:

PRINCIPLE 1

Man has the fundamental right to freedom, equality and adequate conditions of life, in an environment of a quality that permits a life of dignity and well-being, and he bears a solemn responsibility to protect and improve the environment for present and future generations. In this respect, policies promoting or perpetuating apartheid, racial segregation, discrimination, colonial and other forms of oppression and foreign domination stand condemned and must be eliminated.

PRINCIPLE 2

The natural resources of the earth, including the air, water, land, flora and fauna and especially representative samples of natural ecosystems, must be safeguarded for the benefit of present and future generations through careful planning or management, as appropriate.

PRINCIPLE 3

The capacity of the earth to produce vital renewable resources must be maintained and, wherever practicable, restored or improved.

PRINCIPLE 4

Man has a special responsibility to safeguard and wisely manage the heritage of wildlife and its habitat, which are now gravely imperilled by a combination of adverse factors. Nature conservation, including wildlife, must therefore receive importance in planning for economic development.

PRINCIPLE 5

The non-renewable resources of the earth must be employed in such a way as to guard against the danger of their future exhaustion and to ensure that benefits from such employment are shared by all mankind.

PRINCIPLE 6

The discharge of toxic substances or of other substances and the release of heat, in such quantities or concentrations as to exceed the capacity of the environment to render them harmless, must be halted in order to ensure that serious or irreversible damage is not inflicted upon ecosystems. The just struggle of the peoples of ill countries against pollution should be supported.

PRINCIPLE 7

States shall take all possible steps to prevent pollution of the seas by substances that are liable to create hazards to human health, to harm living resources and marine life, to damage amenities or to interfere with other legitimate uses of the sea.

PRINCIPLE 8

Economic and social development is essential for ensuring a favorable living and working environment for man and for creating conditions on earth that are necessary for the improvement of the quality of life.

PRINCIPLE 9

Environmental deficiencies generated by the conditions of under-development and natural disasters pose grave problems and can best be remedied by accelerated development through the transfer of substantial quantities of financial and technological assistance as a supplement to the domestic effort of the developing countries and such timely assistance as may be required.

PRINCIPLE 10

For the developing countries, stability of prices and adequate earnings for primary commodities and raw materials are essential to environmental management, since economic factors as well as ecological processes must be taken into account.

PRINCIPLE 11

The environmental policies of all States should enhance and not adversely affect the present or future development potential of developing countries, nor should they hamper the attainment of better living conditions for all, and appropriate steps should be taken by States and international organizations with a view to reaching agreement on meeting the possible national and international economic consequences resulting from the application of environmental measures.

PRINCIPLE 12

Resources should be made available to preserve and improve the environment, taking into account the circumstances and particular requirements of developing countries and any costs which may emanate- from their incorporating environmental safeguards into their development planning and the need for making available to them, upon their request, additional international technical and financial assistance for this purpose.

PRINCIPLE 13

In order to achieve a more rational management of resources and thus to improve the environment, States should adopt an integrated and coordinated approach to their development planning so as to ensure that development is compatible with the need to protect and improve environment for the benefit of their population.

PRINCIPLE 14

Rational planning constitutes an essential tool for reconciling any conflict between the needs of development and the need to protect and improve the environment.

PRINCIPLE 15

Planning must be applied to human settlements and urbanization with a view to avoiding adverse effects on the environment and obtaining maximum social, economic and environmental benefits for all. In this respect projects which arc designed for colonialist and racist domination must be abandoned.

PRINCIPLE 16

Demographic policies which are without prejudice to basic human rights and which are deemed appropriate by Governments concerned should be applied in those regions where the rate of population growth or excessive population concentrations are likely to have adverse effects on the environment of the human environment and impede development.

PRINCIPLE 17

Appropriate national institutions must be entrusted with the task of planning, managing or controlling the 9 environmental resources of States with a view to enhancing environmental quality.

PRINCIPLE 18

Science and technology, as part of their contribution to economic and social development, must be applied to the identification, avoidance and control of environmental risks and the solution of environmental problems and for the common good of mankind.

PRINCIPLE 19

Education in environmental matters, for the younger generation as well as adults, giving due consideration to the underprivileged, is essential in order to broaden the basis for an enlightened opinion and responsible conduct by individuals, enterprises and communities in protecting and improving the environment in its full human dimension. It is also essential that mass media of communications avoid contributing to the deterioration of the environment, but, on the contrary, disseminates information of an educational nature on the need to project and improve the environment in order to enable mal to develop in every respect.

PRINCIPLE 20

Scientific research and development in the context of environmental problems, both national and multinational, must be promoted in all countries, especially the developing countries. In this connection, the free flow of up-to-date scientific information and transfer of experience must be supported and assisted, to facilitate the solution of environmental problems; environmental technologies should be made available to developing countries on terms which would encourage their wide dissemination without constituting an economic burden on the developing countries.

PRINCIPLE 21

States have, in accordance with the Charter of the United Nations and the principles of international law, the sovereign right to exploit their own resources pursuant to their own environmental policies, and the responsibility to ensure that activities within their jurisdiction or control do not cause damage to the environment of other States or of areas beyond the limits of national jurisdiction.

PRINCIPLE 22

States shall cooperate to develop further the international law regarding liability and compensation for the victims of pollution and other environmental damage caused by activities within the jurisdiction or control of such States to areas beyond their jurisdiction.

PRINCIPLE 23

Without prejudice to such criteria as may be agreed upon by the international community, or to standards which will have to be determined nationally, it will be essential in all cases to consider the systems of values prevailing in each country, and the extent of the applicability of standards which are valid for the most advanced countries but which may be inappropriate and of unwarranted social cost for the developing countries.

PRINCIPLE 24

International matters concerning the protection and improvement of the environment should be handled in a cooperative spirit by all countries, big and small, on an equal footing.

Cooperation through multilateral or bilateral arrangements or other appropriate means is essential to effectively control, prevent, reduce and eliminate adverse environmental effects resulting from activities conducted in all spheres, in such a way that due account is taken of the sovereignty and interests of all States.

PRINCIPLE 25

States shall ensure that international organizations play a coordinated, efficient and dynamic role for the protection and improvement of the environment.

PRINCIPLE 26

Man and his environment must be spared the effects of nuclear weapons and all other means of mass destruction. States must strive to reach prompt agreement, in the relevant international organs, on the elimination and complete destruction of such weapons.

21st plenary meeting
16 June 1972

Declaration on the Right to Development

G.A. res. 41/128, annex, 41 U.N. GAOR Supp. (No. 53) at 186, U.N. Doc. A/41/53 (1986)

http://www1.umn.edu/humanrts/instree/s3drd.htm

The General Assembly,

Bearing in mind the purposes and principles of the Charter of the United Nations relating to the achievement of international co-operation in solving international problems of an economic, social, cultural or humanitarian nature, and in promoting and encouraging respect for human rights and fundamental freedoms for all without distinction as to race, sex, language or religion,

Recognizing that development is a comprehensive economic, social, cultural and political process, which aims at the constant improvement of the well-being of the entire population and of all individuals on the basis of their active, free and meaningful participation in development and in the fair distribution of benefits resulting therefrom,

Considering that under the provisions of the Universal Declaration of Human Rights everyone is entitled to a social and international order in which the rights and freedoms set forth in that Declaration can be fully realized,

Recalling the provisions of the International Covenant on Economic, Social and Cultural Rights and of the International Covenant on Civil and Political Rights,

Recalling further the relevant agreements, conventions, resolutions, recommendations and other instruments of the United Nations and its specialized agencies concerning the integral development of the human being, economic and social progress and development of all peoples, including those instruments concerning decolonization, the prevention of discrimination, respect for and observance of, hum an rights and fundamental freedoms, the maintenance of international peace and security and the further promotion of friendly relations and co-operation among States in accordance with the Charter,

Recalling the right of peoples to self-determination, by virtue of which they have the right freely to determine their political status and to pursue their economic, social and cultural development,

Recalling also the right of peoples to exercise, subject to the relevant provisions of both International Covenants on Human Rights, full and complete sovereignty over all their natural wealth and resources,

Mindful of the obligation of States under the Charter to promote universal respect for and observance of human rights and fundamental freedoms for all without distinction of any kind such as race, colour, sex, language, religion, political or other opinion, national or social origin, property, birth or other status,

Considering that the elimination of the massive and flagrant violations of the human rights of the peoples and individuals affected by situations such as those resulting from colonialism, neo-colonialism, apartheid, all forms of racism and racial discrimination, foreign domination and occupation, aggression and threats against national sovereignty, national unity and territorial integrity and threats of war would contribute to the establishment of circumstances propitious to the development of a great part of mankind,

Concerned at the existence of serious obstacles to development, as well as to the complete fulfilment of human beings and of peoples, constituted, inter alia, by the denial of civil, political, economic, social and cultural rights, and considering that all human rights and fundamental freedoms are indivisible and interdependent and that, in order to promote development, equal attention and urgent consideration should be given to the implementation, promotion and protection of civil, political, economic, social and cultural rights and that, accordingly, the promotion of, respect for and enjoyment of certain human rights and fundamental freedoms cannot justify the denial of other human rights and fundamental freedoms,

Considering that international peace and security are essential elements for the realization of the right to development,

Reaffirming that there is a close relationship between disarmament and development and that progress in the field of disarmament would considerably promote progress in the field of development and that resources released through disarmament measures should be devoted to the economic and social development and well-being of all peoples and, in particular, those of the developing countries,

Recognizing that the human person is the central subject of the development process and that development policy should therefore make the human being the main participant and beneficiary of development,

Recognizing that the creation of conditions favourable to the development of peoples and individuals is the primary responsibility of their States,

Aware that efforts at the international level to promote and protect human rights should be accompanied by efforts to establish a new international economic order,

Confirming that the right to development is an inalienable human right and that equality of opportunity for development is a prerogative both of nations and of individuals who make up nations,

Proclaims the following Declaration on the Right to Development:

ARTICLE I

1. The right to development is an inalienable human right by virtue of which every human person and all peoples are entitled to participate in, contribute to, and enjoy economic, social, cultural and political development, in which all human rights and fundamental freedoms can be fully realized.

2. The human right to development also implies the full realization of the right of peoples to self-determination, which includes, subject to the relevant provisions of both International Covenants on Human Rights, the exercise of their inalienable right to full sovereignty over all their natural wealth and resources.

ARTICLE 2

1. The human person is the central subject of development and should be the active participant and beneficiary of the right to development.

2. All human beings have a responsibility for development, individually and collectively, taking in to account the need for full respect for their human rights and fundamental freedoms as well as their duties to the community, which alone can ensure the free and complete fulfilment of the human being, and they should therefore promote and protect an appropriate political, social and economic order for development.

3. States have the right and the duty to formulate appropriate national development policies that aim at the constant improvement of the well-being of the entire population and of all individuals, on the basis of their active, free and meaningful participation in development and in the fair distribution of the benefits resulting therefrom.

ARTICLE 3

1. States have the primary responsibility for the creation of national and international conditions favourable to the realization of the right to development.

2. The realization of the right to development requires full respect for the principles of international law concerning friendly relations and cooperation among States in accordance with the Charter of the United Nations.

3. States have the duty to co-operate with each other in ensuring development and eliminating obstacles to development. States should realize their rights and fulfil their duties in such a manner as to promote a new international economic order based on sovereign equality, interdependence, mutual interest and co-operation among all States, as well as to encourage the observance and realization of human rights.

ARTICLE 4

1. States have the duty to take steps, individually and collectively, to formulate international development policies with a view to facilitating the full realization of the right to development.

2. Sustained action is required to promote more rapid development of developing countries. As a complement to the efforts of developing countries, effective international co-operation is essential in providing these countries with appropriate means and facilities to foster their comprehensive development.

ARTICLE 5

States shall take resolute steps to eliminate the massive and flagrant violations of the human rights of peoples and human beings affected by situations such as those resulting from apartheid, all forms of racism and racial discrimination, colonialism, foreign domination and occupation, aggression, foreign interference and threats against national sovereignty, national unity and territorial integrity, threats of war and refusal to recognize the fundamental right of peoples to self-determination.

ARTICLE 6

1. All States should co-operate with a view to promoting, encouraging and strengthening universal respect for and observance of all human rights and fundamental freedoms for all without any distinction as to race, sex, language or religion.

2. All human rights and fundamental freedoms are indivisible and interdependent; equal attention and urgent consideration should be given to the implementation, promotion and protection of civil, political, economic, social and cultural rights.

3. States should take steps to eliminate obstacles to development resulting from failure to observe civil and political rights, as well as economic social and cultural rights.

ARTICLE 7

All States should promote the establishment, maintenance and strengthening of international peace and security and, to that end, should do their utmost to achieve general and complete disarmament under effective international control, as well as to ensure that the resources released by effective disarmament measures are used for comprehensive development, in particular that of the developing countries.

ARTICLE 8

1. States should undertake, at the national level, all necessary measures for the realization of the right to development and shall ensure, inter alia, equality of opportunity for all in their access to basic resources, education, health services, food, housing, employment and the fair distribution of income. Effective measures should be undertaken to ensure that women have an active role in the development process. Appropriate economic and social reforms should be carried out with a view to eradicating all social injustices.

2. States should encourage popular participation in all spheres as an important factor in development and in the full realization of all human rights.

ARTICLE 9

1. All the aspects of the right to development set forth in the present Declaration are indivisible and interdependent and each of them should be considered in the context of the whole.

2. Nothing in the present Declaration shall be construed as being contrary to the purposes and principles of the United Nations, or as implying that any State, group or person has a right to engage in any activity or to perform any act aimed at the violation of the rights set forth in the Universal Declaration of Human Rights and in the International Covenants on Human Rights.

ARTICLE 10

Steps should be taken to ensure the full exercise and progressive enhancement of the right to development, including the formulation, adoption and implementation of policy, legislative and other measures at the national and international levels.

World Charter for Nature

28 October 1982

G.A. Res. 37/7 (Annex), U.N.GAOR 37th Sess., U.N. Doc A/37/51

http://www.orgone.org/articles/ax7unwc1.htm

The General Assembly,

Reaffirming the fundamental purposes of the United Nations, in particular the maintenance of international peace and security, the development of friendly relations among nations and the achievement of international cooperation in solving international problems of an economic, social, cultural, technical, intellectual or humanitarian character,

Aware that:

(a) Mankind is a part of nature and life depends on the uninterrupted functioning of natural systems which ensure the supply of energy and nutrients,

(b) Civilization is rooted in nature, which has shaped human culture and influenced all artistic and scientific achievements, and living in harmony with nature gives man the best opportunities for the development of his creativity, and for rest and recreation,

Convinced that:

(a) Every form of life is unique, warranting respect regardless of its worth to man, and, to accord other organisms such recognition, man must be guided by a moral code of action,

(b) Man can alter nature and exhaust natural resources by his action or its consequences and, therefore, must fully recognize the urgency of maintaining the stability and quality of nature and of conserving natural resources,

Persuaded that:

(a) Lasting benefits from nature depend upon the maintenance of essential ecological processes and life support systems, and upon the diversity of life forms, which are jeopardized through excessive exploitation and habitat destruction by man,

(b) The degradation of natural systems owing to excessive consumption and misuse of natural resources, as well as to failure to establish an appropriate economic order among peoples and among States, leads to the breakdown of the economic, social and political framework of civilization,

(c) Competition for scarce resources creates conflicts, whereas the conservation of nature and natural resources contributes to justice and the maintenance of peace and cannot be achieved until mankind learns to live in peace and to forsake war and armaments,

Reaffirming that man must acquire the knowledge to maintain and enhance his ability to use natural resources in a manner which ensures the preservation of the species and ecosystems for the benefit of present and future generations,

Firmly convinced of the need for appropriate measures, at the national and international, individual and collective, and private and public levels, to protect nature and promote international co-operation in this field,

Adopts, to these ends, the present World Charter for Nature, which proclaims the following principles of conservation by which all human conduct affecting nature is to be guided and judged.

I. GENERAL PRINCIPLES

1. Nature shall be respected and its essential processes shall not be impaired.

2. The genetic viability on the earth shall not be compromised; the population levels of all life forms, wild and domesticated, must be at least sufficient for their survival, and to this end necessary habitat shall be safeguarded.

3. All areas of the earth, both land and sea, shall be subject to these principles of conservation; special protection shall be given to unique areas, to representative samples of all the different types of ecosystems and to the habitat of rare or endangered species.

4. Ecosystems and organisms, as well as the land, marine and atmospheric resources that are utilized by man, shall be managed to achieve and maintain optimum sustainable productivity, but not in such a way as to endanger the integrity of those other ecosystems or species with which they coexist.

5. Nature shall be secured against degradation caused by warfare or other hostile activities.

II. FUNCTIONS

6. In the decision-making process it shall be recognized that man's needs can be met only by ensuring the proper functioning of natural systems and by respecting the principles set forth in the present Charter.

7. In the planning and implementation of social and economic development activities, due account shall be taken of the fact that the conservation of nature is an integral part of those activities.

8. In formulating long-term plans for economic development, population growth and the improvement of standards of living, due account shall be taken of the long-term capacity of natural systems to ensure the subsistence and settlement of the populations concerned, recognizing that this capacity may be enhanced through science and technology.

9. The allocation of areas of the earth to various uses shall be planned and due account shall be taken of the physical constraints, the biological productivity and diversity and the natural beauty of the areas concerned.

10. Natural resources shall not be wasted, but used with a restraint appropriate to the principles set forth in the present Charter, in accordance with the following rules:

(a) Living resources shall not be utilized in excess of their natural capacity for regeneration;

(b) The productivity of soils shall be maintained or enhanced through measures which safeguard their long-term fertility and the process of organic decomposition, and prevent erosion and all other forms of degradation;

(c) Resources, including water, which are not consumed as they are used shall be reused or recycled;

(d) Non-renewable resources which are consumed as they are used shall be exploited with restraint, taking into account their abundance, their rational possibilities of converting them for consumption, and the compatibility of their exploitation with the functioning of natural systems.

11. Activities which might have an impact on nature shall be controlled, and the best available technologies that minimize significant risks to nature or other adverse effects shall be used; in particular:

(a) Activities which are likely to cause irreversible damage to nature shall be avoided;

(b) Activities which are likely to pose a significant risk to nature shall be preceded by an exhaustive examination; their proponents shall demonstrate that expected benefits outweigh potential damage to nature, and where potential adverse effects are not fully understood, the activities should not proceed;

(c) Activities which may disturb nature shall be preceded by assessment of their consequences, and environmental impact studies of development projects shall be conducted sufficiently in advance, and if they are to be undertaken, such activities shall be planned and carried out so as to minimize potential adverse effects;

(d) Agriculture, grazing, forestry and fisheries practices shall be adapted to the natural characteristics and constraints of given areas;

(e) Areas degraded by human activities shall be rehabilitated for purposes in accord with their natural potential and compatible with the well-being of affected populations.

12. Discharge of pollutants into natural systems shall be avoided and:

(a) Where this is not feasible, such pollutants shall be treated at the source, using the best practicable means available;

(b) Special precautions shall be taken to prevent discharge of radioactive or toxic wastes.

13. Measures intended to prevent, control or limit natural disasters, infestations and diseases shall be specifically directed to the causes of these scourges and shall avoid averse side-effects on nature.

III. IMPLEMENTATION

14. The principles set forth in the present Charter shall be reflected in the law and practice of each State, as well as at the international level.

15. Knowledge of nature shall be broadly disseminated by all possible means, particularly by ecological education as an integral part of general education.

16. All planning shall include, among its essential elements, the formulation of strategies for the conservation of nature, the establishment of inventories of ecosystems and assessments of the effects on nature of proposed policies and activities; all of these elements shall be disclosed to the public by appropriate means in time to permit effective consultation and participation.

17. Funds, programmes and administrative structures necessary to achieve the objective of the conservation of nature shall be provided.

18. Constant efforts shall be made to increase knowledge of nature by scientific research and to disseminate such knowledge unimpeded by restrictions of any kind.

19. The status of natural processes, ecosystems and species shall be closely monitored to enable early detection of degradation or threat, ensure timely intervention and facilitate the evaluation of conservation policies and methods.

20. Military activities damaging to nature shall be avoided.

21. States and, to the extent they are able, other public authorities, international organizations, **individuals, groups** and corporations shall:

(a) Co-operate in the task of conserving nature through common activities and other relevant actions, including information exchange and consultations;

(b) Establish standards for products and other manufacturing processes that may have adverse effects on nature, as well as agreed methodologies for assessing these effects;

(c) Implement the applicable international legal provisions for the conservation of nature and the protection of the environment;

(d) Ensure that activities within their jurisdictions or control do not cause damage to the natural systems located within other States or in the areas beyond the limits of national jurisdiction;

(e) **Safeguard and conserve nature in areas beyond national jurisdiction.**

22. Taking fully into account the sovereignty of States over their natural resources, each State shall give effect to the provisions of the present Charter through its competent organs and in co-operation with other States.

23. All persons, in accordance with their national legislation, shall have the opportunity to participate, individually or with others, in the formulation of decisions of direct concern to their environment, and shall have access to means of redress when their environment has suffered damage or degradation.

24. Each person has a duty to act in accordance with the provisions of the present Charter; acting individually, in association with others or through participation in the political process, each person shall strive to ensure that the objectives and requirements of the present Charter are met.

Rio Declaration on Environment and Development

Rio de Janeiro, 13 June 1992

U.N.Doc. A/CONF.151/26 (vol. I) (1992) 31 I.L.M. 874 (1992)

http://www.unep.org/Documents/Default.asp?DocumentID=78&ArticleID=1163

The United Nations Conference on Environment and Development,

Having met at Rio de Janeiro from 3 to 14 June 1992,

Reaffirming the Declaration of the United Nations Conference on the Human Environment, adopted at Stockholm on 16 June 1972, and seeking to build upon it,

With the goal of establishing a new and equitable global partnership through the creation of new levels of cooperation among States, key sectors of societies and people,

Working towards international agreements which respect the interests of all and protect the integrity of the global environmental and developmental system,

Recognizing the integral and interdependent nature of the Earth, our home,

Proclaims that:

PRINCIPLE 1

Human beings are at the centre of concerns for sustainable development. They are entitled to a healthy and productive life in harmony with nature.

PRINCIPLE 2

States have, in accordance with the Charter of the United Nations and the principles of international law, the sovereign right to exploit their own resources pursuant to their own environmental and developmental policies, and the responsibility to ensure that activities within their jurisdiction or control do not cause damage to the environment of other States or of areas beyond the limits of national jurisdiction.

PRINCIPLE 3

The right to development must be fulfilled so as to equitably meet developmental and environmental needs of present and future generations.

PRINCIPLE 4

In order to achieve sustainable development, environmental protection shall constitute an integral part of the development process and cannot be considered in isolation from it.

PRINCIPLE 5

All States and all people shall cooperate in the essential task of eradicating poverty as an indispensable requirement for sustainable development, in order to decrease the disparities in standards of living and better meet the needs of the majority of the people of the world.

PRINCIPLE 6

The special situation and needs of developing countries, particularly the least developed and those most environmentally vulnerable, shall be given special priority. International actions in the field of environment and development should also address the interests and needs of all countries.

PRINCIPLE 7

States shall cooperate in a spirit of global partnership to conserve, protect and restore the health and integrity of the Earth's ecosystem. In view of the different contributions to global environmental degradation, States have common but differentiated responsibilities. The developed countries acknowledge the responsibility that they bear in the international pursuit to sustainable development in view of the pressures their societies place on the global environment and of the technologies and financial resources they command.

PRINCIPLE 8

To achieve sustainable development and a higher quality of life for all people, States should reduce and eliminate unsustainable patterns of production and consumption and promote appropriate demographic policies.

PRINCIPLE 9

States should cooperate to strengthen endogenous capacity-building for sustainable development by improving scientific understanding through exchanges of scientific and technological knowledge, and by enhancing the development, adaptation, diffusion and transfer of technologies, including new and innovative technologies.

PRINCIPLE 10

Environmental issues are best handled with participation of all concerned citizens, at the relevant level. At the national level, each individual shall have appropriate access to information concerning the environment that is held by public authorities, including information on hazardous materials and activities in their communities, and the opportunity to participate in decision-making processes. States shall facilitate and encourage public awareness and participation by making information widely available. Effective access to judicial and administrative proceedings, including redress and remedy, shall be provided.

PRINCIPLE 11

States shall enact effective environmental legislation. Environmental standards, management objectives and priorities should reflect the environmental and development context to which they apply. Standards applied by some countries may be inappropriate and of unwarranted economic and social cost to other countries, in particular developing countries.

PRINCIPLE 12

States should cooperate to promote a supportive and open international economic system that would lead to economic growth and sustainable development in all countries, to better address the problems of environmental degradation. Trade policy measures for environmental purposes should not constitute a means of arbitrary or unjustifiable discrimination or a disguised restriction on international trade. Unilateral actions to deal with environmental challenges outside the jurisdiction of the importing country should be avoided. Environmental measures addressing transboundary or global environmental problems should, as far as possible, be based on an international consensus.

PRINCIPLE 13

States shall develop national law regarding liability and compensation for the victims of pollution and other environmental damage. States shall also cooperate in an expeditious and more determined manner to develop further international law regarding liability and compensation for adverse effects of environmental damage caused by activities within their jurisdiction or control to areas beyond their jurisdiction.

PRINCIPLE 14

States should effectively cooperate to discourage or prevent the relocation and transfer to other States of any activities and substances that cause severe environmental degradation or are found to be harmful to human health.

PRINCIPLE 15

In order to protect the environment, the precautionary approach shall be widely applied by States according to their capabilities. Where there are threats of serious or irreversible damage, lack of full scientific certainty shall not be used as a reason for postponing cost-effective measures to prevent environmental degradation.

PRINCIPLE 16

National authorities should endeavour to promote the internalization of environmental costs and the use of economic instruments, taking into account the approach that the polluter should, in principle, bear the cost of pollution, with due regard to the public interest and without distorting international trade and investment.

PRINCIPLE 17

Environmental impact assessment, as a national instrument, shall be undertaken for proposed activities that are likely to have a significant adverse impact on the environment and are subject to a decision of a competent national authority.

PRINCIPLE 18

States shall immediately notify other States of any natural disasters or other emergencies that are likely to produce sudden harmful effects on the environment of those States. Every effort shall be made by the international community to help States so afflicted.

PRINCIPLE 19

States shall provide prior and timely notification and relevant information to potentially affected States on activities that may have a significant adverse transboundary environmental effect and shall consult with those States at an early stage and in good faith.

PRINCIPLE 20

Women have a vital role in environmental management and development. Their full participation is therefore essential to achieve sustainable development.

PRINCIPLE 21

The creativity, ideals and courage of the youth of the world should be mobilized to forge a global partnership in order to achieve sustainable development and ensure a better future for all.

PRINCIPLE 22

Indigenous people and their communities and other local communities have a vital role in environmental management and development because of their knowledge and traditional practices. States should recognize and duly support their identity, culture and interests and enable their effective participation in the achievement of sustainable development.

PRINCIPLE 23

The environment and natural resources of people under oppression, domination and occupation shall be protected.

PRINCIPLE 24

Warfare is inherently destructive of sustainable development. States shall therefore respect international law providing protection for the environment in times of armed conflict and cooperate in its further development, as necessary.

PRINCIPLE 25

Peace, development and environmental protection are interdependent and indivisible.

PRINCIPLE 26

States shall resolve all their environmental disputes peacefully and by appropriate means in accordance with the Charter of the United Nations.

PRINCIPLE 27

States and people shall cooperate in good faith and in a spirit of partnership in the fulfilment of the principles embodied in this Declaration and in the further development of international law in the field of sustainable development.

Source: Report of the United Nations Conference on the Human Environment, Stockholm, 5–16 June 1972 (United Nations publication, Sales No. E.73.II.A.14 and corrigendum), chap. I.

The Earth Charter

http://www.earthcharterusa.org/earth_charter.html

PREAMBLE

We stand at a critical moment in Earth's history, a time when humanity must choose its future. As the world becomes increasingly interdependent and fragile, the future at once holds great peril and great promise. To move forward we must recognize that in the midst of a magnificent diversity of cultures and life forms we are one human family and one Earth community with a common destiny. We must join together to bring forth a sustainable global society founded on respect for nature, universal human rights, economic justice, and a culture of peace. Towards this end, it is imperative that we, the peoples of Earth, declare our responsibility to one another, to the greater community of life, and to future generations.

Earth, Our Home

Humanity is part of a vast evolving universe. Earth, our home, is alive with a unique community of life. The forces of nature make existence a demanding and uncertain adventure, but Earth has provided the conditions essential to life's evolution. The resilience of the community of life and the well-being of humanity depend upon preserving a healthy biosphere with all its ecological systems, a rich variety of plants and animals, fertile soils, pure waters, and clean air. The global environment with its finite resources is a common concern of all peoples. The protection of Earth's vitality, diversity, and beauty is a sacred trust.

The Global Situation

The dominant patterns of production and consumption are causing environmental devastation, the depletion of resources, and a massive extinction of species. Communities are being undermined. The benefits of development are not shared equitably and the gap between rich and poor is widening. Injustice, poverty, ignorance, and violent conflict are widespread and the cause of great suffering. An unprecedented rise in human population has overburdened ecological and social systems. The foundations of global security are threatened. These trends are perilous-but not inevitable.

The Challenges Ahead

The choice is ours: form a global partnership to care for Earth and one another or risk the destruction of ourselves and the diversity of life. Fundamental changes are needed in our values, institutions, and ways of living. We must realize that when basic needs have been met, human development is primarily about being more, not having more. We have the knowledge and technology to provide for all and to reduce our impacts on the environment. The emergence of a global civil society is creating new opportunities to build a democratic and humane world. Our environmental, economic, political, social, and spiritual challenges are interconnected, and together we can forge inclusive solutions.

Universal Responsibility

To realize these aspirations, we must decide to live with a sense of universal responsibility, identifying ourselves with the whole Earth community as well as our local communities. We are at once citizens of different nations and of one world in which the local and global are linked. Everyone shares responsibility for the present and future well-being of the human family and the larger living world. The spirit of human solidarity and kinship with all life is strengthened when we live with reverence for the mystery of being, gratitude for the gift of life, and humility regarding the human place in nature.

We urgently need a shared vision of basic values to provide an ethical foundation for the emerging world community. Therefore, together in hope we affirm the following interdependent principles for a sustainable way of life as a common standard by which the conduct of all individuals, organizations, businesses, governments, and transnational institutions is to be guided and assessed.

PRINCIPLES

I. Respect and Care for the Community of Life

1. Respect Earth and life in all its diversity.

a. Recognize that all beings are interdependent and every form of life has value regardless of its worth to human beings.

b. Affirm faith in the inherent dignity of all human beings and in the intellectual, artistic, ethical, and spiritual potential of humanity.

2. Care for the community of life with understanding, compassion, and love.

a. Accept that with the right to own, manage, and use natural resources comes the duty to prevent environmental harm and to protect the rights of people.

b. Affirm that with increased freedom, knowledge, and power comes increased responsibility to promote the common good.

3. Build democratic societies that are just, participatory, sustainable, and peaceful.

a. Ensure that communities at all levels guarantee human rights and fundamental freedoms and provide everyone an opportunity to realize his or her full potential.

b. Promote social and economic justice, enabling all to achieve a secure and meaningful livelihood that is ecologically responsible.

4. Secure Earth's bounty and beauty for present and future generations.

a. Recognize that the freedom of action of each generation is qualified by the needs of future generations.

b. Transmit to future generations values, traditions, and institutions that support the long-term flourishing of Earth's human and ecological communities.

In order to fulfill these four broad commitments, it is necessary to:

II. Ecological Integrity

4. Protect and restore the integrity of Earth's ecological systems, with special concern for biological diversity and the natural processes that sustain life.

a. Adopt at all levels sustainable development plans and regulations that make environmental conservation and rehabilitation integral to all development initiatives.

b. Establish and safeguard viable nature and biosphere reserves, including wild lands and marine areas, to protect Earth's life support systems, maintain biodiversity, and preserve our natural heritage.

c. Promote the recovery of endangered species and ecosystems.

d. Control and eradicate non-native or genetically modified organisms harmful to native species and the environment, and prevent introduction of such harmful organisms.

e. Manage the use of renewable resources such as water, soil, forest products, and marine life in ways that do not exceed rates of regeneration and that protect the health of ecosystems.

f. Manage the extraction and use of non-renewable resources such as minerals and fossil fuels in ways that minimize depletion and cause no serious environmental damage.

6. Prevent harm as the best method of environmental protection and, when knowledge is limited, apply a precautionary approach.

a. Take action to avoid the possibility of serious or irreversible environmental harm even when scientific knowledge is incomplete or inconclusive.

b. Place the burden of proof on those who argue that a proposed activity will not cause significant harm, and make the responsible parties liable for environmental harm.

c. Ensure that decision making addresses the cumulative, long-term, indirect, long distance, and global consequences of human activities.

d. Prevent pollution of any part of the environment and allow no build-up of radioactive, toxic, or other hazardous substances.

e. Avoid military activities damaging to the environment.

7. Adopt patterns of production, consumption, and reproduction that safeguard Earth's regenerative capacities, human rights, and community well-being.

a. Reduce, reuse, and recycle the materials used in production and consumption systems, and ensure that residual waste can be assimilated by ecological systems.

b. Act with restraint and efficiency when using energy, and rely increasingly on renewable energy sources such as solar and wind.

c. Promote the development, adoption, and equitable transfer of environmentally sound technologies.

d. Internalize the full environmental and social costs of goods and services in the selling price, and enable consumers to identify products that meet the highest social and environmental standards.

e. Ensure universal access to health care that fosters reproductive health and responsible reproduction.

f. Adopt lifestyles that emphasize the quality of life and material sufficiency in a finite world.

8. Advance the study of ecological sustainability and promote the open exchange and wide application of the knowledge acquired.

a. Support international scientific and technical cooperation on sustainability, with special attention to the needs of developing nations. b. Recognize and preserve the traditional knowledge and spiritual wisdom in all cultures that contribute to environmental protection and human well-being. c. Ensure that information of vital importance to human health and environmental protection, including genetic information, remains available in the public domain.

III. Social and Economic Justice

9. Eradicate poverty as an ethical, social, and environmental imperative.

a. Guarantee the right to potable water, clean air, food security, uncontaminated soil, shelter, and safe sanitation, allocating the national and international resources required.

b. Empower every human being with the education and resources to secure a sustainable livelihood, and provide social security and safety nets for those who are unable to support themselves.

c. Recognize the ignored, protect the vulnerable, serve those who suffer, and enable them to develop their capacities and to pursue their aspirations.

10. Ensure that economic activities and institutions at all levels promote human development in an equitable and sustainable manner.

a. Promote the equitable distribution of wealth within nations and among nations.

b. Enhance the intellectual, financial, technical, and social resources of developing nations, and relieve them of onerous international debt.

c. Ensure that all trade supports sustainable resource use, environmental protection, and progressive labor standards.

d. Require multinational corporations and international financial organizations to act transparently in the public good, and hold them accountable for the consequences of their activities.

11. Affirm gender equality and equity as prerequisites to sustainable development and ensure universal access to education, health care, and economic opportunity.

a. Secure the human rights of women and girls and end all violence against them.

b. Promote the active participation of women in all aspects of economic, political, civil, social, and cultural life as full and equal partners, decision makers, leaders, and beneficiaries.

c. Strengthen families and ensure the safety and loving nurture of all family members.

12. Uphold the right of all, without discrimination, to a natural and social environment supportive of human dignity, bodily health, and spiritual well-being, with special attention to the rights of indigenous peoples and minorities.

a. Eliminate discrimination in all its forms, such as that based on race, color, sex, sexual orientation, religion, language, and national, ethnic or social origin.

b. Affirm the right of indigenous peoples to their spirituality, knowledge, lands and resources and to their related practice of sustainable livelihoods.

c. Honor and support the young people of our communities, enabling them to fulfill their essential role in creating sustainable societies.

d. Protect and restore outstanding places of cultural and spiritual significance.

IV. Democracy, Nonviolence, and Peace

13. Strengthen democratic institutions at all levels, and provide transparency and accountability in governance, inclusive participation in decision making, and access to justice.

a. Uphold the right of everyone to receive clear and timely information on environmental matters and all development plans and activities which are likely to affect them or in which they have an interest.

b. Support local, regional and global civil society, and promote the meaningful participation of all interested individuals and organizations in decision making.

c. Protect the rights to freedom of opinion, expression, peaceful assembly, association, and dissent.

d. Institute effective and efficient access to administrative and independent judicial procedures, including remedies and redress for environmental harm and the threat of such harm.

e. Eliminate corruption in all public and private institutions.

e. Strengthen local communities, enabling them to care for their environments, and assign environmental responsibilities to the levels of government where they can be carried out most effectively.

14. Integrate into formal education and life-long learning the knowledge, values, and skills needed for a sustainable way of life.

a. Provide all, especially children and youth, with educational opportunities that empower them to contribute actively to sustainable development.

b. Promote the contribution of the arts and humanities as well as the sciences in sustainability education.

c. Enhance the role of the mass media in raising awareness of ecological and social challenges.

d. Recognize the importance of moral and spiritual education for sustainable living.

15. Treat all living beings with respect and consideration.

a. Prevent cruelty to animals kept in human societies and protect them from suffering.

b. Protect wild animals from methods of hunting, trapping, and fishing that cause extreme, prolonged, or avoidable suffering.

c. Avoid or eliminate to the full extent possible the taking or destruction of non-targeted species.

16. Promote a culture of tolerance, nonviolence, and peace.

a. Encourage and support mutual understanding, solidarity, and cooperation among all peoples and within and among nations.

b. Implement comprehensive strategies to prevent violent conflict and use collaborative problem solving to manage and resolve environmental conflicts and other disputes.

c. Demilitarize national security systems to the level of a non-provocative defense posture, and convert military resources to peaceful purposes, including ecological restoration.

d. Eliminate nuclear, biological, and toxic weapons and other weapons of mass destruction.

e. Ensure that the use of orbital and outer space supports environmental protection and peace.

f. Recognize that peace is the wholeness created by right relationships with oneself, other persons, other cultures, other life, Earth, and the larger whole of which all are a part.

THE WAY FORWARD

As never before in history, common destiny beckons us to seek a new beginning. Such renewal is the promise of these Earth Charter principles. To fulfill this promise, we must commit ourselves to adopt and promote the values and objectives of the Charter.

This requires a change of mind and heart. It requires a new sense of global interdependence and universal responsibility. We must imaginatively develop and apply the vision of a sustainable way of life locally, nationally, regionally, and globally. Our cultural diversity is a precious heritage and different cultures will find their own distinctive ways to realize the vision. We must deepen and expand the global dialogue that generated the Earth Charter, for we have much to learn from the ongoing collaborative search for truth and wisdom.

Life often involves tensions between important values. This can mean difficult choices. However, we must find ways to harmonize diversity with unity, the exercise of freedom with the common good, short-term objectives with long-term goals. Every individual, family, organization, and community has a vital role to play. The arts, sciences, religions, educational institutions, media, businesses, nongovernmental organizations, and governments are all called to offer creative leadership. The partnership of government, civil society, and business is essential for effective governance.

In order to build a sustainable global community, the nations of the world must renew their commitment to the United Nations, fulfill their obligations under existing international agreements, and support the implementation of Earth Charter principles with an international legally binding instrument on environment and development.

Let ours be a time remembered for the awakening of a new reverence for life, the firm resolve to achieve sustainability, the quickening of the struggle for justice and peace, and the joyful celebration of life.

Plan of Implementation for the United Nations World Summit on Sustainable Development

Adopted September 4, 2002 Johannesburg, South Africa.

United Nations, Report of the World Summit on Sustainable Development UN Doc. A/CONF.199/20 (2002)

http://www.johannesburgsummit.org/html/documents/summit_docs/2309_planfinal.htm

I. INTRODUCTION

1. The United Nations Conference on Environment and Development (UNCED), held in Rio de Janeiro in 1992, provided the fundamental principles and the programme of action for achieving sustainable development. We strongly reaffirm our commitment to the Rio principles, the full implementation of Agenda 21 and the Programme for the Further Implementation of Agenda 21. We also commit ourselves to achieving the internationally agreed development goals, including those contained in the United Nations Millennium Declaration and in the outcomes of the major United Nations conferences and international agreements since 1992.

2. The present plan of implementation will further build on the achievements made since UNCED and expedite the realization of the remaining goals. To this end, we commit ourselves to undertaking concrete actions and measures at all levels and to enhancing international cooperation, taking into account the Rio Principles, including, inter alia, the principle of common but differentiated responsibilities as set out in principle 7 of the Rio Declaration on Environment and Development. These efforts will also promote the integration of the three components of sustainable development – economic development, social development and environmental protection – as interdependent and mutually reinforcing pillars. Poverty eradication, changing unsustainable patterns of production and consumption, and protecting and managing the natural resource base of economic and social development are overarching objectives of, and essential requirements for, sustainable development.

3. We recognize that the implementation of the outcomes of the Summit should benefit all, particularly women, youth, children and vulnerable groups. Furthermore, the implementation should involve all relevant actors through partnerships, especially between Governments of the North and South, on the one hand, and between Governments and major groups, on the other, to achieve the widely shared goals of sustainable development. As reflected in the Monterrey Consensus, such partnerships are key to pursuing sustainable development in a globalizing world.

4. Good governance within each country and at the international level is essential for sustainable development. At the domestic level, sound environmental, social and economic policies, democratic institutions responsive to the needs of the people, the rule of law, anti-corruption measures, gender equality and an enabling environment for investment are the basis for sustainable development. As a result of globalization, external factors have become critical in determining the success or failure of developing countries in their national efforts. The gap between developed and developing countries points to the continued need for a dynamic and enabling international economic environment supportive of international cooperation, particularly in the areas of finance, technology transfer, debt and trade, and full and effective participation of developing countries in global decision-making, if the momentum for global progress towards sustainable development is to be maintained and increased.

5. Peace, security, stability and respect for human rights and fundamental freedoms, including the right to development, as well as respect for cultural

diversity, are essential for achieving sustainable development and ensuring that sustainable development benefits all.

5bis We acknowledge the importance of ethics for sustainable development, and therefore we emphasize the need to consider ethics in the implementation of Agenda 21.

II. POVERTY ERADICATION

6. Eradicating poverty is the greatest global challenge facing the world today and an indispensable requirement for sustainable development, particularly for developing countries. Although each country has the primary responsibility for its own sustainable development and poverty eradication and the role of national policies and development strategies cannot be overemphasized, concerted and concrete measures are required at all levels to enable developing countries to achieve their sustainable development goals as related to the internationally agreed poverty-related targets and goals, including those contained in Agenda 21, the relevant outcomes of other United Nations conferences and the United Nations Millennium Declaration. This would include actions at all levels to:

(a) Halve, by the year 2015, the proportion of the world's people whose income is less than $1 a day and the proportion of people who suffer from hunger and, by the same date, to halve the proportion of people without access to safe drinking water;

(b) Establish a world solidarity fund to eradicate poverty and to promote social and human development in the developing countries pursuant to modalities to be determined by the General Assembly, while stressing the voluntary nature of the contributions, the need to avoid duplication of existing United Nations funds, and encouraging the role of the private sector and individual citizens relative to Governments in funding the endeavours;

(c) Develop national programmes for sustainable development and local and community development, where appropriate within country-owned poverty reduction strategies, to promote the empowerment of people living in poverty and their organizations. These programmes should reflect their priorities and enable them to increase access to productive resources, public services and institutions, in particular land, water, employment opportunities, credit, education and health;

(d) Promote women's equal access to and full participation, on the basis of equality with men, in decision-making at all levels, mainstreaming gender perspectives in all policies and strategies, eliminating all forms of violence and discrimination against women, and improving the status, health and economic welfare of women and girls through full and equal access to economic opportunity, land, credit, education and health-care services;

(e) Develop policies and ways and means to improve access by indigenous people and their communities to economic activities, and increase their employment through, where appropriate, such measures as training, technical assistance and credit facilities. Recognize that traditional and direct dependence on renewable resources and ecosystems, including sustainable harvesting, continues to be essential to the cultural, economic and physical well-being of indigenous people and their communities;

(f) Deliver basic health services for all and reduce environmental health threats, taking into account the special needs of children and the linkages between poverty, health and environment, with provision of financial resources, technical assistance and knowledge transfer to developing countries and countries with economies in transition;

(g) Ensure that children everywhere, boys and girls alike, will be able to complete a full course of primary schooling and will have equal access to all levels of education;

(h) Provide access to agricultural resources for people living in poverty, especially women and indigenous communities, and promote, as appropriate, land tenure arrangements that recognize and protect indigenous and common property resource management systems;

(i) Build basic rural infrastructure, diversify the economy and improve transportation and access to markets, market information and credit for the rural poor to support sustainable agriculture and rural development;

(j) Transfer basic sustainable agricultural techniques and knowledge, including natural resource management, to small and medium-scale farmers, fishers and the rural poor, especially in developing countries, including through multi-stakeholder approaches and public-private partnerships aimed at increasing agriculture production and food security;

(k) Increase food availability and affordability, including through harvest and food technology and management, as well as equitable and efficient distribution systems, by promoting, for example, community-based partnerships linking urban and rural people and enterprises;

(l) Combat desertification and mitigate the effects of drought and floods through such measures as improved use of climate and weather information and forecasts, early warning systems, land and natural resource management, agricultural practices and ecosystem conservation in order to reverse current trends and minimize degradation of land and water resources, including through the provision of adequate and predictable financial resources to implement the United Nations Convention to Combat Desertification in Those Countries Experiencing Serious Drought and/or Desertification, particularly in Africa, as one of the tools for poverty eradication;

(m) Increase access to sanitation to improve human health and reduce infant and child mortality, prioritizing water and sanitation in national sustainable development strategies and poverty reduction strategies where they exist.

7. The provision of clean drinking water and adequate sanitation is necessary to protect human health and the environment. In this respect, we agree to halve, by the year 2015, the proportion of people who are unable to reach or to afford safe drinking water (as outlined in the Millennium Declaration) and the proportion of people who do not have access to basic sanitation, which would include actions at all levels to:

(a) Develop and implement efficient household sanitation systems;

(b) Improve sanitation in public institutions, especially schools;

(c) Promote safe hygiene practices;

(d) Promote education and outreach focused on children, as agents of behavioural change;

(e) Promote affordable and socially and culturally acceptable technologies and practices;

(f) Develop innovative financing and partnership mechanisms;

(g) Integrate sanitation into water resources management strategies.

8. Take joint actions and improve efforts to work together at all levels to improve access to reliable and affordable energy services for sustainable development sufficient to facilitate the achievement of the millennium development goals, including the goal of halving the proportion of people in poverty by 2015, and as a means to generate other important services that mitigate poverty, bearing in mind that access to energy facilitates the eradication of poverty. This would include actions at all levels to:

(a) Improve access to reliable, affordable, economically viable, socially acceptable and environmentally sound energy services and resources, taking into account national specificities and circumstances, through various means, such as enhanced rural electrification and decentralized energy systems, increased use of renewables, cleaner liquid and gaseous fuels and enhanced energy efficiency, by intensifying regional and international cooperation in support of national efforts, including through capacity-building, financial and technological assistance and innovative financing mechanisms, including at the micro and meso levels, recognizing the specific factors for providing access to the poor;

(b) Improve access to modern biomass technologies and fuelwood sources and supplies, and commercialize biomass operations, including the use of agricultural residues, in rural areas and where such practices are sustainable;

(c) Promote a sustainable use of biomass and, as appropriate, other renewable energies through improvement of current patterns of use, such as management of resources, more efficient use of fuelwood and new or improved products and technologies;

(d) Support the transition to the cleaner use of liquid and gaseous fossil fuels, where considered more environmentally sound, socially acceptable and cost-effective;

(e) Develop national energy policies and regulatory frameworks that will help to create the necessary economic, social and institutional conditions in the energy sector to improve access to reliable, affordable, economically viable, socially acceptable and environmentally sound energy services for sustainable development and poverty eradication in rural, peri-urban and urban areas;

(f) Enhance international and regional cooperation to improve access to reliable, affordable, economically viable, socially acceptable and environmentally sound energy services, as an integral part of poverty reduction programmes, by facilitating the creation of enabling environments and addressing capacity-building needs, with special attention to rural and isolated areas, as appropriate;

(g) Assist and facilitate on an accelerated basis, with the financial and technical assistance of developed countries, including through public-private partnerships, the access of the poor to reliable, affordable, economically viable, socially acceptable and environmentally sound energy services, taking into account the instrumental role of developing national policies on energy for sustainable development, bearing in mind that in developing countries sharp increases in energy services are required to improve the standards of living of their populations and that energy services have positive impacts on poverty eradication and improve standards of living.

9. Strengthen the contribution of industrial development to poverty eradication and sustainable natural resource management. This would include actions at all levels to:

(a) Provide assistance and mobilize resources to enhance industrial productivity and competitiveness as well as industrial development in developing countries, including the transfer of environmentally sound technologies on preferential terms, as mutually agreed;

(b) Provide assistance to increase income-generating employment opportunities, taking into account the International Labour Organization (ILO) Declaration on Fundamental Principles and Rights at Work;

(c) Promote the development of micro, small and medium-sized enterprises, including by means of training, education and skill enhancement, with a special focus on agro-industry as a provider of livelihoods for rural communities;

(d) Provide financial and technological support, as appropriate, to rural communities of developing countries to enable them to benefit from safe and sustainable livelihood opportunities in small-scale mining ventures;

(e) Provide support to developing countries for the development of safe low-cost technologies that provide or conserve fuel for cooking and water heating;

(f) Provide support for natural resource management for creating sustainable livelihoods for the poor.

10. By 2020, achieve a significant improvement in the lives of at least 100 million slum dwellers, as proposed in the "Cities without slums" initiative. This would include actions at all levels to:

(a) Improve access to land and property, to adequate shelter and to basic services for the urban and rural poor, with special attention to female heads of household;

(b) Use low-cost and sustainable materials and appropriate technologies for the construction of adequate and secure housing for the poor, with financial and technological assistance to developing countries, taking into account their culture, climate, specific social conditions and vulnerability to natural disasters;

(c) Increase decent employment, credit and income for the urban poor, through appropriate national policies, promoting equal opportunities for women and men;

(d) Remove unnecessary regulatory and other obstacles for microenterprises and the informal sector;

(e) Support local authorities in elaborating slum upgrading programmes within the framework of urban development plans and facilitate access, particularly for the poor, to information on housing legislation.

11. Take immediate and effective measures to eliminate the worst forms of child labour as defined in ILO Convention No. 182, and elaborate and implement strategies for the elimination of child labour that is contrary to accepted international standards.

12. Promote international cooperation to assist developing countries, upon request, in addressing child labour and its root causes, inter alia, through social and economic policies aimed at poverty conditions, while stressing that labour standards should not be used for protectionist trade purposes.

III. CHANGING UNSUSTAINABLE PATTERNS OF CONSUMPTION AND PRODUCTION

13. Fundamental changes in the way societies produce and consume are indispensable for achieving global sustainable development. All countries should promote sustainable consumption and production patterns, with the developed countries taking the lead and with all countries benefiting from the process, taking into account the Rio principles, including, inter alia, the principle of common but differentiated responsibilities as set out in principle 7 of the Rio Declaration on Environment and Development. Governments, relevant international organizations, the private sector and all major groups should play an active role in changing unsustainable consumption and production patterns. This would include the actions at all levels set out below.

14. Encourage and promote the development of a 10-year framework of programmes in support of regional and national initiatives to accelerate the shift towards sustainable consumption and production to promote social and economic development within the carrying capacity of ecosystems by addressing and, where appropriate, delinking economic growth and environmental degradation through improving efficiency and sustainability in the use of resources and production processes, and reducing resource degradation, pollution and waste. All countries should take action, with developed countries taking the lead, taking into account the development needs and capabilities of developing countries through mobilization, from all sources, of financial and technical assistance and capacity-building for developing countries. This would require actions at all levels to:

(a) Identify specific activities, tools, policies, measures and monitoring and assessment mechanisms, including, where appropriate, life-cycle analysis and national indicators for measuring progress, bearing in mind that standards applied by some countries may be inappropriate and of unwarranted economic and social cost to other countries, in particular developing countries;

(b) Adopt and implement policies and measures aimed at promoting sustainable patterns of production and consumption, applying, inter alia, the polluter-pays principle described in principle 16 of the Rio Declaration on Environment and Development;

(c) Develop production and consumption policies to improve the products and services provided, while reducing environmental and health impacts, using, where appropriate, science-based approaches, such as life-cycle analysis;

(d) Develop awareness-raising programmes on the importance of sustainable production and consumption patterns, particularly among youth and the relevant segments in all countries, especially in developed countries, through, inter alia, education, public and consumer information, advertising and other media, taking into account local, national and regional cultural values;

(e) Develop and adopt, where appropriate, on a voluntary basis, effective, transparent, verifiable, non-misleading and non-discriminatory consumer information tools to provide information relating to sustainable consumption and production, including human health and safety aspects. These tools should not be used as disguised trade barriers;

(f) Increase eco-efficiency, with financial support from all sources, where mutually agreed, for capacity-building, technology transfer and exchange of technology with developing countries and countries with economies in transition, in cooperation with relevant international organizations.

15. Increase investment in cleaner production and eco-efficiency in all countries through, inter alia, incentives and support schemes and policies directed at establishing appropriate regulatory, financial and legal frameworks. This would include actions at all levels to:

(a) Establish and support cleaner production programmes and centres and more efficient production methods by providing, inter alia, incentives and capacity-building to assist enterprises, especially small and medium-sized enterprises and particularly in developing countries, in improving productivity and sustainable development;

(b) Provide incentives for investment in cleaner production and eco-efficiency in all countries, such as state-financed loans, venture capital, technical assistance and training programmes for small and medium-sized companies while avoiding trade-distorting measures inconsistent with WTO rules;

(c) Collect and disseminate information on cost-effective examples in cleaner production, eco-efficiency and environmental management, and promote the exchange of best practices and know-how on environmentally sound technologies between public and private institutions;

(d) Provide training programmes to small and medium-sized enterprises on the use of information and communication technologies.

16. Integrate the issue of production and consumption patterns into sustainable development policies, programmes and strategies, including, where applicable, into poverty reduction strategies.

17. Enhance corporate environmental and social responsibility and accountability. This would include actions at all levels to:

(a) Encourage industry to improve social and environmental performance through voluntary initiatives, including environmental management systems, codes of conduct, certification and public reporting on environmental and social issues, taking into account such initiatives as the International Organization for Standardization (ISO) standards and Global Reporting Initiative guidelines on sustainability reporting, bearing in mind principle 11 of the Rio Declaration on Environment and Development;

(b) Encourage dialogue between enterprises and the communities in which they operate and other stakeholders;

(c) Encourage financial institutions to incorporate sustainable development considerations into their decision-making processes;

(d) Develop workplace-based partnerships and programmes, including training and education programmes.

18. Encourage relevant authorities at all levels to take sustainable development considerations into account in decision-making, including on national and local development planning, investment in infrastructure, business development and public procurement. This would include actions at all levels to:

(a) Provide support for the development of sustainable development strategies and programmes, including in decision-making on investment in infrastructure and business development;

(b) Continue to promote the internalization of environmental costs and the use of economic instruments, taking into account the approach that the polluter should, in principle, bear the costs of pollution, with due regard to the public interest and without distorting international trade and investment;

(c) Promote public procurement policies that encourage development and diffusion of environmentally sound goods and services;

(d) Provide capacity-building and training to assist relevant authorities with regard to the implementation of the initiatives listed in the present paragraph;

(e) Use environmental impact assessment procedures.

19. Call upon Governments, as well as relevant regional and international organizations and other relevant stakeholders, to implement, taking into account national and regional specificities and circumstances, the recommendations and conclusions of the Commission on Sustainable Development concerning energy for sustainable development adopted at its ninth session, including the issues and options set out below, bearing in mind that in view of the different contributions to global environmental degradation, States have common but differentiated responsibilities. This would include actions at all levels to:

(a) Take further action to mobilize the provision of financial resources, technology transfer, capacity-building and the diffusion of environmentally sound technologies according to the recommendations and conclusions of the Commission on Sustainable Development as contained in section A, paragraph 3, and section D, paragraph 30, of its decision 9/1 on energy for sustainable development;

(b) Integrate energy considerations, including energy efficiency, affordability and accessibility, into socio-economic programmes, especially into policies of major energy-consuming sectors, and into the planning, operation and maintenance of long-lived energy consuming infrastructures, such as the public sector, transport, industry, agriculture, urban land use, tourism and construction sectors;

(c) Develop and disseminate alternative energy technologies with the aim of giving a greater share of the energy mix to renewable energies, improving energy efficiency and greater reliance on advanced energy technologies, including cleaner fossil fuel technologies;

(d) Combine, as appropriate, the increased use of renewable energy resources, more efficient use of energy, greater reliance on advanced energy technologies, including advanced and cleaner fossil fuel technologies, and the sustainable use of traditional energy resources, which could meet the growing need for energy services in the longer term to achieve sustainable development;

(e) Diversify energy supply by developing advanced, cleaner, more efficient, affordable and cost-effective energy technologies, including fossil fuel technologies and renewable energy technologies, hydro included, and their transfer to developing countries on concessional terms as mutually agreed. With a sense of urgency, substantially increase the global share of renewable energy sources with the objective of increasing its contribution to total energy supply, recognizing the role of national and voluntary regional targets as well as initiatives, where they exist, and ensuring that energy policies are supportive to developing countries' efforts to eradicate poverty, and regularly evaluate available data to review progress to this end;

(f) Support efforts, including through provision of financial and technical assistance to developing countries, with the involvement of the private sector, to reduce flaring and venting of gas associated with crude oil production;

(g) Develop and utilize indigenous energy sources and infrastructures for various local uses and promote rural community participation, including local Agenda 21 groups, with the support of the international community, in developing and utilizing renewable energy technologies to meet their daily energy needs to find simple and local solutions;

(h) Establish domestic programmes for energy efficiency, including, as appropriate, by accelerating the deployment of energy efficiency technologies, with the necessary support of the international community;

(i) Accelerate the development, dissemination and deployment of affordable and cleaner energy efficiency and energy conservation technologies, as well as the transfer of such technologies, in particular to developing countries, on favourable terms, including on concessional and preferential terms, as mutually agreed;

(j) Recommend that international financial institutions and other agencies' policies support developing countries, as well as countries with economies in transition, in their own efforts to establish policy and regulatory frameworks which create a level playing field between the following: renewable energy, energy efficiency, advanced energy technologies, including advanced and cleaner fossil fuel technologies, and centralized, distributed and decentralized energy systems;

(k) Promote increased research and development in the field of various energy technologies, including renewable energy, energy efficiency and advanced energy technologies, including advanced and cleaner fossil fuel technologies, both nationally and through international collaboration; strengthen national and regional research and development institutions/centres on reliable, affordable, economically viable, socially acceptable and environmentally sound energy for sustainable development;

(l) Promote networking between centres of excellence on energy for sustainable development, including regional networks, by linking competent centres on energy technologies for sustainable development that could support and promote efforts at capacity-building and technology transfer activities, particularly of developing countries, as well as serve as information clearing houses;

(m) Promote education to provide information for both men and women about available energy sources and technologies;

(n) Utilize financial instruments and mechanisms, in particular the Global Environment Facility (GEF), within its mandate, to provide financial resources to developing countries, in particular least developed countries and small island developing States, to meet their capacity needs for training, technical know-how and strengthening national institutions in reliable, affordable, economically viable, socially acceptable and environmentally sound energy, including promoting energy efficiency and conservation, renewable energy and advanced energy technologies, including advanced and cleaner fossil fuel technologies;

(o) Support efforts to improve the functioning, transparency and information about energy markets with respect to both supply and demand, with the aim of achieving greater stability and predictability and to ensure consumer access to reliable, affordable, economically viable, socially acceptable and environmentally sound energy services;

(p) Policies to reduce market distortions would promote energy systems compatible with sustainable development through the use of improved market signals and by removing market distortions, including restructuring taxation and phasing out harmful subsidies, where they exist, to reflect their environmental impacts, with such policies taking fully into account the specific needs and conditions of developing countries with the aim of minimizing the possible adverse impacts on their development;

(q) Take action, where appropriate, to phase out subsidies in this area that inhibit sustainable development, taking fully into account the specific conditions and different levels of development of individual countries and considering their adverse effect, particularly on developing countries;

(r) Governments are encouraged to improve the functioning of national energy markets in such a way that they support sustainable development, overcome market barriers and improve accessibility, taking fully into account that such policies should be decided by each country, and that its own characteristics and capabilities and level of development should be considered, especially as reflected in national sustainable development strategies, where they exist;

(s) Strengthen national and regional energy institutions or arrangements for enhancing regional and international cooperation on energy for sustainable development, in particular to assist developing countries in their domestic efforts to provide reliable, affordable, economically viable, socially acceptable and environmentally sound energy services to all sections of their populations;

(t) Countries are urged to develop and implement actions within the framework of the ninth session of the Commission on Sustainable Development, including through public-private partnerships, taking into account the different circumstances of countries, based on lessons learned by Governments, international institutions and stakeholders and including business and industry, in the field of access to energy, including renewable energy and energy-efficiency and advanced energy technologies, including advanced and cleaner fossil fuel technologies;

(u) Promote cooperation between international and regional institutions and bodies dealing with different aspects of energy for sustainable development within their existing mandate, bearing in mind paragraph 46 (h) of the Programme of Action for the Further Implementation of Agenda 21, strengthening, as appropriate, regional and national activities for the promotion of education and capacity-building regarding energy for sustainable development;

(v) Strengthen and facilitate, as appropriate, regional cooperation arrangements for promoting cross-border energy trade, including the interconnection of electricity grids and oil and natural gas pipelines;

(w) Strengthen and, where appropriate, facilitate dialogue forums among regional, national and international producers and consumers of energy.

20. Promote an integrated approach to policy-making at the national, regional and local levels for transport services and systems to promote sustainable development, including policies and planning for land use, infrastructure, public transport systems and goods delivery networks, with a view to providing safe, affordable and efficient transportation, increasing energy efficiency, reducing pollution, reducing congestion, reducing adverse health effects and limiting urban sprawl, taking into account national priorities and circumstances. This would include actions at all levels to:

(a) Implement transport strategies for sustainable development, reflecting specific regional, national and local conditions, so as to improve the affordability, efficiency and convenience of transportation, as well as improving urban air quality and health, and reduce greenhouse gas emissions, including through the development of better vehicle technologies that are more environmentally sound, affordable and socially acceptable;

(b) Promote investment and partnerships for the development of sustainable, energy efficient multi-modal transportation systems, including public mass transportation systems and better transportation systems in rural areas, with technical and financial assistance for developing countries and countries with economies in transition.

21. Prevent and minimize waste and maximize reuse, recycling and use of environmentally friendly alternative materials, with the participation of government authorities and all stakeholders, in order to minimize adverse effects on the environment and improve resource efficiency, with financial, technical and other assistance for developing countries. This would include actions at all levels to:

(a) Develop waste management systems, with highest priorities placed on waste prevention and minimization, reuse and recycling, and environmentally sound disposal facilities, including technology to recapture the energy contained in waste, and encourage small-scale waste-recycling initiatives that support urban and rural waste management and provide income-generating opportunities, with international support for developing countries;

(b) Promote waste prevention and minimization by encouraging production of reusable consumer goods and biodegradable products and developing the infrastructure required.

22. Renew the commitment, as advanced in Agenda 21, to sound management of chemicals throughout their life cycle and of hazardous wastes for sustainable development and for the protection of human health and the environment, inter alia, aiming to achieve by 2020 that chemicals are used and produced in ways that lead to the minimization of significant adverse effects on human health and the environment, using transparent science-based risk assessment procedures and science-based risk management procedures, taking into account the precautionary approach, as set out in principle 15 of the Rio Declaration on Environment and Development, and support developing countries in strengthening their capacity for the sound management of chemicals and hazardous wastes by providing technical and financial assistance. This would include actions at all levels to:

(a) Promote the ratification and implementation of relevant international instruments on chemicals and hazardous waste, including the Rotterdam Convention on Prior Informed Consent Procedures for Certain Hazardous Chemicals and Pesticides in International Trade so that it can enter into force by 2003 and the Stockholm Convention on Persistent Organic Pollutants so that it can enter into force by 2004, and encourage and improve coordination as well as supporting developing countries in their implementation;

(b) Further develop a strategic approach to international chemicals management based on the Bahia Declaration and Priorities for Action beyond 2000 of the Intergovernmental Forum on Chemical Safety (IFCS) by 2005, and urge that the United Nations Environment Programme (UNEP), IFCS, other international organizations dealing with chemical management, and other relevant international organizations and actors closely cooperate in this regard, as appropriate;

(c) Encourage countries to implement the new globally harmonized system for the classification and labelling of chemicals as soon as possible with a view to having the system fully operational by 2008;

(d) Encourage partnerships to promote activities aimed at enhancing environmentally sound management of chemicals and hazardous wastes, implementing multilateral environmental agreements, raising awareness of issues relating to chemicals and hazardous waste, and encouraging the collection and use of additional scientific data;

(e) Promote efforts to prevent international illegal trafficking of hazardous chemicals and hazardous wastes and to prevent damage resulting from the transboundary movement and disposal of hazardous wastes in a manner consistent with obligations under relevant international instruments, such as the Basel Convention on the Control of Transboundary Movements of Hazardous Wastes and Their Disposal;

(f) Encourage development of coherent and integrated information on chemicals, such as through national pollutant release and transfer registers;

(g) Promote reduction of the risks posed by heavy metals that are harmful to human health and the environment, including through a review of relevant studies, such as the UNEP global assessment of mercury and its compounds.

IV. PROTECTING AND MANAGING THE NATURAL RESOURCE BASE OF ECONOMIC AND SOCIAL DEVELOPMENT

23. Human activities are having an increasing impact on the integrity of ecosystems that provide essential resources and services for human well-being and economic activities. Managing the natural resources base in a sustainable and integrated manner is essential for sustainable development. In this regard, to reverse the current trend in natural resource degradation as soon as possible, it is necessary to implement strategies which should include targets adopted at the national and, where appropriate, regional levels to protect ecosystems and to achieve integrated management of land, water and living resources, while strengthening regional, national and local capacities. This would include actions at all levels to:

24. Launch a programme of actions, with financial and technical assistance, to achieve the millennium development goal on safe drinking water. In this respect, we agree to halve, by the year 2015, the proportion of people who are unable to reach or to afford safe drinking water as outlined in the Millennium Declaration and the proportion of people without access to basic sanitation, which would include actions at all levels to:

(a) Mobilize international and domestic financial resources at all levels, transfer technology, promote best practice and support capacity-building for water and sanitation infrastructure and services development, ensuring that such infrastructure and services meet the needs of the poor and are gender-sensitive;

(b) Facilitate access to public information and participation, including by women, at all levels, in support of policy and decision-making related to water resources management and project implementation;

(c) Promote priority action by Governments, with the support of all stakeholders, in water management and capacity-building at the national level and, where appropriate, at the regional level, and promote and provide new and additional financial resources and innovative technologies to implement chapter 18 of Agenda 21;

(d) Intensify water pollution prevention to reduce health hazards and protect ecosystems by introducing technologies for affordable sanitation and industrial and domestic wastewater treatment, by mitigating the effects of groundwater contamination, and by establishing, at the national level, monitoring systems and effective legal frameworks;

(e) Adopt prevention and protection measures to promote sustainable water use and to address water shortages.

25. Develop integrated water resources management and water efficiency plans by 2005, with support to developing countries, through actions at all levels to:

(a) Develop and implement national/regional strategies, plans and programmes with regard to integrated river basin, watershed and groundwater management, and introduce measures to improve the efficiency of water infrastructure to reduce losses and increase recycling of water;

(b) Employ the full range of policy instruments, including regulation, monitoring, voluntary measures, market and information-based tools, land-use management and cost recovery of water services, without cost recovery objectives becoming a barrier to access to safe water by poor people, and adopt an integrated water basin approach;

(c) Improve the efficient use of water resources and promote their allocation among competing uses in a way that gives priority to the satisfaction of basic human needs and balances the requirement of preserving or restoring ecosystems and their functions, in particular in fragile environments, with human domestic, industrial and agriculture needs, including safeguarding drinking water quality;

(d) Develop programmes for mitigating the effects of extreme water-related events;

(e) Support the diffusion of technology and capacity-building for non-conventional water resources and conservation technologies, to developing countries and regions facing water scarcity conditions or subject to drought and desertification, through technical and financial support and capacity-building;

(f) Support, where appropriate, efforts and programmes for energy-efficient, sustainable and cost-effective desalination of seawater, water recycling and water harvesting from coastal fogs in developing countries, through such measures as technological, technical and financial assistance and other modalities;

(g) Facilitate the establishment of public-private partnerships and other forms of partnership that give priority to the needs of the poor, within stable and transparent national regulatory frameworks provided by Governments, while respecting local conditions, involving all concerned stakeholders, and monitoring the performance and improving accountability of public institutions and private companies.

26. Support developing countries and countries with economies in transition in their efforts to monitor and assess the quantity and quality of water resources, including through the establishment and/or further development of national monitoring networks and water resources databases and the development of relevant national indicators.

27. Improve water resource management and scientific understanding of the water cycle through cooperation in joint observation and research, and for this purpose encourage and promote knowledge-sharing and provide capacity-building and the transfer of technology, as mutually agreed, including remote-sensing and satellite technologies, particularly to developing countries and countries with economies in transition.

28. Promote effective coordination among the various international and intergovernmental bodies and processes working on water-related issues, both within the United Nations system and between the United Nations and international financial institutions, drawing on the contributions of other international institutions and civil society to inform intergovernmental decision-making; closer coordination should also be promoted to elaborate and support proposals and undertake activities related to the International Year of Freshwater 2003 and beyond.

29. Oceans, seas, islands and coastal areas form an integrated and essential component of the Earth's ecosystem and are critical for global food security and for sustaining economic prosperity and the well-being of many national economies, particularly in developing countries. Ensuring the sustainable development of the oceans requires effective coordination and cooperation, including at the global and regional levels, between relevant bodies, and actions at all levels to:

(a) Invite States to ratify or accede to and implement the United Nations Convention on the Law of the Sea, which provides the overall legal framework for ocean activities;

(b) Promote the implementation of chapter 17 of Agenda 21 which provides the programme of action for achieving the sustainable development of oceans, coastal areas and seas through its programme areas of integrated management and sustainable development of coastal areas, including exclusive economic zones; marine environmental protection; sustainable use and conservation of marine living resources; addressing critical uncertainties for the management of the marine environment and climate change; strengthening international, including regional, cooperation and coordination; and sustainable development of small islands;

(c) Establish an effective, transparent and regular inter-agency coordination mechanism on ocean and coastal issues within the United Nations system;

(d) Encourage the application by 2010 of the ecosystem approach, noting the Reykjavik Declaration on Responsible Fisheries in the Marine Ecosystem and decision 5/6 of the Conference of Parties to the Convention on Biological Diversity;

(e) Promote integrated, multidisciplinary and multisectoral coastal and ocean management at the national level, and encourage and assist coastal States in developing ocean policies and mechanisms on integrated coastal management;

(f) Strengthen regional cooperation and coordination between the relevant regional organizations and programmes, the UNEP regional seas programmes, regional fisheries management organizations and other regional science, health and development organizations;

(g) Assist developing countries in coordinating policies and programmes at the regional and subregional levels aimed at the conservation and sustainable management of fishery resources, and implement integrated coastal area management plans, including through the promotion of sustainable coastal and small-scale fishing activities and, where appropriate, the development of related infrastructure;

(h) Take note of the work of the open-ended informal consultative process established by the United Nations General Assembly in its resolution 54/33 in order to facilitate the annual review by the Assembly of developments in ocean affairs and the upcoming review of its effectiveness and utility to be held at its fifty-seventh session under the terms of the above-mentioned resolution.

30. To achieve sustainable fisheries, the following actions are required at all levels:

(a) Maintain or restore stocks to levels that can produce the maximum sustainable yield with the aim of achieving these goals for depleted stocks on an urgent basis and where possible not later than 2015;

(b) Ratify or accede to and effectively implement the relevant United Nations and, where appropriate, associated regional fisheries agreements or arrangements, noting in particular the Agreement for the Implementation of the Provisions of the United Nations Convention on the Law of the Sea of 10 December 1982 relating to the Conservation and Management of Straddling Fish Stocks and Highly Migratory Fish Stocks and the 1993 Agreement to Promote Compliance with International Conservation and Management Measures by Fishing Vessels on the High Seas;

(c) Implement the 1995 Code of Conduct for Responsible Fisheries, taking note of the special requirements of developing countries as noted in its article 5, and the relevant Food and Agriculture Organization of the United Nations (FAO) international plans of action and technical guidelines;

(d) Urgently develop and implement national and, where appropriate, regional plans of action, to put into effect the FAO international plans of action, in particular the international plan of action for the management of fishing capacity by 2005 and the international plan of action to prevent, deter and eliminate illegal, unreported and unregulated fishing by 2004. Establish effective monitoring, reporting and enforcement, and control of fishing vessels, including by flag States, to further the international plan of action to prevent, deter and eliminate illegal, unreported and unregulated fishing;

(e) Encourage relevant regional fisheries management organizations and arrangements to give due consideration to the rights, duties and interests of coastal States and the special requirements of developing States when addressing the issue of the allocation of share of fishery resources for straddling stocks and highly migratory fish stocks, mindful of the provisions of the United Nations Convention on the Law of the Sea and the Agreement for the Implementation of the Provisions of the United Nations Convention on the Law of the Sea of 10 December 1982 Relating to the Conservation and Management of Straddling Fish Stocks and Highly Migratory Fish Stocks, on the high seas and within exclusive economic zones;

(f) Eliminate subsidies that contribute to illegal, unreported and unregulated fishing and to over-capacity, while completing the efforts undertaken at WTO to clarify and improve its disciplines on fisheries subsidies, taking into account the importance of this sector to developing countries;

(g) Strengthen donor coordination and partnerships between international financial institutions, bilateral agencies and other relevant stakeholders to enable developing countries, in particular the least developed countries and small island developing States and countries with economies in transition, to develop their national, regional and subregional capacities for infrastructure and integrated management and the sustainable use of fisheries;

(h) Support the sustainable development of aquaculture, including small-scale aquaculture, given its growing importance for food security and economic development.

31. In accordance with chapter 17 of Agenda 21, promote the conservation and management of the oceans through actions at all levels, giving due regard to the relevant international instruments to:

(a) Maintain the productivity and biodiversity of important and vulnerable marine and coastal areas, including in areas within and beyond national jurisdiction;

(b) Implement the work programme arising from the Jakarta Mandate on the Conservation and Sustainable Use of Marine and Coastal Biological Diversity of the Convention on Biological Diversity, including through the urgent mobilization of financial resources and technological assistance and the development of human and institutional capacity, particularly in developing countries;

(c) Develop and facilitate the use of diverse approaches and tools, including the ecosystem approach, the elimination of destructive fishing practices, the establishment of marine protected areas consistent with international law and based on scientific information, including representative networks by 2012 and time/area closures for the protection of nursery grounds and periods, proper coastal land use; and watershed planning and the integration of marine and coastal areas management into key sectors;

(d) Develop national, regional and international programmes for halting the loss of marine biodiversity, including in coral reefs and wetlands;

(e) Implement the RAMSAR Convention, including its joint work programme with the Convention on Biological Diversity, and the programme of action called for by the International Coral Reef Initiative to strengthen joint management plans and international networking for wetland ecosystems in coastal zones, including coral reefs, mangroves, seaweed beds and tidal mud flats.

32. Advance implementation of the Global Programme of Action for the Protection of the Marine Environment from Land-based Activities and the Montreal Declaration on the Protection of the Marine Environment from Land-based Activities, with particular emphasis in the period 2002–2006 on municipal wastewater, the physical alteration and destruction of habitats, and nutrients, by actions at all levels to:

(a) Facilitate partnerships, scientific research and diffusion of technical knowledge; mobilize domestic, regional and international resources; and promote human and institutional capacity-building, paying particular attention to the needs of developing countries;

(b) Strengthen the capacity of developing countries in the development of their national and regional programmes and mechanisms to mainstream the objectives of the Global Programme of Action and to manage the risks and impacts of ocean pollution;

(c) Elaborate regional programmes of action and improve the links with strategic plans for the sustainable development of coastal and marine resources, noting in particular areas which are subject to accelerated environmental changes and development pressures;

(d) Make every effort to achieve substantial progress by the next Global Programme of Action conference in 2006 to protect the marine environment from land-based activities.

33. Enhance maritime safety and protection of the marine environment from pollution by actions at all levels to:

(a) Invite States to ratify or accede to and implement the conventions and protocols and other relevant instruments of the International Maritime Organization (IMO) relating to the enhancement of maritime safety and protection of the marine environment from marine pollution and environmental damage caused by ships, including the use of toxic anti-fouling paints and urge IMO to consider stronger mechanisms to secure the implementation of IMO instruments by flag States;

(b) Accelerate the development of measures to address invasive alien species in ballast water. Urge IMO to finalize the IMO International Convention on the Control and Management of Ships' Ballast Water and Sediments.

33bis Governments, taking into account their national circumstances, are encouraged, recalling paragraph 8 of resolution GC (44)/RES/17 of the General Conference of the International Atomic Energy Agency (IAEA) and taking into account the very serious potential for environment and human health impacts of radioactive wastes, to make efforts to examine and further improve measures and internationally agreed regulations regarding safety, while stressing the importance of having effective liability mechanisms in place, relevant to international maritime transportation and other transboundary movement of radioactive material, radioactive waste and spent fuel, including, inter alia, arrangements for prior notification and consultations done in accordance with relevant international instruments.

34. Improve the scientific understanding and assessment of marine and coastal ecosystems as a fundamental basis for sound decision-making, through actions at all levels to:

(a) Increase scientific and technical collaboration, including integrated assessment at the global and regional levels, including the appropriate transfer of marine science and marine technologies and techniques for the conservation and management of living and non-living marine resources and expanding ocean-observing capabilities for the timely prediction and assessment of the state of marine environment;

(b) Establish by 2004 a regular process under the United Nations for global reporting and assessment of the state of the marine environment, including socio-economic aspects, both current and foreseeable, building on existing regional assessments;

(c) Build capacity in marine science, information and management, through, inter alia, promoting the use of environmental impact assessments and environmental evaluation and reporting techniques, for projects or activities that are potentially harmful to the coastal and marine environments and their living and non-living resources;

(d) Strengthen the ability of the Intergovernmental Oceanographic Commission of the United Nations Educational, Scientific and Cultural Organization, FAO and other relevant international and regional and subregional organizations to build national and local capacity in marine science and the sustainable management of oceans and their resources.

35. An integrated, multi-hazard, inclusive approach to address vulnerability, risk assessment and disaster management, including prevention, mitigation, preparedness, response and recovery, is an essential element of a safer world in the twenty-first century. Actions are required at all levels to:

(a) Strengthen the role of the International Strategy for Disaster Reduction and encourage the international community to provide the necessary financial resources to its Trust Fund;

(b) Support the establishment of effective regional, subregional and national strategies and scientific and technical institutional support for disaster management;

(c) Strengthen the institutional capacities of countries and promote international joint observation and research, through improved surface-based monitoring and increased use of satellite data, dissemination of technical and scientific knowledge, and the provision of assistance to vulnerable countries;

(d) Reduce the risks of flooding and drought in vulnerable countries by, inter alia, promoting wetland and watershed protection and restoration, improved land-use planning, improving and applying more widely techniques and methodologies for assessing the potential adverse effects of climate change on wetlands and, as appropriate, assisting countries that are particularly vulnerable to those effects;

(e) Improve techniques and methodologies for assessing the effects of climate change, and encourage the continuing assessment of those adverse effects by the Intergovernmental Panel on Climate Change;

(f) Encourage the dissemination and use of traditional and indigenous knowledge to mitigate the impact of disasters, and promote community-based disaster management planning by local authorities, including through training activities and raising public awareness;

(g) Support the ongoing voluntary contribution of, as appropriate, non-governmental organizations, the scientific community and other partners in the management of natural disasters according to agreed, relevant guidelines;

(h) Develop and strengthen early warning systems and information networks in disaster management, consistent with the International Strategy for Disaster Reduction;

(i) Develop and strengthen capacity at all levels to collect and disseminate scientific and technical information, including the improvement of early warning systems for predicting extreme weather events, especially El Niño/La Niña, through the provision of assistance to institutions devoted to addressing such events, including the International Centre for the Study of the El Niño phenomenon;

(j) Promote cooperation for the prevention and mitigation of, preparedness for, response to and recovery from major technological and other disasters with an adverse impact on the environment in order to enhance the capabilities of affected countries to cope with such situations.

36. Change in the Earth's climate and its adverse effects are a common concern of humankind. We remain deeply concerned that all countries, particularly developing countries including the least developed countries and small island developing States, face increased risks of negative impacts of climate change and recognize that, in this context, the problems of poverty, land degradation, access to water and food and human health remain at the centre of global attention. The United Nations Framework Convention on Climate Change is the key instrument for addressing climate change, a global concern, and we reaffirm our commitment to achieving its ultimate objective of stabilization of greenhouse gas concentrations in the atmosphere at a level that would prevent dangerous anthropogenic interference with the climate system, within a time frame sufficient to allow ecosystems to adapt naturally to climate change, to ensure that food production is not threatened and to enable economic development to proceed in a sustainable manner, in accordance with our common but differentiated responsibilities and respective capabilities. Recalling the United Nations Millennium Declaration, in which heads of State and Government resolved to make every effort to ensure the entry into force of the Kyoto Protocol to the United Nations Framework Convention on Climate Change, preferably by the tenth anniversary of the United Nations Conference on Environment and Development in 2002, and to embark on the required reduction of emissions of greenhouse gases, States that have ratified the Kyoto Protocol strongly urge States that have not already done so to ratify the Kyoto Protocol in a timely manner. Actions at all levels are required to:

(a) Meet all the commitments and obligations under the UNFCCC;

(b) Work cooperatively towards achieving the objectives of the UNFCCC;

(c) Provide technical and financial assistance and capacity building to developing countries and countries with economies in transition in accordance with commitments under the UNFCCC, including the Marrakech accords;

(d) Build and enhance scientific and technological capabilities, inter alia through continuing support to the IPCC for the exchange of scientific data and information especially in developing countries;

(e) Develop and transfer technological solutions;

(f) Develop and disseminate innovative technologies in respect of key sectors of development, particularly energy, and of investment in this regard, including through private sector involvement, market-oriented approaches, as well as supportive public policies and international cooperation;

(g) Promote the systematic observation of the Earth's atmosphere, land and oceans by improving monitoring stations, increasing the use of satellites, and appropriate integration of these observations to produce high-quality data that could be disseminated for the use of all countries, in particular developing countries;

(h) Enhance the implementation of national, regional and international strategies to monitor the Earth's atmosphere, land and oceans including, as appropriate, strategies for integrated global observations, inter alia with the cooperation of relevant international organisations, especially the United Nations specialized agencies in cooperation with the UNFCCC;

(i) Support initiatives to assess the consequences of climate change, such as the Arctic Council initiative, including the environmental, economic and social impacts on local and indigenous communities.

37. Enhance cooperation at the international, regional and national levels to reduce air pollution, including transboundary air pollution, acid deposition and ozone depletion bearing in mind the Rio principles, including, inter alia, the principle that, in view of the different contributions to global environmental degradation, States have common but differentiated responsibilities, with actions at all levels to:

(a) Strengthen capacities of developing countries and countries with economies in transition to measure, reduce and assess the impacts of air pollution, including health impacts, and provide financial and technical support for these activities;

(b) Facilitate implementation of the Montreal Protocol on Substances that Deplete the Ozone Layer by ensuring adequate replenishment of its fund by 2003/2005;

(c) Further support the effective regime for the protection of the ozone layer established in the Vienna Convention for the Protection of the Ozone Layer and the Montreal Protocol, including its compliance mechanism;

(d) Improve access by developing countries to affordable, accessible, cost-effective, safe and environmentally sound alternatives to ozone-depleting substances by 2010, and assist them in complying with the phase-out schedule under the Montreal Protocol, bearing in mind that ozone depletion and climate change are scientifically and technically interrelated;

(e) Take measures to address illegal traffic in ozone-depleting substances.

38. Agriculture plays a crucial role in addressing the needs of a growing global population, and is inextricably linked to poverty eradication, especially in developing countries. Enhancing the role of women at all levels and in all aspects of rural development, agriculture, nutrition and food security is imperative. Sustainable agriculture and rural development are essential to the implementation of an integrated approach to increasing food production and enhancing food security and food safety in an environmentally sustainable way. This would include actions at all levels to:

(a) Achieve the Millennium Declaration target to halve by the year 2015 the proportion of the world's people who suffer from hunger and realize the right to a standard of living adequate for the health and well-being of themselves and their families, including food, including by promoting food security and fighting hunger in combination with measures which address poverty, consistent with the outcome of the World Food Summit and, for States Parties, with their obligations under article 11 of the International Covenant on Economic, Social and Cultural Rights;

(b) Develop and implement integrated land management and water-use plans that are based on sustainable use of renewable resources and on integrated assessments of socio-economic and environmental potentials, and strengthen the capacity of Governments, local authorities and communities to monitor and manage the quantity and quality of land and water resources;

(c) Increase understanding of the sustainable use, protection and management of water resources to advance long-term sustainability of freshwater, coastal and marine environments;

(d) Promote programmes to enhance in a sustainable manner the productivity of land and the efficient use of water resources in agriculture, forestry, wetlands, artisanal fisheries and aquaculture, especially through indigenous and local community-based approaches;

(e) Support the efforts of developing countries to protect oases from silt, land degradation and increasing salinity by providing appropriate technical and financial assistance;

(f) Enhance the participation of women in all aspects and at all levels relating to sustainable agriculture and food security;

(g) Integrate existing information systems on land-use practices by strengthening national research and extension services and farmer organizations to trigger farmer-to-farmer exchange on good practices, such as those related to environmentally sound, low-cost technologies, with the assistance of relevant international organizations;

(h) Enact, as appropriate, measures that protect indigenous resource management systems and support the contribution of all appropriate stakeholders, men and women alike, in rural planning and development;

(i) Adopt policies and implement laws that guarantee well defined and enforceable land and water use rights, and promote legal security of tenure, recognizing the existence of different national laws and/or systems of land access and tenure, and provide technical and financial assistance to developing countries as well as countries with economies in transition that are undertaking land tenure reform in order to enhance sustainable livelihoods;

(j) Reverse the declining trend in public sector finance for sustainable agriculture, provide appropriate technical and financial assistance, and promote private sector investment and support efforts in developing countries and countries with economies in transition to strengthen agricultural research and natural resource management capacity and dissemination of research results to the farming communities;

(k) Employ market-based incentives for agricultural enterprises and farmers to monitor and manage water use and quality, inter alia, by applying such methods as small-scale irrigation and wastewater recycling and reuse;

(l) Enhance access to existing markets and develop new markets for value-added agricultural products;

(m) Increase brown-field redevelopment in developed countries and countries with economies in transition, with appropriate technical assistance where contamination is a serious problem;

(n) Enhance international cooperation to combat the illicit cultivation of narcotic plants, taking into account their negative social, economic and environmental impacts;

(o) Promote programmes for the environmentally sound, effective and efficient use of soil fertility improvement practices and agricultural pest control;

(p) Strengthen and improve coordination of existing initiatives to enhance sustainable agricultural production and food security;

(q) Invite countries that have not done so to ratify the International Treaty on Plant Genetic Resources for Food and Agriculture;

(r) Promote the conservation, and sustainable use and management of traditional and indigenous agricultural systems and strengthen indigenous models of agricultural production.

39. Strengthen the implementation of the United Nations Convention to Combat Desertification in Those Countries Experiencing Serious Drought and/or Desertification, particularly in Africa, to address causes of desertification and land degradation in order to maintain and restore land, and to address poverty resulting from land degradation. This would include actions at all levels to:

(a) Mobilize adequate and predictable financial resources, transfer of technologies and capacity-building at all levels;

(b) Formulate national action programmes to ensure timely and effective implementation of the Convention and its related projects, with the support of the international community, including through decentralized projects at the local level;

(c) Encourage the United Nations Framework Convention on Climate Change, the Convention on Biological Diversity and the Convention to Combat Desertification to continue exploring and enhancing synergies, with due regard to their respective mandates, in the elaboration and implementation of plans and strategies under the respective Conventions;

(d) Integrate measures to prevent and combat desertification as well as to mitigate the effects of drought through relevant policies and programmes, such as land, water and forest management, agriculture, rural development, early warning systems, environment, energy, natural resources, health and education, and poverty eradication and sustainable development strategies;

(e) Provide affordable local access to information to improve monitoring and early warning related to desertification and drought;

(f) Call on the Second Assembly of the Global Environment Facility (GEF) to take action on the recommendations of the GEF Council concerning the designation of land degradation (desertification and deforestation) as a focal area of GEF as a means of GEF support for the successful implementation of the Convention to Combat Desertification; and consequently, consider making GEF a financial mechanism of the Convention, taking into account the prerogatives and decisions of the Conference of the Parties to the Convention, while recognizing the complementary roles of GEF and the Global Mechanism of the Convention in providing and mobilizing resources for the elaboration and implementation of action programmes;

(g) Improve the sustainability of grassland resources through strengthening management and law enforcement and providing financial and technical support by the international community to developing countries.

40. Mountain ecosystems support particular livelihoods, and include significant watershed resources, biological diversity and unique flora and fauna. Many are particularly fragile and vulnerable to the adverse effects of climate change and need specific protection. Actions at all levels are required to:

(a) Develop and promote programmes, policies and approaches that integrate environmental, economic and social components of sustainable mountain development and strengthen international cooperation for its positive impacts on poverty eradication programmes, especially in developing countries;

(b) Implement programmes to address, where appropriate, deforestation, erosion, land degradation, loss of biodiversity, disruption of water flows and retreat of glaciers;

(c) Develop and implement, where appropriate, gender-sensitive policies and programmes, including public and private investments that help eliminate inequities facing mountain communities;

(d) Implement programmes to promote diversification and traditional mountain economies, sustainable livelihoods and small-scale production systems, including specific training programmes and better access to national and international markets, communications and transport planning, taking into account the particular sensitivity of mountains;

(e) Promote full participation and involvement of mountain communities in decisions that affect them and integrate indigenous knowledge, heritage and values in all development initiatives;

(f) Mobilize national and international support for applied research and capacity-building, provide financial and technical assistance for the effective implementation of sustainable development of mountain ecosystems in developing countries and countries with economies in transition, and address the poverty among people living in mountains through concrete plans, projects and programmes, with sufficient support from all stakeholders, taking into account the spirit of the International Year of Mountains, 2002.

41. Promote sustainable tourism development, including non-consumptive and eco-tourism, taking into account the spirit of the International Year of Eco-tourism 2002, the United Nations Year for Cultural Heritage in 2002, the World Eco-tourism Summit 2002 and its Quebec Declaration, and the Global Code of Ethics for Tourism as adopted by the World Tourism Organization in order to increase the benefits from tourism resources for the population in host communities while maintaining the cultural and environmental integrity of the host communities and enhancing the protection of ecologically sensitive areas and natural heritages. Promote sustainable tourism development and capacity-building in order to contribute to the strengthening of rural and local communities. This would include actions at all levels to:

(a) Enhance international cooperation, foreign direct investment and partnerships with both private and public sectors, at all levels;

(b) Develop programmes, including education and training programmes, that encourage people to participate in eco-tourism, enable indigenous and local communities to develop and benefit from eco-tourism, and enhance stakeholder cooperation in tourism development and heritage preservation, in order to improve the protection of the environment, natural resources and cultural heritage;

(c) Provide technical assistance to developing countries and countries with economies in transition to support sustainable tourism business development and investment and tourism awareness programmes, to improve domestic tourism, and to stimulate entrepreneurial development;

(d) Assist host communities in managing visits to their tourism attractions for their maximum benefit, while ensuring the least negative impacts on and risks for their traditions, culture and environment, with the support of the World Tourism Organization and other relevant organizations;

(e) Promote the diversification of economic activities, including through the facilitation of access to markets and commercial information, and participation of emerging local enterprises, especially small and medium-sized enterprises.

42. Biodiversity, which plays a critical role in overall sustainable development and poverty eradication, is essential to our planet, human well-being and to the livelihood and cultural integrity of people. However, biodiversity is currently being lost at unprecedented rates due to human activities; this trend can only be reversed if the local people benefit from the conservation and sustainable use of biological diversity, in particular in countries of origin of genetic resources, in accordance with article 15 of the Convention on Biological Diversity. The Convention is the key instrument for the conservation and sustainable use of biological diversity and the fair and equitable sharing of benefits arising from use of genetic resources. A more efficient and coherent implementation of the three objectives of the Convention and the achievement by 2010 of a significant reduction in the current rate of loss of biological diversity will require the provision of new and additional financial and technical resources to developing countries, and includes actions at all levels to:

(a) Integrate the objectives of the Convention into global, regional and national sectoral and cross-sectoral programmes and policies, in particular in the programmes and policies of the economic sectors of countries and international financial institutions;

(b) Promote the ongoing work under the Convention on the sustainable use on biological diversity, including on sustainable tourism, as a cross-cutting issue relevant to different ecosystems, sectors and thematic areas;

(c) Encourage effective synergies between the Convention and other multilateral environmental agreements, inter alia, through the development of joint plans and programmes, with due regard to their respective mandates, regarding common responsibilities and concerns;

(d) Implement the Convention and its provisions, including active follow-up of its work programmes and decisions through national, regional and global action programmes, in particular the national biodiversity strategies and action plans, and strengthen their integration into relevant cross-sectoral strategies, programmes and policies, including those related to sustainable development and poverty eradication, including initiatives which promote community-based sustainable use of biological diversity;

(e) Promote the wide implementation and further development of the ecosystem approach, as being elaborated in the ongoing work of the Convention;

(f) Promote concrete international support and partnership for the conservation and sustainable use of biodiversity, including in ecosystems, at World Heritage sites and for the protection of endangered species, in particular through the appropriate channelling of financial resources and technology to developing countries and countries with economies in transition;

(g) To effectively conserve and sustainably use biodiversity, promote and support initiatives for hot spot areas and other areas essential for biodiversity and promote the development of national and regional ecological networks and corridors;

(h) Provide financial and technical support to developing countries, including capacity-building, in order to enhance indigenous and community-based biodiversity conservation efforts;

(i) Strengthen national, regional and international efforts to control invasive alien species, which are one of the main causes of biodiversity loss, and encourage the development of effective work programme on invasive alien species at all levels;

(j) Subject to national legislation, recognize the rights of local and indigenous communities who are holders of traditional knowledge, innovations and practices, and, with the approval and involvement of the holders of such knowledge, innovations and practices, develop and implement benefit-sharing mechanisms on mutually agreed terms for the use of such knowledge, innovations and practices;

(k) Encourage and enable all stakeholders to contribute to the implementation of the objectives of the Convention, and in particular recognize the specific role of youth, women and indigenous and local communities in conserving and using biodiversity in a sustainable way;

(l) Promote the effective participation of indigenous and local communities in decision and policy-making concerning the use of their traditional knowledge;

(m) Encourage technical and financial support to developing countries and countries with economies in transition in their efforts to develop and implement, as appropriate, inter alia, national sui generis systems and traditional systems according to national priorities and legislation, with a view to conserving and the sustainable use of biodiversity;

(n) Promote the wide implementation of and continued work on the Bonn Guidelines on Access to Genetic Resources and Fair and Equitable Sharing of Benefits arising out of their Utilization of the Convention, as an input to assist Parties to the Convention when developing and drafting legislative, administrative or policy measures on access and benefit-sharing, and contract and other arrangements under mutually agreed terms for access and benefit-sharing;

(o) Negotiate within the framework of the Convention on Biological Diversity, bearing in mind the Bonn Guidelines, an international regime to promote and safeguard the fair and equitable sharing of benefits arising out of the utilization of genetic resources;

(p) Encourage successful conclusion of existing processes under the World Intellectual Property Organization Intergovernmental Committee on Intellectual Property and Genetic Resources, Traditional Knowledge and Folklore, and in the ad hoc open-ended working group on article 8 (j) and related provisions of the Convention;

(q) Promote practicable measures for access to the results and benefits arising from biotechnologies based upon genetic resources, in accordance with articles 15 and 19 of the Convention, including through enhanced scientific and technical cooperation on biotechnology and biosafety, including the exchange of experts, training human resources and developing research-oriented institutional capacities;

(r) With a view to enhancing synergy and mutual supportiveness, taking into account the decisions under the relevant agreements, promote the discussions, without prejudging their outcome, with regard to the relationships between the Convention and agreements related to international trade and intellectual property rights, as outlined in the Doha Ministerial Declaration;

(s) Promote the implementation of the programme of work of the Global Taxonomy Initiative;

(t) Invite all States which have not already done so to ratify the Convention, the Cartagena Protocol on Biosafety and other biodiversity-related agreements, and invite those that have done so, to promote their effective implementation at the national, regional and international levels and to support developing countries and countries with economies in transition technically and financially in this regard.

43. Forests and trees cover nearly one third of the Earth's surface. Sustainable forest management of both natural and planted forests and for timber and non-timber products is essential to achieving sustainable development and is a critical means to eradicate poverty, significantly reduce deforestation and halt the loss of forest biodiversity and land and resource degradation, and improve food security and access to safe drinking water and affordable energy; highlights the multiple benefits of both natural and planted forests and trees; and contributes to the well-being of the planet and humanity. Achievement of sustainable forest management, nationally and globally, including through partnerships among interested Governments and stakeholders, including the private sector, indigenous and local communities and non-governmental organizations, is an essential goal of sustainable development. This would include actions at all levels to:

(a) Enhance political commitment to achieve sustainable forest management by endorsing it as a priority on the international political agenda, taking full account of the linkages between the forest sector and other sectors through integrated approaches;

(b) Support the United Nations Forum on Forests, with the assistance of the Collaborative Partnership on Forests, as key intergovernmental mechanisms to facilitate and coordinate the implementation of sustainable forest management at the national, regional and global levels, thus contributing, inter alia, to the conservation and sustainable use of forest biodiversity;

(c) Take immediate action on domestic forest law enforcement and illegal international trade in forest products, including in forest biological resources, with the support of the international community, and provide human and institutional capacity-building related to the enforcement of national legislation in those areas;

(d) Take immediate action at the national and international levels to promote and facilitate the means to achieve sustainable timber harvesting, and to facilitate the provision of financial resources and the transfer and development of environmentally sound technologies, and thereby address unsustainable timber-harvesting practices;

(e) Develop and implement initiatives to address the needs of those parts of the world that currently suffer from poverty and the highest rates of deforestation and where international cooperation would be welcomed by affected Governments;

(f) Create and strengthen partnerships and international cooperation to facilitate the provision of increased financial resources, the transfer of environmentally sound technologies, trade, capacity-building, forest law enforcement and governance at all levels, and integrated land and resource management to implement sustainable forest management, including the Intergovernmental Panel on Forests (IPF)/Intergovernmental Forum on Forests (IFF) proposals for action;

(g) Accelerate implementation of the IPF/IFF proposals for action by countries and by the Collaborative Partnership on Forests, and intensify efforts on reporting to the United Nations Forum on Forests to contribute to an assessment of progress in 2005;

(h) Recognize and support indigenous and community-based forest management systems to ensure their full and effective participation in sustainable forest management;

(i) Implement the Convention on Biological Diversity's expanded action-oriented work programme on all types of forest biological diversity, in close cooperation with the Forum, Partnership members and other forest-related processes and conventions, with the involvement of all relevant stakeholders.

44. Mining, minerals and metals are important to the economic and social development of many countries. Minerals are essential for modern living. Enhancing the contribution of mining, minerals and metals to sustainable development includes actions at all levels to:

(a) Support efforts to address the environmental, economic, health and social impacts and benefits of mining, minerals and metals throughout their life cycle, including workers' health and safety, and use a range of partnerships, furthering existing activities at the national and international levels, among interested Governments, intergovernmental organizations, mining companies and workers, and other stakeholders, to promote transparency and accountability for sustainable mining and minerals development;

(b) Enhance the participation of stakeholders, including local and indigenous communities and women, to play an active role in minerals, metals and mining development throughout the life cycles of mining operations, including after closure for rehabilitation purposes, in accordance with national regulations and taking into account significant transboundary impacts;

(c) Foster sustainable mining practices through the provision of financial, technical and capacity-building support to developing countries and countries with economies in transition for the mining and processing of minerals, including small-scale mining, and, where possible and appropriate, improve value-added processing, upgrade scientific and technological information, and reclaim and rehabilitate degraded sites.

V. SUSTAINABLE DEVELOPMENT IN A GLOBALIZING WORLD*

45. Globalization offers opportunities and challenges for sustainable development. We recognize that globalization and interdependence are offering new opportunities to trade, investment and capital flows and advances in technology, including information technology, for the growth of the world economy, development and the improvement of living standards around the world. At the same time, there remain serious challenges, including serious financial crises, insecurity, poverty, exclusion and inequality within and among societies. The developing countries and countries with economies in transition face special difficulties in responding to those challenges and opportunities. Globalization should be fully inclusive and equitable, and there is a strong need for policies and measures at the

* Because the structure of chapter V was changed in the course of negotiations so that its paragraph numbering no longer corresponds to the earlier version contained in document A/CONF.199/L.1, Latin ordinal numbers (bis, ter etc.) are used after paragraph 45 until the end of the chapter in order not to disrupt the paragraph numbering of subsequent chapters which were not so changed.

national and international levels, formulated and implemented with the full and effective participation of developing countries and countries with economies in transition, to help them to respond effectively to those challenges and opportunities. This will require urgent action at all levels to:

(a) Continue to promote open, equitable, rules-based, predictable and non-discriminatory multilateral trading and financial systems that benefit all countries in the pursuit of sustainable development. Support the successful completion of the work programme contained in the Doha Ministerial Declaration and the implementation of the Monterrey Consensus. Welcome the decision contained in the Doha Ministerial Declaration to place the needs and interests of developing countries at the heart of the work programme of the Declaration, including through enhanced market access for products of interest to developing countries;

(b) Encourage ongoing efforts by international financial and trade institutions to ensure that decision-making processes and institutional structures are open and transparent;

(c) Enhance the capacities of developing countries, including the least developed countries, landlocked developing countries and small island developing States, to benefit from liberalized trade opportunities, through international cooperation and measures aimed at improving productivity, commodity diversification and competitiveness, community-based entrepreneurial capacity, and transportation and communication infrastructure development;

(d) Support the International Labour Organization and encourage its ongoing work on the social dimension of globalization, as stated in paragraph 64 of the Monterrey Consensus;

(e) Enhance the delivery of coordinated, effective and targeted trade-related technical assistance and capacity-building programmes, including to take advantage of existing and future market access opportunities, and to examine the relationship between trade, environment and development.

45bis Implement the outcomes of the Doha Ministerial Conference by WTO members, further strengthen trade-related technical assistance and capacity-building, and ensure the meaningful, effective and full participation of developing countries in multilateral trade negotiations by placing their needs and interests at the heart of the WTO work programme.

45ter Actively promote corporate responsibility and accountability, based on the Rio Principles, including through the full development and effective implementation of intergovernmental agreements and measures, international initiatives and public-private partnerships, and appropriate national regulations, and support continuous improvement in corporate practices in all countries.

45quater Strengthen the capacities of developing countries to encourage public/private initiatives that enhance the ease of access, accuracy, timeliness and coverage of information on countries and financial markets. Multilateral and regional financial institutions could provide further assistance for these purposes.

45quinquies Strengthen regional trade and cooperation agreements, consistent with the multilateral trading system, among developed and developing countries and countries with economies in transition, as well as among developing countries, with the support of international finance institutions and regional development banks, as appropriate, with a view to achieving the objectives of sustainable development.

45sexties Assist developing countries and countries with economies in transition in narrowing the digital divide, creating digital opportunities and harnessing the potential of information and communication technologies for development, through technology transfer on mutually agreed terms and the provision of financial and technical support, and in this context support the World Summit on the Information Society.

VI. HEALTH AND SUSTAINABLE DEVELOPMENT

46. The Rio Declaration on Environment and Development states that human beings are at the centre of concerns for sustainable development, and that they are entitled to a healthy and productive life, in harmony with nature. The goals of sustainable development can only be achieved in the absence of a high prevalence of debilitating diseases, while obtaining health gains for the whole population requires poverty eradication. There is an urgent need to address the causes of ill health, including environmental causes, and their impact on development, with particular emphasis on women and children, as well as vulnerable groups of society, such as people with disabilities, elderly persons and indigenous people.

47. Strengthen the capacity of health-care systems to deliver basic health services to all, in an efficient, accessible and affordable manner aimed at preventing, controlling and treating diseases, and to reduce environmental health threats, in conformity with human rights and fundamental freedoms and consistent with national laws and cultural and religious values, taking into account the reports of relevant United Nations conferences and summits and of special sessions of the General Assembly. This would include actions at all levels to:

(a) Integrate the health concerns, including those of the most vulnerable populations, into strategies, policies and programmes for poverty eradication and sustainable development;

(b) Promote equitable and improved access to affordable and efficient health-care services, including prevention, at all levels of the health system, essential and safe drugs at affordable prices, immunization services and safe vaccines, and medical technology;

(c) Provide technical and financial assistance to developing countries and countries with economies in transition to implement the Health for All Strategy, including health information systems and integrated databases on development hazards;

(d) Improve the development and management of human resources in health-care services;

(e) Promote and develop partnerships to enhance health education with the objective of achieving improved health literacy on a global basis by 2010, with the involvement of United Nations agencies, as appropriate;

(f) Develop programmes and initiatives to reduce, by the year 2015, mortality rates for infants and children under 5 by two thirds, and maternal mortality rates by three quarters, of the prevailing rate in 2000, and reduce disparities between and within developed and developing countries as quickly as possible, with particular attention to eliminating the pattern of disproportionate and preventable mortality among girl infants and children;

(g) Target research efforts and apply research results to priority public health issues, in particular those affecting susceptible and vulnerable populations, through the development of new vaccines, reducing exposures to health risks, building on equal access to health-care services, education, training and medical treatment and technology, and addressing the secondary effects of poor health;

(h) Promote the preservation, development and use of effective traditional medicine knowledge and practices, where appropriate, in combination with modern medicine, recognizing indigenous and local communities as custodians of traditional knowledge and practices, while promoting effective protection of traditional knowledge, as appropriate, consistent with international law;

(i) Ensure equal access of women to health-care services, giving particular attention to maternal and emergency obstetric care;

(j) Address effectively, for all individuals of appropriate age, the promotion of their healthy lives, including their reproductive and sexual health, consistent with the commitments and outcomes of recent United Nations conferences and summits, including the World Summit for Children, the United Nations Conference on Environment and Development, the International Conference of Population and Development, the World Summit for Social Development and the Fourth World Conference on Women, and their respective reviews and reports;

(k) Launch international capacity-building initiatives, as appropriate, that assess health and environment linkages and use the knowledge gained to create more effective national and regional policy responses to environmental threats to human health;

(l) Transfer and disseminate, on mutually agreed terms, including through public-private multisector partnerships, technologies for safe water, sanitation and waste management for rural and urban areas in developing countries and countries with economies in transition, with international financial support, taking into account country-specific conditions and gender equality including specific technology needs of women;

(m) Strengthen and promote ILO and World Health Organization (WHO) programmes to reduce occupational deaths, injuries and illnesses, and link occupational health with public health promotion as a means of promoting public health and education;

(n) Improve availability and access for all to sufficient, safe, culturally acceptable and nutritionally adequate food, increase consumer health protection, address issues of micronutrient deficiency, and implement existing internationally agreed commitments and relevant standards and guidelines;

(o) Develop or strengthen, where applicable, preventive, promotive and curative programmes to address non-communicable diseases and conditions, such as cardiovascular diseases, cancer, diabetes, chronic respiratory diseases, injuries, violence and mental health disorders and associated risk factors, including alcohol, tobacco, unhealthy diets and lack of physical activity.

48. Implement, within the agreed time frames, all commitments agreed in the Declaration of Commitment on HIV/AIDS adopted by the General Assembly at its twenty-sixth special session, emphasizing in particular the reduction of HIV prevalence among young men and women aged 15–24 by 25 per cent in the most affected countries by 2005 and globally by 2010, as well as combat malaria, tuberculosis and other diseases by, inter alia:

(a) Implementing national preventive and treatment strategies, regional and international cooperation measures, and the development of international initiatives to provide special assistance to children orphaned by HIV/AIDS;

(b) Fulfilling commitments for the provision of sufficient resources to support the Global Fund to Fight AIDS, Tuberculosis and Malaria, while promoting access to the Fund by countries most in need;

(c) Protecting the health of workers and promoting occupational safety, by, inter alia, taking into account, as appropriate the voluntary ILO code of practice on HIV/AIDS and the world of work, to improve conditions of the workplace;

(d) Mobilizing adequate public and encouraging private financial resources for research and development on diseases of the poor, such as HIV/AIDS, malaria, tuberculosis, directed at biomedical and health research, as well as new vaccine and drug development.

49. Reduce respiratory diseases and other health impacts resulting from air pollution, with particular attention to women and children, by:

(a) Strengthening regional and national programmes, including through public-private partnerships, with technical and financial assistance to developing countries;

(b) Supporting the phasing out of lead in gasoline;

(c) Strengthening and supporting efforts for the reduction of emissions, through the use of cleaner fuels and modern pollution control techniques;

(d) Assisting developing countries in providing affordable energy to rural communities, particularly to reduce dependence on traditional fuel sources for cooking and heating, which affect the health of women and children.

50. Phase out lead in lead-based paints and other sources of human exposure, work to prevent, in particular, children's exposure to lead, and strengthen monitoring and surveillance efforts and the treatment of lead poisoning.

[*Paragraph 51 is deleted*]

VII. SUSTAINABLE DEVELOPMENT OF SMALL ISLAND DEVELOPING STATES

52. Small island developing States are a special case both for environment and development. Although they continue to take the lead in the path towards sustainable development in their countries, they are increasingly constrained by the interplay of adverse factors clearly underlined in Agenda 21, the Programme of Action for the Sustainable Development of Small Island Developing States and the decisions adopted at the twenty-second special session of the General Assembly. This would include actions at all levels to:

(a) Accelerate national and regional implementation of the Programme of Action, with adequate financial resources, including through GEF focal areas, transfer of environmentally sound technologies and assistance for capacity-building from the international community;

(b) Further implement sustainable fisheries management and improve financial returns from fisheries by supporting and strengthening relevant regional fisheries management organizations, as appropriate, such as the recently established Caribbean Regional Fisheries Mechanism and such agreements as the Convention on the Conservation and Management of Highly Migratory Fish Stocks in the Western and Central Pacific Ocean;

(c) Assist small island developing States, including through the elaboration of specific initiatives, in delimiting and managing in a sustainable manner their coastal areas and exclusive economic zones and the continental shelf (including, where appropriate, the continental shelf areas beyond 200 miles from coastal baselines), as well as relevant regional management initiatives within the context of the United Nations Convention on the Law of the Sea and the UNEP regional seas programmes;

(d) Provide support, including for capacity-building, for the development and further implementation of:

(i) Small island developing States-specific components within programmes of work on marine and coastal biological diversity;

(ii) Freshwater programmes for small island developing States, including through the GEF focal areas;

(e) Effectively reduce, prevent and control waste and pollution and their health-related impacts by undertaking by 2004 initiatives aimed at implementing the Global Programme of Action for the Protection of the Marine Environment from Land-based Activities in small island developing States;

(f) Work to ensure that, in the ongoing negotiations and elaboration of the WTO work programme on trade in small economies, due account is taken of small island developing States, which have severe structural handicaps in integrating into the global economy, within the context of the Doha development agenda;

(g) Develop community-based initiatives on sustainable tourism by 2004, and build the capacities necessary to diversify tourism products, while protecting culture and traditions, and effectively conserving and managing natural resources;

(h) Extend assistance to small island developing States in support of local communities and appropriate national and regional organizations of small island developing States for comprehensive hazard and risk management, disaster prevention, mitigation and preparedness, and help relieve the consequences of disasters, extreme weather events and other emergencies;

(i) Support the finalization and subsequent early operationalization, on agreed terms, of economic, social and environmental vulnerability indices and related indicators as tools for the achievement of the sustainable development of the small island developing States;

(j) Assist small island developing States in mobilizing adequate resources and partnerships for their adaptation needs relating to the adverse effects of climate change, sea level rise and climate variability, consistent with commitments under the United Nations Framework Convention on Climate Changes, where applicable;

(k) Support efforts by small island developing States to build capacities and institutional arrangements to implement intellectual property regimes;

53. Support the availability of adequate, affordable and environmentally sound energy services for the sustainable development of small island developing States by, inter alia:

(a) Strengthening ongoing and supporting new efforts on energy supply and services, by 2004, including through the United Nations system and partnership initiatives;

(b) Developing and promoting efficient use of sources of energy, including indigenous sources and renewable energy, and building the capacities of small island developing States for training, technical know-how and strengthening national institutions in the area of energy management;

54. Provide support to SIDS to develop capacity and strengthen:

(a) Health-care services for promoting equitable access to health care;

(b) Health systems for making available necessary drugs and technology in a sustainable and affordable manner to fight and control communicable and non-communicable diseases, in particular HIV/AIDS, tuberculosis, diabetes, malaria and dengue fever;

(c) Efforts to reduce and manage waste and pollution and building capacity for maintaining and managing systems to deliver water and sanitation services, in both rural and urban areas;

(d) Efforts to implement initiatives aimed at poverty eradication, which have been outlined in section II of the present document.

55. Undertake a full and comprehensive review of the implementation of the Barbados Programme of Action for the Sustainable Development of Small Island Developing States in 2004, in accordance with the provisions set forth in General Assembly resolution S-22/2, and in this context requests the General Assembly at its fifty-seventh session to consider convening an international meeting for the sustainable development of small island developing States.

VIII. SUSTAINABLE DEVELOPMENT FOR AFRICA

56. Since the United Nations Conference on Environment and Development, sustainable development has remained elusive for many African countries. Poverty remains a major challenge and most countries on the continent have not benefited fully from the opportunities of globalization, further exacerbating the continent's marginalization. Africa's efforts to achieve sustainable development have been hindered by conflicts, insufficient investment, limited market access opportunities and supply side constraints, unsustainable debt burdens, historically declining ODA levels and the impact of HIV/AIDS. The World Summit on Sustainable Development should reinvigorate the commitment of the international community to address these special challenges and give effect to a new vision based on concrete actions for the implementation of Agenda 21 in Africa. The New Partnership for Africa's Development (NEPAD) is a commitment by African leaders to the people of Africa. It recognizes that partnerships among African countries themselves and between them and with the international community are key elements of a shared and common vision to eradicate poverty, and furthermore it aims to place their countries, both individually and collectively, on a path of sustained economic growth and sustainable development, while participating actively in the world economy and body politic. It provides a framework for sustainable development on the continent to be shared by all Africa's people. The international community welcomes NEPAD and pledges its support to the implementation of this vision, including through utilization of the benefits of South-South cooperation supported, inter alia, by the Tokyo International Conference on African Development. It also pledges support for other existing development frameworks that are owned and driven nationally by African countries and that embody poverty reduction strategies, including poverty reduction strategy papers. Achieving sustainable development includes actions at all levels to:

(a) Create an enabling environment at the regional, subregional, national and local levels in order to achieve sustained economic growth and sustainable development and support African efforts for peace, stability and security, the resolution and prevention of conflicts, democracy, good governance, respect for human rights and fundamental freedoms, including the right to development and gender equality;

(b) Support the implementation of the vision of NEPAD and other established regional and subregional efforts, including through financing, technical cooperation and institutional cooperation, and human and institutional capacity-building at the regional, subregional and national levels, consistent with national policies, programmes and nationally owned and led strategies for poverty reduction and sustainable development, such as, where applicable, poverty reduction strategy papers;

(c) Promote technology development, transfer and diffusion to Africa and further develop technology and knowledge available in African centres of excellence;

(d) Support African countries to develop effective science and technology institutions and research activities capable of developing and adapting to world class technologies;

(e) Support the development of national programmes and strategies to promote education within the context of nationally owned and led strategies for poverty reduction, and strengthen research institutions in education in order to increase the capacity to fully support the achievement of internationally agreed development goals related to education, including those contained in the Millennium Declaration on ensuring that, by 2015, children everywhere, boys and girls alike, will be able to complete a full course of primary schooling, and that girls and boys will have equal access to all levels of education relevant to national needs;

(f) Enhance the industrial productivity, diversity and competitiveness of African countries through a combination of financial and technological support for the development of key infrastructure, access to technology, networking of research centres, adding value to export products, skills development and enhancing market access in support of sustainable development;

(g) Enhance the contribution of the industrial sector, in particular mining, minerals and metals, to the sustainable development of Africa by supporting the development of effective and transparent regulatory and management frameworks and value addition, broad-based participation, social and environmental responsibility and increased market access in order to create an attractive and conducive environment for investment;

(h) Provide financial and technical support to strengthen the capacity of African countries to undertake environmental legislative policy and institutional reform for sustainable development and to undertake environmental impact assessments and, as appropriate, to negotiate and implement multilateral environment agreements;

(i) Develop projects, programmes and partnerships with relevant stakeholders and mobilize resources for the effective implementation of the outcome of the African Process for the Protection and Development of the Marine and Coastal Environment;

(j) Deal effectively with energy problems in Africa, including through initiatives to:

(i) Establish and promote programmes, partnerships and initiatives to support Africa's efforts to implement NEPAD objectives on energy, which seek to secure access for at least 35 per cent of the African population within 20 years, especially in rural areas;

(ii) Provide support to implement other initiatives on energy, including the promotion of cleaner and more efficient use of natural gas and increased use of renewable energy, and to improve energy efficiency and access to advanced energy technologies, including cleaner fossil fuel technologies, particularly in rural and peri-urban areas;

(k) Assist African countries in mobilizing adequate resources for their adaptation needs relating to the adverse effects of climate change, extreme weather events, sea level rise and climate variability, and assist in developing national climate change strategies and mitigation programmes, and continue to take actions to mitigate the adverse effects on climate change in Africa, consistent with the United Nations Framework Convention on Climate Change;

(l) Support African efforts to develop affordable transport systems and infrastructure that promote sustainable development and connectivity in Africa;

(m) Further to paragraph 40 above, address the poverty affecting mountain communities in Africa;

(n) Provide financial and technical support for afforestation and reforestation in Africa and to build capacity for sustainable forest management, including combating deforestation and measures to improve the policy and legal framework of the forest sector.

57. Provide financial and technical support for Africa's efforts to implement the Convention to Combat Desertification at the national level and integrate indigenous knowledge systems into land and natural resources management practices, as appropriate, and improve extension services to rural communities and promote better land and watershed management practices, including through improved agricultural practices that address land degradation, in order to develop capacity for the implementation of national programmes.

58. Mobilize financial and other support to develop and strengthen health systems that aim at:

(a) Promoting equitable access to health-care services;

(b) Making available necessary drugs and technology in a sustainable and affordable manner to fight and control communicable diseases, including HIV/AIDS, malaria and tuberculosis, and trypanosomiasis, as well as non-communicable diseases, including those caused by poverty;

(c) Building capacity of medical and paramedical personnel;

(d) Promoting indigenous medical knowledge, as appropriate, including traditional medicine;

(e) Researching and controlling the Ebola disease.

59. Deal effectively with natural disasters and conflicts, including their humanitarian and environmental impacts, recognizing that conflicts in Africa have hindered and in many cases obliterated both the gains and efforts aimed at sustainable development, with the most vulnerable members of society, particularly women and children, being the most impacted victims, through efforts and initiatives, at all levels, to:

(a) Provide financial and technical assistance to strengthen the capacities of African countries, including institutional and human capacity, including at the local level, for effective disaster management, including observation and early warning systems, assessments, prevention, preparedness, response and recovery;

(b) Provide support to African countries to enable them to better deal with the displacement of people as a result of natural disasters and conflicts, and put in place rapid response mechanisms;

(c) Support Africa's efforts for the prevention and resolution, management and mitigation of conflicts and its early response to emerging conflict situations to avert tragic humanitarian consequences;

(d) Provide support to refugee host countries in rehabilitating infrastructure and environment, including ecosystems and habitats, that were damaged in the process of receiving and settling refugees.

60. Promote integrated water resources development and optimize the upstream and downstream benefits therefrom, the development and effective management of water resources across all uses and the protection of water quality and aquatic ecosystems, including through initiatives at all levels, to:

(a) Provide access to potable domestic water, hygiene education and improved sanitation and waste management at the household level through initiatives to encourage public and private investment in water supply and sanitation that give priority to the needs of the poor, within stable and transparent national regulatory frameworks provided by Governments, while respecting local conditions involving all concerned stakeholders and monitoring the performance and improving the accountability of public institutions and private companies; and develop critical water supply, reticulation and treatment infrastructure, and build capacity to maintain and manage systems to deliver water and sanitation services, in both rural and urban areas;

(b) Develop and implement integrated river basin and watershed management strategies and plans for all major water bodies, consistent with paragraph 25 above;

(c) Strengthen regional, subregional and national capacities for data collection and processing, and for planning, research, monitoring, assessment and enforcement, as well as arrangements for water resource management;

(d) Protect water resources, including groundwater and wetland ecosystems, against pollution, as well as, in cases of most acute water scarcity, support efforts for developing non-conventional water resources, including the energy-efficient, cost-effective and sustainable desalination of seawater, rainwater harvesting and recycling of water.

61. Achieve significantly improved sustainable agricultural productivity and food security in furtherance of the agreed millennium development goals, including those contained in the Millennium Declaration, in particular to halve by 2015 the proportion of people who suffer from hunger, including through initiatives at all levels to:

(a) Support the development and implementation of national policies and programmes, including research programmes and development plans of African countries to regenerate their agricultural sector and sustainably develop their fisheries, and increase investment in infrastructure, technology and extension services, according to country needs. African countries should be in the process of developing and implementing food security strategies, within the context of national poverty eradication programmes, by 2005;

(b) Promote and support efforts and initiatives to secure equitable access to land tenure and clarify resource rights and responsibilities, through land and tenure reform processes which respect the rule of law and are enshrined in national law, and to provide access to credit to all, especially to women, and that enable economic and social empowerment and poverty eradication as well as efficient and ecologically sound utilization of land, and enable women producers to become decision makers and owners in the sector, including the right to inherit land;

(c) Improve market access for goods, including goods originating from African countries, in particular least developed countries, within the framework of the Doha Ministerial Declaration, without prejudging the outcome of the WTO negotiations and also within the framework of preferential agreements;

(d) Provide support for African countries to improve regional trade and economic integration between African countries. Attract and increase investment in regional market infrastructure;

(e) Support livestock development programmes aimed at progressive and effective control of animal diseases.

62. Achieve sound management of chemicals, with particular focus on hazardous chemicals and wastes, inter alia, through initiatives to assist African countries in elaborating national chemical profiles, and regional and national frameworks and strategies for chemical management and establishing chemical focal points.

63. Bridge the digital divide and create digital opportunity in terms of access infrastructure and technology transfer and application, through integrated initiatives for Africa. Create an enabling environment to attract investments, accelerate existing and new programmes and projects to connect essential institutions, and stimulate the adoption of information communication technologies in government and commerce programmes and other aspects of national economic and social life.

64. Support Africa's efforts to attain sustainable tourism that contributes to social, economic and infrastructure development through the following measures:

(a) Implementing projects at the local, national and subregional levels, with specific emphasis on marketing African tourism products, such as adventure tourism, eco-tourism and cultural tourism;

(b) Establishing and supporting national and cross-border conservation areas to promote ecosystem conservation according to the ecosystem approach, and to promote sustainable tourism;

(c) Respecting local traditions and cultures and promoting the use of indigenous knowledge in natural resource management and eco-tourism;

(d) Assisting host communities in managing their tourism projects for maximum benefit, while limiting negative impact on their traditions, culture and environment;

(e) Support the conservation of Africa's biological diversity, the sustainable use of its components and the fair and equitable sharing of the benefits arising out of the utilization of genetic resources, in accordance with commitments that countries have under biodiversity-related agreements to which they are parties, including such agreements as the Convention on Biological Diversity and the Convention on International Trade in Endangered Species of Wild Fauna and Flora, as well as regional biodiversity agreements.

65. Support African countries in their efforts to implement the Habitat Agenda and the Istanbul Declaration through initiatives to strengthen national and local institutional capacities in the areas of sustainable urbanization and human settlements, provide support for adequate shelter and basic services and the development of efficient and effective governance systems in cities and other human settlements, and strengthen, inter alia, the United Nations Human Settlements Programme/UNEP managing water for African cities programme.

VIIBIS OTHER REGIONAL INITIATIVES

66. Important initiatives have been developed within other United Nations regions and regional, subregional and transregional forums to promote sustainable development. The international community welcomes these efforts and the results already achieved, and calls for actions at all levels for their further development, while encouraging interregional, intraregional and international cooperation in this respect, and expresses its support for their further development and implementation by the countries of the regions.

Sustainable Development in Latin America and the Caribbean

67. The Initiative of Latin America and the Caribbean on Sustainable Development is an undertaking by the leaders of that region that, building on the Platform for Action on the Road to Johannesburg 2002, which was approved in Rio de Janeiro in October 2001, recognizes the importance of regional actions towards sustainable development and takes into account the region's singularities, shared visions and cultural diversity. It is targeted towards the adoption of concrete actions in different areas of sustainable development, such as biodiversity, water resources, vulnerabilities and sustainable cities, social aspects (including health and poverty), economic aspects (including energy) and institutional arrangements (including capacity-building, indicators and participation of civil society), taking into account ethics for sustainable development.

68. The Initiative envisages the development of actions among countries in the region that may foster South-South cooperation and may count with the support of groups of countries, as well as multilateral and regional organizations, including financial institutions. Being a framework for cooperation, the Initiative is open to partnerships with governments and all major groups.

Sustainable Development in Asia and the Pacific

69. Bearing in mind the target of halving the number of people who live in poverty by the year 2015, as provided in the Millennium Declaration, the Phnom Penh Regional Platform on Sustainable Development for Asia and the Pacific recognized that the region contains over half of the world's population and the largest number of the world's people living in poverty. Hence, sustainable development in the region is critical to achieving sustainable development at the global level.

70. The Regional Platform identified seven initiatives for follow-up action: capacity-building for sustainable development; poverty reduction for sustainable development; cleaner production and sustainable energy; land management and biodiversity conservation; protection and management of and access to freshwater resources; oceans, coastal and marine resources and sustainable development of small island developing States; and action on atmosphere and climate change. Follow-up actions of these initiatives will be taken through national strategies and relevant regional and subregional initiatives, such as the Regional Action Programme for Environmentally Sound and Sustainable Development and the Kitakyushu Initiative for a Clean Environment, adopted at the Fourth Ministerial Conference on Environment and Development in Asia and the Pacific organized by the Economic and Social Commission for Asia and the Pacific.

Sustainable Development in the West Asia Region

71. The West Asia region is known for its scarce water and limited fertile land resources. The region has made progress to a more knowledge-based production of higher value-added commodities.

72. The regional preparatory meeting endorsed the following priorities: poverty alleviation, relief of debt burden; and sustainable management of natural resources, including, inter alia, integrated water resources management, implementation of programmes to combat desertification, integrated coastal zone management, and land and water pollution control.

Sustainable Development in the Economic Commission for Europe Region

73. The Economic Commission for Europe (ECE) regional ministerial meeting for the World Summit on Sustainable Development recognized that the region has a major role to play and responsibilities in global efforts to achieve sustainable development by concrete actions. The region recognized that different levels of economic development in countries of the region may require the application of different approaches and mechanisms to implement Agenda 21. In order to address the three pillars of sustainable development in a mutually reinforcing way, the region identified its priority actions for the

ECE region for sustainable development in paragraphs 32–46 of a ministerial statement.

74. In furtherance of the region's commitment to sustainable development, there are ongoing efforts at the regional, subregional and transregional levels, including, inter alia, the Environment for Europe process; the fifth ECE ministerial conference, to be held in Kiev in May 2003; the development of an environmental strategy for the 12 countries of Eastern Europe; the Caucasus and Central Asia; the Central Asian Agenda 21; OECD work on sustainable development, the EU sustainable development strategy; and regional and subregional conventions and processes relevant to sustainable development, including, inter alia, the Aarhus Convention, the Alpine Convention, the North American Commission on Environmental Cooperation, the Boundary Waters Treaty, the Iqaluit Declaration of the Arctic Council, the Baltic Agenda 21 and the Mediterranean Agenda 21.

IX. MEANS OF IMPLEMENTATION*

75. The implementation of Agenda 21 and the achievement of the internationally agreed development goals, including those contained in the Millennium Declaration as well as in the present plan of action, require a substantially increased effort, both by countries themselves and by the rest of the international community, based on the recognition that each country has primary responsibility for its own development and that the role of national policies and development strategies cannot be overemphasized, taking fully into account the Rio principles, including, in particular, the principle of common but differentiated responsibilities, which states:

"States shall cooperate in a spirit of global partnership to conserve, protect and restore the health and integrity of the Earth's ecosystem. In view of the different contributions to global environmental degradation, States have common but differentiated responsibilities. The developed countries acknowledge the responsibility that they bear in the international pursuit of sustainable development in view of the pressures their societies place on the global environment and of the technologies and financial resources they command."

The internationally agreed development goals, including those contained in the Millennium Declaration and Agenda 21, as well as in the present plan of action, will require significant increases in the flow of financial resources as elaborated in the Monterrey Consensus, including through new and additional financial resources, in particular to developing countries, to support the implementation of national policies and programmes developed by them, improved trade opportunities, access to and transfer of environmentally sound technologies on a concessional or preferential basis, as mutually agreed, education and awareness-raising, capacity-building, and information for decision-making and scientific capabilities within the agreed time frame required to meet these goals and initiatives. Progress to this end will require that the international community implement the outcomes of major United Nations conferences, such as the programmes of action adopted at the Third United Nations Conference on the Least Developed Countries, and the Global Conference on the Sustainable Development of Small Island Developing States, and relevant international agreements since 1992, particularly those of the International Conference on Financing for Development and the Fourth WTO Ministerial Conference, including building on them as part of a process of achieving sustainable development.

76. Mobilizing and increasing the effective use of financial resources and achieving the national and international economic conditions needed to fulfil internationally agreed development goals, including those contained in the Millennium Declaration, to eliminate poverty, improve social conditions and raise living standards and protect our environment, will be our first step to ensuring that the twenty-first century becomes the century of sustainable development for all.

77. In our common pursuit of growth, poverty eradication and sustainable development, a critical challenge is to ensure the necessary internal conditions for mobilizing domestic savings, both public and private, sustaining adequate levels of productive investment and increasing human capacity. A

* Because the structure of chapter IX was changed in the course of negotiations, so that its paragraph numbering no longer corresponds to the earlier version contained in document A/CONF.199/L.1, Latin ordinal numbers (bis, ter etc.) are used after paragraph 119 until the end of the chapter in order not to disrupt the paragraph numbering of the following chapter, which was not so changed.

crucial task is to enhance the efficacy, coherence and consistency of macroeconomic policies. An enabling domestic environment is vital for mobilizing domestic resources, increasing productivity, reducing capital flight, encouraging the private sector, and attracting and making effective use of international investment and assistance. Efforts to create such an environment should be supported by the international community.

78. Facilitate greater flows of foreign direct investment so as to support the sustainable development activities, including the development of infrastructure, of developing countries, and enhance the benefits that developing countries can draw from foreign direct investment, with particular actions to:

(a) Create the necessary domestic and international conditions to facilitate significant increases in the flow of FDI to developing countries, in particular the least developed countries, which is critical to sustainable development, particularly FDI flows for infrastructure development and other priority areas in developing countries to supplement the domestic resources mobilized by them;

(b) Encourage foreign direct investment in developing countries and countries with economies in transition through export credits that could be instrumental to sustainable development;

79. Recognize that a substantial increase in ODA and other resources will be required if developing countries are to achieve the internationally agreed development goals and objectives, including those contained in the Millennium Declaration. To build support for ODA, we will cooperate to further improve policies and development strategies, both nationally and internationally, to enhance aid effectiveness, with actions to:

(a) Make available the increased ODA commitments announced by several developed countries at the International Conference on Financing for Development. Urge the developed countries that have not done so to make concrete efforts towards the target of 0.7 per cent of GNP as ODA to developing countries, and effectively implement their commitment on ODA to the least developed countries as contained in paragraph 83 of the Programme of Action for the Least Developed Countries for the Decade 2001–2010. We also encourage developing countries to build on progress achieved in ensuring that ODA is used effectively to help achieve development goals and targets in accordance with the outcome of the International Conference on Financing for Development. We acknowledge the efforts of all donors, commend those donors whose ODA contributions exceed, reach or are increasing towards the targets, and underline the importance of undertaking to examine the means and time frames for achieving the targets and goals;

(b) Encourage recipient and donor countries, as well as international institutions, to make ODA more efficient and effective for poverty eradication, sustained economic growth and sustainable development. In this regard, intensify efforts by the multilateral and bilateral financial and development institutions, in accordance with paragraph 43 of the Monterrey Consensus, in particular to harmonize their operational procedures at the highest standards, so as to reduce transaction costs and make ODA disbursement and delivery more flexible and more responsive to the needs of developing countries, taking into account national development needs and objectives under the ownership of recipient countries, and to use development frameworks that are owned and driven by developing countries and that embody poverty reduction strategies, including poverty reduction strategy papers, as vehicles for aid delivery, upon request.

80. Make full and effective use of existing financial mechanisms and institutions, including through actions at all levels to:

(a) Strengthen ongoing efforts to reform the existing international financial architecture, to foster a transparent, equitable and inclusive system that is able to provide for the effective participation of developing countries in the international economic decision-making processes and institutions, as well as for their effective and equitable participation in the formulation of financial standards and codes;

(b) Promote, inter alia, measures in source and destination countries to improve transparency and information about financial flows to contribute to stability in the international financial environment. Measures that mitigate the impact of excessive volatility of short-term capital flows are important and must be considered;

(c) Work to ensure that the funds are made available on a timely, more assured and predictable basis to international organizations and agencies, where appropriate, for their sustainable development activities, programmes and projects;

(d) Encourage the private sector, including transnational corporations, private foundations and civil society institutions, to provide financial and technical assistance to developing countries;

(e) Support new and existing public/private sector financing mechanisms for developing countries and countries with economies in transition, to benefit in particular small entrepreneurs and small, medium-sized and community-based enterprises and to improve their infrastructure, while ensuring the transparency and accountability of such mechanisms.

81. Welcome the successful and substantial third replenishment of the GEF, which will enable it to address the funding requirements of new focal areas and existing ones and continue to be responsive to the needs and concerns of its recipient countries, in particular developing countries, and further encourage GEF to leverage additional funds from key public and private organizations, improve the management of funds through more speedy and streamlined procedures and simplify its project cycle.

82. Explore ways of generating new public and private innovative sources of finance for development purposes, provided that those sources do not unduly burden developing countries, noting the proposal to use special drawing rights allocations for development purposes, as set forth in paragraph 44 of the Monterrey Consensus.

83. Reduce unsustainable debt burden through such actions as debt relief and, as appropriate, debt cancellation and other innovative mechanisms geared to comprehensively address the debt problems of developing countries, in particular the poorest and most heavily indebted ones. Therefore, debt relief measures should, where appropriate, be pursued vigorously and expeditiously, including within the Paris and London Clubs and other relevant forums, in order to contribute to debt sustainability and facilitate sustainable development, while recognizing that debtors and creditors must share responsibility for preventing and resolving unsustainable debt situations, and that external debt relief can play a key role in liberating resources that can then be directed towards activities consistent with attaining sustainable growth and development. Therefore, we support paragraphs 47 through 51 of the Monterrey Consensus dealing with external debt. Debt relief arrangements should seek to avoid imposing any unfair burdens on other developing countries. There should be an increase in the use of grants for the poorest, debt-vulnerable countries. Countries are encouraged to develop national comprehensive strategies to monitor and manage external liabilities as a key element in reducing national vulnerabilities. In this regard, actions are required to:

(a) Implement speedily, effectively and fully the enhanced heavily indebted poor countries (HIPC) initiative, which should be fully financed through additional resources, taking into consideration, as appropriate, measures to address any fundamental changes in the economic circumstances of those developing countries with unsustainable debt burden caused by natural catastrophes, severe terms-of-trade shocks or affected by conflict, taking into account initiatives which have been undertaken to reduce outstanding indebtedness;

(b) Encourage participation in the HIPC initiative of all creditors that have not yet done so;

(c) Bring international debtors and creditors together in relevant international forums to restructure unsustainable debt in a timely and efficient manner, taking into account the need to involve the private sector in the resolution of crises due to indebtedness, where appropriate;

(d) Acknowledge the problems of the debt sustainability of some non-HIPC low-income countries, in particular those facing exceptional circumstances;

(e) Encourage exploring innovative mechanisms to comprehensively address the debt problems of developing countries, including middle-income countries and countries with economies in transition. Such mechanisms may include debt-for-sustainable-development swaps;

(f) Encourage donor countries to take steps to ensure that resources provided for debt relief do not detract from ODA resources intended to be available for developing countries.

84. Recognizing the major role that trade can play in achieving sustainable development and in eradicating poverty, we encourage WTO members to pursue the work programme agreed at the Fourth WTO Ministerial Conference. In order for developing countries, especially the least developed among them, to secure their share in the growth of world trade commensurate with the needs of their economic development, we urge WTO members to take the following actions:

(a) Facilitate the accession of all developing countries, particularly the least developed countries, as well as countries with economies in transition, that apply for membership of WTO, in accordance with the Monterrey Consensus;

(b) Support the Doha work programme as an important commitment on the part of developed and developing countries to mainstream appropriate trade policies in their respective development policies and programmes;

(c) Implement substantial trade-related technical assistance and capacity-building measures and support the Doha Development Agenda Global Trust Fund established after the Fourth WTO Ministerial Conference as an important step forward in ensuring a sound and predictable basis for WTO-related technical assistance and capacity-building;

(d) Implement the New Strategy for WTO Technical Cooperation for Capacity-Building, Growth and Integration;

(e) Fully support the implementation of the Integrated Framework for Trade-Related Technical Assistance to Least Developed Countries, and urge development partners to significantly increase contributions to the Trust Fund of the Framework, in accordance with the Doha Ministerial Declaration.

85. In accordance with the Doha Declaration as well as with relevant decisions taken at Doha, we are determined to take concrete action to address issues and concerns raised by developing countries regarding the implementation of some WTO agreements and decisions, including the difficulties and resource constraints faced by them in fulfilling those agreements.

86. Call upon WTO members to fulfil the commitments made in the Doha Ministerial Declaration, notably in terms of market access, in particular for products of export interest to developing countries, especially least developed countries, by implementing the following actions, taking into account paragraph 45 of the Doha Ministerial Declaration:

(a) Review all special and differential treatment provisions with a view to strengthening them and making them more precise, effective and operational, in accordance with paragraph 44 of the Doha Ministerial Declaration;

(b) Aim to reduce or, as appropriate, eliminate tariffs on non-agricultural products, including the reduction or elimination of tariff peaks, high tariffs and tariff escalation, as well as non-tariff barriers, in particular on products of export interest to developing countries. Product coverage should be comprehensive and without a priori exclusions. The negotiations shall take fully into account the special needs and interests of developing and least developed countries, including through less than full reciprocity in reduction commitments, in accordance with the Doha Ministerial Declaration;

(c) Fulfill, without prejudging the outcome of the negotiations, the commitment for comprehensive negotiations initiated under article 20 of the Agreement on Agriculture as referred to in paragraphs 13 and 14 of the Doha Ministerial Declaration, aiming at substantial improvements in market access, reductions of with a view to phasing out all forms of export subsidies, and substantial reductions in trade-distorting domestic support, while agreeing that the provisions for special and differential treatment for developing countries shall be an integral part of all elements of the negotiations and shall be embodied in the schedules of concession and commitments and, as appropriate, in the rules and disciplines to be negotiated, so as to be operationally effective and to enable developing countries to effectively take account of their development needs, including food security and rural development. Take note of the non-trade concerns reflected in the negotiating proposals submitted by WTO members and confirm that non-trade concerns will be taken into account in the negotiations as provided for in the Agreement on Agriculture, in accordance with the Doha Ministerial Declaration.

87. Call on developed countries that have not already done so to work towards the objective of duty-free and quota-free access for all least developed countries' exports, as envisaged in the Programme of Action for the Least Developed Countries for the Decade 2001–2010, which was adopted in Brussels on 20 May 2001.

88. Commit to actively pursue the WTO work programme to address the trade-related issues and concerns affecting the fuller integration of small, vulnerable economies into the multilateral trading system in a manner commensurate with their special circumstances and in support of their efforts towards sustainable development, in accordance with paragraph 35 of the Doha Declaration.

89. Build the capacity of commodity-dependent countries to diversify exports through, inter alia, financial and technical assistance, international assistance for economic diversification and sustainable resource management, and address the instability of commodity prices and declining terms of trade, as well as strengthen the activities covered by the Second Account of the Common Fund for Commodities to support sustainable development.

90. Enhance the benefits for developing countries, as well as countries with economies in transition, from trade liberalization, including through public-private partnerships, through, inter alia, action at all levels, including through financial support for technical assistance, the development of technology and capacity-building to developing countries to:

(a) Enhance trade infrastructure and strengthen institutions;

(b) Increase developing country capacity to diversify and increase exports to cope with the instability of commodity prices and declining terms of trade;

(c) Increase the value added of developing country exports.

91. Continue to enhance the mutual supportiveness of trade, environment and development with a view to achieving sustainable development through actions at all levels to:

(a) Encourage the WTO Committee on Trade and Environment and the WTO Committee on Trade and Development, within their respective mandates, to each act as a forum to identify and debate developmental and environmental aspects of the negotiations, in order to help achieve an outcome which benefits sustainable development in accordance with the commitments made under the Doha Ministerial Declaration;

(b) Support the completion of the work programme of the Doha Ministerial Declaration on subsidies so as to promote sustainable development and enhance the environment, and encourage reform of subsidies that have considerable negative effects on the environment and are incompatible with sustainable development;

(c) Encourage efforts to promote cooperation on trade, environment and development, including in the field of providing technical assistance to developing countries, between the secretariats of WTO, UNCTAD, UNDP, UNEP and other relevant international environmental and development and regional organizations;

(d) Encourage the voluntary use of environmental impact assessments as an important national-level tool to better identify trade, environment and development interlinkages. Further encourage countries and international organizations with experience in this field to provide technical assistance to developing countries for these purposes.

92. Promote mutual supportiveness between the multilateral trading system and the multilateral environmental agreements, consistent with sustainable development goals, in support of the work programme agreed through WTO, while recognizing the importance of maintaining the integrity of both sets of instruments.

93. Complement and support the Doha Ministerial Declaration and the Monterrey Consensus by undertaking further action at the national, regional and international levels, including through public/private partnerships, to enhance the benefits, in particular for developing countries as well as for countries with economies in transition, of trade liberalization, through, inter alia, actions at all levels to:

(a) Establish and strengthen existing trade and cooperation agreements, consistent with the multilateral trading system, with a view to achieving sustainable development;

(b) Support voluntary WTO compatible market-based initiatives for the creation and expansion of domestic and international markets for environmentally friendly goods and services, including organic products, which maximize environmental and developmental benefits through, inter alia, capacity-building and technical assistance to developing countries;

(c) Support measures to simplify and make more transparent domestic regulations and procedures that affect trade so as to assist exporters, particularly those from developing countries.

94. Address the public health problems affecting many developing and least developed countries, especially those resulting from HIV/AIDS, tuberculosis, malaria and other epidemics, while noting the importance of the Doha Declaration on the TRIPS Agreement and Public Health, in which it has been agreed that the TRIPS Agreement does not and should not prevent WTO members from taking measures to protect public health. Accordingly, while reiterating our commitment to the TRIPS Agreement, we reaffirm that the Agreement can and should be interpreted and implemented in a manner supportive of WTO members' right to protect public health and in particular to promote access to medicines for all.

95. States should cooperate to promote a supportive and open international economic system that would lead to economic growth and sustainable development in all countries to better address the problems of environmental degradation. Trade policy measures for environmental purposes should not constitute a means of arbitrary or unjustifiable discrimination or a disguised restriction on international trade. Unilateral actions to deal with environmental challenges outside the jurisdiction of the importing country should be avoided. Environmental measures addressing transboundary or global environmental problems should, as far as possible, be based on an international consensus.

96. Take steps with a view to the avoidance of and refrain from any unilateral measure not in accordance with international law and the Charter of the United Nations that impedes the full achievement of economic and social development by the population of the affected countries, in particular women and children, that hinders their well-being and that creates obstacles to the full enjoyment of their human rights, including the right of everyone to a standard of living adequate for their health and well-being and their right to food, medical care and the necessary social services. Ensure that food and medicine are not used as tools for political pressure.

97. Take further effective measures to remove obstacles to the realization of the right of peoples to self-determination, in particular peoples living under colonial and foreign occupation, which continue to adversely affect their economic and social development and are incompatible with the dignity and worth of the human person and must be combated and eliminated. People under foreign occupation must be protected in accordance with the provisions of international humanitarian law.

98. In accordance with the Declaration on Principles of International Law concerning Friendly Relations and Cooperation among States in accordance with the Charter of the United Nations, this shall not be construed as authorizing or encouraging any action which would dismember or impair, totally or in part, the territorial integrity or political unity of sovereign and independent States conducting themselves in compliance with the principle of equal rights and self-determination of peoples and thus possessed of a Government representing the whole people belonging to the territory without distinction of any kind.

99. Promote, facilitate and finance, as appropriate, access to and the development, transfer and diffusion of environmentally sound technologies and corresponding know-how, in particular to developing countries and countries with economies in transition on favourable terms, including on concessional and preferential terms, as mutually agreed, as set out in chapter 34 of Agenda 21, including through urgent actions at all levels to:

(a) Provide information more effectively;

(b) Enhance existing national institutional capacity in developing countries to improve access to and the development, transfer and diffusion of environmentally sound technologies and corresponding know-how;

(c) Facilitate country-driven technology needs assessments;

(d) Establish legal and regulatory frameworks in both supplier and recipient countries that expedite the transfer of environmentally sound technologies in a cost-effective manner by both public and private sectors and support their implementation;

(e) Promote the access and transfer of technology related to early warning systems and to mitigation programmes to developing countries affected by natural disasters.

100. Improve the transfer of technologies to developing countries, in particular at the bilateral and regional levels, including through urgent actions at all levels to:

(a) Improve interaction and collaboration, stakeholder relationships and networks between and among universities, research institutions, government agencies and the private sector;

(b) Develop and strengthen networking of related institutional support structures, such as technology and productivity centres, research, training and development institutions, and national and regional cleaner production centres;

(c) Create partnerships conducive to investment and technology transfer, development and diffusion, to assist developing countries, as well as countries with economies in transition, in sharing best practices and promoting programmes of assistance, and encourage collaboration between corporations and research institutes to enhance industrial efficiency, agricultural productivity, environmental management and competitiveness;

(d) Provide assistance to developing countries, as well as countries with economies in transition, in accessing environmentally sound technologies that are publicly owned or in the public domain, as well as available knowledge in the public domain on science and technology, and in accessing the know-how and expertise required in order for them to make independent use of this knowledge in pursuing their development goals;

(e) Support existing mechanisms and, where appropriate, establish new mechanisms for the development, transfer and diffusion of environmentally sound technologies to developing countries and economies in transition.

101. Assist developing countries in building capacity to access a larger share of multilateral and global research and development programmes. In this regard, strengthen and, where appropriate, create centres for sustainable development in developing countries.

102. Build greater capacity in science and technology for sustainable development, with action to improve collaboration and partnerships on research and development and their widespread application among research institutions, universities, the private sector, governments, NGOs and networks, as well as between and among scientists and academics of developing and developed countries, and in this regard encourage networking with and between centres of scientific excellence in developing countries.

103. Improve policy and decision-making at all levels through, inter alia, improved collaboration between natural and social scientists, and between scientists and policy makers, including through urgent actions at all levels to:

(a) Increase the use of scientific knowledge and technology, and increase the beneficial use of local and indigenous knowledge in a manner respectful of the holders of that knowledge and consistent with national law;

(b) Make greater use of integrated scientific assessments, risk assessments and interdisciplinary and intersectoral approaches;

(c) Continue to support and collaborate with international scientific assessments supporting decision-making, including the Intergovernmental Panel on Climate Change, with the broad participation of developing country experts;

(d) Assist developing countries in developing and implementing science and technology policies;

(e) Establish partnerships between scientific, public and private institutions, and by integrating scientists' advice into decision-making bodies in order to ensure a greater role for science, technology development and engineering sectors;

(f) Promote and improve science-based decision-making and reaffirm the precautionary approach as set out in principle 15 of the Rio Declaration on Environment and Development, which states:

"In order to protect the environment, the precautionary approach shall be widely applied by States according to their capabilities. Where there are threats of serious or irreversible damage, lack of full scientific certainty shall not be used as a reason for postponing cost-effective measures to prevent environmental degradation."

104. Assist developing countries, through international cooperation, in enhancing their capacity in their efforts to address issues pertaining to environmental protection including in their formulation and implementation of policies for environmental management and protection, including through urgent actions at all levels to:

(a) Improve their use of science and technology for environmental monitoring, assessment models, accurate databases and integrated information systems;

(b) Promote and, where appropriate, improve their use of satellite technologies for quality data collection, verification and updating, and further improvement of aerial and ground-based observations, in support of their efforts to collect quality, accurate, long-term, consistent and reliable data;

(c) Set up and, where appropriate, further develop national statistical services capable of providing sound data on science education and research and development activities that are necessary for effective science and technology policy-making.

105. Establish regular channels between policy makers and the scientific community for requesting and receiving science and technology advice for the implementation of Agenda 21, and create and strengthen networks for science and education for sustainable development, at all levels, with the aim of sharing knowledge, experience and best practices and building scientific capacities, particularly in developing countries.

106. Use information and communication technologies, where appropriate, as tools to increase the frequency of communication and the sharing of experience and knowledge, and to improve the quality of and access to information and communications technology in all countries, building on the work facilitated by the United Nations Information and Communications Technology Task Force and the efforts of other relevant international and regional forums.

107. Support publicly funded research and development entities to engage in strategic alliances for the purpose of enhancing research and development to achieve cleaner production and product technologies, through, inter alia, the mobilization from all sources of adequate financial and technical resources, including new and additional resources, and encourage the transfer and diffusion of those technologies, in particular to developing countries.

108. Examine issues of global public interest through open, transparent and inclusive workshops to promote a better public understanding of such questions.

108bis Further resolve to take concerted action against international terrorism, which causes serious obstacles to sustainable development.

109. Education is critical for promoting sustainable development. It is therefore essential to mobilize necessary resources, including financial resources at all levels, by bilateral and multilateral donors, including the World Bank and the regional development banks, by civil society and by foundations, to complement the efforts by national governments to pursue the following goals and actions:

(a) Meet the development goal contained in the Millennium Declaration of achieving universal primary education, ensuring that, by 2015, children everywhere, boys and girls alike, will be able to complete a full course of primary schooling;

(b) Provide all children, particularly those living in rural areas and those living in poverty, especially girls, with the access and opportunity to complete a full course of primary education;

110. Provide financial assistance and support to education, research, public awareness programmes and developmental institutions in developing countries and countries with economies in transition in order to:

(a) Sustain their educational infrastructures and programmes, including those related to environment and public health education;

(b) Consider means of avoiding the frequent, serious financial constraints faced by many institutions of higher learning, including universities around the world, particularly in developing countries and countries in transition.

111. Address the impact of HIV/AIDS on the educational system in those countries seriously affected by the pandemic.

112. Allocate national and international resources for basic education as proposed by the Dakar Framework for Action on Education for All and for improved integration of sustainable development into education and in bilateral and multilateral development programmes, and improve integration between publicly funded research and development and development programmes.

113. Eliminate gender disparity in primary and secondary education by 2005, as provided in the Dakar Framework for Action on Education for All, and at all levels of education no later than 2015, to meet the development goals contained in the Millennium Declaration, with action to ensure, inter alia, equal access to all levels and forms of education, training and capacity-building by gender mainstreaming, and by creating a gender-sensitive educational system.

114. Integrate sustainable development into education systems at all levels of education in order to promote education as a key agent for change.

115. Develop, implement, monitor and review education action plans and programmes at the national, subnational and local levels, as appropriate, that reflect the Dakar Framework for Action on Education for All and that are relevant to local conditions and needs leading to the achievement of community development, and make education for sustainable development a part of those plans.

116. Provide all community members with a wide range of formal and non-formal continuing educational opportunities, including volunteer community service programmes, in order to end illiteracy and emphasize the importance of lifelong learning and promote sustainable development.

117. Support the use of education to promote sustainable development, including through urgent actions at all levels to:

(a) Integrate information and communications technology in school curriculum development to ensure its access by both rural and urban communities, and provide assistance particularly to developing countries, inter alia, for the establishment of an appropriate enabling environment required for such technology;

(b) Promote, as appropriate, affordable and increased access to programmes for students, researchers and engineers from developing countries in the universities and research institutions of developed countries in order to promote the exchange of experience and capacity that will benefit all partners;

(c) Continue to implement the work programme of the Commission on Sustainable Development on education for sustainable development;

(d) Recommend to the United Nations General Assembly that it consider adopting a decade of education for sustainable development, starting in 2005.

118. Enhance and accelerate human, institutional and infrastructure capacity-building initiatives, and promote partnerships in that regard that respond to the specific needs of developing countries in the context of sustainable development.

119. Support local, national, subregional and regional initiatives, with action to develop, use and adapt knowledge and techniques and to enhance local, national, subregional and regional centres of excellence for education, research and training in order to strengthen the knowledge capacity of developing countries and countries with economies in transition through, inter alia, the mobilization from all sources of adequate financial and other resources, including new and additional resources;

119bis Provide technical and financial assistance to developing countries, including through the strengthening of capacity-building efforts, such as the United Nations Development Programme capacity 21 programme, to:

(a) Assess their own capacity development needs and opportunities at the individual, institutional and societal levels;

(b) Design programmes for capacity-building and support for local, national and community-level programmes that focus on meeting the challenges of globalization more effectively and attaining the internationally agreed development goals, including those contained in the Millennium Declaration;

(c) Develop the capacity of civil society, including youth, to participate, as appropriate, in designing, implementing and reviewing sustainable development policies and strategies at all levels;

(d) Build and, where appropriate, strengthen national capacities for carrying out effective implementation of Agenda 21.

119ter Ensure access, at the national level, to environmental information and judicial and administrative proceedings in environmental matters, as well as public participation in decision-making, so as to further principle 10 of the Rio Declaration on Environment and Development, taking into full account principles 5, 7 and 11 of the Declaration.

119quater Strengthen national and regional information and statistical and analytical services relevant to sustainable development policies and programmes, including data disaggregated by sex, age and other factors, and encourage donors to provide financial and technical support to developing countries to enhance their capacity to formulate policies and implement programmes for sustainable development.

119quinquies Encourage further work on indicators for sustainable development by countries at the national level, including integration of gender aspects, on a voluntary basis, in line with national conditions and priorities.

119sexties Promote further work on indicators, in conformity with paragraph 3 of decision 9/4 of the Commission on Sustainable Development.

119septies Promote the development and wider use of earth observation technologies, including satellite remote sensing, global mapping and geographic information systems, to collect quality data on environmental impacts, land use and land-use changes, including through urgent actions at all levels to:

(a) Strengthen cooperation and coordination among global observing systems and research programmes for integrated global observations, taking into account the need for building capacity and sharing of data from ground-based observations, satellite remote sensing and other sources among all countries;

(b) Develop information systems that make the sharing of valuable data possible, including the active exchange of Earth observation data;

(c) Encourage initiatives and partnerships for global mapping.

119octies Support countries, particularly developing countries, in their national efforts to:

(a) Collect data that are accurate, long-term, consistent and reliable;

(b) Use satellite and remote-sensing technologies for data collection and further improvement of ground-based observations;

(c) Access, explore and use geographic information by utilizing the technologies of satellite remote sensing, satellite global positioning, mapping and geographic information systems.

119noviens Support efforts to prevent and mitigate the impacts of natural disasters, including through urgent actions at all levels to:

(a) Provide affordable access to disaster-related information for early warning purposes;

(b) Translate available data, particularly from global meteorological observation systems, into timely and useful products.

119diciens Develop and promote the wider application of environmental impact assessments, inter alia, as a national instrument, as appropriate, to provide essential decision-support information on projects that could cause significant adverse effects to the environment.

119undeciens Promote and further develop methodologies at policy, strategy and project levels for sustainable development decision-making at the local and national levels, and where relevant at the regional level. In this regard, emphasize that the choice of the appropriate methodology to be used in countries should be adequate to their country-specific conditions and circumstances, should be on a voluntary basis and should conform to their development priority needs.

X. INSTITUTIONAL FRAMEWORK FOR SUSTAINABLE DEVELOPMENT

120. An effective institutional framework for sustainable development at all levels is key to the full implementation of Agenda 21, the follow-up to the outcomes of the World Summit on Sustainable Development and meeting emerging sustainable development challenges. Measures aimed at strengthening such a framework should build on the provisions of Agenda 21 as well as the 1997 Programme for its further implementation and the principles of the Rio Declaration on Environment and Development and should promote the achievement of the internationally agreed development goals, including those contained in the Millennium Declaration, taking into account the Monterrey Consensus and relevant outcomes of other major United Nations conferences and international agreements since 1992. It should be responsive to the needs of all countries, taking into account the specific needs of developing countries including the means of implementation. It should lead to the strengthening of international bodies and organizations dealing with sustainable development, while respecting their existing mandates, as well as to the strengthening of relevant regional, national and local institutions.

120bis Good governance is essential for sustainable development. Sound economic policies, solid democratic institutions responsive to the needs of the people and improved infrastructure are the basis for sustained economic growth, poverty eradication, and employment creation. Freedom, peace and security, domestic stability, respect for human rights, including the right to development, and the rule of law, gender equality, market-oriented policies, and an overall commitment to just and democratic societies are also essential and mutually reinforcing.

Objectives

121. Measures to strengthen sustainable development institutional arrangements at all levels should be taken within the framework of Agenda 21[1] and should build on developments since UNCED, and should lead to the achievement of, inter alia, the following objectives:

(a) Strengthening commitments to sustainable development;

(b) Integration of the economic, social and environmental dimensions of sustainable development in a balanced manner;

(c) Strengthening of the implementation of Agenda 21, including through the mobilization of financial and technological resources, as well as capacity-building programmes, particularly for developing countries;

(d) Strengthening coherence, coordination and monitoring;

(e) Promoting the rule of law and strengthening of governmental institutions;

(f) Increasing effectiveness and efficiency through limiting overlap and duplication of activities of international organizations, within and outside the United Nations system, based on their mandates and comparative advantages;

(g) Enhancing participation and effective involvement of civil society and other relevant stakeholders in the implementation of Agenda 21, as well as promoting transparency and broad public participation;

(h) Strengthening capacities for sustainable development at all levels, including the local level, in particular those of developing countries;

(i) Strengthening international cooperation aimed at reinforcing the implementation of Agenda 21 and the outcomes of the Summit.

Strengthening the Institutional Framework for Sustainable Development at the International Level

122. The international community should:

(a) Enhance the integration of sustainable development goals as reflected in Agenda 21 and support for implementation of Agenda 21 and the outcomes of the Summit into the policies, work programmes and operational guidelines of relevant United Nations agencies, programmes and funds, GEF and international financial and trade institutions within their mandates, while stressing that their activities should take full account of national programmes and priorities, particularly those of developing countries, as well as, where appropriate, countries with economies in transition, to achieve sustainable development;

(b) Strengthen collaboration within and between the United Nations system, international financial institutions, the Global Environment Facility and WTO, utilizing the United Nations Chief Executives Board for Coordination (CEB), the United Nations Development Group, the Environment Management Group and other inter-agency coordinating bodies. Strengthened inter-agency collaboration should be pursued in all relevant contexts, with special emphasis on the operational level and involving partnership arrangements on specific issues to support, in particular, developing countries' efforts in implementing Agenda 21;

(c) Strengthen and better integrate the three dimensions of sustainable development policies and programmes, and promote the full integration

[1] References in the present chapter to Agenda 21 are deemed to include Agenda 21, the Programme for the Further Implementation of Agenda 21 and the outcomes of the Summit.

of sustainable development objectives into programmes and policies of bodies that have a primary focus on social issues. In particular, the social dimension of sustainable development should be strengthened, inter alia, by emphasizing follow-up to the outcomes of the World Summit for Social Development and its five-year review, and taking into account their reports, and by support to social protection systems;

(d) Fully implement the outcomes of decision I on international environmental governance adopted by the UNEP Governing Council at its seventh special session, and invite the General Assembly at its fifty-seventh session to consider the important but complex issue of establishing universal membership for the Governing Council/Global Ministerial Environment Forum;

(e) Engage actively and constructively in ensuring the timely completion of the negotiations on a comprehensive United Nations convention against corruption, including the question of repatriation of funds illicitly acquired to countries of origin;

(f) Promote corporate responsibility and accountability and the exchange of best practices in the context of sustainable development, including, as appropriate, through multi-stakeholder dialogue, such as through the Commission on Sustainable Development, and other initiatives;

(g) Take concrete action to implement the Monterrey Consensus at all levels.

123. Good governance at the international level is fundamental for achieving sustainable development. In order to ensure a dynamic and enabling international economic environment, it is important to promote global economic governance through addressing the international finance, trade, technology and investment patterns that have an impact on the development prospects of developing countries. To this effect, the international community should take all necessary and appropriate measures, including ensuring support for structural and macroeconomic reform, a comprehensive solution to the external debt problem and increasing market access for developing countries. Efforts to reform the international financial architecture need to be sustained with greater transparency and the effective participation of developing countries in decision-making processes. A universal, rule-based, open, non-discriminatory and equitable multilateral trading system, as well as meaningful trade liberalization, can substantially stimulate development worldwide, benefiting countries at all stages of development.

124. A vibrant and effective United Nations system is fundamental to the promotion of international cooperation for sustainable development and to a global economic system that works for all. To this effect, a firm commitment to the ideals of the United Nations and to the principles of international law and those enshrined in the Charter of the United Nations, and to strengthening the United Nations system and other multilateral institutions and promoting the improvement of their operations, is essential. States should also fulfil their commitment to negotiate and finalize as soon as possible a United Nations convention against corruption in all its aspects, including the question of repatriation of funds illicitly acquired to countries of origin and also to promoting stronger cooperation to eliminate money-laundering.

Role of the General Assembly

125. The General Assembly of the United Nations should adopt sustainable development as a key element of the overarching framework for United Nations activities, particularly for achieving the internationally agreed development goals, including those contained in the Millennium Declaration, and should give overall political direction to the implementation of Agenda 21 and its review.

Role of the Economic and Social Council

126. Pursuant to the relevant provisions of the Charter of the United Nations and Agenda 21 provisions regarding the Economic and Social Council and General Assembly resolutions 48/162 and 50/227, which reaffirmed the Council as the central mechanism for the coordination of the United Nations system and its specialized agencies and supervision of subsidiary bodies, in particular its functional commissions, and to promote the implementation of Agenda 21 by strengthening system-wide coordination, the Council should:

(a) Increase its role in overseeing system-wide coordination and the balanced integration of economic, social and environmental aspects of United Nations policies and programmes aimed at promoting sustainable development;

(b) Organize periodic consideration of sustainable development themes in regard to the implementation of Agenda 21, including the means of implementation. Recommendations in regard to such themes could be made by the Commission on Sustainable Development;

(c) Make full use of its high-level, coordination, operational activities and the general segments to effectively take into account all relevant aspects of the work of the United Nations on sustainable development. In this context, the Council should encourage the active participation of major groups in its high-level segment and the work of its relevant functional commissions, in accordance with the respective rules of procedure;

(d) Promote greater coordination, complementarity, effectiveness and efficiency of activities of its functional commissions and other subsidiary bodies that are relevant to the implementation of Agenda 21;

(e) Terminate the work of the Committee on Energy and Natural Resources for Development and transfer its work to the Commission on Sustainable Development;

(f) Ensure that there is a close link between the role of the Council in the follow-up to the Summit and its role in the follow-up to the Monterrey Consensus, in a sustained and coordinated manner. To that end, the Council should explore ways to develop arrangements relating to its meetings with the Bretton Woods institutions and WTO, as set out in the Monterrey Consensus;

(g) Intensify its efforts to ensure that gender mainstreaming is an integral part of its activities concerning the coordinated implementation of Agenda 21.

Role and Function of the Commission on Sustainable Development

127. The Commission on Sustainable Development should continue to be the high-level commission on sustainable development within the United Nations system and serve as a forum for consideration of issues related to integration of the three dimensions of sustainable development. Although the role, functions and mandate of the Commission as set out in relevant parts of Agenda 21 and adopted in General Assembly resolution 47/191 continue to be relevant, the Commission needs to be strengthened, taking into account the role of relevant institutions and organizations. An enhanced role of the Commission should include reviewing and monitoring progress in the implementation of Agenda 21 and fostering coherence of implementation, initiatives and partnerships.

128. Within that context, the Commission should give more emphasis on actions that enable implementation at all levels, including promoting and facilitating partnerships involving Governments, international organizations and relevant stakeholders for the implementation of Agenda 21.

129. The Commission should:

(a) Review and evaluate progress and promote further implementation of Agenda 21;

(b) Focus on the cross-sectoral aspects of specific sectoral issues and provide a forum for better integration of policies, including through interaction among Ministers dealing with the various dimensions and sectors of sustainable development through the high-level segments;

(c) Address new challenges and opportunities related to the implementation of Agenda 21;

(d) Focus on actions related to implementation of Agenda 21, limiting negotiations in the sessions of the Commission to every two years;

(e) Limit the number of themes addressed in each session.

130. In relation to its role in facilitating implementation, the Commission should emphasize the following:

(a) Review progress and promote the further implementation of Agenda 21. In this context, the Commission should identify constraints on implementation and make recommendations to overcome those constraints;

(b) Serve as a focal point for the discussion of partnerships that promote sustainable development, including sharing lessons learned, progress made and best practices;

(c) Review issues related to financial assistance and transfer of technology for sustainable development, as well as capacity-building, while making full use of existing information. In this regard, the Commission on Sustainable Development could give consideration to more effective use of national reports and regional experience and to this end make appropriate recommendations;

(d) Provide a forum for analysis and exchange of experience on measures that assist sustainable development planning, decision-making and the implementation of sustainable development strategies. In this regard, the Commission could give consideration to more effective use of national and regional reports;

(e) Take into account significant legal developments in the field of sustainable development, with due regard to the role of relevant intergovernmental bodies in promoting the implementation of Agenda 21 relating to international legal instruments and mechanisms.

131. With regard to the practical modalities and programme of work of the Commission, specific decisions on those issues should be taken by the Commission at its next session, when the Commission's thematic work programme will be elaborated. In particular, the following issues should be considered:

(a) Giving a balanced consideration to implementation of all of the mandates of the Commission contained in General Assembly resolution 47/191;

(b) Continuing to provide for more direct and substantive involvement of international organizations and major groups in the work of the Commission;

(c) Give greater consideration to the scientific contributions to sustainable development through, for example, drawing on the scientific community and encouraging national, regional and international scientific networks to be involved in the Commission;

(d) Furthering the contribution of educators to sustainable development, including, where appropriate, in the activities of the Commission;

(e) The scheduling and duration of intersessional meetings.

132. Undertake further measures to promote best practices and lessons learned in sustainable development, and in addition promote the use of contemporary methods of data collection and dissemination, including broader use of information technologies.

Role of International Institutions

133. Stress the need for international institutions both within and outside the United Nations system, including international financial institutions, WTO and GEF, to enhance, within their mandates, their cooperative efforts to:

(a) Promote effective and collective support to the implementation of Agenda 21 at all levels;

(b) Enhance the effectiveness and coordination of international institutions to implement Agenda 21, the outcomes of the World Summit on Sustainable Development, relevant sustainable development aspects of the Millennium Declaration, the Monterrey Consensus and the outcomes of the fourth WTO ministerial meeting, held in Doha in November 2001.

134. Request the Secretary-General of the United Nations, utilizing the United Nations System Chief Executives Board for Coordination, including through informal collaborative efforts, to further promote system-wide inter-agency cooperation and coordination on sustainable development, to take appropriate measures to facilitate exchange of information, and to continue to keep the Economic and Social Council and the Commission informed of actions being taken to implement Agenda 21.

135. Significantly strengthen support for UNDP capacity-building programmes for sustainable development, building on the experience gained from Capacity 21, as important mechanisms for supporting local and national development capacity-building efforts, in particular in developing countries.

136. Strengthen cooperation among UNEP and other United Nations bodies and specialized agencies, the Bretton Woods institutions and WTO, within their mandates.

137. UNEP, UN-Habitat, UNDP and UNCTAD, within their mandates, should strengthen their contribution to sustainable development programmes and the implementation of Agenda 21 at all levels, particularly in the area of promoting capacity-building.

138. To promote effective implementation of Agenda 21 at the international level, the following should also be undertaken:

(a) Streamline the international sustainable development meeting calendar and, as appropriate, reduce the number of meetings, the length of meetings and the amount of time spent on negotiated outcomes in favour of more time spent on practical matters related to implementation;

(b) Encourage partnership initiatives for implementation by all relevant actors to support the outcome of the World Summit on Sustainable Development. In this context, further development of partnerships and partnership follow-up should take note of the preparatory work for the Summit;

(c) Make full use of developments in the field of information and communication technologies.

[Paragraph 139 is deleted]

140. Strengthening of the international institutional framework for sustainable development is an evolutionary process. It is necessary to keep under review relevant arrangements; identify gaps; eliminate duplication of functions; and continue to strive for greater integration, efficiency and coordination of the economic, social and environmental dimensions of sustainable development aiming at the implementation of Agenda 21.

Strengthening Institutional Arrangements for Sustainable Development at the Regional Level

141. Implementation of Agenda 21 and the outcomes of the Summit should be effectively pursued at the regional and subregional levels, through the regional commissions and other regional and subregional institutions and bodies.

142. Intraregional coordination and cooperation on sustainable development should be improved among the regional commissions, United Nations Funds, programmes and agencies, regional development banks, and other regional and subregional institutions and bodies. This should include, as appropriate, support for development, enhancement and implementation of agreed regional sustainable development strategies and action plans, reflecting national and regional priorities.

143. In particular and taking into account relevant provisions of Agenda 21, the regional commissions, in collaboration with other regional and subregional bodies, should:

(a) Promote the integration of the three dimensions of sustainable development into their work in a balanced way, including through implementation of Agenda 21. To this end, the regional commissions should enhance their capacity through internal action and be provided, as appropriate, with external support;

(b) Facilitate and promote a balanced integration of the economic, social and environmental dimensions of sustainable development into the work of regional, subregional and other bodies, for example by facilitating and strengthening the exchange of experiences, including national experience, best practices, case studies and partnership experience related to the implementation of Agenda 21;

(c) Assist in the mobilization of technical and financial assistance, and facilitate the provision of adequate financing for the implementation of regionally and subregionally agreed sustainable development programmes and projects, including addressing the objective of poverty eradication;

(d) Continue to promote multi-stakeholder participation and encourage partnerships to support the implementation of Agenda 21 at the regional and subregional levels.

144. Regionally and subregionally agreed sustainable development initiatives and programmes, such as the New Partnership for Africa's Development (NEPAD) and the interregional aspects of the globally agreed Programme of Action for the Sustainable Development of Small Island Developing States, should be supported.

Strengthening Institutional Frameworks for Sustainable Development at the National Level

145. States should:

(a) Continue to promote coherent and coordinated approaches to institutional frameworks for sustainable development at all national levels, including through, as appropriate, the establishment or strengthening of existing authorities and mechanisms necessary for policy-making, coordination and implementation and enforcement of laws;

(b) Take immediate steps to make progress in the formulation and elaboration of national strategies for sustainable development and begin their implementation by 2005. To this end, as appropriate, strategies should be supported through international cooperation, taking into account the special needs of developing countries, in particular the least developed countries. Such strategies, which, where applicable, could be formulated as poverty reduction strategies that integrate economic, social and environmental aspects of sustainable development, should be pursued in accordance with each country's national priorities.

146. Each country has the primary responsibility for its own sustainable development, and the role of national policies and development strategies cannot be overemphasized. All countries should promote sustainable development at the national level by, inter alia, enacting and enforcing clear and effective laws that support sustainable development. All countries should strengthen governmental institutions, including by providing necessary infrastructure and by promoting transparency, accountability and fair administrative and judicial institutions.

140bis All countries should also promote public participation, including through measures that provide access to information regarding legislation, regulations, activities, policies and programmes. They should also foster full public participation in sustainable development policy formulation and implementation. Women should be able to participate fully and equally in policy formulation and decision-making.

147. Further promote the establishment or enhancement of sustainable development councils and/or coordination structures at the national level, including at the local level, in order to provide a high-level focus on sustainable development policies. In that context, multi-stakeholder participation should be promoted.

148. Support efforts by all countries, particularly developing countries, as well as countries with economies in transition, to enhance national institutional arrangements for sustainable development, including at the local level. That could include promoting cross-sectoral approaches in the formulation of strategies and plans for sustainable development, such as, where applicable, poverty reduction strategies, aid coordination, encouraging participatory approaches and enhancing policy analysis, management capacity and implementation capacity, including mainstreaming a gender perspective in all those activities.

149. Enhance the role and capacity of local authorities as well as stakeholders in implementing Agenda 21 and the outcomes of the Summit and in strengthening the continuing support for local Agenda 21 programmes and associated initiatives and partnerships, and encourage, in particular, partnerships among and between local authorities and other levels of government and stakeholders to advance sustainable development as called for in, inter alia, the Habitat Agenda.

Participation of Major Groups

150. Enhance partnerships between governmental and non-governmental actors, including all major groups, as well as volunteer groups, on programmes and activities for the achievement of sustainable development at all levels.

[Paragraph 151 is deleted]

152. Acknowledge the consideration being given to the possible relationship between environment and human rights, including the right to development, with full and transparent participation of Member States of the United Nations and observer States.

153. Promote and support youth participation in programmes and activities relating to sustainable development through, for example, supporting local youth councils or their equivalent, and by encouraging their establishment where they do not exist.

Decision of the Commission on Sustainable Development Ninth Session (CSD-9)

Report on the Ninth Session, U.N. doc. E/CN.17/2001/19 – E/2001/29, Decision 9/1

http://www.un.org/esa/sustdev/csd/CSD9.htm
http://www.un.org/esa/sustdev/csd/ecn172001-19e.htm#decision9/1

DECISION 9/1

ENERGY FOR SUSTAINABLE DEVELOPMENT

A. General Considerations

1. Energy is central to achieving the goals of sustainable development.

2. The magnitude and scale of energy needs facing the world today in relation to sustainable development can be gauged by the fact that nearly one third of the global population of six billion, mostly living in developing countries, continue to lack access to energy and transportation services. Wide disparities in the levels of energy consumption within and between developed and developing countries exist. Current patterns of energy production, distribution and utilization are unsustainable.

3. The challenge ahead will require adequate, predictable, new and additional financial resources, in accordance with chapter 33 of Agenda 21,[1[1]] and paragraphs 76 to 87 of the Programme for the Further Implementation of Agenda 21,[2[2]] technology transfer and, where appropriate, political will, as well as commitment to innovative ways of applying energy efficient, environmentally sound, and cost-effective technologies and systems to all sectors of the economy. Energy resources are plentiful, and environmentally sound technological options exist and should be made available and facilitated by developed countries to developing countries as well as countries with economies in transition with a view to making energy for sustainable development a reality. Ensuring adequate and affordable access to energy for present and future generations, in an environmentally sound, socially acceptable and economically viable way, will require considerable efforts and substantial investments, including from the private sector. Attention will also need to be given to promoting an enabling environment.

4. In order to make energy systems more supportive of sustainable development objectives, contributions from all stakeholders, as well as increased investments, will be needed. Change will not be driven by resource constraints for a very long time to come. Energy for sustainable development can be achieved by providing universal access to a cost-effective mix of energy resources compatible with different needs and requirements of various countries and regions. This should include giving a greater share of the energy mix to renewable energies, improving energy efficiency and greater reliance on advanced energy technologies, including fossil fuel technologies. Policies relating to energy for sustainable development intended to promote these objectives will address many of the issues of economic and social development as well as facilitate the responsible management of environmental resources.

5. In view of the different contributions to global environmental degradations, States have common but differentiated responsibilities. The choice and implementation of policies to improve the ways to achieve energy for sustainable development basically rest with Governments. However, financial resources play a key role in their implementation. For developing countries, official development assistance (ODA) is a main source of external funding, and substantial new and additional funding for sustainable development and the implementation

1[1] *Report of the United Nations Conference on Environment and Development, Rio de Janeiro, 3–14 June 1997*, vol. I, *Resolutions adopted by the Conference* (United Nations publication, Sales No. E.93.I.8 and corrigenda), resolution 1, annex II.

2[2] General Assembly resolution S-19/3, annex.

of Agenda 21 will be required. A participatory approach involving all relevant stakeholders could facilitate progress. Given that energy is an area with strong interdependencies among countries, international cooperation should be promoted in line with the principle of common but differentiated responsibilities. The way in which energy issues are addressed in a country depends on the national energy situation and needs. Therefore, a range of options and strategies becomes necessary to address the issues involved. Accordingly, a number of options and strategies that could effect a change in the way energy is dealt with are delineated subsequently. The choice of any specific option would obviously depend on the domestic situation.

6. The Commission underlines the importance of principle 16 of the Rio Declaration on Environment and Development[3[3]] in the context of energy policies, taking fully into account the economic, social and environmental conditions of all countries, in particular of developing countries.

B. Issues and Options

7. Governments, as well as relevant regional and international organizations and other relevant stakeholders, are invited to consider the issues and options set out below when dealing with energy, taking into account national and regional specificities and circumstances, bearing in mind the principle of common but differentiated responsibilities.

8. Foremost in the developing countries' priorities is the eradication of poverty for the furtherance of sustainable development. Efforts should therefore be made to ensure that energy policies are supportive to developing countries' efforts to eradicate poverty, with financial assistance, as appropriate. Nevertheless, environmental standards should not be applied in ways that would hinder these efforts.

9. Governments may seek assistance, as appropriate, from relevant regional and international organizations in the formulation and implementation of their domestic energy policies. The international community should support national efforts by promoting capacity-building, technology transfer, investments and other forms of financial resources for developing countries.

[3[3]] *Report of the United Nations Conference on Environment and Development*. . . , resolution 1, annex I.

10. Governments, continuing to have responsibility to develop and apply energy policies to achieve sustainable development, are invited to consider the following options, as appropriate:

(a) Combining, as appropriate, the increased use of renewable energy sources, more efficient use of energy, greater reliance on advanced energy technologies, including advanced fossil fuel technologies, and the sustainable use of traditional energy resources, which could meet the growing needs for energy services in the longer term to achieve sustainable development;

(b) Integrating energy considerations in socio-economic programmes, especially in policy-making of major energy-consuming sectors, such as the public sector, transport, industry, agriculture, urban planning and construction;

(c) Establishing an appropriate enabling environment conducive to attracting investments and supportive of the objectives of sustainable development and to ensuring public participation;

(d) Developing appropriate energy services, particularly in rural areas, through the application of the most cost-effective, socially acceptable and environmentally friendly technologies, the deployment of specific energy service delivery structures and the development of renewable energy resources, including biomass;

(e) Supporting efforts to improve the functioning of energy markets with respect to both supply and demand, with the aim of achieving greater stability and predictability and to ensure consumer access to energy services;

(f) Establish domestic programmes for energy efficiency, including, as appropriate, by accelerating the deployment of energy efficiency technologies, with the necessary support of the international community;

(g) Supporting increased use of renewable energies both in grid-connected and decentralized systems;

(h) Optimizing the efficient use of fossil fuels through the increased development and use of advanced fossil fuel technologies;

(i) Enhancing international cooperation in order to assist countries, in particular developing countries, in their efforts to achieve energy for sustainable development;

(j) All countries should strive to promote sustainable consumption patterns; developed countries should take the lead in achieving sustainable consumption patterns; developing countries should seek to achieve sustainable consumption patterns in their development process, guaranteeing the provision of basic needs for the poor;

(k) Encouraging public-private partnerships with a view to advancing energy for sustainable development;

(l) Facilitating the dissemination of information on environmentally sound technologies and processes to increase awareness of these options and enhance public participation, as appropriate, in decision-making surrounding the provision of these energy services for sustainable development;

(m) Strengthening the role of major groups, including women, inter alia, through participation in decision-making, as appropriate;

(n) Supporting energy conservation programmes in all economic sectors;

(o) Strengthening existing national and local institutions that develop, implement and operate national programmes on energy for sustainable development;

(p) Supporting research, development and demonstration for the above-mentioned activities towards energy for sustainable development, including on transport systems; and enhancing regional and international cooperation in the research and development in these areas.

C. Key Issues

11. Concerning the key issues of energy identified at the first session of the Ad Hoc Open-ended Intergovernmental Group of Experts on Energy and Sustainable Development, the Commission recommends the options and strategies set out below for each key issue. To ensure effective implementation of such key issues, the means of such implementation, namely adequate and predictable new and additional financial resources in accordance with chapter 33 of Agenda 21 and paragraphs 76 to 87 of the Programme for the Further Implementation of Agenda 21, as well as the transfer of environmentally sound technologies and capacity-building, are fundamental.

1. Accessibility of Energy

Challenges

12. Access to energy is crucial to economic and social development and the eradication of poverty. Improving accessibility of energy implies finding ways and means by which energy services can be delivered reliably, affordably and in an economically viable, socially acceptable and environmentally sound manner.

Recommendations

13. Governments, taking into account their national circumstances, are encouraged to:

(a) Establish or strengthen national and regional arrangements for promoting energy accessibility within the country;

(b) Improve access to modern biomass technologies and fuel wood sources and supplies and commercializing biomass operations, including the use of agricultural residues, where such practices are sustainable;

(c) Support the transition to the use of liquid and gaseous fossil fuels, where considered more environmentally sound, socially acceptable and cost-effective;

(d) Develop locally available energy resources for greater energy diversification, where considered more environmentally sound, socially acceptable and cost-effective, with increasing use of renewable energy resources;

(e) Support electricity services based on grid extension and/or decentralized energy technologies, particularly in isolated areas, as appropriate;

(f) Strengthen national and regional research and development institutions/centres on energy for sustainable development, including renewable energy technologies, energy efficiency, advanced energy technologies, including advanced fossil fuel technologies, and sustainable use of traditional energy resources;

(g) Promote an environment which enables the public sector, the private sector and, as appropriate, energy cooperatives, including through public-private partnerships, to engage in the generation, transmission and distribution of electricity at affordable rates and in the transfer of technology;

(h) Develop renewable energy, especially in rural areas, through community-based development methods;

(i) Enhance developing countries' access to environmentally sound and economically viable technologies relating to energy for sustainable development;

(j) Support equal access for women to sustainable and affordable energy technologies through needs assessments, energy planning and policy formulation at the local and national levels.

2. Energy Efficiency

Challenges

14. Energy efficiency can be a win-win solution both for developed and developing countries, but currently energy efficiency has not reached its potential. Barriers to optimizing the energy efficiency potential involve lack of access to technology, capacity-building and financial resources, as well as market related and institutional issues.

Recommendations

15. Governments, taking into account their national circumstances, are encouraged to:

(a) Strengthen public awareness programmes to mobilize all stakeholders;

(b) Promote an enabling environment for encouraging energy service companies for research and investments in energy efficiency;

(c) Provide incentives for energy conservation in all sectors, taking into account domestic priorities;

(d) Develop, as appropriate, at the country and regional level, energy efficiency programmes and policy options;

(e) Strengthen capacity-building, including education and training, ranging from energy planning to technical engineering, to improve the performance of energy and materials use;

(f) Accelerate development and deployment of energy efficiency technologies;

(g) Integrate, as appropriate, energy efficiency considerations into the planning, operation and maintenance of long-lived energy consuming infrastructures, notably transport, urban lay-out, industry, agriculture and tourism;

(h) Increase the efficiency of technologies used in the production and consumption of energy;

(i) Facilitate a movement towards more efficient utilization of energy through equipment manufacturing support programmes, with international cooperation;

(j) Encourage the transfer of energy efficiency technologies, in particular to developing countries, on favourable terms, including on concessional and preferential terms, as mutually agreed;

(k) Strengthen, as appropriate, existing institutions that develop and operate energy efficiency programmes;

(l) Strengthen, as appropriate, existing institutions that compile and disseminate information on energy efficiency programmes and technologies;

(m) Develop and implement measures that make energy efficiency technologies more affordable.

3. Renewable Energy

Challenges

16. The main challenge lies both for developed and developing countries in the development, utilization and dissemination of renewable energy technologies, such as solar, wind, ocean, wave, geothermal, biomass and hydro power, on a scale wide enough to significantly contribute to energy for sustainable development. Despite some progress in promoting renewable energy applications in recent years, inter alia, through the implementation of the World Solar Programme 1996–2005, numerous constraints and barriers including costs continue to exist.

Recommendations

17. Governments, taking into account their national circumstances, are encouraged to:

(a) Develop and implement appropriate national, regional and international policies and measures to create an enabling environment for the development, utilization and distribution of renewable energy sources;

(b) Develop domestic programmes to increase the contribution of renewable energies to total energy consumption;

(c) Encourage the role of the private sector in the development and utilization of renewable energy technologies, through the provision of appropriate incentives and regulation;

(d) Strengthen research, development, demonstration and institutional capacities in the field of renewable energy utilization, as well as the transfer of environmentally sound and advanced technologies;

(e) Promote the utilization of renewable natural resources, such as solar, wind, biomass, geothermal, hydro (including mini-hydro), and ocean (wave, tidal, and thermal energy conversion) to meet part of the energy needs for sustainable development;

(f) Strengthen information networks, compilation and dissemination systems and public awareness programmes on renewable energy sources and technologies;

(g) Develop and use indigenous sources of renewable energy, where appropriate;

(h) Develop and implement measures to make renewable energy technologies more affordable;

(i) Strengthen financial support to developing countries for the promotion of renewable energy.

4. Advanced Fossil Fuel Technologies

Challenges

18. Given that fossil fuels will continue to play a dominant role in the energy mix in the decades to come, the deployment and use of advanced and cleaner fossil fuel technologies should be increased. More efforts should go into supporting the further development and dissemination of those technologies.

Recommendations

19. Governments, taking into account national circumstances, are encouraged to:

(a) Develop and apply more efficient fossil-fuel fired power plants, buildings, appliances and transportation, including cleaner coal and oil technologies;

(b) Increase the use of cleaner fossil fuels to improve efficiency in energy production, distribution and use, where appropriate;

(c) Research, develop and transfer technologies for transforming solid fuels to liquid or gaseous fuels;

(d) Enhance research, development, demonstration and transfer of advanced fossil fuel technologies leading to lower emissions;

(e) Promote research and, where suitable, applications of carbon capture and storage technologies;

(f) Promote cooperation with industries in a voluntary programme framework for cleaner fossil fuel technology deployment;

(g) Develop and implement measures to make advanced fossil fuel technologies more accessible and affordable.

5. Nuclear Energy Technologies

Challenges

20. Nuclear power currently accounts for 16 per cent of the world's electricity generation. However, nuclear energy is associated with a number of concerns, in particular regarding nuclear safety, spent fuel, waste management, transboundary consequences and decommissioning. The choice of nuclear energy rests with countries. Some countries have been using nuclear energy technologies safely and see no inordinate concern in using and developing additional technology for properly managing and controlling spent fuel and other nuclear materials, and some of these countries consider that the use of nuclear energy should be increased. From their perspective, nuclear power is a sustainable energy source with both economical and environmental advantages. In their view, the removal of the option of nuclear power would remove an important element of flexibility and diversity in energy supply. For those countries that choose nuclear energy, the challenge lies in ensuring environmentally sound, socially acceptable and cost-effective solutions and in addressing nuclear safety and spent fuel and waste management as well as public concerns on these issues. Many countries seek the promotion of international cooperation in the peaceful use of nuclear energy. Some other countries have decided to phase out nuclear energy from their energy supply mix. Other countries, including several developed countries as well as small island developing States, do not use nuclear energy and do not consider nuclear energy as an appropriate or acceptable source of energy. Many of these countries are of the view that nuclear energy is not compatible with the objectives of sustainable development, and that risks related to safety, waste management and transport and stranded costs remain unsolved. Some are also of the opinion that the use of nuclear energy in

general should be phased out as soon as practically possible.

Recommendations

21. Governments, taking into account their national circumstances, are encouraged to:

(a) Support their national efforts, including research, and international cooperation as an effective tool in addressing the issues of nuclear safety and spent fuel and waste management;

(b) Strengthen independent national regulatory agencies and promote international cooperation in nuclear safety;

(c) Promote a high level of nuclear safety;

(d) Improve the transparency of nuclear safety-related decisions, inter alia, through public participation, where appropriate;

(e) Promote public education and participation as well as capacity-building of human resources, in the areas of nuclear energy and waste management;

(f) Further develop technological solutions for long-lived radioactive waste;

(g) Address the safety of their nuclear energy installations, as deemed appropriate, after assessment by national regulatory authorities, including consideration of the option of phasing out and closing, as appropriate, such installations;

(h) Recalling paragraph 8 of the Governing Council of the International Atomic Energy Agency (IAEA) resolution GC (44)/RES/17 and taking into account the very serious potential for environment and human health impacts of radioactive wastes, make efforts to examine and further improve measures and internationally agreed regulations regarding safety, while stressing the importance of having effective liability mechanisms in place, relevant to international maritime transportation and other transboundary movement of radioactive material, radioactive waste and spent fuel, including, inter alia, arrangements for prior notification and consultations done in accordance with relevant international instruments.

6. Rural Energy

Challenges

22. To implement the goal accepted by the international community to halve the proportion of people living on less than US$ 1 per day by 2015, access to affordable energy services is a prerequisite. Efforts at finding the most appropriate solution to the energy problems of rural areas are hampered by the enormity of the problem, the limited availability of resources and lack of appropriate technologies, the high investment cost and connection fees and insufficient attention to rural development in general. An effective strategy to address the energy needs of rural populations can be to promote the climbing of the energy ladder. This implies both improving ways of using biomass as well as moving from simple biomass fuels to the most convenient efficient form of energy appropriate to the task at hand, usually liquid or gaseous fuels for cooking and heating and electricity for most other uses.

Recommendations

23. Governments, taking into account their national circumstances, are encouraged to:

(a) Strengthen and, where appropriate, establish policies on energy for rural development, including, as appropriate, regulatory systems to promote access to energy in rural areas;

(b) Develop, where necessary, specific and targeted energy service delivery structures adapted to rural needs;

(c) Promote local energy enterprises as employment opportunities, enhance local private entrepreneurs and develop local dealers to sell/maintain equipment building on local retail networks and relationships;

(d) Take into consideration the health and safety concerns of women and children in rural energy programmes;

(e) Promote research and development of the rural energy situation in support of the achievement of international development priorities, particularly poverty eradication;

(f) Promote a sustainable use of biomass and, as appropriate, other renewable energies through improvement of current patterns of use, such as management of resources, more efficient use of fuelwood and new or improved products and technologies;

(g) Establish financial arrangements to make rural energy services affordable to the poor;

(h) Support local groups and/or non-governmental organizations in the promotion and delivery of newly developed environmentally sound technologies, including solar cooker technology;

(i) Develop and utilize indigenous energy sources and infrastructures for various local uses and promote rural community participation, including local Agenda 21 groups, with the support of the international community, in developing and utilizing renewable energy technologies to meet their daily energy needs to find simple and local solutions;

(j) Promote capacity-building in local societies and remove barriers in the implementation of policies for renewable energy development in rural areas;

(k) Promote efforts to address the disproportionate burdens experienced by women in rural areas, including carrying loads of fuelwood over long distances and suffering adverse health effects from prolonged exposure to open fires.

7. Energy and Transport

Challenges

24. The transport sector is a major energy consuming sector and the sector for which energy consumption is projected to grow at the highest rate. The challenge is to promote an integrated approach to developing transport systems for sustainable development.

Recommendations

25. Governments, taking into account their national circumstances, are encouraged to:

(a) Manage transportation demand;

(b) Implement better transportation practices, including planning, in both urban and rural contexts, particularly towards public transportation systems and rail or water based freight transport;

(c) Increase fuel efficiency for different transportation modes;

(d) Promote the use of cleaner fuels and transport equipment and assist with the implementation of the recommendations of the General Assembly at its nineteenth special session on the progressive phasing out of the use of lead in gasoline, inter alia, by making available information, technical assistance, capacity-building and funding to developing countries, including the time-bound transfer of technology;

(e) Integrate transport policy in other sustainable development policies.

D. Overarching Issues

1. Research and Development

26. The enhancement of research and development at the national, regional and international levels of advanced and cleaner fossil fuel technologies, more efficient energy technologies and renewable energy technologies is important for achieving energy for sustainable development for all. Governments are encouraged to develop policies and incentives and to act as a catalyst to foster private sector investment in this field. Increased energy research should also come from public and private investments or through joint public and private partnerships and/or through international and regional cooperation.

2. Capacity-Building

27. Lack of local capacity is a major obstacle to the expansion of energy services in the developing world. It is important that institutions, infrastructures and human resources in developing countries be strengthened and that technological leadership in developing countries as well as in countries with economies in transition, with special efforts for least developed countries and small island developing States, be enhanced through international public and private cooperation that supports sustainable development objectives. Developed countries, development banks, the United Nations Development Programme (UNDP) and other relevant agencies, including the regional commissions and bilateral development agencies, should focus on capacity-building in development cooperation. A substantially replenished Global Environment Facility (GEF) would, among other things, continue to provide support, within its mandate, for capacity-building and technology transfer to developing countries to advance energy for sustainable development. International financial institutions should, through their lending policies, support capacity-building and technology transfer as well as efforts to identify local needs.

3. Technology Transfer

28. In order to promote energy for sustainable development there is a need for favourable access to and transfer of environmentally sound technologies, in particular to developing countries, through supportive measures that promote technology cooperation and that should enable the transfer of necessary technological know-how and the building up of economic, technical and managerial capabilities for the efficient use and further development of transferred technology. Technology cooperation involves joint efforts by enterprises and Governments, both suppliers of technology and its recipients. Therefore, such cooperation entails an iterative process, involving government, the private sector and research and development facilities, to ensure the best possible results from transfer of technology. Successful long-term partnerships in technology cooperation necessarily require continuing systematic training and capacity-building at all levels over an extended period of time.

4. Information-Sharing and Dissemination

29. Information- and knowledge-sharing on technologies and policies facilitate efforts to achieve energy for sustainable development. Relevant information could direct decision makers to suitable policy and energy supply options. Very often, the lack of such information and knowledge precludes countries from adopting new approaches in energy planning and technology applications. Internet-based information could assist such an exchange of information. Developing countries require the assistance of developed countries in the area of information technology.

5. Mobilization of Financial Resources

30. Financial resources and mechanisms play a key role in the implementation of Agenda 21. In general, the financing for the implementation of Agenda 21 will come from a country's own public and private sectors. For developing countries, ODA is an important source of external funding and new and additional funding for sustainable development and energy for sustainable development and the implementation of Agenda 21 will be required. Hence all financial commitments of Agenda 21, particularly those contained in its chapter 33 and the provisions with regard to new and additional resources that are both adequate and predictable need to be urgently fulfilled. Renewed efforts are essential to ensure that all sources of funding contribute to economic growth, social development and environmental protection in the context of sustainable development and the implementation of Agenda 21. Many Governments have initiated reforms aimed at improving regulatory frameworks and institutional set-ups in order to attract private sector funding. Specific policies have been introduced to induce the flow of investment capital for energy technology for sustainable development. While more sustainable technologies often have lower operating costs than competing solutions, they sometimes require greater initial investments. Particular attention should therefore be paid to the difficulties of financing these essential infrastructure investments in developing countries. Financing from GEF, within its mandate, could also be considered in this context.

6. Making Markets Work Effectively for Sustainable Development

31. Policies to reduce market distortions would promote energy systems compatible with sustainable development through the use of improved market signals and by removing market distortions, including restructuring taxation and phasing out of harmful subsidies, where they exist, to reflect their environmental impacts. Such policies should take fully into account the specific needs and conditions of developing countries, with the aim of minimizing the possible adverse impacts on their development. Governments are encouraged to improve the functioning of national energy markets in such a way that they support sustainable development, overcome market barriers and improve accessibility, taking fully into account that such policies should be decided by each country, and that its own characteristics and capabilities and different levels of development should be considered, especially as reflected in national sustainable development strategies, where they exist.

7. Multi-Stakeholder Approach and Public Participation

32. Energy solutions that are compatible with sustainable development require the participation of all stakeholders and the involvement of the public at large. The capacity of community-based organizations and institutions, including women's groups, to facilitate participatory approaches to energy for sustainable development should be strengthened, taking into account principle 10 of the Rio

Declaration on Environment and Development with full recognition of principles 5, 7 and 11.

E. Regional Cooperation

33. The Commission notes with appreciation the efforts made at the regional level and by interest groups to discuss the key issues and formulate regional positions and programmes of action to promote energy for sustainable development. It welcomes the statements that have resulted from these deliberations, recognizing that they provide valuable inputs to the work of the Commission. Moreover, it encourages the Governments in these regional deliberations to actively promote the implementation of the resulting programmes of action. In particular, the Commission recognized the value of regional cooperation in achieving economies of scale in energy services for sustainable development.

34. From these statements, the Commission recommends implementation of the following regional and subregional endeavours that may require subregional, regional, and international support:

(a) Strengthening national and regional energy institutions or arrangements for enhancing regional and international cooperation on energy for sustainable development, in particular to assist developing countries in their domestic efforts to provide modern energy services to all sections of their populations by:

(i) Conducting in depth studies to promote sustainable development in the energy sector in the region, including the social, economic and environmental situation of the region and energy alternatives that support sustainable development;

(ii) Promoting training and exchange of experience and regarding energy efficiency, renewable energy and advanced fossil-fuel technologies and lessons learned;

(iii) Strengthening regional networks of centres of excellence for the exchange of information and experience in the research, development and application of energy efficiency technologies, advanced fossil fuel and renewable energy;

(iv) Strengthening and, where appropriate, establishing regional information and dissemination capabilities to provide information to the energy service industry on market opportunities and energy infrastructure and information to consumers on the benefits of energy efficiency measures;

(b) Promoting, at the regional level, rural electrification projects, including, renewable energy technologies, and supporting local efforts to provide energy supplies to their basic infrastructures, as well as integrating energy policies into overall rural development strategies, with emphasis on income-generation, taking into account national circumstances;

(c) Strengthening and facilitating, as appropriate, regional cooperation arrangements for promoting cross-border energy trade, including the interconnection of electricity grids and oil and natural gas pipelines;

(d) Strengthening and, where appropriate, facilitating dialogue forums among regional, national and international producers and consumers of energy; and to that effect, the Commission complements the work of existing international energy forums;

(e) Promoting, where appropriate, cooperation among the concerned countries of the region and with the support of the international organizations to improve development and production of hydro-carbon fields through integrated cost reduction, enhanced operational efficiency, and application of advanced and more environmentally sound technology;

(f) Fostering regional cooperation when undertaking research, development and demonstration of energy efficiency, renewable energy and advanced fossil fuel technologies;

(g) Encouraging regional cooperation for capacity-building, including South-South cooperation.

F. International Cooperation

35. The Commission recognizes the critical role that international cooperation, including regional cooperation, can play in assisting countries, particularly developing countries, in their efforts to achieve the goals of sustainable development. In particular, international cooperation can be very effective in capacity-building, education, technology transfer, information-sharing, research and development, and the mobilization of resources, including financial resources, taking into account the above-mentioned key issues and energy sources.

36. The Commission recommends, in particular, international cooperation in the following reas:

1. Take concrete measures to maximize existing and to explore ways to increase financial resources and create innovative financing solutions to support energy for sustainable development, including through debt relief and, where possible, debt cancellation, facilitating foreign investment, action to reverse the downward trend in ODA, and strive to fulfil the commitments undertaken to reach the accepted United Nations target of 0.7 per cent of gross national product (GNP) as soon as possible, the incorporation of energy for sustainable development considerations in bilateral and multilateral development cooperation programmes and in development cooperation programme activities of the international financial institutions and general lending policies, including through addressing the development of energy policy in national poverty eradication policies, where they exist. In this context, consideration should also be given to how, inter alia, ODA can be used to leverage private funds for the development of energy solutions that are compatible with sustainable development, bearing in mind that for developing countries ODA is a main source of external funding.
2. Continuing the dialogue on issues relating to energy for sustainable development within the World Summit on Sustainable Development process, in accordance with General Assembly resolution 55/199.
3. Promoting international public-private partnership cooperation programmes for promoting affordable, energy efficient and advanced fossil fuel and renewable energy technologies.
4. Promote networking between centres of excellence on energy for sustainable development by linking competent centres on energy technologies for sustainable development that could support and promote efforts at capacity-building and technology transfer activities, as well as serve as information clearing houses.
5. Making available grants and loans to developing countries on favourable terms that would permit sharing the cost of the development of energy infrastructure, including rural and remote energy infrastructure, with relevant international lending institutions and private sector investments.
6. Exploring the scope of the use of existing international mechanisms for financing infrastructure development to identify risks and ensure they are managed on a transparent basis, with an effective equitable partnership between investors and host countries, since developing countries do not have institutional structures that are adequately prepared to deal with the scale of commercial risks associated with major energy investments.
7. Supporting the international endeavours to promote equal access and opportunities for women in relation to energy, including credit facilities and involvement in energy policy decision-making processes.

Recommendation of the Council on Environmentally Favourable Energy Options and their Implementation

20 June 1985 – C(85)102

http://webdomino1.oecd.org/horizontal/oecdacts.nsf/Display/994A6A24F7604446C1256E5E00837847?OpenDocument

THE COUNCIL,

Having regard to Article 5 b) of the Convention on the Organisation for Economic Co-operation and Development of 14th December 1960;

Having regard to the Recommendation of the Council of 14th November 1974 on Energy and the Environment [C(74)222] and to the Recommendation of the Council of 12th October 1976, concerning the Reduction of Environmental Impacts from Energy Production and Use [C(76)162(Final)];

Recognising the increasing importance attributed to environmental quality by both governments and the public;

Considering that energy availability and environmental quality are both central factors for economic development and the quality of life, and that these objectives often need to be reconciled in order to find optimum solutions for industrialised society;

Considering that improvement of the efficiency of energy use is already a major contributor to energy, environmental and economic goals, and noting the on-going work of the International Energy Agency on policies to improve energy efficiency and on other work on energy and environment;

Considering that the identification and implementation of environmentally favourable energy options can contribute significantly to both energy and environmental objectives as well as yielding a variety of other economic and social benefits;

Recognising the differences among Member countries with regard to various factors such as the actual state of pollution, the degree of implementation of environmental measures, and the institutional aspects of energy and environmental policy formulation;

On the proposal of the Environment Committee;

I. RECOMMENDS that Member countries, in the context of their long-term environmental and energy policies, identify and promote environmentally favourable energy options consistent with broader social and economic goals by:

a) Achieving closer institutional links between energy and environmental policymaking from the earliest stages and throughout the policy process;

b) Developing further and applying methods of energy and environmental analysis;

c) Encouraging the identification of the net environmental benefits of policies which promote increased energy efficiency;

d) Identifying and reducing barriers to the implementation of environmentally favourable energy options;

e) Allowing the various costs of adequate environmental protection at the different stages of energy production, transformation and use to be reflected in the prices of all forms of energy;

f) Improving the clarity, efficiency and predictability of regulations;

g) Identifying and taking into account, at an early stage of decision-making, the environmental implications of energy-related measures and strategies as well as the energy implications of environmental measures and strategies;

h) Referring to the elements of environmentally favourable energy options, set out below.

II. INSTRUCTS the Environment Committee:

a) To continue to develop its present work on environmentally favourable energy options, including the development of new data and analytical capabilities;

b) To provide for exchange of information on technical and non-technical means of promoting Environmentally Favourable Energy Options;

c) To continue its co-operation with the International Energy Agency in implementing this Recommendation and to take into account on-going work in other international organisations;

d) To assess Member countries' progress in implementing this Recommendation.

III. REQUESTS the International Energy Agency to take this Recommendation into account and to continue its co-operation with the Environment Committee in its work in this field.

ELEMENTS OF ENVIRONMENTALLY FAVOURABLE ENERGY OPTIONS

The following elements are indicative of the types of action which could be undertaken by Member countries, depending on their specific circumstances, in order to implement this Recommendation:

a) Enhanced institutional linking

1. Co-operation between those responsible for energy planning, including long-term supply and demand forecasting, and those responsible for assessing environmental impacts;

2. Establishment of environmental policy "early warning systems" that would alert energy policymakers to issues that are at an early stage of identification and understanding, but that might arouse serious concern in a few years time when these issues are better understood;

3. Development of joint promotional initiatives by energy and environmental agencies to increase public acceptance of measures that further energy and environment objectives, e.g. improving building heating and cooling efficiencies;

4. Closer co-operation in government sponsored research and development on environmental control technologies, environmentally favourable conversion technologies and system impact assessment techniques;

5. Closer consultations between government departments responsible for both energy and environment, and industry involved in energy investments and pollution control equipment manufacturing.

b) Better analytical and data capabilities

1. Improved energy/environment data bases, including energy efficiency and environmental impact indicators;

2. Guidelines and techniques to increase the reliability and comparability of estimates of environmental costs and benefits related to energy;

3. Development of better techniques to compare differing environmental risks of energy technologies;

4. Co-operation among concerned agencies towards a better understanding of the relationships linking economic growth, energy systems and the environment.

c) Promotion of more efficient use of energy from the environmental perspective

1. Encouragement for energy policies designed to achieve investment by industry and individual consumers in more energy-efficient buildings, vehicles and other equipment, and better energy management;

2. Identification and quantification of environmental benefits from improved efficiency of energy use;

3. Better information to consumers on these environmental benefits;

4. Encouragement of co-operation between energy and environmental institutions to identify energy initiatives offering simultaneous high environmental gains and energy savings, and to attempt to quantify the benefits to both energy and environment.

d) Reduction of barriers to environmentally favourable energy options

1. Co-operation between governments to reduce technological and economic barriers, and help to develop, improve and bring onstream new environmentally favourable energy technologies;

2. Improved transparency relating to the cost of energy-using equipment (e.g. specification of running costs) and environmental performance

(e.g. specific pollutant emissions) to enable consumers to make informed and environmentally sensitive decisions;

3. Identification and reduction of institutional barriers;

4. Improvement of public awareness concerning environmentally favourable energy options, and of ability to apply these options in their use of energy, taking into account both energy and environmental benefits.

e) Integration of environmental costs in energy pricing and incentives

1. Identification of energy pricing policies or practices which are not in accordance with the Polluter Pays Principle;

2. Incentives (e.g. tax credits, grants), where appropriate, to undertake environmentally favourable energy investments, which reflect not only energy savings but also environmental benefits.

f) Improved regulations

1. Sufficient flexibility in regulatory schemes to encourage research and innovation of environmentally favourable and economically efficient energy options;

2. Better integration of regulatory procedures at national, regional and local levels;

3. Advance notice of changes in environmental regulations as far as possible, and adequate lead-time to comply with regulations;

4. Consultations at an early stage among concerned parties regarding environmental problems which may require future regulatory changes.

Recommendation of the Council on Improving the Environmental Performance of Public Procurement

23 January 2002 – C(2002)3

http://webdomino1.oecd.org/horizontal/oecdacts.nsf/Display/489622C240A88C27C1256E5F00005189?OpenDocument

THE COUNCIL,

Having regard to Article 5 b) of the Convention on the Organisation for Economic Co-operation and Development of 14th December 1960;

Having regard to Recommendation of the Council on Improving the Environmental Performance of Government [C(96)39/FINAL];

Having regard to the Resolution of the Council on Improving the Environmental Performance of the Organisation for Economic Co-operation and Development [C(96)40/FINAL];

Having regard to the support for the use of green public procurement practices as expressed in the OECD *Environmental Strategies for the First Decade of the 21st Century*, which was adopted by OECD Environment Ministers and endorsed by the OECD Council at Ministerial level in May 2001;

Recognising the importance of governments in demonstrating leadership in progressing toward sustainable development;

Mindful of the commitments made by Member countries in 1992 at the UN Conference on Environment and Development to review and improve government procurement policies in order to move towards more sustainable patterns of consumption and production;

Noting that as a means to improve the environmental performance of public procurement, public authorities in a number of Member countries apply policies and practices which seek to encourage procurement officers to purchase products and services which are less environmentally-damaging (hereafter "greener public purchasing policies");

Noting that greener public purchasing policies constitute a significant element of product-related environmental policies adopted by some Member countries;

Noting that the scale of government purchases is such that greener public purchasing policies can contribute to the development and diffusion of products and services which are less environmentally-damaging;

Noting that greener public purchasing policies can result in more cost-effective procurement practices;

Recognising the need to preserve market openness and to apply the principles of transparent and competitive processes and non-discrimination among potential suppliers;

Considering that measures to improve the environmental performance of public procurement should not constitute unnecessary obstacles to international trade;

Considering that the use of relevant international standards, as well as equivalence and mutual recognition arrangements, could result in enhanced co-ordination amongst Member countries' greener public purchasing policies, and thus could have beneficial environmental and economic effects;

Recognising that greener public purchasing policies depend for their efficiency and effectiveness upon: the use of appropriate methods to account for the environmental costs of products and services including, where appropriate, environmental impacts throughout the lifecycle; co-ordination between procurement, budget, environment and other relevant government officials; co-ordination with other environmental policy measures such as economic instruments (e.g. tradable permits and environmental taxes), performance standards, and information-based measures (e.g. demonstration projects and eco-labels); and, the prevention of false or misleading claims of environmental quality;

Conscious of the need for Member countries to tailor implementation strategies for greener public purchasing policies to fit their individual institutional, social, economic and environmental needs and priorities;

On the proposal of the Environmental Policy Committee:

I. RECOMMENDS that Member countries take greater account of environmental considerations in public procurement of products and services (including, but not limited to, consumables, capital goods, infrastructure, construction and public works), in order to improve the environmental performance of public procurement, and thereby promote continuous improvement in the environmental performance of products and services.

II. RECOMMENDS to this effect that Member countries should:

i) develop greener public purchasing policies in ways which are consistent with Member countries' competition and other relevant national policies, and with their international obligations and commitments;

ii) take the following concrete steps to ensure the incorporation of environmental criteria into public procurement of products and services including, where appropriate, environmental impacts throughout the lifecycle, while ensuring that transparency, non-discrimination and competition are preserved:

(a) provide the appropriate policy framework to incorporate environmental criteria into public procurement of products and services, along with price and performance criteria;

(b) introduce financial, budgeting, and accounting measures to ensure that public procurement policies and practices consider the environmental costs of products and services;

(c) provide information, training and technical assistance to officials involved in the public procurement and use chain, including those who set the performance criteria of products and services, those who are responsible for procurement, and those who use the products and services;

(d) make information and tools that facilitate greener public purchasing available to all levels of government;

(e) disseminate the information needed to facilitate and encourage greener public purchasing decisions, as well as the results and benefits derived from their adoption;

(f) establish procedures for the identification of products and services which meet the objectives of greener public purchasing policies;

(g) encourage the development of indicators to measure and monitor progress made in greener public purchasing;

(h) assess and evaluate greener public purchasing policies in order to ensure that they are economically efficient and environmentally effective.

III. INVITES the Environment Policy Committee to:

i) support efforts by Member countries to develop and apply efficient and effective greener public purchasing policies, for example through the collection and dissemination of information on "best practices" and the development of appropriate indicators;

ii) monitor, assess and report to the Council in 2005 on Member countries' implementation of this Recommendation and on any barriers to further progress.

Recommendation of the Council on Traffic Limitation and Low-Cost Improvement of the Urban Environment

14 November 1974 – C(74)218

http://webdomino1.oecd.org/horizontal/oecdacts.nsf/Display/9189E611B9E61DEDC1256E5F00001113?OpenDocument

THE COUNCIL,

Having regard to Article 5 b) of the Convention on the Organisation for Economic Co-operation and Development of 14th December 1960;

Having regard to the Recommendation of the Council of 26th May 1972 on Guiding Principles concerning International Economic Aspects of Environmental Policies [C(72)128];

Considering that urban areas are the home of a vast and ever growing proportion of Member countries' populations;

Considering that air pollution, noise, congestion and accidents which result from motorised traffic severely hinder attempts to improve the quality of urban life;

Considering that the need to lessen dependence on private automobiles is reinforced by the necessity to conserve energy resources;

Considering that certain measures to reduce the adverse effects of traffic can be implemented on a relatively short time scale and do not necessarily require large capital investment;

Considering that solutions to urban environmental problems cannot be found on a piecemeal basis but require a comprehensive urban policy approach;

On the proposal of the Environment Committee;

I. RECOMENDS that Member countries:

1. Seek to strike a better balance between private and public transportation by encouraging local authorities and other responsible bodies, particularly in congested cities, to expand and improve the quality of transportation services, and to encourage the use of means of transport other than private automobiles whenever these alternative means are or can be made available;

2. Include in the above efforts, traffic management and other measures which can be implemented at relatively low cost – such as bus priority measures, provision of bicycle-ways, car pooling, traffic signal systems, parking control and establishment of car-free areas;

3. Complement the above policies with low-cost measures to improve the quality of the local environment, for example through the creation of small parks and open spaces, pedestrian areas, and conservation of the urban landscape;

4. Support and encourage further experimental projects aimed at demonstrating the feasibility and financial, environmental and urban development implications of the measures referred to above and co-operate in the international dissemination of this experience;

5. In the longer run, seek to reduce the need for transportation through comprehensive land use and transportation planning and through other measures affecting the patterns of human activities.

II. INSTRUCTS the Environment Committee:

1. To continue its examination of national policies and programmes for traffic limitation and its assessments of their costs and effectiveness with emphasis on measures which can be implemented at relatively low cost;

2. To assess the action taken pursuant to this Recommendation and report thereon to the Council;

3. To carry out this work in conjunction with other appropriate bodies of the Organisation and with the European Conference of Ministers of Transport.

European Energy Charter Conference: Final Act, Energy Charter Treaty, Decisions and Energy Charter Protocol on Energy Efficiency and Related Environmental Aspects

The Hague, 17 December 1991

33 I.L.M.360 (1995)

http://www.encharter.org/upload/1/TreatyBook-en.pdf

PREAMBLE

The Contracting Parties to this Treaty,

Having regard to the Charter of Paris for a New Europe signed on 21 November 1990;

Having regard to the European Energy Charter adopted in the Concluding Document of the Hague Conference on the European Energy Charter signed at The Hague on 17 December 1991;

Recalling that all signatories to the Concluding Document of the Hague Conference undertook to pursue the objectives and principles of the European Energy Charter and implement and broaden their co-operation as soon as possible by negotiating in good faith an Energy Charter Treaty and Protocols, and desiring to place the commitments contained in that Charter on a secure and binding international legal basis;

Desiring also to establish the structural framework required to implement the principles enunciated in the European Energy Charter;

Wishing to implement the basic concept of the European Energy Charter initiative which is to catalyse economic growth by means of measures to liberalize investment and trade in energy;

Affirming that Contracting Parties attach the utmost importance to the effective implementation of full national treatment and most favoured nation treatment, and that these commitments will be applied to the Making of Investments pursuant to a supplementary treaty;

Having regard to the objective of progressive liberalization of international trade and to the principle of avoidance of discrimination in international trade as enunciated in the General Agreement on Tariffs and Trade and its Related Instruments and as otherwise provided for in this Treaty;

Determined progressively to remove technical, administrative and other barriers to trade in Energy Materials and Products and related equipment, technologies and services;

Looking to the eventual membership in the General Agreement on Tariffs and Trade of those Contracting Parties which are not currently parties thereto and concerned to provide interim trade arrangements which will assist those Contracting Parties and not impede their preparation for such membership;

Mindful of the rights and obligations of certain Contracting Parties which are also parties to the General Agreement on Tariffs and Trade and its Related Instruments;

Having regard to competition rules concerning mergers, monopolies, anti-competitive practices and abuse of dominant position;

Having regard also to the Treaty on the Non-Proliferation of Nuclear Weapons, the Nuclear Suppliers Guidelines and other international nuclear non-proliferation obligations or understandings;

Recognizing the necessity for the most efficient exploration, production, conversion, storage, transport, distribution and use of energy;

Recalling the United Nations Framework Convention on Climate Change, the Convention on Long-Range Transboundary Air Pollution and its protocols, and other international environmental agreements with energy-related aspects; and

Recognizing the increasingly urgent need for measures to protect the environment, including the decommissioning of energy installations and waste disposal, and for internationally-agreed objectives and criteria for these purposes,

HAVE AGREED AS FOLLOWS:

PART I DEFINITIONS AND PURPOSE

ARTICLE 1 DEFINITIONS

As used in this Treaty:

(1) "Charter" means the European Energy Charter adopted in the Concluding Document of the Hague Conference on the European Energy Charter signed at The Hague on 17 December 1991; signature of the Concluding Document is considered to be signature of the Charter.

(2) "Contracting Party" means a state or Regional Economic Integration Organization which has consented to be bound by this Treaty and for which the Treaty is in force.

(3) "Regional Economic Integration Organization" means an organization constituted by states to which they have transferred competence over certain matters a number of which are governed by this Treaty, including the authority to take decisions binding on them in respect of those matters.

(4) "Energy Materials and Products", based on the Harmonized System of the Customs Co-operation Council and the Combined Nomenclature of the European Communities, means the items included in Annex EM.

(5) "Economic Activity in the Energy Sector" means an economic activity concerning the exploration, extraction, refining, production, storage, land transport, transmission, distribution, trade, marketing, or sale of Energy Materials and Products except those included in Annex NI, or concerning the distribution of heat to multiple premises.

(6) "Investment" means every kind of asset, owned or controlled directly or indirectly by an Investor and includes:

(a) tangible and intangible, and movable and immovable, property, and any property rights such as leases, mortgages, liens, and pledges;

(b) a company or business enterprise, or shares, stock, or other forms of equity participation in a company or business enterprise, and bonds and other debt of a company or business enterprise;

(c) claims to money and claims to performance pursuant to contract having an economic value and associated with an Investment;

(d) Intellectual Property;

(e) Returns;

(f) any right conferred by law or contract or by virtue of any licences and permits granted pursuant to law to undertake any Economic Activity in the Energy Sector.

A change in the form in which assets are invested does not affect their character as investments and the term "Investment" includes all investments, whether existing at or made after the later of the date of entry into force of this Treaty for the Contracting Party of the Investor making the investment and that for the Contracting Party in the Area of which the investment is made (hereinafter referred to as the "Effective Date") provided that the Treaty shall only apply to matters affecting such investments after the Effective Date.

"Investment" refers to any investment associated with an Economic Activity in the Energy Sector and to investments or classes of investments designated by a Contracting Party in its Area as "Charter efficiency projects" and so notified to the Secretariat.

(7) "Investor" means:

(a) with respect to a Contracting Party:

(i) a natural person having the citizenship or nationality of or who is permanently residing in that Contracting Party in accordance with its applicable law;

(ii) a company or other organization organized in accordance with the law applicable in that Contracting Party;

(b) with respect to a "third state", a natural person, company or other organization which fulfils, mutatis mutandis, the conditions specified in subparagraph (a) for a Contracting Party.

(8) "Make Investments" or "Making of Investments" means establishing new Investments, acquiring all or part of existing Investments or moving into different fields of Investment activity.

(9) "Returns" means the amounts derived from or associated with an Investment, irrespective of the form in which they are paid, including profits, dividends, interest, capital gains, royalty payments, management, technical assistance or other fees and payments in kind.

(10) "Area" means with respect to a state that is a Contracting Party:

(a) the territory under its sovereignty, it being understood that territory includes land, internal waters and the territorial sea; and

(b) subject to and in accordance with the international law of the sea: the sea, sea-bed and its subsoil with regard to which that Contracting Party exercises sovereign rights and jurisdiction.

With respect to a Regional Economic Integration Organization which is a Contracting Party, Area means the Areas of the member states of such Organization, under the provisions contained in the agreement establishing that Organization.

(11) (a) "GATT" means "GATT 1947" or "GATT 1994", or both of them where both are applicable.

(b) "GATT 1947" means the General Agreement on Tariffs and Trade, dated 30 October 1947, annexed to the Final Act Adopted at the Conclusion of the Second Session of the Preparatory Committee of the United Nations Conference on Trade and Employment, as subsequently rectified, amended or modified.

(c) "GATT 1994" means the General Agreement on Tariffs and Trade as specified in Annex 1A of the Agreement Establishing the World Trade Organization, as subsequently rectified, amended or modified.

A party to the Agreement Establishing the World Trade Organization is considered to be a party to GATT 1994.

(d) "Related Instruments" means, as appropriate:

(i) agreements, arrangements or other legal instruments, including decisions, declarations and understandings, concluded under the auspices of GATT 1947 as subsequently rectified, amended or modified; or

(ii) the Agreement Establishing the World Trade Organization including its Annex 1 (except GATT 1994), its Annexes 2, 3 and 4, and the decisions, declarations and understandings related thereto, as subsequently rectified, amended or modified.

(12) "Intellectual Property" includes copyrights and related rights, trademarks, geographical indications, industrial designs, patents, layout designs of integrated circuits and the protection of undisclosed information.

(13) (a) "Energy Charter Protocol" or "Protocol" means a treaty, the negotiation of which is authorized and the text of which is adopted by the Charter Conference, which is entered into by two or more Contracting Parties in order to complement, supplement, extend or amplify the provisions of this Treaty with respect to any specific sector or category of activity within the scope of this Treaty, or to areas of co-operation pursuant to Title III of the Charter.

(b) "Energy Charter Declaration" or "Declaration" means a non-binding instrument, the negotiation of which is authorized and the text of which is approved by the Charter Conference, which is entered into by two or more Contracting Parties to complement or supplement the provisions of this Treaty.

(14) "Freely Convertible Currency" means a currency which is widely traded in international foreign exchange markets and widely used in international transactions.

ARTICLE 2 PURPOSE OF THE TREATY

This Treaty establishes a legal framework in order to promote long-term co-operation in the energy field, based on complementarities and mutual benefits, in accordance with the objectives and principles of the Charter.

PART II COMMERCE

ARTICLE 3 INTERNATIONAL MARKETS

The Contracting Parties shall work to promote access to international markets on commercial terms, and generally to develop an open and competitive market, for Energy Materials and Products.

ARTICLE 4 NON-DEROGATION FROM GATT AND RELATED INSTRUMENTS

Nothing in this Treaty shall derogate, as between particular Contracting Parties which are parties to the GATT, from the provisions of the GATT and Related Instruments as they are applied between those Contracting Parties.

ARTICLE 5 TRADE-RELATED INVESTMENT MEASURES

(1) A Contracting Party shall not apply any trade-related investment measure that is inconsistent with the provisions of article III or XI of the GATT; this shall be without prejudice to the Contracting Party's rights and obligations under the GATT and Related Instruments and Article 29.

(2) Such measures include any investment measure which is mandatory or enforceable under domestic law or under any administrative ruling, or compliance with which is necessary to obtain an advantage, and which requires:

(a) the purchase or use by an enterprise of products of domestic origin or from any domestic source, whether specified in terms of particular products, in terms of volume or value of products, or in terms of a proportion of volume or value of its local production; or

(b) that an enterprise's purchase or use of imported products be limited to an amount related to the volume or value of local products that it exports; or which restricts:

(c) the importation by an enterprise of products used in or related to its local production, generally or to an amount related to the volume or value of local production that it exports;

(d) the importation by an enterprise of products used in or related to its local production by restricting its access to foreign exchange to an amount related to the foreign exchange inflows attributable to the enterprise; or

(e) the exportation or sale for export by an enterprise of products, whether specified in terms of particular products, in terms of volume or value of products, or in terms of a proportion of volume or value of its local production.

(3) Nothing in paragraph (1) shall be construed to prevent a Contracting Party from applying the trade-related investment measures described in subparagraphs (2)(a) and (c) as a condition of eligibility for export promotion, foreign aid, government procurement or preferential tariff or quota programmes.

(4) Notwithstanding paragraph (1), a Contracting Party may temporarily continue to maintain trade-related investment measures which were in effect more than 180 days before its signature of this Treaty, subject to the notification and phase-out provisions set out in Annex TRM.

ARTICLE 6 COMPETITION

(1) Each Contracting Party shall work to alleviate market distortions and barriers to competition in Economic Activity in the Energy Sector.

(2) Each Contracting Party shall ensure that within its jurisdiction it has and enforces such laws as are necessary and appropriate to address unilateral and concerted anti-competitive conduct in Economic Activity in the Energy Sector.

(3) Contracting Parties with experience in applying competition rules shall give full consideration to providing, upon request and within available resources, technical assistance on the development and implementation of competition rules to other Contracting Parties.

(4) Contracting Parties may co-operate in the enforcement of their competition rules by consulting and exchanging information.

(5) If a Contracting Party considers that any specified anti-competitive conduct carried out within the Area of another Contracting Party is adversely affecting an important interest relevant to the purposes identified in this Article, the Contracting Party may notify the other Contracting Party and may request that its competition authorities initiate appropriate enforcement action. The notifying Contracting Party shall include in such notification sufficient information to permit the notified Contracting Party to identify the anti-competitive conduct that is the subject of the notification and shall include an offer of such further information and co-operation as the notifying Contracting Party is able to provide. The notified Contracting Party or, as the case may be, the relevant competition authorities may consult with the competition authorities of

the notifying Contracting Party and shall accord full consideration to the request of the notifying Contracting Party in deciding whether or not to initiate enforcement action with respect to the alleged anti-competitive conduct identified in the notification. The notified Contracting Party shall inform the notifying Contracting Party of its decision or the decision of the relevant competition authorities and may if it wishes inform the notifying Contracting Party of the grounds for the decision. If enforcement action is initiated, the notified Contracting Party shall advise the notifying Contracting Party of its outcome and, to the extent possible, of any significant interim development.

(6) Nothing in this Article shall require the provision of information by a Contracting Party contrary to its laws regarding disclosure of information, confidentiality or business secrecy.

(7) The procedures set forth in paragraph (5) and Article 27(1) shall be the exclusive means within this Treaty of resolving any disputes that may arise over the implementation or interpretation of this Article.

ARTICLE 7 TRANSIT

(1) Each Contracting Party shall take the necessary measures to facilitate the Transit of Energy Materials and Products consistent with the principle of freedom of transit and without distinction as to the origin, destination or ownership of such Energy Materials and Products or discrimination as to pricing on the basis of such distinctions, and without imposing any unreasonable delays, restrictions or charges.

(2) Contracting Parties shall encourage relevant entities to co-operate in:

(a) modernising Energy Transport Facilities necessary to the Transit of Energy Materials and Products;

(b) the development and operation of Energy Transport Facilities serving the Areas of more than one Contracting Party;

(c) measures to mitigate the effects of interruptions in the supply of Energy Materials and Products;

(d) facilitating the interconnection of Energy Transport Facilities.

(3) Each Contracting Party undertakes that its provisions relating to transport of Energy Materials and Products and the use of Energy Transport Facilities shall treat Energy Materials and Products in Transit in no less favourable a manner than its provisions treat such materials and products originating in or destined for its own Area, unless an existing international agreement provides otherwise.

(4) In the event that Transit of Energy Materials and Products cannot be achieved on commercial terms by means of Energy Transport Facilities the Contracting Parties shall not place obstacles in the way of new capacity being established, except as may be otherwise provided in applicable legislation which is consistent with paragraph (1).

(5) A Contracting Party through whose Area Energy Materials and Products may transit shall not be obliged to

(a) permit the construction or modification of Energy Transport Facilities; or

(b) permit new or additional Transit through existing Energy Transport Facilities, which it demonstrates to the other Contracting Parties concerned would endanger the security or efficiency of its energy systems, including the security of supply.

Contracting Parties shall, subject to paragraphs (6) and (7), secure established flows of Energy Materials and Products to, from or between the Areas of other Contracting Parties.

(6) A Contracting Party through whose Area Energy Materials and Products transit shall not, in the event of a dispute over any matter arising from that Transit, interrupt or reduce, permit any entity subject to its control to interrupt or reduce, or require any entity subject to its jurisdiction to interrupt or reduce the existing flow of Energy Materials and Products prior to the conclusion of the dispute resolution procedures set out in paragraph (7), except where this is specifically provided for in a contract or other agreement governing such Transit or permitted in accordance with the conciliator's decision.

(7) The following provisions shall apply to a dispute described in paragraph (6), but only following the exhaustion of all relevant contractual or other dispute resolution remedies previously agreed between the Contracting Parties party to the dispute or between any entity referred to in paragraph (6)

and an entity of another Contracting Party party to the dispute:

(a) A Contracting Party party to the dispute may refer it to the Secretary-General by a notification summarizing the matters in dispute. The Secretary-General shall notify all Contracting Parties of any such referral.

(b) Within 30 days of receipt of such a notification, the Secretary-General, in consultation with the parties to the dispute and the other Contracting Parties concerned, shall appoint a conciliator. Such a conciliator shall have experience in the matters subject to dispute and shall not be a national or citizen of or permanently resident in a party to the dispute or one of the other Contracting Parties concerned.

(c) The conciliator shall seek the agreement of the parties to the dispute to a resolution thereof or upon a procedure to achieve such resolution. If within 90 days of his appointment he has failed to secure such agreement, he shall recommend a resolution to the dispute or a procedure to achieve such resolution and shall decide the interim tariffs and other terms and conditions to be observed for Transit from a date which he shall specify until the dispute is resolved.

(d) The Contracting Parties undertake to observe and ensure that the entities under their control or jurisdiction observe any interim decision under subparagraph (c) on tariffs, terms and conditions for 12 months following the conciliator's decision or until resolution of the dispute, whichever is earlier.

(e) Notwithstanding subparagraph (b) the Secretary-General may elect not to appoint a conciliator if in his judgement the dispute concerns Transit that is or has been the subject of the dispute resolution procedures set out in subparagraphs (a) to (d) and those proceedings have not resulted in a resolution of the dispute.

(f) The Charter Conference shall adopt standard provisions concerning the conduct of conciliation and the compensation of conciliators.

(8) Nothing in this Article shall derogate from a Contracting Party's rights and obligations under international law including customary international law, existing bilateral or multilateral agreements, including rules concerning submarine cables and pipelines.

(9) This Article shall not be so interpreted as to oblige any Contracting Party which does not have a certain type of Energy Transport Facilities used for Transit to take any measure under this Article with respect to that type of Energy Transport Facilities. Such a Contracting Party is, however, obliged to comply with paragraph (4).

(10) For the purposes of this Article:

(a) "Transit" means

(i) the carriage through the Area of a Contracting Party, or to or from port facilities in its Area for loading or unloading, of Energy Materials and Products originating in the Area of another state and destined for the Area of a third state, so long as either the other state or the third state is a Contracting Party; or

(ii) the carriage through the Area of a Contracting Party of Energy Materials and Products originating in the Area of another Contracting Party and destined for the Area of that other Contracting Party, unless the two Contracting Parties concerned decide otherwise and record their decision by a joint entry in Annex N. The two Contracting Parties may delete their listing in Annex N by delivering a joint written notification of their intentions to the Secretariat, which shall transmit that notification to all other Contracting Parties. The deletion shall take effect four weeks after such former notification.

(b) "Energy Transport Facilities" consist of high-pressure gas transmission pipelines, high-voltage electricity transmission grids and lines, crude oil transmission pipelines, coal slurry pipelines, oil product pipelines, and other fixed facilities specifically for handling Energy Materials and Products.

ARTICLE 8 TRANSFER OF TECHNOLOGY

(1) The Contracting Parties agree to promote access to and transfer of energy technology on a commercial and non-discriminatory basis to assist effective trade in Energy Materials and Products and Investment and to implement the objectives of the Charter subject to their laws and regulations, and to the protection of Intellectual Property rights.

(2) Accordingly, to the extent necessary to give effect to paragraph (1) the Contracting Parties shall eliminate existing and create no new obstacles to the transfer of technology in the field of Energy Materials and Products and related equipment and services, subject to non-proliferation and other international obligations.

ARTICLE 9 ACCESS TO CAPITAL

(1) The Contracting Parties acknowledge the importance of open capital markets in encouraging the flow of capital to finance trade in Energy Materials and Products and for the making of and assisting with regard to Investments in Economic Activity in the Energy Sector in the Areas of other Contracting Parties, particularly those with economies in transition. Each Contracting Party shall accordingly endeavour to promote conditions for access to its capital market by companies and nationals of other Contracting Parties, for the purpose of financing trade in Energy Materials and Products and for the purpose of Investment in Economic Activity in the Energy Sector in the Areas of those other Contracting Parties, on a basis no less favourable than that which it accords in like circumstances to its own companies and nationals or companies and nationals of any other Contracting Party or any third state, whichever is the most favourable.

(2) A Contracting Party may adopt and maintain programmes providing for access to public loans, grants, guarantees or insurance for facilitating trade or Investment abroad. It shall make such facilities available, consistent with the objectives, constraints and criteria of such programmes (including any objectives, constraints or criteria relating to the place of business of an applicant for any such facility or the place of delivery of goods or services supplied with the support of any such facility) for Investments in the Economic Activity in the Energy Sector of other Contracting Parties or for financing trade in Energy Materials and Products with other Contracting Parties.

(3) Contracting Parties shall, in implementing programmes in Economic Activity in the Energy Sector to improve the economic stability and investment climates of the Contracting Parties, seek as appropriate to encourage the operations and take advantage of the expertise of relevant international financial institutions.

(4) Nothing in this Article shall prevent:

(a) financial institutions from applying their own lending or underwriting practices based on market principles and prudential considerations; or

(b) a Contracting Party from taking measures:

(i) for prudential reasons, including the protection of Investors, consumers, depositors, policy-holders or persons to whom a fiduciary duty is owed by a financial service supplier; or

(ii) to ensure the integrity and stability of its financial system and capital markets.

PART III INVESTMENT PROMOTION AND PROTECTION

ARTICLE 10 PROMOTION, PROTECTION AND TREATMENT OF INVESTMENTS

(1) Each Contracting Party shall, in accordance with the provisions of this Treaty, encourage and create stable, equitable, favourable and transparent conditions for Investors of other Contracting Parties to make Investments in its Area. Such conditions shall include a commitment to accord at all times to Investments of Investors of other Contracting Parties fair and equitable treatment. Such Investments shall also enjoy the most constant protection and security and no Contracting Party shall in any way impair by unreasonable or discriminatory measures their management, maintenance, use, enjoyment or disposal. In no case shall such Investments be accorded treatment less favourable than that required by international law, including treaty obligations. Each Contracting Party shall observe any obligations it has entered into with an Investor or an Investment of an Investor of any other Contracting Party.

(2) Each Contracting Party shall endeavour to accord to Investors of other Contracting Parties, as regards the Making of Investments in its Area, the Treatment described in paragraph (3).

(3) For the purposes of this Article, "Treatment" means treatment accorded by a Contracting Party which is no less favourable than that which it accords to its own Investors or to Investors of any other

Contracting Party or any third state, whichever is the most favourable.

(4) A supplementary treaty shall, subject to conditions to be laid down therein, oblige each party thereto to accord to Investors of other parties, as regards the Making of Investments in its Area, the Treatment described in paragraph (3). That treaty shall be open for signature by the states and Regional Economic Integration Organizations which have signed or acceded to this Treaty. Negotiations towards the supplementary treaty shall commence not later than 1 January 1995, with a view to concluding it by 1 January 1998.

(5) Each Contracting Party shall, as regards the Making of Investments in its Area, endeavour to:

(a) limit to the minimum the exceptions to the Treatment described in paragraph (3);

(b) progressively remove existing restrictions affecting Investors of other Contracting Parties.

(6) (a) A Contracting Party may, as regards the Making of Investments in its Area, at any time declare voluntarily to the Charter Conference, through the Secretariat, its intention not to introduce new exceptions to the Treatment described in paragraph (3).

(b) A Contracting Party may, furthermore, at any time make a voluntary commitment to accord to Investors of other Contracting Parties, as regards the Making of Investments in some or all Economic Activities in the Energy Sector in its Area, the Treatment described in paragraph (3). Such commitments shall be notified to the Secretariat and listed in Annex VC and shall be binding under this Treaty.

(7) Each Contracting Party shall accord to Investments in its Area of Investors of other Contracting Parties, and their related activities including management, maintenance, use, enjoyment or disposal, treatment no less favourable than that which it accords to Investments of its own Investors or of the Investors of any other Contracting Party or any third state and their related activities including management, maintenance, use, enjoyment or disposal, whichever is the most favourable.

(8) The modalities of application of paragraph (7) in relation to programmes under which a Contracting Party provides grants or other financial assistance, or enters into contracts, for energy technology research and development, shall be reserved for the supplementary treaty described in paragraph (4). Each Contracting Party shall through the Secretariat keep the Charter Conference informed of the modalities it applies to the programmes described in this paragraph.

(9) Each state or Regional Economic Integration Organization which signs or accedes to this Treaty shall, on the date it signs the Treaty or deposits its instrument of accession, submit to the Secretariat a report summarizing all laws, regulations or other measures relevant to:

(a) exceptions to paragraph (2); or

(b) the programmes referred to in paragraph (8).

A Contracting Party shall keep its report up to date by promptly submitting amendments to the Secretariat. The Charter Conference shall review these reports periodically.

In respect of subparagraph (a) the report may designate parts of the energy sector in which a Contracting Party accords to Investors of other Contracting Parties the Treatment described in paragraph (3).

In respect of subparagraph (b) the review by the Charter Conference may consider the effects of such programmes on competition and Investments.

(10) Notwithstanding any other provision of this Article, the treatment described in paragraphs (3) and (7) shall not apply to the protection of Intellectual Property; instead, the treatment shall be as specified in the corresponding provisions of the applicable international agreements for the protection of Intellectual Property rights to which the respective Contracting Parties are parties.

(11) For the purposes of Article 26, the application by a Contracting Party of a trade-related investment measure as described in Article 5(1) and (2) to an Investment of an Investor of another Contracting Party existing at the time of such application shall, subject to Article 5(3) and (4), be considered a breach of an obligation of the former Contracting Party under this Part.

(12) Each Contracting Party shall ensure that its domestic law provides effective means for the assertion of claims and the enforcement of rights with

respect to Investments, investment agreements, and investment authorizations.

ARTICLE 11 KEY PERSONNEL

(1) A Contracting Party shall, subject to its laws and regulations relating to the entry, stay and work of natural persons, examine in good faith requests by Investors of another Contracting Party, and key personnel who are employed by such Investors or by Investments of such Investors, to enter and remain temporarily in its Area to engage in activities connected with the making or the development, management, maintenance, use, enjoyment or disposal of relevant Investments, including the provision of advice or key technical services.

(2) A Contracting Party shall permit Investors of another Contracting Party which have Investments in its Area, and Investments of such Investors, to employ any key person of the Investor's or the Investment's choice regardless of nationality and citizenship provided that such key person has been permitted to enter, stay and work in the Area of the former Contracting Party and that the employment concerned conforms to the terms, conditions and time limits of the permission granted to such key person.

ARTICLE 12 COMPENSATION FOR LOSSES

(1) Except where Article 13 applies, an Investor of any Contracting Party which suffers a loss with respect to any Investment in the Area of another Contracting Party owing to war or other armed conflict, state of national emergency, civil disturbance, or other similar event in that Area, shall be accorded by the latter Contracting Party, as regards restitution, indemnification, compensation or other settlement, treatment which is the most favourable of that which that Contracting Party accords to any other Investor, whether its own Investor, the Investor of any other Contracting Party, or the Investor of any third state.

(2) Without prejudice to paragraph (1), an Investor of a Contracting Party which, in any of the situations referred to in that paragraph, suffers a loss in the Area of another Contracting Party resulting from

(a) requisitioning of its Investment or part thereof by the latter's forces or authorities; or

(b) destruction of its Investment or part thereof by the latter's forces or authorities, which was not required by the necessity of the situation,

shall be accorded restitution or compensation which in either case shall be prompt, adequate and effective.

ARTICLE 13 EXPROPRIATION

(1) Investments of Investors of a Contracting Party in the Area of any other Contracting Party shall not be nationalized, expropriated or subjected to a measure or measures having effect equivalent to nationalization or expropriation (hereinafter referred to as "Expropriation") except where such Expropriation is:

(a) for a purpose which is in the public interest;

(b) not discriminatory;

(c) carried out under due process of law; and

(d) accompanied by the payment of prompt, adequate and effective compensation.

Such compensation shall amount to the fair market value of the Investment expropriated at the time immediately before the Expropriation or impending Expropriation became known in such a way as to affect the value of the Investment (hereinafter referred to as the "Valuation Date").

Such fair market value shall at the request of the Investor be expressed in a Freely Convertible Currency on the basis of the market rate of exchange existing for that currency on the Valuation Date. Compensation shall also include interest at a commercial rate established on a market basis from the date of Expropriation until the date of payment.

(2) The Investor affected shall have a right to prompt review, under the law of the Contracting Party making the Expropriation, by a judicial or other competent and independent authority of that Contracting Party, of its case, of the valuation of its Investment, and of the payment of compensation, in accordance with the principles set out in paragraph (1).

(3) For the avoidance of doubt, Expropriation shall include situations where a Contracting Party expropriates the assets of a company or enterprise in its Area in which an Investor of any other Contracting

Party has an Investment, including through the ownership of shares.

ARTICLE 14 TRANSFERS RELATED TO INVESTMENTS

(1) Each Contracting Party shall with respect to Investments in its Area of Investors of any other Contracting Party guarantee the freedom of transfer into and out of its Area, including the transfer of:

(a) the initial capital plus any additional capital for the maintenance and development of an Investment;

(b) Returns;

(c) payments under a contract, including amortization of principal and accrued interest payments pursuant to a loan agreement;

(d) unspent earnings and other remuneration of personnel engaged from abroad in connection with that Investment;

(e) proceeds from the sale or liquidation of all or any part of an Investment;

(f) payments arising out of the settlement of a dispute;

(g) payments of compensation pursuant to Articles 12 and 13.

(2) Transfers under paragraph (1) shall be effected without delay and (except in case of a Return in kind) in a Freely Convertible Currency.

(3) Transfers shall be made at the market rate of exchange existing on the date of transfer with respect to spot transactions in the currency to be transferred. In the absence of a market for foreign exchange, the rate to be used will be the most recent rate applied to inward investments or the most recent exchange rate for conversion of currencies into Special Drawing Rights, whichever is more favourable to the Investor.

(4) Notwithstanding paragraphs (1) to (3), a Contracting Party may protect the rights of creditors, or ensure compliance with laws on the issuing, trading and dealing in securities and the satisfaction of judgements in civil, administrative and criminal adjudicatory proceedings, through the equitable, non-discriminatory, and good faith application of its laws and regulations.

(5) Notwithstanding paragraph (2), Contracting Parties which are states that were constituent parts of the former Union of Soviet Socialist Republics may provide in agreements concluded between them that transfers of payments shall be made in the currencies of such Contracting Parties, provided that such agreements do not treat Investments in their Areas of Investors of other Contracting Parties less favourably than either Investments of Investors of the Contracting Parties which have entered into such agreements or Investments of Investors of any third state.

(6) Notwithstanding subparagraph (1)(b), a Contracting Party may restrict the transfer of a Return in kind in circumstances where the Contracting Party is permitted under Article 29(2)(a) or the GATT and Related Instruments to restrict or prohibit the exportation or the sale for export of the product constituting the Return in kind; provided that a Contracting Party shall permit transfers of Returns in kind to be effected as authorized or specified in an investment agreement, investment authorization, or other written agreement between the Contracting Party and either an Investor of another Contracting Party or its Investment.

ARTICLE 15 SUBROGATION

(1) If a Contracting Party or its designated agency (hereinafter referred to as the "Indemnifying Party") makes a payment under an indemnity or guarantee given in respect of an Investment of an Investor (hereinafter referred to as the "Party Indemnified") in the Area of another Contracting Party (hereinafter referred to as the "Host Party"), the Host Party shall recognize:

(a) the assignment to the Indemnifying Party of all the rights and claims in respect of such Investment; and

(b) the right of the Indemnifying Party to exercise all such rights and enforce such claims by virtue of subrogation.

(2) The Indemnifying Party shall be entitled in all circumstances to:

(a) the same treatment in respect of the rights and claims acquired by it by virtue of the assignment referred to in paragraph (1); and

(b) the same payments due pursuant to those rights and claims, as the Party Indemnified was entitled to receive by virtue of this Treaty in respect of the Investment concerned.

(3) In any proceeding under Article 26, a Contracting Party shall not assert as a defence, counterclaim, right of set-off or for any other reason, that indemnification or other compensation for all or part of the alleged damages has been received or will be received pursuant to an insurance or guarantee contract.

ARTICLE 16 RELATION TO OTHER AGREEMENTS

Where two or more Contracting Parties have entered into a prior international agreement, or enter into a subsequent international agreement, whose terms in either case concern the subject matter of Part III or V of this Treaty,

(1) nothing in Part III or V of this Treaty shall be construed to derogate from any provision of such terms of the other agreement or from any right to dispute resolution with respect thereto under that agreement; and

(2) nothing in such terms of the other agreement shall be construed to derogate from any provision of Part III or V of this Treaty or from any right to dispute resolution with respect thereto under this Treaty,

where any such provision is more favourable to the Investor or Investment.

ARTICLE 17 NON-APPLICATION OF PART III IN CERTAIN CIRCUMSTANCES

Each Contracting Party reserves the right to deny the advantages of this Part to:

(1) a legal entity if citizens or nationals of a third state own or control such entity and if that entity has no substantial business activities in the Area of the Contracting Party in which it is organized; or

(2) an Investment, if the denying Contracting Party establishes that such Investment is an Investment of an Investor of a third state with or as to which the denying Contracting Party:

(a) does not maintain a diplomatic relationship; or

(b) adopts or maintains measures that:

(i) prohibit transactions with Investors of that state; or

(ii) would be violated or circumvented if the benefits of this Part were accorded to Investors of that state or to their Investments.

PART IV MISCELLANEOUS PROVISIONS

ARTICLE 18 SOVEREIGNTY OVER ENERGY RESOURCES

(1) The Contracting Parties recognize state sovereignty and sovereign rights over energy resources. They reaffirm that these must be exercised in accordance with and subject to the rules of international law.

(2) Without affecting the objectives of promoting access to energy resources, and exploration and development thereof on a commercial basis, the Treaty shall in no way prejudice the rules in Contracting Parties governing the system of property ownership of energy resources.

(3) Each state continues to hold in particular the rights to decide the geographical areas within its Area to be made available for exploration and development of its energy resources, the optimalization of their recovery and the rate at which they may be depleted or otherwise exploited, to specify and enjoy any taxes, royalties or other financial payments payable by virtue of such exploration and exploitation, and to regulate the environmental and safety aspects of such exploration, development and reclamation within its Area, and to participate in such exploration and exploitation, inter alia, through direct participation by the government or through state enterprises.

(4) The Contracting Parties undertake to facilitate access to energy resources, inter alia, by allocating in a non-discriminatory manner on the basis of published criteria authorizations, licences, concessions and contracts to prospect and explore for or to exploit or extract energy resources.

ARTICLE 19 ENVIRONMENTAL ASPECTS

(1) In pursuit of sustainable development and taking into account its obligations under those international agreements concerning the environment to which it is party, each Contracting Party shall

strive to minimize in an economically efficient manner harmful Environmental Impacts occurring either within or outside its Area from all operations within the Energy Cycle in its Area, taking proper account of safety. In doing so each Contracting Party shall act in a Cost-Effective manner. In its policies and actions each Contracting Party shall strive to take precautionary measures to prevent or minimize environmental degradation. The Contracting Parties agree that the polluter in the Areas of Contracting Parties, should, in principle, bear the cost of pollution, including transboundary pollution, with due regard to the public interest and without distorting Investment in the Energy Cycle or international trade. Contracting Parties shall accordingly:

(a) take account of environmental considerations throughout the formulation and implementation of their energy policies;

(b) promote market-oriented price formation and a fuller reflection of environmental costs and benefits throughout the Energy Cycle;

(c) having regard to Article 34(4), encourage co-operation in the attainment of the environmental objectives of the Charter and co-operation in the field of international environmental standards for the Energy Cycle, taking into account differences in adverse effects and abatement costs between Contracting Parties;

(d) have particular regard to Improving Energy Efficiency, to developing and using renewable energy sources, to promoting the use of cleaner fuels and to employing technologies and technological means that reduce pollution;

(e) promote the collection and sharing among Contracting Parties of information on environmentally sound and economically efficient energy policies and Cost-Effective practices and technologies;

(f) promote public awareness of the Environmental Impacts of energy systems, of the scope for the prevention or abatement of their adverse Environmental Impacts, and of the costs associated with various prevention or abatement measures;

(g) promote and co-operate in the research, development and application of energy efficient and environmentally sound technologies, practices and processes which will minimize harmful Environmental Impacts of all aspects of the Energy Cycle in an economically efficient manner;

(h) encourage favourable conditions for the transfer and dissemination of such technologies consistent with the adequate and effective protection of Intellectual Property rights;

(i) promote the transparent assessment at an early stage and prior to decision, and subsequent monitoring, of Environmental Impacts of environmentally significant energy investment projects;

(j) promote international awareness and information exchange on Contracting Parties' relevant environmental programmes and standards and on the implementation of those programmes and standards;

(k) participate, upon request, and within their available resources, in the development and implementation of appropriate environmental programmes in the Contracting Parties.

(2) At the request of one or more Contracting Parties, disputes concerning the application or interpretation of provisions of this Article shall, to the extent that arrangements for the consideration of such disputes do not exist in other appropriate international fora, be reviewed by the Charter Conference aiming at a solution.

(3) For the purposes of this Article:

(a) "Energy Cycle" means the entire energy chain, including activities related to prospecting for, exploration, production, conversion, storage, transport, distribution and consumption of the various forms of energy, and the treatment and disposal of wastes, as well as the decommissioning, cessation or closure of these activities, minimizing harmful Environmental Impacts;

(b) "Environmental Impact" means any effect caused by a given activity on the environment, including human health and safety, flora, fauna, soil, air, water, climate, landscape and historical monuments or other physical structures or the interactions among these factors; it also includes effects on cultural heritage or socio-economic conditions resulting from alterations to those factors;

(c) "Improving Energy Efficiency" means acting to maintain the same unit of output (of a good or service) without reducing the quality or performance of the output, while reducing the amount of energy required to produce that output;

(d) "Cost-Effective" means to achieve a defined objective at the lowest cost or to achieve the greatest benefit at a given cost.

ARTICLE 20 TRANSPARENCY

(1) Laws, regulations, judicial decisions and administrative rulings of general application which affect trade in Energy Materials and Products are, in accordance with Article 29(2)(a), among the measures subject to the transparency disciplines of the GATT and relevant Related Instruments.

(2) Laws, regulations, judicial decisions and administrative rulings of general application made effective by any Contracting Party, and agreements in force between Contracting Parties, which affect other matters covered by this Treaty shall also be published promptly in such a manner as to enable Contracting Parties and Investors to become acquainted with them. The provisions of this paragraph shall not require any Contracting Party to disclose confidential information which would impede law enforcement or otherwise be contrary to the public interest or would prejudice the legitimate commercial interests of any Investor.

(3) Each Contracting Party shall designate one or more enquiry points to which requests for information about the above mentioned laws, regulations, judicial decisions and administrative rulings may be addressed and shall communicate promptly such designation to the Secretariat which shall make it available on request.

ARTICLE 21 TAXATION

(1) Except as otherwise provided in this Article, nothing in this Treaty shall create rights or impose obligations with respect to Taxation Measures of the Contracting Parties. In the event of any inconsistency between this Article and any other provision of the Treaty, this Article shall prevail to the extent of the inconsistency.

(2) Article 7(3) shall apply to Taxation Measures other than those on income or on capital, except that such provision shall not apply to:

(a) an advantage accorded by a Contracting Party pursuant to the tax provisions of any convention, agreement or arrangement described in subparagraph (7)(a)(ii); or

(b) any Taxation Measure aimed at ensuring the effective collection of taxes, except where the measure of a Contracting Party arbitrarily discriminates against Energy Materials and Products originating in, or destined for the Area of another Contracting Party or arbitrarily restricts benefits accorded under Article 7(3).

(3) Article 10(2) and (7) shall apply to Taxation Measures of the Contracting Parties other than those on income or on capital, except that such provisions shall not apply to:

(a) impose most favoured nation obligations with respect to advantages accorded by a Contracting Party pursuant to the tax provisions of any convention, agreement or arrangement described in subparagraph (7)(a)(ii) or resulting from membership of any Regional Economic Integration Organization; or

(b) any Taxation Measure aimed at ensuring the effective collection of taxes, except where the measure arbitrarily discriminates against an Investor of another Contracting Party or arbitrarily restricts benefits accorded under the Investment provisions of this Treaty.

(4) Article 29(2) to (6) shall apply to Taxation Measures other than those on income or on capital.

(5) (a) Article 13 shall apply to taxes.

(b) Whenever an issue arises under Article 13, to the extent it pertains to whether a tax constitutes an expropriation or whether a tax alleged to constitute an expropriation is discriminatory, the following provisions shall apply:

(i) The Investor or the Contracting Party alleging expropriation shall refer the issue of whether the tax is an expropriation or whether the tax is discriminatory to the relevant Competent Tax Authority. Failing such referral by the Investor or the Contracting Party, bodies called upon to settle disputes pursuant to Article 26(2)(c) or 27(2) shall make a referral to the relevant Competent Tax Authorities;

(ii) The Competent Tax Authorities shall, within a period of six months of such referral, strive to resolve the issues so referred. Where non-discrimination issues are concerned, the Competent Tax Authorities shall apply the non-discrimination provisions of the relevant tax convention or, if there is no non-discrimination provision in the relevant tax convention applicable to the tax or no such tax convention is in force between the Contracting Parties concerned, they shall apply the non-discrimination principles under the Model Tax Convention on Income and Capital of the Organisation for Economic Co-operation and Development;

(iii) Bodies called upon to settle disputes pursuant to Article 26(2)(c) or 27(2) may take into account any conclusions arrived at by the Competent Tax Authorities regarding whether the tax is an expropriation. Such bodies shall take into account any conclusions arrived at within the six-month period prescribed in subparagraph (b)(ii) by the Competent Tax Authorities regarding whether the tax is discriminatory. Such bodies may also take into account any conclusions arrived at by the Competent Tax Authorities after the expiry of the six-month period;

(iv) Under no circumstances shall involvement of the Competent Tax Authorities, beyond the end of the six-month period referred to in subparagraph (b)(ii), lead to a delay of proceedings under Articles 26 and 27.

(6) For the avoidance of doubt, Article 14 shall not limit the right of a Contracting Party to impose or collect a tax by withholding or other means.

(7) For the purposes of this Article:

(a) The term "Taxation Measure" includes:

(i) any provision relating to taxes of the domestic law of the Contracting Party or of a political subdivision thereof or a local authority therein; and

(ii) any provision relating to taxes of any convention for the avoidance of double taxation or of any other international agreement or arrangement by which the Contracting Party is bound.

(b) There shall be regarded as taxes on income or on capital all taxes imposed on total income, on total capital or on elements of income or of capital, including taxes on gains from the alienation of property, taxes on estates, inheritances and gifts, or substantially similar taxes, taxes on the total amounts of wages or salaries paid by enterprises, as well as taxes on capital appreciation.

(c) A "Competent Tax Authority" means the competent authority pursuant to a double taxation agreement in force between the Contracting Parties or, when no such agreement is in force, the minister or ministry responsible for taxes or their authorized representatives.

(d) For the avoidance of doubt, the terms "tax provisions" and "taxes" do not include customs duties.

ARTICLE 22 STATE AND PRIVILEGED ENTERPRISES

(1) Each Contracting Party shall ensure that any state enterprise which it maintains or establishes shall conduct its activities in relation to the sale or provision of goods and services in its Area in a manner consistent with the Contracting Party's obligations under Part III of this Treaty.

(2) No Contracting Party shall encourage or require such a state enterprise to conduct its activities in its Area in a manner inconsistent with the Contracting Party's obligations under other provisions of this Treaty.

(3) Each Contracting Party shall ensure that if it establishes or maintains an entity and entrusts the entity with regulatory, administrative or other governmental authority, such entity shall exercise that authority in a manner consistent with the Contracting Party's obligations under this Treaty.

(4) No Contracting Party shall encourage or require any entity to which it grants exclusive or special privileges to conduct its activities in its Area in a manner inconsistent with the Contracting Party's obligations under this Treaty.

(5) For the purposes of this Article, "entity" includes any enterprise, agency or other organization or individual.

ARTICLE 23 OBSERVANCE BY SUB-NATIONAL AUTHORITIES

(1) Each Contracting Party is fully responsible under this Treaty for the observance of all provisions of

the Treaty, and shall take such reasonable measures as may be available to it to ensure such observance by regional and local governments and authorities within its Area.

(2) The dispute settlement provisions in Parts II, IV and V of this Treaty may be invoked in respect of measures affecting the observance of the Treaty by a Contracting Party which have been taken by regional or local governments or authorities within the Area of the Contracting Party.

ARTICLE 24 EXCEPTIONS

(1) This Article shall not apply to Articles 12, 13 and 29.

(2) The provisions of this Treaty other than

(a) those referred to in paragraph (1); and

(b) with respect to subparagraph (i), Part III of the Treaty

shall not preclude any Contracting Party from adopting or enforcing any measure

(i) necessary to protect human, animal or plant life or health;

(ii) essential to the acquisition or distribution of Energy Materials and Products in conditions of short supply arising from causes outside the control of that Contracting Party, provided that any such measure shall be consistent with the principles that

(A) all other Contracting Parties are entitled to an equitable share of the international supply of such Energy Materials and Products; and

(B) any such measure that is inconsistent with this Treaty shall be discontinued as soon as the conditions giving rise to it have ceased to exist; or

(iii) designed to benefit Investors who are aboriginal people or socially or economically disadvantaged individuals or groups or their Investments and notified to the Secretariat as such, provided that such measure

(A) has no significant impact on that Contracting Party's economy; and

(B) does not discriminate between Investors of any other Contracting Party and Investors of that Contracting Party not included among those for whom the measure is intended, provided that no such measure shall constitute a disguised restriction on Economic Activity in the Energy Sector, or arbitrary or unjustifiable discrimination between Contracting Parties or between Investors or other interested persons of Contracting Parties. Such measures shall be duly motivated and shall not nullify or impair any benefit one or more other Contracting Parties may reasonably expect under this Treaty to an extent greater than is strictly necessary to the stated end.

(3) The provisions of this Treaty other than those referred to in paragraph (1) shall not be construed to prevent any Contracting Party from taking any measure which it considers necessary:

(a) for the protection of its essential security interests including those

(i) relating to the supply of Energy Materials and Products to a military establishment; or

(ii) taken in time of war, armed conflict or other emergency in international relations;

(b) relating to the implementation of national policies respecting the non-proliferation of nuclear weapons or other nuclear explosive devices or needed to fulfil its obligations under the Treaty on the Non-Proliferation of Nuclear Weapons, the Nuclear Suppliers Guidelines, and other international nuclear non-proliferation obligations or understandings; or

(c) for the maintenance of public order.

Such measure shall not constitute a disguised restriction on Transit.

(4) The provisions of this Treaty which accord most favoured nation treatment shall not oblige any Contracting Party to extend to the Investors of any other Contracting Party any preferential treatment:

(a) resulting from its membership of a free-trade area or customs union; or

(b) which is accorded by a bilateral or multilateral agreement concerning economic co-operation between states that were constituent parts of the former Union of Soviet Socialist Republics pending the establishment of their mutual economic relations on a definitive basis.

ARTICLE 25 ECONOMIC INTEGRATION AGREEMENTS

(1) The provisions of this Treaty shall not be so construed as to oblige a Contracting Party which is party to an Economic Integration Agreement (hereinafter referred to as "EIA") to extend, by means of most favoured nation treatment, to another Contracting Party which is not a party to that EIA, any preferential treatment applicable between the parties to that EIA as a result of their being parties thereto.

(2) For the purposes of paragraph (1), "EIA" means an agreement substantially liberalizing, inter alia, trade and investment, by providing for the absence or elimination of substantially all discrimination between or among parties thereto through the elimination of existing discriminatory measures and/or the prohibition of new or more discriminatory measures, either at the entry into force of that agreement or on the basis of a reasonable time frame.

(3) This Article shall not affect the application of the GATT and Related Instruments according to Article 29.

PART V DISPUTE SETTLEMENT

ARTICLE 26 SETTLEMENT OF DISPUTES BETWEEN AN INVESTOR AND A CONTRACTING PARTY

(1) Disputes between a Contracting Party and an Investor of another Contracting Party relating to an Investment of the latter in the Area of the former, which concern an alleged breach of an obligation of the former under Part III shall, if possible, be settled amicably.

(2) If such disputes can not be settled according to the provisions of paragraph (1) within a period of three months from the date on which either party to the dispute requested amicable settlement, the Investor party to the dispute may choose to submit it for resolution:

(a) to the courts or administrative tribunals of the Contracting Party party to the dispute;

(b) in accordance with any applicable, previously agreed dispute settlement procedure; or

(c) in accordance with the following paragraphs of this Article.

(3) (a) Subject only to subparagraphs (b) and (c), each Contracting Party hereby gives its unconditional consent to the submission of a dispute to international arbitration or conciliation in accordance with the provisions of this Article.

(b) (i) The Contracting Parties listed in Annex ID do not give such unconditional consent where the Investor has previously submitted the dispute under subparagraph (2)(a) or (b).

(ii) For the sake of transparency, each Contracting Party that is listed in Annex ID shall provide a written statement of its policies, practices and conditions in this regard to the Secretariat no later than the date of the deposit of its instrument of ratification, acceptance or approval in accordance with Article 39 or the deposit of its instrument of accession in accordance with Article 41.

(c) A Contracting Party listed in Annex IA does not give such unconditional consent with respect to a dispute arising under the last sentence of Article 10(1).

(4) In the event that an Investor chooses to submit the dispute for resolution under subparagraph (2)(c), the Investor shall further provide its consent in writing for the dispute to be submitted to:

(a) (i) The International Centre for Settlement of Investment Disputes, established pursuant to the Convention on the Settlement of Investment Disputes between States and Nationals of other States opened for signature at Washington, 18 March 1965 (hereinafter referred to as the "ICSID Convention"), if the Contracting Party of the Investor and the Contracting Party party to the dispute are both parties to the ICSID Convention; or

(ii) The International Centre for Settlement of Investment Disputes, established pursuant to the Convention referred to in subparagraph (a)(i), under the rules governing the Additional Facility for the Administration of Proceedings by the Secretariat of the Centre (hereinafter referred to as the "Additional Facility Rules"), if the Contracting Party of the Investor or the Contracting Party party to the dispute, but not both, is a party to the ICSID Convention;

(b) a sole arbitrator or ad hoc arbitration tribunal established under the Arbitration Rules of the United Nations Commission on

International Trade Law (hereinafter referred to as "UNCITRAL"); or

(c) an arbitral proceeding under the Arbitration Institute of the Stockholm Chamber of Commerce.

(5) (a) The consent given in paragraph (3) together with the written consent of the Investor given pursuant to paragraph (4) shall be considered to satisfy the requirement for:

(i) written consent of the parties to a dispute for purposes of Chapter II of the ICSID Convention and for purposes of the Additional Facility Rules;

(ii) an "agreement in writing" for purposes of article II of the United Nations Convention on the Recognition and Enforcement of Foreign Arbitral Awards, done at New York, 10 June 1958 (hereinafter referred to as the "New York Convention"); and

(iii) "the parties to a contract [to] have agreed in writing" for the purposes of article 1 of the UNCITRAL Arbitration Rules.

(b) Any arbitration under this Article shall at the request of any party to the dispute be held in a state that is a party to the New York Convention. Claims submitted to arbitration hereunder shall be considered to arise out of a commercial relationship or transaction for the purposes of article I of that Convention.

(6) A tribunal established under paragraph (4) shall decide the issues in dispute in accordance with this Treaty and applicable rules and principles of international law.

(7) An Investor other than a natural person which has the nationality of a Contracting Party party to the dispute on the date of the consent in writing referred to in paragraph (4) and which, before a dispute between it and that Contracting Party arises, is controlled by Investors of another Contracting Party, shall for the purpose of article 25(2)(b) of the ICSID Convention be treated as a "national of another Contracting State" and shall for the purpose of article 1(6) of the Additional Facility Rules be treated as a "national of another State".

(8) The awards of arbitration, which may include an award of interest, shall be final and binding upon the parties to the dispute. An award of arbitration concerning a measure of a sub-national government or authority of the disputing Contracting Party shall provide that the Contracting Party may pay monetary damages in lieu of any other remedy granted. Each Contracting Party shall carry out without delay any such award and shall make provision for the effective enforcement in its Area of such awards.

ARTICLE 27 SETTLEMENT OF DISPUTES BETWEEN CONTRACTING PARTIES

(1) Contracting Parties shall endeavour to settle disputes concerning the application or interpretation of this Treaty through diplomatic channels.

(2) If a dispute has not been settled in accordance with paragraph (1) within a reasonable period of time, either party thereto may, except as otherwise provided in this Treaty or agreed in writing by the Contracting Parties, and except as concerns the application or interpretation of Article 6 or Article 19 or, for Contracting Parties listed in Annex IA, the last sentence of Article 10(1), upon written notice to the other party to the dispute submit the matter to an ad hoc tribunal under this Article.

(3) Such an ad hoc arbitral tribunal shall be constituted as follows:

(a) The Contracting Party instituting the proceedings shall appoint one member of the tribunal and inform the other Contracting Party to the dispute of its appointment within 30 days of receipt of the notice referred to in paragraph (2) by the other Contracting Party;

(b) Within 60 days of the receipt of the written notice referred to in paragraph (2), the other Contracting Party party to the dispute shall appoint one member. If the appointment is not made within the time limit prescribed, the Contracting Party having instituted the proceedings may, within 90 days of the receipt of the written notice referred to in paragraph (2), request that the appointment be made in accordance with subparagraph (d);

(c) A third member, who may not be a national or citizen of a Contracting Party party to the dispute, shall be appointed by the Contracting Parties parties to the dispute. That member shall be the President of the tribunal. If, within 150 days of the receipt of the notice referred to in paragraph (2), the Contracting Parties are unable to agree on the appointment of a third member, that appointment shall be made, in accordance with subparagraph (d), at the request of either Contracting Party submitted within 180 days of the receipt of that notice;

(d) Appointments requested to be made in accordance with this paragraph shall be made by the Secretary-General of the Permanent Court of International Arbitration within 30 days of the receipt of a request to do so. If the Secretary-General is prevented from discharging this task, the appointments shall be made by the First Secretary of the Bureau. If the latter, in turn, is prevented from discharging this task, the appointments shall be made by the most senior Deputy;

(e) Appointments made in accordance with subparagraphs (a) to (d) shall be made with regard to the qualifications and experience, particularly in matters covered by this Treaty, of the members to be appointed;

(f) In the absence of an agreement to the contrary between the Contracting Parties, the Arbitration Rules of UNCITRAL shall govern, except to the extent modified by the Contracting Parties parties to the dispute or by the arbitrators. The tribunal shall take its decisions by a majority vote of its members;

(g) The tribunal shall decide the dispute in accordance with this Treaty and applicable rules and principles of international law;

(h) The arbitral award shall be final and binding upon the Contracting Parties parties to the dispute;

(i) Where, in making an award, a tribunal finds that a measure of a regional or local government or authority within the Area of a Contracting Party listed in Part I of Annex P is not in conformity with this Treaty, either party to the dispute may invoke the provisions of Part II of Annex P;

(j) The expenses of the tribunal, including the remuneration of its members, shall be borne in equal shares by the Contracting Parties parties to the dispute. The tribunal may, however, at its discretion direct that a higher proportion of the costs be paid by one of the Contracting Parties parties to the dispute;

(k) Unless the Contracting Parties parties to the dispute agree otherwise, the tribunal shall sit in The Hague, and use the premises and facilities of the Permanent Court of Arbitration;

(l) A copy of the award shall be deposited with the Secretariat which shall make it generally available.

ARTICLE 28 NON-APPLICATION OF ARTICLE 27 TO CERTAIN DISPUTES

A dispute between Contracting Parties with respect to the application or interpretation of Article 5 or 29 shall not be settled under Article 27 unless the Contracting Parties parties to the dispute so agree.

PART VI TRANSITIONAL PROVISIONS

ARTICLE 29 INTERIM PROVISIONS ON TRADE-RELATED MATTERS

(1) The provisions of this Article shall apply to trade in Energy Materials and Products while any Contracting Party is not a party to the GATT and Related Instruments.

(2) (a) Trade in Energy Materials and Products between Contracting Parties at least one of which is not a party to the GATT or a relevant Related Instrument shall be governed, subject to subparagraphs (b) and (c) and to the exceptions and rules provided for in Annex G, by the provisions of GATT 1947 and Related Instruments, as applied on 1 March 1994 and practised with regard to Energy Materials and Products by parties to GATT 1947 among themselves, as if all Contracting Parties were parties to GATT 1947 and Related Instruments.

(b) Such trade of a Contracting Party which is a state that was a constituent part of the former Union of Soviet Socialist Republics may instead be governed, subject to the provisions of Annex TFU, by an agreement between two or more such states, until 1 December 1999 or the admission of that Contracting Party to the GATT, whichever is the earlier.

(c) As concerns trade between any two parties to the GATT, subparagraph (a) shall not apply if either of those parties is not a party to GATT 1947.

(3) Each signatory to this Treaty, and each state or Regional Economic Integration Organization acceding to this Treaty, shall on the date of its signature or of its deposit of its instrument of accession provide to the Secretariat a list of all tariff rates and other charges levied on Energy Materials and Products at the time of importation or exportation,

notifying the level of such rates and charges applied on such date of signature or deposit. Any changes to such rates or other charges shall be notified to the Secretariat, which shall inform the Contracting Parties of such changes.

(4) Each Contracting Party shall endeavour not to increase any tariff rate or other charge levied at the time of importation or exportation:

(a) in the case of the importation of Energy Materials and Products described in Part I of the Schedule relating to the Contracting Party referred to in article II of the GATT, above the level set forth in that Schedule, if the Contracting Party is a party to the GATT;

(b) in the case of the exportation of Energy Materials and Products, and that of their importation if the Contracting Party is not a party to the GATT, above the level most recently notified to the Secretariat, except as permitted by the provisions made applicable by subparagraph (2)(a).

(5) A Contracting Party may increase such tariff rate or other charge above the level referred to in paragraph (4) only if:

(a) in the case of a rate or other charge levied at the time of importation, such action is not inconsistent with the applicable provisions of the GATT other than those provisions of GATT 1947 and Related Instruments listed in Annex G and the corresponding provisions of GATT 1994 and Related Instruments; or

(b) it has, to the fullest extent practicable under its legislative procedures, notified the Secretariat of its proposal for such an increase, given other interested Contracting Parties reasonable opportunity for consultation with respect to its proposal, and accorded consideration to any representations from such Contracting Parties.

(6) Signatories undertake to commence negotiations not later than 1 January 1995 with a view to concluding by 1 January 1998, as appropriate in the light of any developments in the world trading system, a text of an amendment to this Treaty which shall, subject to conditions to be laid down therein, commit each Contracting Party not to increase such tariffs or charges beyond the level prescribed under that amendment.

(7) Annex D shall apply to disputes regarding compliance with provisions applicable to trade under this Article and, unless both Contracting Parties agree otherwise, to disputes regarding compliance with Article 5 between Contracting Parties at least one of which is not a party to the GATT, except that Annex D shall not apply to any dispute between Contracting Parties, the substance of which arises under an agreement that:

(a) has been notified in accordance with and meets the other requirements of subparagraph (2)(b) and Annex TFU; or

(b) establishes a free-trade area or a customs union as described in article XXIV of the GATT.

ARTICLE 30 DEVELOPMENTS IN INTERNATIONAL TRADING ARRANGEMENTS

Contracting Parties undertake that in the light of the results of the Uruguay Round of Multilateral Trade Negotiations embodied principally in the Final Act thereof done at Marrakesh, 15 April 1994, they will commence consideration not later than 1 July 1995 or the entry into force of this Treaty, whichever is the later, of appropriate amendments to this Treaty with a view to the adoption of any such amendments by the Charter Conference.

ARTICLE 31 ENERGY-RELATED EQUIPMENT

The provisional Charter Conference shall at its first meeting commence examination of the inclusion of energy-related equipment in the trade provisions of this Treaty.

ARTICLE 32 TRANSITIONAL ARRANGEMENTS

(1) In recognition of the need for time to adapt to the requirements of a market economy, a Contracting Party listed in Annex T may temporarily suspend full compliance with its obligations under one or more of the following provisions of this Treaty, subject to the conditions in paragraphs (3) to (6):

Article 6(2) and (5)

Article 7(4)

Article 9(1)

Article 10(7) specific measures

Article 14(1)(d) related only to transfer of unspent earnings

Article 20(3)

Article 22(1) and (3)

(2) Other Contracting Parties shall assist any Contracting Party which has suspended full compliance under paragraph (1) to achieve the conditions under which such suspension can be terminated. This assistance may be given in whatever form the other Contracting Parties consider most effective to respond to the needs notified under subparagraph (4)(c) including, where appropriate, through bilateral or multilateral arrangements.

(3) The applicable provisions, the stages towards full implementation of each, the measures to be taken and the date or, exceptionally, contingent event, by which each stage shall be completed and measure taken are listed in Annex T for each Contracting Party claiming transitional arrangements. Each such Contracting Party shall take the measure listed by the date indicated for the relevant provision and stage as set out in Annex T. Contracting Parties which have temporarily suspended full compliance under paragraph (1) undertake to comply fully with the relevant obligations by 1 July 2001. Should a Contracting Party find it necessary, due to exceptional circumstances, to request that the period of such temporary suspension be extended or that any further temporary suspension not previously listed in Annex T be introduced, the decision on a request to amend Annex T shall be made by the Charter Conference.

(4) A Contracting Party which has invoked transitional arrangements shall notify the Secretariat no less often than once every 12 months:

(a) of the implementation of any measures listed in its Annex T and of its general progress to full compliance;

(b) of the progress it expects to make during the next 12 months towards full compliance with its obligations, of any problem it foresees and of its proposals for dealing with that problem;

(c) of the need for technical assistance to facilitate completion of the stages set out in Annex T as necessary for the full implementation of this Treaty, or to deal with any problem notified pursuant to subparagraph (b) as well as to promote other necessary market-oriented reforms and modernization of its energy sector;

(d) of any possible need to make a request of the kind referred to in paragraph (3).

(5) The Secretariat shall:

(a) circulate to all Contracting Parties the notifications referred to in paragraph (4);

(b) circulate and actively promote, relying where appropriate on arrangements existing within other international organizations, the matching of needs for and offers of technical assistance referred to in paragraph (2) and subparagraph (4)(c);

(c) circulate to all Contracting Parties at the end of each six month period a summary of any notifications made under subparagraph (4)(a) or (d).

(6) The Charter Conference shall annually review the progress by Contracting Parties towards implementation of the provisions of this Article and the matching of needs and offers of technical assistance referred to in paragraph (2) and subparagraph (4)(c). In the course of that review it may decide to take appropriate action.

PART VII STRUCTURE AND INSTITUTIONS

ARTICLE 33 ENERGY CHARTER PROTOCOLS AND DECLARATIONS

(1) The Charter Conference may authorize the negotiation of a number of Energy Charter Protocols or Declarations in order to pursue the objectives and principles of the Charter.

(2) Any signatory to the Charter may participate in such negotiation.

(3) A state or Regional Economic Integration Organization shall not become a party to a Protocol or Declaration unless it is, or becomes at the same time, a signatory to the Charter and a Contracting Party to this Treaty.

(4) Subject to paragraph (3) and subparagraph (6)(a), final provisions applying to a Protocol shall be defined in that Protocol.

(5) A Protocol shall apply only to the Contracting Parties which consent to be bound by it, and shall not derogate from the rights and obligations of those Contracting Parties not party to the Protocol.

(6) (a) A Protocol may assign duties to the Charter Conference and functions to the Secretariat, provided that no such assignment may be made by an amendment to a Protocol unless that amendment

is approved by the Charter Conference, whose approval shall not be subject to any provisions of the Protocol which are authorized by subparagraph (b).

(b) A Protocol which provides for decisions thereunder to be taken by the Charter Conference may, subject to subparagraph (a), provide with respect to such decisions:

(i) for voting rules other than those contained in Article 36;

(ii) that only parties to the Protocol shall be considered to be Contracting Parties for the purposes of Article 36 or eligible to vote under the rules provided for in the Protocol.

ARTICLE 34 ENERGY CHARTER CONFERENCE

(1) The Contracting Parties shall meet periodically in the Energy Charter Conference (referred to herein as the "Charter Conference") at which each Contracting Party shall be entitled to have one representative. Ordinary meetings shall be held at intervals determined by the Charter Conference.

(2) Extraordinary meetings of the Charter Conference may be held at such times as may be determined by the Charter Conference, or at the written request of any Contracting Party, provided that, within six weeks of the request being communicated to the Contracting Parties by the Secretariat, it is supported by at least one-third of the Contracting Parties.

(3) The functions of the Charter Conference shall be to:

(a) carry out the duties assigned to it by this Treaty and any Protocols;

(b) keep under review and facilitate the implementation of the principles of the Charter and of the provisions of this Treaty and the Protocols;

(c) facilitate in accordance with this Treaty and the Protocols the co-ordination of appropriate general measures to carry out the principles of the Charter;

(d) consider and adopt programmes of work to be carried out by the Secretariat;

(e) consider and approve the annual accounts and budget of the Secretariat;

(f) consider and approve or adopt the terms of any headquarters or other agreement, including privileges and immunities considered necessary for the Charter Conference and the Secretariat;

(g) encourage co-operative efforts aimed at facilitating and promoting market-oriented reforms and modernization of energy sectors in those countries of Central and Eastern Europe and the former Union of Soviet Socialist Republics undergoing economic transition;

(h) authorize and approve the terms of reference for the negotiation of Protocols, and consider and adopt the texts thereof and of amendments thereto;

(i) authorize the negotiation of Declarations, and approve their issuance;

(j) decide on accessions to this Treaty;

(k) authorize the negotiation of and consider and approve or adopt association agreements;

(l) consider and adopt texts of amendments to this Treaty;

(m) consider and approve modifications of and technical changes to the Annexes to this Treaty;

(n) appoint the Secretary-General and take all decisions necessary for the establishment and functioning of the Secretariat including the structure, staff levels and standard terms of employment of officials and employees.

(4) In the performance of its duties, the Charter Conference, through the Secretariat, shall co-operate with and make as full a use as possible, consistently with economy and efficiency, of the services and programmes of other institutions and organizations with established competence in matters related to the objectives of this Treaty.

(5) The Charter Conference may establish such subsidiary bodies as it considers appropriate for the performance of its duties.

(6) The Charter Conference shall consider and adopt rules of procedure and financial rules.

(7) In 1999 and thereafter at intervals (of not more than five years) to be determined by the Charter Conference, the Charter Conference shall thoroughly review the functions provided for in this Treaty in the light of the extent to which the provisions of the Treaty and Protocols have been implemented. At the conclusion of each review the Charter Conference may amend or abolish the functions

specified in paragraph (3) and may discharge the Secretariat.

ARTICLE 35 SECRETARIAT

(1) In carrying out its duties, the Charter Conference shall have a Secretariat which shall be composed of a Secretary-General and such staff as are the minimum consistent with efficient performance.

(2) The Secretary-General shall be appointed by the Charter Conference. The first such appointment shall be for a maximum period of five years.

(3) In the performance of its duties the Secretariat shall be responsible to and report to the Charter Conference.

(4) The Secretariat shall provide the Charter Conference with all necessary assistance for the performance of its duties and shall carry out the functions assigned to it in this Treaty or in any Protocol and any other functions assigned to it by the Charter Conference.

(5) The Secretariat may enter into such administrative and contractual arrangements as may be required for the effective discharge of its functions.

ARTICLE 36 VOTING

(1) Unanimity of the Contracting Parties Present and Voting at the meeting of the Charter Conference where such matters fall to be decided shall be required for decisions by the Charter Conference to:

(a) adopt amendments to this Treaty other than amendments to Articles 34 and 35 and Annex T;

(b) approve accessions to this Treaty under Article 41 by states or Regional Economic Integration Organizations which were not signatories to the Charter as of 16 June 1995;

(c) authorize the negotiation of and approve or adopt the text of association agreements;

(d) approve modifications to Annexes EM, NI, G and B;

(e) approve technical changes to the Annexes to this Treaty; and

(f) approve the Secretary-General's nominations of panelists under Annex D, paragraph (7).

The Contracting Parties shall make every effort to reach agreement by consensus on any other matter requiring their decision under this Treaty. If agreement cannot be reached by consensus, paragraphs (2) to (5) shall apply.

(2) Decisions on budgetary matters referred to in Article 34(3)(e) shall be taken by a qualified majority of Contracting Parties whose assessed contributions as specified in Annex B represent, in combination, at least three-fourths of the total assessed contributions specified therein.

(3) Decisions on matters referred to in Article 34(7) shall be taken by a three-fourths majority of the Contracting Parties.

(4) Except in cases specified in subparagraphs (1)(a) to (f), paragraphs (2) and (3), and subject to paragraph (6), decisions provided for in this Treaty shall be taken by a three-fourths majority of the Contracting Parties Present and Voting at the meeting of the Charter Conference at which such matters fall to be decided.

(5) For purposes of this Article, "Contracting Parties Present and Voting" means Contracting Parties present and casting affirmative or negative votes, provided that the Charter Conference may decide upon rules of procedure to enable such decisions to be taken by Contracting Parties by correspondence.

(6) Except as provided in paragraph (2), no decision referred to in this Article shall be valid unless it has the support of a simple majority of the Contracting Parties.

(7) A Regional Economic Integration Organization shall, when voting, have a number of votes equal to the number of its member states which are Contracting Parties to this Treaty; provided that such an Organization shall not exercise its right to vote if its member states exercise theirs, and vice versa.

(8) In the event of persistent arrears in a Contracting Party's discharge of financial obligations under this Treaty, the Charter Conference may suspend that Contracting Party's voting rights in whole or in part.

ARTICLE 37 FUNDING PRINCIPLES

(1) Each Contracting Party shall bear its own costs of representation at meetings of the Charter Conference and any subsidiary bodies.

(2) The cost of meetings of the Charter Conference and any subsidiary bodies shall be regarded as a cost of the Secretariat.

(3) The costs of the Secretariat shall be met by the Contracting Parties assessed according to their capacity to pay, determined as specified in Annex B, the provisions of which may be modified in accordance with Article 36(1)(d).

(4) A Protocol shall contain provisions to assure that any costs of the Secretariat arising from that Protocol are borne by the parties thereto.

(5) The Charter Conference may in addition accept voluntary contributions from one or more Contracting Parties or from other sources. Costs met from such contributions shall not be considered costs of the Secretariat for the purposes of paragraph (3).

PART VIII FINAL PROVISIONS

ARTICLE 38 SIGNATURE

This Treaty shall be open for signature at Lisbon from 17 December 1994 to 16 June 1995 by the states and Regional Economic Integration Organizations which have signed the Charter.

ARTICLE 39 RATIFICATION, ACCEPTANCE OR APPROVAL

This Treaty shall be subject to ratification, acceptance or approval by signatories. Instruments of ratification, acceptance or approval shall be deposited with the Depositary.

ARTICLE 40 APPLICATION TO TERRITORIES

(1) Any state or Regional Economic Integration Organization may at the time of signature, ratification, acceptance, approval or accession, by a declaration deposited with the Depositary, declare that the Treaty shall be binding upon it with respect to all the territories for the international relations of which it is responsible, or to one or more of them. Such declaration shall take effect at the time the Treaty enters into force for that Contracting Party.

(2) Any Contracting Party may at a later date, by a declaration deposited with the Depositary, bind itself under this Treaty with respect to other territory specified in the declaration. In respect of such territory the Treaty shall enter into force on the ninetieth day following the receipt by the Depositary of such declaration.

(3) Any declaration made under the two preceding paragraphs may, in respect of any territory specified in such declaration, be withdrawn by a notification to the Depositary. The withdrawal shall, subject to the applicability of Article 47(3), become effective upon the expiry of one year after the date of receipt of such notification by the Depositary.

(4) The definition of "Area" in Article 1(10) shall be construed having regard to any declaration deposited under this Article.

ARTICLE 41 ACCESSION

This Treaty shall be open for accession, from the date on which the Treaty is closed for signature, by states and Regional Economic Integration Organizations which have signed the Charter, on terms to be approved by the Charter Conference. The instruments of accession shall be deposited with the Depositary.

ARTICLE 42 AMENDMENTS

(1) Any Contracting Party may propose amendments to this Treaty.

(2) The text of any proposed amendment to this Treaty shall be communicated to the Contracting Parties by the Secretariat at least three months before the date on which it is proposed for adoption by the Charter Conference.

(3) Amendments to this Treaty, texts of which have been adopted by the Charter Conference, shall be communicated by the Secretariat to the Depositary which shall submit them to all Contracting Parties for ratification, acceptance or approval.

(4) Instruments of ratification, acceptance or approval of amendments to this Treaty shall be deposited with the Depositary. Amendments shall enter into force between Contracting Parties having ratified, accepted or approved them on the ninetieth day after deposit with the Depositary of instruments of ratification, acceptance or approval by at least three-fourths of the Contracting Parties. Thereafter the amendments shall enter into force for any other Contracting Party on the ninetieth day after that

Contracting Party deposits its instrument of ratification, acceptance or approval of the amendments.

ARTICLE 43 ASSOCIATION AGREEMENTS

(1) The Charter Conference may authorize the negotiation of association agreements with states or Regional Economic Integration Organizations, or with international organizations, in order to pursue the objectives and principles of the Charter and the provisions of this Treaty or one or more Protocols.

(2) The relationship established with and the rights enjoyed and obligations incurred by an associating state, Regional Economic Integration Organization, or international organization shall be appropriate to the particular circumstances of the association, and in each case shall be set out in the association agreement.

ARTICLE 44 ENTRY INTO FORCE

(1) This Treaty shall enter into force on the ninetieth day after the date of deposit of the thirtieth instrument of ratification, acceptance or approval thereof, or of accession thereto, by a state or Regional Economic Integration Organization which is a signatory to the Charter as of 16 June 1995.

(2) For each state or Regional Economic Integration Organization which ratifies, accepts or approves this Treaty or accedes thereto after the deposit of the thirtieth instrument of ratification, acceptance or approval, it shall enter into force on the ninetieth day after the date of deposit by such state or Regional Economic Integration Organization of its instrument of ratification, acceptance, approval or accession.

(3) For the purposes of paragraph (1), any instrument deposited by a Regional Economic Integration Organization shall not be counted as additional to those deposited by member states of such Organization.

ARTICLE 45 PROVISIONAL APPLICATION

(1) Each signatory agrees to apply this Treaty provisionally pending its entry into force for such signatory in accordance with Article 44, to the extent that such provisional application is not inconsistent with its constitution, laws or regulations.

(2) (a) Notwithstanding paragraph (1) any signatory may, when signing, deliver to the Depositary a declaration that it is not able to accept provisional application. The obligation contained in paragraph (1) shall not apply to a signatory making such a declaration. Any such signatory may at any time withdraw that declaration by written notification to the Depositary.

(b) Neither a signatory which makes a declaration in accordance with subparagraph (a) nor Investors of that signatory may claim the benefits of provisional application under paragraph (1).

(c) Notwithstanding subparagraph (a), any signatory making a declaration referred to in subparagraph (a) shall apply Part VII provisionally pending the entry into force of the Treaty for such signatory in accordance with Article 44, to the extent that such provisional application is not inconsistent with its laws or regulations.

(3) (a) Any signatory may terminate its provisional application of this Treaty by written notification to the Depositary of its intention not to become a Contracting Party to the Treaty. Termination of provisional application for any signatory shall take effect upon the expiration of 60 days from the date on which such signatory's written notification is received by the Depositary.

(b) In the event that a signatory terminates provisional application under subparagraph (a), the obligation of the signatory under paragraph (1) to apply Parts III and V with respect to any Investments made in its Area during such provisional application by Investors of other signatories shall nevertheless remain in effect with respect to those Investments for twenty years following the effective date of termination, except as otherwise provided in subparagraph (c).

(c) Subparagraph (b) shall not apply to any signatory listed in Annex PA. A signatory shall be removed from the list in Annex PA effective upon delivery to the Depositary of its request therefor.

(4) Pending the entry into force of this Treaty the signatories shall meet periodically in the provisional Charter Conference, the first meeting of which shall be convened by the provisional Secretariat referred to in paragraph (5) not later than 180 days after the

opening date for signature of the Treaty as specified in Article 38.

(5) The functions of the Secretariat shall be carried out on an interim basis by a provisional Secretariat until the entry into force of this Treaty pursuant to Article 44 and the establishment of a Secretariat.

(6) The signatories shall, in accordance with and subject to the provisions of paragraph (1) or subparagraph (2)(c) as appropriate, contribute to the costs of the provisional Secretariat as if the signatories were Contracting Parties under Article 37(3). Any modifications made to Annex B by the signatories shall terminate upon the entry into force of this Treaty.

(7) A state or Regional Economic Integration Organization which, prior to this Treaty's entry into force, accedes to the Treaty in accordance with Article 41 shall, pending the Treaty's entry into force, have the rights and assume the obligations of a signatory under this Article.

ARTICLE 46 RESERVATIONS

No reservations may be made to this Treaty.

ARTICLE 47 WITHDRAWAL

(1) At any time after five years from the date on which this Treaty has entered into force for a Contracting Party, that Contracting Party may give written notification to the Depositary of its withdrawal from the Treaty.

(2) Any such withdrawal shall take effect upon the expiry of one year after the date of the receipt of the notification by the Depositary, or on such later date as may be specified in the notification of withdrawal.

(3) The provisions of this Treaty shall continue to apply to Investments made in the Area of a Contracting Party by Investors of other Contracting Parties or in the Area of other Contracting Parties by Investors of that Contracting Party as of the date when that Contracting Party's withdrawal from the Treaty takes effect for a period of 20 years from such date.

(4) All Protocols to which a Contracting Party is party shall cease to be in force for that Contracting Party on the effective date of its withdrawal from this Treaty.

ARTICLE 48 STATUS OF ANNEXES AND DECISIONS

The Annexes to this Treaty and the Decisions set out in Annex 2 to the Final Act of the European Energy Charter Conference signed at Lisbon on 17 December 1994 are integral parts of the Treaty.

ARTICLE 49 DEPOSITARY

The Government of the Portuguese Republic shall be the Depositary of this Treaty.

ARTICLE 50 AUTHENTIC TEXTS

In witness whereof the undersigned, being duly authorized to that effect, have signed this Treaty in English, French, German, Italian, Russian and Spanish, of which every text is equally authentic, in one original, which will be deposited with the Government of the Portuguese Republic.

Done at Lisbon on the seventeenth day of December in the year one thousand nine hundred and ninety-four.

Additional Protocol to the Energy Charter Treaty on Energy Efficiency and Related Matters

http://www.encharter.org/index.jsp

PREAMBLE

THE CONTRACTING PARTIES to this Protocol,

Having regard to the European Energy Charter adopted in the Concluding Document of the Hague Conference on the European Energy Charter, signed at The Hague on 17 December 1991; and in particular to the declarations therein that co-operation is necessary in the field of energy efficiency and related environmental protection;

Having regard also to the Energy Charter Treaty, opened for signature from 17 December 1994 to 16 June 1995;

Mindful of the work undertaken by international organizations and fora in the field of energy efficiency and environmental aspects of the energy cycle;

Aware of the improvements in supply security, and of the significant economic and environmental gains, which result from the implementation of cost-effective energy efficiency measures; and aware of their importance for restructuring economies and improving living standards;

Recognizing that improvements in energy efficiency reduce negative environmental consequences of the energy cycle including global warming and acidification;

Convinced that energy prices should reflect as far as possible a competitive market, ensuring market-oriented price formation, including fuller reflection of environmental costs and benefits, and recognizing that such price formation is vital to progress in energy efficiency and associated environmental protection;

Appreciating the vital role of the private sector including small and medium-sized enterprises in promoting and implementing energy efficiency measures, and intent on ensuring a favourable institutional framework for economically viable investment in energy efficiency;

Recognizing that commercial forms of co-operation may need to be complemented by intergovernmental co-operation, particularly in the area of energy policy formulation and analysis as well as in other areas which are essential to the enhancement of energy efficiency but not suitable for private funding; and

Desiring to undertake co-operative and coordinated action in the field of energy efficiency and related environmental protection and to adopt a Protocol providing a framework for using energy as economically and efficiently as possible:

HAVE AGREED AS FOLLOWS:

PART I INTRODUCTION

ARTICLE 1 SCOPE AND OBJECTIVES OF THE PROTOCOL

(1) This Protocol defines policy principles for the promotion of energy efficiency as a considerable source of energy and for consequently reducing adverse Environmental Impacts of energy systems. It furthermore provides guidance on the development of energy efficiency programmes, indicates areas of co-operation and provides a framework for the development of co-operative and coordinated action. Such action may include the prospecting for, exploration, production, conversion, storage, transport, distribution, and consumption of energy, and may relate to any economic sector.

(2) The objectives of this Protocol are:

(a) the promotion of energy efficiency policies consistent with sustainable development;

(b) the creation of framework conditions which induce producers and consumers to use energy as economically, efficiently and environmentally soundly as possible, particularly through the organization of efficient energy markets and a fuller reflection of environmental costs and benefits; and

(c) the fostering of co-operation in the field of energy efficiency.

ARTICLE 2 DEFINITIONS

As used in this Protocol:

(1) "Charter" means the European Energy Charter adopted in the Concluding Document of the Hague Conference on the European Energy Charter signed at The Hague on 17 December 1991; signature of the Concluding Document is considered to be signature of the Charter.

(2) "Contracting Party" means a state or Regional Economic Integration Organization which has consented to be bound by this Protocol and for which the Protocol is in force.

(3) "Regional Economic Integration Organization" means an organization constituted by states to which they have transferred competence over certain matters a number of which are governed by this Protocol, including the authority to take decisions binding on them in respect of those matters.

(4) "Energy Cycle" means the entire energy chain, including activities related to prospecting for, exploration, production, conversion, storage, transport, distribution and consumption of the various forms of energy, and the treatment and disposal of wastes, as well as the decommissioning, cessation or closure of these activities, minimizing harmful Environmental Impacts.

(5) "Cost-Effectiveness" means to achieve a defined objective at the lowest cost or to achieve the greatest benefit at a given cost.

(6) "Improving Energy Efficiency" means acting to maintain the same unit of output (of a good or service) without reducing the quality or performance of the output, while reducing the amount of energy required to produce that output.

(7) "Environmental Impact" means any effect caused by a given activity on the environment, including human health and safety, flora, fauna, soil, air, water, climate, landscape and historical monuments or other physical structures or the interactions among these factors; it also includes effects on cultural heritage or socio-economic conditions resulting from alterations to those factors.

PART II POLICY PRINCIPLES

ARTICLE 3 BASIC PRINCIPLES

Contracting Parties shall be guided by the following principles:

(1) Contracting Parties shall co-operate and, as appropriate, assist each other in developing and implementing energy efficiency policies, laws and regulations.

(2) Contracting Parties shall establish energy efficiency policies and appropriate legal and regulatory frameworks which promote, inter alia:

(a) efficient functioning of market mechanisms including market-oriented price formation and a fuller reflection of environmental costs and benefits;

(b) reduction of barriers to energy efficiency, thus stimulating investments;

(c) mechanisms for financing energy efficiency initiatives;

(d) education and awareness;

(e) dissemination and transfer of technologies;

(f) transparency of legal and regulatory frameworks.

(3) Contracting Parties shall strive to achieve the full benefit of energy efficiency throughout the Energy Cycle. To this end they shall, to the best of their competence, formulate and implement energy efficiency policies and co-operative or coordinated actions based on Cost-Effectiveness and economic efficiency, taking due account of environmental aspects.

(4) Energy efficiency policies shall include both short-term measures for the adjustment of previous practices and long-term measures to improve energy efficiency throughout the Energy Cycle.

(5) When co-operating to achieve the objectives of this Protocol, Contracting Parties shall take into

account the differences in adverse effects and abatement costs between Contracting Parties.

(6) Contracting Parties recognize the vital role of the private sector. They shall encourage action by energy utilities, responsible authorities and specialised agencies, and close co-operation between industry and administrations.

(7) Co-operative or coordinated action shall take into account relevant principles adopted in international agreements, aimed at protection and improvement of the environment, to which Contracting Parties are parties.

(8) Contracting Parties shall take full advantage of the work and expertise of competent international or other bodies and shall take care to avoid duplication.

ARTICLE 4 DIVISION OF RESPONSIBILITY AND COORDINATION

Each Contracting Party shall strive to ensure that energy efficiency policies are coordinated among all of its responsible authorities.

ARTICLE 5 STRATEGIES AND POLICY AIMS

Contracting Parties shall formulate strategies and policy aims for Improving Energy Efficiency and thereby reducing Environmental Impacts of the Energy Cycle as appropriate in relation to their own specific energy conditions. These strategies and policy aims shall be transparent to all interested parties.

ARTICLE 6 FINANCING AND FINANCIAL INCENTIVES

(1) Contracting Parties shall encourage the implementation of new approaches and methods for financing energy efficiency and energy-related environmental protection investments, such as joint venture arrangements between energy users and external investors (hereinafter referred to as "Third Party Financing").

(2) Contracting Parties shall endeavour to take advantage of and promote access to private capital markets and existing international financing institutions in order to facilitate investments in Improving Energy Efficiency and in environmental protection related to energy efficiency.

(3) Contracting Parties may, subject to the provisions of the Energy Charter Treaty and to their other international legal obligations, provide fiscal or financial incentives to energy users in order to facilitate market penetration of energy efficiency technologies, products and services. They shall strive to do so in a manner that both ensures transparency and minimizes the distortion of international markets.

ARTICLE 7 PROMOTION OF ENERGY EFFICIENT TECHNOLOGY

(1) Consistent with the provisions of the Energy Charter Treaty, Contracting Parties shall encourage commercial trade and co-operation in energy efficient and environmentally sound technologies, energy-related services and management practices.

(2) Contracting Parties shall promote the use of these technologies, services and management practices throughout the Energy Cycle.

ARTICLE 8 DOMESTIC PROGRAMMES

(1) In order to achieve the policy aims formulated according to Article 5, each Contracting Party shall develop, implement and regularly update energy efficiency programmes best suited to its circumstances.

(2) These programmes may include activities such as the:

(a) development of long-term energy demand and supply scenarios to guide decision-making;

(b) assessment of the energy, environmental and economic impact of actions taken;

(c) definition of standards designed to improve the efficiency of energy using equipment, and efforts to harmonize these internationally to avoid trade distortions;

(d) development and encouragement of private initiative and industrial co-operation, including joint ventures;

(e) promotion of the use of the most energy efficient technologies that are economically viable and environmentally sound;

(f) encouragement of innovative approaches for investments in energy efficiency improvements, such as Third Party Financing and co-financing;

(g) development of appropriate energy balances and data bases, for example with data on energy demand at a sufficiently detailed level and on technologies for Improving Energy Efficiency;

(h) promotion of the creation of advisory and consultancy services which may be operated by public or private industry or utilities and which provide information about energy efficiency programmes and technologies, and assist consumers and enterprises;

(i) support and promotion of cogeneration and of measures to increase the efficiency of district heat production and distribution systems to buildings and industry;

(j) establishment of specialized energy efficiency bodies at appropriate levels, that are sufficiently funded and staffed to develop and implement policies.

(3) In implementing their energy efficiency programmes, Contracting Parties shall ensure that adequate institutional and legal infrastructures exist.

PART III INTERNATIONAL CO-OPERATION

ARTICLE 9 AREAS OF CO-OPERATION

The co-operation between Contracting Parties may take any appropriate form. Areas of possible co-operation are listed in the Annex.

PART IV ADMINISTRATIVE AND LEGAL ARRANGEMENTS

ARTICLE 10 ROLE OF THE CHARTER CONFERENCE

(1) All decisions made by the Charter Conference in accordance with this Protocol shall be made by only those Contracting Parties to the Energy Charter Treaty who are Contracting Parties to this Protocol.

(2) The Charter Conference shall endeavour to adopt, within 180 days after the entry into force of this Protocol, procedures for keeping under review and facilitating the implementation of its provisions, including reporting requirements, as well as for identifying areas of co-operation in accordance with Article 9.

ARTICLE 11 SECRETARIAT AND FINANCING

(1) The Secretariat established under Article 35 of the Energy Charter Treaty shall provide the Charter Conference with all necessary assistance for the performance of its duties under this Protocol and provide such other services in support of the Protocol as may be required from time to time, subject to approval by the Charter Conference.

(2) The costs of the Secretariat and Charter Conference arising from this Protocol shall be met by the Contracting Parties to this Protocol according to their capacity to pay, determined according to the formula specified in Annex B to the Energy Charter Treaty.

ARTICLE 12 VOTING

(1) Unanimity of Contracting Parties Present and Voting at the meeting of the Charter Conference where such matters fall to be decided shall be required for decisions to:

(a) adopt amendments to this Protocol; and

(b) approve accessions to this Protocol under Article 16.

Contracting Parties shall make every effort to reach agreement by consensus on any other matter requiring their decision under this Protocol. If agreement cannot be reached by consensus, decisions on non-budgetary matters shall be taken by a three-fourths majority of Contracting Parties Present and Voting at the meeting of the Charter Conference at which such matters fall to be decided.

Decisions on budgetary matters shall be taken by a qualified majority of Contracting Parties whose assessed contributions under Article 11(2) represent, in combination, at least three-fourths of the total assessed contributions.

(2) For purposes of this Article, "Contracting Parties Present and Voting" means Contracting Parties to this Protocol present and casting affirmative or negative votes, provided that the Charter Conference may decide upon rules of procedure to enable such decisions to be taken by Contracting Parties by correspondence.

(3) Except as provided in paragraph (1) in relation to budgetary matters, no decision referred to in this Article shall be valid unless it has the support of a simple majority of Contracting Parties.

(4) A Regional Economic Integration Organization shall, when voting, have a number of votes equal to the number of its member states which are Contracting Parties to this Protocol; provided that such an Organization shall not exercise its right to vote if its member states exercise theirs, and vice versa.

(5) In the event of persistent arrears in a Contracting Party's discharge of financial obligations under this Protocol, the Charter Conference may suspend that Contracting Party's voting rights in whole or in part.

ARTICLE 13 RELATION TO THE ENERGY CHARTER TREATY

(1) In the event of inconsistency between the provisions of this Protocol and the provisions of the Energy Charter Treaty, the provisions of the Energy Charter Treaty shall, to the extent of the inconsistency, prevail.

(2) Article 10(1) and Article 12(1) to (3) shall not apply to votes in the Charter Conference on amendments to this Protocol which assign duties or functions to the Charter Conference or the Secretariat, the establishment of which is provided for in the Energy Charter Treaty.

PART V FINAL PROVISONS

ARTICLE 14 SIGNATURE

This Protocol shall be open for signature at Lisbon from 17 December 1994 to 16 June 1995 by the states and Regional Economic Integration Organizations whose representatives have signed the Charter and the Energy Charter Treaty.

ARTICLE 15 RATIFICATION, ACCEPTANCE OR APPROVAL

This Protocol shall be subject to ratification, acceptance or approval by signatories. Instruments of ratification, acceptance or approval shall be deposited with the Depositary.

ARTICLE 16 ACCESSION

This Protocol shall be open for accession, from the date on which the Protocol is closed for signature, by states and Regional Economic Integration Organizations which have signed the Charter and are Contracting Parties to the Energy Charter Treaty, on terms to be approved by the Charter Conference. The instruments of accession shall be deposited with the Depositary.

ARTICLE 17 AMENDMENTS

(1) Any Contracting Party may propose amendments to this Protocol.

(2) The text of any proposed amendment to this Protocol shall be communicated to Contracting Parties by the Secretariat at least three months before the date on which it is proposed for adoption by the Charter Conference.

(3) Amendments to this Protocol, texts of which have been adopted by the Charter Conference, shall be communicated by the Secretariat to the Depositary which shall submit them to all Contracting Parties for ratification, acceptance or approval.

(4) Instruments of ratification, acceptance or approval of amendments to this Protocol shall be deposited with the Depositary. Amendments shall enter into force between Contracting Parties having ratified, accepted or approved them on the thirtieth day after deposit with the Depositary of instruments of ratification, acceptance or approval by at least three-fourths of the Contracting Parties. Thereafter the amendments shall enter into force for any other Contracting Party on the thirtieth day after that Contracting Party deposits its instrument of ratification, acceptance or approval of the amendments.

ARTICLE 18 ENTRY INTO FORCE

(1) This Protocol shall enter into force on the thirtieth day after the date of deposit of the fifteenth instrument of ratification, acceptance or approval thereof, or of accession thereto, by a state or Regional Economic Integration Organization which is a signatory to the Charter and a Contracting Party to the Energy Charter Treaty or on the same date as the Energy Charter Treaty enters into force, whichever is later.

(2) For each state or Regional Economic Integration Organization for which the Energy

Charter Treaty has entered into force and which ratifies, accepts, or approves this Protocol or accedes thereto after the Protocol has entered into force in accordance with paragraph (1), the Protocol shall enter into force on the thirtieth day after the date of deposit by such state or Regional Economic Integration Organization of its instrument of ratification, acceptance, approval or accession.

(3) For the purposes of paragraph (1), any instrument deposited by a Regional Economic Integration Organization shall not be counted as additional to those deposited by member states of such Organization.

ARTICLE 19 RESERVATIONS

No reservations may be made to this Protocol.

ARTICLE 20 WITHDRAWAL

(1) At any time after this Protocol has entered into force for a Contracting Party, that Contracting Party may give written notification to the Depositary of its withdrawal from the Protocol.

(2) Any Contracting Party which withdraws from the Energy Charter Treaty shall be considered as also having withdrawn from this Protocol.

(3) The effective date of withdrawal under paragraph (1) shall be ninety days after receipt of notification by the Depositary. The effective date of withdrawal under paragraph (2) shall be the same as the effective date of withdrawal from the Energy Charter Treaty.

ARTICLE 21 DEPOSITARY

The Government of the Portuguese Republic shall be the Depositary of this Protocol.

ARTICLE 22 AUTHENTIC TEXTS

In witness whereof the undersigned, being duly authorized to that effect, have signed this Protocol in English, French, German, Italian, Russian and Spanish, of which every text is equally authentic, in one original, which will be deposited with the Government of the Portuguese Republic.

Done at Lisbon on the seventeenth day of December in the year one thousand nine hundred and ninety-four.

North American Agreement on Environmental Cooperation

Washington 9 and 14 September, 1993; Ottawa 12 and 14 1993; and Mexico City 8 and 14 September 1993

32 I.L.M. 1480 (1993)

http://www.naaec.gc.ca/eng/index_e.htm

PREAMBLE

The Government of Canada, the Government of the United Mexican States and the Government of the United States of America:

CONVINCED of the importance of the conservation, protection and enhancement of the environment in their territories and the essential role of cooperation in these areas in achieving sustainable development for the well-being of present and future generations;

REFFIRMING the sovereign right of States to exploit their own resources pursuant to their own environmental and development policies and their responsibility to ensure that activities within their jurisdiction or control do not cause damage to the environment of other States or of areas beyond the limits of national jurisdiction;

RECOGNIZING the interrelationship of their environments;

ACKNOWLEDGING the growing economic and social links between them, including the North American Free Trade Agreement (NAFTA);

RECONFIRMING the importance of the environmental goals and objectives of the NAFTA, including enhanced levels of environmental protection;

EMPHASIZING the importance of public participation in conserving, protecting and enhancing the environment;

NOTING the existence of differences in their respective natural endowments, climatic and geographical conditions, and economic, technological and infrastructural capabilities;

REAFFIRMING the *Stockholm Declaration on the Human Environment* of 1972 and the *Rio Declaration on Environment and Development* of 1992;

RECALLING their tradition of environmental cooperation and expressing their desire to support and build on international environmental agreements and existing policies and laws, in order to promote cooperation between them; and

CONVINCED of the benefits to be derived from a framework, including a Commission, to facilitate effective cooperation on the conservation, protection and enhancement of the environment in their territories;

HAVE AGREED as follows:

PART ONE OBJECTIVES

Article 1: Objectives

The objectives of this Agreement are to:

(a) foster the protection and improvement of the environment in the territories of the Parties for the well-being of present and future generations;

(b) promote sustainable development based on cooperation and mutually supportive environmental and economic policies;

(c) increase cooperation between the Parties to better conserve, protect, and enhance the environment, including wild flora and fauna;

(d) support the environmental goals and objectives of the NAFTA;

(e) avoid creating trade distortions or new trade barriers;

(f) strengthen cooperation on the development and improvement of environmental laws, regulations, procedures, policies and practices;

(g) enhance compliance with, and enforcement of, environmental laws and regulations;

(h) promote transparency and public participation in the development of environmental laws, regulations and policies;

(i) promote economically efficient and effective environmental measures; and

(j) promote pollution prevention policies and practices.

PART TWO OBLIGATIONS

Article 2: General Commitments

1. Each Party shall, with respect to its territory:

(a) periodically prepare and make publicly available reports on the state of the environment;

(b) develop and review environmental emergency preparedness measures;

(c) promote education in environmental matters, including environmental law;

(d) further scientific research and technology development in respect of environmental matters;

(e) assess, as appropriate, environmental impacts; and

(f) promote the use of economic instruments for the efficient achievement of environmental goals.

2. Each Party shall consider implementing in its law any recommendation developed by the Council under Article 10(5)(b).

3. Each Party shall consider prohibiting the export to the territories of the other Parties of a pesticide or toxic substance whose use is prohibited within the Party's territory. When a Party adopts a measure prohibiting or severely restricting the use of a pesticide or toxic substance in its territory, it shall notify the other Parties of the measure, either directly or through an appropriate international organization.

Article 3: Levels of Protection

Recognizing the right of each Party to establish its own levels of domestic environmental protection and environmental development policies and priorities, and to adopt or modify accordingly its environmental laws and regulations, each Party shall ensure that its laws and regulations provide for high levels of environmental protection and shall strive to continue to improve those laws and regulations.

Article 4: Publication

1. Each Party shall ensure that its laws, regulations, procedures and administrative rulings of general application respecting any matter covered by this Agreement are promptly published or otherwise made available in such a manner as to enable interested persons and Parties to become acquainted with them.

2. To the extent possible, each Party shall:

a. publish in advance any such measure that it proposes to adopt; and

b. provide interested persons and Parties a reasonable opportunity to comment on such proposed measures.

Article 5: Government Enforcement Action

1. With the aim of achieving high levels of environmental protection and compliance with its environmental laws and regulations, each Party shall effectively enforce its environmental laws and regulations through appropriate governmental action, subject to Article 37, such as:

(a) appointing and training inspectors;

(b) monitoring compliance and investigating suspected violations, including through on-site inspections;

(c) seeking assurances of voluntary compliance and compliance agreements;

(d) publicly releasing non-compliance information;

(e) issuing bulletins or other periodic statements on enforcement procedures;

(f) promoting environmental audits;

(g) requiring record keeping and reporting;

(h) providing or encouraging mediation and arbitration services;

(i) using licenses, permits or authorizations;

(j) initiating, in a timely manner, judicial, quasi-judicial or administrative proceedings to seek appropriate sanctions or remedies for violations of its environmental laws and regulations;

(k) providing for search, seizure or detention; or

(l) issuing administrative orders, including orders of a preventative, curative or emergency nature.

2. Each party shall ensure that judicial, quasi-judicial or administrative enforcement proceedings are available under its law to sanction or remedy violations of its environmental laws and regulations.

3. Sanctions and remedies provided for a violation of a Party's environmental laws and regulations shall, as appropriate:

(a) take into consideration the nature and gravity of the violation, any economic benefit derived from the violation by the violator, the economic condition of the violator, and other relevant factors; and

(b) include compliance agreements, fines, imprisonment, injunctions, the closure of facilities, and the cost of containing or cleaning up pollution.

Article 6: Private Access to Remedies

1. Each Party shall ensure that interested persons may request the Party's competent authorities to investigate alleged violations of its environmental laws and regulations and shall give such requests due consideration in accordance with law.

2. Each Party shall ensure that persons with a legally recognized interest under its law in a particular matter have appropriate access to administrative, quasi-judicial or judicial proceedings for the enforcement of the Party's environmental laws and regulations.

3. Private access to remedies shall include rights, in accordance with the Party's law, such as:

(a) to sue another person under that Party's jurisdiction for damages;

(b) to seek sanctions or remedies such as monetary penalties, emergency closures or orders to mitigate the consequences of violations of its environmental laws and regulations;

(c) to request the competent authorities to take appropriate action to enforce that Party's environmental laws and regulations in order to protect the environment or to avoid environmental harm; or

(d) to seek injunctions where a person suffers, or may suffer, loss, damage or injury as a result of conduct by another person under that Party's jurisdiction contrary to that Party's environmental laws and regulations or from tortious conduct.

Article 7: Procedural Guarantees

1. Each Party shall ensure that its administrative, quasi-judicial and judicial proceedings referred to in Articles 5(2) and 6(2) are fair, open and equitable, and to this end shall provide that such proceedings:

(a) comply with due process of law;

(b) are open to the public, except where the administration of justice otherwise requires;

(c) entitle the parties to the proceedings to support or defend their respective positions and to present information or evidence; and

(d) are not unnecessarily complicated and do not entail unreasonable charges or time limits or unwarranted delays.

2. Each Party shall provide that final decisions on the merits of the case in such proceedings are:

(a) in writing and preferably state the reasons on which the decisions are based;

(b) made available without undue delay to the parties to the proceedings and, consistent with its law, to the public; and

(c) based on information or evidence in respect of which the parties were offered the opportunity to be heard.

3. Each Party shall provide, as appropriate, that parties to such proceedings have the right, in accordance with its law, to seek review and, where warranted, correction of final decisions issued in such proceedings.

4. Each Party shall ensure that tribunals that conduct or review such proceedings are impartial and independent and do not have any substantial interest in the outcome of the matter.

PART THREE COMMISSION FOR ENVIRONMENTAL COOPERATION

Article 8: The Commission

1. The Parties hereby establish the Commission for Environmental Cooperation.

2. The Commission shall comprise a Council, a Secretariat and a Joint Public Advisory Committee.

SECTION A: THE COUNCIL

Article 9: Council Structure and Procedures

1. The Council shall comprise cabinet-level or equivalent representatives of the Parties, or their designees.

2. The Council shall establish its rules and procedures.

3. The Council shall convene:

(a) at least once a year in regular session; and

(b) in special session at the request of any Party.

Regular sessions shall be chaired successively by each Party.

4. The Council shall hold public meetings in the course of all regular sessions. Other meetings held in the course of regular or special sessions shall be public where the Council so decides.

5. The Council may:

(a) establish, and assign responsibilities to, *ad hoc* or standing committees, working groups or expert groups;

(b) seek the advice of non-governmental organizations or persons, including independent experts; and

(c) take such other action in the exercise of its functions as the Parties may agree.

6. All decisions and recommendations of the Council shall be taken by consensus, except as the Council may otherwise decide or as otherwise provided in this Agreement.

7. All decisions and recommendations of the Council shall be made public, except as the Council may otherwise decide or as otherwise provided in this Agreement.

Article 10: Council Functions

1. The Council shall be the governing body of the Commission and shall:

(a) serve as a forum for the discussion of environmental matters within the scope of this Agreement;

(b) oversee the implementation and develop recommendations on the further elaboration of this Agreement and, to this end, the Council shall, within four years after the date of entry into force of this Agreement, review its operation and effectiveness in the light of experience;

(c) oversee the Secretariat;

(d) address questions and differences that may arise between the Parties regarding the interpretation or application of this Agreement;

(e) approve the annual program and budget of the Commission; and

(f) promote and facilitate cooperation between the Parties with respect to environmental matters.

2. The Council may consider, and develop recommendations regarding:

(a) comparability of techniques and methodologies for data gathering and analysis, data management and electronic data communications on matters covered by this Agreement;

(b) pollution prevention techniques and strategies;

(c) approaches and common indicators for reporting on the state of the environment;

(d) the use of economic instruments for the pursuit of domestic and internationally agreed environmental objectives;

(e) scientific research and technology development in respect of environmental matters;

(f) promotion of public awareness regarding the environment;

(g) transboundary and border environmental issues, such as the long-range transport of air and marine pollutants;

(h) exotic species that may be harmful;

(i) the conservation and protection of wild flora and fauna and their habitat, and specially protected natural areas;

(j) the protection of endangered and threatened species;

(k) environmental emergency preparedness and response activities;

(l) environmental matters as they relate to economic development;

(m) the environmental implications of goods throughout their life cycles;

(n) human resource training and development in the environmental field;

(o) the exchange of environmental scientists and officials;

(p) approaches to environmental compliance and enforcement;

(q) ecologically sensitive national accounts;

(r) eco-labelling; and

(s) other matters as it may decide.

3. The Council shall strengthen cooperation on the development and continuing improvement of environmental laws and regulations, including by:

(a) promoting the exchange of information on criteria and methodologies used in establishing domestic environmental standards; and

(b) without reducing levels of environmental protection, establishing a process for developing recommendations on greater compatibility of environmental technical regulations, standards and conformity assessment procedures in a manner consistent with the NAFTA.

4. The Council shall encourage:

(a) effective enforcement by each Party of its environmental laws and regulations;

(b) compliance with those laws and regulations; and

(c) technical cooperation between the Parties.

5. The Council shall promote and, as appropriate, develop recommendations regarding:

(a) public access to information concerning the environment that is held by public authorities of each Party, including information on hazardous materials and activities in its communities, and opportunity to participate in decision-making processes related to such public access; and

(b) appropriate limits for specific pollutants, taking into account differences in ecosystems.

6. The Council shall cooperate with the NAFTA Free Trade Commission to achieve the environmental goals and objectives of the NAFTA by:

(a) acting as a point of inquiry and receipt for comments from non-governmental organizations and persons concerning those goals and objectives;

(b) providing assistance in consultations under Article 1114 of the NAFTA where a Party considers that another Party is waiving or derogating from, or offering to waive or otherwise derogate from, an environmental measure as an encouragement to establish, acquire, expand or retain an investment of an investor, with a view to avoiding any such encouragement;

(c) contributing to the prevention or resolution of environment-related trade disputes by:

(i) seeking to avoid disputes between the Parties,

(ii) making recommendations to the Free Trade Commission with respect to the avoidance of such disputes, and

(iii) identifying experts able to provide information or technical advice to NAFTA committees, working groups and other NAFTA bodies;

(d) considering on an ongoing basis the environmental effects of the NAFTA; and

(e) otherwise assisting the Free Trade Commission in environment-related matters.

7. Recognizing the significant bilateral nature of many transboundary environmental issues, the Council shall, with a view to agreement between the Parties pursuant to this Article within three years on obligations, consider and develop recommendations with respect to:

(a) assessing the environmental impact of proposed projects subject to decisions by a competent government authority and likely to cause significant adverse transboundary effects, including a full evaluation of comments provided by other Parties and persons of other Parties;

(b) notification, provision of relevant information and consultation between Parties with respect to such projects; and

(c) mitigation of the potential adverse effects of such projects.

8. The Council shall encourage the establishment by each Party of appropriate administrative procedures pursuant to its environmental laws to permit another Party to seek the reduction, elimination or mitigation of transboundary pollution on a reciprocal basis.

9. The Council shall consider and, as appropriate, develop recommendations on the provision by a Party, on a reciprocal basis, of access to and rights and remedies before its courts and administrative agencies for persons in another Party's territory who have suffered or are likely to suffer damage or injury caused by pollution originating in its

territory as if the damage or injury were suffered in its territory.

SECTION B: THE SECRETARIAT

Article 11: Secretariat Structure and Procedures

1. The Secretariat shall be headed by an Executive Director, who shall be chosen by the Council for a three-year term, which may be renewed by the Council for one additional three-year term. The position of Executive Director shall rotate consecutively between nationals of each Party. The Council may remove the Executive Director solely for cause.

2. The Executive Director shall appoint and supervise the staff of the Secretariat, regulate their powers and duties and fix their remuneration in accordance with general standards to be established by the Council. The general standards shall provide that:

(a) staff shall be appointed and retained, and their conditions of employment shall be determined, strictly on the basis of efficiency, competence and integrity;

(b) in appointing staff, the Executive Director shall take into account lists of candidates prepared by the Parties and by the Joint Public Advisory Committee;

(c) due regard shall be paid to the importance of recruiting an equitable proportion of the professional staff from among the nationals of each Party; and

(d) the Executive Director shall inform the Council of all appointments.

3. The Council may decide, by a two-thirds vote, to reject any appointment that does not meet the general standards. Any such decision shall be made and held in confidence.

4. In the performance of their duties, the Executive Director and the staff shall not seek or receive instructions from any government or any other authority external to the Council. Each Party shall respect the international character of the responsibilities of the Executive Director and the staff and shall not seek to influence them in the discharge of their responsibilities.

5. The Secretariat shall provide technical, administrative and operational support to the Council and to committees and groups established by the Council, and such other support as the Council may direct.

6. The Executive Director shall submit for the approval of the Council the annual program and budget of the Commission, including provision for proposed cooperative activities and for the Secretariat to respond to contingencies.

7. The Secretariat shall, as appropriate, provide the Parties and the public information on where they may receive technical advice and expertise with respect to environmental matters.

8. The Secretariat shall safeguard:

(a) from disclosure information it receives that could identify a non-governmental organization or person making a submission if the person or organization so requests or the Secretariat otherwise considers it appropriate; and

(b) from public disclosure any information it receives from any non-governmental organization or person where the information is designated by that non-governmental organization or person as confidential or proprietary.

Article 12: Annual Report of the Commission

1. The Secretariat shall prepare an annual report of the Commission in accordance with instructions from the Council. The Secretariat shall submit a draft of the report for review by the Council. The final report shall be released publicly.

2. The report shall cover:

(a) activities and expenses of the Commission during the previous year;

(b) the approved program and budget of the Commission for the subsequent year;

(c) the actions taken by each Party in connection with its obligations under this Agreement, including data on the Party's environmental enforcement activities;

(d) relevant views and information submitted by non-governmental organizations and persons, including summary data regarding submissions, and any other relevant information the Council deems appropriate;

(e) recommendations made on any matter within the scope of this Agreement; and

(f) any other matter that the Council instructs the Secretariat to include.

3. The report shall periodically address the state of the environment in the territories of the Parties.

Article 13: Secretariat Reports

1. The Secretariat may prepare a report for the Council on any matter within the scope of the annual program. Should the Secretariat wish to prepare a report on any other environmental matter related to the cooperative functions of this Agreement, it shall notify the Council and may proceed unless, within 30 days of such notification, the Council objects by a two-thirds vote to the preparation of the report. Such other environmental matters shall not include issues related to whether a Party has failed to enforce its environmental laws and regulations. Where the Secretariat does not have specific expertise in the matter under review, it shall obtain the assistance of one or more independent experts of recognized experience in the matter to assist in the preparation of the report.

2. In preparing such a report, the Secretariat may draw upon any relevant technical, scientific or other information, including information:

(a) that is publicly available;

(b) submitted by interested non-governmental organizations and persons;

(c) submitted by the Joint Public Advisory Committee;

(d) furnished by a Party;

(e) gathered through public consultations, such as conferences, seminars and symposia; or

(f) developed by the Secretariat, or by independent experts engaged pursuant to paragraph 1.

3. The Secretariat shall submit its report to the Council, which shall make it publicly available, normally within 60 days following its submission, unless the Council otherwise decides.

Article 14: Submissions on Enforcement Matters

1. The Secretariat may consider a submission from any non-governmental organization or person asserting that a Party is failing to effectively enforce its environmental law, if the Secretariat finds that the submission:

(a) is in writing in a language designated by that Party in a notification to the Secretariat;

(b) clearly identifies the person or organization making the submission;

(c) provides sufficient information to allow the Secretariat to review the submission, including any documentary evidence on which the submission may be based;

(d) appears to be aimed at promoting enforcement rather than at harassing industry;

(e) indicates that the matter has been communicated in writing to the relevant authorities of the Party and indicates the Party's response, if any; and

(f) is filed by a person or organization residing or established in the territory of a Party.

2. Where the Secretariat determines that a submission meets the criteria set out in paragraph 1, the Secretariat shall determine whether the submission merits requesting a response from the Party. In deciding whether to request a response, the Secretariat shall be guided by whether:

(a) the submission alleges harm to the person or organization making the submission;

(b) the submission, alone or in combination with other submissions, raises matters whose further study in this process would advance the goals of this Agreement;

(c) private remedies available under the Party's law have been pursued; and

(d) the submission is drawn exclusively from mass media reports.

Where the Secretariat makes such a request, it shall forward to the Party a copy of the submission and any supporting information provided with the submission.

3. The Party shall advise the Secretariat within 30 days or, in exceptional circumstances and on notification to the Secretariat, within 60 days of delivery of the request:

(a) whether the matter is the subject of a pending judicial or administrative proceeding, in which case the Secretariat shall proceed no further; and

(b) of any other information that the Party wishes to submit, such as

(i) whether the matter was previously the subject of a judicial or administrative proceeding, and

(ii) whether private remedies in connection with the matter are available to the person or organization making the submission and whether they have been pursued.

Article 15: Factual Record

1. If the Secretariat considers that the submission, in the light of any response provided by the Party, warrants developing a factual record, the Secretariat shall so inform the Council and provide its reasons.

2. The Secretariat shall prepare a factual record if the Council, by a two-thirds vote, instructs it to do so.

3. The preparation of a factual record by the Secretariat pursuant to this Article shall be without prejudice to any further steps that may be taken with respect to any submission.

4. In preparing a factual record, the Secretariat shall consider any information furnished by a Party and may consider any relevant technical, scientific or other information:

(a) that is publicly available;

(b) submitted by interested non-governmental organizations or persons;

(c) submitted by the Joint Public Advisory Committee; or

(d) developed by the Secretariat or by independent experts.

5. The Secretariat shall submit a draft factual record to the Council. Any Party may provide comments on the accuracy of the draft within 45 days thereafter.

6. The Secretariat shall incorporate, as appropriate, any such comments in the final factual record and submit it to the Council.

7. The Council may, by a two-thirds vote, make the final factual record publicly available, normally within 60 days following its submission.

SECTION C: ADVISORY COMMITTEES

Article 16: Joint Public Advisory Committee

1. The Joint Public Advisory Committee shall comprise 15 members, unless the Council otherwise decides. Each Party or, if the Party so decides, its National Advisory Committee convened under Article 17, shall appoint an equal number of members.

2. The Council shall establish the rules of procedure for the Joint Public Advisory Committee, which shall choose its own chair.

3. The Joint Public Advisory Committee shall convene at least once a year at the time of the regular session of the Council and at such other times as the Council, or the Committee's chair with the consent of a majority of its members, may decide.

4. The Joint Public Advisory Committee may provide advice to the Council on any matter within the scope of this Agreement, including on any documents provided to it under paragraph 6, and on the implementation and further elaboration of this Agreement, and may perform such other functions as the Council may direct.

5. The Joint Public Advisory Committee may provide relevant technical, scientific or other information to the Secretariat, including for purposes of developing a factual record under Article 15. The Secretariat shall forward to the Council copies of any such information.

6. The Secretariat shall provide to the Joint Public Advisory Committee at the time they are submitted to the Council copies of the proposed annual program and budget of the Commission, the draft annual report, and any report the Secretariat prepares pursuant to Article 13.

7. The Council may, by a two-thirds vote, make a factual record available to the Joint Public Advisory Committee.

Article 17: National Advisory Committees

Each Party may convene a national advisory committee, comprising members of its public, including representatives of non-governmental organizations and persons, to advise it on the implementation and further elaboration of this Agreement.

Article 18: Governmental Committees

Each Party may convene a governmental committee, which may comprise or include representatives of federal and state or provincial governments, to advise it on the implementation and further elaboration of this Agreement.

SECTION D: OFFICIAL LANGUAGES

Article 19: Official Languages

The official languages of the Commission shall be English, French and Spanish. All annual reports under Article 12, reports submitted to the Council under Article 13, factual records submitted to the Council under Article 15(6) and panel reports under Part Five shall be available in each official language at the time they are made public. The Council shall establish rules and procedures regarding interpretation and translation.

PART FOUR COOPERATION AND PROVISION OF INFORMATION

Article 20: Cooperation

1. The Parties shall at all times endeavor to agree on the interpretation and application of this Agreement, and shall make every attempt through cooperation and consultations to resolve any matter that might affect its operation.

2. To the maximum extent possible, each Party shall notify any other Party with an interest in the matter of any proposed or actual environmental measure that the Party considers might materially affect the operation of this Agreement or otherwise substantially affect that other Party's interests under this Agreement.

3. On request of any other Party, a Party shall promptly provide information and respond to questions pertaining to any such actual or proposed environmental measure, whether or not that other Party has been previously notified of that measure.

4. Any Party may notify any other Party of, and provide to that Party, any credible information regarding possible violations of its environmental law, specific and sufficient to allow the other Party to inquire into the matter. The notified Party shall take appropriate steps in accordance with its law to so inquire and to respond to the other Party.

Article 21: Provision of Information

1. On request of the Council or the Secretariat, each Party shall, in accordance with its law, provide such information as the Council or the Secretariat may require, including:

(a) promptly making available any information in its possession required for the preparation of a report or factual record, including compliance and enforcement data; and

(b) taking all reasonable steps to make available any other such information requested.

2. If a Party considers that a request for information from the Secretariat is excessive or otherwise unduly burdensome, it may so notify the Council. The Secretariat shall revise the scope of its request to comply with any limitations established by the Council by a two-thirds vote.

3. If a Party does not make available information requested by the Secretariat, as may be limited pursuant to paragraph 2, it shall promptly advise the Secretariat of its reasons in writing.

PART FIVE CONSULTATION AND RESOLUTION OF DISPUTES

Article 22: Consultations

1. Any Party may request in writing consultations with any other Party regarding whether there has been a persistent pattern of failure by that other Party to effectively enforce its environmental law.

2. The requesting Party shall deliver the request to the other Parties and to the Secretariat.

3. Unless the Council otherwise provides in its rules and procedures established under Article 9(2), a third Party that considers it has a substantial interest in the matter shall be entitled to participate in the consultations on delivery of written notice to the other Parties and to the Secretariat.

4. The consulting Parties shall make every attempt to arrive at a mutually satisfactory resolution of the matter through consultations under this Article.

Article 23: Initiation of Procedures

1. If the consulting Parties fail to resolve the matter pursuant to Article 22 within 60 days of delivery of a request for consultations, or such other period as the consulting Parties may agree, any such Party may request in writing a special session of the Council.

2. The requesting Party shall state in the request the matter complained of and shall deliver the request to the other Parties and to the Secretariat.

3. Unless it decides otherwise, the Council shall convene within 20 days of delivery of the request and shall endeavor to resolve the dispute promptly.

4. The Council may:

(a) call on such technical advisers or create such working groups or expert groups as it deems necessary,

(b) have recourse to good offices, conciliation, mediation or such other dispute resolution procedures, or

(c) make recommendations,

as may assist the consulting Parties to reach a mutually satisfactory resolution of the dispute. Any such recommendations shall be made public if the Council, by a two-thirds vote, so decides.

5. Where the Council decides that a matter is more properly covered by another agreement or arrangement to which the consulting Parties are party, it shall refer the matter to those Parties for appropriate action in accordance with such other agreement or arrangement.

Article 24: Request for an Arbitral Panel

1. If the matter has not been resolved within 60 days after the Council has convened pursuant to Article 23, the Council shall, on the written request of any consulting Party and by a two-thirds vote, convene an arbitral panel to consider the matter where the alleged persistent pattern of failure by the Party complained against to effectively enforce its environmental law relates to a situation involving workplaces, firms, companies or sectors that produce goods or provide services:

(a) traded between the territories of the Parties; or

(b) that compete, in the territory of the Party complained against, with goods or services produced or provided by persons of another Party.

2. A third Party that considers it has a substantial interest in the matter shall be entitled to join as a complaining Party on delivery of written notice of its intention to participate to the disputing Parties and the Secretariat. The notice shall be delivered at the earliest possible time, and in any event no later than seven days after the date of the vote of the Council to convene a panel.

3. Unless otherwise agreed by the disputing Parties, the panel shall be established and perform its functions in a manner consistent with the provisions of this Part.

Article 25: Roster

1. The Council shall establish and maintain a roster of up to 45 individuals who are willing and able to serve as panelists. The roster members shall be appointed by consensus for terms of three years, and may be reappointed.

2. Roster members shall:

(a) have expertise or experience in environmental law or its enforcement, or in the resolution of disputes arising under international agreements, or other relevant scientific, technical or professional expertise or experience;

(b) be chosen strictly on the basis of objectivity, reliability and sound judgment;

(c) be independent of, and not be affiliated with or take instructions from, any Party, the Secretariat or the Joint Public Advisory Committee; and

(d) comply with a code of conduct to be established by the Council.

Article 26: Qualifications of Panelists

1. All panelists shall meet the qualifications set out in Article 25(2).

2. Individuals may not serve as panelists for a dispute in which:

(a) they have participated pursuant to Article 23(4); or

(b) they have, or a person or organization with which they are affiliated has, an interest, as set out in the code of conduct established under Article 25(2)(d).

Article 27: Panel Selection

1. Where there are two disputing Parties, the following procedures shall apply:

(a) The panel shall comprise five members.

(b) The disputing Parties shall endeavor to agree on the chair of the panel within 15 days after the Council votes to convene the panel. If the disputing Parties are unable to agree on the chair within this period, the disputing Party chosen by lot shall select within five days a chair who is not a citizen of that Party.

(c) Within 15 days of selection of the chair, each disputing Party shall select two panelists who are citizens of the other disputing Party.

(d) If a disputing Party fails to select its panelists within such period, such panelists shall be selected by lot from among the roster members who are citizens of the other disputing Party.

2. Where there are more than two disputing Parties, the following procedures shall apply:

(a) The panel shall comprise five members.

(b) The disputing Parties shall endeavor to agree on the chair of the panel within 15 days after the Council votes to convene the panel. If the disputing Parties are unable to agree on the chair within this period, the Party or Parties on the side of the dispute chosen by lot shall select within 10 days a chair who is not a citizen of such Party or Parties.

(c) Within 30 days of selection of the chair, the Party complained against shall select two panelists, one of whom is a citizen of a complaining Party, and the other of whom is a citizen of another complaining Party. The complaining Parties shall select two panelists who are citizens of the Party complained against.

(d) If any disputing Party fails to select a panelist within such a period, such panelist shall be selected by lot in accordance with the citizenship criteria of subparagraph (c).

3. Panelists shall normally be selected from the roster. Any disputing Party may exercise a peremptory challenge against any individual not on the roster who is proposed as a panelist by a disputing Party within 30 days after the individual has been proposed.

4. If a disputing Party believes that a panelist is in violation of the code of conduct, the disputing Parties shall consult and, if they agree, the panelist shall be removed and a new panelist shall be selected in accordance with this Article.

Article 28: Rules of Procedure

1. The Council shall establish Model Rules of Procedure. The procedures shall provide:

(a) a right to at least one hearing before the panel;

(b) the opportunity to make initial and rebuttal written submissions; and

(c) that no panel may disclose which panelists are associated with majority or minority opinions.

2. Unless the disputing Parties otherwise agree, panels convened under this Part shall be established and conduct their proceedings in accordance with the Model Rules of Procedure.

3. Unless the disputing Parties otherwise agree within 20 days after the Council votes to convene the panel, the terms of reference shall be:

"To examine, in light of the relevant provisions of the Agreement, including those contained in Part Five, whether there has been a persistent pattern of failure by the Party complained against to effectively enforce its environmental law, and to make findings, determinations and recommendations in accordance with Article 31(2)."

Article 29: Third Party Participation

A party that is not a disputing Party, on delivery of a written notice to the disputing Parties and to the Secretariat, shall be entitled to attend all hearings, to make written and oral submissions to the panel and to receive written submissions of the disputing Parties.

Article 30: Role of Experts

On request of a disputing Party, or on its own initiative, the panel may seek information and technical advice from any person or body that it deems appropriate, provided that the disputing Parties so agree and subject to such terms and conditions as such Parties may agree.

Article 31: Initial Report

1. Unless the disputing Parties otherwise agree, the panel shall base its report on the submissions and arguments of the Parties and on any information before it pursuant to Article 30.

2. Unless the disputing Parties otherwise agree, the panel shall, within 180 days after the last panelist is selected, present to the disputing Parties an initial report containing:

(a) findings of fact;

(b) its determination as to whether there has been a persistent pattern of failure by the Party complained against to effectively enforce its environmental law, or any other determination requested in the terms of reference; and

(c) in the event the panel makes an affirmative determination under subparagraph (b), its recommendations, if any, for the resolution of the dispute, which normally shall be that the Party complained against adopt and implement an action plan sufficient to remedy the pattern of non-enforcement.

3. Panelists may furnish separate opinions on matters not unanimously agreed.

4. A disputing party may submit written comments to the panel on its initial report within 30 days of presentation of the report.

5. In such an event, and after considering such written comments, the panel, on its own initiative or on the request of any disputing Party, may:

(a) request the views of any participating Party;

(b) reconsider its report; and

(c) make any further examination that it considers appropriate.

Article 32: Final Report

1. The panel shall present to the disputing Parties a final report, including any separate opinions on matters not unanimously agreed, within 60 days of presentation of the initial report, unless the disputing Parties otherwise agree.

2. The disputing Parties shall transmit to the Council the final report of the panel, as well as any written views that a disputing Party desires to be appended, on a confidential basis within 15 days after it is presented to them.

3. The final report of the panel shall be published five days after it is transmitted to the Council.

Article 33: Implementation of Final Report

If, in its final report, a panel determines that there has been a persistent pattern of failure by the Party complained against to effectively enforce its environmental law, the disputing Parties may agree on a mutually satisfactory action plan, which normally shall conform with the determinations and recommendations of the panel. The disputing Parties shall promptly notify the Secretariat and the Council of any agreed resolution of the dispute.

Article 34: Review of Implementation

1. If, in its final report, a panel determines that there has been a persistent pattern of failure by the Party complained against to effectively enforce its environmental law, and:

(a) the disputing Parties have not agreed on an action plan under Article 33 within 60 days of the date of the final report, or

(b) the disputing Parties cannot agree on whether the Party complained against is fully implementing

(i) an action plan agreed under Article 33,

(ii) an action plan deemed to have been established by a panel under paragraph 2, or

(iii) an action plan approved or established by a panel under paragraph 4,

any disputing Party may request that the panel be reconvened. The requesting Party shall deliver the request in writing to the other Parties and to the Secretariat. The Council shall reconvene the panel on delivery of the request to the Secretariat.

2. No Party may make a request under paragraph 1(a) earlier than 60 days, or later than 120 days, after the date of the final report. If the disputing Parties have not agreed to an action plan and if no request was made under paragraph 1(a), the last action plan, if any, submitted by the Party complained against to the complaining Party or Parties within 60 days of the date of the final report, or such other period as the disputing Parties may agree, shall be deemed to have been established by the panel 120 days after the date of the final report.

3. A request under paragraph 1(b) may be made no earlier than 180 days after an action plan has been:

(a) agreed under Article 33;

(b) deemed to have been established by a panel under paragraph 2; or

(c) approved or established by a panel under paragraph 4;

and only during the term of any such action plan.

4. Where a panel has been reconvened under paragraph 1(a), it:

(a) shall determine whether any action plan proposed by the Party complained against is sufficient to remedy the pattern of non-enforcement and

(i) if so, shall approve the plan, or

(ii) if not, shall establish such a plan consistent with the law of the Party complained against, and

(b) may, where warranted, impose a monetary enforcement assessment in accordance with Annex 34,

within 90 days after the panel has been reconvened or such other period as the disputing Parties may agree.

5. Where a panel has been reconvened under paragraph 1(b), it shall determine either that:

(a) the Party complained against is fully implementing the action plan, in which case the panel may not impose a monetary enforcement assessment, or

(b) the Party complained against is not fully implementing the action plan, in which case the panel shall impose a monetary enforcement assessment in accordance with Annex 34,

within 60 days after it has been reconvened or such other period as the disputing Parties may agree.

6. A panel reconvened under this Article shall provide that the Party complained against shall fully implement any action plan referred to in paragraph 4(a)(ii) or 5(b), and pay any monetary enforcement assessment imposed under paragraph 4(b) or 5(b), and any such provision shall be final.

Article 35: Further Proceeding

A complaining Party may, at any time beginning 180 days after a panel determination under Article 34(5)(b), request in writing that a panel be reconvened to determine whether the Party complained against is fully implementing the action plan. On delivery of the request to the other Parties and the Secretariat, the Council shall reconvene the panel. The panel shall make the determination within 60 days after it has been reconvened or such other period as the disputing Parties may agree.

Article 36: Suspension of Benefits

1. Subject to Annex 36A, where a Party fails to pay a monetary enforcement assessment within 180 days after it is imposed by a panel:

(a) under Article 34(4)(b), or

(b) under Article 34(5)(b), except where benefits may be suspended under paragraph 2(a),

any complaining Party or Parties may suspend, in accordance with Annex 36B, the application to the Party complained against of NAFTA benefits in an amount no greater than that sufficient to collect the monetary enforcement assessment.

2. Subject to Annex 36A, where a panel has made a determination under Article 34(5)(b) and the panel:

(a) has previously imposed a monetary enforcement assessment under Article 34(4)(b) or established an action plan under Article 34(4)(a)(ii); or

(b) has subsequently determined under Article 35 that a Party is not fully implementing an action plan;

the complaining Party or Parties may, in accordance with Annex 36B, suspend annually the application to the Party complained against of NAFTA benefits in an amount no greater than the monetary enforcement assessment imposed by the panel under Article 34(5)(b).

3. Where more than one complaining Party suspends benefits under paragraph 1 or 2, the combined suspension shall be no greater than the amount of the monetary enforcement assessment.

4. Where a Party has suspended benefits under paragraph 1 or 2, the Council shall, on the delivery of a written request by the Party complained against to the other Parties and the Secretariat, reconvene the panel to determine whether the monetary enforcement assessment has been paid or collected, or whether the Party complained against is fully implementing the action plan, as the case may be. The panel shall submit its report within 45 days after it has been reconvened. If the panel determines that the assessment has been paid or collected, or that the Party complained against is fully implementing the action plan, the suspension of benefits under paragraph 1 or 2, as the case may be, shall be terminated.

5. On the written request of the Party complained against, delivered to the other Parties and the Secretariat, the Council shall reconvene the panel to determine whether the suspension of benefits by the complaining Party or Parties pursuant to paragraph 1 or 2 is manifestly excessive. Within 45 days of the request, the panel shall present a report to the disputing Parties containing its determination.

PART SIX GENERAL PROVISIONS

Article 37: Enforcement Principle

Nothing in this Agreement shall be construed to empower a Party's authorities to undertake environmental law enforcement activities in the territory of another Party.

Article 38: Private Rights

No Party may provide for a right of action under its law against any other Party on the ground that another Party has acted in a manner inconsistent with this Agreement.

Article 39: Protection of Information

1. Nothing in this Agreement shall be construed to require a Party to make available or allow access to information:

(a) the disclosure of which would impede its environmental law enforcement; or

(b) that is protected from disclosure by its law governing business or proprietary information, personal privacy or the confidentiality of governmental decision making.

2. If a Party provides confidential or proprietary information to another Party, the Council, the Secretariat or the Joint Public Advisory Committee, the recipient shall treat the information on the same basis as the Party providing the information.

3. Confidential or proprietary information provided by a Party to a panel under this Agreement shall be treated in accordance with the rules of procedure established under Article 28.

Article 40: Relation to Other Environmental Agreements

Nothing in this Agreement shall be construed to affect the existing rights and obligations of the Parties under other international environmental agreements, including conservation agreements, to which such Parties are party.

Article 41: Extent of Obligations

Annex 41 applies to the Parties specified in that Annex.

Article 42: National Security

Nothing in this Agreement shall be construed:

(a) to require any Party to make available or provide access to information the disclosure of which it determines to be contrary to its essential security interests; or

(b) to prevent any Party from taking any actions that it considers necessary for the protection of its essential security interests relating to

(i) arms, ammunition and implements of war, or

(ii) the implementation of national policies or international agreements respecting the non-proliferation of nuclear weapons or other nuclear explosive devices.

Article 43: Funding of the Commission

Each Party shall contribute an equal share of the annual budget of the Commission, subject to the availability of appropriated funds in accordance with the Party's legal procedures. No Party shall be obligated to pay more than any other Party in respect of an annual budget.

Article 44: Privileges and Immunities

The Executive Director and staff of the Secretariat shall enjoy in the territory of each Party such privileges and immunities as are necessary for the exercise of their functions.

Article 45: Definitions

1. For purposes of this Agreement:

A Party has not failed to **"effectively enforce its environmental law"** or to comply with Article 5(1) in a particular case where the action or inaction in question by agencies or officials of that Party:

(a) reflects a reasonable exercise of their discretion in respect of investigatory, prosecutorial, regulatory or compliance matters; or

(b) results from *bona fide* decisions to allocate resources to enforcement in respect of other environmental matters determined to have higher priorities;

"non-governmental organization" means any scientific, professional, business, non-profit, or public interest organization or association which is neither affiliated with, nor under the direction of, a government;

"persistent pattern" means a sustained or recurring course of action or inaction beginning after the date of entry into force of this Agreement;

"province" means a province of Canada, and includes the Yukon Territory and the Northwest Territories and their successors; and

"territory" means for a Party the territory of that Party as set out in Annex 45.

2. For purposes of Article 14(1) and Part Five:

(a) **"environmental law"** means any statute or regulation of a Party, or provision thereof, the primary purpose of which is the protection of the environment, or the prevention of a danger to human life or health, through

(i) the prevention, abatement or control of the release, discharge, or emission of pollutants or environmental contaminants,

(ii) the control of environmentally hazardous or toxic chemicals, substances, materials and wastes, and the dissemination of information related thereto, or

(iii) the protection of wild flora or fauna, including endangered species, their habitat, and specially protected natural areas

in the Party's territory, but does not include any statute or regulation, or provision thereof, directly related to worker safety or health.

(b) For greater certainty, the term **"environmental law"** does not include any statute or regulation, or provision thereof, the primary purpose of which is managing the commercial harvest or exploitation, or subsistence or aboriginal harvesting, of natural resources.

(c) The primary purpose of a particular statutory or regulatory provision for purposes of subparagraphs (a) and (b) shall be determined by reference to its primary purpose, rather than to the primary purpose of the statute or regulation of which it is part.

3. For purposes of Article 14(3), **"judicial or administrative proceeding"** means:

(a) a domestic judicial, quasi-judicial or administrative action pursued by the Party in a timely fashion and in accordance with its law. Such actions comprise: mediation; arbitration; the process of issuing a license, permit, or authorization; seeking an assurance of voluntary compliance or a compliance agreement; seeking sanctions or remedies in an administrative or judicial forum; and the process of issuing an administrative order; and

(b) an international dispute resolution proceeding to which the Party is party.

PART SEVEN FINAL PROVISIONS

Article 46: Annexes

The Annexes to this Agreement constitute an integral part of the Agreement.

Article 47: Entry into Force

This Agreement shall enter into force on January 1, 1994, immediately after entry into force of the NAFTA, on an exchange of written notifications certifying the completion of necessary legal procedures.

Article 48: Amendments

1. The Parties may agree on any modification of or addition to this Agreement.

2. When so agreed, and approved in accordance with the applicable legal procedures of each Party, a modification or addition shall constitute an integral part of this Agreement.

Article 49: Accession

Any country or group of countries may accede to this Agreement subject to such terms and conditions as may be agreed between such country or countries and the Council and following approval in accordance with the applicable legal procedures of each country.

Article 50: Withdrawal

A Party may withdraw from this Agreement six months after it provides written notice of withdrawal to the other Parties. If a Party withdraws, the Agreement shall remain in force for the remaining Parties.

Article 51: Authentic Texts

The English, French, and Spanish texts of this Agreement are equally authentic.

IN WITNESS WHEREOF, the undersigned, being duly authorized by the respective Governments, have signed this Agreement.

North American Free Trade Agreement

Chapter 6 Energy and Basic Petrochemicals
32 I.L.M. 289 (1993)

http://www.nafta-sec-alena.org/DefaultSite/legal/index_e.aspx?articleid=124

ARTICLE 601: PRINCIPLES

1. The Parties confirm their full respect for their Constitutions.

2. The Parties recognize that it is desirable to strengthen the important role that trade in energy and basic petrochemical goods plays in the free trade area and to enhance this role through sustained and gradual liberalization.

3. The Parties recognize the importance of having viable and internationally competitive energy and petrochemical sectors to further their individual national interests.

ARTICLE 602: SCOPE AND COVERAGE

1. This Chapter applies to measures relating to energy and basic petrochemical goods originating in the territories of the Parties and to measures relating to investment and to the cross-border trade in services associated with such goods, as set forth in this Chapter.

2. For purposes of this Chapter, energy and basic petrochemical goods refer to those goods classified under the Harmonized System as:

a) subheading 2612.10;

b) headings 27.01 through 27.06;

c) subheading 2707.50;

d) subheading 2707.99 (only with respect to solvent naphtha, rubber extender oils and carbon black feedstocks);

e) headings 27.08 and 27.09;

f) heading 27.10 (except for normal paraffin mixtures in the range of C9 to C15);

g) heading 27.11 (except for ethylene, propylene, butylene and butadiene in purities over 50 percent);

h) headings 27.12 through 27.16;

i) subheadings 2844.10 through 2844.50 (only with respect to uranium compounds classified under those subheadings);

j) subheading 2845.10; and

k) subheading 2901.10 (only with respect to ethane, butanes, pentanes, hexanes, and heptanes).

3. Except as specified in Annex 602.3, energy and petrochemical goods and activities shall be governed by the provisions of this Agreement.

ARTICLE 603: IMPORT AND EXPORT RESTRICTIONS

1. Subject to the further rights and obligations of this Agreement, the Parties incorporate the provisions of the *General Agreement on Tariffs and Trade* (GATT), with respect to prohibitions or restrictions on trade in energy and basic petrochemical goods. The Parties agree that this language does not incorporate their respective protocols of provisional application to the GATT.

2. The Parties understand that the provisions of the GATT incorporated in paragraph 1 prohibit, in any circumstances in which any other form of quantitative restriction is prohibited, minimum or maximum export-price requirements and, except as permitted in enforcement of countervailing and antidumping orders and undertakings, minimum or maximum import-price requirements.

3. In circumstances where a Party adopts or maintains a restriction on importation from or exportation to a non-Party of an energy or basic petrochemical good, nothing in this Agreement shall be construed to prevent the Party from:

a) limiting or prohibiting the importation from the territory of any Party of such energy or basic petrochemical good of the nonParty; or

b) requiring as a condition of export of such energy or basic petrochemical good of the Party to the territory of any other Party that the good be consumed within the territory of the other Party.

4. In the event that a Party adopts or maintains a restriction on imports of an energy or basic petrochemical good from non-Party countries, the Parties, on request of any Party, shall consult with a view to avoiding undue interference with or distortion of pricing, marketing and distribution arrangements in another Party.

5. Each Party may administer a system of import and export licensing for energy or basic petrochemical goods provided that such system is operated in a manner consistent with the provisions of this Agreement, including paragraph 1 and Article 1502 (Monopolies and State Enterprises).

6. This Article is subject to the reservations set out in Annex 603.6.

ARTICLE 604: EXPORT TAXES

No Party may adopt or maintain any duty, tax or other charge on the export of any energy or basic petrochemical good to the territory of another Party, unless such duty, tax or charge is adopted or maintained on:

a) exports of any such good to the territory of all other Parties; and

b) any such good when destined for domestic consumption.

ARTICLE 605: OTHER EXPORT MEASURES

Subject to Annex 605, a Party may adopt or maintain a restriction otherwise justified under Articles XI:2(a) or XX(g), (i) or (j) of the GATT with respect to the export of an energy or basic petrochemical good to the territory of another Party, only if:

a) the restriction does not reduce the proportion of the total export shipments of the specific energy or basic petrochemical good made available to that other Party relative to the total supply of that good of the Party maintaining the restriction as compared to the proportion prevailing in the most recent 36 month period for which data are available prior to the imposition of the measure, or in such other representative period on which the Parties may agree;

b) the Party does not impose a higher price for exports of an energy or basic petrochemical good to that other Party than the price charged for such good when consumed domestically, by means of any measure such as licenses, fees, taxation and minimum price requirements. The foregoing provision does not apply to a higher price that may result from a measure taken pursuant to subparagraph (a) that only restricts the volume of exports; and

c) the restriction does not require the disruption of normal channels of supply to that other Party or normal proportions among specific energy or basic petrochemical goods supplied to that other Party, such as, for example, between crude oil and refined products and among different categories of crude oil and of refined products.

ARTICLE 606: ENERGY REGULATORY MEASURES

1. The Parties recognize that energy regulatory measures are subject to the disciplines of:

a) national treatment, as provided in Article 301;

b) import and export restrictions, as provided in Article 603; and

c) export taxes, as provided in Article 604.

2. Each Party shall seek to ensure that in the application of any energy regulatory measure, energy regulatory bodies within its territory avoid disruption of contractual relationships to the maximum extent practicable, and provide for orderly and equitable implementation appropriate to such measures.

ARTICLE 607: NATIONAL SECURITY MEASURES

Subject to Annex 607, no Party may adopt or maintain a measure restricting imports of an energy or basic petrochemical good from, or exports of an energy or basic petrochemical good to, another Party under Article XXI of the GATT or under Article 2102 (National Security), except to the extent necessary to:

a) supply a military establishment of a Party or enable fulfillment of a critical defense contract of a Party;

b) respond to a situation of armed conflict involving the Party taking the measure;

c) implement national policies or international agreements relating to the non-proliferation of nuclear weapons or other nuclear explosive devices; or

d) respond to direct threats of disruption in the supply of nuclear materials for defense purposes.

ARTICLE 608: MISCELLANEOUS PROVISIONS

1. The Parties agree to allow existing or future incentives for oil and gas exploration, development and related activities in order to maintain the reserve base for these energy resources.

2. Annex 608.2 applies only to the Parties specified in that Annex with respect to other agreements relating to trade in energy goods.

ARTICLE 609: DEFINITIONS

For purposes of this Chapter:

consumed means transformed so as to qualify under the rules of origin set out in Chapter Four (Rules of Origin), or actually consumed;

cross-border trade in services means "crossborder trade in services" as defined in Article 1213 (Cross-Border Trade in Services Definitions);

energy regulatory measure means any measure by federal or sub-federal entities that directly affects the transportation, transmission or distribution, purchase or sale, of an energy or basic petrochemical good;

enterprise means "enterprise" as defined in Article 1139 (Investment-Definitions);

enterprise of a Party means "enterprise of a Party" as defined in Article 1139;

facility for independent power production means a facility that is used for the generation of electric energy exclusively for sale to an electric utility for further resale;

first hand sale refers to the first commercial transaction affecting the good in question;

investment means investment as defined in Article 1139;

restriction means any limitation, whether made effective through quotas, licenses, permits, minimum or maximum price requirements or any other means;

total export shipments means the total shipments from total supply to users located in the territory of the other Party; and

total supply means shipments to domestic users and foreign users from:

a) domestic production;

b) domestic inventory; and

c) other imports, as appropriate.

Transboundary Impact Assessment Overarching Principles

Oaxaca, Mexico 13 October 1995

Council Resolution 95-7

http://www.cec.org/files/pdf/COUNCIL/95-07e_EN.pdf

These principles are intended to inform and guide the Council as it develops more specific recommendations and considerations pursuant to Article 10(7) of the *North American Agreement on Environmental Cooperation.*

1. *Pollution does not respect borders*

• As part of the same environment, States need to work together to achieve national objectives concerning conservation, environmental protection and environmental enhancement.

• Recognizing that environmental effects extend across borders, States should promote communication, cooperation and information sharing on projects and developments within their jurisdictions.

• A State which is likely to be adversely affected by an activity taking place in another State is best equipped to determine which environmental impacts are of concern to itself and its citizens and should make these known to that State.

2. *Good neighborliness*

• Good neighborliness embraces Principle 2 of the *1992 Rio Declaration.*

• Good neighborliness embraces Article 10(7) of the *North American Agreement on Environmental Cooperation.*

• Good neighborliness is a willingness to cooperate with neighboring States to seek to inform a potentially affected State of relevant data and a willingness to take appropriate steps to address the legitimate concerns of those potentially impacted by the activities in another State.

• Good neighborliness provides a potentially affected State with the opportunity to contribute comments and information to the environmental assessment process.

3. *Respect for national and subnational processes*

• Recognizing the unique circumstances giving rise to environmental impact assessment laws and practices, any new procedures or mechanisms proposed should respect the integrity of national and subnational processes and instruments.

4. *Cost effectiveness and efficiency*

• Any procedure or mechanism developed should be efficient and cost effective, maximizing wherever possible the utilization of existing processes, structures or mechanisms.

5. *Complementarity*

• Any procedure or mechanism developed should complement or build on successful procedures or mechanisms in place at various levels of government.

6. *Public participation*

• Consistent with national and subnational regimes, any mechanism or procedure developed should ensure that the public has adequate information and the opportunity to participate in a meaningful manner in such mechanisms or procedures.

Additional Protocol to the American Convention on Human Rights in the Area of Economic Social and Cultural Rights, "Protocol of San Salvador"

San Salvador, 17 November 17 1988,

http://www.oas.org/juridico/english/Treaties/a-52.html

ARTICLE 11 RIGHT TO A HEALTHY ENVIRONMENT

1. Everyone shall have the right to live in a healthy environment and to have access to basic public services.

2. The States Parties shall promote the protection, preservation, and improvement of the environment.

Action Plan of the Council of Andean Community Ministers of Energy, Electricity, Hydrocarbons and Mines

Bogotá, Colombia, 19 June 2003

www.comunidadandina.org/ingles/services/energy_2.htm

1. To incorporate the interconnection of natural gas as a new element of Andean energy integration policy.

2. To foster the harmonization of contracting procedures for hydrocarbon and mining projects, among others, in a context of full respect for each Member Country's autonomy in this area.

3. To approve the Work Plan presented by the Working Group of Regulatory Agencies (GTOR) to advance electric interconnection and domestic energy markets in the subregion and to report its progress to the Council of Ministers of Energy, Electricity, Hydrocarbons and Mines.

4. To support the activities that are being carried out as part of the IIRSA in the energy sector and to reinforce Andean Community participation.

5. To promote and boost the use of alternative energy sources in the subregion and to share existing experiences.

6. Given the impact of the energy sector in improving the living conditions of the subregion's inhabitants, it is essential to link up this subject with the formulating and execution of the Andean social agenda.

7. To point out to the Advisory Council of Treasury or Finance Ministers, Central Bank Presidents and heads of Planning Institutions that in harmonizing macroeconomic policies within the Andean integration process, due consideration should be given to the impact of these policies on the integration of the energy sector.

8. To promote actions for balancing the development of the electric, hydrocarbon and mining sectors within a framework of sustainable development.

9. To bolster the transfer of technology to companies in the region and to expedite the participation of national companies in providing energy and mining services.

10. Based on an evaluation of the legal contexts and of the policies in effect today in the Andean Community and its five Member Countries that affect the promotion and operation of energy clusters and energy services, to prepare an inventory and a preliminary evaluation of domestic and transnational enterprises operating in the subregion and to identify concrete opportunities to consolidate existing clusters and promote new networks and complexes for cooperation among firms at the national and subregional levels. Furthermore, to request the Andean Community General Secretariat to prepare public policy options – for consideration by the Ministers – aimed at promoting and developing energy services and energy clusters in the subregion.

11. To request the Andean Community General Secretariat to prepare scenarios and proposals on negotiating objectives and strategies that will make it possible to implement the proposed policies for developing energy services and energy clusters. These scenarios and proposals should cover energy services and other subjects that are vitally important for ensuring the viability of those polices and should be submitted for consideration by the energy and trade authorities of the Andean countries.

12. To recommend that the Member Countries back the proposal on the objectives, negotiating methods and classification of energy services put forward by Venezuela during the WTO negotiations and the attendance of that country at the forthcoming meeting of the "Friends of Energy Group," to be held on July 8, 2003 in Geneva, and its active participation in the successive negotiations concerning energy services in the WTO.

13. To recommend that the Member Countries form national inter-institutional teams to follow up on the energy services negotiations and to support the negotiating teams of the Andean missions in Geneva.

14. To foster the establishment of common Andean positions in negotiating with third parties, particularly the United States of America, given the characteristics of the oil and gas market and the region's competitive possibilities.

VI. SELECT NATIONAL LEGISLATION ILLUSTRATIVE OF SUSTAINABLE ENERGY LAW INNOVATIONS

AFRICA

Convention of the African Energy Commission

PREAMBLE

The Member States of the Organization of African Unity;

RECOGNIZING that severe energy shortages in many African countries have constrained industrial development efforts for many years in spite of the enormous conventional energy potential as well as vast deposits of new and renewable energy resources;

REALIZING the fact that Africa must harness its energy resources and make them available to meet the energy needs of its peoples in order to be able to develop and provide an alternative to deforestation and use of firewood as a primary source of energy;

RECALLING the various Resolutions and Declarations wherein it had been stipulated that the integrated economic development of the African continent is an essential condition for the achievement of the objectives of the Organization of African Unity;

RECALLING FURTHER the Lagos Plan of Action adopted in 1980, the Cairo Agenda for Action adopted in 1995 and the Resolutions of the First Pan African Energy Ministers' Conferences adopted in Tunis in 1995, of the First and Second Regional Conference of African Ministers Responsible for the Development and Utilization of Mineral and Energy Resources held in Accra in 1995 and Durban in 1997, which, *inter alia*, advocate the need for accelerated socio-economic development in Africa, including the sustainable development and exploitation of energy resources, respectively;

RECALLING ALSO the Regulation and Decision adopted by the Council of Ministers meeting in its Seventy-Second and Seventy-Third Ordinary Sessions in Lomé, Togo, from 6 to 8 July 2000 and Tripoli, Libya, from 22 to 26 February 2001 endorsing the principle of establishing the African Energy Commission, Regulation CM/OAU/AEC/ Regl. 1 (VII), Para.5 and CM/Dec.559 (LXXXIIIII), respectively, as well as the recommendations of the Conference of African Ministers of Energy held in Algiers, Algeria, from 23 to 24 April 2001;

RECOGNIZING the need to co-ordinate the actions of the African countries to develop their energy resources and deal jointly with the various problems relating to their efficient and rational exploitation and utilization, in order to ensure socio-economic development;

REAFFIRMING the provisions of the Treaty Establishing the African Economic Community, in general, and Article 54 (2) (f), in particular wherein it has been provided that Member States of the African Economic Community shall, in the co-ordination and harmonization of their policies and programmes in the field of energy, "establish an adequate mechanism of concerted action and co-ordination for the collective solution of the energy development problems within the community. . . .";

HAVE AGREED as follows:

CHAPTER I GENERAL PROVISIONS

ARTICLE 1 DEFINITIONS

In this Convention, unless the context requires otherwise,

(a) "AFREC" shall mean the African Energy Commission

(b) "Board" shall mean the Executive Board established by Article 6 of this Convention;

(c) "Conference" shall mean the Conference of Ministers or Authorities responsible for Energy established by Article 6 of this Convention;

(d) "Energy" shall mean new and renewable or non-renewable resource of energy in the natural state or processed, harnessed by humankind.

(e) "Treaty" shall mean the Treaty Establishing the African Economic Community

(f) "Regional Economic Community" or RECs shall mean any African regional economic community established, inter alia, to co-ordinate energy development on a regional or sub-regional basis and in compliance with the Treaty's definition.

(g) "Member State" shall mean a Member State of the African Energy Commission established by this Convention.

ARTICLE 2 ESTABLISHMENT

1. There shall be established within the Organization of African Unity, the African Energy Commission.

2. It shall be composed of each Member States of the OAU.

ARTICLE 3 GUIDING PRINCIPLES

For the purpose of this Convention, the Member States solemnly affirm and declare their adherence to the following principles:

(a) Development of the use of energy to promote and support rapid economic and social development, eradication of poverty, combat desertification and improve the standard and quality of life throughout the Member States;

(b) Co-operation in the area of energy among Member States, particularly through joint development of energy resources and identification and promotion of regional and/or sub-regional projects;

(c) Development and utilization of sustainable and environmentally sound energy;

(d) Acceleration of the implementation of the Abuja Treaty through the integrated, co-ordinated and harmonized development and utilization of energy and the development and implementation of energy policies and programmes;

(e) Promotion of research and development, and the encouragement of transfer of technology in the energy sector;

(f) Enhancement of integration, collective self-reliance, security and reliability of energy supply among Member States;

(g) Inter-state, sub-regional and regional co-operation in training and development of human resources in the energy field;

(h) Harmonization of standards and procedures in the energy sector;

(i) Promotion of trade and technical assistance in energy among Member States;

(j) Promotion of partnership among enterprises and institutions of Member States through, inter alia, the creation of favourable conditions for that purpose;

(k) Equitable cost-sharing in the implementation of this Convention in a spirit of good governance and transparency;

(l) Peaceful settlement of disputes;

ARTICLE 4 FUNCTIONS OF AFREC

AFREC shall have the following functions, namely to:

(a) Map out energy development policies, strategies and plans based on sub-regional, regional and continental development priorities and recommend their implementation;

(b) Design, create and up date an energy continental data base and facilitate rapid dissemination of information and exchange of information among Member States, as well as among the Regional Economic Communities (RECs);

(c) Advise and encourage the development of human resources in the energy sector in particular, through training;

(d) Mobilize financial resources to provide to Member States and the Regional Economic Communities with all the necessary assistance for the development of their energy sectors;

(e) Encourage research and development in the energy sector;

(f) Develop trade and transit of energy goods and services among Member States, particularly through the identification and removal of barriers;

(g) Provide technical assistance to Member States, Regional Economic Communities and other stake holders in the African energy sectors;

(h) Recommend the use of harmonized standards and procedures in the energy sector;

(i) Establish the necessary mechanisms for the exploitation and utilization of energy resources of the continent in an optimal manner with the aim of complimentarity;

(j) Undertake the harmonisation and rationalization of energy development and utilization programmes;

(k) Promote among Member States the identification and the adoption and implementation of effective measures to prevent environmental pollution particularly in the exploitation, transportation, storage, distribution, and utilization of the continent's energy resources the control of the system and mechanism for the pricing and tarification of energy;

(l) Work towards the realization of added value to energy resources in Member States;

(m) Assist in the development and utilization of new and renewable sources of energy;

(n) Provide assistance in feasibility study for energy projects and its adverse impact on the environment;

(o) Perform any other activity that may be necessary for realization of the above objectives;

ARTICLE 5 HEADQUARTERS OF AFREC

The Headquarters of AFREC shall be in Algiers, in the People's Democratic Republic of Algeria.

ARTICLE 6 STRUCTURE

The organs of the AFREC shall be:

(a) The Conference of Ministers or Authorities responsible for Energy;

(b) The Executive Board;

(c) The Secretariat;

(d) The Technical Advisory Body; and

(e) Other subsidiary organs that may be established in accordance with the provisions of this Convention.

CHAPTER II MANAGEMENT

ARTICLE 7 THE CONFERENCE – POWERS AND DUTIES

1. The Conference shall be the highest authority of the Commission.

2. It shall meet in ordinary session once every two (2) years at the Headquarters of the Commission or in any Member State upon the recommendation of the Conference. It may meet in extra-ordinary session at the request of the Executive Board or a Member State and subject to the concurrence of at least two-thirds of the Member States of the Commission.

3. Without prejudice to the generality of the foregoing, the Conference shall, in particular.

(a) Discuss the general policy and approve the work programmes of the Commission and evaluate their implementation;

(b) Consider and approve the Commission's budget and examine the auditors' report;

(c) Adopt its Rules of Procedure;

(d) Approve the Commission's Staff Rules and Regulations and Financial Rules and Regulations;

(e) Elect its Bureau;

(f) Approve, on the proposal of the Executive Board the appointment and removal of the Executive Director of the Commission, in accordance with this Convention and the internal regulations;

(g) Elect Member States to serve on the Executive Board of the Commission;

(h) Approve the organizational structure of the Secretariat.

ARTICLE 8 EXECUTIVE BOARD

1. The Board shall serve for a period of two years.

2. It shall hold one ordinary meeting every year at the Headquarters of the Commission or in any Member State upon the recommendation of the Board. It may also meet in extra-ordinary session under conditions to be specified in the Rules of Procedure of the Commission;

3. It shall be composed as follows:

(a) Fifteen senior energy experts representing Member States, elected on the basis of the OAU criteria for geographical representation and on a rotational basis;

(b) Senior energy expert of the Organization of African Unity representing the Secretary- General;

(c) One duly appointed representative of each of the RECs, *ex-officio*;

(d) One duly appointed representative of the Union of Producers, Conveyors and Distributors of Electric Power in Africa (UPEDEA), *ex-officio*;

(e) A senior energy expert of the African Development Bank, *ex-officio*;

(f) A senior energy expert of the United Nations Economic Commission for Africa, *ex-officio;*

(g) The Executive Director who shall serve as the Secretary of the Board.

4. The Board shall be answerable to the Conference.

5. Without prejudice to the generality of the foregoing, the Board shall, in particular, be responsible for the following:

(a) Prepare and submit the provisional work programmes, studies, projects, and the Commission's annual budget for the consideration of the Conference;

(b) Submit a periodic report on the activities of the Commission to the Conference;

(c) Determine the terms and conditions of service of the staff of the Commission;

(d) Prepare for the meetings of the Conference;

(e) Recommend the appointment and the removal of the Executive Director of the Commission;

(f) Perform any other function that may be assigned to it by the Conference.

ARTICLE 9 THE SECRETARIAT – POWERS AND DUTIES

1. The Secretariat of the Commission shall be headed by the Executive Director. He/she shall be assisted by the necessary staff.

2. The Secretariat shall in particular:

(a) Provide Secretarial services to all the sessions of the Commission's organs;

(b) Be responsible for the day to day management of the Commission;

(c) Follow-up on the implementation of decisions of the Conference and the Board;

(d) Keep in custody the documents, files and other data relating or relevant to the work of the Commission;

(e) Keep an inventory of the energy resources, requirements, legislation, and programmes of Member States, RECs and other parties;

(f) Prepare of Agenda, documents and provisional work programmes for consideration by the Board;

(g) Prepare and submit the draft Programme-Budget, annual report, balance sheet and financial statements for submission to the Conference for its consideration and appropriate action, subject to previous study by the Executive Board;

(h) Prepare and submit reports on the activities of the Commission;

(i) Convene meetings, symposiums, exhibitions as well as groups and panels of experts it considers necessary for the implementation of its work programmes and of the activities entrusted to it by the Conference or the Executive Board;

(j) Initiate studies, collect and analyse information and data;

(k) Perform any other duty that may be entrusted to it by the Conference and/or the Executive Board;

ARTICLE 10 THE EXECUTIVE DIRECTOR – FUNCTIONS

1. The Executive Director, appointed for a renewable mandate of four years, shall direct the affairs of the Secretariat and is responsible for the performance of its duties.

2. He/she is the accounting officer of the Commission and is responsible for the proper administration of the budget.

3. Without any prejudice to the generality of the foregoing, the Executive Director shall, in particular,

(a) Follow-up and ensure the implementation of the decisions of the Conference and the Executive Board.

(b) Provide secretarial services to the Conference and the Executive Board;

(c) Act as the legal representative of the Commission;

(d) Appoint and remove in accordance with conditions to be laid down in the internal regulations, the administrative and technical personnel of the Secretariat; and

(e) Ensure the geographical and equitable distribution of the Secretariat's personnel;

(f) Performing other functions that may be assigned to it by the Conference.

ARTICLE 11 TECHNICAL ADVISORY BODY

1. The Technical Advisory Body shall comprise the RECs, Joint Secretariat of the OAU/ECA/ADB/UN Agencies operating in the energy sector such as UNEP, UNDP, UNDESA, UNIDO, FAO and UNESCO as well as relevant regional and sub-regional entities dealing with energy as the World Energy Council (WEC).

2. It shall be a consultative forum on energy policies, programmes, projects and related activities. It shall provide, more particularly, advisory and technical assistance to the Commission.

ARTICLE 12 RULES OF PROCEDURE

The Commission shall determine its own rules of procedure. The Rules will provide, inter alia, for the quorum and the procedures for decision making by the Commission.

ARTICLE 13 OBSERVERS

The Conference may establish modalities, in the Rules of Procedure, for granting Observer status and for the participation of invited guests in its sessions.

ARTICLE 14 OBLIGATIONS

1. In the performance of their duties, the Executive Director and the staff shall not receive instructions from any Government or from any other authority external to organization. They shall refrain from any action which might reflect on their position as international officials responsible only to the Organization.

2. Each Member State undertakes to respect the exclusive character of the responsibilities of the Executive Director and the staff and not to seek to influence them in the discharge of their responsibilities.

CHAPTER III ASSETS, FINANCIAL RESOURCES AND AUDIT

ARTICLE 15 ASSETS OF THE COMMISSION

The assets of the Commission shall consist of acquisitions by gift or purchase.

ARTICLE 16 FINANCIAL RESOURCES

1. The Budget of the Commission approved by the Conference shall, subject to such Financial Rules and Regulations as may be adopted, be administered by the Executive Director of the Commission under the supervision of the Board.

2. The financial resources of the Commission shall consist of,

(a) Annual contributions by the Member States;

(b) Special contributions from the Member States;

(c) The Commission's remuneration for any services that it renders;

(d) Gifts, bequests and other donations

(e) Other sources as may be approved by the Board.

ARTICLE 17 AUDIT

The books of accounts of the Commission shall be audited by external auditors approved by the Conference.

ARTICLE 18 PAYMENT OF CONTRIBUTIONS

1. Members of the Commission undertake to pay their assessed contributions regularly;

2. Any Member with outstanding arrears of contributions to the regular budget of the Commission equal to or greater than its assessed contribution for the previous two complete fiscal years shall be deprived of the right to take the floor, to vote and to present candidates for any post in any of the organs of the Commission.

CHAPTER IV MISCELLANEOUS PROVISIONS

ARTICLE 19 STATUS, PRIVILEGES AND IMMUNITIES

The Commission, its property and assets and staff shall enjoy in the territory of each State party to this

Constitution the privileges and immunities provided for in the OAU General Convention on Privileges and Immunities. In this regard, the Commission shall conclude with the Member State in whose territory its Headquarters is established a Host Agreement.

ARTICLE 20 AMENDMENT

1. Any Member State may submit its written proposals for the amendment of this Convention to the Executive Director who shall transmit the same to all the Member States of the Commission, within a period not exceeding three months following the receipt by the Secretariat of the proposed amendment.

2. The proposed amendment shall not be submitted to the Conference for consideration until all the members have been duly notified of it and a period of one year has elapsed.

3. Such an amendment shall require approval by at least two-thirds of all the Member States.

ARTICLE 21 CESSATION OF MEMBERSHIP

1. Any State which desires to withdraw or renounce its Membership shall forward a written notification to the Executive Director. At the end of one year from the date of such notification, if not withdrawn, the Convention shall cease to apply with respect to the renouncing State, which, shall thereby cease to be a Member.

2. A member that has submitted a notice of withdrawal in accordance with sub-article (1) of this Article shall, during the period of notice, exercise all the rights and obligations of a member in accordance with the provisions of this Convention.

3. The Conference shall have the power to suspend, under conditions to be specified, any member from the Commission where it decides by two thirds majority of the votes of all members that such a member has failed to discharge its obligations in accordance with the provisions of this Convention.

ARTICLE 22 OFFICIAL LANGUAGES

The official languages of the Commission shall be those of the Organization of African Unity.

ARTICLE 23 SPECIAL RELATIONS WITH REGIONAL ECONOMIC COMMUNITIES AND INTERNATIONAL ORGANIZATIONS

The Commission may enter into such co-operation agreements with the Regional Economic Communities and International Organizations as the Conference may decide, on the recommendation of the Board.

ARTICLE 24 SUBSIDIARY BODIES

The Conference may establish such subsidiary bodies and ad-hoc working groups, as it may deem necessary.

ARTICLE 25 DEPOSITORY OF THE CONVENTION

1. The instruments of ratification or accession to this Convention shall be deposited with the Secretary-General of the OAU.

2. The Secretary-General of the Organization of African Unity shall transmit certified copies of this Convention and information concerning ratification, acceptance and approval of, or accession to this Convention to all States.

3. The functions of the Secretariat of the Commission shall, prior to its establishment, be performed by the interim structure established by Article 26 of this Convention, which shall, in collaboration with the General Secretariat of the Organization of African Unity, convene the first meeting of the Conference.

ARTICLE 26 TRANSITIONAL ARRANGEMENTS

Following the adoption of this Convention by the Member States of the OAU, and pending its entry into force, the General Secretariat of the OAU shall, in close cooperation and consultation with the host country and the members of the Bureau of the Conference of African Ministers of Energy, undertake the necessary measures to appoint the required staff and to set up an interim structure in order to facilitate the speedy establishment of AFREC in accordance with this Convention.

ARTICLE 27 RATIFICATION, ACCESSION AND ENTRY INTO FORCE

1. This Convention shall be open for signature and ratification or accession by any Member State of the OAU.

2. This Convention shall come into force thirty days after fifteen instruments of ratification have been deposited.

3. For any State acceding subsequently, this Convention shall come into force in respect of that State on the date of the deposit of its instrument of ratification or accession.

4. The Secretary General of the OAU shall inform all Member Sates of the entry into force of this Convention.

IN FAITH WHEREOF, WE the representatives of Member States of the Organization of African Unity have signed this Convention.

Done at Lusaka, Zambia, on 11 July, 2001

CONVENTION OF THE AFRICAN ENERGY COMMISSION

Done at Lusaka, Zambia, on 11 July, 2001

1. People's Democratic Republic of Algeria

....

2. Republic of Angola

....

3. Republic of Benin

....

4. Republic of Botswana

....

5. Burkina Faso

....

6. Republic of Burundi

....

7. Republic of Cameroon

....

8. Republic of Cape Verde

....

9. Central African Republic

....

10. Republic of Chad

....

11. Islamic Federal Republic of the Comoros

....

12. Republic of the Congo

....

13. Republic of Côte d'Ivoire

....

14. Democratic Republic of Congo

....

15. Republic of Djibouti

....

16. Arab Republic of Egypt

....

17. State of Eritrea

....

18. Federal Democratic Republic of Ethiopia.

....

19. Republic of Equatorial Guinea

....

20. Republic of Gabon

....

21. Republic of The Gambia

....

22. Republic of Ghana

....

23. Republic of Guinea

....

24. Republic of Guinea Bissau.

....

25. Republic of Kenya

....

26. Kingdom of Lesotho

....

27. Republic of Liberia

....

28. Great Socialist People's Libyan Arab Jamahiriya

....

29. Republic of Madagascar

....

30. Republic of Malawi

....

31. Republic of Mali

....

32. Islamic Republic of Mauritania

....

33. Republic of Mauritius

....

34. Republic of Mozambique

....

35. Republic of Namibia

....

36. Republic of Niger

....

37. Federal Republic of Nigeria

....

38. Republic of Rwanda

....

39. Sahrawi Arab Democratic Republic

....

40. Republic of Sao Tome and Principe

....

41. Republic of Senegal

....

42. Republic of Seychelles

....

43. Republic of Sierra Leone

....

44. Republic of Somalia

....

45. Republic of South Africa

....

46. Republic of Sudan

....

47. Kingdom of Swaziland

....

48. United Republic of Tanzania

....

49. Republic of Togo

....

50. Republic of Tunisia

....

51. Republic of Uganda

....

52. Republic of Zambia

....

53. Republic of Zimbabwe

....

African Convention on the Conservation of Nature and Natural Resources

15 September 1968

1976 U.N.T.S. 4

http://www.iucn.org/themes/wcpa/wpc2003/pdfs/outputs/africa/africa_pasconvention.pdf

ARTICLE XVI Inter-State Co-operation

1. The Contracting States shall co-operate:

(a) whenever such co-operation is necessary to give effect to the provisions of this convention, and

(b) whenever any national measure is likely to affect the natural resources of any other State.

2. The Contracting States shall supply the Organization of African Unity with:

(a) the text of laws, decrees, regulations and instructions in force in their territories, which are intended to ensure the implementation of this Convention;

(b) reports on the results achieved in applying the provisions of this Convention; and

(c) all the information necessary for the complete documentation of matters dealt with by this Convention if requested.

3. If so requested by Contracting States, the Organization of African Unity shall organize any meeting which may be necessary to dispose of any matters covered by this Convention. Requests for such meetings must be made by at least three of the Contracting States and be approved by two thirds of the States which it is proposed should participate in such meetings.

4. Any expenditure arising from this Convention, which devolves upon the Organization of African Unity shall be included in its regular budget, unless shared by the Contracting States or otherwise defrayed.

Integrated Energy Plan for the Republic of South Africa

Department of Minerals and Energy

19 March 2003

GLOSSARY

bpd	Barrels (oil) per day
Capacity load factor	The percentage output of a plant compared with the maximum possible on a continuous basis.
Energy Intensity	Ratio of the energy required to produce a Rand of product-here measured nationally as PJ/Rbillion.
GWhr	Giga Watt hour – a measure of energy. (1GWhr is equivalent to 3.6×10^{12} Joules)
IEA	International Energy Agency
KWh	kilo Watt hour – measure of energy, usually electricity.
Levelised cost	Levelised cost where capital is levelised over the life of a plant taking the annual production (average annual production factor) into account. It is derived by dividing the total cost of building and operating the plant over its life by the net production output over the same time period taking into account inflation.
Net discount rate	The discount rate can be defined as the required rate of return by investors in a company in real terms. The net discount rate is the return after subtracting inflation.
ppm	Parts per million
PJ	Peta Joules (10^{15} Joules)
Program	Computer instruction set.
MGJ	Million Giga Joules – measure of energy
MW	Mega Watts – measure of power
Mwe	Mega Watts electrical – measure of power
Reserves	Reserves are economically exploitable in this case energy sources, eg coal, oil, gas and hydro.
Resources	Resources are in this case energy sources, eg coal, oil, gas and hydro, but not at this stage economically exploitable.
tcf	Trillion cubic feet – standard term to measure natural gas volume.

Energy is a necessary but insufficient requirement for development.

INTEGRATED ENERGY PLAN OVERVIEW

- Energy supply will remain reliant on coal for at least the next two decades.
- Diversify energy supply through increased use of natural gas and new and renewable energies.
- Continue investigations into nuclear options as a future new energy source.
- Promote the use of energy efficiency management and technologies.
- Maximise load factors on electricity generation plant to lower levelised lifecycle costs.
- Lessen reliance on imported liquid fuels by exploring and developing oil and gas deposits.
- Increase existing oil refineries capacity when appropriate rather than greenfields development.
- Continue with existing synfuel plants and supplement with natural gas as feedstock.
- New electricity generation will remain coal based with potential for hydro, natural gas and nuclear capacity.

• Ensure environmental considerations in energy supply, transformation and end use.

• Promote universal access to clean and affordable energy, with emphasis on household energy supply being co-ordinated with provincial and local integrated development programmes.

• Introduce policy, legislation and regulation for the promotion of renewable energy and energy efficiency measures and mandatory provision of energy data.

• Undertake integrated energy planning on an ongoing basis.

1. INTRODUCTION

Energy is one of the key elements in production processes. A lack or shortage of energy has a serious effect on the economy and gross domestic growth. By virtue of its size and economic importance, the energy sector periodically requires considerable investments in new and replacement supply capacity. Historically, such decisions were primarily driven by concerns regarding maintaining supply security, without giving full consideration to the economic, environmental and social impacts of all alternatives. As a consequence, the tendency has been towards the construction of large-scale capital-intensive supply facilities and the neglect of alternatives that might have been more cost effective in the long term, and had greater employment benefits and more favourable environmental impacts. Consequently, the policy espoused in the White Paper[1] stated that;

The Department of Minerals and Energy will ensure that an integrated resource planning approach is adopted for large investment decisions by energy suppliers and service providers, in terms of which comprehensive evaluations of the economic, social and environmental implications of all feasible supply and demand side investments will have to be undertaken.

Over the recent years, the contribution of different sectors to the country's Gross Domestic Product has changed significantly. In the past two years the industrial policy has shifted towards a greater focus on knowledge-intensive sectors and human resource development, placing less emphasis on comparative advantage based on natural endowments[2]. Primary production like agriculture and mining now contribute less to the economy than the tertiary or services sector. The tertiary sector now contributes almost two-thirds of our gross domestic product. This implies a lowering of overall energy intensity, as generally the energy required per unit product (measured in Rands) is less for the tertiary sector compared with the primary sector. This shift is similar to what has occurred in most industrialising nations. This does not mean that agriculture and mining are becoming unimportant, but that the energy sector may re-focus efforts on how to further exploit South Africa's endowments. Such re-focusing may be based on integrated energy planning.

According to the White Paper, integrated energy planning is a process that entails the following technical functions:

• interpreting the requirements of national economic, social and environmental policies for the energy sector;

• analysing energy needs in terms of how their fulfilment will contribute towards attaining national economic and social goals;

• analysing the potential of energy supply systems and demand side management to meet current and potential future energy needs. This would include analyses of individual supply sub-sectors and the linkages between sub-sectors;

• analysing energy sector linkages to the macro-economy;

• analysing the potential effects on the energy sector of global and technological developments;

• evaluating the effects of legislative, institutional and industry structure arrangements on energy supply and demand; and

• specifying, sourcing and presenting data on energy supply and demand, energy sector institutions, and linkages with economic and social factors in order to provide a statistical description of the energy sector's historic evolution and current impact on economic and social development.

The integrated energy planning process is a relatively new tool world-wide and is still under evolutionary development. There are many documents

[1] White Paper on the Energy Policy of the Republic of South Africa, December 1998

[2] South Africa – Locomotive for African Growth?, UNECA

internationally that address integrated energy planning, but a dearth of explicit integrated energy plans. The development of the energy plan addressed here is the first for South Africa. As such, it has been a learning process and some aspects addressed above have been absent from the process because of time constraints. Moreover, the process has identified a number of gaps and deficiencies. These gaps and deficiencies are scheduled to be addressed during the follow-up process.

The energy plan addressed here is based on the scenario modelling done for the Department of Minerals and Energy and Eskom by the Energy Research Institute of the University of Cape Town. Details of scenario development, energy supply, demand, economic and environmental modelling may be found in the final report[3] – approximately 400 pages. This document summarises and analyses that report. Details of the methodology are addressed in Section 4.

As addressed above, the purpose of the integrated energy plan or strategy is to balance energy demand with supply resources in concert with safety, health and environmental considerations. An integrated energy plan or strategy is not a precise blueprint for the energy sector, but is a framework within which specific energy development decisions can be made.

The format of this text will be to:

a) briefly describe an overview of the current energy sector;

b) briefly describe available energy resources;

c) describe the modelling methodology of the energy planning process;

d) summarise and discuss the results of the modelling process;

e) based on the results develop an integrated energy plan;

f) identify the gaps in the current process; and

g) discuss the furtherance of the integrated energy planning process.

2. ENERGY SECTOR OVERVIEW

The first step of integrated energy planning is to assess the present situation in the context of current consumptions and trends.

[3] "*Energy Outlook 2002*", Energy Research Institute, University of cape Town.

2.1 ENERGY FLOWS

The flow of energy from its source, through transformation, transport to final use has a number of conversion losses as determined by the laws of physics. The flow of energy from production to final use is illustrated in Figure 1, where the portion of use and conversion losses are indicated approximately to scale.

Note the dominance of coal in the primary energy supply. Biomass (renewable energy) features relatively highly, it being mostly fuel wood in rural areas where accurate and reliable data is difficult to obtain.

2.2 PRIMARY ENERGY SUPPLY

The primary energy supply for the South Africa energy sector is dominated by coal – Figure 2 – it being plentiful and inexpensive by international standards. The total primary energy supply is approximately 4 782 PJ for the year 2000.

Most of South Africa's liquid fuel requirements are imported in the form of crude oil. Approximately 30% of South Africa's liquid fuel requirements are sourced from coal via Sasol. Further, 100% of South Africa's current natural gas production (Mossel Bay) is converted into liquid fuels, supplying 8% of national liquid fuel requirements.

With respect to forthcoming new primary energy supply, it is pertinent to state that natural gas is scheduled to be delivered to South Africa from Mozambique during the year 2004. The initial capacity of the gas transmission pipeline is 120 MGJ per year. To place this into perspective, the 120 MGJ per year is equivalent to approximately 3 800 MW, which assuming a 50% conversion efficiency to electricity, is equivalent to 1 900 MWe or approximately one half an Eskom ("six-pack") electricity generation station. Approximately one third of the natural gas coming from Mozambique is scheduled to be used by Sasol as a replacement for coal as a feedstock, another one third is scheduled to replace the syngas in Sasol's existing gas market, and the remaining one third is to go into Sasol's expansion of the gas market.

2.3 ENERGY DEMAND

The final energy demand during the year 2000 was 2363 PJ. Liquid fuels, coal and electricity are the

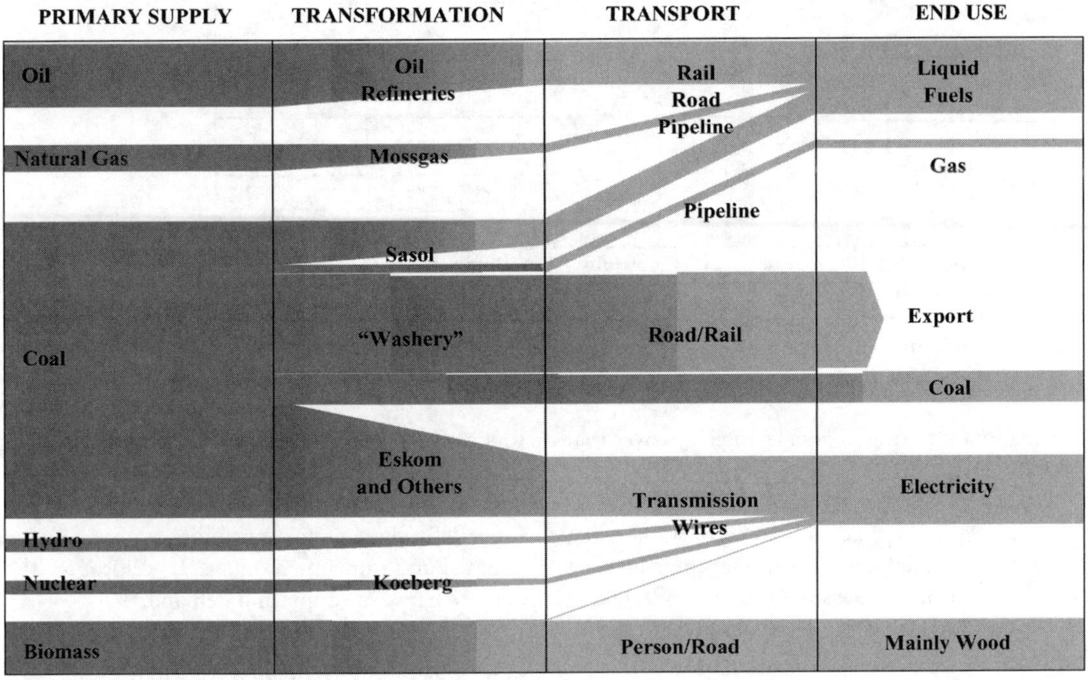

Figure 1: Energy flow from primary energy supply to final use – roughly to scale.

main forms of the end use of energy, dominating biomass and other forms of energy – Figure 3.

Biomass and other energy accounted for only ~8% of energy demand, mainly rural use of firewood that is currently not being renewed.

The historic energy demand by sector is shown in Figure 4. A comparison of energy consumption between 1992 and 2000 shows that: residential use has remained almost constant, commerce and public service has fallen 25%, agriculture has fallen 18%, transport has risen 27%, mining and quarrying has fallen 15% and industry risen 22%.

The underlying reasons for these changes are not yet apparent, except to say that the historic trends in energy demand for mining and quarrying and industry are consistent with the gold mining output falling (gold mining uses more energy than all other mining) and the increase in tertiary industry activities.

By international standards, South Africa has a high energy intensity, that is a high energy input per unit of gross national product (GDP). This is because of low energy costs and an abundance of mineral deposits have led to an emphasis on primary extraction and processing, which is inherently energy intensive. Table 1 indicates South Africa's energy intensity between 1993 and 2000, where post 1995, GDP rises and final energy consumption falls

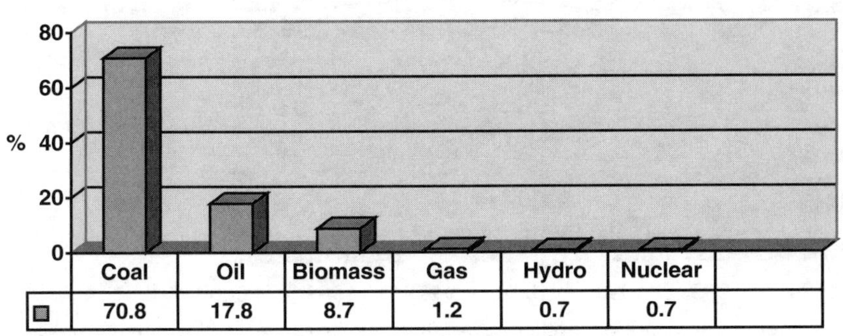

Figure 2: South Africa primary energy supply by energy carrier for the year 2000.

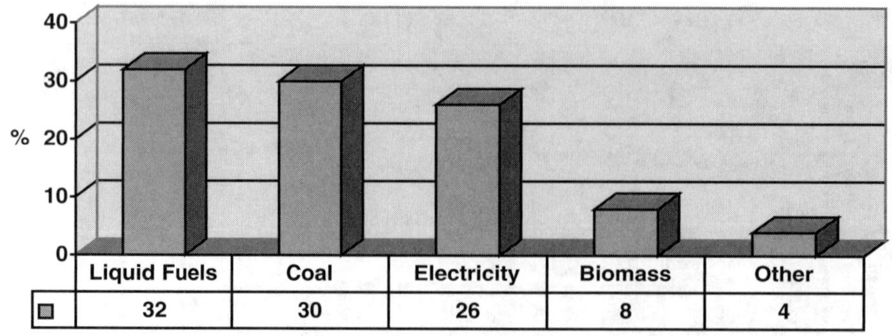

Figure 3: South Africa final energy demand by energy carrier for the year 2000.

reusing in a lowering of energy intensity over that period.

The lowering of energy intensity reflects the swing away from primary industry to tertiary industry. Preliminary studies have shown that there is scope for energy efficiency measures, that is, undertaking the same functions using less energy, with a preliminary savings potential of approximately 20%. As energy comprises approximately 15% of gross domestic product, there is potential for energy efficiency measures to contribute to an approximately 3% GDP growth.

2.4 ENERGY TRANSFORMATION CAPACITY BY SECTOR

A large portion of the primary energy is transformed into other forms of energy more appropriate for final use. The two major energy transformation sectors concern the generation of electricity and the production of liquid fuels (including petrol, diesel and paraffin) from coal, crude oil and gas. Sufficient capacity in these sectors, including a provision for planned and unplanned outages, is critical for the balance between supply and demand.

2.4.1 Electricity Generation Capacity

South Africa currently has approximately 37,000 MWe of generating capacity, of which 87% is coal fired – see Table 2. Table 2 excludes imported electricity, for example from the Cahora Bassa hydro scheme.

Note that the pumped storage unit is a net energy loss system, its purpose being to store energy generated during off-peak periods for conversion back to electricity during peak periods. On the other hand, a pumped storage system could make the overall system more efficient by the judicious storage of

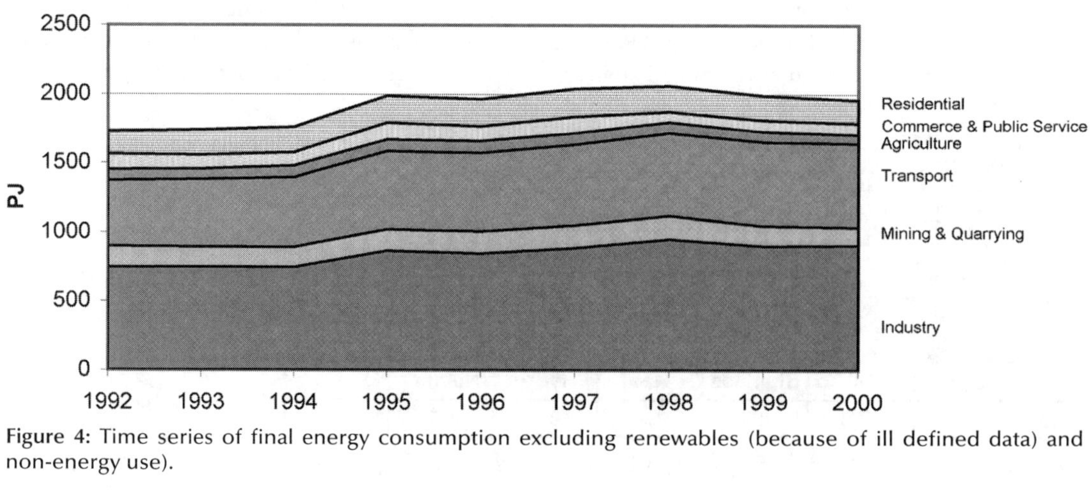

Figure 4: Time series of final energy consumption excluding renewables (because of ill defined data) and non-energy use).

Table 1: National energy intensities between 1993 and 2000

	1993	1994	1995	1996	1997	1998	1999	2000
GDP- all industries at basic prices R billion (constant 1995 prices)	472	486	500	521	534	538	549	571
Total final energy consumption (renewable and waste excluded) PJ	1766	1789	2016	1996	2071	2098	2026	2003
Energy intensity (total energy consumtion/GDP) PJ/R billion	3.74	3.68	4.03	3.83	3.88	3.90	3.69	3.51

energy during low cost periods for use during high cost periods.

Eskom produces 92% of South Africa's electricity requirements, the remainder being provided through local authorities, industry and imports via the South African Power Pool. Eskom's generation capacity, assuming a 50 year life per plant, is indicated in Figure 5. The solid line in Figure 4 indicates electricity actual and projected demand.

The capacity is primarily coal-fired and the graph indicates that current plant is scheduled to be operational until at least the year 2020. The projected demand line indicates that further electricity generation plant will be required at approximately year 2007. It is pertinent to note that whilst current concerns relate to new capacity to accommodate growth in demand, after the year 2020 and for the following three decades, generating capacity to replace the existing 37 000 MWe will need to be addressed. Current concerns may seem trivial when compared with the foreseen task after the year 2020.

Current peak electricity demand is approximately 31 500 MWe (July 2002), and national installed capacity is approximately 37 000 MWe. According to the Baseline Simulated scenario (see anon), which assumes a 10% reserve margin, South Africa will be short on capacity by 2005–2007, unless demand side management or new plant is built. Assuming the 10% reserve margin on a gross capacity of 37 000 MWe, the current net capacity is 33 300 MWe, which is only 1 800 MWe (that is the size of Koeberg) above the peak demand. Given the time to commission new plant, the current electricity generation system could soon be viewed as vulnerable.

Table 2: South Africa electricity generation capacity

Energy Source	Capacity /MWe
Coal	32,202
Nuclear	1,840
Pumped Storage	1,580
Hydro	667
Gas Turbine	662
Bagasse	105
Total	**37,056**

Table 3: Oil refineries' capacity[4]

Facility	Barrels/day (crude or equivalent)
Calref (Cape Town: Caltex)	100 000
Sapref (Durban: BP/Shell)	180 000
Genref (Durban: Engen)	105 000
Natref (Sasolburg: Sasol/Total)	86 000
Sasol CTL	150 000
Mossgas GTL	45 000
Total	**666 000**

2.4.2 Oil Refineries Capacity

Oil refineries capacities are indicated in Table 3.

Current refinery output is approximately 493 000 bpd and South African final demand about 427 000 bpd. The surplus production, mainly diesel, is exported.

In this sector, there is currently a mismatch between petrol/diesel production and demand. Because of the almost fixed ratio between petrol and diesel production quantities (ranges approximately between 60:40 to 40:60), and in order to meet the demand for petrol, South Africa currently

[4] SAPIA Annual Report 2001

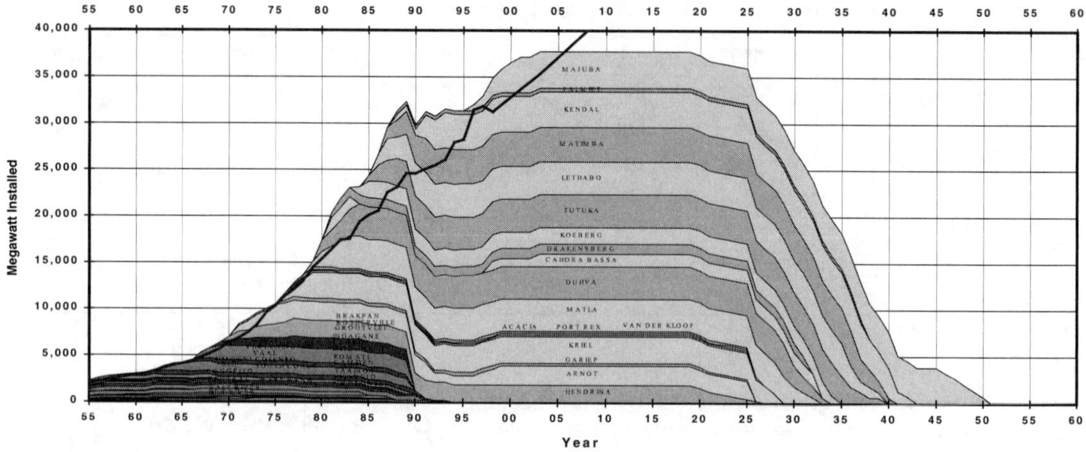

Figure 5: Eskom Electricity generating capacity as a function of time – the solid line indicates actual and projected demand.

produces a surplus of diesel. During year 2001[5], the consumption of petrol and diesel was 10 340 million litres and 6 448 million litres respectively. During the period 2000/01, diesel sales grew by 3.4% in contrast with petrol sales declining by 0.5%. During year 1998, exports of petrol and diesel were 2178 million litres and 4782 million litres respectively. Imbalances in petrol and diesel production and demand is addressed through exports (mainly diesel) and imports (for example petrol during 2001 as an aftermath of the refinery fire).

3. ENERGY RESOURCES

South Africa's major energy resource is coal, which is plentiful and inexpensive to exploit. Hence the current dominance of coal in the energy supply composition. The other main energy sources are addressed in Table 4.

South Africa also imports energy (electricity, soon natural gas) from neighbouring countries. An estimation of energy resources in southern African countries is addressed in Table 5. The majority of South Africa's crude oil is imported, mostly sourced from the middle-east, primarily Saudi Arabia and Iran who account for approximately 81% of imported crude oil.

[5] SAPIA Annual Report 2002

4. INTEGRATED ENERGY PLANNING METHODOLOGY

Under the methodology of integrated energy and resource planning, calculations were done under likely scenarios. Two basic scenarios were used: a "Baseline" or business as usual scenario, and a "Siyaphambili" (we are going forward) scenario that promoted diversification of supply and environmental improvement.

With respect to environmental aspects, the Treasury and the Department of Environmental Affairs and Tourism are currently investigating the financial internalisation of environmental externalities. Because these internalisation of externalities have not yet been quantified, environmental aspects were primarily addressed here through efficiency measures and renewable energy. When these internalisation of externalities have been quantified, they will be included in the modelling.

The two scenarios were used both in a simulated and an optimised mode. The simulated mode is where options are prescribed. The optimised mode is where the options are selected on a least cost basis.

Detailed descriptions of the two scenarios (for both the simulated and optimised modes) are addressed in Table 6, where the specifics for each are itemised.

In summary, the:

"Baseline Simulated" scenario is "business-as-usual", continuing present trends based on coal;

Table 4: Estimation of South Africa's untapped potential energy reserves/resources

Energy Carrier	Reserve/Resource	Comment
Coal	55 billion tonnes	Coal technology well developed and inexpensive. Coal resources/reserves are currently under re-appraisal.
Oil	Potential reserves (P90): 40 million barrels. Potential (resource): 5 billion barrels.	Oribi/Oryx audited remaining reserves 12 million barrels plus Sable field reserves of 150 million barrels sufficient for four years production. Untested deep-water potential.
Natural Gas	Reserves (P50): 1.3 tcf	F-A/E-M and satellites audited (P50) 0.5 tcf and 11.8 million barrels condensate plus Ibhubesi field.
	Potential (resource): 25 tcf	Upside potential of untested areas.
Uranium	261 000 Tonnes	Uranium beneficiation (conversion and enrichment) and fuel fabrication are done outside the country.
Hydro	~300 MWe potential	South Africa classified as a "water stressed" country and therefore has limited potential for hydro-power.
Renewable	Undefined	Largely untapped solar based resource that is variable depending on weather conditions. Non-commercial biomass energy mainly used in rural areas and is currently not being replenished. Technologies not fully developed and expensive.

"Baseline Optimised" optimises that scenario on least cost, taking into account energy efficiency and fuel switching;

"Siyaphambili Simulated" scenario promotes fuel diversification away from coal, prescribing other energy technologies at set times; and

"Siyaphambili Optimised" optimises that scenario based on least cost, using energy efficiency and fuel switching.

The energy and resource plan addressed here is based on the scenario modelling done for the Department of Minerals and Energy and Eskom by the Energy Research Institute of the University of Cape Town. The key parameters and drivers were decided by specialists at the public participation workshops.

It should also be born in mind that the further the projections are made into the future, the less reliable the outputs of the scenarios become. Hence, the energy planning process should be seen as an ongoing process that should be updated periodically.

The general assumptions and constraints of the calculations for the four scenarios are given in Table 7. These parameters were agreed at the initial public workshop and by the Steering Core Group during October 2001. These parameters can be altered but, because of the model structure, to vary

Table 5: Estimation of regional energy resources

Country	Reserves/Resources	Comment
Mozambique	Gas: ~2.0 tcf proven ~5 tcf potential	Pipeline to South Africa currently under construction – schedule completion 2004 – with an initial carrying capacity of 120 MGJ/y.
	Hydro: ~5 0000 MWe	Cahora Bassa 1800 MWe the majority of which is assigned to Eskom. Mepanda Uncua potential ~2 200MWe
DRC	Hydro	Potential for approximately 50 000–100 000 MWe of hydro generated electricity at Inga.
	Gas: > 50 bcf proven Oil: > 200 million barrels	
Zimbabwe	No oil and gas reserves	
	Coal	Large coal reserves and potential for coal bed methane.
Namibia	Gas: 1.2 tcf proven Upside potential 7 tcf	Investigations currently underway to import gas to the western Cape.
Angola	Oil: 5.4 billion barrels proven Gas: > 20 tcf	

Table 6: Scenario descriptions

Baseline simulated	Baseline optimised	Siyaphambili simulated	Siyiphambili optimised
General			
Business as usual – external costs excluded	Business as usual, but can select technologies to obtain lowest costs – external costs excluded.	Deliberate policy to diversity supply and improve the environment – external costs excluded.	Similar to simulated, but can select technologies to obtain lowest costs – external costs excluded.
No regional co-operation	Regional co-operation if economic	More regional co-operation	More regional co-operation if economic
No active energy efficiency	Energy efficiency if it reduces costs	Drive to increase energy efficiency and demand side management	Drive to increase energy efficiency and demand side management
Fuel switching only to follow current trends.	Burn fuel directly in end use thermal applications, if economic.	Fuel switching only to follow current trends and limited fuel switching from coal to gas.	Burn fuel directly in end use thermal applications, if economic, but with no increase in use of coal over the simulated case.
Electricity			
Coal continues to dominate	Any technology on cost alone:	New technologies before coal	Can chose on cost from any:
Mothballed coal fired power stations brought back into operation	• Conventional coal without FGD • Combine cycle gas turbine	• mothballed stations • Combine cycle gas turbine • Imported hydro	• conventional coal with FGD • Fluidised bed coal combustion • Combined cycle gas turbine
New coal fired stations without flue gas desulphurisation FGD	• Imported hydro • Nuclear • Solar	• Pebble bed modular reactor • Fluidised bed coal • Peaking gas turbine	• Imported hydro • Nuclear • Wind and solar
Some combined cycle gas turbine	• Wind • Municipal waste	• Wind and solar Thereafter a conventional coal-fired station with FGD	• Municipal waste
New pumped storage and gas turbines for peaking power			

Liquid Fuels			
Keep existing sulphur levels Mossgas ends 2008	Keep existing sulphur levels	Low sulphur fuels	Mandatory low sulphur
New refineries built to meet demand, if necessary	Least cost to build new refineries or import refined product. Sasol uses coal or gas to liquid fuels technology	New refineries build to meet demand if necessary Sasol used gas to liquid technology	Least cost to build new refineries or import refined product.
Natural Gas			
No increase in use except for electricity generation	Increase if economic	Gas provide 5% primary energy	Gas used if economic
Residential Sector			
Current trends continue	More electrification if economic	More demand. Electrification increases. More electricity for cooking, heating appliances	More demand and more electrification if economic
Commercial Sector			
No increase in energy efficiency	Some increase in energy efficiency	Increased energy efficiency	Increased energy efficiency
Transport			
No taxi recapitalisation	Taxi recapitalisation if economic	Taxi recapitalisation More electric trains	Taxi recapitalisation if economic More electric trains if economic

Table 7 General assumptions and constraints pertaining to the calculations made in the scenarios' development

General Assumptions

- Twenty year planning period (2001 to 2020)
- Process performance data and costs and commodity prices at 1 January 2001 values
- $1 = R8 (1 Jan 2001)
- Net discount Rate: 11%
- Inflation rate: 5.5% (SARB target 3–6%)
- Population Growth: 2000 = 44 Million, 2010 = 50 Million (1.3%p.a.), 2020 = 57 Million (0.87% p.a.)
- GDP Growth: 2.8% average annual growth over period
- Gas generally available from SA, Namibia andMozambique at $2.5 / GJ escalating at SA PPI.
- 20% coal price increase for Sasol from 2008.
- At least 15% Sasol coal/liquid process replaced by gas/liquid process by 2015
- Coal supplied to industrial and other processes, except electricity generation, at R6/GJ

General Constraints

- All energy projects must be South African or joint ventures with South African partners.
- All energy projects must be technologically feasible, economically viable and with adequate accuracy of costs.

some of the parameters would require considerable reworking of the calculations.

Although the validity of the results was unaffected, it is currently a time consuming process to change input parameters (such as rate of exchange, discount rate etc). To advance the process for future work, the calculation programs should be optimised to allow more ready facilities to change driver parameters and baseline data both up-front and over the planning period.

The calculations for the scenario development were undertaken using the MARKAL and LEAP computer models. To do so, it was necessary to:

- configure the model structure and the reference energy system for South African conditions
- research, collect and collate required data, including energy and economic data
- configure the database on which the calculations were done
- determine the primary planning assumptions and scenarios
- populate and refine the reference energy system
- undertake the calculations and analyse the results
- iterate the process on advice from the Steering Core Group and sector experts.

This process normally takes approximately two to three years, including the collection of the appropriate data. The current modelling process (for which much of the data was already available), excluding the training to operate the models, was undertaken over a period of 8 months. The current structure for the use of the models is less than optimum, but did allow the production of results within a short period of time. For future work (see below) the use of the models needs to be optimised.

The processes, including the scenarios and data, were reviewed by local experts at the Workshops and were found to conform to requirements. The model structure, the reference energy system and the modelling process were reviewed by international experts (the International Energy Agency's Energy Technology Systems Analysis Programme and others) and found to conform to international standards.

The integrated energy and resource planning process takes into account physical, technical, resource and economic considerations. The modelling process cannot by itself account for matters pertaining to sociological effects, political imperatives, global changes etc.

5. INTEGRATED ENERGY PLANNING PROCESS

The integrated energy plan addresses energy demand balanced with energy supply, transformation, economics and environmental considerations in concourse with available resources. By addressing the integrated energy plan under the umbrella of the scenarios, it is possible to take into account

Table 8: Energy supply/demand results for the four scenarios (Electricity and oil Capacity expansion plans for each of the 4 scenarios)

Baseline simulated	Baseline optimised	Siyaphambili simulated	Siyaphambili optimised
Electricity Generation Based on coal as primary fuel source: • builds 3556MWe mothballed PF Stations from 2007 • Four sites for new 6×640MWe dry-cooled coal-fired plants with FGD from 2013 • 1×750MWe CCGT plants in 2014 • Four sites with each 3×333MWe pumped storage plants from 2011 • 5×240MWe simple cycle gas turbines (oil) for peaking built at max rate of one pa. from 2011 • No new hydro imports, nuclear, renewable energy sources are built	• Builds 3556MWe mothballed PF Stations from 2011 • Builds Four 6×640MWe dry-cooled coal-fired stations without FGD from 2015. • Build pumped storage plants from 2011 • No new hydro imports, nuclear, renewable energy sources are built	New technologies built before new coal options as specified: • 3556MWe mothballed PF Stations from 2007 at a max rate of 500MWe/a • 3×750MWe CCGT plants in 2005, 2006, 2007 using Kudu gas • 1×750MWe CCGT using Pande gas in 2014 • Builds part of the four sites with each 3×333MWe pumped storage plants from 2011 • 2684MWe imported Hydro Electricity from 2008 at max rate of 550MWe/a • 125MWe PBMR in 2005 followed by 250MWe/a from 2008 with a max of 1375MWe. • 2333MWe new FBC built at max rate of 466MWe/a from 2015 • 5×240MWe simple gas turbines (oil) for peaking at max rate of 1 pa from 2020 • 5% of electricity generation supplied by renewable options as specified by DME • New 6×640MWe dry-cooled coal-fired plants with FGD are only considered once previous alternatives are built	• Builds 3556MWe mothballed PF Stations at a max rate of 500MWe/a from 2018 • Builds 1×750MWe CCGT using Pande gas from 2014 • Builds pumped storage plants from 2011. • Builds 2333MWe new FBC built at max rate of 466MWe/a from 2020 • Builds 5×240MWe simple gas turbines (oil) for peaking built at max rate of one pa from 2020 • No new hydro imports, nuclear, renewable energy sources are built

(continued)

Table 8: (*continued*)

Baseline simulated	Baseline optimised	Siyaphambili simulated	Siyaphambili optimised
Liquid Fuels			
• All the oil refineries increase their capacity to 307 million bbl/year • Imports of finished liquid fuel products to meet increased demand.	• All the oil refineries increase their capacity to 307 million bbl/year • Imports of finished liquid fuel products to meet increased demand	• All the oil refineries increase their capacity to 307 million bbl/year • Imports of finished liquid fuel products to meet increased demand.	• All the oil refineries increase their capacity to 307 million bbl/year • Imports of finished liquid fuel products to meet increased demand.
Energy Demand			
No active fuel switching or energy efficiency measures	• Moderate uptake of efficient practice, high during times of low capacity, from 2005 onward. • General switching to coal and some biomass away from electricity and oil. Increasing the system efficiency. • In the transport sector there is switching from oil to electricity. Partial taxi-recapitalisation takes place. Generally there is also a move away from petrol to more efficient diesel vehicles.	Moderate fuel switching to gas, and switching from petrol to diesel due to petrol taxi recapitalisation.	• High uptake of energy efficient practice especially during times of low power plant capacity from 2005 onward. Fuel switching away from oil and electricity to natural gas. At the end of the period there is some switching from electricity to oil, when the marginal cost is of electricity is high. At the beginning of the period there was some fuel switching from oil to electricity, especially in the transport sector. • In the transport sector there is partial petrol taxi recapitisation, and a move toward electric trains, especially during the beginning of the period. Generally there is also a move away from petrol to more efficient diesel vehicles.

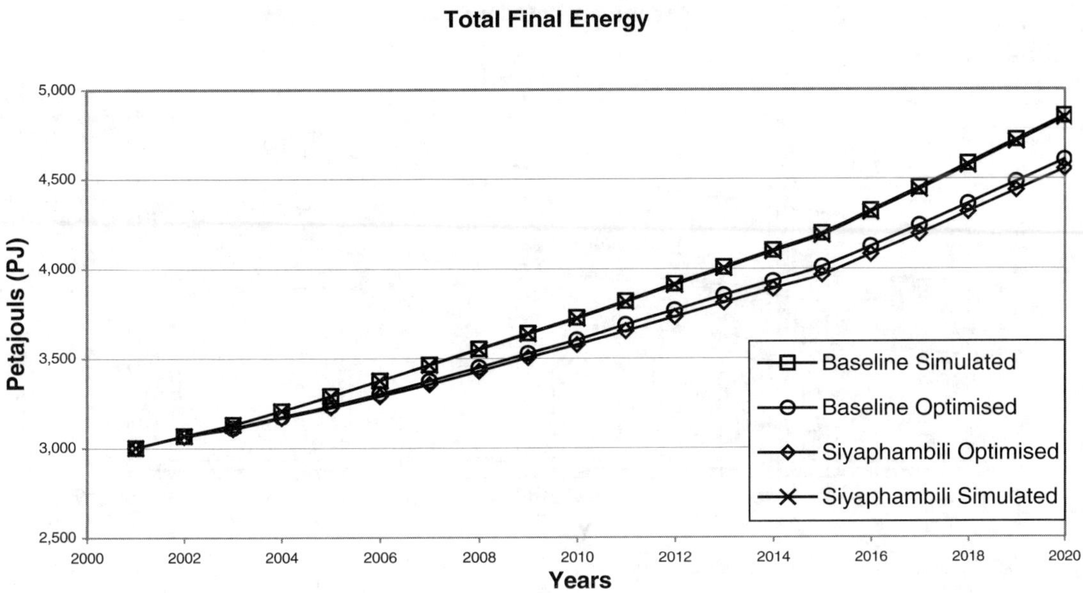

Figure 6: Total final energy demand per year projection (including non-energy use) – note that the Y axis starts at 2 500 PJ to emphasise the differences between each scenario (ERI, 2002).

the various consequences of each scenario. The output of each scenario is addressed in Section 5.1. The consequences are detailed in the following sections.

5.1 PLAN DESCRIPTIONS

The calculations were done according to the methods outline above for the four scenarios and the outcomes generated the energy plans that are summarised in Table 8. This Table summarises the outputs of the scenarios for electricity generation, liquid fuel production and energy demand trends.

5.2 ENERGY DEMAND

For the above scenarios, the calculated overall final energy demand projections are displayed in Figure 6.

The total final energy demand includes non-end-use-energy applications (eg the conversion of coal to chemicals) of approximately 690 PJ per year.

Note that the total primary demand varies by approximately only 7% between the scenarios by the year 2020, because the major drivers for energy demand are GDP and population growth and these are the same for all scenarios. Moreover, over the planning horizon, the average primary energy consumption rises by approximately 58% – or approximately 3% per year.

The activities for which energy is required remains the same for all four scenarios, however the total final energy demand differs because of different technologies and efficiencies used in each scenario.

The sector energy demand can be gleaned by expanding the final energy demand for the Baseline Simulated scenario – Figure 7. The major sectors of energy use are industry and transport. The largest increases are for; transport 75%, other 70%, industry 75% and Commerce 65% – over the planning horizon.

The other three sectors show a moderate increase; residential 29%, non-energy 35%, and agriculture 13% – over the planning horizon.

5.3 PRIMARY ENERGY SUPPLY

To accommodate the above energy demands, overall energy supply projections have been calculated and illustrated in Figure 8.

Note that the total primary energy supply varies by approximately only 12% between the scenarios

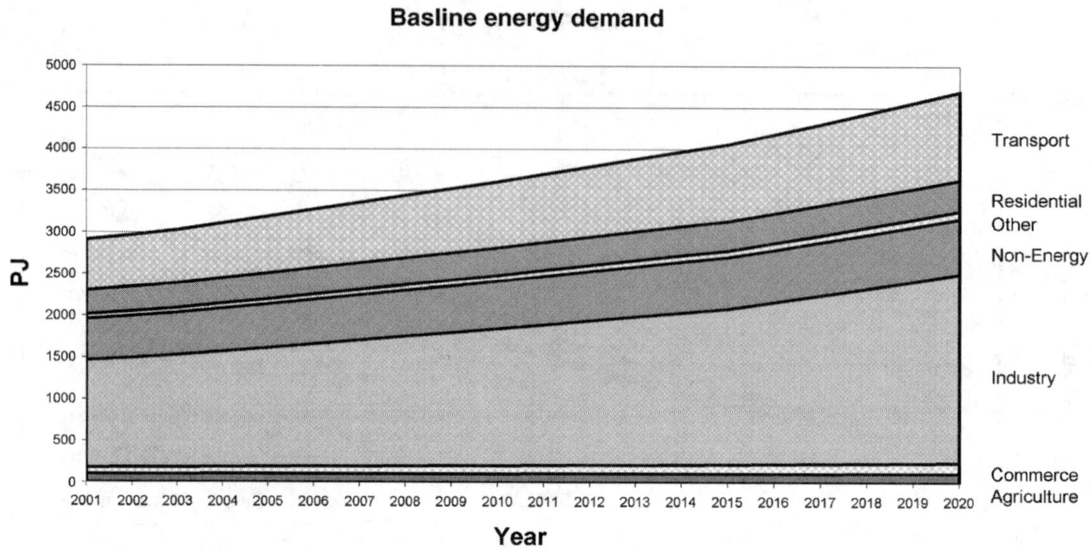

Figure 7: Final energy demand by sector (ERI).

by the year 2020 to meet the same energy service demand. This variation is because of the selection of final energy options which require less processing (with lower transformation efficiency losses), such as coal or natural gas versus electricity or liquid fuels. The result is a potential decrease in primary energy demand that is greater than the decrease in final energy demand. The average increase in primary energy supply over the planning horizon is approximately 60% – or approximately 3% per year.

The total energy supply differs because of different efficiencies of the technologies used in each scenario, for example when one uses natural gas as final energy (for thermal requirements) instead of electricity, then there is less need to transform a primary energy into electricity with its commensurate losses in energy.

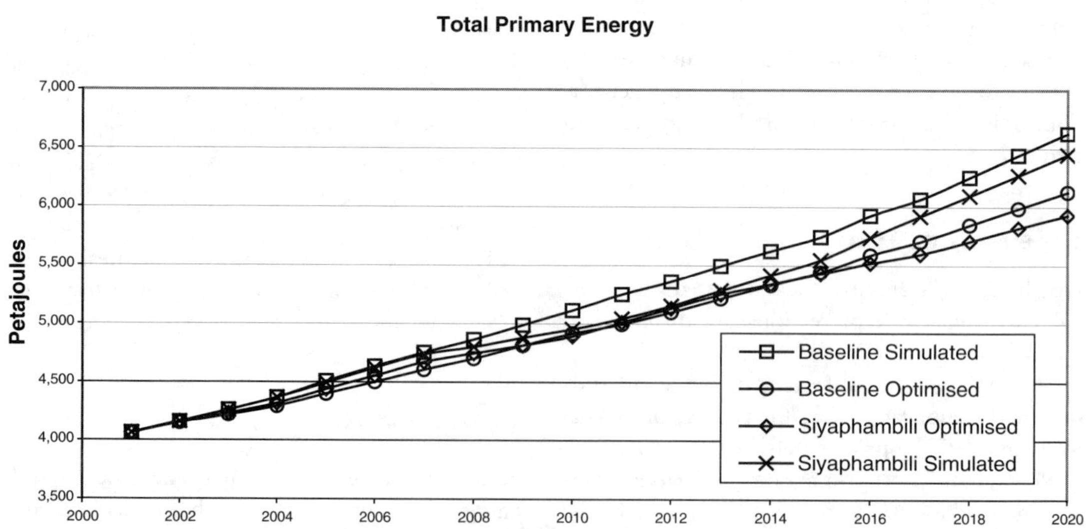

Figure 8: Primary energy supply projections under the scenarios – note that the Y axis starts at 3 500 PJ to emphasise the differences between each scenario (ERI, 2002).

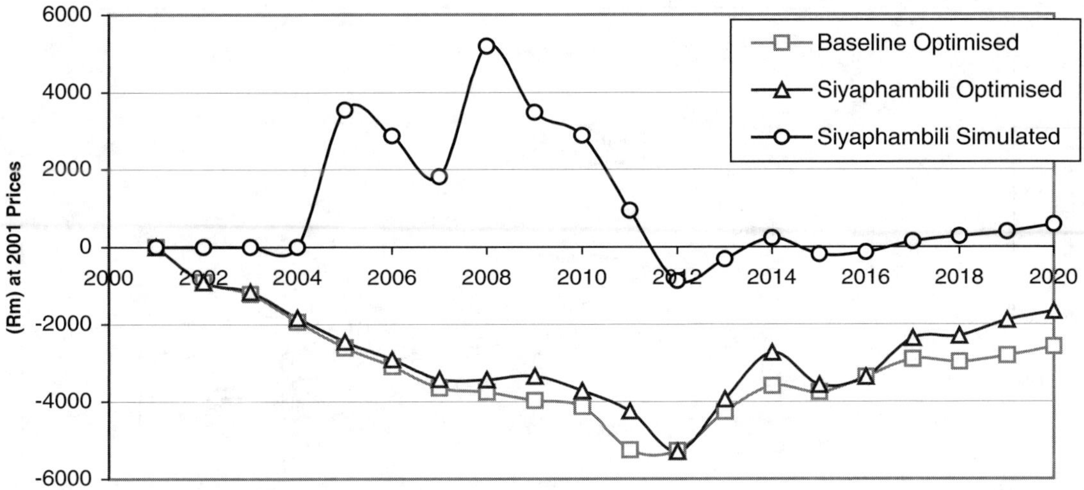

Figure 9: Total energy costs, discounted at 11%, for the three scenarios compared with Baseline Simulated (ERI, 2002).

5.4 ENERGY COSTS

Projected energy costs can be gleaned from calculating the overall costs of energy supply and then addressing the factors that contribute to the variation in costs for each scenario. The total net discounted energy costs relative to the Baseline Simulated scenarios are projected in Figure 9. Positive costs mean costs greater than the Baseline Simulated scenario and negative costs means costs less than the Baseline Simulated scenario. Remember that the Baseline Simulated describes the "business-as-usual" scenario based on coal – it is the reference case for all scenarios.

The Siyaphambili Simulated plan is more expensive than the Baseline Simulated plan because expensive options (gas combined cycle plants, renewable energy, PBMR, imported electricity) are implemented early instead of coal.

The Siyaphambili Optimised plan is less expensive than the Baseline Simulated plan because the implementation of energy efficiency measures and fuel switching (oil to electricity and gas, and some electricity to gas) delays the onset of new plant (electricity generation and liquid fuel refineries). At the end of the projection period, the marginal costs of electricity increase because the plan can only invest in certain new plant (renewable energy, pebble bed modular reactor). The result is that at the end of this period there is a switch away from expensive[6] electricity to imported oil.

The Baseline Optimised plan is less expensive than the Baseline Simulated (and slightly less expensive than the Siyaphambili Optimised plan) because the implementation of energy efficiency measures and fuel switching (electricity and oil to coal) delays the onset of new plant (electricity generation and liquid fuel refineries).

Note that the three scenarios show a trend to become more expensive (when compared with the Baseline Simulated scenario towards of the planning horizon as more expensive energy supply options take effect.

As the modelling process optimises the "optimised" scenarios for least cost, it is to be expected that these two scenarios are the least expensive.

Another factor pertaining to energy costs is the manner in which plant is used. For example, the load factor for electricity generation – Figure 10. It is immediately obvious that as the load factor rises the levelised costs decrease markedly. Therefore, to minimise the levelised unit costs, it is apparent that electricity generation units/stations and refineries should be run at their maximum

[6] Under the Siyaphambili Optimised Scenario, cheap coal is not an option for electricity generation and the imported hydro is expensive and limited.

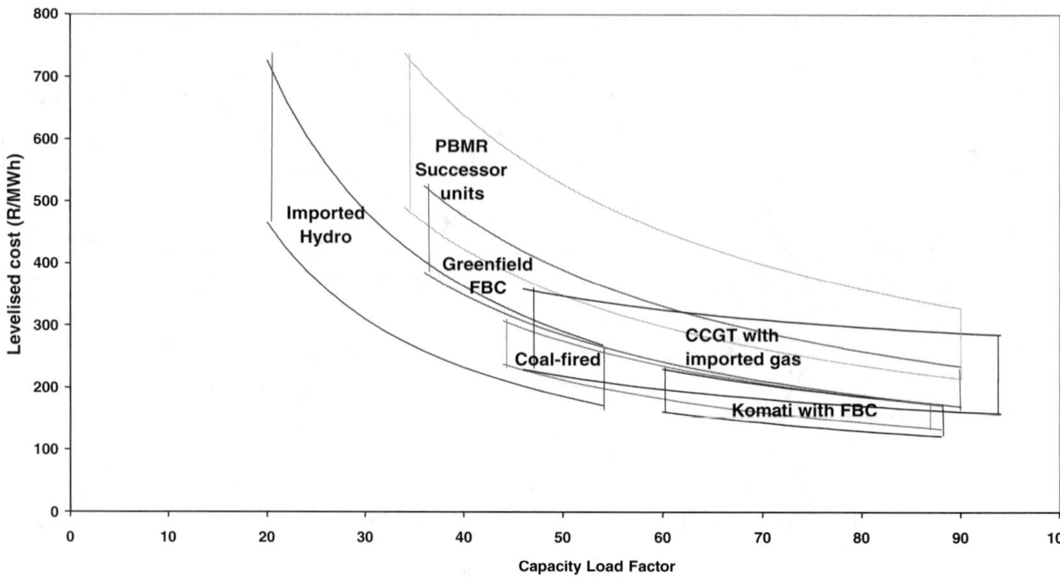

Figure 10: Lifetime levelised costs of new base load electricity generation supply-side options – from "An Integrated Electricity Outlook For South Africa" – Eskom/NER (2002).

appropriate load factors consistent with appropriate margins for planned and unplanned outages.

Other calculations have confirmed that running plant at highest possible capacity load factors and "resting" spare capacity will lower overall electricity generation costs.

Figure 10 also indicates the levelised cost regimes for various electricity generation technologies, namely:

- Pebble bed modular reactor (PBMR) successor units
- Imported hydro
- Greenfield fluidised bed coal combustion (FBC)
- Combined cycle gas turbine (CCGT) with imported gas
- Current coal fired technology
- De-mothballed Komati electricity generation station with fluidised bed coal combustion (FBC)

Clearly the lowest cost option is the re-activation of mothballed plant.

With regard to liquid fuel production comparisons, the approach will be to use a levelised cost[7] methodology to enable different technologies, plant productions and lifetimes to be compared on an equal footing.

Based on this life-cycle costing approach with nominal return on investment (11% net discount rate), Figure 11 illustrates the calculated Rand per barrel of refined product as a function of plant production load factor for three averaged cases of new gas-to-liquid, new oil refinery and new coal-to liquid.

The first point of note is that as may be expected the unit cost falls as the plants are producing nearer their maximum capacity. This is similar to electricity generation as discussed above. This is a clear illustration that it is inefficient and cost ineffective to have too much spare capacity on a national basis. Due care should be given to permitting production capacity in line with national needs, with sufficient spare capacity for maintenance and planned expansion to meet demand.

Moreover, the calculations indicate that at high load factors, the unit cost of refined product for a new coal-to liquid plant is less than new oil refinery, which in turn is less than new gas-to-liquid plant. On the other hand, at low load factors, a new

[7] Levelised cost where capital is levelised over the life of a plant taking the annual production (average annual production factor) into account. It is derived by dividing the total cost of building and operating the plant over its life by the net production output over the same time period taking into account inflation.

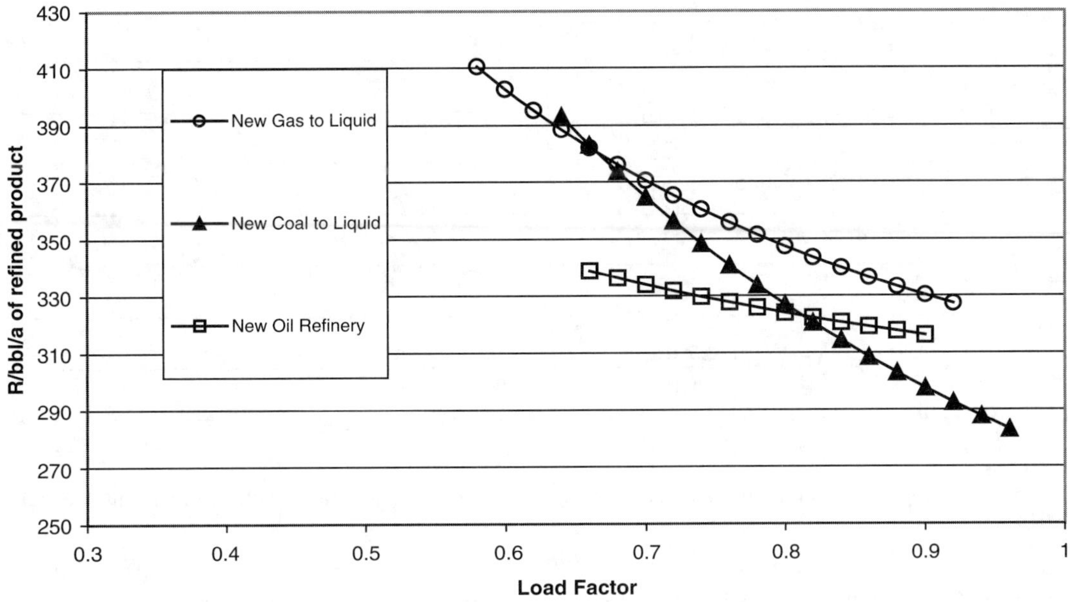

Figure 11: Costs of new liquid fuel production options based on the following assumptions: Brent crude $US 24.09/barrel (5.8 GJ/barrel), sulphur content 10 ppm by year 2015, Gas at $2.5/GJ and coal at R6/GJ, levelised over a 25 year period lifetime (ERI).

refinery plant has lower unit costs than both the coal-to-liquid and gas-to-liquid plants.

The reason for this counter-intuitive outcome is that if the plants are operated at high load factors, then, notwithstanding the higher capital and operational expenses of the synthetic fuel plants, the fuel feedstock costs for coal and gas are lower than that for oil – see below.

	New Oil Refinery R/bbl	New Coal to Liquid R/bbl	New Gas to Liquid R/bbl
Levelised Plant Capex	44.97	178.63	110.00
Total O&M Cost	18.29	61.12	103.90
Total Fuel Cost	251.84	43.83	116.95
Total Cost	315.10	283.58	330.85
Capacity Load Factor	*Full capacity: Refinery 92%*	*Coal to Liquid 96%,*	*Gas to Liquid 93%*

On the other hand, at low capacity load factors, the synthetic fuel plants have a higher levelised cost.

Given the increase in oil price, deterioration of the Rand/Dollar exchange rate and feedstock costs, coal-to-liquid would appear to be a more economic option than a new refinery on a levelised costs basis. This relationship could change when comparing costs on another basis.

5.5 CARBON DIOXIDE EMISSIONS

The environmental component was addressed through carbon dioxide emissions – a critical factor pertaining to global climate change considerations and the implementation of the Kyoto Protocol. The total carbon dioxide emission reductions for the three scenarios relative to the Baseline Simulated are illustrated in Figure 12.

The reduction of carbon dioxide emissions generally increases over time for all three scenarios of Baseline Optimised, Siyaphambili Optimised and Siyaphambili Simulated when compared with the Baseline Simulated scenario. However, from approximately year 2015 onwards, the Siyaphambili Optimised scenario decreases its carbon dioxide emissions (increases savings) significantly more than the other scenarios because the use of coal (both for power generation and as an end use fuel) is retarded.

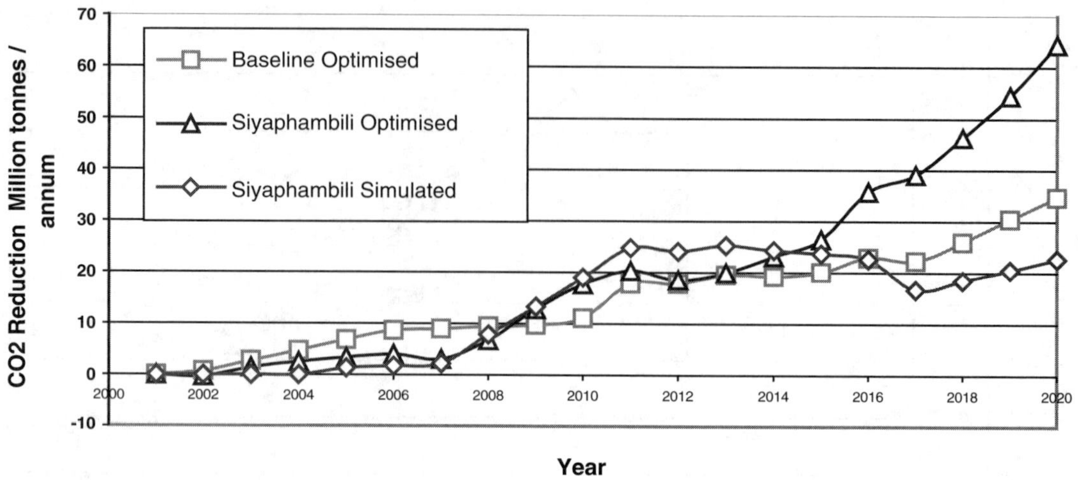

Figure 12: Carbon dioxide emission reductions, for the three scenarios compared with Baseline Simulated (ERI, 2002).

5.6 ENERGY SUPPLY RESERVES/RESOURCES

The availability of sufficient energy reserves/ resources is the other side to the energy planning equation. Without sufficient energy reserves/ resources, supply side options to meet demand will be severely strained.

5.6.1 Energy Reserves/Resources

The four scenarios addressed require sufficient energy supply resources to implement. Table 9 addresses the availability of energy supply resources for the four scenarios.

Energy transformation usually requires water (eg coal to electricity – 1.8 litre per kWh). South Africa is classified as a "water stressed" country, therefore the conversion of coal/oil/gas energy may be limited by the provision of process water. This condition may however be resolved by using dry cooling systems even though they have inherently lower physical efficiency and higher cost.

From the above, it may be concluded that the energy plan is not unreasonably constricted by the current availability of energy and water resources over the current planning horizon.

Table 9: Energy Resources

Energy Carrier	Resource Availability
Coal	There are sufficient coal reserves/resources to supply all scenarios for the planning horizon and beyond.
Natural Gas	There is insufficient certified natural gas reserves in South Africa for the planning horizon for a major switch to gas. These gas reserves can be supplemented by natural gas reserves in neighbouring countries. Further exploration is necessary in the region to firm-up resource estimates. (See discussion below regarding the ratio of natural gas and coal reserves.)
Oil	Currently only approximately 5% of crude is supplied from indigenous reserves, the remainder is imported. Although there are some prospects of deep-water oil deposits off the west coast, these are yet to be confirmed. Hence, South Africa remains reliant on imported oil for the foreseeable future.
Hydro	There are limited unused hydro reserves in South Africa (approximately 300 MWe) with other opportunities for pumped storage. Imported hydro electricity still requires development.
Renewables	South Africa has large areas of untapped reserves of solar (especially in the central regions) and wind (mainly on the coast) energy.
Nuclear	There are sufficient uranium reserves in South Africa, but currently the material must be exported to be processed into usable fuel.

Table 10: Gas/coal reserves and resources ratio

	Reserves	Unit	Energy Content	Energy Content PJ
Coal reserves	55	billion tonnes	22 MJ/kg	1,210,000
Coal resources	115	billion tonnes	22 MJ/kg	2,530,000
Natural gas reserves	5	tcf	41 MJ/m3	5,802
Natural gas resources	20	tcf	41 MJ/m3	23,206
Coal: South Africa	Gas reserves as a function of coal reserves 0.5%			
Gas: SA/Nam/Moz	Gas resources as a function of coal resources 0.9%			

5.6.2 Coal/Natural Gas Ratio

The current euphoria (primarily on an environmental basis) regarding a potential shift to natural gas as a significant contributor to energy supply needs to be placed in the context of available local and regional gas reserves. The potential contribution that natural gas can make to the overall primary energy supply portfolio is currently limited as the energy content of natural gas reserves/resources is significantly lower than those of coal, even on an optimistic assessment of gas reserves. Table 10 indicates the energy content of current coal and gas reserves and potential coal and gas resources.

Table 10 indicates that the energy content of the known gas reserves is only 0.5% of known coal reserves. Even if the gas reserves were 20 tcf (and compared with coal reserves of 55 billion tonnes), then the gas reserves would amount to only 1.9% of coal reserves. On the other hand, the equivalent ratio for gas and coal resources is 0.9%.

Hence, it is manifest that under these circumstances gas is unlikely to form any major component of primary energy supply over any extended period when compared with coal. There is however no reason why natural gas cannot take a momentary high profile in energy supply, especially if imported gas (including liquefied natural gas sources from outside southern Africa) is considered.

5.7 DISCUSSION OF RESULTS

The investigations were aimed at sustainable energy options, the development of the economy, poverty alleviation, energy efficiency, environmental protection and renewable technologies.

In all scenarios, the most economic energy strategy for the next twenty years uses coal as the main primary energy source. Moreover, the use of coal and other forms of energy can be enhanced through the implementation of programmes for improved energy efficiency.

Diversifying transformation processes away from coal as primary fuel source will result in a more expensive option for the economy. However, if this strategy is tempered with economic implementation and more efficient use of energy, it will to some extent, offset the additional cost of diversification.

5.7.1 Energy Demand

The two simulated scenarios show a greater energy demand projection than the two optimised scenarios. The lower projected energy demand is because of energy efficiency measures including fuel switching (eg. end use burning fuel for thermal applications rather than first converting into electricity and then later using electricity to generate low grade heat).

Increased energy efficiency reduces energy demand significantly with a substantial decrease in cost to the energy system. In addition, strategies aimed at switching some thermal energy requirements from electricity to coal or gas would result in significant savings to the economy by deferring investment in expensive new electricity supply options, as well as being physically more energy efficient. It is more economic to switch from electricity to coal rather than gas if environmental externalities are not considered.

Implementing energy efficiency measures and fuel switching for end thermal use can result in the following savings:

- Implementing moderate energy efficiency and switching to coal in the Baseline scenario results in a decrease in cumulative energy demand of 2533 PJ by 2020 with a present value cumulative cost saving of approximately R62 billion over the 20 years. Further there is a cumulative reduction of 294 Mega tonnes of carbon dioxide emissions by 2020.

• Implementing moderate energy efficiency and fuel switching to gas in the Siyaphambili scenario results in a decrease in cumulative energy demand of 2981 PJ by 2020 with a present value cumulative cost saving of approximately R75 billion over the 20 years. In this case there is a marginal increase of 131 Mega tonnes of carbon dioxide emissions by 2020 because more environmentally friendly generation technologies are deferred beyond the planning horizon.

Improvements in existing devices, new technologies and changes in energy usage patterns are likely to cause:

• Increased production of hybrid cars (regenerative braking, hydrogen, fuel cell technology, battery etc.)

• Increased usage of electricity for mass transit systems for public and freight transport

There is significant potential for the Black Economic Empowerment options, job creation and poverty alleviation through:

• Development of energy service companies

• Provision of low cost, cleaner energy to industry to attract investment and sustain energy intensive industries (e.g. gold mines)

• Reduction of household energy costs by supplying an optimal energy and appliance mix

5.7.2 Energy Transformation

Although in some circumstances electricity may be the energy carrier of preference because of its ease of use, it may not always be the most physically efficient energy source.

Implementing energy efficiency including switching devices from electricity to coal or gas (especially where thermal energy as an end use is required) will result in reduced demand for electricity. In the Baseline and Siyaphambili scenarios, moderate implementation of energy efficiency programmes and switching from electricity usage to coal and gas results in a cumulative reduction from current projections in demand for electricity of 141 PJ and 193 PJ respectively by 2020.

All scenarios show that electricity generation based on coal remains the most economic available to South Africa under current national environmental legislation. Alternative electricity generation technologies have been identified to diversify supply and environmental concerns. These are ranked approximately in increasing economic cost to the economy over coal-fired electricity generation plant (fitted with Flue Gas Desulphurisation):

• Importing Hydro electricity from plants located in neighbouring States such as Mozambique (inclusive of Transmission costs and taking account of losses);

• Options using coal with Fluidised Bed Boiler Technologies;

• Gas combined cycle technologies using natural gas, both local production and that imported from neighbouring states;

• New nuclear technologies such as the Pebble Bed Modular Reactor, pending feasibility analyses;

• Renewable technologies using wind and solar.

The current expanding gas industry is displacing inter alia electricity as a thermal end use. Such an arrangement is more physically efficient and cost effective (as manifest by the conversions from other forms of energy to gas). It may be argued that, considering the insignificant natural gas reserves when compared with coal (natural gas energy reserves are currently only at best 2% of those of coal), and that for thermal requirements it is more efficient to burn gas at the end user rather than first convert it into electricity then produce heat, the use of natural gas for electricity generation should be done sparingly. Moreover, switching from electricity to gas will alleviate the demand on electricity and defer the requirement for increased supply capacity.

With respect to liquid fuel production, with the recent increased refinery capacity and the levelising in demand over the past four years, there appears to be no immediate need for further refinery capacity nationwide. On the other hand, refinery capacity in the centre of the country produces less than the demand, and refined products need to be transported inland. In this case, limited pipeline capacity may be a confounding factor.

Major shifts in petrol/diesel consumption, for example the taxi re-capitalisation programme, may affect supply parameters. The taxi industry currently uses approximately 15% of petrol (approximately 10 000 million litres) consumption nationwide. Converting that to diesel would comprise about 25% of current diesel exports (~4 700 million litres per year). Therefore, the taxi recapitalisation programme could be accommodated by exporting less diesel and at the same time free-up 15% of current petrol consumption and delay the need for further refining capacity.

As addressed earlier, based on levelised costs, it may be more economic to produce liquid fuels from new coal-to-liquid plant than from new refineries using imported oil. Moreover, it is more economic to import finished liquid fuel products than to build any new refinery capacity. As new refinery capacity is not urgent at this stage, such options should be further investigated.

Nuclear Pebble Bed Modular Reactor and renewable energy supply options are not economic for grid electricity generation when compared with non-coal supply options such as imported hydro, gas (assuming price increase with South African PPI) combined cycle plants and fluidised bed technologies within the next twenty years. These technologies are not included for electricity generation in the Siyaphambili Optimised scenario.

Implementing plans for renewable energy supply by installing 300 MWe of wind electricity generation by 2010 increases the total present cost of the Siyaphambili plan by R1,038,000. However, there is a reduction of 7.86 million tons of carbon dioxide emissions over the 20 year period.

Bio-diesel production will have marginal effect on the plan, replacing at most 1% to 2% of diesel production by 2020.

5.7.3 Additional Considerations

The major shift from the business-as-usual scenario is the additional use of renewable energies and the promotion energy efficiency measures.

Renewable energy currently forms approximately 8% of South Africa's primary energy supply, nearly all of that being non-commercial energy in the form of fire wood in the rural areas – that is not being renewed. South Africa is endowed with large resources of renewable energy potential that can be harnessed to contribute significantly to the national energy supply with minimal impacts on the environment. The cardinal conundrum regarding renewable energy is the introduction of initially expensive new energy technologies into a low priced energy environment. Energy efficiency measures are generally cost effective with pay-back periods of one to three years being acceptable depending on the circumstances. Similar to renewable energy, energy efficiency measures need to be kick-started.

The introduction of renewable energy technologies and energy efficiency measures is confounded by the managed liberalisation of the energy market and the multitude of private sector players expected to participate. In order to achieve a cross-sector goal, the government needs to regulate the sector accordingly.

6. INTEGRATED ENERGY PLAN

The integrated energy plan has been developed by channelling economic data through two scenarios based on assumptions and constraints determined by a group of specialists. Remembering that an integrated energy plan or strategy is not a precise blueprint for the energy sector but is a framework within which specific energy policy and development decisions can be made, and in recognising the need to balance the requirement of low cost energy with other imperatives such as social development, environment and security of supply, analysis of the results of the scenarios has lead to the following conclusions.

Coal Dominance: Notwithstanding the different scenarios, coal remains the dominant primary energy source over the planning horizon. In all circumstances where cost is the major driver, coal generally emerges as the least expensive option. The use of such coal energy presupposes the increased use of clean coal technologies. Moreover, coal remains the largest indigenous energy resource currently available.

Diversification: Notwithstanding coal's continued dominance, it is important to diversify energy resources to other energy forms such as natural gas and renewable energies to improve supply security, improve environmental performance and facilitate regional development. This diversification to other energy sources will have associated cost implications that must be traded off against other benefits on a project-by-project basis.

Energy Efficiency: Improved economic and environmental performance are brought about by sustained energy efficiency measures, including end use fuel switching. Energy efficiency measures are effective in both the "business as usual" scenario (that resulted in cost savings of up to R62 billion and carbon dioxide savings of up to 294 million tonnes) and the Siyaphambili scenario (that resulted in a decrease in cumulative energy demand of 2981 PJ with a present value cumulative cost saving of approximately R75 billion over the planning horizon).

Renewable Energies: Although the introduction of renewable energies has higher costs over the planning horizon, it is important to promote renewables for environmental reasons and for diversification of supply and to establish an infra-structure in South Africa that can develop to the extent where renewable energies can contribute significantly to energy supply on an economic basis. For grid connected electricity, it is important to bear in mind that wind and solar generation cannot produce electricity in response to demand. These technologies only produce when the source (wind or solar) is available. This increases the system costs, as extra storage is necessary if such is the only source of energy. Wind energy is at least 300% more expensive than new coal fired plant. So the large scale use of wind energy will be costly for the economy. However, there are renewable energy sources that are economic in the South African energy sector, such as biomass, especially in industry. South Africa's current target for renewable energy is 10 000 GWhr by the year 2012.

Nuclear: The technical and economic feasibility studies into the Pebble Bed Modular Reactor should be completed to determine if it could be a viable future source of electricity generation and the possible beneficial role that it could play in diversification of supply, replacement of fossil fuel as its use diminishes, contributing to the problem of global climate change by lowering carbon dioxide emissions and the possibility of establishing a nuclear export industry

Natural Gas: The diversification of energy supply by the increased use of natural gas has been shown to improve environmental performance, with the potential for regional development and security of supply. The increased use of gas will have associated cost implications that must be traded off against other benefits on a project-by-project basis. The end use of natural gas for thermal applications is physically the most efficient use of the energy contained in the gas. There may however be the need for large anchor customers, such as electricity generating stations, to catalyse the introduction of natural gas into a region. Moreover, when considering the quantity of current coal reserves and current an prospective gas reserves, natural gas in unlikely to become a serious competitor of primary energy supply over any extended period when compared with coal.

Exploration: Notwithstanding the dollar price base of oil, increasing the oil and gas reserve/resource base will increase security of supply and contribute to foreign exchange savings. Therefore the current oil and gas exploration measures should be expanded.

Oil Refineries Expansion: It is more cost effective to expand existing refinery capacity than to build green-fields plant, even taking into account the capital requirements for low sulphur fuels. The importation of refined product should be undertaken during the period when demand exceeds capacity until importation reaches levels where it becomes economically viable to expand the existing plant. Currently strain is put on the system due to a relatively high petrol to diesel ratio. (Petrol to diesel ratios close to one are more economic for refineries to produce.) The calculations show that this balance can be rectified with current trends in the transport sector for more diesel driven vehicles and the petrol to diesel taxi recapitalisation.

Synthetic Liquid Fuels: The outputs of the scenarios indicate that production of synthetic liquid fuels from gas appears uneconomic in comparison with a new oil refinery. On the other hand, it appears that at high load factors, synthetic fuels from coal could be economic when compared with new refinery capacity. These findings contradict findings in other investigations and the fact that globally investment in gas-to-liquids is taking place but not coal-to-liquids. The production of synthetic liquid fuels needs to be investigated further.

Electricity Generation: Coal based electricity generation remains the least cost option during the planning horizon. However, there is potential for hydro, natural gas and nuclear generation capacity that will have associated cost implications that must be traded off against other benefits on a project-by-project basis. The use of natural gas to generate electricity should be considered sparingly because of limited reserves and the higher efficiencies obtainable by burning gas directly at the point of application for thermal applications. Moreover, switching from electricity to gas will

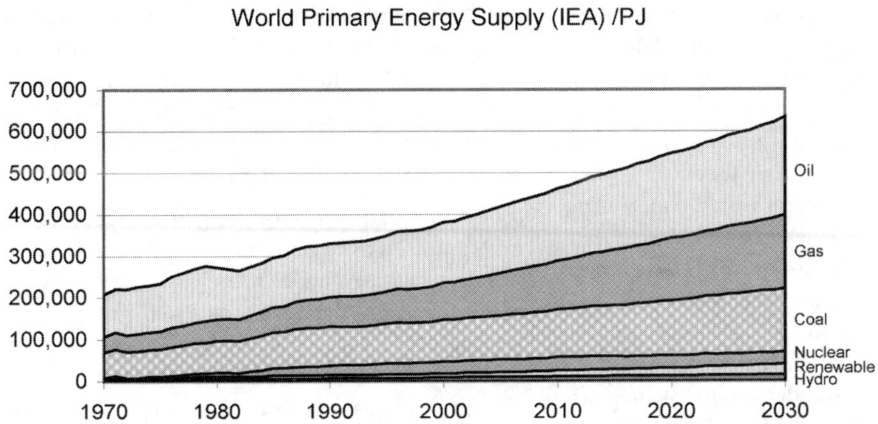

Figure 13: International Energy Agency's (IEA) forecasts for world primary energy supply.

alleviate the demand on electricity and defer the requirement for increased supply capacity. However, a gas-fired power electricity generation station could provide a base-load for gas to be introduced into a region.

Universal Access: Although addressed only implicitly in the integrated energy planning process, the programme for universal access to affordable, clean and appropriate energy gives rise to a number of concerns – the most important being the conversion of non-commercial energy to commercial energy especially in the rural areas. Energy demand rises with increased energisation (especially electrification) in households. Such energisation programmes should be linked to the integrated development programmes both at provincial and local level. The synergy between regional/local development and energy supply would enable sustainable growth.

Load Factors: Calculations for both the electricity sector and the oil refining sector have indicated that running plant at highest possible load factors – and "resting" spare capacity – will lower overall generation costs. Therefore, to minimise the levelised unit costs, it is apparent that electricity generation units/stations and oil refineries should be run at their maximum appropriate load factors consistent with appropriate margins. This factor also mitigates against the construction of too much spare capacity in these sectors and the need for suitable planning to match demand.

Reserves/Resources: There are sufficient energy and water resources currently available so that the integrated energy plan is not constricted over the current planning horizon.

Governance: It will be a major shift to increase significantly the use of renewable energies and to promote energy efficiency measures. Such goals require government intervention that in the first instance will be undertaken through the promulgation of a *White Paper on Renewable Energy and Clean Energy Development*, the introduction of an Energy Bill[8] and electricity regulatory amendments to be administered by the National Electricity Regulator.

7. COMPARISON WITH INTERNATIONAL ENERGY AGENCY PERSPECTIVES

It is pertinent at this stage to assess the above with the International Energy Agency's perspectives.

Notwithstanding the diversification of South Africa's energy supply from coal through the increased use of natural gas and renewable energies, and the increasing implementation of energy efficiency measures, the major source of primary energy remains coal over the next two decades. This of course presupposes the wider use of clean coal technologies.

The above is in concert with the International Energy Agency's forecast – Figure 13.

[8] (Energy Bill addresses a National Energy Advisory Committee, National Energy Data Base and Information System, Integrated Energy Planning, Renewable Energy, Energy Efficiency, Energy and safety Health and Environment, Energy Research)

According to the World Energy Outlook 2002 the International Energy Agency has projected that fossil fuels will remain the primary source of energy, meeting more that 90% of the increase in energy demand by year 2030. However the demand for natural gas will rise more strongly than for any other fossil fuel – again this is in concert with the increasing part that natural gas will play in South Africa. The consumption of coal will also grow but at a slower pace than that of oil and gas. Whereas the World Energy Outlook states that the role of nuclear power will decline, because few nuclear reactors will be build and some will be retired, the outlook in South Africa for the Pebble Bed Modular Reactor is still contingent on the ongoing feasibility studies. In line with the World Energy Outlook, renewable energies will play an increasing role in energy supply.

The World Energy Outlook states that energy demand will rise fastest in developing countries (such as South Africa) and that transport uses will outstrip all other uses.

Increases in coal production are likely to be concentrated where extraction, processing and transportation are lowest – in South Africa, Australia, China, India, Indonesia, North America and Latin America.

8. IDENTIFIED GAPS

The present integrated energy planning is the first such process to be undertaken in South Africa and was primarily based on basic techno-economic modelling. Notwithstanding the legitimacy of the results as projections, the undertaking has, however, identified a number of gaps (that are being addressed for future endeavours) that include:

(a) Governance: The present process did not consider in any detail the legislative, regulatory and institutional aspects in the energy sector for the implementation of the recommendations. Where decisions are based on considerations other than only economic, and in a changing environment where previous monopolies are being replaced by a multitude of players, the government needs to intervene for example to facilitate the expansion of renewable energy and energy efficiency measures.

(b) Stakeholder Participation: The present process included inputs from the Department of Trade and Industry, Treasury, Department of Environmental Affairs and Tourism as well as other interested and affected parties through two workshops. Future endeavours should intensify the participation of relevant government departments as well as other stakeholders, especially when it comes to fixing assumptions such as growth rates etc.

(c) Energy Data: The modelling processes required large amounts of accurate energy and other (eg economic growth, exchange rates, population growth, sector inflations) data. Some data were not available (eg the provision of energy data is not currently mandatory) and some available data were inconsistent. Data quantities vary from source to source, and energy balances are not well disaggregated. The exception is electricity, which is well described by Eskom.

(d) Models Programs: During the current integrated energy planning process, the development of optimal calculation programs were traded off against the need to expedite results. This has been identified is a major gap in the current process. To advance the process, the calculation programs should be optimised to allow more ready facilities to change driver parameters and baseline data both up-front and over the planning period.

(e) Environmental Externalities: The present process did not explicitly include environmental externalities because of the uncertainty of current policy developments in this regard, reliable local data and uncertainty as to how such external costs would be constituted in a policy void.

(f) Environmental Funding: Environmental funding (especially international funding) was not included in the modelling because; policy regarding national environmental taxing/funding is not yet resolved and some uncertainties with international funding.

(g) Industry Restructuring: The effect of privatisation costs and security of supply was not addressed directly. The calculations were based on providing the most economic energy system for the country. This was assumed to be realisable, and did not take into account investment patterns of various sectors. This means that the calculated result might require policy instruments beyond simple deregulation.

(h) Other: For example the trade off between least cost energy production and other factors such as job creation and social development.

The gaps listed above are scheduled to be addressed in Phase II of the integrated energy planning programme.

9. FURTHERANCE OF INTEGRATED ENERGY PLANNING

The core of any planning process is the ability to accurately predict the principle drivers or parameters of any enterprise. It should also be borne in mind that the projections of the drivers become less tenable and consequently the outputs of the scenarios the less reliable the further in time one projects. Hence, integrated energy planning is a process that is updated periodically to address:

(a) changing market circumstances;

(b) re-appraised energy resources;

(c) changing global considerations;

(d) changing driver parameters (eg growth rates, exchange rates, discount rates);

(e) changing energy demand profiles; and

(f) cost benefit analyses of individual energy projects.

The cycle time of such a process is approximately eighteen months.

As an output of this first South African integrated energy plan, a number of gaps have been identified – Section 8 – that will be addressed in the second phase. Gaps that are currently undergoing deliberation include:

(a) Energy data gaps that are being addressed in the forthcoming reassessment of South Africa's energy data base and information system and the forthcoming Energy Bill.

(b) Re-appraisal of South Africa's coal reserves and resources.

The integrated energy plan provides a strategy framework with which certain trade-offs need to be made on a project-by-project basis. Notwithstanding program limitations, the current model with its extensive data base can provide a decision making support tool to assist in project-by-project trade-offs.

The current work has identified the significant potential for reducing the cost of an energy project while increasing it's health and environmental performance. The computer based model can now also be used to investigate specific policies and measures for energy efficiency, energisation, large scale energy investments and the potential of new technologies, such as energy efficient appliances. The model also does this in the context of the whole energy system, thus looking at the total effect of a measure, in terms of costs and environmental loading.

In furthering the integrated energy planning process, the current study will be appraised and inter alia the above gaps addressed.

The Law on Energy Conservation of the People's Republic of China

(Approved at the 28th Session of the Standing Committee of the Eighth National People's Congress on November 1, 1997)

Presidential Mandate of the People's Republic of China No. 90

The Law on Energy Conservation of the People's Republic of China was approved at the 28th session of the Standing Committee of the Eighth National People's Congress of the People's Republic of China on November 1, 1997. It is promulgated and shall come into force from January 1, 1998.

JIANG Zemin
President of the People's Republic of China
November 1, 1997

CHAPTER 1 GENERAL PROVISIONS

Article 1 This law is formulated in order to promote energy conservation throughout society, improve the efficiency of energy utilization, achieve economic benefits, protect the environment, secure national economic and social development, and meet the requirement everyday life of people.

Article 2 The term energy used in this Law refers to various resources including coal, crude oil, natural gas, power, coke, coal gas, heat, oil products, liquid petroleum gas, biomass, and other resources from which useful energy can be derived directly or through processing and conversion.

Article 3 The term energy conservation used in this Law means: enhancing energy use management; adopting measures which are technologically feasible, economically rational, and environmentally and socially acceptable; reducing loss and waste in the chain of energy production and consumption, all to achieve the efficient and rational use of energy.

Article 4 Energy conservation is a long term strategy for national economic development.

The State Council and the governments of provinces, autonomous regions and municipalities directly under the central government should: strengthen their efforts in energy conservation; restructure industry, enterprises, products, and energy consumption patterns; promote technological progress for energy conservation; reduce energy consumption per unit of economic output and energy consumption per physical unit of product; improve the exploitation, processing, conversion, transmission, and distribution of energy; and encourage the national economy to develop in an energy-efficient manner.

The state encourages the development and utilization of new and renewable sources of energy.

Article 5 The state makes energy conservation policy and compiles energy conservation plans which shall be incorporated into the national social and economic development plan, consistent with economic development and environmental protection.

Article 6 The state encourages and supports the research and dissemination of energy conservation science and technology, enhances understanding of and education for energy conservation, popularizes scientific knowledge about energy conservation, and improves citizens' awareness of energy conservation.

Article 7 All organizations and individuals should fulfill energy conservation obligations and have the right to report any wasteful energy behavior.

The people's governments at all levels provides awards to organizations and individuals for outstanding achievements in energy conservation or research and popularization of energy conservation science and technology.

Article 8 The authorized energy conservation agencies of the State Council are responsible for energy conservation supervision and management on a national basis. Other agencies of the State Council supervise energy conservation efforts within their areas of responsibility.

Energy conservation management authorities of local governments at and above the county level supervise and manage energy conservation within their jurisdictions. Relevant authorities of local people's governments at and above the county level supervise and manage energy conservation within their jurisdictions.

CHAPTER 2 ENERGY CONSERVATION MANAGEMENT

Article 9 The State Council and local governments at various levels should enhance their leadership in energy conservation, and on an annual basis deploy, coordinate, supervise, review, and promote energy conservation efforts.

Article 10 The State Council and People's governments of provinces, autonomous regions, and municipalities directly under the central government should, according to the principle of giving importance to energy conservation and energy exploitation, putting energy conservation first, choose in an optimal way energy conservation and energy exploitation investment projects, and develop energy investment plans, based on a technical, economic, and environmental assessment of energy conservation and energy exploitation.

Article 11 The State Council and People's governments of provinces, autonomous regions, and municipalities directly under the central government shall arrange energy conservation funds from capital construction and technical retrofit funds to support rational energy utililization and exploitation of new and renewable energy sources.

People's governments at municipal and county levels shall arrange energy conservation funds according to their situation in order to support rational energy utililization and exploitation of new and renewable energy sources.

Article 12 Special assessment of rational energy utilization should be included in the feasibility analysis reports of fixed capital investment projects.

The design and construction of fixed capital investment projects should comply with the standards of rational energy use and regulations of energy conservation design.

Regulatory and supervisory authorities shall not approve the construction or completion of projects which do not meet the standards of rational energy use and regulations for energy conservation design. Completed projects which do not meet these standards and regulations should not be certified.

Article 13 New industrial projects which employ backward technology, consume excessive amounts of energy, and waste energy significantly are prohibited from being constructed. The energy conservation management authorities of the State Council, in cooperation with other relevant agencies of the State Council, develop lists of prohibited industrial projects that consume excessive amounts of energy, and develop specific enforcement methods.

Article 14 The administrative agency of the State Council in charge of standardization formulates national standards of energy conservation.

In the absence of the aforementioned national standards, relevant departments of the State Council formulate sectoral energy conservation standards by legal means and report them for filing to the responsible department of the State Council.

Energy conservation standards should be technically advanced, economically rational, and subject to continuous improvement and perfection.

Article 15 The authorized energy conservation agencies of the State Council, in association with the relevant agencies of the State Council, should enhance supervision of sectors producing large numbers of widely used energy-consuming products, and urge them to apply energy conservation measures, make efforts to improve product design and manufacturing technology, and reduce energy consumption per physical unit of production within these sectors.

Article 16 The responsible energy conservation management authorities at and above the provincial level, in coordination with the relevant departments at the same level, shall set limits in terms of energy consumption per physical unit of product, for products which are energy-intensive to produce.

Limits on energy consumption per physical unit of product shall be set scientifically and rationally.

Article 17 The state applies a system for discontinuing backward, over energy-intensive energy-consuming products and equipment.

The authorized energy conservation agencies of the State Council, in association with relevant agencies of the State Council, determines and promulgates an inventory of overly energy-intensive energy-consuming products and equipment to be discontinued. The authorized energy conservation agencies of the State Council, in association with relevant agencies of the State Council, formulates a detailed method of enforcement and implementation.

Article 18 Enterprises may voluntarily apply to the product quality supervision and management agencies of the State Council or to the certification agencies assigned by sectoral agencies authorized by products quality supervision and management agencies of the State Council, in accordance with relevant national product certification regulations, for energy saving quality certification for their energy-consuming products. After successful certification, a certificate of energy saving quality shall be issued, and labels of energy saving quality certification can be affixed on the energy-using products and their packaging.

Article 19 The statistical agencies of the People's governments at and above county level, in association with relevant agencies at the same level, organize statistics on energy consumption and utilization, publicize periodically statistical bulletins, and report energy consumption per physical unit of product for major energy consuming products, etc.

Article 20 The state shall enhance energy conservation management in key energy-consuming entities. Key energy-consuming entities are defined as:

(1) Energy-consuming entities with total annual energy consumption above 10,000 tons of coal equivalent;

(2) Energy-consuming entities with total annual energy consumption between 5,000 and 10,000 tons of coal equivalent, as determined by relevant agencies of the State Council, or energy conservation management agencies of people's governments of provinces, autonomous regions, and municipalities directly under the central government.

Energy conservation management agencies of governments at and above the county level shall coordinate with other relevant agencies to supervise and examine the energy utilization situation of key energy-consuming entities. They may, by legal means, delegate to appropriate organizations the authority and responsibility for conducting energy efficiency examinations and measurements.

The responsible energy conservation management agencies of the State Council, in association with relevant agencies of the State Council, formulate energy conservation requirements, energy conservation measures, and management methods for key energy-consuming entities.

CHAPTER 3 RATIONAL UTILIZATION OF ENERGY

Article 21 Based on the principle of rational energy use, energy-using entities shall strengthen energy conservation management capabilities, formulate and implement energy conservation technical measures, and reduce energy consumption.

Energy-using entities shall provide energy conservation education and organize conservation training for relevant employees.

Employees who have not received any energy conservation education and training shall not be allowed to work in a position of operation of an energy-using facility.

Article 22 Energy-using entities should enhance energy audit and management, and establish and improve energy consumption statistics and systems of analysis of energy consumption.

Article 23 Energy-using entities should establish energy conservation responsibility system, and grant awards to groups and individuals who make achievements in energy conservation.

Article 24 Entities producing energy-intensive products should comply with legal limits for energy consumption per physical unit of product.

Entities in which energy consumption per physical unit significantly exceeds established limits shall be required to provide corrective measures within a given period of time. This period will be determined by the energy conservation management agencies of People's governments at or above the county level based on their authority, delegated by the State Council.

Article 25 Entities or individuals producing and selling energy-using products shall stop producing and selling energy-using products that the state has determined will be discontinued or discarded. Use of discontinued or discarded energy-using equipment beyond within the time limit set by energy conservation management departments and relevant departments of the State Council is prohibited. It is prohibited to transfer the discarded equipment to other users.

Article 26 Organizations and individuals producing energy-using products shall display energy conservation labels or indicators on product specifications and product identification.

Article 27 Organizations and individuals producing energy-using products shall not use forged certificates or labels of energy conservation quality, or use misleading-leading information on the label.

Article 28 In accordance with national regulations, key energy-using organizations shall submit reports of energy use periodically. These reports shall include information on energy consumption, energy efficiency, analyses of energy conservation benefits, and energy conservation measures taken or applied.

Article 29 Key energy-using organizations shall establish energy management positions, select energy management personnel with appropriate energy conservation expertise, practical experience, and technical qualification above the level of engineer, and report for filing to energy conservation management organizations of governments above county level.

Energy management personnel shall supervise and examine their employers' performance of energy use.

Article 30 Employees as well as rural and urban residents shall comply with national regulations to meter and pay for energy used, including electricity, coal gas, natural gas and coal produced by enterprises. It is prohibited to use energy for free or charged at a fixed fee.

Article 31 Energy producing and supplying organizations shall provide energy to energy-using organizations in accordance with legislation, regulation, and contract obligation.

CHAPTER 4 TECHNOLOGICAL PROGRESS OF ENERGY CONSERVATION

Article 32 The state encourages and supports the development of energy conservation technology, determines the priority and direction for developing advanced energy conservation technology, establishes and completes energy conservation technology service systems, and creates and regulates the energy conservation technology market.

Article 33 The state coordinates and implements key energy conservation scientific research and demonstration projects and recommends energy conservation projects for public education and popularization. The state also directs enterprises, utilities, and individuals to employ advanced energy conservation processes, technologies, equipment, and material.

The state formulates preferential policies to support energy conservation projects for demonstration and public education.

Article 34 The state encourages the introduction of advanced foreign energy conservation technology and equipment, and prohibits the introduction of outdated foreign energy-using technology, equipment, and materials.

Article 35 Energy conservation funding for energy conservation technology research shall be arranged within the scientific research funds allocated by the State Council and governments of provinces, autonomous regions, and municipalities under the direct control of the central government.

Article 36 On the basis of national industrial policy and energy conservation technology policy, governments at different levels above the county level shall coordinate with relevant organizations to promote scientific and optimized production methods with the characteristics of energy conservation.

Article 37 In accordance with relevant legislation, administrative laws and regulations, the design and construction of buildings shall employ building structures, materials, appliances, and products with energy conservation features in order to improve thermal and insulating performance, and to reduce energy consumption for heating, cooling, and lighting.

Article 38 Based on the principle that solutions shall be flexible and adaptable to a variety of conditions and situations, energy development shall be diverse, consistent with other national objectives, and benefits optimized for taking into account comprehensive resource utilization. Governments at various levels shall enhance rural energy development and develop and utilize biogas, solar energy, wind energy, hydro energy, geothermal energy, and other renewable and new energy sources.

Article 39 With respect to the following common energy conservation technologies, the state will:

(1) Encourage cogeneration and district heating, increase the capacity factor of cogeneration units, develop heat-cascading technology, encourage combined heat, power, and cooling technology, as well as combined heat, power and coal gas technology, and promote comprehensive efficiency in thermal energy applications;

(2) Achieve more-efficient operation of electric motors, fans, pumping equipment and systems; develop adjustable speed motor drives for energy conservation, along with electric-electronic power saving technology; develop, produce, and popularize high-quality and low-cost energy-efficient appliances and equipment; and increase the efficiency of electric power utilization;

(3) Develop and popularize the use of clean coal technologies, including fluidized bed combustion, smokeless combustion, and gasification and liquefaction systems appropriate for domestic coals in order to increase coal utilization efficiency;

(4) Develop and popularize general energy conservation technologies that are mature and that have demonstrated, significant benefits.

Article 40 Each economic and management sector shall formulate sectoral energy conservation technology policies, develop and popularize new energy conservation technologies, techniques, equipment, and materials, limit or discontinue use of old and outdated technologies, techniques, equipment, and materials with high energy consumption rates.

Article 41 The energy conservation management department in the State Council, in coordination with relevant departments of the State Council, shall: formulate common and sectorally detailed energy conservation technology indicators, requirements, and measures, modify them in ways consistent with technological and economic goals and needs, increase energy use efficiency, reduce energy consumption, and help the nation step-by-step to achieve advanced international levels of energy utilization.

CHAPTER 5 LEGAL LIABILITY

Article 42 New, energy-intensive industrial projects prohibited by national mandate and in violation of Article 13 of this law shall be noted by the energy conservation management organizations of the people's government above county level and reported to the people's government. Reporting shall be made at the governmental level with authority to terminate operations and energy use, within their capacity as determined by the State Council.

Article 43 Organizations with high energy consumption levels in product production in violation of Article 24 of this law, and that significantly exceed the energy consumption limits per unit of production, and that do not correct the violation within the allotted time limit or that fail to meet the proposed corrective measures shall be noted by the energy conservation management organizations of the people's government above the county level and reported to the people's government at the level of authority to order suspension and closing of violators' facilities, within the capacity stipulated by the State Council.

Article 44 Those who produce and sell discontinued energy-using products as defined by the state and that violate Article 25 of this Law shall be ordered to stop producing and selling said product by the supervisory management organizations of people's government above the county level. Income obtained from the sale or use of energy-using products that have been discontinued by the state shall be confiscated. Fines equal to one to five times the income so obtained may be levied. Industrial and commercial authorities of the people's governments above the county level may suspend violators' business licenses.

Article 45 Operators of energy-using equipment discontinued by the state and in violation of Article 25 of this Law shall be forced to stop this activity by the energy conservation management organizations of people's government above county level, and their energy using equipment shall be confiscated. Serious violations shall be noted by the energy conservation management organizations of the people's governments above county level and reported to authorities with the power to suspend or shut down operations, consistent with their capacity as authorized by the State Council.

Article 46 Those who transfer discarded energy-using equipment to others and violate Article 25 of this Law shall have their income confiscated by the product quality supervisory and administrative authorities of people's government above county level, and will receive fines of one to five times the value of the income.

Article 47 Producers not displaying energy consumption indicators on product specifications and production identification in violation of Article 26 of this Law shall correct this violation within a time limit stipulated by the product quality supervisory and administrative authorities of people's government above county level, and fined up to 50,000 Yuan.

Article 48 Producers who use forged energy conservation quality certificates or distort or provide misleading information in violation of Article 27 of this Law shall be ordered to make public amends to the product quality supervisory and administrative authorities of the people's government above the county level. Income illegally obtained in this fashion shall be confiscated and the producers may be fined one to five times the amount of income so obtained.

Article 49 Government civil servants who abuse their power, neglect their responsibilities, or commit fraud or acts of corruption for personal gain shall be cited for criminal liabilities. In the case that their behavior constitutes criminal offense, these individuals shall receive administrative punishment.

CHAPTER 6 SUPPLEMENTARY PROVISIONS

Article 50 This Law shall go into force from January 1, 1998.

China

Utility Demand-side management in China Opportunities and Policy Options

Compiled by
Dr. Hu Zhaoguang and Dr. Zhou Fuqiu, et al.

1. Law on Energy Conservation (promulgated on November 1, 1997, effective January 1, 1998)

Selected Provisions:

Article 5 The state makes energy conservation policies and compiles energy conservation plans, which shall be incorporated into the national social and economic development plan, consistent with economic development and environmental protection.

Article 9 the State Council and local governments at various levels should enhance their leadership in energy conservation, and on an annual basis deploy, coordinate, supervise, review, and promote energy conservation efforts.

Article 10 The State Council and People's governments of provinces, autonomous regions, and municipalities directly under the central government should, according to the principle of giving importance to energy conservation and energy exploitation, putting energy conservation first, choose in an optimal way energy conservation and energy exploitation investment projects, and develop energy investment plans, based on a technical, economic, and environmental assessment of energy conservation and energy exploitation.

Article 11 The State Council and People's governments of provinces, autonomous regions, and municipalities directly under the central government shall arrange energy conservation funds from capital construction and technical retrofit funds to support rational energy utilization and exploitation of new and renewable energy sources.

Article 12 Special assessment of rational energy utilization should be included in the feasibility analysis reports of fixed capital investment projects.

Article 13 New Industrial projects that employ backward technology, consume excessive amounts of energy, and waste energy significantly are prohibited from being constructed.

Article 14 The administrative agency of the State Council in charge of standardization formulates national standards of energy conservation.

Article 15 The authorized energy conservation agencies of the State Council, in association with relevant agencies of the State Council, should enhance supervision of sectors producing large numbers of widely used energy-consuming products, and urge them to apply energy conservation measures, make efforts to improve product design and manufacturing technology, and reduce energy consumption per physical unit of production within these sectors.

Article 16 The responsible energy conservation management authorities at and above the provincial level, in coordination with relevant departments at the same level, shall set limits in terms of energy consumption per physical unit of product, for products which are energy-intensive to produce.

Article 17 The state applies a system for discontinuing backward, over energy-intensive energy-consuming products and equipment.

Article 18 Enterprises may voluntarily apply to the product quality supervision and management agencies of the State Council of to the relevant certification agencies, in accordance with relevant national product certification regulations, for energy saving quality certification for their energy-consuming products.

Article 19 The statistical agencies of the People's governments at and above county level, in association with relevant agencies at the same level, organize statistics on energy consumption and utilization, publicize periodically statistical bulletins, and report energy consumption per physical unit of production for major energy consuming products, etc.

Article 20 The state shall enhance energy conservation management in key energy-consuming entities. The responsible energy conservation management agencies of the State Council, in association with relevant agencies of the State Council, formulate energy conservation requirements, energy conservation measures, and management methods for key energy-consuming entities.

Article 21 Based on the principles of rational energy use, energy-using entities shall strengthen energy conservation management capabilities, formulate and implement energy conservation technical measures, and reduce energy consumption.

Article 22 Energy-using entities shall enhance energy audit and management, and establish and improve energy consumption statistics and systems of analysis in energy conservation.

Article 23 Energy-using entities should establish energy conservation responsibility system, and grant awards to groups and individuals who make achievements in energy conservation.

Article 24 Entities producing energy-intensive products should comply with legal limits for energy consumption per physical unit of product.

Article 25 Entities or individuals producing or selling energy-using products shall stop producing and selling energy-using products that the state has determined will be discontinued or discharged.

Article 26 Organizations and individuals producing energy-using products shall display energy conservation labels or indicators on product specifications and product identification.

Article 27 Organizations and individuals producing energy-using products shall not used forged certificates or labels of energy conservation quality, or use misleading information on the label.

Article 28 In accordance with national regulations, key energy-using organizations shall submit reports of energy use periodically.

Article 29 Key energy-using organizations shall establish energy management positions and select qualified energy management personnel.

Article 30 Employees as well as rural and urban residents shall comply with national regulations to meter and pay for energy used. It is prohibited to use energy for free or charged at a fixed fee.

Article 40 Each economic and management sector shall formulate sectoral energy conservation technology policies, develop and popularize new energy conservation technologies, techniques, equipment and materials, limit or discontinue use of old and outdated technologies, techniques, equipment and materials with high energy consumption rates.

Article 41 The energy conservation management department in the State Council, in coordination with relevant departments of the State Council, shall: formulate common and sectorally detailed energy conservation technology indicators, requirements, and measures, modify them in ways consistent with technological and economic goals and needs, increase energy use efficiency, reduce energy consumption, and help the nation step-by-step to achieve advanced international levels of energy utilization.

3. Electric Power Law (promulgated and effective on July 2, 1983)

Selected Provisions:

Article 9 The State shall encourage the adoption of advanced technology and management techniques in the course of electric power construction, production, supply and consumption, and shall reward units or individuals that have made significant achievements in research, development and/or application of advanced technology and management techniques.

Article 24 With respect to supply and consumption of electric power, the State shall implement the management principles of safe, economical and planned power consumption. The procedures for supply and consumption of electric power are subject to formulation by the State Council pursuant to the provisions hereof.

Article 31 A consumer should install a metering device [to measure] its power consumption. The amount of electric power consumed as adopted by the consumer should conform to the amount as recorded by a metering device that has been approved according to law by a meter rating organization. The design, installation and operations management of a consumer's device [for measurement of] consumed electricity should comply with standards [established by] the State or electric power industry standards.

Article 32 No consumer may endanger the supply or safe use of electricity or disturb the regular order of electric power supply and consumption. In the event of such threat to the supply or safe use of electricity or disturbance to the regular order of electric power supply and consumption, the Power Supply Enterprise has the right to halt [such abuse].

Article 33 A Power Supply Enterprise should assess electric power fees to its consumers in accordance with the electricity price ratified by the State and the recorded [usage] as shown by the metering device in use. A consumer should pay electric power fees in accordance with the electricity price ratified by the State and the recorded [usage] as shown by the metering device in use.

Article 34 Power Supply Enterprises and electricity consumers should obey the relevant regulations of the State and take effective measures to implement safe, economical and planned consumption of electric power.

Article 41 The State shall implement electricity pricing [system based on] different types of usage and different [consumption] times. The standard for defining usage types and the method of calculating consumption times are subject to determination by the State Council.

Article 42 The standards for assessment of fees based on a consumer's increased capacity are to be formulated jointly by the State Council's Electricity Department and its department in charge of pricing administration.

Article 44 No unit or individual may add any surcharge to electricity fees except as may be otherwise stipulated by law or administration regulation . . . When collecting electricity fees, no power supply enterprise may collect other fees on behalf of others.

Article 49 Local people's governments at the county level and above and their departments for comprehensive economic administration should, when allocating quotas for electricity consumption, preserve an appropriate ration between the consumption of electricity [earmarked] for agriculture and by rural communities [in general], and should give priority to electricity consumption for the purposes of flood diversion, drought protection, and seasonal agricultural activities required for production in rural communities. Electric Power Enterprises should carry out the above provision in their allocation of electricity consumption, and may not reduce electric power quotas for [other] agriculture of rural communities.

Law on the Prevention and Control of Atmospheric Pollution (promulgated Sept. 5, 1987; revised in April 2001).

Article 19 Enterprises shall give priority to the adoption of clean production techniques that are instrumental to high efficient use of energy and to reducing the discharge of pollutants so as to decrease the generation of atmospheric pollutants.

Article 25 The relevant departments under the State Council and the local people's governments at various levels shall adopt measures to improve the urban energy structure and popularize the production and utilization of clean energy.

Article 30 Where any newly built or expanded thermal power plants and other large or medium-sized enterprise that discharge sulfur dioxide more than the prescribed standards for pollutants discharge or the quota of total control allow, supporting facilities for desulphurization and dust removal must be installed or other measures for controlling the discharge of sulfur dioxide or for dust removal must be adopted.

In the acid rain control areas or sulfur dioxide pollution control areas, if an existing enterprise discharges atmospheric pollutants more than the standards for pollutants discharge allow, the discharge of atmospheric pollutants of the enterprise shall be controlled within a time limit.

Construction Law (promulgated Nov. 1, 1997, effective March 1, 1998)

Article 4 The state supports construction sciences research to improve the designing level and encourage energy conservation and environmental protection, advocate for the use of advanced technologies, equipment and processes, new building materials and modern management methods.

Rules on Electric Power Supply and Use, State Council Order No. 196, issued April 17, 1996, effective September 1, 1996.

Article 5 The state [government] will implement, for the electric power supply and sue, the management principle of using the electric power in a safe, saving and planned way. Power Enterprises and Users shall obey the relevant regulations, take effective measures and make the works in respect of using the electric power in a safe, saving and planned way to be well done.

Article 26 Users shall install [their] power consumption metering devices. The capacity and energy consumption shall be determined by the records of a power consumption metering device recognized by a measurement verification organization pursuant to the laws. Such metering device shall be installed at the boundary point between the titles of a power supply facility and a power receiving facility.

Article 27 Power Enterprises shall compute the electricity charges payable by their Users according to the electricity rates approved by the state [government] and the consumption records measured by a metering device.

Article 29 The electric power administrative departments of the people's governments above county level shall implement the state industrial policies and shall work out the plan of electric power use in accordance with the principle of overall planning and all-around consideration, securing key [Users] and supplying power to those that are outstanding [profit-making Users]. Both Power Enterprises and Users should lay down their own projections in respect of power saving, should promote and utilize new technology, new materials, new techniques and new equipment in connection with power saving so as to reduce electric power consumption.

Article 30 No User shall have any following actions hazardous to the safety of power supply or use and actions disturbing the order of normal power supply and use: (1) voluntarily changing the type of power use; (2) voluntarily overconsuming the capacity as provided in a [power supply and use] contract; (3) voluntarily overconsuming [the capacity or energy] amounts as allocated pursuant to a [power supply and use] plan.

Power Conservation Management Provisions, State Economic and Trade Commission and State Planning and Development Commission (promulgated and effective December 29, 2000)

These joint regulations cover power energy efficiency improvements and rational electricity use.

Chapter Three: Power Demand Side Management

Article 15 Defines DSM as power management measures that meet the same power performance through improving power efficiency and optimizing power utilization at the side of end users while reducing power consumption and demand, with a view to energy conservation and environmental protection.

Article 16 Requires economic and trade commissions to facilitate DSM efforts. Measures shall be taken to conduct load management at the side of end users, extend interruptible load management and direct load management, so as to make full utilization of off-peak power supplies.

Article 17 Encourages a range of power conservation technologies.

Article 18 Power planning and integrated resources planning should include DSM.

Article 19 Efforts should be made to expand the application of double-layer rate systems by gradually raising basic rates and reducing kilowatt-hour rates; expedite the extension of time-of-use rates and expand the time difference; research, develop and extend interruptible load rates.

Article 20 Power users that apply power saving electric products recommended or certified by the state may apply to provincial pricing and power administrative bodies for reduction or exemption from capacity charge. Key power saving technologies and products shall be entitled to preferential tax policies promulgated by the state.

Article 21 Utilities shall enhance efforts to popularize and facilitate DSM. The cost of these [education] efforts may be covered by their management budget.

Provincial Regulations Implementing the National Law on Energy Conservation

[None]

Management Method for Key Energy Use Organizations, State Economic and Trade Commission (March 1999)

[None]

Regulations on Developing Combined Heat and Power, State Development and Planning Commission, State Economic and Trade Commission, Ministry of Construction and former MFI

Regulates CHP technical indicators and exempts from grid fees new or expanded CHPs that meet the technical indicators.

Regulations on the Formulation and Assessment of the "Chapter on Energy Conservation" in Feasibility Studies of Fixed Asset Investment Projects (effective January 1, 1998).

Article 2 Feasibility studies of fixed asset investment projects shall include a "Chapter on Energy Conservation" which shall be assessed by qualified construction firms.

Article 3 The "Chapter on Energy Conservation" shall analyze the energy consumption level of construction, equipment and processes of the project of the project, as well as efficiency and energy consumption indexes of energy-using products.

Article 4 State industrial policies, state and sectoral standards of energy conservation shall be implemented in newly constructed, transformed and expanded projects.

Article 5 Specific requirements for rational utilization of energy and energy conservation contained in existing construction and technical standards shall be revised every five years.

Top Level Power Supply Enterprise Qualification Standards (Tentative), State Power Corporation (issued in 2001)

These standards clearly stipulate that top-level power supply enterprises must take active steps to launch DSM programs in a planned and effective manner.

Promotion Law of Renewable Energy Development and Utilization, the People's Republic of China

(Draft for Advice)

March, 2004

CHAPTER 1 GENERAL PRINCIPLES

Article 1 [Purpose of the Law] The purpose of this law is to push the development and utilization of renewable energy, improve energy structure, protect environment and accelerate the sustainable development of economy and society.

Article 2 [Applicable Area] The renewable energy in this law refers to small-scale hydropower (50 thousand KW or below), wind, solar energy, biomass, geothermal energy, ocean energy and other categories of resources in the nature that can continuously reproduce and be utilized as useful energy directly or after processing and conversion.

Article 3 [Universal Obligation] Any corporation and individual within the territory of the People's Republic of China has the right and obligation to utilize renewable energy.

Article 4 [Universal Principle] The government implements the principle of the combination of government-promotion and market-orientation for the development and utilization of renewable energy.

The government allows all forms of market participant with different ownership to participate in the renewable energy development in China, and encourages the investment diversity.

Article 5 [Rural Energy] The government encourages rural and remote areas to give priority to the development and utilization of renewable energy, in order to satisfy the local energy demand for the purpose of living and production.

Article 6 [R&D, Dissemination and Education] The government encourages and supports the research and popularization of the technologies for renewable energy development and utilization, diffusion and dissemination the renewable energy knowledge, as well as improving the public awareness of importance of the renewable energy development and utilization.

Article 7 [Environment Protection] The development and utilization of renewable energy should avoid the pollution and destruction to the environment.

Article 8 [Sector Guidance] The government should design the renewable energy development plan, technology criterion and product standard to strengthen the guidance and management of the renewable energy industry in China.

Article 9 [Honor and Award] Governments at different levels should offer financial and policy support to corporations and individuals that develop and utilize renewable energy, and honor or award those that make significant contributions.

Article 10 [Management Agency] The principal energy management agency of the State Council is in charge of the comprehensive management of the national renewable energy development and utilization. The relevant agencies of the State Council, within their respective incumbent responsibilities, are in charge of the related management of the renewable energy development and utilization.

The principal energy management agency of above-county local People's government is in charge of the local management of the renewable energy development and utilization within its administrative area. The relevant agencies in the local government, within their respective incumbent responsibilities, are in charge of the related management of the renewable energy development and utilization.

CHAPTER 2 RESOURCES MANAGEMENT AND DEVELOPMENT PLAN

Article 11 [Resources Survey] The principal energy management agency of the State Council is responsible for organizing the national renewable energy resources survey and management.

The relevant agencies of the State Council, within their respective responsibilities, are in charge of the survey of relevant renewable energy resources, and report the survey results to the principal energy management agency of the State Council.

The principal energy management agency of above-county local People's government is responsible for organizing the local survey of renewable energy resources within its administrative area, and survey results should be reported to one-level-upper government energy management agency for records.

The survey results of renewable energy resources should be open to the public.

Article 12 [Resources Management] Corporations and individuals should obtain the rights of developing and utilizing renewable energy resources according to relevant national regulations.

Article 13 [Plan System] The State Council designs the plan for national renewable energy development and incorporates it into the national scheme for economic and social development.

Provincial people's government should design the plan for local renewable energy development based on the general requirements of national renewable energy development plan, and incorporates it into the local scheme for economic and social development.

Article 14 [Plan Principle] The design of the renewable energy development plan should accord with the general requirements of national energy development plan, and follow the principles of the combination of near-term development and utilization and long-term development, the combination of fully utilizing the resources and optimizing the energy structure, the combination of collective development and scattered development, and the combination of technology advancement and industrialization development.

Article 15 [Plan Content] The renewable energy development plan should include the overall objective of the renewable energy development and utilization, structure and scale, distribution and emphasis, industry development, investment and profit, policy and ensuring measures, and so on. The plan should be open to the public.

Article 16 [Plan correspondence] Other national energy development plans should correspond with the renewable energy development plan.

Article 17 [Management of Project Construction] The government manages the construction of renewable energy projects by different level and classification. The rights of developing and operating important construction projects on renewable energy power generation and biomass liquid fuels should be permitted by the principal energy management agency of the State Council. For other non-important renewable energy power generation and biomass liquid fuels projects, the developing and operating rights should be permitted by the principal energy management agency of above-county people's government. The rights are obtained in ways of bidding, auction or agreement based on the principles of openness, impartiality and justice.

Renewable energy projects for heat and gas are developed and operated by enterprises and individuals independently according to relevant national regulations.

Article 18 [Project Check and Accept] The renewable energy construction projects should be put into production and operation after being eligibly checked and accepted according to the relevant national regulations.

Article 19 [Safe Production] The construction and operation of renewable energy projects should comply with the relevant regulations in terms of national safe production and environment protection.

CHAPTER 3 INDUSTRY GUIDANCE AND TECHNOLOGY ADVANCEMENT

Article 20 [Industry Catalogue] The principal energy management agency of the State council should, based on the national renewable energy development plan, regularly issue the guidance catalogue for the development of renewable energy industry.

The People's governments of provinces, self-governing areas and municipalities issue local guidance catalogue for the development of renewable energy industry according to national renewable energy development plan and local practical situations.

Article 21 [Standard and Criterion] The standardization management agency of the State Council should design the national standard for renewable energy technology and product.

For those without the national standard mentioned in the previous paragraph, the relevant agencies of the State Council should design corresponding industry standards and report them to the standardization management agency of the State Council for records.

Other industry standards designed by relevant agencies of the State Council should be beneficial to the development and utilization of renewable energy.

Article 22 [Testing and Certification] The principal energy management agency of the State Council should coordinate with other management agencies in charge of technology supervision, product testing and certification to construct national testing, inspecting and certification centers for renewable energy products.

Article 23 [Education, R&D] The government should increase the input to the research and development of renewable energy technology, as well as the education in this field.

The people's government at different levels and relevant agencies should arrange special fund for the research and development of renewable energy technology in their science and technology development plans.

The science and technology management agency of the State Council and other administrative agencies should support the establishment of national experiment and research, development and application centers for renewable energy technology.

The education management agency of the State Council should incorporate renewable energy knowledge and technology courses into general and professional education, and support the establishment of technology training system.

Corporations including national news and publication, broadcasting and filming, culture and relevant social groups have the obligation to disseminate the technology and knowledge about renewable energy development and utilization.

Article 24 [Industry Development] The government encourages enterprises and individuals to develop and manufacture advanced and applicable renewable energy technology equipments.

Article 25 [Industry Association] The People's government at different levels should bring industry association into playing an active role in pushing the development and utilization of renewable energy.

CHAPTER 4 DISSEMINATION AND APPLICATION

Article 26 [Market Ensure] The government implements the renewable energy quota system to regulate the proportion of renewable energy in energy production or consumption and to establish the renewable energy quota trading market. Detailed measures will be designed by the State Council.

Article 27 [Grid-connected Power Generation] The government encourages and supports all forms of grid-connected renewable energy power generation.

Areas with the relevant resources and development and utilization qualifications should develop small-scale hydropower, wind power and biomass power.

Urban landfill plants should install gas reclaim equipments, and eligible ones should install power generation equipments. Urban incinerating plants should install power generation equipments.

The government encourages the installation and utilization of solar power generation system on urban and rural buildings and traffic equipments.

The Government encourages the attempt and demonstration of grid-connected power generation technologies using solar, geothermal, ocean and other renewable energies.

Article 28 [Grid-connected] Grid corporations must purchase all eligible grid-connected renewable energy electricity at full price.

Grid corporations must offer convenience for renewable energy power generation projects to access grid. For the renewable energy delivering projects constructed by the permission of the government, renewable energy power generation enterprises should invest and construct the parts from substation to the first transmitting tower, and power grid enterprises invest and construct other parts.

Article 29 [Off-grid Power Generation] The government supports the development of renewable energy independent power generation systems in remote areas and areas that grid is hard to cover, to satisfy the local power demand for living or production.

The government encourages enterprises and individuals to construct renewable energy independent power generation systems in areas that grid has already covered.

Grid corporations are responsible for the operation and management of the renewable energy independent power generation systems invested and constructed by the government.

Article 30 [Fuels] The government encourages the clean and efficient development and utilization of biomass fuels.

[Gas and Heat] The government encourages the utilization of biomass energy to supply gas and heat. Enterprises supplying gas and heat should offer convenience for the gas and heat produced by renewable energy to be grid-connected. For the gas and heat that cannot be grid-connected, investors are responsible for the operation and management independently.

[Liquid Fuels] The government encourages the production and utilization of biomass liquid fuels using non-food and non-edible oil plants as sources.

For the areas that annual output or sales of biomass liquid fuels exceeds 100-thousand tons, oil-selling enterprises should construct equipments for the store and sale of biomass liquid fuels, which will offer convenience for the sale of biomass liquid fuels.

For other areas without the qualifications defined in the previous paragraph, enterprises producing biomass liquid fuels are responsible for the operation and management of their product independently.

Article 31 [Solar thermal utilization] The government encourages corporations and individuals to use solar water system.

The construction management agency of the State Council should coordinate with relevant agencies to design the technological standard and product criterion for the integration of solar water system with buildings.

The construction management agency of above-county People's government should, in accordance with urban and rural construction plan, design detailed measures to promote the utilization of solar water system.

For areas that the annual sunlight exceeds 1500 hours, project construction corporations must install solar water systems or leave space for pipelines and solar water system installation on newly built 10-storey or lower residences, hotels, restaurants, hospitals, schools as well as public buildings invested or construction-organized by government.

Real estate developers and property management enterprises must offer convenience for dwellers to install solar water systems according with national technological standard and product criterion, and must not refuse to do so for any reason.

Article 32 [Rural Energy] The government encourages the development and utilization of renewable energy in rural areas.

The People's government at different levels should, coordinating with environmental construction and sanitarian comprehensive management and according to local resources characteristics and detailed situations, support the development, diffusion and utilization of renewable energies, such as small-scale hydropower, biogas, solar energy and so on.

The government encourages the efficient and clean utilization of stalks to generate power and supply gas or heat collectively.

The government encourages collective livestock farms to construct equipments for biogas reclaim and utilization.

CHAPTER 5 PRICE MANAGEMENT

Article 33 [Grid-connected power generation] The price of grid-connected renewable-energy-source electricity is decided by the government in way of approving, bidding, or designing classified catalogue.

Government approving price is applied to the projects invested and constructed by government, and projects using bilateral or multilateral donation, as well as government concession projects. Bidding price is applied to projects that government is responsible for inviting public bidding and implementation. Classified catalogue price is applied to other renewable energy projects.

Classified catalogue price is calculated and decided by the price management agency of the State Council according to the advanced cost level of same kind of power generation projects, and is open to the public regularly.

[Price Apportionment] The cost of renewable energy power generation is apportioned among national electricity users. Grid corporations purchase the increased cost of renewable energy power generation, and make a settlement at provincial level with the Renewable Energy Development Fund.

Article 34 [Off-grid Power Generation] For the renewable-energy-source independent power generation systems managed by grid corporations in the article 29, they apply the terminal sale price in the same area.

The margin between the income of selling electricity and the fees of maintaining and managing the independent power generation system is subsidized by the Renewable Energy Fund.

Article 35 [Heat and gas supply] The renewable-energy-source heat and gas connected to urban pipeline net applies the local price of heat and gas.

Article 36 [Liquid Fuels] The purchase price of biomass liquid fuels is decided by the price management agency of the State Council. The price margin higher than same kind of common oil fuels is subsidized by the Renewable Energy Development Fund.

Article 37 [Independent Management] The renewable-energy-source electricity, heat and liquid fuels managed independently by corporations and individuals apply agreement price.

CHAPTER 6 ECONOMIC INCENTIVE

Article 38 [Fund Establishment and Sources] The government establishes the Renewable Energy Development Fund, which comprises the following:

1. The appreciated selling price of electricity and oil;
2. Central government fiscal fund;
3. Profit from the Fund;
4. Donations;
5. Others.

Article 39 [Fund Purpose] The Renewable Energy Development Fund is mainly used for:

1. Subsidy for the price margin of renewable energy electricity;
2. Subsidy for the renewable energy development and utilization in rural areas;
3. Subsidy for the investment and operation of off-grid power generation systems in remote areas;
4. Subsidy for the price margin of biomass liquid fuels;
5. Subsidy for resources reconnaissance, the construction of management system for technology and product, and technology diffusion;
6. Subsidy for technology research and development, introduction and demonstration, and pilot projects;
7. Support the localization of the production of renewable energy equipments;
8. Dissemination and education, training, international cooperation and communication.

The State Council is responsible for designing measures separately to establish and manage the Renewable Energy Development Fund.

Article 40 [Credit Measures] Policy bank should offer favorable credit to the renewable energy development and utilization projects. Commercial banks should offer credit support to the renewable energy development and utilization projects.

Article 41 [Tax Measures] The government offers favorable tax to the development and utilization renewable energy listed in the industry guidance catalogue.

[Equipment Value-added Tax] The government reduces or exempts the tax for the production and sale of renewable energy development and utilization equipments.

[Product Value-added Tax] The government reduces or exempts the tax for the production of electricity, heat or clean fuels using renewable energy.

[Other Taxes] The government offers favorable deed tax to commercial residence installed with solar water system or solar power generation system.

The tax management agency of the State Council will design the detailed favorable tax measures.

CHAPTER 7 LEGAL RESPONSIBILITIES

Article 42 The People's governments at different levels and related responsible personnel that disobey the provisions on obligations and responsibilities in this law should bear corresponding legal responsibilities.

Article 43 For grid corporations that disobey the article 28 and do not purchase eligible renewable energy electricity at full price and offer convenience for renewable energy projects to access grid, the national principal energy management agency orders them to correct before a time limit. Those that refuse to correct are fined between 500 thousand to 1 million Yuan.

If grid corporations disobeying the regulations make renewable energy power generation enterprises suffer economic loss, they are responsible for the compensation.

Article 44 For grid corporations that disobey the article 29 and do not offer related service to the independent power stations managed by them, the national principal energy management agency orders them to correct before a time limit. Those that refuse to correct are fined between 500 thousand to 1 million Yuan.

Article 45 For selling oil enterprises that disobey the 4th paragraph of article 30 and do not construct equipments for the store and sale of biomass liquid fuels, the national principal energy management agency orders them to correct before a time limit. Those that refuse to correct are fined between 500 thousand to 1 million Yuan.

Article 46 For projects construction enterprises that disobey the 4th paragraph of article 31 and do not install solar water heating system or leave space for pipeline installation are fined lower than 100 thousand Yuan by above-county local People's government.

Article 47 For real estate developers and property management enterprises that disobey the 5th paragraph of article 31 and hinder dwellers to install solar water heating and power generation systems, the principal energy management agency of above-county local People's government orders them to correct before a time limit. Those that refuse to correct are fined lower than 100 thousand Yuan.

CHAPTER 8 EXPLANATORY NOTE

Article 48 This Law will come into force since Year Month Day.

Japan

Law Concerning the Rational Use of Energy

22 June 1979, Law No.49
Revised in 10 December 1983
Revised in 31 March 1993
Revised in 12 November 1993
Revised in 9 April 1997
Revised in 5 June 1998

CHAPTER I. GENERAL PROVISIONS

Article 1

(Purpose)

This law was enacted for the purpose of contributing to the sound development of the national economy by setting up necessary measures for the rational use of energy by factories, buildings, machinery and equipment, and other necessary measures, etc. for promoting comprehensively the rational use of energy in order to ensure the effective use of fuel resources which will meet the economic and social environment of energy at home and abroad.

Article 2

(Definitions)

"Energy" in this law means fuel, heat produced by such fuel and electricity (excluding the electricity which is used in place of the electricity obtained by converting the power obtained by converting the heat produced by such fuel and is determined by a government ordinance; hereinafter that same).

2. "Fuel" in this law means those products usable for combustion such as crude oil, gasoline, heavy oil or other petroleum products as designated by the Ordinance of the Ministry of International Trade and Industry (hereinafter referred to as "MITI Ordinance"), or inflammable natural gas, coal, coke or other coal products as designated by the MITI Ordinance.

CHAPTER I-2. FUNDAMENTAL POLICIES, ETC.

Article 3

(Fundamental Polices)

The Minister of International Trade and Industry (hereinafter referred to as "Minister") shall determine and make public fundamental policies concerning the rational use of energy (hereinafter referred to as "Fundamental Policies") for the purpose of promoting comprehensively the rational use of energy at a factory or other place of business (hereinafter referred to simply as "Factory"), buildings, machinery and equipment.

2. The Fundamental Policies shall, in order to rationalize the use of energy, define fundamental matters concerning the measures to be taken by energy users, fundamental matters concerning the policies for promoting the rational use of energy and other matters concerning the rational use of energy in consideration of a long-term outlook of energy supply and demand, technical levels for the rational use of energy or other circumstances.

3. The Minister's Fundamental Policies shall be approved by a cabinet meeting

4. Before the Minister determines Fundamental Policies, the Minister shall have a consultation with the Minister of Construction as to the part of the Fundamental Policies regarding the construction, maintenance and security of buildings, and with the Minister of Transport as to the part regarding the performance of motor vehicles in relation to energy consumption.

5. The Minister shall, when necessary in accordance with changes in the circumstances described in Paragraph 2, revise the Fundamental Policies.

6. The provisions of Paragraph 1 through Paragraph 4 apply to the amendment of the Fundamental Policies according to the provisions of the preceding paragraph.

Article 3-2

(Effort on the Part of Energy Users)

Energy users shall make efforts to rationalize their energy use in compliance with the Fundamental Policies.

CHAPTER II. MEASURES FOR FACTORIES, ETC.

SECTION 1. MEASURES FOR FACTORIES

Article 4

(Matters to Be Used as Standards for Judgment by Enterprise)

The Minister shall determine and make public the matters given below and the matters to be used as the standards for judgment, regarding the objective of rational use of energy and the measures to be taken systematically to achieve such objective, by the enterprise which uses energy at the Factory (hereinafter referred to as "Enterprise") in order to promote the rational use of energy at the Factory properly and effectively.

1. Rationalization of fuel combustion.
2. Rationalization of heating, cooling and heat transfer.
3. Prevention of heat loss by radiation, conduction, etc.
4. Recovery of waste heat.
5. Rationalization of heat conversion into power, etc.
6. Prevention of electricity loss by resistance, etc.
7. Rationalization of conversion of electricity into power, heat, etc.

2. The matters to be used as the standards for judgment as provided in the preceding paragraph shall reflect the consideration of a long-term outlook of energy supply and demand, technical level for the rational use of energy or other circumstances, and shall be revised when necessary in accordance with charges in these circumstances.

Article 5

(Guidance and Advice)

The competent minister may, in the event that it is deemed necessary in order to ensure the rational use of energy at a Factory, provide an Enterprise with guidance and advice for the implementation of the matters to be used as the standards for judgment enumerated in each item of Paragraph 1 of the preceding article, in consideration of such matters as provided in such paragraph.

Article 6

(Designation of Type 1 Designated Energy Management Factory)

The Minister may designate those Factories which are used for the operation of the manufacturing industry or other industry determined by a government ordinance and whose consumption of fuel and heat produced by such fuel (hereinafter referred to as "Fuel, etc.") per year (which means the period from April 1 to March 31 the following year; hereinafter the same) is the amount determined by a government ordinance or more as those especially needing the promotion of rational use of Fuel, etc., and those Factories which are used for such operation and whose consumption of electricity per year is the amount determined by a government ordinance or more as those especially needing the promotion of rational use of electricity, respectively.

2. The enterprise which establishes a Factory used for an operation belonging to the industry determined by a government ordinance as provided in the preceding paragraph shall, in the event that the consumption of Fuel, etc. or electricity at such Factory in the preceding year is the amount determined by a government ordinance or more report to the Minister the matters determined by an MITI Ordinance concerning the condition of use of Fuel, etc. or electricity at such Factory in accordance with the provisions of an MITI Ordinance. However, the above is not applicable to the Factories designated as those especially needing the promotion of rational use of Fuel, etc. in accordance with the provisions

of such paragraph (hereinafter referred to as "Type 1 Designated Heat Management Factory") or the Factories designated as those especially needing the promotion of rational use of electricity in accordance with such provisions (hereinafter referred to as "Type 1 Designated Electricity Management Factory").

3. The enterprise (hereinafter referred to as "Type 1 Designated Enterprise") which establishes a Type 1 Designated Heat Management Factory or Type 1 Designated Electricity Management Factory (hereinafter referred to collectively as "Type 1 Designated Energy Management Factory") may file an application with the Minister for the cancellation of the designation pursuant to the provisions of Paragraph 1 in accordance with the provisions of an MITI Ordinance, in the event that any one of the following situations arises with respect to such Factory:

1. Such Factory ceases the operation belonging to the industry determined by a government ordinance as provided in Paragraph 1.
2. Such Factory loses the possibility of reaching or exceeding the amount of the consumption per year of Fuel, etc. or electricity determined by a government ordinance as provided in Paragraph 1.

4. If an application is filed as provided in the preceding paragraph and the Minister finds that such application has a sufficient reason, the Minister shall cancel, without delay, the designation made in accordance with the provisions of Paragraph 1. The above also applies to a case where the Minister finds that any one of the situations described in such paragraph arises with respect to such Factory even if no such application is filed.

5. If the Minister makes a designation in accordance with the provisions of Paragraph 1 or cancels such a designation in accordance with the provisions of the preceding paragraph, the Minister shall notify such designation or cancellation to the minister or ministers responsible for the operation undertaken at the Factory concerned.

Article 7

(Energy Manager)

The Type 1 Designated Enterprise shall, in accordance with the stipulations of an MITI Ordinance, appoint an energy manager for each Type 1 Designated Energy Management Factory from among those who have received an energy manager license, pursuant to the standards determined by a government ordinance.

2. When the Type 1 Designated Enterprise appoints an energy manager, it shall report such appointment to the Minister within thirty days of the date of such appointment in accordance with the stipulations of an MITI Ordinance. This applies to a case where the energy manager dies or is dismissed.

Article 8

(Licensing of Energy Manager)

There shall be two types of license for energy manager, heat manager and electricity manager licenses, which will be issued by the Minister to the individuals coming under one of the following items:

1. Those passing the examination for energy manager;
2. Those recognized by the Minister as having the knowledge and experience equal to or exceeding those of the individuals described in the preceding item.

2. The procedures for granting an energy manager license shall be determined by an MITI Ordinance.

Article 8-2

(Examination for Energy Manager)

The examination for energy managers shall be carried out by the Minister for both types of licenses.

2. The Minister may designate an organization (hereinafter referred to as the "Designated Examination Body") to carry out the affairs concerning the examination for energy manager (hereinafter referred to as "Examination Affairs").

3. The subjects of the examination for energy managers, procedures for taking such examination and any other details related to such examination shall be determined by an MITI Ordinance.

Article 9

(Duties of Energy Manager)

The energy manager shall, at a Type 1 Designated Heat Management Factory, be responsible for maintaining the facilities for the consumption of Fuel, etc., improving and supervising the method of using Fuel, etc. and conducting all other work as provided by an MITI Ordinance for the rational use of Fuel, etc., or shall, at a Type 1 Designated Electricity Management Factory, be responsible for maintaining the facilities for the consumption of electricity, improving and supervising the method of using electricity and conducting all other work as provided by an MITI Ordinance for the rational use of electricity.

Article 10

(Obligations of Energy Manager, etc.)

The energy manager shall faithfully carry out their duties.

2. The Type 1 Designated Enterprise shall respect the opinions of the energy manager about the performance of his or her duties concerning the rational use of energy.

3. The employee in the Type 1 Designated Energy Management Factory shall follow any instruction given by the energy manager as necessary one in the performance of such duties.

Article 10-2

(Formulation of Medium-to-Long Term Plan)

The Type 1 Designated Enterprise shall every year, in accordance with the stipulations of an MITI Ordinance, formulate a medium-to-long term plan for achieving the objective of rational use of energy determined in the matters to be used as the standards for judgment as provided in Paragraph 1 of Article 4 regarding Type 1 Designated Energy Management Factory, and shall submit such a plan to the competent minister.

2. The competent minister may set a necessary guideline to serve for the proper formulation of such plan as provided in the preceding paragraph by the Type 1 Designated Enterprise.

3. The competent minister shall, if the competent minister sets guideline as provided in the preceding paragraph, make such guideline public.

Article 11

(Periodical Report)

The Type 1 Designated Enterprise shall, every year in accordance with the stipulations of an MITI Ordinance, report to the Minister the matters determined by an MITI Ordinance concerning the consumption of Fuel, etc. and other conditions of consumption of Fuel, etc. (including the matters relating to the efficiency of use of Fuel, etc.) and conditions with respect to the installation, modification and abolition of the facilities for the consumption of Fuel, etc. and facilities for the rational use of Fuels, etc. at the Type 1 Designated Heat Management Factory, and concerning the consumption of electricity and other conditions of consumption of electricity (including the matters relating to the efficiency of use of electricity) and conditions with respect to the installation, modification and abolition of the facilities for the consumption of electricity, and facilities for the rational use of electricity at the Type 1 Designated Electricity Management Factory.

Article 12

(Instructions and Orders concerning Rationalization Plan)

The competent minister may, if the minister finds the rational use of energy at the Type 1 Designated Energy Management Factory to be greatly insufficient in consideration of the matters to be used as the standards for judgment as provided in Paragraph 1 of Article 4, give the Type 1 Designated Enterprise which operates such Type 1 Designated Energy Management Factory an instruction to prepare and submit a plan of rational use of energy (hereinafter referred to as "Rationalization Plan") by indicating the basis for such finding.

2. The competent minister may, if the minister finds the submitted Rationalization Plan to be inadequate for realizing the satisfactorily rational use of energy at the Type 1 Designated Energy Management Factory concerned, instruct the Type 1 Designated Enterprise to revise such Rationalization Plan.

3. The competent ministry may, if the minister finds that the Type 1 Designated Enterprise has not implemented the Rationalization Plan, instruct such Type 1 Designated Enterprise to implement such Rationalization Plan properly.

4. The competent minister may, if the Type 1 Designated Enterprise has failed to follow the instruction as provided in the preceding three paragraphs, make public the fact of such failure.

5. The competent minister may, if the Type 1 Designated Enterprise has failed to take the measures included in the instruction as provided in

Paragraphs 1 to 3 with no good reason, order such Type 1 Designated Enterprise to take such measures after consulting with the council determined by a government ordinance.

Article 12-2

(Designation of Type 2 Designated Energy Management Factory)

The Minister may designate those Factories other than the Type 1 Designated Heat Management Factory whose consumption of Fuel, etc. per year is the amount determined by a government ordinance or more as those especially needing the promotion of rational use of Fuel, etc. in a manner similar to the case of the Type 1 Designated Heat Management Factory, and those Factories other than the Type 1 Designated Electricity Management Factory whose consumption of electricity per year is the amount determined by a government ordinance or more as those especially needing the promotion of rational use of electricity in a manner similar to the case of the Type 1 Designated Electricity Management Factory, respectively.

2. The enterprise which establishes a Factory shall, in the event that the consumption of Fuel, etc. or electricity at such Factory in the preceding year is the amount determined by a government ordinance as provided in the preceding paragraph or more, report to the Minister the matters determined by an MITI Ordinance concerning the condition of use of Fuel, etc. or electricity at such Factory in accordance with the provisions of an MITI Ordinance. However, the above is not applicable to the Type 1 Designated Energy Management Factory, the Factories which shall report concerning the condition of use of Fuel, etc. or electricity in accordance with the provisions of Paragraph 2 of Article 6, the Factories designated as those especially needing the promotion of rational use of Fuel, etc. in a manner similar to the case of the Type 1 Designated Heat Management Factory in accordance with the provisions of the preceding paragraph (hereinafter referred to as "Type 2 Designated Heat Management Factory") and the Factories designated as those especially needing the promotion of rational use of electricity in a manner similar to the case of the Type 1 Designated Electricity Management Factory in accordance with such provisions (hereinafter referred to as "Type 2 Designated Electricity Management Factory").

3. The enterprise (hereinafter referred to as "Type 2 Designated Enterprise") which establishes a Type 2 Designated Heat Management Factory or Type 2 Designated Electricity Management Factory (hereinafter referred to collectively as "Type 2 Designated Energy Management Factory") may file an application with the Minister for the cancellation of the designation pursuant to the provisions of Paragraph 1 in accordance with the provisions of an MITI Ordinance, in the event that any one of the following situations arises with respect to such Factory:

1. Such factory ceases its operation.
2. Such factory loses the possibility of reaching or exceeding the amount of the consumption per year of Fuel, etc. or electricity determined by a government ordinance as provided in Paragraph 1.

4. If an application is filed as provided in the preceding paragraph and the Minister finds that such application has a sufficient reason, the Minister shall cancel, without delay, the designation made in accordance with the provisions of Paragraph 1. The above also applies to a case where the Minister finds that any one of the situations described in such paragraph arises with respect to such Factory even if no such application is filed.

5. The Minister shall, in the event that the consumption per year of Fuel, etc. at a Type 2 Designated Heat Management Factory reaches or exceeds the amount determined by a government ordinance as provided in Article 6, Paragraph 1 or in the event that the consumption per year of electricity reaches or exceeds the amount determined by a government ordinance as provided in such paragraph and if the Minister designates such Factory as those especially needing the promotion of rational use of Fuel, etc. or those especially needing the promotion of rational use of electricity, respectively, in accordance with the provisions of such paragraph, cancel the designation of such Factory in accordance with Paragraph 1.

6. The Ministry shall, if the Minister makes a designation in accordance with the provisions of Paragraph 1 or cancels such designation in accordance with the provisions of the preceding two paragraphs, notify the minister in charge of the undertaking of such Factory of such designation or cancellation.

Article 12-3

(Energy Management Officer)

The Type 2 Designated Enterprise shall, in accordance with the stipulations of an MITI Ordinance, appoint an energy management officer for each Type 2 Designated Energy Management Factory from among the persons given below:

1. Those who have completed the training course concerning the necessary knowledge and skill regarding rational use of energy which is offered by the Minister or the person designated by the Minister (hereinafter referred to as "Designated Training Course Body") in accordance with the stipulations of an MITI Ordinance.
2. Those who hold a license of energy manager.

2. The Type 2 Designated Enterprise shall, for each period determined by an MITI Ordinance, cause the person who meets the condition of Item 1 of the preceding paragraph and is appointed an energy management officer to take the training course for improving the ability of energy management officers which is offered by the Minister or a Designated Training Course Body in accordance with the stipulations of an MITI Ordinance.

3. The Type 2 Designated Enterprise shall report to the Minister the appointment, death or dismissal of an energy management officer in accordance with the stipulations of an MITI Ordinance.

4. The provisions of Article 9 and Paragraph 1 of Article 10 shall also apply to energy management officers, the provisions of Paragraph 2 of such article, to Type 2 Designated Enterprises and the provisions of Paragraph 3 of such article, to the employees of Type 2 Designated Energy Management Factories. In such a case, "energy manager" in Paragraphs 2 and 3 of Article 10 shall read "energy management officer."

Article 12-4

(Recording)

The Type 2 Designated Enterprise shall provide its Type 2 Designated Energy Management Factory with books, and, in accordance with the stipulations of an MITI Ordinance, shall record the consumption of Fuel, etc. and other conditions of use of Fuel, etc. and the situation of the installment, replacement and scrapping of the equipment consuming Fuel, etc. and the equipment for rational use of Fuel, etc. at its Type 2 Designated Heat Management Factory and the consumption of electricity and other conditions of use of electricity and the situation of the installment, replacement and scrapping of the equipment consuming electricity and the equipment for rational use of electricity at its Type 2 Designated Electricity Management Factory.

Article 12-5

(Recommendation)

The competent minister shall, if the minister finds the rational use of energy at the Type 2 Designated Energy Management Factory to be greatly insufficient in consideration of the matters to be used as the standards for judgment as provided in Paragraph 1 of Article 4, give the Designated Enterprise which operates such Type 2 Designated Energy Management Factory a recommendation that necessary measures be taken for the rational use of energy by indicating the basis for such finding.

SECTION 2. DESIGNATED EXAMINATION BODY

Article 12-6

(Designation)

The designation described in Paragraph 2 of Article 8-2 shall be made by the application of a person or organization desiring to handle Examination Affairs, in accordance with the stipulations of an MITI Ordinance.

2. The Minister shall not be directly involved in Examination Affairs after the Minister has made a designation under the provisions the provisions of Paragraph 2 of Article 8-2.

Article 12-7

(Disqualification Clause)

Any person or organization coming under one of the following items shall not be eligible for any designation described in Paragraph 2 of Article 8-2:

1. The person or organization who has had his or her or its designation canceled in accordance with the provisions of Paragraph 2 of Article 12-17 within the last two (2) years.

2. The organization which has any officer conducting its affairs who comes under one of the following items:

A. Any person who was punished for violating this law or for ignoring the measures taken in accordance with this law and is within two (2) years from the completion of the execution of such punishment or the date when such person was excused from such punishment.

B. Any person who was dismissed in accordance with the provisions of Article 12-13 within the last two (2) years.

Article 12-8

(Standard for Designation)

The Minister shall not make a designation if another person or organization has already been designated in accordance with the provisions of Paragraph 2 of Article 8-2, and unless the Minister finds that the application for designation under such paragraph conforms to each of the following items:

1. The plan for conducting Examination Affairs, including the matters of staffing, facilities, method of implementation of Examination Affairs and other matters, shall be adequate to conduct Examination Affairs properly;

2. The accounting system and technical level shall be sufficient to implement properly the plan for conducting Examination Affairs described in the preceding item;

3. The applicant shall be a juridical person incorporated in accordance with the provisions of Article 34 of the Civil Code (Low No. 89, 1896);

4. If the applicant is to be engaged in any other affair than Examination Affairs, too, such other affair shall not make Examination Affairs unfair.

Article 12-9

(Examination Affairs Regulations)

The Designated Examination Body shall prescribe regulations for implementing Examination Affairs (hereinafter referred to as "Examination Affairs Regulations") and shall have such Examination Affairs Regulations approved by the Minister. The approval of the Minister shall also be obtained for any revision of such Examination Affairs Regulations.

2. The matters to be prescribed in the Examination Affairs Regulations shall be defined by an MITI Ordinance.

3. The Minister may, if the Minister finds that the Examination Affairs Regulations as approved in accordance with the provisions of Paragraph 1 have become inadequate for the fair implementation of Examination Affairs, order the Designated Examination Body concerned to revise such Examination Affairs Regulations.

Article 12-10

(Suspension or Discontinuance of Examination Affairs)

The Designated Examination Body shall not suspend or discontinue all or part of Examination Affairs without the permission of the Minister.

Article 12-11

(Business Plan, etc.)

The designated Examination Body shall prepare a business plan and budget for each business year prior to the start of that year (without delay after designation in the business year to which the date of designation obtained in accordance with the provisions of Paragraph 2 of Article 8-2 belongs) and obtain the approval of the Minister to such business plan and budget. The approval of the Minister shall also be obtained for any revision of such business plan and budget.

2. The Designated Examination Body shall prepare and submit to the Minister a business report and settlement of accounts for each business year within three (3) months of the end of that business year.

Article 12-12

(Election and Dismissal of Officers)

The election or dismissal of officers of the Designated Examination Body shall not be effective without the approval of the Minister.

Article 12-13

(Order for Dismissal of Officers)

The Minister may, if the officer of the Designated Examination Body has violated this law (including measures taken in accordance with this law) or the Examination Affairs Regulations, or has conducted any seriously inappropriate act with respect to Examination Affairs, order the Designated Examination Body concerned to dismiss such officer.

Article 12-14

(Examination Commissioner for Energy Managers)

The Designated Examination Body shall have an examination commissioner for energy managers (hereinafter referred to as "Examination Commissioner") conduct Examination Affairs if such Examination Affairs are concerned with a judgment as to whether or not the applicant has enough knowledge and ability as an energy manager.

2. The Designated Examination Body shall elect the Examination Commissioner from among those with the qualifications stipulated by an MITI Ordinance.

3. When it has elected its Examination Commissioner, the Designated Examination Body shall report such election to the Minister in accordance with the stipulations of an MITI Ordinance. It shall also report to the Minister when any change occurs in the status of the Examination Commissioner.

4. The provisions of the preceding article shall also apply to the Examination Commissioner.

Article 12-15

(Secrecy Obligation, etc.)

Any officer or staff (including the Examination Commissioner; the same in the next paragraph) of the Designated Examination Body or any other person who was such officer or staff shall not disclose any secret information known to him or her with regard to Examination Affairs.

2. Any officer or staff of the Designated Examination Body engaged in Examination Affairs shall be regarded as staff engaged in public services by laws and regulations as to the application of penal regulations of the Penal Code (Law No. 45, 1907) or other laws.

Article 12-16

(Order for Conformity, etc.)

The Minister may, if the Minister finds that the Designated Examination Body no longer conforms to any one of the items of Article 12-8 (except Item 3; hereinafter the same in this paragraph), order such Designated Examination Body to take measures to make it conform to such item.

2. In addition to the provisions of the preceding paragraph, the Minister may, if the Minister finds it necessary in order to enforce this law, issue to the Designated Examination Body orders necessary for supervision with regard to Examination Affairs.

Article 12-17

(Cancellation of Designation, etc.)

The Minister shall cancel the designation made in accordance with Paragraph 2 of Article 8-2 if the Designated Examination Body no longer conforms to Item 3 of Article 12-8.

2. The Minister may, if the Designated Examination Body comes under any one of the following items, cancel the designation made in accordance with Paragraph 2 of Article 8-2 or order such Designated Examination Body to suspend all or part of Examination Affairs for a certain period of time:

If the Designated Examination Body violates the pro visions of this section;

If the Designated Examination Body comes under Item 2 of Article 12-7;

If the Designated Examination Body conducts Examination Affairs not pursuant to the Examination Affairs Regulations approved by the Minister under Paragraph 1 of Article 12-9;

If the Designated Examination Body fails to follow the order as provided in Paragraph 3 of Article 12-9 or in Article 12-13 (including the case where the provisions of Article 12-13 are applied under Item 4 of Article 12-14) or as provided in the preceding Article;

If the Designated Examination Body obtained by improper means the designation as described in Paragraph 2 of Article 8-2.

Article 12-18

(Preparation of Book)

The Designated Examination Body shall prepare a book and record in such book the matters concerning Examination Affairs as provided in an MITI Ordinance.

2. The book referred to in the preceding paragraph shall be kept in accordance with the stipulations of an MITI Ordinance.

Article 12-19

(Examination Affairs Conducted by the Minister, etc.)

The Minister shall conduct all or part of Examination Affairs in person when the Designated Examination Body suspends all or part of Examination Affairs with the permission granted in accordance with the provisions of Article 12-10, or when the Minister orders the Designated Examination Body to suspend all or part of Examination Affairs in accordance with the provisions of Paragraph 2 of Article 12-17, or when the Minister finds it necessary in the event that it becomes necessary for the Designated Examination Body to conduct all or part of Examination Affairs due to an act of God or any other reason.

2. The MITI Ordinance shall determine the procedures for transferring Examination Affairs or any other necessary matters in the case where the Minister conducts all or part of Examination Affairs in person in accordance with the provisions of the preceding paragraph, or where the Designated Examination Body discontinues all or part of Examination Affairs with the permission as provided in Article 12-10, or where the Minister cancels the designation of the Designated Examination Body in accordance with the provisions of Article 12-17.

Article 12-20

(Public Notice)

The Minister shall make public notice through the official gazette the fact concerning the following cases:

1. When the Minister grants a designation in accordance with Paragraph 2 of Article 8-2;

2. When the Minister grants a permission described in Article 12-10;

3. When the Minister cancels the designation in accordance with the provisions of Article 12-17, or when the Minister orders the suspension of all or part of Examination Affairs in accordance with the provisions of Paragraph 2 of the same Article;

4. When the Minister conducts all or part of Examination Affairs in person in accordance with the provisions of Paragraph 1 of the preceding article, or when the Minister decides to conduct no longer all or part of Examination Affairs that the Minister has been conducting.

SECTION 3. DESIGNATED TRAINING COURSE BODY

Article 12-21

(Designation)

The designation described in Item 1 of Paragraph 1 of Article 12-3 shall be made by the application of a person or organization desiring to handle the training course provided in such item and Paragraph 2 of such Article (hereinafter in this section and in Article 27-3 referred to as the "Training Course"), in accordance with the stipulations of an MITI Ordinance.

2. The provisions of Article 12-7 (except b of Item 2), Article 12-8 and Article 12-17 shall also apply to the designation provided in Item 1 of Paragraph 1 of Article 12-3, and the provisions of Article 12-9, Article 12-11, Paragraph 2 of Article 12-15, Article 12-16 and Article 12-18 shall also apply to a Designated Training Course Body.

In this case, "if another person or organization has not been designated in accordance with the provisions of Paragraph 2 of Article 8-2, and unless the Minister finds that the application for designation under such paragraph conforms to each of the below-mentioned provisions, the designation shall not be made" in Article 12-8 shall read "if another person or organization has not been designated in accordance with the provisions of Paragraph 2 of Article 8-2, and unless the Minister finds that the application for designation under Item 1 of Paragraph 1 of Article 12-3 conforms to each of the below-mentioned provisions, the designation shall not be made," "Examination Affairs" in Items 1, 2 and 4 of Article 12-8, Paragraphs 1 and 3 of Article 12-9, Paragraph 2 of Article 12-15, Paragraph 2 of Article 12-16, Paragraph 2 of Article 12-17 and Paragraph 1 of Article 12-18 shall read "Training Course Affairs," "Examination Affairs Regulations" in Article 12-9 and Item 3 of Paragraph 2 of Article 12-17 shall read "Training Course Regulations," "Paragraph 2 of Article 8-2" in Paragraph 1 of Article 12-11 shall read "Item 1 of Paragraph 1 of Article 12-3," and "Article 12-13 (including the case where the provisions of Article 12-13 are applied under Paragraph 4 of Article 12-14) or the under the provision of the preceding Article is violated" in Item 4 of Paragraph 2 of Article 12-17 shall read "or."

Article 12-22

(Suspension or Discontinuance of Training Course Affairs)

The Designated Training Course Body shall, if it suspends or discontinues all or part of its Training Course Affairs, report to the Minister such suspension or discontinuance within the period determined by an MITI Ordinance.

Article 12-23

(Public Notice)

The Minister shall make public notice through the official gazette the fact concerning the following cases:

1. When the Minister grants a designation in accordance with Item 1 of Paragraph 1 of Article 12-3;

2. When the Minister cancels a designation in accordance with the provisions of Article 12-17 applied as provided in Paragraph 2 of Article 12-21, or orders the suspension of all or part of the Training Course Affairs in accordance with the provisions of Paragraph 2 of such Article applied as provided in such paragraph;

3. When the Minister receives a report in accordance with the provisions of the preceding Article.

CHAPTER III. MEASURES FOR BUILDINGS

Article 13

(Efforts by Owner)

Any person who plans to construct a building (hereinafter referred to as "Owner") shall endeavor to contribute to the rational use of energy relating to such building by taking the following measures properly, paying attention to the stipulations of the Fundamental Policies:

1. Measures to prevent the loss of heat through the outer walls, windows, etc. of such building;

2. Measures to ensure an efficient use of energy relating to air conditioning equipment installed in such building and such other building equipment as provided by a government ordinance (hereinafter referred to as "Air Conditioning Equipment, etc.").

Article 14

(Matters to Be Used as Standards for Judgment by Owner)

The Minister and the Minister of Construction shall determine and make public matters to be used as standards for judgment by the Owner concerning the measures described in each item of the preceding Article in order to implement properly and effectively the rational use of energy relating to buildings.

2. The provisions of Paragraph 2 of Article 4 shall also apply to the matters to be used as standards for judgment as provided in the preceding paragraph.

Article 15

(Guidance and Advice for Buildings, etc.)

The Minister of Construction may, if the Minister of Construction finds it necessary to ensure the proper implementation of the measures as described in each item of Article 13 with regard to buildings (excluding houses; hereinafter the same in this paragraph and Paragraph 1 of the following Article), give guidance and advice to the Owner on matters relevant to the design and construction of such buildings in consideration of the matters to be used as standards for judgment as provided in Paragraph 1 of the preceding Article.

2. The Minister of Construction shall, if the Minister of Construction finds it necessary to ensure the proper implementation of the measures as described in each item of Article 13 with regard to houses, determine and make public guidelines for the design and construction of houses to prevent the loss of heat through the outer walls, windows, etc. of houses and to achieve the efficient use of energy relating to Air Conditioning Equipment, etc. installed in houses, in conformity with the matters to be used as standards for judgment as provided in Paragraph 1 of the preceding Article.

Article 15-2

(Instructions for Designated Building)

The Minister of Construction may, if the Minister of Construction finds that the measures to prevent the loss of heat through the outer walls, windows, etc. of such a building as comes under the requirements of the scale as provided by a government ordinance (hereinafter referred to as "Designated Building") and the measures to achieve the efficient use of energy relating to Air Conditioning Equipment, etc. installed in a Designated Building are seriously insufficient in light of the matters to be used as standards for judgment as provided in Paragraph 1 of Article 14, give the person who plans to construct a Designated Building (hereinafter referred to as "Designated Owner") instructions concerning that portion of the matters relating to the design and construction of such Designated Building which is concerned about the measures to prevent the loss of heat through the outer walls, windows, etc. of such Designated Building and the measures to achieve the efficient use of energy relating to Air Conditioning Equipment, etc. installed in such Designated Building, by indicating the basis for such finding.

2. The Minister of Construction may, if the Designated Owner has failed to follow the instructions given as provided in the preceding paragraph without any good reason, make public the fact of such failure.

Article 16

(Guidance and Advice Regarding Building Materials)

The Minister may, if the Minister finds it especially necessary to ensure that buildings conform to the matters to be used as standards for judgment as provided in Paragraph 1 of Article 14 or to the guidelines as provided in Paragraph 2 of Article 15, give to the person or organization manufacturing building materials to be used in preventing the loss of heat through the outer walls, windows, etc. of buildings guidance and advice necessary for improving and indicating the quality of such building materials regarding heat insulation properties, in consideration of such matters to be used as standards for judgment or such guidelines.

CHAPTER IV. MEASURES FOR MACHINERY AND EQUIPMENT

Article 17

(Efforts by Manufacturer)

Any person who undertakes the manufacture or import of machinery or equipment that consumes energy (hereinafter referred to as "Manufacturer, etc.") shall endeavor to contribute to the rational use of energy relating to the machinery or equipment manufactured or imported by improving the performance of such machinery or equipment relative to the energy consumption by such machinery or equipment, paying attention to the Fundamental Policies.

Article 18

(Matters to Be Used as Standards for Judgment by Manufacturer, etc.)

For some machinery or equipment consuming energy, such as motor vehicles (limited, in this paragraph, to those motor vehicles stipulated by a government ordinance as especially requiring the improvement of performance as provided in the preceding Article) or other machinery or equipment used in large quantities in Japan and consuming a considerable amount of energy in their operation which are stipulated by a government ordinance as especially requiring the improvement of performance (hereinafter referred to as "Designated Machinery"), the Minister (the Minister and the Minister of Transport in the case of motor vehicles; hereinafter the same in this chapter and Paragraph 5 of Article 25) shall determine and make public the matters to be used as standards for judgment by Manufacturers, etc. with regard to the improvement of such performance for each Designated Machinery.

2. The matters to be used as standards for judgment as provided in the preceding paragraph shall be determined in consideration of the performance of such Designated Machinery whose performance as provided in the preceding Article is the best, future prospects for the technical development of such Designated Machinery and other circumstances, and shall be amended as needed according to changes in these circumstances.

Article 19

(Recommendation and Order for Improvement of Performance)

The Minister may, if the Minister finds it necessary to improve to a considerable extent the performance of the Designated Machinery manufactured or imported by a Manufacturer, etc. whose production or import of Designated Machinery comes under the requirements determined by a government ordinance in accordance with the provisions of Article 17, in light of the matters to be used as standards for judgment as provided in Paragraph 1 of the preceding Article, make recommendations to such Manufacturer, etc. on the improvement of such performance of such Designated Machinery manufactured or imported by such Manufacturer, etc.

2. The Minister may, if the Manufacturer, etc. fails to follow the recommendations made as provided in the preceding paragraph, make such failure public.

3. The Minister may, in the event that the Manufacturer, etc. who has received the recommendations as provided in Paragraph 1 fails to take measures relating to such recommendations without good reason, if the Minister finds that such failure will cause great damage to the rational use of energy by such Designated Machinery, order such Manufacturer, etc. to take measures relating to such recommendations after consulting a council determined by a government ordinance.

Article 20

(Product Labeling)

The Minister shall determine and make notification of the matters enumerated below for each Designated Machinery as to the Designated Machinery (excluding household Articles as provided in Item 1 of Paragraph 1 of Article 2 of the Household Articles Quality Labeling Law (Law No. 104, 1962); hereinafter the same in this Article and in the following Article):

1. Matters to be labeled by the Manufacturer, etc. with respect to the energy consumption efficiency of the Designated Machinery (the value calculated in accordance with the provisions of an MITI Ordinance (in the case of motor vehicles, an MITI Ordinance and an ordinance of the Ministry of Transport) as the performance of the Designated Machinery in relation to energy consumption; hereinafter the same);

2. Matters to be observed by the Manufacturer, etc., such as the method of product labeling or other aspects regarding the labeling of energy consumption efficiency.

Article 21

(Recommendation and Orders regarding Product Labeling)

The Minister may, if the Minister finds that the Manufacturer, etc. has failed to label the energy consumption efficiency of Designated Machinery in accordance with the notification made as provided in the preceding Article, recommend that such Manufacturer, etc. should label the energy consumption efficiency of the Designated Machinery manufactured or imported by such Manufacturer, etc. in accordance with such notification.

2. The Minister may, if the Manufacturer, etc. has failed to follow the recommendation made as provided in the preceding paragraph, make public the fact of such failure.

3. The Minister may, if the Minister finds that the failure of the Manufacturer, etc. to take measures in compliance with the recommendation made as provided in Paragraph 1 will be seriously harmful

to the rational use of energy relating to the Designated Machinery concerned, order such Manufacturer, etc. to take measures in compliance with such recommendation after listening to the opinions of a council determined by a government ordinance.

CHAPTER IV-2. AFFAIRS FOR RATIONAL USE OF ENERGY OF THE NEW ENERGY AND INDUSTRIAL DEVELOPMENT ORGANIZATION

Article 21-2

(Affairs for Rational Use of Energy)

The New Energy and industrial Development Organization (hereinafter referred to as "Organization") shall conduct, in addition to conducting the affairs as provided in Paragraph 1 and 2 of Article 39 of the Law concerning the Promotion of Development and Introduction of Alternative Energies (Law No. 71, 1980; hereinafter referred to as "Alternative Energies Law"), the following affairs in order to promote the rational use of energy:

1. To develop the technology for the rational use of energy whose industrial use is especially needed from the standpoint of the national economy;
2. To provide subsidies as the funds needed in the introduction of the technology for the rational use of energy whose diffusion is especially necessary;
3. To provide guidance on the collection and distribution of information regarding the rational use of energy and on the technology for the rational use of energy;
4. To conduct all affairs pertinent to the affairs enumerated in each of the preceding items.

Article 21-3

(Special Rules regarding the Alternative Energies Law)

When the Organization conducts its affairs in accordance with the provisions of the preceding Article, "Items 1 and 9 of Paragraph 1 of the preceding Article" in Paragraph 1 of Article 40 of the Alternative Energies Law shall read "Items 1 and 9 of Paragraph 1 of the preceding Article and Item 1 of Article 21-2 of the Law concerning the Rational Use of Energy (hereinafter referred to as "Rational Use Law")", "Paragraph 1 of Article 39" in Paragraph 1 of Article 41 of the Alternative Energies Law shall read "Paragraph 1 of Article 39 and Article 212 of the Rational Use Law", "this law" in Paragraph 2 of Article 53 and Paragraph 1 of Article 54 of the Alternative Energies Law shall read "this law or the Rational Use Law", and "Paragraph 1 of Article 39" in Item 3 of Article 59 of the Alternative Energies Law shall read "Paragraph 1 of Article 39 and Article 21-2 of the Rational Use Law".

CHAPTER V. MISCELLANEOUS PROVISIONS

Article 22

(Budgetary Measures, etc.)

The state shall endeavor to take budgetary, financial and tax measures necessary to promote the rational use of energy, etc.

Article 23

(Promotion of Science and Technology)

The state shall endeavor to take necessary measures in order to promote science and technology helpful to the rational use of energy, etc., such as the promotion of research and development and provision of the results of such research and development.

Article 24

(Measures for Increasing Public Awareness, etc.)

The state shall endeavor through educational, publicity and other activities, to increase public awareness regarding the rational use of energy and to secure public cooperation in performing such activities.

Article 24-2

(Consideration by Local Public Bodies in Educational Activities, etc.)

Local public bodies shall, in performing educational activities, public relations activities, etc., give consideration as much as possible so that such activities contribute to the better understanding of the public about the rational use of energy, etc.

Article 25

(Reports and On-site Inspections)

The Minister may, to the extent necessary for enforcing the provisions of Paragraph 1 and 4 of Article 6 and Paragraphs 1 and 4 of Article 12-2, request any person or Enterprise engaged in the industry determined by a government ordinance as provided in Paragraph 1 of Article 6 to submit a report concerning the operating conditions at such person's Factory, in accordance with the stipulations of a government ordinance.

2. The competent minister may, to the extent necessary for enforcing the provisions of Article 12 and Article 12-5, request the Type 1 Designated Enterprise or Type 2 Designated Enterprise to submit a report concerning the operating conditions of the Type 1 Designated Energy Management Factory or Type 2 Designated Energy Management Factory, or have ministry staff visit the Type 1 Designated Energy Management Factory or Type 2 Designated Energy Management Factory to inspect equipment consuming energy, books, documents or other materials, in accordance with the stipulations of a government ordinance.

3. The Minister may, to the extent necessary for enforcing the provisions of Sections 2 and 3 of Chapter II, request the Designated Examination Body or Designated Training Course Body to submit a report concerning the conditions of its affairs or accounts, or have ministry staff visit the office of the Designated Examination Body or Designated Training Course Body to inspect book, documents or other materials.

4. The Minister of Construction may, to the extent necessary for enforcing the provisions of Article 15-2, request the Designated Owner to submit a report concerning the matters with regard to the design and construction of the Designated Building, or have ministry staff visit such Designated Building or its construction site to inspect such Designated Building, construction equipment, documents or other materials, in accordance with the stipulations of a government ordinance.

5. The Minister may, to extent necessary for enforcing the provisions of Articles 19 and 21, request the Manufacturer, etc. of Designated Machinery to submit a report concerning the operating conditions relating to Designated Machinery, or have ministry staff visit the office, factory or warehouse of such Manufacturer, etc. of Designated Machinery to inspect such Designated Machinery, books, documents or other materials, in accordance with the stipulations of a government ordinance.

6. Any ministry staff member conducting on-site inspections as provided in Paragraph 2 through the preceding paragraph shall carry with him or her an identity card indicating his or her authority and show such card to the person concerned.

7. The authorization to conduct on-site inspections as provided in Paragraphs 2 through 5 shall not be construed as the authority to carry out criminal investigations.

Article 25-2

(Fee)

Any person desiring to take the examination for energy manager, or any person desiring to obtain the recognition provided in Item 2 of Paragraph 1 of Article 8, or any person desiring to receive the license of energy manager after having passed the examination for energy manager conducted by a Designated Examination Body, or any person desiring to renew the license of energy manager, or any person desiring to take the training course provided in Item 1 of Paragraph 1 of Article 12-3 (excluding the training course offered by a Designated Training Course Body), or any person desiring to take the training course provided in Paragraph 2 of such Article (excluding the training course offered by a Designated Training Course Body) shall pay a fee in the amount stipulated by a government ordinance in consideration of the actual expenses.

2. The fee provided in the preceding paragraph shall be treated as the revenue of the Designated Examination Body when such a fee is paid by a person taking the examination for energy manager, or as the revenue of the National Treasury in all other cases.

Article 25-3

(Hearings)

The Minister shall, when the Minister takes measures in accordance with the provisions of Article

12-13 (including the case where these provisions apply as provided in Paragraph 4 of Article 12-14) or of Article 12-17 (including the case where these provisions apply as provided in Paragraph 2 of Article 12-21), hold a public hearing for the person involved, providing a sufficient advance notice.

2. The advance notice as provided in the preceding paragraph shall include the data, place and agenda of the public hearing.

At the public hearing, the Minister shall give the person involved in the measures concerned and other interested parties the opportunity to submit supporting evidence and to express their opinions.

Article 25-4

(Appeal against Measures Taken by Designated Examination Body, etc.)

Any person who has a complaint against the disposition with respect to Examination Affairs adopted by a Designated Examination Body (excluding disposition concerning examination results) or against a forbearance of such Designated Examination Body may request the Minister to review such disposition or forbearance in accordance with that Administrative Appeal Law (Law NO. 160, 1962).

Article 26

(Mandate of Interim Measures to Orders)

In the event that an order is enacted, revised or repealed in accordance with this law, necessary interim measures (including interim measures concerning penal regulations) may be determined by such order, to the extent considered to be reasonably necessary as the result of such enactment, revision or repeal.

Article 27

(Competent Minister)

The competent ministers in this law shall be the Minister of International Trade and Industry and any other minister having jurisdiction over the operation of the Factory concerned.

2. The authorization as provided in this law may be delegated to the senior official of a regional bureau or office or department in accordance with the stipulations of a government ordinance.

CHAPTER VI. PENAL REGULATIONS

Article 27-2

Any person who has violated the provisions of Paragraph 1 of Article 12-15 shall be punished by imprisonment with hard labor not exceeding one (1) year or a fine not exceeding one million (1,000,000) yen.

Article 27-3

In a case of violation of the order to suspend Examination Affairs or Training Course Affairs issued as provided in Paragraph 2 of Article 12-17 (including the case where these provisions apply as provided in Paragraph 2 of Article 12-21), the officer of staff member of the Designated Examination Body or Designated Training Course Body who has committed such violation shall be punished by imprisonment with hard labor not exceeding one (1) year or a fine not exceeding one million (1,000,000) yen.

Article 28

Any person who comes under one of the following items shall be punished by a fine not exceeding one million (1,000,000) yen;

1. Any person who has violated the provisions of Paragraph 1 of Article 7 or Paragraph 1 of Article 12-3;

2. Any person who has violated the provisions of Paragraph 5 of Article 12, Paragraph 3 of Article 19 or Paragraph 3 of Article 21.

Article 29

Any person who comes under one of the following items shall be punished by a fine not exceeding three hundred thousand (300,000) yen:

1. Any person who has failed to report in accordance with the provisions of Paragraph 2 of Article 6 or Paragraph 2 of Article 12-2, or who has submitted a false report;

2. Any person who has failed to report in accordance with the provisions of Paragraph 1 of Article 10-2;

3. Any person who has failed to report in accordance with the provisions of Article 11 or Paragraph 2, 4 or 5 of Article 25, or who has submitted a false report, or any person who has refused,

obstruct or evade the inspection as provided in Paragraph 2, 4 or 5 of Article 25.

4. Any person who has failed to provide books or record or has made a false record in violation of the provisions of Article 12-4;

5. Any person having reported in accordance with the provisions of Recording 2 of Article 6, a Type 1 Designated Enterprise, any person having reported in accordance with the provisions of Paragraph 2 of Article 12-2 or a Type 2 Designated Enterprise that has failed to report in accordance with the provisions of Paragraph 1 of Article 25 or that have submitted a false report.

Article 29-2

Any officer or staff member of the Designated Examination Body or Designated Training Course Body who has committed any of the violations enumerated in the following items shall be punished by a fine not exceeding three hundred thousand (300,000) yen:

1. When such person or staff member has discontinued all of the Examination Affairs without permission as provided in Article 12-10;

2. When such person or staff member has not prepared any books nor has entered no records in book or has made false records in the book in violation of the provisions of Paragraph 1 of Article 12-18 (including the case where these provisions apply as provided in Paragraph 2 of Article 12-21), or has not kept any books in violation of the provisions of Paragraph 2 of Article 12-18 (including the case where these provisions apply as provided in Paragraph 2 of Article 12-21);

3. When such person or staff member has failed to report in accordance with the provisions of Article 12-22 or has submitted a false report;

4. When such person or staff member has failed to report in accordance with the provisions of Paragraph 3 of Article 25 or has submitted a false report, or has refused, obstruct or evade the inspection in accordance with the same paragraph.

Article 30

In the event that a representative of a juridical person or proxy, servant or other employee of a juridical person or person has committed a violation as provided in Article 28 or 29 in connection with the affairs of such juridical person or person, not only such representative or proxy, servant or other employee but also such juridical person or person shall be subjected to an applicable punishment as provided in this Article.

Article 31

Any person who has failed to report in accordance with the provisions of Paragraph 2 of Article 7 or Paragraph 3 of Article 12-3 or has submitted a false report shall be punished by a fine not exceeding two hundred thousand (200,000) yen.

Supplementary Provisions

(Omitted)

Fundamental Policies for Rational Use of Energy

Adopted at the Cabinet Meeting on 6 July 1993
Ordinance No. 361 of the Ministry of International Trade and Industry on 15 July 1993

Japan has to rely on imports for most of its domestic demand for fuel resources. In such a situation, the country's energy consumption is increasing at a high level with the development of the national economy in recent years – which had led to expansion in production, distribution and consumption – and with changing people's lifestyles. However, there is the constant possibility of a global crisis in energy supply and demand. On the other hand, global warming, which is mainly caused by energy use and resulting generation of carbon dioxide, is posing a grave problem that may have ill effects on the very basis of our survival.

With this in mind, these Fundamental Policies prescribe the matters needed for the comprehensive promotion of rational use of energy at factories or workshops (hereinafter referred simply to as "factories") and buildings and for machines, etc.

In carrying out these matters, we should pay attention to the fact that energy consumption is affected by the development of the national economy and by the efforts to promote the rational use of energy.

Industrial structures, corporate behaviors, traffic systems and changes in people's lifestyles and other social factors also have an impact on energy consumption.

The target of these Policies is to generally reduce Japan's energy consumption in 2000 and 2010 to the levels of the long-term outlook for energy supply and demand which was considered in the formulation process of the supply target of petroleum alternative energy (Ordinance No. 470 of the Ministry of International Trade and Industry of 1990).

I. FUNDAMENTAL MATTERS CONCERNING THE MEASURES TO BE TAKEN BY ENERGY USERS, ETC. FOR THE RATIONAL USE OF ENERGY

1. Measures to be taken by those who use energy at factories for business purposes

(1) Those who use energy at factories for business purposes shall make efforts to reduce the basic unit of energy consumption by taking the following measures:

1) In installing energy-consuming units, to choose those units which have a high energy consumption efficiency and allow an efficient use;

2) To make efforts to renew and improve existing limits and to introduce additional units for among others controlling energy use of such existing units in order to increase energy consumption efficiency and to use such units efficiently;

3) To establish management standards regarding the operation, maintenance, inspection, etc. of energy-consuming units and to manage such units according to such management standards;

4) To make proper and full use of energy managers and to take other measures in order to improve the energy management system at factories in general;

5) To examine the method of effectively using the surplus energy hard to use at factories and to make efforts to realize such effective use if possible;

(2) Those who are engaged in energy supply business shall carry out the matters prescribed in (1)

above in order to increase energy conversion efficiency. They shall also make efforts to operate energy supply facilities efficiently and to minimize energy loss during transport in such a way as to attain the best energy consumption efficiency of such facilities as a whole according to changing demand;

2. Measures to be taken by the builders of buildings

Those who build buildings shall in order to prevent heat loss through the outer walls, windows, etc. of such buildings and to ensure an efficient energy use for air-conditioning units, etc. installed in such buildings, adopt proper designing and construction work and install such air-conditioning units, etc. as have a high energy consumption efficiency and allow an efficient use.

3. Measures to be taken by the owners, etc. of buildings

(1) The owners of buildings shall make efforts to carry out the following matters taking account of the conditions, investment effects, etc. of such buildings:

1) To make efforts to renew and improve existing energy-consuming units and to introduce additional units for, among others, controlling energy use of such existing units in order to increase energy consumption efficiency and to use such units efficiently;

2) To do a proper management for keeping the function of buildings in order to prevent heat loss through the outer walls, windows, etc. of such buildings and to ensure an efficient energy use for air-conditioning units, etc, installed in such buildings and to examine repairing and other necessary measures to keep or improve such functions;

(2) The owners of buildings or those who are in charge of the management of energy-consuming units in such buildings under a contract with such owners shall make efforts to manage such units properly by establishing management standards regarding the operation, maintenance, inspection, etc. of such units and to improve the energy management system for such buildings, including a system for cooperation with tenants.

4. Measures to be taken by the manufacturers of construction materials

Those who are engaged in the manufacture of the construction materials used to prevent heat loss through the outer walls, windows, etc. of buildings shall make efforts to bring into wide use construction materials having a high insulation through the development and manufacture of construction materials having a high insulation, labeling of insulation-related quality, improvement of easiness in construction work, etc.

5. Measures to be taken by the manufacturers, etc. of machines and apparatuses

(1) Those who are engaged in the manufacture of energy-consuming machines and apparatuses shall make efforts to do their business activities laying stress on improvement in the energy consumption efficiency of the machines and apparatuses they manufacture at the respective stages of development, designing, prototype manufacture and mass production and to develop and introduce such technology as allows the efficient use of such machines and apparatuses according to the situations of users.

(2) Those who are engaged in the manufacture, import or sale of energy-consuming machines and apparatuses shall provide information helpful to the proper selection by consumers and take other necessary measures in order to increase the ratio of such products as have a better' energy consumption efficiency and allow a more efficient use.

6. Measures to be taken by the users of machines and apparatuses

Those who use automobiles, air-conditioning appliances, water heaters, lighting appliances, office appliances or other energy-consuming machines and apparatuses shall select those products having a high energy consumption efficiency and allowing efficient use as much as possible and shall make efforts to use such machines and apparatuses efficiently by keeping the functions of such machines and apparatuses through proper management, by preventing unnecessary energy consumption or by taking other measures.

7. Development and diffusion of technology helpful to rational use of energy

Those who use energy at factories for business purposes, who are engaged in the designing or construction of buildings, who are engaged in the manufacture of machines and apparatuses and other entrepreneurs shall make efforts to develop and bring into wide use such technology as help improve the method of using, and help increase the energy consumption efficiency of energy-consuming units, etc., such technology as help prevent heat loss through the outer walls, windows, etc. of buildings and help realize the efficient use of energy for air-conditioning units, etc. installed in buildings, and such other technology as is helpful to the rational use of energy.

8. Introduction and diffusion of energy supply-demand systems helpful to the efficient use of energy in areas

In order to promote the rational use of energy in Japan, it has an important meaning to realize an efficient energy use of energy users in respective areas as a whole through effective use of waste heat, use of unused energy, etc. In light of this, those who are engaged in energy supply business shall make efforts to introduce and bring into wide use the optimum energy supply-demand system, taking account of the situation of energy supply sources, structure of energy supply-demand, etc. in such areas. Those who use energy shall cooperate in the introduction and diffusion of such energy supply-demand system as much as possible.

II. FUNDAMENTAL MATTERS CONCERNING POLICIES FOR PROMOTING RATIONAL USE OF ENERGY

1. Measures to be taken by the central and local governments themselves as energy users, etc.

The central and local governments shall, in a case where they are themselves energy users, are engaged in energy supply business or become the builders, designers or owners of buildings, take the initiative in taking the measures prescribed in "I. Fundamental matters concerning the measures to be taken by energy users, etc. for the rational use of energy" (heremafter referred to as the "specific matters") and make efforts to contribute to the rational use of energy.

2. Support to capital investment, etc.

The government shall, in order to support the measures to install the units helpful to the rational use of energy and other measures helpful to the rational use of energy taken according to the specific matters, make efforts to take financial and other necessary measures and shall supply sufficient information relating to such measures.

3. Support to energy management

The government shall, in order to support the measures to Improve energy management systems and use machines and apparatuses efficiently and other measures taken according to the specific matters, make efforts to develop and secure the engineers engaged in the rational use of energy and to diffuse technical knowledge relating to the rational use of energy.

4. Support to technical development

The government shall, in order to support the development of technology helpful to the rational use of energy done according to the specific matters, make efforts to take financial and other necessary measures and shall supply sufficient information relating to such measures.

5. Support to the introduction and diffusion of optimum energy supply-demand systems in areas

The government and the New Energy and Industrial Development Organization (hereinafter referred to as the "Organization") shall, in order to support the introduction and diffusion of such energy supply-demand systems as contribute to an efficient energy use of energy users in respective areas as a whole through effective use of waste heat, use of unused energy, etc., make efforts to take financial and other necessary measures and shall supply sufficient information relating to such measures.

6. Promotion of research and development, etc.

In order to promote the rational use of energy, it has an important meaning to foster science and technology helpful to the rational use of energy. In light of this, the government and the Organization shall make efforts to promote research and development and to bring the results of such research and development into wide use.

7. Education, public relations, etc. to people

In order to effectively advance the rational use of energy, it is essential to have all people understand and take part in the activities for it. In light of this, the government shall make efforts to increase people's understanding of the rational use of energy through educational activities, public relations activities, etc.

III. DATE OF IMPLEMENTATION

These Fundamental Policies shall be implemented as from 1 August 1993.

Enforcement Ordinance for the Law Concerning Rational Use of Energy

(Translated by ECCJ)

Government Ordinance No. 267 of September 29, 1979

Partial Amendment, March 25, 1981
Partial Amendment, February 21, 1984
Partial Amendment, March 20, 1987
Partial Amendment, March 22, 1989
Partial Amendment, March 25, 1991
Partial Amendment, July 9, 1993
Partial Amendment, March 24, 1994
Partial Amendment, April 18, 1994
Partial Amendment, September 7, 1994
Partial Amendment, March 6, 1996
Partial Amendment, March 24, 1997
Partial Amendment, August 28, 1998

Article 1

(Definition)

Electricity to be specified by a government ordinance pursuant to Article 2, Paragraph 1, of the Law Concerning Rational Use of Energy (hereinafter referred to as the "Law") means electricity which is produced by power generating facilities that produce such electricity as is used in place of electricity obtained by converting power gained through the conversion of heat using fuel as a heat source and which meets either one of the following requirements:

(1) A person who has produced electricity will use such electricity for himself; or

(2) A person who has received a supply of electricity from a person who supplies such electricity will use such electricity.

Article 1-2

(Types of Business)

Types of business to be specified by a government ordinance pursuant to Article 6, Paragraph 1, of the Law shall be as prescribed below:

(1) Manufacturing (including article processing and repairing business);

(2) Mining;

(3) Electricity supply;

(4) Gas supply; and

(5) Heat supply.

Article 2

(Consumption of Fuels, Etc. and Electricity Relating to Designation of Type 1 Designated Energy Management Factory)

A numerical value to be specified by a government ordinance with regard to the annual consumption of fuels and heat produced using these fuels as heat sources (hereinafter referred to as "fuels, etc.") pursuant to Article 6, Paragraph 1, of the Law shall be 3,000 kiloliters in terms of the consumption of fuels, etc. as converted into the quantity of crude oil by such a method as is specified in the Ordinance of the Ministry of International Trade and Industry (hereinafter referred to as the "consumption of fuels, etc. in oil equivalent").

2. A numerical value to be specified by a government ordinance with regard to the annual consumption of electricity pursuant to Article 6, Paragraph 1, of the Law shall be 12,000,000 kilowatt-hours.

Article 3

(Energy Manager Appointment Criteria)

The criteria to be specified by a government ordinance pursuant to Article 7, Paragraph 1, of the Law shall be as prescribed below.

(1) Those type 1 designated heat management factories which fall under the coke manufacturing, electric power supply, gas supply or heat supply business sector shall appoint energy managers in the number stated in the right column of the table below from among those who have heat manager's licenses according to the appropriate consumption of fuels, etc. in oil equivalent for the previous fiscal year stated in the left column of the table below.

Less than 100,000 kiloliters	One (1)
Over 100,000 kiloliters	Two (2)

(2) Those type 1 designated heat management factories other than those specified under the preceding item shall appoint energy managers in the number stated in the right column of the table below from among those who have heat manager's licenses according to the appropriate consumption of fuels, etc. in oil equivalent for the previous fiscal year stated in the left column of the table below.

Less than 20,000 kiloliters	One (1)
Over 20,000 kiloliters to less than 50,000 kiloliters	Two (2)
Over 50,000 kiloliters to less than 100,000 kiloliters	Three (3)
Over 100,000 kiloliters	Four (4)

(3) Those type 1 designated electricity management factories shall appoint energy managers in the number stated in the right column of the table below from among those who have electricity manager's licenses according to the appropriate electricity consumption for the previous fiscal year stated in the left column of the table below.

Less than 200,000,000 kilowatt-hours	One (1)
Over 200,000,000 kilowatt-hours to less than 500,000,000 kilowatt-hours	Two (2)
Over 500,000,000 kilowatt-hours	Three (3)

Article 4

(Deliberative Councils to Take Counsel in Issuing Order to Type 1 Specified Business Operators)

Deliberative councils to be specified by a government ordinance pursuant to Article 12, Paragraph 5, of the Law shall be those stated in the right column of the table below to correspond to the ministers stated in the left column of the table.

Minister of International Trade and Industry	Advisory Committee for Energy
Minister of Finance	Tobacco Industries Council in the case of factories which are used for businesses belonging to the tobacco or salt manufacturing industry
	Central Council on Alcoholic Beverages in the case of factories which are used for business belonging to alcoholic beverage manufacturing industry
Minister of Health and Welfare	Central Pharmaceutical Affairs Council
Minister of Agriculture, Forestry and Fisheries	Food and Marketing Council
Minister of Transport	Council for Transport Technology

Article 4-2

(Consumption of Fuels, Etc. and Electricity Relating to Designation of Type 2 Designated Energy Management Factory)

A numerical value to be specified by a government ordinance with regard to the annual consumption of fuels, etc. pursuant to Article 12-2, Paragraph 1, of the Law shall be 1,500 kiloliters in terms of the consumption of fuels, etc. in oil equivalent.

2. A numerical value to be specified by a government ordinance with regard to the annual consumption of electricity pursuant to Article 12-2, Paragraph 1, of the Law shall be 6,000,000 kilowatt-hours.

Article 5

(Air Conditioners, etc.)

Building facilities to be specified by a government ordinance (hereinafter referred to as "air conditioners, etc.") pursuant to Article 13, Paragraph 2, of the Law shall be as prescribed below:

(1) Air conditioners and other machines and ventilation systems;

(2) Lighting fixtures;

(3) Water heaters; and

(4) Elevators.

Article 6

(Scale Requirements for Specified Buildings)

Requirements to be specified by a government ordinance pursuant to Article 15-2, Paragraph 1, of the Law shall be such that the total floor space (in the case of an extension, addition or reconstruction, the floor space of such extension, addition or reconstructed portion) is more than 2,000 square meters.

Article 7

(Specified Equipment)

Machines and appliances to be specified by a government ordinance pursuant to Article 18, Paragraph 1, of the Law shall be as prescribed below:

(1) Passenger cars {including only those cars which use gasoline as fuel, have a seating capacity of 10 persons or less and whose types are designated pursuant to Article 75, Paragraph 1, of the Vehicles for Road Transportation Law (Law No. 185 of 1951) and excluding those two-wheeled vehicles (including those with sidecars) and caterpillar tractors};

(2) Air conditioners (including only those air conditioners which can be used for heating purposes and excluding those air conditioners which have a cooling capacity of 27 kilowatts or more, water-cooled air conditioners and other types of air conditioners which are specified in the Ordinance of the Ministry of International Trade and Industry);

(3) Lighting fixtures which use only fluorescent lamps as their main light source (excluding the explosion-proof type lighting fixtures and those other pieces of lighting apparatus which are specified in the Ordinance of the Ministry of International Trade and Industry);

(4) Television sets (including only those television sets which are provided with Braun tubes and used in an alternating-current electrical line and excluding those television sets for industrial use);

(5) Copying machines (including only dry indirect electrostatic type copying machines and excluding color copying machines and other copying machines which are specified in the Ordinance of the Ministry of International Trade and Industry);

(6) Electronic computers (excluding those computers which are specified as those having advanced processing capability in the Ordinance of the Ministry of International Trade and Industry);

(7) Magnetic disk memory devices (excluding those magnetic disk memory devices with a storage capacity of 200 megabytes or less);

(8) Automobile trucks {including only those trucks which use gasoline as fuel, whose total vehicle weight is 2.5 tons or less as specified in Article 40, Paragraph 3, of the Vehicles for Road Transportation Law, and whose types are designated pursuant to Article 75, Paragraph 1, of the same law, and excluding those two-wheeled vehicles (including those with sidecars) and caterpillar tractors}; and

(9) Videotape recorders (including only those videotape recorders which are used in an alternating-current electrical line, and excluding videotape recorders for industrial use and those videotape recorders which are specified in the Ordinance of the Ministry of International Trade and Industry).

Article 8

(Production or Import Volume Requirements Pertaining to Manufacturers, etc. of Specified Equipment)

Requirements to be specified by a government ordinance pursuant to Article 19, Paragraph 1, of the Law shall be such that the annual production or import volume (including imports relating to shipments for the domestic market) is greater than the quantity stated in the right column of the table below according to the classification of specified equipment stated in the left column of the table.

(1) Passenger cars	2,000
(2) Air conditioners	500
(3) Lighting fixtures which use only fluorescent lamps as their main light source	30,000
(4) Television sets	10,000
(5) Copying machines	500
(6) Electronic computers	200
(7) Magnetic disk memory devices	5,000
(8) Automobile trucks	2,000
(9) Videotape recorders	5,000

Article 9

(Deliberative Councils to Take Counsel in Issuing Order to Manufacturers, etc. of Specified Equipment)

Deliberative councils to be specified by a government ordinance pursuant to Article 19, Paragraph 3, and Article 21, Paragraph 3, of the Law shall be the Advisory Committee for Energy in the case of the Minister of International Trade and Industry, and the Council for Transport Technology in the case of the Minister of Transport.

Article 10

(Reporting on Operational Conditions)

The Minister of International Trade and Industry may, in accordance with the provisions of Article 25, Paragraph 1, of the Law, cause a person who carries on any of the businesses falling under the types of business specified in Article 1-2 or an operator of any such business to report on the following particulars as to a factory in operation:

(1) Production volume and productive capacity pertaining to the business;

(2) Energy consumption and anticipated energy consumption; and

(3) Conditions of energy consuming equipment.

Article 11

(Reporting and On-the-Spot Inspection)

The competent Minister may, in accordance with the provisions of Article 25, Paragraph 2, of the Law, cause a type 1 specified business operator or a type 2 specified business operator to report on the following particulars as to a type 1 designated energy management factory or a type 2 designated energy management factory in operation:

(1) Energy consumption and other energy use information;

(2) Conditions of energy consuming equipment; and

(3) Conditions of equipment pertaining to rationalization of energy uses and other matters concerning rationalization of energy uses.

2. The competent Minister may, in accordance with the provisions of Article 25, Paragraph 2, of the Law, cause the personnel to enter a type 1 designated energy management factory or a type 2 designated energy management factory and make an inspection of energy consuming equipment, equipment pertaining to rationalization of energy uses and equipment related thereto, fuels, etc. in use, account books and other related documents.

Article 12

The Minister of Construction may, in accordance with the provisions of Article 25, Paragraph 4, of the Law, cause a specified owner, with regard to a specified building which he intends to construct, to report on the following particulars among those matters concerning the design and construction of such specified building:

(1) Particulars concerning measures to prevent heat loss through external walls, windows, etc. of the specified building; and

(2) Particulars concerning measures to achieve an efficient use of energy concerning air conditioners, etc. to be installed in the specified building.

2. The Minister of Construction may, in accordance with the provisions of Article 25, Paragraph 4, of the Law, cause the personnel to enter a specified building or the construction site of a specified building and make an inspection of the external walls, windows, etc. of such specified building, air conditioners, etc. to be installed in such specified building, construction materials to be used therefor, design drawings, and other related documents.

Article 13

The Minister of International Trade and Industry (the Minister of International Trade and Industry and the Minister of Transport in the case of cars; to be so understood in this article) may, in accordance with the provisions of Article 25, Paragraph 5, of the Law, cause persons who carry on the business of manufacturing or importing specified equipment (hereinafter referred to "manufacturing business operators") to report on the following particulars as to specified equipment for manufacturing or importing:

(1) Production or import volume and shipments for the domestic market;

(2) Energy consumption efficiency and particulars pertaining to improvement thereof; and

(3) Labeling of energy consumption efficiency.

2. The Minister of International Trade and Industry may, in accordance with the provisions of Article 25, Paragraph 5, of the Law, cause the personnel to enter the offices, factories or warehouses of the specified equipment manufacturing business operators and make an inspection of such specified equipment for manufacturing or importing, equipment for the manufacture of such specified equipment, equipment for measuring the energy consumption efficiency of such specified equipment, and related account books and documents.

Article 14

(Fees)

The amount of fees to be paid in accordance with the provisions of Article 25-2, Paragraph 1, of the Law shall be as prescribed in the table below.

Persons obligated to pay	Amount
(1) Persons who intend to take an examination for an energy manager's license	19,200 yen
(2) Persons who intend to obtain certification pursuant to the provisions of Article 8, Paragraph 1, Item (2), of the Law	4,900 yen
(3) Persons who have passed an examination for an energy manager's license given by the designated examination institution and hence intends to obtain the issuance of an energy manager's license	3,700 yen
(4) Persons who intends to obtain a reissue of an energy manager's license	2,600 yen

Article 15

(Delegation of Powers)

The powers of the Minister of International Trade and Industry pursuant to the provisions of Article 6, Paragraphs 1 to 4, Article 7, Paragraph 2, Article 10-2, Paragraph 1, Article 11, Article 12-2, Paragraphs 1–5, Article 12-3, Paragraph 3, and Article 25, Paragraph 1, of the Law may be delegated to the Director-General of the Regional Bureau of International Trade and Industry which has jurisdiction over the district where factories are located, and the powers of the Minister of Transport pursuant to the provisions of Article 10-2, Paragraph 1, and Article 11, of the Law may be delegated to the Director-General of the District Transport Bureau (including the Manager of the District Maritime Administration Department) which has jurisdiction over the district where factories are located.

Excerpt from Supplementary Provisions (Government Ordinance No. 267 of September 29, 1979)

1. This Government Ordinance shall come into force on the enforcement date of the Law (October 1, 1979).

2. The following Government Ordinances shall be abrogated:

(1) Enforcement Ordinance for the Heat Management Law (Government Ordinance No. 298 of 1951); and

(2) Ordinance on Fees for an Energy Manager's License

Excerpt from Supplementary Provisions (Government Ordinance No. 38 of March 25, 1981)

This Government Ordinance shall come into force on April 1, 1981.

(Omitted)

Supplementary Provisions (Government Ordinance No. 17 of February 21, 1984)

1. This Government Ordinance shall come into force on the promulgation date.

2. The application of the penal clauses to any act performed before the enforcement of this Government Ordinance shall still be treated in compliance with the previous practice.

Supplementary Provisions (Government Ordinance No. 19 of February 21, 1984)

This Government Ordinance shall come into force on March 9, 1984.

Excerpt from Supplementary Provisions (Government Ordinance No. 49 of March 20, 1987)

1. This Government Ordinance shall come into force on April 1, 1987.

Excerpt from Supplementary Provisions (Government Ordinance No. 59 of March 22, 1989)

1. This Government Ordinance shall come into force on April 1, 1989.

Excerpt from Supplementary Provisions (Government Ordinance No. 49 of March 25, 1991)

1. This Government Ordinance shall come into force on April 1, 1991.

Excerpt from Supplementary Provisions (Government Ordinance No. 248 of July 9, 1993)

Article 1

(Date of Enforcement)

This Government Ordinance shall come into force on the enforcement date of the Part of the Law Concerning the Improvement of Related Laws for the Advancement of the Energy Supply and Demand Structure (August 1, 1993).

Excerpt from Supplementary Provisions (Government Ordinance No. 77 of March 24, 1994)

1. This Government Ordinance shall come into force on April 1, 1994.

Supplementary Provisions (Government Ordinance No. 129 of April 18, 1994)

This Government Ordinance shall come into force on the promulgation date.

Supplementary Provisions (Government Ordinance No. 286 of September 7, 1994)

This Government Ordinance shall come into force on the promulgation date.

Supplementary Provisions (Government Ordinance No. 29 of March 6, 1996)

This Government Ordinance shall come into force on the promulgation date.

Excerpt from Supplementary Provisions (Government Ordinance No. 67 of March 24, 1997)

1. This Government Ordinance shall come into force on April 1, 1997.

Supplementary Provisions (Government Ordinance No. 293 of August 28, 1998)

This Government Ordinance shall come into force on the enforcement date of the Law for Partial Amendments to the Law Concerning Rational Use of Energy (April 1, 1999).

Enforcement Regulations for the Law Concerning Rational Use of Energy

(Translated by ECCJ)

Ministerial Ordinance No.74 of September 29, 1979

Partial Amendment, March 9, 1984
Partial Amendment, July 30, 1993
Partial Amendment, December 13, 1993
Partial Amendment, April 18, 1994
Partial Amendment, September 7, 1994
Partial Amendment, January 25, 1996
Partial Amendment, March 6, 1996
Partial Amendment, February 26, 1997
Partial Amendment, April 9, 1997
Partial Amendment, March 30, 1998
Partial Amendment, January 25, 1999

Article 1

(Definition)

The terms used in this Ministerial Ordinance shall be treated in compliance with the definitions of the terms used in the Law Concerning Rational Use of Energy (hereinafter referred to as the "Law") and the Enforcement Ordinance for the Law Concerning Rational Use of Energy (hereinafter referred to as the "Enforcement Ordinance").

Article 2

(Fuel Types)

Petroleum products to be specified by the Ordinance of the Ministry of International Trade and Industry pursuant to Article 2, Paragraph 2, of the Law shall be naphtha, kerosene, gas oil and petroleum gas (including liquefied petroleum gas; hereinafter to be so understood).

2. Coal products to be specified by the Ordinance of the Ministry of International Trade and Industry pursuant to Article 2, Paragraph 2, of the Law shall be coke oven gas and blast furnace gas.

Article 3

(Conversion Methods)

The methods for converting the consumption of fuels, etc. into the amount of crude oil, specified in Article 2, Paragraph 1, of the Enforcement Ordinance, shall be as prescribed below:

(1) In the case of fuels mentioned in the left column of *Annexed Table 1*, the quantities given in the same column shall be converted to those stated in the right column of the table;

(2) In the case of fuels, etc. other than those fuels specified in the preceding item, the quantity equivalent to ten million kilojoules of heating value shall be counted as 0.258 kiloliter of crude oil.

Article 4

(Notification of Usage of Fuels, etc. or Electricity Relating to Designation of Type 1 Designated Energy Management Factory)

Notification pursuant to the provisions of Article 6, Paragraph 2, of the Law shall be made by submitting two copies of a notification made out on Form 1 no later than the end of April each year.

Article 5

Particulars to be specified by the Ordinance of the Ministry of International Trade and Industry pursuant to Article 6, Paragraph 2, of the Law shall, in the case of a type 1 designated heat management factory, be the consumption of fuels, etc. for the previous fiscal year (in case the consumption of fuels, etc. in the following fiscal year and thereafter apparently will not exceed the numerical value under Article 2, Paragraph 1, of the Enforcement Ordinance, notice to that effect and the consumption of fuels, etc. for the previous fiscal year).

2. Particulars to be specified by the Ordinance of the Ministry of International Trade and Industry pursuant to Article 6, Paragraph 2, of the Law shall, in the case of a type 1 designated electricity management factory, be the consumption of electricity for the previous fiscal year (in case the consumption of electricity in the following fiscal year and thereafter apparently will not exceed the numerical value under Article 2, Paragraph 2, of the Enforcement Ordinance, notice to that effect and the consumption of electricity for the previous fiscal year).

Article 6

(Request for Cancellation of Designation Relating to Type 1 Designated Energy Management Factory)

Request specified under Article 6, Paragraph 3, of the Law shall be made by submitting two copies of a letter of request made out on Form 2.

Article 7

(Appointment of Energy Managers)

Appointment of energy managers specified in Article 7, Paragraph 1, of the Law shall be made as prescribed below:

(1) Appointment shall be made within six (6) months of the day that reasons for the appointment of energy managers have arisen; and

(2) Persons who have been appointed as energy managers or energy management officers at other type 1 designated energy management factories or type 2 designated energy management factories shall not be appointed.

Article 8

(Notification of Appointment, etc. of Energy Managers)

Notification pursuant to the provisions of Article 7, Paragraph 2, of the Law shall be made by submitting two copies of a notification made out on Form 3 no later than the end of May of the fiscal year after the fiscal year in which the day that energy managers have been appointed, died or dismissed from service belongs.

Article 8-2

(Notification by Electronic Information Processing Organization)

Notification pursuant to the provisions of Article 7, Paragraph 2, of the Law may be made by using an electronic information processing organization which connects an electronic computer (including input/output devices) in use at the Ministry of International Trade and Industry through a telecommunications line with the input/output devices in use by a person who intends to make notification.

2. Notification pursuant to the provisions of the preceding paragraph shall be deemed to have arrived at the Ministry of International Trade and Industry when it has been recorded in a file provided in the electronic computer mentioned in the same paragraph.

3. Notification pursuant to the provisions of the preceding paragraph shall be deemed to have been made by submitting documents specified in the provisions of the preceding article prescribing that such notification shall be made by submitting such documents.

Article 8-3

A person who intends to make notification under Paragraph 1 of the preceding article shall input in Form 3-2 those particulars to be notified in accordance with the provisions of Article 7, Paragraph 2, of the Law.

Article 8-4

Input under the preceding article shall be made in compliance with such a method as is specified in Annex 1 to the Japanese Industrial Standard (hereinafter referred to as the "JIS") X0208 pursuant to the Industrial Standardization Law (Law No. 184 of 1949).

2. Input under the preceding article shall be made by using those graphic characters specified in the JIS X0201 and X0208 and the "carriage return (CR)"

and the "line feed (LF)" from among those control characters specified in the JIS X0211.

Article 8-5

(Notifier's Code)

A person who intends to make notification in accordance with the provisions of Article 8-2, Paragraph 1, shall give notification to that effect to the Minister of International Trade and Industry by submitting in advance a document made out on Form 3-3 stating his name, notifier's identification code and other necessary particulars.

2. The Minister of International Trade and Industry shall, upon receipt of a document under the preceding paragraph, issue a notifier's code to the person who has submitted such document.

3. The person who has made notification under Paragraph 1 of this article shall, when there is change as to the particulars notified or when he intends to discontinue the use of the notifier's code, promptly serve a notice to that effect made out on Form 3-4 or 3-5 upon the Minister of International Trade and Industry.

Article 9

(Duties of Energy Manager)

Duties to be specified by the Ordinance of the Ministry of International Trade and Industry pursuant to Article 9 of the Law shall be as prescribed below:

(1) In the case of a type 1 designated heat management factory, maintenance of equipment pertaining to rationalization of use of fuels, etc.;

(2) In the case of a type 1 designated electricity management factory, maintenance of equipment pertaining to rationalization of electric energy uses; and

(3) Preparation of reports under Article 10 and preparation of documents associated with reporting under Article 25, Paragraph 2, of the Law.

Article 9-2

(Submission of Medium-to-Long-Term Plan)

Submission of a plan pursuant to the provisions of Article 10-2, Paragraph 1, of the Law shall be made by sending in two copies of a plan made out on Form 3-6 no later than the end of May each year.

Article 10

(Periodical Reporting)

Reporting pursuant to the provisions of Article 11 of the Law shall, in the case of a type 1 designated heat management factory, be made by sending in two copies of a report made out on Form 4 no later than the end of May each year.

2. Reporting pursuant to the provisions of Article 11 of the Law shall, in the case of a type 1 designated electricity management factory, be made by sending in two copies of a report made out on Form 5 no later than the end of May each year.

Article 11

Particulars to be specified by the Ordinance of the Ministry of International Trade and Industry pursuant to Article 11 of the Law shall, in the case of a type 1 designated heat management factory, be the following matters for the previous fiscal year:

(1) Consumption of fuels, etc. by types and total consumption thereof;

(2) Installation, remodeling or removal of energy consuming equipment, and operation thereof;

(3) Installation, remodeling or removal of equipment pertaining to rationalization of use of fuels, etc., and operation thereof;

(4) Compliance with the standards of judgment specified under Article 4, Paragraph 1, of the Law Concerning Rationalization of Use of Fuels, Etc., and other measures taken for rationalization of use of fuels, etc.;

(5) Production volume (including equivalent value; hereinafter to be so understood); and

(6) Efficiency of use of fuels, etc. (in case the factory concerned is a type 1 designated electricity management factory, efficiency of use of fuels, etc. and energy consumption efficiency).

2. Particulars to be specified by the Ordinance of the Ministry of International Trade and Industry pursuant to Article 11 of the Law shall, in the case of a type 1 designated electricity management factory,

be the following matters for the previous fiscal year:

(1) Consumption of electricity;

(2) Installation, remodeling or removal of electricity consuming equipment, and operation thereof;

(3) Installation, remodeling or removal of equipment pertaining to rationalization of electric energy uses, and operation thereof;

(4) Compliance with the standards of judgment specified under Article 4, Paragraph 1, of the Law Concerning Rationalization of Electric Energy Uses, and other measures taken for rationalization of electric energy uses;

(5) Production volume; and

(6) Electric energy consumption efficiency.

Article 11-2

(Notification of Usage of Fuels, etc. or Electricity Relating to Designation of Type 2 Designated Energy Management Factory)

Notification pursuant to the provisions of Article 12-2, Paragraph 2, of the Law shall be made by submitting two copies of a notification made out on Form 5-2 no later than the end of April each year.

Article 11-3

Particulars to be specified by the Ordinance of the Ministry of International Trade and Industry pursuant to Article 12-2, Paragraph 2, of the Law shall, in the case of a type 2 designated heat management factory, be the consumption of fuels, etc. for the previous fiscal year (in case the consumption of fuels, etc. in the following fiscal year and thereafter apparently will not exceed the numerical value under Article 4-2, Paragraph 1, of the Enforcement Ordinance, notice to that effect, reasons therefor and the consumption of fuels, etc. for the previous fiscal year).

2. Particulars to be specified by the Ordinance of the Ministry of International Trade and Industry pursuant to Article 12-2, Paragraph 2, of the Law shall, in the case of a type 2 designated electricity management factory, be the consumption of electricity for the previous fiscal year (in case the consumption of electricity in the following fiscal year and thereafter apparently will not exceed the numerical value under Article 4-2, Paragraph 2, of the Enforcement Ordinance, notice to that effect, reasons therefor and the consumption of electricity for the previous fiscal year).

Article 11-4

(Request for Cancellation of Designation Relating to Type 2 Designated Energy Management Factory)

Request specified under Article 12-2, Paragraph 3, of the Law shall be made by submitting two copies of a letter of request made out on Form 5-3.

Article 11-5

(Appointment of Energy Management Officers)

Appointment of energy management officers pursuant to the provisions of Article 12-3, Paragraph 1, of the Law shall be made as prescribed below:

(1) Persons described in the right column of the table below shall be appointed as energy management officers according to the classification of type 2 designated energy management factories stated in the left column of the table.

Type 2 designated heat management factory	Persons who have completed the training course under Article 12-3, Paragraph 1, Item (1), of the Law, on knowledge and skills necessary for rationalization of use of fuels, etc., or who have heat manager's licenses.
Type 2 designated electricity management factory	Persons who have completed the training course under Article 12-3, Paragraph 1, Item (1), of the Law, on knowledge and skills necessary for rationalization of electric energy uses, or who have electricity manager's licenses.

(2) Appointment shall be made within six (6) months of the day that reasons for the appointment of energy managers have arisen; and

(3) Persons who have been appointed as energy managers or energy management officers at other type 1 designated energy management factories

or type 2 designated energy management factories shall not be appointed.

Article 11-6

(Training Courses for Knowledge and Technical Improvement)

A period to be specified by the Ordinance of the Ministry of International Trade and Industry pursuant to Article 12-3, Paragraph 2, of the Law shall be three (3) years counting from the first day of the fiscal year after the fiscal year in which the day belongs that a person appointed as energy management officer has taken the training course specified in Paragraph 1, Item (1), of the same article (in case the person appointed as energy management officer has taken the training course specified in Paragraph 2 of the same article, the day that he has taken the latest of those training courses). However, if the person appointed as energy management officer falls under one of the categories described hereunder, the said period shall be one (1) year counting from the first day of the fiscal year after the fiscal year in which the day belongs that he was appointed as energy management officer:

(1) Person who has been appointed as energy management officer on and after the day when two years have passed counting from the first day of the fiscal year after the fiscal year in which the day of taking the training course specified in Article 12-3, Paragraph 1, Item (1), of the Law belongs; or

(2) Person who has been appointed as energy management officer on and after the day when two years have passed counting from the first day of the fiscal year after the fiscal year in which the day belongs that he took the latest of those training courses specified in Article 12-3, Paragraph 2, of the Law.

Article 11-7

(Notification of Appointment, Etc. of Energy Management Officers)

Notification pursuant to the provisions of Article 12-3, Paragraph 3, of the Law shall be made by submitting two copies of a notification made out on Form 5-4 no later than the end of May of the fiscal year after the fiscal year in which the day that energy management officers have been appointed, died or dismissed from service belongs.

Article 11-8

(Duties of Energy Management Officers)

Duties to be specified by the Ordinance of the Ministry of International Trade and Industry under Article 9 of the Law, as also applicable in Article 12-3, Paragraph 4, of the Law, shall be as prescribed below:

(1) In the case of a type 2 designated heat management factory, maintenance of equipment pertaining to rationalization of use of fuels, etc.;

(2) In the case of a type 2 designated electricity management factory, maintenance of equipment pertaining to rationalization of electric energy uses; and

(3) Keeping of account books under Article 12-4 of the law and preparation of documents associated with reporting under Article 25, Paragraph 2, of the Law.

Article 11-9

(Recording)

In an account book specified in Article 12-4 of the Law the following particulars for the previous month shall be recorded by the end of each month in the case of a type 2 designated heat management factory:

(1) Amount of fuels, etc. purchased by types, amount of byproducts generated, amount of fuels, etc. sold and consumption of fuels, etc.;

(2) Installation, remodeling or removal of energy consuming equipment, and operation thereof;

(3) Consumption of fuels, etc., by types by each unit of energy consuming equipment;

(4) Installation, remodeling or removal of equipment pertaining to rationalization of use of fuels, etc., and operation thereof;

(5) Measures taken for rationalization of use of fuels, etc.

2. In an account book specified in Article 12-4 of the Law the following particulars for the previous month shall be recorded by the end of each month in the case of a type 2 designated electricity management factory:

(1) Amount of electricity purchased, amount of electricity self-generated, amount of electricity sold and consumption of electricity;

(2) Installation, remodeling or removal of electric energy consuming equipment, and operation thereof;

(3) Installation, remodeling or removal of equipment pertaining to rationalization of electric energy uses and operation thereof;

(4) Measures taken for rationalization of electric energy uses.

Article 12

(Exception of Specified Equipment)

Air conditions to be specified by the Ordinance of the Ministry of International Trade and Industry pursuant to Article 7, Item (2), of the Enforcement Ordinance shall be those mentioned below:

(1) Air conditioners of construction without an electric motor for compression;

(2) Air conditioners of such construction as to use energy sources other than electricity as heat sources for heating purposes;

(3) Air conditioners of such construction as to have temperature control or dusting capability for air-conditioning purposes to maintain the performance of machines and appliances or to keep food and drink in a hygienically good state of preservation;

(4) Air conditions of such construction as to cool outside air wholly and send cold air into rooms;

(5) Spot air conditioners;

(6) Air conditioners designed for use in vehicles and other means of transportation;

(7) Air conditions of such construction as to have ducts at air inlet and outlet of outside heat exchanger; and

(8) Separate type air conditioners of such construction as to connect two or more indoor units to one outdoor unit.

2. Lighting fixtures, which use only fluorescent lamps as their main light source, to be specified by the Ordinance of the Ministry of International Trade and Industry pursuant to Article 7, Item (3), of the Enforcement Ordinance shall be those mentioned below:

(1) Heat-resisting type lighting fixtures;

(2) Lighting fixtures of dustproof construction;

(3) Corrosion-resistant type lighting fixtures;

(4) Lighting fixtures designed for use in vehicles and other means of transportation; and

(5) Lighting fixtures which use fluorescent lamps of less than 40 size (excluding pendant lighting apparatus for household use and fluorescent desk lamps).

3. Copying machines to be specified by the Ordinance of the Ministry of International Trade and Industry pursuant to Article 7, Item (5), of the Enforcement Ordinance shall be those mentioned below:

(1) Copying machines of such construction to make a duplicate copy of something on copying paper of A2 or larger in size;

(2) Copying machines of such construction as to make 86 sheets or more of duplicate copies per minute;

(3) Copying machines structurally integrated with printer in one-piece construction; and

(4) Copying machines structurally integrated with facsimile machines in one-piece construction.

4. Electronic computers to be specified by the Ordinance of the Ministry of International Trade and Industry pursuant to Article 7, Item (6), of the Enforcement Ordinance shall be those whose composite theoretical performance (appropriate performance values stated in the right column of *Annexed Table 2* for the appropriate electronic computer described in the left column of the table) is 3,000 mega-operations per second.

5. Videotape recorders to be specified by the Ordinance of the Ministry of International Trade and Industry pursuant to Article 7, Item (9), of the Enforcement Ordinance shall be those mentioned below:

(1) Videotape recorders of such construction as to process voice and image electric signals digitally;

(2) Videotape recorders of such construction as to process electric signals for images consisting of 1,125 scanning lines or more;

(3) Videotape recorders of such construction as to process electric signals for images consisting of 400 horizontal resolution power lines or more and without satellite broadcasting receiving capability;

(4) Videotape recorders of such construction as to have two or more videotape players; and

(5) Videotape recorders of such construction as to have playback feature only.

Article 13

(Energy Consumption Efficiency)

Energy consumption efficiency of specified equipment specified in Article 20, Item (1), of the Law shall be the appropriate numerical value stated in the right column of *Annexed Table 2* for specified equipment mentioned in the left column of the table.

Article 14

(Certificate of Identification)

A certificate under Article 25, Paragraph 6, of the Law shall be made out on Form 6.

Article 15

(Following Procedure by Flexible Disks)

Submission of documents mentioned in the left column of the table below may be made by sending in flexible disks stating the particulars to be declared therein on the appropriate forms mentioned in the right column of the table and by submitting flexible disk submission slips made out on Form 7.

Notification (Article 4)	Form 8
Letter of request (Article 6)	Form 9

Article 16

(Construction of Flexible Disks)

Flexible disks under the preceding article shall be those which fall under either one of the following categories:

(1) 90-millimeter flexible disk cartridge conforming to the JIS X6221; or

(2) 90-millimeter flexible disk cartridge conforming to the JIS X6223.

Article 17

(Flexible Disk Recording Methods)

Recording of the particulars in a flexible disk pursuant to the provisions of Article 15 shall be made by any of the method described below:

(1) For a track format, the method specified in the JIS X6222 when the particulars are recorded in the flexible disk under Item (1) of the preceding article, or the method specified in the JIS X6225 when particulars are recorded in the flexible disk under Item (2) of the same article;

(2) For a volume and file configuration, the method specified in the JIS X0605; or

(3) For character coded representation, the method specified in Annex 1 to the JIS X0208.

2. Recording of the particulars in a flexible disk pursuant to the provisions of Article 15 shall be made by using those graphic characters specified in the JIS X0201 and X0208 and the "carriage return (CR)" and the "line feed (LF)" from among those control characters specified in the JIS X0211.

Article 18

(Document to Be Pasted Up on Flexible Disk)

In a flexible disk under *Article 15*, a document stating the following particulars shall be pasted on the labeling area specified in the JIS X6221 or X6223:

(1) Name of person to submit;

and

(2) Date of submission.

ANNEXED TABLE 1 (RELATING TO ARTICLE 3)

Crude oil 1 kiloliter	1 kiloliter
Gasoline 1 kiloliter	0.91 kiloliter
Naphtha 1 kiloliter	0.86 kiloliter
Kerosene 1 kiloliter	0.96 kiloliter
Gas oil 1 kiloliter	0.99 kiloliter
Fuel oil	
(a) Fuel oil A 1 kiloliter	1.01 kiloliter
(b) Fuel oil B 1 kiloliter	1.04 kiloliter
(c) Fuel oil C 1 kiloliter	1.06 kiloliter

Petroleum gas	
(a) Liquefied petroleum gas (LPG) 1 ton	1.30 kiloliter
(b) Petroleum-based hydrocarbon gas 1 thousand cubic meters	1.02 kiloliter
Inflammable natural gas	
(a) Liquefied natural gas (natural gas liquefied with nitrogen, moisture and other impurities separated) 1 ton	1.41 kiloliter
(b) Coal mine firedamp drainage gas 1 thousand cubic meters	0.93 kiloliter
(c) Other inflammable natural gas 1 thousand cubic meters	1.06 kiloliter
Coal 1 ton	
(a) Coking (stock) coal	0.82 kiloliter
(b) Steaming (thermal) coal	0.66 kiloliter
(c) Anthracite (Kilkenny coal)	0.70 kiloliter
Coal coke 1 ton	0.78 kiloliter
Coke oven gas 1 thousand cubic meters	0.52 kiloliter
Blast furnace gas Ten thousand cubic meters	0.86 kiloliter

ANNEXED TABLE 2 (RELATING TO ARTICLE 12)

1. Computers with single computing element only

Theoretical performance of such computing element

2. Computers with two or more computing elements all of which operate individually

Largest of the theoretical performance values of such computing elements

3. Computers with two or more computing elements all of which operate simultaneously and which share the same memory device (excluding those falling under Paragraph 4)

Sum total of the largest of the theoretical performance values of such computing elements plus all the numerical values obtainedby multiplying the theoretical performance of other computing elements by 0.75

4. Computers with two or more computing elements all of which operate simultaneously, which share the same memory device and which meet all of the requirements described hereunder:

A. Composite theoretical performance calculated in 3 does not exceed 194mega-operations per second;

B. Theoretical performance of individual computing elements or a group of computing elementsdoes not exceed 30 mega-operations per second;

C. Individual computing elements or groups of computing elements are connected with one singlechannel to the memory device;

D. Computing elements or computing element groups which are allowed to use one single channel simultaneously are one in number.

Sum total of the largest of the theoretical performance values of such computing elements plus the numerical values obtained bymultiplying the theoretical performance of each one of other computing elements by 0.75, and divided by the square root of the number of computing elements orcomputing element groups sharing the same memory device with one single channel

5. Computers with two or more computing elements all of which operate simultaneously and which do not share the same memory device

Sum total of the largest of the theoretical performance values of such computing elements plus all the numerical values obtainedby multiplying the theoretical performance of other computing elements by any of the appropriate coefficients given hereunder:

A. For the 2nd through the 32nd computing elements when arranged in descending order oftheoretical performance of computing elements:

(1) 0.75 when the sum total of the maximum data speeds of all the channels with which the saidcomputing elements are connected (expressed in terms of megabytes per second; to be referred simply as the "maximum dataspeed" in Paragraph 5) is 20 megabytes or more per second;

- *Numerical value obtained by dividing the sum total of the maximum data speedsby 20 and multiplying the result by 0.75 when the sum total of the maximum data speeds is less than 20 megabytes per second;providing that the said coefficient shall be 0.75 in the case of computing elements whose composite theoretical performance exceeds 50mega-operations per second and which fall under the 2nd to the 12th;*

B. For the 33rd through the 64th computing elements when arranged indescending order of theoretical performance:

- *0.6 when the sum total of the maximum data speeds is 20 megabytes or more persecond;*
- *Numerical value obtained by dividing the sum total of the maximum data speedsby 20 and multiplying the result by 0.6 when the sum total of the maximum data speeds is less than 20 megabytes persecond;*

C. For the 65th through the 256th computing elements when arranged in descending order oftheoretical performance:

- *0.45 when the sum total of the maximum data speeds is 20 megabytes or moreper second;*
- *Numerical value obtained by dividing the sum total of the maximum data speedsby 20 and multiplying the result by 0.45 when the sum totalof the maximum data speeds is less than 20 megabytes per second;*

D. For the computing elements from the256th upward when arranged in descending order of theoretical performance:

- *0.3 when the sum total of the maximum data speeds is 20 megabytes or more persecond;*
- *Numerical value obtained by dividing the sum total ofthe maximum data speeds by 20 and multiplying the result by 0.3 when the sum total of the maximum data speeds is less than 20 megabytesper second;*

6. Computers both with two or more computing elements all of which operate simultaneously andwhich share the same memory device and with two or more computing elements or groups of computing elements which do not share the samememory device

Numerical values obtained through the following calculation procedure:

A. Obtain the theoretical performance of two or more computing elements all of which operatesimultaneously and which share the same memory device in accordance with Paragraph 3 or 4;

B. Sum total of the largest of the theoretical performance values of such computing elements whichdo not share the theoretical performance or memory device obtained in the above A plus all the numerical values obtained by multiplyingthe theoretical performance of other computing elements by any of the appropriate coefficients given hereunder:

(1) For the 2nd through the 32nd computing elements when arranged in descending order oftheoretical performance of computing elements or computing element groups:

1. 0.75 when the sum total of the maximum data speeds of all the channels with which the saidcomputing elements or computing element groups are connected (expressed in terms of megabytes per second; to be referred simply asthe "maximum data speed" in Paragraph 6) is 20 megabytes or more per second;

2. Numerical value obtained by dividing the sum total of the maximum data speeds by 20 andmultiplying the result by 0.75 when the sum total of the maximum data speeds is less than 20 megabytes per second; providing thatthe said coefficient shall be 0.75 in the case of computing elements or computing element groups whose composite theoretical performanceexceeds 50 mega-operations per second and which fall under the 2nd to the 12th;

(2) For the 33rd through the 64th computing elements when arranged in descending order oftheoretical performance of computing elements or computing element groups:

1. 0.6 when the sum total of the maximum data speeds is 20 megabytes or more persecond;

2. Numerical value obtained by dividing the sum total of the maximum data speeds by 20 andmultiplying the result by 0.6 when the sum total of the maximum data speeds is less than 20 megabytes persecond;

(3) For the 65th through the 256th computing elements when arranged in descending order oftheoretical performance of computing elements or computing element groups:

1. 0.45 when the sum total of the maximum data speeds is 20 megabytes or more persecond;

2. Numerical value obtained by dividing the sum total of the maximum data speeds by 20 andmultiplying the result by 0.45 when the sum total of the maximum data speeds is less than 20 megabytes persecond;

(4) For the computing elements from the 256th upward when arranged in descending order oftheoretical performance of computing elements or computing element groups:

1. 0.3 when the sum total of the maximum data speeds is 20 megabytes or more persecond;

2. Numerical value obtained by dividingthe sum total of the maximum data speeds by 20 and multiplying the result by 0.3 when the sum total of the maximum data speeds is lessthan 20 megabytes per second.

7. Computers with two or more computing elements (excluding those falling under any of the categories under Paragraphs 2 to 6)

Largest of the theoretical performance values of computing elements operating independently or a combination of computingelements operating simultaneously. The theoretical performance of a combination of computing elements operating simultaneously shall be the numerical valuesobtained under Paragraphs 3 through 6.

REMARKS

1. Theoretical performance shall be the largest of all the numerical values obtained by multiplying the effective computing speed calculated for the length of each operand by the correction coefficient (value obtained by dividing such operand length by 96 and adding one-third). However, the effective computing speed shall apply to computing elements which are able to perform logical operations other than one single logical\break operation.

2. Effective computing speed shall be as prescribed below. However, in the case of computing elements capable of performing the same arithmetic operation twice or more in one single cycle, the execution time (shortest of the time required for each operation as expressed in terms of seconds; to be so understood) shall be the numerical value obtained by dividing one single cycle time by the frequency of operations per cycle.

A. For the computing elements performing fixed-point arithmetic operations only, the following values apply:

(1) In the case of the elements capable of executing addition instruction, the inverse number of the numerical value obtained by multiplying the addition instruction execution time by 3;

(2) In the case of the elements not capable of executing addition instruction, the inverse number of the multiplication instruction execution time;

(3) In the case of the elements not capable of executing addition and multiplication instructions, the inverse number of the shortest of the arithmetic operation execution time.

B. For the computing elements performing floating-point arithmetic operations only, the following values apply:

(1) In the case of the elements capable of executing addition instruction but not capable of executing multiplication instruction, the inverse number of the addition instruction execution time;

(2) In the case of the elements capable of executing multiplication instruction but not capable of executing addition instruction, the inverse number of the multiplication instruction execution time;

(3) In the case of the elements capable of executing addition and multiplication instructions, the inverse number of the addition instruction execution time or the inverse number of the multiplication instruction execution time, whichever is larger;

(4) In the case of the elements not capable of executing both addition and multiplication instructions but capable of executing division instruction, the inverse number of the division instruction execution time;

(5) In the case of the elements not capable of executing addition, multiplication and division instructions but capable of executing inverse number arithmetic operation instruction, the inverse number of the inverse number arithmetic operation instruction execution time;

(6) In the case of the elements not capable of executing addition, multiplication, division and reverse number arithmetic operation instructions, zero.

C. For the computing elements performing fixed-point and floating-point arithmetic operations, the numerical values calculated by the method specified in (A) shall apply to the portion relating to fixed-point arithmetic and those calculated by the method specified in (B) shall apply to the portion relating to floating-point arithmetic.

D. For the computing elements not capable of performing arithmetic operation but capable of performing logical operation as one single logical operation, the following values apply:

(1) In the case of the elements capable of performing exclusive-OR operation, the inverse number of the numerical value obtained by multiplying the exclusive-OR operation execution time by 3;

(2) In the case of the elements not capable of performing exclusive-OR operation, the inverse number of the numerical value obtained by multiplying the shortest of the logical operation execution time by 3.

E. For the computing elements capable of performing logical operations other than one single logical operation, the applicable value shall be the numerical value obtained by multiplying the maximum frequency of operations executable in one second by the number of bits for performing such logical operations and by dividing the result by 64.

ANNEXED TABLE 3 (RELATING TO ARTICLE 13)

1. Air conditioners (excluding those air conditioners under Paragraph 3(13) of Annexed Table 1 to the Enforcement Ordinance for the Household Goods Quality Labeling Law)

1. For cooling energy consumption efficiency,the numerical value obtained by dividing the numerical valueexpressed in watts of cooling capacity measured by the method specified in cooling capacity tests of the-JIS B8616 or C9612 by the numerical value expressed in watts of cooling power consumption measured by themethod specified in cooling power consumption tests of the JIS B8616 or C9612.2. For heating energyconsumption efficiency, the numerical value obtained by dividing the numerical value expressed inwatts of heating capacity measured by the methodspecified in heat pump standard heating capacity tests of the JIS B8616 or in standard heatingcapacity tests of the JIS C9612 by the numerical value expressed in watts of heating powerconsumption measured by the method specified in heat pump standard heating capacity tests of the JISB8616 or in standard heating capacity tests of the JIS C9612.

2. Lighting fixtures which use only fluorescent lamps astheir main light source (excluding fluorescent desk lamps under Paragraph 3(25) of Annexed Table 1 to the Enforcement Ordinance for theHousehold Goods Quality Labeling Law)

The numerical value obtained by dividing the numerical valueexpressed in lumen of total luminous fluxmeasured by such a method as is specified by the Minister of International Trade and Industry in accordance with the method specifiedin the JIS C7601 by the numerical value expressed in watts of power consumption measuredby the method specified in input tests of the JIS C8105.

3. Copying machines

The numerical value expressed in watt-hours of hourly power consumption measured by the method-specified by the Minister of International Trade and Industry.

4. Electronic computers

The numerical value expressed in watts of power consumption measured by the method specified by the Minister of International Trade and Industry.

5. Magnetic disk memory devices

The numerical value obtained by dividing the numerical value expressed in watts of power consumptionmeasured by the method specified by the Minister of International Trade and Industry by the numerical value expressed megabytes ofstorage capacity.

6. Videotape recorders

The numerical value expressed in watts of power consumption measured by the method specified by the Minister of International Trade and Industry.

SUPPLEMENTARY PROVISIONS

1. This Ministerial Ordinance shall come into force on the enforcement date (October 1, 1979).

2. The Enforcement Ordinance for the Heat Management Law (Ministry of International Trade and Industry Ordinance No. 60 of 1951) shall be abrogated.

3. For the purposes of applying the provisions of Article 5, Item (1), to those factories which may have been designated, in accordance with the provisions of Article 6, Paragraph 1, of the Law, as the factories where the rationalization of electric energy uses should be particularly needed during a period from the enforce date of the Law until August 31, 1980, "within six (6) months of the day that reasons for the appointment of energy managers have arisen" under the said item shall read "no later than February 28, 1981."

SUPPLEMENTARY PROVISIONS

This Ministerial Ordinance shall come into force on the date of promulgation and apply as from February 21, 1984. In this case, "Article 4, Item (2)" in the revised provisions of Article 9, Paragraph 2, shall read "Article 5, Item (2)" for the period from February 21, 1984 through March 8 the same year."

SUPPLEMENTARY PROVISIONS

This Ministerial Ordinance shall come into force on the enforcement date of the Part of the Law Concerning the Improvement of Related Laws for the Advancement of the Energy Supply and Demand Structure (August 1, 1993).

SUPPLEMENTARY PROVISIONS

This Ministerial Ordinance shall come into force on the date of promulgation.

SUPPLEMENTARY PROVISIONS

This Ministerial Ordinance shall come into force on February 26, 1997. However, with regard to reports to be submitted no later than the end of May 1997, "reasons for failure, if any, to improve the energy consumption rate by 1% or more on the yearly average" in Form 4 Schedules 5 and 7 and Form 5 Schedule 5 shall read "reasons for a decrease in the energy consumption rate over the year, if any."

SUPPLEMENTARY PROVISIONS

This Ministerial Ordinance shall come into force on April 1, 1999.

Act on the Promotion of the Development, Use and Dissemination of New and Renewable Energy

Wholly Amended by Act No. 5446, Dec. 13, 1997   Amended by Act No. 6672, Mar. 25, 2002

Article 1 (Purpose)

The purpose of this Act is to contribute to the sound development of national economy and the promotion of national welfare by diversifying energy resources through promoting the technological development and use or dissemination of new and renewable energy, and reducing the discharge of gases harmful to human bodies or environments by activating the new and renewable energy industry. *<Amended by Act No. 6672, Mar. 25, 2002>*

Article 2 (Definition)

The definition of terms used in this Act shall be as follows:

1. The term "new and renewable energy" means other energy resources than petroleum, coal, atomic energy, or natural gas, which fall under one of the following subparagraphs:

(a) Solar energy;

(b) Biomass;

(c) Wind energy;

(d) Small hydro power;

(e) Fuel cell;

(f) Energy from liquefied or gasified coal, and from gasified heavy residue;

(g) Ocean energy;

(h) Waste;

(i) Geothermal energy;

(j) Hydrogen; and

(k) Other sources of energy prescribed by the Presidential Decree;

2. The term "heavy residue" means such final residuals after a refining of crude oil, as the vacuum residue and asphalt generated from a vacuum distillation process and the cokes, tar, pitch, etc. generated from the process of thermal cracking;

3. The term "new and renewable energy facilities" means the facilities producing or utilizing the new and renewable energy, which are determined by the Ordinance of the Ministry of Commerce, Industry and Energy;

4. The term "certification" means verifying that the new and renewable energy facilities satisfy the international or domestic performance and standard;

5. The term "new and renewable energy power generation" means the generation of electricity by utilizing the new and renewable energy; and

6. The term "operator of new and renewable energy power generation business" means a business operator to carry on the new and renewable energy power generation business, who is an operator of the electric generation business under subparagraph 4 of Article 2 of the Electric Utility Act, or an installer of the electric installations for private use under subparagraph 17 of the same Article and same paragraph.

[This Article Wholly Amended by Act No. 6672, Mar. 25, 2002]

Article 3 (Policy and Encouragement, etc.)

The Government shall devise a policy for the promotion of the technological development and use or dissemination of new and renewable energy, and encourage, protect and foster the voluntary technological development, use and dissemination of new and renewable energy by local governments, government-invested institutions under the Framework Act on the Management of Government-Invested Institutions (hereinafter referred to as "government-invested institutions"), public agencies, or enterprises, etc.

Article 4 (Basic Plan on Technological Development and Use or Dissemination of New and Renewable Energy)

(1) The Minister of Commerce, Industry and Energy shall establish a basic plan for the promotion of technological development, use and dissemination of new and renewable energy (hereinafter referred to as the "basic plan") through deliberation of the New and Renewable Energy policy Council referred to in Article 7. *<Amended by Act No. 6672, Mar. 25, 2002>*

(2) The basic plan shall have a duration of ten years or more, and include the following matters: *<Amended by Act No. 6672, Mar. 25, 2002>*

1. Objective and duration of the basic plan;

2. Objective of the technological development, use and dissemination of new and renewable energy by resource;

2-2. Objective of the ratio occupied by the quantity of new and renewable energy power generation in the gross quantity of power generation;

3. Method of promoting the basic plan;

4. Assessment of technological level, prospect of dissemination, and prospective effect of new and renewable energy;

5. Support schemes on the technological development, use and dissemination of new and renewable energy; and

6. Other matters deemed necessary by the Minister of Commerce, Industry and Energy for the achievement of objectives of the basic plan.

(3) The Minister of Commerce, Industry and Energy may modify the basic plan, if deemed necessary in light of technological development trends in new and renewable energy, changes in the supply and demand of energy, or other circumstances. *<Amended by Act No. 6672, Mar. 25, 2002>*

Article 5 (Yearly Execution Program)

(1) The Minister of Commerce, Industry and Energy shall, in order to achieve objectives specified in the basic plan, devise and perform an execution program on the technological development, use and dissemination of new and renewable energy for each year (hereinafter referred to as an "execution program"), and a power supply by the new and renewable energy power generation for each type of new and renewable energy technologies. *<Amended by Act No. 6672, Mar. 25, 2002>*

(2) Where the Minister of Commerce, Industry and Energy intends to formulate and implement an execution program, he shall consult in advance the head of related central administrative agency. *<Amended by Act No. 6672, Mar. 25, 2002>*

(3) Where the Minister of Commerce, Industry and Energy has worked out an execution program, he shall make public notice thereof. *<Amended by Act No. 6672, Mar. 25, 2002>*

Article 6 (Prior Consultations on Plans for Technological Development, etc. of New and Renewable Energy)

Where a State agency, local government, government-invested institution, public agency, or other person prescribed by the Presidential Decree intends to formulate and implement a plan for the technological development, use and dissemination of new and renewable energy, he shall in advance consult with the Minister of Commerce, Industry and Energy, under the conditions as prescribed by the Presidential Decree. *<Amended by Act No. 6672, Mar. 25, 2002>*

Article 7 (New and Renewable Energy Policy Council)

(1) For the purpose of deliberating on important matters concerning the technological development, use and dissemination of new and renewable energy, the New and Renewable Energy Policy Council (hereinafter referred to as the "Council") shall be established in the Ministry of Commerce, Industry and Energy. *<Amended by Act No. 6672, Mar. 25, 2002>*

(2) The Council shall deliberate on the following matters: *<Amended by Act No. 6672, Mar. 25, 2002>*

1. Matters on the formulation and alteration of the basic plan: *Provided*, That any alteration in the matters as prescribed in the Presidential Decree, from among the details of the basic plan, shall be excluded;

2. Important matters concerning the technological development, use and dissemination of new and renewable energy;

2-2. Matters on the standard price for electricity supplied by the new and renewable energy power generation, and its alterations; and

3. Other matters deemed necessary by the Minister of Commerce, Industry and Energy.

(3) The composition and operation of the Council and other necessary matters shall be prescribed by the Presidential Decree.

Article 8 (Creation of Project Expenses for Technological Development, Use and Dissemination of New and Renewable Energy)

The Government shall appropriate in its expenditure budget for each fiscal year the project expenses needed to implement an execution program.

Article 9 (Use of Created Project Expenses)

The Minister of Commerce, Industry and Energy shall use the project expenses created pursuant to Article 8 for the projects falling under any of the following subparagraphs: *<Amended by Act No. 6672, Mar. 25, 2002>*

1. Survey of resources of new and renewable energy, and demand for its technology, and compilation of statistics thereon;

2. Research and development of new and renewable energy;

3. Technological assessment and post-management of new and renewable energy;

4. Collection, analysis, and provision of technological information on new and renewable energy;

5. Guidance, education, and publicity of technology related to new and renewable energy;

6. Use and dissemination of new and renewable energy, and model project;

7. International cooperation related to new and renewable energy; and

8. Other projects necessary for the technological development, use and dissemination of new and renewable energy, which are prescribed by the Presidential Decree.

Article 10 (Execution of Projects)

(1) The Minister of Commerce, Industry and Energy may, where he deems it necessary for efficiently promoting the projects under subparagraphs of Article 9, enter into an agreement with a person falling under any of the following subparagraphs, and have him undertake such projects: *<Amended by Act No. 6672, Mar. 25, 2002>*

1. Specific research institutions under the Support of Specific Research Institutions Act;

2. Research institutes attached to the enterprises under the Technology Development Promotion Act;

3. Industrial technology research cooperatives under the Act on the Support of the Industrial Technology Research Cooperatives;

4. Universities or junior colleges under the Higher Education Act;

5. State or public research institutions;

6. State agencies, local governments, government-invested institutions, and public agencies; or

7. Other persons recognized by the Minister of Commerce, Industry and Energy as competent to perform technological developments.

(2) The Minister of Commerce, Industry and Energy may contribute all or part of the expenses required for technological development, or projects for use and dissemination under paragraph (1). *<Amended by Act No. 6672, Mar. 25, 2002>*

(3) Matters necessary for the payment, use and management of the contribution under paragraph (2) shall be prescribed by the Presidential Decree.

Article 11 (Investment Recommendation and Making Liable for Use of New and Renewable Energy, etc.)

(1) Where the Minister of Commerce, Industry and Energy deems it necessary to promote the technological development, use and dissemination of new and renewable energy, he may recommend a person carrying on the energy-related industry to operate the business under each subparagraph of Article 9, or invest therein or contribute thereto. *<Amended by Act No. 6672, Mar. 25, 2002>*

(2) Where the Minister of Commerce, Industry and Energy deems it necessary for promoting the use

and dissemination of new and renewable energy, he may make persons use the new and renewable energy obligatorily with regard to the structures newly built by a State agency, a local government, a government-invested institution, and other persons as prescribed by the Presidential Decree under the conditions as prescribed by the Presidential Decree. *<Amended by Act No. 6672, Mar. 25, 2002>*

(3) The Minister of Commerce, Industry and Energy may recommend the factory, business place, or collective housing complex, etc., for which it is adequate to use new and renewable energy, to use new and renewable energy as designated by him, or to install the facilities to use it. *<Amended by Act No. 6672, Mar. 25, 2002>*

Article 11-2 (Certification, etc. of New and Renewable Energy Facilities)

(1) Any person who intends to manufacture or import and sell the new and renewable energy facilities may obtain a certification for the new and renewable energy facilities from an agency as determined by the Minister or Commerce, Industry and Energy (hereinafter referred to as the "certification institute").

(2) Any person who intends to obtain a certification for the new and renewable energy facilities under paragraph (1) shall file an application for a certification for the relevant new and renewable energy facilities with the certification institute.

(3) When any person applies for a certification under paragraph (2), he shall undergo a performance test and inspection performed by the performance examination agency as determined by the Minister of Commerce, Industry and Energy (hereinafter referred to as the "performance examination agency"), and submit to the certification institute a record of test results and a written inspection results issued by the performance examination agency.

(4) The Minister of Commerce, Industry and Energy shall designate, as the certification institute, the center for new and renewable energy development and dissemination under Article 16, and a person deemed to be adequate for an certification, from among other persons carrying on the promotional business of technical development, use and dissemination of new and renewable energy.

(5) The certification institute shall, upon receipt of an application for certification for the new and renewable energy facilities under paragraph (2), examine it pursuant to the criteria for certification examination as determined by the Ordinance of the Ministry of Commerce, Industry and Energy based upon a record of test results and a written inspection results issued by the performance examination agency, and thereafter, shall grant a certification to the new and renewable energy facilities satisfying the relevant criteria.

(6) The scope of duties, certification procedures, post management of certification of the certification institute, the designation procedures for the performance examination agency, and other matters necessary for certification shall be prescribed by the Ordinance of the Ministry of Commerce, Industry and Energy.

[This Article Newly Inserted by Act No. 6672, Mar. 25, 2002]

Article 11-3 (Indication, etc. of Certification of New and Renewable Energy Facilities)

(1) Any person who has obtained a certification for new and renewable energy facilities under Article 11-2 may either indicate a certification on the relevant new and renewable energy facilities, or give publicity to a receipt of certification.

(2) Any person who has failed to obtain a certification for new and renewable energy facilities shall not make an indication of certification under paragraph (1) or any indication similar thereto, or give any publicity to the effect as if he has received a certification.

[This Article Newly Inserted by Act No. 6672, Mar. 25, 2002]

Article 11-4 (Cancellation of Designation as Certification Institute or Performance Examination Agency)

(1) The certification institute shall, when any person has obtained a certification by falsity and other illegal means, cancel such certification, and if it has discovered that any new and renewable energy facilities, which have been manufactured, or imported and sold after obtaining a certification, failed to satisfy the certification examination criteria under Article 11-2 (5), it may cancel such certification.

(2) The Minister of Commerce, Industry and Energy may, when the performance examination agency falls under any of the following subparagraphs, either cancel such designation under the conditions as prescribed by the Presidential Decree, or order to suspend the whole or part of business, with fixing a period not exceeding one year: *Provided*, That when falling under subparagraph 1, he shall cancel such designation:

1. When having obtained the designation by falsity and other illegal means;
2. When having failed to commence the inspection business for not less than one year from the date of obtaining the designation without any justifiable reasons, or suspended the inspection business for not less than one consecutive year; or
3. When coming not to satisfy the designation criteria.

(3) The Minister of Commerce, Industry and Energy shall hold a hearing when he intends to cancel the designation of a performance examination agency under paragraph (2).

[This Article Newly Inserted by Act No. 6672, Mar. 25, 2002]

Article 11-5 (Fees)

The certification institute or the performance examination agency may charge a fee to a person who applies for a certification or performance examination.

[This Article Newly Inserted by Act No. 6672, Mar. 25, 2002]

Article 11-6 (Public Notification of Price for New and Renewable Energy Power Generation and Support for Differences)

(1) The Minister of Commerce, Industry and Energy shall notify publicly the standard price by source of power generation which is supplied by the new and renewable energy power generation.

(2) The Minister of Commerce, Industry and Energy shall, where the power trade price for the electricity supplied by the new and renewable energy power generation (referring to the power trade price under Article 33 of the Electric Utility Act) is lower than the standard price notified publicly under paragraph (1), make a preferential support from the Electrical Industry Foundation Fund under Article 48 of the Electric Utility Act for the difference between the standard price and the power trade prices, to the new and renewable energy power generation businessman who has supplied the relevant electricity.

[This Article Newly Inserted by Act No. 6672, Mar. 25, 2002]

Article 11-7 (Application for Ruling)

A new and renewable energy power generation businessman may apply for a ruling to the Electrical Affairs Commission under Article 53 of the Electric Utility Act in case where a consultation with an operator of the electric transmission business under subparagraph 6 of Article 2 of the same Act or an operator of the electric distribution business under subparagraph 8 of the same Article is not achieved or is impossible, in supplying the electricity generated by new and renewable energy power generation through the facilities of transmission or distribution to the Korea Power Exchange under Article 35 of the same Act or the electricity users.

[This Article Newly Inserted by Act No. 6672, Mar. 25, 2002]

Article 12 (Sale, etc. of State or Public Property)

(1) The State or a local government may, where deemed necessary for the projects related to the technological development, use and dissemination of new and renewable energy, sell or lease, under a private contract, the State or public property to the person operating the project related to the technological development and use or dissemination of new and renewable energy, notwithstanding the provisions of the State Properties Act or the Local Finance Act.

(2) When the person who has purchased or leased the land from the State or a local government under paragraph (1) fails to carry out the project for technological development and use or dissemination of new and renewable energy within two years from the date of such purchase or lease, the State or local government may repurchase it or revoke the lease contract.

Article 13 (Model Project)

The Minister of Commerce, Industry and Energy may, where deemed necessary for promoting the use or dissemination of new and renewable energy for which a technology has been developed, operate a model project such as a model supply project, a model housing complex creation project, etc., under the conditions as prescribed by the Presidential Decree. <*Amended by Act No. 6672, Mar. 25, 2002*>

Article 14 (Financial Measures, etc.)

Where it is deemed appropriate, the Government shall take necessary measures, such as financial or tax support, to a person who is recommended pursuant to Article 11 or has to comply with liabilities, a person conducting the technological development and use or dissemination of new and renewable energy, or a person who has obtained an certification for new and renewable energy facilities under Article 11-2. <*Amended by Act No. 6672, Mar. 25, 2002*>

Article 15 (Education and Publicity on New and Renewable Energy)

The Government shall endeavor to seek the understanding and cooperation from the people with regard to the technological development, use and dissemination of new and renewable energy, through education and publicity.

Article 16 (Center for New and Renewable Energy Development and Dissemination)

(1) The Minister of Commerce, Industry and Energy may establish the center for new and renewable energy development and dissemination (hereinafter referred to as the "center") in the institute as prescribed by the Presidential Decree in order to professionally and efficiently promote the technical development, use and dissemination of new and renewable energy, and have it perform the projects falling under each of the following subparagraphs:

1. Support and management of the executors of the technological development, use and dissemination of new and renewable energy under Article 10 (1);

2. Support and management of the model project of new and renewable energy under Article 13;

3. Education and publicity of new and renewable energy under Article 15;

4. Projects for foreign and domestic investigation and research and international cooperation for new and renewable energy; and

5. Other projects required for the promotion of technological development, use and dissemination of new and renewable energy, which are entrusted by the Minister of Commerce, Industry and Energy.

(2) The Minister of Commerce, Industry and Energy may render the fund contribution and other necessary supports in the execution of projects under paragraph (1) by the center.

(3) Matters concerning the organization, manpower, budget and operation of the center shall be determined by the Ordinance of the Ministry of Commerce, Industry and Energy.

[This Article Wholly Amended by Act No. 6672, Mar. 25, 2002]

Article 17 (Delegation of Authority)

Part of the authority of the Minister of Commerce, Industry and Energy under this Act may be delegated to the Special Metropolitan City Mayor, Metropolitan City Mayor, or *Do* governor, under the conditions as prescribed by the Presidential Decree. <*Amended by Act No. 6672, Mar. 25, 2002*>

Article 18 (Legal Fiction as Public Official in Applying Penal Provisions)

Any officers or employees of the certification institute and performance examination agency engaged in the duties of certification and performance examination shall be deemed to be public officials in applying Articles 129 through 132 of the Criminal Act.

[This Article Newly Inserted by Act No. 6672, Mar. 25, 2002]

Article 19 (Fine for Negligence)

(1) Any person falling under any of the following subparagraphs shall be punished by the fine for negligence not exceeding 10 million won:

1. A person who has obtained an certification by falsity and other illegal means; and

2. A person who has made an indication of certification or that similar thereto or a publicity as if he obtained a certification, without obtaining any certification from the certification institute in violation of Article 11-3 (2).

(2) Fine for negligence under paragraph (1) shall be imposed and collected by the Minister of Commerce, Industry and Energy under the conditions as prescribed by the Presidential Decree.

(3) Any person who is dissatisfied with a disposition of fine for negligence under paragraph (2) may raise an objection to the Minister of Commerce, Industry and Energy within 30 days from the date of receiving a notice of such disposition.

(4) Where any person subjected to a disposition of a fine for negligence pursuant to paragraph (2) makes objections pursuant to paragraph (3) the Minister of Commerce, Industry and Energy shall notify the competent court thereof without delay, and the court in receipt of such a notice shall bring the case to trial under the Non-Contentious Case Litigation Procedure Act.

(5) If neither an objection is raised nor is a fine for negligence paid within the period as prescribed in paragraph (3), it shall be collected by referring to the practices of dispositions on default of national taxes.

[This Article Newly Inserted by Act No. 6672, Mar. 25, 2002]

ADDENDA

(1) (Enforcement Date) This Act shall enter into force six months after the date of its promulgation.

(2) (Transitional Measures concerning Policy Deliberation Commission on Technological Development of New and Renewable Energy) The Policy Deliberation Commission on the Technological Development of New and Renewable Energy pursuant to the previous provisions at the time this Act enters into force shall be considered as the Council referred to in this Act.

(3) Omitted.

ADDENDUM ***<Act No. 6672, Mar. 25, 2002>***

This Act shall enter into force six months after the date of its promulgation.

Energy Efficiency Building Code for Commercial Buildings in Sri Lanka

Final Draft Prepared for Ceylon Electricity Board

Prepared by Lawrence Berkeley National Laboratory, Berkeley, California, USA, and Dessau Soprin, Montreal Quebec, Canada
September 2000

ACKNOWLEDGEMENTS

This *Energy Efficiency Building Code for Commercial Buildings in Sri Lanka* was developed with the support of the World Bank. The project was initiated by Prof. Nimal de Silva, Chairman Urban Development Authority and P. A. M. Deraniyagala, Chairman Ceylon Electricity Board, to whom a debt of gratitude is owed for their guidance. The project was managed by the CEB Demand Side Management Branch: M. S. Jayalath (Deputy General Manager), K. K. U. B. Adikaram (Project Manager) and D. G. K. Ranasinghe. The Project Consultants were Econoler International (Canada), Lawrence Berkeley National Laboratory (USA), and Infotechs I/D/E/A/S (Sri Lanka), with Louis-Philippe Lavoie as Team Leader. The Steering Committee members were D. C. Wijeratne (Chair), Prof. Lal Balasooriya, M. Zubair, W. J. L. S. Fernando, Prasanna Silva, M. S. Jayalath & B. B. Perera. Substantial expert guidance and assistance was provided by professionals who served as Technical Subcommittee members: *Ventilation and Air Conditioning*: Wijitha Perera, C. L. E. Koelmeyer, J. O. Yatawara; *Lighting*: Sharmila Dhanapala, S. Ranasinghe, Noel Joseph; *Electric Power and Distribution*: Ranil Seneratna, D. B. Yatawara, D. G. R. Fernando; *Building Envelope*: Dr. Samitha Manawadu; Jaliya Kumarasinghe, Arch. Mahinda Withanaarachchi & Arch. Harsha Fernando *Service Water Heating*: K. D. C. E. Wickramaratne, Lakshman Jayasuriya, Parakrama Jayasinghe. The following individuals from LBNL performed technical analysis and authored the code: John Busch, Steve Greenberg, Francis Rubinstein, Andrea Denver, Esther Rawner, Ellen Franconi, Joe Huang, and Danielle Neils. Logistical support was provided by Irani Oluka Mayadunne and B. K. D. S. Samarasinghe.

1. INTRODUCTION

1.1 Purpose

1.1.1 To encourage energy efficient design or retrofit of commercial buildings so that they may be constructed, operated, and maintained in a manner that reduces the use of energy without constraining the building function, the comfort, health, or the productivity of the occupants and with appropriate regard for economic considerations.

1.1.2 To provide criterion and minimum standards for energy efficiency in the design or retrofit of commercial buildings and provide methods for determining compliance with them.

1.1.3 To encourage energy efficient designs that exceed these criterion and minimum standards.

1.2 Scope

1.2.1 This energy efficiency building code (EEBC) sets forth the requirements for design or retrofit of commercial buildings used primarily for human occupancy.

1.2.2 The requirements pertain to commercial buildings such as offices, hotels, shopping complexes, hospitals, and others that are not primarily for residential or industrial use.

1.2.3 This EEBC covers the following building elements: exterior envelope, systems for ventilation and air-conditioning, electric power and distribution, lighting, and service water heating.

1.2.4 All commercial buildings meeting ANY of the following criteria must meet the requirements of this EEBC:

(a) Four stories or higher

(b) Floor area of 2,000 m^2 or greater

(c) Building enclosed volume of 5,600 m^3 or greater

(d) Electrical peak demand of 125 kVA or greater

(e) Air-conditioning cooling capacity of 350 kW (output)

1.2.5 Residential and industrial buildings are exempted.

1.2.6 This EEBC covers only the energy performance aspects of the building and not other aspects such as health and safety. This in no way replaces other requirements of building design, construction, or occupancy that may apply. All other codes and regulations pertaining to buildings are still in effect.

1.2.7 This EEBC assumes professional expertise in building design and construction for the covered areas and systems. It is not intended as a design manual on energy efficient design practice.

2. LIGHTING

2.1 General Principles of Energy Efficient Lighting Practice

Lighting is one of the single largest consumers of energy (kilowatt-hours) in a building. A number of lighting technologies are available that can significantly reduce the amount of energy needed for lighting. In addition to consuming energy, the lighting load can also have an impact on the cooling load as lighting generates heat. The effect of added lighting load on a building's cooling requirements is particularly significant for warm climates.

This code will limit the maximum allowable lighting load for the building lighting system as well as place lower limits on the acceptable efficiencies of commonly used lighting components (lamps and ballasts). An energy efficient light system can provide a flexible, effective, and pleasing visual environment for a space and, at the same time, minimize energy consumption.

2.2 Scope

2.2.1 Spaces Covered. The rooms, spaces and areas covered by this section include:

(a) Interior spaces of buildings

(b) Building exterior areas including facade lighting, entrances, exits, loading docks, etc.

(c) Roads, grounds and other exterior areas including open-air covered areas where lighting is installed and is powered by the building electrical service.

2.2.2 Spaces Exempted. The following rooms, spaces, areas and equipment exempted from this section include:

(a) Commercial greenhouses

(b) Lighting power for theatrical productions, television broadcasting, those portions of entertainment facilities such as stage areas in hotel ballrooms, night-clubs, discos and casinos where lighting is an essential technical element of the function performed.

(c) Specialized luminaire for medical and dental purposes.

(d) Outdoor athletic facilities

(e) Exterior lighting of public monuments

(f) Special lighting needs of research laboratories.

(g) Lighting used solely for indoor plant growth during the hours of 10:00 PM and 6:00 am

(h) Emergency lighting that is automatically OFF during normal operation

(i) High-risk security areas identified by local ordinances or regulation or by security or safety personnel requiring additional lighting.

2.2.3 Light Source Selection. The use of incandescent or tungsten halogen lamps for general lighting should be discouraged. General lighting should ordinarily be provided with fluorescent lamps. Although incandescent and tungsten halogen light sources are often the least expensive to install, they are energy inefficient and are usually less cost effective than efficient sources such as fluorescent lighting. Incandescent lamps use more energy to supply a given light level than fluorescent or high

Table 2-1: Recommended illuminance levels and glare indices

	Illuminance (Lux)[a]			
	Recommended	Low	High	Limiting glare index[b]
HOTELS				
Bathrooms	150	100	200	
Bed rooms, general	75	50	100	
Bed rooms, reading	300	200	500	
Corridors, elevators and stairs	150	100	200	
Front desk	500	300	750	
Lobby, reading and working area	300	200	500	
Lobby, general lighting	150	100	200	
OFFICES				
Accounting	300	200	500	19
Audio visual areas	300	200	500	19
Conference areas	300	200	500	16
General and private offices	300	200	500	19
Libraries	300	200	500	19
Lobbies, lounges and reception areas	150	100	200	19
Off-set printing and duplicating area	300	200	500	19
HOSPITALS				
Consulting areas, general	300	200	500	
Consulting areas, examination	500	300	750	
Corridors, general	150	100	200	
Ward corridors, day	200	150	300	
Ward corridors, night		5	10	
Laboratories, general	300	200	500	
Laboratories, examination	500	300	750	
Nurses stations	300	200	500	
Ward bed head		30	50	
Ward bed head, reading	150	100	200	
Surgeries, general	300	200	500	
Surgeries, waiting rooms	150	100	200	
BANKS				
Lobby, general	150	100	200	19
Lobby, writing area	300	200	500	19
Tellers' stations	500	300	750	19
SHOPS & STORES				
Conventional with counters	300	200	500	19
Conventional with wall display	300	200	500	19
Self service	300	200	500	19
Supermarkets	500	300	750	22

[a] The recommended values are for "average" age workers (age 30–70) performing important tasks. The low value is appropriate for younger workers performing non-critical tasks. The high value should be used for older workers or workers more than 30 years old performing critical tasks.

[b] See Chartered Institution for Building Services Engineers (CIBSE) Code for Interior Lighting, London, Great Britain, 1994. for definition of glare index.

intensity discharge (HID) sources. Furthermore, they must be replaced much more frequently. Consequently, the life cycle cost of fluorescent and HID sources is usually lower than that of incandescent lamps even though the initial installed costs may be higher. This is especially true of commercial buildings which typically have long lighting operation hours (compared to residences).

Use compact fluorescent lamps in "downlights" in ceilings under 4 meters. For "high bay" applications (ceilings over 4 meters), use high pressure sodium or metal halide lamps.

2.2.4 General and Task Lighting Considerations. It is energy wasteful to provide the maximum required light level everywhere throughout a facility. The middle illuminance level, for a given task, in Table 2-1 below will provide adequate lighting for most of the people and tasks. Where a person or task requires a higher light level, task lighting should be

Table 2-2: Minimum lamp efficacy linear fluorescent lamps (0.6 to 1.2 meters)

Lamp length (mm)	Lamp power (watts)	Diameter (mm)	Minimum lamp efficacy (lumens/Watt)
600	18	26	55
1200	36	26	66
1500	58	26	66

provided. Fluorescent lighting is an ideal and efficacious source for general lighting in commercial buildings. Task lighting can be provided by CFL, halogen, and incandescent sources. Table 2-1 provides recommendations for the illuminance levels in different portions of a building.

2.3 Recommended Illuminance Levels.

2.3.1 Lighting needs in most buildings vary according to specific space type. For example, low light levels are acceptable for corridors while higher light levels should be used for desk locations. The following table is a list of recommended illuminance levels for different building and space types. This table should be used as guidance for designing lighting systems in commercial buildings.

2.4 Lighting Equipment Efficiency Levels

2.4.1 Fluorescent. Use the most efficient lamp that is cost-effective for the application. Table of fluorescent lamps minimum efficacies (lumens/W). The lamp efficacy shall not be below the values indicated in Table 2-2 for linear fluorescent lamps and in Table 2-3 & 2-4 for compact fluorescent lamps. Note that the lamp efficacy is the efficacy of the lamp alone. It does not include the ballast losses. It is found by dividing the lamp's rated light output (in lumens) by the rated lamp power (watts). For the system LPD limits (which include both lamp and ballast) see section 2.5.

Table 2-3: Minimum lamp efficacy integral-type compact fluorescent lamps

Lamp power (watts)	Minimum lamp efficacy (lumens/Watt)
9	42
11	52
15	57
20	57
23	62

Table 2-4: Minimum lamp efficacy modular-type compact fluorescent lamps

Lamp power (Watts)	Minimum lamp efficacy (lumens/Watt)	Ballast loss (Watts)
7	54	6
10	57	6
11	78	5
13	66	5
18	63	7

2.4.1.1 Fluorescent ballast loss maxima. For linear fluorescent lamp ballasts, the ballast losses shall not exceed the values given in Table 2-5.

2.4.2 Incandescent. The lamp efficacy for incandescent lamps should not be below the efficacies listed in Table 2-6.

2.4.3 High Intensity Discharge. The lamp efficacy for High Intensity Discharge lamps (e.g. sodium, metal halide, mercury) should not be below the efficacies listed in Table 2-7, and the ballast losses for HID lamps should not exceed the values in Table 2-7.

2.4.4 Fluorescent Luminaire. Where fixture manufacturer information is available, use the most efficient fixtures appropriate to the application. The efficiency of a lighting fixture is given by its Light Output Ratio (L.O.R.) which is defined as the ratio

Table 2-5: Maximum allowed ballast loss for linear fluorescent lamps

Ballast type	Maximum allowed ballast loss (W)
Electromagnetic	
For 18 W single-lamp	8
For 36 W single-lamp	8
Electronic	
For 18 W single-lamp	4
For 18 W two-lamp	6
For 36 W single-lamp	4
For 36 W two-lamp	7

Table 2-6: Incandescent lamp – minimum lamp efficacy

Lamp power (watts)	Minimum lamp efficacy (lumens/Watt)
40	10.6
60	12.0
75	12.7
100	13.6

Table 2-7: HID lamp – minimum lamp efficacy and maximum allowed ballast loss

Lamp power (Watts)	Minimum lamp efficacy (lumens/Watt)	Maximum allowed ballast loss (Watts)
50	57	10
70	64	15
100	53	15
150	76	20
175	70	22
250	74	26
320	67	28
400	68	30
1000	104	60
1500	98	85

of the lumens from the luminaire divided by the sum of the individual lumen values of the lamps inside the luminaire. For most fixtures used in commercial buildings, this information is available from the fixture manufacturer.

For general-purpose fluorescent lighting systems, use fixtures that have an L.O.R. of at least 0.50. Exceptions to this would be a space with critical glare control needs (high-end graphics workstation, for example).

2.4.5 Emergency and Exit Lighting. Exit sign luminaire operating at greater than 20 Watts shall have a minimum source efficacy of 35 lumens per Watt. Where possible, LEDs should be used in exit signs.

Emergency lighting includes all of egress lighting, illuminated exit signs, and all other lights specified as necessary to provide the required illumination. Emergency lights systems shall be so designed and installed that failure of any individual lighting element, such as the burning out of a light bulb, cannot leave any space that requires emergency illumination in total darkness. Switches installed in emergency lighting circuits shall be so arranged that only authorized persons will have control of emergency lighting.

Table 2-8: Maximum allowed lighting power density

Building Type	Maximum allowed lighting power limits (Watts/m^2)
General Commercial Building	13
Commercial Storage Building	9
Medical Buildings and Clinics	16
Office Building	16
Hotels/Motels	
Guest rooms and corridors	17
Public, banquet, and exhibit areas	20
Food Service	16
Shops	22
Schools	19
All Others	9

Table 2-9: Maximum allowed lighting power for building exteriors

Application	Maximum allowed power limits (W/linear m)
Building entrance (with canopy)	
Low Traffic (hospital, office, school)	32.4 (of canopied area)
High Traffic (retail, hotel, airport, theater)	64.8 (of canopied area)
Building entrance (without canopy)	98.4 (of door width)
Building Exit	65.6 (of door width)
Loading	
Loading Area	3.0 (W/m^2)
Loading Door	50.0 (of door width)

2.5 Maximum Allowable Power for Illumination Systems

The lighting power density (LPD) for building lighting systems shall not exceed the values given in Table 2-8. LPD is calculated by dividing the total connected load for all lighting systems in the building by the gross lighted floor area of the building. For building types not listed in Table 2-8, selection of a reasonable equivalent is permitted.

2.6 Building Exterior Lighting Power

2.6.1 Building exterior and grounds lighting power densities. The connected lighting power shall not exceed the power limits specified in Tables 2-9

Table 2-10: Maximum allowed lighting power for roads/grounds

Application	Maximum Allowed Power Limits (W/m^2)
Storage and work area	2.0
Areas for casual use (picnic grounds, gardens, parks, landscaped areas)	1.0
Driveways,/walkways	
Private	1.0
Public	1.5
Parking Lots	
Private	1.2
Public	1.8

Table 2-11: Power credits for certain types of lighting controls

Type of Control	Type of Space	Factor
Occupant sensor (with separate sensor for each space)	Any space < or = 23 m^2 enclosed by ceiling to floor partitions: any size classroom, corridor, conference or waiting room	0.20
	Rooms of any size that are used exclusively for storage	0.60
	Rooms > 23 m^2	0.10
Automatic time switch control device	Room < or = 23 m^2 and with a timed manual override at each switch location and controlling only the lights in the area enclosed by ceiling-height partitions	0.05

and 2-10 for each of the listed building exterior applications. Trade-offs between applications are not permitted.

2.7 Lighting Controls

2.7.1 Area Controls. The simplest way to improve lighting efficiency is to turn off lights when they are not in use. All lighting systems must have switching or control capabilities to allow lights to be turned off when they are not needed.

(a) All spaces enclosed by walls or ceiling height partitions shall be provided with one manually operated on/off lighting control (switch) for each space. Each space must have its own switching; gang switching of several spaces is not permitted.

(b) The total number of switches shall not be less than one switch per 1000 Watts controlled load.

(c) All manually operated switching devices must be located so that personnel can see the controlled area when operating the switch(es). In public areas, such as lobbies, concourses, etc., the switches may be located in areas accessible to authorized personnel only.

2.7.2 Exceptions. Continuously illuminated areas within a building, for reasons of security or emergency egress, are exempt from the switching requirements as long as the maximum lighting power density used for this purpose does not exceed 0.05 watts per square meter.

2.7.3 Exterior Lighting. Exterior lighting shall be automatically controlled by a photosensor or timer.

2.7.4 Daylighted Area Control. Electric lighting in enclosed areas greater than 23 square meters that are "daylit areas[1]", must be switched so that the lighting in these areas can be controlled separately from the non-daylit areas. It is acceptable to achieve control of the daylit area by shutting off at least 50% of the lamps within the daylit area. This must be done by a control dedicated to serving only luminaires in the daylit area.

Separate control of daylit areas is not required when there is not enough daylight to be used effectively (e.g., if a window is so obstructed by adjacent structures, trees, or other natural objects that the effective use of daylighting is not feasible).

2.7.5 Lighting Controls Credits. To encourage the use of lighting controls beyond the mandatory switching requirements of Section 2.6.1, the connected lighting power within a building may be adjusted to take credit for the benefits of certain types of automatic lighting controls. The lighting control credit is a multiplier that reduces the amount of energy used for lighting, giving a lower adjusted lighting power. In order to qualify for a lighting power density reduction, the control device must control all of the fixtures for which the credit is claimed. At least 50% of the light output of the controlled luminaire must fall within the applicable type of space listed in Table 2-9. The list of the type of lighting controls that qualify for these credits is shown in Table 2-9.

The lighting control credits listed in Tables 2-11 and 2-12 have the effect of reducing the actual lighting power for those portions of the building where the credit applies by the amount listed in the tables. The credits therefore make it easier to meet the allowed lighting power requirement.

[1] "Daylit Area" is the space on the floor that is daylit by vertical glazing. The daylit area has a length of 1.5 meters, or the distance on the floor, perpendicular to the glazing, to the nearest 0.5 meters or higher opaque partition, whichever is less; and the width of the window plus 0.2 meters on each side or the distance to an opaque partition, whichever is least.

Table 2-12: Power credits for automatic daylighting controls

	Stepped dimming controls			Continuous dimming controls		
Glazing Properties	WWR < 20%	WWR 20% to 40%	WWR > 40%	WWR < 20%	WWR 20% to 40%	WWR > 40%
VLT ≥ 60%	0.20	0.30	0.40	0.30	0.40	0.40
VLT ≥ 35 and < 60%	0	0.20	0.30	0	0.30	0.40
VLT < 35%	0	0	0.20	0	0	0.40

In order to qualify for power savings adjustment, the control system or device must control all of the fixtures in the areas for which the credit is claimed. At least 50% of the light output of the controlled luminaire must fall within the applicable space listed in the table. Credits may not be combined.

2.7.6 Hotel and motel guest rooms shall have a master switch at the door that turns off all permanently wired lighting fixtures except for security lighting, if required.

2.8 Submission Procedure

2.8.1 The Engineer or Architect responsible for the lighting installation shall provide a complete set of plans to the Building Owner showing the installed lighting devices and including the following information.

(a) The design standard service illuminance.

(b) The number of each type of lighting device

(c) The total wattage of each type of lighting device, including nominal rating and control losses.

(d) The installed lighting load for interior and exterior.

3. VENTILATION AND AIR CONDITIONING

3.1 Load Calculations

3.1.1 Calculation Procedures. Cooling system design loads for the purpose of sizing systems and equipment shall be determined in accordance with the procedures described in the latest edition of the ASHRAE Handbook or other equivalent publications.

3.1.2 Indoor Design Conditions. The indoor conditions of an air-conditioned space shall be designed for a dry bulb temperature of 24°C ± 1°C and relative humidity of 55% ± 5%. Further energy savings could be achieved by raising the dry bulb temperature limit during operation without compromising occupant comfort.

3.1.3 Outdoor Design Conditions. Dry bulb temperature of 32°C and wet bulb temperature of 27°C.

3.1.4 Ventilation and Exhaust. Outdoor air ventilation rates shall comply with ASHRAE Standard 62, 1999 (ANSI/ASHRAE 62-1999, Ventilation for Acceptable Indoor Air Quality). Outdoor air quantities may exceed those shown in Standard 62 if required because of special occupancy or process requirements or source control of air contamination.

3.2 System and Equipment Sizing

3.2.1 AC systems and equipment shall be sized to provide no more than the space and system loads calculated in accordance with sub-section 3.1 above, consistent with available equipment capacity.

3.2.2 Where chillers are used and when the design load is greater than 700 kW, the equipment shall have a minimum of two separate refrigerant circuits to meet the required load.

3.2.3 Multiple units of the same equipment type, such as multiple chillers, with combined capacities exceeding the design load may be specified to operate concurrently only if controls are provided that sequence or otherwise optimally control the operation of each unit based on load.

3.2.4 Capacity of any individual unit shall not be less than 20kW (output), excepting backup units for specified areas.

3.3 Fan System Design Criteria

3.3.1 General. The following design criteria apply to all AC fan systems used for comfort ventilating and/or air conditioning. For the purposes of this sub-section, the energy demand of a fan system is the sum of the demand of all fans that are required to operate at design conditions to supply air from the cooling source to the conditioned space(s) and return it back to the source or exhaust it to the outdoors.

3.3.2 EXCEPTIONS. Systems with total fan system nameplate motor power of 4 kW or less.

3.3.3 Constant Volume Fan Systems. For fan systems that provide a constant air volume whenever the fans are operating, there shall be at least 590 L/s of supply air volume per kW of total input power required by the motors for the combined fan system at design conditions.

3.3.4 Variable Air Volume (VAV) Fan Systems. For fan systems that are able to vary system air volume automatically as a function of load, there shall be at least 420 L/s of supply air volume per kW of total input power required by the motors for the combined fan system at design conditions.

3.4 Pumping System Design Criteria

3.4.1 General. The following design criteria apply to all pumping systems used for comfort air conditioning. For the purposes of this sub-section, the energy demand of a pumping system is the sum of the demand of all pumps that are required to operate at design conditions to supply fluid from the cooling source to the conditioned space(s) or heat transfer device(s) and return it back to the source.

3.4.2 Friction Rate. Piping systems shall be designed at friction pressure loss rate of no more than 2 metre of water per 100 equivalent metre of pipe, subject to the velocity in the system pipe lines not exceeding 2.5 m/s. Lower friction rates may be required for proper noise or corrosion control.

3.4.3 Sizing, Selection, and System Design. The following aspects of pumping systems should be designed to minimize life-cycle system costs. Pipe size, components, and layout should be optimized to reduce system pressure drops, thus reducing the pump and motor sizes required. Once the operating flow and pressure are established, the pump should be carefully selected for maximum efficiency, and not less than 70%. The flow rate should never exceed 110% of design flow. Once the pump shaft power requirement is determined, the motor with the highest efficiency at the design load should be selected that meets or exceeds the values in Table 5-3 Minimum Motor Efficiencies. The motor horsepower rating should not exceed 125% of the calculated maximum load being served. If a standard rated motor is not available within the range, the next largest standard motor size may be used. It is recommended that pump speeds be less than 1500 rpm. Variable-speed pumps should be considered for variable-flow systems, especially for large systems. Variable-flow chilled water systems should also be evaluated (either variable flow through the chiller, as allowed by many manufacturers; or primary-secondary pumping systems with constant chiller flow and variable building system flow).

3.4.4 Variable Flow. Pumping systems that serve control valves designed to modulate or step open and closed as a function of load, shall be designed for variable fluid flow. Flow may be varied using variable-speed driven pumps, staged multiple pumps, or pumps riding their characteristic curves.

3.4.5 EXCEPTIONS:

(a) Systems where a minimum flow greater than 50% of the design flow is required for the proper operation of equipment served by the system, such as some chillers.

(b) Systems that serve no more than one control valve.

3.5 Separate Air Distribution Systems

3.5.1 Zones with Non-Simultaneous Operation. Zones that are expected to operate non-simultaneously for more than 300 hours per year shall be served by separate air distribution systems. As an alternative, off-hour controls shall be provided in accordance with Section 3.7.3.

3.5.2 Zones with Special Process Requirements. Zones with special process temperature and/or humidity requirements shall be served by separate air distribution systems from those serving zones requiring only comfort cooling, or shall include supplementary provisions so that the primary systems may be specifically controlled for comfort purposes only.

3.5.3 EXCEPTIONS. Zones requiring comfort cooling only, which are served by a system primarily used for process temperature and humidity control, need not be served by a separate system if the total supply air to these zones is no more than 25% of the total system supply air, or the total conditioned floor area of the zones is less than 100 m^2.

Table 3-1: Piping insulation

Piping system type	Fluid temp range (°C)	Insulation thickness for nominal pipe sizes (mm): Runouts up to 50 mm	25 mm and less	32 mm to 50 mm	63 mm & above
Chilled water	4.5–13	13	13	25	38
Refrigerant or brine	Below 4.5	25	25	38	50

Notes: 1. The insulation thickness is based on insulation having thermal resistance in the range of 28 to 32 m^2 K/W per metre of thickness on a flat surface at a mean temperature of 24°C. See 4.8.2 and 4.8.3 for insulation materials with thermal resistance outside this range.
2. These thicknesses are based on energy efficiency considerations only. Issues such as water vapor permeability or surface condensation may require vapor retarders or additional insulation.

3.5.4 Zones with Different Load Characteristics. Separate air distribution systems should be considered for areas of the building having substantially different cooling characteristics, such as perimeter zones in contrast to interior zones.

3.6 Temperature Controls

3.6.1 System Control. Each AC system shall include at least one temperature control.

3.6.2 Zone Controls. The supply of cooling energy to each zone shall be controlled by individual thermostatic controls responding to temperature within the zone.

3.6.3 Thermostats. Zone controls should be set no lower than indoor design conditions (24°C). Temperature sensors shall be located in the zone or the return air path.

3.7 Off-Hour Controls

3.7.1 Equipment Shutdown During Non-Use. AC systems shall be equipped with automatic controls capable of accomplishing a reduction of energy use through equipment shutdown, or increase in the temperature set point, during periods of non-use or alternative use of the spaces served by the system.

3.7.2 EXCEPTIONS:

(a) Systems serving areas that are expected to operate continuously.

(b) Equipment with a connected load of 2 kW or less may be controlled by readily accessible manual off-hour controls.

3.7.3 Outside Air Control During Non-Use. Outdoor air supply and exhaust systems shall be provided with motorized or gravity dampers or other means of automatic volume shutoff or reduction during periods of non-use of alternative use of the spaces served by the system.

3.7.4 EXCEPTIONS:

(a) Systems serving areas that are expected to operate continuously.

(b) Systems that have a design air flow of 500 L/s or less.

(c) Gravity and other non-electrical ventilation systems may be controlled by readily accessible manual damper controls.

(d) Where restricted by process requirements such as combustion-air intakes.

3.7.5 Zones with Non-Simultaneous Operation. Systems that serve zones that can be expected to operate non-simultaneously for more than 300 hours per year shall include isolation devices and controls to shut off the supply of cooling to each zone independently. For central systems and plants, controls and devices shall be provided to allow stable system and equipment operation for any length of time while serving only the smallest isolation area served by the system or plant. Isolation is not required for zones expected to operate continuously. For buildings where occupancy patterns are not known at the time of the system design, such as speculative buildings, isolation areas may be predesigned. Zones may be grouped into a single isolation area provided the total conditioned floor area does not exceed 250 m^2 per group nor include more than one floor.

3.8 Piping Insulation

3.8.1 Chilled Water Piping. All AC system chilled water piping shall be thermally insulated in accordance with Table 3-1 not only to reduce heat gain from the outside, but also to avoid condensation on

Table 3-2: Minimum duct seal level

	Duct type			
	Supply			
Duct location	< 500 Pa[a]	≥ 500 Pa[a]	Exhaust	Return
Outside conditioned space	1	1	none	1
Unconditioned spaces	2	1	none	3
Indirectly conditioned spaces[b]	3	2	3	None
Cooled spaces	None	3[c]	3[c]	None

[a] Duct design static pressure classification. Unless otherwise shown in design documents, ductwork between the supply fan and variable air volume boxes shall be considered 500 Pa pressure classification, while all other ductwork of any application shall be considered 250 Pa pressure classification.
[b] Includes return-air plenums.
[c] Ducts within the conditioned space to which they supply air or from which they exhaust air need not be sealed.

Seal Levels:

1. All joints, longitudinal seams, and at all duct wall penetrations. Pressure-sensitive tape shall not be used as the primary sealant.
2. All joints and longitudinal seams. Pressure-sensitive tape shall not be used as the primary sealant.
3. Transverse joints only.

Definitions: Longitudinal seams are joints oriented in the direction of airflow. *Transverse joints* are connections of two duct sections oriented perpendicular to airflow. *Duct wall penetrations* are openings made by any screw or fastener. Spiral lock joints in round and flat oval duct need not be sealed. All other connections are considered joints, including but not limited to spin-ins, lateral taps and other branch connections, access door frames and jambs, duct connections to equipment, etc.

the surface of the installation. The insulation shall be suitably protected from damage. Reference is to be made to the insulation manufacturer's catalogue.

3.8.2 EXCEPTIONS. Piping insulation shall not be required in any of the following areas:

(a) Piping that conveys fluids that have a design temperature above 20°C. Note that if the indoor design conditions are exceeded, insulation may be required on higher temperature piping to prevent condensation.

(b) Piping that conveys fluids that have not been heated or cooled through the use of fossil fuels or electricity.

3.8.3 Chilled Water Piping. For material with thermal resistance greater than 32 m^2 K/W per metre of thickness, the minimum insulation thickness, t (mm), is given by:

$$t = \frac{28 \times \text{thickness in Table 3-1}}{\text{Actual R value}}$$

3.8.4 Chilled Water Piping. For material with thermal resistance less than 28 m^2 K/W per metre of thickness, the minimum insulation thickness, t (mm), is given by:

$$t = \frac{32 \times \text{thickness in Table 3-1}}{\text{Actual R value}}$$

3.9 Air Handling System Insulation

3.9.1 AC System Ducts and Plenums. All air-handling ducts and plenums installed as part of an AC air distribution system shall be thermally insulated.

3.9.2 EXCEPTIONS. Duct insulation is not required in any of the following cases:

(a) Factory installed plenums, casings, or ductwork furnished as a part of AC equipment, provided that they are either insulated at the factory or installed in a conditioned space.

(b) Exhaust air ducts.

(c) Outdoor air ducts.

(d) Return air ducts within conditioned space.

3.9.3 Thermal Resistance Requirement. The minimum thermal resistance, R (m^{2}K/W), of the

Table 3-3: AC equipment standard rating conditions (°C)

Fluid	Water-cooled water chillers	Air-cooled water chillers	Water-cooled unitary AC	Air-cooled unitary AC	Cooling towers
Leaving chilled water	6.7	6.7	N/A	N/A	N/A
Entering chilled water	12.2	12.2	N/A	N/A	N/A
Leaving cooling water	35.0	N/A	35.0	N/A	31.0
Entering cooling water	29.4	N/A	29.4	N/A	36.5
Condenser air inlet	N/A	35.0	N/A	35.0	N/A
Evaporator air inlet	N/A	N/A	27 DB/19.5 WB	27 DB/19.5 WB	N/A
Cooling tower air inlet	N/A	N/A	N/A	N/A	27.0 WB

insulation, excluding film resistance shall be:

$$R = \frac{\Delta T}{47.3}$$

where ΔT = design temperature differential between the air in the duct and the surrounding air in K

3.10 Air Handling System Ducts

3.10.1 Ductwork and plenums shall be sealed in accordance with Table 3-2 and with standard industry practice as defined in SMACNA 1995 (Sheet Metal and Air Conditioning Contractors' National Association, HVAC Duct Construction Standards – Metal & Flexible, 1995).

3.11 AC Equipment

3.11.1 Minimum Equipment Performance. Equipment shall meet or exceed the minimum performance shown in Table 3-4 when tested at the standard rating conditions shown in Table 3-3. Note that except for the cooling towers, the rating conditions are those used internationally (for ease of comparison) rather than being typical of Sri Lanka conditions. VAC designers should determine equipment load profiles and obtain applied part-load values (APLVs) from the manufacturers to better estimate the actual energy use of the equipment as it will be used. With the load and APLV information, designers should then select equipment based on minimizing life-cycle cost of the system.

3.11.2 Excessive compressor cycling at part-load conditions shall not be controlled by either hot gas bypass or other evaporator pressure regulator control systems unless the system is designed with multiple steps of unloading. The capacity of the hot gas bypass shall be limited to not more than 50% of the total capacity in systems up to 70 kW of rated capacity, and to not more than 25% of the total capacity in systems over 70 kW of rated capacity.

3.11.3 Water-to-water heat recovery systems (double-bundle chillers) should be used for water heating only after carrying out an energy balance, cost-benefit analysis and life-cycle costing. Such systems to produce hot water at temperatures exceeding 42°C are discouraged.

3.11.4 Designers are encouraged to consider cooling towers with 2-speed or variable-speed fans, which are often very cost-effective.

3.12 Testing, Adjusting, Balancing and Commissioning

3.12.1 Air system balancing shall be accomplished in a manner to minimise throttling losses and then fan speed shall be adjusted to meet design flow conditions.

Table 3-4: Minimum efficiencies for AC equipment

Equipment type	Size	Minimum COP[a] (full load)
Air-cooled chiller	All	2.8
Reciprocating water-cooled chiller	All	4.2
Centrifugal water-cooled chiller	All	5.4
Rotary screw/scroll water-cooled chiller	All	4.4
Unitary air-cooled air conditioners	All	2.4
Unitary water-cooled air conditioners	All	4.0
Cooling towers	All	3.5 L/s/kW[b]

[a] Coefficient of Performance = refrigeration output/ power input (dimensionless)
[b] Maximum flow rate of cooling tower at rating conditions in Table 3-3 divided by motor nameplate output power.

3.12.2 Hydronic system balancing shall be accomplished in a manner to minimise throttling losses and then the pump impeller shall be trimmed or pump speed shall be adjusted to meet design flow conditions.

3.12.3 AC control systems shall be tested to assure that control elements are calibrated, adjusted, and in proper working condition.

3.12.4 Systems larger than 350 kW of cooling shall be commissioned in accordance with the procedures in ASHRAE Guideline1-1996, The HVAC Commissioning Process.

3.13 Water Treatment

3.13.1 The make-up water for systems larger than 350 kW of cooling shall be analyzed by a recognized authority to determine the chemical characteristics of the water. This procedure shall be repeated once within every 365 days from the date of the commissioning of the plant to verify whether the chemical characteristics have changed.

3.13.2 Appropriate water treatment equipment shall be specified and installed to minimize the possibility of corrosion to the water cooling circuits, scale formation, and biological growth as well as the presence of suspended solids and sludge formation. The reduction in the quantity of water to be bled from the water circuit shall also be addressed with the intent to reduce water usage and pumping energy costs.

3.13.3 Water treatment may be in the form of automatically dosing chemicals, magnetic de-scalers, filtration equipment, ozone dosing, or a combination of these methods.

3.13.4 Water treatment shall be in accordance with procedures detailed in ASHRAE 1995 HVAC Applications Handbook, Chapter 44 (Corrosion Control and Water Treatment), or other equivalent publications.

3.14 Maintenance

(a) An operating and maintenance manual shall be provided to the owner. The manual shall include basic data relating to the operation and maintenance of AC systems and equipment, including but not limited to original copies of manufacturers' O & M manuals for all pieces of equipment. Required routine maintenance actions shall be clearly identified. Where applicable, AC controls information such as diagrams, schematics, control sequence descriptions, and maintenance and calibration information shall be included.

(b) The owner should implement a preventive maintenance program and schedule periodic maintenance on all the critical items of the air-conditioning system such as compressors, cooling towers, pumps, condensers, air handlers, controls, filters, and piping.

3.15 Submission Procedure

3.15.1 Plans provided to the Building Owner by a Chartered Engineer with adequate experience in the field of refrigeration and air-conditioning or a Full Member of ASHRAE shall contain the following:

(a) The cooling capacity in kW of each air-handling unit and air-conditioning plant.

(b) The capacity in L/s of each fan.

(c) The location and capacity of each fresh air intake.

(d) Supply, exhaust and return duct work distinctly coloured for clarity.

(e) A summary of the air-conditioning load calculations and equipment performance figures.

4. BUILDING ENVELOPE

4.1 General Principles of Energy Efficient Envelope Design

Solar heat gain through building envelope constitutes a substantial share of the cooling load in a building that will have to be eventually removed by the air-conditioning system at the expense of energy and utility bills. To minimize solar heat gain into a building is, therefore, a primary consideration in the design of energy-efficient buildings in Sri Lanka. Among the architectural techniques for achieving this are siting and orientation of rectangular buildings to avoid exposure of long axis to east and west, use of light colored exterior wall and roof surfaces, appropriate shading of fenestration, and employing moderate glass window areas. Opaque wall sections and roofs should incorporate thermal insulation materials to minimize heat gains. Air leakage through the building envelope into or from conditioned space should be minimized.

4.2 System Performance Criteria for Exterior Walls

4.2.1 The total Overall Thermal Transfer Value (OTTV) for the exterior walls of a building shall not exceed 90 W/m^2. OTTV is a system performance criterion that allows trade-offs among opaque wall and window areas and their thermal and solar characteristics to achieve an overall minimum performance. OTTV is calculated for each individual façade and then for the building taking the weighted average of the individual façade OTTVs.

4.2.2 OTTV for an individual façade is calculated using following formula:

$$OTTV_i = TD_{EQ}\forall(1 - WWR)U_W + \Delta T(WWR)U_F + SF(WWR)SC\ CF \quad (4\text{-}1)$$

Where the terms are defined as:

- $OTTV_i$ = overall thermal transmittance value for the ith specific wall orientation and construction combination, (W/m^2)
- TD_{EQ} = equivalent indoor-outdoor temperature difference through the opaque wall section, (19.3°C)
- $\forall$ = solar absorptance of the exterior opaque wall (dimensionless)
- WWR = window-to-wall ratio, using the gross wall area in the denominator, (dimensionless).
- U_W = thermal transmittance of opaque wall section, ($W/m^{2\circ}C$)
- T = temperature difference through the window section, (3.6°C)
- U_F = thermal transmittance of window section, ($W/m^{2\circ}C$)
- SF = solar factor, defined as the average hourly value of solar energy incident on vertical windows, (186 W/m^2)
- SC = shading coefficient of the fenestration system as given in Section 4.3, (dimensionless)
- CF = solar correction factor for the orientation of the fenestration as given in Table 4-1, dimensionless

Table 4-1: Solar correction factors (CF) (dimensionless)

South	North	East	West	SE	NE	SW	NW
0.95	0.79	1.34	0.90	1.15	1.07	0.93	0.85

Replacing the constants suitable for Sri Lanka into Equation 4-1 above,

$$OTTV_i = 19.3\forall(1 - WWR)U_W + 3.6\ WWR\ U_F + 186\ WWR\ SC\ CF \quad (4\text{-}2)$$

4.2.3 The OTTV for the total exterior gross wall area of the building is a weighted average of the $OTTV_i$'s computed for the individual façades. For a building with N individual façades, OTTV shall be determined by:

$$OTTV = \frac{(A_1\ OTTV_1 + A_2\ OTTV_2 + \cdots + A_N\ OTTV_N)}{(A_1 + A_2 + \cdots + A_N)} \quad (4\text{-}3)$$

4.3 Shading Coefficient

4.3.1 Shading coefficient is defined as the ratio of the solar heat gain through the fenestration system under consideration to the solar heat gain through an unshaded clear 3mm thick glass. The fenestration system is defined as the combination of glazing and any external shading devices affixed to the building.

$$SC = \frac{\text{solar heat gain of fenestration system}}{\text{solar heat gain of unshaded clear 3mm glass}} \quad (4\text{-}4)$$

In general, the SC of the fenestration system is the product of the SC of the glass and the SC of the

Table 4-2: Shading coefficient (SC) for horizontal overhang projections

	Orientation							
R1	South	North	East	West	SE	NE	SW	NW
0.2	0.69	0.77	0.80	0.76	0.75	0.79	0.72	0.76
0.4	0.53	0.68	0.68	0.59	0.61	0.68	0.56	0.64
0.6	0.45	0.63	0.58	0.50	0.52	0.61	0.47	0.56
0.8	0.39	0.59	0.50	0.43	0.45	0.54	0.41	0.51
1.0	0.37	0.56	0.43	0.40	0.40	0.50	0.38	0.48
1.2	0.36	0.54	0.39	0.37	0.37	0.46	0.36	0.46
1.4	0.35	0.53	0.35	0.36	0.35	0.44	0.35	0.44
1.6	0.34	0.52	0.32	0.35	0.33	0.42	0.34	0.43
1.8	0.33	0.51	0.29	0.34	0.31	0.40	0.34	0.42
2.0	0.33	0.50	0.27	0.33	0.30	0.38	0.33	0.42

Table 4-3: Shading coefficient (SC) for vertical side-fin projections

	Orientation							
R2	South	North	East	West	SE	NE	SW	NW
0.2	0.80	0.80	0.87	0.84	0.83	0.83	0.82	0.82
0.4	0.75	0.75	0.83	0.79	0.79	0.79	0.77	0.77
0.6	0.71	0.70	0.79	0.75	0.75	0.75	0.73	0.73
0.8	0.69	0.68	0.77	0.73	0.73	0.73	0.71	0.71
1.0	0.67	0.66	0.75	0.71	0.71	0.71	0.69	0.68
1.2	0.67	0.66	0.75	0.71	0.71	0.70	0.69	0.68
1.4	0.66	0.64	0.74	0.70	0.70	0.69	0.68	0.67
1.6	0.66	0.64	0.73	0.70	0.70	0.69	0.68	0.67
1.8	0.66	0.64	0.73	0.69	0.69	0.68	0.67	0.67
2.0	0.65	0.63	0.72	0.69	0.69	0.68	0.67	0.66

external shading device.

$$SC = SC_{glass}\,SC_{shade} \qquad (4\text{-}5)$$

4.3.2 SC for glass shall be based on manufacturers' recommended value at an incidence angle of 45 degrees.

4.3.3 SC for external shading projections (e.g., horizontal, vertical, eggcrate) shall be determined from Tables 4-2 through 4-4 (*or its closest approximation*), where R1 is the ratio of the horizontal projection depth to the window height and R2 is the ratio of the vertical projection depth to the window width. Any distance between the top of the window and the bottom of the horizontal projection should be added to the window height in calculating R1. Any distance between the sides of the window and the fin projections (on both sides if applicable) should be added to the window width in calculating R2.

$$R1 = \frac{\text{depth of horizontal projection}}{\text{height of window}} \qquad (4\text{-}6)$$

$$R2 = \frac{\text{depth of vertical projection}}{\text{width of window}} \qquad (4\text{-}7)$$

4.4 Roofs

4.4.1 The maximum allowable thermal transmittance (U-value in W/m^2-°C) of the roof assembly is

Table 4-4: Shading coefficient (SC) for horizontal and vertical "egg-crate" projections

		Orientation							
R1	R2	South	North	East	West	SE	NE	SW	NW
0.2	0.2	0.52	0.60	0.72	0.62	0.62	0.66	0.57	0.61
0.2	0.4	0.31	0.46	0.53	0.41	0.42	0.49	0.36	0.44
0.2	0.6	0.21	0.36	0.40	0.27	0.31	0.38	0.24	0.32
0.2	0.8	0.17	0.30	0.28	0.18	0.23	0.29	0.18	0.24
0.2	1.0	0.13	0.25	0.18	0.13	0.15	0.22	0.13	0.19
0.4	0.2	0.48	0.55	0.65	0.58	0.56	0.60	0.53	0.56
0.4	0.4	0.27	0.42	0.50	0.37	0.38	0.46	0.32	0.39
0.4	0.6	0.20	0.34	0.37	0.25	0.28	0.36	0.23	0.30
0.4	0.8	0.15	0.28	0.26	0.16	0.20	0.27	0.15	0.22
0.4	1.0	0.22	0.37	0.30	0.23	0.26	0.34	0.23	0.30
0.6	0.2	0.43	0.50	0.62	0.53	0.53	0.56	0.48	0.52
0.6	0.4	0.25	0.40	0.47	0.35	0.36	0.43	0.30	0.37
0.6	0.6	0.18	0.31	0.35	0.23	0.26	0.33	0.20	0.27
0.6	0.8	0.24	0.39	0.34	0.26	0.29	0.37	0.25	0.32
0.6	1.0	0.18	0.32	0.23	0.19	0.21	0.28	0.19	0.26
0.8	0.2	0.42	0.48	0.60	0.52	0.51	0.54	0.47	0.50
0.8	0.4	0.23	0.37	0.44	0.33	0.34	0.41	0.28	0.35
0.8	0.6	0.26	0.42	0.41	0.28	0.34	0.42	0.27	0.35
0.8	0.8	0.20	0.34	0.28	0.21	0.24	0.31	0.21	0.28
0.8	1.0	0.15	0.27	0.20	0.15	0.17	0.24	0.15	0.21
1.0	0.2	0.40	0.45	0.58	0.49	0.49	0.52	0.44	0.47
1.0	0.4	0.29	0.46	0.50	0.35	0.39	0.48	0.32	0.40
1.0	0.6	0.22	0.37	0.35	0.24	0.28	0.36	0.23	0.31
1.0	0.8	0.16	0.29	0.24	0.17	0.20	0.27	0.17	0.23
1.0	1.0	0.13	0.25	0.17	0.13	0.15	0.21	0.13	0.19
1.2	0.2	0.36	0.51	0.60	0.45	0.48	0.55	0.41	0.48
1.2	0.4	0.25	0.41	0.43	0.31	0.34	0.42	0.28	0.36
1.2	0.6	0.18	0.32	0.32	0.20	0.25	0.32	0.19	0.26
1.2	0.8	0.15	0.28	0.21	0.16	0.18	0.24	0.15	0.22
1.2	1.0	0.11	0.22	0.13	0.11	0.12	0.18	0.11	0.17

Table 4-5: Maximum U-value for roofs (W/m^2-°C)

Exterior roof surface solar absorptance (∀)	Roof assembly mass	
	≤ 100 kg/m^2	>100 kg/m^2
Light (∀ < 0.4)	0.7	1.5
Medium (0.4 < ∀ < 0.6)	0.3	0.5
Dark (∀ > 0.6)	0.2	0.3

shown in Table 4-5, which is a function of the weight of construction materials of the roof assembly in kg/m^2 and external surface color. For purposes of this document, the roof assembly includes only the horizontal elements, not the structural or vertical elements.

4.5 Air Leakage

4.5.1 The requirements of this section are limited to those building elements separating exterior ambient conditions from interior building conditioned air space.

4.5.2 The following areas of the building envelope shall be sealed, caulked, gasketed, or weather-stripped to minimize air leakage:

(a) joints around fenestration and doors

(b) junctions between walls and foundations, between walls at building corners, between walls and structural floors or roofs, and between walls and roof or wall panels

(c) openings at penetrations of utility services through roofs, walls, and floors

(d) site built fenestration and doors

(e) building assemblies used as ducts or plenums

(f) joints, seams, and penetrations of vapor retarders

(g) all other openings in the building envelope

4.5.3 Fenestration and doors shall be designed to limit air leakage such that the air infiltration rate not exceed 5.0 L/s m^2 for glazed swinging entrance doors and for revolving doors, and 2.0 L/s m^2 for all other fenestration and door products.

4.6 Submission Procedure

4.6.1 The following shall be provided to the building owner by the engineer or architect:

(a) OTTV calculations for the exterior walls and supporting data and drawings

(b) U-value calculations for the roof and supporting data and drawings

(c) Plan to minimize air leakage and supporting data

5. ELECTRIC POWER AND DISTRIBUTION

5.1 Scope

5.1.1 This section applies to all building electrical systems, except required extra low voltage systems, if wired separately.

5.1.2 The following sub-sections address only energy-efficiency issues and not other aspects of design, installation, operation, and maintenance of building electrical power and distribution systems.

5.1.3 For existing buildings at the stage of rewiring, all criteria under 5.2 should apply.

5.2 Electrical Distribution System

5.2.1 Supply connection exceeding 1000 kVA shall have built-in recording facility to record demand (kVA), energy consumption (kWh), and total power factor in permanently installed energy meter. The metering shall also display current (A in each phase and the neutral), voltage (V between phases and between each phase and neutral), and total harmonic distortion (THD of current) as a percentage of total current.

5.2.2 Supply connection not exceeding 1000 kVA but over 125 kVA shall have built-in recording facility to record demand (kVA), energy consumption (kWh), and total power factor.

5.2.3 Supply connection not exceeding 125 kVA shall have built-in recording facility to record energy consumption (kWh).

5.2.4 Check Metering. Buildings whose maximum demand is greater than 250 kVA shall have the electrical distribution system designed so that energy consumption can be check-metered. The electrical power feeders for each facility for which check-metering is required shall be subdivided in accordance with the following categories:

(a) Lighting and socket outlets.

(b) Air-conditioning systems and equipment.

(c) Other load centers with probable high energy consumption, such as kitchen, laundry, and restaurants in hotels or surgery rooms in hospitals.

5.2.5 Tenant Submetering. Multiple-Tenant Buildings shall have submetering for each tenant. Each tenant having a maximum demand of 100 kVA or more shall have provision to permit check-metering the tenant load as per 5.2.4 above. Common air-conditioning systems need not meet these tenant check-metering requirements.

5.2.6 Additional Metering. The designer and user should consider additional metering where it would be useful for analysis to improve efficiency in the end-use loads and the distribution systems serving them.

5.2.7 Power Factor Correction. All electricity supplies exceeding 100 A, 3 phase shall maintain their power factor between 0.98 lag and unity at the point of connection. Loads should have power factor correction at the point of use (capacitors on motors and lighting fixtures with ballasts; harmonic filters on non-linear loads); if necessary further correction equipment at the main switchboard should be provided to meet the overall requirement.

5.2.8 Neutral Current. Building loads should be balanced such that the fundamental component of the neutral current in any three-phase installation does not exceed 10% of the design current of the entire installation when the design current is being supplied.

5.2.9 Conductor Sizing. Every effort should be made to size electrical conductors so as to minimize life-cycle costs. Designers may use British Standard 7450 (*Method of Determination of Economic Optimization of Power Cable Size*) for guidance.

Table 5-1: 11 kV Transformer, 3-phase, oil immersed

Transformer capacity, kVA	Maximum allowable losses at full load (% load loss + no-load loss)
100	2.5
160	2.3
250	2.1
400	1.5
630	1.4
800	1.4
1000	1.2

Reference conditions: 100% of nameplate load at temperature of 75°C.

Table 5-2: 33 kV Transformer, 3-phase, oil immersed

Transformer capacity, kVA	Maximum allowable losses at full load (% load loss + no-load loss)
100	2.7
160	2.2
250	1.8
400	1.5
630	1.5
800	1.5
1000	1.2

Reference conditions: 100% of nameplate load at temperature of 75°C.

5.3 Transformers

5.3.1 All transformers that are part of the building electrical distribution system should be selected to minimise the combination of no-load, part-load, and full-load losses, without compromising the electrical system operation and reliability requirements.

5.3.2 If the total capacity of such transformers exceeds 250 kVA, a calculation of total estimated annual operating costs of the transformer losses shall be made and compared to the cost of more-efficient transformers. This calculation shall be based on estimated hours of transformer operation at projected loading conditions, and the associated transformer losses. Based on this analysis, transformer(s) with the lowest life-cycle cost shall be selected.

5.3.3 Three-phase oil-immersed transformers shall be selected based on maximum allowable losses in Table 5-1 and 5-2.

5.3.4 EXCEPTIONS:

(a) Transformers below 100 kVA and above 1000 kVA

(b) AC and DC drive transformers

(c) All rectifier transformers and transformers designed for higher harmonics

(d) Autotransformers

(e) Non-distribution transformers, such as UPS (Uninterruptible Power supply) transformers

(f) Special impedence transformers applied for special cases.

(g) Grounding or testing transformers.

Table 5-3: Minimum efficiencies for three-phase induction motors

Motor output KW	Required efficiency (%)		Recommended efficiency (%)	
	2 Pole	4 Pole	2 Pole	4 Pole
1.1	82.2	83.8	85.5	86.5
1.5	84.1	85.0	86.5	86.5
2.2	85.6	86.4	86.5	89.5
3.0	86.7	87.4	87.2	89.5
4.0	87.6	88.3	89.5	89.5
5.5	88.5	89.2	89.5	91.0
7.5	89.5	90.1	90.2	91.7
11.0	90.6	91.0	91.0	93.0
15.0	91.3	91.8	92.4	93.0
18.5	91.8	92.2	93.0	93.6
22.0	92.2	92.6	93.0	94.1
30.0	92.9	93.2	93.6	94.1
37.0	93.3	93.6	93.6	94.5
45.0	93.7	93.9	94.1	95.0
55.0	94.0	94.2	94.5	95.0
75.0	94.6	94.7	95.0	95.4

Reference Conditions: Nominal full-load efficiences per IEC 34-2 test procedure.

5.4 Electric Motors

All permanently wired electric motors that serve the building shall meet the requirements of this Section.

5.4.1 Three-phase induction motors shall have a nominal full-load motor efficiency not less than shown as "Required" in Table 5-3.

5.4.2 System designers should select motors to minimize the life-cycle cost of the motordriven system. Such analysis will often result in the use of motors of a higher efficiency than required herein. The "Recommended" efficiencies in Table 5-3 provide a suggested improved efficiency level for motor selection. Designers should perform a life-cycle cost analysis to select the proper motor.

5.4.3 Motor types and sizes not covered by Table 5-3 are not regulated as to efficiency by this section. However, designers should also use highly efficient motors for other categories not specifically covered by this standard. Such categories include smaller and larger polyphase motors, polyphase motors of 6 and 8 poles, and single-phase motors.

5.4.4 Motor nameplates shall list the minimum and the nominal full-load motor efficiencies and the full-load power factor.

5.4.5 Motor horsepower rating shall not exceed 200% of the calculated maximum load being served.

5.4.6 Motor Rewinding. Motor users should insist on proper rewinding practices for any rewound motors. If the following practices cannot be assured, the damaged motor should be replaced with a new, efficient one rather than suffer the significant efficiency penalty associated with typical rewind practices. At a minimum, the following practices (taken from "Guidelines for Maintaining Motor Efficiency During Rebuilding", Electrical Apparatus Service Association, St. Louis, MO, USA) should be followed for rewinding:

(a) Conduct a stator core loss test before and after stripping.

(b) Repair or replace defective laminations.

(c) Calibrate all test equipment and measuring devices at least annually against standards traceable to the National Standard.

(d) Measure and record winding resistance and room temperature.

(e) Measure and record no-load amps and voltage during the final test.

(f) Have a quality assurance program.

(g) Have and use, at a minimum, the following test equipment: ammeter, voltmeter, wattmeter, ohmmeter, megohmmeter, and high potential tester.

(h) Have a three-phase power supply for running motors at rated voltage.

(i) Balance the rotor.

(j) Do not heat stators above 350°C.

(k) Do not sandblast the iron core.

(l) Do not knurl, peen, or paint bearing fits.

(m) Do not use an open flame for stripping.

(n) Do not grind the laminations or file the slots.

(o) Do not increase the air gap.

(p) Do not increase the resistance of the windings.

(q) Do not make mechanical modifications without the customer's prior approval. This includes but is not limited to changing fans, types of bearings, shaft material, and seals.

(r) Do not change the winding design.

5.5 Submission Procedure

Building owners shall be provided with written information that provides basic data relating to the design, operation, and maintenance of the electrical distribution system for the building. This shall include:

(a) A single-line diagram of the building electrical system, inclusive of all the metering equipment.

(b) Floor plans showing locations of equipment, distribution gear, power factor correction equipment, and the metering equipment.

(c) Schematic diagrams of electrical control systems used for power saving (if any).

(d) Manufactures data sheets as to confirm the maximum losses allowed by the clause 5.3.3 (applicable only for consumers) & for motors by the clause 5.4.1.

6. SERVICE WATER HEATING

6.1 Scope

6.1.1 This section applies to all service water heating *systems and equipment.*

6.1.2 The following sub-sections address only energy-efficiency issues and not other aspects of design, installation, operation, and maintenance of service water heating systems.

6.2 Sizing of Systems

6.2.1 Service water heating system design loads for the purpose of sizing systems and equipment shall follow manufacturers' recommendations.

6.3 Water Heating Equipment Efficiency

6.3.1 All water heating equipment, hot water supply boilers used solely for heating potable water, pool heaters, and hot water storage tanks shall meet the criteria listing in Table 6-1.

Table 6-1: Minimum energy efficiency of water heating equipment

Equipment type	Minimum efficiency
Electric resistance water heaters	5.9 + 5.3V SL (W)
Gas storage water heaters	78% E_T
Gas instantaneous water heaters	78% E_T
Gas hot water supply boilers	77% E_T
Oil hot water supply boilers	80% E_T
Dual fuel gas/oil hot water supply boilers	80% E_T

6.3.2 Electric resistance water heaters are strongly discouraged except as backup for other SHW systems. Electric heat pump water heaters have considerably higher energy efficiency than electric resistance water heaters, particularly in Sri Lankan climate conditions.

6.3.3 Efficiency for electric resistance water heaters is given in terms of maximum Standby Loss (SL), where V is the measured volume in liters. SL is the maximum watts based on a 38.9°C temperature difference between stored water and ambient requirements.

6.3.4 Minimum efficiency for oil and gas-fired water heaters is given in terms of Thermal Efficiency (E_T), which includes thermal losses from the heater shell.

6.3.5 Where appropriate, solar water heating systems should be considered to supply all or part of service hot water demand. Solar water heaters shall have a minimum efficiency of 60% and have a minimum insulation R-value of 2.2 ((m^2- °C)/W) behind the collector plate.

6.4 Service Water Heating Piping Insulation

6.4.1 The following hot water piping shall be insulated to levels shown in Table 6-2.

Table 6-2: Minimum pipe insulation thickness (cm)

Fluid design operating temp. range (°C)	Insulation conductivity		Nominal pipe size	
	Conductivity (W/m-°C)	Mean rating temp. (°C)	<25 mm	≥ 25 mm
41	0.032–0.040	38	1.3	2.5

(a) Recirculating system piping, including the supply and return piping of a circulating tank type water heater

(b) The first 2.4 meters of outlet piping for a constant temperature nonrecirculating storage system

(c) The inlet pipe between the storage tank and a heat trap in a nonrecirculating storage system

(d) Pipes that are externally heated

6.4.2 For insulation outside the stated conductivity range, the minimum thickness (T) shall be determined with the following formula:

$$T = r[(1 + t/r)^{K/k} - 1] \qquad (6\text{-}1)$$

where

T = minimum thickness (cm)
R = actual outside radius of pipe (cm)
t = insulation thickness listed in Table 6-2 for applicable pipe size
K = conductivity of alternate material at mean 38°C mean rating temp.
k = 0.040

6.5 Service Water Heating System Controls

6.5.1 Temperature controls shall be provided to limit point-of-use water temperatures not to exceed 50°C.

6.5.2 Temperature controls shall be provided to limit the maximum temperature of water delivered to wash basin faucets in public restrooms to 43°C.

6.5.3 Systems designed to maintain usage temperatures in hot water pipes, such as recirculating hot water systems, shall be equipped with automatic time switches or other controls that can be set to switch off the usage temperature maintenance system during extended periods when hot water is not required.

6.5.4 When used to maintain storage tank water temperature, recirculating pumps shall be equipped with controls limiting operation to a period from the start of the heating cycle to a maximum of 5 minutes after the end of the heating cycle.

6.6 Heat Traps

6.6.1 Vertical pipe risers serving storage water heaters and storage tanks not having integral heat traps and serving a nonrecirculating system shall have heat traps on both the inlet and outlet piping as close as practical to the storage tank. A heat trap is a means to counteract the natural convection of heated water in a vertical pipe run. The means is either a device specifically designed for the purpose or an arrangement of tubing that forms a loop of 360 degrees or piping that from the point of connection to the water heater (inlet or outlet) includes a length of piping directed downward before connection to the vertical piping of the supply water or hot water distribution system, as applicable.

6.7 Submission Procedure

6.7.1 The Engineer responsible for the service hot water system installation shall provide a complete details to the Building Owner including the following information:

(a) Input energy consumption rate (kW/kcal)

(b) Design operating temperature range

(c) For boilers, maximum design pressure, tested pressure (Pa)

(d) Type of fuel is used

(e) Listing of equipment

(f) Storage tank capacity (liters)

(g) Maximum draw off rate (liters/sec).

Uzbekistan

Law on the Rational Use of Energy (1997)[1]

1 GENERAL PROVISIONS

ARTICLE 1 PURPOSE OF THE LAW

The present Law establishes a general legal framework to secure the conservation of national energy resources and the efficient use of energy and industrial potential.

ARTICLE 2 LEGISLATIVE ACTS ON RATIONAL ENERGY USE

Activities in the field of rational energy use are regulated by the present Law and by other legislative acts of the Republic of Uzbekistan.

Activities in the field of rational energy use in the Republic of Karakalpakstan are also regulated by legislative acts of the Republic Karakalpakstan.

ARTICLE 3 SCOPE OF THE LAW

Within the scope of the present Law are activities by legal and natural persons relating to extraction, production, refining, storage, transport, transmission, distribution and consumption (hereinafter will be referred to as production and consumption) of thermal and electric energy (hereinafter will be referred to as energy).

Legal regulation in the field of rational energy use is aimed at:

- ensuring the efficient and environmentally sound use of energy in its production and consumption;
- stimulating the development and application of energy efficient technologies, extraction and production of less expensive petroleum products, natural gas, coal and other types of natural fuel (hereinafter will be referred to as fuel);
- ensuring accuracy and uniformity of measurements, as well as accounting of energy produced and consumed in terms of both quality and quantity; and
- execution of supervision and control by the state over the efficiency of energy production and consumption, as well as over the state of energy equipment and energy supply and consumption systems.

ARTICLE 4 STANDARDIZATION

Energy efficiency characteristics shall be established for energy producing and using equipment in accordance with legislatively established procedure.

Energy efficiency characteristics shall be put in standards to indicate the efficiency of energy use in its production and consumption; also put in the relevant standards shall be energy consumption characteristics for technological processes, provision of heat and hot water supply, cooling, provision of electricity supply, lighting of buildings and works.

Observing standards, technical rules and norms concerning the efficiency of energy use shall be mandatory for all energy producers, suppliers and users.

Energy quality shall meet the requirements established by the relevant standards.

ARTICLE 5 OBJECTS AND SUBJECTS OF STANDARDIZATION

Objects of standardization as regards rational energy use are energy, equipment and products that produce energy or transform one its type into another, transport means, construction, road and agricultural machinery, lighting devices, heat supply, cooling and ventilation systems, consumer goods, as well as thermal insulation and construction materials.

[1] This unofficial English translation was prepared by the Uzbekistan Energy Centre, Tashkent, Uzbekistan.

Subjects of standardization are sets and values of energy expenditure characteristics of energy production and consumption, technological processes and services.

ARTICLE 6 STATE SUPERVISION AND CONTROL OVER OBSERVANCE OF ENERGY EFFICIENCY AND ENERGY QUALITY CHARACTERISTICS

The Uzbekistan State Centre of Standardization, Metrology and Certification at the Cabinet of Ministers (Uzgosstandart) and other responsible bodies shall be commissioned, in accordance with established procedure, with the task of xecuting the state supervision and control over the observance of energy efficiency and energy quality characteristics set by respective standards and norms.

ARTICLE 7 STANDARDIZED ENERGY CONSUMPTION CHARACTERISTICS

Standardized energy consumption characteristics for the objects listed in Article 5 of the present Law shall be established by the Government of the Republic of Uzbekistan or by other bodies duly authorized by the Government to this effect.

For Energy producing and using equipment, standardized energy consumption characteristics shall be included in its registration certificates, duty and repair maps, and exploitative documents. Standardized energy consumption characteristics for heat supply, ventilaltion and cooling of buildings and works shall be included in th relevant construction rules and standards. Standardized energy consumption characteristics are subject to revision and correction in every five years on the basis of up-to-date technological developments.

ARTICLE 8 CERTIFICATION

The following are subject to compulsory certification as regards the compliance with the relevant energy efficiency characteristics:

- energy resources;
- production of consumer goods and provision of services; and
- energy producing and using equipment and products.

The compliance of equipment produced with the requirements set by the relevant standard as regards energy efficiency requirements shall be stated by the producer by means of energy labelling.

ARTICLE 9 METROLOGY

In energy production and consumption, as well as certification, the state metrology supervision and control are mandatory.

The state metrology supervision and control over the efficiency of energy use include a complex of actions and standards that aim at ensuring the measurement uniformity in energy production and consumption.

Objects of the state metrology supervision and control in energy production and consumption are the following:

- measurement means;
- information measurement systems;
- standard composition and property samples of substances and materials;
- complexes and units for accounting energy and energy carriers;
- measurement techniques; and
- other objects that are provided for by metrology standards and rules.

The execution of the state metrology supervision and control over the observance of energy efficiency standards shall be commissioned to Uzgosstandart.

2 CORNERSTONES OF STATE REGULATION OF RATIONAL ENERGY USE

ARTICLE 10 MAIN ELEMENTS OF THE STATE POLICY IN THE FIELD OF RATIONAL ENERGY USE

Main elements of the state policy in the field of rational energy use are the following:

- implementation of national, regional and sectoral targeted programmes and projects;
- stabilization of energy production and consumption at the level necessary for the intensive development of national economy.

• optimization of energy production and consumption conditions, organization of energy accounting;

• stimulating production of energy efficient equipment and less energy intensive goods;

• putting energy efficiency characteristics in standards for energy producing and using equipment and goods;

• institution of control by the state over energy quality, energy efficiency of production and energy intensity of produce;

• introduction of energy audit of enterprises and organizations;

• rendering energy examination of products, facilities in operation and under reconstruction, also of equipment and technologies;

• establishment of energy efficiency demonstration zones for implementing high energy efficiency projects;

• stimulating the development of energy efficient and environmentally sound technologies and manufactures; and

• organization of energy production and consumption monitoring.

ARTICLE 11 POWERS OF THE GOVERNMENT OF THE REPUBLIC OF UZBEKISTAN IN IMPLEMENTING THE STATE POLICY ON RATIONAL ENERGY USE

In order to implement the state policy elements in the field of rational energy use, the Government of the Republic of Uzbekistan shall:

• develop and implement programmes and projects that are aimed at the rational use of energy;

• coordinate activities by ministries, authorities, enterprises, organizations and institutions, as well as the Government of the Republic of Karakalpakstan, regional administrations and the city administration of Tashkent in the development and implementation of energy conservation programmes and projects;

• promote the implementation of projects that are aimed at practical application of energy efficient machinery and goods, energy efficient technologies, management practices and scientific research in this field, also utilization of secondary energy resources and waste; of technologies employing the use of solar energy, wind and natural energy of watercourses (hereinafter will be referred to as renewable energy sources);

• further the development of adequate industrial base for manufacturing energy metering, accounting and control devices, as well as energy efficient and environmentally safe equipment;

• license activities in the field of energy audit and examination;

• give permission to introduce specific energy consumption regimes;

• foster the creation of a system for personnel training and skills improving in the field of rational energy use and energy equipment operation;

• inform the public about the efficiency of energy use; and

• exercise its other powers in accordance with domestic law.

ARTICLE 12 NATIONAL, REGIONAL AND SECTORAL TARGETED PROGRAMMES AND PROJECTS

National, regional and sectoral targeted programmes and projects in the field of rational energy use are compulsory in implementing the state policy towards improving energy efficiency.

Initiators of the development of national, regional and sectoral targeted programmes and projects are, respectively:

• the Government of the Republic of Uzbekistan;

• ministries and institutions; and

• the Government of the Republic of Karakalpakstan, regional administrations and the city administration of Tashkent.

National, regional and sectoral targeted programmes and projects are developed with a duration of five years or for a longer term, adopted by the Government of the Republic of Uzbekistan and are of priority in implementation. Responsibilities for their implementation shall be assumed by the Government of the Republic of Uzbekistan, ministries and institutions, and local state authorities, respectively.

ARTICLE 13 ENERGY AUDIT

Energy audits shall be carried out to assess the efficiency of energy production and consumption.

Compulsorily audited shall be all enterprises, organizations and institutions consuming energy resources in an amount of more than six thousand tons of equivalent fuel per annum or more than one thousand tons of motor fuel.

The order and terms for the audits shall be determined by the Government of the Republic of Uzbekistan.

ARTICLE 14 ENERGY EXAMINATION

Energy examination of design documents of new and revamped facilities, technologies and equipment is mandatory.

Energy examination shall be carried out according to the relevant procedure established by the Government of the Republic of Uzbekistan.

ARTICLE 15 ENERGY ACCOUNTING

The whole amount of energy produced and consumed is subject to compulsory accounting.

The order of priority and procedures of installing energy metering devices, also rules for using electricity, heat, natural gas and refined products shall be defined by the Government of the Republic of Uzbekistan.

Energy accounting shall be carried out following rules to be laid down in the relevant standards.

The responsibility for accuracy of energy accounting shall lay on management of enterprises, organizations and institutions, or on other officials in charge.

ARTICLE 16 ENERGY PRODUCTION AND CONSUMPTION MONITORING

Monitoring over the amount and breakdown of energy produced and consumed, as well as over its using in a rational way shall be organized and carried out by the State Committee for Projection and Statistics at the Cabinet of Ministers of the Republic of Uzbekistan according to the relevant procedure to be established by the Government of the Republic of Uzbekistan.

3 ECONOMIC MECHANISMS OF RATIONAL ENERGY USE

ARTICLE 17 FINANCING OF TARGETED PROGRAMMES AND PROJECTS

Financing to national, regional and sectoral targeted programmes and projects in the field of rational energy use will be provided out of economic activity revenues of the enterprises that are benefit from having implemented energy efficiency programmes and projects, also out of special non-budget funds, domestic or foreign investments, budget means and other sources, in accordance with legislatively established procedure.

ARTICLE 18 INTERSECTORAL ENERGY CONSERVATION FUND

With a view to financially support the implementation of the state policy in the field of rational energy use, the Government of the Republic of Uzbekistan shall establish a non-budget intersetoral energy conservation fund (hereinafter will be referred to as the Fund).

The sources to form the Fund can be:

- returns on financing provided and also other income resulting from financial and economic activities by the Fund;
- part of financial benefits from implementing national, regional and sectoral targeted programmes and projects in the field of rational energy use;
- voluntary contributions by natural and legal persons, including foreign ones;
- means resulting from having applied economic sanctions in cases of wasteful energy use; and
- any other form of income, if not contrary to the effective law.

ARTICLE 19 INCENTIVES TO ENERGY PRODUCERS AND USERS

In order to encourage using energy in an efficient way, the Government of the Republic of Uzbekistan will provide the following incentives to legal and natural persons:

- funding through state financing on favourable terms of national, regional and sectoral targeted programmes and projects in the field of rational energy use;

- providing funds for pursuing intersectoral R&D and manufacturing pilot series of energy efficient equipment;
- reduced customs duties and taxes levied on importing certain equipment, devices and materials whose use can increase substantially the efficiency of energy use; and other incentives within its competence.

The Government of the Republic of Uzbekistan has the right to apply reduced energy supply rates in respect of those legal and natural persons which:

- have decreased energy consumption as against the relevant rates established;
- produce competitive products whose energy intensity is lower than that set by the relevant standard;
- only use fuel as a raw material for producing consumer goods.

With the aim to shorten the recovery of investments into energy conservation technologies, for manufactures of equipment, devices thermal insulation materials and units, energy efficient consumer goods and services, as well as for those legal and natural persons that are involved in putting in practice and operation of the above, abated taxation established in accordance with the effective law.

Legal and natural persons which carry out work on improving electricity and heat supply systems, equipping residential buildings, apartments, enterprises, organizations and institutions with energy consumption metering devices, controls and regulations, improving thermal insulation, or involved in other activities aimed at decreasing energy consumption, using secondary energy resources and also indigenous types of fuel and industrial residues for heating purposes, can be subsidized by the Fund.

ARTICLE 20 USE OF RENEWABLE ENERGY SOURCES

Non-utility facilities for producing heat and electricity are entitled to supply energy to the utility grid in an amount and schedule that ensure an optimum operation schedule of grids and sources of centralized energy supply and are agreed upon with the energy supplier operating the grid. Energy suppliers shall be obligated to take the energy from the above mentioned non-utility developers in their grids at a transaction rate charged in accordance with established procedure.

For energy facilities that use renewable energy sources or utilize secondary resources and wastes and have been constructed under a programme or project in the field of rational energy use, prices of heat and electricity should serve to expedite as much as agreed upon with the Government of the Republic of Uzbekistan the pay-back of investments into those facilities.

With a view to stimulating the efficient use of energy, seasonal prices of refined products and boiler fuel, seasonal electric and heat supply service rates, as well as differential daily electric service rates shall be set according to a procedure to be established by the Government of the Republic of Uzbekistan.

ARTICLE 21 RESPONSIBILITY FOR WASTEFUL USE OF ENERGY

Legal and natural persons involved in energy production and consumption shall keep the set energy efficiency of production, produce and services, precluding direct energy losses and the manufacturing of energy inefficient products.

The present Law provides for applying economic sanctions, according to the effective law, in the event of:

- non-observance of energy quality characteristics;
- direct energy losses detected by either instrumental or normative method;
- production of goods whose energy efficiency characteristics do not meet the requirements laid down in the relevant standards;
- metering irregularities;
- use of uncertified energy equipment or energy supply system and grid elements; and
- failure to recover the set percent of secondary energy resources available.

The fact of having applied an economic sanction against a legal person does not release it from indemnification for the injury.

Responsibilities of natural persons for wasting energy are established by law.

Losses inflicted by an energy supplier on its consumers as a result of an interrupt in energy supply for which no provision was made in the relevant agreement is subject to being indemnified in accordance with legislatively established procedure.

4 FINAL PROVISIONS

ARTICLE 22 INTERNATIONAL COOPERATION IN THE FIELD OF RATIONAL ENERGY USE

The main lines of international cooperation in the field of rational energy use are, as follows:

- mutually beneficial exchange of energy efficient technologies with foreign and international organizations;
- implementation in the Republic of joint interstate projects aimed at improving energy efficiency;
- participation in international projects in the field of rational energy use; and
- harmonization of national energy efficiency standards with international ones, as well as achieving mutual recognition of certification results.

ARTICLE 23 INTERNATIONAL AGREEMENTS

In the event of inconsistency between a provision of this Law and a provision of an international agreement to which the Republic of Uzbekistan is party, the provision of that international agreement shall prevail.

ARTICLE 24 RESPONSIBILITY FOR INFRINGING LEGISLATIVE ACTS ON RATIONAL ENERGY USE

Persons that have infringed the law on rational energy use shall carry the responsibility in accordance with established procedure.

European Union

Commission Decision of 23 December 2003

Setting Up an Executive Agency, the 'Intelligent Energy Executive Agency', to Manage Community Action in the Field of Energy in Application of Council Regulation (EC) No 58/2003

THE COMMISSION OF THE EUROPEAN COMMUNITIES,

Having regard to the Treaty establishing the European Community,

Having regard to Council Regulation (EC) No 58/2003 of 19 December 2002 laying down the statute for executive agencies to be entrusted with certain tasks in the management of Community programmes ([1]), and in particular Article 3(1) thereof,

Whereas:

(1) In the framework of the sustainable development strategy, the European Union has taken measures aimed at promoting and developing renewable energy and energy efficiency in order to contribute in a balanced way to achieving the following general objectives: security of energy supply, competitiveness and environmental protection.

(2) These measures include Decision No 1230/2003/EC of the European Parliament and of the Council of 26 June 2003 adopting a multiannual programme for action in the field of energy: 'Intelligent Energy – Europe' (2003–2006) ([2]), the areas of action of which are the development of renewable energy and energy efficiency, including in the transport sector, and their promotion in developing countries.

(3) Regulation (EC) No 58/2003 empowers the Commission to set up executive agencies in accordance with the general statute laid down by that Regulation and to entrust them with certain management tasks relating to one or more Community programmes.

(4) The purpose of empowering the Commission to set up executive agencies is to allow it to focus on core activities and functions which cannot be outsourced, without relinquishing control over, or ultimate responsibility for, activities managed by those executive agencies.

(5) Management of the Intelligent Energy – Europe programme involves implementation of technical projects which do not entail political decision-making and requires a high level of technical and financial expertise throughout the project cycle.

(6) The delegation to an executive agency of tasks related to programme implementation is possible with a clear separation between programming, establishing priorities and evaluating the programme, which would be carried out by the Commission, and project implementation, which would be entrusted to the executive agency.

(7) A cost-benefit analysis carried out for that purpose has showed that certain management tasks, such as budget implementation, technical and financial monitoring of projects and the dissemination and use of results could be carried out by an executive agency more efficiently whilst ensuring the implementation by the Commission of the Intelligent Energy – Europe programme in accordance with the Decision adopting the programme, as well as the programme's work programme and the guidelines adopted by the Commission with the assistance of the Management Committee provided for in Article 8 of the Decision.

[1] OJ L 11, 16.1.2003, p. 1.
[2] OJ L 176, 15.7.2003, p. 29.

(8) The use of an executive agency would mean that the new programme, which is significantly larger than its predecessor, could be managed more efficiently.

(9) The performance of the identified tasks by an executive agency would allow the Commission to focus on strategic and regulatory questions, whilst increasing Community aid to multinational actions in the Member States. This is the best way to achieve the energy objectives set in the various legislative texts and other measures in the areas of renewable energy and energy efficiency, including in the transport sector.

(10) The implementation of the Commission's priorities and, in particular, the sustainable development strategy may result in measures being adopted as part of the Community policy in the areas cited entailing Commission action which could be implemented by the agency. Provision should be made for the possibility of assigning additional management and implementation tasks to the agency.

(11) The measures provided for by this Decision are in accordance with the opinion of the Committee of the Executive Agencies,

HAS DECIDED AS FOLLOWS:

ARTICLE 1 ESTABLISHMENT OF THE AGENCY

1. An executive agency (hereinafter referred to as 'the Agency') for the management of Community action in the field of energy, the statute of which is laid down in Council Regulation (EC) No 58/2003, is hereby established.

2. The name of the Agency shall be the 'Intelligent Energy Executive Agency'.

ARTICLE 2 LOCATION

The agency shall be located in Brussels.

ARTICLE 3 DURATION

The Agency is hereby established for a period beginning on 1 January 2004 and ending on 31 December 2008.

ARTICLE 4 OBJECTIVES AND TASKS

1. Under the Community programme Intelligent Energy – Europe, established by Decision No 1230/2003/EC, the Agency is responsible for implementing the tasks concerning Community aid under the programme, except for programme evaluation, monitoring of legislation and strategic studies, or any other action which comes under the exclusive competence of the Commission. It shall be responsible for the following tasks:

(a) managing all the phases in the lifetime of specific projects in the context of implementing the Community programme Intelligent Energy – Europe on the basis of Decision 1230/2003/EC and the work programme provided for in this Decision and adopted by the Commission following the advice of the executive committee of the programme, as well as the necessary checks to that end, by adopting the relevant decisions where the Commission has empowered it to do so;

(b) adopting the instruments of budget implementation for revenue and expenditure and carrying out, where the Commission has empowered it to do so, all the operations necessary to manage the Community programme and, in particular, those linked to the award of contracts and grants;

(c) gathering, analysing and passing on to the Commission all the information needed to guide the implementation of the Community programme, as well as any other information or report for the Commission provided for in the work programme or in the instrument of delegation.

2. The Agency may be charged by the Commission following the opinion of the committee as established by Article 24 of Regulation (EC) No 58/2003, to carry out tasks of the same type under other Community programmes, within the meaning of Article 2 of that Regulation, as the programme referred to in paragraph 1, provided that these programmes or projects remain within the limits of the development of renewable energy and energy efficiency, including in the transport sector, and their promotion and provided that they do not constitute a significant increase of the tasks of the Agency.

3. The Commission decision delegating authority to the Agency shall set out in detail all the tasks entrusted to it and shall be adapted in the light of any additional tasks which may be entrusted to the Agency. The Commission decision will be transmitted, for information, to the committee established by Article 24 of Regulation (EC) No 58/2003.

ARTICLE 5 ORGANISATIONAL STRUCTURE

1. The Agency shall be managed by a Steering Committee and a Director appointed by the Commission.

2. The members of the Steering Committee shall be appointed for three years.

3. The Director shall be appointed for five years.

ARTICLE 6 GRANTS

The Agency shall receive a grant which shall be entered in the general budget of the European Communities from the funds allocated to the Community programme Intelligent Energy – Europe and, where appropriate, other Community programmes or actions entrusted to the Agency for implementation pursuant to Article 4(2).

ARTICLE 7 SUPERVISION AND REPORTING REQUIREMENT

The Agency shall be subject to supervision by the Commission and shall report regularly on progress in implementing the programmes for which it is responsible in accordance with the arrangements and at the intervals stipulated in the instrument of delegation.

ARTICLE 8 IMPLEMENTATION OF THE ADMINISTRATIVE BUDGET

The Agency shall implement its administrative budget in accordance with the provisions of the standard Financial Regulation.

Done at Brussels, 23 December 2003.

For the Commission
Loyola DE PALACIO
Vice-President

Directive of the European Parliament and of the Council on the Promotion of Cogeneration Based on a Useful Heat Demand in the Internal Energy Market

Brussels, 22.7.2002 COM (2002) 415 final

2002/0185 (COD)

Explanatory Memorandum

1. INTRODUCTION

This proposal, building on the dual objectives of contributing both to security of energy supply and to climate change polices, arises from the need for reinforced efforts to promote high-efficiency cogeneration[1] in the internal energy market.

In its Green Paper on security of energy supply[2], the Commission highlighted the following points:

• the European Union is extremely dependent on its external energy supplies, with imports currently accounting for 50% of requirements. This figure is projected to rise to 70% by 2030 if current trends persist.

• at present greenhouse gas emissions in the European Union are on the rise making it difficult to respond to the challenge of climate change and to meet the commitments under the Kyoto Protocol.

• the European Union has relatively limited scope to influence energy supply conditions. Efforts will have to focus on orienting the demand for energy in a way that respects the EU's Kyoto commitments and is mindful of security of supply.

These observations provide strong arguments for developing new Community policies and measures aimed at curbing energy demand and reducing greenhouse gas emissions. Even the level of greenhouse gas emissions in EU in 1999 was the same or just below the level of 1990, it is still a great challenge to meet the Kyoto target. Due to the efficient use of the fuel, the simultaneous production of heat and power can offer energy savings and avoided CO_2 emissions compared with separate production of heat and power. This need for policy action on co-generation at EU level was reinforced in the Commissions Communication on the implementation of the European Climate Change Programme[3].

Cogeneration is a highly efficient technique to provide electricity and heat for the European energy market. Promotion of cogeneration is a part of the strategy for efficient use of energy and supplementary to the strategy of increased use of renewables. However cogeneration is not a target in itself but can be an efficient tool to generate energy savings and to pursue the targets of reductions in CO_2 emissions by replacing separate production of heat and electricity.

As cogeneration is linking together the production of heat and electricity, it is important to ensure that the produced electricity and heat meet real demands. The electricity can be transmitted into a market place and sold where it is needed, the heat however cannot easily by transported or stored, and therefore the cogeneration process must be based in time and place of a real need for heat. The real need for useful heat is the cornerstone of efficient cogeneration, because if the produced heat is not meeting a real demand the advantages of cogeneration disappear. Furthermore the promotion of cogeneration should not lead to encouragement of increased heat consumption.

In the Commission's cogeneration strategy[4] from 1997, an overall indicative Community target of

[1] The terms cogeneration and combined heat and power (CHP) have the same meaning

[2] COM(2000) 769 "Towards a European Strategy for Energy Supply".

[3] COM(2001) 580 final

[4] COM(97) 514 final "A Community strategy to promote combined heat and power (CHP) and to dismantle barriers to its development".

doubling the share of electricity production from cogeneration in total EU electricity production from 9% in 1994 to 18% by 2010 was set. Nevertheless, despite the promising potential for cogeneration, no significant increase in the share of cogeneration has been seen in the past years. An overall indicative target of 18% provides a benchmark against which to measure progress. Once a stable framework has been established, based on common definitions and methodologies, and the potential of Member States assessed, the Commission could examine the possibility of indicative objectives for each Member State.

A stable framework based on common definitions and methodologies provides the best possible foundation for promotion of cogeneration based on an economically justified heat demand also taking into account the deep complexity of the matter.

2. OBJECTIVE AND SCOPE OF THE PROPOSED DIRECTIVE

The overriding objective of this proposal is to create a framework, which can support and facilitate the installation and proper functioning of electrical cogeneration plants where a useful heat demand exists or is foreseen. This overall objective translates into two specific aims:

- *In the short term*, a cogeneration Directive should serve as an instrument to consolidate existing and, where feasible, promote new high-efficiency cogeneration installations in the internal energy market. In order to create a level playing field, regulatory certainty and in some cases financial support are vital for cogeneration. This applies to the current transitional phase of the liberalisation process, where the internal energy market is not fully completed and where internalisation of external costs is not reflected in energy prices.

- *In the medium to long term*, a cogeneration Directive should serve as a means to create the necessary framework that will ensure that high-efficiency cogeneration, alongside other environmentally friendly supply options, constitutes a key element when decisions on investment in new production capacity are made. By creating a supportive framework, such cogeneration can contribute to the establishment of more diversified and energy efficient supply systems in the Community.

In order to exploit the potential for cogeneration regulatory certainty and appropriate mechanisms that address the lack of internalisation of external costs are needed. The proposed Directive lays down a framework, which addresses these issues through a set of common principles for the promotion of cogeneration.

The practical application of the framework will to a large extent be the responsibility of the individual Member States, given the heterogeneous nature of the cogeneration sector across Europe and the need to take account of national and climatic circumstances. However the Commission could have an important role in facilitating that EU objectives on cogeneration are met.

It is necessary to stress the importance of the different climatic and industrial conditions in Member States for development of cogeneration providing different possibilities for using the produced heat, and taking into account the thermodynamic efficiency of the engines and systems employed. The consequences in practice of the thermodynamic efficiency for electricity production could be illustrated for a steam turbine. If the heat output is needed at a temperature of 200°C it is not possible to produce as much electricity in the turbine as if the heat output is needed at 60°C.

These considerations lead to creation of three classes of cogeneration reflecting thermodynamic considerations as well as a division of cogeneration into market segments facing different barriers to overcome:

- **Industrial applications** of heat, that usually require steam or hot water above 140°C;

- **Central Heating applications** that require warm water between 40°C and 140°C;

- **Agricultural applications:** for example in order to heat greenhouses, the temperature of the warm water could be below 40°C, but in the case of heating pools in aquaculture the need is only of 15–25°C. Justification of useful heat at this temperature level should be considered very careful in order not to increase fuel consumption.

The climatic differences among Member States is one of the most important factors explaining the huge differences of penetration of cogeneration and underline the relevance of the principle of subsidiarity. This proposal for Directive does not aim to ensure the same level of penetration of cogeneration in all Member States. The aim is to promote cogeneration wherever an economically justified potential is identified in order to save energy and reduce CO_2-emission.

The proposed Directive builds in some respects on the recently adopted Directive 2001/77/EC on the promotion of electricity from renewable energy sources[5]. Renewables and cogeneration are in some areas faced with similar problems such as for example lack of internalisation of external costs, the need to provide regulatory certainty concerning grid issues and administrative procedures. However it has to be stressed that there are important differences between cogeneration and renewable energy. Cogeneration is not a source of energy, it is a highly efficient process to transform energy from one source usually fossil fuel but also renewables into electricity and heat.

The proposal covers the following main elements:

• *Guarantee of origin* of electricity produced from cogeneration following the "disclosure" requirements on Directives concerning commons rules for the internal markets in electricity and natural gas;

• provisions obliging Member States to analyse *national potentials for highefficiency cogeneration and barriers to their realisation*;

• provisions for *evaluating the experiences gained with the application and coexistence of different support mechanisms* for cogeneration used by Member States;

• provisions laying down the principles for the *interaction between cogeneration producers and the electricity grid*; furthermore to facilitate grid access for cogeneration units using renewable energy sources and microcogeneration plants below 1 MW

• provisions requiring Member States to *evaluate current administrative procedures* with a view to reducing the administrative barriers to the development of cogeneration.

[5] Directive 2001/77/EC of the European Parliament and of the Council of 27 September 2001 on the promotion of electricity produced from renewable energy sources in the internal electricity market. OJ L 283 of 27.10.2001, p. 33.

3. CURRENT STATUS FOR COGENERATION IN THE EU

3.1 Problems to Face

In an open market to be developed in Europe, cogeneration has to face several problems in order to take advantage of the useful heat demands and propose the construction of new plants or carry on exploiting the existing ones. These are mainly the following:

1. High prices for fuels, usually due to the fact that they are smaller fuel users than the large traditional electricity producers.

2. Problems linked to the access to the electricity market, especially if they are small producers.

3. The installation costs per kilowatt are usually higher than in a large electrical plant

4. The amount of operating hours of the installation will usually be lower than for larger baseload plants because it will be linked to the real use of heat in the associated installations. In an industrial cogeneration plant, the working hours will be the hours that the industrial associated process works, for example not at night hours or on weekends. In the case of cogeneration for central heating some facilities may have to stop during summer time.

3.2 Reasons for Political Support

The following reasons justify a political support for high efficient cogeneration:

1. *High efficiency* means less fuel consumption and less CO_2 and other emissions and thereby a contribution to sustainable development.

2. Avoided losses on the electrical grid because these installations usually are close to the consumption point on the electrical grid.

3. Increasing competition among electricity producers because cogeneration technology allows new actors to enter the market of electricity generation.

4. Opportunity to *create new enterprises*, notably SME's, joint ventures and other collaboration formulas among the stakeholders (industrial, electrical, technological and so on).

5. Facilitation of *the link between the population and the territory*, mainly in less favorised, isolated or ultraperipherical areas.

3.3 Statistic overview

According to the latest cogeneration statistics from Eurostat[6] presented in Table 1, the overall share of cogeneration electricity in total EU electricity production was 11%[7] in 1998 compared with 9% in 1994.

In the cogeneration statistics it is important to avoid counting in electricity, that has not been produced in cogeneration mode. For this purpose the cogeneration statistics are developing and new methodologies have to be adopted. This directive would establish a methodology, which only takes into account electricity gained from cogeneration, the residual heat of which has been used efficiently.

Taking into account the previous considerations, the available statistics show substantial differences across the EU. Denmark, Finland and the Netherlands are the countries with the highest market penetration with cogeneration accounting in some case for more than 50% of total electricity generation. In contrast, in countries like France, Greece and Ireland cogeneration only plays a marginal role with contributions around 2%. However, if the cogeneration share is related to the amount of thermal based electricity production, the market shares of cogeneration in some case change significantly. Then countries like Sweden, Austria and France report cogeneration shares of 96%, 76% and 23% respectively.

Roughly 40% of electricity from cogeneration is produced for public supply purposes, often in connection with district heating networks. The remaining 60% are generated by auto-producers, normally for industrial processes. In terms of installed capacity, the electrical capacity of cogeneration in the EU increased with 14% between 1994 and 1998 from 63 GW to 72 GW. In absolute terms, Germany was in 1998 with 22 GW cogeneration electrical capacity by far the country with most cogeneration capacity in the EU followed by Italy (9,5 GW), Netherlands (8,5 GW), Denmark (7 GW) and Finland (5 GW).

The development in the use of fuels for cogeneration shows a trend towards cleaner fuels thus enhancing the environmental benefits of cogeneration. Natural gas is the most used fuel in cogeneration production with a share of 45% in 1998 compared with 30% in 1994. In contrast, the use of hard coal and lignite has declined from 30% to 20% between 1994–1998. Renewables accounted for 13% in 1998. Within the Eurostat definition of renewables for cogeneration both biodegradable and non-biodegradable municipal solid waste have until now been included. However, in the light of the definition of waste for renewables in the Directive for the promotion of electricity from renewables, it would be coherent to establish data as well for the biodegradable part alone.

The absence of more recent figures means, however, that the above figures should be treated by some caution. Since 1998, the cogeneration sector has reported stagnating or even declining market trends in several EU countries. This lack of progress in promoting new cogeneration is to large extent results from the existence of a number of barriers, which hampers the development of cogeneration.

A study on the administrative obstacles to decentralised cogeneration[8] has analysed the situation in France, Netherlands and the United Kingdom. The study identifies economic barriers to decentralised cogeneration such as low prices for excess electricity sold to the grid, high connection costs, high costs of grid reinforcement charged on the cogeneration developer, high costs for use of the distribution system, complex and lengthy administrative procedures, lack of recognition of the benefits to the network of embedded generation etc. Another study[9] has evaluated the impact of the liberalisation of the electricity market on the cogeneration and district heating and cooling sector through analyses of the economic viability of such plants. The study concludes that new efficient gas fired cogeneration technologies in principle should be competitive to new

[6] "Combined Heat and Power production (CHP) in the EU – Summary of statistics 1994–1998", Eurostat 2001.

[7] There is discussion among experts as to whether the Eurostat cogeneration statistics overestimate the real share of cogeneration because electricity produced in non-cogeneration mode in some cases might be counted as cogeneration electricity. The actual cogeneration share at Community level may therefore be somewhat lower than 11%. Eurostat has for the next collection of cogeneration statistics adopted a new methodology designed to better identify real cogeneration production.

[8] "The Administrative obstacles to the development of decentralised cogeneration", Cogen Europe et.al. SAVE programme 1999.

[9] "Evaluation of the impact of the European electricity market on the CHP, district heating and cooling sector", Cowi Consulting Engineers and Planners et.al., SAVE programme, 2000.

Table 1: Historical data on CHP in member states and CHP as a percentage of thermal and total electricity generation

Member state	1994**			1996			1997			1998		
	CHP electricity GWh	Portion of thermal electricity %	Portion of total electricity %	CHP electricity GWh	Portion of thermal electricity %	Portion of total electricity %	CHP electricity GWh	Portion of thermal electricity %	Portion of total electricity %	CHP electricity GWh	Portion of thermal electricity %	Portion of total electricity %
Belgium	2448	8,0	3,4	3000	9,5	3,9	3069	10,2	3,9	3410	9,6	4,1
Denmark	21874	56,2	54,5	29260	55,9	54,6	26562	62,7	59,9	25591	66,9	62,3
Germany	47752	13,5	9,0	37817	10,3	6,8	36834	10,3	6,7	41770	11,3	7,5
Greece	819	2,2	2,0	886	2,3	2,1	968	2,5	2,2	981*	2,3	2,1
Spain	8537	11,1	5,3	13390	17,5	7,7	18567	18,9	9,8	21916	22,2	11,2
France	8506	24,5	1,8	9864	22,0	1,9	10663	26,2	2,1	12660	22,7	2,5
Ireland	259	1,6	1,5	357	2,0	1,9	457	2,4	2,3	404	2,0	1,9
Italy	26477	14,7	11,4	31383	16,2	12,9	40164	20,1	16,0	44856	21,6	17,3
Luxembourg							120	37,1	9,5	320	87,7	22,5
Netherlands	31543	41,7	39,5	36410	45,1	42,7	41502	49,6	47,9	47835	55,4	52,6
Austria	11721	66,0	21,4	13539	70,3	24,7	14025	71,7	24,7	14268	76,2	24,8
Portugal	3111	15,1	9,9	2845	14,5	8,2	2949	14,1	8,6	3288	12,8	8,4
Finland	20312	59,0	30,9	22536	59,3	32,5	23051	64,0	33,3	25128	75,6	35,8
Sweden	9257	85,0	6,4	10241	70,9	7,3	9301	91,4	6,2	9544	95,5	6,0
UK	11619	5,0	3,6	15108	6,1	4,3	16762	7,0	4,9	18644	7,4	5,2
EU-15	204235	17,6	9,0	226336	18,3	9,4	244994	19,8	10,1	270615	21,0	10,9

* Eurostat estimation

** The German figures are for 1995.

Source: "Combined Heat and Power production (CHP) in the EU – Summary of statistics 1994–1998", Eurostat 2001

efficient condensing power plants. However, if the electricity prices do not reflect real costs (including internalisation of external costs), only large gas fired cogeneration plants are competitive. If an assumed rate on environmental benefits of 10 EUR per saved ton CO_2 is included in the calculation some additional medium-sized gas fired cogeneration plants would be feasible. If the price on the Nordic power market from May 2000 of 15 EUR/MWh is applied none of the cogeneration plants analysed would be feasible on purely economic criteria[10].

Due to its widespread use in cogeneration production, the price of natural gas is another important parameter influencing the economic viability of cogeneration. The opening of gas markets to competition should in principle lead to lower gas prices. However, many cogeneration producers have during the past years experienced fluctuating and often high gas prices due to i.a. gas prices being linked to the oil price. Moreover, Article 18(2) of Directive 98/30/EC[11], which allows Member States to restrict the access of cogeneration producers to the internal gas market, is another potential barrier for cogeneration. However, the Commission's proposal for amendment of the gas Directive[12] envisages that this provision would disappear. Ensuring access to the gas market for all cogeneration producers is important as gas fired cogeneration allows for the highest possible fuel efficiency thus benefiting both the environment and the Community's energy balance. From an internal market point of view it is also important to create a level playing field where cogeneration producers and other power producers enjoy the same basic rights with regard to access to the gas market across the Community.

As described above, barriers to cogeneration continue to exist both in the electricity and gas markets.

[10] It should be noted that these calculations are based on cogeneration plants with district heating with assumed operating hours of 4.500 per year. Industrial cogeneration plants with a more constant heat demand can have up to 8.000 operating hours per year, which normally makes them economically more viable.

[11] Directive 98/30/EC of the European parliament and of the Council of 22 June 1998 concerning common rules for the internal market in natural gas. OJ L 204 of 21.07.1998, p. 1.

[12] "Proposal for a Directive of the European Parliament and of the Council amending Directives 96/92/EC and 98/30/EC concerning common rules for the internal market in electricity and natural gas", COM(2001) 125 final.

Many cogeneration producers have experienced increasing gas input prices combined with decreasing electricity output prices thus putting the economic viability of cogeneration under threat. Both markets are still in a transitional phase with asymmetric market openings across the EU, increased market uncertainty, more focus on short-term decisions, and lack of internalisation of external costs. Such a market environment is generally detrimental to smaller and less competitive operators such as cogeneration producers. Altogether, the current market conditions have contributed to a situation where many existing cogeneration plants have came under pressure and where incentives to upgrade existing capacity or invest in new capacity are significantly reduced.

4. FOCUSED PUBLIC SUPPORT OF COGENERATION BASED ON USEFUL HEAT DEMAND IN THE EUROPEAN INTERNAL MARKET

The purpose of this directive, according to the subsidiarity principle, is to introduce a common and transparent framework in order to focus Member States public support for cogeneration process based on useful heat demand according to the national circumstances and energy policies, in the framework of the European competition rules. This Directive sets up common definitions of electricity from cogeneration in order to develop the same methodological background for member state support schemes. The aim of this methodology is also to ensure impacts on the internal electricity market from support schemes are transparent.

As the large cogeneration installations have easier access to more favourable financing and fuel prices direct support for production of cogenerated electricity should be concentrated to electricity produced either in installations with a capacity below an indicative threshold value of 50 MW (e) or in larger installations but then only the amount of electricity produced by the capacity below such an indicative threshold. The reason for this is not to disqualify larger installations but to avoid overcompensation of the larger installations. Larger installation would still have support for the production based on the first 50 MW, but will not receive additional support for the rest of the production. If direct support to the production of cogenerated electricity is based on a fixed amount per MWh produced, the support should not be applied to production above the indicative threshold value. Member States should use the following considerations in design of support schemes:

1. Support schemes for production of cogenerated electricity should be limited to the electricity produced in one process together with a useful heat production.

2. The economic support to the electricity production should be focused to develop the necessary economic incentive to operate efficient cogeneration plants on the basis of economically justified heat demand.

3. Direct support for production should in principle be focused on the share of cogenerated electricity produced *either* in installations with a capacity below an indicative threshold value that should be set at 50 MW(e) or lower, *or* in larger installations but then only the amount of electricity produced by the capacity below such a threshold value.

4. The cogeneration plants should be designed and sized for the actual heat demand present or foreseen with certainty.

5. ELEMENTS OF THE PROPOSED DIRECTIVE

5.1 Definition of Cogeneration

Cogeneration is currently defined in different ways across the Community. Some definitions are only intended to identify and measure cogeneration for statistical purposes. Other definitions are related to the eligibility of cogeneration for national support schemes. Sometimes such eligibility criteria are linked with quantifications of the benefits of cogeneration measured in terms of energy savings or CO_2 savings. In addition, defining cogeneration is complicated by certain cogeneration technologies that allow cogeneration units to switch between cogeneration and generation of separate electricity or heat.

For the purpose of this Directive, it is necessary to create a common basis for the definition of cogeneration. In principle, it would be desirable to lay down a single harmonised definition of cogeneration to be used across the Community for all purposes. However, the Commission is mindful that most Member States have already adopted different national definitions of cogeneration developed for various purposes and often adapted to national circumstances. To take account of these two opposite concerns, this Directive introduces a two-step approach consisting of:

(1) a harmonised basic definition of electricity from cogeneration (Annex II to the Directive)

(2) a methodology to define high-efficiency cogeneration (Annex III to the Directive)

The basic definition will serve as a means to eliminate the current ambiguity resulting from the different definitions of cogeneration. This will create certainty that the basic concept of cogeneration is understood and measured in the same way across the Community. The basic definition will be used for cogeneration statistics and for monitoring purposes at Community level. As a second step, the Directive provides a methodology to be used to determine the quality[13] – expressed in terms of energy savings – of the cogeneration production identified under the basic definition in step 1. The latter will be applied to promotional aspects, notably certification of origin, identification of national cogeneration potentials and, where appropriate, eligibility for financial support.

5.2 Guarantee of the Origin of Electricity from Cogeneration

In order to fulfil the obligations on information about the primary energy sources used on the production of the electricity, as set up on the "disclosure" provisions at the amending directives 96/92/EC and 98/30/EC concerning common rules for the internal markets in electricity and gas, this Directive sets up a mechanism, which will ensure that producers and others with an interest in cogeneration can request a guarantee of the origin of electricity from cogeneration.

Under the proposal the guarantee of origin must specify the fuel source used, the use of the heat generated together with the electricity and the dates and places of production. The guarantee of origin must also specify the national reference values used to define high-efficiency cogeneration.

[13]The term "quality cogeneration" is sometimes used to describe cogeneration providing a high level of energy savings or CO_2 savings. For the purpose of this Directive the term "high-efficiency cogeneration" is considered to be a more precise indicator of what is meant when referring to the benefits of cogeneration.

It is not the aim at this stage of development of cogeneration and statistic knowledge to establish any other connection between the Guarantee of origin of electricity from cogeneration and the system of Guarantee of origin of electricity produced from renewable energy sources, than introducing the same procedures to be established by Member States. The high efficient cogeneration plants using fossil fuels produce at least 5–10% less CO_2 than in the situation of separate production, while electricity from renewables produce almost no CO_2. It is therefore obvious that the 'CO_2 reduction value' of 1 kWh cogenerated electricity is much smaller than the 'CO_2 reduction value' of 1 kWh renewable electricity.

It is important for reasons of transparency and for monitoring purposes that cogeneration is defined and counted in the same way across the EU. This proposal therefore introduces in Annex II a harmonised methodology to be used for the basic definition of cogeneration. This methodology is largely based on a recently revised methodology used by Eurostat for collection of EU-wide cogeneration statistics[14]. The new Eurostat methodology essentially implies that in cogeneration units with annual overall efficiency higher or equal to 75%, the total electricity generation is considered to be cogeneration electricity. In cogeneration units with an annual overall efficiency below 75%, calculations must be made in order to subtract electricity that is not produced in a cogeneration process.

To address the concerns expressed by some experts that a 75% threshold in some cases may be too low, the methodology set out in Annex II adds a separate threshold of 85% to be applied to cogeneration units, which can switch to operation in non-cogeneration mode. Such units below an overall annual efficiency of 85% will be subjected to additional calculations to identify the actual cogeneration production. With this approach, the risk of certifying non-cogeneration as cogeneration electricity is judged to be minimal.

5.3 Efficiency Criteria

To secure that only cogeneration that offers actual benefits compared with separate production of heat and power is promoted under this Directive, it essential that an appropriate mechanism to determine these benefits exists. The proposal therefore provides in Annex III a methodology for determining the benefits of cogeneration.

The benefits of cogeneration can be expressed in terms of energy savings or CO_2 savings. In most cases, a cogeneration installation that provides energy savings will also offer CO_2 savings. However, the choice of fuel for cogeneration will have an impact on the amount of CO_2 savings. The concept of cogeneration is basically about saving energy by using the fuel input in a highly efficiency manner to generate both electricity and heat. For the purpose of this Directive energy savings are therefore considered the most suitable indicator to express the benefits of cogeneration. By using this indicator, the Directive focuses on the energy efficiency characteristics of cogeneration and it remains fuel neutral thus allowing for a diversified mix of fuels in the cogeneration sector. However, under the reporting requirements the Commission could make an assessment of the environmental benefits, including the CO_2 emission savings.

To determine the energy savings from cogeneration, the basic definition of cogeneration as set out in Annex II cannot stand alone because it only identifies cogeneration without quantifying the potential energy savings. It is therefore necessary to develop additional criteria to determine the energy savings from cogeneration production as defined under the basic definition provided in Annex II. To define high-efficiency cogeneration the fuel used to produce a given amount of heat and power by cogeneration must be quantified and compared with the fuel that would have been necessary to produce the same amount of heat and power via separate generation. This implies that for the comparison assumptions must be made as to what kind of separate production cogeneration displaces.

One option would be to lay down in the Directive harmonised references for separate production of heat and power that any given cogeneration production should be compared with. However, defining such references is a highly complex exercise, especially for new production where empirical data is not available and assumptions must be made about the future fuels, technologies and expected efficiencies. In addition, the differences in the energy mix across the Community also make it difficult to establish a single harmonized reference, which can be applied to all Member States. This has led the

[14]This revised methodology was adopted by Member States at the last meeting of the Eurostat Working Group on Combined Heat and Power Statistics on 2 April 2001.

Commission to conclude that at this stage it is necessary to provide a common methodology for calculating the energy savings from cogeneration. However, it will be up to Member States to define, on the basis of the framework provided in Annex III, the exact national efficiency reference values to be used in the calculation. Member States will be asked to present a well-documented analysis of the choice of reference values, which must be published and forwarded to the Commission. The Commission will evaluate the efficiency reference values adopted by Member States and on that basis consider the scope for further harmonisation.

For the application of the efficiency criteria, the proposal distinguishes between new and existing production. Electricity from *new cogeneration* production should – within the same fuel category – be compared with the best new state-of-the-art power production technology that it is assumed to displace. By comparing efficiencies within similar fuel categories, the assessment of the benefits of cogeneration remains fuel neutral and focuses entirely on the energy efficiency characteristics of cogeneration. On the heat side, new cogeneration should normally be compared with an indicative heat efficiency reference value of 90% although lower efficiency references may be used for some fuels. Altogether, new cogeneration production should provide energy savings of at least 10% to qualify as high-efficiency cogeneration. Small-scale cogeneration and cogeneration based on renewable energy sources may qualify with a reduced level of energy savings. Electricity from *existing cogeneration* should be compared with the average efficiency of the existing national fossil-based electricity production. Nuclear and renewable electricity is excluded from the mix, as they in an actual market situation are normally not displaced by cogeneration electricity. On the heat side, existing cogeneration should be compared with the average efficiency of the existing national heat generation mix. Existing cogeneration production should provide energy savings of at least 5%to qualify as high-efficiency cogeneration.

5.4 National Potentials for High-Efficiency Cogeneration

Setting targets helps to quantify and subsequently monitor what the Community and individual Member States wish to achieve in the field of cogeneration. The Commission has therefore considered whether indicative national targets for the market share of cogeneration should be set for all Member States at Community level. On the other hand, the national market frameworks for cogeneration across the EU are very disparate with regard to for instance market potential for cogeneration, national energy mix, availability of fuels, industrial structure, demand for heating and/or cooling etc. This means that the conditions for promoting a specific energy efficiency technology like cogeneration in the national heat and electricity markets are very different. At this stage the establishment of indicative targets for each Member State would be technically difficult. However, the Commission could examine the possibility and need for such targets on the basis of the first reporting from Member States on the national potentials for high efficiency cogeneration. The Commission considers that initially the focus should be on stimulating effective promotional policies and measures in favour of cogeneration. The Directive will therefore initiate a compulsory procedure aimed at activating the existing national potentials for high-efficiency cogeneration.

Member States will be obliged to carry out well-documented analyses of the national potentials for cogeneration. To ensure that the analyses are carried out in a systematic and comparable manner, which will allow the Commission and the general public to monitor the implementation of the Directive, Annex IV to the Directive sets out a number of criteria and elements that must be covered in the analyses. The criteria include inter alia a requirement to consider the likely fuels for cogeneration with special emphasis on the scope for promoting renewable energy sources in the national heat markets via cogeneration and an obligation to examine aspects relating to cogeneration technologies, cost effectiveness and timeframes.

Annex IV also requires a breakdown of the cogeneration potential into at least three main categories. The categories "Industrial cogeneration", "Heating cogeneration" and "Agricultural cogeneration" refer to the different applications of the heat output. Member States will also be obliged to make a separate analysis of national barriers to cogeneration and to report regularly on progress towards realising national potentials and measures taken to promote cogeneration. To allow monitoring and assessment of progress at regular intervals reliable cogeneration statistics are necessary. The Directive therefore introduces an obligation for Member States to submit cogeneration statistics on an annual basis to the Commission. It is envisaged that this data collection in practice will be a continuation of the current practice where Member States submit national cogeneration statistics to Eurostat.

5.5 Support Schemes

A variety of different national support schemes for cogeneration are currently in operation or in the process of implementation. Such schemes include inter alia direct price support (feed-in tariffs), tax exemptions or reductions, green certificates and investment aid.

While the justification for financial support of cogeneration will disapear as the external costs are fully internalised in the market, support for cogeneration will in many cases be justifiable in the short to medium term. In order to reflect this aspect public support schemes should include the phase-out principle In order to realise the potential benefits from the installation and proper functioning of electrical cogeneration plants where a heat demand exists or is foreseen, continuation and reinforcement of support schemes in favour of cogeneration will therefore often be necessary within the limits set by the EC Treaty and in particular its Articles 87 and 88. The Community has, however, a clear interest in ensuring that support is successful in promoting high-efficient cogeneration. Under the Directive, the Commission will therefore be obliged to evaluate the application of the different support schemes for cogeneration used in Member States and to present a report on the experiences gained with the application and coexistence of different support mechanisms.

5.6 Grid System Issues

To function properly, the internal electricity market has to provide a level playing field for all existing and potential new producers of electricity. In this context, objective, transparent and non-discriminatory rules and procedures in relation to grid system issues can facilitate the market penetration of cogeneration. Regulatory certainty about grid system issues is of particular importance for cogeneration given that cogeneration producers in many cases are smaller and independent operators that are vulnerable to costs and conditions in this field.

Cogeneration producers are generally faced with the same difficulties as producers of electricity from renewable energy sources in relation to grid system issues. As a consequence, this proposal in many respects bases itself on the same provisions as those contained in Directive 2001/77/EC. This implies that the proposal has provisions, which guarantee the transmission and distribution of electricity produced from cogeneration. Grid connection and grid reinforcement is another area where barriers to cogeneration in some cases exist as described in section 3. To address such barriers, the proposal contains provisions requiring transmission system operators and distribution system operators to set up and publish standard rules relating to grid connection and reinforcement. Such rules must be based on objective, transparent and non-discriminatory criteria.

Due to the link between electricity production and the heat demand, cogeneration producers sometimes need to purchase additional electricity to back-up or top-up the producer's own generation. Excess electricity must also sometimes be sold, when production exceeds consumption. Special markets for balancing and regulating power are gradually emerging. However, not all cogeneration producers are currently eligible customers with access to such markets. Until the electricity market is fully opened, it is therefore necessary with specific provisions to ensure that the tariffs offered to cogeneration producers without market access that need to purchase electricity are set according to objective, transparent and non-discriminatory criteria. For reasons of transparency and for monitoring purposes, it is also proposed that benchmarking analyses on tariffs offered to cogeneration both for the purchase of additional electricity and for the selling of excess electricity are undertaken.

5.7 Administrative Procedures

It has been pointed out by organisations representing cogeneration developers that administrative procedures represent a barrier to the further development of cogeneration. Such barriers can for instance be the length of the procedure, the requirements necessary to meet, or high costs associated with the authorisation procedure.

Directive 96/92/EC provides the basic rules in this respect, notably with regard to authorisation procedures. Nevertheless, these general rules may not always be sufficient for smaller producers such as for example many independent cogeneration producers for whom administrative and planning procedures can be a serious barrier.

In many respects, harmonised rules in this area could contribute towards promoting cogeneration. On the other hand, administrative and planning procedures vary significant across the Community reflecting very different administrative and constitutional set-ups. Taking this into consideration and with due regard to the principle of subsidiarity, this proposal does therefore not contain provisions for such harmonised rules.

Nevertheless, reinforced efforts to minimise administrative barriers are needed. It is therefore proposed that Member States or the competent bodies appointed by the Member States evaluate existing legislative frameworks with a view to reducing barriers to cogeneration, streamlining and expediting procedures and ensuring that rules are objective, transparent and non-discriminatory. Member States will be obliged to report the results of the evaluation and indicate, where appropriate, action taken to remove barriers.

6. JUSTIFICATION FOR ACTION AT COMMUNITY LEVEL

6.1 Current Political Context

In the Green Paper on the security of energy supply[15], the Commission outlines the prospective energy situation in the EU for the coming decades. The Green Paper emphasises the need to reinforce efforts to reduce energy demand as a means to both reduce the dependence on external suppliers and to contribute to solving climate change problems. Clear rules for cogeneration, which allows plants to work properly with its fuel saving characteristics, can contribute to both policy objectives.

The Commission in its proposal for amendment of the electricity and gas directives[16] emphasised that a fully opened market needs an internalisation of external costs to ensure a true level playing field. According to for example the ExternE study[17], CHP provokes with the same fuel at least two times less socio-environmental damages compared with conventional electricity production. As long as external costs are not fully integrated into energy prices, the Commission will promote initiatives that seek to rectify this imbalance. Such initiatives should seek to compensate the extra costs of the cogeneration producer compared to the costs involved in separate production of heat and electricity. At the present market conditions such compensation should seek to rectify the above mentioned imbalance and to avoid that the extra costs result in higher prices of the cogenerated heat and electricity compared to the separately produced. Compensation of extra costs should be adjusted in order to reflect the need for compensation for the different sizes of installations, types of technologies and fuels. Larger cogeneration plants have less need for compensation than the smaller ones.

The Commission in its Communication on the completion of the internal market[18] underlined that the creation of the internal market for electricity and gas in many respects has shown to have had positive environmental effects in terms of e.g. increased operating efficiency and switch to cleaner fuels. However, it was also stressed that falling energy prices might not be conducive to the development of energy efficiency and renewables. Waiting for the internal energy market to be fully completed could involve many risks because opportunities for cogeneration could be lost in the meantime. The Commission therefore announced in the above-mentioned Communication that it intends to prepare, in 2002, proposals with respect to cogeneration.

Art.2 of the EC Treaty calls for a sustainable development of the economy of the Community. *Art.6 of the EC Treaty* reinforced these objectives of sustainable development by integrating environment policy into other Community policies. In addition, the Commission's Communication on sustainable development[19] presented at the European Council

[15] "Towards a European strategy for the security of energy supply", COM(2000) 769.

[16] "Proposal for a Directive of the European Parliament and of the Council amending Directives 96/92/EC and 98/30/EC concerning common rules for the internal market in electricity and natural gas", COM(2001) 125 final.

[17] "ExternE – Externalities of Energy", EC, DG Research, Brussels, 1999.

[18] "Completing the internal energy market", COM(2001) 125 final

[19] "A Sustainable Europe for a Better world: a European Union Strategy for Sustainable Development" COM(2001) 264.

in Göteborg in June 2001 identified greenhouse gas emissions as a one of the major obstacles to sustainable development. The European Council in Göteborg[20] adopted a strategy for sustainable development and added an environmental dimension to the Lisbon process on economic and social renewal.

To address climate change, the Commission recently adopted a Communication on implementation of the European Climate Change Programme[21], in which it announced its intention to put forward a proposal for a cogeneration Directive in 2002. Moreover, a proposal for a Directive on greenhouse gas emission trading[22] has also recently been adopted by the Commission. When such a market is in full operation, a price on CO_2 emissions will in effect be disclosed whereby an important step towards internalisation of external costs will have been taken. Furthermore introduction of such a market will also be a step towards eliminating the justification of national economic support schemes for promoting cogeneration. However, as long as a well-functioning market reflecting the price of CO_2 emissions is not in operation, cogeneration is particular vulnerable to competition from less clean energy producers and will therefore often need specific promotion. In response to the Commission's energy efficiency action plan[23], the Council identified promotion of cogeneration as one of the short-term priority actions in the follow-up on the action plan[24]. The European Parliament called on the Commission to submit proposals for common rules for the promotion of cogeneration[25].

In the recently revised Community guidelines on state aid for environmental protection[26], provisions were included, which allow under certain conditions financial support to cogeneration. In order to qualify under the guidelines, the environmental benefits of the concerned cogeneration scheme must be documented.

6.2 Additional Impact of Action at Community Level

Member States are becoming increasingly interdependent in the field of energy, notably as regards the internal energy market and the common commitment to reduce greenhouse gas emissions following the ratification of the Kyoto Protocol. Policy decisions on cogeneration in one Member State can have an impact on the energy markets in other member States. Member States are also faced with common competition rules of the Treaty, including the recently revised Community guidelines on state aid for environmental protection, which also define the national room of manoeuvre in the field of cogeneration. In addition, the current lack of progress in the cogeneration market demonstrates that it is doubtful that the potential for cogeneration can be realised via initiatives at Member State level alone.

This has led the Commission to conclude that cogeneration policies at Member State level need to be complemented by legislative action at Community level. This Directive will create the necessary legislative framework whereby efforts at all levels can be concentrated on promoting high-efficiency cogeneration. The Directive will serve as a means to reduce the current market uncertainty surrounding cogeneration and provide important stimuli for cogeneration in individual Member States by establishing a coherent Community framework. Given the need to take account of the different national circumstances for cogeneration and to respect the principle of subsidiarity, it will to a large extent be left to Member States to decide how to operate within this overall Community framework for cogeneration.

Legislative action at Community level will ensure that a set of common principles for the promotion of cogeneration is developed. The definition of high-efficiency cogeneration is an example of an area where Community action is necessary to ensure a coherent methodology for promoting cogeneration so as to avoid market distortions. Moreover, common principles for high-efficiency cogeneration can also ensure that financial support for cogeneration is prioritised in such a way that support is allocated to the most efficient production.

[20] "Presidency Conclusions – Göteborg European Council 15 and 16 June 2001": SI(2001)500.
[21] COM(2001) 580 final.
[22] "Proposal for a framework Directive for greenhouse gas emissions trading within the European Community", COM(2001) 581.
[23] "Action Plan to improve energy efficiency in the European Community", COM(2000)247 final.
[24] Doc. 13407/1/00 ENER – COM (2000) 247 final.
[25] Resolution on the Action Plan to improve energy efficiency in the European Community, A5-0054/2001.
[26] "Community guidelines on State aid for environmental protection", OJ C 37, 03.02.2001 pages 3–15.

Table 2: Energy savings calculated for different cycles in the EU, TJ

	1994*	1996	1997	1998
Combined cycle	139349	240175	309744	385842
Total backpressure steam turbine	329604	321296	326528	278328
Condensing steam turbine with heat recovery	83645	258982	247361	236937
Gas turbine with heat recovery	79041	91287	128305	149877
Internal combustion engine	36684	71375	103506	124823
Others	1068	4015	2585	138
Total EU-15	**669391**	**987130**	**1118029**	**1175946**

* German figures are for 1995.
Source: "Combined Heat and Power production (CHP) in the EU – summary of statistics 1994–1998", Eurostat, 2001.

It is also of common Community interest to work towards the creation of a level playing field within the internal energy market. Establishing an objective, non-discriminatory and transparent framework for cogeneration producers in relation to grid system issues is an important question with a clear Community dimension. Creation of a level playing field is also relevant from a competition point of view as it could contribute to ensuring a certain number of market players in the internal energy market. Community action in favour of independent, and often small-scale, power producers such as cogeneration could thereby indirectly contribute to stimulating competition in the internal electricity market.

From a security of energy supply perspective, the Community also has an interest in promoting high-efficiency cogeneration as an element in its overall strategy to reduce energy demand. Promotion of cogeneration using indigenous energy sources such as bioenergy, waste and geothermal energy is particularly important in this context.

In respect of the future Community a Directive on promotion of cogeneration provides the Candidate Countries with possibilities to improve security of supply based on the existence of large heat markets and existing support programmes.

Finally, cogeneration can due to its high fuel efficiency and reduced environmental impact contribute to Community policies on sustainable development, notably in relation to the need for increased use of clean energy and measures to reduce energy demand. In the context of climate change, the Community has a clear interest in putting forward concrete proposals aimed at reducing the emission of greenhouse gases. A Directive on the promotion of cogeneration will therefore be one of the elements in the package of measures needed to comply with the Kyoto Protocol to the United Nations Framework Convention on Climate Change and any policy package to meet further commitments.

7. IMPACT OF THE PROPOSED DIRECTIVE

7.1 Potential Energy Savings

In its summary report on cogeneration statistics, Eurostat presents the following calculation of the estimated primary energy savings achieved by different types of cogeneration plants in the years 1994 to 1998.

According to Eurostat the absolute primary energy savings from cogeneration in 1998 amounted to 1176 PJ, or 28 Mtoe. This corresponds to 2% of total EU gross inland consumption of primary energy. The Eurostat calculation is based on an assumed average efficiency of separate electricity generation of 36%, an average efficiency of separate heat generation of 85% and an overall efficiency of CHP plants of 75% in 1998

7.2 Impact on Security of Energy Supply

Import dependency and rising import ratios may lead to concern about the risk of interruption to or difficulties in supply. However, it would be simplistic and wrong to conceive security of supply as merely a question of reducing import dependency and boosting domestic production. Security of supply calls for a wide range of policy initiatives aimed at, inter alia, diversification of sources and technologies and improved international relations.

From an *import dependency* point of view, cogeneration would be beneficial, if the import of fuel to the EU were to be reduced compared with separate production of electricity and heat. However cogeneration schemes do not automatically trigger a reduction in energy imports. When it follows, the benefits from a security of supply point of view can be of varying size. If a more *diversified fuel mix* results from a cogeneration project than from separate production, the security of supply will be increased. Local production of electricity may also enhance *security of electricity supply*, since it ensures that electricity is produced in many different regions of a country where heat is needed. These regions become more self sufficient in power supply and less vulnerable to power failures. Most large industries with a steam demand are very sensitive to power failures for their industrial production and see their own electricity generation as an increased security of electricity supply.

If cogeneration takes place in a district heating system the *security of heat supply* is increased, considering that a large cogeneration installation always has stand-by capacity to back-up failures in individual units, something that a small heat installation can rarely afford.

The *physical security* of a cogeneration plant as regards sabotage and terrorist attacks also needs to be considered, especially following the 11 September 2001 attack on the USA. Cogeneration production would take place in a large number of plants, whereas electricity production in the reference case would take place in a few, large, centralized power plants, which are more likely targets for terrorists because of the larger impact of an attack. Cogeneration production would thus normally increase the physical security of the power system.

7.3 Cost-Effectiveness of the Measure

New high-efficiency and well-designed cogeneration installations dimensioned on the basis of a relatively stable heat demand and operated for a reasonable amount of hours over the year are generally considered to be a cost-effective energy solution.

Nevertheless, determining the costs-effectiveness of this proposal must necessarily be subject to many uncertainties and assumptions. In this context, a key issue is to define the reference case with which the cost-effectiveness of cogeneration is compared. The huge differences in the calculation of CO_2 savings from cogeneration referred to in section 6.2 illustrate the impact of applying different assumptions to the calculation of CO_2 savings or to calculations of cost-effectiveness.

In the context of the European Climate Change Programme reference was made to an estimated savings potential from a cogeneration Directive of 65 Mt CO_2eq of which 12 Mt CO_2eq could be achieved at costs of between €20 and €50 per tonne[27]. However, the document subsequently underlines that actual reductions are subject to uncertainties because the proposed Directive will leave the choice of implementation strategy and specific support mechanisms in favour of cogeneration to the Member States.

It should also be noted that these cost estimates are based on the assumption that the reference to cogeneration is a gas economy with combined cycle gas turbines with electrical efficiencies of 55%. In other words, this is the assumption that generates the most conservative estimates as to the cost-effectiveness of cogeneration. If other references were used, cogeneration would be more cost-effective.

The fact that this Directive will only promote high-efficiency cogeneration installations that make optimal use of the fuel input is also likely to improve the overall cost-effectiveness of the measure. In addition, it should be kept in mind that promotion of cogeneration is not only aimed at reducing greenhouse gas emissions, but also at saving energy. Important additional benefits with regard to energy savings and security of energy supply must therefore also be taken into account when judging the cost-effectiveness of the measure.

8. RELEVANCE FOR THE CANDIDATE COUNTRIES

Community action promoting cogeneration is also very important for the Candidate Countries of in particular Central and Eastern Europe where cogeneration, and especially district heating, for many years has been an important component in the energy supply system. Most of the Central and Eastern European Countries have cogeneration shares of at least 10% of electricity production and some substantially higher[28]. District heating is even more widespread in Central and Eastern Europe with district heating networks in most major cities and

[27] "Communication from the Commission on implementation of the first phase of the European Climate Change Programme", COM(2001) 580 final.

[28] "The European Cogeneration Review", Cogen Europe, 1999.

markets shares for district heating in the range between 13–70%[29]. According to Euroheat & Power[30] almost 40% of the inhabitants of Central and Eastern Europe are customers of district heating representing 41 million users compared with around 20 million in the EU.

The energy sectors in most of the countries in Central and Eastern Europe are generally characterised by a high heat demand and a considerable potential for energy savings. The general conditions of many district heating systems in Central and Eastern Europe is not good with sometimes oversized capacities and old district heating networks in need of refurbishment. This often results in relatively low system efficiencies. At the same time, district heating is sometimes faced with competition from other energy sources. Community action to promote cogeneration could therefore provide a stable and supportive framework for cogeneration and district heating in this region.

In this context, it could be of particular importance to protect the existing district heating infrastructure, which has come under threat due to lack of renovation and competition from individual heating. A cogeneration Directive could provide guidance and incentives to promote high-efficiency cogeneration on the basis of i.a. the existing infrastructure and the documented experiences with cogeneration and district heating in the region. Modernisation of the district heating networks and shift to cogeneration instead of heat-only boilers could in many cases be important elements in future efforts to improve energy efficiency in the Candidate Countries.

9. CONSULTATION DURING THE PREPARATION OF THE PROPOSAL

This proposal follows a consultation and preparation phase involving a number of different meetings and working groups.

Member States and representatives of European associations and non-governmental organisations were invited to a formal consultation meeting organised by the Commission services on 26 November 2001. At this meeting Member States and stakeholders were given the opportunity to present their views and positions on the possible elements of a cogeneration Directive. A background document circulated prior to the meeting formed the basis for the consultation. A number of Member States and stakeholder organizations have subsequently submitted written comments on the Directive.

Specific consultation with experts from industry, associations and research institutes took place on 12 November 2001 in the form of a workshop devoted exclusively to discussing technical issues relating to the definition and certification of cogeneration.

Another workshop focussing on the future outlook for cogeneration in Europe was organised on 25 October 2001 where representatives from Member States and Candidate Countries as well as industry were invited.

Finally, Community action in favour of cogeneration was also subject to discussions in two separate working groups under the European Climate Change Programme working from mid-2000 to mid-2001. In these working groups work was conducted through a co-operative effort involving representatives from the Commission's different departments, the Member States, industry and environmental groups.

10. CONTENTS OF THE PROPOSAL

Article 1 defines the purpose of the proposal.

Article 2 sets out the scope of the proposed Directive.

Article 3 lays down technical definitions.

Article 4 contains provisions for guarantee of origin of electricity from cogeneration, in line with the "disclosure" provisions on common rules for the internal markets in electricity and natural gas.

Article 5 obliges Member States to development criteria to determine the energy efficiency of cogeneration on the basis of a common methodology.

Article 6 obliges Member States to publish reports with analyses of national potentials for high-efficiency cogeneration and national barriers to their realisation.

Article 7 contains provisions for the evaluation of support schemes for cogeneration.

Article 8 concerns grid system issues.

[29] "District Heat in Europe – Country by Country 2001 Survey", Euroheat & Power, 2001.

[30] "District Heat in Europe – 1999 Survey", Euroheat & Power, 1999.

Article 9 obliges Member States to evaluate the scope for reducing administrative barriers to cogeneration.

Article 10 concerns reporting requirements under the Directive.

Annex I lists the cogeneration technologies covered by the proposal

Annex II sets out the methodology to be used for the basic definition of cogeneration.

Annex III outlines a methodology for determining the efficiency of cogeneration production.

Annex IV lists the criteria to be followed when analysing national potentials for high-efficiency cogeneration.

Proposal for a Directive of the European Parliament and of the Council on the Promotion of Cogeneration Based on a Useful Heat Demand in the Internal Energy Market

THE EUROPEAN PARLIAMENT AND THE COUNCIL OF THE EUROPEAN UNION,

Having regard to the Treaty establishing the European Community, and in particular Article 175 thereof,

Having regard to the proposal from the Commission[31]

Having regard to the opinion of the Economic and Social Committee[32]

Having regard to the opinion of the Committee of the Regions[33]

Acting in accordance with the procedure laid down in Article 251 of the Treaty[34]

Whereas:

(1) The potential for use of cogeneration as a measure to save energy is underused in the Community at present. Promotion of high-efficiency cogeneration based on a useful heat demand is a Community priority given the potential benefits of cogeneration with regard to saving primary energy and reducing emissions, in particular of greenhouse gases. In addition, efficient use of energy by cogeneration can also contribute positively to the security of energy supply and to the competitive situation of the European Union and its Member States. It is therefore necessary to take measures to ensure that the potential is better exploited within the framework of the internal energy market.

(2) Directive 96/92/EC of the European Parliament and of the Council of 19 December 1996 concerning common rules for the internal market in electricity[35] provides for an important step in the completion of the internal market in electricity. At its meeting in Lisbon on 23 and 24 March 2000, the European Council called for rapid work to be undertaken to complete the internal market in both electricity and gas and to speed up liberalisation in these sectors with a view to achieving a fully operational internal market. In response, the Commission adopted on 13 March 2001 a package of measures on completing the internal energy market, including a proposal for a Directive amending Directives 96/92/EC and 98/30/EC concerning common rules for the internal market in electricity and natural gas[36].

(3) The Green Paper[37] on security of energy supply points out that the European Union is extremely dependent on its external energy supplies currently accounting for 50% of requirements and projected to rise to 70% by 2030 if current trends persists. Import dependency and rising import ratios may lead to concern about the risk of interruption to or difficulties in supply. However, it would be simplistic and wrong to conceive security of supply as merely a question of reducing import dependency and boosting domestic production. Security of supply calls for a wide range of policy initiatives aimed at, inter alia, diversification of sources and technologies and improved international relations. The Green Paper emphasized furthermore that security of energy supply is essential for a future sustainable development. The Green Paper concludes that the adoption of new measures to reduce energy demand is essential both in terms of reducing the import dependence and in order to limit greenhouse gas emissions.

(4) The Commission's Communication "A Sustainable Europe for a better world – A European Union Strategy for Sustainable Development"[38] presented at the Gothenburg European Council on 15 and

[31]OJ C . . . . , ... , p.
[32]OJ C . . . . , ... , p.
[33]OJ C . . . . , ... , p.
[34]OJ C . . . . , ... , p.
[35]OJ L 27, 30.1.1997, p.20.

[36]COM(2001) 125 final.
[37]COM(2000) 769 final
[38]COM(2001) 264 final

16 June 2001 identified climate change as one of the principal barriers to sustainable development and emphasised the need for increased use of clean energy and clear action to reduce energy demand.

(5) The increased correct use of cogeneration constitutes an important part of the package of measures needed to comply with the Kyoto Protocol to the United Nations Framework Convention on Climate Change, and of any policy package to met further commitments. The Commission in its Communication on the implementation of the first phase of the European Climate Change Programme[39] identified promotion of cogeneration as one of the measures needed to reduce the greenhouse gas emissions from the energy sector and announced its intention to present a proposal for a Directive on the promotion of cogeneration in 2002.

(6) The increased correct use of cogeneration is a priority as outlined in the Communication "A Community strategy to promote combined heat and power (CHP) and to dismantle barriers to its development"[40]. This was endorsed by the Council in its resolution of 18 December 1997 on a Community strategy to promote combined heat and power[41], and by the European Parliament in its resolution of 23 April 1998 on the Community strategy to promote combined heat and power[42].

(7) The Council in its Conclusions of 30 May 2000 and of 5 December 2000[43] endorsed the Commission's Action Plan on energy efficiency[44] and identified promotion of cogeneration as one of the short-term priority areas. The European Parliament in its resolution of 7 February 2001[45] on the Action Plan on energy efficiency called on the Commission to submit proposals establishing common rules for the promotion of cogeneration, where this makes environmental sense.

(8) Council Directive 96/61/EC of 24 September 1996 concerning integrated pollution prevention and control[46], Directive 2001/80/EC of the European Parliament and of the Council on the limitation of emissions of certain pollutants into the air from large combustion plants[47] and Directive 2000/76/EC of the European Parliament and of the Council on the incineration of waste[48] all recite the need to evaluate the potential for cogeneration in new installations.

(9) High efficiency cogeneration is in this directive defined by the energy savings obtained by combined production in stead of separate production of heat and electricity. For existing plants energy savings of more than 5%, and for new plants energy savings of more than 10% qualify for the term 'high efficiency cogeneration'. To maximise the energy savings and to avoid that energy savings are lost through incorrect operation of the cogeneration plants the greatest attention must be paid to the functioning conditions of these plants, mainly to ensure that the heat production is being properly used.

(10) It is important for monitoring purposes and for reasons of transparency to adopt a harmonised basic definition of cogeneration. Where cogeneration installations are equipped to generate separate electricity or heat production, such production should be excluded from the definition of cogeneration.

(11) To ensure that only cogeneration that provides benefits in terms of primary energy savings is promoted, it is necessary to develop additional criteria to determine and quantify the energy efficiency of the cogeneration production identified under the basic definition. To avoid distortions of the internal energy market, national efficiency reference values used to define high-efficiency cogeneration should be adopted on the basis of a common methodology.

(12) The definitions of cogeneration and of high-efficiency cogeneration used in this Directive do not prejudge the use of different definitions in national legislation, for purposes other than those set out in this Directive. It is appropriate to borrow the definitions contained in Directive 96/92/EC of the European Parliament and of the Council of 19 December 1996 concerning common rules for the internal market of electricity[49] and in Directive 2001/77/EC of the European Parliament and of the Council of 27 September 2001 on the promotion of electricity

[39] COM(2001) 580 final
[40] COM(97) 514 final
[41] OJ C 4, 8.1.1998, p. 1
[42] A4-0145/98
[43] Council Conclusions 8835/00 (30 May 2000) and Council Conclusions 1400/00 (5 December 2000).
[44] COM(2000) 247 final
[45] A5-0054/2001.
[46] OJ L 257, 10.10.1996, p. 26

[47] OJ L 309, 27.11.2001, p. 1
[48] OJ L 332, 28.12.2000, p. 91
[49] OJ L 27, 30.01.1997, p.20

produced from renewable energy sources in the internal electricity market.[50]

(13) To increase transparency for the consumer's choice between electricity from cogeneration and electricity produced on the basis of other techniques, guarantee of origin of high efficiency cogeneration is necessary.

(14) To ensure increased market penetration of cogeneration in the medium term, it is appropriate to require all Member States to adopt and publish a report analyzing the national potential for high-efficiency cogeneration and to include a separate analysis of barriers to cogeneration in the report. The Commission, on the basis of these reports and the progress made in achieving the global indicative Community target of 18% of electricity consumption from cogeneration by 2010, should consider whether it is appropriate to establish indicative objectives for each Member State. Special considerations should be given to analysing the scope for increased use of renewable energy sources in the national heat markets via cogeneration.

(15) Public support should be consistent with the provisions of the Community guidelines on State aid for environmental protection[51]. These guidelines currently allow certain types of public support if it can be shown that the measures are beneficial in terms of protection of the environment because the conversion efficiency is particularly high, because the measures will allow energy consumption to be reduced or because the production process will be less damaging to the environment. Such support will in some cases be necessary to further exploit the potential for cogeneration, in particular to take account of the need to internalise external costs.

(16) Public support schemes for promoting cogeneration should focus on support for cogeneration based on a useful heat demand and avoid encouragement of increased heat demand in order to avoid increase of fuel consumption and CO_2 emissions. Member States should take steps to prevent public financial support for electricity from cogeneration from being used to subsidise heat production, thereby creating incentives for being less careful about the proper use of the heat output. Without prejudice to the Community Guidelines on State aid for environmental protection, direct support for production should in principle be focused on the share of cogenerated electricity produced either in installations with a capacity below a threshold value that should be set at 50 MW(e) or lower or in larger installations but then only the amount of electricity produced by the capacity below such a threshold value.

(17) Member States operate different mechanisms of support for cogeneration at the national level, including investment aid, tax exemptions or reductions, green certificates and direct price support schemes. The Commission intends to monitor the situation and report on experiences gained with the application of national support schemes.

(18) Grid connection costs and tariffs related to the transmission and distribution of electricity from cogeneration and tariffs related to the purchase of additional electricity sometimes needed by cogeneration producers should be set according to objective, transparent and non-discriminatory criteria taking into account the costs and benefits of cogeneration. Especially for cogeneration installations using renewables and small ones with capacity below 1 MW(e), costs and administrative burdens in relation to connection to the electricity grid constitute considerable barriers for further development.

(19) The specific structure of the cogeneration sector, which includes many small and medium-sized producers, should be taken into account, especially when reviewing the administrative procedures for obtaining permission to construct cogeneration capacity.

(20) Within the purpose of this Directive to create a framework for promoting cogeneration it is important to emphasise the need for a stabile economical and administrative environment for investments in new cogeneration installations. Member States are encouraged to address this need by designing support schemes with a duration period of at least 4 years and by avoiding frequent changes in administrative procedures etc. Member States are furthermore encouraged to ensure that public support schemes respect the phase-out principle.

(21) The overall efficiency and sustainability of cogeneration is dependent on the many factors such as technology used, fuel types, load curves, the size, and also on the properties of the heat. Use of heat as high pressure steam for industrial processes

[50]OJ L 283, 27.10.2001, p.33
[51]OJ C 37, 03.02.2001, pages 3–15

provides limits of the electrical efficiency of the cogeneration installation because of the high temperature level for the heat (above 140°C). Use of heat for central heating purposes, demanding a lower temperature level (from 40°C to 140°C) than the industrial use, allows a higher electrical efficiency of the cogeneration installation. Use of heat for agricultural heating, such as warming of greenhouses and aquaculture pools, provides an even lower level of temperature (below 40°C) and improves thereby the possibilities to increase the electrical efficiency. This Directive reflects these considerations by introducing three classes of cogeneration in order to ensure that evaluation of electrical efficiency of different cogeneration installations take the different heat temperature levels into consideration.

(22) In accordance with the principles of subsidiarity and proportionality as set out in Article 5 of the Treaty, general principles providing a framework for the promotion of cogeneration in the internal energy market should be set at Community level, but the detailed implementation should be left to Member States, thus allowing each Member State to choose the regime, which corresponds best to its particular situation. This Directive confines itself to the minimum required in order to achieve those objectives and does not go beyond what is necessary for that purpose.

HAVE ADOPTED THIS DIRECTIVE:

ARTICLE 1 PURPOSE

The purpose of this Directive is to create a framework for promotion of cogeneration based on useful heat demand in the internal energy market. Implementation of this Directive shall take into account the specific national circumstances especially concerning climatic and economic conditions.

ARTICLE 2 SCOPE

This Directive shall apply to cogeneration as defined in Article 3. Annex I provides a list of different types of cogeneration units covered by this Directive.

ARTICLE 3 DEFINITIONS

For the purpose of this Directive, the following definitions shall apply:

(a) "cogeneration" shall mean the generation in one process of thermal energy and electrical and/or mechanical energy. For practical reasons and based on the fact, that the use of the heat output for different purposes requires different temperature levels of the heat, and that these differences influence efficiencies of the cogeneration, cogeneration shall be divided into three classes: "industrial cogeneration", "heating cogeneration" and "agricultural cogeneration";

(b) "industrial cogeneration" shall mean the generation in one process of electrical and/or mechanical energy and thermal energy useful for industrial production generally with heat temperatures of 140°C or higher;

(c) "heating cogeneration" shall mean the generation in one process of electrical and/or mechanical energy and thermal energy useful for heating purposes in district heating systems or directly in buildings generally with heat temperatures between 40°C and 140°C;

(d) "agricultural cogeneration" shall mean the generation in one process of electrical and/or mechanical energy and thermal energy useful for agricultural heating of greenhouses, aquaculture plants and similar applications generally with heat temperatures between 15°C and 40°C;

(e) "useful heat" is heat produced in a cogeneration process to satisfy an economically justified demand, on the basis of the efficiency criteria laid down in Annex III, point c. 2; useful heat could via a secondary process be used to generate useful cooling;

(f) "electricity from cogeneration" shall mean electricity generated in accordance with the methodology laid down in Annex II and in a process linked to production of useful heat;

(g) "district heating" shall mean a system supplying commercially heat in the form of hot water or steam to users via a distribution network;

(h) "district cooling" shall mean a system supplying chilled water or hot water or steam to chillers via a distribution network;

(i) "back-up electricity" shall mean the electricity that has to be supplied through the electricity grid whenever the cogeneration process is disrupted or out of order;

(j) "top-up electricity" shall mean the electricity that has to be supplied through the electricity grid in cases where the electricity demand is greater than the electrical output of the cogeneration process.

(k) "heat efficiency" shall mean annual useful heat output divided by the fuel input used for heat produced in a cogeneration process and for gross electricity production. In the case of cogeneration with district heating useful heat output is measured at the point of outlet to the heat distribution network decreased by a realistic estimation of losses in the distribution network. In the case of other cogeneration applications useful heat output is measured at the point of use;

(l) "electrical efficiency" shall mean annual electricity production measured at the point of outlet of the main generators divided by the fuel input used for heat produced in a cogeneration process and gross electricity production;

(m) "overall efficiency" shall mean the annual sum of electricity production and useful heat output divided by the fuel input used for heat produced in a cogeneration process and gross electricity production;

(n) "efficiency" shall mean efficiency calculated on the basis of Net Calorific Values of fuels (lower calorific value) which means that the latent heat of vaporisation of moisture is not included;

(o) "high efficiency cogeneration" shall mean cogeneration meeting the criteria outlined in Annex III;

(p) "efficiency reference value for separate production" shall mean efficiency of the alternative separate productions of heat and electricity that the cogeneration process is assumed to displace.

(q) "Power to Heat Ratio" shall mean the relation of electrical energy to useful thermal energy;

(r) "cogeneration unit" shall mean a unit mainly intended for cogeneration processes as defined under point a); when a cogeneration unit generates only electrical energy or only thermal energy it is still to be defined as a cogeneration unit, but its output shall not be considered cogeneration for the purpose of this Directive.

(s) "cogeneration installation" shall mean an installation made up of one or more cogeneration units. A cogeneration installation may include equipment where it is possible to generate only electrical energy or only thermal energy. The output from such equipment shall not be considered cogeneration for the purpose of this Directive;

(t) "new cogeneration units" shall mean cogeneration units having started operation on, or after, 1 January 2004;

(u) "existing cogeneration units" shall mean cogeneration units having started operation before 1 January 2004.

In addition, the definitions in Directive 96/92/ and in Directive 2001/77/EC shall apply.

ARTICLE 4 GUARANTEE OF ORIGIN OF ELECTRICITY FROM COGENERATION

1. Member States shall no later than two years after the entry into force of this Directive ensure that the origin of electricity produced in cogeneration units can be guaranteed as such within the meaning of this Directive according to objective, transparent and non-discriminatory criteria laid down by each Member State. Member States shall ensure that this guarantee of origin of the electricity is issued to this effect in response to a request.

2. Member States shall designate no later than one year after the entry into force of this Directive one or more competent bodies, independent of generation and distribution activities, to supervise the issue of the guarantee of origin referred in paragraph 1 Member States or the competent bodies shall put in place appropriate mechanisms to ensure that the guarantee of origin are both accurate and reliable and they shall outline in the report referred to in Article 6(3) the measures taken to ensure the reliability of the certificate system

3. Guarantee of origin shall:

- specify the fuel source from which the electricity was produced, specify the use of the heat generated together with the electricity and finally specify the dates and places of production;
- specify the quantity of electricity from cogeneration that the guarantee represents;
- specify the efficiency reference values for separate production of electricity and heat, and the efficiency of cogeneration in accordance with Article 5;
- enable producers of electricity from cogeneration to demonstrate that the electricity they sell is

produced from cogeneration within the meaning of this Directive.

Member States may include additional information on the guarantee of origin

4. Guarantee of origin, issued according to paragraph 2, shall be mutually recognised by the Member States, exclusively as proof of the elements referred in paragraph 3. Any refusal to recognise a certificate of origin as such proof, in particular for reasons relating to the prevention of fraud, must be based on objective, transparent and non-discriminatory criteria. In the event of refusal to recognise a certificate of origin, the Commission may compel the refusing party to recognise it, particularly with regard to objective, transparent and non-discriminatory criteria on which such recognition is based.

ARTICLE 5 EFFICIENCY CRITERIA

1. Member States shall no later than two years after the entry into force of this Directive ensure that the efficiency of cogeneration production, defined in terms of achievement of primary energy savings can be determined in accordance with Annex III.

2. For the purpose of determining the efficiency of cogeneration, Member States shall not later than two years after the entry into force of this Directive adopt:

(a) efficiency reference values for separate production of heat and electricity to be used for the calculation of primary energy savings from cogeneration in accordance with the methodology set out in Annex III.

(b) principles for defining the national efficiency reference values for separate production of heat and electricity based on a well-documented analysis of the most realistic references in each Member State.

3. Member States shall review the national efficiency reference values for separate production of heat and electricity every 5 years to take account of technological developments and changes in the distribution on energy sources. Where changes in the national efficiency reference values for separate production are made, the new reference values shall be published and shall be notified to the Commission.

4. The Commission shall evaluate the criteria for determining the efficiency of cogeneration adopted by the Member States pursuant to (paragraph 2). After having consulted the Member States, the Commission shall in the report referred to in Article 10 (1), consider the scope for a harmonised methodology that Member States could follow in order to determine the efficiency of cogeneration production.

ARTICLE 6 NATIONAL POTENTIALS FOR HIGH-EFFICIENCY COGENERATION

1. Member States shall establish an analysis of the national potential for high-efficiency cogeneration.

2. The analysis shall comply with the criteria listed in Annex IV. It shall be based on well-documented scientific data and shall distinguish between applications of cogeneration in at least the following categories:

- industrial cogeneration
- heating cogeneration
- agricultural cogeneration

3. Member States shall include in the analysis a separate analysis of barriers, which may prevent the realisation of the national potential for high-efficiency cogeneration. In particular, this analysis shall consider barriers relating to the prices of and access to fuels, barriers in relation to grid system issues, barriers in relation to administrative procedures, and barriers relating to the lack of internalisation of the external costs in energy prices.

4. Member States shall for the first time not later than two years after the entry into force of this Directive and thereafter every three years evaluate progress towards increasing the share of high-efficiency cogeneration. Member States shall also evaluate measures taken to promote high-efficiency cogeneration and indicate to what extent the measures are consistent with national climate change commitments.

5. On the basis of the reports referred to in paragraphs 1, 3 and 4, the Commission shall assess how much progress Member States have made towards realizing their national potentials for high-efficiency cogeneration.

The Commission shall publish its conclusions in the report referred to in Article 10, for the first time not later than four years after the entry into force of this Directive and thereafter every three years.

ARTICLE 7 SUPPORT SCHEMES

1. Member States shall ensure that support for cogeneration production is based on the useful heat demand, in the light of opportunities available for reducing energy demand through other economically feasible measures like energy efficiency measures.

2. Without prejudice to Articles 87 and 88 of the Treaty, the Commission shall evaluate the application of support mechanisms used in Member States according to which a producer of cogeneration receives, on the basis of regulations issued by public authorities, direct or indirect support, which could have the effect of restricting trade.

The Commission shall consider whether those mechanisms contribute to the pursuit of the objectives set out in Articles 6 and 174(1) of the Treaty.

3. The Commission shall in the report referred to in Article 10 present a well-documented analysis on experience gained with the application and coexistence of the different support mechanisms referred to in paragraph 2. The report shall assess the success, including cost-effectiveness, of the support systems in promoting the use of high-efficiency cogeneration in conformity with the national potentials referred to in Article 6. The report shall further review to what extent the support schemes have contributed to the creation of stable conditions for investments in cogeneration.

ARTICLE 8 ELECTRICITY GRID SYSTEM ISSUES

1. Without prejudice to the maintenance of the reliability and safety of the grid, Member States shall take the necessary measures to ensure that transmission system operators and distribution system operators in their territory guarantee the transmission and distribution of electricity produced from cogeneration.

2. Member States shall establish a legal framework or require transmission system operators and distribution system operators to set up and publish standard rules on the bearing of the costs of technical adaptations, such as grid connections and grid reinforcements, which are necessary in order to integrate new producers feeding into the grid electricity produced from cogeneration.

Member States shall establish a legal framework or require transmission system operators and distribution system operators to set up and publish standard rules relating to the sharing of costs of system installations, such as grid connections and reinforcements, between all system users benefiting from them.

The sharing shall be enforced by a mechanism based on objective, transparent and non-discriminatory criteria taking into account the benefits which initially and subsequently connected producers as well as transmission system operators and distribution system operators derive from the connections.

The rules shall be based on objective, transparent and non-discriminatory criteria taking particular account of all the costs and benefits associated with the connection of the producers to the grid. The rules may provide for different types of connection.

3. Member States may require transmission system operators and distribution system operators to bear, in full or in part, the costs referred to in paragraph 2.

4. Transmission system operators and distribution system operators shall be required to provide any new producer wishing to be connected with a comprehensive and detailed estimate of the costs associated with the connection.

5. Member States shall ensure that the charging of transmission and distribution fees does not discriminate against electricity from cogeneration. Where appropriate, Member States shall put in place a legal framework or require transmission system operators and distribution system operators to ensure that fees charged for the transmission and distribution of electricity from installations using cogeneration reflect realisable cost benefits resulting from the installation's connection to the network. Such cost benefits may arise from the direct use of the low-voltage grid.

6. Unless the cogeneration producer is an eligible customer under national legislation within the meaning of Article 17 (2) of Directive 96/92/EC, Member States shall take the necessary measures to ensure that the tariffs for the purchase of electricity

to back-up or top-up electricity generation are set on the basis of published tariffs and terms and conditions. Such tariffs and terms and conditions shall be fixed or approved in accordance with objective, transparent and non-discriminatory criteria by an independent regulatory authority prior to their entry into force.

7. Member States shall designate one or more competent bodies, which may be an independent regulatory authority, to monitor and benchmark the tariffs and terms and conditions offered to cogeneration producers when back-up or top-up electricity is purchased or when excess electricity is sold. The body shall publish for the first time three years after the entry into force of this Directive and thereafter every third year a report outlining the findings of these assessments. The report shall be forwarded to the Commission.

8. Member States shall particularly facilitate access to the grid system of electricity produced from cogeneration units using renewables energy sources and installations with a capacity less than 1 MW_e, as set out in Annex III, a).

ARTICLE 9 ADMINISTRATIVE PROCEDURES

1. Member States or the competent bodies appointed by the Member States shall evaluate the existing legislative and regulatory framework with regard to authorisation procedures or the other procedures laid down in Article 4 of Directive 96/92/EC, which are applicable to cogeneration installations, with a view to:

(a) encouraging the design of cogeneration installations to match economically justified demands for heat output and avoiding production of more heat than useful heat.

(b) reducing the regulatory and non-regulatory barriers to an increase in cogeneration;

(c) streamlining and expediting procedures at the appropriate administrative level; and

(d) ensuring that the rules are objective, transparent and non-discriminatory, and take fully into account the particularities of the various cogeneration technologies.

2. Member States shall – where this is appropriate in the context of national legislation – provide an indication of the stage reached specifically in:

(a) co-ordination between the different administrative bodies as regards deadlines, reception and treatment of applications for authorisations;

(b) the drawing up of possible guidelines for the activities referred to in paragraph 1, and the feasibility of a fast-track planning procedure for cogeneration producers; and

(c) the designation of authorities to act as mediators in disputes between authorities responsible for issuing authorisations and applicants for authorisations.

3. The Commission shall, in the report referred to in Article 11 and on the basis of the Member States' reports referred to in Article 10(1), assess best practices with a view to achieving the objectives referred to in paragraph 1.

ARTICLE 10 MEMBER STATES' REPORTING

1. Member States shall, not later than two years after the entry into force of this Directive, publish a report with the following content:

(a) efficiency reference values for separate production of heat and electricity referred to in Article 5 (2);

(b) principles for defining the national efficiency reference values for separate production of heat and electricity referred to in Article 5 (2);

(c) analysis of national potential for high efficiency cogeneration referred to in Article 6(1);

(d) analysis of barriers, which may prevent the realisation of the national potential for high efficiency cogeneration referred to in Article 6 (3);

(e) examination of the measures taken to facilitate access to the grid system of electricity produced from cogeneration and, inter alia, the feasibility of introducing two-way metering for cogeneration units installed in residential buildings;

(f) evaluation of the existing legislative and regulatory framework referred to in Article 9(1) and 9(2).

2. Member States shall not later than two years after the entry into force of this Directive and hereafter every three years publish a report on progress towards increasing the share of high efficiency cogeneration referred to in Article 6(4);

3. Member States shall submit to the Commission on an annual basis statistics on national electricity and heat production from cogeneration, in accordance with the methodology shown in Annex II.

They shall also submit annual statistics on cogeneration capacities and fuels used for cogeneration.

ARTICLE 11 COMMISSION REPORTING

On the basis of the reports submitted pursuant to Article 8(7) and Article 10 (1) and (3), the Commission shall review the application of this Directive and submit to the European Parliament and to the Council not later than four years after the entry into force of this Directive and thereafter every six years, a progress report on the implementation of this Directive.

In particular, the report shall:

(a) consider the scope for further harmonisation of the criteria to determine the efficiency of cogeneration.

(b) consider progress towards realising national potentials for high-efficiency cogeneration referred to in Article 6.

(c) assess the extent to which rules and procedures defining the framework conditions for cogeneration in the internal energy market are set on the basis of objective, transparent and non-discriminatory criteria taking due account of the benefits of cogeneration.

(d) examine the experiences gained with the application and coexistence of different support mechanisms for cogeneration.

(e) review reference values for separate production on the basis of the current technologies

If appropriate, the Commission shall submit with the report further proposals to the European Parliament and the Council.

ARTICLE 12 TRANSPOSITION

Member States shall bring into force the laws, regulations and administrative provisions necessary to comply with this Directive not later than two years after the entry into force of this Directive. They shall forthwith inform the Commission thereof.

When Member States adopt these measures, they shall contain a reference to this Directive or shall be accompanied by such a reference on the occasion of their official publication. The Member States shall lay down the methods of making such reference.

ARTICLE 13 ENTRY INTO FORCE

This Directive shall enter into force on the twentieth day following that of its publication in the Official Journal of the European Communities.

ARTICLE 14 ADDRESSEES

This Directive is addressed to the Member States.

Done at Brussels,

For the Council
The President

ANNEX I COGENERATION TECHNOLOGIES COVERED BY THE DIRECTIVE

a. Combined cycle gas turbine with heat recovery

b. Steam backpressure turbine

c. Steam extraction condensing turbine

d. Gas turbine with heat recovery

e. Internal combustion engine

f. Microturbines

g. Stirling engines

h. Fuel cells

i. Steam engines

j. Organic Rankine cycles

k. Any other type of technology or combination thereof falling under the definitions laid down in Article 3.

ANNEX II DEFINITION OF ELECTRICITY FROM COGENERATION

Values used for calculation of electricity from cogeneration shall be determined on the basis of the expected or actual operation of the unit under realistic conditions.

(a) Electricity production from cogeneration shall be considered equal to total annual electricity production of the unit.

- in cogeneration units of type b), d), e), f), g), and h) referred to in Annex I, with an annual overall efficiency higher or equal to 75%, and
- in cogeneration units of type a) and c) referred to in Annex I with an annual overall efficiency higher or equal to 85%.

(b) Calculations shall be made in order to separate electricity from cogeneration and electricity not produced in a cogeneration process. In cogeneration units with an annual overall efficiency below 75% (cogeneration units of type b), d), e), f), g), and h) referred to in Annex I) or with an annual overall efficiency below 85% (cogeneration units of type a) and c) referred to in Annex I) The following formula shall be used:

$$E_{CHP} = Q_{net} \cdot C$$

where

E_{CHP} is the amount of electricity from cogeneration

C is the power to heat ratio

Q_{net} is the net heat production from a cogeneration process (defined as total heat production minus any heat produced in separate boilers)

If the actual power to heat ratio of a cogeneration unit is not known, the following default values may be used for units of type a), b), c), d), and e) referred to in Annex I provided that the calculated cogeneration electricity is less or equal to total electricity production of the unit:

	Default power to heat capacity ratio, C	
Type of the unit	**District heating**	**Industrial**
Combined cycle gas turbine with heat recovery	0,95	0,75
Steam backpressure turbine	0,45	0,30
Steam condensing extraction turbine	0,45	0,30
Gas turbine with heat recovery	0,55	0,40
Internal combustion engine	0,75	0,60

Subject to prior notification to the Commission, Member States may use other default values for power to heat ratios than the ones provided in this Annex. Such alternative default values shall be published by Member States.

If Member States introduce default values for power to heat ratios for units of type f), g), h), i), j) and k) referred to in Annex I, such default values shall be published and shall be notified to the Commission.

(c) Subject to prior approval by the Commission, Member States may use other methods than the one provided for in paragraph b) of this annex to subtract possible electricity production not produced in a cogeneration process from the reported figures.

ANNEX III METHODOLOGY FOR DETERMINING THE EFFICIENCY OF COGENERATION PRODUCTION

Values used for calculation of efficiency of cogeneration production and primary energy savings shall be determined on the basis of the expected or actual operation of the unit under realistic conditions.

(a) High-Efficiency Cogeneration

For the purpose of this Directive high-efficiency cogeneration production shall fulfil the following criteria:

- production from new cogeneration units shall provide primary energy savings of at least 10% compared with the references for separate production of heat and power;
- production from existing cogeneration units shall provide primary energy savings of at least 5% compared with the references for separate production of heat and power;
- production from cogeneration units using renewable energy sources and from cogeneration installations with an installed capacity below 1 MWe providing primary energy savings in the range 0–5% may qualify as high-efficiency cogeneration;
- Member States may introduce principles whereby production from cogeneration units below the thresholds referred to in this Annex may be considered to be partially fulfilling the efficiency criteria. If such principles are applied, appropriate methodologies for determining the

reduced efficiency of such production, calculated in proportion to the reduced primary energy savings, shall be developed by the Member State and shall be notified to the Commission. In such cases, the reduced efficiency of the cogeneration production shall be clearly displayed on the certificate of origin.

(b) Calculation of Primary Energy Savings

The amount of primary energy savings provided by cogeneration production defined in accordance with Annex II to this Directive shall be calculated on the basis of the following formula:

$$PES = \left(1 - \frac{1}{\frac{CHP\ H\eta}{Ref\ H\eta} + \frac{CHP\ E\eta}{Ref\ E\eta}}\right) \times 100\%$$

Where:

PES	is primary energy savings
CHP Hη	is the heat efficiency of the cogeneration production
Ref Hη	is the heat efficiency of the reference for separate heat production
CHP Eη	is the electrical efficiency of the cogeneration production
Ref Eη	is the electrical efficiency of the reference for separate electricity production

Subject to prior notification to the Commission, Member States may use other formula leading to the same results to calculate the primary energy savings from cogeneration. In the cases where alternative formulas are used, such formula shall be published by the Member State.

(c) Efficiency Reference Values for Separate Production of Heat and Electricity

The principles for defining the references for separate production of heat and electricity referred to in Article 5(2) and in the formula set out in paragraph b) of this Annex shall establish the operating efficiency of the separate heat and electricity production that cogeneration is assumed to displace.

To define the efficiency reference values, the following principles shall be applied:

(1) For *new cogeneration units* as defined in Article 3, the comparison with new separate electricity production shall be based on the principle that similar fuel categories are compared. The following indicative efficiency reference values for new separate electricity production may be used:

Indicative efficiency reference values for new separate electricity production

Fuel category	Operating efficiency
Natural gas	55%
Coal	42%
Oil	42%
Renewables and waste	22–35%

In the case of cogeneration units connected at the electricity distribution system, the reference values provided in the above table may be lowered with 5–10% to take account of avoided network losses.

(2) For *new cogeneration units* as defined in Article 3, the indicative efficiency reference value of new separate heat production shall be an operating efficiency of 90%.

In the case of heat production based on oil or coal, the efficiency reference value may be lowered to 85%. In the case of heat production based on renewable energy sources or waste, the efficiency reference value may be lowered to 80%. In the case of high temperature steam used for industrial processes, the reference values for separate heat production may be lowered to 80%.

(3) For *existing cogeneration units* as defined in Article 3, the efficiency reference value for separate electricity production shall be based on the average operating efficiency of the national fossil-fuelled electricity production. Where appropriate, possible crossborder trade in electricity having an impact on the reference values may be taken into account.

(4) For *existing cogeneration units* as defined in Article 3 the efficiency reference value for separate heat production shall be based on the average operating efficiency of the national heat production mix.

(5) Subject to prior notification to the Commission, Member States may include additional aspects in the national criteria for determining the efficiency of cogeneration.

ANNEX IV CRITERIA FOR ANALYSIS OF NATIONAL POTENTIALS FOR HIGH-EFFICIENCY COGENERATION

(a) The analysis of the national potential for high-efficiency cogeneration shall identify suitable heating and/or cooling demands and shall distinguish between application of cogeneration in at least the following main categories:

- Industrial cogeneration
- Heating cogeneration
- Agricultural cogeneration

(b) For each of the three categories referred to under a), the analysis shall consider:

- The type of fuels that are likely to be used to realise the cogeneration potentials, including specific considerations on the potential for increasing the use of renewable energy sources in the national heat markets via cogeneration.
- The type of cogeneration technologies as listed in Annex I that are likely to be used to realise the national potential.
- The type of separate production of heat and electricity that high-efficiency cogeneration is likely to substitute.
- A division of the potential into modernisation of existing capacity and construction of new capacity.

(c) The analysis shall include appropriate mechanisms to assess the cost effectiveness – in terms of primary energy savings – of increasing the share of high-efficiency cogeneration in the national energy mix. The analysis of cost effectiveness shall also take into account national commitments accepted in the context of the climate change commitments accepted by the Community pursuant to the Kyoto Protocol to the United Nations Framework Convention on Climate Change.

(d) The analysis of the national cogeneration potential shall specify the potentials in relation to the timeframes 2010, 2015 and 2020 and include appropriate cost estimates for each of the timeframes.

Directive 2003/87/EC of the European Parliament and of the Council of 13 October 2003 Establishing a Scheme for Greenhouse Gas Emission Allowance Trading within the Community and Amending Council Directive 96/61/EC

(Text with EEA relevance)

THE EUROPEAN PARLIAMENT AND THE COUNCIL OF THE EUROPEAN UNION,

Having regard to the Treaty establishing the European Community, and in particular Article 175(1) thereof,

Having regard to the proposal from the Commission[1],

Having regard to the opinion of the European Economic and Social Committee[2],

Having regard to the opinion of the Committee of the Regions[3],

Acting in accordance with the procedure laid down in Article 251 of the Treaty[4],

Whereas:

(1) The Green Paper on greenhouse gas emissions trading within the European Union launched a debate across Europe on the suitability and possible functioning of greenhouse gas emissions trading within the European Union. The European Climate Change Programme has considered Community policies and measures through a multi-stakeholder process, including a scheme for greenhouse gas emission allowance trading within the Community (the Community scheme) based on the Green Paper. In its Conclusions of 8 March 2001, the Council recognised the particular importance of the European Climate Change Programme and of work based on the Green Paper, and underlined the urgent need for concrete action at Community level.

(2) The Sixth Community Environment Action Programme established by Decision No 1600/2002/EC of the European Parliament and of the Council[5] identifies climate change as a priority for action and provides for the establishment of a Community-wide emissions trading scheme by 2005. That Programme recognises that the Community is committed to achieving an 8% reduction in emissions of greenhouse gases by 2008 to 2012 compared to 1990 levels, and that, in the longerterm, global emissions of greenhouse gases will need to be reduced by approximately 70% compared to 1990 levels.

(3) The ultimate objective of the United Nations Framework Convention on Climate Change, which was approved by Council Decision 94/69/EC of 15 December 1993 concerning the conclusion of the United Nations Framework Convention on Climate Change[6], is to achieve stabilisation of greenhouse gas concentrations in the atmosphere at a level which prevents dangerous anthropogenic interference with the climate system.

(4) Once it enters into force, the Kyoto Protocol, which was approved by Council Decision 2002/358/EC of 25 April 2002 concerning the approval, on behalf of the European Community, of the Kyoto Protocol to the United Nations Framework Convention on Climate Change and the joint fulfilment of commitments thereunder[7], will commit the Community and its Member States to reducing their aggregate anthropogenic emissions of greenhouse gases listed in Annex A to the Protocol

[1] OJ C 75 E, 26.3.2002, p. 33.
[2] OJ C 221, 17.9.2002, p. 27.
[3] OJ C 192, 12.8.2002, p. 59.
[4] Opinion of the European Parliament of 10 October 2002 (not yet published in the Official Journal), Council Common Position of 18 March 2003 (OJ C 125 E, 27.5.2003, p. 72), Decision of the European Parliament of 2 July 2003 (not yet published in the Official Journal) and Council Decision of 22 July 2003.
[5] OJ L 242, 10.9.2002, p. 1.
[6] OJ L 33, 7.2.1994, p. 11.
[7] OJ L 130, 15.5.2002, p. 1.

by 8% compared to 1990 levels in the period 2008 to 2012.

(5) The Community and its Member States have agreed to fulfil their commitments to reduce anthropogenic greenhouse gas emissions under the Kyoto Protocol jointly, in accordance with Decision 2002/358/EC. This Directive aims to contribute to fulfilling the commitments of the European Community and its Member States more effectively, through an efficient European market in greenhouse gas emission allowances, with the least possible diminution of economic development and employment.

(6) Council Decision 93/389/EEC of 24 June 1993 for a monitoring mechanism of Community CO_2 and other greenhouse gas emissions[8], established a mechanism for monitoring greenhouse gas emissions and evaluating progress towards meeting commitments in respect of these emissions. This mechanism will assist Member States in determining the total quantity of allowances to allocate.

(7) Community provisions relating to allocation of allowances by the Member States are necessary to contribute to preserving the integrity of the internal market and to avoid distortions of competition.

(8) Member States should have regard when allocating allowances to the potential for industrial process activities to reduce emissions.

(9) Member States may provide that they only issue allowances valid for a five-year period beginning in 2008 to persons in respect of allowances cancelled, corresponding to emission reductions made by those persons on their national territory during a three-year period beginning in 2005.

(10) Starting with the said five-year period, transfers of allowances to another Member State will involve corresponding adjustments of assigned amount units under the Kyoto Protocol.

(11) Member States should ensure that the operators of certain specified activities hold a greenhouse gas emissions permit and that they monitor and report their emissions of greenhouse gases specified in relation to those activities.

(12) Member States should lay down rules on penalties applicable to infringements of this Directive and ensure that they are implemented. Those penalties must be effective, proportionate and dissuasive.

(13) In order to ensure transparency, the public should have access to information relating to the allocation of allowances and to the results of monitoring of emissions, subject only to restrictions provided for in Directive 2003/4/EC of the European Parliament and of the Council of 28 January 2003 on public access to environmental information[9].

(14) Member States should submit a report on the implementation of this Directive drawn up on the basis of Council Directive 91/692/EEC of 23 December 1991 standardising and rationalising reports on the implementation of certain Directives relating to the environment[10].

(15) The inclusion of additional installations in the Community scheme should be in accordance with the provisions laid down in this Directive, and the coverage of the Community scheme may thereby be extended to emissions of greenhouse gases other than carbon dioxide, *inter alia* from aluminium and chemicals activities.

(16) This Directive should not prevent any Member State from maintaining or establishing national trading schemes regulating emissions of greenhouse gases from activities other than those listed in Annex I or included in the Community scheme, or from installations temporarily excluded from the Community scheme.

(17) Member States may participate in international emissions trading as Parties to the Kyoto Protocol with any other Party included in Annex B thereto.

(18) Linking the Community scheme to greenhouse gas emission trading schemes in third countries will increase the cost-effectiveness of achieving the Community emission reductions target as laid down in Decision 2002/358/EC on the joint fulfilment of commitments.

(19) Project-based mechanisms including Joint Implementation (JI) and the Clean Development Mechanism (CDM) are important to achieve the goals of both reducing global greenhouse gas emissions and increasing the costeffective functioning

[8] OJ L 167, 9.7.1993, p. 31. Decision as amended by Decision 1999/296/EC (OJ L 117, 5.5.1999, p. 35).

[9] OJ L 41, 14.2.2003, p. 26.

[10] OJ L 377, 31.12.1991, p. 48.

of the Community scheme. In accordance with the relevant provisions of the Kyoto Protocol and Marrakech Accords, the use of the mechanisms should be supplemental to domestic action and domestic action will thus constitute a significant element of the effort made.

(20) This Directive will encourage the use of more energyefficient technologies, including combined heat and power technology, producing less emissions per unit of output, while the future directive of the European Parliament and of the Council on the promotion of cogeneration based on useful heat demand in the internal energy market will specifically promote combined heat and power technology.

(21) Council Directive 96/61/EC of 24 September 1996 concerning integrated pollution prevention and control[11] establishes a general framework for pollution prevention and control, through which greenhouse gas emissions permits may be issued. Directive 96/61/EC should be amended to ensure that emission limit values are not set for direct emissions of greenhouse gases from an installation subject to this Directive and that Member States may choose not to impose requirements relating to energy efficiency in respect of combustion units or other units emitting carbon dioxide on the site, without prejudice to any other requirements pursuant to Directive 96/61/EC.

(22) This Directive is compatible with the United Nations Framework Convention on Climate Change and the Kyoto Protocol. It should be reviewed in the light of developments in that context and to take into account experience in its implementation and progress achieved in monitoring of emissions of greenhouse gases.

(23) Emission allowance trading should form part of a comprehensive and coherent package of policies and measures implemented at Member State and Community level. Without prejudice to the application of Articles 87 and 88 of the Treaty, where activities are covered by the Community scheme, Member States may consider the implications of regulatory, fiscal or other policies that pursue the same objectives. The review of the Directive should consider the extent to which these objectives have been attained.

[11]OJ L 257, 10.10.1996, p. 26.

(24) The instrument of taxation can be a national policy to limit emissions from installations temporarily excluded.

(25) Policies and measures should be implemented at Member State and Community level across all sectors of the European Union economy, and not only within the industry and energy sectors, in order to generate substantial emissions reductions. The Commission should, in particular, consider policies and measures at Community level in order that the transport sector makes a substantial contribution to the Community and its Member States meeting their climate change obligations under the Kyoto Protocol.

(26) Notwithstanding the multifaceted potential of market-based mechanisms, the European Union strategy for climate change mitigation should be built on a balance between the Community scheme and other types of Community, domestic and international action.

(27) This Directive respects the fundamental rights and observes the principles recognised in particular by the Charter of Fundamental Rights of the European Union.

(28) The measures necessary for the implementation of this Directive should be adopted in accordance with Council Decision 1999/468/EC of 28 June 1999 laying down the procedures for the exercise of implementing powers conferred on the Commission[12].

(29) As the criteria (1), (5) and (7) of Annex III cannot be amended through comitology, amendments in respect of periods after 2012 should only be made through codecision.

(30) Since the objective of the proposed action, the establishment of a Community scheme, cannot be sufficiently achieved by the Member States acting individually, and can therefore by reason of the scale and effects of the proposed action be better achieved at Community level, the Community may adopt measures, in accordance with the principle of subsidiarity as set out in Article 5 of the Treaty. In accordance with the principle of proportionality, as set out in that Article, this Directive does not go beyond what is necessary in order to achieve that objective,

[12]OJ L 184, 17.7.1999, p. 23.

HAVE ADOPTED THIS DIRECTIVE:

ARTICLE 1 SUBJECT MATTER

This Directive establishes a scheme for greenhouse gas emission allowance trading within the Community (hereinafter referred to as the 'Community scheme') in order to promote reductions of greenhouse gas emissions in a cost-effective and economically efficient manner.

ARTICLE 2 SCOPE

1. This Directive shall apply to emissions from the activities listed in Annex I and greenhouse gases listed in Annex II.

2. This Directive shall apply without prejudice to any requirements pursuant to Directive 96/61/EC.

ARTICLE 3 DEFINITIONS

For the purposes of this Directive the following definitions shall apply:

(a) 'allowance' means an allowance to emit one tonne of carbon dioxide equivalent during a specified period, which shall be valid only for the purposes of meeting the requirements of this Directive and shall be transferable in accordance with the provisions of this Directive;

(b) 'emissions' means the release of greenhouse gases into the atmosphere from sources in an installation;

(c) 'greenhouse gases' means the gases listed in Annex II;

(d) 'greenhouse gas emissions permit' means the permit issued in accordance with Articles 5 and 6;

(e) 'installation' means a stationary technical unit where one or more activities listed in Annex I are carried out and any other directly associated activities which have a technical connection with the activities carried out on that site and which could have an effect on emissions and pollution;

(f) 'operator' means any person who operates or controls an installation or, where this is provided for in national legislation, to whom decisive economic power over the technical functioning of the installation has been delegated;

(g) 'person' means any natural or legal person;

(h) 'new entrant' means any installation carrying out one or more of the activities indicated in Annex I, which has obtained a greenhouse gas emissions permit or an update of its greenhouse gas emissions permit because of a change in the nature or functioning or an extension of the installation, subsequent to the notification to the Commission of the national allocation plan;

(i) 'the public' means one or more persons and, in accordance with national legislation or practice, associations, organisations or groups of persons;

(j) 'tonne of carbon dioxide equivalent' means one metric tonne of carbon dioxide (CO_2) or an amount of any other greenhouse gas listed in Annex II with an equivalent global-warming potential.

ARTICLE 4 GREENHOUSE GAS EMISSIONS PERMITS

Member States shall ensure that, from 1 January 2005, no installation undertakes any activity listed in Annex I resulting in emissions specified in relation to that activity unless its operator holds a permit issued by a competent authority in accordance with Articles 5 and 6, or the installation is temporarily excluded from the Community scheme pursuant to Article 27.

ARTICLE 5 APPLICATIONS FOR GREENHOUSE GAS EMISSIONS PERMITS

An application to the competent authority for a greenhouse gas emissions permit shall include a description of:

(a) the installation and its activities including the technology used;

(b) the raw and auxiliary materials, the use of which is likely to lead to emissions of gases listed in Annex I;

(c) the sources of emissions of gases listed in Annex I from the installation; and

(d) the measures planned to monitor and report emissions in accordance with the guidelines adopted pursuant to Article 14.

The application shall also include a non-technical summary of the details referred to in the first subparagraph.

ARTICLE 6 CONDITIONS FOR AND CONTENTS OF THE GREENHOUSE GAS EMISSIONS PERMIT

1. The competent authority shall issue a greenhouse gas emissions permit granting authorisation to emit greenhouse gases from all or part of an installation if it is satisfied that the operator is capable of monitoring and reporting emissions.

A greenhouse gas emissions permit may cover one or more installations on the same site operated by the same operator.

2. Greenhouse gas emissions permits shall contain the following:

(a) the name and address of the operator;

(b) a description of the activities and emissions from the installation;

(c) monitoring requirements, specifying monitoring methodology and frequency;

(d) reporting requirements; and

(e) an obligation to surrender allowances equal to the total emissions of the installation in each calendar year, as verified in accordance with Article 15, within four months following the end of that year.

ARTICLE 7 CHANGES RELATING TO INSTALLATIONS

The operator shall inform the competent authority of any changes planned in the nature or functioning, or an extension, of the installation which may require updating of the greenhouse gas emissions permit. Where appropriate, the competent authority shall update the permit. Where there is a change in the identity of the installation's operator, the competent authority shall update the permit to include the name and address of the new operator.

ARTICLE 8 COORDINATION WITH DIRECTIVE 96/61/EC

Member States shall take the necessary measures to ensure that, where installations carry out activities that are included in Annex I to Directive 96/61/EC, the conditions of, and procedure for, the issue of a greenhouse gas emissions permit are coordinated with those for the permit provided for in that Directive. The requirements of Articles 5, 6 and 7 of this Directive may be integrated into the procedures provided for in Directive 96/61/EC.

ARTICLE 9 NATIONAL ALLOCATION PLAN

1. For each period referred to in Article 11(1) and (2), each Member State shall develop a national plan stating the total quantity of allowances that it intends to allocate for that period and how it proposes to allocate them. The plan shall be based on objective and transparent criteria, including those listed in Annex III, taking due account of comments from the public. The Commission shall, without prejudice to the Treaty, by 31 December 2003 at the latest develop guidance on the implementation of the criteria listed in Annex III.

For the period referred to in Article 11(1), the plan shall be published and notified to the Commission and to the other Member States by 31 March 2004 at the latest. For subsequent periods, the plan shall be published and notified to the Commission and to the other Member States at least 18 months before the beginning of the relevant period.

2. National allocation plans shall be considered within the committee referred to in Article 23(1).

3. Within three months of notification of a national allocation plan by a Member State under paragraph 1, the Commission may reject that plan, or any aspect thereof, on the basis that it is incompatible with the criteria listed in Annex III or with Article 10. The Member State shall only take a decision under Article 11(1) or (2) if proposed amendments are accepted by the Commission. Reasons shall be given for any rejection decision by the Commission.

ARTICLE 10 METHOD OF ALLOCATION

For the three-year period beginning 1 January 2005 Member States shall allocate at least 95% of the allowances free of charge. For the five-year period beginning 1 January 2008, Member States shall allocate at least 90% of the allowances free of charge.

ARTICLE 11 ALLOCATION AND ISSUE OF ALLOWANCES

1. For the three-year period beginning 1 January 2005, each Member State shall decide upon the total quantity of allowances it will allocate for that

period and the allocation of those allowances to the operator of each installation. This decision shall be taken at least three months before the beginning of the period and be based on its national allocation plan developed pursuant to Article 9 and in accordance with Article 10, taking due account of comments from the public.

2. For the five-year period beginning 1 January 2008, and for each subsequent five-year period, each Member State shall decide upon the total quantity of allowances it will allocate for that period and initiate the process for the allocation of those allowances to the operator of each installation. This decision shall be taken at least 12 months before the beginning of the relevant period and be based on the Member State's national allocation plan developed pursuant to Article 9 and in accordance with Article 10, taking due account of comments from the public.

3. Decisions taken pursuant to paragraph 1 or 2 shall be in accordance with the requirements of the Treaty, in particular Articles 87 and 88 thereof. When deciding upon allocation, Member States shall take into account the need to provide access to allowances for new entrants.

4. The competent authority shall issue a proportion of the total quantity of allowances each year of the period referred to in paragraph 1 or 2, by 28 February of that year.

ARTICLE 12 TRANSFER, SURRENDER AND CANCELLATION OF ALLOWANCES

1. Member States shall ensure that allowances can be transferred between:

(a) persons within the Community;

(b) persons within the Community and persons in third countries, where such allowances are recognised in accordance with the procedure referred to in Article 25 without restrictions other than those contained in, or adopted pursuant to, this Directive.

2. Member States shall ensure that allowances issued by a competent authority of another Member State are recognised for the purpose of meeting an operator's obligations under paragraph 3.

3. Member States shall ensure that, by 30 April each year at the latest, the operator of each installation surrenders a number of allowances equal to the total emissions from that installation during the preceding calendar year as verified in accordance with Article 15, and that these are subsequently cancelled.

4. Member States shall take the necessary steps to ensure that allowances will be cancelled at any time at the request of the person holding them.

ARTICLE 13 VALIDITY OF ALLOWANCES

1. Allowances shall be valid for emissions during the period referred to in Article 11(1) or (2) for which they are issued.

2. Four months after the beginning of the first five-year period referred to in Article 11(2), allowances which are no longer valid and have not been surrendered and cancelled in accordance with Article 12(3) shall be cancelled by the competent authority.

Member States may issue allowances to persons for the current period to replace any allowances held by them which are cancelled in accordance with the first subparagraph.

3. Four months after the beginning of each subsequent fiveyear period referred to in Article 11(2), allowances which are no longer valid and have not been surrendered and cancelled in accordance with Article 12(3) shall be cancelled by the competent authority.

Member States shall issue allowances to persons for the current period to replace any allowances held by them which are cancelled in accordance with the first subparagraph.

ARTICLE 14 GUIDELINES FOR MONITORING AND REPORTING OF EMISSIONS

1. The Commission shall adopt guidelines for monitoring and reporting of emissions resulting from the activities listed in Annex I of greenhouse gases specified in relation to those activities, in accordance with the procedure referred to in Article 23(2), by 30 September 2003. The guidelines shall be based on the principles for monitoring and reporting set out in Annex IV.

2. Member States shall ensure that emissions are monitored in accordance with the guidelines.

3. Member States shall ensure that each operator of an installation reports the emissions from that installation during each calendar year to the

competent authority after the end of that year in accordance with the guidelines.

ARTICLE 15 VERIFICATION

Member States shall ensure that the reports submitted by operators pursuant to Article 14(3) are verified in accordance with the criteria set out in Annex V, and that the competent authority is informed thereof.

Member States shall ensure that an operator whose report has not been verified as satisfactory in accordance with the criteria set out in Annex V by 31 March each year for emissions during the preceding year cannot make further transfers of allowances until a report from that operator has been verified as satisfactory.

ARTICLE 16 PENALTIES

1. Member States shall lay down the rules on penalties applicable to infringements of the national provisions adopted pursuant to this Directive and shall take all measures necessary to ensure that such rules are implemented. The penalties provided for must be effective, proportionate and dissuasive. Member States shall notify these provisions to the Commission by 31 December 2003 at the latest, and shall notify it without delay of any subsequent amendment affecting them.

2. Member States shall ensure publication of the names of operators who are in breach of requirements to surrender sufficient allowances under Article 12(3).

3. Member States shall ensure that any operator who does not surrender sufficient allowances by 30 April of each year to cover its emissions during the preceding year shall be held liable for the payment of an excess emissions penalty. The excess emissions penalty shall be EUR 100 for each tonne of carbon dioxide equivalent emitted by that installation for which the operator has not surrendered allowances. Payment of the excess emissions penalty shall not release the operator from the obligation to surrender an amount of allowances equal to those excess emissions when surrendering allowances in relation to the following calendar year.

4. During the three-year period beginning 1 January 2005, Member States shall apply a lower excess emissions penalty of EUR 40 for each tonne of carbon dioxide equivalent emitted by that installation for which the operator has not surrendered allowances. Payment of the excess emissions penalty shall not release the operator from the obligation to surrender an amount of allowances equal to those excess emissions when surrendering allowances in relation to the following calendar year.

ARTICLE 17 ACCESS TO INFORMATION

Decisions relating to the allocation of allowances and the reports of emissions required under the greenhouse gas emissions permit and held by the competent authority shall be made available to the public by that authority subject to the restrictions laid down in Article 3(3) and Article 4 of Directive 2003/4/EC.

ARTICLE 18 COMPETENT AUTHORITY

Member States shall make the appropriate administrative arrangements, including the designation of the appropriate competent authority or authorities, for the implementation of the rules of this Directive. Where more than one competent authority is designated, the work of these authorities undertaken pursuant to this Directive must be coordinated.

ARTICLE 19 REGISTRIES

1. Member States shall provide for the establishment and maintenance of a registry in order to ensure the accurate accounting of the issue, holding, transfer and cancellation of allowances. Member States may maintain their registries in a consolidated system, together with one or more other Member States.

2. Any person may hold allowances. The registry shall be accessible to the public and shall contain separate accounts to record the allowances held by each person to whom and from whom allowances are issued or transferred.

3. In order to implement this Directive, the Commission shall adopt a Regulation in accordance with the procedure referred to in Article 23(2) for a standardised and secured system of registries in the form of standardised electronic databases containing common data elements to track the issue, holding, transfer and cancellation of allowances, to provide

for public access and confidentiality as appropriate and to ensure that there are no transfers incompatible with obligations resulting from the Kyoto Protocol.

ARTICLE 20 CENTRAL ADMINISTRATOR

1. The Commission shall designate a Central Administrator to maintain an independent transaction log recording the issue, transfer and cancellation of allowances.

2. The Central Administrator shall conduct an automated check on each transaction in registries through the independent transaction log to ensure there are no irregularities in the issue, transfer and cancellation of allowances.

3. If irregularities are identified through the automated check, the Central Administrator shall inform the Member State or Member States concerned who shall not register the transactions in question or any further transactions relating to the allowances concerned until the irregularities have been resolved.

ARTICLE 21 REPORTING BY MEMBER STATES

1. Each year the Member States shall submit to the Commission a report on the application of this Directive. This report shall pay particular attention to the arrangements for the allocation of allowances, the operation of registries, the application of the monitoring and reporting guidelines, verification and issues relating to compliance with the Directive and on the fiscal treatment of allowances, if any. The first report shall be sent to the Commission by 30 June 2005. The report shall be drawn up on the basis of a questionnaire or outline drafted by the Commission in accordance with the procedure laid down in Article 6 of Directive 91/692/EEC. The questionnaire or outline shall be sent to Member States at least six months before the deadline for the submission of the first report.

2. On the basis of the reports referred to in paragraph 1, the Commission shall publish a report on the application of this Directive within three months of receiving the reports from the Member States.

3. The Commission shall organise an exchange of information between the competent authorities of the Member States concerning developments relating to issues of allocation, the operation of registries, monitoring, reporting, verification and compliance.

ARTICLE 22 AMENDMENTS TO ANNEX III

The Commission may amend Annex III, with the exception of criteria (1), (5) and (7), for the period from 2008 to 2012 in the light of the reports provided for in Article 21 and of the experience of the application of this Directive, in accordance with the procedure referred to in Article 23(2).

ARTICLE 23 COMMITTEE

1. The Commission shall be assisted by the committee instituted by Article 8 of Decision 93/389/EEC.

2. Where reference is made to this paragraph, Articles 5 and 7 of Decision 1999/468/EC shall apply, having regard to the provisions of Article 8 thereof.

The period laid down in Article 5(6) of Decision 1999/468/EC shall be set at three months.

3. The Committee shall adopt its rules of procedure.

ARTICLE 24 PROCEDURES FOR UNILATERAL INCLUSION OF ADDITIONAL ACTIVITIES AND GASES

1. From 2008, Member States may apply emission allowance trading in accordance with this Directive to activities, installations and greenhouse gases which are not listed in Annex I, provided that inclusion of such activities, installations and greenhouse gases is approved by the Commission in accordance with the procedure referred to in Article 23(2), taking into account all relevant criteria, in particular effects on the internal market, potential distortions of competition, the environmental integrity of the scheme and reliability of the planned monitoring and reporting system.

From 2005 Member States may under the same conditions apply emissions allowance trading to installations carrying out activities listed in Annex I below the capacity limits referred to in that Annex.

2. Allocations made to installations carrying out such activities shall be specified in the national allocation plan referred to in Article 9.

3. The Commission may, on its own initiative, or shall, on request by a Member State, adopt monitoring and reporting guidelines for emissions from activities, installations and greenhouse gases which are not listed in Annex I in accordance with the procedure referred to in Article 23(2), if monitoring and reporting of these emissions can be carried out with sufficient accuracy.

4. In the event that such measures are introduced, reviews carried out pursuant to Article 30 shall also consider whether Annex I should be amended to include emissions from these activities in a harmonised way throughout the Community.

ARTICLE 25 LINKS WITH OTHER GREENHOUSE GAS EMISSIONS TRADING SCHEMES

1. Agreements should be concluded with third countries listed in Annex B to the Kyoto Protocol which have ratified the Protocol to provide for the mutual recognition of allowances between the Community scheme and other greenhouse gas emissions trading schemes in accordance with the rules set out in Article 300 of the Treaty.

2. Where an agreement referred to in paragraph 1 has been concluded, the Commission shall draw up any necessary provisions relating to the mutual recognition of allowances under that agreement in accordance with the procedure referred to in Article 23(2).

ARTICLE 26 AMENDMENT OF DIRECTIVE 96/61/EC

In Article 9(3) of Directive 96/61/EC the following subparagraphs shall be added:

Where emissions of a greenhouse gas from an installation are specified in Annex I to Directive 2003/87/EC of the European Parliament and of the Council of 13 October 2003 establishing a scheme for greenhouse gas emission allowance trading within the Community and amending Council Directive 96/61/EC* in relation to an activity carried out in that installation, the permit shall not include an emission limit value for direct emissions of that gas unless it is necessary to ensure that no significant local pollution is caused.

For activities listed in Annex I to Directive 2003/87/EC, Member States may choose not to impose requirements relating to energy efficiency in respect of combustion units or other units emitting carbon dioxide on the site.

Where necessary, the competent authorities shall amend the permit as appropriate.

The three preceding subparagraphs shall not apply to installations temporarily excluded from the scheme for greenhouse gas emission allowance trading within the Community in accordance with Article 27 of Directive 2003/87/EC.

* OJ L 275, 25.10.2003, p. 32.

ARTICLE 27 TEMPORARY EXCLUSION OF CERTAIN INSTALLATIONS

1. Member States may apply to the Commission for installations to be temporarily excluded until 31 December 2007 at the latest from the Community scheme. Any such application shall list each such installation and shall be published.

2. If, having considered any comments made by the public on that application, the Commission decides, in accordance with the procedure referred to in Article 23(2), that the installations will:

(a) as a result of national policies, limit their emissions as much as would be the case if they were subject to the provisions of this Directive;

(b) be subject to monitoring, reporting and verification requirements which are equivalent to those provided for pursuant to Articles 14 and 15; and

(c) be subject to penalties at least equivalent to those referred to in Article 16 (1) and (4) in the case of non-fulfilment of national requirements;

it shall provide for the temporary exclusion of those installations from the Community scheme.

It must be ensured that there will be no distortion of the internal market.

ARTICLE 28 POOLING

1. Member States may allow operators of installations carrying out one of the activities listed in Annex I to form a pool of installations from the same activity for the period referred to in Article 11(1) and/or the first five-year period referred to in Article 11(2) in accordance with paragraphs 2 to 6 of this Article.

2. Operators carrying out an activity listed in Annex I who wish to form a pool shall apply to the

competent authority, specifying the installations and the period for which they want the pool and supplying evidence that a trustee will be able to fulfil the obligations referred to in paragraphs 3 and 4.

3. Operators wishing to form a pool shall nominate a trustee:

(a) to be issued with the total quantity of allowances calculated by installation of the operators, by way of derogation from Article 11;

(b) to be responsible for surrendering allowances equal to the total emissions from installations in the pool, by way of derogation from Articles 6(2)(e) and 12(3); and

(c) to be restricted from making further transfers in the event that an operator's report has not been verified as satisfactory in accordance with the second paragraph of Article 15.

4. The trustee shall be subject to the penalties applicable for breaches of requirements to surrender sufficient allowances to cover the total emissions from installations in the pool, by way of derogation from Article 16(2), (3) and (4).

5. A Member State that wishes to allow one or more pools to be formed shall submit the application referred to in paragraph 2 to the Commission. Without prejudice to the Treaty, the Commission may within three months of receipt reject an application that does not fulfil the requirements of this Directive. Reasons shall be given for any such decision. In the case of rejection the Member State may only allow the pool to be formed if proposed amendments are accepted by the Commission.

6. In the event that the trustee fails to comply with penalties referred to in paragraph 4, each operator of an installation in the pool shall be responsible under Articles 12(3) and 16 in respect of emissions from its own installation.

ARTICLE 29 FORCE MAJEURE

1. During the period referred to in Article 11(1), Member States may apply to the Commission for certain installations to be issued with additional allowances in cases of *force majeure*. The Commission shall determine whether *force majeure* is demonstrated, in which case it shall authorise the issue of additional and non-transferable allowances by that Member State to the operators of those installations.

2. The Commission shall, without prejudice to the Treaty, develop guidance to describe the circumstances under which *force majeure* is demonstrated, by 31 December 2003 at the latest.

ARTICLE 30 REVIEW AND FURTHER DEVELOPMENT

1. On the basis of progress achieved in the monitoring of emissions of greenhouse gases, the Commission may make a proposal to the European Parliament and the Council by 31 December 2004 to amend Annex I to include other activities and emissions of other greenhouse gases listed in Annex II.

2. On the basis of experience of the application of this Directive and of progress achieved in the monitoring of emissions of greenhouse gases and in the light of developments in the international context, the Commission shall draw up a report on the application of this Directive, considering:

(a) how and whether Annex I should be amended to include other relevant sectors, *inter alia* the chemicals, aluminium and transport sectors, activities and emissions of other greenhouse gases listed in Annex II, with a view to further improving the economic efficiency of the scheme;

(b) the relationship of Community emission allowance trading with the international emissions trading that will start in 2008;

(c) further harmonisation of the method of allocation (including auctioning for the time after 2012) and of the criteria for national allocation plans referred to in Annex III;

(d) the use of credits from project mechanisms;

(e) the relationship of emissions trading with other policies and measures implemented at Member State and Community level, including taxation, that pursue the same objectives;

(f) whether it is appropriate for there to be a single Community registry;

(g) the level of excess emissions penalties, taking into account, *inter alia*, inflation;

(h) the functioning of the allowance market, covering in particular any possible market disturbances;

(i) how to adapt the Community scheme to an enlarged European Union;

(j) pooling;

(k) the practicality of developing Community-wide benchmarks as a basis for allocation, taking into account the best available techniques and cost-benefit analysis.

The Commission shall submit this report to the European Parliament and the Council by 30 June 2006, accompanied by proposals as appropriate.

3. Linking the project-based mechanisms, including Joint Implementation (JI) and the Clean Development Mechanism (CDM), with the Community scheme is desirable and important to achieve the goals of both reducing global greenhouse gas emissions and increasing the cost-effective functioning of the Community scheme. Therefore, the emission credits from the project-based mechanisms will be recognised for their use in this scheme subject to provisions adopted by the European Parliament and the Council on a proposal from the Commission, which should apply in parallel with the Community scheme in 2005. The use of the mechanisms shall be supplemental to domestic action, in accordance with the relevant provisions of the Kyoto Protocol and Marrakesh Accords.

ARTICLE 31 IMPLEMENTATION

1. Member States shall bring into force the laws, regulations and administrative provisions necessary to comply with this Directive by 31 December 2003 at the latest. They shall forthwith inform the Commission thereof. The Commission shall notify the other Member States of these laws, regulations and administrative provisions.
When Member States adopt these measures, they shall contain a reference to this Directive or be accompanied by such a reference on the occasion of their official publication. The methods of making such reference shall be laid down by Member States.

2. Member States shall communicate to the Commission the text of the provisions of national law which they adopt in the field covered by this Directive. The Commission shall inform the other Member States thereof.

ARTICLE 32 ENTRY INTO FORCE

This Directive shall enter into force on the day of its publication in the *Official Journal of the European Union.*

ARTICLE 33 ADDRESSEES

This Directive is addressed to the Member States.
Done at Luxembourg, 13 October 2003.

For the European Parliament	*For the Council*
The President	*The President*
P. COX	G. ALEMANNO

ANNEX I CATEGORIES OF ACTIVITIES REFERRED TO IN ARTICLES 2(1), 3, 4, 14(1), 28 AND 30

1. Installations or parts of installations used for research, development and testing of new products and processes are not covered by this Directive.

2. The threshold values given below generally refer to production capacities or outputs. Where one operator carries out several activities falling under the same subheading in the same installation or on the same site, the capacities of such activities are added together.

Activities	**Greenhouse gases**
Energy activities	
Combustion installations with a rated thermal input exceeding 20 MW (except hazardous or municipal waste installations)	Carbon dioxide
Mineral oil refineries	Carbon dioxide
Coke ovens	Carbon dioxide
Production and processing of ferrous metals	
Metal ore (including sulphide ore) roasting or sintering installations	Carbon dioxide
Installations for the production of pig iron or steel (primary or secondary fusion) including continuous casting, with a capacity exceeding 2,5 tonnes per hour	Carbon dioxide
Mineral industry	
Installations for the production of cement clinker in rotary kilns with a production capacity exceeding 500 tonnes per day or lime in rotary kilns with a production capacity	Carbon dioxide

exceeding 50 tonnes per day or in other furnaces with a production capacity exceeding 50 tonnes per day	
Installations for the manufacture of glass including glass fibre with a melting capacity exceeding 20 tonnes per day	Carbon dioxide
Installations for the manufacture of ceramic products by firing, in particular roofing tiles, bricks, refractory bricks, tiles, stoneware or porcelain, with a production capacity exceeding 75 tonnes per day, and/or with a kiln capacity exceeding 4 m^3 and with a setting density per kiln exceeding 300 kg/m^3	Carbon dioxide
Other activities	
Industrial plants for the production of	
(a) pulp from timber or other fibrous materials	Carbon dioxide
(b) paper and board with a production capacity exceeding 20 tonnes per day	Carbon dioxide

ANNEX II GREENHOUSE GASES REFERRED TO IN ARTICLES 3 AND 30

Carbon dioxide (CO_2)

Methane (CH_4)

Nitrous Oxide (N_2O)

Hydrofluorocarbons (HFCs)

Perfluorocarbons (PFCs)

Sulphur Hexafluoride (SF_6)

ANNEX III CRITERIA FOR NATIONAL ALLOCATION PLANS REFERRED TO IN ARTICLES 9, 22 AND 30

1. The total quantity of allowances to be allocated for the relevant period shall be consistent with the Member State's obligation to limit its emissions pursuant to Decision 2002/358/EC and the Kyoto Protocol, taking into account, on the one hand, the proportion of overall emissions that these allowances represent in comparison with emissions from sources not covered by this Directive and, on the other hand, national energy policies, and should be consistent with the national climate change programme. The total quantity of allowances to be allocated shall not be more than is likely to be needed for the strict application of the criteria of this Annex. Prior to 2008, the quantity shall be consistent with a path towards achieving or over-achieving each Member State's target under Decision 2002/358/EC and the Kyoto Protocol.

2. The total quantity of allowances to be allocated shall be consistent with assessments of actual and projected progress towards fulfilling the Member States' contributions to the Community's commitments made pursuant to Decision 93/389/EEC.

3. Quantities of allowances to be allocated shall be consistent with the potential, including the technological potential, of activities covered by this scheme to reduce emissions. Member States may base their distribution of allowances on average emissions of greenhouse gases by product in each activity and achievable progress in each activity.

4. The plan shall be consistent with other Community legislative and policy instruments. Account should be taken of unavoidable increases in emissions resulting from new legislative requirements.

5. The plan shall not discriminate between companies or sectors in such a way as to unduly favour certain undertakings or activities in accordance with the requirements of the Treaty, in particular Articles 87 and 88 thereof.

6. The plan shall contain information on the manner in which new entrants will be able to begin participating in the Community scheme in the Member State concerned.

7. The plan may accommodate early action and shall contain information on the manner in which early action is taken into account. Benchmarks derived from reference documents concerning the best available technologies may be employed by Member States in developing their National Allocation Plans, and these benchmarks can incorporate an element of accommodating early action.

8. The plan shall contain information on the manner in which clean technology, including energy efficient technologies, are taken into account.

9. The plan shall include provisions for comments to be expressed by the public, and contain information on the arrangements by which due account

will be taken of these comments before a decision on the allocation of allowances is taken.

10. The plan shall contain a list of the installations covered by this Directive with the quantities of allowances intended to be allocated to each.

11. The plan may contain information on the manner in which the existence of competition from countries or entities outside the Union will be taken into account.

ANNEX IV PRINCIPLES FOR MONITORING AND REPORTING REFERRED TO IN ARTICLE 14(1)

Monitoring of carbon dioxide emissions

Emissions shall be monitored either by calculation or on the basis of measurement.

Calculation

Calculations of emissions shall be performed using the formula:

Activity data × Emission factor × Oxidation factor

Activity data (fuel used, production rate etc.) shall be monitored on the basis of supply data or measurement.

Accepted emission factors shall be used. Activity-specific emission factors are acceptable for all fuels. Default factors are acceptable for all fuels except non-commercial ones (waste fuels such as tyres and industrial process gases). Seam-specific defaults for coal, and EU-specific or producer country-specific defaults for natural gas shall be further elaborated. IPCC default values are acceptable for refinery products. The emission factor for biomass shall be zero.

If the emission factor does not take account of the fact that some of the carbon is not oxidised, then an additional oxidation factor shall be used. If activity-specific emission factors have been calculated and already take oxidation into account, then an oxidation factor need not be applied.

Default oxidation factors developed pursuant to Directive 96/61/EC shall be used, unless the operator can demonstrate that activity-specific factors are more accurate.

A separate calculation shall be made for each activity, installation and for each fuel.

Measurement

Measurement of emissions shall use standardised or accepted methods, and shall be corroborated by a supporting calculation of emissions.

Monitoring of emissions of other greenhouse gases

Standardised or accepted methods shall be used, developed by the Commission in collaboration with all relevant stakeholders and adopted in accordance with the procedure referred to in Article 23(2).

Reporting of emissions

Each operator shall include the following information in the report for an installation:

A. Data identifying the installation, including:

- Name of the installation;
- Its address, including postcode and country;
- Type and number of Annex I activities carried out in the installation;
- Address, telephone, fax and email details for a contact person; and
- Name of the owner of the installation, and of any parent company.

B. For each Annex I activity carried out on the site for which emissions are calculated:

- Activity data;
- Emission factors;
- Oxidation factors;
- Total emissions; and
- Uncertainty.

C. For each Annex I activity carried out on the site for which emissions are measured:

- Total emissions;
- Information on the reliability of measurement methods; and
- Uncertainty.

D. For emissions from combustion, the report shall also include the oxidation factor, unless oxidation has already been taken into account in the development of an activity-specific emission factor.

Member States shall take measures to coordinate reporting requirements with any existing reporting requirements in order to minimise the reporting burden on businesses.

ANNEX V CRITERIA FOR VERIFICATION REFERRED TO IN ARTICLE 15

General Principles

1. Emissions from each activity listed in Annex I shall be subject to verification.

2. The verification process shall include consideration of the report pursuant to Article 14(3) and of monitoring during the preceding year. It shall address the reliability, credibility and accuracy of monitoring systems and the reported data and information relating to emissions, in particular:

(a) the reported activity data and related measurements and calculations;

(b) the choice and the employment of emission factors;

(c) the calculations leading to the determination of the overall emissions; and

(d) if measurement is used, the appropriateness of the choice and the employment of measuring methods.

3. Reported emissions may only be validated if reliable and credible data and information allow the emissions to be determined with a high degree of certainty. A high degree of certainty requires the operator to show that:

(a) the reported data is free of inconsistencies;

(b) the collection of the data has been carried out in accordance with the applicable scientific standards; and

(c) the relevant records of the installation are complete and consistent.

4. The verifier shall be given access to all sites and information in relation to the subject of the verification.

5. The verifier shall take into account whether the installation is registered under the Community eco-management and audit scheme (EMAS).

Methodology

Strategic Analysis

6. The verification shall be based on a strategic analysis of all the activities carried out in the installation. This requires the verifier to have an overview of all the activities and their significance for emissions.

Process Analysis

7. The verification of the information submitted shall, where appropriate, be carried out on the site of the installation. The verifier shall use spot-checks to determine the reliability of the reported data and information.

Risk Analysis

8. The verifier shall submit all the sources of emissions in the installation to an evaluation with regard to the reliability of the data of each source contributing to the overall emissions of the installation.

9. On the basis of this analysis the verifier shall explicitly identify those sources with a high risk of error and other aspects of the monitoring and reporting procedure which are likely to contribute to errors in the determination of the overall emissions. This especially involves the choice of the emission factors and the calculations necessary to determine the level of the emissions from individual sources. Particular attention shall be given to those sources with a high risk of error and the abovementioned aspects of the monitoring procedure.

10. The verifier shall take into consideration any effective risk control methods applied by the operator with a view to minimising the degree of uncertainty.

Report

11. The verifier shall prepare a report on the validation process stating whether the report pursuant to Article 14(3) is satisfactory. This report shall specify all issues relevant to the work carried out. A statement that the report pursuant to Article 14(3) is satisfactory may be made if, in the opinion of the verifier, the total emissions are not materially misstated.

Minimum Competency Requirements for the Verifier

12. The verifier shall be independent of the operator, carry out his activities in a sound and objective professional manner, and understand:

(a) the provisions of this Directive, as well as relevant standards and guidance adopted by the Commission pursuant to Article 14(1);

(b) the legislative, regulatory, and administrative requirements relevant to the activities being verified; and

(c) the generation of all information related to each source of emissions in the installation, in particular, relating to the collection, measurement, calculation and reporting of data.

Directive 2001/77/EC of the European Parliament and of the Council of 27 September 2001

On the Promotion of Electricity Produced from Renewable Energy Sources in the Internal Electricity Market

THE EUROPEAN PARLIAMENT AND THE COUNCIL OF THE EUROPEAN UNION,

Having regard to the Treaty establishing the European Community, and in particular Article 175(1) thereof,

Having regard to the proposal from the Commission[1],

Having regard to the opinion of the Economic and Social Committee[2],

Having regard to the opinion of the Committee of the Regions[3],

Acting in accordance with the procedure laid down in Article 251 of the Treaty[4],

Whereas:

(1) The potential for the exploitation of renewable energy sources is underused in the Community at present. The Community recognises the need to promote renewable energy sources as a priority measure given that their exploitation contributes to environmental protection and sustainable development. In addition this can also create local employment, have a positive impact on social cohesion, contribute to security of supply and make it possible to meet Kyoto targets more quickly. It is therefore necessary to ensure that this potential is better exploited within the framework of the internal electricity market.

(2) The promotion of electricity produced from renewable energy sources is a high Community priority as outlined in the White Paper on Renewable Energy Sources (hereinafter referred to as 'the White Paper') for reasons of security and diversification of energy supply, of environmental protection and of social and economic cohesion. That was endorsed by the Council in its resolution of 8 June 1998 on renewable sources of energy[5], and by the European Parliament in its resolution on the White Paper.[6]

(3) The increased use of electricity produced from renewable energy sources constitutes an important part of the package of measures needed to comply with the Kyoto Protocol to the United Nations Framework Convention on Climate Change, and of any policy package to meet further commitments.

(4) The Council in its conclusions of 11 May 1999 and the European Parliament in its resolution of 17 June 1998 on electricity from renewable energy sources[7] have invited the Commission to submit a concrete proposal for a Community framework on access for electricity produced from renewable energy sources to the internal market. Furthermore, the European Parliament in its resolution of 30 March 2000 on electricity from renewable energy sources and the internal electricity market[8] underlined that binding and ambitious renewable energy targets at the national level are essential for obtaining results and achieving the Community targets.

(5) To ensure increased market penetration of electricity produced from renewable energy sources in the medium term, all Member States should be required to set national indicative targets for the consumption of electricity produced from renewable sources.

[1] OJ C 311 E, 31.10.2000, p. 320 and OJ C 154 E, 29.5.2001, p. 89.
[2] OJ C 367, 20.12.2000, p. 5.
[3] OJ C 22, 24.1.2001, p. 27.
[4] Opinion of the European Parliament of 16 November 2000 (OJ C 223, 8.8.2001, p. 294), Council Common Position of 23 March 2001 (OJ C 142, 15.5.2001, p. 5) and Decision of the European Parliament of 4 July 2001 (not yet published in the Official Journal). Council Decision of 7 September 2001.

[5] OJ C 198, 24.6.1998, p. 1.
[6] OJ C 210, 6.7.1998, p. 215.
[7] OJ C 210, 6.7.1998, p. 143.
[8] OJ C 378, 29.12.2000, p. 89.

(6) These national indicative targets should be consistent with any national commitment made as part of the climate change commitments accepted by the Community under the Kyoto Protocol.

(7) The Commission should assess to what extent Member States have made progress towards achieving their national indicative targets, and to what extent the national indicative targets are consistent with the global indicative target of 12% of gross domestic energy consumption by 2010, considering that the White Paper's indicative target of 12% for the Community as a whole by 2010 provides useful guidance for increased efforts at Community level as well as in Member States, bearing in mind the need to reflect differing national circumstances. If necessary for the achievement of the targets, the Commission should submit proposals to the European Parliament and the Council which may include mandatory targets.

(8) Where they use waste as an energy source, Member States must comply with current Community legislation on waste management. The application of this Directive is without prejudice to the definitions set out in Annex 2a and 2b to Council Directive 75/442/EEC of 15 July 1975 on waste[9]. Support for renewable energy sources should be consistent with other Community objectives, in particular respect for the waste treatment hierarchy. Therefore, the incineration of non-separated municipal waste should not be promoted under a future support system for renewable energy sources, if such promotion were to undermine the hierarchy.

(9) The definition of biomass used in this Directive does not prejudge the use of a different definition in national legislation, for purposes other than those set out in this Directive.

(10) This Directive does not require Member States to recognise the purchase of a guarantee of origin from other Member States or the corresponding purchase of electricity as a contribution to the fulfilment of a national quota obligation. However, to facilitate trade in electricity produced from renewable energy sources and to increase transparency for the consumer's choice between electricity produced from non-renewable and electricity produced from renewable energy sources, the guarantee of origin of such electricity is necessary. Schemes for the guarantee of origin do not by themselves imply a right to benefit from national support mechanisms established in different Member States. It is important that all forms of electricity produced from renewable energy sources are covered by such guarantees of origin.

(11) It is important to distinguish guarantees of origin clearly from exchangeable green certificates.

(12) The need for public support in favour of renewable energy sources is recognised in the Community guidelines for State aid for environmental protection[10], which, amongst other options, take account of the need to internalise external costs of electricity generation. However, the rules of the Treaty, and in particular Articles 87 and 88 thereof, will continue to apply to such public support.

(13) A legislative framework for the market in renewable energy sources needs to be established.

(14) Member States operate different mechanisms of support for renewable energy sources at the national level, including green certificates, investment aid, tax exemptions or reductions, tax refunds and direct price support schemes. One important means to achieve the aim of this Directive is to guarantee the proper functioning of these mechanisms, until a Community framework is put into operation, in order to maintain investor confidence.

(15) It is too early to decide on a Community-wide framework regarding support schemes, in view of the limited experience with national schemes and the current relatively low share of price supported electricity produced from renewable energy sources in the Community.

(16) It is, however necessary to adapt, after a sufficient transitional period, support schemes to the developing internal electricity market. It is therefore appropriate that the Commission monitor the situation and present a report on experience gained with the application of national schemes. If necessary, the Commission should, in the light of the conclusions of this report, make a proposal for a Community framework with regard to support schemes for electricity produced from renewable energy sources. That proposal should contribute to the achievement of the national indicative targets, be compatible with

[9] OJ L 194, 25.7.1975, p. 39. Directive as last amended by Commission Decision 96/350/EC (OJ L 135, 6.6.1996, p. 32).

[10] OJ C 37, 3.2.2001, p. 3.

the principles of the internal electricity market and take into account the characteristics of the different sources of renewable energy, together with the different technologies and geographical differences. It should also promote the use of renewable energy sources in an effective way, and be simple and at the same time as efficient as possible, particularly in terms of cost, and include sufficient transitional periods of at least seven years, maintain investors' confidence and avoid stranded costs. This framework would enable electricity from renewable energy sources to compete with electricity produced from non-renewable energy sources and limit the cost to the consumer, while, in the medium term, reduce the need for public support.

(17) Increased market penetration of electricity produced from renewable energy sources will allow for economies of scale, thereby reducing costs.

(18) It is important to utilise the strength of the market forces and the internal market and make electricity produced from renewable energy sources competitive and attractive to European citizens.

(19) When favouring the development of a market for renewable energy sources, it is necessary to take into account the positive impact on regional and local development opportunities, export prospects, social cohesion and employment opportunities, especially as concerns small and medium-sized undertakings as well as independent power producers.

(20) The specific structure of the renewable energy sources sector should be taken into account, especially when reviewing the administrative procedures for obtaining permission to construct plants producing electricity from renewable energy sources.

(21) In certain circumstances it is not possible to ensure fully transmission and distribution of electricity produced from renewable energy sources without affecting the reliability and safety of the grid system and guarantees in this context may therefore include financial compensation.

(22) The costs of connecting new producers of electricity from renewable energy sources should be objective, transparent and non-discriminatory and due account should be taken of the benefit embedded generators bring to the grid.

(23) Since the general objectives of the proposed action cannot be sufficiently achieved by the Member States and can therefore, by reason of the scale or effects of the action, be better achieved at Community level, the Community may adopt measures, in accordance with the principle of subsidiarity as set out in Article 5 of the Treaty. Their detailed implementation should, however, be left to the Member States, thus allowing each Member State to choose the regime which corresponds best to its particular situation. In accordance with the principle of proportionality, as set out in that Article, this Directive does not go beyond what is necessary in order to achieve those objectives,

HAVE ADOPTED THIS DIRECTIVE:

ARTICLE 1 PURPOSE

The purpose of this Directive is to promote an increase in the contribution of renewable energy sources to electricity production in the internal market for electricity and to create a basis for a future Community framework thereof.

ARTICLE 2 DEFINITIONS

For the purposes of this Directive, the following definitions shall apply:

(a) '*renewable energy sources*' shall mean renewable non-fossil energy sources (wind, solar, geothermal, wave, tidal, hydropower, biomass, landfill gas, sewage treatment plant gas and biogases);

(b) '*biomass*' shall mean the biodegradable fraction of products, waste and residues from agriculture (including vegetal and animal substances), forestry and related industries, as well as the biodegradable fraction of industrial and municipal waste;

(c) '*electricity produced from renewable energy sources*' shall mean electricity produced by plants using only renewable energy sources, as well as the proportion of electricity produced from renewable energy sources in hybrid plants also using conventional energy sources and including renewable electricity used for filling storage systems, and excluding electricity produced as a result of storage systems;

(d) '*consumption of electricity*' shall mean national electricity production, including autoproduction, plus imports, minus exports (gross national electricity consumption).

In addition, the definitions in Directive 96/92/EC of the European Parliament and of the Council of 19 December 1996 concerning common rules for the internal market of electricity[11] shall apply.

ARTICLE 3 NATIONAL INDICATIVE TARGETS

1. Member States shall take appropriate steps to encourage greater consumption of electricity produced from renewable energy sources in conformity with the national indicative targets referred to in paragraph 2. These steps must be in proportion to the objective to be attained.

2. Not later than 27 October 2002 and every five years thereafter, Member States shall adopt and publish a report setting national indicative targets for future consumption of electricity produced from renewable energy sources in terms of a percentage of electricity consumption for the next 10 years. The report shall also outline the measures taken or planned, at national level, to achieve these national indicative targets. To set these targets until the year 2010, the Member States shall:

- take account of the reference values in the Annex,
- ensure that the targets are compatible with any national commitments accepted in the context of the climate change commitments accepted by the Community pursuant to the Kyoto Protocol to the United Nations Framework Convention on Climate Change.

3. Member States shall publish, for the first time not later than 27 October 2003 and thereafter every two years, a report which includes an analysis of success in meeting the national indicative targets taking account, in particular, of climatic factors likely to affect the achievement of those targets and which indicates to what extent the measures taken are consistent with the national climate change commitment.

4. On the basis of the Member States' reports referred to in paragraphs 2 and 3, the Commission shall assess to what extent:

- Member States have made progress towards achieving their national indicative targets,
- the national indicative targets are consistent with the global indicative target of 12% of gross national energy consumption by 2010 and in particular with the 22,1% indicative share of electricity produced from renewable energy sources in total Community electricity consumption by 2010.

The Commission shall publish its conclusions in a report, for the first time not later than 27 October 2004 and thereafter every two years. This report shall be accompanied, as appropriate, by proposals to the European Parliament and to the Council.

If the report referred to in the second subparagraph concludes that the national indicative targets are likely to be inconsistent, for reasons that are unjustified and/or do not relate to new scientific evidence, with the global indicative target, these proposals shall address national targets, including possible mandatory targets, in the appropriate form.

ARTICLE 4 SUPPORT SCHEMES

1. Without prejudice to Articles 87 and 88 of the Treaty, the Commission shall evaluate the application of mechanisms used in Member States according to which a producer of electricity, on the basis of regulations issued by the public authorities, receives direct or indirect support, and which could have the effect of restricting trade, on the basis that these contribute to the objectives set out in Articles 6 and 174 of the Treaty.

2. The Commission shall, not later than 27 October 2005, present a well-documented report on experience gained with the application and coexistence of the different mechanisms referred to in paragraph 1. The report shall assess the success, including cost-effectiveness, of the support systems referred to in paragraph 1 in promoting the consumption of electricity produced from renewable energy sources in conformity with the national indicative targets referred to in Article 3(2). This report shall, if necessary, be accompanied by a proposal for a Community framework with regard to support schemes for electricity produced from renewable energy sources.

Any proposal for a framework should:

(a) contribute to the achievement of the national indicative targets;

(b) be compatible with the principles of the internal electricity market;

(c) take into account the characteristics of different sources of renewable energy, together

[11] OJ L 27, 30.1.1997, p. 20.

with the different technologies, and geographical differences;

(d) promote the use of renewable energy sources in an effective way, and be simple and, at the same time, as efficient as possible, particularly in terms of cost;

(e) include sufficient transitional periods for national support systems of at least seven years and maintain investor confidence.

ARTICLE 5 GUARANTEE OF ORIGIN OF ELECTRICITY PRODUCED FROM RENEWABLE ENERGY SOURCES

1. Member States shall, not later than 27 October 2003, ensure that the origin of electricity produced from renewable energy sources can be guaranteed as such within the meaning of this Directive according to objective, transparent and non-discriminatory criteria laid down by each Member State. They shall ensure that a guarantee of origin is issued to this effect in response to a request.

2. Member States may designate one or more competent bodies, independent of generation and distribution activities, to supervise the issue of such guarantees of origin.

3. A guarantee of origin shall:

- specify the energy source from which the electricity was produced, specifying the dates and places of production, and in the case of hydroelectric installations, indicate the capacity;
- serve to enable producers of electricity from renewable energy sources to demonstrate that the electricity they sell is produced from renewable energy sources within the meaning of this Directive.

4. Such guarantees of origin, issued according to paragraph 2, should be mutually recognised by the Member States, exclusively as proof of the elements referred to in paragraph 3. Any refusal to recognise a guarantee of origin as such proof, in particular for reasons relating to the prevention of fraud, must be based on objective, transparent and non-discriminatory criteria. In the event of refusal to recognise a guarantee of origin, the Commission may compel the refusing party to recognise it, particularly with regard to objective, transparent and non-discriminatory criteria on which such recognition is based.

5. Member States or the competent bodies shall put in place appropriate mechanisms to ensure that guarantees of origin are both accurate and reliable and they shall outline in the report referred to in Article 3(3) the measures taken to ensure the reliability of the guarantee system.

6. After having consulted the Member States, the Commission shall, in the report referred to in Article 8, consider the form and methods that Member States could follow in order to guarantee the origin of electricity produced from renewable energy sources. If necessary, the Commission shall propose to the European Parliament and the Council the adoption of common rules in this respect.

ARTICLE 6 ADMINISTRATIVE PROCEDURES

1. Member States or the competent bodies appointed by the Member States shall evaluate the existing legislative and regulatory framework with regard to authorisation procedures or the other procedures laid down in Article 4 of Directive 96/92/EC, which are applicable to production plants for electricity produced from renewable energy sources, with a view to:

- reducing the regulatory and non-regulatory barriers to the increase in electricity production from renewable energy sources,
- streamlining and expediting procedures at the appropriate administrative level, and
- ensuring that the rules are objective, transparent and non-discriminatory, and take fully into account the particularities of the various renewable energy source technologies.

2. Member States shall publish, not later than 27 October 2003, a report on the evaluation referred to in paragraph 1, indicating, where appropriate, the actions taken. The purpose of this report is to provide, where this is appropriate in the context of national legislation, an indication of the stage reached specifically in:

- coordination between the different administrative bodies as regards deadlines, reception and treatment of applications for authorisations,
- drawing up possible guidelines for the activities referred to in paragraph 1, and the feasibility of

a fast-track planning procedure for producers of electricity from renewable energy sources, and

• the designation of authorities to act as mediators in disputes between authorities responsible for issuing authorisations and applicants for authorisations.

3. The Commission shall, in the report referred to in Article 8 and on the basis of the Member States' reports referred to in paragraph 2 of this Article, assess best practices with a view to achieving the objectives referred to in paragraph 1.

ARTICLE 7 GRID SYSTEM ISSUES

1. Without prejudice to the maintenance of the reliability and safety of the grid, Member States shall take the necessary measures to ensure that transmission system operators and distribution system operators in their territory guarantee the transmission and distribution of electricity produced from renewable energy sources. They may also provide for priority access to the grid system of electricity produced from renewable energy sources. When dispatching generating installations, transmission system operators shall give priority to generating installations using renewable energy sources insofar as the operation of the national electricity system permits.

2. Member States shall put into place a legal framework or require transmission system operators and distribution system operators to set up and publish their standard rules relating to the bearing of costs of technical adaptations, such as grid connections and grid reinforcements, which are necessary in order to integrate new producers feeding electricity produced from renewable energy sources into the interconnected grid.

These rules shall be based on objective, transparent and non-discriminatory criteria taking particular account of all the costs and benefits associated with the connection of these producers to the grid. The rules may provide for different types of connection.

3. Where appropriate, Member States may require transmission system operators and distribution system operators to bear, in full or in part, the costs referred to in paragraph 2.

4. Transmission system operators and distribution system operators shall be required to provide any new producer wishing to be connected with a comprehensive and detailed estimate of the costs associated with the connection. Member States may allow producers of electricity from renewable energy sources wishing to be connected to the grid to issue a call for tender for the connection work.

5. Member States shall put into place a legal framework or require transmission system operators and distribution system operators to set up and publish their standard rules relating to the sharing of costs of system installations, such as grid connections and reinforcements, between all producers benefiting from them.

The sharing shall be enforced by a mechanism based on objective, transparent and non-discriminatory criteria taking into account the benefits which initially and subsequently connected producers as well as transmission system operators and distribution system operators derive from the connections.

6. Member States shall ensure that the charging of transmission and distribution fees does not discriminate against electricity from renewable energy sources, including in particular electricity from renewable energy sources produced in peripheral regions, such as island regions and regions of low population density.

Where appropriate, Member States shall put in place a legal framework or require transmission system operators and distribution system operators to ensure that fees charged for the transmission and distribution of electricity from plants using renewable energy sources reflect realisable cost benefits resulting from the plant's connection to the network. Such cost benefits could arise from the direct use of the low-voltage grid.

7. Member States shall, in the report referred to in Article 6(2), also consider the measures to be taken to facilitate access to the grid system of electricity produced from renewable energy sources. That report shall examine, *inter alia*, the feasibility of introducing two-way metering.

ARTICLE 8 SUMMARY REPORT

On the basis of the reports by Member States pursuant to Article 3(3) and Article 6(2), the Commission shall present to the European Parliament and the Council, no later than 31 December 2005 and

thereafter every five years, a summary report on the implementation of this Directive.
This report shall:

- consider the progress made in reflecting the external costs of electricity produced from non-renewable energy sources and the impact of public support granted to electricity production,

- take into account the possibility for Member States to meet the national indicative targets established in Article 3(2), the global indicative target referred to in Article 3(4) and the existence of discrimination between different energy sources.

If appropriate, the Commission shall submit with the report further proposals to the European Parliament and the Council.

ARTICLE 9 TRANSPOSITION

Member States shall bring into force the laws, regulations and administrative provisions necessary to comply with this Directive not later than 27 October 2003. They shall forthwith inform the Commission thereof.
When Member States adopt these measures, they shall contain a reference to this Directive or shall be accompanied by such a reference on the occasion of their official publication. The methods of making such reference shall be laid down by the Member States.

ARTICLE 10 ENTRY INTO FORCE

This Directive shall enter into force on the day of its publication in the *Official Journal of the European Communities.*

ARTICLE 11 ADDRESSEES

This Directive is addressed to the Member States.
Done at Brussels, 27 September 2001.

For the European Parliament
The President
N. FONTAINE

For the Council
The President
C. PICQUÉ

ANNEX

Reference values for Member States' national indicative targets for the contribution of electricity produced from renewable energy sources to gross electricity consumption by 2010*

This Annex gives reference values for the fixing of national indicative targets for electricity produced from renewable energy sources ('RES-E'), as referred to in Article 3(2):

	RES-E TWh 1997**	RES-E% 1997***	RES-E% 2010***
Belgium	0,86	1,1	6,0
Denmark	3,21	8,7	29,0
Germany	24,91	4,5	12,5
Greece	3,94	8,6	20,1
Spain	37,15	19,9	29,4
France	66,00	15,0	21,0
Ireland	0,84	3,6	13,2
Italy	46,46	16,0	25,0[1]
Luxembourg	0,14	2,1	5,7[2]
Netherlands	3,45	3,5	9,0
Austria	39,05	70,0	78,1[3]
Portugal	14,30	38,5	39,0[4]
Finland	19,03	24,7	31,5[5]
Sweden	72,03	49,1	60,0[6]
United Kingdom	7,04	1,7	10,0
Community	338,41	13,9%	22%****

* In taking into account the reference values set out in this Annex, Member States make the necessary assumption that the State aid guidelines for environmental protection allow for the existence of national support schemes for the promotion of electricity produced from renewable energy sources.
** Data refer to the national production of RES-E in 1997.
*** The percentage contributions of RES-E in 1997 and 2010 are based on the national production of RES-E divided by the gross national electricity consumption. In the case of internal trade of RES-E (with recognised certification or

origin registered) the calculation of these percentages will influence 2010 figures by Member State but not the Community total.

**** Rounded figure resulting from the reference values above.

1 *Italy* states that 22% would be a realistic figure, on the assumption that in 2010 gross national electricity consumption will be 340 TWh. When taking into account the reference values set out in this Annex, Italy has assumed that gross national electricity production from renewable energy sources will attain up to 76 TWh in 2010. This figure includes the contribution of the non-biodegradable fraction of municipal and industrial waste used in compliance with Community legislation on waste management.

In this respect, the capability to reach the indicative target as referred to in this Annex, is contingent, *inter alia*, upon the effective level of the national demand for electric energy in 2010.

2 Taking into account the indicative reference values set out in this Annex, *Luxembourg* takes the view that the objective set for 2010 can be achieved only if:

- total electricity consumption in 2010 does not exceed that of 1997,
- wind-generated electricity can be multiplied by a factor of 15,
- biogas-generated electricity can be multiplied by a factor of 208,
- electricity produced from the only municipal waste incinerator in Luxembourg, which in 1997 accounted for half the electricity produced from renewable energy sources, can be taken into account in its entirety,
- photovoltaically generated electricity can be raised to 80 GWh, and

in so far as the above points can be achieved from the technical standpoint in the time allowed.

In the absence of natural resources, an additional increase in electricity generated by hydroelectric power stations is ruled out.

3 *Austria* states that 78,1% would be a realistic figure, on the assumption that in 2010 gross national electricity consumption will be 56,1 TWh. Due to the fact that the production of electricity from renewable sources is highly dependent on hydropower and therefore on the annual rainfall, the figures for 1997 and 2010 should be calculated on a long-range model based on hydrologic and climatic conditions.

4 *Portugal*, when taking into account the reference values, set out in this Annex, states that to maintain the 1997 share of electricity produced from renewable sources as an indicative target for 2010 it was assumed that:

- it will be possible to continue the national electricity plan building new hydro capacity higher than 10 MW,
- other renewable capacity, only possible with financial state aid, will increase at an annual rate eight times higher than has occurred recently.

These assumptions imply that new capacity for producing electricity from renewable sources, excluding large hydro, will increase at a rate twice as high as the rate of increase of gross national electricity consumption.

5 In the *Finnish* action plan for renewable energy sources, objectives are set for the volume of renewable energy sources used in 2010. These objectives have been set on the basis of extensive background studies. The action plan was approved within the Government in October 1999.

According to the Finnish action plan, the share of electricity produced from renewable energy sources by 2010 would be 31%. This indicative target is very ambitious and its realisation would require extensive promotion measures in Finland.

6 When taking into account the reference values set out in this Annex, *Sweden* notes that the possibility of reaching the target is highly dependent upon climatic factors heavily affecting the level of hydropower production, in particular variations in pluviometry, timing of rainfall during the year and inflow. The electricity produced from hydropower can vary substantially. During extremely dry years production may amount to 51 TWh, whereas in wet years it could amount to 78 TWh. The figure for 1997 should thus be calculated with a long-range model based on scientific facts on hydrology and climatic change.

It is a generally applied method in countries with important shares of hydropower production to use water inflow statistics covering a time span of 30 to 60 years. Thus, according to the Swedish methodology and based on conditions during the period 1950–1999, correcting for differences in total hydropower production capacity and inflow over the years, average hydropower production amounts to 64 TWh which corresponds to a figure for 1997 of 46%, and in this context Sweden considers 52% to be a more realistic figure for 2010.

Furthermore, the ability of Sweden to achieve the target is limited by the fact that the remaining unexploited rivers are protected by law. Moreover, the ability of Sweden to reach the target is heavily contingent upon:

- the expansion of combined heat and power (CHP) depending on population density, demand for heat and technology development, in particular for black liquor gasification, and
- authorisation for wind power plants in accordance with national laws, public acceptance, technology development and expansion of grids.

Proposal for a Directive of the European Parliament and of the Council on the Energy Performance of Buildings

(presented by the Commission)

Brussels, 11.5.2001 COM(2001) 226 final 2001/0098 (COD)

Explanatory Memorandum

1. INTRODUCTION

In its Green Paper "Towards a European Strategy for Energy Supply"[1] the Commission highlighted three main points:

- The European Union will become increasingly dependent on external energy sources; enlargement will reinforce this trend. Based on current forecasts, if measures are not taken, import dependence will reach 70% in 2030, compared to 50% today.
- At present, greenhouse gas emissions in the European Union are on the rise, making it difficult to respond to the challenge of climate change and to meet its commitments under the Kyoto Protocol. Moreover, the commitments made in the Kyoto Protocol must be regarded as a first step; climate change is a longterm battle involving the entire international community.
- The European Union has very limited scope to influence energy supply conditions. It is essentially on the demand side that the EU can intervene, mainly by promoting energy savings in buildings and in the transport sector.

These observations provide strong reasons to economise the use of energy wherever possible. The residential and tertiary[2] sectors have been shown to be the largest overall end users, mainly for heating, lighting, appliances and equipment. Numerous studies and practical experience show that there is a large potential for energy savings here, probably larger than in any other sector[3]. Member State and Community efforts to realise this potential need, therefore, to be intensified.

The Green Paper concludes in this regard that, in general, the Community programmes for the support and promotion of new technologies have not succeeded to bring about the application of new standards on energy efficiency in buildings in many Member States. Therefore, more emphasis should now be placed on concrete measures such as the establishment of a clear legislative framework to reduce growth in demand.

The scope for energy saving in the buildings sector and possible measures to realise the large potential here have also been important topics in the European Climate Change Programme[4].

Community action also makes the issue of energy demand management and energy savings a commitment in Candidate countries where, in general, a very large potential for energy savings exists in the residential and tertiary sectors.

2. OBJECTIVE AND SCOPE OF PROPOSED DIRECTIVE

The basic objective underlying this draft Directive is to promote the improvement of the energy performance of buildings within the EU, ensuring in so far as possible that only such measures as are the most cost-effective are undertaken.

Given the low turn-over rate of buildings (lifetime of 50 to more than 100 years) it is clear

[1] COM(2000)769 of 29 November 2000.

[2] Tertiary includes offices, wholesale and retail trade, hotels, restaurants, schools, hospitals, sports halls, indoor swimming pools, etc. but excludes industrial buildings.

[3] Mesures d'Utilisation Rationelle de l'Energie (MURE) Database, European Commission 1998.

[4] COM(2000)88 final of 8 March 2000.

that the largest potential for improving energy performance in the short and medium term is in the existing stock of buildings. The proposed Directive lays down a framework that will lead to increased co-ordination between Member States of legislation in this field. The practical application of the framework, however, will remain primarily the responsibility of the individual Member States.

The proposal covers four main elements:

(A) Establishment of a general framework of a common methodology for calculating the *integrated* energy performance of buildings.

(B) Application of minimum standards on the energy performance to new buildings and to certain existing buildings when they are renovated.

(C) Certification schemes for new and existing buildings on the basis of the above standards and public display of energy performance certificates and recommended indoor temperatures and other relevant climatic factors in public buildings and buildings frequented by the public.

(D) Specific inspection and assessment of boilers and heating/cooling installations.

A Common Methodology for Integrated Energy Performance Standards

There is a strong tendency towards an integrated approach in building standards and codes that are being developed in and outside the EU (e.g. in the U.S., Australia, Canada and New Zealand). Such an approach can integrate, in addition to the quality of insulation of the building, heating installations, cooling installations, energy for ventilation, lighting installations, position and orientation of the building, heat recovery, active solar gains and other renewable energy sources. With today's highly insulated new buildings and the trend towards low energy houses, these additional factors play an increasingly large role and should therefore be included in regulatory provisions. Such an integrated approach will give more flexibility to designers to meet energy reduction standards in the most cost-effective way. An integrated approach for the energy performance of buildings has to varying degrees already been applied in D, F, UK, I and NL and some other Member States intend to do the same. In some cases it is mandatory. A common approach on this basis would contribute to a more level playing field as regards the efforts made by Member States to achieve energy savings in the buildings sector. It would also facilitate the comparison of buildings throughout the EU for prospective users and make it easier for designers and constructors to apply standards in other Member States.

A common methodology could then form the basis for integrated minimum energy performance standards for different building categories to be adopted by the Member States, reflecting local circumstances, particularly climatic differences.

Application of these Standards to New Buildings and to Certain Existing Buildings when They Are Being Renovated

New residential buildings and dwellings as well as new buildings in the tertiary sector should meet the minimum energy performance standards based on an integrated methodology. Furthermore these standards should also be applied to larger (i.e., greater than 1000 m^2) existing buildings, when the buildings undergo larger renovations. It should be noted that the indoor climate conditions should be given due consideration when these standards are applied.

Certification Schemes for New and Existing Buildings on the Basis of the Above Methodology

One of the main reasons for market imperfections as regards investment in energy efficiency on the rental market is the fact that the owner and renter of a building, dwelling or office have different interests. As the renter normally pays the energy bill, the incentive for the owner to invest in energy efficiency is weak. The best way to make these investments more attractive is to provide clear and reliable information to prospective renters. Clear information will influence the rent that can be asked and therefore will be an incentive for owners to make investments in the energy efficiency of buildings and houses. Therefore, to facilitate the transfer of this information on the energy performance of buildings and apartments, energy certificates for new and existing buildings and dwellings should be available when these are constructed, sold or rented out. This certification, which should not be more than 5 years old, should be based on the same integrated approach as used for the minimum standards for new

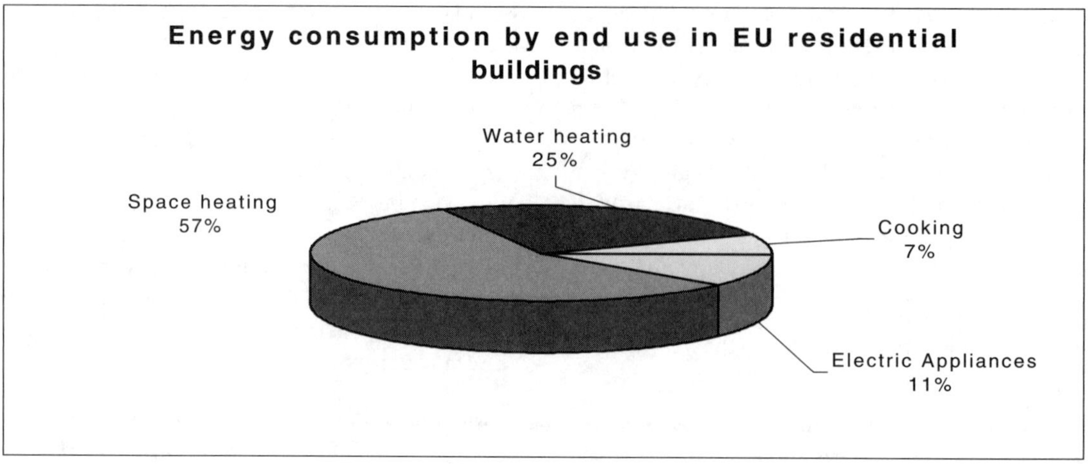

Figure 1: Energy consumption in the residential sector [5].

buildings and should include accompanying advice on how to improve the energy performance of the building.

In the case of public authority buildings and certain privately owned or occupied buildings frequented by the public, energy certificates not more than 5 years old must be prominently and permanently displayed for the public. Public authority buildings and buildings frequented by the general public are able to demonstrate efficient technology and to set examples by incorporating energy efficiency measures into the renovation of such buildings. Appropriate measures can make the public aware of the energy performance of these buildings and also provide recommendations to improve them. This is best done by means of a certification procedure.

In addition, for public authority buildings and buildings frequented by the general public, in order to inform the public and to promote the proper use of heating, air-conditioning and ventilation systems, certain information should be clearly displayed.

The displayed information should include the range of indoor temperatures and, when local climatic conditions require it, other relevant climatic factors such as relative humidity, that are recommended by the authorities for that specific type of building. This will help to avoid unnecessary use of energy and to safeguard comfortable indoor climatic conditions (thermal comfort) in relation to the outside temperature.

The current inside temperature and, when appropriate other relevant climatic factors, should also be displayed and indicated by means of a reliable device or devices.

Certification for new buildings is at present mandatory in DK, D and UK. For existing buildings, only Denmark has a mandatory scheme but several Member States have voluntary programs.

In Denmark, a calculation on the basis of the database of 3.5 years of certification of 160,000 houses showed a total cost of the certification of ca 25 M€ and identified potential savings measures of ca 125 M€. These measures reduced the costs for energy for the consumers by 20M€ each year. In this particular case, certification, together with the implementation of identified measures, provided a more than 13% return on investments.

Specific Inspection and Assessment of Heating/Cooling Installations

Heating installations are recognized to be a key issue as regards energy efficiency. Boilers with an effective output of more than 10 kW, the power necessary for smaller households with accumulation capacity, up to boilers for blocks of flats, offices, etc. should be regularly inspected to improve their operating conditions. Such an inspection is compulsory in 10 Member States whilst the others apply voluntary schemes and information programs.

[5] COM (2000)769 of 29 November 2000

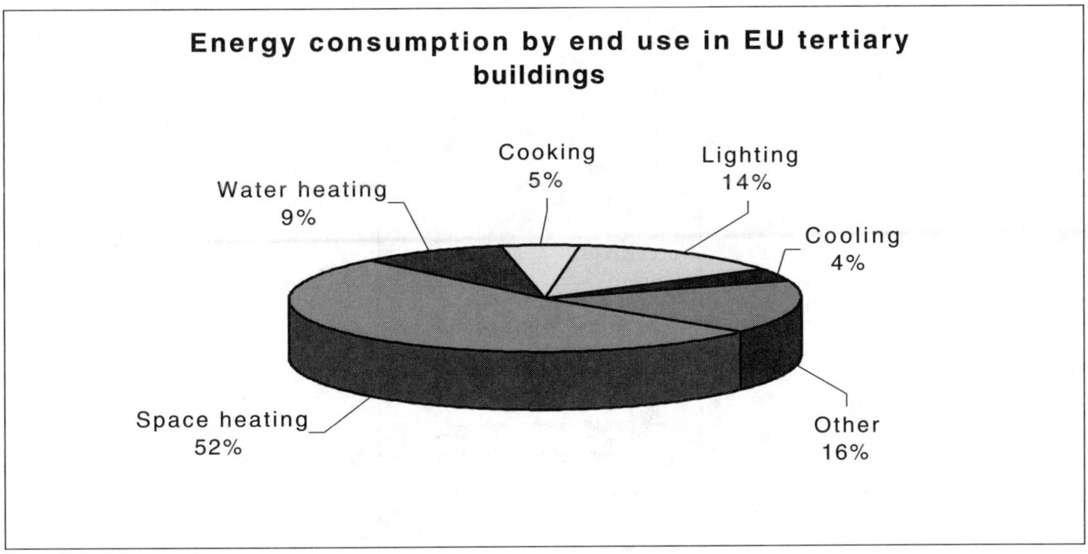

Figure 2: Energy consumption in the tertiary sector [6].

In the case of boilers more than 15 years old, the entire heating installation should be inspected and advice should be given to the users on alternative solutions which could reduce energy consumption.

Similar measures need to be taken as regards cooling systems, in particular in larger buildings.

3. ENERGY CONSUMPTION IN THE BUILDINGS SECTOR

The total final energy consumption in the EU in 1997 was about 930 Mtoe. A simplified breakdown of this demand shows the importance of buildings in this context: 40.7% of total energy demand is used in the residential and tertiary sectors, most of it for building-related energy services (see Table 1). It should also be pointed out that approximately 10% of the consumed energy in buildings comes from renewable energy sources (RES).

Space heating is by far the largest energy end-use of households in Member States (57%), followed by water heating (25%). Electrical appliances and lighting make up 11% of the sector's total energy consumption (see Figure 1). For the tertiary sector (see Figure 2) the importance of space heating is somewhat lower (52% of total consumption of the sector), while energy consumption for lighting and office equipment and "other" (which is mainly office equipment) are 14% and 16%, respectively.

[6] *Ibid*

4. POTENTIAL SAVINGS THROUGH ENERGY EFFICIENCY MEASURES IN THE BUILDING SECTOR

4.1 Scope of the Initiative

Aspects of energy in buildings used for heating, hot water, cooling and lighting purposes will be addressed in the present initiative. It should be noted that this document covers the building envelope, including windows, and installed equipment such as heating, air-conditioning and ventilation. It does not cover measures for non-installed equipment such as domestic appliances (including cooking), which together are responsible for 18% of the total energy consumption in the residential sector. In the tertiary sector, lighting, which accounts for 14% of the sector's energy consumption, is for the most part installed equipment and therefore included. Non-installed equipment is estimated to account for around 20% of the tertiary sector's consumption, due partially to the large share of office equipment. For non-installed equipment, specific policies such as labelling, mandatory minimum efficiency requirements, voluntary agreements, etc.

Table 1: European Union final energy demand by sector and by fuel in 1997 (Mtoe)[7]

Final energy demand by sector/Final energy demand by fuel	Buildings (residential + tertiary)	% of total final energy demand	Industry	% of total final energy demand	Transport	% of total final energy demand	Total	% of total final energy demand
Solid fuels	8,7	0,9%	37,2	4,0%	0,0	0,0%	45,9	4,9%
Oil	101	10,8%	45,6	4,9%	283,4	30,5%	430,1	46,2%
Gas	129,1	13,9%	86,4	9,3%	0,3	0,0%	215,9	23,2%
Electricity (incl. 14% from RES)	98	10,5%	74,3	8,0%	4,9	0,5%	177,2	19,0%
Derived heat	16,2	1,7%	4,2	0,5%	0,0	0,0%	20,4	2,2%
Renewables	26,1	2,8%	15,0	1,6%	0,0	0,0%	41,1	4,4%
Total	**379,2**	**40,7%**	**262,7**	**28,2%**	**288,6**	**31,0%**	**930,5**	**100,0%**

[7] "Energy in Europe – European Union Energy Outlook to 2020", Special Issue November 1999, the Shared Analysis Project, European Commission.

Table 2: Thermal insulation and glazing in some EU Member States

Insulation Type	FIN	S	DK	IRL	UK	D	NL	B	F	L	A	P	GR
No insulation			1	13	10		14	21	21	55	39	23	77
Loft/roof insulation	100	100	76	72	90	42	53	43	71	35	37		16
Cavity wall insulation	100	100	65	42	25	24	47	42	68	2	26		12
Floor insulation	100	100	63	22	4	15	27	14	24	5	11		6
Double glazing	100	100	91	33	61	88	78	62	52	20	53	3	8

have been implemented or are envisaged in the Action Plan for Energy Efficiency[8].

4.2 Global Savings Potential

As regards energy in buildings that is used for heating, hot water, air-conditioning or lighting purposes, a savings potential[9] of around 22% of present consumption is estimated to exist and can be realised by the year 2010[10]. As stated in the European Climate Change Progress Report, this figure has been based on the assumption of a normal rate of retrofitting and rehabilitation for existing buildings, a net increase in the building stock of around 1.5%/year, and a successively increasing share in the use of best available technologies in buildings[11].

In its Green Paper "Towards a European Strategy for Energy Supply"[12] the Commission re-states the indicative target from the Council Resolution of 7 December 1998[13]: to improve energy intensity of final consumption by a further 1 percentage point per year over that which would have been otherwise attained. For the building sector, meeting this indicative target would result in avoided energy consumption of over 55 Mtoe, equivalent to avoided CO_2 emissions of around 100 Mt/year or around 20 % of the EU Kyoto commitment. Meeting this target would also realise two-thirds of the available savings potential in the sector, while making allowance for price fluctuations and possible "rebound effects"[14]. However, for this to be achieved effective action is required.

4.3 Savings Potential through Improvements of the Building Envelope

In 1995 there were approximately 150 million residential dwellings in the 15 EU Member States. About 32 % of the current stock was built prior to 1945, about 40 % between 1945 and 1973–75, and about 28 % since 1973–75[15]. On average 56 % of the residential buildings are owner-occupied, ranging from almost 40% in Germany to almost 80% in Spain. 66% of the dwellings in the EU-15 are in single family houses, with 80 % and more in Germany, Ireland, Luxembourg and the United Kingdom.

The most recent available EUROSTAT survey on residential energy consumption (published in 1999) shows significant differences in terms of insulation measures carried out among Member States, connected partially but not wholly to the varying climatic conditions between countries. Measures implemented are shown in Table 2. The figures indicate the percentage of those participating in the questionnaire who had implemented measures[16].

[8]"Action Plan to improve Energy Efficiency in the European Community" COM(2000)247 final.

[9]In this context, savings potential is generally defined in terms of investments in energy-efficient technology having a pay-back period of eight years or less, allowing a high rate of return compared to alternative investments, including investments in energy production.

[10]"*Mesures d'Utilisation Rationnelle de l'Energie (MURE)*" Database, European Commission *1998. Op, Cit.*

[11]ECCP Progress Report (2000), http://europa.eu.int/comm/environment/climat/eccp/htm

[12]COM(2000)769 of 29 November 2000. *Op. Cit.*

[13]Council Resolution of 7 December 1998 on energy efficiency in the European Community (98/C 394/01).

[14]Studies using the PRIMES model and Ecofys bottom-up approach indicate that the cost-effective potential for emission reduction could be between 130 Mt/year and 160 Mt/year, respectively.

[15]Sciotech (1998), "Electrical Heating and Cooling of Residential Dwellings", study financed by the SAVE Programme of the EC.

[16]"Energy Consumption in Households", p.23. EUROSTAT 1999. The figures are indicative to the extent that insulation quality is not taken into account and methodology may vary somewhat between Member States. Complete data from Italy, Portugal and Spain are not yet available.

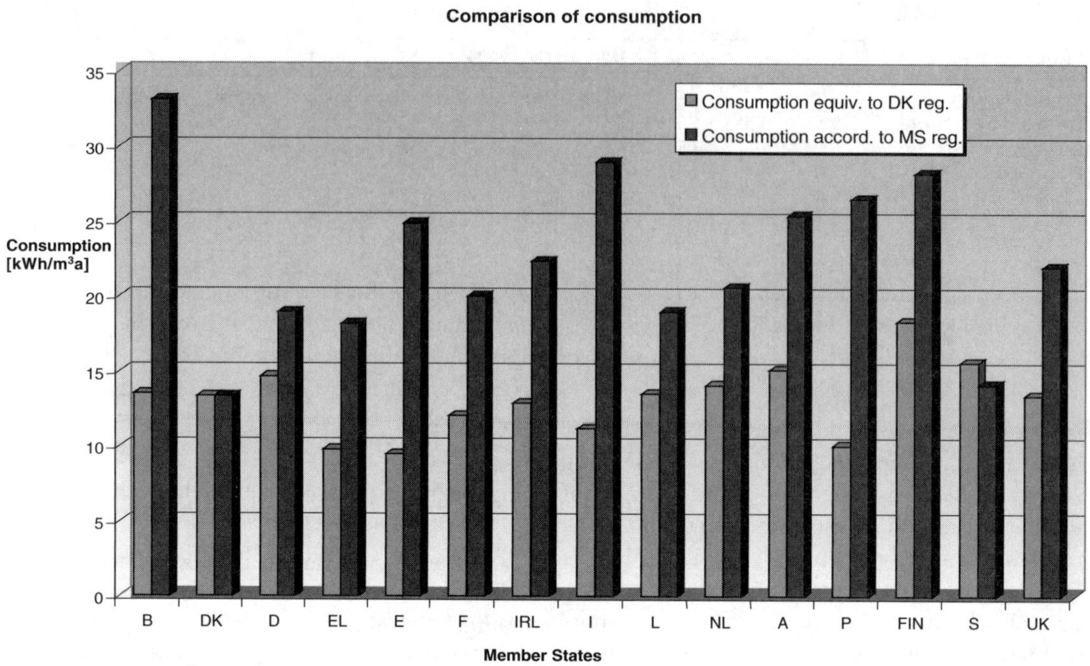

Figure 3: Energy consumption in Member States according to their existing national building regulations compared to the Danish model regulation adjusted for climatic differences[18,19].

While there has been some improvement compared with the results of earlier surveys, large differences remain between Member States.

The current average heat loss in the EU for new buildings is presently about half of what it is for the pre-1945 housing stock[17]. The total energy used in new dwellings is 60 % of that used in old dwellings. An upgrade of thermal insulation regulations and improved efficiency for installed equipment for existing dwellings, bringing them close to current buildings codes, would help to realise this important savings potential, making it a very desirable and in most cases a cost-effective option.

A comparison of thermal building regulations in the European Union has been carried out. The comparison below shows that rather extreme differences exist in building regulations even after these have been made comparable by correcting for climatic differences using so-called "degree days". The comparison is made by using the model building regulation of Denmark and applying it to each Member State after climatic correction. Consumption as measured by the application of this model building code is, in many cases, dramatically lower than with existing national thermal insulation codes (see Figure 3).

Figure 3 illustrates that a European initiative intended to improve the energy performance of buildings by promoting improved Member State thermal insulation regulations to a level already attained by some Member States could result in substantial energy savings for the EU as a whole.

It should also be pointed out that the above calculations are based on the assumption that the theoretical standards are effectively applied in practice.

[17] 55W/m^2 compared with 100 W/m^2.

[18] FhG-ISI (1999), A Comparison of Thermal Building Regulations in the European Union,MURE Database Case Study N° 1, Study carried out inthe framework of the MURE project, financed by the SAVE Programme of the EC, *http://www.mure2.com/Mr-/fr5.htm*

[19] Simplified calculation, not taking into account solar heat recovery, internal heat sources, ventilation losses; exclusion ofheating system efficiencies or energy and insulation cost differences. In cases where several codes exist in the same Member State, only one code has been chosen. In some cases, regional codes are stricter than national codes.

4.4 Savings Potential of Boilers

Directive 92/42/EEC has introduced minimum efficiency requirements for residential hot water boilers, thus ensuring that all new boilers have a reasonable efficiency. However, SAVE studies have indicated that there are, in the EU, more than 10 million boilers more than 20 years old. The savings potential which could be realised by the replacement of these old boilers is calculated by itself to result in reduced consumption by over over 10 Mtoe or around 5% of the energy used for heating in the residential sector.

The annual overall efficiency of boilers is improved by the correct matching of the boiler to the heating installation (radiator system), by reducing stand-by losses, by the use of control devices and by the correct sizing of the boiler for the building and climate. Old boilers have much lower nominal and part-load efficiencies and most of them are oversized for various reasons, including the economic incentive for the installer to promote larger and more expensive boilers. The combination of oversizing, high stand-by losses and low efficiency results in an overall efficiency which is 35% below that of new boilers, which are properly dimensioned and installed, and which comply with existing EU minimum efficiency standards.

It should be pointed out that the benefit of a new, modern boiler, assessed only on the basis of its nominal efficiency, is often not sufficient to justify the cost of replacement of a boiler which is still running. An integrated calculation should therefore be made which includes the above-mentioned factors in the life-cycle cost of the new boiler and in the alternative cost (and risk) of retaining the existing boiler.

4.5 Savings Potential of Other Installed Equipment

Lighting consumes about 9 Mtoe, or around 4% of total energy in the residential sector, where the majority of lighting fixtures are not permanently installed in the building. In the tertiary sector, where the large majority of lighting is provided by fluorescent lighting which is installed in the building, lighting consumes around 18 Mtoe, or 14% of the sector's energy, as has been pointed out. A large potential savings exists in lighting, especially in the tertiary sector. Savings in the order of between 30% and 50% could be achieved with the use of the most efficient components, the use of control systems and the integration of daylighting and related technologies. These savings, of between 6 Mtoe and 9 Mtoe, represent a significant share of the available potential in the building sector. The recently launched EU GreenLight Programme demonstrates that most of the energy savings in lighting are highly cost-effective.

Air-conditioning is a rapidly growing consumption activity in the residential and tertiary sectors. The total consumption of energy for air-conditioning, which is about 3 Mtoe, or 0,7% of total final energy consumption in the two sectors combined, will double by 2020 if current trends persist. The cost-effective savings potential is about 25%. Much could be achieved by 2010 if the right policy measures are in place at an early stage, including minimum efficiency requirements for air-conditioning equipment.

4.6 Potential for Environmental-Friendly Energy Generation Installations

In many buildings, there is a promising potential for reducing CO_2 emissions and saving energy by means of an integrated approach, whereby traditional energy savings on the building envelope are combined with environmental-friendly energy generation. While this sort of energy generation could in many cases be decentralised and on-site, connection to existing district heating/cooling networks can also be an important means to improve a building's overall energy performance.

Environmental-friendly energy generation installations relevant to the buildings sector can broadly be divided into three main groups:

- Renewable energy sources
- Combined heat and power (CHP) and district heating/cooling
- Heat pumps (only in specific cases and under certain conditions)

Renewable Energy Sources (RES)

On 10 May 2000 the Commission adopted a proposal for a Directive on the promotion of electricity from renewable energy sources[20], which was taken

[20] COM(2000)279 final.

as a matter of priority by The European Parliament and the French and Swedish Presidencies. It is expected that in 2001 this proposal will result in a regulatory framework for electricity from renewable energy sources, including indicative targets for the Member States.

The present proposal addresses the specific potential benefits of integrating RES installations into buildings, covering not only electricity but, equally important, heat generation.

The Green Paper "Towards a European Strategy for the Security of Energy Supply"[21] underscores the importance of developing new and renewable energy sources. It cites the White Paper on RES[22], which estimates that a total installed capacity of 100 million m^2 of solar collectors can be achieved by 2010 (the installed capacity was 9,0 million m^2 in 1998[23]). In a follow-up report on the White Paper[24], which contains more detailed break-downs of the different sectors and technologies, it has been estimated that a large proportion of these solar collectors could be for domestic hot water production (50%), space heating (11 %) and large collective solar heating systems (19%), all relevant to the buildings sector. Photovoltaics is expected in the White Paper to contribute with a total installed capacity of 3000 MW_p by 2010 (from today's level of around 200 MW_p) of which most is expected to come from grid connected installations integrated into the structure of the buildings (roofs or facades). To reach this potential, however, there is a need for more effective measures and incentives[25].

With regard to biomass, solid biofuels such as logwood, woodchips and pellets are already used, in particular in the residential sector, for heating and hot water. The applications can be both for individual single-family heating and central heating units in large buildings and apartment blocks and, according to the above-mentioned follow-up report on the White Paper, they can provide substantial capacity by 2010.

Combined Heat and Power (CHP) and District Heating/Cooling

Combined heat and power (CHP), suitable for individual buildings and groups of buildings, is another generation technology, which can make a positive contribution to the overall energy performance of a building. Due to the efficient use of the fuel used[26] both for electricity and heat production, CHP is an energy-efficient solution that saves fuel and thereby also contributes to reducing CO_2 emissions.

Increased use of CHP in the buildings sector could make a major contribution to meeting the indicative Community target of doubling the total share for CHP electricity production to 18% by 2010[27]. CHP is applicable mostly in larger buildings such as apartment blocks, hospitals, hotels, leisure centres, airports, shopping centres, and other large office buildings. In the medium to long-term, micro cogeneration units for installation in the residential sector may also offer an additional potential. Connection to existing district heating or cooling networks will often offer an energy efficient option to meet the heating or cooling demand of a building. Where such systems are in operation, connecting more buildings to the network must be a priority. District heating/cooling is also a supply option to consider when planning and developing new residential areas.

Heat Pumps

Heat pumps are yet another supply option, which, under certain circumstances, could contribute positively to saving energy in buildings. Heat pumps can have high efficiencies and are applicable in some cases both for single and multi-family dwellings for space heating. Apart from Sweden, the market penetration for heat pumps in most EU countries is modest. The high investment costs compared with

[21] COM(2000)769 of 29 November 2000, *Op. Cit.*

[22] "Energy for the Future: Renewable Sources of Energy", White Paper for a Community Strategy and Action Plan, COM(1997)599 final.

[23] Eurostat

[24] "Ex-ante Evaluation on the Impact of the Community Strategy and Action Plan for renewable Energy Sources", ALTENER Contract N° 4.1030/T/98-020.

[25] In the city of Barcelona for example, under a special ordinance that came into effect on 1 August 2000, most new buildings will have to be fitted with solar panels unless it can be proved that a particular building cannot produce at least 25% of its hot water requirements from solar panels.

[26] According to EUROSTAT, the EU average overall efficiency of CHP plants was in 1998 74.9% compared with an average conversion efficiency of 39.4 % in conventional power generation (CHP Statistics (1994–98) Draft Summary Report and EUROSTAT figures on conventional power generation in Commission Staff Working Paper "Completing the internal energy market", SEC(2001)438).

[27] European Cogeneration Review, July 1999.

other technologies are seen as a major barrier but costs are falling and efficiencies improving.

Promotion of decentralised energy generation in buildings should for all three of the above categories be carried out in a way whereby both demand and supply measures are analysed in an integrated manner. For example, use of energy-efficient or CO_2-free supply forms in buildings with very poor insulation should generally not be encouraged.

4.7 Savings Potential in Terms of Building Design and Orientation: The Bioclimatic Dimension

It is estimated that taking full account of existing bioclimatic or ecological dimensions when designing and locating buildings can reduce energy requirements significantly over the lifetime of a building. In certain cases, buildings which already meet high thermal insulation standards can reduce energy demand by up to 60 % by using proper passive solar design, optimised active solar systems for domestic hot water and space heating, improved daylighting and natural cooling and solar/glare control. New buildings can be constructed in this manner with one-fourth of present space heating requirements[28]. Even with existing buildings, where the design and location are already fixed, this savings potential can be significant if favourable conditions exist and are properly exploited.

The concept of bioclimatic design and construction includes strategies for enhancing all physical parameters and improving heating, cooling, ventilation and lighting.

A strategy for heating and cooling implies that measures are taken which, for example, maximise the use and accumulation of passive solar heat during the heating season or minimise it during the cooling season, depending on the relative lengths of the two. It includes such factors as positioning the house in such a way as to design and expose the maximum external surface area possible to the sun (or, for cooling, to protect it from the sun). It also includes taking into account prevailing wind conditions, potential and existing shading from trees, and heating and cooling accumulation potentials of surrounding terrain and bodies of water, for heat/cooling pumps and similar uses.

A strategy for lighting includes optimising the use of natural daylight to complement and reduce the need for artificial lighting. This is done by allowing for the use of daylighting techniques, including the geometry of windows, light diffusion, prism technology and similar measures.

4.8 Concluding Remarks

Energy savings in the buildings sector involves many different economic and technical aspects as described above. In several Member States these aspects have been integrated into a single system to describe the energy performance of a building. With such an integrated approach the different aspects that should be incorporated into the standards for new buildings can be expressed in simple energy performance indicators. Moreover, such an approach allows added flexibility regarding details, giving designers greater choice in meeting minimum standards. In order to achieve a certain degree of harmonisation of assessment of buildings for designers and users throughout the EU, a common methodology based on such an integrated approach should be pursued.

While all Member States apply minimum standards, especially for new buildings, considerable differences exist in the level of energy performance required in these standards. These differences indicate a large potential for improvement and the need for measures to be taken to realise this potential in the most cost-effective way.

Nevertheless it should be recognised that the largest potential for energy saving is in the renovation of existing buildings. In order to address this issue, the most appropriate measure seems to be to introduce certification of buildings in order to raise awareness, and at the same time remedy the major market imperfection that owners have no incentives to invest in buildings they rent out. Special attention should be given to the effective replacement of heating installations. Moreover, buildings should meet higher standards as regards energy performance when they are renovated. As educational information to the general public, the certification of public authority buildings or certain other buildings with high energy consumption which are frequented by the public should be displayed in the buildings, along with recommended and current indoor temperatures and relevant climatic factors.

[28] IEA (2000), IEA Solar Heating and Cooling Study, SHC, Paris.

5. JUSTIFICATION FOR ACTION AT COMMUNITY LEVEL

5.1 Current Political Context

Art.2 of the EC Treaty calls for a sustainable development of the economy of the Community. *Art.6 of the EC Treaty* reinforced these objectives of sustainable development by integrating environment policy into other Community policies. The Cardiff European Council in 1998 reaffirmed the need for integration of environment into energy policy. *Art. 175* sets the framework for adopting measures with environmental objectives.

The UN Framework Convention on Climate Change requires the parties to adopt policies and to take measures to reduce and limit greenhouse gas emissions in order to stabilise their emissions by 2000 at the 1990 level. This non-binding commitment has been supplemented by the Community 8% reduction commitment as laid down in the Kyoto Protocol of 1997. Whereas the building sector can already provide a substantial contribution to the Community efforts to meet the Kyoto target in the relatively few years left before 2012, it should play an even more important role in the period beyond 2012, where the Commission's proposal for a Sixth Environmental Action Programme foresees a 20–40% reduction by the year 2020. On 8 March 2000, the Commission adopted the Communication on "EU policies and measures to reduce greenhouse gas emissions: Towards a European Climate Change Programme (ECCP)"[29]. The ECCP is based on the May 1999 Communication "Preparing for implementation of the Kyoto Protocol"[30] and follows up suggestions originally given by the Environment Council in June 1998 and in October 1999. The latter urged the Commission to put forward a list of priority actions for common and co-ordinated policies and measures as early as possible in 2000 and to prepare appropriate policy proposals.

In view of the expected increase in emissions in the absence of further measures and the challenge that the majority of Member States may face in meeting their commitments under the EU burden sharing agreement, a reinforcement of policies and measures at EU level becomes an important supplement to national climate strategies.

In its "Green Paper on the security of energy supply"[31] the Commission outlines the prospective energy situation in the EU for 2010 and beyond. One of the essential observations in this Communication is that the EU will in the short and medium term have a decreasing possibility to influence the supply side of energy. However as the EU is one of the main consumer areas it should do its utmost, notably on the demand side, to reduce the strong dependence on external suppliers.

The informal ECOFIN Council in its meeting on 9 September 2000 stressed the need for acceleration of the implementation of EU action plans in the field of energy savings measures and diversification in order to reduce the oil dependency of our economies.

In response to the Commission's Action Plan on Energy Efficiency, the Energy Council has adopted two Conclusions during the year 2000. One was adopted on 30 May 2000 and the other on 5 December 2000[32,33]. In both the Commission is invited to undertake initiatives, notably in the residential and tertiary sectors, including building certification, improved thermal insulation and improved installed equipment and other installations.

5.2 Additional impact of action at Community level

Under paragraph 4.3 above, the substantial differences which exist between the performance of Member States in the field of energy savings in the building sector have been displayed, along with the most promising measures.

Therefore, the proposal for a new legally binding instrument must be seen in the light of the objective of increasing energy performances of buildings in all Member States in the European Union. Reduction of Co2 emissions and security of energy supply are issues of common responsibility for the Member States and therefore a legal initiative at Community level is justified. In some Member States the current building standards date from the late seventies whilst others have recently made substantial improvements in this important sector. It should,

[29] COM(2000)88 final. *Op. Cit.*

[30] Commission Communication to the Council and the Parliament "Preparing for implementation of the Kyoto Protocol" COM (1999)230.

[31] Green Paper "Towards a European strategy for the security of energy supply", COM(2000) 769. *Op. Cit.*

[32] Council Conclusion 8835/00.

[33] Council Conclusion 14000/00.

therefore, be emphasised that as a first step one of the purposes of this proposal is to achieve a convergence of building standards, including thermal insulation standards towards those of Member States which already have relatively ambitious levels.

The target of improved energy efficiency in buildings has already been set out in earlier existing legal instruments. Among the main existing Community legislation for the building sector are the "Boilers Directive" (92/42/EEC), the "Construction Products Directive" (89/106/EEC) and the "buildings" articles in the "SAVE" Directive 93/76/EEC.

The latter Directive requires Member States to draw up and implement programmes in six specific fields in order to improve energy efficiency. These programmes can be in the form of laws, regulations, economic and administrative instruments, information, education and voluntary agreements.

However, it should be pointed out that this 93/76 Directive was agreed in another political context, before the conclusion of the Kyoto Protocol and before the recent new doubts about the growing dependence of the EU on supply from other global actors. Although this Directive has made a contribution, it has not proven to be completely adequate in reaching the important objective of improving the energy performance of buildings to the degree which is judged to be economically and technically feasible.

The above developments underline the Community dimension of energy efficiency and justify the establishment of more concrete action at Community level that can complement or reinforce existing national measures in this field. It also should be pointed out that a Community approach will create an economy of scale in the internal market for products, components and installations that will improve energy performance of buildings. Moreover, where market imperfections make it necessary to intervene with legal measures such as mandatory certification for the promotion of energy efficiency, a Community approach will give a better guarantee for a level playing field for consumers and industry that e.g. occupy, rent, construct or sell those buildings in the internal market.

5.3 Relevance of the initiative for the Accession Countries

In its 1999 survey of household energy consumption, EUROSTAT included many Central and Eastern European Countries[34]. In most of these CEE countries, more than two-thirds of the population live in urban areas. The share of owner-occupied dwellings is on average higher than in EU-15. It is often between 80 and 90 %, and only in Poland, the Czech Republic and Latvia is it lower than 55 %.

In most CEE countries the percentage of energy consumption used for space heating is more than 70% of total household energy consumption. In most of these countries, central heating systems (either individual for each dwelling, collective for multi-family houses or district heating for blocks of buildings) are clearly the most common way of heating.

Especially buildings in large-panel construction, which were mostly constructed from the late 60's up to the 90's, are characterised by a very high heat demand, which is 2 to 3 times higher per square meter than that of the EU, mostly due to poor insulation standards.

The transformation of the economies of the CEECs has already led to a considerable increase in energy prices for households, especially for district heating. The realisation of the energy savings potentials in the building sector in these countries, in addition to environmental and security of supply benefits, is also important in reducing the negative economic impact on household economies of price increases.

6. CONTENTS OF THE PROPOSAL

Article 1 defines the purpose and scope of the proposal.

Article 2 defines the terms and concepts used in the proposal.

Article 3 lays down the requirements for Member States to establish a methodology for an integrated calculation of the energy performance of buildings. A framework for such a methodology has been outlined in the annex to the proposed Directive.

Article 4 obliges Member States to set minimum standards for the energy performance of new buildings and to update them regularly; and to assess the

[34] "Energy Consumption in Households 1999" EUROSTAT 1999. *Op.cit.* The investigated CEE countries have been Albania, Bulgaria, Czech Republic, Estonia, Hungary, Latvia, Lithuania, Romania, Slovak Republic, Slovenia and Poland.

feasibility of installing alternative energy supply systems for large new buildings.

Article 5 obliges Member States to apply the appropriate standards for energy performance to large existing buildings when these buildings undergo major renovations, provided certain cost and cost-effectiveness criteria are met.

Article 6 provides for an energy certificate not older than 5 years to be made available for buyers and renters of new and existing buildings at the point of construction, sale or rental. For public authority buildings and buildings frequented by the public such a certification should take place at least every 5 years and the energy certificate must be placed in a prominent place and made clearly visible to the general public. In addition, for such public buildings, recommended indoor temperatures and, when appropriate other climatic conditions, should be clearly displayed along with indications of the actual current indoor temperature and climatic conditions.

Article 7 lays down specific requirements for a regular inspection of boilers connected to a one-off inspection and assessment of the total heating installation when these boilers have been installed more than 15 years.

Article 8 requires that central air-conditioning systems shall be regularly inspected.

Article 9 requires Member States to put in place a system that ensures that certification and inspection are carried out by qualified and independent personnel.

Article 10 & 11 concern the comitology procedure for adapting the annex of the proposed Directive to technical progress or incorporating future agreed standards.

Article 12 & 13 concern the administrative provisions of the proposal.

The Annex to the proposal contains the main aspects to be taken into account when calculating the energy performance of buildings and requirements for inspection of boilers and central air conditioning systems.

Proposal for a Directive of the European Parliament and of the Council on the Energy Performance of Buildings

THE EUROPEAN PARLIAMENT AND THE COUNCIL OF THE EUROPEAN UNION,

Having regard to the Treaty establishing the European Community, and in particular Article 175 thereof,

Having regard to the proposal from the Commission, where several codes exist in the same Member State, Only one code has been chosen. In some cases, regional codes are stricter than national codes.

Having regard to the opinion of the Economic and Social Committee,

Having regard to the opinion of the Committee of the Regions,

Acting in accordance with the procedure laid down in Article 251 of the Treaty,

Whereas:

(1) Article 6 of the Treaty requires environmental protection requirements to be integrated into the definition and implementation of Community policies and actions.

(2) The natural resources, to whose prudent and rational utilisation Article 174 of the Treaty refers, include oil products, natural gas and solid fuels, which are essential sources of energy but also the leading sources of carbon dioxide emissions.

(3) Increased energy efficiency constitutes an important part of the package of policies and measures needed to comply with the Kyoto Protocol, and should appear in any policy package to meet further commitments.

(4) Demand management of energy is an important tool enabling the Community to influence the global energy market and hence the security of energy supply in the medium and long term.

(5) The Council in its Conclusions of 30 May 2000 and of 5 December 2000[35] endorsed the Commission's Action Plan on Energy Efficiency and requested specific measures in the building sector.

(6) The residential and tertiary sector, the major part of which is buildings, accounts for more than 40% of final energy consumption in the Community and is expanding, a trend which is bound to increase its energy consumption and hence also its carbon dioxide emissions.

(7) Directive 93/76/EEC of 13 September 1993 to limit carbon dioxide emissions by improving energy efficiency (SAVE)[36], which requires Member States to develop, implement and report on programmes in the field of energy efficiency in the building sector, is now starting to show some important benefits. However, a complementary legal instrument is needed to lay down more concrete actions with a view to achieving the great unrealised potential for energy savings and reducing the large differences between Member States' results in this sector.

(8) Directive 89/106/EEC[37] on the approximation of laws, regulations and administrative provisions of the Member States relating to construction products requires that the construction works and its heating, cooling and ventilation installations must be designed and built in such a way that the amount of energy required in use shall be low, having regard to the climatic conditions of the location and the occupants.

(9) The energy performance of buildings should be calculated on the basis of a methodology that integrates, in addition to thermal insulation also other factors that play an increasingly important role such as heating/air-conditioning installations, application of renewable energy sources and design of the building. A common approach to this process, carried out by qualified personnel, will

[35] Council Conclusion 8835/00 (30 May 2000) and Council Conclusion 14000/00 (5 December 2000).

[36] OJ L 237, 22.09.1993, p. 28.

[37] OJ L 40, 11.02.1989, p. 12.

contribute to a level playing field as regards efforts made in Member States to energy saving in the buildings sector and would introduce transparency for prospective owners or users with regard to the energy performance in the Community property market.

(10) Buildings will have an impact on long-term energy consumption and new buildings should therefore meet minimum energy performance standards tailored to the local climate. As the application of alternative energy supply systems is generally not explored to its full potential, a systematic assessment of the feasibility of such systems for new buildings above a certain size is appropriate.

(11) Major renovations of existing buildings above a certain size should be regarded as an opportunity to take cost effective measures to enhance energy performance.

(12) By providing objective information on the energy performance of buildings when they are constructed, sold or rented out, energy certification will help to improve transparency of the property market and thus encourage investment in energy savings. It should also facilitate the use of incentive systems. Public authority buildings and buildings frequently visited by the public should set an example by taking environmental and energy considerations into account and therefore, should be subject to energy certification on a regular basis. The dissemination to the public of this information on energy performance should be enhanced by clearly displaying these energy certificates. Moreover, the displaying of officially recommended indoor temperatures, together with the actual measured temperature, should discourage the misuse of heating, air-conditioning and ventilation systems. This will contribute to avoiding unnecessary use of energy and to safeguard comfortable indoor climatic conditions (thermal comfort) in relation to the outside temperature.

(13) Regular maintenance of boilers and of central air conditioning systems by qualified personnel contributes to maintaining their correct adjustment in accordance with the product specification and in that way will ensure optimal performance from an environmental, safety and energy point of view. An independent assessment of the total heating installation is appropriate whenever replacement could be considered on the basis of cost effectiveness.

(14) In accordance with the principles of subsidiarity and proportionality as set out in Article 5 of the Treaty, general principles providing for a system of energy performance standards and its objectives should be established at Community level, but the detailed implementation should be left to Member States, thus allowing each Member State to choose the regime which corresponds best to its particular situation. This Directive confines itself to the minimum required in order to achieve those objectives and does not go beyond what is necessary for that purpose.

(15) Provision should be made for the possibility of rapidly adapting the methodology of calculation in the field of energy performance of buildings to technical progress and to future developments in standardisation.

(16) Since the measures necessary for the implementation of this Directive are measures of general scope within the meaning of Article 2 of Council Decision 1999/468/EC of 28 June 1999 laying down the procedures for the exercise of implementing powers conferred on the Commission[38], they should be adopted by use of the regulatory procedure provided for in Article 5 of that Decision,

HAVE ADOPTED THIS DIRECTIVE:

ARTICLE 1

A common framework is hereby created to promote the improvement of the energy performance of buildings within the Community, taking into account climatic and local conditions.

This Directive lays down requirements as regards:

(a) the general framework of a common methodology for calculating the integrated energy performance of buildings,

(b) the application of minimum standards on the energy performance of new buildings,

(c) the application of minimum standards on the energy performance of large existing buildings that are subject to major renovation,

[38] OJ L 184, 17.07.1999, p. 23.

(d) energy certification of buildings, and for public buildings, prominent display of this certification and other relevant information, and

(e) regular inspection, of boilers and of central air-conditioning systems in buildings and in addition an assessment of the heating installation in which the boilers are older than 15 years.

ARTICLE 2

For the purpose of this Directive, the following definitions shall apply:

(1) *building*: a building as a whole or, in the residential sector, parts of the building which have been designed to be used separately such as apartments or semi-detached houses;

(2) *energy performance of a building*: the total energy efficiency of a building, reflected in one or more numeric indicators which have been calculated, taking into account insulation, installation characteristics, design and positioning, own energy generation and other factors that influence the net energy demand;

(3) *minimum energy performance standard of a building*: a regulated minimum requirement as regards the energy performance of buildings;

(4) *energy performance certificate of a building*: an officially recognised certificate in which the result of the calculation of the energy performance of a building according to the methodology set out in the Annex has been laid down;

(5) *public buildings*: buildings occupied by public authorities or frequently visited and used by the general public, such as: schools, hospitals, public transport buildings, indoor sports centres, indoor swimming pools and retail trade services buildings larger than 1000 m2;

(6) *CHP (combined heat and power*: the simultaneous conversion of primary fuels into mechanical or electrical energy and heat;

(7) *air conditioning system*: installation designed to cool and condition the ambient air;

(8) *boiler*: the combined boiler body and burner-unit designed to transmit to water the heat released from burning;

(9) *effective rated output (expressed in kW)*: the maximum calorific output laid down and guaranteed by the manufacturer as being deliverable during continuous operation while complying with the useful efficiency indicated by the manufacturer;

(10) *useful efficiency (expressed in %)*: the ratio between the heat output transmitted to the boiler water and the product of the net calorific value at constant fuel pressure and the consumption expressed as a quantity of fuel per unit time;

(11) *heat pump*: installation that extracts heat from the surrounding environment and supplies it to the controlled environment.

ARTICLE 3

Member States shall adopt a methodology of calculation of the energy performance of buildings of which the general framework is set out in the Annex. This methodology shall be further developed and defined in accordance with the procedure referred to in article 11(2).

The energy performance of a building shall be expressed in a transparent and simple manner and may include a CO_2 emission indicator.

ARTICLE 4

Member States shall take the necessary measures to ensure that new buildings which are intended to be regularly used meet minimum energy performance standards, calculated according to the methodology framework set out in the Annex. These standards should include general indoor climate requirements in order to avoid possible negative effects such as inadequate ventilation. These energy performance standards shall be updated at least every five years in order to reflect technical progress in the building sector. Member States may exclude historic buildings, temporary buildings, industrial sites, workshops and residential buildings which are not used as normal residences.

For new buildings with a total surface area over 1000 m^2, Member States shall ensure that the technical, environmental and economic feasibility of installing decentralised energy supply systems based on renewable energy, CHP, district heating or, under certain conditions, heat pumps, is assessed before the building permit is granted. The result of such an assessment shall be available to all stakeholders for consultation.

ARTICLE 5

Member States shall take the necessary measures to ensure that the energy performance of existing buildings with a total surface area over 1000 m^2 which are being renovated, are upgraded in order to meet minimum energy performance standards in so far as these are technically feasible and involve additional costs that can on the basis of the current average mortgage rate be recovered within a period of 8 years by the accrued energy savings.

This principle shall apply in all those cases where the total cost of the renovation is higher than 25 % of the existing insured value of the building.

ARTICLE 6

1. Member States shall ensure that, when buildings are constructed, sold or rented out, an energy performance certificate, being not older than 5 years, is made available to the prospective buyer or tenant.

Member States may exclude historic buildings, temporary buildings, industrial sites, workshops and residential buildings which are not used as normal residences

2. The energy performance certificate for buildings shall provide relevant information for prospective users. It shall include reference values such as current legal standards and best practice in order to make it possible for consumers to compare and assess the energy performance of the building. The certificate shall be accompanied by recommendations for the improvement of the energy performance.

3. Member States shall require for public buildings an energy performance certificate, which is not older than 5 years, to be placed in a prominent place clearly visible to the general public.

In addition, for public buildings the following information shall be clearly displayed:

(a) the range of indoor temperatures and, when appropriate, other relevant climatic factors such as relative humidity, that are recommended by the authorities for that specific type of building.

(b) the current indoor temperature and other relevant climatic factors indicated by means of a reliable device or devices.

ARTICLE 7

Member States shall lay down the necessary measures to establish a regular inspection of boilers of an effective output of more than 10 kW of which the requirements are set out in the Annex. These requirements shall be further developed and defined in accordance with the procedure referred to in article 11(2).

ARTICLE 8

Member States shall lay down the necessary measures to establish a regular inspection of central air conditioning systems of an effective output of more than 12 kW of which the requirements are set out in the Annex. These requirements shall be further developed and defined in accordance with the procedure referred to in article 11(2).

ARTICLE 9

Member States shall ensure that the certification of buildings and inspection of heating and air-conditioning systems are carried out by qualified and independent personnel.

ARTICLE 10

Any amendments necessary in order to adapt the Annex to technical progress shall be adopted in accordance with the procedure referred to in Article 11(2).

ARTICLE 11

1. The Commission shall be assisted by the committee established by Article 10 of Council Directive 92/75/EEC[39], hereinafter referred to as the "committee", composed of representatives of the Member States and chaired by the representative of the Commission.

2. Where reference is made to this paragraph, the regulatory procedure laid down in Article 5 of Decision 1999/468/EC shall apply, in compliance with Article 7 and Article 8 thereof.

3. The period provided for in Article 5(6) of Decision 1999/468/EC shall be three months.

[39] OJ L 297, 13.10.1992, p. 16.

ARTICLE 12

1. Member States shall bring into force the laws, regulations and administrative provisions to comply with this Directive by 31 December 2003 at the latest.

When Member States adopt those provisions, they shall contain a reference to this Directive or shall be accompanied by such reference on the occasion of their official publication. Member States shall determine how such reference is to be made.

2. Member States shall communicate to the Commission the provisions of national law which they adopt in the field covered by this Directive.

ARTICLE 13

This Directive shall enter into force on the twentieth day following that of its publication in the *Official Journal of the European Communities.*

ARTICLE 14

This Directive is addressed to the Member States.

Done at Brussels,

For the European Parliament	*For the Council*
The President	*The President*

ANNEX

A. Framework for the Calculation of Energy Performances of Buildings (Article 3)

1. The methodology of calculation of energy performances of buildings shall integrate the following aspects:

(a) thermal insulation (of building shell and installations)

(b) heating installation and hot water supply

(c) air-conditioning installation

(d) ventilation system

(e) lighting installation

(f) position and orientation of houses and apartments

2. The positive influence of the following aspects shall in this calculation be taken into account:

(a) solar systems and other heating and electricity systems based on renewable energy sources

(b) electricity produced by CHP and/or district heating systems

3. Buildings should for the purpose of this calculation at least be classified into the following categories:

(a) single family houses of different types

(b) apartment blocks

(c) offices

(d) education buildings

(e) hospitals

(f) hotels and restaurants

(g) wholesale and retail trade services buildings

(h) other types of energy consuming buildings

B. Requirements for the Inspection of Boilers (Article 7)

The inspection of boilers shall have regard to energy consumption and limiting carbon dioxide emissions.

Boilers of an effective output of more than 100 kW shall be inspected at least every 2 years

For heating installations with boilers of an effective rated output of more than 10 kW which are older than 15 years, Member States shall lay down the necessary measures to establish a one-off inspection of the whole heating installation. On the basis of this inspection, which shall include an assessment of the boiler efficiency at full and part load and the boiler sizing compared to the heating requirements of the building, the competent authorities shall provide advice to the users on the replacement of the boilers and on alternative solutions.

C. Requirements for the Inspection of Central Air Conditioning Systems (Article 8)

The inspection of central air conditioning systems shall have regard to energy consumption and limiting carbon dioxide emissions.

On the basis of this inspection, which shall include an assessment of the air-conditioning efficiency at full and part load and the sizing compared to the cooling requirements of the building, the competent authorities shall provide advice to the users on possible improvement or replacement of the air-conditioning system and on alternative solutions.

Germany

Act on Granting Priority to Renewable Energy Sources

(Renewable Energy Sources Act)

BREAKTHROUGH FOR RENEWABLE ENERGY SOURCES – PRIORITY LAW IS PASSED

– by Federal Environment Minister Jürgen Trittin –

A decisive breakthrough in the development of sustainable energy provision has been achieved with the adoption of the Renewable Energy Sources Act ("Act on Granting Priority to Renewable Energy Sources"). Having been passed by the German Bundestag on February 25, 2000, the act received the approval of the Bundesrat (upper chamber) on 17 March.

Although the previous law, the Electricity Feed Act (*Stromeinspeisungsgesetz;* StrEG)[1], was successful, it had to be replaced. There were a number of reasons for updating the legislation: the growth of the green electricity output beyond the five percent ceiling previously set for support entitlement, the need for a national distribution of costs beyond the regions, the lack of planning and investment security, and the adjustments required for compliance with EU directives. The Federal Government had to act fast as more and more renewable energy investment projects were being shelved.

Replacing the Electricity Feed Act, the Renewable Energy Sources Act (*Erneuerbare-Energien-Gesetz;* EEG) regulates the prioritisation of grid-supplied electricity from renewable sources. It specifies mechanisms for implementing the option of granting priority to renewable power generation envisaged in the EU Directive on the internal market in electricity. Energy utilities will also now benefit from the compensation for supplying the grid with electricity from renewable sources.

By guaranteeing compensatory payments down to the last pfennig per kWh, the act restores a secure climate for investment. This remunerative arrangement is made available for a period of up to twenty years per plant, with the exception of hydroelectricity installations, which require longer amortisation periods. In addition, we have incorporated degressive steps, starting in 2002, for plants coming on line then. The law also offers scope for altering the compensation rates for future installations if necessary. This remuneration system does not mean the abandonment of market principles, but only creates the security needed for investment under present market conditions. There is adequate provision to safeguard the future existence of all the plants already in operation.

The new act has abolished the regulation contained in the Electricity Feed Act which limits the uptake at preferential rates of electricity from renewable energy sources to a maximum share of five percent of overall output. Instead, we have introduced a nation-wide cost-sharing arrangement. The act should put an end to any fears of excessive financial burdens. The contribution resulting from the new cost-sharing mechanism amounts to a mere 0.05 cent per kWh. Even if, as we hope, there is powerful growth in renewable energy sources, this would still only rise to 0.1 cent per kWh in a few years time. That, indeed, is a small price to pay for the development of this key sector.

The compensation to which suppliers are entitled is now geared to costs. The compensation rates differ between energy forms and also depend on the size of installations. We have raised these rates significantly in the case of biomass and photovoltaics. The German Federal Environment Ministry is authorised to issue an ordinance to define the term biomass in this context.

[1] also referred to as Act on the Sale of Electricity to the Grid

Note: This translation was made by the language service of the *Deutscher Bundestag.* The titles of documents referred to in this text may differ slightly from the titles used by the Federal Environment Ministry and the alternatives have been given in the footnotes.

As for wind energy, we have set different rates on the basis of a technology-neutral yield reference model. Special conditions have been set for offshore wind turbines. Due to the higher specific costs initially incurred, they can benefit from a high rate over a longer period: 9.10 cent per kWh over nine years. This arrangement also applies to offshore installations outside the twelvemile zone.

The new law (EEG) complies with EU criteria by setting time limits on compensation, establishing cost-oriented rates, differentiating according to energy source, plant size and location, introducing a degressive structure and insisting on regular reviews.

It opens up great opportunities not only to enhance our future energy-mix but also in terms of skilled jobs and exports. The wind energy sector has so far led the way in Germany by creating more than 20,000 jobs. This act gives biomass exploitation in particular every chance of embarking on a similar phase of dynamic growth.

In this way, emissions of the climate-damaging greenhouse gas CO_2 can be reduced by about three percent by 2010 through the generation of green electricity alone. The EEG is a law that will give a major boost to renewable energy forms, enabling them to increase their contribution to overall energy production to at least ten percent by 2010.

ACT ON GRANTING PRIORITY TO RENEWABLE ENERGY SOURCES

SECTION 1 PURPOSE

The purpose of this Act is to facilitate a sustainable development of energy supply in the interest of managing global warming and protecting the environment and to achieve a substantial increase in the percentage contribution made by renewable energy sources to power supply in order at least to double the share of renewable energy sources in total energy consumption by the year 2010, in keeping with the objectives defined by the European Union and by the Federal Republic of Germany.

SECTION 2 SCOPE OF APPLICATION

(1) This Act deals with the purchase of, and the compensation to be paid for, electricity generated exclusively from hydrodynamic power, wind energy, solar radiation energy, geothermal energy, gas from sanitary landfills, sewage treatment plants, mines, or biomass within the territorial scope of this Act or within Germany's exclusive economic zone, by utility companies which operate grids for public power supply (grid operators). The Federal Ministry for Environment, Nature Conservation and Nuclear Safety shall be authorised to lay down rules – in agreement with the Federal Ministry of Food, Agriculture and Forestry as well as the Federal Ministry of Economics and Technology – by adopting an ordinance, which shall be subject to approval by the German Bundestag. Said ordinance shall specify what substances and technical processes used in connection with biomass fall within the scope of application of this Act; in addition, the ordinance shall lay down the relevant environmental standards.

(2) This Act shall not apply to electricity

1. produced by hydro-electric power plants and installations fuelled by gas from landfills or sewage treatment plants with an installed electrical capacity of over 5 megawatts, or by installations in which electricity is generated from biomass, with an installed electrical capacity of over 20 megawatts, and

2. produced by installations of which over 25 per cent is owned by the Federal Republic of Germany or one of Germany's federal states, and

3. produced by installations for the generation of electricity from solar radiation energy, with an installed electrical capacity of over five megawatts. In the case of installations for the generation of electricity from solar radiation energy which are not attached to or built on structures which are primarily used for purposes other than the generation of electricity from solar radiation energy, the upper capacity limit specified in the first sentence above shall be 100 kilowatts.

(3) New installations shall be installations which were commissioned after [add: date of entry into force of this Act]. Reactivated or modernised installations shall be considered as new installations if major components of the installations were replaced. Modernisation work shall be deemed to be major if the modernisation costs amount to at least 50 percent of the investment cost required to build a completely new installation. Existing

installations shall be installations which were commissioned prior to [add: date of entry into force of this Act].

SECTION 3 OBLIGATION TO PURCHASE AND PAY COMPENSATION

(1) Grid operators shall be obliged to connect to their grids electricity generation installations as defined in Section 2 above, to purchase electricity available from these installations as a priority, and to compensate the suppliers of this electricity in accordance with the provisions in Sections 4 to 8 below. This obligation shall apply to the grid operator whose grid is closed to the location of the electricity generation installation, providing that the grid is technically suitable to feed in this electricity. A grid shall be considered to be technically suitable even if – notwithstanding the priority to be granted pursuant to the first sentence above – a grid operator needs to upgrade its grid at reasonable economic expense to feed in the electricity; in this case, the grid operator shall be obliged to upgrade its grid without delay if this is requested by a party interested in feeding in electricity. Grid data and data of the electricity generation installation shall be disclosed where this is necessary for the grid operator and the party interested in feeding in electricity to do their planning and to determine the technical suitability of a grid.

(2) Pursuant to Sections 4 to 8 below, the upstream transmission grid operator shall be obliged to purchase, and pay compensation for, the amount of energy purchased by the grid operator in accordance with clause (1) above. If there is no domestic transmission grid in the area serviced by the grid operator entitled to sell electricity, the next closest domestic transmission grid operator shall be obliged to purchase and pay compensation for this electricity as specified in the first sentence above.

SECTION 4 COMPENSATION TO BE PAID FOR ELECTRICITY GENERATED FROM HYDRODYNAMIC POWER, GAS FROM LANDFILLS, MINES, AND SEWAGE TREATMENT PLANTS

The compensation to be paid for electricity generated from hydrodynamic power and gas from landfills, mines and sewage treatment plants shall amount to at least 7.67 cent per kilowatt-hour. In the case of electricity generation installations with an electrical capacity of over 500 kilowatts, this shall apply only to that part of the total amount of electricity fed in during a given accounting year which corresponds to the ratio of 500 kilowatts to the total capacity of the installation in kilowatts; the capacity shall be calculated as the annual average of the mean effective electrical capacity measured in the various months of the year. The price to be paid for other electricity shall be at least 6.65 cent per kilowatt-hour.

SECTION 5 COMPENSATION TO BE PAID FOR ELECTRICITY GENERATED FROM BIOMASS

(1) The following compensation shall be paid for electricity generated from biomass:

1. At least 10.23 cent per kilowatt-hour in the case of installations with an installed electrical capacity of up to 500 kilowatts.

2. At least 9.21 cent per kilowatt-hour in the case of installations with an installed electrical capacity of up to 5 megawatts.

3. At least 8.70 cent per kilowatt-hour in the case of installations with an installed effective electrical capacity of over 5 megawatts; however, this provision shall not be effective before the date of the entry into force of the ordinance specified in the second sentence of Section 2(1).

The first clause of the second sentence in Section 4 above shall apply *mutatis mutandis.*

(2) As of 1 January 2002, the minimum compensation amounts specified in (1) above shall be reduced by one per cent annually for new installations commissioned as of this date; the amounts payable shall be rounded to one decimal.

SECTION 6 COMPENSATION TO BE PAID FOR ELECTRICITY GENERATED FROM GEOTHERMAL ENERGY

The following compensation shall be paid for electricity generated from geothermal energy:

1. At least 8.95 cent per kilowatt-hour if the installation involved has an installed electrical capacity of up to 20 megawatts, and

2. At least 7.16 cent per kilowatt-hour if the installation involved has an installed electrical capacity of over 20 megawatts.

The first clause of the second sentence in Section 4 above shall apply *mutatis mutandis.*

SECTION 7 COMPENSATION TO BE PAID FOR ELECTRICITY GENERATED FROM WIND ENERGY

(1) The compensation to be paid for electricity generated from wind energy shall be at least 9.10 cent per kilowatt-hour for a period of five years starting from the date of commissioning. Hence, the compensation to be paid for installations which, during this period of time, achieve 150 per cent of the reference yield calculated for the reference installation as described in the Annex to this Act shall be at least 6.19 cent per kilowatt-hour. For other installations, the period mentioned in the first sentence above shall be prolonged by two months for every 0.75 per cent which their yield stays below 150 per cent of the reference yield. If the electricity is generated by installations which are located at least three nautical miles seawards from the baselines used to demarcate territorial waters and if these installations are commissioned no later than 31 December 2006, the periods specified in the first sentence and in the second sentence above shall be nine years.

(2) For existing installations, the date of commissioning as defined in the first sentence of (1) above shall be [add: the date of the entry into force of this Act]. For these installations, the period defined in the first 3 sentences of (1) above shall be reduced by half of the operating life of an installation as of [add: the date of the entry into force of this Act]; in any case, however this period shall not be less than four years starting from [add: the date of the entry into force of this Act]. If P-V curves are not available for such installations, an authorised institution as defined in the Annex may perform the necessary calculations on the basis of the design documents of the type of installation concerned.

(3) As of 1 January 2002, the minimum compensation amounts specified in (1) above shall be reduced by 1.5 per cent annually for new installations commissioned as of this date; the amounts payable shall be rounded to one decimal.

(4) For the, implementation of the provisions in (1) above, the Federal Ministry of Economics and Technology shall be authorised to adopt an ordinance laying down rules for the calculation of the reference yield.

SECTION 8 COMPENSATION TO BE PAID FOR ELECTRICITY GENERATED FROM SOLAR RADIATION ENERGY

(1) The compensation to be paid for electricity generated from solar radiation energy shall be at least 50.62 cent per kilowatt-hour. As of 1 January 2002, the minimum compensation paid shall be reduced by 5 per cent annually for new electricity generation installations commissioned as of this date; the amounts payable shall be rounded to one decimal.

(2) The obligation to pay compensation as specified in (1) above shall not apply to photovoltaic installations which are commissioned after 31 December of the year following the year in which photovoltaic installations which are eligible for compensation under this Act reach a total installed capacity of 350 megawatts. Prior to the discontinuation of the obligation to pay compensation as specified in (1) above, the German Bundestag shall adopt a follow-up compensation scheme which shall enable installation operators to manage their installations cost-effectively, taking into consideration the decline of marginal unit cost achieved by then in the field of system engineering.

SECTION 9 COMMON PROVISIONS

(1) The minimum compensation amounts specified in Sections 4 to 8 shall be payable for newly commissioned installations for a period of 20 years after the year of commissioning, except for installations which generate electricity from hydrodynamic power. For installations which were commissioned prior to the entry into force of this Act, the year 2000 shall be considered to be the year of commissioning.

(2) If electricity generated from various installations is billed via a common metering device, the calculation of the amounts of the different rates of compensation payable shall be based on the maximum effective capacity of each individual installation. If electricity is generated from several wind energy converters, the calculation of the compensation shall – notwithstanding the first sentence above – be based on the cumulative values of these installations.

SECTION 10 GRID COSTS

(1) The costs associated with connecting installations as specified 1 in Section 2 above to the technically and economically most suitable grid connecting point shall be borne by the installation operators. The implementation of this connection must comply with the grid operator's technical requirements in a given case and with the provisions laid down in Section 16 of the *Energiewirtschaftsgesetz* (Energy Management Act) of 24 April 1998 (Federal Law Gazette 1, p. 730). The installation operator shall be entitled to have the connection implemented either by the grid operator or by a qualified third party.

(2) The costs associated with upgrading the grid exclusively in order to connect new installations in accordance with Section 2 for accepting and transmitting energy fed into the grid for public power supply shall be borne by the grid operator whose grid will have to be upgraded. The grid operator shall specify the concrete investment required by presenting the costs in detail. The grid operators shall be entitled to add the costs borne by them when determining the charges for the use of the grid.

(3) Any disputes shall be settled by a clearing centre which shall be established within the Federal Ministry of Economics and Technology, with the involvement of the parties concerned.

SECTION 11 NATION-WIDE EQUALISATION SCHEME

(1) Transmission grid operators shall be obliged to record any differences in the amount of energy purchased and compensation payments made under Section 3 above and to equalise such differences amongst themselves as specified in (2) below.

(2) By 31 March of each year, the transmission grid operators shall determine the amount of energy purchased in accordance with Section 3 above and the percentage share which this amount represents relative to the overall amount of energy delivered to final consumers either directly by the operator or indirectly via downstream grids. If transmission grid operators have purchased amounts of energy that are greater than this average share, they shall be entitled to sell energy to, and receive compensation from, the other transmission grid operators in accordance with Sections 3 to 8 above, until these other grid operators have purchased a volume of energy which is equal to the average share mentioned above.

(3) Monthly instalments shall be paid in accordance with the equalisation amounts and payments to be expected.

(4) Utility companies which deliver electricity to final consumers shall be obliged to purchase and pay compensation for that part of the electricity which their regular transmission grid operator purchased in accordance with the provisions of (2) above. The first sentence shall not apply to utility companies if, relative to the total amount of electricity they deliver, at least 50 per cent of the electricity delivered is electricity as defined in Section 2 (1) in conjunction with (2) above. The part of the electricity to be purchased by a utility company in accordance with the first sentence shall be related to the amount of electricity delivered by the utility company concerned and shall be determined in such a way that each utility company will receive a relatively equal share. The compulsory amount to be purchased (part) shall be calculated as the ratio of the total amount of electricity fed into the grid under Section 3 to the total amount of electricity sold to final consumers; furthermore, it is necessary to deduct from this sum the amount of electricity delivered by utility companies in accordance with the second sentence above. The compensation as specified in the first sentence above shall be calculated as the average compensation per kilowatt-hour paid by all grid operators two quarters earlier in accordance with Section 3. Electricity purchased in accordance with the first sentence shall not be sold at the compensation paid in accordance with the fifth sentence, if that electricity is marketed as electricity pursuant to Section 2 or as comparable electricity.

(5) Each grid operator shall be obliged to make available in good time to the other grid operators the data required to perform the calculations referred to in (1) and (2) above. Each grid operator shall be entitled to request that the other grid operators have their data audited by a chartered accountant or a sworn auditor appointed by mutual agreement. If no agreement can be reached, the chartered accountant or sworn auditor shall be appointed by the President of the Higher Regional Court which has jurisdiction at the seat of

the grid operator eligible to receive equalisation payments.

SECTION 12 PROGRESS REPORT

By 30 June, every two years after the entry into force of this Act, the Federal Ministry of Economics and Technology shall submit a report – drafted in consultation with the Federal Ministry for Environment, Nature Conservation and Nuclear Safety as well as the Federal Ministry of Food, Agriculture and Forestry – on the progress achieved in terms of the market introduction and the cost development of power generation installations as specified in Section 2; and by 1 January, every two years after the year of entry into force of this Act, the Ministry shall, where necessary, propose adjustments of the compensation amounts specified in Sections 4 to 8 and of their reduction rates, in keeping with technological progress and market developments with regard to new installations; furthermore, the Ministry shall propose a prolongation of the period for calculating the yield of a wind energy converter as specified in the Annex, based on the experience made with the period defined in this Act.

ANNEX

1. The reference installation shall be a wind energy converter of a specific type for which a yield at the level of the reference yield can be calculated on the basis of P-V curve (powerwind speed curve) measured by an authorised institution at the reference site.

2. The reference yield shall be the amount of electricity which each specific type of wind energy converter, including the respective hub heights, would yield during five years of operation – calculated on the basis of measured P-V curves – if it were built at the reference site.

3. The type of a wind energy converter shall be defined by the model designation, the swept rotor area, the rated power output and the hub height as specified by the manufacturer.

4. The reference site shall be a site determined by means of a Rayleigh distribution with a mean annual wind speed of 5.5 metres per second at a height of 30 metres, a logarithmic wind shear profile and a roughness length of 0.1 metres.

5. The P-V curve shall be the correlation between wind speed and power output (irrespective of hub height) determined for each type of wind energy converter. P-V curves shall be determined in accordance with the standard procedure defined in the *Technische Richtlinien für Windenergieanlagen* (Technical Guidelines for Wind Energy Converters), rev. 13, as of 1 January 2000, published by *Fördergesellschaft Windenergie e. V.* (FGW), Hamburg, or in the Power Performance Measurement Procedure, version 1, published in September 1997 by the Network of European Measuring Institutes (MEASNET), Brussels/Belgium,. P-V curves which were determined by means of a comparable procedure prior to 1 January 2000 can also be used instead of P-V curves as specified in the second sentence, providing that the construction of wind energy converters of the type to which they apply is not initiated within the territorial scope of this Act after 31 December 2001.

6. Measurements of the P-V curves and calculations of the reference yields of different types of wind energy converters at reference sites shall be carried out for the purposes of this Act by institutions which are accredited for the measurement of P-V curves as defined in (5) above in accordance with the General Criteria for the Operation of Test Laboratories (DIN EN 45001) of May 1990. The names of these institutions shall be published in the Federal Official Gazette by the Federal Ministry of Economics and Technology for the information of interested parties.

EXPLANATORY MEMORANDUM

A. GENERAL PROVISIONS

For the sake of protecting the environment and managing global warming as well as guaranteeing a reliable energy supply, the German Federal Government and the German Bundestag – in agreement with the European Union – have set themselves the objective of at least doubling the percentage share of renewable energy sources in total energy supply by the year 2010. This objective is related to the envisaged commitment on the part of the Federal Republic of Germany to reduce greenhouse gas emissions by 21 per cent by the year 2010 in the framework of the European Union's burden sharing as laid down in the Kyoto Protocol to the Framework. Climate Convention of the United Nations; and this objective is linked to the German Federal Government's objective to reduce carbon dioxide emissions by 25 per cent by the year 2005, relative to 1990.

In order to attain this objective, it is necessary to mobilise the so-called new renewable energy sources. Traditional hydrodynamic power from large dams accounts for the overwhelming share of the renewable energy sources used today. For geographical reasons, the utilisation potential of hydrodynamic power is largely exhausted. For this reason, it is necessary additionally to generate electricity from wind energy, solar radiation energy, biomass, and hydrodynamic power of rivers in order to attain the objective set for Europe as a whole by the year 2010. To this end, the currently used potential of these energy sources will have to grow fivefold.

In order to translate this objective into reality, the European Commission has proposed a number of energy policy measures in its communication entitled "The Energy Policy Dimension of Climate Change", in which renewable energy sources play a key role. The purpose of the Act on Granting Priority to Renewable Energy Sources (Renewable Energy Sources Act) is intended to help attain these objectives and to implement the European Union's "Campaign for a Breakthrough of Renewable Energy Sources". In view of growing meteorological evidence of a warming of the Earth's atmosphere and the increase in the frequency of natural disasters world-wide, prompt action by the legislator is indispensable in the interest of protecting the environment and managing global warming.

Currently, renewables are unevenly and insufficiently used, although many renewable energy sources are available in large quantities. Despite their considerable economic potential, they account for an extremely low share of the total, statistically identified gross domestic energy consumption. If we fail to cover a much larger share of our energy requirements by means of renewable energy sources, there will be two consequences: not only will we find it more and more difficult to meet our obligations in the fields of environmental protection and global warming management, at both European and international level, but we will also miss out on major economic development opportunities. Renewables are domestic energy sources, which can help to reduce our dependence on energy imports, thereby making our energy supply more reliable. Currently, the EU depends on energy imports to cover approximate 50 per cent of its energy consumption; and there is a risk that this figure will rise to 60 per cent by the year 2010 and 70 per cent by the year 2020 if we do not tap the, potential of renewable energy sources.

Greater use of renewable energy sources will create jobs, especially in the sector of small and medium-sized enterprises, which play a crucial role in the economic structure of the Federal Republic of Germany. Small and medium-sized enterprises are not only an important factor in crafts and trades; they also provide an impetus for a variety of industries, including the metal industry, electrical engineering, mechanical engineering, engine and equipment engineering, as well as the building materials industry. The stimulation of the use of biomass for electricity generation associated with the adoption of this Act will also provide a major impetus for an economic recovery of the agricultural sector. Furthermore, the production and use of renewable energy sources will promote sustainable regional development, which will help to improve the social and economic cohesion within the Community and to harmonise living conditions within the Federal Republic of Germany.

In three European countries – Germany, Denmark and Spain – national legislation has been adopted to introduce minimum prices for feeding into grids electricity generated from renewable energy sources. It is owing exclusively to the national legislation of these three countries that the European Union witnessed the emergence of a wind turbine manufacturing industry which offers cutting-edge technology in the world market today. This also proved that it was wrong to assume that the introduction of minimum price systems would hamper productivity, because in all the three countries mentioned above the introduction of wind energy converters was based on minimum prices guaranteed by law. This has stimulated a market development – initially in the wind energy sector – which led to an efficient industry with considerable export opportunities, which has created jobs for over 20,000 people in Germany alone. As a result of the associated economics of scale and the global competition initiated among manufacturers of wind energy converters, production costs as well as the compensation paid in real terms have been successfully reduced by 50 per cent since 1991. Owing to technological progress, there is growing demand in the world market; in the next ten years, demand for wind energy converters alone may amount to over 100.000 megawatts. Against this background, the market introduction of renewable energy sources should not be underestimated in terms of its importance for industrial policy, not least because it can be safely assumed in view of global climate problems that there will be rapidly growing demand world-wide. It can be expected that the impact which the Renewable Energy Sources Act will have on other sectors in which renewable energy sources are used will be similar to the effects which it will have on the wind energy sector.

In the past, the *Stromeinspeisungsgesetz für Erneuerbare Energien* (Act on Feeding into the Grid Electricity Generated from Renewable Energy Sources)[1], which entered into force on 1 January 1991, has mainly provided an impetus for the wind energy sector because the compensation rates laid down in the Act made this possible. By the end of 1999, i.e. nine years after the entry into force of the Act, as much as approximately 4.400 megawatts had been installed within the territorial scope of the Act accounting for about one-third of the capacity installed world-wide. For hydroelectric power plants below the capacity limit of five megawatts laid down in this Act, the compensation rates specified have been more or less sufficient to permit cost-effective operation. Nevertheless, the Act has not brought about a level of utilisation of the existing potential that would be comparable to the use of wind energy because there are still many licensing obstacles that are beyond the scope of this Act; at least the Act has helped to stabilise the potential of hydro-electric power plants which was partially jeopardized before the entry into force of this Act. However, the compensation rates have not been sufficient to stimulate a large-scale market introduction of electricity generated from other sources, especially photovoltaic cells and biomass. For this reason, the compensation rates have been modified in the Renewable Energy Sources Act, which replaces Electricity Feed Act[1], in order to promote large-scale generation of electricity from all kinds of renewable energy sources.

However, the adoption of the Renewable Energy Sources Act has also become necessary for other reasons:

- The coupling of the current compensation rates to the development of the power rates can no longer be maintained without risking a disruption in the use of renewable energy sources. The non-simultaneity of liberalisation in the various national electricity markets of the European Union without any practicable reciprocity clauses between markets that are already fully liberalised and others which are still protected; the abundance of capacity which was created without risk during the days of territorial monopolies and which has been largely written off; the fact that the "unbundling" of electricity generation, transmission and distribution is far from being implemented; the competitive advantages enjoyed by the German utility corporations due to the fact that they can use their tax-free nuclear provisions (which by now amount to over € 35 billion) at their discretion for investments: for all of these reasons, it is not likely that a price will settle down in the electricity market which will reflect the actual medium-term and long-term costs of electrical power supply. For this reason, it is initially necessary to set fixed prices for renewable energy sources in order to safeguard a continuous increase in the use of renewable energy sources, which is undeniably necessary.

- The Electricity Feed Act[1] currently in force has led to an unequal distribution of burdens among the utility companies which are obliged to pay compensation. The percentage "capping" of the amount of electricity that can be fed into the grid, which was introduced with the second amendment of 1998, needs adjusting because this upper limit brings the utilisation of wind energy in the northern German region already close to the point of market introduction. The purpose of the Renewable Energy Sources Act is therefore to abolish this upper limit, while at the same time introducing an non-bureaucratic mechanism that will evenly distribute extra cost among all utility companies.

- Since the previous Electricity Feed Act[1] was aimed at utility companies which could act as producers, regional grid operators and distributors at the same time, it is now necessary because of the new energy management legislation to redefine both the addressee of electricity to be fed into the grid and the company obliged to pay compensation.

The compensation scheme defined in the Renewable Energy Sources Act is based on the systematic approach introduced in the Electricity Feed Act[1] and guided by the recommendations presented by the European Commission in its White Paper on "Energy for the Future: Renewable Sources of Energy" as well as the relevant resolutions adopted by the European Parliament. The compensation rates specified in the Renewable Energy Sources Act have been determined by means of scientific studies, subject to the proviso that the rates identified should make it possible for an installation – when managed efficiently – to be operated cost-effectively, based on the use of state-of-the-art technology and depending on the renewable energy sources naturally available in a given geographical environment. However, there is no guarantee that the cost of a given installation will be covered.

In some cases, the cost of the production of renewable energy sources is still much higher than the production cost of conventional energy sources. This is largely due to the fact that the overwhelming share of the external costs associated with the generation of electricity from conventional energy sources is not reflected in the price; instead, these costs are borne by the general public and by future generations. In addition, conventional energy sources still benefit from substantial governmental subsidies which keep their price artificially low. Another reason for the higher costs is the structural discrimination of new technologies. Their lower market share does not allow economies of scale to become effective. Lower production volumes lead to higher unit cost and thus reduce competitiveness, which in turn prevents higher production volumes, like in a vicious circle.

For this reason, the purpose of this Act is not only to protect the operation of existing installations but also to break this vicious circle and to stimulate a dynamic development in all fields of electricity generation from renewable energy sources. In combination with measures aimed at internalising external costs, the purpose of this pricing regime is to bring renewable energy sources closer to conventional energy sources in terms of their competitiveness. In order to continue to facilitate major improvements in technological efficiency, the compensation rates specified in the Renewable Energy Sources Act vary, depending on the energy sources, the sites and the installation sizes involved; furthermore, they will decline over time and will remain in effect for a limited period of time. The fact that the rates will be reviewed every two years guarantees that they will be updated continuously and at short intervals to reflect market and cost trends.

The German Bundestag and the German Federal Government feel – in line with the established practice of the European Court of Justice – that the Renewable Energy Sources Act does not constitute aid granted by a Member State or through state resources as defined in Article 87 of the Treaty Establishing the European Community (ECT).

In accordance with the wording of Article 87 ECT, the European Court of Justice has consistently ruled that the only benefits which can be regarded as state aid as defined in the Treaty are benefits which are granted – directly or indirectly – from state resources. This obviously does not apply to the Renewable Energy Sources Act. It does not imply any benefits in cash or kind to be made available – either directly or indirectly or subsequently by public authorities, nor does it imply any renunciation of tax revenues or other payments in cash or in kind owed to the public sector. Instead, the compensation payments made are straightforward financial transfers which, in accordance with the 'polluter pays' principle laid down in Community law, are used directly to cover electricity production costs. In a case involving a similar pricing regime, the European Court of Justice therefore stated quite clearly that a measure which is characterised by the fact that minimum prices are set with the objective of benefiting the seller of a product exclusively at the expense of the consumer did not constitute state aid.

In addition, compensation paid under this Act cannot be state aid from a terminological perspective because operators of installations for the generation of electricity from renewable energy sources are not granted any benefits; instead, the Act compensates disadvantages which such operators have in comparison with conventional electricity producers. After all, most of the social and ecological follow-up costs associated with conventional electricity generation are currently not borne by the operators of such installations but by the general public, the taxpayers and future generations. The Renewable Energy Sources Act merely reduces this competitive advantage which conventional electricity generators have vis-à-vis operators generating electricity from renewable energy sources which cause only limited external costs.

In no other field is the introduction of a pricing regime at the expense of polluters more legitimate and more justifiable than in the field of energy supply because of the ecological damage associated with conventional electricity generation. The Renewable Energy Sources Act, which is designed to promote the market introduction of emission-free and sustainable energy sources to substitute for conventional energy sources, provides for strictly consistent, equal burden sharing among all power suppliers. This is in keeping with the 'polluter pays' principle established in environmental protection. This principle is part and parcel of the primary law laid down in the EC Treaty, which in its Article 6 stipulates compliance with ecological interests.

The Renewable Energy Sources for which the Act provides compensation payments cannot be obtained anywhere at lower prices. For this reason, the pricing scheme specified in the Act is not an instrument for artificially supporting the "commodity" kilowatt-hour of electricity generated from renewable energy sources; instead, the prices specified in the Act will permit operators to manage their installations cost-effectively in the first place.

The key regulatory element contained in the Renewable Energy Sources Act is the obligation to purchase electricity generated from renewable energy sources, based on the amount of electricity generated during a calendar year. calculated as a ratio of the total amount of electricity sold. Such obligations are usually imposed when the movement of goods poses serious risks to external interests and when those who are responsible for such risks are not expected to take any voluntary action or sufficient action to prevent such risks. The consumption of electricity in the free market poses such risks to the climate and to the environment. Hence, the Renewable Energy Sources Act can be characterised as a protective standard. Such standards are quite commonly used without this constituting state aid: The fact that it is prohibited to sell alcoholic beverages to adolescents, for instance, does not constitute state aid for non-alcoholic beverages. And systematically reducing the price of lead-free petrol despite higher production costs does Dot constitute state aid; instead, it is a buying and investing incentive based on the 'polluter pays' principle.

The provisions of the Renewable Energy Sources Act are based on Directive 96/92/EC of the European Parliament and the Council of 19 December 1996 concerning common rules for the internal market in electricity, in particular Articles 3 (2), 7 (5), 8 (3) and (4), as well as Art. 11 (3); furthermore, these provisions are designed to implement Article 20a of the German Constitution, which stipulates that, as a responsibility vis-à-vis future generations, natural resources must be protected because they are the very basis of human survival; and finally, the provisions are aimed at implementing the environmental protection objectives laid down in Articles 2, 6, and 10 of the Treaty Establishing the European Community.

B. SPECIAL PROVISIONS

Section 1

Paragraph 1

Paragraph 1 specifies the purpose of this Act. The Act is designed to achieve sustainable energy supply in the interest of protecting the environment and managing global warming. Hence, it is an instrument for the implementation of the objectives agreed in the United Nations Framework Climate Convention and for the implementation of the climate strategies pursued by the European Union and the Federal Republic of Germany.

Paragraph 2

The objective of doubling the percentage share of renewable energy sources in total energy supply was already stipulated in the European Commission's White Paper on "Energy for the Future: Renewable Sources of Energy", and it has been confirmed by the Council of Ministers. The German Federal Government has also endorsed this objective. And the Renewable Energy Sources Act is evidence of the German Bundestag's explicit support of this objective.

In the next few decades, renewable energy sources will have to make relevant contributions to energy supply and thus to global warming management. Hence, in the interest of sustainable energy supply, it will be necessary in the next decade to double or triple the contribution made by renewable energy sources to electricity generation. The European

Commission feels that renewable energy sources should account for 23.5 per cent of total European power supply by the year 20 1 0. Germany – where renewable energy sources currently account for approximately six per cent of the national power supply – is far below the European average.

Section 2

Paragraph 1

Paragraph 1 provides a positive list of the renewable energy sources to which this Act applies. Like the Electricity Feed Act[1], it covers hydrodynamic power, wind energy, landfill gas, gas from sewage treatment plants, and biomass.

The term "solar energy", which was still used in the Electricity Feed Act[1], has been replaced by "solar radiation energy", which is correct in ten-ns of physics. The installations which this term refers to include in particular photovoltaic installations and installations for solar thermal electricity generation.

Geothermal energy, which had not been covered by the Electricity Feed Act[1], has been added to the scope of application of this Act in order to render the vast potential of geothermal energy accessible for use.

The use of mine gas for electricity generation will improve the carbon dioxide and methane balance, relative to the release of these substances into the atmosphere without utilising them. For this reason, mine gas was included in the scope of application of this Act.

In this Act – like in the Electricity Feed Act[1]– hydrodynamic power means the use of original, renewable hydrodynamic power in run-of-river and storage power stations fed exclusively from natural water resources.

The term "biomass" has not been conclusively defined. However, with a view to the purpose of this Act as specified in Section 1, it certainly does not include fossil fuels such as oil, coal and gas which will not be renewed within reasonable periods of time. The term "biomass" comprises solid, liquid and gaseous fuels which originate in recently harvested crops including timber and harvest residues, as well as waste wood and organic waste from food production and animal husbandry.

This Act maintains the principle of exclusive use introduced in the Electricity Feed Act[1] According to this principle, privileges under the Act will be granted only to those forms of electricity generation which are based exclusively on the use of the energy sources specified, unless the generation of electricity from renewable energy sources is only possible in the presence of priming or supporting fuels. As a general rule, it is not in keeping with the principle of exclusive use if materials such as harbour sludge, surfacetreated railway sleepers, particle boards with synthetic components or other types of contaminated waste wood are used for the generation of electricity. In accordance with the purpose of this Act as specified in Section 1, the key criterion is that the electricity generation process used should not compromise the environment or the climate. In order not to rule out from the very beginning processes which make ecological and economic sense but which are still under development, und in order to correct misguided developments where necessary, the Federal Ministry for the Environment, Nature Conservation and Nuclear Safety will be in charge of monitoring and reviewing developments; and the Ministry is authorised to adopt provisions which will specify what substances and technical processes in the biomass segment fall into the scope of application of the Act, and what environmental standards will have to be observed. What is important for the legislator in the final analysis is that the various processes used should make sure that the harmful substances contained in the biomass will, as far as possible, be accumulated in the residues instead of being released to the environment via the atmosphere or water.

In all other respects, the provisions of the *Gesetz zum Schutz vor schädlichen Umwelteinwirkungen durch Luftverunreinigungen, Geräusche, Erschütterungen und ähnliche Vorgänge (Bundesimmissionsschutzgesetz* – Act for the Protection against Harmful Environmental Effects Caused by Air Pollution, Noise, Vibration and Similar Factors Federal Ambient Pollution Control Act)[2] as well as the relevant implementing regulations will apply. In addition, an implementing regulation for the *Kreislaufwirtschqfts- und Abfallgesetz* (Recycling and Waste Management Act)[3], which will deal with the treatment of waste wood, is in the process of being prepared.

[2] also referred to as Federal Immission Control Act

[3] also referred to as Closed Substance Cycle and Waste Management Act

The scope of application of the Act also covers biogas which is generated elsewhere and fed into the gas network when such biogas is used for electricity generation, providing that proof is furnished of the origin of this gas and providing that there are calculations which prove that the energy content of the gas quantity used is equal to the energy content of the biogas quantity fed into the network.

The scope of application of the Act is extended to include the exclusive economic area located outside the 12-mile zone in order to facilitate the implementation of offshore wind projects in this area.

The term "grid operator" is used as defined in the *Gesetz aber die Elektrizitäts- und Gasversorgung* (Electricity and Gas Supply Act). It should be emphasised that only operators of public supply grids are obliged to purchase and pay compensation for electricity fed into their grids.

Paragraph 2

Paragraph 2 specifies electricity generation installations which are excluded from the scope of application of this Act. Like the Electricity Feed Act[1] the present Act does not cover large scale hydro-electric power plants, as well as large installations generating electricity from landfill gas and gas from sewage treatment plants. On the one hand, this is because it can be assumed that large-scale installations can be operated cost-effectively even without being included in the scope of application of this Act; and on the other hand, it is intended that especially decentralised smaller installations should become the pillar of future energy supply.

As far as electricity generation from biomass is concerned, this Act covers a wider range of installations than previous legislation. The scope of application covers biomass installations with a capacity of up to 20 megawatts in order to tap additional potential and mobilise efficiency reserves.

In addition, physically separate installations will be treated separately in terms of the scope of application, even if they use a common line to feed in electricity.

In the interest of equal treatment, the scope of application now also covers installations operated by electricity producers which had been excluded in the past. The "unbundling" of the activities of producers, regional grid operators and distributors, which the new energy legislation calls for, legally puts producers of electricity from renewable energy sources on an equal footing with conventional electricity producers. As a result, all producers will be motivated to invest in renewable energy sources.

In addition, there is a limitation for installations used for the generation of electricity from solar radiation energy. The purpose of this limitation is to prevent a continuation of the sealing of open spaces. The building structures specified in the Act which are covered by the rules on compensation include roofs, facades, noise protection walls and in some cases also embankments not exclusively designed for the purpose of electricity generation from solar radiation energy.

Paragraph 3

Paragraph 3 defines the terms "existing installations" and "new installations" as used in this Act. These definitions are particularly relevant for wind energy converters. Hence, the yardstick for determining the investment cost associated with the construction of a new installation is only the cost incurred above the foundation level.

Section 3

Paragraph 1

The obligation to connect electricity generators, purchase their electricity and pay compensation for the electricity purchased is now incumbent upon the grid operator whose grid is geographically closest to the electricity generator. This makes more economic sense than the reference to supply areas found in the provisions of the Electricity Feed Act[1].

The grid operators still are the right addressees for the obligation to connect electricity generators, purchase electricity, and pay compensation for, the electricity purchased because they own a natural monopoly which in practice is not jeopardised by the deglomeration of utility companies and the liberalisation of the electricity market.

It is clearly stated that the obligation to purchase, and pay compensation for, electricity is not limited to "excess electricity": instead, this obligation applies to the entire amount of electricity offered to the grid operator.

In line with the European Union's Internal Market for Electricity Directive, the Act stipulates that renewable energy sources should be granted priority when purchasing and paying compensation for electricity. Consequently, grid operators cannot refuse to purchase and pay compensation for electricity generated from renewable energy sources by stating that the power supply requirements of their grids are already fully met by means of conventionally generated electricity. For the same reason, it will only be necessary to expand the grid if the grid's power supply requirements are already fully met by means of electricity generated from renewable energy sources. This will tend to be the exception to the rule. For this reason, it is justified that the grid operator in this rare case will be obliged to upgrade the grid if an eligible electricity generator, as defined in this Act, wants to feed in electricity. In keeping with the, principle of proportionality, this obligation on the part of the grid operators is limited by what is economically no longer reasonable.

Since both grid operators and electricity generators interested in feeding in electricity have to carry out complex planning processes and take decisions affecting the use of their assets, both are obliged to provide to the other the data required.

Paragraph 2

The transmission grid operator which is upstream from the grid operator as defined in paragraph 2 is obliged to accept the electricity purchased by the grid operator under this Act, and to pay compensation for this electricity as specified in Sections 4 to 8.

Sections 4 to 8

The compensation scheme laid down for all renewable energy sources which are within the scope of application of this Act is guided by the principle that operators of optimised installations for the generation of electricity from renewable energy sources should generally be enabled to run these installations cost-effectively when these are managed efficiently. The most important factors included in the calculation of the compensation rates are the investment cost, the operating cost, the metering cost and the cost of capital for a specific type of installation relative to the service life, as well as the market return on capital employed.

In order to limit the administrative effort required – especially for the parties feeding electricity into the grid from small decentralised installations, but also for grid operators and governmental authorities – the Act upholds the principle of applying a uniform compensation rate nation-wide because this dispenses with the need for examining the cost or controlling the economic efficiency of electricity generating installations on a case-by-case basis. Such a lump-sum approach cannot and will not guarantee that a profitable compensation will be paid in every single case. For this reason, the compensation rates specified in this Act are minimum amounts; hence, higher compensation rates can be paid as a means of systematically promoting specific technologies. In this way, it is possible to attain the objectives pursued by this Act more effectively than by exclusively applying the lump-sum provisions contained in this Act.

It is up to the Federal Ministry of Economics and Technology – in agreement with the Federal Ministry for the Environment, Nature Conservation and Nuclear Safety and the Federal Ministry of Food, Agriculture and Forestry – to monitor developments in this field and, where necessary, to propose differentiated adjustments of the compensation rates to be paid for new installations in accordance with Section 12 of this Act.

In order to allow for technological progress and the expected reduction of costs, the compensation rates will be subject to nominal degressive annual reductions as of the year 2002; these reductions – which will apply across the board to all electricity generating installations built in the same year – will amount to 1 per cent for biomass, 1.5 per cent for wind energy, and 5 per cent for photovoltaic energy. As far as installations for the generation of electricity from hydrodynamic power, landfill gas, mine gas and gas from sewage treatment plants are concerned, on the other hand, their cost reduction potential has already largely been exhausted. The remaining cost-cutting potential will be adequately covered by the inflation rate. Currently, there is no need to introduce specific provisions for geothermal electricity generating installations because it will take some years before such systems will be operational.

With the exception of wind energy converters, existing and newly built installations will be treated alike. This general rule does not apply to wind energy converters because under the former Electricity Feed Act[1], the latter have already benefited from compensation payments which have permitted a cost-effective operation of such installations at suitable sites. For this reason, the period of time during which the higher initial compensation rate applies is reduced from five to four years for existing wind energy converters. This should be sufficient to safeguard existing installations.

Section 4

The provisions contained in the Electricity Feed Act[1] with regard to electricity generation from hydrodynamic power, landfill gas and gas from sewage treatment plants have essentially been maintained because they have proven to be effective in the past; the scope of these provisions was extended to include installations generating electricity from mine gas.

Section 5

The use of biomass for the purpose of electricity generation represents a hitherto inadequately used potential to supply energy in a way which does not lead to an adverse impact on the climate. At the same time, biomass provides additional perspectives for the domestic agriculture and forestry. The compensation rates have to be increased substantially above the rates laid down in the Electricity Feed Act[1] in order to enable operators of biomass installations to operate their installations cost-effectively, thereby initiating a dynamic development. Compensation rates differ in accordance with the electrical capacity of installations in order to give due account to the fact that the power production costs of smaller decentralised installations are higher.

The provision to the effect that compensation will not be paid before the entry into force of the ordinance applies only to electricity generating installations with a capacity of over five megawatts. Compensation for electricity from installations with a capacity less than 5 megawatts will be paid after the entry into force of this Act.

Section 6

The use of geothermal energy for the purpose of electricity generation depends on the presence of a reliable legal setting for investors; the purpose of the provisions in Section 6 is to create such a setting.

Section 7

The previous provisions applying in the field of wind energy systems did not give due account to the differences prevailing between various sites. In the amended version of the relevant provisions, different compensation rates are specified; irrespective of the type of technology used, the rates vary as a function of site profitability. Compared to the previous provisions, the new provisions – when applied to electricity generating installations over a service life of twenty years – on balance lead to the following results: at very good sites, compensation rates will be reduced to 6.9 cent per kilowatt-hour; at sites with average wind conditions, the rates will be stabilised at 8.4 cent per kilowatt-hour, and at inland sites, the rates will be moderately increased to 8.8 cent per kilowatt-hour. The purpose of these new provisions is to avoid payment of compensation rates that are higher than what is required for a cost-effective operation of such installations, and to create an incentive for installing wind energy converters at inland sites. Compensation rates differ because of the different periods of time during which the initial compensation rates will be paid. In addition, the higher initial compensation rate will facilitate the financing of wind energy converters which was increasingly being questioned by credit institutions when the previous provisions were in force.

The period during which the higher initial compensation rate will be paid is calculated by means of a comparison with a reference installation. This calculation is based on the P-V curve of the reference installation, determined either in accordance with the technical guidelines for wind energy converters published by *Fördergesellschaft Windenergie* (FGW Association for the Promotion of Wind Energy) or in accordance with the Power Performance Measurement Procedure defined by the Network of European Measuring Institutes (MEASNET), which was funded by the European Commission. The purpose of the provisions concerning the key features to be used to determine identical installation models is first of all to prevent manipulation by turbine manufacturers or operators; and secondly, the provisions are designed to clarify that it will not be necessary to repeat the calculation every time the installation is modified.

The following example may help to illustrate how to calculate the prolongation of the period during which the higher initial compensation rate will be paid: A site with a reference yield of 144 is six percentage points below the reference level of 150. Divided by 0.75 per cent of the reference yield, as specified in the provisions of Section 7 (1), these six percentage points give 8, which must then be multiplied by 2 months, again as specified in the provisions. The result is 16 months, which must be added to the basic period of five years. Hence, the higher compensation rate will be paid for a period of 6 years and 4 months.

The electricity production costs of offshore wind energy converters are expected to decrease substantially in the future. At present, however, the investment cost is much higher than the cost of onshore installations due to the lack of experience, higher expenses for new converter models, complicated foundation work and the lack of economies of scale. The purpose of the special provisions for offshore installations, which will be in effect for a limited period of time, is to make up for this shortcoming and to create incentives for investments. The relevant provisions apply to wind energy converters which are located at least three nautical miles seawards from the baselines. However, the resulting line is not completely identical with the seaward demarcation line of the former three-mile zone.

Section 8

Paragraph 1

In the long term, the use of solar radiation energy holds the greatest potential for providing energy supply, which does not have an adverse impact on the climate. This energy source both requires sophisticated technology and will attain considerable economic importance in the future. The relatively high compensation rate is due to the fact that, because of insufficient demand, these electricity generating installations are currently not yet produced in sufficient quantities.

As soon as this Act has created sufficient demand, the large production volumes which will result can be expected to lead to a substantial reduction in manufacturing cost, and hence, in electricity production cost, so that the compensation rates can be allowed to decrease rapidly. In addition to the real reduction of compensation payments due to inflation, the development described above is anticipated in this Act by stipulating degressive compensation rates. For electricity generating installations which will become operational after 1 January 2003 and in subsequent years, the compensation rates – for newly commissioned installations only – will once again be reduced degressively by five percent.

In combination with the "100,000 Roofs Programme", the provisions in Section 8 (1) lead to compensation payments which for the first time make electricity generation from solar radiation energy an attractive option for private investors; however, in many cases, the compensation specified does not permit a profitable operation of such installations at all times. The level of compensation has also been influenced by the compensation rates currently paid in Spain. In this context, it should be borne in mind that solar radiation intensity is much greater in Spain than in Germany.

Paragraph 2

For electricity generated from solar radiation energy, the obligation to pay the compensation rates specified in Section 8 (2) will end as of 31 December of the year following the year in which the total installed capacity of photovoltaic installations which are eligible to receive compensation under the present Act surpasses the limit of 350 megawatts. The waiting period of twelve months has been introduced in order not to create any uncertainty in the market and to enable market players to prepare for a smooth transition. The limit of 350 megawatts was calculated by adding the 300-megawatt target of the "100,000 Roofs Programme" to the capacity of the currently installed base.

In the framework of the present Act, the German Bundestag will introduce provisions for compensation payments to be made during the follow-up period to ensure that cost-effective operation of photovoltaic installations will be possible – giving due account of the decline in the marginal unit cost achieved by then – and to ensure that the photovoltaic sector will grow at an increasing pace.

Section 9

Paragraph 1

The fact that compensation payments are limited to a period of 20 years is in keeping with calculation formulas and amortisation cycles commonly used in the energy sector. Only in the case of hydroelectric power is this period usually not sufficient to safeguard the profitability of the installations.

The fact that the period during which compensation will be paid for electricity generated from already existing installations is calculated as of 1 January 2000 is designed to protect the installed base of operators of such existing installations.

Paragraph 2

If electricity supplied from several wind energy converters is billed on the basis of a single metering device, these electricity generating installations will be treated as a single entity for the purpose of determining the level, of the compensation to be paid.

Section 10

Paragraph 1

The provisions concerning the connection charges are designed to avoid legal disputes, and hence, to provide transparency and legal certainty.

If another grid, which is not used for public power supply, is located between an electricity generating installation and a grid whose operator is obliged to purchase electricity under the provisions of this Act, the electricity generating installation can be connected to this other grid if this is technically feasible. This will help to avoid cost which would not make any economic sense.

Paragraph 2

In line with the rules introduced in Denmark in 1997 with the approval of the European Commission, the cost associated with upgrading the grid – which also involves the necessary grid expansion – will have to be borne by the grid operator. For the sake of transparency, the grid operators will be obliged to present detailed calculations of the investments required because these expenses can be included by grid operators when calculating their service charges.

Paragraph 3

A clearing centre, which will be attached to the Federal Ministry of Economics and Technology, will be established for the settlement of disputes. The parties concerned include in particular the associations of grid operators and of operators of electricity generating installations as defined in Section 2 of this Act.

Section 11

Section 11 must be seen in close connection with Section 3. The provisions laid down in both sections, taken together, constitute a multi-level equalising system for electricity purchases and compensation payments.

Level 1, which is dealt with in Section 3 (1), provides for the connect-Ion of an electricity generating installation to the next closest suitable grid. This grid will usually be a local low-voltage grid. However, if the installation to be connected is a large wind farm, the grid may, also be a higher voltage grid, or even a transmission grid. The operator of the grid concerned will be obliged to purchase, and pay compensation for, the electricity delivered.

Level 2, which is dealt with in Section 3 (2), provides for the purchase of, and compensation payments to be made for, electricity by the upstream transmission grid operator. If the grid to which an installation is connected is already a transmission grid, there will be no upstream transmission grid. In that case, level 2 will not apply.

Level 3, which is dealt with in Section 11 (1) to (3), provides for fair nation-wide equalisation among transmission grid operators in terms of electricity volumes purchased and compensation payments made. This provision is designed to remedy a shortcoming in the former Electricity Feed Act[1] as a result of which the electricity purchases to be made under the Electricity Feed Act[1] in some regions were far above average. The equalisation provision in the present Act is aimed at the operators of transmission grids because this is a small group with a limited number of players which will easily be able to handle the transactions associated with the equalisation scheme and which will also be able to monitor each other. After the implementation of the equalisation procedure, each transmission grid operator will carry the same percentage share of electricity (fed in under this Act), relative to the total amount of electricity transmitted via the grid of the operator concerned.

Level 4, which is dealt with in Section 11 (4), provides for another step to be taken. Pursuant to the provisions in this paragraph, transmission grid operators will evenly distribute the electricity purchased under this Act among electricity distributors operating within their sales territory, and the latter will be obliged to pay the same compensation rates for this electricity nation-wide. The result of this provision is that each utility company which supplies electricity will have to purchase the same percentage share of electricity and pay the same percentage share of the compensation due. Level 4 ideally complements the principle of deglomeration for utility companies insofar as that it imposes a similar obligation on electricity distributors which are responsible for energy production methods that jeopardise the climate and the environment.

The obligation to purchase, and pay compensation for, electricity as specified in Section 11 (4) will not apply to utility companies if over half of the electricity they deliver is generated from renewables because – again in accordance with the 'polluter pays' principle – such companies have already done enough to protect the environment and manage global warming.

Electricity purchased at the compensation rates specified in Sections 4 to 8 must not be marketed as electricity from renewable energy sources at prices which are below the average compensation rates. In other words, when electricity which was fed into the grid under the provisions of this Act is marketed, the compensation rates paid will be regarded as the electricity generation costs to which other cost items (e.g. grid operating charges, licence fees, eco-tax and value-added tax) have to be added in order to obtain the market price. The purpose of this provision is to combat price dumping in the renewables electricity market. There is a risk of price dumping because the overwhelming share of the electricity to be purchased under this Act will be purchased by the large utility companies which still have a dominant position in the market. The reference period for calculating the average compensation rate will be the period two quarters earlier. During the first quarter after the entry into force of the Renewable Energy Sources Act, the compensation payments made under the Electricity Feed Act[1] can be used *mutates mutandis.*

The purpose of the provisions in Section 11 (5) is to ensure transparency with regard to electricity purchases and compensation payments by grid operators which are obliged under this Act to connect electricity generators to their grids; and to equalise among transmission grid operators the amounts of electricity purchased and the compensation payments made.

Section 12

These provisions are designed to monitor the market penetration achieved and the technological progress made by installations for the generation of electricity from renewable energy sources and, where necessary, to adjust the level of the compensation rates.

Adjustments of compensation rates will have to be announced early enough prior to their introduction. However, such adjustments can only apply to new installations; otherwise, there would be no reliable basis for operators of installations to make their investments, and it would be impossible for credit institutions involved in financing such installations to estimate the cost of such investments.

Amending the Renewable Energy Sources Act

The Government Draft of 17 December 2003[1] in Detail

Berlin, 17 December 2003

The Renewable Energy Sources Act as a successful instrument of environmental and energy policies is being further developed: One of the Federal Government's main policy objectives is to ensure establishment of sustainable energy supply systems. In this context, it is necessary to secure the energy supply of future generations and take account of ecological targets and economic growth at the same time. One major element of this strategy is to considerably increase the share of renewable energies in energy supply with a view to securing finite energy resources and advancing environmental and climate protection.

The Renewable Energy Sources Act is one of the central elements of the Federal Government's environmental and energy policy. It was adopted by the German *Bundestag* on 29 March 2000 and came into effect on 1 April 2000. The Renewable Energy Sources Act has helped to considerably improve the grid feeding and payment systems introduced in favour of renewable energies under the Electricity Feed Act in 1991 by adjusting them to conditions on the liberalised electricity market. Nevertheless the progress report of 2002 clearly shows that modifications are necessary, despite the great success of the act.

Given the Federal Government's medium- and long-term objectives, renewable energies will only be truly competitive if they continue to receive targeted support into the foreseeable future.

[1] This overview provides an outline of the amendment of the Renewable Energy Sources Act explaining the Federal Cabinet's decision adopting the government draft of 17 December 2003. This government draft can be used to deepen understanding of the subject matter as well as of the individual provisions. Now the draft is due to go through the parliamentary process. If cleared in a speedy manner by the *Bundestag* and the *Bundesrat*, the new Renewable Energy Sources Act may come into force as early as spring 2004 – possibly with amendments due to the parliamentary process.

In relation to the act currently in force, the following important amendments have been made:

Purpose of the act: The Amending Act regulates in detail the objective embedded in the existing Renewable Energy Sources Act to double the share of renewable energies in electricity supply by 2010. By that year, renewable energies are to provide at least 12.5% of total electricity supply. The medium-term objective for 2020 is to increase the share to at least 20%. Thus, the framework for expanding renewable energies has been clearly set for all parties involved. The aim is to reduce the costs of energy supply for the national economy by integrating long-term external effects.

EU Directive on renewable energy sources: The amendment to the Renewable Energy Sources Act also serves to implement the EU Directive on the promotion of renewable energy sources of September 2001. For this reason, the Renewable Energy Sources Act will now be amended to include the whole spectrum of renewable energy sources. The principle of exclusive use is retained, i.e. the payment of fees under the Renewable Energy Sources Act will only be possible if the electricity was produced exclusively in plants using renewable energy sources. This means, for example, that electricity produced from co-incinerating the biodegradable fraction of waste will be included in the definition of renewable energies, but without being paid for under the Renewable Energy Sources Act.

Scope of application/principle of priority: The Renewable Energy Sources Act provides for the connection to the general power grid of plants producing electricity from renewable energies and from mine gas on the territory of the Federal Republic of Germany including its exclusive economic zone. The act also provides for the priority purchase, transmission and payment of the electricity by the system operators as well as for a nation-wide compensation scheme for the electricity purchased and paid for.

Electricity produced in plants of which at least 25% are owned by the Federal Republic of Germany or by one of its *Länder* will be paid for when the Renewable Energy Sources Act enters into force. Thus, another potential, so far insufficiently used, has been opened up for the use of renewable energies.

Definitions: The Amendment Act introduces a number of definitions for terms which in the past have led to ambiguities and legal disputes. Thus clarity is established in the interest of all parties to which the act applies. A plant is defined as a separate technical installation producing electricity from renewable energies or from mine gas. The definition of commissioning is relevant for determining the date from which the claim for payment arises. The capacity of a plant is defined as the effective electrical capacity which the plant can produce at the grid connection point.

Improved integration into the grid of plants using renewable energies: A increase in the share of renewable energies in power generation makes it necessary to integrate plants using renewable energies into the general power grid.

Under the new act, the operators of plants using renewable energies and the grid system operators are enabled to agree on a production management scheme in their mutual interest.

This is particularly relevant for upgrading the grid and the balancing power. Such an arrangement requires the consent by both the plant operators and the grid system operators; both parties may profit from this possibility. The total costs for electricity production and distribution can thus be lowered, which finally results in lower consumer prices.

Fees for electricity produced from onshore wind farms: The basic rate for wind energy in 2004 is lowered by 0.5 cents per kilowatt-hours compared to 2003. The effects of lowering the low rate of payment can be seen in particular in extremely suitable coastal sites, which is intended to avoid potential over-production. The initial rate of payment is lowered by 0.1 cent per kWh. Plants commissioned in 2004 receive a starting payment of 8.7 cents per kWh and a final rate of 5.5 cents per kWh.

Special incentives are provided in particular for repowering in costal areas where older and small-sized plants are to be replaced by modern high-performance plants. Plants situated in low-wind sites will no longer receive payment under the Renewable Energy Sources Act; the limit has been established at 65% of the reference yield. The degression for new plants will be increased from 1.5% to 2% in order to optimise costs.

Fees for electricity produced from offshore wind farms: The Amending Act aims at a speedy development of offshore wind power. For electricity produced in offshore wind power installations, a high rate of payment of 9.1 cents per kWh will apply for a period of at least 12 years, with a possible prolongation of this period, subject to distance from the coastline and water depth. A high rate of fees will apply to offshore installations commissioned by 2010 (previously 2006). The high-rate period is twelve years in the 12-sea-mile zone and in the exclusive economic zone up to a water depth of 20 meters. This period is increased for installations erected far from the coastline and at great water depths: the period will be increased by 0.5 months for each sea mile exceeding twelve sea miles and by 1.7 months for each additional meter of water depth. Electricity produced by offshore wind energy installations licensed after 1 January 2005 in the exclusive economic zone will only be paid for if they are situated outside protected areas and bird sanctuaries. Thus, incentives to interfere with these protection areas are avoided. Degression for offshore installations will start in 2008.

Fees for electricity produced from biomass: The Renewable Energy Sources Act currently in force provides for 9.5 cents per kWh at a first capacity level of 500 kW (for plants commissioned in 2004). As the rate of payment for smaller plants is clearly too low under the present regime, as various studies have shown, a new capacity level of 150 kWh is introduced with a higher rate of payment at 11.5 cents per kWh. The higher rate will apply to electricity produced from biomass plants commissioned after 31 December 2003 from the date of entry into force of the Act.

Bonuses for renewable raw materials: The fee rates are increased by 2.5 cents per kWh where electricity is generated exclusively from plants or parts of plants as required by the Biomass Ordinance and/or from liquid manure. Thus, the higher costs arising from the use of renewable raw materials are taken into account. This is a prerequisite for exploiting further potentials of biomass, once the potentials of waste wood and biowaste have been used up. The bonus for renewable raw materials will apply to both existing and new installations.

Bonus for innovative technologies: The fee rates are increased by an additional 1 cent per kWh, where the electricity is produced using innovative technologies with often higher efficiencies. This includes in particular fuel cells. But the rate of payment will also be increased by one cent per kWh for the efficient production of electricity in combined heat and power generation plants. Bonuses are granted for plants with a maximum capacity of 5 MW. A degressive minimum rate of payment of 2% p.a. is introduced for new plants. This rate will be applied to plants commissioned as of 1 January 2005, for a period of 15 years (previously 20 years).

Fees for electricity produced from solar radiation: The basic rate for electricity produced from solar energy will be 45.7 cents per kWh. Where the installations are attached to or built on top of a building, the fees are increased by 11.7 cents/kWh for an installed capacity of up to 30 kW, by 8.9 cents/kWh for the installed capacity of 30 kW or over and by 8.3 cents/kWh for an installed capacity of 100 kW (the fees are thus adjusted to the successfully completed 100,000-roofs photovoltaic programme). For facade-mounted installations, the fees are increased by an additional 5 cents/kWh. The payment of fees for solar electricity is fixed for a period of 20 years for each installation.

In the case of installations that are not attached to or built on top of a building structure, fees may only be claimed where these installations were commissioned within the scope of a local development plan within the meaning of Article 30 of the Federal Building Code or in an area for which a procedure pursuant to Article 38(1) of the Federal Building Code was carried out. This is to ensure that environmentally sensitive areas are not built on and that maximum acceptance can be achieved among the local population.

The act regulating the fees payable for the production of electricity from solar radiation (preliminary act) can enter into force as early as 1 January, 2004. This preliminary act amending the Renewable Energy Sources Act has been fully integrated into the revision of the Renewable Energy Sources Act.

Fees for electricity produced from geothermal power: For electricity produced from geothermal power, further capacity levels are included at 5 MW and 10 MW, carrying higher payment rates (only one capacity level at 20 MW under the present regime; the first plants being developed are considerably smaller, and their electricity production costs are higher). This development is of particular importance since geothermal plants produce base load and peak load electricity. The fee rate for plants commissioned prior to 1 January 2010 is 15 cents per kWh for a capacity of up to 5 MW, 14 cents per kWh up to 10 MW, 8.95 cents per kWh up to 20 MW and 7.16 cents per kWh for a capacity exceeding 20 MW. Since the technology is still in its teething stages, the newly introduced degressive rate of 1% p.a. will only apply to plants commissioned in 2010 and later.

Fees for electricity produced from large-scale hydropower: Under certain prerequisites fees will now be paid for electricity from large-scale hydroelectric power plants with an installed electrical capacity of between 5 MW and 150 MW. Such plants must be modernized or expanded by 31 December 2012. Such modernisation or expansion must lead to an increase in the electrical capacity of at least 15% and must improve the ecological status. As a rule, only the additional share of electricity produced due to the modernisation is paid for. The payment of fees for electricity produced by large-scale hydroelectric power plants is limited to a period of 15 years.

Electricity produced in small-scale hydroelectric power plants: The Amending Act maintains fees to be paid for electricity produced in hydroelectric power plants with a capacity of up to 5 MW. This also applies to small plants with a capacity of 500 kW, if they have been recently constructed near existing barrage weirs or dams and are likely to bring about a positive ecological status. Small plants with a capacity of up to 500 kW which will not be operated in combination with barrage weirs or dams, will only fall within the scope of the Renewable Energy Sources Act if the plants are licensed prior to 31 December 2005. This is to ensure that there are no additional interventions in small natural rivers and streams. The fees are 7.67 cents per kWh for a capacity of up to 500 kW and 6.65 cents per kWh for a capacity of up to 5 MW. As for all other types of energy source, degressive rates will apply to new hydroelectric power plants. This degression is 1% annually for electricity produced in small-scale hydroelectric power plants.

Fees for electricity produced from landfill gas, sewage treatment plant gas and mine gas: A degressive minimum rate of 2% p.a. will be introduced for new plants as of 2005. In 2004, the fees are 7.67 cents per kWh for a capacity of up to 500 kW, and 6.65 cents per kWh for up to 5 MW. Fees at 6.65 cents per kWh are also paid for electricity produced from mine gas in plants above a capacity of 5 MW. In order to boost fuel cell technology, the rate of payment is increased by 1 cent per kWh where the electricity is produced by this innovative technology. The fees previously paid for electricity from landfill gas is now limited to 15 years for plants commissioned after 31 December 2006 (previously 20 years).

Nation-wide compensation scheme: The transmission system operators will continue to run a compensation scheme for electricity quantities for which fees have been paid pursuant to the Renewable Energy Sources Act. To facilitate such compensation, the grid system operators are now obliged to determine the quantities of electricity purchased and the amount of the fees paid. The electricity quantities are to be transmitted in accordance with a profile commensurate with the actual quantity fed in – thus saving costs. As the costs arising due to the Renewable Energy Sources Act continue to be broadly redistributed before reaching the final supplier, the final consumer only pays a small fee for electricity produced pursuant to the Renewable Energy Sources Act.

Transparency: To increase transparency, the Amending Act includes a requirement for operators to publish the energy quantities and the payments made in respect to the individual technologies for renewable energy production. More transparency is also to be achieved with regard to the publication of differential costs and the costs of the Renewable Energy Sources Act. The transmission system operators are to deduct from their fee payments received the charges for the use of the grid avoided in accordance with the rules of good professional practice. Thus, decentralised feeding methods are used, and the total costs of the system are reduced.

Provisions for special cases: The provisions for special cases applying to electricity-intensive enterprises of the manufacturing industry will be extended, and the time restrictions suspended. Electricity-intensive enterprises of the manufacturing industry may be included in the above mentioned provisions if their electricity consumption is higher than 10 GWh (so far 100 GWh) and if the ratio of the electricity costs to the gross value added exceeds 15% (so far 20%). The special-case increase of the share redistributed pursuant to the Renewable Energy Sources Act amounts to a maximum of 10% for the other electricity consumers.

FINANCIAL IMPACT

The present draft bill provides for lower fees for electricity from onshore wind farms. In addition, the draft bill provides for an annual degression of fees for all capacity levels in new plants, with the exception of geothermal power plants and offshore wind power installations, where the degression will apply at a later point in time. The rates of degression are adjusted to the efficiency potentials of the different capacities. Thus, significant incentives are given to lower the costs and increase the efficiency. The new act gives way to the expectation that the real differential costs will fall below the costs which would have arisen if the existing regime had remained in force unchanged.

The aim is to achieve the competitiveness and viability of renewable energies in the market in the medium and long-term. The fees paid for most renewable energies have in nominal terms been decreasing since 2002, as a consequence of the degression rules; in addition, the real price trends must be considered. Where the charges for conventional electricity will increase in the next few years, the difference in cost between energy from renewable sources and energy from non-renewable sources will further decrease. However, slightly increasing cost differences still have to be expected, which are borne by the electricity consumers as part of the electricity prices. In the long-term, this trend may be reversed, and electricity from renewables may become more competitive as the costs of the electricity thus generated fall below the costs of conventionally produced electricity.

The Ecological Tax Reform: Introduction, Continuation and Further Development to an Ecological Financial Reform

January 2003

With its ecological tax reform, the **German Government's is aiming** to encourage **energy saving** and **efficient energy use**, and to promote **renewable energies**. These pillars of **the new direction in energy policy** – together with the phase-out of nuclear power – are crucial for **climate protection** and for **creating new jobs**. Following the introduction of the ecological tax reform in 1999, the decision was taken to continue the reform until at least 2003. Furthermore, the Act on the Further Development of the Ecological Tax Reform entered into force in 2003, and **the expansion to an ecological financial reform** was initiated.

Fossil energies are scarce and limited. **The prices for their use are too low in the long term** because they only reflect a share of their "true" costs. Consequently they offer **too little incentive to exhaust existing energy saving potential, to further expand renewable energies and to develop and use energy-saving products and production processes**. In contrast, employers and employees are burdened with excessive non-wage costs, in particular social insurance contributions. This has a negative impact on Germany's competitiveness and contributes to the relatively high unemployment.

The tax burden on the labour factor is therefore being reduced and shifted to the environmental consumption factor. In this way **two problems can be tackled at the same time**. Energy taxes are being introduced or increased in small, calculable stages and pension contributions are being reduced and stabilised. **The ecological tax reform is therefore almost revenue-neutral** since its revenue is returned to industry and to private individuals by lowering other levies. This measure, which extends beyond one legislative period, enables the German Government to create reliable framework conditions for investment and purchasing decisions.

This measure represents a **historic reversal in taxation policy**, which up until now increased mineral oil tax for purely fiscal reasons, at the same time placing an ever-greater burden on wages in the form of higher social security contributions. This change in direction not only implies an important foundation for advancing climate protection. As energy saving primarily calls for labour-intensive activities (thermal insulation; development, production, installation and maintenance of new highly efficient technologies with corresponding export opportunities), the ecological tax reform also plays a role in **bringing down unemployment**. This is fostered by reduced and stabilised non-wage costs, plus a wave of investment and innovation and the reduction in energy imports for which German money has previously flowed abroad. This money can now be used to create jobs in Germany: intelligent engineering is putting an end to energy wasting.

1999: With the introduction and continuation of the ecological tax reform Germany is following the recommendations from the European Commission and the Organisation for Economic Cooperation and Development. By following the examples set by other EU countries such as Denmark, Italy, the Netherlands, Austria, Sweden and Great Britain Germany is also contributing to tax harmonisation within Europe.

The Act on the Introduction of the Ecological Tax Reform increased the price of energy from 1 April 1999. The mineral oil tax was raised by:

- 6 pfennigs per litre (3.07 ct) on motor fuel
- 4 pfennigs per litre (2.05 ct) on light heating oil
- 32 pfennigs per kilowatt-hour (0.164 ct) on natural gas.

In addition

- an electricity tax of 2 pfennigs (1,02 ct) per kilowatt-hour was introduced.

At the same time, the pension contributions, and consequently the non-wage costs, were cut by

0.8 percent, the reduction being equally split between employers and employees. This lowers the additional non-wage costs for employees and employees receive a higher net wage.

2000–2003: The Act on the Continuation of the Ecological Tax Reform regulates the gradually increasing taxation in four further stages from 2000 to 2003. The details of this Act are as follows:

Increase in the mineral oil tax

- by 6 pfennigs per litre (3.07 ct) on motor fuel on 1 January each year from 2000 to 2003; with an additional tax of 3 pfennigs (1.57 ct) per litre on non-low sulphur fuels (sulphur content over 50 ppm, equivalent to 50 mg/kg) from 1 November 2001 and from 1 January 2003. At this latter date, the limit value will be decreased to 10 ppm (sulphur-free fuels)
- a one-off increase on heavy heating oil of 0.5 pfennigs (0.256 ct) per kilogram on 1 January 2000.

Increase in electricity tax

- by 0.5 pfennings (0.256 ct) per kilowatt-hour on 1 January each year from 2000 to 2003.

Low sulphur and sulphur-free fuels significantly reduce emissions from traffic and facilitate the development and use of more efficient engine technology. The EU requirements regarding the reduction in the sulphur content (50 ppm from 2005) were thus already met in 2001, and from 2003 the sulphur content will fall considerably below the EU level. Announcing the proposed step at an early stage ensures there is a sufficient supply of these fuels. They can be used in any make of car without the need for any technical alterations. This extra tax premium will not lead to an additional burden; instead it will bring about a market shift towards tax-privileged low-sulphur and sulphur-free fuels.

The basic structure of taxation and special regulations remain intact during the continuation. A reduced rate of 20% of the regular tax rate will still apply for **the manufacturing sector and forestry and agriculture** (aquaculture, fish farming and disabled persons' workshops were also included from 2000), on condition that the basic amount of DM 1000 (€ 511) per energy source (based on electricity and heating fuels) is exceeded. All other sectors of industry and services are subject to the full tax rate. Furthermore, there is the additional option for the manufacturing industry alone to apply for a tax cap ("Spitzenausgleich"). As long as the burden from increased tax rates (disregarding the mineral oil tax on motor fuel and heavy heating oil) is 1.2 times greater than the tax relief from the reduction in pension contributions, enterprises will, on application, be refunded the full differential amount. This gives due consideration to the competitiveness of energy-intensive enterprises and there is no question of production being transferred to locations abroad which do not at present have high energy taxes. In view of the ecological objective and the far-reaching tax exemption of industry, however, the intention to provide incentives should always be borne in mind. Furthermore, a reduced and limited tax rate of 50 pfennigs (25.6 ct)/litre is applicable retroactively from 1 January 2001 for diesel used for **agriculture and forestry** (agricultural diesel).

Since 2000 the entire **local public transport system** (buses, school buses, trains and group taxis) must only pay half the rate of increase of the mineral oil tax on fuels (3 pfennigs [1.53 ct] per litre p.a.). The **public track and rail system** (trains, trams, trolleybuses, local trains, underground, magnetic-levitation trains) also enjoy as before a 50% reduced tax rate for ecological reasons. The tax rate for the **use of natural gas in the transport sector** remains significantly below the tax rate for diesel and petrol until at least 2009.

Night storage heating systems installed before 1 April 1999 will only be subject to half ofthe increased rate of the electricity tax for social welfare reasons.

In order to give efficient technologies a competitive boost, efficient **combined heat and power plants** (cogeneration and use of electricity and heat) with a utilisation rate of 70% or more are fully exempt from the existing mineral oil tax. The option of choosing between annual and monthly utilisation rates – introduced as part of the continuation of the ecological tax reform (previously the only option was the annual utilisation rate) – will benefit, for example, public utilities, which can mainly only sell their heat in winter.

Highly efficient gas-steam power plants with an electric efficiency factor of at least 57.5% that were completed and began operating after 31 December 1999 will have full exemption from the existing mineral oil tax and the eco-tax for five years after first generation. In almost all other European countries the energy used in electricity generation is not subject to any taxation. Germany is therefore removing distortion of competition and thus taking into account the changed conditions in a liberalised electricity market. This will in particular remove the competitive disadvantage in comparison to coal and nuclear fuels, which can be used untaxed for electricity generation. Instead all electricity is taxed. Gas–steam power plants can play an essential role in providing an environmentally sound replacement capacity for nuclear power plants.

The previous maximum output of 0.7 megawatts per plant for exemption from the electricity tax for the autoproducers' own use has been raised to 2 MW. Tax exemption for **contracting concepts** has been adapted accordingly. This represents an important incentive for an efficient and decentralised energy supply, e.g. in the form of small cogeneration plants. In addition, electricity from **renewable energy sources** intended for autoproducers' own use is exempt from the electricity tax. The previous maximum output (0.7 MW per plant) has been abolished; in the case of hydropower, the maximum output has been raised from the previous 5 MW to 10 MW per plant. Furthermore, electricity that is generated from renewable energy sources and which is taken from a grid fed solely by such energy sources or from a corresponding circuit is exempt from the electricity tax.

The revenues from the ecological tax reform will be almost fully returned (over 90%) to the taxpayers. The largest share of revenues serves the gradual reduction and stabilisation of employer and employee pension contributions from 20.3% in 1998 to 19.5% in 2003. Without the eco-tax, these contributions would be 21.2% in 2003 (diagram 2). Several hundred million euro per year are being used to promote renewable energies (DM 200 million in both 1999 and 2000: DM 300 million in 2001: € 190 million in both 2002 and 2003: € 200 million in 2004: € 220 million in 2005 and € 230 million in 2006.) **Together with the above tax reductions for the benefit of the environment, over 20% of the revenue serves environmental protection.** Around EUR 1 billion will be allocated from 2003 to consolidate the Federal budget.

The following table provides an overview of the expected revenue and contains data on how much higher pension contributions would be without the ecological tax reform:

Year	Volume of revenue	Reduction
1999	€ 4.3 billion	0.6 percent
2000	€ 8.8 billion	1.0 percent
2001	€ 11.8 billion	1.3 percent
2002	€ 14.6 billion	1.5 percent
2003	€ 18.8 billion	1.7 percent

Several leading economic research institutes have confirmed that the ecological tax reform, with its gradually increasing stages, is a practical and effective concept. In a study on the overall social impacts of the ecological tax reform the German Institute for Economic Research (DIW), together with other institutions, identified clear signs of the **desired ecological effects.** Energy consumption is decreasing; by 2005 CO_2 emissions can be reduced by 2–3%. In contrast, economic development is barely affected, while the impacts on the labour market are positive, with the creation of 250,000 new jobs by 2003.

The ecological tax reform combined with the particularly sharp increase in crude oil prices in 2000 and the US dollar exchange rate, and the resulting public discussion, have already led to increased awareness of energy-saving behaviour. In particular in the transport sector there are **clear indications of a trend reversal. Fuel consumption fell for the first time in three consecutive years (2000–2002)**, as compared to the almost constant increases in the past. According to figures from the Federal Statistical Office, fuel consumption in road traffic decreased by 1.1 percent in 2000 compared to the previous year; a further reduction of 1.5 percent was measured in 2001, and this rate continued to decline in 2002. The biggest contribution to this development was petrol sales, which fell by 2.9 percent in 2000 and 3.8 percent in 2001 (1999: −0.2 percent). A slight increase was determined for diesel, which was, however, much weaker than 1999 (+3.7 percent) with +1.2 percent in both 2000 and 2001. The reasons given for this decrease are an efficient and more reserved driving behaviour due to the higher petrol prices and lower, specific consumption values of new vehicles. Consumption is once again playing a prominent role when advertising and purchasing vehicles.

In addition, the **number of environmentally friendly natural gas-powered cars has increased to 13,000.** This is as much due to tax concessions for

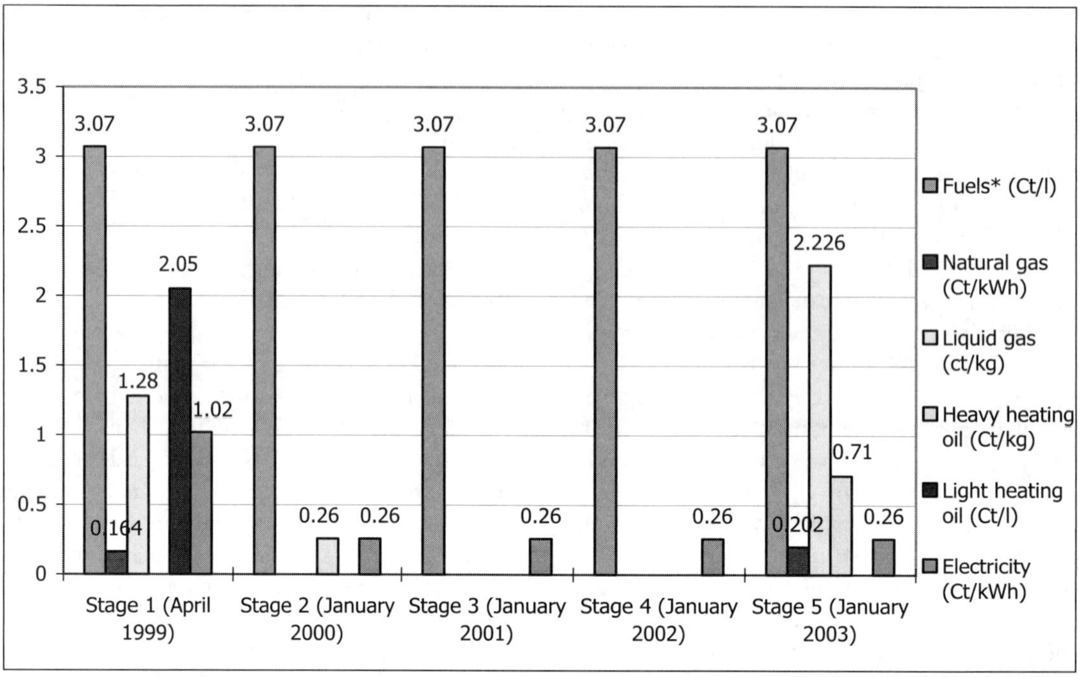

Diagram 1: Rate increases as part of the ecological tax reform. Source: Ökosteuer – sparen oder zahlen?, Federal Environmental Agency (UBA), November 2002

* from 1 November 2001 for low-sulphur, from 1 January 2003 for sulphur-free fuels rounded figures

the use of natural gas in the traffic sector as to the commitment to setting up a nationwide natural gas filling system by 2006.

Another consequence of the ecological tax reform is an **increase in the number of passengers travelling by public transport.** The number of rail passengers increased by 2% in 2000, and those making use of car-sharing agencies increased by as much as 25% in the first half of 1999. Following a downward trend in the number of passengers using local public transport up to 1998, a 0.4 percent increase was determined in 1999, 0.8% in 2000 and a further 0.8% in 2001.

Manufacturers of solar thermal plants for warm water treatment have recorded two-digit growth rates – a boom in renewable energies also thanks to the eco-tax on heating fuels and to the market incentive programme for renewable energies financed by the eco-tax.

The climate, the environment, the job market and innovative enterprises benefit from the ecological tax reform, as it makes it possible to avoid the high external costs resulting from car traffic, shifts this traffic to more environmentally sound modes of transport and reduces energy consumption and the related environmental pollution by means of alternative fuels.

2003: The Act on the Further Development of the Ecological Tax Reform entered into force on 1 January 2003. This will dismantle **environmentally harmful tax reductions** and will adapt taxes on natural and fluid gas and on heavy heating oil.

By cutting down the existing tax reductions, additional revenue of EUR 1.4 billion will be generated. Furthermore, around EUR 2.8 billion are to be collected from the fifth stage of the ecological tax reform (decided on in 1999) by the increase in the electricity tax and fuel taxes (see diagram 1).

From the total annual tax revenue of EUR 18.8 billion, around EUR 17 billion (over 90%) will continue to be paid into pension insurance funds. Thus the eco-tax as before will play a role in stabilising pension contributions. Without this revenue, a **pension contribution rate of 19.5%** would not be tenable due to the demographic development – in

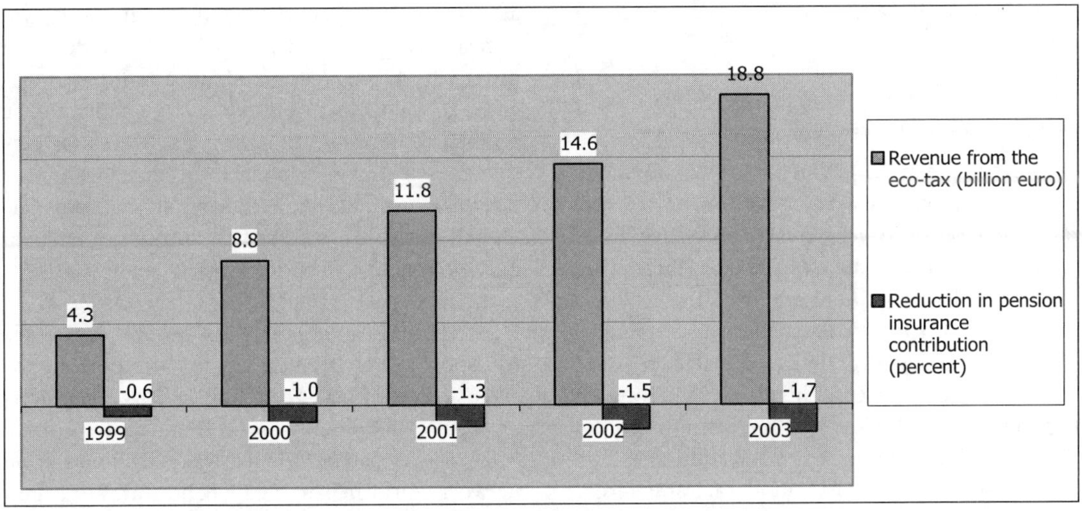

Diagram 2: Eco-tax revenue and reduction in pension insurance contributions. Source: BMF 2002. 1999 to 2001: actual values, 2002 and 2003: prognosis

fact, **without the eco-tax, this rate would be 21.2%.** In 1998 it was still 20.3% (see diagram 2). Together with fundamental reforms, revenue from the eco-tax can thus contribute to the long-term safeguarding of the pension insurance system. The eco-tax therefore continues to ensure that the labour factor remains affordable for enterprises and that social insurance contributions by employees remain stable at a lower level than in 1998.

EUR 190 million are being invested in the promotion of renewable energies as part of the market incentive programme. An additional EUR 150 million p.a. from 2003 will be used to promote building remediation and EUR 10 million will be used to assist the phase-out of old night storage heating systems. Thus **part of this revenue is benefiting the environment.**

Only EUR 1 billion will be used for budget consolidation. This is a temporary and thus justifiable deviation from the principle of strict revenue-neutrality of the ecological tax reform. Fundamentally, this reform thus **continues to represent a shift of the tax burden from the labour factor to the energy consumption factor.**

The Act on the Further Development of the Ecological Tax Reform provides for the following concrete measures:

• Increase in the eco-tax rates for the manufacturing industry and for agriculture and forestry – from a previous reduced rate of 20% for electricity, heating oil and natural gas to a reduced rate of 60% of the regular eco-tax rate

• Modification of the tax cap ("Spitzenausgleich"): if the tax burden on an enterprise in the manufacturing sector exceeds the relief on pension insurance contributions brought about by the eco-tax, 95% of the excess tax will be reimbursed (previously 100%)

• Increase in the tax rate for night storage heating systems installed before 1 April 1999 – from 50% (1.02 ct/kWh) to 60% (1.23 ct/kWh) of the regular electricity tax rate; abolishment of tax relief on 1 January 2007

• Adaptation of the regular mineral oil tax rate for natural gas when used as a heating fuel to 0.55 ct/kWh (previously 0.3476 ct/kWh), for liquid gas to EUR 60.60/1000 kg (previously EUR 38.34/1000 kg) and for heavy heating oil to EUR 25/1000 kg (previously EUR 17.89/1000 kg); efficient heat-power cogeneration plants and gas–steam power plants are exempt

• Extension of the tax reduction for natural gas in the transport sector to 31 December 2020 (previously 31 December 2009)

• Extension of the tax reduction for mineral oils used to heat greenhouses and closed growing rooms to 31 December 2004 (previously 31 December 2002)

• Use of EUR 150 million for a building remediation programme

• Use of EUR 10 million to assist the phase-out of night storage heating systems.

The increase in the tax rates for the manufacturing industry and for agriculture/forestry to a less favourable rate leads to increased incentives for effective energy use. Industry has had sufficient time over around four years to adjust to the ecological tax reform. It is therefore tenable and appropriate within the framework of the ecological tax reform to dismantle subsidies for industry, which amounted to around € 3.9 billion in 2002 alone (according to the subsidies report) by € 380 million (almost 10 percent) per annum. A moderate amendment to tax breaks will correct possible distortions in competition. This will modify **the tax cap**, which is especially relevant for energy-intensive enterprises. Previously, an enterprise had the right to reimbursement of the differential amount assuming it paid 1.2-times (from 2003: 1-times) more eco-tax than the reduction in pension insurance contributions. This means there was actually no relevant extra burden. If these rates were now merely reduced less than before, the steering effect would be limited because this would also result in higher reimbursement amounts. The tax cap was therefore reduced from 100% to 95%. There is now a real incentive for efficient energy use even for energy-intensive enterprises in the manufacturing sector.

The **dismantling of tax reductions for night storage heating systems** and the expiry of these reductions in 2007 is progress from an ecological perspective, since most of the energy used here is wasted. This inefficient method of heating runs counter to the principles of energy saving and efficient energy use, and to the phase-out of nuclear power. The promotion of these heaters is therefore being gradually abolished. Funds of EUR 10 million p.a. are being invested for this modernisation to promote the switch to efficient heating systems.

Tax relief from the mineral oil tax for glass constructions such as greenhouses and closed growing rooms remains in place until 2004. This is primarily justified by similar tax reductions for competitors in the Netherlands.

Adapting the natural gas tax rate to 0.55 ct/kWh can be viewed as problematic at first glance. In view of the energy content, natural gas had a strong tax advantage over light heating oil, which is also used to heat rooms. This advantage has been reduced in order to achieve a systematic taxation that is oriented to the CO_2 output and energy content. The ecological advantage of natural gas from a tax perspective will, however, continue to exist to a limited degree. In addition, this tax adaptation creates further incentives to save energy and to use efficient heat-power cogeneration plants. In this way, investment in energy saving leads to quick profits.

The ecological **advantage of natural gas in the transport sector** is taken fully into account by the extension of the tax reduction to 2020. The users of these cars only pay around half of the normal fuel price. A nationwide natural gas filling station network will be in place by 2006. Both are important prerequisites for the German automobile industry to be able to take the offensive in offering and selling natural gas-powered vehicles in series.

The coalition agreement provides for a **further review of the ecological tax reform** by 2004 at the latest. The purpose of this review is to decide whether and if so how to proceed. The key issue for the German Environment Ministry is, however, anchoring this in a broader ecological financial reform which also dismantles further subsidies which are ecologically harmful and for which the economic benefits are doubtful. This has also been laid down in the coalition agreement. A first step along this path has now been taken.

In addition to the above measures, the coalition agreement of 16 October 2002 also specifies the following measures as part of an **ecological financial reform:**

• Reduction in the VAT rate for rail passenger transport from 16% to 7% from 2005

• Abolition of VAT exemption for air traffic to other EU countries

• Supporting the taxation of kerosene at European level

• Further development of motor vehicle tax both ecologically and in a manner which is neutral in its effect on revenue, with CO_2 as basis for assessment

• Programme to support the building of "passive" (zero-energy) houses with 30,000 accommodation units

• Further reductions in subsidies for the German coal industry.

Furthermore, the German Cabinet decided on **the Act on the Dismantling of Tax Reductions and Exemption Regulations** on 20 November 2002. This Act provides for an increase in the flat-rate taxation for the use of private vehicles from 1% per month to 1.5% of the domestic list price, and the continuation of the eco-premium when aligning the owner-occupied homes premium ("Eigenheimzulage") for existing and new buildings, and provides for a focus on families with children.

As far as environmentally harmful subsidies are concerned, such as billions of euros for the coal industry, the question arises, and rightly so, as to why citizens are expected to still pay even higher taxes to finance them.

Further **information on the ecological tax reform** can be found on the Internet at

http://www.bmu.de/oekologische-steuerreform,

http://www.umweltbundesamt.de/uba-infodaten/daten/oekosteuer.htm,

http://www.bundestag.de

and http://www.bundesfinanzministerium.de (legislative texts),

applications for funding of renewable energies and energy-saving measures can be downloaded at

http://www.bmwi.de,

http://www.bafa.de,

http://www.bawi.de/ and

http://www.kfw.de.

An overview of all funding options can be found at

http://www.bmu.de and

http://bine.fiz-karlsruhe.de/bine/indexnew.html.

Further information on energy saving can be found at

www.bmu.de/klimaschutz,

http://www.bmu.de/energiespartipps,

http://www.co2online.de and

http://www.deutsche-energie-agentur.de/.

Republic of Lithuania

Republic of Lithuania Law on Energy

16 May 2002 No. IX-884 Vilnius

CHAPTER ONE GENERAL PROVISIONS

ARTICLE 1. PURPOSE OF THE LAW

1. The Law on Energy regulates general energy activities, the basic principles of energy development and management, energy and energy resources efficiency. Peculiarities of activities of individual energy systems and of relations between energy enterprises and consumers shall be established by other laws.

2. Provisions of other laws regulating energy activities shall be applicable to the extent they are not contrary to this Law.

ARTICLE 2. TERMS AND DEFINITIONS

As used in this Law:

1. "**Energy sector**" means a section of the economy embracing the energy sector activities.

2. "**Energy sector activities**" means economic activities embracing prospecting for, extraction, processing, production, storage, transportation, transmission, distribution, supply of, trade in and marketing of energy resources and energy, operation of energy facilities and installations.

3. "**Energy**" means electricity and thermal energy. Energy shall be regarded as a good. For the purposes of this Law, natural gas shall also be treated as energy.

4. "**Energy systems**" means energy areas directly connected with any type of energy resources or energy: electricity, heat, nuclear energy, natural gas, solid fuel, oil, petroleum products, renewable energy resources.

5. "**Energy resources**" means natural resources and products of their processing used for energy production.

6. "**Renewable energy resources**" means natural resources: potential hydro energy, solar energy, wind energy, biomass energy and energy which flows out from the centre to the surface of the earth (geothermal energy). The origin and renewal of this type of energy is conditioned by processes created by nature or human activity; it may be consumed or used for energy production.

7. "**Indigenous energy resources**" means energy resources available in the country, except for imported resources and their products.

8. "**Efficiency**" means the rate of efficient use of energy resources and energy.

9. "**Security of supply**" means reliability and technical safety of energy resources or energy supply.

10. "**Energy enterprise**" means an enterprise engaged in energy activities.

11. "**Operation of energy equipment**" means technological management of energy equipment, its technical maintenance, repairs, measurement, testing, work related to putting it into operation and adjustment.

12. "**Energy facilities**" means power plants and boiler houses; electricity networks and associated equipment; natural gas systems; natural gas storage facilities; liquefied natural gas import, export terminals and storage facilities; main oil pipelines, networks for the transport of energy products; oil refining facilities; oil and oil product terminals and storage facilities; heat supply networks and the associated equipment.

13. "**Energy facilities of national importance**" means power plants and boiler houses with a capacity of 50 MW or more; electricity transmission networks of 110 kV voltage or more and associated equipment; main oil pipelines; natural gas storage facilities with a capacity of 25 000 000 m^3 or more; liquefied natural gas import terminals and storage

facilities; main oil pipelines; networks for the transport of energy products; oil refineries with the annual crude oil refining capacity amounting to 20 000 tons and over; crude oil, oil product terminals and storage facilities for 10 000 m^3 and more; nuclear energy facilities; energy facilities the national importance whereof is recognised by the Government.

14. **"Energy equipment"** means a technical construction (mechanism, machine, apparatus, line, the accessories thereof) designed for the prospecting, extraction, processing/refining, generation/production, storage, transport, transmission, and distribution of energy resources and/or energy.

15. **"Emergency in the energy sector"** means a period of disruption of normal supply of energy resources or energy to energy enterprises and customers, where the supply is disrupted to the extent that energy enterprises prove unable to timely forecast and manage the disruptions by economic methods and the supply of energy resources or energy to energy enterprises and customers has to be regulated by the Government, its authorised institution or a municipal institution.

16. **"Energy transmission"** means transport of energy via transmission networks or main oil pipelines.

17. **"Energy distribution"** means transport of energy via the distribution networks.

18. **"Energy supply"** means energy delivery and/or sale to the customers.

19. **"Public service obligations"** means imposition in the cases prescribed by law, upon the decision of the Government or its authorised institution, of obligations relating to security of energy supply.

20. **"Main oil pipeline, networks for the transport of energy products "** means high-pressure pipelines, connected constructions and installations for transmitting oil to oil terminals and storage facilities or to oil refineries and for transmitting petroleum products to export, import terminals and storage facilities.

21. **"Main gas pipeline"** means high-pressure pipelines, connected constructions and equipment for transmitting natural gas from undertakings to natural gas storage facilities and distribution networks of towns and settlements or to gas-consuming installation up to the natural gas distribution stations inclusive.

22. **"Energy customer"** means a legal or natural person who purchases energy.

23. **"Regulated customer"** means a customer having no right to choose the energy supplier.

24. **"State control of the energy sector"** means control of safety of energy facilities, operation of energy equipment, security and efficiency of supplies.

25. **"Audit of the energy sector"** means inspection and evaluation of the state of energy equipment, technological equipment and processes in terms of energy efficiency as well as the choice of energy resources or energy saving means.

26. **"Technical safety"** means the entirety of requirements prescribed under this Law and other legal acts for energy facilities and equipment ensuring their reliability and safety.

CHAPTER TWO ENERGY SECTOR ACTIVITIES AND MANAGEMENT

ARTICLE 3. OBJECTIVES OF REGULATION OF ENERGY ACTIVITIES

The principal objectives of regulation of state energy sector activities shall be as follows:

(1) security of energy supplies;

(2) energy resources and energy efficiency;

(3) reduction of adverse effects of energy activities on the environment;

(4) promotion of fair competition;

(5) promotion of consumption of indigenous and renewable energy resources.

ARTICLE 4. INSTITUTIONS MANAGING THE ENERGY SECTOR

1. In the Republic of Lithuania State management of the energy sector shall be carried out according to the procedure established by this Law by:

(1) the Government or its authorised institution;

(2) the Ministry of Economy;

(3) the Ministry of the Environment;

(4) municipalities.

2. The main tasks of the State and municipal institutions, managing the energy sector, regulating and controlling the energy sector activities shall be as follows:

(1) ensuring optimum structure of the state energy sector;

(2) creating preconditions for efficient energy sector activities;

(3) ensuring uninterrupted energy supply and stability of the established quality parameters;

(4) promoting energy and energy resources efficiency;

(5) promoting consumption of indigenous and renewable energy resources;

(6) encouraging enterprises to carry out energy audits.

ARTICLE 5. COMPETENCE OF THE GOVERNMENT

1. When carrying out State management of the energy sector, the Government shall:

(1) formulate and implement State policy in the energy sector;

(2) submit the National Energy Strategy to the Seimas for approval;

(3) approve the plan and programmes for the implementation of the National Energy Strategy;

(4) declare an emergency in the energy sector;

(5) have the right to regulate the principles of price setting when the prices are subject to state regulation.

2. When carrying out State management of the energy sector, the Government or its authorised institution shall:

(1) establish the procedure for supplying the customers with energy and/or energy resources in case of an emergency in the energy sector;

(2) make a decision regarding construction of energy sector facilities crossing the state borders;

(3) approve the rules for licensing activities in the energy sector;

(4) establish the procedure for licensing trade in unprepacked petroleum products;

(5) establish the procedure of supply, export and import of energy and energy resources;

(6) draw up the list of activities in the energy sector subject to authorisation as well as rules and terms of issuing the said authorisations;

(7) establish the procedure of installation and maintenance of energy accounting and metering devices;

(8) in the cases prescribed by law shall have the right to impose public service obligations on enterprises engaged in energy activities;

(9) establish the procedure of purchasing the electricity generated from renewable energy resources and at CHP power plants;

(10) approve the mandatory standard terms of energy transmission, distribution and supply contracts for the regulated customers and natural persons;

(11) approve the rules of protection of energy facilities, electricity supply lines and pipelines;

(12) fulfil other functions established by this and other laws.

ARTICLE 6. COMPETENCE OF THE MINISTRY OF ECONOMY

The Ministry of Economy shall:

(1) implement the State policy in the energy sector;

(2) develop international cooperation in the energy sector;

(3) draft and approve legal acts regulating the issues of security of supply, installation, operation, technical safety, efficiency of energy facilities and equipment as well as other technical issues;

(4) draft, revise the draft National Energy Strategy (hereinafter referred to as the Strategy) and submit it to the Government;

(5) draft the Strategy implementation plan and programmes, coordinate their implementation;

(6) approve the rules for the transmission, distribution, supply and consumption of energy and energy resources;

(7) establish the procedure for building up, maintenance, accumulation and use of stocks of energy resources;

(8) lay down quality requirements for energy consumed in the country;

(9) establish the procedure and terms for the connection of energy facilities (networks, equipment, systems) of the customers and producers to the operating facilities of energy enterprises (networks, equipment, systems);

(10) in conjunction with the Ministry of the Environment establish the procedure and terms for the planning of construction of energy facilities of national importance;

(11) establish the procedure of state control of the energy sector and control of the customers' energy equipment;

(12) establish the procedure, volume and terms of furnishing of the information relating to the energy activities to state institutions, agencies and third parties;

(13) approve the list of positions and professions of the employees listed in Article 21(1) of this Law, establish the qualification requirements for the said employees, approve the list of the employees engaged in the operation of energy facilities, construction and operation of energy installations who are subject to performance evaluation and establish the procedure for conducting the evaluation;

(14) have the right to lay down efficiency requirements for the equipment in Article 20 of this Law and the efficiency control procedure;

(15) fulfil other functions established by this Law and other laws or assigned by the Government.

ARTICLE 7. COMPETENCE OF THE MINISTRY OF THE ENVIRONMENT

The Ministry of the Environment shall:

(1) decide issues relating to environmental protection, construction and fulfil functions within its competence;

(2) organise and carry out monitoring of environmental effects in increased pollution areas of energy sector activities;

(3) in conjunction with the Ministry of Economy lay down quality requirements for the energy resources used and intended to be used in the country and submit recommendations for the use thereof;

(4) take part in the drawing up of renewable energy resources programmes.

ARTICLE 8. COMPETENCE OF MUNICIPALITIES

Within its territory a municipality shall:

(1) regulate the supply of customers with heat within the competence laid down by laws;

(2) make arrangements for the lighting of the territories used for public needs;

(3) grant, according to the nomenclature approved by the Government, licences for retail trade in unprepacked petroleum products;

(4) grant, according to the procedure approved by the Ministry of Economy, authorisations for trade in liquefied petroleum gas;

(5) upon the declaration of an emergency in the energy sector, implement the plan approved by the Government or its authorised institution for the supply of customers with energy and/or energy resources, ensure the implementation of other decisions of the Government;

(6) take part in the preparation of educational public information tools promoting energy and energy resources efficiency.

CHAPTER THREE DEVELOPMENT OF THE ENERGY SECTOR

ARTICLE 9. NATIONAL ENERGY STRATEGY

1. The Strategy shall determine energy development trends for a twenty year period.

2. The Strategy shall be approved by the Seimas upon the recommendation of the Government.

3. The Strategy shall cover all energy systems, it shall be subject to revision at least every 5 years. The Strategy shall be prepared, revised and implemented with State budget and other funds.

4. The Strategy shall provide for:

(1) the safety of the national energy sector;

(2) forecasts of demand, import and export of energy resources;

(3) forecast of energy production demand;

(4) improvement of the energy sector structure;

(5) structure of energy resources consumption and its forecasts;

(6) forecasts and means of reduction of the energy sector's adverse effect upon the environment;

(7) development of consumption of renewable and indigenous resources;

(8) energy efficiency;

(9) necessary investment;

(10) evaluation and building up of reserves of energy resources;

(11) energy market development;

(12) directions of improvement of energy sector management;

(13) improvement of pricing;

(14) other issues relating to energy sector development.

5. The Government shall approve a five-year strategy implementation plan and programmes of action.

6. The Strategy shall be implemented according to their respective competence by the State and/or municipal institutions, agencies, the Energy Agency and other enterprises.

ARTICLE 10. ENERGY AGENCY

1. The Energy Agency is a State enterprise. Its founder is the Ministry of Economy.

2. Upon the assignment of the Ministry of Economy, the Energy Agency shall fulfil the following main functions:

(1) carry out the measures of the Strategy implementation plan;

(2) implement the programme for the improvement of energy efficiency and its action plan;

(3) carry out the supervision and monitoring of the implementation of foreign assistance programmes and projects in the energy sector;

(4) promote efficiency of energy resources and energy efficiency as well as the use renewable energy resources and provide information relating thereto.

3. The Energy Agency shall also fulfil the functions prescribed by this Law and other laws or assigned by the Ministry of the Economy.

ARTICLE 11. CONSTRUCTION OF ENERGY FACILITIES

1. Energy facilities shall be constructed in accordance with the procedure laid down in the Law on Construction, Law on Territorial Planning, Law on Environmental Protection and other legal acts. Energy facilities of national importance shall be developed according to the provisions of the Strategy. General or special plans for the supply of customers with energy and energy resources shall be drafted on the basis of the Strategy.

2. Energy enterprises shall take part in drafting and developing plans of balanced and efficient supply, distribution, transmission of energy and shall plan the development of energy facilities of national importance. The energy enterprises engaged in energy transmission, distribution shall develop energy transmission, distribution facilities within the territory of their operation.

3. Energy enterprises engaged in the activities the prices whereof are regulated shall co-ordinate prospective investment with the State Prices and Energy Control Commission (hereinafter – the Commission). Where such investment of the energy enterprises is not co-ordinated with the Commission, it may not be recognised as reasonable for revising the State-regulated prices.

4. The energy facilities belonging to energy enterprises but located on the land or in the buildings of other owners may, where possible, be reconstructed or relocated by agreement between the owner of the land or buildings and the energy enterprise. In such case the owner of the land or building shall defray the reconstruction or relocation costs incurred by the energy enterprises. The ownership of the reconstructed or relocated energy facilities shall remain unchanged.

ARTICLE 12. ENERGY SECTOR ACTIVITIES

1. Energy enterprises shall carry out their activities in such a manner as to ensure safe, efficient and environment friendly energy production, supply, transmission, distribution up to the connection point of the supplied energy metering equipment to the customer's system, not exceeding the set State-regulated prices. Energy enterprises which supply heat to multi-family apartment houses shall supply

heat to the apartments, unless the consumers request otherwise.

2. An energy enterprise shall transmit, distribute, supply energy to the customers in accordance with the rules for the transmission, distribution, supply and consumption of energy. An energy enterprise shall have the right according to the procedure established by legal acts to suspend the supply of customers with energy only in the cases prescribed by law.

3. Within the territory of their operation the energy enterprises shall connect, according to the established procedure, the energy generating and/or consuming equipment of the energy generators, customers to the operating energy transmission or distribution networks. The connection costs shall be covered by the appropriate generators or customers according to the set tariffs. The connection work shall be carried out under a mandatory contract between the energy enterprise and energy generator or customer.

4. The energy enterprises which own or in any other lawful way control energy transmission or distribution networks and systems shall provide transmission or distribution services to a third party under objective, non-discriminatory conditions, taking account of the technical possibilities of the networks and systems.

5. The energy enterprises which own or in any other lawful way control energy facilities operating in the common energy system shall cooperate and operate in the common operating mode as well as fulfil instructions given by the networks or system operator. The operator shall be appointed by granting the licences according to the established procedure.

6. Interrelations among the energy enterprises as well as their relations with the customers of energy resources or energy shall be based on contracts. Contracts for the supply, transmission and distribution of energy shall be public. Energy shall be supplied, transmitted or distributed to the regulated customers and natural persons upon conclusion of a contract in accordance with the mandatory standards.

7. Energy enterprises transmitting, distributing energy shall be entitled to inspect, according to the established procedure, conformity of the customers' energy equipment with technical safety requirements.

8. Following the close of the year, the costs of the licensed activities of energy enterprises operating in the electricity, heat, natural gas systems shall be audited within a four month period and the auditor's report shall be submitted to the Commission.

9. Energy enterprises shall participate in the drafting of the methods of setting regulated prices, methods of calculating connection charges for energy facilities, rules for energy transmission, distribution, other legal acts regulating the installation, operation, safety of energy equipment and other technical issues.

ARTICLE 13. PECULIARITIES OF ACTIVITIES IN THE ENERGY SECTOR, QUALITY OF ENERGY AND ENERGY RESOURCES

1. The territory of activities of energy transmission, distribution enterprises shall be defined in the licences.

2. The energy or energy resources consumed in the country must meet the set energy and energy resources quality and composition requirements.

ARTICLE 14. TRANSFER OF IMMOVABLE PROPERTY FOR USE

1. Land for the construction of energy facilities shall be leased or otherwise transferred for use according to the procedure established by laws. For the construction of energy production, transmission and distribution facilities State-owned land shall be sold or leased according to the procedure established by the Government without holding an auction.

2. Private land may be used for the construction of energy facilities by agreement between the energy enterprise and the land owner. Where an agreement is not reached, land may be taken for public needs in accordance with the procedure and under the conditions established by laws.

3. Protection zones shall be established for the purpose of ensuring protection and operation of energy facilities. Construction, planting of greenery and land works shall be restricted in the zones. Easements benefiting land and other immovable property located in the protection zone shall be

established by the energy facilities protection rules, other legal acts. Owners or users of the immovable property located in the protection zone must grant the energy enterprises access to the energy facilities owned or operated by them in order to perform modernisation or maintenance works. Losses inflicted in protection zones by the activities of the energy enterprises shall be covered by the energy enterprise which owns the energy facility in the immovable property located in the protection zone.

CHAPTER FOUR REGULATION OF THE ENERGY SECTOR

ARTICLE 15. PRICES

1. Prices in the energy sector shall be contract and state regulated prices. Prices shall be regulated by setting prices for services or energy, establishing their price caps or the procedure of regulation. The tariffs and principles of regulation of state regulated prices shall be laid down in the laws of appropriate energy systems.

2. When setting the state regulated prices, provisions have to be made for obligatory expenses for extraction of energy resources, energy production, purchasing, transmission, distribution and supply as well as for the development of the energy sector and energy efficiency, the use of local and renewable resources, implementation of public service obligations and the set profit rate.

3. State regulated prices must be announced publicly, not later than one month before the of their introduction unless other laws provide other wise, and shall be applied from the 1st day of the month.

ARTICLE 16. LICENCES AND AUTHORISATIONS

1. Activities in the energy sector shall be subject to licences or authorisations. The types of licences activities shall be set out in the laws on the energy sector and other laws. A list of activities subject to licensing shall be approved by the Government.

2. Activities in the energy sector without a licence or an authorisation where these are required shall be unlawful.

ARTICLE 17. THE STATE CONTROL COMMISSION FOR PRICES AND ENERGY

1. The Commission is a state institution financed with the state budget of Lithuania. Its regulations shall be approved, on the recommendation of the Ministry of Economy, by the Government. The Commission shall be a legal person.

2. The Commission shall be composed of five members. Its Chairman and four members shall be appointed by the President of the Republic, on the recommendation of the Prime Minister, for a period of 5 years.

3. Persons of high moral character who are nationals of the Republic of Lithuania, having a university degree or its equivalent, shall be eligible to serve as members of the Commission.

4. The Chairman and members of the Commission shall be dismissed from office:

(1) upon expiry of their term of office;

(2) upon their resignation;

(3) when elected or appointed to another position;

(4) when a conviction rendered against them becomes effective;

(5) when it transpires that they have committed a grave breach of the requirements for the position held;

(6) for violation of official ethics;

(7) when for health reasons they are no longer able to hold the position;

(8) upon loss of the nationality of the Republic of Lithuania.

5. The Commission shall perform the following functions:

(1) approve the methodology for setting state regulated prices;

(2) set state regulated price caps;

(3) control the application of state regulated prices and tariffs;

(4) approve charges for connection of energy facilities (networks, systems and equipment);

(5) have the right to introduce unilaterally state regulated prices where energy enterprises are not in compliance with the requirements for setting of these prices;

(6) when setting the state regulated prices shall take account of the return on investment and justification for operating expenditure;

(7) approve the purchase price for electricity generated from renewable energy resources;

(8) grant, suspend and revoke licences for transmission, distribution, storage and supply of energy, and check the licensed activities of energy enterprises;

(9) have the right to submit proposals to the Government, the Ministry of Economy and municipalities in respect of the licensed activities of energy enterprises;

(10) have the right to obligate energy enterprises to conclude contracts for transmission, distribution or supply of energy where energy enterprises refuse to a third party to provide services or to supply energy to customers;

(11) perform other functions provided for in legal acts.

6. The Commission shall be responsible for the decisions taken. The decisions of the Commission shall be adopted by a roll-call vote. The decisions of the Commission may be appealed following the procedure prescribed by law.

7. At the close of a calendar year, the Commission shall, within four months, draft its annual report, make it public and submit it to the President of the Republic, the Seimas and the Government.

8. The Commission Administration shall be formed for the performance of the functions of the Commission. The functions of the Administration of the Commission and its employees shall be defined in the regulations of the Commission.

9. Unless this Law provides otherwise, the Law on Budgetary Institutions shall apply to the activities of the Commission.

ARTICLE 18. STATE CONTROL OF THE ENERGY SECTOR

1. State control of energy facilities and equipment shall be exercised within the whole territory of the Republic of Lithuania irrespective of their form of ownership.

2. State control of energy shall be exercised, in accordance with the prescribed procedure, by the State Energy Inspectorate under the Ministry of Economy (hereinafter "the State Energy Inspectorate").

3. The State Energy Inspectorate shall be a state institution. Its founder is be the Ministry of Economy. The regulations of the State Energy Inspectorate shall be approved by the Ministry of Economy.

4. The State Energy Inspectorate:

(1) shall grant, suspend and revoke, following the established procedure, authorisations for energy activities and control compliance with the terms and conditions of the activities specified in the authorisations;

(2) shall check, following the established procedure, technical safety and maintenance of energy facilities and equipment, reliability of production, transmission, distribution and supply of energy and energy resources and their efficiency;

(3) shall carry out inquiries into accidents of energy facilities and equipment and disruptions of their functioning, take part in inquiries into accidents at work, conduct inquiries into domestic accidents related to the use of energy;

(4) shall monitor compliance with special requirements during installation and reconstruction of energy equipment as well as their conformity and suitability for use;

(5) shall organise performance evaluation of energy specialists and managers referred to in Article 21(2);

(6) shall monitor compliance with the prescribed energy quality requirements;

(7) shall monitor state and reserve stocks of energy resources;

(8) shall have a right to verify the information supplied by energy enterprises to state institutions;

(9) shall perform the functions set out in this Law and other legislation.

5. The State Energy Inspectorate shall be responsible for the decisions taken. The decisions of the State Energy Inspectorate may be appealed following the procedure established by law.

6. Monitoring and state supervision of physical safety of nuclear facilities and accounting of nuclear materials shall be carried out by the State Nuclear Safety Inspectorate. The competence of the State

Nuclear Safety Inspectorate shall be established by the Law on Nuclear Energy.

7. The State Energy Inspectorate shall not monitor compliance of the employees with the requirements prescribed by legal acts on safety and health.

ARTICLE 19. PROVISION OF INFORMATION

1. The state institutions and agencies, for the performance of the functions assigned to them, shall have a right to obtain the relevant information from energy enterprises. Energy enterprises shall provide, in accordance with the established procedure, information to state and municipal institutions, agencies, appropriate associations and third parties.

2. The Government or institutions authorised by it shall provide information relating to energy to the European Commission, other countries and international organisations.

3. Energy enterprises owning or otherwise controlling energy facilities of national importance must inform the Ministry of Economy about the beginning of construction or commissioning of these facilities.

4. Energy enterprises shall, within the limits of their competence, provide energy consumers within the territory of their operation, information about efficiency of energy resources and energy, safe and effective use of energy facilities and equipment, about energy facilities and installations under construction or reconstruction, about energy tariffs and the services provided to energy consumers.

ARTICLE 20. EFFICIENCY OF ENERGY RESOURCES AND ENERGY

1. The major guidelines for efficiency of energy resources and energy shall be set out in the Strategy, while measures for the implementation of the guidelines shall be defined in the increased energy efficiency and other programmes.

2. The imported, manufactured and sold hot-water boilers with the nominal heating power in the range of 4 to 400 kW, fired with liquid fuel or gas, must conform to the prescribed efficiency requirements.

3. The imported, manufactured and sold heat generators for heating premises and/or water in the new or existing buildings used for non-industrial purposes must conform to the prescribed efficiency requirements.

4. The imported, manufactured and sold domestic appliances which use electricity and other types of energy must have appropriate energy efficiency labelling.

5. Enterprises having boilers and equipment using other energy resources with the nominal heating power of more than 0.4 MW shall check efficiency of energy resources of these equipment in accordance with the established procedure.

ARTICLE 21. QUALIFICATIONS AND PERFORMANCE EVALUATION OF THE STAFF

1. The employees engaged in the construction and operation of energy facilities and equipment must have adequate qualifications and training. Their training programmes must include questions relating to efficiency of energy and energy resources.

2. The employees engaged in the construction and operation of energy facilities and equipment must undergo performance evaluation following the procedure specified in Article 6(13) and subparagraph 5 of Article 18(4) of this Law.

ARTICLE 22. RESERVE STOCKS OF ENERGY

Energy enterprises having heat or electricity facilities with the heating power of more than 5MW and producing heat and electricity for sale must maintain reserve energy stocks. Reserve energy stocks shall be built, maintained and renewed with the funds of energy enterprises and other funds. Energy reserve stocks must be at a level corresponding to at least one month's consumption.

ARTICLE 23. ENERGY ACCOUNTING

1. The produced, transmitted, distributed, sold, exported and exported or transmitted by transit energy must be accounted.

2. Energy must be accounted by energy measuring instruments registered with the Register of Measuring Instruments of the Republic of Lithuania. Newly installed energy measuring instruments must conform with the specifications of measuring instruments used in the Member States of the European Union.

3. Energy measuring instruments shall be installed and operated by energy enterprises owning or otherwise controlling energy facilities of transmission, distribution or storage with their own funds.

4. Energy measuring instruments between energy facilities shall be installed and maintained by energy enterprises owning or otherwise controlling energy facilities of transmission with their own funds.

ARTICLE 24. ENERGY TRANSIT

1. Transit of energy or energy resources (hereinafter "transit") shall be carried out under contracts concluded between the energy enterprises controlling energy facilities of origin, final destination and transmission of energy or energy supply in accordance with the provisions of the Energy Charter Treaty and taking account of the capacities of the transmission facilities and priorities of national needs.

2. Enterprises controlling energy transmission facilities shall supply information to the Commission and the Ministry of Economy about each request for transit, the concluded transit contracts and refusals to conclude them. A refusal to conclude a transit contract must be duly substantiated.

CHAPTER FIVE EMERGENCY IN THE ENERGY SECTOR

ARTICLE 25. EMERGENCY IN THE ENERGY SECTOR

1. A state of emergency in the energy sector shall be declared where electricity, natural gas or petroleum products are in short supply affecting the security and health of the population or the functioning of economy of the country.

2. A state of emergency in the energy sector shall be declared by a resolution of the Government. After a state of emergency or war has been declared in accordance with the procedure prescribed by law, a state of emergency in the energy sector shall be declared without a special resolution of the Government.

3. Energy enterprises must inform, in accordance with the established procedure, the municipalities and the Ministry of Economy about shortages in energy supply and about the measures for restoring the supply.

4. After an emergency in the energy sector has been declared, supply of energy and energy resources to the customers may be restricted or suspended by the Government or an institution authorised by it in accordance with the prescribed procedure. In the event of an emergency in the energy sector energy enterprises acting in accordance with the instructions of the Government, the institutions authorised by it, and of the mayors of regional/city municipalities shall not be liable for the losses caused to the customers by reason of the restrictions in the supply or suspension of energy or energy resources.

5. To provide energy supplies to the consumers in the event of an emergency in the energy sector, state stocks of petroleum products shall be built in accordance with the procedure provided by law.

6. After an emergency in the energy sector has been declared, enterprises producing, transmitting, transporting, loading and unloading crude oil or petroleum products, natural gas, fuel oil and electricity must first satisfy the needs of domestic consumers.

7. After an emergency in the energy sector has been declared, legal and natural persons must act in accordance with the instructions of the Government, institutions authorised by it and the mayors of regional/city municipalities. Where, in the event of an emergency in the energy sector, energy enterprises fail to act in accordance with the instructions, the Government or a municipality council shall have a right, while the emergency in the energy sector lasts, to remove the governing bodies of these enterprises and appoint temporarily their own representatives to act as administrators. Representatives of the Government or a municipal institution, while performing the functions of the heads of the boards or the administration of the enterprises, shall act in accordance with the laws of the Republic of Lithuania and the powers vested in them by the Government.

8. After an emergency in the energy sector has been declared the Government or institutions authorised by it shall have a right to regulate export, import of and trade in crude oil, petroleum products, energy and energy resources as well as to control and restrict, taking account of the market conditions, the unreasonably high prices of petroleum products, energy and resources of energy sold and services provided.

CHAPTER SIX HEARING OF COMPLAINTS. LIABILITY

ARTICLE 26. HEARING OF COMPLAINTS

1. The National Council for Consumer Protection under the Ministry of Justice shall hold a preliminary extra-judicial hearing of complaints by natural persons concerning application of unfair conditions in the sale or service agreements.

2. The State Energy Inspectorate shall hold a preliminary extra-judicial hearing of complaints concerning malfunctioning of energy facilities and breakdowns of equipment and metering instruments, breaches of the requirements of maintenance, energy quality, accounting of and payment for energy, accidents, interruption, suspension or restriction of energy supply.

3. The Commission shall hold a preliminary extra-judicial hearing of complaints concerning acts or omissions of energy enterprises in supply, distribution, transmission, storing of energy, failure to grant them a right to use networks and systems, connection, balancing of energy supply flows, application of prices and tariffs.

ARTICLE 27. LIABILITY

Persons shall be held liable under law for violations of this Law.

CHAPTER SEVEN FINAL PROVISIONS

ARTICLE 28. PROCEDURE OF ENFORCEMENT OF THIS LAW

1. Energy enterprises shall buy out or operate, following the procedure prescribed by the Government or an institution authorised by it, energy facilities acquired at the expense of the customers (legal and natural persons), installed for common use prior to the entry of this Law into force and intended for transmission and/or distribution of energy.

2. Energy enterprises shall provide information to the State Tax Inspectorate under the Ministry of Finance or to the municipalities about energy facilities which, though in use, are not recorded and have no owners or whose owners are unknown (hereinafter "derelict energy facilities"). The State Tax Inspectorate under the Ministry of Finance or the municipalities shall, following the procedure established by the Government, include the derelict energy facilities in the records and take measures to find the owners of these facilities. The State Tax Inspectorate under the Ministry of Finance or a municipal institution, at the close of four months from the day when the facility was included in the register, shall file an application with court to transfer the derelict energy facility into the ownership of the state or a municipality. The derelict energy facilities which have been transferred by a court decision into the ownership of the state or a municipality, shall, by a decision of the State or the municipality council, be sold, leased or given into any other form of use to an energy transmission or energy distribution enterprise operating within their territory.

3. The provisions of paragraph 2 of this Article shall not apply to energy facilities which have been acquired in good faith and are in lawful control even where their administrators have not yet acquired the right of ownership to these facilities by prescription.

4. After entry of this Law into force, when appointing members of the Commission for the first time, two members of the Commission shall be appointed for a term of three years.

ARTICLE 29. ENTRY INTO FORCE

1. With the exception of paragraphs 2, 3 and 4 of Article 20, this Law shall enter into force on 1 July 2002.

2. Paragraphs 2, 3, and 4 of Article 20 shall enter into force on 1 January 2004.

ARTICLE 30. LAWS REPEALED

1. Upon entry into force of this Law the following laws shall be repealed:

(1) Law of the Republic of Lithuania on Energy (*Official Gazette* 1995, No. 32-743);

(2) Law Amending Article 20 of the Law on Energy (*Official Gazette* 1996, No.32-791);

(3) Law of the Republic of Lithuania on Securing the Interests of the State by Providing Lithuanian Economy with Crude Oil and Petroleum Products

in an Emergency (*Official Gazette* 1997, No. 53-1227);

(4) Law of the Republic of Lithuania Amending Article 15 of the Law on Energy (*Official Gazette* 1997, No. 64-1494);

(5) Law of the Republic of Lithuania Amending Articles 1, 9, 11, 12, 16, 17, 19, 20 and 22 (*Official Gazette* 1997; No. 96-2425);

(6) Law of the Republic of Lithuania Amending Articles 1, 3, 4, 5, 6, 8, 9, 11, 12, 13, 14, 15 and 17 of the Law on Energy (*Official Gazette* 1998, No. 34-899);

(7) Law of the Republic of Lithuania Amending Article 1 of the Law on Energy (*Official Gazette* 1998, No. 103-2837);

(8) Law of the Republic of Lithuania Amending Article 15 of the Law on Energy (*Official Gazette* 1998, No. 105-2899);

(9) Law of the Republic of Lithuania Amending Articles 10 and 14 of the Law on Energy (*Official Gazette* 1999, No. 86-2563);

(10) Law of the Republic of Lithuania Amending Article 17 of the Law on Energy (*Official Gazette* 2000, No. 28-757);

(11) Law of the Republic of Lithuania Amending Article 14 of the Law on Energy (*Official Gazette* 2000, No. 58-1709).

I promulgate this Law passed by the Seimas

President of the Republic
VALDAS ADAMKUS

Netherlands

Act of 2 July 1998 Providing Rules in Relation to the Production, Transmission and Supply of Electricity

(Electricity Act)[including all amendments pursuant to the Gas Act 26463 and the Electricity Production Sector (Transition) Act 27250]

We, Beatrix, by the Grace of God Queen of the Netherlands, Princess of Orange-Nassau, etc. etc. etc.

To all who shall see or have read to them these presents, greetings! Give notice:

As We have considered that it is desirable, in part for the implementation of Directive No. 96/92/EC of the European Parliament and the Council of the European Union of 19 December 1996 concerning community rules for the internal market in electricity (OJEC 1997, L27), to extend the possibilities for the generation, supply, import and export of electricity and for the use of electricity works connected to grids and, for that purpose to introduce new regulations relating to the production, transmission and supply of electricity, taking into consideration the importance of the reliable, sustainable and efficient supply of electricity;

We therefore, having consulted the Council of State, and in general consultation with both Houses of Parliament, have approved and understood as We approve and understand in these presents:

CHAPTER 1. GENERAL PROVISIONS

§1. DEFINITIONS

Section 1

(1) For the purposes of this Act and the provisions based upon it, the following definitions shall apply:

(a) "Our Minister": Our Minister of Economic Affairs;

(b) "connection": one or more connections between a grid and immovable property, as referred to in sections 16 (a) to 16 (d) of the Valuation of Immovable Property Act or, alternatively, between a grid and another grid with a different voltage;

(c) "customer": a natural person or legal entity that has at his disposal a connection to a grid;

(d) "captive customer": a customer that has at his disposal a connection to a grid with:

(i) a total maximum transmission value of more than 3.80 A and an available electrical capacity of no more than 2 MW per connection in the period up to and including 31 December 2001; or

(ii) a total maximum transmission value of 3.80 A in the period up to and including 31 December 2003;

(e) "Director of DTe": the Director of the Office of Energy Regulation [*Dienst uitvoering en toezicht Energie*], referred to in section 5(2);

(f) "supplier": an organizational unit concerned with the supply of electricity;

(g) "producer": an organizational unit concerned with the generation of electricity;

(h) "trader": an organisational unit concerned with entering into agreements for the purchase and sale of electricity;

(i) "grid": one or more connections for the transmission of electricity together with the transformer stations, switching stations, distributing stations and substations belonging to it, excepting in so far as these connections and auxiliary units are located within the installation belonging to a producer or a customer;

(j) "national high-voltage grid": the grid referred to in section 10(1);

(k) "grid manager": a company designated in accordance with sections 10, 13 or 14 to manage one or more grids;

(l) "licence holder": a holder of a supply licence, as referred to in section 54;

(m) "Directive": Directive No. 96/92/EC of the European Parliament and the Council of the European Union of 19 December 1996 concerning community rules for the internal market in electricity (OJEC 1997, L27);

(n) "Notification Directive": Directive No. 98/34/EC of the European Parliament and the Council of the European Union of 22 June 1998 concerning a notification procedure in respect of standards and technical guidelines and rules in relation to services in the information society (OJEC L 204)

(o) "programme responsibility": the responsibility of customers, other than captive customers, and licence holders to draw up plans with regard to the production, transmission, and the use of electricity, or to have such plans drawn up, for the grid managers and to act in accordance with such plans, subject to the conditions referred to in section 31;

(p) "system services": the services provided by the grid manager of the national high-voltage grid to ensure the safe and effective transmission of electricity across all the grids, to solve large-scale disruption in the transmission of electricity and to maintain or restore the balance of energy on all the grids;

(q) "black-start provision": the provision required to power up an electricity generating facility's own energy supply in the event of a power failure on the grid, after which the generation of electricity can be resumed;

(r) "affiliated company": an associated enterprise, in terms of section 41 of the Seventh Directive No. 83/349/EEC of the Council of 13 June 1983, based on section 54(3)(g) of the Treaty, in respect of the consolidated annual reports of an associated enterprise in terms of section 3(3)(1) thereof or an enterprise which belongs to the same shareholders.

(2) For the purposes of applying the provisions of or pursuant to this Act, a customer, other than a captive customer, shall be deemed to be an organisational unit concerned mainly with public transport by underground railway, tram or trolley bus, with mining activities, with the supervision of public lighting or traffic control installations, or, alternatively, with sewerage, water purification or the transport and distribution of water shall be deemed to be a customer, albeit not a captive customer, provided that:

(a) this unit has at its disposal various connections, due solely to the technical nature of its operations;

(b) the total electrical power provided to the unit for its operations amounts to more than 2 MW; and

(c) the operations of this unit are carried out in a physically integrated manner.

(3) The period, in which a consumer, as referred to in section 1(d)(i) and (1)(d)(ii), shall be deemed to be a consumer, may be amended by Ministerial Order.

(4) In deviation from subsection (1), a company, which in the main concerns itself with the transportation of people or goods by train, shall be deemed to be a customer, not a captive customer, even if it is not connected to a grid.

§2. ENERGY REPORT

Section 2

(1) At least once every four years Our Minister shall approve a report providing guidelines for the decisions to be taken by the government in the following four years, in so far as the importance of the reliable, sustainable and efficient supply of electricity must or may be taken into consideration. Our Minister shall involve administrative bodies, institutions and organisations, which in his opinion have the greatest interest in the topics to be dealt with, in the preparation of an Energy Report.

(2) In so far as the Energy Report relates to matters that are the responsibility of Our Minister for Housing, Spatial Planning and the Environment, the report shall be approved only after consultation with the said Minister.

(3) The Energy Report shall include at least:

(a) an analysis of the developments on the national and international energy markets and the effects of these on the reliable, sustainable and efficient operation of the energy economy;

(b) an analysis of changes in the use of energy resources in the generation of electricity and the way in which and the extent to which a sustainable energy economy is developing;

(c) an analysis of the development of market forces in the supply of energy;

(d) a summary of the intended results regarding the promotion of the reliable, sustainable, efficient and environmentally responsible operation of the energy economy and of the ways in which these results are to be achieved in the respective four-year period;

(e) an analysis of other aspects, which may be deemed to be important in relation to energy policy in general.

Section 3

(1) Once the Energy Report has been approved, Our Minister shall give notice of this by submitting the report to the two Houses of Parliament.

(2) Our Minister shall announce the approval of the Energy Report in the *Netherlands Government Gazette*[1] and shall indicate in his announcement how interested parties may take cognisance of the contents of the Energy Report.

Section 4

(1) The Energy Report shall apply with effect from a date to be determined by Order of Our Minister.

(2) The Order shall not be made less than eight weeks after the Energy Report has been presented to the two Houses of Parliament, in accordance with section 3(1).

(3) If within eight weeks of the submission of the Energy Report notice is given by or on behalf of one of the Houses of Parliament that it wishes to hold a public debate on the Energy Report then the Order shall not be issued less than six months after the presentation of the Energy Report or else after the debates, if these are completed at an earlier date.

CHAPTER 2. THE NETHERLANDS ELECTRICITY REGULATORY SERVICE

Section 5

(1) The Office of Energy Regulation[2] (the "DTe") shall be established as a chamber of the Netherlands Competition Authority.[3]

(2) The DTe shall have a Director as its head.

(3) DTe's task shall be to carry out activities relating to the implementation of this Act and to supervise compliance with this Act, with the exception of Chapter 8, Section 1a.

(4) The officers of DTe, appointed by order of the Director of DTe, shall be charged with the supervision of compliance with the provisions of or pursuant to the Act, with the exception of Chapter 8, Section 1a.

(5) Notice of an order, as referred to in section 5(4), shall be given by publication in the *Netherlands Government Gazette.*

(6) The Director of DTe may issue binding instructions in relation to compliance with this Act.

Section 5a

(1) In the event of a contravention of the provisions of or pursuant to sections 5(6), 36 or 37, the Director of the Service may impose an obligation subject to a penalty. The Director of the Service may amend or revoke an obligation that is subject to a penalty.

(2) The purpose of the obligation, subject to a penalty, shall be to reverse the contravention or to prevent further contraventions or repetitions of the contravention.

(3) The decision in which an obligation subject to a penalty is imposed shall at least state:

(a) the substance of the obligation and the period for which this applies;

(b) the legal provision, in respect of which the obligation is imposed;

[1] *Staatscourant*

[2] *Dienst uitvoering en toezicht Energie*

[3] *Nederlandse mededingingsautoriteit*

(c) the legal entity or natural person to whom the obligation applies.

(4) The Director of the Service shall draw up policy rules with regard to the exercising of the powers referred to in subsection (1).

(5) A decision, as referred to in subsection (1), after it has been published, shall be available for inspection at the offices of the Service. Notice of the decision shall be given in the *Netherlands Government Gazette.*[4] Information that may not the published, in accordance with section 10 of the Government Information (Public Access) Act,[5] shall not be available for inspection.

Section 6

(1) The Director of DTe shall carry out the tasks and exercise the powers granted to him under this Act and the Gas Act on the responsibility of Our Minister.

(2) Before Our Minister issues instructions with regard to the exercising of the powers granted to the Director of DTe under this Act and the Gas Act, he shall invite the Director General of the Netherlands Competition Authority to give his opinion on the Minister's intentions.

(3) Our Minister shall lay down as policy rules general instructions to the Director of DTe regarding the exercise of the powers granted to him under this Act and the Gas Act.

(4) These policy rules shall be promulgated by publication in the *Netherlands Government Gazette.*

Section 7

(1) The Director of DTe may demand from a producer, a supplier, a trader or a grid manager any data and information he requires for the performance of the duties assigned to him under this Act and the Gas Act.

(2) A person who is called upon to supply data and information shall be required to provide all cooperation which can reasonably assist the Director of DTe in the exercising of his powers within a reasonable period to be determined by the Director of DTe.

(3) Data and information relating to a producer, a supplier, a trader or a grid manager, which are obtained in connection with any activities for the purpose of implementing this Act, may be used only for the application of this Act or the Gas Act.

Section 8

The Director-General of the Netherlands Competition Authority may issue general and special instructions with regard to the exercising of the duties and powers assigned to the Director of DTe under this Act and the Gas Act if, in the opinion of the Director General, a definition of terms used in the application of the Competition Act[6] may or must be given.

Section 9

(1) The Director of DTe shall report annually by 1 May to Our Minister on DTe's activities in the previous year.

(2) Our Minister shall bring the report together with his findings and the recommendations made to him by the Director of DTe to the notice of the two Houses of Parliament by 1 July of the same year.

CHAPTER 3. TRANSMISSION OF ELECTRICITY

§1. APPOINTMENT OF GRID MANAGERS

Section 10

(1) The national high-voltage grid shall consist of the grids which are intended for the transmission of electricity at a voltage of 220 kV or more and which are operated accordingly, together with the grids that cross the national borders with a voltage of 500 V or more.

(2) The legal entity with a right to use more than half of the circuit length of the national high-voltage grid shall appoint for the management of the grid a private or public limited liability company as the grid manager, after consulting the other legal entities with rights to the use of that grid.

(3) A legal entity with a right to use a grid, other than the national high-voltage grid, shall appoint for the management of that grid one or more other private or public limited liability companies as the grid manager.

[4] *Staatscourant*
[5] *Wet openbaarheid van bestuur*
[6] *Mededingingswet*

(4) Without prejudice to the provisions of sections 14(1) and 14(2), an appointment, as referred to in sections 14(2) and 14(3), shall apply for a period of ten years, commencing on the date on which Our Minister gives his assent to the appointment, in accordance with section 12(2).

Section 11

(1) A producer or a supplier shall not be appointed as a grid manager.

(2) The Articles of Association of the grid manager, other than the grid manager of the national high-voltage grid, shall in any event include:

(a) the appointment of a Supervisory Board;

(b) the provision that the members of the Board of Management and the majority of the members of the Supervisory Board shall not have any direct or indirect affiliation to a producer, a supplier or a shareholder of the grid manager;

(c) the provision that at least the decisions of the Board of Management of the legal entity, as referred to in section 164(1) or 274 (1) of Book 2 of the Netherlands Civil Code, shall be subject to the approval of the Supervisory Board; and

(d) the provision that the shareholders of the grid manager shall refrain from any involvement in the performance of the duties assigned to the grid manager, in accordance with sections 16(1) or 16(2).

Section 11a

(1) Sections 268 up to and including 274 of Book 2 of the Netherlands Civil Code shall apply to the company designated to manage the national high-voltage grid and its Articles of Association shall be drawn up accordingly.

(2) The company, designated to manage the national high-voltage grid, is not permitted to amend its Articles of Association until Our Minister has approved the amendment. Our Minister shall withhold his approval if the Articles of Association, following the amendment, do not comply with this section.

(3) A producer, supplier, trader, legal entity or natural person employed by a producer, supplier or trader, may not hold shares in the company designated as the grid manager of the national high-voltage grid.

(4) A producer, supplier, trader, legal entity or natural person, as referred to in subsection (3), who holds or acquires shares in the company designated as the grid manager of the national high-voltage grid, is obliged to sell such shares in the company and to transfer them to third parties.

(5) Persons other than the company, designated as the grid manager of the national high-voltage grid, are prohibited from acquiring assets which together form part of the national high-voltage grid, or part thereof, and the owner of the national high-voltage grid, or part of thereof, is prohibited from vesting rights to that grid in favour of parties other than the grid manager of the national high-voltage grid, unless Our Minister approves of the acquisition or such vesting of rights. The acquisition of assets and the vesting of rights to these in contravention of the first sentence shall be null and void.

(6) The management and the majority of the Supervisory Board of the company, designated as the manager of the national high-voltage grid, shall have no direct or indirect association with a producer, a supplier, a trader or a shareholder of this company.

(7) A member of the Supervisory Board of the company designated to manage the national high-voltage grid shall not be appointed until the Minister of Economic Affairs has approved the proposed appointment.

(8) Our Minister shall not give his approval in accordance with subsections (3) or (5) until four weeks have passed since both Houses of Parliament were informed of his intention to do so.

Section 12

(1) Immediately on its appointment the grid manager shall inform Our Minister of its name and address and the names and addresses of its shareholders and shall send the Minister a description of the grid that will be managed by it. At least once a year, the grid manager shall inform Our Minister of any changes to the names or addresses and shall send him a description of changes to the grid managed by it.

(2) The appointment shall require the assent of Our Minister. The Minister shall withhold his assent, or may attach conditions to such assent, if section 11 has not been complied with, or if the appointed grid manager is not in a position to comply adequately

with an obligation, as referred to in section 7, to perform a duty, as referred to in sections 16(1) or 16(2), or to comply with a prohibition, as referred to in section 17 or section 18.

(3) If Our Minister attaches conditions to his assent, these shall serve only to eliminate the shortcoming identified, as referred to in subsection (2).

Section 13

(1) If a legal entity, as referred to in sections 10(2) or 10(3) fails to appoint a grid manager within twelve weeks of this section coming into effect, within four weeks of the construction of a grid or else immediately after a previous appointment is withdrawn or lapses, Our Minister shall appoint a private or public limited liability company as the grid manager of that grid.

(2) If Our Minister determines that there has been a failure to comply with section 11 or if Our Minister determines that a grid manager is not or will not be able adequately to perform a duty, as referred to in sections 16(1) or 16(2) or to comply with a prohibition, as referred to in sections 17 and 18, he may instruct the grid manager concerned to make such provisions as the Minister deems necessary.

(3) If the grid manager fails to comply with an instruction, as referred to in subsection (2), Our Minister may substitute the appointment of the grid manager concerned by the appointment of another company as the grid manager.

Section 14

(1) A legal entity, as referred to in sections 10(2) or 10(3), may substitute the appointment of a grid manager with the appointment of another private or public limited liability company as the grid manager, taking into account a reasonable period of notice.

(2) In the event of a merger or a division, or the dissolution or bankruptcy of the company appointed as the grid manager, the appointment as grid manager shall lapse by law and the legal entities referred to in sections 10(1) and 10(2) shall immediately appoint another company as the grid manager. This company may be the same company as that previously appointed as the grid manager.

(3) The legal entities, referred to in sections 10(2) and 10(3), shall appoint a private or public limited liability company as the grid manager for the period immediately following the period referred to in section 10(4). This company may be the same company as that previously appointed as the grid manager.

(4) Sections 10 to 13 shall apply likewise to the appointment of the grid manager, as referred to in subsections (1), (2) or (3).

Section 15

(1) The Order, referred to in section 10(3), shall not apply in so far as this relates to a grid with a maximum voltage of 0.4 kV and a maximum usage of 0.1 GWh per annum, and if a third party other than the supplier of the grid manager is entitled to use that grid.

(2) At the request of a legal entity, as referred to in section 10(3), Our Minister may grant an exemption from the Order, referred to in section 10(3), in so far as this relates to a grid to which a limited number of other natural persons or legal entities, other than the said legal entity, are connected and:

(a) the grid is intended to supply electricity to this legal entity or, alternatively, to support the central operating processes of this legal entity; or

(b) the grid is intended to supply a number of co-operating legal entities with electricity and the co-operation of these legal entities has the aim of bringing about the reliable, sustainable, efficient and environmentally responsible management of energy in their facilities; or

(c) quality standards apply to the grid, which significantly deviate from the conditions laid down by the Director of DTe, in accordance with section 36; or

(d) this legal entity is not a grid manager and is not affiliated to a group of companies with a grid manager and:

(i) it enters into an agreement with the grid manager of the grid to which its grid is connected to ensure that the said grid manager is not obstructed in the performance of his duties; and

(ii) it provides whoever requests such with a connection to the grid in question or, alternatively, it makes an offer to transmit electricity on behalf of the applicant using the said grid, subject to reasonable tariffs and conditions, as well as the regulations referred to in subsection (3).

(3) An exemption may be granted, subject to regulations with regard to the performance of the duties, referred to in sections 16(1), and with regard to the tariffs and other conditions applicable to this.

(4) Our Minister may withdraw an exemption, if the person to whom the exemption has been granted:

(a) no longer satisfies the conditions, referred to in subsection (2);

(b) acts contrary to the regulations, referred to in subsection (3);

(c) on applying for exemption, supplied incorrect or incomplete data and if supplying correct or complete data would have resulted in a different decision in respect of the application.

§2. DUTIES AND OBLIGATIONS OF THE GRID MANAGER

Section 16

(1) Within the framework of the management of the grids in the area assigned to him, in accordance with section 36, the grid manager shall have the duty:

(a) to ensure the operation and maintenance of the grids managed by him;

(b) to ensure, in the most effective manner, the safety and reliability of the grids and of the transmission of electricity across the grids;

(c) to construct, repair, replace or extend the grids;

(d) to maintain sufficient reserve capacity for the transmission of electricity;

(e) to provide third parties with a connection to the grids and to make a meter available to them, at their request, in accordance with section 23;

(f) to carry out the transmission of electricity on behalf of third parties, in accordance with section 24;

(g) to promote the safe use of appliances and installations that consume electricity;

(h) to measure the quantity of electricity generated in the manner referred to in section 53(2)(e), input into the grid by a producer, and to provide the producer with this data.

(2) In addition to the duties referred to in subsection (1), the manager of the national high-voltage grid shall also have the duty:

(a) to make such technical provisions and carry out such system services as are necessary to guarantee the transmission of electricity over all grids in a safe and efficient manner;

(b) to use the technical facilities and system services, referred to under (a), also for the benefit of the other grid managers;

(c) in accordance with subsection (7) of this chapter, to carry out the transmission of electricity on behalf of third parties by using the national high-voltage grid, to export such electricity from the Netherlands to customers or suppliers abroad or, alternatively, to import such electricity from abroad for customers or suppliers in the Netherlands;

(d) to take measures to ensure the security of supply of electricity;

(e) to bring about or maintain a market with the purpose of bringing together the supply of and demand for electricity, if Our Minister should decide to do so, in accordance with the conditions, referred to in section 31, and subject to regulations to be determined by Ministerial Order.

(3) It is prohibited for any person other than the respective grid manager to perform a duty, as referred to in subsections (1) or (2), except in so far as this relates to the construction of a grid that extends beyond the national borders, as referred to in subsection (6), or the construction, management and maintenance of a grid, as referred to in section 15(2) or, alternatively the implementation of a procedure, as referred to in section 20(3).

(4) Producers, suppliers, traders and shareholders shall refrain from any interference with the performance of the duties with which a grid manager is charged, in accordance with subsection (1) and (2).

(5) Subject to retention by the grid manager of his responsibility for the full and proper performance of his duties in respect of the management of the grids, the duties, as referred to in subsections (1)(a) and (1)(c), may be carried out by a legal entity that is not appointed as a grid manager.

(6) If a third party other than the grid manager of the national high-voltage grid has constructed a

grid that extends beyond the national borders, the grid manager of the national high-voltage grid shall be charged with the management of the said grid, subject to the provisions of or pursuant to this Act. If a third party other than the grid manager of the national high-voltage grid is entitled to use a grid that is part of the national highvoltage grid, in accordance with section 10(1), he shall be obliged to give the grid manager of the national high-voltage grid his full co-operation so that the grid manager can carry out his duties, in accordance with subsections (1) and (2).

Section 17

The grid manager, or a legal entity in which the grid manager has a participating interest, as referred to in section 24(c) of Book 2 of the Netherlands Civil Code, may not supply goods or services resulting in competition between them and third parties, unless this relates to carrying out activities in respect of:

(a) the performance of the duties referred to in sections 16(1) and 16(2), either for himself or for other grid managers, or on behalf of third parties entitled to use a grid;

(b) the construction, management or maintenance of cables and pipelines outside of buildings for the transmission of gas, heat, cold or water; or

(c) the provision and maintenance of grids for the use of related services by third parties.

Section 18

(1) If a group company, as referred to in section 24(b) of Book 2 of the Netherlands Civil Code, affiliated to the grid manager in a group, carries out activities which the grid manager may not himself carry out, in accordance with section 17, the grid manager or a legal entity in which the grid manager has a participating interest, as referred to in section 17, may not give such a group company preferential treatment over others with which the said group company is in competition or grant to the said group company any other privileges beyond those that are customary in normal business practice.

(2) The following shall in any event be regarded as treatment preferential to a group company, as referred to in subsection (1), or as granting privileges beyond those that are customary in normal business practice:

(a) supplying a group company with data relating to customers, other than captive customers, who have submitted an application, as referred to in sections 23 or 24;

(b) supplying goods or services to a group company for a consideration which is lower than the costs which may reasonably be attributed to such goods or services; or

(c) permitting the use by a group company of the name and logo of the grid manager in such a way that there is a danger of creating public confusion with regard to the origin of goods or services.

(3) The grid manager shall include with its annual accounts a statement to the effect that the financial relationships between the grid manager and the group companies, referred to in subsection (1), comply with the provisions of subsection (1). The grid manager shall make a copy of its annual accounts, the accompanying notes and the accompanying statement available for inspection by the public in each of its offices and shall send a copy thereof to the Director of DTe.

Section 19

The grid manager shall use the data issued to him in relation to captive customers solely for carrying out the duties assigned to the grid manager under this Act, on the understanding that such data may also be used to collect payments on behalf of the licence holder for the supply of electricity.

§3. CONSTRUCTION, REPAIR, EXTENSION OR REPLACEMENT OF GRIDS

Section 20

(1) A grid that has been or is being constructed, repaired, replaced or extended by a grid manager in an area assigned to it, in accordance with sections 31(1)(d) and 36, shall be deemed to be a public utility for the purposes of the Public Works (Removal of Impediments in Bye-Laws) Act and the Public Works (Removal of Impediments in Private Law) Act.

(2) Rules governing the manner in which consideration shall be given to the construction of a grid or the laying of pipelines or cables for the transmission of gas or heat may be determined by General

Administrative Order in relation to areas to be allocated, with due regard to the importance of the reliable, sustainable and efficient supply of energy.

(3) The measures, referred to in subsection (2), may entail that a grid may only be constructed and a licence, as referred to in section 24, may only be issued as the outcome of a public procedure in which interested parties may submit tenders for the contract and submit offers for the construction of a grid or the laying of pipelines or cables for the transmission of gas or heat.

Section 21

(1) Once every two years the grid manager shall provide the Director of DTe with the most accurate possible estimates of the total capacity required for the transmission of electricity over the grids managed by him for each of the first seven years after the year in which the estimates are made. In doing so, the grid manager shall also state the assumptions on which these estimates are based and shall make any distinctions deemed important.

(2) At the same time the grid manager shall provide an explanation, on the basis of these estimates, of the way in which he will provide for the total capacity required for the transmission of electricity over the grids managed by him in the first seven years after the year in which the estimates are made.

(3) Further rules regarding the content of the data to be provided in accordance with subsections of (1) and (2) shall be determined in by Ministerial Order.

Section 22

(1) If, in the opinion of the Director of DTe, it appears from the data, referred to in section 21, or by other means that a grid manager is not or will not be able to provide for the total capacity required for the transmission of electricity over the grids managed by him efficiently or in sufficient quantities, he shall notify Our Minister of this after consultation with the manager of the national high-voltage grid and the manager of the grid in question.

(2) Once he has received such notification, Our Minister may order the grid manager in question to take measures to ensure that the transmission of electricity is carried out in sufficient quantities or in an efficient manner in compliance with the provisions of or pursuant to this Act.

(3) Our Minister is authorised to impose administrative penalties to enforce the order referred to in subsection (2).

§4. CONNECTION TO THE GRID AND THE TRANSMISSION OF ELECTRICITY

Section 23

(1) The grid manager shall be required to provide any person who requests such with a connection to the grid managed by him at tariffs and subject to other conditions, in accordance with the provisions of paragraphs 5 and 6 of this chapter.

(2) The grid manager shall refrain from any form of discrimination in relation to those to whom he has an obligation, as referred to in subsection (1).

Section 24

(1) The grid manager shall be required to make an offer to any person who requests such in relation to the transmission of electricity, making use of the grid managed by him, and at tariffs and subject to conditions, in accordance with paragraphs 5 and 6 of this chapter.

(2) The requirement, referred to subsection (1) shall not apply in so far as the grid manager within reason has no capacity available for the transmission requested.

(3) The grid manager shall refrain from any form of discrimination in relation to those to whom he has an obligation, as referred to in subsection (1).

Section 25 expired

Section 26

(1) The Director of DTe may decide, if requested, that capacity for the transmission of electricity shall be allocated with priority to applicants designated by him for the transmission of a certain quantity of electricity, to be decided by him, and for a period, to be decided by him, if:

(a) the application relates to a grid that extends beyond the national borders, as referred to in section 16 (6); or

(b) the reserving of capacity for the transmission of electricity contributes to the proper functioning of the electricity market.

(2) In taking a decision, as referred to in subsection (1), the Director of DTe may stipulate conditions and tariffs for the transmission of electricity that deviate from the conditions and tariffs determined in accordance with sections 36 and 41.

(3) The Director of DTe shall take a decision, as referred to in the subsection (1) and subsection (1)(a), taking into consideration the importance of the economically sound construction and operation of grids extending beyond the national borders, the importance of access by third parties to the respective grids extending beyond the national borders and the importance of promoting cross-border trade.

(4) The decision, referred to in subsection (1) may not result in limitations on the capacity that the grid manager of the national high-voltage grid reserves for the essential transmission of electricity within the framework of mutual assistance and support with a view to maintaining the integrity of the grids or the capacity designated, in accordance with section 13 of the Electricity Production Sector (Transition) Act.

(5) A decision, as referred to in subsection (1), shall be published in the *Netherlands Government Gazette.*

Section 26a

(1) Grid managers shall apply conditions that are reasonable, objective and non-discriminatory.

(2) Conditions, as referred to in Articles 236 and 237 of Book 6 of the Netherlands Civil Code shall be deemed to be unreasonable.

(3) Conditions shall be deemed to be reasonable if this is shown by the nature or content of the condition or process by which the condition in question came into existence.

§5. TARIFF STRUCTURES AND CONDITIONS

Section 27

The grid managers shall send to the Director of DTe a joint proposal in relation to the tariff structures, which describes the manner in which the components and the method of calculating the tariff for connecting customers to a grid, the tariff for transmitting electricity on behalf of customers, including the import, export and forwarding of electricity, and the tariff applicable to the system services and the energy balance.

Section 28

(1) The tariff, at which customers shall be connected to a grid, shall relate exclusively to:

(a) breaking the grid of the respective grid manager to connect the customer's installation to the said grid;

(b) the installation of facilities to secure the grid of the respective grid manager and to ensure its continued security; and

(c) bringing about and maintaining a connection between the place at which the grid has been broken and the grid's security facility.

(2) The tariff, as referred to in subsection (1), shall be charged to every customer connected by a grid manager to a grid managed by a grid manager.

Section 29

(1) The tariff, at which the transmission of electricity shall be carried out on behalf of customers, shall relate to the receipt of electricity by the customer, irrespective of the location at which the electricity is generated and the connection at which the electricity enters the Dutch grid, or to the input of electricity by the customer, irrespective of the location at which the electricity is received.

(2) The tariff, as referred to in subsection (1), shall be charged to every customer connected by a grid manager to a grid managed by a grid manager.

(3) Our Minister shall determine the tariff base for the element of the tariff not related to transmission, as referred to in subsection (1), before 1 July 1999. The element of the tariff not related to transmission, as referred to in subsection (1), shall be expressed as an amount in guilders.

(4) In addition to the provisions of or in accordance with subsections (1), (2) and (3), regulations may be determined by General Administrative Order with regard to the tariff at which the transmission of electricity shall be carried out on behalf of customers, designated in the Order, or, alternatively, for the transmission of electricity, as described therein.

(5) The tariff, referred to in subsection (1) shall serve *inter alia* to cover the cost of obligations entered into by the designated company prior to the repeal of the Electricity Act of 1989 for the

construction of a connection for the transmission of electricity between the Netherlands and Norway.

Section 30

(1) The tariff for the carrying out of system services relates to:

(a) the reserve and control power;

(b) the black-start provision; and

(c) the other system services.

(2) The tariff, as referred to in subsection (1), shall be charged to every customer connected by a grid manager to a grid managed by a grid manager.

(3) The tariff, referred to in subsection (1), shall be expressed as an amount per unit of electricity generated or, alternatively, consumed, measured in kWh.

(4) It may be decided by General Administrative Order that the tariff, referred to in subsection (1), shall be charged to the customer, referred to in subsection (2), and to every customer who generates and inputs into the grid a quantity of electricity or, alternatively, uses a quantity of electricity at his own facility. In this case, the tariff shall be expressed as an amount per unit of electricity generated or, alternatively, consumed, measured in kWh.

Section 31

(1) The grid managers jointly shall send to the Director of DTe a proposal with regard to the conditions applicable to:

(a) the relationship between grid managers, and between grid managers and customers, in relation to the operation of the grids, the provision of a connection to the grid and the transmission of electricity across the grid;

(b) the relationship between grid managers, and between grid managers and customers, in relation to the measurement of data with regard to the transmission of electricity and the exchange of measurement data;

(c) the relationship between the grid manager of the national high-voltage grid, on the one hand, and customers and other grid managers, on the other hand, with regard to system services;

(d) the allocation of areas to grid managers;

(e) arrangements in relation to the co-operation between the grid managers with regard to the carrying out of duties, as referred to in sections 36(1)(a), 36(1)(b) and 36(1)(c), as well as with regard to ensuring the grid management of all grids and the transmission of electricity in exceptional circumstances;

(f) the quality criteria to be met by grid managers in respect of their services, which shall include, in any event, compliance with the technical specifications, eliminating disruptions to the transmission of electricity, customer service and providing compensation in the case of serious disruptions.

(2) In any event, the conditions applicable to programme responsibility shall be included in the conditions, referred to in subsection (1)(c), and shall include the provision that programme responsibility may be transferred to another natural person or legal entity, with the exception of the grid manager.

(3) The conditions, referred to in subsection (1)(a) shall in any event included a scheme for determining the capacity for transmitting electricity through cross-border grids and for allocating available capacity on these grids, which shall also include the auctioning of capacity or, alternatively, the allocation of capacity by some other method in line with the market, and the allocation of capacity that a customer does not use. The conditions include provisions necessary with a view to preventing obstacles to the proper operation of market forces.

(4) The capacity that may be allocated by means of an auction or another method in line with the market is subject to a maximum of the total capacity for the transmission of electricity through cross-border grids, after the deduction of:

(a) the capacity reserved by the grid manager of the national high-voltage grid to carry out the essential transmission of electricity within the framework of mutual assistance and support with a view to maintaining the integrity of the grids;

(b) the capacity allocated in accordance with section 13 of the Electricity Production Sector (Transition) Act; and

(c) the capacity that the Director of the Service has allocated to certain applicants for the transmission of electricity, in accordance with section 26.

(5) The grid manager of the national high-voltage grid shall use the proceeds of the auction or another method of allocating capacity in line with the market and in accordance with the scheme, referred to in subsection (3), to remove limitations to the transmission capacity of cross-border grids or, alternatively, for other purposes to be determined by the Director of the Service.

(6) The grid manager of the national high-voltage grid shall keep separate accounts for the proceeds of the auction or the allocation of capacity by another method in line with the market. Section 43 shall apply *mutates mutandis.*

(7) Our Minister, supplementary to the conditions referred to in subsection (1)(b), may determine further rules with regard to the measurement and the provision of data, as referred to in section 16(1)(h), which may stipulate that the data may be issued to parties other than the producers of the electricity referred to therein.

Section 31a

(1) It is prohibited for a customer, supplier or trader, whether or not indirectly or subject to conditions, to have at his disposal transmission capacity on the cross-border grid in excess of 400 MW.

(2) Having transmission capacity at one's disposal, as referred to in subsection (1), shall be understood to mean that the transmission capacity shall be at the disposal of the customer, supplier or trader himself or, alternatively, together with others, who as part of the group, in terms of section 24b of Book 2 of the Netherlands Civil Code, act on behalf of the customer, supplier or trader, who, in terms of section 24c of Book 2 of the Netherlands Civil Code, have a participating interest in the customer, supplier or trader, or who are affiliated to the customer, supplier or trader in any other manner.

(3) With a view to the performance of the agreements, referred to in section 2 of the Electricity Production Sector (Transition) Act, at the request of the production companies, referred to in the said section, Our Minister may determine that the transmission capacity shall be allocated in a manner that deviates from subsections (1) and (2), provided the total transmission capacity on the national high-voltage grid in favour of production companies does not exceed 1600 MW. Our Minister may stipulate that the allocation, referred to in the first sentence, shall be subject to regulations.

(4) On the basis of a proposal made by the Director of thc Scrvicc, Our Minister may amend the quantity of 400 MW, referred to in subsection (1), if the development of the electricity market gives cause for this.

(5) Chapters 6, 7, 8, with the exception of paragraphs 2, 9, 11 and 12 of the Competition Act, shall apply *mutates mutandis* in the event of contraventions of this section.

Section 32

(1) The grid manager of the national high-voltage grid, or at least one-third of the other grid managers, may request the grid managers to submit a joint proposal to amend the tariff structures or the conditions, as referred to in sections 27 and 31, together with a statement of the reasons why, in their opinion, such an amendment is necessary.

(2) If an amendment of the tariff structures or the conditions, as referred to in sections 27 and section 31, is deemed necessary, in the opinion of the Director of DTe, he shall send a draft decision amending the tariff structures or the conditions to all the grid managers jointly.

(3) A proposal or a draft decision amending the tariff structures or the conditions shall include the items, as referred to in sections 27 or 31, whose amendment has been requested.

Section 33

(1) The grid managers shall jointly hold consultations with organisations representing parties on the electricity market with regard to proposals in respect of the tariff structures and conditions, as referred to in sections 27, 31 and 32(1).

(2) In the proposals sent to the Director of DTe, the grid managers shall provide a joint statement of the conclusions they attach to the views raised by the organisations, referred to in subsection (1).

Section 34

(1) On the first occasion, after this section comes into effect, the grid managers shall send their joint proposals with regard to the tariff structures and conditions, referred to in sections 27 and 31, to the

Director of Dte within four weeks following the date on which this section takes effect.

(2) The grid managers shall send a joint proposal with regard to amendments to the tariff structures and conditions to the Director of DTe within 12 weeks after the date on which a request is made, as referred to in section 32(1).

(3) The grid managers jointly shall inform the Director of DTe of their views with regard to a draft decision amending the tariff structures or the conditions within twelve weeks following the date on which the draft decision was sent to them, in accordance with section 32(2).

Section 35

If a proposal, as referred to in sections 27, 31 or 32(1), is not sent to the Director of DTe within the period, referred to in section 34(2), every grid manager shall be entitled to send him a proposal with regard to the tariff structures or conditions within four weeks after the date on which this period expires.

Section 36

(1) The Director of DTe shall determine the tariff structures and conditions, taking into consideration:

(a) the joint proposal submitted by the grid managers, as referred to in sections 27, 31 or 32, and the results of the consultations, referred to in section 33(1);

(b) the importance of the reliable, sustainable, efficient and environmentally responsible supply of electricity;

(c) the importance of promoting the development of trade on the electricity market;

(d) the importance of promoting efficiency amongst customers; and

(e) the importance of good quality service provision by grid managers.

(2) The Director of DTe shall not approve the conditions until, subject to section 7(2) of the Directive, he has ascertained that the conditions will guarantee the interoperability of the grids and that they are objective and not discriminatory and, insofar as this is necessary in accordance with the Notification Directive, that the Commission of the European Community has been informed of the conditions in their draft form and that the applicable periods, referred to in section 9 of the Notification Directive, have expired.

(3) If a proposal, as referred to in sections 27, 31 or 32, is in conflict with the interests, referred to in subsections (1)(b), (1)(c), (1)(d) or (1)(e), in the opinion of the Director of DTe, the Director of DTe shall instruct the grid managers jointly to amend the proposal in such a manner that this conflict is eliminated. Section 4(15) of the General Administrative Law Act shall apply *mutatis mutandis.*

(4) If the grid managers do not amend the proposal jointly within four weeks, on the instructions of the Director of DTe, as referred to in subsection (3), the Director of DTe shall determine the tariff structures or the conditions, after amending these in such a manner that they accord with the interests, referred to in subsections (1)(b) to (1)(e), and with the requirements, referred to in subsection (2).

Section 37

(1) After the period, referred to in section 35, has expired, the Director of DTe shall determine the tariff structures and conditions, taking into consideration the proposals of the grid managers and subject to sections 36(1) and 36(2). If a proposal, as referred to in section 35, has not been sent to the Director of DTe within the specified period, he shall determine the tariff structures or the conditions of his own accord, subject to sections 36(1) and 36(2).

(2) If the grid managers do not inform the Director of DTe jointly of their view of a draft decision, as referred to in section 34(3), within the period referred to in section 34(3), he shall determine the tariff structures or the conditions of his own accord, subject to sections 36(1) and 36(2).

Section 38

(1) The tariff structures and the conditions shall take effect on a date to be determined by the Director of DTe and shall apply for an indefinite period.

(2) Notice shall be given of decisions with regard to the determining of the tariff structures and conditions, as well as amendments thereto, by publication of these decisions in the *Netherlands Government Gazette*;

(3) Every grid manager shall have a copy of the tariff structures and conditions available for inspection by third parties at its offices.

(4) After the conditions have been determined, these shall apply as the minimum requirements for the technical design and operation of installations and grids, as referred to in section 7(2) of the Directive.

Section 39

(1) Grid managers shall send the Director of DTe a report on their compliance with the quality criteria, as referred to in section 31(1)(f), before 1 November of each year.

(2) The Director of DTe shall announce the findings that he derives from reports, as referred to in subsection (1), in the report, referred to in section 9.

§6. TARIFFS AND ACCOUNTS OF THE GRID MANAGER

Section 40

(1) Taking into consideration the tariff structures, determined in accordance with section 36, and in accordance with section 41, every grid manager shall send to the Director of DTe before 1 October a proposal with regard to the maximum tariffs that the said grid manager may charge for a connection to a grid, or for the transmission of electricity or, alternatively, if this relates to the grid manager of the national high-voltage grid, in addition a proposal for the carrying out of system services and the maintenance of the energy balance.

(2) A proposal, as referred to in subsection (1), may also relate to an exceptional and notable investment in the expansion of the grids managed by the grid manager in question.

Section 41

The Director of DTe shall determine the tariffs, which may differ in the case of the various grid managers, taking into consideration the importance of promoting efficient operations and cost reductions to the advantage of customers and by means of market forces and, in doing so, shall apply the following formula:

$$p_t = \left(1 + \frac{cpi - x_t}{100}\right) p_{t-1}, \text{ where:}$$

p_t = the tariffs that will apply in the period t;
p_{t-1} = the tariffs that applied in the period preceding t;
cpi = the relative changes in the consumer price index (for all households), calculated using the quotient of this price index, published in the fourth month prior to the period t, and this price index, published in the sixteenth month prior to period t; as determined on a monthly basis by the Central Bureau of Statistics;
x_t = the discount to promote efficiency in the business operations of grid managers.

(2) The Director of DTe shall determine the discount to promote efficient operations for a minimum period of three years and a maximum period of five years.

(3) The Director of DTe shall consult with the grid managers jointly and with organisations representing parties on the electricity market with regard to the determination of the discount to promote efficient operations and, in the decision in which the discount is determined, he shall indicate the findings that he derived from the results of these consultations.

(4) If a proposal is not sent to the Director of DTe within the period, referred to in section 40, he shall determine the tariffs for the respective grid manager of his own accord, subject to subsection (1).

Section 42

(1) The tariffs shall take effect on a date to be decided by the Director of DTe and shall apply until 1 January of the year, following the date on which the decision takes effect, in which the tariffs are set.

(2) If the tariffs for the following year have not been determined on 1 January, the tariffs shall apply up until the date on which the decision comes into effect, in which the tariffs are set for the following year.

(3) Every grid manager shall have available at his offices for inspection by the public a copy of the tariffs applicable in his case.

Section 43

(1) A grid manager shall be obliged to keep separate accounts in respect of the management of the grids, in accordance with his duties, as referred to in section 16. If the grid manager carries out activities, as referred to in section 17, he shall keep separate accounts, whether or not on a consolidated basis.

(2) The separate accounts shall include:

(a) a balance sheet and a profit-and-loss account;

(b) a specification of the allocation of assets and liabilities, and income and expenditure, as referred to in subsection (1), in which, in particular, the costs, income and quantities of at least the functions, referred to in section 27 to section 30, shall be stated; and

(c) an explanation of the policies applied in relation to depreciation.

(3) The grid manager shall state in the accounts the methods and criteria applied in drawing up the accounts.

(4) The allocation of costs to activities, as referred to in subsection (1), shall be carried out on the basis of the *de facto* use of financial and other resources for these activities.

(5) Changes to the policies for depreciation, referred to in subsection (2), shall be reported in the accounts together with the reasons for these changes.

(6) In the notes to the annual accounts, each affiliated company with which a grid manager has entered into a contract, the income or costs of which exceed an amount of NLG 10 million, shall be reported. In addition, the number of contracts per company shall be reported.

(7) If a grid manager is not already required, in accordance with a legal obligation, to publish its annual accounts or an equivalent financial statement, it shall make these annual accounts or this financial statement available for inspection by the public at its head office.

§7. IMPORT AND EXPORT OF ELECTRICITY

Section 44

(1) Once every three months, as well as in response to a request to that effect, the grid manager of the national high-voltage grid shall report to Our Minister all the requests it has received for the transmission of electricity from another country to the Netherlands or from the Netherlands to another country.

(2) More detailed rules relating to the reporting, referred to in subsection (1), shall be set out in a Ministerial Order.

Section 45

(1) The grid manager of the national high-voltage grid shall be obliged to make an offer to transmit electricity from another country to a customer, who will use the electricity in question himself, if the customer requests this, or, alternatively, to a supplier who requests this on behalf of the customer, if:

(a) this customer consumes more electricity than the quantity stipulated in a Ministerial Order; and

(b) this customer, assuming that he is domiciled in the other country, may be deemed to qualify as a customer, as referred to in section 19(3) of the Directive, in accordance with the law of that country.

(2) The grid manager of the national high-voltage grid shall be obliged to make an offer for the transmission of electricity from another country to a supplier, if the supplier requests this, if this supplier is a licence holder and if the supplier may be deemed to quality as a supplier, as referred to in section 19(3) of the Directive, in accordance with the law of that country.

(3) The grid manager of the national high-voltage grid shall be obliged to make an offer to transmit electricity if, in accordance with section 48, an exemption has been granted for the transmission of the electricity requested or, the Commission of the European Community has obliged the grid manager to carry out the transmission of electricity requested, in accordance with section 19(5)(b) of the Directive.

(4) Customers, and suppliers, agreements or countries, to which subsection (1) or subsection (2) apply, shall be designated by Ministerial Order.

(5) If the other country is not a Member State of the European Union, a qualified customer shall be understood to be a customer or supplier who, in accordance with the law of that country, is entitled to import electricity from another country.

Section 46

If the customer or the supplier, as referred to in section 45(1) and section 45(2), in respect of whom it has not been determined by Ministerial Order, as referred to in section 45(4), that section 45(1) shall apply, may not be deemed to be a qualified customer, as referred to in section 19(3) of the Directive, in the other country, the grid manager of the national high-voltage grid shall be prohibited from making an offer to transmit electricity from that country to the customer or supplier in question. This prohibition shall not apply in the cases referred to in section 45(3).

Section 47

(1) A customer or supplier, who requests electricity to be transmitted, as referred to in section 45(1) or section 45(2), shall provide the grid manager with such information as he requires to assess whether or not, and to what extent, the customer or supplier domiciled in the Netherlands may be deemed to be a qualified customer, in accordance with the law of the other country. In any event, he shall state the country in which the electricity in question was generated and, in so far as this relates to the customer, referred to in section 45(1), the amount of electricity that the customer consumes annually.

(2) The grid manager of the national high-voltage grid shall use the data and all other information, referred to in section 19(4) of the Directive, in making his assessment, referred to in subsection (1).

Section 48

(1) Our Minister may grant exemption from the prohibition, referred to in section 46, at the request of a customer or a supplier, if there is reason to believe that the transmission of electricity in question shall not result in disturbance of the equilibrium on the electricity markets, taking into account the data that the applicant is required to provide, as stipulated by Ministerial Order.

(2) In his assessment of an application for exemption, Our Minister shall take into account whether a prohibition on carrying out the transmission of electricity in question is necessary and proportionate in the light of the aim thereof, and whether the prohibition would affect the development of trade to an extent that would conflict with the interests of the Community, as referred to in section 3(3) of the Directive.

(3) Our Minister may revoke an exemption, if the person to whom the exemption was granted submitted incorrect or incomplete data in applying for an exemption and the submission of correct or complete data would have resulted in a different decision in relation to the application.

Section 49

A customer or supplier, whose transaction, as referred to in of section 19(5)(b) of the Directive, is refused, may petition Our Minister to exercise his powers, as referred to in the same subsection of the Directive.

Section 50

(1) If it should transpire that the person who has made a request, as referred to in section 45(1) or section 45(2), in doing so provided the grid manager of the national high-voltage grid with incorrect or incomplete data and this grid manager would not have made an offer for the transmission in question, in accordance with section 46, if he had been provided with the correct and complete data, the grid manager of the national high-voltage grid shall cease the transmission of electricity carried out on behalf of the applicant and shall declare the agreement in respect of this transmission to be void.

(2) If the grid manager of the national high-voltage grid has declared an agreement to be void, in accordance with subsection (1), the person who requests the transmission in question, on submitting a new request, as referred to in section 45(1) or section 45(2), shall be required to include declarations from the customer or the supplier, stating that the electricity to be transmitted is intended for him, and from the producer, stating that the electricity to be transmitted shall be generated by him.

(3) Subsection (2) shall apply *mutatis mutandis*, if the grid manager of the national high-voltage grid becomes aware of the incorrectness or incompleteness of the data after he has fulfilled his obligation under the contract for the transmission of electricity and after the grid manager has informed the person who requested the transmission of electricity in question or, alternatively, if Our Minister has revoked an exemption, as referred to in section 48.

(4) If subsection (2) is applicable, the grid manager of the national high-voltage grid shall not make an offer for the transmission of electricity, as referred to in section 45(1) or section 45(2), until he has received the written declarations.

§8. SETTLEMENT OF DISPUTES

Section 51

Disputes, as referred to in section 20(3) of the Directive, shall be settled, in accordance with the Competition Act, by the Director-General of the Netherlands Competition Authority, as referred to in section 2 of that Act.

Section 52

In the event of a dispute in relation to electricity transmission within the framework of an agreement which extends across national borders, the Director-General shall not be competent to deal with the dispute, in so far as the grid manager of a grid located in another Member State of the European Union refuses to carry out the said transmission or sets tariffs and conditions for the said transmission of electricity to which the applicant does not agree.

CHAPTER 4. SUPPLY OF ELECTRICITY

§1. SUPPLY LICENCE

Section 53

(1) Supplying electricity without a licence to captive customers is prohibited.

(2) This prohibition shall not apply to the supply of electricity:

(a) if the electricity is generated by an installation, which is operated for the account and risk of the captive customer, whether alone or, for a proportional share, together with other captive customers, and the captive customer consumes the electricity supplied;

(b) by a supplier established outside of the Netherlands who supplies electricity to no more than 500 captive customers, as referred to in section 1(1)(d)(ii), who reside in areas adjacent to the national border of the Netherlands;

(c) for supply purposes, as referred to in section 20(1)(i) of the Directive, if the customer is part of the same legal entity as the producer that generates the electricity or is a subsidiary thereof, as referred to in section 24(a) of Book 2 of the Netherlands Civil Code, and the customer consumes the electricity supplied; or

(d) if the electricity is provided, other than commercially, in accordance with rules to be determined by Ministerial Order.

(e) generated by a hydroelectric power station for the generation of electricity with a voltage of less than 15 MW, an installation for the generation of electricity by means of wind energy or solar energy, or an installation in which biomass is processed thermally without additional burning or the addition of synthetic substances and is converted into electricity.

Section 54

(1) On request, Our Minister shall grant a supply licence if the applicant demonstrates satisfactorily that adequate provision has been made to meet the obligation to supply electricity to captive customers, as referred to in section 56(1).

(2) Such provisions shall be understood to include the conditions stipulated by the applicant in relation to the supply of electricity to captive customers and the treatment of complaints in respect of such supply.

(3) The conditions, referred to in subsection (2), shall also include the quality criteria to which licence holders must adhere in providing their services. These criteria shall relate, in any event, to compliance with technical specifications, eliminating disruptions to the supply of electricity, customer service and providing compensation in the event of serious disruptions.

(4) Section 39 shall apply *mutatis mutandis* to licence holders.

Section 55

(1) A supply licence shall be valid up to and including 31 December 2006 or, alternatively, until the date on which the amended period, as referred to in section 1(3), expires.

(2) The supply licence shall indicate the area in which the licence holder may supply electricity to captive customers.

(3) A supply licence may be amended if the institution of a procedure, as referred to in section 20(3), gives cause for the issuing of a new supply licence.

(4) To guarantee the interests served by this Act and, in particular, the interest of captive customers to be assured of the supply of electricity, subject to reasonable conditions, Our Minister may attach conditions to a supply licence and amend such conditions.

§2. TARIFFS AND THE OBLIGATION TO SUPPLY ELECTRICITY

Section 56

(1) The licence holder shall be obliged to supply electricity within the area for which the supply licence is granted to every captive customer domiciled in that area and who requests such, at a tariff set in accordance with the provisions of section 58 and subject to paragraph 3 of this chapter.

(2) Subsection (1) shall not apply if the licence holder cannot reasonably be required to supply electricity to the captive customer in question.

Section 57

(1) Subject to subsection (2) and with due regard to section 58, each licence holder shall send Our Minister a proposal with regard to the maximum tariffs that the said licence holder may charge captive customers for the supply of electricity, to whom this licence holder is obliged to supply electricity, in accordance with section 56(1).

(2) Our Minister shall determine the tariff base for the supply-related component of the tariffs, as referred to in subsection (1), before 1 July 1999. The component of the tariffs not related to supply, referred to in subsection (1), shall be expressed as an amount in guilders

(3) The proposal, referred to in subsection (1), may comprise tariffs that differ for each time unit and for each consumption pattern.

Section 58

(1) The tariffs, as referred to in section 57(1), shall be determined by Our Minister with due regard to:

(a) the importance of the reliable, sustainable, efficient and environmentally responsible supply of electricity, including the importance of promoting efficient business operations and cost reductions in favour of customers by means of market forces, and the importance of ensuring that captive customers are guaranteed a supply of electricity subject to reasonable conditions, in particular, as a result of the effect of the efficient management of their businesses by licence holders, which partly entails the procurement of electricity and energy sources for generating electricity; and

(b) the formula $p_t = (1 + \frac{cpi - x_t}{100}) p_{t-1}$, where:

p_t = the tariffs that will apply in the period t;

p_{t-1} = the tariffs that applied in the period preceding t;

cpi = the relative changes in the consumer price index (for all households), calculated using the quotient of this price index, published in the fourth month prior to the period t, and this price index, published in the sixteenth month prior to period t, as determined on a monthly basis by the Central Bureau of Statistics;

x_t = the discount to promote efficiency in the business operations of licence holders, in so far as this relates to the procurement of electricity and the services in relation to the supply of electricity.

(2) Our Minister shall determine the discount to promote efficient operations for a minimum period of three years and a maximum period of five years, on the understanding that he may adjust the discount at most four times in each calendar year if the *de facto* development of electricity procurement prices on that part of the market comprised by customers, other than captive customers, gives cause for this.

(3) The Director of DTe shall consult with the licence holders and with organisations representing captive customers with regard to the determination of the discount to promote efficient operations. In the decision in which the discount is determined, Our Minister shall state the conclusions that he drew from the results of these consultations.

(4) If a proposal is not sent to Our Minister within the period, referred to in section 57(1), he shall determine the tariff of his own accord, after taking into consideration subsection (1) and subsection (2).

Section 59

(1) The tariffs shall take effect on a date to be decided by Our Minister and shall apply until 1 January of the year following the date on which the decision, in which the tariffs are determined, takes effect.

(2) If the tariffs for the following year have not been determined on 1 January, the tariffs shall apply up until the date on which the decision, in which the tariffs are determined for the following year, comes into effect.

(3) Every licence holder shall have available for inspection by the public at his offices a copy of the tariffs applicable in his case, as referred to in section 58.

(4) Every licence holder shall have available for inspection by the public at his offices a copy of the tariff structures, conditions and tariffs, determined in accordance with section 56 and section 41, applicable to the grid managers which manage grids in the area for which the supply licence has been granted.

Section 60

(1) The licence holder shall be prohibited from charging the protected customers towards which it has an obligation to supply electricity under section 56 at higher rates than those determined in accordance with section 58, unless the licence holder supplies the captive customer in question, at his request, with electricity generated by one of the methods, referred to in section 53(2)(e).

(2) The licence holder is prohibited from supplying electricity to a captive customer domiciled in an area in respect of which a supply licence has been granted to a different supplier, unless this relates to the supply of electricity, generated by one of the methods, referred to in section 53(2)(e)

§3. OTHER OBLIGATIONS

Section 61

(1) The licence holder is forbidden to include in an agreement for the supply of electricity to a captive customer provisions intended to prevent the generation of electricity by the captive customer.

(2) A provision included in an agreement for the supply of electricity to a captive customer in contravention of subsection (1) shall be void.

Section 62

The licence holder shall keep separate accounts relating to the supply of electricity to captive customers.

Section 63

The licence holder shall use data issued to him in relation to captive customers exclusively for carrying out the duties assigned to him under this Act, on the understanding that these data may also be used to collect payments for the connection to a grid or for the transmission of electricity on behalf of the grid manager.

Section 64

(1) Once every two years the licence holder shall provide the Director of DTe with the most accurate possible estimates of the total electricity requirement of the captive customers to which the licence holder is obliged to supply electricity in accordance with section 56(1), for each of the first five years after the year in which the estimates are made. The licence holder shall also state the assumptions on which these estimates are based and make any important distinctions.

(2) At the same time the licence holder shall state on the basis of the estimates the manner in which the licence holder will ensure the supply of electricity to the captive customers to which the licence holder is obliged to supply electricity, in accordance with section 56(1), for each of the first five years after the year in which the estimates are made.

Section 65

(1) If, in the opinion of the Director of DTe, it shall appear from the information referred to in section 64 or by other means that a licence holder is not or will not be able to ensure an adequate and efficient supply of electricity to captive customers to whom he is obliged to supply electricity, in accordance with section 56(1), he shall notify Our Minister of this.

(2) Once he has received such notification, Our Minister may order the licence holder in question to take steps to ensure that the adequate and efficient

supply of electricity to the captive customers in question in compliance with the provisions of or pursuant to this Act.

(3) These steps may include the preferential supply of electricity to the captive customers.

(4) The State shall not be liable for costs or losses incurred by implementing the order to take appropriate steps.

Section 66

Further regulations shall be introduced by Ministerial Order in respect of:

(a) the content of an application for a supply licence and the details to be supplied;

(b) the manner in which a supply licence application is to be submitted and dealt with;

(c) the manner in which the obligation, referred to in section 62, shall be fulfilled;

(d) the content of the information to be provided, in accordance with section 64;

(e) temporary provisions and procedures for the revocation of a supply licence.

§4. WITHDRAWAL OF THE SUPPLY LICENCE

Section 67

Our Minister may withdraw a supply licence if:

(a) the licence holder so requests;

(b) the licence holder does not comply satisfactorily with the obligation to supply electricity to captive customers, as referred to in section 56(1);

(c) the licence holder does not comply with the conditions attached to the supply licence;

(d) the licence holder sets tariffs for the supply of electricity to captive customers which are higher than the tariffs determined in accordance with section 58;

(e) the licence holder does not take the mandatory steps, referred to in section 65(2);

(f) the licence holder supplied incorrect or incomplete data in his application and the supply of correct or complete data would have led to a different decision in respect of the application;

(g) the licence holder for other reasons may no longer be deemed to be in a position to perform the licensed activity or to comply with the conditions stipulated in the supply licence.

CHAPTER 5. SUSTAINABLE PROVISION OF ELECTRICITY

§1. DUTIES RELATING TO ENERGY CONSERVATION AND THE PROMOTION OF SUSTAINABLE ENERGY

Section 68

(1) Producers and suppliers have the duty, partly with regard to the importance of protecting the environment, as referred to in section 3(2) of the Directive, of promoting the efficient and environmentally responsible production or use of electricity by their own companies and by customers.

(2) Every producer or supplier that supplies an average of 10 GWh or more per year shall report once every two years before 1 March to Our Minister on the way in which it has carried out its duty, as referred to in subsection (1), in the two years prior to the year in which the report is submitted.

§2. REVERSE SUPPLY OF ELECTRICITY

Section 69

(1) The licence holder is obliged to accept an offer for the supply of electricity, if a captive customer makes this offer and the said customer generates electricity by means of a combined heat and power plant.

(2) The licence holder is obliged to accept an offer for the supply of electricity, if a captive customer makes such an offer and this customer generates electricity by means of a hydroelectric power station or an installation in which biomass is processed thermally without additional burning or the addition of synthetic substances and is converted into electricity, and such an installation or power station has a maximum capacity of 2 MW.

(3) If a customer generates electricity by means of wind energy or solar energy, the licence holder, to whom a licence has been granted for the area in which this customer is established, is obliged to accept an offer for the supply of electricity, provided this installation has a maximum capacity of 8 MW in

the period up to and including 31 December 2001, or a maximum capacity of 600 kW in the period up to and including 31 December 2003, or, alternatively, up until the date on which the amended period, as referred to in section 1(3), expires.

Section 70

Before 1 October and subject to the provisions of section 71, every licence holder shall send Our Minister a proposal with regard to the payment owing to this licence holder for the supply of electricity generated in the manner referred to in section 69.

Section 71

(1) Our Minister shall determine the payment, referred to in section 70, taking into consideration:

(a) the importance of the reliable, sustainable, efficient and environmentally responsible supply of electricity; and

(b) The formula $v_t = p_t - (\frac{y_t}{100})\, p_t$, where:

v_t = the payment that will apply in the period t;

p_t = the tariff for the supply of electricity to private homes, determined in accordance with section 58, that will apply in the period t;

y_t = the deduction of the average added value of the electricity supply services provided by all licence holders, which shall apply in the period t.

(2) Our Minister shall determine the deduction of the average added value of the electricity supply services provided by all licence holders.

(3) The Director of DTe shall consult with the licence holders and with organisations representing captive customers, who generate electricity in the manner referred to in section 69, in relation to the determination of the deductible amount, referred to in subsection (2). In the decision, in which the deductible amount is determined, Our Minister shall state the conclusions that he has drawn from the results of such consultation.

(4) If a proposal, as referred to in section 70, is not sent to Our Minister in time, he shall determine the payment of his own accord, after taking into consideration subsection (1) and subsection (2).

Section 72

(1) The payment shall take effect on a date to be determined by Our Minister and shall apply until 1 January of the year following the date on which the decision took effect, in which the payment was determined.

(2) If the payment for the following year has not been determined on 1 January, the payment shall apply up until the date on which the decision comes into effect, in which the tariffs are set for the following year.

(3) Every licence holder shall have available for inspection by the public at its offices a copy of the payment applicable in his case.

§3. INCENTIVES FOR THE PRODUCTION OF SUSTAINABLE ENERGY

Section 73

(1) In order to stimulate the production of sustainable energy in accordance with the provisions of or pursuant to this paragraph, Our Minister may set up a system for the issuing and revoking of certificates.

(2) The following definitions shall apply to this paragraph and the provisions based upon this paragraph:

(a) "certificate": a transferable document showing that in a stated year a producer has generated or will generate a stated amount of sustainable electricity, expressed in kWh;

(b) "sustainable electricity": electricity generated using a hydro-electric power station for generating electricity with a capacity of less than 15 MW or by means of wind power, solar energy, or installations in which biomass is processed thermally without additional burning or the addition of synthetic substances and with conversion into electricity.

Section 74

Our Minister shall grant, on request, a certificate for the amount of sustainable electricity that the licence holder can show that it has generated or will generate, using an energy source referred to in section 73(2)(b), and has transmitted or will transmit to a supplier or customer domiciled in the Netherlands.

Section 75

(1) Every customer shall be obliged to present to Our Minister before a date to be set by General

Administrative Order as many certificates as are required for the year in question, in accordance with or pursuant to subsection (2).

(2) The number of certificates, which a customer is required to present in a year, shall be determined by applying a formula to be set out in a General Administrative Order, which shall stipulate that certificates shall be presented for a stated factor of the total quantity of electricity supplied in a year.

Section 76

Our Minister shall set a surcharge on the tariffs for the transmission of electricity that shall be payable if by a date to be determined by General Administrative Order a customer does not fulfil, or does not fulfil adequately, the obligation referred to in section 75(1).

Section 77

Further regulations shall be determined by General Administrative Order in respect of:

(a) the information to be supplied to Our Minister by producers, suppliers, customers or grid managers;

(b) the procedure for compliance with the obligation to produce certificates, referred to in section 75(1);

(c) the trade in, revocation, registration, cancellation and safe-keeping of certificates;

(d) the calculation of the surcharge, referred to in section 76, in respect of each certificate which is not presented, contrary to the obligation referred to in section 75(1);

(e) the procedure for determining and imposing the surcharge on the tariffs for the transmission of electricity;

(f) the payment by a grid manager to Our Minister of the sums obtained by applying the surcharge to the tariffs for the transmission of electricity.

CHAPTER 6. OTHER GENERAL PROVISIONS

§1. PROVISION OF INFORMATION

Section 78

(1) Our Minister may require a producer, a supplier, a trader or a grid manager to submit the data and information he needs for the implementation of this Act.

(2) Any person who is requested to supply data and information shall be required to cooperate in every manner that may within reason be demanded by Our Minister in the exercising of his powers and shall do so within a reasonable period to be decided by Our Minister.

(3) Data or information relating to a producer, a supplier, a trader or a grid manager, which Our Minister has obtained in relation to any operations in the performance of any of his duties, may be used only for the performance of that duty.

Section 79

A grid manager or a licence holder, who in the performance of his duties gains access to data which he knows or may reasonably assume to be of a confidential nature is obliged to maintain the confidentiality of such data, except in so far as the sections of this Act require him to report the said data or the necessity to report such data arises from his duties.

Section 80

(1) Within four years of the promulgation of this Act in the *Netherlands Bulletin of Acts and Decrees*,[7] Our Minister shall send both Houses of Parliament a report on the effectiveness and the effects of this Act in practice.

(2) In any event, the report shall consider the manner in which the implementation and the supervision of compliance with this report have been organised, in accordance with the Competition Act.

Section 81

(1) On the first occasion that a General Administrative Order is approved, in accordance with sections 1, 20, 68, 75, 76, 77, 93 or 99, the said Order shall not be proposed until a draft has been presented to both Houses of Parliament. Within four weeks after the presentation of the Order, one of the Houses of Parliament or a fifth of all the members, in accordance with Constitution, of one of the Houses may express the wish to introduce legislation in respect of the item regulated in the draft Order by an Act of

[7] *Staatsblad*

Parliament. In this case, a Bill to this effect shall be presented as soon as possible.

(2) A General Administrative Order, approved in accordance with sections 29, 30, 84 or 85, or, alternatively, with the purpose of amending a General Administrative Order, approved in accordance with sections 1, 20, 68, 75, 76, 77, 93 or 99, shall take effect at the earliest four weeks after the date of publication of the *Netherlands Bulletin of Acts and Decrees* in which it is published. Both Houses of Parliament shall be informed of its publication without delay.

§2. APPEALS

Section 82

(1) An interested party may lodge an appeal against a decision taken under this Act with the Trade and Industry Appeals Tribunal,[8] except in the case of a decision, as referred to in section 76 and sections 98 to 101. In so far as a decision taken in accordance with section 27 or section 31 may be deemed to be a binding regulation, an interested party, by way of departure from section 8:2 of the General Administrative Law Act, may appeal to the Industrial Appeals Court.

(2) If an appeal is lodged against a decision, in accordance with section 76, the Court in Rotterdam shall be the competent Court, contrary to section 8(7) of the General Administrative Law Act.

(3) If an appeal is lodged against a decision, in accordance with sections 98 to 101, the Court in Arnhem shall be the competent Court, contrary to section 8(7) of the General Administrative Law Act.

§3. EXCEPTION IN RESPECT OF THE AUTHORITY TO ISSUE REGULATIONS

Section 83

The provincial councils and municipal councils are not authorised to issue regulations in respect of the transmission and generation of electricity in the interests of electricity supply.

§4. FURTHER REGULATIONS FOR THE IMPLEMENTATION OF EC DECISIONS

Section 84

For the implementation of a decision based on the treaty establishing the European Community, rules may be laid down by General Administrative Order relating to:

(a) the tariffs and conditions that grid managers charge or, alternatively, take into account in carrying out the transmission of electricity with the use of a grid that extends beyond national borders;

(b) the conditions that a grid manager or a supplier sets in the interests of safety and efficiency in relation to the supply of electricity or the connection of appliances or installations that use electricity.

§5. CONTRIBUTIONS

Section 85

(1) In accordance with rules to be determined by or in accordance with a General Administrative Order, an amount to be determined by Our Minister shall be payable for the granting of assent, as referred to in section 12(2), an appointment, as referred to in section 13, an exemption, as referred to in section 15(2), a decision, as referred to in section 26, or a licence, as referred to in section 54, or a certificate, as referred to in section 74, which payment shall amount at most to the cost incurred in relation to the assent, appointment, exemption, decision, licence or the certificate.

(2) In accordance with the regulations, referred to in subsection (1), grid managers and licence holders may be charged for the cost incurred in carrying out the duties and exercising the powers, referred to in section 22, sections 27 to 43, sections 57 to 59 section 65 and sections 70 to 72.

(3) If payment is not made within the period stipulated in a General Administrative Order, Our Minister may collect the amount owing, increased with the legal interest and costs incurred for issuing a demand for payment and for collection by means of a writ. The writ shall be served at the expense of the person who owes the amount and shall give rise to an enforceable order, as defined in Book Two of the Netherlands Code of Civil Procedure.

[8] *College van Beroep voor het bedrijfsleven*

(4) For a period of six weeks after the date on which the writ is served objections may be raised to the writ by issuing the State with a writ of summons. An objection shall adjourn the execution of the writ. At the request of the State, the Court may revoke the adjournment of execution.

§6. ACCOUNTS OF PRODUCERS AND SUPPLIERS

Section 86

(1) A producer or a supplier, other than a licence holder, is obliged to keep separate accounts for the production of electricity with the use of his installations and the supply of electricity to customers, other than captive customers. If the producer or supplier carries out other activities than those relating to the production or supply of electricity, he shall also keep separate accounts for these activities, whether or not on a consolidated basis.

(2) Section 43, subsections (2) to (7), shall apply *mutatis mutandis* to the accounting and annual accounts of the producer or supplier.

(3) Subsections (1) and (2) shall not apply to:

(a) customers, as referred to in section 69; or

(b) suppliers that supply electricity on a non-commercial basis.

§7. APPLICABLE LAW

Section 86a

(1) Agreements in relation to the transmission or supply of electricity shall be subject to Dutch law.

(2) Only Dutch courts shall be competent to hear disputes relating to agreements concerning the transmission or supply of electricity.

(3) Any provisions of agreements in respect of the transmission or supply of electricity that do not comply with the provisions of subsections (1) and (2) of this section shall be null and void.

(4) Subsections (1) to (3) of this section shall not apply to agreements relating to the supply of electricity that a supplier or trader enters into with a person with a connection to a grid with a total maximum transmission value of more than 3·80 A and an available electrical capacity of at least 2 MW per connection.

(5) The application of this section is restricted by mandatory provisions of international law.

CHAPTER 7. AMENDMENT OF OTHER ACTS

Section 87

Section 1 of the Economic Offences Act is amended as follows:

(1) In subsection (i)[9] the following is inserted alphabetically: the Electricity Act 1998, sections 7(2), 12(1), 16, 18(3), 21, 46, 47(1), 53(1), 56, 60, 62, 64, 69, 78(2), 79 and 84.

(2) The phrase referring to the Electricity Act of 1989 in subsection (iv)[10] is deleted.

Section 88

The Energy Distribution Act is amended as follows:

A

Section 1 is amended as follows:

(1) The phrase "distribution of electricity or gas: the supply of electricity or gas to consumers within the framework of the public provision thereof" is replaced by:
""distribution of electricity": the supply of electricity to captive customers, as referred to in section 56 of the Electricity Act of 1998"; ""distribution of gas": the supply of gas to consumers within the framework of the public provision thereof".

(2) The following is inserted after the definition of "distribution of heat": " "user of electricity": a customer, as referred to in section 1(1)(c) of the Electricity Act of 1998";

(3) The definition of a "distribution company" is replaced by: "an organisational unit concerned in full or in part with the supply of electricity in relation to the distribution thereof or with the distribution of gas or heat".

B

Section 2 is amended as follows:

(1) In subsection (b) "electricity" is deleted.

[9]Numbered in the Dutch text of the Act as "1°".
[10]Numbered in the Dutch text of the Act as "4°".

(2) In subsection (c) "consumers of electricity, gas or heat" is replaced by: "consumers for whom the distribution company carries out the distribution of electricity, gas or heat".

C

Chapter 3 is deleted.

D

Section 10 is amended as follows:

(1) In subsection (1), after "is charged for the" shall be inserted: "in relation to the distribution".

(2) A subsection (6) shall be added, which shall read as follows:

> "(6) If a distribution company and an electricity user agree that the electricity to be supplied to the user shall be generated in full or in part in an environmentally responsible manner, the distribution company may stipulate that the payment it shall charge for supplying electricity to that consumer in relation to the distribution thereof shall be increased by a sum to cover the costs incurred by generating electricity in one of the ways referred to in section 36(c)(7)(a) of the Environmental Taxes Act,[11] in so far as such costs exceed the costs incurred by other methods of generating electricity."

E

Section 12 is amended as follows:

(1) In subsection (1) the comma at the end of subsection (d) shall be replaced by "or". At the end of subsection (e) "or" shall also be replaced by a full stop. Finally, subsection (f) shall be deleted.

(2) In the first sentence of subsection (3), the words "and the activities relating to the use of electricity, gas or heat, supplied by the distribution company, or with the production of electricity, gas or heat" shall be deleted.

(3) In the first sentence of subsection (6), the words "by an accountant, as referred to in section 393(1) of Book 2 of the Netherlands Civil Code" shall be deleted.

F

In section 13 "electricity," shall be deleted.

G

Section 16 shall read:

Section 16

> Works that have been or are being carried out for the distribution of gas or heat shall be deemed to be works for the public good for the application of the Public Works (Removal of Impediments in Local and Regional Regulations) Act and the Public Works (Removal of Impediments in Private Law) Act.

Section 89

[Contains amendments to the Act of 18 December 1997, amending a number of tax laws of 1998 (fiscal strengthening of the environment) (*Staatsblad* 732)]

Section 90

[Contains amendments to the Schedule, referred to in Section 20 of the Administrative Law (Industrial Organisation) Act.[12]]

CHAPTER 8. TRANSITIONAL AND FINAL PROVISIONS

§1. GENERAL TRANSITIONAL PROVISIONS

Section 91

After section 103 has taken effect, the permanent regulations for electricity provision, referred to in section 14 of the Electricity Act of 1989 and approved by the Ministerial Order of 1 February 1994 by Our Minister and the Minister for Housing, Spatial Planning and the Environment shall be based only on section 2(a) of the Spatial Planning Act.[13]

Section 92

(1) Up to and including 31 December 2002 every change to the shares of a producer who was a licence holder, as referred to in section 1 of the Electricity Act of 1989, or its legal successor, shall require the approval of Our Minister.

(2) Our Minister may withhold his assent, if the change to the ownership of the shares of the

[11] *Wet belastingen op milieutoeslag*

[12] *Wet bestuursrechtsspraak bedrijfsorganisatie.*

[13] *Wet op de Ruimtelijke Ordening*

producer would lead to a situation where a natural person or legal entity would be entitled to shares of the producer and such a natural person or legal entity was not of the group that held shares in a producer, or its legal successor, which was a licence holder, as referred to in section 1 of the Electricity Act of 1989.

(3) Sections 10(28) to 10(31) of the General Administrative Law Act shall apply *mutatis mutandis* to the granting of assent in respect of the change.

Section 93

(1) If a change occurs in the ownership of the grid in question or in the shares of a legal entity to which the grid in question belongs, in the period from 1 July 1996 to the date on which the grid manager, as referred to in section 10, is appointed, it shall be a requirement for the appointment of the grid manager that Our Minister has no objections to the appointment.

(2) If, in the period between 1 July 1996 and the date on which the application is submitted, a change occurs in the ownership of the shares of a supplier, who applies for a licence, it shall be a requirement for the appointment of the grid manager that Our Minister has no objections to the appointment.

(3) The assent of Our Minister shall be required for every change to the ownership of a grid or of the shares of a grid manager or of a licence holder.

(4) Our Minister may withhold his assent, if the change to the ownership of any grid or of the shares of a grid manager or of a licence holder would lead to a situation where a natural person or legal entity would be entitled to shares of the grid manager or the licence holder and such a natural person or legal entity was not of the group that held shares in a grid manager.

(5) If Our Minister withholds his assent and the intended change to the ownership of a grid or of the shares proceeds, Our Minister may appoint a different legal person as the grid manager of the grid managed by the grid manager in question or, alternatively, Our Minister may revoke the licence.

(6) Sections 10(28) to 10(31) of the General Administrative Law Act shall apply *mutatis mutandis* to the granting of assent in respect of the change.

Section 94

A meter, which is the property of a producer or of a supplier and which was installed on the premises of a customer prior to the date on which section 10 took effect, shall be managed as of that date by the grid manager who carries out the transmission of electricity on behalf of the said customer.

Section 95

(1) Supply licences, as referred to in section 54, shall be granted for the first time after section 54 takes effect to distribution companies or their legal successors, which supplied electricity to consumers on 1 July 1996 within the framework of public electricity provision.

(2) The preferential rights, referred to in subsection (1), shall lapse if a distribution company or its legal successor does not submit an application for a supply licence within 16 weeks after the date on which section 54 takes effect.

(3) The prohibition, referred to in section 53(1), shall not apply to suppliers other than those referred to in subsection (1), who supply electricity to captive customers on the date on which this Act is published in the *Netherlands Government Gazette*, in so far as this relates to the supply of electricity to the said captive customers or their legal successors.

(4) Up until the date on which a supply licence takes effect in the particular area, sections 12 and 27 of the Electricity Act of 1989, as applicable on the date of publication of this Act in the *Netherlands Government Gazette*, shall continue to apply to distribution companies which supplied electricity to consumers in that area within the framework of public electricity provision.

§1. LICENCES FOR THE SUPPLY OF ELECTRICITY TO SMALL CONSUMERS

Section 95a

(1) It is prohibited to supply electricity to customers with a connection to a grid with a total maximum

transmission value of less than 3·80 A without a licence.

(2) The prohibition of subsection (1) of this section shall not apply to the supply of electricity:

(a) if the electricity is generated by means of an installation that is operated at the risk and expense of the customer, alone or, for a proportional share, together with other customers, and the customer consumes the electricity generated;

(b) by an electricity supplier domiciled outside the Netherlands to no more than 500 customers, referred to in subsection (1) of this section, residing in areas on the Dutch borders;

(c) for supply purposes, as referred to in section 20(1)(i) of the Directive, if the customer forms part of the same legal person as the producer that generated the electricity, or is a subsidiary of that legal person, as referred to in section 24a, Book 2 of the Civil Code, and the customer consumes the electricity supplied; or

(d) if the electricity is supplied for purposes other than commercial purposes, in compliance with rules to be imposed by Ministerial Order.

Section 95b

(1) A licence holder is required to provide for the supply of electricity to all customers, as referred to in section 95a(1), on request, in a reliable manner, for reasonable rates and subject to reasonable conditions.

(2) The holder of a licence shall provide the Director of the Service every year with a statement of the tariffs that he charges and the conditions that he uses in supplying electricity to customers, as referred to in section 95a(1).

(3) If the Director of the Service is of the opinion that the tariffs that the licence holders charge are unreasonable, because the effects of this on efficient operations, which includes the procurement of electricity and energy sources intended for the generation of such electricity, results in insufficient cost reductions, he may determine a maximum tariff that suppliers may charge for the supply of electricity to customers, as referred to in section 95a.

(4) After determining the maximum tariff, referred to in subsection (3), the tariffs for the supply of electricity to customers, as referred to in section 95a, which exceed the maximum tariff, shall by law be set at the maximum tariff.

(5) By General Administrative Order further regulations may be introduced for determining whether the tariffs, referred to in subsection (2), are unreasonable and for determining the maximum tariff, referred to in subsection (3). The General dministrative Order shall not take effect earlier than four weeks after the date on which it is published in the *Bulletin of Act and Decrees,*[14] in which it is promulgated. Both Houses of Parliament shall be notified of the publication thereof without delay.

(6) Subsections (2) up to and including (6) shall be repealed as of a date to be determined by Royal Decree. The Royal Decree shall not be approved before four weeks have passed after the draft was presented to both Houses of Parliament.

Section 95c

(1) *Our Minister shall issue a licence, on request, if the* applicant provides satisfactory evidence that it:

(a) has the required organisational, financial and technical qualities for the effective performance of its duties; and

(b) can reasonably be expected to comply with the obligations stipulated in this section.

(2) Further rules relating to the content and procedures for licence applications, and the criteria referred to in subsection (1)(a) of this section shall be provided by General Administrative Order.

Section 95d

(1) Our Minister may issue a licence subject to conditions and restrictions.

(2) Our Minister may amend the conditions and restrictions attached to a licence.

(3) A licence may be transferred to another licence holder only with the consent of Our Minister.

[14] *Staatsblad*

(4) Section 95c shall apply mutatis mutandis to the granting of consent in accordance with subsection 3 of this section.

Section 95e

1) Our Minister may withdraw a licence:

a) at the licence holder's request;

b) if the licence holder fails to comply satisfactorily with the obligation, referred to in section 95b;

c) if the licence holder fails to comply with the conditions or restrictions attached to the licence;

d) if the licence holder provided inaccurate or incomplete information with its application, and the provision of accurate or complete information would have led to a different decision on the application;

e) in Our Minister's opinion, the licence holder can no longer be deemed capable, on other grounds, of compliance with the licensed activity or the conditions of the licence.

2) Further rules with regard to the temporary provisions and procedures for the withdrawal of a licence may be imposed by General Administrative Order.

Section 95f

(1) Section 79 shall apply *mutatis mutandis* to licence holders.

(2) Licence holders shall use the information provided to them in relation to customers, as referred to in section 95a, only for the purpose of implementing the duties assigned to them in accordance with this Act, on the understanding that such information may also be used for the purpose of collecting payment, on behalf of the grid manager, for a connection to a grid or for the transmission of electricity.

(3) Section 19 shall apply *mutatis mutandis* to the collection of payment by the grid manager for the supply of electricity to customers, as referred to in section 95a(1).

Section 95g

(1) The officials, designated by a decision of Our Minister, shall responsible for supervision of compliance with the provisions of or pursuant to this section.

(2) Decisions, as referred to in subsection (1) of this section, shall be promulgated in the *Netherlands Government Gazette.*

Section 95h

Our Minister is authorised to impose administrative penalties to enforce compliance with the obligations in accordance with or pursuant to this section.

Section 95i

Section 45(2) and section 46 shall apply *mutatis mutandis* to suppliers that are licence holders.

§2. SETTLEMENT OF ACCOUNTS IN THE ELECTRICITY PRODUCTION SECTOR

Sections 96–102 expired

§3. FINAL PROVISIONS

Section 103

(1) Sections 15 to 21 of the Electricity Act of 1989 are revoked.

(2) The Electricity Act of 1989 is repealed.

Section 104

(1) The sections of this Act shall come into effect at a moment to be determined by Royal Decree and may differ in respect of the various sections or parts thereof.

(2) Sections 45 to 50 shall expire on 19 February 2006 or, alternatively, at an earlier time to be determined by Royal Decree.

(3) Section 89 shall come into effect at a moment to be determined by Royal Decree with retrospective effect up to and including 1 January 1998.

(4) Chapter 4 shall be repealed as of 1 January 2004 or as of the date on which the period in which a customer, as referred to in section 1(2)(o), is deemed to be a captive customer expires, in accordance with a decision, as referred to in section 1(3).

(5) Paragraph 8(1)(a) shall take effect as of the date on which chapter 4 is repealed or as of an earlier date to be determined by Royal Decree.

Section 105

This Act shall be cited as the Electricity Act, stating the year and the *Netherlands Government Gazette* in which it is promulgated.

Charge and order that this shall be published in the *Netherlands Government Gazette* and that all Ministries, authorities, boards and civil servants to whom it pertains shall see to the precise implementation thereof.

Issued in The Hague on the second day of July 1998.

Beatrix

Issued on the sixteenth of July 1998

The Minister of Economic Affairs,

G. J. Wijers

The Minister of Justice,

W. Sorgdrager

United Kingdom of Great Britain and Northern Ireland

Sustainable Energy Act 2003

2003 Chapter 30

An **Act** to make provision about the development and promotion of a **sustainable energy** policy; to amend the Utilities **Act** 2000; and for connected purposes. [30th October 2003]

BE IT ENACTED by the Queen's most Excellent Majesty, by and with the advice and consent of the Lords Spiritual and Temporal, and Commons, in this present Parliament assembled, and by the authority of the same, as follows: –

1. ANNUAL REPORTS ON PROGRESS TOWARDS SUSTAINABLE ENERGY AIMS

(1) The Secretary of State must in each calendar year, beginning with 2004, publish a report ("a **sustainable energy** report") on the progress made in the reporting period towards –

(a) cutting the United Kingdom's carbon emissions;

(b) maintaining the reliability of the United Kingdom's **energy** supplies;

(c) promoting competitive **energy** markets in the United Kingdom; and

(d) reducing the number of people living in fuel poverty in the United Kingdom.

(2) "The reporting period", for the purposes of subsection (1), means the year ending with 23 February in the calendar year in question.

(3) Accordingly, the report must be published in that calendar year within the period beginning with 24 February and ending with 31 December ("the publication period").

(4) A **sustainable energy** report may either be published as a single report or published in a number of parts during the publication period, and any such report or part may be contained in a document containing other material.

(5) A **sustainable energy** report must be based on such information as is available to the Secretary of State when the report is completed (except that if it is published in parts, each of those parts must be based on such information as is so available when that part is completed).

(6) For the purposes of this section a person is to be regarded as living in fuel poverty if he is a member of a household living on a lower income in a home which cannot be kept warm at a reasonable cost.

2. ENERGY EFFICIENCY OF RESIDENTIAL ACCOMMODATION: SECRETARY OF STATE

(1) The Secretary of State must within one week beginning with the coming into force of this section designate under this subsection at least one **energy** efficiency aim.

(2) For the purposes of this section an "**energy** efficiency aim" is an aim which –

(a) is contained in a published document;

(b) relates to the **energy** efficiency of residential accommodation in England; and

(c) is compatible with Community obligations and any other international obligations of the United Kingdom.

(3) The Secretary of State may, at any time after designation under subsection (1), designate under this subsection a further **energy** efficiency aim or aims.

(4) Where an **energy** efficiency aim is for the time being designated under this section, the Secretary of State must take reasonable steps to achieve the aim.

(5) In deciding which steps to take for the purposes of subsection (4), the Secretary of State must consider steps relating to the heating, cooling,

ventilation, lighting and insulation of residential accommodation.

(6) A designation under this section may be withdrawn, but not if its withdrawal would result in there being no **energy** efficiency aim designated under this section.

(7) If an **energy** efficiency aim designated under this section ceases to meet the condition in subsection (2)(c) it ceases to be designated under this section, but if this results in there being no **energy** efficiency aim so designated the Secretary of State must without delay designate a new **energy** efficiency aim.

(8) A designation of an aim under this section, or a withdrawal or cessation of such a designation, must be published in such way as the Secretary of State considers appropriate: a designation may be contained in the same published document as the aim itself.

(9) In this section "residential accommodation" has the meaning given by section 1 of the Home **Energy** Conservation **Act** 1995 (c. 10).

3. ENERGY EFFICIENCY OF RESIDENTIAL ACCOMMODATION: NATIONAL ASSEMBLY FOR WALES

(1) The National Assembly for Wales ("the Assembly") must within one week beginning with the coming into force of this section designate under this subsection at least one **energy** efficiency aim.

(2) For the purposes of this section an "**energy** efficiency aim" is an aim which –

(a) is contained in a published document;

(b) relates to the **energy** efficiency of residential accommodation in Wales; and

(c) is compatible with Community obligations and any other international obligations of the United Kingdom.

(3) The Assembly may, at any time after designation under subsection (1), designate under this subsection a further **energy** efficiency aim or aims.

(4) Where an **energy** efficiency aim is for the time being designated under this section, the Assembly must (using the powers it has apart from this section) take reasonable steps to achieve the aim.

(5) In deciding which steps to take for the purposes of subsection (4), the Assembly must consider steps relating to the heating, cooling, ventilation, lighting and insulation of residential accommodation.

(6) A designation under this section may be withdrawn, but not if its withdrawal would result in there being no **energy** efficiency aim designated under this section.

(7) If an **energy** efficiency aim designated under this section ceases to meet the condition in subsection (2)(c) it ceases to be designated under this section, but if this results in there being no **energy** efficiency aim so designated the Assembly must without delay designate a new **energy** efficiency aim.

(8) A designation of an aim under this section, or a withdrawal or cessation of such a designation, must be published in such way as the Assembly considers appropriate: a designation may be contained in the same published document as the aim itself.

(9) In this section "residential accommodation" has the meaning given by section 1 of the Home **Energy** Conservation **Act** 1995 (c. 10).

4. ENERGY EFFICIENCY OF RESIDENTIAL ACCOMMODATION: ENERGY CONSERVATION AUTHORITIES

(1) In this section an "**energy** efficiency direction" means a direction requiring each **energy** conservation authority to which it applies to take such **energy** conservation measures as that authority considers to be –

(a) likely to result in achieving, by a date specified in the direction, an improvement so specified (which may be expressed as a percentage) in the **energy** efficiency of residential accommodation in that authority's area; and

(b) practicable and cost-effective.

(2) For the purposes of this section, "the **energy** efficiency" of residential accommodation in an **energy** conservation authority's area has such meaning as

may be specified in an order made by the Secretary of State.

(3) The Secretary of State may, after consulting the Local Government Association, give an **energy** efficiency direction which applies –

(a) to one or more named **energy** conservation authorities in England;

(b) to all **energy** conservation authorities in England; or

(c) to a particular description of **energy** conservation authority in England.

(4) The National Assembly for Wales ("the Assembly") may, after consulting the Welsh Local Government Association, give an **energy** efficiency direction which applies –

(a) to one or more named **energy** conservation authorities in Wales;

(b) to all **energy** conservation authorities in Wales; or

(c) to a particular description of **energy** conservation authority in Wales.

(5) With effect from the giving of an **energy** efficiency direction –

(a) each **energy** conservation authority to which the direction applies must comply with the direction, using the powers it has apart from this section; and

(b) the Home **Energy** Conservation **Act** 1995 (c. 10) ("HECA") shall cease to apply in relation to each such authority.

(6) In deciding which measures to take for the purposes of complying with an **energy** efficiency direction, an authority must give preference to measures which it considers would also contribute to –

(a) achieving the objective mentioned in paragraph (d) of section 2(2) of the Warm Homes and **Energy** Conservation **Act** 2000 (c. 31) by the target date for the time being specified under that paragraph;

(b) achieving any interim objectives for the time being specified under paragraph (c) of section 2(2) of that **Act** by the target date so specified.

(7) Different **energy** efficiency directions may be given in relation to different **energy** conservation authorities or different descriptions of such authority.

(8) The Secretary of State may after consulting the Local Government Association, and the Assembly may after consulting the Welsh Local Government Association, alter the date or the improvement (or both) for the time being specified in an **energy** efficiency direction given by the Secretary of State or (as the case may be) by the Assembly.

(9) An **energy** efficiency direction may be revoked, but only if each authority to which it applies either –

(a) is subject to a new **energy** efficiency direction taking effect immediately on the revocation; or

(b) no longer exists at the time of the revocation.

(10) The Secretary of State may give to **energy** conservation authorities in England, and the Assembly may give to **energy** conservation authorities in Wales, such guidance as he or it considers appropriate in relation to the exercise of an **energy** conservation authority's functions under this section.

(11) An **energy** conservation authority must have regard to any such guidance.

(12) The Secretary of State may by order –

(a) amend this section so as to alter the body which must be consulted by him;

(b) make transitional provision in relation to HECA's ceasing to apply in relation to an **energy** conservation authority in England.

(13) The Assembly may by order –

(a) amend this section so as to alter the body which must be consulted by it;

(b) make transitional provision in relation to HECA's ceasing to apply in relation to an **energy** conservation authority in Wales.

(14) Any power to make an order under this section is exercisable by statutory instrument which, in the case of an order made by the Secretary of State, shall be subject to annulment in pursuance of a resolution of either House of Parliament.

(15) In this section the following expressions have the meaning given by section 1 of HECA –

"**energy** conservation authority";

"residential accommodation";

"area", in relation to an **energy** conservation authority;

"**energy** conservation measures".

5. CHP TARGETS

(1) Before the end of 2003, the Secretary of State must make a statement –

(a) specifying one or more CHP targets; and

(b) specifying the period that each CHP target is for.

(2) At any time after making the statement mentioned in subsection (1), the Secretary of State may make a further statement doing either or both of the following –

(a) specifying as mentioned in that subsection;

(b) revoking a CHP target contained in an earlier statement under this section.

(3) A CHP target is the percentage of the amount of electricity for government use in the period the target is for that the Secretary of State considers will be capable, at a reasonable cost to the government, of being supplied from CHP electricity.

(4) For the purposes of this section –

"amount of electricity for government use in the period the target is for" means the amount of electricity that the Secretary of State estimates that the government will use in that period;

"CHP electricity" means electricity that –

(a) is generated by a generating station which is operated for the purposes of producing heat, or a cooling effect, in association with electricity; and

(b) satisfies any other requirements specified in an order made by the Secretary of State.

(5) The Secretary of State may by order –

(a) specify the departments and other bodies which (taken together) are to constitute "the government" for the purposes of this section;

(b) provide for the exclusion from any estimation of the amount of electricity that the government will use in a period of –

(i) the use of electricity for purposes specified in the order or in circumstances so specified;

(ii) the use of electricity by any part of the government specified in the order.

(6) One of the periods specified under subsection (1)(b) must –

(a) begin with 1 January 2010; and

(b) end with 31 December 2010.

(7) The Secretary of State must lay any statement made under this section before Parliament.

(8) Any power to make an order under this section is exercisable by statutory instrument which shall be subject to annulment in pursuance of a resolution of either House of Parliament.

(9) No proceedings may be brought to enforce any CHP target contained in a statement made under this section or otherwise to review any **act** done, or any failure to **act**, in relation to any such CHP target.

6. DUTY OF GAS AND ELECTRICITY MARKETS AUTHORITY TO CARRY OUT IMPACT ASSESSMENTS

After section 5 of the Utilities **Act** 2000 (c. 27) insert –

"5A DUTY OF AUTHORITY TO CARRY OUT IMPACT ASSESSMENT

(1) This section applies where –

(a) the Authority is proposing to do anything for the purposes of, or in connection with, the carrying out of any function exercisable by it under or by virtue of Part 1 of the 1986 **Act** or Part 1 of the 1989 **Act**; and

(b) it appears to it that the proposal is important;

but this section does not apply if it appears to the Authority that the urgency of the matter makes it impracticable or inappropriate for the Authority to comply with the requirements of this section.

(2) A proposal is important for the purposes of this section only if its implementation would be likely to do one or more of the following –

(a) involve a major change in the activities carried on by the Authority;

(b) have a significant impact on persons engaged in the shipping, transportation or supply of gas conveyed through pipes or in the generation, transmission, distribution or supply of electricity;

(c) have a significant impact on persons engaged in commercial activities connected with the shipping, transportation or supply of gas conveyed through pipes or with the generation, transmission, distribution or supply of electricity;

(d) have a significant impact on the general public in Great Britain or in a part of Great Britain; or

(e) have significant effects on the environment.

(3) Before implementing its proposal, the Authority must either –

(a) carry out and publish an assessment of the likely impact of implementing the proposal; or

(b) publish a statement setting out its reasons for thinking that it is unnecessary for it to carry out an assessment.

(4) An assessment carried out under this section must –

(a) include an assessment of the likely effects on the environment of implementing the proposal; and

(b) relate to such other matters as the Authority considers appropriate.

(5) In determining the matters to which an assessment under this section should relate, the Authority must have regard to such general guidance relating to the carrying out of impact assessments as it considers appropriate.

(6) An assessment carried out under this section may take such form as the Authority considers appropriate.

(7) Where the Authority publishes an assessment under this section –

(a) it must provide an opportunity of making representations to the Authority about its proposal to members of the public and other persons who, in the Authority's opinion, are likely to be affected to a significant extent by the proposal's implementation;

(b) the published assessment must be accompanied by a statement setting out how representations may be made; and

(c) the Authority must not implement its proposal unless the period for making representations about the proposal has expired and it has considered all the representations that were made in that period.

(8) Where the Authority is required (apart from this section) –

(a) to consult about a proposal to which this section applies, or

(b) to give a person an opportunity of making representations about it,

the requirements of this section are in addition to, but may be performed contemporaneously with, the other requirements.

(9) Every report under section 5(1) must set out –

(a) a list of the assessments under this section carried out during the financial year to which the report relates; and

(b) a summary of the decisions taken during that year in relation to proposals to which assessments carried out in that year or previous financial years relate.

(10) The publication of anything under this section must be in such manner as the Authority considers appropriate for bringing it to the attention of the persons who, in the Authority's opinion, are likely to be affected if its proposal is implemented.

(11) References in sections 4AA, 4AB and 4A of the 1986 **Act** to functions of the Authority under Part 1 of that **Act** include references to any functions of the Authority under this section that are exercisable in relation to a proposal to do anything for the purposes of, or in connection with, the carrying out of any function of the Authority under Part 1 of the 1986 **Act**.

(12) References in sections 3A, 3B and 3C of the 1989 **Act** to functions of the Authority under Part 1 of that **Act** include references to any functions of the Authority under this section that are exercisable in relation to a proposal to do anything for the purposes of, or in connection with, the carrying out of any function of the Authority under Part 1 of the 1989 **Act**."

7. USE OF CERTAIN MONEY HELD BY GAS AND ELECTRICITY MARKETS AUTHORITY

(1) If the Secretary of State so directs, the person prescribed under section 33(1)(b) of the Electricity **Act** (collection of fossil fuel levy) must pay an

amount into the Consolidated Fund out of money that has been paid under section 33(5A) of that Act.

(2) The total of the amounts directed to be paid under this section must not exceed £60,000,000.

(3) At any time which falls after the giving of a direction under this section, the Secretary of State is under a duty to spend the required amount for the purpose of promoting the use of **energy** from renewable sources.

(4) "The required amount", for the purposes of subsection (3), is an amount of money equal to the total of the amounts that at the time in question have been paid into the Consolidated Fund under subsection (1), less the total of any amounts that the Secretary of State has already spent under subsection (3).

(5) In subsection (3) "renewable sources" means sources of **energy** other than fossil fuel or nuclear fuel.

(6) In subsection (5) "fossil fuel" means coal, substances produced directly or indirectly from coal, lignite, natural gas, crude liquid petroleum, or petroleum products (and "natural gas" and "petroleum products" have the same meanings as in the **Energy Act** 1976 (c. 76)).

(7) The Secretary of State's duty under subsection (3) is without prejudice to any power or duty of his apart from this section to spend money for the purpose mentioned in that subsection.

(8) In this section –

(a) "the Electricity Act" means the Electricity Act 1989 (c. 29); and

(b) the references to section 33 of that Act are to that section as it has effect in England and Wales.

8. FINANCIAL PROVISION

There shall be paid out of money provided by Parliament –

(a) any expenditure of the Secretary of State under this Act; and

(b) any increase attributable to this Act in the sums which under any other Act are payable out of money so provided.

9. CITATION, EXTENT AND COMMENCEMENT

(1) This Act may be cited as the **Sustainable Energy Act** 2003.

(2) Except as provided in subsections (3) and (4), this Act extends to England and Wales, Scotland and Northern Ireland.

(3) Sections 2, 3, 4, 5 and 7 extend to England and Wales only.

(4) Section 6 extends to England and Wales and to Scotland.

(5) Sections 2, 4 (so far as it relates to England) and 5 shall come into force on such day as the Secretary of State may by order made by statutory instrument appoint.

(6) Sections 3 and 4 (so far as it relates to Wales) shall come into force on such day as the National Assembly for Wales may by order made by statutory instrument appoint.

(7) The other provisions of this Act shall come into force at the end of two months beginning with the day on which it is passed.

(8) An order under subsection (5) or (6) may appoint different days for different purposes.

Climate Change Levy

2003 No. 604

The Climate Change Levy (General) (Amendment) Regulations 2003

Made, 11th March 2003
Laid before the House of Commons, 11th March 2003
Coming into force, 1st April 2003

The Commissioners of Customs and Excise, in exercise of the powers conferred on them by section 30 of and Schedule 6 paragraphs 19, 20A, 22, 41, 125, 146 and 149A to the Finance Act 2000[1], hereby make the following Regulations:

1. These Regulations may be cited as the **Climate Change** Levy (General) (Amendment) Regulations 2003 and come into force on 1 April 2003.

2. The **Climate Change** Levy (General) Regulations 2001[2] are amended as follows.

3. In regulation 2(1), substitute "the Schedules" for "the Schedule" and omit the expression ""Schedule" refers to the Schedule to these Regulations;".

4. In regulations 5(1)(b), 8(g), 12(1), 12(2), 27(3)(b), 33, 34(3), 35(3), 36(3), 38(1), 38(3), 39(2), 43(4), 59(2)(b) and 60(1)(h), substitute "Schedule 1" for each reference to "the Schedule" or "The Schedule".

5. In regulation 6A in the meaning given for "transitional accounting period", substitute "first current accounting year" for "first accounting year".

6. In regulations 6D(2)(a) and 6E(1)(e), substitute "transitional accounting period" for "transitional period".

7. In regulation 6E(1)(d), insert "accounting period" immediately after "transitional".

8. Insert after regulation 8(c) –

"(ca) any record required by or under Part IV(A) (combined heat and power stations);".

9. Renumber regulation 46(1) as regulation 46 and insert after the meaning given for "exempt renewable supplies" –

""MWh" is an abbreviation for megawatt-hour;

"relevant Authority" refers to the Gas and Electricity Markets Authority or, in relation to electricity produced or supplied in Northern Ireland or produced in the Republic of Ireland, the Director General of Electricity Supply for Northern Ireland;".

10. Omit regulations 46(2), 46(3) and 46(4).

11. In regulation 47(2) –

(a) insert immediately before the meaning given for "declared net capacity" –

" "biomass" means fuel used in a generating station of which at least 98 per cent. of the energy content is derived from plant or animal matter, or substances derived directly or indirectly therefrom (whether or not such matter or substances are waste) and includes agricultural, forestry or wood wastes or residues, sewage and energy crops (provided that such plant or animal matter is not or is not derived directly from or indirectly from fossil fuel);"

(b) in the meaning given for "renewable sources" –

(i) insert "peat," immediately after "other than";

(ii) insert "(a) biomass, and (b)" between "includes" and "waste".

12. In regulations 47(3) and 47(9), insert "biomass or" immediately before each use of the word "waste".

13. Insert after regulation 47(5) –

"(5A) Where the renewable sources used to fuel a generating station includes biomass (whether or not the generating station is fuelled by biomass in combination with other renewable sources or fossil fuel) paragraph (9) applies in order to calculate the amount of renewable source electricity which is to be regarded as generated from that biomass in any period specified by the relevant Authority.".

14. Omit regulation 47(14).

15. Insert after regulation 48(1) –

"(1A) The relevant Authority must only issue a levy exemption certificate on the basis of the most accurate figures for electricity produced in a generating station that the person who generates that electricity makes known to the Authority.

(1B) The relevant Authority must disregard any figures that are made known to it or of which it becomes aware after the end of the second month following the end of the month in which the electricity is produced.".

16. Insert after regulation 48(3) –

"(4) The relevant Authority need not issue a Renewables LEC as respects a quantity of electricity less than 1 MWh.

However the relevant Authority may aggregate or disaggregate such quantities relating to the same generating station, certifying each complete MWh as appropriate.

(5) The relevant Authority need not issue a Renewables LEC unless it is satisfied that the Renewables LEC, if issued, would represent electricity consumed or to be consumed in the United Kingdom.

For this purpose, the relevant Authority may have regard in particular to whether any part of that electricity is or may be allocated by the operator of the generating station or a supplier for consumption outside the United Kingdom.

(6) A Renewables LEC must be regarded for all purposes of this Part as only relating to the actual electricity in relation to which it was issued.".

17. Substitute for "the relevant levy exemption certificates" in regulations 49(4)(a)(iii) and 49(4)(b)(iii) the expression "any relevant Renewables LEC (and, if different from the relevant recipient, the identity of any person to whom entitlement to that Renewables LEC is transferred)".

18. Substitute "Renewables LEC" for "LEC" in regulations 48(2), 48(3), 49(1) and 49(3).

19. Insert after Part IV –

"PART IV(A) COMBINED HEAT AND POWER STATIONS

Interpretation of Part IV(A)

51A. For the purposes of this Part and Schedule 2–

"authorised person" (except for the purposes of Schedule 2, paragraph 7(a)) refers to a person authorised by the relevant Authority;

"CHP declaration contract" refers to the contract mentioned in paragraph 20A(1)(b) of the Act[3];

"CHP Relief Condition" refers to paragraphs 2 to 7 and paragraph 12 of Schedule 2;

"exemption certificate" refers to a full-exemption certificate or a part-exemption certificate (see paragraphs 148(2) and 148(3) of the Act and the **Climate Change** Levy (Combined Heat and Power Stations) Exemption Certificate Regulations 2001[4]);

"fully exempt CHP" refers to a fully exempt combined heat and power station (see paragraph 148(2) of the Act);

"indirect supplies" refers to supplies in relation to which provision is made by paragraph 20A(1) of the Act (exemption for supply made by electricity utility of CHP electricity)[5];

"MWh" is an abbreviation for megawatt-hour;

"operator" refers to the person who operates a station[6] or who generates or produces electricity in that station;

"outputs" or "output" refers to the meaning given by paragraph 148(9) of the Act (electricity or motive power produced in a station, and (a) heat or steam, or (b) air, or water, that has been heated or cooled);

"partly exempt CHP" refers to a partly exempt combined heat and power station (see paragraph 148(3) of the Act);

"QPO" means qualifying power output[7];

"QPO electricity" refers to electricity that –

(a) has been produced in a fully exempt CHP;

(b) has been produced in a partly exempt CHP and supplied from it without causing the limit referred to in paragraph 16(2) of the Act[8] to be exceeded;

"station" refers to a fully or partly exempt CHP;

"relevant Authority" refers to the Gas and Electricity Markets Authority or, in relation to electricity produced or supplied in Northern Ireland or produced in the Republic of Ireland, the Director General of Electricity Supply for Northern Ireland.

Certification of Electricity Produced in a Combined Heat and Power Station

51B. – (1) The relevant Authority may certify that a given MWh of electricity is QPO electricity.

(2) The relevant Authority must only certify on the basis of the most accurate figures for electricity produced in an individual station that the station's operator makes known to the Authority.

(3) The relevant Authority must disregard any figures that are made known to it or of which it becomes aware after the end of the second month following the end of the month in which the electricity is produced.

(4) Paragraph (3) does not apply to regulation 51D, regulation 51E or Schedule 2 paragraph 11 (wrongly certified electricity and periodic reconciliation).

(5) The station's operator must only make known figures for the purposes of paragraph (2) that are made in accordance with the metering requirements of CHPQA Guidance Note 15 Version 1, published by the Department for Environment, Food and Rural Affairs[9].

(6) The relevant Authority must for the purposes of paragraphs (1) and (2) –

(a) regard electricity production in a station as being referable to the calendar year in which the electricity is produced, and

(b) regard the production of any of that electricity that constitutes QPO electricity as being spread evenly throughout that calendar year.

(7) The relevant Authority must not certify any electricity produced in a station when no exemption certificate is in force for that station.

(8) Where the relevant Authority certifies under paragraph (1), it must issue a levy exemption certificate ("CHP LEC") as respects that electricity.

(9) A CHP LEC must be regarded for all purposes of this Part and Schedule 2 as only relating to the actual electricity in relation to which it was issued.

(10) Each CHP LEC must carry a unique identifying reference.

51C. – (1) The relevant Authority must neither certify electricity nor issue a CHP LEC as respects any electricity under any of the following circumstances.

(2) The first circumstance is where the quantity of electricity in question is less than 1 MWh.

However the relevant Authority may aggregate or disaggregate such quantities relating to the same station, certifying each complete MWh as appropriate.

(3) The second circumstance is where the relevant Authority is not satisfied that the CHP LEC, if issued, would represent electricity consumed or to be consumed in the United Kingdom.

For this purpose, the relevant Authority may have regard in particular to whether any part of that electricity is or may be allocated by the operator or a supplier for consumption outside the United Kingdom.

(4) The third circumstance is any one or more of the following –

(a) the operator not providing the relevant Authority with such information, particulars, records and declarations as the relevant Authority may require for the purposes of this Part or Schedule 2;

(b) the operator not providing the relevant Authority with any updated readings the relevant Authority may require from any relevant electricity meter;

(c) any authorised person not being granted, on request, access at any reasonable time to the station in question;

(d) any authorised person not being permitted, on request and having been granted access to the station –

(i) to inspect or test anything that is at the station and connected with the production or supply of any relevant electricity, and

(ii) to inspect any records that are at that station and so connected;

(e) any authorised person not, on request, being granted access to any premises at any reasonable time to take updated readings from any relevant electricity meter;

(f) the operator having been notified of an assessment to a civil penalty or to penalty interest in relation to an event subject to this Part or Schedule 2 and, irrespective of any relevant review or appeal, that amount being unrecovered (for assessments, see paragraphs 106 and 111 of the Act; for review and appeal, see Part XI of the Act);

(g) any one or more of sub-paragraphs (a) to (e) not being satisfied within such time as the relevant Authority considers reasonable for the purpose in question;

(h) the relevant Authority for any reason not being satisfied that the electricity in question should be certified as QPO electricity.

51D. – (1) If the relevant Authority becomes aware that it has issued a CHP LEC in relation to –

(a) production when no exemption certificate was in force for the relevant station, or

(b) production in relation to which there is a breach of regulation 51B(5) (metering standards),

it shall as soon as practicable both restrict the validity of that CHP LEC to indirect supplies (see regulations 51I to 51M) and notify that restriction to the person to whom it was issued (see regulation 51B(8)).

(2) A CHP LEC so restricted is referred to in the remainder of this Part and in Schedule 2 as a "restricted CHP LEC" and any other CHP LEC is referred to as an "unrestricted CHP LEC" (but see also Schedule 2 paragraphs 8(3), 11(5) and 13(2)).

51E. – (1) The relevant Authority shall, in carrying out its functionsunder this Part, have regard to the proper administration of CCL[10].

(2) The relevant Authority shall in particular, and as appropriate, act in accordance with and have regard to Schedule 2 paragraphs 8, 10 and 11.

(3) The relevant Authority must keep a record of each CHP LEC for 6 years from the date of issue.

The record must show the person to whom it was issued, whether the CHP LEC is unrestricted or restricted, and any indirect supply of the electricity to which the CHP LEC is relevant (see regulation 51J(3)).

CCL Treatment Dependent on Certification

51F. Electricity shall not be regarded as QPO electricity for the purposes of regulation 4(1)(a) of the **Climate Change** Levy (Electricity and Gas) Regulations 2001[11] (direct supplies of electricity by utility from fully exempt CHP) unless it remains the subject of an unrestricted CHP LEC.

51G. – (1) Electricity shall not be regarded as QPO electricity for any of the following purposes unless it remains the subject of an unrestricted CHP LEC –

(a) the outputs of a station referred to in paragraph 15(1) of the Act (supplies to CHP exempt if to be used in producing station's outputs);

(b) the electricity referred to in paragraphs 16(1)(a), 17(3) and 17(4) of the Act (supplies from partly exempt CHP are exempt from CCL if specified limit not exceeded; self-supplies from station exempt if producer not auto-generator).

(2) Each of the following exemptions shall only be given effect subject to the CHP Relief Condition (see regulation 51H(1)) being fulfilled as follows –

(a) for paragraph 15(1) of the Act, the Condition must be fulfilled in relation to any QPO electricity that is a relevant output for the purposes of that paragraph (supplies to CHP exempt if for use in producing station's outputs);

(b) for paragraph 16(2) of the Act, the Condition must be fulfilled in relation to any QPO electricity referred to in that paragraph (supplies from partly exempt CHP are exempt from CCL if specified limit not exceeded);

(c) for paragraph 17(2) of the Act, the Condition must be fulfilled in relation to any QPO electricity that is the subject of the supply referred to in that paragraph (self-supply by auto-generator exempt);

(d) for paragraph 17(3) or 17(4) of the Act, the Condition must be fulfilled in relation to any QPO electricity that is electricity for the purposes of that paragraph (self-supplies from fully or partly exempt CHP exempt from CCL if producer not auto-generator).

51H. – (1) Schedule 2 has effect and, accordingly, the CHP Relief Condition binds any person who –

(a) represents to a supplier entitlement to the exemption from CCL provided for by paragraph 15(1) of the Act (supplies of taxable commodities to stations, and see also paragraph (4));

(b) does not account for CCL on a supply because an exemption is provided for by paragraph 16(2), 17(3) or 17(4) of the Act (supplies from partly exempt CHP and self-supplies from fully or partly exempt CHP);

(c) does not account for CCL on a supply because an exemption is provided for by paragraph 17(2) of the Act (self-supply by autogenerator) (but only if the electricity in question is QPO electricity).

(2) Paragraph 1 and regulations 51F and 51G only apply in relation to supplies that are treated as taking place on or after 1 April 2003 (see paragraphs 25 to 39 of the Act, time of supply).

(3) Regulations 51F and 51G apply in addition to regulation 60(1)(hb) (penalties relating to CHP Relief Condition)).

(4) Part III and Schedule 1 apply independently of this Part (certification, etc. in relation to excluded, exempt, half-rate and reduced-rate supplies).

Supplies Pursuant to CHP Declaration Contract

51I. Electricity is only "CHP electricity" for the purposes of paragraphs 20A and 20B of the Act (exemption for indirect supplies) if it remains the subject of an unrestricted CHP LEC or a restricted CHP LEC.

51J. – (1) Any electricity that is the subject of a CHP LEC shall be regarded as never having been CHP electricity capable of being the subject of exempt CHP supplies for the purposes of paragraph 20A of the Act (indirect supplies) if one or more of the conditions prescribed in the following paragraphs are not fulfilled.

(2) The electricity must only be allocated to a supply to a person who intends it to be consumed in the United Kingdom.

(3) Should the electricity be allocated to some supply pursuant to some CHP declaration contract, the supplier must inform the relevant Authority of this fact and of the relevant CHP LEC's unique identifying reference (see regulation 51B(10)).

(4) At any time up to 6 years after the day the electricity is produced, any supplier of that electricity must on request and within such time as the relevant Authority considers reasonable provide that Authority with readily legible records relating to and detailing –

(a) the supplies that supplier received or made of that electricity,

(b) the relevant suppliers or recipients of any supplies that supplier received or made of that electricity,

(c) the relevant CHP LECs and, if different from the relevant supplier or recipient, the identity of any person from or to whom entitlement to the CHP LEC was obtained or transferred.

51K. Supplies shall not be regarded as exempt CHP supplies for the purposes of paragraph 20A of the Act unless –

(a) the supplier provides the recipient with a written notice for the duration of the CHP declaration contract, updated as necessary, setting out how to identify those supplies of electricity that –

(i) are or will be made under the CHP declaration contract, and

(ii) are or will be referred to on a **climate change** levy accounting document (or an invoice) issued in respect of those supplies;

(b) the supplier retains a copy of each such notice for 6 years starting from the day after it is provided to the recipient;

(c) the supplier provides a copy of any such notice to the Commissioners no later than 14 days after the Commissioners request one.

51L. The exemption provided for by paragraph 20A(1) of the Act (indirect supplies) shall only be given effect if the supplier, and each other person (if any) who is an operator in relation to any CHP electricity allocated by the supplier to supplies under the CHP declaration contract in question, has delivered a copy of the notice referred to in paragraph 20A(1)(d) of the Act (agreement to fulfil conditions) to the relevant Authority.

51M. – (1) A supply of electricity is exempt from the levy chargeable under paragraph 5(1) of the

Act, and electricity is "CHP electricity" for the purposes of paragraphs 20A and 20B of the Act, only if paragraph (2) is satisfied in relation to that electricity.

(2) The electricity must not have been produced when the station that produced it has received State aid exceeding any relevant limit in the "Community guidelines on State aid for environmental protection (2001/C 37/03)[12]."

20. Insert immediately after regulation 60(1)(h) –

"(ha) regulation 51B(5);

(hb) regulation 51H(1) and paragraph 2, 3(1), 3(3), 3(4), 3(5), 4, 5, 6, 7, 11(2) or 12(1) of Schedule 2;".

21. Renumber the existing Schedule "Schedule 1".

22. Insert as Schedule 2 –

"SCHEDULE 2

Regulation 51H(1)

The CHP Relief Condition

Introduction

1. These obligations are for the purpose of ensuring the correct application of CCL to the outputs of a fully exempt or a partly exempt combined heat and power station.

CHP LEC and Outputs Record

2. A person to whom regulation 51H(1) applies must for the purposes of that regulation keep and maintain a discrete, proper, accurate and true record (the "CHP outputs record") of –

(a) any relevant supply of electricity constituting an output of the station in question for the purposes of paragraph 15(1) of the Act (supplies to stations);

(b) any relevant supply in relation to which CCL is not accounted for because of an exemption provided for by paragraph 16(2), 17(3) or 17(4) of the Act (supplies from partly exempt CHP and self-supplies);

(c) any relevant supply in relation to which CCL is not accounted for because of an exemption provided for by paragraph 17(2) of the Act (self-supply by autogenerator) (but only if the electricity in question is QPO electricity).

3. – (1) That record must also identify separately, according to the following categories, each MWh of QPO electricity that is an output of the station in question and allocate to each such MWh a CHP LEC issued in respect of QPO electricity.

(2) The categories are –

(a) self-supplies of the electricity;

(b) supplies made to the person who consumes the electricity;

(c) supplies made to a person who makes a supply of the electricity.

(3) A CHP LEC (or any part of it) that remains allocated to a supply must not be allocated to any other supply.

(4) The allocation must be made no later than the 120th day following when the supply is treated as taking place.

(5) Any restricted CHP LEC must be identified as such in the record no later than the 30th day after the one on which the notification that the relevant Authority has restricted its validity to indirect supplies is received (see regulation 51D and paragraph 11(5)).

4. That record must also show the quantity of all electricity that is an output of the station in question but in relation to which no CHP LEC is issued (including for this purpose, and discretely identified, any renewable source electricity (see Part IV) or electricity produced when no exemption certificate is in force for the station).

5. That record must show –

(a) when each relevant supply of electricity is treated as taking place and the recipient of each such supply;

(b) the CHP LEC (if any) relating to that electricity and, if different from the recipient, the identity of any person to whom entitlement to the CHP LEC is transferred;

(c) the date (or dates) on which each other event to which it relates occurs;

(d) the date on which each entry to the record is made.

6. That record must be kept for 6 years starting from each reconciliation day to which it is relevant (see paragraphs 10 and 13(3)).

7. Subject to paragraph 6, that record must be made available on request and at any reasonable time to a person authorised by –

(a) the Secretary of State, or

(b) the relevant Authority.

8. – (1) This paragraph applies when paragraphs 2 to 7 are not fully met.

(2) The relevant Authority may refuse to certify or issue any CHP LEC in relation to electricity produced in the station (see regulations 51B(1) and 51B(8)).

(3) The relevant Authority may also restrict the validity of any relevant and as yet unrestricted CHP LEC to indirect supplies, in which case the relevant Authority must as soon as practicable notify that restriction to the person to whom it was issued (see regulation 51B(8)).

A CHP LEC is relevant for this purpose if it has not been reconciled in accordance with this Schedule (see paragraph 13(1)).

Reconciliation of Outputs

9. For the purposes of the following paragraphs, regard a completed calendar year as one for which 31 December is passed and an incompleted calendar year as one for which 31 December is not passed.

10. – (1) The reconciliation day for a completed calendar year is the earlier of –

(a) the first day of the month in the subsequent calendar year in which regulation 3(2) of the **Climate Change** Levy (Combined Heat and Power Stations) Exemption Certificate Regulations 2001[13] is met in relation to the station (current CHPQA certificate sent to Secretary of State by 30 June);

(b) the day in the subsequent calendar year on which revocation of the current exemption certificate takes effect pursuant to regulation 4(2) of those Regulations (station ceases to operate, current CHPQA certificate not sent to Secretary of State by 30 June, or relevant written request to Secretary of State).

(c) The "reconciliation span" relating to this reconciliation day spans 1 January in the completed calendar year to the day before the reconciliation day, inclusive.

(2) A reconciliation day for an incompleted calendar year is any day in that incompleted calendar year on which revocation of the current exemption certificate takes effect pursuant to regulation 4(2) of those Regulations.

The "reconciliation span" relating to any such reconciliation day spans 1 January in that calendar year to the day before that reconciliation day, inclusive.

(3) The relevant Authority shall act in accordance with paragraph 11 no later than the 90th day following a reconciliation day, subject as appropriate to regulations 51C and 51D (relevant Authority neither certifying electricity nor issuing CHP LEC, or relevant Authority dealing with incorrect certification).

(4) A reconciliation day in paragraph (2) may arise irrespective of any overlap between the reconciliation span in that paragraph with the reconciliation span in paragraph (1).

11. – (1) The relevant Authority shall determine whether insufficient or excessive CHP LECs have been issued and remain unrestricted as respects each reconciliation span, having proper regard to the difference between –

(a) the quantity of QPO electricity actually produced in the station during that reconciliation span, and

(b) the quantity of QPO electricity represented by the CHP LECs issued as respects electricity produced in the station during that reconciliation span and remaining unrestricted.

(2) If the relevant Authority determines that insufficient CHP LECs have been issued and remain unrestricted as respects a reconciliation span, it must –

(a) to the extent of that insufficiency, and

(b) as respects that reconciliation span,

issue additional CHP LECs (see regulation 51B(8)) as respects the QPO electricity outputs of the station.

Any such CHP LEC must, within 60 days of issue, be allocated by the person referred to in paragraph 2 to relevant and appropriate supplies identified in the record as taking place in that reconciliation span.

(3) If the relevant Authority determines that excessive CHP LECs have been issued and remain unrestricted as respects a reconciliation span, it must act in accordance with paragraphs (4) and (5), as appropriate.

(4) If the reconciliation day arises because regulation 3(2) of the **Climate Change** Levy (Combined Heat and Power Stations) Exemption Certificate Regulations 2001 is met (see paragraph 10(1)(a)), the relevant Authority must treat the excess CHP LECs as being prospectively referable to figures made known to it by the operator for the purposes of regulation 51B(2) as respects production in the station after the relevant reconciliation day.

(5) If the relevant reconciliation day arises because the exemption certificate is revoked (see paragraph 10(1)(b)), the relevant Authority must restrict the validity of any excess CHP LECs to indirect supplies, in which case it must as soon as practicable notify that restriction to the person to whom the CHP LEC in question was issued or to any person appearing to control the station (see regulation 51B(8)).

The relevant Authority must ensure that those CHP LECs remaining unrestricted afterwards (and not yet reconciled, see paragraph 13(1)) collectively represent QPO electricity produced in the station during the reconciliation span.

(6) For the purposes of this paragraph, the relevant Authority must regard calendar year 2003 as beginning on 1 April 2003.

(7) For the purposes of regulation 51B(6) (QPO electricity referable to calendar year), the relevant Authority must not regard electricity referable to before 1 April 2003 as QPO electricity.

Monitoring and Balancing Obligation

12. – (1) The CHP outputs record must never show or indicate as respects a reconciliation span –

(a) a deficit of unrestricted CHP LECs in relation to the total quantity of QPO electricity identified in the record pursuant to paragraph 3(2)(a) and 3(2)(b) (self-supplies and supplies to consumers);

(b) a deficit of unrestricted plus restricted CHP LECs in relation to the total quantity of QPO electricity identified pursuant to paragraph 3(2)(a), 3(2)(b) and 3(2)(c) (self-supplies, supplies to consumers and supplies to others).

(2) Each deficit representing 1 MWh shall be regarded as a separate breach of this paragraph for the purposes of regulation 60(1)(hb) (penalties).

(3) Paragraph (1) has effect subject to paragraphs 3(4), 3(5), 11(2) and 11(5).

(4) Paragraph (1) continues to apply after a CHP LEC is reconciled (see paragraph 13(1)).

Interpretation

13. – (1) A CHP LEC is "reconciled" for the purposes of this Schedule only if –

(a) it is the subject of a reconciliation span in relation to which the relevant Authority has performed its functions under paragraph 10(3), and

(b) it is allocated, if required, in accordance with paragraph 11(2).

(2) A CHP LEC the validity of which is restricted under paragraph 8(3) or 11(5) may be regarded as a restricted CHP LEC for the purposes of regulations 51I to 51M.

(3) The CHP outputs record is relevant to a reconciliation day to the extent that it records (or is required to record) events taking place during the reconciliation span relating to that reconciliation day (see paragraphs 6, 10(1) and 10(2)).

(4) See also regulation 51A.".

M J ELAND
Commissioner of Customs and Excise

New King's Beam House, London SE1 9PJ
11 March 2003

EXPLANATORY NOTE

(This note is not part of the Regulations)

These Regulations come into force on 1 April 2003 and amend the **Climate Change** Levy (General) Regulations 2001 (S.I. 2001/838) (the "General Regulations").

Combined Heat and Power Stations

Regulations 19, 20 and 22 insert new provisions into the General Regulations.

Those inserted by regulation 19 provide for electricity produced in a combined heat and power station to be so certified by the Gas and Electricity Markets Authority (or the Director General of Electricity Supply for Northern Ireland). The existing favourable CCL[14] treatment afforded to such electricity becomes subject to such certification. The new CCL exemption[15] for supplies of such electricity that are not made from the relevant station are subjected to these certification requirements as well as to other formalities. These formalities parallel those that already apply to the exemption for renewable source electricity[16], but with an additional requirement relating to conformity with the Community guidelines on State aid for environmental protection[17].

Regulation 22 inserts certain record-keeping and reconciliation requirements on which favourable CCL treatment is made to depend. These requirements are for the better, quantitative application of the favourable CCL treatment afforded to electricity produced in combined heat and power stations.

Regulation 20 inserts relevant penalty provisions.

The CHPQA Guidance Note 15 Version 1 referred to in regulation 19 (inserted regulation 51B(5)) is available on the World Wide Web at http://chpqa.com or from the CHPQA Administrator, telephone 01235 432868.

Renewable Source Electricity

Supplies of renewable source electricity can be exempt from CCL.Biomass is prescribed as, and peat is excluded from being, a renewable source by the amendments made to the General Regulations by regulations 11 to 13. The provisions inserted by regulations 15 to 16 refine the existing certification process for renewable source electricity. Accurate figures for electricity production must now be finalised no later than 2 months after the month of production. The levy exemption certificates (Renewables LECs) are to be regarded as only relating to a given batch of electricity, may be issued in just multiples of 1 megawatt-hour and may be withheld if the quantity of electricity in question is for consumption outside the United Kingdom.

Consequential Amendments and Corrections

Regulations 3 to 10, 14, 17, 18 and 21 make consequentialamendments and typographical corrections.

Notes

[1] 2000 c. 17; paragraph 147 of Schedule 6 to the Finance Act 2000 provides that in that Schedule the Commissioners means the Commissioners of Customs and Excise. Paragraphs 20A and 149A inserted respectively by section 123 and section 124 of the Finance Act 2002 (c. 23).*back*

[2] S.I. 2001/838; amended by S.I. 2002/1152.*back*

[3] Regulation 2(1) of S.I. 2001/838, which these Regulations amend, provides that "the Act" refers to Schedule 6 to the Finance Act 2000.*back*

[4] S.I. 2001/486.*back*

[5] Paragraph 20A (and paragraph 20B) inserted by section 123 of the Finance Act 2002 (c. 23).*back*

[6] See S.I. 2001/486.*back*

[7] See S.I. 2001/1140.*back*

[8] See S.I. 2001/1140 regulation 5(2) (specified limit above which supplies of electricity from partly exempt CHP not exempt).*back*

[9] Version 1 posted on 31 January 2003 and available at http://www.chpqa.com. The metering requirements are in GN 15.7.*back*

[10] Regulation 2(1) of S.I. 2001/838, which these Regulations amend, provides that "CCL" refers to **climate change** levy.*back*

[11] S.I. 2001/1136.*back*

[12] OJ C 37, 3.2.2001, p. 3; available also on the World Wide Web at http://europa.eu.int.*back*

[13] S.I. 2001/486.*back*

[14] **Climate change** levy.*back*

[15] See S.I. 2003/603 (C. 31); the day appointed for the exemption is 1 April 2003.*back*

[16] See Part IV of the General Regulations.*back*

[17] OJ C 37, 3.2.2001, p. 3; available also on the World Wide Web at http://europa.eu.int.*back*

NORTH AMERICA

United States

Energy Policy Act of 1992

http://energy.navy.mil/publications/law_us/92epact/hr776toc.htm

TITLE I ENERGY EFFICIENCY

SUBTITLE A BUILDINGS

Sec. 101. Building Energy Efficiency Standards

(a) IN GENERAL. – Title III of the Energy Conservation and Production Act (42 U.S.C. 6831 et seq.) is amended –

(1) in section 303 –

(A) by striking paragraph (9);

(B) by redesignating paragraphs (10), (11), (12), and (13) as paragraphs (9), (10), (11), and (12), respectively; and

(C) by adding at the end the following new paragraphs –

"(13) The term 'Federal building energy standards' means energy consumption objectives to be met without specification of the methods, materials, or equipment to be employed in achieving those objectives, but including statements of the requirements, criteria, and evaluation methods to be used, and any necessary commentary.

"(14) The term 'voluntary building energy code' means a building energy code developed and updated through a consensus process among interested persons, such as that used by the Council of American Building Officials; the American Society of Heating, Refrigerating, and Air-Conditioning Engineers; or other appropriate organizations.

"(15) The term 'CABO' means the Council of American Building Officials.

"(16) The term 'ASHRAE' means the American Society of Heating, Refrigerating, and Air-Conditioning Engineers."; and

(2) by striking sections 304, 306, 308, 309, 310, and 311 and inserting the following:

"SEC. 304. UPDATING STATE BUILDING ENERGY EFFICIENCY CODES

"(a) CONSIDERATION AND DETERMINATION RESPECTING RESIDENTIAL BUILDING ENERGY CODES. –

(1) Not later than 2 years after the date of the enactment of the Energy Policy Act of 1992, each State shall certify to the Secretary that it has reviewed the provisions of its residential building code regarding energy efficiency and made a determination as to whether it is appropriate for such State to revise such residential building code provisions to meet or exceed CABO Model Energy Code, 1992.

"(2) The determination referred to in paragraph (1) shall be –

"(A) made after public notice and hearing;

"(B) in writing;

"(C) based upon findings included in such determination and upon the evidence presented at the hearing; and

"(D) available to the public.

"(3) Each State may, to the extent consistent with otherwise applicable State law, revise the provisions of its residential building code regarding energy efficiency to meet or exceed CABO Model Energy Code, 1992, or may decline to make such revisions.

"(4) If a State makes a determination under paragraph (1) that it is not appropriate for such State to revise its residential building code, such State shall submit to the Secretary, in writing, the reasons for such determination, and such statement shall be available to the public.

"(5)(A) Whenever CABO Model Energy Code, 1992, (or any successor of such code) is revised, the Secretary shall, not later than 12 months after such revision, determine whether such revision would improve energy efficiency in residential buildings. The Secretary shall publish notice of such determination in the Federal Register.

"(B) If the Secretary makes an affirmative determination under subparagraph (A), each State shall, not later than 2 years after the date of the publication of such determination, certify that it has reviewed the provisions of its residential building code regarding energy efficiency and made a determination as to whether it is appropriate for such State to revise such residential building code provisions to meet or exceed the revised code for which the Secretary made such determination.

"(C) Paragraphs (2), (3), and (4) shall apply to any determination made under subparagraph (B).

"(b) CERTIFICATION OF COMMERCIAL BUILDING ENERGY CODE UPDATES. – (1) Not later than 2 years after the date of the enactment of the Energy Policy Act of 1992, each State shall certify to the Secretary that it has reviewed and updated the provisions of its commercial building code regarding energy efficiency. Such certification shall include a demonstration that such State's code provisions meet or exceed the requirements of ASHRAE Standard 90.1-1989.

"(2)(A) Whenever the provisions of ASHRAE Standard 90.1-1989 (or any successor standard) regarding energy efficiency in commercial buildings are revised, the Secretary shall, not later than 12 months after the date of such revision, determine whether such revision will improve energy efficiency in commercial buildings. The Secretary shall publish a notice of such determination in the Federal Register.

"(B)(i) If the Secretary makes an affirmative determination under subparagraph (A), each State shall, not later than 2 years after the date of the publication of such determination, certify that it has reviewed and updated the provisions of its commercial building code regarding energy efficiency in accordance with the revised standard for which such determination was made. Such certification shall include a demonstration that the provisions of such State's commercial building code regarding energy efficiency meet or exceed such revised standard.

"(ii) If the Secretary makes a determination under subparagraph (A) that such revised standard will not improve energy efficiency in commercial buildings, State commercial building code provisions regarding energy efficiency shall meet or exceed ASHRAE Standard 90.1-1989, or if such standard has been revised, the last revised standard for which the Secretary has made an affirmative determination under subparagraph (A).

"(c) EXTENSIONS. – The Secretary shall permit extensions of the deadlines for the certification requirements under subsections (a) and (b) if a State can demonstrate that it has made a good faith effort to comply with such requirements and that it has made significant progress in doing so.

"(d) TECHNICAL ASSISTANCE. – The Secretary shall provide technical assistance to States to implement the requirements of this section, and to improve and implement State residential and commercial building energy efficiency codes or to otherwise promote the design and construction of energy efficient buildings.

"(e) AVAILABILITY OF INCENTIVE FUNDING. – (1) The Secretary shall provide incentive funding to States to implement the requirements of this section, and to improve and implement State residential and commercial building energy efficiency codes. In determining whether, and in what amount, to provide incentive funding under this subsection, the Secretary shall consider the actions proposed by the State to implement the requirements of this section, to improve and implement residential and commercial building energy efficiency codes, and to promote building energy efficiency through the use of such codes.

"(2) There are authorized to be appropriated such sums as may be necessary to carry out this subsection.

"SEC. 305. FEDERAL BUILDING ENERGY EFFICIENCY STANDARDS.

"(a)(1) IN GENERAL. – Not later than 2 years after the date of the enactment of the Energy Policy Act of 1992, the Secretary, after consulting with appropriate Federal agencies, CABO, ASHRAE, the National Association of Home Builders, the Illuminating Engineering Society, the American Institute of Architects, the National Conference of the States on Building Codes and Standards, and other appropriate persons, shall establish, by rule, Federal building energy standards that require in new Federal buildings those energy efficiency measures that are technologically feasible and economically justified. Such standards shall become effective no later than 1 year after such rule is issued.

"(2) The standards established under paragraph (1) shall –

"(A) contain energy saving and renewable energy specifications that meet or exceed the energy saving and renewable energy specifications of CABO Model Energy Code, 1992 (in the case of residential buildings) or ASHRAE Standard 90.1-1989 (in the case of commercial buildings);

"(B) to the extent practicable, use the same format as the appropriate voluntary building energy code; and

"(C) consider, in consultation with the Environmental Protection Agency and other Federal agencies, and where appropriate contain, measures with regard to radon and other indoor air pollutants.

"(b) REPORT ON COMPARATIVE STANDARDS. – The Secretary shall identify and describe, in the report required under section 308, the basis for any substantive difference between the Federal building energy standards established under this section (including differences in treatment of energy efficiency and renewable energy) and the appropriate voluntary building energy code.

"(c) PERIODIC REVIEW. – The Secretary shall periodically, but not less than once every 5 years, review the Federal building energy standards established under this section and shall, if significant energy savings would result, upgrade such standards to include all new energy efficiency and renewable energy measures that are technologically feasible and economically justified.

"(d) INTERIM STANDARDS. – Interim energy performance standards for new Federal buildings issued by the Secretary under this title as it existed before the date of the enactment of the Energy Policy Act of 1992 shall remain in effect until the standards established under subsection (a) become effective.

"SEC. 306. FEDERAL COMPLIANCE.

"(a) PROCEDURES. – (1) The head of each Federal agency shall adopt procedures necessary to assure that new Federal buildings meet or exceed the Federal building energy standards established under section 305.

"(2) The Federal building energy standards established under section 305 shall apply to new buildings under the jurisdiction of the Architect of the Capitol. The Architect shall adopt procedures necessary to assure that such buildings meet or exceed such standards.

"(b) CONSTRUCTION OF NEW BUILDINGS. – The head of a Federal agency may expend Federal funds for the construction of a new Federal building only if the building meets or exceeds the appropriate Federal building energy standards established under section 305.

"SEC. 307. SUPPORT FOR VOLUNTARY BUILDING ENERGY CODES.

"(a) IN GENERAL. – Not later than 1 year after the date of the enactment of the Energy Policy Act of 1992, the Secretary, after consulting with the Secretary of Housing and Urban Development, the Secretary of Veterans Affairs, other appropriate Federal agencies, CABO, ASHRAE, the National Conference of States on Building Codes and Standards, and any other appropriate building codes and standards organization, shall support the upgrading of voluntary building energy codes for new residential and commercial buildings. Such support shall include –

"(1) a compilation of data and other information regarding building energy efficiency standards and codes in the possession of the Federal Government, State and local governments, and industry organizations;

"(2) assistance in improving the technical basis for such standards and codes;

"(3) assistance in determining the cost-effectiveness and the technical feasibility of the energy efficiency measures included in such standards and codes; and

"(4) assistance in identifying appropriate measures with regard to radon and other indoor air pollutants.

"(b) REVIEW. – The Secretary shall periodically review the technical and economic basis of voluntary building energy codes and, based upon ongoing research activities –

"(1) recommend amendments to such codes including measures with regard to radon and other indoor air pollutants;

"(2) seek adoption of all technologically feasible and economically justified energy efficiency measures; and

"(3) otherwise participate in any industry process for review and modification of such codes.

"SEC. 308. REPORTS.

"The Secretary, in consultation with the Secretary of Housing and Urban Development, the Secretary of Veterans Affairs, and other appropriate Federal agencies, shall report annually to the Congress on activities conducted pursuant to this title. Such report shall include –

"(1) recommendations made under section 307(b) regarding the prevailing voluntary building energy codes;

"(2) a State-by-State summary of actions taken under this title; and

"(3) recommendations to the Congress with respect to opportunities to further promote building energy efficiency and otherwise carry out the purposes of this title.".

(b) CONFORMING AMENDMENT. – The table of contents of such Act is amended by striking the items relating to sections 304, 306, 308, 309, 310 and 311, and inserting in lieu thereof the following –

"Sec. 304. Updating State building energy efficiency codes.

"Sec. 305. Federal building energy efficiency standards.

"Sec. 306. Federal compliance.

"Sec. 307. Support for voluntary building energy codes.

"Sec. 308. Reports."

(c) FEDERAL MORTGAGE REQUIREMENTS –

(1) AMENDMENT TO CRANSTON-GONZALEZ NATIONAL AFFORDABLE HOUSING ACT. – Section 109 of the Cranston-Gonzalez National Affordable Housing Act (42 U.S.C. 12709) is amended to read as follows:

"SEC. 109. ENERGY EFFICIENCY STANDARDS.

"(a) ESTABLISHMENT. –

"(1) IN GENERAL. – The Secretary of Housing and Urban Development and the Secretary of Agriculture shall, not later than 1 year after the date of the enactment of the Energy Policy Act of 1992, jointly establish, by rule, energy efficiency standards for –

"(A) new construction of public and assisted housing and single family and multifamily residential housing (other than manufactured homes) subject to mortgages insured under the National Housing Act; and

"(B) new construction of single family housing (other than manufactured homes) subject to mortgages insured, guaranteed, or made by the Secretary of Agriculture under title V of the Housing Act of 1949.

"(2) CONTENTS. – Such standards shall meet or exceed the requirements of the Council of American Building Officials Model Energy Code, 1992 (hereafter in this section referred to as 'CABO Model Energy Code, 1992'), or, in the case of multifamily high rises, the requirements of the American Society of Heating, Refrigerating, and Air-Conditioning Engineers Standard 90.1-1989 (hereafter in this section referred to as 'ASHRAE Standard 90.1-1989'), and shall be cost-effective with respect to construction and operating costs on a life-cycle cost basis. In developing such standards, the Secretaries shall consult with an advisory task force composed of homebuilders, national, State, and local housing agencies (including public housing agencies), energy agencies, building code organizations and agencies, energy efficiency organizations, utility organizations, low-income housing organizations, and other parties designated by the Secretaries.

"(b) MODEL ENERGY CODE. – If the Secretaries have not, within 1 year after the date of the enactment of the Energy Policy Act of 1992, established energy efficiency standards under subsection (a), all new construction of housing specified in such subsection shall meet the requirements of CABO Model Energy Code, 1992, or, in the case of multifamily high rises, the requirements of ASHRAE Standard 90.1-1989.

"(c) REVISIONS OF MODEL ENERGY CODE. – If the requirements of CABO Model Energy Code, 1992, or, in the case of multifamily high rises, ASHRAE Standard 90.1-1989, are revised at any time, the Secretaries shall, not later than 1 year after such revision, amend the standards established under subsection (a) to meet or exceed the requirements of such revised code or standard unless the Secretaries determine that compliance with such revised code or standard would not result in a significant increase in energy efficiency or would not be technologically feasible or economically justified.".

(2) AMENDMENT TO TITLE 38, UNITED STATES CODE. – Section 3704 of title 38, United States Code, is amended by adding at the end thereof the following new subsection:

"(g) A loan for the purchase or construction of new residential property, the construction of which began after the energy efficiency standards under section 109 of the Cranston-Gonzalez National Affordable Housing Act (42 U.S.C. 12709), as amended by section 101(c) of the Energy Policy Act of 1992, take effect, may not be financed through the assistance of this chapter unless the new residential property is constructed in compliance with such standards.".

Sec. 102. Residential Energy Efficiency Ratings.

(a) RATINGS. – Title II of the National Energy Conservation Policy Act (42 U.S.C. 8211 et seq.) is amended by adding at the end the following new part:

"PART 6 – RESIDENTIAL ENERGY EFFICIENCY RATING GUIDELINES

"SEC. 271. VOLUNTARY RATING GUIDELINES.

"(a) IN GENERAL. – Not later than 18 months after the date of the enactment of the Energy Policy Act of 1992, the Secretary, in consultation with the Secretary of Housing and Urban Development, the Secretary of Veterans Affairs, representatives of existing home energy rating programs, and other appropriate persons, shall, by rule, issue voluntary guidelines that may be used by State and local governments, utilities, builders, real estate agents, lenders, agencies in mortgage markets, and others, to enable and encourage the assignment of energy efficiency ratings to residential buildings.

"(b) CONTENTS OF GUIDELINES. – The voluntary guidelines issued under subsection (a) shall –

"(1) encourage uniformity with regard to systems for rating the annual energy efficiency of residential buildings;

"(2) establish protocols and procedures for –

"(A) certification of the technical accuracy of building energy analysis tools used to determine energy efficiency ratings;

"(B) training of personnel conducting energy efficiency ratings;

"(C) data collection and reporting;

"(D) quality control; and

"(E) monitoring and evaluation;

"(3) encourage consistency with, and support for, the uniform plan for Federal energy efficient mortgages, including that developed under section 946 of the Cranston-Gonzalez National Affordable Housing Act (42 U.S.C. 12712 note) and pursuant to sections 105 and 106 of the Energy Policy Act of 1992;

"(4) provide that rating systems take into account local climate conditions and construction practices, solar energy collected on-site, and the benefits of peak load shifting construction practices, and not discriminate among fuel types; and

"(5) establish procedures to ensure that residential buildings can receive an energy efficiency rating at the time of sale and that such rating is communicated to potential buyers.

"SEC. 272. TECHNICAL ASSISTANCE.

"Not later than 2 years after the date of the enactment of the Energy Policy Act of 1992, the Secretary shall establish a program to provide technical assistance to State and local organizations to encourage the adoption of and use of residential energy efficiency rating systems consistent with the voluntary guidelines issued under section 271.

"SEC. 273. REPORT.

"Not later than 3 years after the date of the enactment of the Energy Policy Act of 1992, the Secretary shall transmit to the President and the Congress a final report containing –

"(1) a description of actions taken by the Secretary and other Federal agencies to implement this part;

"(2) a description of the action taken by States, local governments, and other organizations to implement the voluntary guidelines issued under section 271 and any problems encountered in implementing such guidelines; and

"(3) recommendations on the feasibility of requiring, as a prerequisite to receiving federally assisted, guaranteed, or insured mortgages, the achievement of a minimum energy efficiency rating.".

(b) CONFORMING AMENDMENT. – The table of contents for such Act is amended by adding at the end of title II the following:

"PART 6 RESIDENTIAL ENERGY EFFICIENCY RATINGS

"Sec. 271. Voluntary rating guidelines.

"Sec. 272. Technical assistance.

"Sec. 273. Report.".

Sec. 103. Energy Efficient Lighting and Building Centers.

(a) PURPOSE. – The purpose of this section is to encourage energy efficiency in buildings through the establishment of regional centers to promote energy efficient lighting, heating and cooling, and building design.

(b) GRANTS FOR ESTABLISHMENT. – Not later than 18 months after the date of the enactment of this Act, the Secretary shall make grants to nonprofit institutions, or to consortiums that may include nonprofit institutions, State and local governments, universities, and utilities, to establish or enhance one regional building energy efficiency center (hereafter in this section referred to as a "regional center") in each of the 10 regions served by a Department of Energy regional support office.

(c) PERMITTED ACTIVITIES. – Each regional center established under this section may –

(1) provide information, training, and technical assistance to building professionals such as architects, designers, engineers, contractors, and building code officials, on building energy efficiency methods and technologies, including lighting, heating and cooling, and passive solar;

(2) operate an outreach program to inform such building professionals of the benefits and opportunities of energy efficiency, and of the services of the center;

(3) provide displays demonstrating building energy efficiency methods and technologies, such as lighting, windows, and heating and cooling equipment;

(4) coordinate its activities and programs with other institutions within the region, such as State and local governments, utilities, and educational institutions, in order to support their efforts to promote building energy efficiency;

(5) serve as a clearinghouse to ensure that information about new building energy efficiency technologies, including case studies of successful applications, is disseminated to end-users in the region;

(6) study the building energy needs of the region and make available region-specific energy efficiency information to facilitate the adoption of cost-effective energy efficiency improvements;

(7) assist educational institutions in establishing building energy efficiency engineering and technical programs and curricula; and

(8) evaluate the performance of the center in promoting building energy efficiency.

(d) APPLICATION. – Any nonprofit institution or consortium interested in receiving a grant under this section shall submit to the Secretary an application in such form and containing such information as the Secretary may require. A lighting or building energy center in existence on the date of the enactment of this section which is owned and operated by a nonprofit institution or a consortium as described in subsection (b) shall be eligible for a grant under this section.

(e) SELECTION CRITERIA. – The Secretary shall select recipients of grants under this section on the basis of the following criteria:

(1) The capability of the grant recipient to establish a board of directors for the regional center composed of representatives from utilities, State and local governments, building trade and professional organizations, manufacturers, and nonprofit energy and environmental organizations.

(2) The demonstrated or potential resources available to the grant recipient for carrying out this subsection.

(3) The demonstrated or potential ability of the grant recipient to promote building energy efficiency by carrying out the activities specified in subsection (c).

(4) The activities which the grant recipient proposes to carry out under the grant.

(f) REQUIREMENT OF MATCHING FUNDS. –

(1) FEDERAL SHARE. – The Federal share of a grant under this section shall be no more than 50 percent of the costs of establishing, and no more than 25 percent of the cost of operating the regional center.

(2) NON-FEDERAL CONTRIBUTIONS. – No grant may be made under this section in any fiscal year unless the recipient of such grant enters into such agreements with the Secretary as the Secretary may require to ensure that such recipient will provide the necessary non-Federal contributions. Such non-Federal contributions may be provided by utilities, State and local governments, nonprofit institutions, foundations, corporations, and other non-Federal entities.

(g) TASK FORCE. – The Secretary shall establish a task force to –

(1) advise the Secretary on activities to be carried out by grant recipients;

(2) review and evaluate programs carried out by grant recipients; and

(3) make recommendations regarding the building energy efficiency center grant program.

(h) MEMBERSHIP TERMS AND ADMINISTRATION OF TASK FORCE. –

(1) IN GENERAL. – The task force shall be composed of approximately 20 members, appointed by the Secretary, with expertise in the area of building energy efficiency, including representatives from –

(A) State or local energy offices;

(B) utilities;

(C) building construction trade or professional associations;

(D) architecture, engineering or professional associations;

(E) building component or equipment manufacturers;

(F) from national laboratories;

(G) building code officials or professional associations; and

(H) nonprofit energy or environmental organizations.

(2) GEOGRAPHIC REPRESENTATION. – The Secretary shall ensure that there is broad geographical representation among task force members.

(3) TERMS. – Members shall be appointed for a term of 3 years. A vacancy in the task force shall be filled in the manner in which the original appointment was made.

(4) PAY. – Members shall serve without pay. Each member shall receive travel expenses, including per diem in lieu of subsistence, in accordance with sections 5702 and 5703 of title 5, United States Code.

(5) CHAIRPERSON. – The Chairperson and Vice Chairperson of the task force shall be elected by the members.

(6) MEETINGS. – The task force shall meet biannually and at the call of the Chairperson.

(7) INAPPLICABILITY OF TERMINATION DATE. – Section 14 of the Federal Advisory Committee Act shall not apply to the task force.

(i) REPORT. – The Secretary shall transmit annually to the Congress a report on the activities of regional centers established under this section, including the degree to which matching funds are being leveraged from private sources to establish and operate such centers.

(j) AUTHORIZATION OF APPROPRIATIONS. – There is authorized to be appropriated for purposes of carrying out this section, to remain available until expended, not more than $10,000,000 for each of fiscal years 1994, 1995, and 1996.

Sec. 104. Manufactured Housing Energy Efficiency.

(a) AMENDMENTS TO CRANSTON-GONZALEZ NATIONAL AFFORDABLE HOUSING ACT. – Section

943(d)(1) of the Cranston-Gonzalez National Affordable Housing Act (Public Law 101-625; 109 Stat. 4413) is amended –

(1) in subparagraph (D), by striking "thermal insulation, energy efficiency";

(2) by redesignating subparagraphs (E), (F), (G), and (H) as subparagraphs (F), (G), (H), and (I), respectively; and

(3) by inserting after subparagraph (D) the following new subparagraph:

> "(E) consult with the Secretary of Energy and make recommendations regarding additional or revised standards for thermal insulation and energy efficiency applicable to manufactured housing;".

(b) DUTIES OF THE SECRETARY. – The Secretary of Housing and Urban Development shall assess the energy performance of manufactured housing and make recommendations to the National Commission on Manufactured Housing established under section 943 of the Cranston-Gonzalez National Affordable Housing Act regarding any thermal insulation and energy efficiency improvements applicable to manufactured housing which are technologically feasible and economically justified. The Secretary shall also test the performance and determine the cost effectiveness of manufactured housing constructed in compliance with the standards established under such section.

(c) EXCEPTION TO FEDERAL PREEMPTION. – If the Secretary of Housing and Urban Development has not issued, within 1 year after the date of the enactment of this Act, final regulations pursuant to section 604 of the National Manufactured Housing Construction and Safety Standards Act of 1974 (42 U.S.C. 5403) that establish thermal insulation and energy efficiency standards for manufactured housing that take effect before January 1, 1995, then States may establish thermal insulation and energy efficiency standards for manufactured housing if such standards are at least as stringent as thermal performance standards for manufactured housing contained in the Second Public Review Draft of BSR/ASHRAE 90.2P entitled "Energy Efficient Design of Low-Rise Residential Buildings" and all public reviews of Independent Substantive Changes to such document that have been approved on or before the date of the enactment of this Act.

Sec. 105. Energy Efficient Mortgages.

(a) DEFINITION OF ENERGY EFFICIENT MORTGAGE. – Section 104 of the Cranston-Gonzalez National Affordable Housing Act (42 U.S.C. 12704) is amended by adding at the end the following new paragraph:

> "(24) The term 'energy efficient mortgage' means a mortgage that provides financing incentives for the purchase of energy efficient homes, or that provides financing incentives to make energy efficiency improvements in existing homes by incorporating the cost of such improvements in the mortgage.".

(b) UNIFORM MORTGAGE FINANCING PLAN FOR ENERGY EFFICIENCY. – Section 946 of the Cranston-Gonzalez National Affordable Housing Act (42 U.S.C. 12712 note) is amended –

(1) in subsection (a), by striking "mortgage financing incentives for energy efficiency" and inserting "energy efficient mortgages (as such term is defined in section 104 of this Act)"; and

(2) in subsection (b) –

(A) in the second sentence, by inserting ", but not be limited to," after "include"; and

(B) by inserting after the period at the end of the following new sentence: "The Task Force shall determine whether notifying potential home purchasers of the availability of energy efficient mortgages would promote energy efficiency in residential buildings, and if so, the Task Force shall recommend appropriate notification guidelines, and agencies and organizations referred to in the preceding sentence are authorized to implement such guidelines.".

Sec. 106. Energy Efficient Mortgages Pilot Program.

(a) ESTABLISHMENT OF PILOT PROGRAM. –

(1) IN GENERAL. – Not later than 6 months after the date of enactment of this Act, the Secretary of Housing and Urban Development (hereafter referred to as the "Secretary") shall establish an energy efficient mortgage pilot program in 5 States, to promote the purchase of existing energy efficient residential

buildings and the installation of cost-effective improvements in existing residential buildings.

(2) PILOT PROGRAM. – The pilot program established under this subsection shall include the following criteria, where applicable:

(A) ORIGINATION. – The lender shall originate a housing loan that is insured under title II of the National Housing Act in accordance with the applicable requirements.

(B) APPROVAL. – The mortgagor's base loan application shall be approved if the mortgagor's income and credit record is found to be satisfactory.

(C) COST OF IMPROVEMENTS. – The cost of cost-effective energy efficiency improvements shall not exceed the greater of –

(i) 5 percent of the property value (not to exceed $8,000); or

(ii) $4,000.

(3) AUTHORITY FOR MORTGAGEES. – In granting mortgages under the pilot program established pursuant to this subsection, the Secretary shall grant mortgagees the authority –

(A) to permit the final loan amount to exceed the loan limits established under title II of the National Housing Act by an amount not to exceed 100 percent of the cost of the cost-effective energy efficiency improvements, if the mortgagor's request to add the cost of such improvements is received by the mortgagee prior to funding of the base loan;

(B) to hold in escrow all funds provided to the mortgagor to undertake the energy efficiency improvements until the efficiency improvements are actually installed; and

(C) to transfer or sell the energy efficient mortgage to the appropriate secondary market agency, after the mortgage is issued, but before the energy efficiency improvements are actually installed.

(4) PROMOTION OF PILOT PROGRAM. – The Secretary shall encourage participation in the energy efficient mortgage pilot program by –

(A) making available information to lending agencies and other appropriate authorities regarding the availability and benefits of energy efficient mortgages;

(B) requiring mortgagees and designated lending authorities to provide written notice of the availability and benefits of the pilot program to mortgagors applying for financing in those States designated by the Secretary as participating under the pilot program; and

(C) requiring each applicant for a mortgage insured under title II of the National Housing Act in those States participating under the pilot program to sign a statement that such applicant has been informed of the program requirements and understands the benefits of energy efficient mortgages.

(5) TRAINING PROGRAM. – Not later than 9 months after the date of enactment of this Act, the Secretary, in consultation with the Secretary of Energy, shall establish and implement a program for training personnel at relevant lending agencies, real estate companies, and other appropriate organizations regarding the benefits of energy efficient mortgages and the operation of the pilot program under this subsection.

(6) REPORT. – Not later than 18 months after the date of enactment of this Act, the Secretary shall prepare and submit a report to the Congress describing the effectiveness and implementation of the energy efficient mortgage pilot program as described under this subsection, and assessing the potential for expanding the pilot program nationwide.

(b) EXPANSION OF PROGRAM. – Not later than the expiration of the 2-year period beginning on the date of the implementation of the energy efficient mortgage pilot program under this section, the Secretary of Housing and Urban Development shall expand the pilot program on a nationwide basis and shall expand the program to include new residential housing, unless the Secretary determines that either such expansion would not be practicable, in which case the Secretary shall submit to the Congress, before the expiration of such period, a report explaining why either expansion would not be practicable.

(c) DEFINITIONS. – For purposes of this section:

(1) The term "base loan" means any mortgage loan for a residential building eligible for insurance under title II of the National Housing Act or title 38, United States Code, that does not include the cost of cost-effective energy improvements.

(2) The term "cost-effective" means, with respect to energy efficiency improvements to a residential building, improvements that result in the total present value cost of the improvements (including any maintenance and repair expenses) being less

than the total present value of the energy saved over the useful life of the improvement, when 100 percent of the cost of improvements is added to the base loan. For purposes of this paragraph, savings and cost-effectiveness shall be determined pursuant to a home energy rating report sufficient for purposes of the Federal National Mortgage Association and the Federal Home Loan Mortgage Corporation, or by other technically accurate methods.

(3) The term "energy efficient mortgage" means a mortgage on a residential building that recognizes the energy savings of a home that has cost-effective energy saving construction or improvements (including solar water heaters, solar-assisted air conditioners and ventilators, super-insulation, and insulating glass and film) and that has the effect of not disqualifying a borrower who, but for the expenditures on energy saving construction or improvements, would otherwise have qualified for a base loan.

(4) The term "residential building" means any attached or unattached single family residence.

(d) RULE OF CONSTRUCTION. – This section may not be construed to affect any other programs of the Secretary of Housing and Urban Development for energy-efficient mortgages. The pilot program carried out under this section shall not replace or result in the termination of such other programs.

(e) REGULATIONS. – The Secretary shall issue any regulations necessary to carry out this section not later than the expiration of the 180-day period beginning on the date of the enactment of this Act. The regulations shall be issued after notice and opportunity for public comment pursuant to the provisions of section 553 of title 5, United States Code (notwithstanding subsections (a)(2), (b)(B), and (d)(3) of such section).

(f) AUTHORIZATION OF APPROPRIATIONS. – There are authorized to be appropriated such sums as may be necessary to carry out this section.

SUBTITLE B UTILITIES

Sec. 111. Encouragement of Investments in Conservation and Energy Efficiency by Electric Utilities.

(a) AMENDMENT TO THE PUBLIC UTILITY REGULATORY POLICIES ACT. – The Public Utility Regulatory Policies Act of 1978 (P.L.95-617; 92 Stat. 3117; 16 U.S.C. 2601 and following) is amended by adding the following at the end of section 111(d):

"(7) INTEGRATED RESOURCE PLANNING. – Each electric utility shall employ integrated resource planning. All plans or filings before a State regulatory authority to meet the requirements of this paragraph must be updated on a regular basis, must provide the opportunity for public participation and comment, and contain a requirement that the plan be implemented.

"(8) INVESTMENTS IN CONSERVATION AND DEMAND MANAGEMENT. – The rates allowed to be charged by a State regulated electric utility shall be such that the utility's investment in and expenditures for energy conservation, energy efficiency resources, and other demand side management measures are at least as profitable, giving appropriate consideration to income lost from reduced sales due to investments in and expenditures for conservation and efficiency, as its investments in and expenditures for the construction of new generation, transmission, and distribution equipment. Such energy conservation, energy efficiency resources and other demand side management measures shall be appropriately monitored and evaluated.

"(9) ENERGY EFFICIENCY INVESTMENTS IN POWER GENERATION AND SUPPLY. – The rates charged by any electric utility shall be such that the utility is encouraged to make investments in, and expenditures for, all cost-effective improvements in the energy efficiency of power generation, transmission and distribution. In considering regulatory changes to achieve the objectives of this paragraph, State regulatory authorities and nonregulated electric utilities shall consider the disincentives caused by existing ratemaking policies, and practices, and consider incentives that would encourage better maintenance, and investment in more efficient power generation, transmission and distribution equipment.".

(b) PROTECTION FOR SMALL BUSINESS. – The Public Utility Regulatory Policies Act of 1978 (P.L.95-617; 92 Stat. 3117; 16 U.S.C. 2601 and following) is amended by inserting the following new paragraph at the end of subsection 111(c):

"(3) If a State regulatory authority implements a standard established by subsection (d)(7) or (8), such authority shall –

"(A) consider the impact that implementation of such standard would have on small businesses engaged in the design, sale, supply, installation or servicing of energy conservation, energy efficiency or other demand side management measures, and

"(B) implement such standard so as to assure that utility actions would not provide such utilities with unfair competitive advantages over such small businesses.".

(c) EFFECTIVE DATE. – Section 112(b) of such Act is amended by inserting "(or after the enactment of the Comprehensive National Energy Policy Act in the case of standards under paragraphs (7), (8), and (9) of section 111(d)" after "Act" in both places such word appears in paragraphs (1) and (2).

(d) DEFINITIONS. – Section 3 of such Act is amended by adding the following new paragraphs at the end thereof:

"(19) The term 'integrated resource planning' means, in the case of an electric utility, a planning and selection process for new energy resources that evaluates the full range of alternatives, including new generating capacity, power purchases, energy conservation and efficiency, cogeneration and district heating and cooling applications, and renewable energy resources, in order to provide adequate and reliable service to its electric customers at the lowest system cost. The process shall take into account necessary features for system operation, such as diversity, reliability, dispatchability, and other factors of risk; shall take into account the ability to verify energy savings achieved through energy conservation and efficiency and the projected durability of such savings measured over time; and shall treat demand and supply resources on a consistent and integrated basis.

"(20) The term 'system cost' means all direct and quantifiable net costs for an energy resource over its available life, including the cost of production, distribution, transportation, utilization, waste management, and environmental compliance.

"(21) The term 'demand side management' includes load management techniques.".

(e) REPORT. – Not later than 2 years after the date of the enactment of this Act, the Secretary shall transmit a report to the President and to the Congress containing –

(1) a survey of all State laws, regulations, practices, and policies under which State regulatory authorities implement the provisions of paragraphs (7), (8), and (9) of section 111(d) of the Public Utility Regulatory Policies Act of 1978;

(2) an evaluation by the Secretary of whether and to what extent, integrated resource planning is likely to result in –

(A) higher or lower electricity costs to an electric utility's ultimate consumers or to classes or groups of such consumers;

(B) enhanced or reduced reliability of electric service; and

(C) increased or decreased dependence on particular energy resources; and

(3) a survey of practices and policies under which electric cooperatives prepare integrated resource plans, submit such plans to the Rural Electrification Administration and the extent to which such integrated resource planning is reflected in rates charged to customers.

The report shall include an analysis prepared in conjunction with the Federal Trade Commission, of the competitive impact of implementation of energy conservation, energy efficiency, and other demand side management programs by utilities on small businesses engaged in the design, sale, supply, installation, or servicing of similar energy conservation, energy efficiency, or other demand side management measures and whether any unfair, deceptive, or predatory acts exist, or are likely to exist, from implementation of such programs.

Sec. 112. Energy Efficiency Grants to State Regulatory Authorities.

(a) ENERGY EFFICIENCY GRANTS. – The Secretary is authorized in accordance with the provisions of this section to provide grants to State regulatory authorities in an amount not to exceed $250,000 per authority, for purposes of encouraging demand-side management including energy conservation, energy efficiency and load management techniques and for meeting the requirements of paragraphs (7), (8), and (9) of section 111(d) of the Public

Utility Regulatory Policies Act of 1978 and as a means of meeting gas supply needs and to meet the requirements of paragraphs (3) and (4) of section 303(b) of the Public Utility Regulatory Policies Act of 1978. Such grants may be utilized by a State regulatory authority to provide financial assistance to nonprofit subgrantees of the Department of Energy's Weatherization Assistance Program in order to facilitate participation by such subgrantees in proceedings of such regulatory authority to examine energy conservation, energy efficiency, or other demand-side management programs.

(b) PLAN. – A State regulatory authority wishing to receive a grant under this section shall submit a plan to the Secretary that specifies the actions such authority proposes to take that would achieve the purposes of this section.

(c) SECRETARIAL ACTION. – (1) In determining whether, and in what amount, to provide a grant to a State regulatory authority under this section the Secretary shall consider, in addition to other appropriate factors, the actions proposed by the State regulatory authority to achieve the purposes of this section and to consider implementation of the ratemaking standards established in –

(A) paragraphs (7), (8) and (9) of section 111(d) of the Public Utility Regulatory Policies Act of 1978; or

(B) paragraphs (3) and (4) of section 303(b) of the Public Utility Regulatory Policies Act of 1978.

(2) Such actions –

(A) shall include procedures to facilitate the participation of grantees and nonprofit subgrantees of the Department of Energy's Weatherization Assistance Program in proceedings of such regulatory authorities examining demand-side management programs; and

(B) shall provide for coverage of the cost of such grantee and subgrantees' participation in such proceedings.

(d) RECORDKEEPING. – Each State regulatory authority that receives a grant under this section shall keep such records as the Secretary shall require.

(e) DEFINITION. – For purposes of this section, the term "State regulatory authority" shall have the same meaning as provided by section 3 of the Public Utility Regulatory Policies Act of 1978 in the case of electric utilities, and such term shall have the same meaning as provided by section 302 of the Public Utility Regulatory Policies Act of 1978 in the case of gas utilities, except that in the case of any State without a statewide ratemaking authority, such term shall mean the State energy office.

(g) AUTHORIZATION. – There are authorized to be appropriated $5,000,000 for each of the fiscal years 1994, 1995 and 1996 to carry out the purposes of this section.

Sec. 113. Tennessee Valley Authority Least-Cost Planning Program.

(a) IN GENERAL. – The Tennessee Valley Authority shall conduct a least-cost planning program in accordance with this section.

(b) CONDUCT OF PROGRAM. –

(1) IN GENERAL. – In conducting a least-cost planning program under subsection (a), the Tennessee Valley Authority shall employ and implement a planning and selection process for new energy resources which evaluates the full range of existing and incremental resources (including new power supplies, energy conservation and efficiency, and renewable energy resources) in order to provide adequate and reliable service to electric customers of the Tennessee Valley Authority at the lowest system cost.

(2) PLANNING AND SELECTION PROCESS. – The planning and selection process referred to in paragraph (1) shall –

(A) take into account necessary features for system operation, including diversity, reliability, dispatchability, and other factors of risk;

(B) take into account the ability to verify energy savings achieved through energy conservation and efficiency and the projected durability of such savings measured over time; and

(C) treat demand and supply resources on a consistent and integrated basis.

(3) SYSTEM COST DEFINED. – As used in paragraph (1), the term "system cost" means all direct and quantifiable net costs for an energy resource over its available life, including the cost of production, transportation, utilization, waste management, environmental compliance, and, in the case of imported energy resources, maintaining access to foreign sources of supply.

(c) PARTICIPATION BY DISTRIBUTORS. –

(1) IN GENERAL. – In conducting a least-cost planning program under subsection (a), the Tennessee Valley Authority shall –

(A) provide an opportunity for distributors of the Tennessee Valley Authority to recommend cost-effective energy efficiency opportunities, rate structure incentives, and renewable energy proposals for inclusion in such program; and

(B) encourage and assist such distributors in the planning and implementation of cost-effective energy efficiency options.

(2) ASSISTANCE. – The Tennessee Valley Authority shall provide appropriate assistance to distributors under paragraph (1)(B). Such assistance shall, where cost effective, be provided by the Tennessee Valley Authority acting through, or in cooperation with, an association of distributors. Such assistance may include publications, workshops, conferences, one-on-one assistance, financial assistance, equipment loans, technology assessment studies, marketing studies, and other appropriate mechanisms to transfer information on energy efficiency and renewable energy options and programs to customers.

(d) PUBLIC REVIEW AND COMMENT. – Before the selection and addition of a major new energy resource on the Tennessee Valley Authority system, the Tennessee Valley Authority shall provide an opportunity for public review and comment and shall include a description of any such action in an annual report to the President and Congress.

(e) EXEMPTION FROM CERTAIN REQUIREMENTS. – The Tennessee Valley Authority shall not be subject to the least-cost planning requirements contained in section 111(d) of the Public Utility Regulatory Policies Act of 1978 or any similar requirement which might arise out of the Tennessee Valley Authority's electric power transactions with the Southeastern Power Administration.

Sec. 114. Amendment of Hoover Power Plant Act.

Title II of the Hoover Power Plant Act of 1984 (42 U.S.C. 7275-7276, Public Law 98-381) is amended to read as follows:

"TITLE II – INTEGRATED RESOURCE PLANNING

"Sec. 201. Definitions.

"Sec. 202. Regulations to require integrated resource planning.

"Sec. 203.Technical assistance.

"Sec. 204. Integrated resource plans.

"Sec. 205. Miscellaneous provisions.

"SEC. 201. DEFINITIONS.

"As used in this title:

"(1) The term 'Administrator' means the Administrator of the Western Area Power Administration.

"(2) The term 'integrated resource planning' means a planning process for new energy resources that evaluates the full range of alternatives, including new generating capacity, power purchases, energy conservation and efficiency, cogeneration and district heating and cooling applications, and renewable energy resources, in order to provide adequate and reliable service to its electric customers at the lowest system cost. The process shall take into account necessary features for system operation, such as diversity, reliability, dispatchability, and other factors of risk; shall take into account the ability to verify energy savings achieved through energy conservation and efficiency and the projected durability of such savings measured over time; and shall treat demand and supply resources on a consistent and integrated basis.

"(3) The term 'least cost option' means an option for providing reliable electric services to electric customers which will, to the extent practicable, minimize life-cycle system costs, including adverse environmental effects, of providing such service. To the extent practicable, energy efficiency and renewable resources may be given priority in any least-cost option.

"(4) The term 'long-term firm power service contract' means any contract for the sale by Western Area Power Administration of firm capacity, with or without energy, which is to be delivered over a period of more than one year.

"(5) The terms 'customer' or 'customers' means any entity or entities purchasing firm capacity with or without energy, from the Western Area Power

Administration under a long-term firm power service contract. Such terms include parent-type entities and their distribution or user members.

"(6) For any customer, the term 'applicable integrated resource plan' means the integrated resource plan approved by the Administrator under this title for that customer.

"SEC. 202. REGULATIONS TO REQUIRE INTEGRATED RESOURCE PLANNING.

"(a) REGULATIONS. – Within 1 year after the enactment of this section, the Administrator shall, by regulation, revise the Final Amended Guidelines and Acceptance Criteria for Customer Conservation and Renewable Energy Programs published in the Federal Register on August 21, 1985 (50 F.R. 33892), or any subsequent amendments thereto, to require each customer purchasing electric energy under a long-term firm power service contract with the Western Area Power Administration to implement, within 3 years after the enactment of this section, integrated resource planning in accordance with the requirements of this title.

"(b) CERTAIN SMALL CUSTOMERS. – Notwithstanding subsection (a), for customers with total annual energy sales or usage of 25 Gigawatt Hours or less which are not members of a joint action agency or a generation and transmission cooperative with power supply responsibility, the Administrator may establish different regulations and apply such regulations to customers that the Administrator finds have limited economic, managerial, and resource capability to conduct integrated resource planning. The regulations under this subsection shall require such customers to consider all reasonable opportunities to meet their future energy service requirements using demand-side techniques, new renewable resources and other programs that will provide retail customers with electricity at the lowest possible cost, and minimize, to the extent practicable, adverse environmental effects.

"SEC. 203. TECHNICAL ASSISTANCE.

"The Administrator may provide technical assistance to customers to, among other things, conduct integrated resource planning, implement applicable integrated resource plans, and otherwise comply with the requirements of this title. Technical assistance may include publications, workshops, conferences, one-to-one assistance, equipment loans, technology and resource assessment studies, marketing studies, and other mechanisms to transfer information on energy efficiency and renewable energy options and programs to customers. The Administrator shall give priority to providing technical assistance to customers that have limited capability to conduct integrated resource planning.

"SEC. 204. INTEGRATED RESOURCE PLANS.

"(a) REVIEW BY WESTERN AREA POWER ADMINISTRATION. – Within 1 year after the enactment of this section, the Administrator shall, by regulation, revise the Final Amended Guidelines and Acceptance Criteria for Customer Conservation and Renewable Energy Programs published in the Federal Register on August 21, 1985 (50 F.R. 33892), or any subsequent amendments thereto, to require each customer to submit an integrated resource plan to the Administrator within 12 months after such regulations are amended. The regulation shall require a revision of such plan to be submitted every 5 years after the initial submission. The Administrator shall review the initial plan in accordance with a schedule established by the Administrator (which schedule will provide for the review of all initial plans within 24 months after such regulations are amended), and each revision thereof within 120 days after his receipt of the plan or revision and determine whether the customer has in the development of the plan or revision, complied with this title. Plan amendments may be submitted to the Administrator at any time and the Administrator shall review each such amendment within 120 days after receipt thereof to determine whether the customer in amending its plan has complied with this title. If the Administrator determines that the customer, in developing its plan, revision, or amendment, has not complied with the requirements of this title, the customer shall resubmit the plan at any time thereafter. Whenever a plan or revision or amendment is resubmitted the Administrator shall review the plan or revision or amendment within 120 days after his receipt thereof to determine whether the customer has complied with this title.

"(b) CRITERIA FOR APPROVAL OF INTEGRATED RESOURCE PLANS. – The Administrator shall approve an integrated resource plan submitted as required under subsection (a) if, in developing the plan, the customer has:

"(1) Identified and accurately compared all practicable energy efficiency and energy supply resource options available to the customer.

"(2) Included a 2-year action plan and a 5-year action plan which describe specific actions the customer will take to implement its integrated resource plan.

"(3) Designated 'least-cost options' to be utilized by the customer for the purpose of providing reliable electric service to its retail consumers and explained the reasons why such options were selected.

"(4) To the extent practicable, minimized adverse environmental effects of new resource acquisitions.

"(5) In preparation and development of the plan (and each revision or amendment of the plan) has provided for full public participation, including participation by governing boards.

"(6) Included load forecasting.

"(7) Provided methods of validating predicted performance in order to determine whether objectives in the plan are being met.

"(8) Met such other criteria as the Administrator shall require.

"(c) USE OF OTHER INTEGRATED RESOURCE PLANS. – Where a customer or group of customers are implementing integrated resource planning under a program responding to Federal, State, or other initiatives, including integrated resource planning considered and implemented pursuant to section 111(d) of the Public Utility Regulatory Policies Act of 1978, in evaluating that customer's integrated resource plan under this title, the Administrator shall accept such plan as fulfillment of the requirements of this title to the extent such plan substantially complies with the requirements of this title.

"(d) COMPLIANCE WITH INTEGRATED RESOURCE PLANS. – Within 1 year after the enactment of this section, the Administrator shall, by regulation, revise the Final Amended Guidelines and Acceptance Criteria for Customer Conservation and Renewable Energy Programs published in the Federal Register on August 21, 1985 (50 F.R. 33892), or any subsequent amendments thereto, to require each customer to fully comply with the applicable integrated resource plan and submit an annual report to the Administrator (in such form and containing such information as the Administrator may require) describing the customer's progress to the goals established in such plan. After the initial review under subsection (a) the Administrator shall periodically conduct reviews of a representative sample of applicable integrated resource plans and the customer's implementation of the applicable integrated resource plan to determine if the customers are in compliance with their plans. If the Administrator finds a customer out-of-compliance, the Administrator shall impose a surcharge under this section on all electric energy purchased by the customer from the Western Area Power Administration or reduce such customer's power allocation by 10 percent, unless the Administrator finds that a good faith effort has been made to comply with the approved plan.

"(e) ENFORCEMENT. –

"(1) NO APPROVED PLAN. – If an integrated resource plan for any customer is not submitted before the date 12 months after the guidelines are amended as required under this section or if the plan is disapproved by the Administrator and a revised plan is not resubmitted by the date 9 months after the date of such disapproval, the Administrator shall impose a surcharge of 10 percent of the purchase price on all power obtained by that customer from the Western Area Power Administration after such date. The surcharge shall remain in effect until an integrated resource plan is approved for that customer. If the plan is not submitted for more than one year after the required date, the surcharge shall increase to 20 percent for the second year (or any portion thereof prior to approval of the plan) and to 30 percent thereafter until the plan is submitted or the contract for the purchase of power by such customer from the Western Area Power Administration terminates.

"(2) FAILURE TO COMPLY WITH APPROVED PLAN. – After approval by the Administrator of an applicable integrated resource plan for any customer, the Administrator shall impose a 10 percent surcharge on all power purchased by such customer from the Western Area Power Administration whenever the Administrator determines that such customer's activities are not consistent with the applicable integrated resource plan. The surcharge shall remain in effect until the Administrator determines that the customer's activities are consistent with the applicable integrated resource plan. The surcharge shall be increased to 20 percent if the customer's activities are out of compliance for more than one year and to 30 percent after more than 2 years, except that no surcharge shall be imposed if the customer demonstrates, to the satisfaction of the Administrator, that a good faith effort has been made to comply with the approved plan.

"(3) REDUCTION IN POWER ALLOCATION. – In the case of any customer subject to a surcharge under paragraph (1) or (2), in lieu of imposing such surcharge the Administrator may reduce such customer's power allocation from the Western Area Power Administration by 10 percent. The Administrator shall provide by regulation the terms and conditions under which a power allocation terminated under this subsection may be reinstated.

"(f) INTEGRATED RESOURCE PLANNING COOPERATIVES. – With the approval of the Administrator, customers within any State or region may form integrated resource planning cooperatives for the purposes of complying with this title, and such customers shall be allowed an additional 6 months to submit an initial integrated resource plan to the Administrator.

"(g) CUSTOMERS WITH MORE THAN 1 CONTRACT. – If more than one long-term firm power service contract exists between the Administrator and a customer, only one integrated resource plan shall be required for that customer under this title.

"(h) PROGRAM REVIEW. – Within 1 year after January 1, 1999, and at appropriate intervals thereafter, the Administrator shall initiate a public process to review the program established by this section. The Administrator is authorized at that time to revise the criteria set forth in section 204(b) to reflect changes, if any, in technology, needs, or other developments.

"SEC. 205. MISCELLANEOUS PROVISIONS.

"(a) ENVIRONMENTAL IMPACT STATEMENT. – The provisions of the National Environmental Policy Act of 1969 shall apply to actions of the Administrator implementing this title in the same manner and to the same extent as such provisions apply to other major Federal actions significantly affecting the quality of the human environment.

"(b) ANNUAL REPORTS. – The Administrator shall include in the annual report submitted by the Western Area Power Administration (1) a description of the activities undertaken by the Administrator and by customers under this title and (2) an estimate of the energy savings and renewable resource benefits achieved as a result of such activities.

"(c) STATE REGULATED INVESTORDOWNED UTILITIES. – Any State regulated electric utility (as defined in section 3(18) of the Public Utility Regulatory Policies Act of 1978) shall be exempt from the provisions of this title.

"(d) RURAL ELECTRIFICATION ADMINISTRATION REQUIREMENTS. – Nothing in this title shall require a customer to take any action inconsistent with a requirement imposed by the Rural Electrification Administration".

Sec. 115. Encouragement of Investments in Conservation and Energy Efficiency by Gas Utilities.

(a) DEFINITIONS. – Section 302 of the Public Utility Regulatory Policies Act of 1978 (15 U.S.C. 3202) is amended by adding the following at the end thereof:

"(9) The term 'integrated resource planning' means, in the case of a gas utility, planning by the use of any standard, regulation, practice, or policy to undertake a systematic comparison between demand-side management measures and the supply of gas by a gas utility to minimize life-cycle costs of adequate and reliable utility services to gas consumers. Integrated resource planning shall take into account necessary features for system operation such as diversity, reliability, dispatchability, and other factors of risk and shall treat demand and supply to gas consumers on a consistent and integrated basis.

"(10) The term 'demand-side management' includes energy conservation, energy efficiency, and load management techniques.".

(b) IN GENERAL. – Section 303(b) of the Public Utility Regulatory Policies Act of 1978 (15 U.S.C. 3202) is amended by inserting at the end the following new paragraphs:

"(3) INTEGRATED RESOURCE PLANNING. – Each gas utility shall employ, in order to provide adequate and reliable service to its gas customers at the lowest system cost. All plans or filings of a State regulated gas utility before a State regulatory authority to meet the requirements of this paragraph shall (A) be updated on a regular basis, (B) provide the opportunity for public participation and comment, (C) provide for methods of validating predicted performance, and (D) contain a requirement that the plan be implemented after approval of the State regulatory authority. Subsection (c) shall not apply to this paragraph to the extent that it could be construed to require the State regulatory authority to extend the record of a State proceeding in submitting reports to the Federal Government.

"(4) INVESTMENTS IN CONSERVATION AND DEMAND MANAGEMENT. – The rates charged by any State regulated gas utility shall be such that the utility's prudent investments in, and expenditures for, energy conservation and load shifting programs and for other demand-side management measures which are consistent with the findings and purposes of the Energy Policy Act of 1992 are at least as profitable (taking into account the income lost due to reduced sales resulting from such programs) as prudent investments in, and expenditures for, the acquisition or construction of supplies and facilities. This objective requires that (A) regulators link the utility's net revenues, at least in part, to the utility's performance in implementing cost-effective programs promoted by this section; and (B) regulators ensure that, for purposes of recovering fixed costs, including its authorized return, the utility's performance is not affected by reductions in its retail sales volumes.".

(c) IMPACT ON SMALL BUSINESS. – Section 303 of such Act is amended by inserting the following new subsection at the end thereof:

"(d) SMALL BUSINESS IMPACTS. – If a State regulatory authority implements a standard established by subsection (b) (3) or (4), such authority shall –

"(1) consider the impact that implementation of such standard would have on small businesses engaged in the design, sale, supply, installation, or servicing of energy conservation, energy efficiency, or other demand-side management measures, and

"(2) implement such standard so as to assure that utility actions would not provide such utilities with unfair competitive advantages over such small businesses.".

(d) EFFECTIVE DATE. – Section 303(a) of such Act is amended by inserting "(or after the enactment of the Energy Policy Act of 1992 in the case of standards under paragraphs (3), and (4) of subsection (b))" after "Act" and by striking out "standard established by subsection (b)(2)" in paragraph (2) and inserting "standards established by paragraphs (2), (3) and (4) of subsection (b)".

(e) REPORT. – The report under section 111(e) of this Act transmitted by the Secretary of Energy to the President and to the Congress shall contain a survey of all State laws, regulations, practices, and policies under which State regulatory authorities implement the provisions of paragraphs (3) and (4) of section 303(b) of the Public Utility Regulatory Policies Act of 1978. The report shall include an analysis, prepared in conjunction, with the Federal Trade Commission, of the competitive impact of implementation of energy conservation, energy efficiency, and other demand side management programs by gas utilities on small businesses engaged in the design, sale, supply, installation, or servicing of similar energy conservation, energy efficiency, or other demand-side management measures and whether any unfair, deceptive, or predatory acts or practices exist, or are likely to exist, from implementation of such programs.

SUBTITLE C APPLIANCE AND EQUIPMENT ENERGY EFFICIENCY STANDARDS

Sec. 121. Energy Efficiency Labeling for Windows and Window Systems.

(a) IN GENERAL. – (1) The Secretary shall, after consulting with the National Fenestration Rating Council, industry representatives, and other appropriate organizations, provide financial assistance to support a voluntary national window rating program that will develop energy ratings and labels for windows and window systems.

(2) Such rating program shall include –

(A) specifications for testing procedures and labels that will enable window buyers to make more informed purchasing decisions about the energy efficiency of windows and window systems; and

(B) information (which may be disseminated through catalogs, trade publications, labels, or other mechanisms) that will allow window buyers to assess the energy consumption and potential cost savings of alternative window products.

(3) Such rating program shall be developed by the National Fenestration Rating Council according to commonly accepted procedures for the development of national testing procedures and labeling programs.

(b) MONITORING. – The Secretary shall monitor and evaluate the efforts of the National Fenestration Rating Council and, not later than one year after the date of the enactment of this Act, make a determination as to whether the program developed by the Council is consistent with the objectives of subsection (a).

(c) ALTERNATIVE SYSTEM. – (1) If the Secretary makes a determination under subsection (b) that a voluntary national window rating program consistent with the objectives of subsection (a) has not been developed, the Secretary shall, after consultation with the National Institute of Standards and Technology, develop, not later than two years after such determination, test procedures under section 323 of the Energy Policy and Conservation Act (42 U.S.C. 6293) for windows and window systems.

(2) Not later than one year after the Secretary develops test procedures under paragraph (1), the Federal Trade Commission (hereafter in this section referred to as the "Commission") shall prescribe labeling rules under section 324 of such Act (42 U.S.C. 6294) for those windows and window systems for which the Secretary has prescribed test procedures under paragraph (1) except that, with respect to any type of window or window system (or class thereof), the Secretary may determine that such labeling is not technologically feasible or economically justified or is not likely to assist consumers in making purchasing decisions.

(3) For purposes of sections 323, 324, and 327 of such Act, each product for which the Secretary has established test procedures or labeling rules pursuant to this subsection shall be considered a new covered product under section 322 of such Act (42 U.S.C. 6292) to the extent necessary to carry out this subsection.

(4) For purposes of section 327(a) of such Act, the term "this part" includes this subsection to the extent necessary to carry out this subsection.

Sec. 122. Energy Conservation Requirements for Certain Commercial and Industrial Equipment.

(a) DEFINITIONS. – Section 340 of the Energy Policy and Conservation Act (42 U.S.C. 6311) is amended –

(1) in paragraph (1) –

(A) by redesignating subparagraph (B) as subparagraph (G); and

(B) by inserting after subparagraph (A) the following:

"(B) Small commercial package air conditioning and heating equipment.

"(C) Large commercial package air conditioning and heating equipment.

"(D) Packaged terminal air-conditioners and packaged terminal heat pumps.

"(E) Warm air furnaces and packaged boilers.

"(F) Storage water heaters, instantaneous water heaters, and unfired hot water storage tanks."; and

(2) in paragraph (2)(B) –

(A) by striking out "pumps)" and inserting in lieu thereof "pumps, small and large commercial package air conditioning and heating equipment, packaged terminal air-conditioners, packaged terminal heat pumps, warm air furnaces, packaged boilers, storage water heaters, instantaneous water heaters, and unfired hot water storage tanks)"; and

(B) by striking out clauses (v) and (xi) and redesignating clauses (vi), (vii), (viii), (ix), (x), (xii), (xiii), and (xiv) as clauses (v), (vi), (vii), (viii), (ix), (x), (xi), and (xii), respectively; and

(3) by adding at the end the following:

"(8) The term 'small commercial package air conditioning and heating equipment' means air-cooled, water-cooled, evaporatively-cooled, or water source (not including ground water source) electrically operated, unitary central air conditioners and central air conditioning heat pumps for commercial application which are rated below 135,000 Btu per hour (cooling capacity).

"(9) The term 'large commercial package air conditioning and heating equipment' means air-cooled, water-cooled, evaporatively-cooled, or water source (not including ground water source) electrically operated, unitary central air conditioners and central air conditioning heat pumps for commercial application which are rated at or above 135,000 Btu per hour and below 240,000 Btu per hour (cooling capacity).

"(10)(A) The term 'packaged terminal air conditioner' means a wall sleeve and a separate unencased combination of heating and cooling assemblies specified by the builder and intended for mounting through the wall. It includes a prime source of refrigeration, separable outdoor louvers, forced ventilation, and heating availability by builder's choice of hot water, steam, or electricity.

"(B) The term 'packaged terminal heat pump' means a packaged terminal air conditioner that utilizes reverse cycle refrigeration as its prime heat source and should have supplementary heat source available to builders with the choice of hot water, steam, or electric resistant heat.

"(11)(A) The term 'warm air furnace' means a self-contained oil- or gas-fired furnace designed to supply heated air through ducts to spaces that require it and includes combination warm air furnace/electric air conditioning units but does not include unit heaters and duct furnaces.

"(B) The term 'packaged boiler' means a boiler that is shipped complete with heating equipment, mechanical draft equipment, and automatic controls; usually shipped in one or more sections.

"(12)(A) The term 'storage water heater' means a water heater that heats and stores water within the appliance at a thermostatically controlled temperature for delivery on demand. Such term does not include units with an input rating of 4000 Btu per hour or more per gallon of stored water.

"(B) The term 'instantaneous water heater' means a water heater that has an input rating of at least 4000 Btu per hour per gallon of stored water.

"(C) The term 'unfired hot water storage tank' means a tank used to store water that is heated externally.

"(13)(A) The term 'electric motor' means any motor which is a general purpose T-frame, single-speed, foot-mounting, polyphase squirrel-cage induction motor of the National Electrical Manufacturers Association, Design A and B, continuous rated, operating on 230/460 volts and constant 60 Hertz line power as defined in NEMA Standards Publication MG1-1987.

"(B) The term 'definite purpose motor' means any motor designed in standard ratings with standard operating characteristics or standard mechanical construction for use under service conditions other than usual or for use on a particular type of application and which cannot be used in most general purpose applications.

"(C) The term 'special purpose motor' means any motor, other than a general purpose motor or definite purpose motor, which has special operating characteristics or special mechanical construction, or both, designed for a particular application.

"(D) The term 'open motor' means a motor having ventilating openings which permit passage of external cooling air over and around the windings of the machine.

"(E) The term 'enclosed motor' means a motor so enclosed as to prevent the free exchange of air between the inside and outside of the case but not sufficiently enclosed to be termed airtight.

"(F) The term 'small electric motor' means a NEMA general purpose alternating current single-speed induction motor, built in a two-digit frame number series in accordance with NEMA Standards Publication MG 1-1987.

"(G) The term 'efficiency' when used with respect to an electric motor means the ratio of an electric motor's useful power output to its total power input, expressed in percentage.

"(H) The term 'nominal full load efficiency' means the average efficiency of a population of motors of duplicate design as determined in accordance with NEMA Standards Publication MG 1-1987.

"(14) The term 'ASHRAE' means the American Society of Heating, Refrigerating, and Air Conditioning Engineers.

"(15) The term 'IES' means the Illuminating Engineering Society of North America.

"(16) The term 'NEMA' means the National Electrical Manufacturers Association.

"(17) The term 'IEEE' means the Institute of Electrical and Electronics Engineers.

"(18) The term 'energy conservation standard' means –

"(A) a performance standard that prescribes a minimum level of energy efficiency or a maximum quantity of energy use for a product; or

"(B) a design requirement for a product."

(b) TEST PROCEDURES. – (1) Section 343(a) of such Act (42 U.S.C. 6314) is amended –

(A) by striking out paragraph (1) and inserting in lieu thereof the following:

"(1) The Secretary may conduct an evaluation of a class of covered

equipment and may prescribe test procedures for such class in accordance with the provisions of this section."; and

(B) by adding at the end the following new paragraphs:

"(4)(A) With respect to small commercial package air conditioning and heating equipment, large commercial package air conditioning and heating equipment, packaged terminal air conditioners, packaged terminal heat pumps, warm-air furnaces, packaged boilers, storage water heaters, instantaneous water heaters, and unfired hot water storage tanks to which standards are applicable under section 342, the test procedures shall be those generally accepted industry testing procedures or rating procedures developed or recognized by the Air-Conditioning and Refrigeration Institute or by the American Society of Heating, Refrigerating and Air Conditioning Engineers, as referenced in ASHRAE/IES Standard 90.1 and in effect on June 30, 1992.

"(B) If such an industry test procedure or rating procedure for small commercial package air conditioning and heating equipment, large commercial package air conditioning and heating equipment, packaged terminal air conditioners, packaged terminal heat pumps, warm-air furnaces, packaged boilers, storage water heaters, instantaneous water heaters, or unfired hot water storage tanks is amended, the Secretary shall amend the test procedure for the product as necessary to be consistent with the amended industry test procedure or rating procedure unless the Secretary determines, by rule, published in the Federal Register and supported by clear and convincing evidence, that to do so would not meet the requirements for test procedures described in paragraphs (2) and (3) of this subsection.

"(C) If the Secretary prescribes a rule containing such a determination, the rule may establish an amended test procedure for such product that meets the requirements of paragraphs (2) and (3) of this subsection. In establishing any amended test procedure under this subparagraph or subparagraph (B), the Secretary shall follow the procedures and meet the requirements specified in section 323(e).

"(5)(A) With respect to electric motors to which standards are applicable under section 342, the test procedures shall be the test procedures specified in NEMA Standards Publication MG1-1987 and IEEE Standard 112 Test Method B for motor efficiency, as in effect on the date of the enactment of the Energy Policy Act of 1992.

"(B) If the test procedure requirements of NEMA Standards Publication MG-1987 and IEEE Standard 112 Test Method B for motor efficiency are amended, the Secretary shall amend the test procedures established by subparagraph (A) to conform to such amended test procedure requirements unless the Secretary determines, by rule, published in the Federal Register and supported by clear and convincing evidence, that to do so would not meet the requirements for test procedures described in paragraphs (2) and (3) of this subsection.

"(C) If the Secretary prescribes a rule containing such a determination, the rule may establish amended test procedures for such electric motors that meets the requirements of paragraphs (2) and (3) of this subsection. In establishing any amended test procedure under this subparagraph or subparagraph (B), the Secretary shall follow the procedures and meet the requirements specified in section 323(e).".

(2) The second subsection designated as subsection (d) of section 343 of such Act (42 U.S.C. 6314(d)(1)) is amended in paragraph (1) in the material preceding subparagraph (A), by inserting after "180 days" the following: "(or, in the case of small commercial package air conditioning and heating

equipment, large commercial package air conditioning and heating equipment, packaged terminal air conditioners, packaged terminal heat pumps, warm-air furnaces, packaged boilers, storage water heaters, instantaneous water heaters, and unfired hot water storage tanks, 360 days)".

(c) LABELING. – Section 344 of such Act (42 U.S.C. 6315) is amended –

(1) in subsection (a), by striking out "may" and inserting in lieu thereof "shall";

(2) in subsection (c), by striking out "may" in the material preceding paragraph (1) and inserting in lieu thereof "shall";

(3) by redesignating subsections (d), (e), (f), (g), (h), and (i) as subsections (f), (g), (h), (i), (j), and (k), respectively; and

(4) by inserting after subsection (c), the following new subsections:

"(d) Subject to subsection (h), not later than 12 months after the Secretary establishes test procedures for electric motors under section 343, the Secretary shall prescribe labeling rules under this section applicable to electric motors taking into consideration NEMA Standards Publication MG1-1987. Such rules shall provide that the labeling of any electric motor manufactured after the 12-month period beginning on the date the Secretary prescribes such labeling rules, shall –

"(1) indicate the energy efficiency of the motor on the permanent nameplate attached to such motor;

"(2) prominently display the energy efficiency of the motor in equipment catalogs and other material used to market the equipment; and

"(3) include such other markings as the Secretary determines necessary solely to facilitate enforcement of the standards established for electric motors under section 342.

"(e) Subject to subsection (h), not later than 12 months after the Secretary establishes test procedures for small commercial package air conditioning and heating equipment, large commercial package air conditioning and heating equipment, packaged terminal air conditioners, packaged terminal heat pumps, warm-air furnaces, packaged boilers, storage water heaters, instantaneous water heaters, and unfired hot water storage tanks under section 343, the Secretary shall prescribe labeling rules under this section for such equipment. Such rules shall provide that the labeling of any small commercial package air conditioning and heating equipment, large commercial package air conditioning and heating equipment, packaged terminal air conditioner, packaged terminal heat pump, warm-air furnace, packaged boiler, storage water heater, instantaneous water heater, and unfired hot water storage tank manufactured after the 12-month period beginning on the date the Secretary prescribes such rules shall –

"(1) indicate the energy efficiency of the equipment on the permanent nameplate attached to such equipment or other nearby permanent marking;

"(2) prominently display the energy efficiency of the equipment in new equipment catalogs used by the manufacturer to advertise the equipment; and

"(3) include such other markings as the Secretary determines necessary solely to facilitate enforcement of the standards established for such equipment under section 342.".

(d) STANDARDS. – Section 342 of such Act is amended to read as follows:

"STANDARDS

"SEC. 342. (A) SMALL AND LARGE COMMERCIAL PACKAGE AIR CONDITIONING AND HEATING EQUIPMENT, PACKAGED TERMINAL AIR CONDITIONERS AND HEAT PUMPS, WARM-AIR FURNACES, PACKAGED BOILERS, STOGAGE WATER HEATERS, INSTANTANEOUS WATER HEATERS, AND UNFIRED HOT WATER STORAGE TANKS. – (1) Each small commercial package air conditioning and heating equipment manufactured on or after January 1, 1994, shall meet the following standard levels:

"(A) The minimum seasonal energy efficiency ratio of air-cooled three-phase electric central air conditioners and central air conditioning heat pumps less than 65,000 Btu per hour (cooling capacity), split systems, shall be 10.0.

"(B) The minimum seasonal energy efficiency ratio of air-cooled three-phase electric central air conditioners and central air conditioning heat pumps less than 65,000 Btu per hour (cooling capacity), single package, shall be 9.7.

"(C) The minimum energy efficiency ratio of air-cooled central air conditioners and central air conditioning heat pumps at or above 65,000 Btu per hour (cooling capacity) and less than 135,000 Btu per hour (cooling capacity) shall be 8.9 (at a standard rating of 95 degrees F db).

"(D) The minimum heating seasonal performance factor of air-cooled three-phase electric central air conditioning heat pumps less than 65,000 Btu per hour (cooling capacity), split systems, shall be 6.8.

"(E) The minimum heating seasonal performance factor of air-cooled three-phase electric central air conditioning heat pumps less than 65,000 Btu per hour (cooling capacity), single package, shall be 6.6.

"(F) The minimum coefficient of performance in the heating mode of air-cooled central air conditioning heat pumps at or above 65,000 Btu per hour (cooling capacity) and less than 135,000 Btu per hour (cooling capacity) shall be 3.0 (at a high temperature rating of 47 degrees F db).

"(G) The minimum energy efficiency ratio of water-cooled, evaporatively-cooled and water-source central air conditioners and central air conditioning heat pumps less than 65,000 Btu per hour (cooling capacity) shall be 9.3 (at a standard rating of 95 degrees F db, outdoor temperature for evaporatively cooled equipment, and 85 degrees Fahrenheit entering water temperature for water-source and water-cooled equipment).

"(H) The minimum energy efficiency ratio of water-cooled, evaporatively-cooled and water-source central air conditioners and central air conditioning heat pumps at or above 65,000 Btu per hour (cooling capacity) and less than 135,000 Btu per hour (cooling capacity) shall be 10.5 (at a standard rating of 95 degrees F db, outdoor temperature for evaporatively cooled equipment, and 85 degrees Fahrenheit entering water temperature for water source and water-cooled equipment).

"(I) The minimum coefficient of performance in the heating mode of water-source heat pumps less than 135,000 Btu per hour (cooling capacity) shall be 3.8 (at a standard rating of 70 degrees Fahrenheit entering water).

"(2) Each large commercial package air conditioning and heating equipment manufactured on or after January 1, 1995, shall meet the following standard levels:

"(A) The minimum energy efficiency ratio of air-cooled central air conditioners and central air conditioning heat pumps at or above 135,000 Btu per hour (cooling capacity) and less than 240,000 Btu per hour (cooling capacity) shall be 8.5 (at a standard rating of 95 degrees F db).

"(B) The minimum coefficient of performance in the heating mode of air-cooled central air conditioning heat pumps at or above 135,000 Btu per hour (cooling capacity) and less than 240,000 Btu per hour (cooling capacity) shall be 2.9.

"(C) The minimum energy efficiency ratio of water- and evaporatively-cooled central air conditioners and central air conditioning heat pumps at or above 135,000 Btu per hour (cooling capacity) and less than 240,000 Btu per hour (cooling capacity) shall be 9.6 (according to ARI Standard 360-86).

"(3) Each packaged terminal air conditioner and packaged terminal heat pump manufactured on or after January 1, 1994, shall meet the following standard levels:

"(A) The minimum energy efficiency ratio (EER) of packaged terminal air conditioners and packaged terminal heat pumps in the cooling mode shall be 10.0 – (0.16 × Capacity [in thousands of Btu per hour at a standard rating of 95 degrees F db, outdoor temperature]). If a unit has a capacity of less than 7,000 Btu per hour, then 7,000 Btu per hour shall be used in the calculation. If a unit has a capacity of greater than 15,000 Btu per hour, then 15,000 Btu per hour shall be used in the calculation.

"(B) The minimum coefficient of performance (COP) of packaged terminal heat pumps in the heating mode shall be 1.3 + (0.16 × the minimum cooling EER as specified in subparagraph (A)) (at a standard rating of 47 degrees F db).

"(4) Each warm air furnace and packaged boiler manufactured on or after January 1, 1994, shall meet the following standard levels:

"(A) The minimum thermal efficiency at the maximum rated capacity of gas-fired warm-air furnaces with capacity of 225,000 Btu per hour or more shall be 80 percent.

"(B) The minimum thermal efficiency at the maximum rated capacity of oil-fired warm-air furnaces with capacity of 225,000 Btu per hour or more shall be 81 percent.

"(C) The minimum combustion efficiency at the maximum rated capacity of gas-fired packaged boilers with capacity of 300,000 Btu per hour or more shall be 80 percent.

"(D) The minimum combustion efficiency at the maximum rated capacity of oil-fired packaged boilers with capacity of 300,000 Btu per hour or more shall be 83 percent.

"(5) Each storage water heater, instantaneous water heater, and unfired water storage tank manufactured on or after January 1, 1994, shall meet the following standard levels:

"(A) Except as provided in subparagraph (G), the maximum standby loss, in percent per hour, of electric storage water heaters shall be 0.30 + (27/Measured Storage Volume [in gallons]).

"(B) Except as provided in subparagraph (G), the maximum standby loss, in percent per hour, of gas- and oil-fired storage water heaters with input ratings of 155,000 Btu per hour or less shall be 1.30 + (114/Measured Storage Volume [in gallons]). The minimum thermal efficiency of such units shall be 78 percent.

"(C) Except as provided in subparagraph (G), the maximum standby loss, in percent per hour, of gas- and oil-fired storage water heaters with input ratings of more than 155,000 Btu per hour shall be 1.30 + (95/Measured Storage Volume [in gallons]). The minimum thermal efficiency of such units shall be 78 percent.

"(D) The minimum thermal efficiency of instantaneous water heaters with a storage volume of less than 10 gallons shall be 80 percent.

"(E) Except as provided in subparagraph (G), the minimum thermal efficiency of instantaneous water heaters with a storage volume of 10 gallons or more shall be 77 percent. The maximum standby loss, in percent/hour, of such units shall be 2.30 + (67/Measured Storage Volume [in gallons]).

"(F) Except as provided in subparagraph (G), the maximum heat loss of unfired hot water storage tanks shall be 6.5 Btu per hour per square foot of tank surface area.

"(G) Storage water heaters and hot water storage tanks having more than 140 gallons of storage capacity need not meet the standby loss or heat loss requirements specified in subparagraphs (A) through (C) and subparagraphs (E) and (F) if the tank surface area is thermally insulated to R-12.5 and if a standing pilot light is not used.

"(6)(A) If ASHRAE/IES Standard 90.1, as in effect on the date of enactment of the Energy Policy Act of 1992, is amended with respect to any small commercial package air conditioning and heating equipment, large commercial package air conditioning and heating equipment, packaged terminal air conditioners, packaged terminal heat pumps, warm-air furnaces, packaged boilers, storage water heaters, instantaneous water heaters, or unfired hot water storage tanks, the Secretary shall establish an amended uniform national standard for that product at the minimum level for each effective date specified in the amended ASHRAE/IES Standard 90.1, unless the Secretary determines, by rule published in the Federal Register and supported by clear and convincing evidence, that adoption of a uniform national standard more stringent than such amended ASHRAE/IES Standard 90.1 for such product would result in significant additional conservation of energy and is technologically feasible and economically justified.

"(B)(i) If the Secretary issues a rule containing such a determination, the rule shall establish such amended standard. In determining whether a standard is economically justified for the purposes of subparagraph (A), the Secretary shall, after receiving views and comments furnished with respect to the proposed standard, determine whether the benefits of the standard exceed its burdens by, to the greatest extent practicable, considering –

"(I) the economic impact of the standard on the manufacturers and on the consumers of the products subject to such standard;

"(II) the savings in operating costs throughout the estimated average life of the product in the type (or class) compared to any increase in the price of, or in the initial charges for, or maintenance expenses of, the products which are likely to result from the imposition of the standard;

"(III) the total projected amount of energy savings likely to result directly from the imposition of the standard;

"(IV) any lessening of the utility or the performance of the products likely to result from the imposition of the standard;

"(V) the impact of any lessening of competition, as determined in writing by the Attorney General, that is likely to result from the imposition of the standard;

"(VI) the need for national energy conservation; and

"(VII) other factors the Secretary considers relevant.

"(ii) The Secretary may not prescribe any amended standard under this paragraph which increases the maximum allowable energy use, or decreases the minimum required energy efficiency, of a covered product. The Secretary may not prescribe an amended standard under this subparagraph if the Secretary finds (and publishes such finding) that interested persons have established by a preponderance of the evidence that a standard is likely to result in the unavailability in the United States in any product type (or class) of performance characteristics (including reliability), features, sizes, capacities, and volumes that are substantially the same as those generally available in the United States at the time of the Secretary's finding. The failure of some types (or classes) to meet this criterion shall not affect the Secretary's determination of whether to prescribe a standard for other types or classes.

"(C) A standard amended by the Secretary under this paragraph shall become effective for products manufactured –

"(i) with respect to small commercial package air conditioning and heating equipment, packaged terminal air conditioners, packaged terminal heat pumps, warm-air furnaces, packaged boilers, storage water heaters, instantaneous water heaters, and unfired hot water storage tanks, on or after a date which is two years after the effective date of the applicable minimum energy efficiency requirement in the amended ASHRAE/IES standard referred to in subparagraph (A); and

"(ii) with respect to large commercial package air conditioning and heating equipment, on or after a date which is three years after the effective date of the applicable minimum energy efficiency requirement in the amended ASHRAE/IES standard referred to in subparagraph (A);

except that an energy conservation standard amended by the Secretary pursuant to a rule under subparagraph (B) shall become effective for products manufactured on or after a date which is four years after the date such rule is published in the Federal Register.

"(b) ELECTRIC MOTORS. – (1) Except for definite purpose motors, special purpose motors, and those motors exempted by the Secretary under paragraph (2), each electric motor manufactured (alone or as a component of another piece of equipment) after the 60-month period beginning on the date of the enactment of this subsection, or in the case of an electric motor which requires listing or certification by a nationally recognized safety testing laboratory, after the 84-month period beginning on such date, shall have a nominal full load efficiency of not less than the following:

"Nominal Full-Load Efficiency
Open Motors Closed Motors
"Number of poles = 6 4 2 6 4 2

Motor Horsepower
1 80.0 82.5 80.0 82.5 75.5
1.5 84.0 84.0 82.5 85.5 84.0 82.5
2 85.5 84.0 84.0 86.5 84.0 84.0
3 86.5 86.5 84.0 87.5 87.5 85.5
5 87.5 87.5 85.5 87.5 87.5 87.5
7.5 88.5 88.5 87.5 89.5 89.5 88.5
10 90.2 89.5 88.5 89.5 89.5 89.5
15 90.2 91.0 89.5 90.2 91.0 90.2
20 91.0 91.0 90.2 90.2 91.0 90.2
25 91.7 91.7 91.0 91.7 92.4 91.0
30 92.4 92.4 91.0 91.7 92.4 91.0
40 93.0 93.0 91.7 93.0 93.0 91.7
50 93.0 93.0 92.4 93.0 93.0 92.4
60 93.6 93.6 93.0 93.6 93.6 93.0
75 93.6 94.1 93.0 93.6 94.1 93.0
100 94.1 94.1 93.0 94.1 94.5 93.6
125 94.1 94.5 93.6 94.1 94.5 94.5
150 94.5 95.0 93.6 95.0 95.0 94.5
200 94.5 95.0 94.5 95.0 95.0 95.0

"(2)(A) The Secretary may, by rule, provide that the standards specified in paragraph (1) shall not apply to certain types or classes of electric motors if –

"(i) compliance with such standards would not result in significant energy savings because such motors cannot be used in most general purpose applications or are very unlikely to be used in most general purpose applications; and

"(ii) standards for such motors would not be technologically feasible or economically justified.

"(B) Not later than one year after the date of the enactment of this subsection, a manufacturer seeking an exemption under this paragraph with respect to a type or class of electric motor developed on or before the date of the enactment of such subsection shall submit a petition to the Secretary requesting such exemption. Such petition shall include evidence that the type or class of motor meets the criteria for exemption specified in subparagraph (A).

"(C) Not later than two years after the date of the enactment of this subsection, the Secretary shall rule on each petition for exemption submitted pursuant to subparagraph (B). In making such ruling, the Secretary shall afford an opportunity for public comment.

"(D) Manufacturers of types or classes of motors developed after the date of the enactment of this subsection to which standards under paragraph (1) would be applicable may petition the Secretary for exemptions from compliance with such standards based on the criteria specified in subparagraph (A).

"(3)(A) The Secretary shall publish a final rule no later than the end of the 24-month period beginning on the effective date of the standards established under paragraph (1) to determine if such standards should be amended. Such rule shall provide that any amendment shall apply to electric motors manufactured on or after a date which is five years after the effective date of the standards established under paragraph (1). "(B) The Secretary shall publish a final rule no later than 24 months after the effective date of the previous final rule to determine whether to amend the standards in effect for such product. Any such amendment shall apply to electric motors manufactured after a date which is five years after –

"(i) the effective date of the previous amendment; or

"(ii) if the previous final rule did not amend the standards, the earliest date by which a previous amendment could have been effective.".

(e) ADMINISTRATION, PENALTIES, ENFORCEMENT, AND PREEMPTION. – (1) Section 345(a) of such Act (42 U.S.C. 6316(a)) is amended –

(A) in the material preceding paragraph (1) –

(i) by inserting after "to this part" the following: "(other than the equipment specified in subparagraphs (B), (C), (D), (E), and (F) of section 340(1))"; and

(ii) by striking out "and sections 328" and inserting in lieu thereof ", the provisions of subsections (l) through (s) of section 325, and sections 327";

(B) in paragraph (1) –

(i) by striking out "and 324" and inserting in lieu thereof ", 324, and 325"; and

(ii) by striking out "343 and 344, respectively" and inserting in lieu thereof "343, 344, and 342, respectively";

(C) in paragraph (3), by striking out "and" at the end thereof;

(D) in paragraph (4), by striking out the period and inserting in lieu thereof a semicolon; and

(E) by adding after paragraph (4) the following new paragraphs:

"(5) section 327(a) shall be applied, in the case of electric motors, as if the National Appliance Energy Conservation Act of 1987 was the Energy Policy Act of 1992;

"(6) section 327(b)(1) shall be applied as if electric motors were fluorescent lamp ballasts and as if the National Appliance Energy Conservation Amendments of 1988 were the Energy Policy Act of 1992;

"(7) section 327(b)(4) shall be applied as if electric motors were fluorescent lamp ballasts and as if paragraph (5) of section 325(g) were section 342; and

"(8) notwithstanding any other provision of law, a regulation or other requirement adopted by a State or subdivision of a State contained in a State or local building code for new construction concerning the energy efficiency or energy use of an electric motor covered under this part is not superseded by the standards for such electric motor established or prescribed under section 342(b) if such regulation or requirement is identical to the standards established or prescribed under such section.".

(2) Section 345 of such Act (42 U.S.C. 6316) is amended by adding at the end the following new subsections:

"(b)(1)The provisions of section 326(a),(b), and (d), section 327(a), and sections 328 through 336 shall apply with respect to the equipment specified in subparagraphs (B), (C), (D), (E), and (F) of section 340(1) to the same extent and in the same manner as they apply in part B. In applying such provisions for the purposes of such equipment, paragraphs (1), (2), (3), and (4) of subsection (a) shall apply.

"(2)(A) A standard prescribed or established under section 342(a) shall, beginning on the effective date of such standard, supersede any State or local regulation concerning the energy efficiency or energy use of a product for which a standard is prescribed or established pursuant to such section.

"(B) Notwithstanding subparagraph (A), a standard prescribed or established under section 342(a) shall not supersede a standard for such a product contained in a State or local building code for new construction if –

"(i) the standard in the building code does not require that the energy efficiency of such product exceed the applicable minimum energy efficiency requirement in amended ASHRAE/IES Standard 90.1; and

"(ii) the standard in the building code does not take effect prior to the effective date of the applicable minimum energy efficiency requirement in amended ASHRAE/IES Standard 90.1.

"(C) Notwithstanding subparagraph (A), a standard prescribed or established under section 342(a) shall not supersede the standards established by the State of California set forth in Table C-6, California Code of Regulations, Title 24, Part 2, Chapter 2-53, for water-source heat pumps below 135,000 Btu per hour (cooling capacity) that become effective on January 1, 1993.

"(D) Notwithstanding subparagraph (A), a standard prescribed or established under section 342(a) shall not supersede a State regulation which has been granted a waiver by the Secretary. The Secretary may grant a waiver pursuant to the terms, conditions, criteria, procedures, and other requirements specified in section 327(d) of this Act.

"(c) With respect to any electric motor to which standards are applicable under section 342(b), the Secretary shall require manufacturers to certify, through an independent testing or certification program nationally recognized in the United States, that such motor meets the applicable."

(3) Section 345 of such Act (42 U.S.C. 6316) is amended by striking out the section heading and inserting in lieu thereof "ADMINISTRATION, PENALTIES, ENFORCEMENT, AND PREEMPTION".

(f) TECHNICAL AMENDMENTS. – (1) Section 340(3) of such Act is amended by striking out "(3) the" and inserting in lieu thereof the following: "(3) The".

(2) Section 343 of such Act (42 U.S.C. 6314) is amended by redesignating the first subsection designated as subsection (d) as subsection (c).

(3) The table of contents of such Act is amended –

(A) by striking out the item relating to section 342 and inserting in lieu thereof the following new item: "Sec. 342. Standards.";

and

(B) by striking the item for section 345 and inserting in lieu thereof the following new item: "Sec. 345. Administration, penalties, enforcement, and preemption.".

Sec. 123. Energy Conservation Requirements for Certain Lamps and Plumbing Products.

(a) STATEMENT OF PURPOSE. – Section 2 of the Energy Policy and Conservation Act (42 U.S.C. 6201) is amended –

(1) in paragraph (6), by striking out "and" at the end;

(2) in paragraph (7), by striking out the period at the end and inserting in lieu thereof "; and"; and

(3) by adding at the end the following new paragraph:

"(8) to conserve water by improving the water efficiency of certain plumbing products and appliances.".

(b) DEFINITIONS. – Section 321(a) of the Energy Policy and Conservation Act (42 U.S.C. 6291(a)) is amended –

(1) by striking out the subsection designation;

(2) in paragraph (1) –

(A) in subparagraph (A), by inserting before the semicolon the following: "or, with respect to showerheads, faucets, water closets, and urinals, water"; and

(B) in subparagraph (B), by striking out "ballasts" and inserting in lieu thereof the following: "ballasts, general service fluorescent lamps, incandescent reflector lamps, showerheads, faucets, water closets, and urinals";

(3) in paragraph (6) –

(A) in subparagraph (A), by inserting ", or, in the case of showerheads, faucets, water closets, and urinals, water use," after "energy use"; and

(B) in subparagraph (B) –

(i) by striking out "and (14)" and inserting in lieu thereof "(15), (16), (17), and (19)"; and

(ii) by striking out "325(o)" and inserting in lieu thereof "325(r)";

(4) in paragraph (7), by inserting after "to be consumed annually" the following: ", and in the case of showerheads, faucets, water closets, and urinals, the aggregate retail cost of water and wastewater treatment services likely to be incurred annually,"; and

(5) by adding at the end the following new paragraphs:

"(30)(A) Except as provided in subparagraph (E), the term 'fluorescent lamp' means a low pressure mercury electric-discharge source in which a fluorescing coating transforms some of the ultraviolet energy generated by the mercury discharge into light, including only the following:

"(i) Any straight-shaped lamp (commonly referred to as 4-foot medium bi-pin lamps) with medium bi-pin bases of nominal overall length of 48 inches and rated wattage of 28 or more.

"(ii) Any U-shaped lamp (commonly referred to as 2-foot U-shaped lamps) with medium bi-pin bases of nominal overall length between 22 and 25 inches and rated wattage of 28 or more.

"(iii) Any rapid start lamp (commonly referred to as 8-foot high output lamps) with recessed double contact bases of nominal overall length of 96 inches and 0.800 nominal amperes, as defined in ANSI C78.1-1978 and related supplements.

"(iv) Any instant start lamp (commonly referred to as 8-foot slimline lamps) with single pin bases of nominal overall length of 96 inches and rated wattage of 52 or more, as defined in ANSI C78.3–1978 (R1984) and related supplement ANSI C78.3a-1985.

"(B) The term 'general service fluorescent lamp' means fluorescent lamps which can be used to satisfy the majority of fluorescent applications, but does not include any lamp designed and marketed for the following nongeneral lighting applications:

"(i) Fluorescent lamps designed to promote plant growth.

"(ii) Fluorescent lamps specifically designed for cold temperature installations.

"(iii) Colored fluorescent lamps.

"(iv) Impact-resistant fluorescent lamps.

"(v) Reflectorized or aperture lamps.

"(vi) Fluorescent lamps designed for use in reprographic equipment.

"(vii) Lamps primarily designed to produce radiation in the ultra-violet region of the spectrum.

"(viii) Lamps with a color rendering index of 82 or greater.

"(C) Except as provided in subparagraph (E), the term 'incandescent lamp' means a lamp in which light is produced by a filament heated to incandescence by an electric current, including only the following:

"(i) Any lamp (commonly referred to as lower wattage nonreflector general service lamps, including any tungsten-halogen lamp) that has a rated wattage between 30 and 199 watts, has an E26 medium screw base, has a rated voltage or voltage range that lies at least partially within 115 and 130 volts, and is not a reflector lamp.

"(ii) Any lamp (commonly referred to as a reflector lamp) which is not colored or designed for rough or vibration service applications, that contains an inner reflective coating on the outer bulb to direct the light, an R, PAR, or similar bulb shapes (excluding ER or BR) with E26 medium screw bases, a rated voltage or voltage range that lies at least partially within 115 and 130 volts, a diameter which exceed 2.75 inches, and is either –

"(I) a low(er) wattage reflector lamp which has a rated wattage between 40 and 205 watts; or

"(II) a high(er) wattage reflector lamp which has a rated wattage above 205 watts.

"(iii) Any general service incandescent lamp (commonly referred to as a high- or higher wattage lamp) that has a rated wattage above 199 watts (above 205 watts for a high wattage reflector lamp).

"(D) The term 'general service incandescent lamp' means any incandescent lamp (other than a miniature or photographic lamp) that has an E26 medium screw base, a rated voltage range at least partially within 115 and 130 volts, and which can be used to satisfy the majority of lighting applications, but does not include any lamps specifically designed for –

"(i) traffic signal, or street lighting service;

"(ii) airway, airport, aircraft, or other aviation service;

"(iii) marine or marine signal service;

"(iv) photo, projection, sound reproduction, or film viewer service;

"(v) stage, studio, or television service;

"(vi) mill, saw mill, or other industrial process service;

"(vii) mine service;

"(viii) headlight, locomotive, street railway, or other transportation service;

"(ix) heating service;

"(x) code beacon, marine signal, lighthouse, reprographic, or other communication service;

"(xi) medical or dental service;

"(xii) microscope, map, microfilm, or other specialized equipment service;

"(xiii) swimming pool or other underwater service;

"(xiv) decorative or showcase service;

"(xv) producing colored light;

"(xvi) shatter resistance which has an external protective coating; or

"(xvii) appliance service.

"(E) The terms 'fluorescent lamp' and 'incandescent lamp' do not include any lamp excluded by the Secretary, by rule, as a result of a determination that standards for such lamp would not result in significant energy savings because such lamp is designed for special applications or has special characteristics not available in reasonably substitutable lamp types.

"(F) The term 'incandescent reflector lamp' means a lamp described in subparagraph (C)(ii).

"(G) The term 'average lamp efficacy' means the lamp efficacy readings taken over a statistically significant period of manufacture with the readings averaged over that period.

"(H) The term 'base' means the portion of the lamp which connects with the socket as described in ANSI C81.61-1990.

"(I) The term 'bulb shape' means the shape of lamp, especially the glass bulb with designations for bulb shapes found in ANSI C79.1-1980 (R1984).

"(J) The term 'color rendering index' or 'CRI' means the measure of the degree of color shift objects undergo when illuminated by a light source as compared with the color of those same objects when illuminated by a reference source of comparable color temperature.

"(K) The term 'correlated color temperature' means the absolute temperature of a blackbody whose chromaticity most nearly resembles that of the light source.

"(L) The term 'IES' means the Illuminating Engineering Society of North America.

"(M) The term 'lamp efficacy' means the lumen output of a lamp divided by its wattage, expressed in lumens per watt (LPW).

"(N) The term 'lamp type' means all lamps designated as having the same electrical and lighting characteristics and made by one manufacturer.

"(O) The term 'lamp wattage' means the total electrical power consumed by a lamp in watts, after the initial seasoning period referenced in the appropriate IES standard test procedure and including, for fluorescent, arc watts plus cathode watts.

"(P) The terms 'life' and 'lifetime' mean length of operating time of a statistically large group of lamps between first use and failure of 50 percent of the group in accordance with test procedures described in the IES Lighting Handbook-Reference Volume.

"(Q) The term 'lumen output' means total luminous flux (power) of a lamp in lumens, as measured in accordance with applicable IES standards as determined by the Secretary.

"(R) The term 'tungsten-halogen lamp' means a gas-filled tungsten filament incandescent lamp containing a certain proportion of halogens in an inert gas.

"(S) The term 'medium base compact fluorescent lamp' means an integrally ballasted fluorescent lamp with a medium screw base and a rated input voltage of 115 to 130 volts and which is designed as a direct replacement for a general service incandescent lamp.

"(31)(A) The term 'water use' means the quantity of water flowing through a showerhead, faucet, water closet, or urinal at point of use, determined in accordance with test procedures under section 323.

"(B) The term 'ASME' means the American Society of Mechanical Engineers.

"(C) The term 'ANSI' means the American National Standards Institute.

"(D) The term 'showerhead' means any showerhead (including a handheld showerhead), except a safety shower showerhead.

"(E) The term 'faucet' means a lavatory faucet, kitchen faucet, metering faucet, or replacement aerator for a lavatory or kitchen faucet.

"(F) The term 'water closet' has the meaning given such term in ASME A112.19.2M-1990, except such term does not include fixtures designed for installation in prisons.

"(G) The term 'urinal' has the meaning given such term in ASME A112.19.2M-1990, except such term does not include fixtures designed for installation in prisons.

"(H) The terms 'blowout', 'flushometer tank', 'low consumption', and 'flushometer valve' have the meaning given such terms in ASME A112.19.2M-1990.".

(c) COVERAGE. – Section 322(a) of such Act (42 U.S.C. 6292(a)) is amended –

(1) by redesignating paragraph (14) as paragraph (19); and

(2) by inserting after paragraph (13) the following new paragraphs:

"(14) General service fluorescent lamps and incandescent reflector lamps.

"(15) Showerheads, except safety shower showerheads.

"(16) Faucets.

"(17) Water closets.

"(18) Urinals.".

(d) TEST PROCEDURES. – Section 323 of such Act (42 U.S.C. 6293) is amended –

(1) in subsection (b) –

(A) in paragraph (3), by inserting after "energy use," the following "water use (in the case of showerheads, faucets, water closets and urinals),";

(B) in paragraph (4) –

(i) by inserting "or, in the case of showerheads, faucets, water closets, or urinals, water use" after "energy use";

(ii) by inserting after "such cycle" the following: ", or in the case of showerheads, faucets, water closets, or urinals, representative average unit costs of water and wastewater treatment service resulting from the operation of such products during such cycle"; and

(iii) by inserting ", water, and wastewater treatment" before the period at the end of the second sentence; and

(C) by adding at the end the following new paragraphs:

"(6) With respect to fluorescent lamps and incandescent reflector lamps to which standards are applicable under subsection (i) of section 325, the Secretary shall prescribe test procedures, to be carried out by accredited test laboratories, that take into consideration the applicable IES or ANSI standard.

"(7)(A) Test procedures for showerheads and faucets to which standards are applicable under subsection (j) of section 325 shall be the test procedures specified in ASME A112.18.1M-1989 for such products.

"(B) If the test procedure requirements of ASME A112.18.1M-1989 are revised at any time and approved by ANSI, the Secretary shall amend the test procedures established by subparagraph (A) to conform to such revised ASME/ANSI requirements unless the Secretary determines, by rule, that to do so would not meet the requirements of paragraph (3).

"(8)(A) Test procedures for water closets and urinals to which standards are applicable under subsection (k) of section 325 shall be the test procedures specified in ASME A112.19.6-1990 for such products.

"(B) If the test procedure requirements of ASME A112.19.6-1990 are revised at any time and approved by ANSI, the Secretary shall amend the test procedures established by subparagraph (A) to conform to such revised ASME/ANSI requirements unless the Secretary determines, by rule, that to do so would not meet the requirements of paragraph (3).";

(2) in paragraphs (1) and (2) of subsection (c), by inserting "or, in the case of showerheads, faucets, water closets, and urinals, water use" after "efficiency" each place it appears;

(3) in subsection (c)(2), in the material preceding subparagraph (A), by inserting "or established" after "prescribed"; and

(4) in subsection (e) –

(A) in paragraph (1), by striking out "or measured energy use" and inserting in lieu thereof ", measured energy use, or measured water use";

(B) in paragraph (2), by striking out "energy efficiency or energy use" each place it appears and inserting in lieu thereof "energy efficiency, energy use, or water use"; and

(C) in paragraph (3), by striking out "energy efficiency or energy use" and inserting in lieu thereof "energy efficiency, energy use, or water use".

(e) LABELING. – Section 324 of such Act (42 U.S.C. 6294) is amended –

(1) in subsection (a)(2), by adding at the end the following new subparagraphs:

"(C)(i) Not later than 18 months after the date of the enactment of the Energy Policy Act of 1992, the Commission shall prescribe labeling rules under this section applicable to general service fluorescent lamps, medium base compact fluorescent lamps, and general service incandescent lamps. Except as provided in clause (ii), such rules shall provide that the labeling of any general service fluorescent lamp, medium base compact fluorescent lamp, and general service incandescent lamp manufactured after the 12-month period beginning on the date of the publication of such rule shall indicate conspicuously on the packaging of the lamp, in a manner prescribed by the Commission under subsection (b), such information as the Commission deems necessary to enable consumers to select the most energy efficient lamps which meet their requirements. Labeling information for incandescent lamps shall be based on performance when operated at 120 volts input, regardless of the rated lamp voltage.

"(ii) If the Secretary determines that compliance with the standards specified in section 325(j) for any lamp will result in the discontinuance of the manufacture of such lamp, the Commission may exempt such lamp from the labeling rules prescribed under clause (i).

"(D)(i) Not later than one year after the date of the enactment of the Energy Policy Act of 1992, the Commission shall prescribe labeling rules under this section for showerheads and faucets to which standards are applicable under subsection (j) of section 325. Such rules shall provide that the labeling of any showerhead or faucet manufactured after the 12-month period beginning on the date of the publication of such rule shall be consistent with the marking and labeling requirements of ASME A112.18.1M-1989, except that each showerhead and flow restricting or controlling spout-end device shall bear a permanent legible marking indicating the flow rate, expressed in gallons per minute (gpm) or gallons per cycle (gpc), and the flow rate value shall be the actual flow rate or the maximum flow rate specified by the standards established in subsection (j) of section 325.

"(ii) If the marking and labeling requirements of ASME A112.18.1M-1989 are revised at any time and approved by ANSI, the Commission shall amend the labeling rules established pursuant to clause (i) to be consistent with such revised ASME/ANSI requirements unless such requirements are inconsistent with the purposes of this Act or the requirement specified in clause (i) requiring each showerhead and flow restricting or controlling spout-end device to bear a permanent legible marking indicating the flow rate of such product.

"(E)(i) Not later than one year after the date of the enactment of the Energy Policy Act of 1992, the Commission shall prescribe labeling rules under this section for water closets and urinals to which standards are applicable under subsection (k) of section 325. Such rules shall provide that the labeling of any water closet or urinal manufactured after the 12-month period beginning on the date of the publication of such rule shall be consistent with the marking and labeling requirements of ASME A112.19.2M-1990, except that each fixture (and flushometer valve associated with such fixture) shall bear a permanent legible marking indicating the water use, expressed in gallons per flush (gpf), and the water use value shall be the actual water use or the maximum water use specified by the standards established in subsection (k) of section 325.

"(ii) If the marking and labeling requirements of ASME A112.19.2M-1990 are revised at any time and approved by ANSI, the Commission shall amend the labeling rules established pursuant to clause (i) to be consistent with such revised ASME/ANSI requirements unless such requirements are inconsistent with the purposes of this Act or the requirement specified in clause (i) requiring each fixture and flushometer valve to bear a permanent legible marking indicating the water use of such fixture or flushometer valve.

"(iii) Any labeling rules prescribed under this subparagraph before January 1, 1997, shall provide that, with respect to any gravity tank-type white 2-piece toilet which has a water use greater than 1.6 gallons per flush (gpf), any printed matter distributed or displayed in connection with such product (including packaging and point of sale material, catalog material, and print advertising) shall include, in a conspicuous manner, the words 'For Commercial Use Only'.";

(2) in subsection (a)(3),by striking out "(14)" and inserting in lieu thereof "(19)";

(3) in subsection (b)(1)(B), by striking out "(14)" and inserting in lieu thereof "(13), and paragraphs (15) through (19)";

(4) in paragraphs (3) and (5) of subsection (b), by striking out "(14)" and inserting in lieu thereof "(19)"; and

(5) in subsection (c) –

(A) in paragraph (7), by striking out "paragraph (13) of section 322" and inserting in lieu thereof "paragraphs (13), (14), (15), (16), (17), and (18) of section 322(a)"; and

(B) by adding at the end the following:

"(8) If a manufacturer of a covered product specified in paragraph (15) or (17) of section 322(a) elects to provide a label for such covered product conveying the estimated annual operating cost of such product or the range of estimated annual operating costs for the type or class of such product –

"(A) such estimated cost or range of costs shall be determined in accordance with test procedures prescribed under section 323;

"(B) the format of such label shall be in accordance with a format prescribed by the Commission; and

"(C) such label shall be displayed in a manner, prescribed by the Commission, to be likely to assist consumers in making purchasing decisions and appropriate to carry out the purposes of this Act.".

(f) STANDARDS. – Section 325 of such Act (42 U.S.C. 6295) is amended –

(1) by redesignating subsections (i) through (q) as subsections (l) through (t);

(2) by inserting after subsection (h) the following:

"(i) GENERAL SERVICE FLUORESCENT LAMPS AND INCANDESCENT REFLECTOR LAMPS. – (1)(A) Each of the following general service fluorescent lamps and incandescent reflector lamps manufactured after the effective date specified in the tables listed in this paragraph shall meet or exceed the following lamp efficacy and CRI standards:

"FLUORESCENT LAMPS

Minimum
Average
Nominal Lamp Effective
Lamp Minimum Efficacy Date
"Lamp Type Wattage CRI (LPW) (Months)
4-foot medium bi-pin >35W 69 75.0 36
35W 45 75.0 36
2-foot U-shaped >35W 69 68.0 36
35W 45 64.0 36
8-foot slimline 65W 69 80.0 18

65W 45 80.0 18
8-foot high output >100W 69 80.0 18
100W 45 80.018

"INCANDESCENT REFLECTOR LAMPS
Minimum
Average
"Nominal Lamp Effective
Lamp Efficacy Date
Wattage (LPW) (Months)
40–50 10.5 36
51–66 11.0 36
67–85 12.5 36
86–115 14.0 36
116–155 14.5 36
156–205 15.0 36

"(B) For the purposes of the tables set forth in subparagraph (A), the term 'effective date' means the last day of the month set forth in the table which follows the date of the enactment of the Energy Policy Act of 1992.

"(2) Notwithstanding section 332(a)(5) and section 332(b), it shall not be unlawful for a manufacturer to sell a lamp which is in compliance with the law at the time such lamp was manufactured.

"(3) Not less than 36 months after the date of the enactment of this subsection, the Secretary shall initiate a rulemaking procedure and shall publish a final rule not later than the end of the 54-month period beginning on the date of the enactment of this subsection to determine if the standards established under paragraph (1) should be amended. Such rule shall contain such amendment, if any, and provide that the amendment shall apply to products manufactured on or after the 36-month period beginning on the date such final rule is published.

"(4) Not less than eight years after the date of the enactment of this subsection, the Secretary shall initiate a rulemaking procedure and shall publish a final rule not later than nine years and six months after the date of the enactment of this subsection to determine if the standards in effect for fluorescent lamps and incandescent lamps should be amended. Such rule shall contain such amendment, if any, and provide that the amendment shall apply to products manufactured on or after the 36-month period beginning on the date such final rule is published.

"(5) Not later than the end of the 24-month period beginning on the date labeling requirements under section 324(a)(2)(C) become effective, the Secretary shall initiate a rulemaking procedure to determine if the standards in effect for fluorescent lamps and incandescent lamps should be amended so that they would be applicable to additional general service fluorescent and general service incandescent lamps and shall publish, not later than 18 months after initiating such rulemaking, a final rule including such amended standards, if any. Such rule shall provide that the amendment shall apply to products manufactured after a date which is 36 months after the date such rule is published.

"(6)(A) With respect to any lamp to which standards are applicable under this subsection or any lamp specified in section 346, the Secretary shall inform any Federal entity proposing actions which would adversely impact the energy consumption or energy efficiency of such lamp of the energy conservation consequences of such action. It shall be the responsibility of such Federal entity to carefully consider the Secretary's comments.

"(B) Notwithstanding section 325(n)(1), the Secretary shall not be prohibited from amending any standard, by rule, to permit increased energy use or to decrease the minimum required energy efficiency of any lamp to which standards are applicable under this subsection if such action is warranted as a result of other Federal action (including restrictions on materials or processes) which would have the effect of either increasing the energy use or decreasing the energy efficiency of such product.

"(7) Not later than the date on which standards established pursuant to this subsection become effective, or, with respect to high-intensity discharge lamps covered under section 346, the effective date of standards established pursuant to such section, each manufacturer of a product to which such standards are applicable shall file with the Secretary a laboratory report certifying compliance with the applicable standard for each lamp type. Such report shall include the lumen output and wattage consumption for each lamp type as an average of measurements taken over the preceding 12-month period. With respect to lamp types which are not manufactured during the 12-month period preceding the date such standards become effective, such report shall be filed with the Secretary not later than the date which is 12 months after the date manufacturing is commenced and shall include the lumen output and wattage consumption for each such lamp type as an average of measurements taken during such 12-month period.

"(j) STANDARDS FOR SHOWERHEADS AND FAUCETS. – (1) The maximum water use allowed for any showerhead manufactured after January 1, 1994, is 2.5 gallons per minute when measured at a flowing water pressure of 80 pounds per square inch. Any such showerhead shall also meet the requirements of ASME/ANSI A112.18.1M-1989, 7.4.3(a).

"(2) The maximum water use allowed for any of the following faucets manufactured after January 1, 1994, when measured at a flowing water pressure of 80 pounds per square inch, is as follows:

"Lavatory faucets = 2.5 gallons per minute

"Lavatory replacement aerators = 2.5 gallons per minute

"Kitchen faucets = 2.5 gallons per minute

"Kitchen replacement aerators = 2.5 gallons per minute

"Metering faucets = 0.25 gallons per cycle

"(3)(A) If the maximum flow rate requirements or the design requirements of ASME/ANSI Standard A112.18.1M-1989 are amended to improve the efficiency of water use of any type or class of showerhead or faucet and are approved by ANSI, the Secretary shall, not later than 12 months after the date of such amendment, publish a final rule establishing an amended uniform national standard for that product at the level specified in the amended ASME/ANSI Standard A112.18.1M and providing that such standard shall apply to products manufactured after a date which is 12 months after the publication of such rule, unless the Secretary determines, by rule published in the Federal Register, that adoption of a uniform national standard at the level specified in such amended ASME/ANSI Standard A112.18.1M –

"(i) is not technologically feasible and economically justified under subsection (o);

"(ii) is not consistent with the maintenance of public health and safety; or

"(iii) is not consistent with the purposes of this Act.

"(B)(i) As part of the rulemaking conducted under subparagraph (A), the Secretary shall also determine if adoption of a uniform national standard for any type or class of showerhead or faucet more stringent than such amended ASME/ANSI Standard A112.18.1M –

"(I) would result in additional conservation of energy or water;

"(II) would be technologically feasible and economically justified under subsection (o); and

"(III) would be consistent with the maintenance of public health and safety.

"(ii) If the Secretary makes an affirmative determination under clause (i), the final rule published under subparagraph (A) shall waive the provisions of section 327(c) with respect to any State regulation concerning the water use or water efficiency of such type or class of showerhead or faucet if such State regulation –

"(I) is more stringent than amended ASME/ANSI Standard A-112.18.1M for such type or class of showerhead or faucet and the standard in effect for such product on the day before the date on which a final rule is published under subparagraph (A); and

"(II) is applicable to any sale or installation of all products in such type or class of showerhead or faucet.

"(C) If, after any period of five consecutive years, the maximum flow rate requirements of the ASME/ANSI standard for showerheads are not amended to improve the efficiency of water use of such products, or after any such period such requirements for faucets are not amended to improve the efficiency of water use of such products, the Secretary shall, not later than six months after the end of such five-year period, publish a final rule waiving the provisions of section 327(c) with respect to any State regulation concerning the water use or water efficiency of such type or class of showerhead or faucet if such State regulation –

"(i) is more stringent than the standards in effect for such type of class of showerhead or faucet; and

"(ii) is applicable to any sale or installation of all products in such type or class of showerhead or faucet.

"(k) STANDARDS FOR WATER CLOSETS AND URINALS. – (1)(A) Except as provided in subparagraph (B), the maximum water use allowed in gallons per flush for any of the following water closets manufactured after January 1, 1994, is the following:

"Gravity tank-type toilets 1.6 gpf.

"Flushometer tank toilets 1.6 gpf.

"Electromechanical hydraulic toilets 1.6 gpf.

"Blowout toilets 3.5 gpf.

"(B) The maximum water use allowed for any gravity tank-type white 2-piece toilet which bears an adhesive label conspicuous upon installation consisting of the words 'Commercial Use Only' manufactured after January 1, 1994, and before January 1, 1997, is 3.5 gallons per flush.

"(C) The maximum water use allowed for flushometer valve toilets, other than blowout toilets, manufactured after January 1, 1997, is 1.6 gallons per flush.

"(2) The maximum water use allowed for any urinal manufactured after January 1, 1994, is 1.0 gallons per flush.

"(3)(A) If the maximum flush volume requirements of ASME Standard A112.19.6-1990 are amended to improve the efficiency of water use of any low consumption water closet or low consumption urinal and are approved by ANSI, the Secretary shall, not later than 12 months after the date of such amendment, publish a final rule establishing an amended uniform national standard for that product at the level specified in amended ASME/ANSI Standard A112.19.6 and providing that such standard shall apply to products manufactured after a date which is one year after the publication of such rule, unless the Secretary determines, by rule published in the Federal Register, that adoption of a uniform national standard at the level specified in such amended ASME/ANSI Standard A112.19.6 –

"(i) is not technologically feasible and economically justified under subsection (o);

"(ii) is not consistent with the maintenance of public health and safety; or

"(iii) is not consistent with the purposes of this Act.

"(B)(i) As part of the rulemaking conducted under subparagraph (A), the Secretary shall also determine if adoption of a uniform national standard for any type or class of low consumption water closet or low consumption urinal more stringent than such amended ASME/ANSI Standard A112.19.6 for such product –

"(I) would result in additional conservation of energy or water;

"(II) would be technologically feasible and economically justified under subsection (o); and

"(III) would be consistent with the maintenance of public health and safety.

"(ii) If the Secretary makes an affirmative determination under clause (i), the final rule published under subparagraph (A) shall waive the provisions of section 327(c) with respect to any State regulation concerning the water use or water efficiency of such type or class of low consumption water closet or low consumption urinal if such State regulation –

"(I) is more stringent than amended ASME/ANSI Standard A-112.19.6 for such type or class of low consumption water closet or low consumption urinal and the standard in effect for such product on the day before the date on which a final rule is published under subparagraph (A); and

"(II) is applicable to any sale or installation of all products in such type or class of low consumption water closet or low consumption urinal.

"(C) If, after any period of five consecutive years, the maximum flush volume requirements of the ASME/ANSI standard for low consumption water closets are not amended to improve the efficiency of water use of such products, or after any such period such requirements for low consumption urinals are not amended to improve the efficiency of water use of such products, the Secretary shall, not later than six months after the end of such five-year period, publish a final rule waiving the provisions of section 327(c) with respect to any State regulation concerning the water use or water efficiency of such type or class of water closet or urinal if such State regulation –

"(i) is more stringent than the standards in effect for such type or class of water closet or urinal; and

"(ii) is applicable to any sale or installation of all products in such type or class of water closet or urinal.";

(3) in subsection (l) (as redesignated by paragraph (1) of this subsection) –

(A) in paragraphs (1) and (2), by striking out "(14)" and inserting in lieu thereof "(19)"; and

(B) in paragraphs (1) and (3), by striking out "(l) and (m)" and inserting in lieu thereof "(o) and (p)";

(4) in subsection (m) (as redesignated by paragraph (1) of this subsection), by striking out "(h)" and inserting in lieu thereof "(i)";

(5) in subsection (n) (as redesignated by paragraph (1) of this subsection) –

(A) in paragraph (1) –

(i) by striking out "and in paragraph (13)" and inserting in lieu thereof ", and in paragraphs (13) and (14)"; and

(ii) by striking out "(h)" and inserting in lieu thereof "(i)";

(B) in paragraph (2)(C), by striking out "(l)(2)(B)(i)(II)" and inserting in lieu thereof "(o)(2)(B)(i)(II)"; and

(C) in paragraph (3)(B), by inserting "general service fluorescent lamps, incandescent reflector lamps," after "fluorescent lamp ballasts,";

(6) in subsection (o) (as redesignated by paragraph (1) of this subsection) –

(A) in paragraph (1), by inserting "or, in the case of showerheads, faucets, water closets, or urinals, water use," after "energy use,";

(B) in paragraph (2)(A), by inserting ", or, in the case of showerheads, faucets, water closets, or urinals, water efficiency," after "energy efficiency";

(C) in paragraph (2)(B)(i)(III), by inserting ", or as applicable, water," after "energy";

(D) in paragraph (2)(B)(i)(VI), by inserting "and water" after "energy";

(E) in paragraph (2)(B)(iii), by striking out "energy savings" and inserting "energy, and as applicable water, savings"; and

(F) in paragraph (3)(B), by inserting ", in the case of showerheads, faucets, water closets, or urinals, water, or" after "energy or"; and

(7) in subsection (p)(3)(A) (as redesignated by paragraph (1) of this subsection) –

(A) by striking out "(l)(2)" and inserting in lieu thereof "(o)(2)"; and

(B) by striking out "(l)(4)" and inserting in lieu thereof "(o)(4)".

(g) REQUIREMENTS OF MANUFACTURERS. – Section 326 of such Act (42 U.S.C. 6296) is amended –

(1) in subsection (b)(4), by inserting "or water use" after "consumption"; and

(2) in subsection (d)(1), by striking out "or energy use" and inserting in lieu thereof ", energy use, or, in the case of showerheads, faucets, water closets, and urinals, water use".

(h) EFFECT ON OTHER LAW. – Section 327 of such Act (42 U.S.C. 6297) is amended –

(1) in subsection (a) –

(A) in paragraph (1), in the material preceding subparagraph (A), by inserting "or water use" after "energy consumption";

(B) in paragraph (1)(A), by inserting ", water use," after "energy consumption";

(C) in paragraph (1)(B), by striking out "or energy efficiency" and inserting in lieu thereof ", energy efficiency, or water use"; and

(D) by amending paragraph (2) to read as follows:

"(2) For purposes of this section, the following definitions apply:

"(A) The term 'State regulation' means a law, regulation, or other requirement of a State or its political subdivisions. With respect to showerheads, faucets, water closets, and urinals, such term shall also mean a law, regulation, or other requirement of a river basin commission that has jurisdiction within a State.

"(B) The term 'river basin commission' means –

"(i) a commission established by interstate compact to apportion, store, regulate, or otherwise manage or coordinate the management of the waters of a river basin; and

"(ii) a commission established under section 201(a) of the Water Resources Planning Act (42 U.S.C. 1962b(a)).";

(2) in subsection (b) –

(A) in the material preceding paragraph (1), by striking out "or energy use of the covered product" and inserting in lieu thereof ", energy use, or water use of the covered product";

(B) by inserting before the semicolon at the end of paragraph (1) the following: ", or in the case of any portion of any regulation which establishes requirements for fluorescent or incandescent lamps, flow rate requirements for showerheads or faucets, or water use requirements for water closets or urinals, was prescribed or enacted before the date of the enactment of the Energy Policy Act of 1992";

(C) in paragraph (4), by inserting before the semicolon at the end the following: ", or is a regulation (or portion thereof) regulating fluorescent or incandescent lamps other than those to which section 325(i) is applicable, or is a regulation (or portion thereof) regulating showerheads or faucets other than those to which section 325(j) is applicable or regulating lavatory faucets (other than metering faucets) for installation in public places, or is a regulation (or portion thereof) regulating water closets or urinals other than those to which section 325(k) is applicable";

(D) in paragraph (5), by striking out "or";

(E) in paragraph (6), by striking out the period at the end and inserting "; or"; and

(F) by adding at the end the following new paragraph:

"(7) is a regulation (or portion thereof) concerning the water efficiency or water use of low consumption flushometer valve water closets.";

(3) in subsection (c) –

(A) in the material preceding paragraph (1) –

(i) by inserting ", subparagraphs (B) and (C) of section 325(j)(3), and subparagraphs (B) and (C) of section 325(k)(3)" after "section 325(b)(3)(A)(ii)"; and

(ii) by striking out "or energy use" and inserting in lieu thereof the following: ", energy use, or water use";

(B) in paragraph (1), by inserting before the semicolon at the end the following: ", except that a State regulation (or portion thereof) regulating fluorescent or incandescent lamps other than those for which section 325(i) is applicable shall be effective only until the effective date of a standard that is prescribed by the Secretary and is applicable to such lamps";

(C) in paragraph (2), by striking out "or";

(D) in paragraph (3), by striking out the period at the end and inserting a semicolon; and

(E) by adding at the end the following new paragraphs:

"(4) is a regulation concerning the water use of lavatory faucets adopted by the State of New York or the State of Georgia before the date of the enactment of the Energy Policy Act of 1992;

"(5) is a regulation concerning the water use of lavatory or kitchen faucets adopted by the State of Rhode Island prior to the date of the enactment of the Energy Policy Act of 1992; or

"(6) is a regulation (or portion thereof) concerning the water efficiency or water use of gravity tank-type low consumption water closets for installation in public places, except that such a regulation shall be effective only until January 1, 1997.";

(4) in subsection (d)(1) –

(A) in subparagraph (A) –

(i) by inserting "or river basin commission" after "Any State"; and

(ii) by striking out "or energy efficiency" and inserting in lieu thereof ", energy efficiency, or water use";

(B) in subparagraph (B) –

(i) by striking out "State has" and inserting "State or river basin commission has"; and

(ii) by inserting "or water" after "energy";

(C) in subparagraph (C) –

(i) in the material preceding clause (i) and in clause (ii), by inserting "or water" after "energy" each place it appears; and

(ii) by inserting before the period at the end the following: ", and, with respect to a State regulation for which a petition has been submitted to the Secretary which provides for any energy conservation standard or requirement with respect to water use of a covered product, within the context of the water supply and groundwater management plan, water quality program, and comprehensive plan (if any) of the State or river basin commission for improving, developing, or conserving a waterway affected by water supply development"; and

(5) in subsection (d)(5)(B), by striking clause (i) and inserting the following:

"(i) there exists within the State an energy emergency condition or, if the State regulation provides for an energy conservation standard or other requirement with respect to the water use of a covered product for which there is a Federal energy conservation standard under subsection (j) or (k) of section 325, a water emergency condition, which –

"(I) imperils the health, safety, and welfare of its residents because of the inability of the State or utilities within the State to provide adequate quantities of gas or electric energy or, in the case of a water emergency condition, water or wastewater treatment, to its residents at less than prohibitive costs; and

"(II) cannot be substantially alleviated by the importation of energy or, in the case of a water emergency condition, by the importation of water, or by the use of interconnection agreements; and".

(i) INCENTIVE PROGRAMS. – Section 337 of such Act (42 U.S.C. 6307) is amended –

(1) by striking out "337." and inserting "337. (a) IN GENERAL. –"; and

(2) by adding at the end the following:

"(b) STATE AND LOCAL INCENTIVE PROGRAMS. – (1) The Secretary shall, not later than one year after the date of the enactment of this subsection, issue recommendations to the States for establishing State and local incentive programs designed to encourage the acceleration of voluntary replacement, by consumers, of existing showerheads, faucets, water closets, and urinals with those products that meet the standards established for such products pursuant to subsections (j) and (k) of section 325.

"(2) In developing such recommendations, the Secretary shall consult with the heads of other federal agencies, including the Administrator of the Environmental Protection Agency; State officials; manufacturers, suppliers, and installers of plumbing products; and other interested parties.".

Sec. 124. High-Intensity Discharge Lamps, Distribution Transformers, and Small Electric Motors.

(a) STANDARDS. – Section 346 of the Energy Policy and Conservation Act (42 U.S.C. 6317) is amended to read as follows:

"ENERGY CONSERVATION STANDARDS FOR HIGH-INTENSITY DISCHARGE LAMPS, DISTRIBUTION TRANSFORMERS, AND SMALL ELECTRIC MOTORS

"Sec. 346. (a)(1) The Secretary shall, within 30 months after the date of the enactment of the Energy Policy Act of 1992, prescribe testing requirements for those high-intensity discharge lamps and distribution transformers for which the Secretary makes a determination that energy conservation standards would be technologically feasible and economically justified, and would result in significant energy savings.

"(2) The Secretary shall, within 18 months after the date on which testing requirements are prescribed by the Secretary pursuant to paragraph (1), prescribe, by rule, energy conservation standards for those high-intensity discharge lamps and distribution transformers for which the Secretary prescribed testing requirements under paragraph (1).

"(3) Any standard prescribed under paragraph (2) with respect to high-intensity discharge lamps shall apply to such lamps manufactured 36 months after the date such rule is published.

"(b)(1) The Secretary shall, within 30 months after the date of the enactment of the Energy Policy Act of 1992, prescribe testing requirements for those small electric motors for which the Secretary makes a determination that energy conservation standards would be technologically feasible and economically justified, and would result in significant energy savings.

"(2) The Secretary shall, within 18 months after the date on which testing requirements are prescribed by the Secretary pursuant to paragraph (1), prescribe, by rule, energy conservation standards for those small electric motors for which the Secretary prescribed testing requirements under paragraph (1).

"(3) Any standard prescribed under paragraph (2) shall apply to small electric motors manufactured 60 months after the date such rule is published or, in the case of small electric motors which require listing or certification by a nationally recognized testing laboratory, 84 months after such date. Such standards shall not apply to any small electric motor which is a component of a covered product under section 322(a) or a covered equipment under section 340.

"(c) In establishing any standard under this section, the Secretary shall take into consideration the criteria contained in section 325(n).

"(d) The Secretary shall, within six months after the date on which energy conservation standards are prescribed by the Secretary for high-intensity discharge lamps and distribution transformers pursuant to subsection (a)(2) and small electric motors pursuant to subsection (b)(2), prescribe labeling requirements for such lamps, transformers, and small electric motors.

"(e) Beginning on the date which occurs six months after the date on which a labeling rule is prescribed for a product under subsection (d), each manufacturer of a product to which such a rule applies shall provide a label which meets, and is displayed in accordance with, the requirements of such rule.

"(f)(1) After the date on which a manufacturer must provide a label for a product pursuant to subsection (e) –

"(A) each such product shall be considered, for purposes of paragraphs (1) and (2) of section 332(a), a new covered product to which a rule under section 324 applies; and

"(B) it shall be unlawful for any manufacturer or private labeler to distribute in commerce any new product for which an energy conservation standard is prescribed under subsection (a)(2) or (b)(2) which is not in conformity with the applicable energy conservation standard.

"(2) For purposes of section 333(a), paragraph (1) of this subsection shall be considered to be a part of section 332.".

(b) TECHNICAL AMENDMENT. – The table of contents of such Act is amended by striking out the item for section 346 and inserting in lieu thereof the following new item:

"Sec. 346. Energy conservation standards for high-intensity discharge lamps, distribution transformers, and small electric motors.".

(c) STUDY OF UTILITY DISTRIBUTION TRANSFORMERS. – The Secretary shall evaluate the practicability, cost-effectiveness, and potential energy savings of replacing, or upgrading components of, existing utility distribution transformers during routine maintenance and, not later than 18 months after the date of the enactment of this Act, report the findings of such evaluation to the Congress with recommendations on how such energy savings, if any, could be achieved.

Sec. 125. Energy Efficiency Information for Commercial Office Equipment.

(a) IN GENERAL. – (1) The Secretary shall, after consulting with the Computer and Business Equipment Manufacturers Association and other interested organizations, provide financial and technical assistance to support a voluntary national testing and information program for those types of commercial office equipment that are widely used and for which there is a potential for significant energy savings as a result of such program.

(2) Such program shall –

(A) consistent with the objectives of paragraph (1), determine the commercial office equipment to be covered under such program;

(B) include specifications for testing procedures that will enable purchasers of such commercial office equipment to make more informed decisions about the energy efficiency and costs of alternative products; and

(C) include information, which may be disseminated through catalogs, trade publications, labels, or other mechanisms, that will allow consumers to assess the energy consumption and potential cost savings of alternative products.

(3) Such program shall be developed by an appropriate organization (composed of interested parties) according to commonly accepted procedures for the development of national testing procedure and labeling programs.

(b) MONITORING. – The Secretary shall monitor and evaluate the efforts to develop the program described in subsection (a) and, not later than three years after the date of the enactment of this Act, shall make a determination as to whether such program is consistent with the objectives of subsection (a).

(c) ALTERNATIVE SYSTEM. – (1) If the Secretary makes a determination under subsection (b) that a voluntary national testing and information program for commercial office equipment consistent with the objectives of subsection (a) has not been developed, the Secretary shall, after consultation with the National Institute of Standards and Technology, develop, not later than two years after such determination, test procedures under section 323 of the Energy Policy and Conservation Act (42 U.S.C. 6293) for such commercial office equipment.

(2) Not later than one year after the Secretary develops test procedures under paragraph (1), the Federal Trade Commission (hereafter in this section referred to as the "Commission") shall prescribe labeling rules under section 324 of such Act (42 U.S.C. 6294) for commercial office equipment for which the Secretary has prescribed test procedures under paragraph (1) except that, with respect to any type of commercial office equipment (or class thereof), the Secretary may determine that such labeling is not technologically feasible or economically justified or is not likely to assist consumers in making purchasing decisions.

(3) For purposes of sections 323, 324, and 327 of such Act, each product for which the Secretary has established test procedures or labeling rules pursuant to this subsection shall be considered a new covered product under section 322 of such Act (42 U.S.C. 6292) to the extent necessary to carry out this subsection.

(4) For purposes of section 327(a) of such Act, the term "this part" includes this subsection to the extent necessary to carry out this subsection.

Sec. 126. Energy Efficiency Information for Luminaires.

(a) IN GENERAL. – (1) The Secretary shall, after consulting with the National Electric Manufacturers Association, the American Lighting Association, and other interested organizations, provide financial and technical assistance to support a voluntary national testing and information program for those types of luminaires that are widely used and for which there is a potential for significant energy savings as a result of such program.

(2) Such program shall –

(A) consistent with the objectives of paragraph (1), determine the luminaires to be covered under such program;

(B) include specifications for testing procedures that will enable purchasers of such luminaires to make more informed decisions about the energy efficiency and costs of alternative products; and

(C) include information, which may be disseminated through catalogs, trade publications, labels, or other mechanisms, that will allow consumers to assess the energy consumption and potential cost savings of alternative products.

(3) Such program shall be developed by an appropriate organization (composed of interested parties) according to commonly accepted procedures for the development of national testing procedures and labeling programs.

(b) MONITORING. – The Secretary shall monitor and evaluate the efforts to develop the program described in subsection (a) and, not later than three years after the date of the enactment of this Act, shall make a determination as to whether the program developed is consistent with the objectives of subsection (a).

(c) ALTERNATIVE SYSTEM. – (1) If the Secretary makes a determination under subsection (b) that a voluntary national testing and information program for luminaires consistent with the objectives of subsection (a) has not been developed, the Secretary shall, after consultation with the National Institute of Standards and Technology, develop, not later than two years after such determination, test procedures under section 323 of the Energy Policy and Conservation Act (42 U.S.C. 6293) for such luminaires.

(2) Not later than one year after the Secretary develops test procedures under paragraph (1), the Federal Trade Commission (hereafter in this section referred to as the "Commission") shall prescribe labeling rules under section 324 of such Act (42 U.S.C. 6294) for those luminaires for which the Secretary has prescribed test procedures under paragraph (1) except that, with respect to any type of luminaire (or class thereof), the Secretary may determine that such labeling is not technologically feasible or economically justified or is not likely to assist consumers in making purchasing decisions.

(3) For purposes of sections 323, 324, and 327 of such Act, each product for which the Secretary has established test procedures or labeling rules pursuant to this subsection shall be considered a new covered product under section 322 of such Act (42

U.S.C. 6292) to the extent necessary to carry out this subsection.

(4) For purposes of section 327(a) of such Act, the term "this part" includes this subsection to the extent necessary to carry out this subsection.

Sec. 127. Report on the Potential of Cooperative Advanced Appliance Development.

(a) IN GENERAL. – Not later than 18 months after the date of the enactment of this Act, the Secretary shall, in consultation with the Administrator of the Environmental Protection Agency, utilities, and appliance manufacturers, prepare and submit to the Congress, a report on the potential for the development and commercialization of appliances which are substantially more efficient than required by Federal or State law.

(b) IDENTIFICATION OF HIGH-EFFICIENCY APPLIANCES. – The report submitted under subsection (a) shall identify candidate high-efficiency appliances which meet the following criteria:

(1) The potential exists for substantial improvement in the appliance's energy efficiency, beyond the minimum established in Federal and State law.

(2) There is the potential for significant energy savings at the national or regional level.

(3) Such appliances are likely to be cost-effective for consumers.

(4) Electric, water, or gas utilities are prepared to support and promote the commercialization of such appliances.

(5) Manufacturers are unlikely to undertake development and commercialization of such appliances on their own, or development and production would be substantially accelerated by support to manufacturers.

(c) RECOMMENDATIONS AND PROPOSALS. – The report submitted under subsection (a) shall also –

(1) describe the general actions the Secretary or the Administrator of the Environmental Protection Agency could take to coordinate and assist utilities and appliance manufacturers in developing and commercializing highly efficient appliances;

(2) describe specific proposals for Department of Energy or Environmental Protection Agency assistance to utilities and appliance manufacturers to promote the development and commercialization of highly efficient appliances;

(3) identify methods by which Federal purchase of highly efficient appliances could assist in the development and commercialization of such appliances; and

(4) identify the funding levels needed to develop and implement a Federal program to assist in the development and commercialization of highly efficient appliances.

Sec. 128. Evaluation of Utility Early Replacement Programs for Appliances.

Within 18 months after the date of the enactment of this Act, the Secretary, in consultation with the Administrator of the Environmental Protection Agency, utilities, and appliance manufacturers, shall evaluate and report to the Congress on the energy savings and environmental benefits of programs which are directed to the early replacement of older, less efficient appliances presently in use by consumers with existing products which are more efficient than required by Federal law. For the purposes of this section, the term "appliance" means those consumer products specified in section 322(a).

SUBTITLE D INDUSTRIAL

Sec. 131. Energy Efficiency in Industrial Facilities.

(a) GRANT PROGRAM. –

(1) IN GENERAL. – The Secretary shall make grants to industry associations to support programs to improve energy efficiency in industry. In order to be eligible for a grant under this subsection, an industry association shall establish a voluntary energy efficiency improvement target program.

(2) AWARDING OF GRANTS. – The Secretary shall request project proposals and provide annual grants on a competitive basis. In evaluating grant proposals under this subsection, the Secretary shall consider –

(A) potential energy savings;

(B) potential environmental benefits;

(C) the degree of cost sharing;

(D) the degree to which new and innovative technologies will be encouraged;

(E) the level of industry involvement;

(F) estimated project cost-effectiveness; and

(G) the degree to which progress toward the energy improvement targets can be monitored.

(3) ELIGIBLE PROJECTS. – Projects eligible for grants under this subsection may include the following:

(A) Workshops.

(B) Training seminars.

(C) Handbooks.

(D) Newsletters.

(E) Data bases.

(F) Other activities approved by the Secretary.

(4) LIMITATION ON COST SHARING. – Grants provided under this subsection shall not exceed $250,000 and each grant shall not exceed 75 percent of the total cost of the project for which the grant is made.

(5) AUTHORIZATION. – There are authorized to be appropriated such sums as are necessary to carry out this subsection.

(b) AWARD PROGRAM. – The Secretary shall establish an annual award program to recognize those industry associations or individual industrial companies that have significantly improved their energy efficiency.

(c) REPORT ON INDUSTRIAL REPORTING AND VOLUNTARY TARGETS. – Not later than one year after the date of the enactment of this Act, the Secretary shall, in consultation with affected industries, evaluate and report to the Congress regarding the establishment of Federally mandated energy efficiency reporting requirements and voluntary energy efficiency improvement targets for energy intensive industries. Such report shall include an evaluation of the costs and benefits of such reporting requirements and voluntary energy efficiency improvement targets, and recommendations regarding the role of such activities in improving energy efficiency in energy intensive industries.

Sec. 132. Process-Oriented Industrial Energy Efficiency.

(a) DEFINITIONS. – For the purposes of this section –

(1) the term "covered industry" means the food and food products industry, lumber and wood products industry, petroleum and coal products industry, and all other manufacturing industries specified in Standard Industrial Classification Codes 20 through 39 (or successor classification codes);

(2) the term "process-oriented industrial assessment" means –

(A) the identification of opportunities in the production process (from the introduction of materials to final packaging of the product for shipping) for –

(i) improving energy efficiency;

(ii) reducing environmental impact; and

(iii) designing technological improvements to increase competitiveness and achieve cost-effective product quality enhancement;

(B) the identification of opportunities for improving the energy efficiency of lighting, heating, ventilation, air conditioning, and the associated building envelope; and

(C) the identification of cost-effective opportunities for using renewable energy technology in the production process and in the systems described in subparagraph (B); and

(3) the term "utility" means any person, State agency (including any municipality), or Federal agency, which sells electric or gas energy to retail customers.

(b) GRANT PROGRAM. –

(1) USE OF FUNDS. – The Secretary shall, to the extent funds are made available for such purpose, make grants to States which, consistent with State law, shall be used for the following purposes:

(A) To promote, through appropriate institutions such as universities, nonprofit organizations, State and local government entities, technical centers, utilities, and trade organizations, the use of energy-efficient technologies in covered industries.

(B) To establish programs to train individuals (on an industry-by-industry basis) in conducting process-oriented industrial assessments and to encourage the use of such trained assessors.

(C) To assist utilities in developing, testing, and evaluating energy efficiency programs and technologies for industrial customers in covered industries.

(2) CONSULTATION. – States receiving grants under this subsection shall consult with utilities and representatives of affected industries, as appropriate,

in determining the most effective use of such funds consistent with the requirements of paragraph (1).

(3) ELIGIBILITY CRITERIA. – Not later than 1 year after the date of the enactment of this Act, the Secretary shall establish eligibility criteria for grants made pursuant to this subsection. Such criteria shall require a State applying for a grant to demonstrate that such State –

(A) pursuant to section 111(a) of the Public Utility and Regulatory Policies Act of 1978 (16 U.S.C. 2621(a)), has considered and made a determination regarding the implementation of the standards specified in paragraphs (7) and (8) of section 111(d) of such Act (with respect to integrated resources planning and investments in conservation and demand management); and

(B) by legislation or regulation –

(i) allows utilities to recover the costs prudently incurred in providing process-oriented industrial assessments; and

(ii) encourages utilities to provide to covered industries –

(I) process-oriented industrial assessments; and

(II) financial incentives for implementing energy efficiency improvements.

(4) ALLOCATION OF FUNDS. – Grants made pursuant to this subsection shall be allocated each fiscal year among States meeting the criteria specified in paragraph (3) who have submitted applications 60 days before the first day of such fiscal year. Such allocation shall be made in accordance with a formula to be prescribed by the Secretary based on each State's share of value added in industry (as determined by the Census of Manufacturers) as a percentage of the value added by all such States.

(5) RENEWAL OF GRANTS. – A grant under this subsection may continue to be renewed after 2 consecutive fiscal years during which a State receives a grant under this subsection, subject to the availability of funds, if –

(A) the Secretary determines that the funds made available to the State during the previous 2 years were used in a manner required under paragraph (1); and

(B) such State demonstrates, in a manner prescribed by the Secretary, utility participation in programs established pursuant to this subsection.

(6) COORDINATION WITH OTHER FEDERAL PROGRAMS. – In carrying out the functions described in paragraph (1), States shall, to the extent practicable, coordinate such functions with activities and programs conducted by the Energy Analysis and Diagnostic Centers of the Department of Energy and the Manufacturing Technology Centers of the National Institute of Standards and Technology.

(c) OTHER FEDERAL ASSISTANCE. –

(1) ASSESSMENT CRITERIA. – Not later than 2 years after the date of the enactment of this Act, the Secretary shall, by contract with nonprofit organizations with expertise in process-oriented industrial energy efficiency technologies, establish and, as appropriate, update criteria for conducting process-oriented industrial assessments on an industry-by-industry basis. Such criteria shall be made available to State and local government, public utility commissions, utilities, representatives of affected process-oriented industries, and other interested parties.

(2) DIRECTORY. – The Secretary shall establish a nationwide directory of organizations offering industrial energy efficiency assessments, technologies, and services consistent with the purposes of this section. Such directory shall be made available to State governments, public utility commissions, utilities, industry representatives, and other interested parties.

(3) AWARD PROGRAM. – The Secretary shall establish an annual award program to recognize utilities operating outstanding or innovative industrial energy efficiency technology assistance programs.

(4) MEETINGS. – In order to further the purposes of this section, the Secretary shall convene annual meetings of parties interested in process-oriented industrial assessments, including representatives of State government, public utility commissions, utilities, and affected process-oriented industries.

(d) REPORT. – Not later than 2 years after the date of the enactment of this Act, and annually thereafter, the Secretary shall submit to the Congress a report which –

(1) identifies barriers encountered in implementing this section;

(2) makes recommendations for overcoming such barriers;

(3) documents the results achieved by the programs established and grants awarded pursuant to this section;

(4) reviews any difficulties encountered by industry in securing and implementing energy efficiency technologies recommended in process-oriented industrial assessments or otherwise identified as a result of programs established pursuant to this section; and

(5) recommends methods for further promoting the distribution and implementation of energy efficiency technologies consistent with the purposes of this section.

(e) AUTHORIZATION OF APPROPRIATIONS. – There are authorized to be appropriated such sums as may be necessary to carry out the purposes of this section.

Sec. 133. Industrial Insulation and Audit Guidelines.

(a) VOLUNTARY GUIDELINES FOR ENERGY EFFICIENCY AUDITING AND INSULATING. – Not later than 18 months after the date of the enactment of this Act, the Secretary, after consultation with utilities, major industrial energy consumers, and representatives of the insulation industry, shall establish voluntary guidelines for –

(1) the conduct of energy efficiency audits of industrial facilities to identify cost-effective opportunities to increase energy efficiency; and

(2) the installation of insulation to achieve cost-effective increases in energy efficiency in industrial facilities.

(b) EDUCATIONAL AND TECHNICAL ASSISTANCE. – The Secretary shall conduct a program of educational and technical assistance to promote the use of the voluntary guidelines established under subsection (a).

(c) REPORT. – Not later than 2 years after the date of the enactment of this Act, and biennially thereafter, the Secretary shall report to the Congress on activities conducted pursuant to this section, including –

(1) a review of the status of industrial energy auditing procedures; and

(2) an evaluation of the effectiveness of the guidelines established under subsection (a) and the responsiveness of the industrial sector to such guidelines.

SUBTITLE E STATE AND LOCAL ASSISTANCE

Sec. 141. Amendments to State Energy Conservation Program.

(a) STATE BUILDINGS ENERGY INCENTIVE FUND. –

(1) IN GENERAL. – Section 363 of the Energy Policy and Conservation Act (42 U.S.C. 6323) is amended by adding at the end the following new subsection:

"(f) If the Secretary determines that a State has demonstrated a commitment to improving the energy efficiency of buildings within such State, the Secretary may, beginning in fiscal year 1994, provide up to $1,000,000 to such State for deposit into a revolving fund established by such State for the purpose of financing energy efficiency improvements in State and local government buildings. In making such determination the Secretary shall consider whether –

"(1) such State, or a majority of the units of local government with jurisdiction over building energy codes within such State, has adopted codes for energy efficiency in new buildings that are at least as stringent as American Society of Heating, Refrigerating, and Air-Conditioning Engineers Standard 90.1–1989 (with respect to commercial buildings) and Council of American Building Officials Model Energy Code, 1992 (with respect to residential buildings);

"(2) such State has established a program, including a revolving fund, to finance energy efficiency improvement projects in State and local government facilities and buildings; and

"(3) such State has obtained funding from non-Federal sources, including but not limited to, oil overcharge funds, State or local government appropriations, or utility contributions (including rebates) equal to or greater than three times the amount provided by the Secretary under this subsection for deposit into such revolving fund.".

(2) AUTHORIZATION OF APPROPRIATIONS. – Section 365(f) of such Act (42 U.S.C. 6325(f)) is amended –

(A) by striking "(f) For the purpose" and inserting the following: "(f)(1) Except as provided in paragraph (2), for the purpose"; and

(B) by inserting at the end the following:

"(2) For the purposes of carrying out section 363(f), there is authorized to be appropriated for fiscal year 1994 and each fiscal year thereafter such sums as may be necessary, to remain available until expended.".

(b) TRAINING OF BUILDING DESIGNERS AND CONTRACTORS; BUILDING RETROFIT STANDARDS; FEASIBILITY; RURAL RENEWABLE ENERGY. – Subsection 362(d) of the Energy Policy and Conservation Act (42 U.S.C. 6322(d)) is amended –

(1) in paragraph (12) by striking "and";

(2) by redesignating paragraph (13) as paragraph (17); and

(3) by inserting after paragraph (12) the following new paragraphs:

"(13) programs(enlisting appropriate trade and professional organizations in the development and financing of such programs) to provide training and education (including, if appropriate, training workshops, practice manuals, and testing for each area of energy efficiency technology) to building designers and contractors involved in building design and construction or in the sale, installation, and maintenance of energy systems and equipment to promote building energy efficiency improvements;

"(14) programs for the development of building retrofit standards and regulations, including retrofit ordinances enforced at the time of the sale of a building;

"(15) support for prefeasibility and feasibility studies for projects that utilize renewable energy and energy efficiency resource technologies in order to facilitate access to capital and credit for such projects;

"(16) programs to facilitate and encourage the voluntary use of renewable energy technologies for eligible participants in Federal agency programs, including the Rural Electrification Administration and the Farmers Home Administration; and"

(c) STATE ENERGY CONSERVATION PLAN REQUIREMENT. –

(1) IN GENERAL. – Section 362(c)(5) of the Energy Policy and Conservation Act (42 U.S.C. 6322(c)(5)) is amended by striking "; and" and by inserting the following: "and to turn such vehicle left from a one-way street onto a one-way street at a red light after stopping; and".

(2) EFFECTIVE DATE. – The amendment made by paragraph (1) shall take effect January 1, 1995.

(d) STUDY REGARDING IMPACT OF PERMITTING RIGHT AND LEFT TURNS ON RED LIGHTS. –

(1) IN GENERAL. – The Administrator of the National Highway Traffic Safety Administration, in consultation with State agencies with jurisdiction over traffic safety issues, shall conduct a study on the safety impact of the requirement specified in section 362(c)(5) of the Energy Policy and Conservation Act (42 U.S.C. 6322(c)(5)), particularly with respect to the impact on pedestrian safety.

(2) REPORT. – The Administrator shall report the findings of the study conducted under paragraph (1) to the Congress and the Secretary not later than 2 years after the date of the enactment of this Act.

Sec. 142. Amendments to Low-Income Weatherization Program.

(a) PRIVATE SECTOR INVESTMENTS IN LOW-INCOME WEATHERIZATION. – Part A of title IV of the Energy Conservation and Production Act (42 U.S.C. 6861 et seq.) is amended by inserting after section 414 the following new sections:

"SEC. 414A. PRIVATE SECTOR INVESTMENTS.

"(a) IN GENERAL. – The Secretary shall, to the extent funds are made available for such purpose, provide financial assistance to entities receiving funding from the Federal Government or from a State through a weatherization assistance program under section 413 or section 414 for the development and initial implementation of partnerships, agreements, or other arrangements with utilities, private sector interests, or other institutions, under which non-Federal financial assistance would be made available to support programs which install energy efficiency improvements in low-income housing.

"(b) USE OF FUNDS. – Financial assistance provided under this section may be used for –

"(1) the negotiation of such partnerships, agreements and other arrangements;

"(2) the presentation of arguments before State or local agencies;

"(3) expert advice on the development of such partnerships, agreements, and other arrangements; or

"(4) other activities reasonably associated with the development and initial implementation of such arrangements.

"(c) CONDITIONS. – (1) Financial assistance provided under this section to entities other than States shall, to the extent practicable, coincide with the timing of financial assistance provided to such entities under section 413 or section 414.

"(2) Not less than 80 percent of amounts provided under this section shall be provided to entities other than States.

"(3) A recipient of financial assistance under this section shall have up to three years to complete projects undertaken with such assistance.

"SEC. 414B. TECHNICAL TRANSFER GRANTS.

"(a) IN GENERAL. – The Secretary may, to the extent funds are made available, provide financial assistance to entities receiving funding from the Federal Government or from a State through a weatherization assistance program under section 413 or section 414 for –

"(1) evaluating technical and management measures which increase program and/or private entity performance in weatherizing low-income housing;

"(2) producing technical information for use by persons involved in weatherizing low-income housing;

"(3) exchanging information; and

"(4) conducting training programs for persons involved in weatherizing low-income housing.

"(b) CONDITIONS. – (1) Not less than 50 percent of amounts provided under this section shall be awarded to entities other than States.

"(2) A recipient of financial assistance under this section may contract with nonprofit entities to carry out all or part of the activities for which such financial assistance is provided.".

(b) USE OF SOLAR THERMAL WATER HEATERS AND WOOD-BURNING HEATING APPLIANCES FOR LOW-INCOME WEATHERIZATION. – Section 412(9) of the Energy Conservation and Production Act (42 U.S.C. 6862(9)) is amended –

(1) by moving subparagraph (G) 2-ems to the right and by striking "and";

(2) by redesignating subparagraph (H) as subparagraph (J); and

(3) by inserting after subparagraph (G), the following:

"(H) solar thermal water heaters;

"(I) wood-heating appliances; and".

(c) CLERICAL AMENDMENT. – The table of contents for part A of title IV of the Energy Conservation and Production Act is amended by inserting after the item related to section 414 the following items:

"Sec. 414A. Private sector investments.

"Sec. 414B. Technical transfer grants.".

Sec. 143. Energy Extension Service Program.

(a) REPEAL. – The National Energy Extension Service Act, title V of Public Law 95-39, is repealed.

(b) CONFORMING AMENDMENT. – Section 103 of the Energy Reorganization Act of 1974 (42 U.S.C. 5813(7)) is amended –

(1) by striking paragraph (7); and

(2) by redesignating paragraphs (8), (9), (10), (11), and (12) as paragraphs (7), (8), (9), (10), and (11), respectively.

SUBTITLE F FEDERAL AGENCY ENERGY MANAGEMENT

Sec. 151. Definitions.

For purposes of this subtitle –

(1) the term "agency" means has the meaning given such term in section 551(1) of title 5, United States Code, except that such term does not include the United States Postal Service;

(2) the term "facility energy supervisor" means the employee with responsibility for the daily operations of a Federal facility, including the management, installation, operation, and maintenance of energy systems in Federal facilities which may include more than one building;

(3) the term "trained energy manager" means a person who has demonstrated proficiency, or who has

completed a course of study in the areas of fundamentals of building energy systems, building energy codes and applicable professional standards, energy accounting and analysis, life-cycle cost methodology, fuel supply and pricing, and instrumentation for energy surveys and audits;

(4) the term "Task Force" means the Interagency Energy Management Task Force established under section 547 of the National Energy Conservation Policy Act (42 U.S.C. 8257); and

(5) the term "energy conservation measures" has the meaning given such term in section 551(4) of the National Energy Conservation Policy Act.

Sec. 152. Federal Energy Management Amendments.

(a) PURPOSE. – Section 542 of the National Energy Conservation Policy Act (42 U.S.C. 8252) is amended by inserting after "use of energy" the following: "and water, and the use of renewable energy sources,".

(b) REQUIREMENTS FOR FEDERAL AGENCIES. – Section 543 of such Act (42 U.S.C. 8253(a)) is amended –

(1) in the section heading by striking "GOALS" and inserting "REQUIREMENTS";

(2) in subsection (a) by striking "GOAL" and inserting "REQUIREMENT";

(3) in subsection (a)(1), by striking the period at the end and inserting the following: "and so that the energy consumption per gross square foot of its Federal buildings in use during the fiscal year 2000 is at least 20 percent less than the energy consumption per gross square foot of its Federal buildings in use during fiscal year 1985."; and

(4) by redesignating subsection (b) as subsection (d) and inserting after subsection (a) the following:

"(b) ENERGY MANAGEMENT REQUIREMENT FOR FEDERAL AGENCIES. – (1) Not later than January 1, 2005, each agency shall, to the maximum extent practicable, install in Federal buildings owned by the United States all energy and water conservation measures with payback periods of less than 10 years, as determined by using the methods and procedures developed pursuant to section 544.

"(2) The Secretary may waive the requirements of this subsection for any agency for such periods as the Secretary may determine if the Secretary finds that the agency is taking all practicable steps to meet the requirements and that the requirements of this subsection will pose an unacceptable burden upon the agency. If the Secretary waives the requirements of this subsection, the Secretary shall notify the Congress promptly in writing with an explanation and a justification of the reasons for such waiver.

"(3) This subsection shall not apply to an agency's facilities that generate or transmit electric energy or to the uranium enrichment facilities operated by the Department of Energy.

"(4) An agency may participate in the Environmental Protection Agency's 'Green Lights' program for purposes of receiving technical assistance in complying with the requirements of this section.

"(c) EXCLUSIONS. – (1) An agency may exclude, from the energy consumption requirements for the year 2000 established under subsection (a) and the requirements of subsection (b)(1), any Federal building or collection of Federal buildings, and the associated energy consumption and gross square footage, if the head of such agency finds that compliance with such requirements would be impractical. A finding of impracticability shall be based on the energy intensiveness of activities carried out in such Federal buildings or collection of Federal buildings, the type and amount of energy consumed, the technical feasibility of making the desired changes, and, in the cases of the Departments of Defense and Energy, the unique character of certain facilities operated by such Departments.

"(2) Each agency shall identify and list, in each report made under section 548(a), the Federal buildings designated by it for such exclusion. The Secretary shall review such findings for consistency with the impracticability standards set forth in paragraph (1), and may within 90 days after receipt of the findings, reverse a finding of impracticability. In the case of any such reversal, the agency shall comply with the energy consumption requirements for the building concerned.".

(c) IMPLEMENTATION. – Section 543(d) of such Act (as redesignated by subsection (b)(4) of this section) is amended –

(1) in the material preceding paragraph (1), by striking out "To achieve the goal established in subsection (a)," and inserting in lieu thereof the following: "The Secretary shall consult with the Secretary of Defense and the Administrator of General Services in developing guidelines for the implementation of this part. To meet the requirements of this section,";

(2) by striking out paragraph (1) and inserting in lieu thereof the following:

"(1) prepare and submit to the Secretary, not later than December 31, 1993, a plan describing how the agency intends to meet such requirements, including how it will –

"(A) designate personnel primarily responsible for achieving such requirements;

"(B) identify high priority projects through calculation of payback periods;

"(C) take maximum advantage of contracts authorized under title VIII of this Act, of financial incentives and other services provided by utilities for efficiency investment, and of other forms of financing to reduce the direct costs to the Government; and

"(D) otherwise implement this part;";

(3) in paragraph (2), by inserting before the semicolon at the end the following: "and update such surveys as needed, incorporating any relevant information obtained from the survey conducted pursuant to section 550";

(4) by striking out paragraph (3) and inserting in lieu thereof the following:

"(3) using such surveys, determine the cost and payback period of energy and water conservation measures likely to achieve the requirements of this section;

"(4) install energy and water conservation measures that will achieve the requirements of this section through the methods and procedures established pursuant to section 544; and"; and

(5) by redesignating paragraph (4) as paragraph (5).

(d) LIFE CYCLE COST METHODS ANDPROCEDURES. – Section 544 of such Act (42 U.S.C. 8254) is amended –

(1) in subsection (a), in the material preceding paragraph (1), by striking out "National Bureau of Standards," and inserting in lieu thereof "National Institute of Standards and Technology,"; and

(2) in subsection (b)(2), by striking "agency shall" and all that follows through the period at the end and inserting the following: "agency shall, after January 1, 1994, fully consider the efficiency of all potential building space at the time of renewing or entering into a new lease.".

(e) IDENTIFICATION OF FUNDS. – Section 545 of such Act (42 U.S.C. 8255) is amended to read as follows:

"SEC. 545. BUDGET TREATMENT FOR ENERGY CONSERVATION MEASURES.

"The President shall transmit to the Congress, along with each budget that is submitted to the Congress under section 1105 of title 31, United States Code, a statement of the amount of appropriations requested in such budget, if any, on an individual agency basis, for –

"(1) electric and other energy costs to be incurred in operating and maintaining agency facilities; and

"(2) compliance with the provisions of this part, the Energy Policy and Conservation Act (42 U.S.C. 6201 et seq.), and all applicable Executive orders, including Executive Order 12003 (42 U.S.C. 6201 note) and Executive Order 12759 (56 Fed. Reg. 16257).".

(f) INCENTIVE PROGRAM. – Section 546 of such Act (42 U.S.C. 8256) is amended –

(1) by striking "(a) IN GENERAL. –" and inserting in lieu thereof "(a) CONTRACTS. – (1)";

(2) by redesignating subsection (b) as paragraph (2) and amending it to read as follows:

"(2) The Secretary shall, not later than 18 months after the date of the enactment of the Energy Policy Act of 1992 and after consultation with the Director of the Office of Management and Budget, the Secretary of Defense, and the Administrator of General Services, develop appropriate procedures and methods for use by agencies to implement the incentives referred to in paragraph (1).";

(3) by striking out subsection (c); and

(4) by adding at the end the following new subsections:

"(b) FEDERAL ENERGY EFFICIENCY FUND. – (1) The Secretary shall establish a Federal Energy

Efficiency Fund to provide grants to agencies to assist them in meeting the requirements of section 543.

"(2) Not later than June 30, 1993, the Secretary shall issue guidelines to be followed by agencies submitting proposals for such grants. All agencies shall be eligible to submit proposals for grants under the Fund.

"(3) The Secretary shall award grants from the Fund after a competitive assessment of the technical and economic effectiveness of each agency proposal. The Secretary shall consider the following factors in determining whether to provide funding under this subsection:

"(A) The cost-effectiveness of the project.

"(B) The amount of energy and cost savings anticipated to the Federal Government.

"(C) The amount of funding committed to the project by the agency requesting financial assistance.

"(D) The extent that a proposal leverages financing from other non-Federal sources.

"(E) Any other factor which the Secretary determines will result in the greatest amount of energy and cost savings to the Federal Government.

"(4) There are authorized to be appropriated, to remain available to be expended, to carry out this subsection not more than $10,000,000 for fiscal year 1994, $50,000,000 for fiscal year 1995, and such sums as may be necessary for fiscal years thereafter.

"(c) UTILITY INCENTIVE PROGRAMS. – (1) Agencies are authorized and encouraged to participate in programs to increase energy efficiency and for water conservation or the management of electricity demand conducted by gas, water, or electric utilities and generally available to customers of such utilities.

"(2) Each agency may accept any financial incentive, goods, or services generally available from any such utility, to increase energy efficiency or to conserve water or manage electricity demand.

"(3) Each agency is encouraged to enter into negotiations with electric, water, and gas utilities to design cost-effective demand management and conservation incentive programs to address the unique needs of facilities utilized by such agency.

"(4) If an agency satisfies the criteria which generally apply to other customers of a utility incentive program, such agency may not be denied collection of rebates or other incentives.

"(5)(A) An amount equal to fifty percent of the energy and water cost savings realized by an agency (other than the Department of Defense) with respect to funds appropriated for any fiscal year beginning after fiscal year 1992 (including financial benefits resulting from energy savings performance contracts under title VIII and utility energy efficiency rebates) shall, subject to appropriation, remain available for expenditure by such agency for additional energy efficiency measures which may include related employee incentive programs, particularly at those facilities at which energy savings were achieved.

"(B) Agencies shall establish a fund and maintain strict financial accounting and controls for savings realized and expenditures made under this subsection. Records maintained pursuant to this subparagraph shall be made available for public inspection upon request.

"(d) FINANCIAL INCENTIVE PROGRAM FOR FACILITY ENERGY MANAGERS. – (1) The Secretary shall, in consultation with the Task Force established pursuant to section 547, establish a financial bonus program to reward, with funds made available for such purpose, outstanding Federal facility energy managers in agencies and the United States Postal Service.

"(2) Not later than June 1, 1993, the Secretary shall issue procedures for implementing and conducting the award program, including the criteria to be used in selecting outstanding energy managers and contributors who have –

"(A) improved energy performance through increased energy efficiency;

"(B) implemented proven energy efficiency and energy conservation techniques, devices, equipment, or procedures;

"(C) developed and implemented training programs for facility energy managers, operators, and maintenance personnel;

"(D) developed and implemented employee awareness programs;

"(E) succeeded in generating utility incentives, shared energy savings contracts, and other federally approved performance based energy savings contracts;

"(F) made successful efforts to fulfill compliance with energy reduction mandates, including the provisions of section 543; and

"(G) succeeded in the implementation of the guidelines established under section 159.

"(3) There is authorized to be appropriated to carry out this subsection not more than $250,000 for each of the fiscal years 1993, 1994, and 1995.

(g) REPORTS. – Section 548 of such Act (42 U.S.C. 8258) is amended –

(1) in subsection (b)(1), by striking "including" and all that follows through the semicolon and inserting the following: "including –

"(A) a copy of the list of the exclusions made under sections 543(a)(2) and 543(c)(3); and

"(B) a statement detailing the amount of funds awarded to each agency under section 546(b), the energy and water conservation measures installed with such funds, the projected energy and water savings to be realized from installed measures, and, for each installed measure for which the projected energy and water savings reported in the previous year were not realized, the percentage of such projected savings that was not realized, the reasons such savings were not realized, and proposals for, and projected costs of, achieving such projected savings in the future;"; and

(2) by adding at the end the following new subsection:

"(c) OTHER REPORT. – The Secretary, in consultation with the Administrator of General Services, shall –

"(1) conduct a study and evaluate legal, institutional, and other constraints to connecting buildings owned or leased by the Federal Government to district heating and district cooling systems; and

"(2) not later than 18 months after the date of the enactment of this subsection, transmit to the Congress a report containing the findings and conclusions of such study, including recommendations for the development of streamlined processes for the consideration of connecting buildings owned or leased by the Federal Government to district heating and cooling systems.".

(h) DEMONSTRATION OF NEW TECHNOLOGY; SURVEY OF ENERGY SAVING POTENTIAL. – Such Act is amended –

(1) by redesignating section 549 as section 551; and

(2) by inserting the following new sections after section 548:

"SEC. 549. DEMONSTRATION OF NEW TECHNOLOGY.

"(a) DEMONSTRATION PROGRAM. – Not later than January 1, 1994, the Secretary, in cooperation with the Administrator of General Services, shall establish a demonstration program to install, in federally owned facilities or federally assisted housing, energy conservation measures for which the Secretary has determined that such installation would accelerate commercial viability. In those cases where technologies are determined to be equivalent, priority shall be given to those technologies that have received or are receiving Federal financial assistance.

"(b) SELECTION CRITERIA. – In addition to the determination under subsection (a), the Secretary shall select, in cooperation with the Administrator of General Services, proposals to be funded under this section on the basis of –

"(1) cost-effectiveness;

"(2) technical feasibility and system reliability in a working environment;

"(3) lack of market penetration in the Federal sector;

"(4) the potential needs of the proposing Federal agency for the technology, projected over 5 to 10 years;

"(5) the potential Federal sector market, projected over 5 to 10 years;

"(6) energy efficiency; and

"(7) other environmental benefits, including the projected reduction of greenhouse gas emissions and indoor air pollution.

"(c) PROPOSALS. – Federal agencies may submit to the Secretary, for each fiscal year, proposals for projects to be funded by the Secretary under this section. Each such proposal shall include –

"(1) a description of the proposed project emphasizing the innovative use of technology in the Federal sector;

"(2) a description of the technical reliability and cost-effectiveness data expected to be acquired;

"(3) an identification of the potential needs of the Federal agency for the technology;

"(4) a commitment to adopt the technology, if the project establishes its technical reliability and life cycle cost-effectiveness, to supply at least 10 percent of the Federal agency's potential needs identified under paragraph (3);

"(5) schedules and milestones for installing additional units; and

"(6) a technology transfer plan to publicize the results of the project.

"(d) PARTICIPATION BY GSA. – The Secretary may only select a project for funding under this section which is proposed to be carried out in a building under the jurisdiction of the General Services Administration if the project will be carried out by the Administrator of General Services. If such project involves a total expenditure in excess of $1,600,000, no appropriation shall be made for such project unless such project has been approved by a resolution adopted by the Committee on Public Works and Transportation of the House of Representatives and the Committee on Environment and Public Works of the Senate.

"(e) STUDY. – The Secretary shall conduct a study to evaluate the potential use of the purchasing power of the Federal Government to promote the development and commercialization of energy efficient products. The study shall identify products for which there is a high potential for Federal purchasing power to substantially promote their development and commercialization, and shall include a plan to develop such potential. The study shall be conducted in consultation with utilities, manufacturers, and appropriate nonprofit organizations concerned with energy efficiency. The Secretary shall report to the Congress on the results of the study not later than two years after the date of the enactment of this Act.

"(f) AUTHORIZATION OF APPROPRIATIONS. – There are authorized to be appropriated to the Secretary for carrying out this section $5,000,000 for each of the fiscal years 1993, 1994, and 1995.

"SEC. 550. SURVEY OF ENERGY SAVING POTENTIAL.

"(a) IN GENERAL. – The Secretary shall, in consultation with the Interagency Energy Management Task Force established under section 547, carry out an energy survey for the purposes of –

"(1) determining the maximum potential cost effective energy savings that may be achieved in a representative sample of buildings owned or leased by the Federal Government in different areas of the country;

"(2) making recommendations for cost effective energy efficiency and renewable energy improvements in those buildings and in other similar Federal buildings; and

"(3) identifying barriers which may prevent an agency's ability to comply with section 543 and other energy management goals.

"(b) IMPLEMENTATION. – (1) The Secretary shall transmit to the Committee on Energy and Natural Resources and the Committee on Governmental Affairs of the Senate and the Committee on Energy and Commerce, the Committee on Government Operations, and the Committee on Public Works and Transportation of the House of Representatives, within 180 days after the date of the enactment of the Energy Policy Act of 1992, a plan for implementing this section.

"(2) The Secretary shall designate buildings to be surveyed in the project so as to obtain a sample of the buildings of the types and in the climates that is representative of buildings owned or leased by Federal agencies in the United States that consume the major portion of the energy consumed in Federal buildings. Such sample shall include, where appropriate, the following types of Federal facility space:

"(A) Housing.

"(B) Storage.

"(C) Office.

"(D) Services.

"(E) Schools.

"(F) Research and Development.

"(G) Industrial.

"(H) Prisons.

"(I) Hospitals.

"(3) For purposes of this section, an improvement shall be considered cost effective if the cost of the energy saved or displaced by the improvement exceeds the cost of the improvement over the remaining life of a Federal building or the remaining term of a lease of a building leased by the Federal Government as determined by the life cycle costing methodology developed under section 544.

"(c) PERSONNEL. – (1) In carrying out this section, the Secretary shall utilize personnel who are –

"(A) employees of the Department of Energy; or

"(B) selected by the agencies utilizing the buildings which are being surveyed under this section.

"(2) Such personnel shall be detailed for the purpose of carrying out this section without any reduction of salary or benefits.

"(d) REPORT. – As soon as practicable after the completion of the project carried out under this section, the Secretary shall transmit a report of the findings and conclusions of the project to the Committee on Energy and Natural Resources and the Committee on Governmental Affairs of the Senate, the Committee on Energy and Commerce, the Committee on Government Operations, and the Committee on Public Works and Transportation of the House of Representatives, and the agencies who own the buildings involved in such project. Such report shall include an analysis of the probability of each agency achieving the 20 percent reduction goal established under section 543(a) of the National Energy Conservation Policy Act (42 U.S.C. 8253(a)).".

(i) TECHNICAL AMENDMENTS. – (1) Section 548 of such Act (42 U.S.C. 8258) is amended –

(A) in subsection (a)(2), by striking "546(b)" and inserting in lieu thereof "546(a)(2)"; and

(B) in subsection (b), in the material preceding paragraph (1), by striking "annually," and insert the following: ", not later than April 2 of each year,".

(2) The table of contents of such Act is amended by striking the item for section 549 and inserting in lieu thereof the following new items:

"Sec. 549. Demonstration of new technology.

"Sec. 550. Survey of energy saving potential.

"Sec. 551. Definitions.".

(3) Section 3 of the Federal Energy Management Improvement Act of 1988 (42 U.S.C. 8253 note) is hereby repealed.

Sec. 153. General Services Administration Federal Buildings Fund.

Section 210(f) of the Federal Property and Administrative Services Act of 1949 (40 U.S.C. 490(f)), is amended –

(1) in paragraph (1), by inserting "(to be known as the Federal Buildings Fund)" after "a fund"; and

(2) by adding at the end the following new paragraphs:

"(7)(A) The Administrator is authorized to receive amounts from rebates or other cash incentives related to energy savings and shall deposit such amounts in the Federal Buildings Fund for use as provided in subparagraph (D).

"(B) The Administrator may accept, from a utility, goods or services which enhance the energy efficiency of Federal facilities.

"(C) In the administration of any real property for which the Administrator leases and pays utility costs, the Administrator may assign all or a portion of energy rebates to the lessor to underwrite the costs incurred in undertaking energy efficiency improvements in such real property if the payback period for such improvement is at least 2 years less than the remainder of the term of the lease.

"(D) The Administrator may, in addition to amounts appropriated for such purposes and without regard to paragraph (2), obligate for energy management improvement programs –

"(i) amounts received and deposited in the Federal Buildings fund under subparagraph (A);

"(ii) goods and services received under subparagraph (B); and

"(iii) amounts the Administrator determines are not needed for other authorized projects and are otherwise available to implement energy efficiency programs.

"(8)(A) The Administrator is authorized to receive amounts from the sale of recycled materials and shall deposit such amounts in the Federal Buildings fund for use as provided in subparagraph (B).

"(B) The Administrator may, in addition to amounts appropriated for such purposes and without regard to paragraph (2), obligate amounts received and deposited in the Federal Buildings Fund under subparagraph (A) for programs which –

"(i) promote further source reduction and recycling programs; and

"(ii) encourage employees to participate in recycling programs by providing funding for child care.".

Sec. 154. Report by General Services Administration.

Not later than one year after the date of the enactment of this Act, and annually thereafter, the Administrator of General Services shall report to the Committee on Governmental Affairs and the Committee on Energy and Natural Resources of the Senate and the Committee on Energy and Commerce, the Committee on Government Operations, and the Committee on Public Works and Transportation of the House of Representatives on the activities of the General Services Administration conducted pursuant to this subtitle.

Sec. 155. Energy Savings Performance Contracts.

(a) IN GENERAL. – Section 801 of the National Energy Conservation Policy Act (42 U.S.C. 8287) is amended –

(1) by striking "The head" and inserting the following:

"(a) IN GENERAL. – (1) The head"; and

(2) by inserting at the end the following:

"(2)(A) Contracts under this title shall be energy savings performance contracts and shall require an annual energy audit and specify the terms and conditions of any government payments and performance guarantees. Any such performance guarantee shall provide that the contractor is responsible for maintenance and repair services for any energy related equipment, including computer software systems.

"(B) Aggregate annual payments by an agency to both utilities and energy savings performance contractors, under an energy savings performance contract, may not exceed the amount that the agency would have paid for utilities without an energy savings performance contract (as estimated through the procedures developed pursuant to this section) during contract years. The contract shall provide for a guarantee of savings to the agency, and shall establish payment schedules reflecting such guarantee, taking into account any capital costs under the contract.

"(C) Federal agencies may incur obligations pursuant to such contracts to finance energy conservation measures provided guaranteed savings exceed the debt service requirements.

"(D) A federal agency may enter into a multiyear contract under this title for a period not to exceed 25 years, without funding of cancellation charges before cancellation, if –

"(i) such contract was awarded in a competitive manner pursuant to subsection (b)(2), using procedures and methods established under this title;

"(ii) funds are available and adequate for payment of the costs of such contract for the first fiscal year;

"(iii) 30 days before the award of any such contract that contains a clause setting forth a cancellation ceiling in excess of $750,000, the head of such agency gives written notification of such proposed contract and of the proposed cancellation ceiling for such contract to the appropriate authorizing and appropriating committees of the Congress; and

"(iv) such contract is governed by part 17.1 of the Federal Acquisition Regulation promulgated under section 25 of the Office of Federal Procurement Policy Act (41 U.S.C. 421) or the applicable rules promulgated under this title.

"(b) IMPLEMENTATION. – (1)(A) The Secretary, with the concurrence of the Federal Acquisition Regulatory Council established under section 25(a) of the Office of Federal Procurement Policy Act, not later than 180 days after the date of the enactment of the Energy Policy Act of 1992, shall, by rule, establish appropriate procedures and methods for use by Federal agencies to select, monitor, and terminate contracts with energy service contractors in accordance with laws governing Federal procurement that will achieve the intent of this section in a cost-effective manner. In developing such procedures and methods, the Secretary, with the concurrence of the Federal Acquisition Regulatory Council, shall determine which existing regulations are inconsistent with the intent of this section and shall formulate substitute regulations consistent with laws governing Federal procurement.

"(B) The procedures and methods established pursuant to subparagraph (A) shall be the procedures and contracting methods for selection, by an agency, of a contractor to provide energy savings performance services. Such procedures and methods shall provide for the calculation of energy savings based on sound engineering and financial practices.

"(2) The procedures and methods established pursuant to paragraph (1)(A) shall –

"(A) allow the Secretary to –

"(i) request statements of qualifications, which shall, at a minimum, include prior experience and capabilities of contractors to perform the proposed types of energy savings services and financial and performance information, from firms engaged in providing energy savings services; and

"(ii) from the statements received, designate and prepare a list, with an update at least annually, of those firms that are qualified to provide energy savings services;

"(B) require each agency to use the list prepared by the Secretary pursuant to subparagraph (A)(ii) unless the agency elects to develop an agency list of firms qualified to provide energy savings performance services using the same selection procedures and methods as are required of the Secretary in preparing such lists; and

"(C) allow the head of each agency to –

"(i) select firms from the list prepared pursuant to subparagraph (A)(ii) or the list prepared by the agency pursuant to subparagraph (B) to conduct discussions concerning a particular proposed energy savings project, including requesting a technical and price proposal from such selected firms for such project;

"(ii) select from such firms the most qualified firm to provide energy savings services based on technical and price proposals and any other relevant information;

"(iii) permit receipt of unsolicited proposals for energy savings performance contracting services from a firm that such agency has determined is qualified to provide such services under the procedures established pursuant to paragraph (1)(A), and require agency facility managers to place a notice in the Commerce Business Daily announcing they have received such a proposal and invite other similarly qualified firms to submit competing proposals; and

"(iv) enter into an energy savings performance contract with a firm qualified under clause (iii), consistent with the procedures and methods established pursuant to paragraph (1)(A).

"(3) A firm not designated as qualified to provide energy savings services under paragraph (2)(A)(i) or paragraph (2)(B) may request a review of such decision to be conducted in accordance with procedures to be developed by the board of contract appeals of the General Services Administration. Procedures developed by the board of contract appeals under this paragraph shall be substantially equivalent to procedures established under section 111(f) of the Federal Property and Administrative Services Act of 1949 (40 U.S.C. 759(f)).

"(c) SUNSET AND REPORTING REQUIREMENTS. – (1) The authority to enter into new contracts under this section shall cease to be effective five years after the date procedures and methods are established under subsection (b).

"(2) Beginning one year after the date procedures and methods are established under subsection (b), and annually thereafter, for a period of five years after such date, the Comptroller General of the United States shall report on the implementation of this section. Such reports shall include, but not be limited to, an assessment of the following issues:

"(A) The quality of the energy audits conducted for the agencies.

"(B) The government's ability to maximize energy savings.

"(C) The total energy cost savings accrued by the agencies that have entered into such contracts.

"(D) The total costs associated with entering into and performing such contracts.

"(E) A comparison of the total costs incurred by agencies under such contracts and the total costs incurred under similar contracts performed in the private sector.

"(F) The number of firms selected as qualified firms under this section and their respective shares of awarded contracts.

"(G) The number of firms engaged in similar activity in the private sector and their respective market shares.

"(H) The number of applicant firms not selected as qualified firms under this section and the reason for their nonselection.

"(I) The frequency with which agencies have utilized the services of government labs to perform any of the functions specified in this section.

"(J) With the respect to the final report submitted pursuant to this paragraph, an assessment of whether the contracting procedures developed pursuant to this section and utilized by agencies have been effective and whether continued use of such procedures, as opposed to the procedures provided by existing public contract law, is necessary for implementation of successful energy savings performance contracts.".

(b) DEFINITION. – Section 804 of such Act (42 U.S.C. 8287c) is amended –

(1) in the material preceding paragraph (1), by striking "title-" and inserting "title, the following definitions apply:";

(2) in paragraph (1), by striking "the" and inserting "The" and by striking ", and" and inserting a period;

(3) in paragraph (2), by striking "the term" and inserting "The term"; and

(4) by adding at the end the following:

"(3) The terms 'energy savings contract' and 'energy savings performance contract' mean a contract which provides for the performance of services for the design, acquisition, installation, testing, operation, and, where appropriate, maintenance and repair, of an identified energy conservation measure or series of measures at one or more locations. Such contracts –

"(A) may provide for appropriate software licensing agreements; and

"(B) shall, with respect to an agency facility that is a public building as such term is defined in section 13(1) of the Public Buildings Act of 1959 (40 U.S.C. 612(1)), be in compliance with the prospectus requirements and procedures of section 7 of the Public Buildings Act of 1959 (40 U.S.C. 606).

"(4) The term "energy conservation measures" has the meaning given such term in section 551(4).".

(c) TECHNICAL AND CONFORMING AMENDMENTS. – (1) The title heading for title VIII of such Act is amended to read as follows:
(2) The table of contents of such Act is amended by striking the item relating to title VIII and inserting the following: "ENERGY SAVINGS PERFORMANCE CONTRACTS".

Sec. 156. Intergovernmental Energy Management Planning and Coordination.

(a) CONFERENCE WORKSHOPS. – The Administrator of General Services, in consultation with the Secretary and the Task Force, shall hold regular, biennial conference workshops in each of the 10 standard Federal regions on energy management, conservation, efficiency, and planning strategy. The Administrator shall work and consult with the Department of Energy and other Federal agencies to plan for particular regional conferences. The Administrator shall invite Department of Energy, State, local, tribal, and county public officials who have responsibilities for energy management or may have an interest in such conferences and shall seek the input of, and be responsive to, the views of such officials in the planning and organization of such workshops.

(b) FOCUS OF WORKSHOPS. – Such workshops and conferences shall focus on the following (but may include other topics):

(1) Developing strategies among Federal, State, tribal, and local governments to coordinate energy management policies and to maximize available intergovernmental energy management resources within the region regarding the use of governmental facilities and buildings.

(2) The design, construction, maintenance, and retrofitting of governmental facilities to incorporate energy efficient techniques.

(3) Procurement and use of energy efficient products.

(4) Dissemination of energy information on innovative programs, technologies, and methods which have proven successful in government.

(5) Technical assistance to design and incorporate effective energy management strategies.

(c) ESTABLISHMENT OF WORKSHOP TIMETABLE. – As a part of the first report to be submitted pursuant to section 154, the Administrator shall set forth the schedule for the regional energy management workshops to be conducted under this section. Not less than five such workshops shall be held by September 30, 1993, and at least one such workshop shall be held in each of the 10 Federal regions every two years beginning on September 30, 1993.

Sec. 157. Federal Agency Energy Management Training.

(a) ENERGY MANAGEMENT TRAINING. – (1) Each executive department described under section 101 of title 5, United States Code, the Environmental Protection Agency, the National Aeronautics and Space Administration, the General Services Administration, and the United States Postal Service shall establish and maintain a program to ensure that facility energy managers are trained energy managers. Such programs shall be managed –

(A) by the department or agency representative on the Task Force; or

(B) if a department or agency is not represented on the Task Force, by the designee of the head of such department or agency.

(2) Departments and agencies described in paragraph (1) shall encourage appropriate employees to participate in energy manager training courses. Employees may enroll in courses of study in the areas described in section 151(3) including, but not limited to, courses offered by –

(A) private or public educational institutions;

(B) Federal agencies; or

(C) professional associations.

(b) REPORT TO TASK FORCE. – (1) Each department and agency described in subsection (a)(1) shall, not later than 60 days following the date of the enactment of this Act, report to the Task Force the following information:

(A) Those individuals employed by such department or agency on the date of the enactment of this Act who qualify as trained energy managers.

(B) The General Schedule (GS) or grade level at which each of the individuals described in subparagraph (A) is employed.

(C) The facility or facilities for which such individuals are responsible or otherwise stationed.

(2) The Secretary shall provide a summary of the reports described in paragraph (1) to the Congress as part of the first report submitted under section 548 of the National Energy Conservation Policy Act (42 U.S.C. 8258) after the date of the enactment of this Act.

(c) REQUIREMENTS AT FEDERAL FACILITIES. – (1) Not later than one year after the date of the enactment of this Act, the departments and agencies described under subsection (a)(1) shall upgrade their energy management capabilities by –

(A) designating facility energy supervisors;

(B) encouraging facility energy supervisors to become trained energy managers; and

(C) increasing the overall number of trained energy managers within such department or agency to a sufficient level to ensure effective implementation of this Act.

(2) Departments and agencies described in subsection (a)(1) may hire trained energy managers to be facility energy supervisors. Trained energy managers, including those who are facility supervisors as well as other trained personnel, shall focus their efforts on improving energy efficiency in the following facilities –

(A) department or agency facilities identified as most costly to operate or most energy inefficient; or

(B) other facilities identified by the department or agency head as having significant energy savings potential.

(d) ANNUAL REPORT TO SECRETARY AND CONGRESS. – Each department and agency listed in subsection (a)(1) shall report to the Secretary on the status and implementation of the requirements of this section. The Secretary shall include a summary of each such report in the annual report to Congress as required under section 548(b) of the National Energy Conservation Policy Act (42 U.S.C. 8258).

Sec. 158. Energy Audit Teams.

(a) ESTABLISHMENT. – The Secretary shall assemble from existing personnel with appropriate expertise, and with particular utilization of the national laboratories, and make available to all Federal agencies, one or more energy audit teams which shall be equipped with instruments and other advanced equipment needed to perform energy audits of Federal facilities.

(b) MONITORING PROGRAMS. – The Secretary shall also assist in establishing, at each site that has utilized an energy audit team, a program for monitoring the implementation of energy efficiency improvements based upon energy audit team recommendations, and for recording the operating history of such improvements.

Sec. 159. Federal Energy Cost Accounting and Management.

(a) GUIDELINES. – Not later than 120 days after the date of the enactment of this Act, the Director of the Office of Management and Budget, in cooperation with the Secretary, the Administrator of General Services, and the Secretary of Defense, shall establish guidelines to be employed by each Federal agency to assess accurate energy consumption for all buildings or facilities which the agency owns, operates, manages or leases, where the Government pays utilities separate from the lease and the Government operates the leased space. Such guidelines are to be used in reports required under section 548 of the National Energy Conservation Policy Act (42 U.S.C. 8258). Each agency shall implement such guidelines no later than 120 days after their establishment. Each facility energy manager shall maintain energy consumption and energy cost records for review by the Inspector General, the Congress, and the general public.

(b) CONTENTS OF GUIDELINES. – Such guidelines shall include the establishment of a monitoring system to determine –

(1) which facilities are the most costly to operate when measured on an energy consumption per square foot basis or other relevant analytical basis;

(2) unusual or abnormal changes in energy consumption; and

(3) the accuracy of utility charges for electric and gas consumption.

(c) FEDERALLY LEASED SPACE ENERGY REPORTING REQUIREMENT. – The Administrator of General Services shall include, in each report submitted under section 154, the estimated energy cost of leased buildings or space in which the Federal Government does not directly pay the utility bills.

Sec. 160. Inspector General Review and Agency Accountability.

(a) AUDIT SURVEY. – Not later than 120 days after the date of the enactment of this Act, each Inspector General created to conduct and supervise audits and investigations relating to the programs and operations of the establishments listed in section 11(2) of the Inspector General Act of 1978 (5 U.S.C. App.), and the Chief Postal Inspector of the United States Postal Service, in accordance with section 8E(f)(1) as established by section 8E(a)(2) of the Inspector General Act Amendments of 1988 (Public Law 100-504) shall –

(1) identify agency compliance activities to meet the requirements of section 543 of the National Energy Conservation Policy Act (42 U.S.C. 8253) and any other matters relevant to implementing the goals of such Act; and

(2) determine if the agency has the internal accounting mechanisms necessary to assess the accuracy and reliability of energy consumption and energy cost figures required under such section.

(b) PRESIDENTS COUNCIL ON INTEGRITY AND EFFICIENCY REPORT TO CONGRESS. – Not later than 150 days after the date of the enactment of this Act, the President's Council on Integrity and Efficiency shall submit a report to the Committee on Energy and Natural Resources and the Committee on Governmental Affairs of the Senate, the Committee on Energy and Commerce, the Committee on Government Operations, and the Committee on Public Works and Transportation of the House of Representatives, on the review conducted by the Inspector General of each agency under this section.

(c) INSPECTOR GENERAL REVIEW. – Each Inspector General established under section 2 of the Inspector General Act of 1978 (5 U.S.C. App.) is encouraged to conduct periodic reviews of agency compliance with part 3 of title V of the National Energy Conservation Policy Act, the provisions of this subtitle, and other laws relating to energy consumption. Such reviews shall not be inconsistent with the performance of the required duties of the Inspector General's office.

Sec. 161. Procurement and Identification of Energy Efficient Products.

(a) PROCUREMENT. – The Administrator of General Services, the Secretary of Defense, and the Director of the Defense Logistics Agency, each shall undertake a program to include energy efficient products in carrying out their procurement and supply functions.

(b) IDENTIFICATION PROGRAM. – The Administrator of General Services, the Secretary of Defense, and the Director of the Defense Logistics Agency, in consultation with the Secretary of Energy, each shall implement, in conjunction with carrying out their procurement and supply functions, a program to identify and designate those energy efficient products that offer significant potential savings, using, to the extent practicable, the life cycle cost methods and procedures developed under section 544 of the National Energy Conservation Policy Act (42 U.S.C. 8254). The Secretary of Energy shall, to the extent necessary to carry out this section and after consultation with the aforementioned agency heads, provide estimates of the degree of relative energy efficiency of products.

(c) GUIDELINES. – The Administrator for Federal Procurement Policy, in consultation with the Administrator of General Services, the Secretary of Energy, the Secretary of Defense, and the Director of the Defense Logistics Agency, shall issue guidelines to encourage the acquisition and use by all Federal agencies of products identified pursuant to this section. The Secretary of Defense and the Director of the Defense Logistics Agency shall consider, and place emphasis on, the acquisition of such products as part of the Agency's ongoing review of military specifications.

(d) REPORT TO CONGRESS. – Not later than December 31 of 1993 and of each year thereafter, the Secretary of Energy, in consultation with the Administrator for Federal Procurement Policy, the Administrator of General Services, the Secretary of Defense, and the Director of the Defense Logistics Agency, shall report on the progress, status, activities, and results of the programs under subsections (a), (b), and (c). The report shall include –

(1) the types and functions of each product identified under subsection (b), and efforts undertaken by the Administrator of General Services, the Secretary of Defense, and the Director of the Defense Logistics Agency to encourage the acquisition and use of such products;

(2) the actions taken by the Administrator of General Services, the Secretary of Defense, and the Director of the Defense Logistics Agency to identify products under subsection (b), the barriers which inhibit implementation of identification of such products, and recommendations for legislative action, if necessary;

(3) progress on the development and issuance of guidelines under subsection (c);

(4) an indication of whether energy cost savings technologies identified by the Advanced Building Technology Council, under section 809(h) of the National Housing Act (12 U.S.C. 1701j–2), have been used in the identification of products under subsection (b);

(5) an estimate of the potential cost savings to the Federal Government from acquiring products identified under subsection (b) with respect to which energy is a significant component of life cycle cost, based on the quantities of such products that could be utilized throughout the Government; and

(6) the actual quantities acquired of products described in paragraph (5).

Sec. 162. Federal Energy Efficiency Funding Study.

(a) STUDY. – The Secretary shall, in consultation with the Secretary of the Treasury, the Director of the Office of Management and Budget, the Administrator of General Services, and such other individuals and organizations as the Secretary deems appropriate, conduct a detailed study of options for the financing of energy and water conservation measures required under part 3 of title V of the National Energy Conservation Policy Act (42 U.S.C. 8251 et seq.) and all applicable Executive orders. Such study shall, taking into account the unique characteristics of Federal agencies, consider and analyze –

(1) the Federal financial investment necessary to comply with such requirements;

(2) the use of revolving funds and other funding mechanisms which offer stable, long-term financing of energy and water conservation measures; and

(3) the means for capitalizing such funds.

(b) REPORT TO CONGRESS. – Not later than 180 days after the date of the enactment of this Act, the Secretary shall submit to the Congress a report containing the results of the study required under subsection (a).

Sec. 163. United States Postal Service Energy Regulations.

(a) IN GENERAL. – The Postmaster General shall issue regulations to ensure the reliable and accurate accounting of energy consumption costs for all buildings or facilities which it owns, leases, operates, or manages. Such regulations shall –

(1) establish a monitoring system to determine which facilities are the most costly to operate on an energy consumption per square foot basis or other relevant analytical basis;

(2) identify unusual or abnormal changes in energy consumption; and

(3) check the accuracy of utility charges for electricity and gas consumption.

(b) IDENTIFICATION OF ENERGY EFFICIENCY PRODUCTS. – The Postmaster General shall actively undertake a program to identify and procure energy efficiency products for use in its facilities. In carrying out this subsection, the Postmaster General shall, to the maximum extent practicable, incorporate energy efficient information available on Federal Supply Schedules maintained by the General Services Administration and the Defense Logistics Agency.

Sec. 164. United States Postal Service Building Energy Survey and Report.

(a) IN GENERAL. – The Postmaster General shall conduct an energy survey, as defined in section 551(5) of the National Energy Conservation Policy Act, for the purposes of –

(1) determining the maximum potential cost effective energy savings that may be achieved in a representative sample of buildings owned or leased by the United States Postal Service in different areas of the country;

(2) making recommendations for cost effective energy efficiency and renewable energy improvements in those buildings and in other similar United States Postal Service buildings; and

(3) identifying barriers which may prevent the United States Postal

Service from complying with energy management goals, including Executive Orders No. 12003 and 12579.

(b) IMPLEMENTATION. – (1) The Postmaster General shall transmit to the Committee on Governmental Affairs and the Committee on Energy and Natural Resources of the Senate, and the Committee on Energy and Commerce and the Committee on Post Office and Civil Service of the House of Representatives, within 180 days after the date of the enactment of this Act, a plan for implementing this section.

(2) The Postmaster General shall designate buildings to be surveyed in the project so as to obtain a sample of United States Postal Service facilities of the types and in the climates that consume the major portion of the energy consumed by the United States Postal Service.

(3) For the purposes of this section, an improvement shall be considered cost effective if the cost of the energy saved or displaced by the improvement exceeds the cost of the improvement over the remaining life of the facility or the remaining term of a lease of a building leased by the United States Postal Service.

(c) REPORT. – As soon as practicable after the completion of the project carried out under this section, the Postmaster General shall transmit a report of the findings and conclusions of the survey to the Committee on Governmental Affairs and the Committee on Energy and Natural Resources of the Senate, and the Committee on Energy and Commerce and the Committee on Post Office and Civil Service of the House of Representatives.

Sec. 165. United States Postal Service Energy Management Report.

Not later than one year after the date of the enactment of this Act, and not later than January 1 of each year thereafter, the Postmaster General shall submit a report to the Committee on Governmental Affairs and the Committee on Energy and Natural

Resources of the Senate and the Committee on Energy and Commerce and the Committee on Post Office and Civil Service of the House of Representatives on the United States Postal Service's building management program as it relates to energy efficiency. The report shall include, but not be limited to –

(1) a description of actions taken to reduce energy consumption;

(2) future plans to reduce energy consumption;

(3) an assessment of the success of the energy conservation program;

(4) a statement of energy costs incurred in operating and maintaining all United States Postal Service facilities; and

(5) the status of the energy efficient procurement program established under section 163.

Sec. 166. Energy Management Requirements for the United States Postal Service.

(a) ENERGY MANAGEMENT REQUIREMENTS FOR POSTAL FACILITIES. – (1) The Postmaster General shall, to the maximum extent practicable, ensure that each United States Postal Service facility meets the energy management requirements for Federal buildings and agencies specified in section 543 of the National Energy Conservation Policy Act (42 U.S.C. 8253).

(2) The Postmaster General may exclude from the requirements of such section any facility or collection of facilities, and the associated energy consumption and gross square footage if the Postmaster General finds that compliance with the requirements of such section would be impracticable. A finding of impracticability shall be based on the energy intensiveness of activities carried out in such facility or collection of facilities, the type and amount of energy consumed, or the technical feasibility of making the desired changes. The Postmaster General shall identify and list in the report required under section 165 the facilities designated by it for such exclusion.

(b) IMPLEMENTATION STEPS – In carrying subsection (a), the Postmaster General shall –

(1) not later than 1 year after the date of the enactment of this Act, prepare or update, as appropriate, a plan (which may be submitted as part of the first report submitted under section 165) –

(A) describing how this section will be implemented;

(B) designating personnel primarily responsible for achieving the requirements of this section; and

(C) identifying high priority projects;

(2) perform energy surveys of United States Postal Service facilities as necessary to achieve the requirements of this section;

(3) install those energy conservation measures that will attain the requirements of this section in a cost-effective manner as defined in section 544 of the National Energy Conservation Policy Act (42 U.S.C. 8254); and

(4) ensure that the operation and maintenance procedures applied under this section are continued.

Sec. 167. Government Contract Incentives.

(a) ESTABLISHMENT OF CRITERIA. – Each agency, in consultation with the Federal Acquisition Regulatory Council, shall establish criteria for the improvement of energy efficiency in Federal facilities operated by Federal Government contractors or subcontractors.

(b) PURPOSE OF CRITERIA. – The criteria established under subsection (a) shall be used to encourage Federal contractors, and their subcontractors, which manage and operate federally-owned facilities, to adopt and utilize energy conservation measures designed to reduce energy costs in Government-owned and contractor-operated facilities and which are ultimately borne by the Federal Government.

Sec. 168. Energy Management Requirements for Congressional Buildings.

(a) IN GENERAL. – The Architect of the Capitol (hereafter in this section referred to as the "Architect") shall undertake a program of analysis and, as necessary, retrofit of the Capitol Building, the Senate Office Buildings, the House Office Buildings, and the Capitol Grounds, in accordance with subsection (b).

(b) PROGRAM. –

(1) LIGHTING. –

(A) IMPLEMENTATION. –

(i) IN GENERAL. – Not later than 18 months after the date of the enactment of this Act and subject to the availability of funds to carry out this section, the

Architect shall begin implementing a program to replace in each building described in subsection (a) all inefficient office and general use area fluorescent lighting systems with systems that incorporate the best available design and technology and that have payback periods of 10 years or less, as determined by using methods and procedures established under section 544(a) of the National Energy and Conservation Policy Act (42 U.S.C. 8254(a)).

(ii) REPLACEMENT OF INCANDESCENT LIGHTING. – Whenever practicable in office and general use areas, the Architect shall replace incandescent lighting with efficient fluorescent lighting.

(B) COMPLETION. – Subject to the availability of funds to carry out this section, the program described in subparagraph (A) shall be completed not later than 5 years after the date of the enactment of this Act.

(2) EVALUATION AND REPORT. –

(A) IN GENERAL. – Not later than 6 months after the date of the enactment of this Act, the Architect shall submit to the Speaker of the House of Representatives and the President pro tempore of the Senate a report evaluating potential energy conservation measures for each building described in subsection (a) in the areas of heating, ventilation, air conditioning equipment, insulation, windows, domestic hot water, food service equipment, and automatic control equipment.

(B) COSTS. – The report submitted under subparagraph (A) shall detail the projected installation cost, energy and cost savings, and payback period of each energy conservation measure, as determined by using methods and procedures established under section 544(a) of the National Energy Conservation Policy Act (42 U.S.C. 8254(a)).

(3) REVIEW AND APPROVAL OF ENERGY CONSERVATION MEASURES. – The Committee on Public Works and Transportation of the House of Representatives and the Committee on Rules and Administration of the Senate shall review the energy conservation measures identified in accordance with paragraph (2) and shall approve any such measure before it may be implemented.

(4) UTILITY INCENTIVE PROGRAMS. – In carrying out this section, the Architect is authorized and encouraged to –

(A) accept any rebate or other financial incentive offered through a program for energy conservation or demand management of electricity, water, or gas that –

(i) is conducted by an electric, natural gas, or water utility;

(ii) is generally available to customers of the utility; and

(iii) provides for the adoption of energy efficiency technologies or practices that the Architect determines are cost-effective for the buildings described in subsection (a); and

(B) enter into negotiations with electric and natural gas utilities to design a special demand management and conservation incentive program to address the unique needs of the buildings described in subsection (a).

(5) USE OF SAVINGS. – The Architect shall use an amount equal to the rebate or other savings from the financial incentive programs under paragraph (4)(A), without additional authorization or appropriation, for the implementation of additional energy and water conservation measures in the buildings under the jurisdiction of the Architect.

(c) AUTHORIZATION OF APPROPRIATIONS. – There are authorized to be appropriated such sums as are necessary to carry out this section.

SOUTH AMERICA

Chile

Law on Geothermal Energy Concessions

Law N° 19.657 Ministry Of Mining

(Nonofficial Translation)

SECTION I GENERAL PROVISIONS

Article 1. The provisions set forth in this law shall govern:

(a) Geothermal energy;

(b) The concessions and tenders for the exploration or exploitation of geothermal energy;

(c) Constitution of the necessary easements required for the exploration or exploitation of geothermal energy;

(d) Safety conditions to be maintained while carrying out geothermal activities;

(e) The relationships between holders of concessions, the Government, owners of surface lands, holders of mining properties and parties to oil operation contracts or companies authorized by law to prospect or develop hydrocarbons, holders of water exploitation rights, in all matters relating to the exploration or exploitation of geothermal energy, and

(f) Government responsibilities related to geothermal energy.

Article 2. The provisions set forth in this law shall not apply to thermal waters, whether mineral or not, used for sanitary, tourism or recreational purposes.

The exploitation and drawdown of thermal waters referred to in the above subparagraph shall be governed by the provisions set forth in Statutory Decree N° 237, year 1931, or by the general or special regulations which, in each case, shall be applicable.

The scope of this law shall cover the continental, insular and Antarctic territory, including inland waters, territorial sea and exclusive economic zone.

Article 3. Geothermal energy shall mean the energy obtained from the natural heat of the earth, which may be drawn from steam, water, gases – except for hydrocarbons – or through fluids artificially injected for such purposes.

Article 4. Geothermal energy, regardless of the location, form or conditions of its manifestation or existence, is state property, susceptible to exploration and exploitation, upon obtaining a concession, in the form set out and in compliance with the requirements under the law.

Article 5. The concession of geothermal energy is a property right in rem, different and independent from the property of surface land holdings, despite having the same owner, opposable against the Government and any person, assignable and transferable, subject to any act or contract.

The holder of a geothermal energy concession holds a property right over such concession, protected by the surety set forth in Article 19 of the Constitution and in other legal rules that are applicable to the same right.

Upon obtaining a concession in conformity with the regulations set forth in this law, the holder thereof shall have the right to keep such concession and shall not be deprived thereof except on the grounds of forfeiture or expiration as contemplated in the law itself.

Any constructions, facilities and other objects permanently destined by the owner thereof to the investigation, exploration or exploitation of geothermal energy, as appropriate, which may be necessary to carry out the activities inherent to the concession shall be deemed accessory properties under such concession, provided such accessory properties are located within the leased area.

Article 6. The geothermal energy concession may be for exploration or exploitation. Any time the law refers to a geothermal energy concession, it is deemed to include both types of concessions.

Exploration operations are all the activities that are carried out in order to ascertain the geothermal energy potentialities of an area, including drilling and measurement of geothermal gradient wells and deep wildcat wells. In consequence, exploration concessions grant the right to carry out studies, measurements and other research to determine the existence of sources of geothermal resources, their physical and chemical characteristics, geographic extension, and suitability and conditions for exploitation thereof.

Exploitation concessions consist in a series of drilling, construction, startup and operation activities within a system designed for drawing, production, and transformation of geothermal fluids into thermal or electric energy. In consequence, exploitation concessions grant the right to utilize and develop the geothermal energy existing within its boundaries.

Article 7. The territorial extension of the geothermal energy concession constitutes a solid cubic volume having a top surface which horizontally forms a right angled parallelogram, where two of its sides are U.T.M. North-South oriented, and its depth is indefinite within the vertical planes limiting the same.

The length and width of the parallelogram shall be, for exploration concessions, multiple integers of one thousand meters, and for exploitation concessions, multiple integers of one hundred meters.

In any event, the ratio between length and width of the parallelogram shall not exceed ten to one.

The surface area of each exploration concession shall not exceed one hundred thousand hectares, or twenty thousand hectares, in the case of exploitation concessions.

The area of the geothermal energy concession shall be set out in the Decree of constitution thereof.

The object of the geothermal energy concession shall be the total amount of such energy existing within its limits.

Article 8. The Ministry of Mining shall be responsible for the application, control and enforcement of this law and regulations therein, notwithstanding the authorities conferred upon the National Energy Commission and other agencies specifically mentioned in the regulations thereof.

The Ministry of Mining shall be responsible for the inspection and enforcement of the regulations in this law and the rules being issued, and fulfillment of the obligations of concession holders, as provided in the concession decrees.

Article 9. The production, transportation, distribution, the concession regime and the rate regime of electric power derived from geothermal energy and the Government's responsibilities in that regard shall be governed, as appropriate, by the regulations set forth in Statutory Decree N° 1, Ministry of Mining, June 22nd, 1982.

SECTION II OF THE CONCESSIONS

Article 10. Every natural Chilean person and every corporate body organized under Chilean laws shall be entitled to apply for geothermal energy concessions and to participate in a public bidding for granting such concessions.

Article 11. Applications for geothermal energy concessions which are filed directly or submitted through public tenders shall contain and be accompanied by at least the following references and background information:

(a) Name, nationality and legal address of the applicant, and, as appropriate, of the person filing such application on behalf of another person. In the event of natural persons, the profession or specific trade and civil status thereof shall be indicated as well;

(b) The location, extension and dimensions of the land holding in which respect the concession is being applied for and map thereof, indicating UTM coordinates and vortexes, and precisely identifying the Region, Province, and Municipality thereof. If the leased property shall extend over more than one Region, Province or Municipal Governments, such identification shall include all

Regions, Provinces or Municipal Governments included, and

(c) The general, technical and economic information of the geothermal energy exploration or exploitation project, and projected investment for its implementation.

Article 12. The Ministry of Mining may request, from any public authority or agency, the reports deemed relevant to avoid or foresee conflicts of rights or interests between an applicant for a geothermal energy concession and the holders of other rights in the area applied for, for better resolution of the application for such geothermal energy concession.

The authorities from which reports are requested shall furnish such reports within a period of sixty calendar days, counted as from the date when such requirement had been received from the Ministry of Mining. Upon expiry of such period without having received such report, it shall be deemed to be in favor of granting such concession.

Article 13. An abridgment of the application for geothermal energy concessions shall be published in the Official Gazette, only once, on the 1st or the 15th or on the following business day if any of these two days were to be a holiday, of the month following the filing date of such application to the Ministry of Mining, in an outstanding advertisement. Such outstanding advertisement shall be published twice in a nationwide newspaper, and in a regional newspaper circulating in the territories covered by the concession being applied for, within the month following the date of filing such application.

The abridgment shall include the identification of the applicant or petitioner; type of concession being applied for; purpose of such concession, and location, extension and dimensions of the area covered thereby.

In the case of areas with difficult access, the abridgment shall be additionally communicated through three radio messages broadcasted in the sector. These messages shall be broadcasted within the same month referred to in the first subparagraph of this Article. The legal representative of the broadcasting means or any person appointed thereby, shall place on record the broadcasting of such messages, indicating date and hour, in a record having characteristics to be determined by the Rules and Regulations. This record shall be public, for any person to examine it.

Article 14. The holder of the exploration concession shall have an exclusive right to the Government's grant of the exploitation concession over the respective exploration area. This right may be used during the period of effectiveness of such exploration concession and up to two years after expiry thereof. The right set forth in this subparagraph shall be transferable in every respect.

In the event of an application for a exploration concession, or a exploitation concession in respect of which the right referred to in the above subparagraph shall not be in order, other natural or corporate persons may request such concession over the property included in the original application, within a term of forty-five calendar days, counted as from publication in the Official Gazette of the abridgement of such application.

Article 15. Upon expiry of the forty-five calendar day term set out in the second subparagraph of the above Article, and there being no other applications for such concession, the Ministry of Mining shall resolve whether to grant or deny such concession, unless any claims or objections are filed in accordance with the provisions under Article 18.

If, within the same term period, other concession applications are filed covering part or the whole territorial extension already applied for, the Ministry of Mining shall call for public bids to grant one or more concessions on the area in question, within a period of ninety days, counted as from expiry of such period.

Notwithstanding the above, the Ministry of Mining may, at any time, call for public bids for granting one or more concessions of geothermal energy from unlikely sources.

Article 16. Notwithstanding the stipulations in the preceding Articles, and except as provided in the first subparagraph in Article 14, the geothermal energy concessions bearing on a probable source shall be always granted by the Ministry of Mining upon a call for public bidding. This bidding process shall be carried out once a year at the government's initiative or upon the petition of one or more private persons.

In the event one or more private persons shall apply for a geothermal energy concession of probable source, the Ministry of Mining shall call for public bids within a period of ninety days, counted as from the date of filing the respective application.

For the purposes of this law, probable sources of geothermal energy are any spontaneously outcropping waters having some heat inside the earth, and the surrounding geographical area which shall not surpass the surface areas indicated in subparagraph fourth in Article 7 for a exploration or exploitation concession.

Probable sources of geothermal energy shall be identified in a special regulation to be issued by the Ministry of Mining within a term of one hundred and twenty days, counted as from the date of publication of this law.

This identification shall include specification of the Region, Province, and Commune where such sources are located, the U.T.M. coordinates of their vortexes and estimated surfaces of such sources, expressed in hectares.

Notwithstanding to the above, for the purposes of this law, the following shall be deemed probable sources of geothermal energy: Jurasi, Untupujo, Chiriguaya, Surire, Polloquere, Enquelca, Berenguela, Quiritari, Puchuldiza, Chuzmiza, Pampa Lirima, Colpagua, Mamiña, Pica, Ascotán, El Tatio, Alitar, Aguas Calientes, Tilopozo, and Tuyaito. The regulation mentioned in this Article shall set forth the geographical areas encompassed in each of these probable sources.

Article 17. The public bidding called by the Ministry of Mining for the purposes of this Section shall include two stages. First, the technical qualification of bidders, and secondly, the appraisal of the economic bids. All bidders selected in the first technical qualification stage shall be entitled to submit bids in the second stage, and the successful bidder shall be chosen according to the price offered thereby for the concession.

All natural or corporate persons who wish to participate in the bidding process called by the Ministry of Mining for granting a geothermal energy concession shall meet the following requirements, as a minimum:

(a) To have capital assets amounting to a minimum of five thousand Unidades de Fomento (UF)*, or minimum capital of ten thousand Unidades de Fomento in the case of corporate persons, and

(b) To accompany the general, technical and economic information of the project for the geothermal energy exploration or exploitation concession and the information on the projected investment for implementation thereof.

The bidding conditions may set forth the authority of the Ministry of Mining to reject, with expression of cause, all the bids and consequently declare the bid void.

The call for bids shall be published in the manner set forth in Article 13.

For the appointment of the successful bidder, the proceedings shall follow the provisions set forth in Article 19.

Article 18. Notwithstanding the legal actions that they may be entitled to, as appropriate, within a period of forty-five calendar days counted as from publication of the abridged application or of the advertisement calling for bids, the owners of surface lands, holders of mining claims or water rights, holders of exploration or exploitation rights on liquid or gaseous hydrocarbons or lithium, or the holders of rights to territorial areas covered by the respective geothermal energy concessions may, by submitting the instruments and information evidencing their title, file with the Ministry of Mining the claims and objections of such that may cause them detriment.

The Ministry of Mining shall inform the petitioner on the claims and objections filed, granting the petitioner a period of sixty calendar days counted as from the date of reception of such communication, for the petitioner to make any statements deemed convenient for its rights. Upon expiry of this sixty-day period, with or without the applicant's reply, the Ministry of Mining shall resolve on the concession application, if appropriate, within the term provided under Article 19.

If such claims or objections shall have been filed upon a call for public bids for granting a geothermal energy concession, the Ministry of Mining shall resolve as appropriate within a period of sixty calendar days, counted as from expiry of the due date set

* Chilean peso-denominated monetary index the value of which is determined monthly by the Central Bank of Chile for each day of the immediately succeeding month according to variations in the CPI during the immediately preceding month.

forth in the first subparagraph. Should the Ministry fail to resolve within such term period, the call for bids shall be deemed null and void.

In any event, the right to file claims or objections referred to in this Article shall not be used whenever the application for a exploitation concession shall have been preceded by a exploration concession over all or part of the same surface area.

Article 19. If no claims or objections shall have been asserted, or if such claims or objections shall have been resolved, the Ministry of Mining, through Supreme Decree, shall determine the merits for the concession application or decide on the call for bids, as appropriate, upon the report issued by the Comisión Nacional de Energía (National Energy Commission). For this, the Ministry of Mining shall have a ninety calendar day period counted, in the case of a concession application, as from the expiry of the sixty-day term set forth in the second subparagraph of the preceding Article, and in the case of a call for bids, as from expiry of the period provided in the third subparagraph of that same provision. In absence of any objections or claims, the ninety-day term shall be counted as from expiry of the term provided in the first subparagraph in Article 15, in the case of a concession application, and as from the opening of bids, in the case of a call for bids.

The Supreme Decree rejecting an application for a concession or declaring void a public tender called for granting a geothermal energy concession shall be well-founded.

Article 20. The decree granting the exploration concession shall contain, as essential references, the following: a) term of the concession; b) holder to whom such concession is granted; c) location, with U.T.M. coordinates of vortexes and extension of the concession, and d) general, technical, and economic information on the geothermal energy exploration project and the projected investment for implementation thereof.

The decree granting a exploitation concession shall contain, as essential references, the following: a) the holder such concession is granted to b) location of the U.T.M. coordinates of the vortexes, and extension of the concession, and c) projected investment.

Copy of any such decree shall be submitted to the Servicio Nacional de Geología y Minería de Chile (Chilean National Geology and Mining Service), which shall keep a record of the granted concessions and their geographical location determined in U.T.M. coordinates.

In qualified cases, and upon the request of the holder of exploration or exploitation concessions, the Ministry of Mining may modify the conditions for such concession, promulgating for such purposes, a new decree.

Article 21. Geothermal energy concessions shall become effective on the date of publication in the Official Gazette of the Supreme Decree granting such concessions.

SECTION III OF THE RIGHTS OF HOLDERS OF CONCESSIONS

Article 22. Solely the holders of exploration or exploitation concessions, as appropriate, shall be entitled to carry out exploration or exploitation activities, respectively, of the geothermal energy found at the area of the respective concessions.

No geothermal energy concessions shall be granted in respect of land properties which are subject to another geothermal energy concession, the existence of which shall be previously inquired by requesting a report from the Chilean National Geology and Mining Service.

Article 23. Notwithstanding the recourses and actions provided by law, the applicants of a geothermal energy concession and bidders in a tender called for awarding any such concessions, may claim before the Minister of Mining against any acts or deeds affecting their rights which may have occurred during the processing of the application or call for bids. Equally, such applicants or bidders may contest before the referred authority, the rejection of such application or decision on the bidding. The term to assert the claims shall be fifteen calendar days counted as from the date of acknowledgement of the act or deed giving rise to such claim.

The Minister shall issue its decision based on a well-founded report from a Commission. Such Commission shall be formed by the Undersecretary of Mining, Chief Legal Advisor for the Ministry of Mining, and the National Director of Geology and Mining.

Such well-founded report shall be submitted within a maximum period of ten calendar days, except if additional reports are required to make such decision, case which shall be placed on record in the claim records. In this case, the period shall be extended by a maximum of ten additional days.

The filing or assertion of the claim shall suspend the term periods referred to in Article 19 to decide on the concession application or bidding process which shall have been called for granting such concession.

The claims referred to in this Article which are filed after the date when the processing of the Supreme Decree granting the concession is complete, shall be dismissed flatly.

Article 24. Geothermal energy concessions may be assigned to third parties, in whole or in part. Such transfer shall be made through public deed.

Upon execution of such public deed of assignment, the new holder of a concession shall surrogate the previous holder thereof, solely by operation of law, in the liabilities and rights under the concession.

The geothermal energy concession and machinery and other personal property destined to the execution or implementation thereof may be furnished as surety.

Article 25. Concessions shall be transferable because of death. Heirs shall inform the Ministry of Mining, merely for registration purposes, the death of the principal, holder of a concession, within a term of sixty calendar days counted as from the death thereof. Within the same term, the heirs' representative before the Ministry and their intention to continue or cease in the exercise of their rights shall be stated.

Article 26. As from the date of effectiveness of the geothermal energy concession and in order to facilitate exploration or exploitation operations, as the case may be, the surface land holdings where the territorial extension covered by the concession is located shall be subject to the following easements:

1. Easements to occupy all the required area of such land holdings, with works and facilities for exploration and exploitation of geothermal energy; communication systems, ports, and piping, constructions and other supplementary works;

2. Easements set out in benefit of electric services licensee companies, according to the applicable legislation, and

3. Rights of way for traffic and location of roads, railways, piping, tunnels, inclined planes, cableways, conveyor belts, and any other systems used for connecting such concession to public roads, railroad stations, airports, ports, and geothermal energy commercial or industrial production stores and consumption centers.

If easements shall affect any houses or ancillary spaces or land holdings planted with vineyards or orchards, such easements shall only be constituted by mutual agreement with the owner of the surface land holding.

The constitution of easements, exercise thereof and the corresponding indemnities for any damages caused thereby to the owner of the lands or any other person shall be determined by mutual agreement between the interested parties, to be recorded in public deed, or by judicial resolution, issued in conformity with the preliminary procedures. However, once the preliminary proceedings are carried out, the continuation thereof may be requested and decreed in conformity with the rules of ordinary procedure, if well-founded motives exist therefore. The application wherein the substitution of the proceeding is requested shall be processed as an incidental plea. The provisions set forth in Article 125, Mining Code shall be applicable.

For the easements provided in this Article to be opposable against third parties such easements shall be registered with the Registry of Mortgages and. Encumbrances of the Registro de Hipotecas y Gravámenes del Conservador de Bienes Raíces (Registrar of Property, Mines and Real Estate).

Such easements shall not be utilized for purposes other than those inherent to the respective concession and for which they shall have been constituted and shall cease whenever such utilization is completed.

Article 27. The holder of geothermal energy concessions shall have, by the sole operation of law, and in the measure required for exercising such concessions, the right to develop, consume and exercise on an ongoing basis, the underground waters outcropping in the exploration or exploitation works. This right of utilization is inherent to the geothermal energy concession and shall expire therewith.

Within a six month term, counted as from the outcropping of underground waters, the holder of a geothermal energy concession shall inform the Dirección General de Aguas (General Bureau of Waters) in respect of the location of the tapping point, the technical characteristics of drawdown and the flows that have been drawn.

Upon termination of the geothermal utilization of the waters referred to in the first subparagraph of this Article, the holder of the geothermal energy concession shall become the owner of the respective exploitation right and may dispose of the waters, as long as the geothermal energy concession is in effect. The same regulation shall be applied to other geothermal fluids.

Waters proceeding from the exercise of a geothermal energy concession, referred to in subparagraphs first and third, once abandoned to a natural stream, shall be subject to the provisions in the Código de Aguas (Code of Waters) and, as appropriate, to the regulations governing spillage of pollutant matter into such streams.

The utilization of waters other than those referred to in the first subparagraph in this Article, shall abide by the regulations in the Código de Aguas (Code of Waters) and other applicable regulations.

Article 28. In land holdings covered by a geothermal energy concession, mining claims, water rights may be constituted or underground water exploration permits may be granted. Equally, management leases may be granted or special operating contracts may be entered into in the case of substances that are not subject to mining claims, in conformity with Article 7, Mining Code. Likewise, the Government or government-owned companies may explore or develop such substances in land holdings covered by a geothermal concession.

If activities under mining claims, concessions for exploration underground waters or water rights, management leases or special operating contracts which have been started after the constitution of a geothermal concession shall affect the exercise of such concession, the holders thereof shall carry out, at their sole charge, any works required to correct any difficulties or else indemnify the holder of such geothermal concession for any proprietary damages that are actually caused thereto.

Geothermal energy concessions may be granted on land properties where mining claims exist or water rights have been constituted, or in the case of substances that are not subject to mining claims under the provisions of Article 7, Mining Code, or whereon management concessions have been granted or special operating contracts have been entered into. If the activities inherent to geothermal energy concessions affect the exercise of such mining claims or special operating contracts or management leases on substances not subject to licensing or water rights, the holder of a geothermal energy concession shall carry out, at its sole charge, any works required to remedy any difficulties or else indemnify the holders of such concessions, water rights, management leases or special operating contracts for the proprietary damages actually caused thereto.

Article 29. If, on account of the exploitation of geothermal energy, the existence of a substance which may be licensed and which shall be the object of a mining property shall be detected, the mining or retrieval of which shall be obtained as a consequence of the exploitation of geothermal energy, the holder of the geothermal energy exploitation concession shall notify this fact to the owner of such mining property, who may demand recovery thereof, provided such owner of such mining property shall previously pay the holder of the geothermal concession any expenses and investment in modifications and supplementary works to be incurred in for such mining, retrieval and its delivery, in which case such owner shall equally pay any indemnities for damages caused on account of the execution of such modifications and supplementary works. These latter works shall be the property of the owner of the mining property. Nevertheless, if such holder of the mining property refuses to take delivery of such substances, the holder of the geothermal concession shall become the owner thereof.

The same rule shall apply, as appropriate, to the Government in respect of substances which are not subject to concessions.

Article 30. Any difficulties arising between two or more holders of concessions on account of the regulations set forth in Articles 27 and 28 or of their respective operations shall be subject to the decision of an arbitrator selected from among those mentioned in Article 223, final subparagraph, Código Orgánico de Tribunales (Organic Code of Courts).

Article 31. The holder of geothermal energy concessions may defend its concession by any means provided by law, against both the Government and private persons, exercising for such purposes the actions that may be in order, such as actions for recovery of possessions based on title or possessory actions, and collect, in addition, any relevant indemnities.

The holder of a concession may impetrate from a competent judge any precautionary measures, legal proceedings or pre-judicial measures destined to preserve and defend its concession.

SECTION IV OF THE DUTIES OF CONCESSION HOLDERS

Article 32. The geothermal energy exploitation concession shall be confirmed by compliance with the obligations set upon the concession holders in the Decree of Concession and by payment of an annual license fee as taxable profit. This license fee shall be equivalent to one tenth of an Unidad Tributaria Mensual[1] (Monthly Tax Unit) for each complete hectare of territorial area covered by such concession.

Payment of the license fee shall be made in advance and in March, each year, at any bank or agency authorized to collect taxes.

Upon expiry of the term period set forth in the above subparagraph, payment of license fees shall have a surcharge of 10% on its value plus an additional 5% for every month of delay.

The amount of the first license fee shall be proportional to the time elapsed between the date when the exploitation concession was granted and the last day of the following February. Once the first license fee has been paid, license fee payments shall continue yearly, on the date and in the manner provided in the second subparagraph.

Refunding of license fees paid for concessions that subsequently expire, fall due or are wholly or partially waived, on any grounds, shall not be in order.

Article 33. An amount equal to the proceeds from the license fees referred to in the previous Article shall be distributed among the Regions and Communes of the country as follows:

(a) 70% of such amount shall be ratably included in the yearly installment of the Fondo Nacional de Desarrollo Regional (National Fund for Regional Exploitation), in the Presupuesto Nacional (National Budget), that the Region or Regions where the concession is located are entitled to.

(b) The remaining 30% shall be paid to the Municipalities of the Communes where the geothermal energy exploitation concessions are located.

In the event that a geothermal energy concession is located on the territory of two or more Regions or two or more Communes, the Servicio Nacional de Geología y Minería (National Geology and Mining Service) shall determine the ratable amount corresponding to each, by dividing the amount ratably to the surface of each Region or Commune covered by such concession.

The Treasurer's Office shall dispose of the funds referred to in this Article to the Regions and Municipalities, as appropriate, within the next month following collection of license fees.

Article 34. The General Treasurer's Office of the Republic shall report, in April each year, to the Ministry of Mining in respect of the geothermal exploitation license fees that are still outstanding, for the purposes of the provisions set forth in Article 39.

SECTION V OF THE EXPLORATION AND EXPLOITATION OPERATIONS BY HOLDERS OF GEOTHERMAL ENERGY CONCESSIONS

Article 35. Holders of exploration concessions shall, yearly in the month of March and throughout the term of effectiveness of such concessions, report to the Ministry of Mining the confirmed progress during the preceding calendar year in the implementation of the project submitted in accordance with Article 11.

Article 36. The term of effectiveness of geothermal energy exploration concessions shall be two years, counted as from the date of effectiveness of the Concession Decree.

Notwithstanding, holders of concessions shall, prior to the last six months of the term of effectiveness set out in the previous subparagraph, request from the Ministry of Mining, for a single instance, the extension of such concession term for a period

[1] Unidad Tributaria Mensual = Monthly Tax Unit, the value of which is present by the IRS.

of two years, counted as from the end of the first period, by vouching for a progress of no less than 25% in the implementation of the investment set forth in letter c), Article 11. The Ministry of Mining shall approve or reject such extension on well-founded grounds, and inform such approval or well-founded rejection to the holder of such concession through written notice, addressed thereto within a period of no more than three months counted as from the date such extension was requested. This same notice shall be sent to the Servicio Nacional de Geología y Minería (National Geology and Mining Service) and to the Comisión Nacional de Energía (National Energy Commission).

Article 37. Holders of exploitation concessions shall inform the Ministry of Mining, during March each year, about the commercial or industrial exploitation activities carried out during the preceding calendar year.

Article 38. In the event two or more exploitation concessions are utilizing the same geothermal fluid yield reservoir, the respective holders of such concessions shall agree upon the technical procedures for their joint exploitation. In lack of agreement, such procedures shall be determined, upon request of any such holders, by an arbitrating arbitrator who shall settle the matter ensuring an optimal exploitation of the resources and safeguarding the rights of such holders of concessions.

SECTION VI OF THE TERMINATION OF GEOTHERMAL ENERGY CONCESSIONS

Article 39. The geothermal exploitation concession shall irrevocably expire, and solely by operation of law, if the holder of a concession shall fail to pay two consecutive license fees. This expiration shall occur at twelve o'clock on the night of March 31st, in the year when the second license fee payment is defaulted.

The Ministry of Mining shall inform this circumstance to the National Geology and Mining Service, and to the Comisión Nacional de Energía (National Energy Commission).

Article 40. The qualified judge for the territory where the geothermal energy concession is located, or any of such judges, if more than one exists, shall be competent to declare the exploitation concession terminated, upon a request from the Ministry of Mining, if the holder of a concession, having paid a license fee, shall have failed to carry out the exploitation activities under its concession, being capable to do so under reasonable profitability conditions, with the purpose of obtaining profits or additional advantages through the exploitation of other energy sources.

The judge shall hear and decide upon this request in accordance with the procedure set forth in Section XI, Book III, Code of Civil Procedure.

The judgement declaring the concession terminated shall be published, in abstract, in the Official Gazette. The judge shall arrange this publication, chargeable to the Ministry of Mining.

Article 41. The geothermal energy concession may be partially or wholly waived through public deed executed by the holder of a concession. Authorized copy of such deed shall be submitted to the Ministry of Mining within a period of one month counted as from the date of execution thereof. Failure to timely perform this obligation shall render such waiver non opposable for the sole purposes of making such holder's money liabilities due and payable.

In the event of partial waiver of the concession, payment of the annual license fee required from the holder of a concession shall be reduced by the corresponding ratable amount, as from the year following such waiver.

Article 42. In the event of expiration, termination or waiver of a geothermal energy concession, the holder of such concession shall be entitled to remove the equipment, facilities and works owned thereby, within a term of one year counted as from the date of expiration, termination or waiver, or as from the date of notification of such expiration, except if, before the due date of such term, the holder of such concession shall have requested an extension thereof, extension which shall solely be granted once and for a term of up to one year.

In the event the equipment, facilities and works shall not be removed within the period set forth in the previous subparagraph, they shall be deemed abandoned by the owner thereof.

SECTION VII FINAL PROVISIONS

Article 43. Any infringement of the provisions set forth in this law that shall not be expressly penalized herein, shall be penalized by a fine or penalty, as taxable profit, ranging from five to one hundred Unidades Tributarias Mensuales (Monthly Tax Units). The Ministry of Mining shall administratively apply such penalty, and resolution thereof shall have the right of execution.

The affected holder may file a claim before the ordinary justice against such penalties imposed by the Ministry. Such claim shall be filed within a term of thirty days, counted as from the date of remittance of the certified letter whereby the application of such penalty is notified. Justice shall hear of the claim briefly and summarily.

Article 44. Any person subtracting geothermal energy from a holder of a concession shall incur, regardless of the value of such subtraction, in the penalties provided in number 1, Article 446, Penal Code. In the event of recurrence, the procedure provided in Article 451, Penal Code, shall be applied.

Article 45. Let the following text be added to the third subparagraph in Article 2, Organic Law N° 9.618 of Empresa Nacional del Petróleo (National Oil Company), after the full stop (.), which becomes a period in the same paragraph (.): "Finally, the Company may participate, through companies wherein the company holds a share of less than 50% of equity capital, in activities relating to geothermal energy, being allowed for such purposes, to file applications for concessions, participate in tenders, provide any type of services to holders of concessions for carrying out the geothermal energy exploration and exploitation activities, and in general, carry out any industrial and commercial operations relating to the exploration and exploitation of such energy. Such companies may equally have the purpose of utilization of outcropping underground waters in the geothermal exploration and exploitation activities.".

Transitory Article. Natural or corporate persons evidencing geothermal research or exploration activities, carried out before the effectiveness of this law, which befall on a specific geographical area, shall have the exclusive right, for a period of one year counted as from the publication of this law, to apply for a geothermal energy concession from the Ministry of Mining."

Index